Lecture Notes in Computer Science   8927

Commenced Publication in 1973
Founding and Former Series Editors:
Gerhard Goos, Juris Hartmanis, and Jan van Leeuwen

More information about this series at http://www.springer.com/series/7412

Lourdes Agapito · Michael M. Bronstein
Carsten Rother (Eds.)

Computer Vision – ECCV 2014 Workshops

Zurich, Switzerland, September 6–7 and 12, 2014
Proceedings, Part III

Springer

Editors
Lourdes Agapito
University College London
London
UK

Michael M. Bronstein
University of Lugano
Lugano
Switzerland

Carsten Rother
Technische Universität Dresden
Dresden
Germany

Videos to this book can be accessed at
http://www.springerimages.com/videos/978-3-319-16198-3

ISSN 0302-9743   ISSN 1611-3349   (electronic)
Lecture Notes in Computer Science
ISBN 978-3-319-16198-3   ISBN 978-3-319-16199-0   (eBook)
DOI 10.1007/978-3-319-16199-0

Library of Congress Control Number: 2015933663

LNCS Sublibrary: SL6 – Image Processing, Computer Vision, Pattern Recognition, and Graphics

Springer Cham Heidelberg New York Dordrecht London

Springer International Publishing AG Switzerland is part of Springer Science+Business Media
(www.springer.com)

Foreword

Welcome to Zurich !

As you know, the European Conference on Computer Vision is one of the top conferences on computer vision. It was first held in 1990 in Antibes (France) with subsequent conferences in Santa Margherita Ligure (Italy) in 1992, Stockholm (Sweden) in 1994, Cambridge (UK) in 1996, Freiburg (Germany) in 1998, Dublin (Ireland) in 2000, Copenhagen (Denmark) in 2002, Prague (Czech Republic) in 2004, Graz (Austria) in 2006, Marseille (France) in 2008, Heraklion (Greece) in 2010, and Firenze (Italy) in 2012. Many people have worked hard to turn the 2014 edition into as great a success. We hope you will find this a mission accomplished.

The Chairs have decided to adhere to the classical single-track scheme. In terms of the time ordering, we have decided to largely follow the Firenze example (typically starting with poster sessions, followed by oral sessions), which offers a lot of flexibility to network and is more forgiving for the not-so-early-birds and hardcore gourmets.

A large conference like ECCV requires the help of many. They made sure you again get a full program including the main conference, tutorials, workshops, exhibits, demos, proceedings, video streaming/archive, and web descriptions. We want to cordially thank all those volunteers! Please have a look at the conference website to see their names (http://eccv2014.org/people/). We also thank our generous sponsors. You will see their logos around at several occasions during the week, and also prominently on the ECCV 2014 website (http://eccv2014.org/). Their support has been vital to keep prices low and to enrich the program. And it is good to see such level of industrial interest in what our community is doing!

Please do not forget to take advantage of your free travel pass. It allows you to crisscross our splendid city with its fabulous public transportation.

We hope you will enjoy ECCV 2014 to the full.

Also, willkommen in Zürich!

September 2014

Marc Pollefeys
Luc Van Gool

Preface

Welcome to the Workshop proceedings of the 13th European Conference on Computer Vision, held during September 6–12, 2014 in Zurich, Switzerland. We are delighted that the main ECCV 2014 was accompanied by 28 workshops.

We received 38 workshop proposals on diverse computer vision topics. The evaluation process was not easy because of the high quality of the submissions, and the final 28 selected workshops complemented the main conference program. Nearly all of the workshops were running for a full day, with the exception of two half-day workshops and one two-day workshop. In the end, the addressed workshop topics constituted a good mix between novel current trends and traditional issues, without forgetting to address the fundamentals of the computational vision area.

We would like to thank all the Workshop Organizers for their hard work and for making the workshop sessions a great success. We hope that participants enjoyed the workshops, together with the associated papers included in these volumes.

Kind regards / mit freundlichen Grüßen,

November 2014

Michael M. Bronstein
Lourdes Agapito
Carsten Rother

Organization

General Chairs

Luc Van Gool   ETH Zurich, Switzerland
Marc Pollefeys   ETH Zurich, Switzerland

Program Chairs

Tinne Tuytelaars   Katholieke Universiteit Leuven, Belgium
Bernt Schiele   MPI Informatics, Saarbrücken, Germany
Tomas Pajdla   Czech Technical University Prague,
                                 Czech Republic
David Fleet   University of Toronto, Canada

Local Arrangement Chairs

Konrad Schindler   ETH Zurich, Switzerland
Vittorio Ferrari   University of Edinburgh, UK

Workshop Chairs

Lourdes Agapito   University College London, UK
Carsten Rother   Technische Universität Dresden, Germany
Michael M. Bronstein   University of Lugano, Switzerland

Tutorial Chairs

Bastian Leibe   RWTH Aachen, Germany
Paolo Favaro   University of Bern, Switzerland
Christoph H. Lampert   IST, Austria

Poster Chair

Helmut Grabner   ETH Zurich, Switzerland

Publication Chairs

Mario Fritz   MPI Informatics, Saarbrücken, Germany
Michael Stark   MPI Informatics, Saarbrücken, Germany

Demo Chairs

Davide Scaramuzza   University of Zurich, Switzerland
Jan-Michael Frahm   University of North Carolina at Chapel Hill, USA

Exhibition Chair

Tamar Tolcachier   University of Zurich, Switzerland

Industrial Liason Chairs

Alexander Sorkine-Hornung   Disney Research Zurich, Switzerland
Fatih Porikli   ANU, Australia

Student Grant Chair

Seon Joo Kim   Yonsei University, Korea

Air Shelters Accommodation Chair

Maros Blaha   ETH Zurich, Switzerland

Website Chairs

Lorenz Meier   ETH Zurich, Switzerland
Bastien Jacquet   ETH Zurich, Switzerland

Internet Chair

Thorsten Steenbock   ETH Zurich, Switzerland

Student Volunteer Chairs

Andrea Cohen   ETH Zurich, Switzerland
Ralf Dragon   ETH Zurich, Switzerland
Laura Leal-Taixé   ETH Zurich, Switzerland

Finance Chair

Amael Delaunoy   ETH Zurich, Switzerland

Conference Coordinator

Susanne H. Keller   ETH Zurich, Switzerland

Workshop Organizers

W01 - Where Computer Vision Meets Art (VISART)

Gustavo Carneiro   The University of Adelaide, Australia
Alessio Del Bue   Italian Institute of Technology, Italy
Joao Paulo Costeira   Instituto Superior Tecnico, Lisbon, Portugal

W02 - Computer Vision in Vehicle Technology with Special Session on Micro Aerial Vehicles

David Geronimo   KTH, Sweden
Friedrich Fraundorfer   Technische Universität München
Davide Scaramuzza   University of Zurich, Switzerland

W03 - Spontaneous Facial Behavior Analysis

Guoying Zhao   University of Oulu, Finland
Stefanos Zafeiriou   Imperial College London, UK
Matti Pietikäinen   University of Oulu, Finland
Maja Pantic   Imperial College London, UK

W04 - Consumer Depth Cameras for Computer Vision

Andrea Fossati   ETH Zurich, Switzerland
Jürgen Gall   University of Bonn, Germany
Miles Hansard   Queen Mary University London, UK

W05 - ChaLearn Looking at People: Pose Recovery, Action/Interaction, Gesture Recognition

Sergio Escalera   Computer Vision Center, UAB and University
                                     of Barcelona, Catalonia, Spain
Jordi González   Universitat Autònoma de Barcelona and Computer
                                     Vision Center, Catalonia, Spain
Xavier Baró   Universitat Oberta de Catalunya and Computer
                                     Vision Center, Catalonia, Spain
Isabelle Guyon   Clopinet, Berkeley, California, USA
Jamie Shotton   Microsoft Research Cambridge, UK

W06 - Video Event Categorization, Tagging, and Retrieval toward Big Data

Thomas S. Huang	University of Illinois at Urbana-Champaign, USA
Tieniu Tan	Chinese Academy of Sciences, China
Yun Raymond Fu	Northeastern University, Boston, USA
Ling Shao	University of Sheffield, UK
Jianguo Zhang	University of Dundee, UK
Liang Wang	Chinese Academy of Sciences, China

W07 - Computer Vision with Local Binary Patterns Variants

Abdenour Hadid	University of Oulu, Finland
Stan Z. Li	Chinese Academy of Sciences, China
Jean-Luc Dugelay	Eurecom, France

W08 - Reconstruction Meets Recognition Challenge (RMRC)

Nathan Silberman	New York University, USA
Raquel Urtasun	University of Toronto, Canada
Andreas Geiger	MPI Intelligent Systems, Germany
Derek Hoiem	University of Illinois at Urbana-Champaign, USA
Sanja Fidler	University of Toronto, Canada
Antonio Torralba	Massachusetts Institute of Technology, USA
Rob Fergus	New York University, USA
Philip Lenz	Karlsruher Institut für Technologie, Germany
Jianxiong Xiao	Princeton, USA

W09 - Visual Object Tracking Challenge

Roman Pflugfelder	Austrian Institute of Technology, Austria
Matej Kristan	University of Ljubljana, Slovenia
Ales Leonardis	University of Birmingham, UK
Jiri Matas	Czech Technical University in Prague, Czech Republic

W10 - Computer Vision + ONTology Applied Cross-disciplinary Technologies (CONTACT)

Marco Cristani	University of Verona, Italy
Robert Ferrario	ISTC-CNR, Trento, Italy
Jason Corso	SUNY Buffalo, USA

W11 - Visual Perception of Affordances and Functional Visual Primitives for Scene Analysis

Karthik Mahesh Varadarajan   Technical University of Vienna, Austria
Alireza Fathi   Stanford University, USA
Jürgen Gall   University of Bon, Germany
Markus Vincze   Technical University of Vienna, Austria

W12 - Graphical Models in Computer Vision

Michael Yang   Leibniz University Hannover, Germany
Qinfeng (Javen) Shi   University of Adelaide, Australia
Sebastian Nowozin   Microsoft Research Cambridge, UK

W13 - Human-Machine Communication for Visual Recognition and Search

Adriana Kovashka   University of Texas at Austin, USA
Kristen Grauman   University of Texas at Austin, USA
Devi Parikh   Virginia Tech, USA

W14 - Light Fields for Computer Vision

Jingyi Yu   University of Delaware, USA
Bastian Goldluecke   Heidelberg University, Germany
Rick Szeliski   Microsoft Research, USA

W15 - Computer Vision for Road Scene Understanding and Autonomous Driving

Bart Nabbe   Toyota, USA
Raquel Urtasun   University of Toronto, Canada
Matthieu Salzman   NICTA, Australia
Lars Petersson   NICTA, Australia
Jose Alvarez   NICTA, Australia
Fatih Porikli   NICTA, Australia
Gary Overett   NICTA, Australia
Nick Barnes   NICTA, Australia

W16 - Soft Biometrics

Abdenour Hadid   University of Oulu, Finland
Paulo Lobato Correia   University of Lisbon, Portugal
Thomas Moeslund   Aalborg University, Denmark

W17 - THUMOS Challenge: Action Recognition with a Large Number of Classes

Jingen Liu	SRI International, USA
Yu-Gang Jiang	Fudan University, China
Amir Roshan Zamir	UCF, USA
George Toderici	Google, USA
Ivan Laptev	Inria, France
Mubarak Shah	UCF, USA
Rahul Sukthankar	Google Research, USA

W18 - Transferring and Adapting Source Knowledge (TASK) in Computer Vision (CV)

Antonio M. Lopez	Computer Vision Center and Universitat Autónoma de Barcelona, Spain
Kate Saenko	University of Massachusetts Lowell, USA
Francesco Orabona	Toyota Technological Institute Chicago, USA
José Antonio Rodríguez	Xerox Research EuroFrance
David Vázquez	Computer Vision Cente, Spain
Sebastian Ramos	Computer Vision Center and Universitat Autónoma de Barcelona, Spain
Jiaolong Xu	Computer Vision Center and Universitat Autónoma de Barcelona, Spain

W19 - Visual Surveillance and Re-identification

Shaogang Gong	Queen Mary University of London, UK
Steve Maybank	Birkbeck College, University of London, UK
James Orwell	Kingston University, UK
Marco Cristani	University of Verona, Italy
Kaiqi Huang	National Laboratory of Pattern Recognition, China
Shuicheng Yan	National University of Singapore, Singapore

W20 - Color and Photometry in Computer Vision

Theo Gevers	University of Amsterdam, The Netherlands
Arjan Gijsenij	Akzo Nobel, The Netherlands
Todd Zickler	Harvard University, USA
Jose M. Alvarez	NICTA, Australia

W21 - Storytelling with Images and Videos

Gunhee Kim	Disney Research, USA
Leonid Sigal	Disney, USA
Kristen Grauman	University of Texas at Austin, USA
Tamara Berg	University of North Carolina at Chapel Hill, USA

W22 - Assistive Computer Vision and Robotics

Giovanni Maria Farinella	University of Catania, Italy
Marco Leo	CNR- Institute of Optics, Italy
Gerard Medioni	USC, USA
Mohan Triverdi	UCSD, USA

W23 - Computer Vision Problems in Plant Phenotyping

Hanno Scharr	Forschungszentrum Jülich, Germany
Sotirios Tsaftaris	IMT Lucca, Italy

W24 - Human Behavior Understanding

Albert Ali Salah	Boğaziçi University, Turkey
Louis-Philippe Morency	University of Southern California, USA
Rita Cucchiara	University of Modena and Reggio Emilia, Italy

W25 - ImageNet Large-Scale Visual Recognition Challenge (ILSVRC2014)

Olga Russakovsky	Stanford University, USA
Jon Krause	Stanford University, USA
Jia Deng	University of Michigan, USA
Alex Berg	University of North Carolina at Chapel Hill, USA
Fei-Fei Li	Stanford University, USA

W26 - Non-Rigid Shape Analysis and Deformable Image Alignment

Alex Bronstein	Tel-Aviv University, Israel
Umberto Castellani	University of Verona, Italy
Maks Ovsjanikov	Ecole Polytechnique, France

W27 - Video Segmentation

Fabio Galasso	MPI Informatics Saarbrücken, Germany
Thomas Brox	University of Freiburg, Germany
Fuxin Li	Georgia Institute of Technology, Germany
James M. Rehg	Georgia Institute of Technology, USA
Bernt Schiele	MPI Informatics Saarbrücken, Germany

W28 - Parts and Attributes

Rogerio S. Feris	IBM, USA
Christoph H. Lampert	IST, Austria
Devi Parikh	Virginia Tech, USA

Contents – Part III

W20 - Color and Photometry in Computer Vision

W22 - Assistive Computer Vision and Robotics (ACVR)

W18 - Transferring and Adapting Source Knowledge (TASK) in Computer Vision (CV)

Automatic Expansion of a Food Image Dataset Leveraging Existing Categories with Domain Adaptation

Yoshiyuki Kawano and Keiji Yanai[✉]

Department of Informatics, The University of Electro-Communications,
1-5-1 Chofugaoka, Chofu-shi, Tokyo 182-8585, Japan
{kawano-y,yanai}@mm.inf.uec.ac.jp

Abstract. In this paper, we propose a novel effective framework to expand an existing image dataset automatically leveraging existing categories and crowdsourcing. Especially, in this paper, we focus on expansion on food image data set. The number of food categories is uncountable, since foods are different from a place to a place. If we have a Japanese food dataset, it does not help build a French food recognition system directly. That is why food data sets for different food cultures have been built independently so far. Then, in this paper, we propose to leverage existing knowledge on food of other cultures by a generic "foodness" classifier and domain adaptation. This can enable us not only to built other-cultured food datasets based on an original food image dataset automatically, but also to save as much crowd-sourcing costs as possible. In the experiments, we show the effectiveness of the proposed method over the baselines.

Keywords: Dataset expansion · Food image · Foodness · Domain adaptation · Crowd-sourcing · Adaptive SVM

1 Introduction

Recently, needs for food image recognition become larger, since food habit recording services for smartphones are spreading widely for everyday health care. For food habit recording, conventional ways such as inputing food names by texts or selecting food items from menus are very tedious, which sometimes prevent users from using such systems regularly. Then, several works on food recognition have been proposed so far [1–5] to make it easy to use food habit recording. In these works, the number of food categories is 100 at most, which is not enough for practical use. In fact, all of the foods we eat in our everyday life cannot be covered with only one hundred food categories, and the number of foods which can be recognized should be increased much more.

On the other hand, in these years, large-scale image classification is paid attention, and many methods for that have been proposed recently [6–9]. Due to these works, the number of categories to be recognized have been increased

© Springer International Publishing Switzerland 2015
L. Agapito et al. (Eds.): ECCV 2014 Workshops, Part III, LNCS 8927, pp. 3–17, 2015.
DOI: 10.1007/978-3-319-16199-0_1

up to 1000. For example, in ImageNet Large Scale Visual Recognition Challenge (ILSVRC), the number of categories to be classified is 1000. The data set for ImageNet Challenge is a subset of ImageNet [10], which is known as the largest visual database where the number of categories are more than 20,000. Large-scale image data sets such as ImageNet cannot be created by researchers by themselves. Most of them use crowd-sourcing Web services such as Amazon Mechanical Turk to build them semi-automatically.

In this paper, we propose a novel framework to expand an existing image dataset automatically leveraging existing categories. Especially, in this paper, we focus on expansion on food image data set.

While ImageNet covers comprehensive concepts, our target is restricted to foods. In ImageNet, annotation of each concept is gathered independently. On the other hand, since foods look more similar to each other, visual knowledge on foods of a certain country is expected to help collect annotations of food photos of the other countries. Then, in this paper, we propose a novel effective framework which utilizes knowledge on food of other countries by domain adaptation.

Basically, we gather food image candidates on novel food categories from the Web, and select good photos and add bounding boxes by using crowd-sourcing. In general, raw Web images include many noise images which are irrelevant to a given keyword. Especially, in this work, non-food images can be regarded as noise images. To exclude them from the gather images, we filter and re-rank Web images related to a given food category by using visual knowledge extracted from the existing food dataset.

Firstly, we built a generic "foodness" classifier from a Japanese food data set, UEC-Food100 [4]. We cluster all the food categories in the exist food image set into several food groups the member of which are similar to each other in terms of image feature vectors, and we train SVMs regarding each food group independently. Then, we evaluate unknown images using the trained SVMs on the food groups, and regards the maximum value of the output values of all the SVM as the "foodness" value of the given image. We can decide if a given image of a unknown category is a food photo or not based on the "foodness" value. In addition, because we select the maximum value from all the output valued of food groups, we estimate the most related food group to a given photo.

After "foodness" filtering, we obtain a food photo set. However, it might include food photos irrelevant to the given food keyword. Secondly, we select and re-rank more relevant images from the images judged as food photos by using transfer learning with visually similar categories in the source food photo data set. As a method of transfer learning, we use Adaptive SVM (A-SVM) [11] which can learn a discriminative hyper-plane in the target domain taking into account source-domain training data. In this work, the labeled data of the source categories which are visually similar to the target food photos are used as source-domain training data. As an initial target-domain training data, we use upper-ranked photos by a unsupervised image ranking method, VisualRank (VR) [12]. Then, we select food candidate images to be submitted for the crowd-sourcing by applying a trained A-SVM. By the experiments, the precision of the food candidate photos by A-SVM has been proved to outperformed the results by only VisualRank and by normal standard SVM.

The contributions of this paper are as follows:

(1) Propose a novel framework to extend an existing image dataset with a generic "foodness" classifier and domain transfer learning.
(2) Three-step crowd-sourcing: selecting representative sample images, excluding noise photos, and drawing bounding boxes.
(3) Evaluate and compare accuracy of built food datasets and costs regarding the proposed method and two baselines.
(4) Apply the proposed framework in a large scale, and build a new 256-category food dataset based on the existing 100-category food dataset automatically.

2   Related Works

In the existing work on food recognition, the target foods are limited to the foods which are common in a certain country. For example, US food [1,3,13], Chinese food [2] and Japanese food [4,14]. From this observation, it is assumed that these food datasets were built to implementing food recognition systems the target of which are only the foods in the specific countries.

In addition, in the above-mentioned works, the number of target food categories is limited to 100 at most. From a practical point of view, 100 food categories is not enough for recognizing everyday foods for generic people. In fact, the number of foods we eat in our everyday life is much more than one hundred, and the number of foods which can be recognized should be increased much more.

Then, in this work, to make it easy to add the number of food categories and to implement food image recognition systems for other country foods or all the country foods, we propose a method to use an existing food dataset to build additional or another food dataset automatically by applying transfer learning.

On the Web, there are various kinds and huge amounts of images. It is very easy to collect images associated with a given keyword using Web API such as Bing Image Search API, Flickr API and Twitter API. However, raw Web images contain many noise images which are irrelevant to the given keyword. Therefore, many works on re-rank Web images regarding the given keyword have been proposed since ten years ago [15,16]. Most of these works employed object recognition methods to select relevant images to given keywords from "raw" images collected from the Web using Web image search engines.

After spreading Amazon Mechanical Turk (AMT) which is the world-largest crowd-sourcing Web platform, it is commonly used for a task to select relevant images. AMT enables us to build a very huge-scale image dataset such as ImageNet [10], to build a middle- or large-scale dataset with bounding boxes [17], and to add attributes to a large-scale dataset [18].

In some works, AMT was incorporated into object recognition procedures, which was called "humans in the loop". Vijayanarasimhan et al.[17] proposed to combine active learning of object detectors and AMT crowd-sourcing tasks to draw bounding boxes as a loop procedure to raise accuracy of object detection gradually. On the other hand, Branson et al.[19] proposed complementary use of AMT with object classifiers by giving AMT workers simple easy questions to tackle difficult fine-grained object classification.

In addition, thanks to crowd-sourcing, many kinds of image datasets have released such as "bird"[20], "aircraft"[21], and "flower"[22]. They are intended to be built for fine-grained visual categorization research.

In this work, we use AMT as a crowd-sourcing service to select relevant images and add bounding boxes to selected food images. The objective is similar to [17]. However, while Vijayanarasimhan et al.[17] collected relevant images and their bounding boxes on each category independently, we collect images using knowledge of the known categories in the existing database with a "foodness" classifier and transfer learning.

In addition, as a pre-step of image selection, we prepare a task to ask the best representative photos regarding the given category. Some small number of representative photos are used to be shown workers as example photos to raise the accuracy of the image selection step.

3   Proposed Method

In this paper, we propose a novel framework to expand an existing image dataset automatically. The proposed framework consists of two stages: (1) the image selection stage, and (2) the crowd-sourcing stage.

In the image selection stage, we collect images from the Web with the given category names, and filter out noise images using a "foodness" classifier and adaptive SVM [11], both of which we train using knowledge of the existing food image database.

Then, in the crowd-sourcing stage, we crowdsource three kinds of tasks. First one is selecting representative images for the given new food category, the second one is discriminating relevant images from noise ones, and the third one is drawing bounding boxes on each of the selected images.

The processing flow of the proposed framework is shown in Fig.1. Each of the processing steps is explained as follows:

(1) Collect target food images associated with the given new food category from the Web.
(2) Evaluate "foodness" on each of the collected images, and select only high "foodness" images.
(3) Rank the selected food images with VisualRank, and train adaptive SVMs(A-SVM) [11] with upper ranked images as pseudo positive samples.
(4) Evaluate collected images again by A-SVM.
(5) Crowdsource a task to select representative samples from the top 30 images in terms of A-SVM scores
(6) Crowdsource a task to discriminate relevant images from noise images for the images ranked higher by A-SVM
(7) Crowdsource a task to draw bounding boxes on the selected images.
(8) Add the annotated food images to a food image dataset.

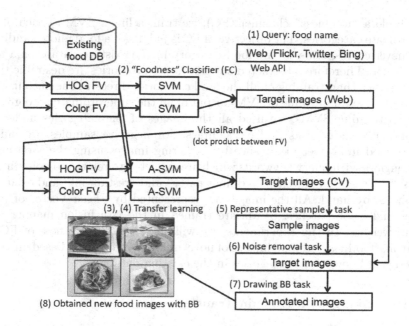

Fig. 1. Processing flow of the proposed framework

3.1 Foodness Classifier

We construct a "Foodness" Classifier (FC) for discriminating and evaluating food images. FC evaluates if the given image is a food photo or not. We use FC to remove noise images from the images gathered from the Web.

We construct a FC from the existing multi-class food image dataset. Regarding feature extraction and coding, we adopt the same way as our mobile food recognition system [14]. Firstly, we train linear SVMs [23] in the one-vs-rest strategy for each category of the existing multi-class food image dataset. As image features, we adopt HOG patches [24] and color patches. Regarding foods, rotation and scale invariance is not so important. We regard fast extraction as more important, since we originally use these features for mobile food recognition. Both descriptors are coded by Fisher Vector (FV) [9,25], and they are integrated in the late fusion manner. We perform multi-class image classification in the cross-validation using the trained liner SVMs, and we build a confusion matrix according to the classification results.

Secondly, we make some category groups based on confusion matrix of multi-class classification results. This is inspired by Bergamo et al.'s work [26]. They grouped a large number of categories into superordinate groups the member categories of which are confusing to each other recursively. In the same way, we perform confusion-matrix-based clustering for all the food categories. We intend to obtain superordinate categories such as meat, sandwiches, noodle and salad automatically.

To build a "foodness" classifier (FC), we train a linear SVM of each of the superordinate categories. The objective of FC is judging if a food photo candidate which never corresponds to any food category in the existing dataset is a food photo or not. Therefore, abstracted superordinate categories are desirable to be trained, rather than training of all the food categories directly. The output value of FC is the maximum value of SVM output of all the superordinate food groups.

When training SVMs, we used all the images of the categories under the superordinate category as positive samples. For negative samples, we built a negative food image set in advance by gathering images using the Web image search engines with query keywords which are expected to related to noise images such as "street stall", "kitchen", "dinner party" and "restaurant" and excluding food photos by hand. All the images are represented by Fisher Vector of HOG patches and color patches. SVMs are trained in the late fusion manner with uniform weights. In the experiments, we will show the effectiveness of FC for evaluating "foodness" of food images of novel unknown categories based on visual knowledge of known food categories in the existing database.

3.2   Re-ranking with Domain Transfer

After "foodness" filtering, most of the remaining images are food images. However, they might includes other kinds of foods than the given food category. Since the objective of the proposed framework is collecting food images of novel unknown categories. To filtering out other food images than the target food category, we adopt discriminative approach with pseudo-positive samples in the similar way as Schroff et al.[16], since we have no labeled samples on the given novel category initially.

To get pseudo-positive samples, we rank the remaining images by the VisualRank [12] method. In addition, we use adaptive SVM [11] to leverage visual knowledge of the existing food image database. Because VisualRank is a unsupervised method to rank images which have many visually similar images in the upper ranking, it is useful to select relevant images from a noisy image dataset. However, it has drawback to narrow diversity of images. To compensate it, we use a domain adaptation method to leverage the existing food image database for classifying novel unknown food images.

VisualRank. To select pseudo-positive images, we apply VisualRank [12] to the top N images in term of "foodness" scores. We set N as 300 in the experiments. For computing VisualRank scores, we obtained similarity matrix S as being dot product of Fisher Vectors (concatenated vectors of HOG FV and Color FV) instead of the number of matched local features. It has been proved that dot-product of FV can be regarded as a good similarity measure, and dot-product of L2-normalized vectors is equivalent to the cosine similarity [9,27]. In addition, according to the following equation, we normalize each element s of similarity matrix S so that $s_{normalized}$ varies within only $[0, 1]$ range, because the value of elements of FV can be negative.

$$s_{\text{normalized}} = \frac{s - s_{min}}{s_{max} - s_{min}} \qquad (1)$$

where s_{max} and s_{min} are maximum and minimum values among all the elements of similarity matrix S. Next, we column-normalized S for computation of Visual-Rank. Regarding a bias vector v, we assign only the top m images with uniform weights in the same way as [12]. We set m as 100 in the experiments. Note that, we use the same Gaussian Mixture Model(GMM)s for FV coding estimated in the the previous step. This mean that the descriptors of unknown category are not modeled independently.

We calculate VisualRank score r in the following equation:

$$r = \alpha * Sr + (1 - \alpha) * v, \qquad (2)$$

where α is a damping factor where we set it to 0.85 according to [12].

Selection of Source Domain Samples and Target Domain Samples. To train and apply adaptive SVM [11], we need to prepare source-domain labeled samples as well as target-domain labeled samples. Because for both domains we need to prepare positive and negative samples, totally we prepare four kinds of samples for training of A-SVM.

As target-domain positive samples, we use the top M images in terms of the VisualRank scores, while as target-domain negative samples, we use the images with lower "foodness" scores in the initial image set gathered from the Web. In the experiments, we selected at most 300 images the "foodness" score of which were less than -0.6. Because the objective of this A-SVM-based re-ranking step is excluding noise images from the initial image set, not classifying generic images into one of food categories, we use negative samples which are peculiar to the given food category.

As source-domain positive samples, we use all the samples in the most related food group to the given new food category. As mentioned in the previous subsection, a "foodness" classifier can estimate the most related food group as well as a "foodness" score. We select the most frequent food group among the top 100 "foodness" images in the initial image set as the most related food group to the given new food category. As source-domain negative sample, we use the same negative food image set used in the previous step of a "foodness" classifier.

In the next step, we select positive samples to exclude noise images, and select effective negative samples for training. Regarding source-domain samples, in general, the distribution of source-domain samples are wider than one of target-domain samples. Regarding target-domain samples, they are unreliable and tend to include outliers, since target-domain samples are selected automatically by a "foodness" classifier and VisualRank. Then we select the samples which are closed to target-domain samples as source-domain samples, and the samples which are closed to other target-domain samples as target-domain samples according to the following heuristics:

- Select the target-domain positive samples each of which has more than 3 positive samples among the nearest 5 samples over the space of all the target-domain (positive and negative) samples.
- Select the target-domain negative samples each of which has 5 negative samples among the nearest 5 samples over the target-domain space.
- Select the source-domain positive samples which are included in the union set of 7 closest source-domain all (positive and negative) samples to each of the selected target-domain positive samples.
- Select the source-domain negative samples which are included in the union set of 7 closest source-domain all samples to each of the selected target-domain positive samples.

This process is called "Sample Selection (SS)" in the section on experiments.

After source/target-domain positive/negative samples are selected finally, we train the adaptive SVM, and apply the trained model to re-rank the images in the image set after filtering by the "foodness" classifier. We use only higher-ranked images for crowd-sourcing tasks.

3.3   Crowd-Sourcing

The final objective is obtaining a novel food image dataset with bounding boxes. In the previous steps, we applied "foodness" filtering and adaptive SVM re-ranking. However, the obtained food imageset is not perfect, and has no bounding box information. As the final steps, we crowdsource the following three kinds of tasks: (1) selecting representative sample images, (2) removing irrelevant images, and (3) drawing bounding boxes. As a crowd-sourcing service, we use Amazon Mechanical Turk (AMT).

Representative Image Selection Task. We assumes that AMT workers do not have knowledge about various kinds of foods. Therefore, it cannot be expected to obtain highly accurate results without any preparations. Then, we prepare a task to select representative sample images as a pre-process step.

In this task, we ask AMT workers to select less than 10 representative images to the given food category from the top 30 image of A-SVM output scores, after studying about the given food category by visiting Wikipedia, Google Web search and Google Web image search with the name of the given food category as a query word. We design the task page so that AMT workers cannot submit the results without clicking the Web links to Wikipedia and Google sites. After collecting results from 5 workers, we select the top 5 or 7 images as representative samples based on the number of votes by the workers. In the experiments, we set one HIT (Human Intelligence Task, which is a task unit in AMT.) of this task as 0.06$.

Noise Removal Task. In this task, we ask AMT workers to annotate if the shown images are relevant to the given food category or not. In the task page, we show the representation images selected in the previous task. We believe this will be helpful for works who have never seen the target food. In one HIT, we use randomly-selected 25 images in the higher rank of the A-SVM scores. To prevent irresponsible worker, if there are more than four unchecked images, the result cannot be submitted. The results will be combined based on the majority voting. In the experiments, we requested each HIT for 5 workers. We set 1 HIT as 0.03$.

Drawing Bounding Box Task. As the final task, we ask AMT workers to draw bounding boxes on the selected food images until the previous step. One HIT contains ten image annotation. In this step, worker can still mark irrelevant images as "noise" in the same way as the noise removal task, if they discover. After obtaining the results, we combine them by averaging the position of bounding boxes excluding images with no bounding boxes and too small bounding boxes. We add the finally selected images with bounding box to a new food image database as a ground-truth data. In the experiments, we requested each HIT for 4 workers. We set one HIT as 0.05$.

4 Experiments

In this section, we perform the following three experiments to evaluate the effectiveness of the proposed method.

- Performance comparison on food image filtering by a "foodness" classifier and adaptive SVM to leverage knowledge of the existing food dataset
- Evaluation of the final results after crowd-sourcing and analysis of crowdsourcing cost.

Before evaluation, we describe a dataset, feature representation and initial food image collection from the Web. As an existing food dataset, we use "UEC-Food100" dataset [4] which consists 14361 food photos. Its number of food categories is 100, most of which are Japanese food categories. When building a "foodness" classifier (FC), we clustered 100 food categories into 13 food groups based on confusion matrix as shown in Tab.1. Note that the type of food groups in the table are named by hand for explanation.

As feature representation, we used 32-dim HOG local patches (8 orientations, 2x2) and 24-dim color local patches (mean and variance of RGB, 2x2) both of which are densely sampled from an image at difference 2 scales. After applying PCA, local descriptors are coded into Fisher Vector with GMM codebook (k=64) and a level-1 spatial pyramid (SPM) [28]. The GMM was estimated from the existing food dataset in advance.

Regarding initial food image collection from Web, we collected food images via Flickr API, Twitter API and Bing Image Search API based on query words associated with the given food category. We collected more than 600 images for each category. As query words, we used the words of both local language and English. We excluded duplicated URLs using a URL hash table after putting together all the image URLs gathered from three different APIs.

Table 1. 13 food groups and their member foods

type of food group	food categories
noodles	udon nooles, dipping noodles, ramen
yellow color	omlet, potage, steamed egg hotchpotch
soup	miso soup, pork miso soup, Japaneses tofu and vegetable chowder
fried	takoyaki, Japaneses-style pancake, fried noodle
deep fried	croquette, sirloin cutlet, fried chicken
salad	green salad, macaroni salad, macaroni salad
bread	sandwiches, raisin bread, roll bread
seafood	sashimi, sashimi bowl, sushi
rice	rice, pilaf, fried rice
fish	grilled salmon, grilled pacific saury, dried fish
boiled	seasoned beef with potatoes
and	simmered ganmodoki
seasoned	seasoned beef with potatoes
sauteed	sauteed vegetables, go-ya chanpuru, kinpira-style sauteed burdock
sauce	stew, curry, stir-fried shrimp in chili sauce

4.1   Evaluation on Image Filtering Results

For evaluation, we collected 35 categories of food image sets including 5 country foods with 7 categories for each country. All the 35 categories do not overlap with the categories in "UEC-FOOD100". We evaluated the precision of the top 300 food images (Precision@300) for each category. Note that we regarded badly-conditioned food images as being irrelevant. For example, an image with very small food region and an image in which only small portion of original food region is visible are not relevant.

We compare Precision@300 after filtering by the following six methods: (1) VisualRank with Fisher Vector, (2) "foodness" classifier (FC), (3) normal SVM using only target-domain training samples without "Sample Selection (SS)" after FC filtering (4) normal SVM using only target-domain training samples with SS after FC filtering (5) adaptive SVM using both source/target-domain training samples without SS after FC filtering, and (6) adaptive SVM using both source/target-domain training samples with SS after FC filtering. The last method (FC + A-SVM(SS)) corresponds to the proposed methods. Note that "Sample Selection (SS)" means the step to select of training samples for A-SVM or SVM (see Sec. 3.2), and VisualRank is still used for positive sample selection in (4)(5)(6)(7).

Tab.2 shows average Precision@300 of the results after filtering by each of the seven methods over 5 country foods and all 35 kinds of foods. Overall, the proposed methods outperformed other six baseline methods for all the regional foods.

Compared between VR and other supervised methods, the precision value by unsupervised VisualRank is not so good as the results by supervised discriminative classifiers such as FC and FC+A-SVM. In fact, FC improved Precision by about 20.0 points compared to VisualRank. This indicates that using

Table 2. Precision@300 of the food images ranked by six methods. The bottom method† is the proposed methods.

no	Method	American	Japanese	Chinese	Thai	Indonesian	Average
(1)	VisualRank(VR)	58.47	54.95	60.66	62.19	58.71	59.00
(2)	"Foodness" (FC)	78.00	75.33	77.61	82.85	78.61	78.48
(3)	FC + SVM	84.52	82.90	84.80	88.80	81.95	84.60
(4)	FC + SVM(SS)	85.57	83.38	85.09	89.23	82.23	85.10
(5)	FC + A-SVM	86.95	85.71	86.19	89.66	82.71	86.24
(6)	FC + A-SVM(SS)†	**89.61**	**87.76**	**87.76**	**91.38**	**84.09**	**88.12**

Table 3. Precision@200 of "pseudo-positive samples" which is provided to SVM or A-SVM as positive target samples

no	Method	American	Japanese	Chinese	Thai	Indonesian	Average
(A)	only FC	79.21	77.00	80.21	83.78	83.00	80.64
(B)	FC+VR	85.00	83.78	85.78	89.14	86.21	85.98

existing categories helps improve filtering accuracy much, although they are different from the newly collected categories.

To use supervised methods such as SVM and A-SVM, we selected pseudo-positive samples from the top 300 images ranked by FC with Visual Rank(VR), and we used the top 200 images ranked by VR as pseudo-positive samples in the after steps. Tab. 3 shows the precision at the top 200 images before and after applying VR. Compared with two results, Precision@200 was improved by 5.34 points, which shows the effectiveness of applying VR after FC.

In case of FC+SVM, we used only target-domain training samples where positive samples are selected by VisualRank from the unlabeled samples, and manually-constructed common negative samples are used as negative samples. Although FC+SVM employs supervised SVM, the step itself is unsupervised because positive samples are "pseudo-positive" samples collected automatically. Even without supervision, FC+SVM improved by about 6 points compared to FC in terms of Precision@300. After adding training sample selection (SS) for SVM, the Precision was slightly improved.

FC+A-SVM and FC+A-SVM(SS) introduced a transfer learning method, adaptive SVM, which takes into account source-domain training samples as well. From their results, introducing domain transfer helps improve accuracy of image filtering, and the proposed method (FC+A-SVM(SS)) has achieved the best result, which proves the effectiveness of the proposed method.

Fig.2 shows the top 3 food categories in terms of Precision@300 among all the 35 categories, "mango pudding", "loco moco" and "fried shrimp with shell" in the left column, and three source-domain samples in the corresponding food groups. The images in each food group are used as source-domain positive samples when training adaptive SVM. The target-domain images looks similar to source-domain images in terms of color, shape or ingredients. All the foods in the first row in the figure are light-yellow, the foods in the second row have brown-colored source, and the foods in the bottom row have fried ingredients.

mango
pudding

omlet

potage

steamed egg
hotchpotch

loco moco

curry

stew

egg sunny-side
up

salt pepper
fried shrimp
with shell

fried shrimp

fried chicken

croquette

Fig. 2. The target-domain food images in the left column, and three source-domain samples in the most related food groups

Table 4. Evaluation by workers on representative samples images (%)

	useful	so so	useless
noise removal task	89.59%	7.90%	2.52 %
drawing bounding box task	91.68%	7.02%	1.31 %

From these results, the new category images can be classified with visually similar images of the existing categories in the most related food group by using transfer learning. This is a part of the contributions of this work.

4.2 Evaluation Accuracy and Costs of Crowdsourcing

We evaluate the effectiveness of showing representative samples to workers, accuracy of obtained image sets and crowdsourcing costs.

Workers' Evaluation on Representative Samples. We prepared a task to select representative sample images as a pre-process step. Selected representation images were shown in the page of noise removal task and drawing bounding box task in order to teach workers what relevant food photos look like. To evaluate its effectiveness, we asked workers in each HIT if sample images shown in the HIT page are useful, so so or useless. As a result, 3495 and 5359 answers are obtained in noise removal task and annotation bounding box task. Tab.4 shows the ratio of each answer, which shows the effectiveness of showing representative samples in both noise removal task and annotation bounding box task.

Evaluation of Accuracy and Costs. To evaluate accuracy and costs including crowdsourcing, we constructed three kinds of datasets by the following different combination of filtering steps: (1) FC + drawing bounding box task (BB task), (2) FC + A-SVM(SS) + BB task, and (3) FC + A-SVM(SS) + noise removal

Table 5. Precision of food images on dataset by difference 3 methods

	precision	gain
FC + BB task	91.10	-
FC + A-SVM + BB task	94.19	+3.09
FC + A-SVM + NR task + BB task	97.83	+3.64

Table 6. Recovery ratio(%) and costs($) to get annotated 100 images

	noise removal		bounding box		total
	recovery ratio	cost	recovery ratio	cost	total
FC + BB task	-	-	64.2	3.11	3.11
FC + A-SVM + BB task	-	-	74.7	2.68	2.68
FC + A-SVM + NR task + BB task	80.9	0.74	86.7	2.31	3.16

task (NR task) + BB task. In case of (1) and (2), workers have to mark irrelevant images as "noise" in addition to drawing bounding boxes to relevant images in the BB task, because the noise removal task is not included. The combination (1) is the simplest, and in (2) adaptive SVM was added. The last combination where noise removal task is prepared as an independent task is equivalent to the proposed framework. Note that all the combination includes representative sample selection task.

Tab.5 shows the precision of food images on the constructed dataset after crowsourcing by each combination. The precision by "FC+BB task" was 91.1%, while the precision by "FC+A-SVM(SS)+BB task" was 94.19%. Introducing A-SVM(SS) improved 3.09%, while it improved about 10% regarding the precision of filtered image sets before crowdsoucing. Although both combinations employs human annotation via crowdsourcing, the difference in precision appeared after crowdsourcing. This is estimated to come from the accuracy of dataset to supply workers. From this observation, to get more accurate results from crowdsourcing, more accurate data should be provided to crowdsourcing workers.

Compared between "FC+A-SVM(SS)+BB task" and "FC+A-SVM(SS)+NR task+BB task", separating noise removal task from drawing bounding box improved the precision, although provided datasets are the same. This indicates that crowdsourcing tasks (HITs) should be include only one kinds of jobs. Of course, increase of the number of crowdsourcing steps means increase of economical costs. We compare costs among the three cases in the next.

Tab.6 shows the recovery ratio and cost for the three combinations. The recovery ratio means the ratio of the number of the images which were finally annotated with correct bounding boxes over the number of provided images to workers for crowdsourced annotation. If the recovery ratio is low, many irrelevant samples are provided to workers, which means economical costs increase. "Costs" shown in the table means the money ($) paid for AMT to get 100 annotated images. To avoid wasting money, the recovery rate should be high, hopefully close to 100%.

"FC+BB task" was apparently a bad strategy, because the total cost is high and the accuracy of the obtained results shown in Tab.5 is worst. "FC+A-SVM+BB" performed the best among the three strategies in terms of cost. Adding the noise removal task, the cost increased, because the number of crowdsourcing steps also increased. However, the precision of the final obtained results was the best as shown in Tab.5. That shows that there is a trade-off between cost and accuracy. It depends on the policy when building a dataset. Of course, Tab.6 shows just one case. If a unit price for HIT of each task is changed, the result of cost analysis will be changed. Regarding cost, more accurate data should be provided to crowdsourcing workers to raise the recovery rate. To do that, introducing "foodness" classifier and adaptive SVM is very effective.

5   Conclusions

In this paper, we proposed a novel framework to expand an existing image dataset automatically employing generic classifiers and domain adaptation to leverage visual knowledge in the existing dataset. Especially, in this paper, we focused on expansion on food image data set. In the experiments, we showed the effectiveness of the proposed method over baselines in terms of the proposed image filtering methods and the proposed procedure for crowdsourcing.

For future work, we will make further analysis on the difference between a hand-collected food image dataset and an automatically collected dataset by the proposed framework. In addition, we plan to extend the framework to other categories than foods such as clothes and animal.

We have released a new large-scale food photo dataset, UEC-FOOD 256, collected by the proposed framework at http://foodcam.mobi/dataset/. It includes 256 kinds of foods from various countries such as French, Italian, US, Chinese, Thai, Vietnamese, Japanese and Indonesia.

References

1. Yang, S., Chen, M., Pomerleau, D., Sukthankar, R.: Food recognition using statistics of pairwise local features. In: CVPR (2010)
2. Chen, M., Yang, Y., Ho, C., Wang, S., Liu, S., Chang, E., Yeh, C., Ouhyoung, M.: Automatic chinese food identification and quantity estimation. In: SIGGRAPH Asia 2012 Technical Briefs (2012)
3. Bosch, M., Zhu, F., Khanna, N., Boushey, C.J., Delp, E.J.: Combining global and local features for food identification in dietary assessment. In: ICIP (2011)
4. Matsuda, Y., Yanai, K.: Multiple-food recognition considering co-occurrence employing manifold ranking. In: ICPR (2012)
5. Kawano, Y., Yanai, K.: Real-time mobile food recognition system. In: Proc. of IEEE CVPR International Workshop on Mobile Vision (IWMV) (2013)
6. Vedaldi, A., Zisserman, A.: Efficient additive kernels via explicit feature maps. IEEE Trans. on PAMI 34(3), 480–492 (2012)
7. Wang, J., Yang, J., Yu, K., Lv, F., Huang, T., Gong, Y.: Locality-constrained linear coding for image classification. In: CVPR, pp. 3360–3367 (2010)

8. Zhou, X., Yu, K., Zhang, T., Huang, T.S.: Image classification using super-vector coding of local image descriptors. In: Daniilidis, K., Maragos, P., Paragios, N. (eds.) ECCV 2010, Part V. LNCS, vol. 6315, pp. 141–154. Springer, Heidelberg (2010)
9. Perronnin, F., Sánchez, J., Mensink, T.: Improving the fisher kernel for large-scale image classification. In: Daniilidis, K., Maragos, P., Paragios, N. (eds.) ECCV 2010, Part IV. LNCS, vol. 6314, pp. 143–156. Springer, Heidelberg (2010)
10. Deng, J., Dong, W., Socher, R., Li, L.J., Li, K., Fei-Fei, L.: ImageNet: a large-scale hierarchical image database. In: CVPR (2009)
11. Yang, J., Yan, R., Hauptmann, A.G.: Cross-domain video concept detection using adaptive svms. In: ACM MM (2007)
12. Jing, Y., Baluja, S.: Visualrank: Applying pagerank to large-scale image search. IEEE Trans. on PAMI (2008)
13. Chen, M., Dhingra, K., Wu, W., Yang, L., Sukthankar, R., Yang, J.: PFID: Pittsburgh fast-food image dataset. In: ICIP, pp. 289–292 (2009)
14. Kawano, Y., Yanai, K.: Rapid mobile food recognition using fisher vector. In: ACPR (2013)
15. Yanai, K., Barnard, K.: Probabilistic web image gathering. In: ACM SIGMM WS Multimedia Information Retrieval, pp. 57–64 (2005)
16. Schroff, F., Criminisi, A., Zisserman, A.: Harvesting image databases from the web. In: ICCV (2007)
17. Vijayanarasimhan, S., Grauman, K.: Large-scale live active learning: training object detectors with crawled data and crowds. In: CVPR, pp. 1449–1456 (2011)
18. Patterson, G., Hays, J.: Sun attribute database: discovering, annotating, and recognizing scene attributes. In: CVPR, pp. 2751–2758 (2012)
19. Branson, S., Wah, C., Schroff, F., Babenko, B., Welinder, P., Perona, P., Belongie, S.: Visual recognition with humans in the loop. In: Daniilidis, K., Maragos, P., Paragios, N. (eds.) Computer Vision - ECCV 2010, vol. 6314, pp. 438–451. Springer, Heidelberg (2010)
20. Welinder, P., Branson, S., Mita, T., Wah, C., Schroff, F., Belongie, S., Perona, P.: Caltech-ucsd birds 200. Technical report, California Institute of Technology (2010)
21. Maji, S., Kannala, J., Rahtu, E., Blaschko, M., Vedaldi, A.: Fine-grained visual classification of aircraft. Technical report, arXiv (2013)
22. : Oxford flower 102. http://www.robots.ox.ac.uk/~vgg/data/flowers/
23. Fan, R.E., Chang, K.W., Hsieh, C.J., Wang, X.R., Lin, C.J.: LIBLINEAR: A library for large linear classification. The Journal of Machine Learning Research 9, 1871–1874 (2008)
24. Dalal, N., Triggs, B.: Histograms of oriented gradients for human detection. In: CVPR (2005)
25. Perronnin, F., Dance, C.: Fisher kernels on visual vocabularies for image categorization. In: CVPR (2007)
26. Bergamo, A., Torresani, L.: Meta-class features for large-scale object categorization on a budget. In: CVPR (2012)
27. Perronnin, F., Liu, Y., Sánchez, J., Poirier, H.: Large-scale image retrieval with compressed fisher vectors. In: CVPR (2010)
28. Lazebnik, S., Schmid, C., Ponce, J.: Beyond bags of features: spatial pyramid matching for recognizing natural scene categories. In: CVPR. vol. 2, pp. 2169–2178. IEEE (2006)

A Testbed for Cross-Dataset Analysis

Tatiana Tommasi[✉] and Tinne Tuytelaars

ESAT-PSI/VISICS - iMinds, KU Leuven, Belgium
ttommasi@east.kuleuven.be

Abstract. Despite the increasing interest towards domain adaptation and transfer learning techniques to generalize over image collections and overcome their biases, the visual community misses a large scale testbed for cross-dataset analysis. In this paper we discuss the challenges faced when aligning twelve existing image databases in a unique corpus, and we propose two cross-dataset setups that introduce new interesting research questions. Moreover, we report on a first set of experimental domain adaptation tests showing the effectiveness of iterative self-labeling for large scale problems.

Keywords: Dataset bias · Domain adaptation · Iterative self-labeling

1 Introduction

In the last two decades computer vision research has lead to the development of many efficient ways to describe and code the image content, and to the definition of several highly performing pattern recognition algorithms. In this evolution a key role was held by different image collections defined both as source of training samples and as evaluation instruments. The plethora of datasets obtained as legacy from the past, together with the modern increasing amount of freely available images from the Internet, pose new challenges and research questions. On one side there is a growing interest for *large scale data* [5,30], i.e. how to mine a huge amount of information and how to use it to tackle difficult problems that were not solvable or not even thinkable before [4]. On the other side there is the *dataset bias* problem [20,32,33]. Every finite image collection tends to be biased due to the acquisition process (used camera, lighting condition, etc.), preferences over certain types of background, post-processing elaboration (e.g. image filtering), or annotator tendencies (e.g. chosen labels). As a consequence the same object category in two datasets can appear visually different, while two different labels can be assigned to the exact same image content. Moreover, not all the datasets cover the same set of classes, thus the definition of what an object "is not" changes depending on the considered collection. The existing curated image datasets were created for a wide variety of tasks, but always with the general purpose of capturing the real visual world. Although each collection ends up covering only a limited part of it, by reorganizing the content of many collections we can define a rich knowledge repository.

© Springer International Publishing Switzerland 2015
L. Agapito et al. (Eds.): ECCV 2014 Workshops, Part III, LNCS 8927, pp. 18–31, 2015.
DOI: 10.1007/978-3-319-16199-0_2

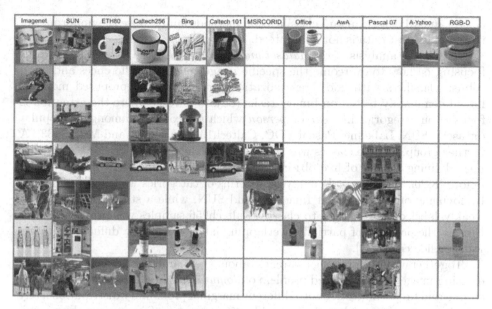

Fig. 1. We show here one image example extracted from each of the 12 datasets (columns) for 7 object categories (rows): mug, bonsai, fire hydrant, car, cow, bottle, horse. The empty positions indicate that the corresponding dataset is not annotated for the considered class.

In this work we discuss the challenges faced when aligning twelve existing image datasets (see Figure 1) and we propose two data setups that can be used both as large scale testbeds for cross-dataset analysis and as a information source for efficient automatic annotation tools.

The rest of the paper is organized as follows. Section 2 gives a brief overview of related works that focused on the dataset bias problem and that proposed domain adaptation solutions. Section 3 introduces the cross-dataset collection, while section 4 reports on the results of a preliminary evaluation of domain adaptation methods over it. We conclude the paper in section 5 pointing to possible directions of future research.

2 Related Work

The existence of several data related issues in any area of automatic classification technology was first discussed by Hand in [17] and [18]. The first sign of peril in image collections was indicated in presenting the Caltech256 dataset [16] where the authors recognized the danger of learning ancillary cues of the image collection (e.g. characteristic image size) instead of intrinsic features of the object categories. However, only recently this topic has been really put under the spotlight for computer vision tasks by Torralba and Efros [33]. Their work pointed out the idiosyncrasies of existing image datasets: the evaluation of cross-dataset performance revealed that standard detection and classification methods fail because the uniformity of training and test data is not guaranteed.

This initial analysis of the *dataset bias* problem gave rise to a series of works focusing on how to overcome the specific image collection differences and learn robust classifiers with good generalization properties. The proposed methods have been mainly tested on binary tasks (object vs rest) where the attention is focused on categories like *car* or *person* which are common among six popular datasets: SUN, Labelme, Pascal VOC, Caltech101, Imagenet, and MSRC [33]. A further group of three classes was soon added to the original set (*bird, chair* and *dog*) defining a total of five object categories over the first four datasets listed before [8,20]. A larger scale analysis in terms of categories was proposed in [28] by focusing on 84 classes of Imagenet and SUN, while a study on how to use weakly labeled Bing images to classify Caltech256 samples was proposed in [1]. Finally the problem of partially overlapping label sets among different datasets was considered in [32].

Together with the growing awareness about the characteristic signature of each existing image set, the related problem of *domain shift* has also emerged. Given a source and target image set with different marginal probability distributions, any learning method trained on the first will present lower performance on the second. In real life settings it is often impossible to have full control on how the test images will differ from the original training data and an adaptation procedure to remove the domain shift is necessary. An efficient (and possibly unsupervised) solution is to learn a shared representation that eliminates the original distribution mismatch. Different methods based on subspace data embedding [11,13], metric [29, 31] and vocabulary learning [27] have been presented. Recently several works have also demonstrated that deep learning architectures may produce domain invariant descriptors through highly non-linear transformation of the original features [6]. Domain adaptation algorithms have been mostly evaluated on the Office dataset [29] containing 31 office-related object categories from three domains. A subset of the Caltech256 dataset was later included defining a setting with 10 classes and four different data sources [13].

Despite their close relation, visual domain and dataset bias are not the same. Domain adaptation solutions have been used to tackle the dataset bias problem, but domain discovery approaches have shown that a single dataset may contain several domains [19] while a single domain may be shared across several datasets [15]. Moreover, the domain shift problem is generally considered under the covariate shift assumption with a fixed set of classes shared by the domains and analogous conditional distributions. On the other hand, different image datasets may contain different object classes.

Currently the literature misses a standard testbed for large scale cross-dataset analysis. We believe that widening the attention from few shared classes to the whole dataset structures can reveal much about the nature of the biases, and on the effectiveness of the proposed algorithmic solutions. Moreover it allows to extend the experience gained by years of research on each image collection to the others. Finally, the use of multiple sources has proven to be beneficial in reducing the domain shift and improve transfer learning for new tasks [26].

3   A Large Scale Cross-Dataset Testbed

In this section we describe the steps taken to define the proposed large scale cross-dataset testbed. We start with a brief description of the considered image datasets (section 3.1) and we give an overview of the merging process (section 3.2), presenting two data setups (section 3.3).

3.1   Collection Details

We focus on twelve datasets that were created and used before for object categorization.

ETH80 [23] was created to facilitate the transition from object identification (recognize a specific given object instance) to categorization (assign the correct class label to an object instance never seen before). It contains 8 categories and 10 toy objects for every category. Each object is captured against a blue background and it is represented by 41 images from viewpoints spaced equally over the upper viewing hemisphere.

Caltech101 [10] contains 101 object categories and was the first large scale collection proposed as a testbed for object recognition algorithms. Each category contain a different number of samples going from a minimum of 31 to a maximum of 800. The images have little or no clutter with the objects centered and presented in a stereotypical pose.

Caltech256 [16]. Differently from the previous case the images in this dataset were not manually aligned, thus the objects appear in several different poses. This collection contains 256 categories with a minimum of 80 and a maximum of 827 images.

Bing [1] contains images downloaded from the Internet for the same set of 256 object categories of the previous collection. Text queries give as output several noisy images which are not removed, resulting in a weakly labeled collection. The number of samples per class goes from a minimum of 197 to a maximum of 593.

Animals with Attributes (AwA) [22] presents a total of 30475 images of 50 animal categories. Each class is associated to a 85-element vector of numeric attribute values that indicate general characteristics shared between different classes. The animals appear in different pose and at different scales in the images.

a-Yahoo [9]. As the previous one, this dataset was collected to explore attribute descriptions. It contains 12 object categories with a minimum of 48 and a maximum of 366 samples per class.

MSRCORID [24]. The Microsoft Research Cambridge Object Recognition Image Database contains a set of digital photographs grouped into 22 categories spanning over objects (19 classes) and scenes (3 classes).

PascalVOC2007 [7]. The Pascal Visual Object Classes dataset contain 20 object categories and a total of 9963 images. Each image depicts objects in realistic scenes and may contain instances of more than one category. This dataset was used as testbed for the Pascal object recognition and detection challenges in 2007.

SUN [34] contains a total of 142165 pictures[1] and it was created as a comprehensive collection of annotated images covering a large variety of environmental scenes, places and objects. Here the objects appears at different scales and positions in the images and many of the instances are partially occluded making object recognition and categorization very challenging.

Office [29]. This dataset contains images of 31 object classes over three domains: the images are either obtained from the Amazon website, or acquired with a high resolution digital camera (DSLR), or taken with a low resolution webcam. The collection contains a total of 4110 images with a minimum of 7 and a maximum of 100 samples per domain and category.

RGB-D [21] is similar in spirit to ETH80 but it was collected with a Kinect camera, thus each RGB image is associated to a depth map. It contains images of 300 objects acquired under multiple views and organized into 51 categories.

Imagenet [5]. At the moment this collection contains around 21800 object classes organized according to the Wordnet hierarchy.

3.2   Merging Challenges

There are two main challenges that must be faced when organizing and using at once all the data collections listed before. One is related to the alignment of the object classes and the other is the need for a shared feature representation.

Composing the datasets in a single corpus turned out to be quite difficult. Even if each image is labeled with an object category name, the class alignment is tricky due to the use of different words to indicate the very same object, for instance *bike* vs *bicycle* and *mobilephone* vs *cellphone*. Sometimes the different nuance of meaning of each word are not respected: *cup* and *mug* should indicate two different objects, but the images are often mixed; *people* is the plural of *person*, but images of this last class often contain more than one subject. Moreover, the choice of different ontology hierarchical levels (*dog* vs *dalmatian* vs *greyhound*, *bottle* vs *water-bottle* vs *wine-bottle*) complicates the combination. Psychological studies demonstrated that humans prefer entry-level categories when naming visual objects [25], thus when combining the datasets we chose "natural" labels that correspond to intermediate nodes in the Wordnet hierarchy. For instance, we used *bird* to associate humming bird, pigeon, ibis, flamingo, flamingo head, rooster, cormorant, ostrich and owl, while *boat* covers kayak, ketch, schooner, speed boat, canoe and ferry. In the cases in which we combine only two classes we keep both their names, e.g. *cup & mug*.

In the alignment process we came across a few peculiar cases. Figure 2 shows samples of three classes in Imagenet. The category *chess board* does not exist at

---

[1] Here we consider the version available in December 2013 at http://labelme.csail.mit. edu/Release3.0/Images/users/antonio/static_sun_database/ and the list of objects reported at http://groups.csail.mit.edu/vision/SUN/.

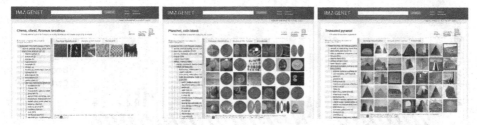

Fig. 2. Three cases of Imagenet categories. Left: some images in class *chess* are wrongly labeled. Middle: the class *planchet* or coin blank contains images that can be more easily labeled as *coin*. Right: the images highlighted with a red square in the class *truncated pyramid* do not contain a pyramid (best viewed in color and with magnification).

bat		saddle		skateboard
Caltech256	SUN	Caltech256	SUN	SUN

Fig. 3. Three categories with labeling issues. The class *bat* has different meanings both across datasets and within a dataset. A *saddle* can be a seat to ride a horse or a part of a bicycle. A *skateboard* and a *snowboard* may be visually similar, but they are not the same object.

the moment, but there are three classes related to the word *chess*: chess master, chessman or chess piece, chess or cheat or bromus secalinus (we use "or" here to indicate different labels associated to the same synset). This last category contains only few images but some of them are not correctly annotated. The categories *coin* and *pyramid* are still not present in Imagenet. For the first, the most closely related class is *planchet* or *coin blank*, which contains many example of what would be commonly named as a coin. For the second, the most similar *truncated pyramid* contains images of some non-truncated pyramids as well as images not containing any pyramids at all. In general, it is important to keep in mind that several of the Imagenet pictures are weakly labeled, thus they cannot be considered as much more reliable than the corresponding Bing images. Imagenet users are asked to clean and refine the data collection by indicating whether an image is a typical or wrong example.

We noticed that the word *bat* usually indicates the flying mammal except in SUN where it refers to the baseball and badminton bat. A *saddle* in Caltech256 is the supportive structure for a horse rider, while in SUN it is a bicycle seat. Tennis shoes and sneakers are two synonyms associated to the same synset in Imagenet, while they correspond to two different classes in Caltech256. In SUN, there are two objects annotated as skateboards, but they are in fact two snowboards. Some

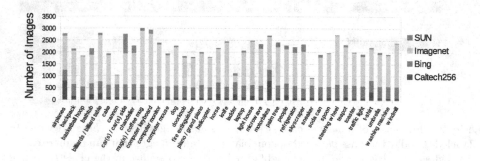

Fig. 4. Stack histogram showing the number of images per class of our cross-dataset dense setup

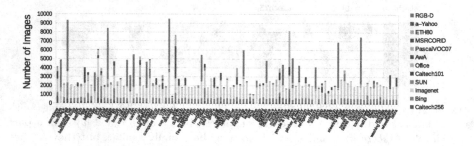

Fig. 5. Stack histogram showing the number of images per class of our cross-dataset sparse setup (best viewed in color and with magnification)

examples are shown in Figure 3. We disregarded all these ambiguous cases and we do not consider them in the final combined setups.

Although many descriptors have been extracted and evaluated separately on each image collection, the considered features usually differ across datasets. Public repositories with pre-calculated features exist for Caltech101 and Caltech256, Bing and Caltech256, and for a set of five classes out of four datasets[2]. Here we consider the group of twelve datasets listed in the previous section and extracted the same feature from all of them defining a homogeneous reference representation for cross-dataset analysis.

3.3   Data Setups and Feature Descriptor

Dense set. Among the considered datasets, the ones with the highest number of categories are Caltech256, Bing, SUN and Imagenet. In fact the last two are open

---

[2] Available respectively at http://files.is.tue.mpg.de/pgehler/projects/iccv09/, http://vlg.cs.dartmouth.edu/projects/domainadapt/, http://undoingbias.csail.mit.edu/

collections progressively growing in time. Overall they share 114 categories: some of the 256 object categories are missing at the moment in Imagenet but they are present in SUN (e.g. desk-globe, fire-hydrant) and vice-versa (e.g. butterfly, pram). Out of this shared group, 40 classes (see Figure 4) contain more than 20 images per dataset and we selected them to define a dense cross-dataset setup. We remark that each image in SUN is annotated with the list of objects visible in the depicted scene: we consider an image as a sample of a category if the category name is in the mentioned list.

Sparse set. A second setup is obtained by searching over all the datasets for the categories which are shared at least by four collections and that contain a minimum of 20 samples. We allow a lower number of samples only for the classes shared by more than four datasets (i.e. from the fifth dataset on the images per category may be less than 20). These conditions are satisfied by 105 object categories in Imagenet overlapping with 95 categories of Caltech256 and Bing, 89 categories of SUN, 35 categories of Caltech101, 17 categories of Office, 18 categories of RGB-D, 16 categories of AwA and PascalVOC07, 13 categories of MSRCORID, 7 categories of ETH80 and 4 categories of a-Yahoo. The histogram in Figure 5 shows the defined sparse set and the number of images per class: the category *cup & mug* is shared across nine datasets, making it the most popular one.

Representation. Dense SIFTs are among the most widely used features in several computer vision tasks, thus we decided to use this descriptor and we adopted the same extraction protocol proposed in the Imagenet development kit[3] by running their code over the twelve considered datasets. Each image is resized to have a max size length of no more than 300 pixels and SIFT descriptors are computed on 20x20 overlapping patches with a spacing of 10 pixels. Images are further downsized (to 1/2 and 1/4 of the side length) and more descriptors are computed. We publicly release both the raw descriptors and the Bag of Words (BOW) representation. We used the visual vocabulary of 1000 words provided with the mentioned kit: it was built over the images of the 1000 classes of the ILSVRC2010 challenge[4] by clustering a random subset of 10 million SIFT vectors.

4   A First Experimental Evaluation

Given the wide variability within and between the considered collections the defined setups can be used for several tasks. Some of the datasets come with extra side information (e.g. attributes, point clouds, bounding boxes) and this opens many possibilities for the evaluation of different (transfer) learning methods across the datasets. Here we kick the experimental analysis off with an initial study on domain adaptation methods.

---

[3] www.image-net.org/download-features
[4] http://www.image-net.org/challenges/LSVRC/2010/

Subspace Methods. Subspace domain adaptation approaches presented high performance in the unsupervised setting where the labeled source data are used to classify on unlabeled target samples. In particular the LANDMARK method proposed in [14] was indicated as a reliable technique to overcome the dataset bias [12]. This approach consists of three steps. (1) A subset of the source data is selected by choosing the samples that are distributed most similarly to the target. This process is executed by solving a quadratic programming problem and it is repeated to consider different similarity levels among the domains by changing the bandwidth σ_q of a Gaussian RBF kernel. (2) Each data subset works then as an auxiliary source to learn a domain invariant representation with the GFK algorithm [13]. Thus, for each sample $\mathbf{x} \in \mathcal{R}^D$ and each scale q we obtain a mapping $\Phi_q(\mathbf{x}) \in \mathcal{R}^d$ to a subspace with $d < D$. (3) Finally a classification model is learned on the auxiliary data by combining the different obtained representations with a multi-kernel SVM. Overall the method needs several parameters: a threshold to binarize the solution of the quadratic problem and identify the landmarks in the source, a set of σ_q values and the subspace dimensionality d.

The GFK algorithm represents each domain in a d dimensional linear subspace and embeds them onto a Grassmann manifold. The geodesic flow on the manifold parametrizes the path connecting the subspaces and it is used to define the mapping Φ to a domain invariant feature as mentioned above.

Self-labeling. Instead of subselecting the source, a different domain adaptation approach can be defined by subselecting and using the target samples while learning the source model. This technique is known as self-labeling [2,3] and starts by annotating the target with a classifier trained on the source. The target samples for which the source model presents the highest confidence are then used together with the source samples in the following training iteration.

When dealing with large scale problems self-labeling appears much more suited than the LANDMARK method. The main reason is in the high computational complexity of solving a quadratic problem over a source set with thousands of samples and repeating this operation several times over different similarity scales among the domains.

We consider here a naïve multiclass self-labeling method and we indicate it as SELF LAB in the following. A one-vs-all SVM model is trained on the source data with the C parameter chosen by cross validation. At each iteration the model is used to classify on the target data and the images assigned to every class are ranked on the basis of their output margin. Only the images with a margin higher than the average are selected and sorted by the difference between the first and the second higher margin over the classes. The top samples in the obtained list per class are then used in training with the pseudo-labels assigned to them in the previous iteration. In this way the sample selection process comes as a side-product of the classification together with a re-ranking of the SVM output margins. Moreover this approach directly exploits the multiclass nature of the domains which is generally disregarded when focusing only on how to reduce the mismatch among their marginal distributions.

Table 1. Classification rate results (%) on the Office-Caltech dataset. Here A,C,D,W stand respectively for Amazon, Caltech, Dslr, Webcam and e.g. A-C indicates the source:A, target:C pair. The results of NO ADAPT, GFK and LANDMARK are reported from [14]. The last column contains the average results per row. Best results per column in bold.

	A-C	A-D	A-W	C-A	C-D	C-W	W-A	W-C	W-D	AVG
NO ADAPT [14]	41.7	41.4	34.2	51.8	54.1	46.8	31.1	31.5	70.7	44.8
GFK [14]	42.2	42.7	40.7	44.5	43.3	44.7	31.8	30.8	75.6	44.0
LANDMARK [14]	**45.5**	**47.1**	**46.1**	**56.7**	**57.3**	49.5	**40.2**	35.4	75.2	**50.3**
SELF LAB	43.6	43.3	45.8	55.8	41.4	**53.2**	39.9	**36.1**	**82.8**	49.1

In our implementation we considered the target selection at a single scale by using a simple linear SVM, but it can also be extended to multiple scales considering non-linear kernels. For the experiments we set the number of iterations and the number of selected target samples per class respectively to 10 and 2. In this way a maximum of 20 target samples per class are used to define the training model.

A First Test on the Office-Caltech Dataset. Up to now the Office-Caltech dataset is the most widely used testbed for domain adaptation with its 4 domains and 10 shared object classes. The images of this collection were released together with SURF BOW features and subspace domain adaptation methods showed particularly high performance over it. To have a sanity check on the performance of SELF LAB we run it on this dataset following the setup used in [14].

In Table 1 we show the performance of SELF LAB, reporting the results presented in [14] as baselines. Here NO ADAPT corresponds to learning only on the source data for training. We can see that the proposed naïve self-labeling approach performs better than NO ADAPT and GFK on average, and it is only slightly worse than LANDMARK, despite being less computationally expensive. On the downside SELF LAB has only a minimal safeguard against negative transfer (that can be improved by better thresholding the SVM output margins or tuning the number of iterations), and it suffers from it in the Caltech-Dslr case (C-D), but GFK seems to have a similar behavior that affects all the cases with Caltech as source. Overall this analysis indicates the value of SELF LAB as a useful basic domain adaptation method.

A Larger Scale Evaluation. We repeat the evaluation described before on three of the datasets in the proposed dense set: Imagenet, Caltech256 and SUN. We leave out Bing, postponing the study of noisy source/target domains for future work. We consider the SIFT BOW features and 5 splits per dataset each containing respectively 5534 images for Imagenet, 2875 images for SUN and 4366 images for Caltech256 over 40 classes. Every split is then equally divided in two parts for training (source) and test (target). We use linear SVM for NO ADAPT with the best C value obtained by cross-validation on each source. The same C value is then used for SVM in combination with the GFK kernel and we tune the subspace dimensionality on the target reporting the best obtained

Table 2. Average classification rate results (%) over 5 splits for cross-dataset classification on 40 classes of three datasets: I, C, S stands respectively for Imagenet, Caltech256 and SUN. With *ss* we indicate the column containing the source-to-source results; see the text for the definition of *drop*. Best average source-to-target and drop results in bold.

		NO ADAPT			GFK				LANDMARK				SELF LAB			
	ss	I	C	S	*drop*	I	C	S	*drop*	I	C	S	*drop*	I	C	S	*drop*
I	30.9	-	22.1	13.0	43.0	-	24.8	13.4	38.2	-	24.7	13.0	39.2	-	24.0	13.5	39.2
C	48.9	18.9	-	9.8	70.6	19.1	-	10.5	69.7	17.5	-	9.9	70.6	21.4	-	11.7	66.1
S	29.5	9.4	7.4	-	71.5	9.3	8.0	-	70.5	9.1	8.7	-	71.9	11.2	9.2	-	65.4
AVG		13.5			61.7	14.2			59.5	13.6			60.6	**15.0**			**56.9**

results. A similar approach[5] is adopted to choose the subspace dimensionality for LANDMARK while the C value for the multi-kernel SVM is optimized over the source through a cross-validation between the landmark and non-landmark samples (see [14] for more details). For both GFK and LANDMARK we use the original implementation provided by the authors. A rough idea about the computational complexity of the methods can be obtained by their running time on a modern desktop computer (2.8GHz cpu, 4Gb of ram, 1core): for a single Caltech-SUN split and fixing d=100, LANDMARK needs 1695s for the source sample selection process on one scale. GFK kernel calculation and the subsequent source training and target classification run in 7s, while SELF LAB performs 10 iterations in 110s.

We show the obtained recognition rate results in Table 2. The table is divided in four parts, each for one of the considered four methods (NO ADAPT, GFK, LANDMARK and SELF LAB). Here the training and the test datasets are respectively specified in each row and column. We indicate with *ss*, *st* the source-to-source and source-to-target results. The classification performance drop among them is $drop = (ss - st) * 100/ss$. In the last row of the table we present both the average drop value for each method and the average source-to-target results. The obtained accuracy confirms the existence of the dataset bias which is particularly severe when passing from object-centric (Imagenet and Caltech) to scene images (SUN). The considered domain adaptation methods appear only minimally effective to alleviate it indicating the difficulty of the task. SELF LAB shows here the best advantage with respect to NO ADAPT.

Although a more in-depth analysis is needed, these preliminary results already give an indication of how the domain adaptation and dataset bias scenario may change when we consider large scale problems. In general a large amount of

---

[5] The original feature dimensionality is 1000 and for GFK we tuned the subspace dimensionality in d=[10,20,30, ...,500]. On average over all the source-target combinations the GFK performance increases with d and reaches a plateau for $d > 200$. For LANDMARK the source sample selection threshold is chosen in [0.0001, 0.0005, 0.001] and for time constraints we restricted the range for the subspace dimensionality to two values d=[100,300]. The source and target domains are compared at five scales q=[-2, -1, 0, 1, 2] with $\sigma_q = 2^q \sigma_0$ where σ_0 is equal to the median distance over all pairwise data points.

data calls for methods able to deal efficiently with them. Moreover, a high number of images per class together with high intra-class variability may reduce the mismatch among the corresponding marginal data distributions. However, the relation among the classes in two datasets can still be different. This pushes towards discriminative approaches able to deal with differences in the conditional distributions of the data.

5   Conclusions

In this paper we discussed the challenges faced when aligning twelve existing image datasets and we proposed two data setups that can be used as testbed for cross-dataset analysis. We extracted dense SIFT descriptors from the images and we created a useful feature repository for future research. We consider this as the first step of a wider project (official webpage: https://sites.google.com/site/crossdataset/) that will continue by both extracting new features and running several cross-dataset classification tests. The preliminary experimental analysis presented here has already indicated the value of self-labeling as a possible baseline for this task. Besides offering new challenges to domain adaptation methods, the proposed setups introduce also new research questions on how to deal with different forms of weak supervision or whether it is possible to transfer attributes and depth information across datasets. Moreover, it may be interesting to understand if the dataset alignment could be done automatically.

To conclude, we believe that exploring the common aspects and the specific characteristics of each collection will not only reveal more about the dataset bias problem, but it will also allow to improve the generalization capabilities of learning methods and mitigate the need for manual image annotation.

Acknowledgments. The authors acknowledge the support of the FP7 EC project AXES and FP7 ERC Starting Grant 240530 COGNIMUND.

References

1. Bergamo, A., Torresani, L.: Exploiting weakly-labeled web images to improve object classification: a domain adaptation approach. In: NIPS (2010)
2. Bruzzone, L., Marconcini, M.: Domain adaptation problems: A dasvm classification technique and a circular validation strategy. IEEE Trans. PAMI **32**(5), 770–787 (2010)
3. Chen, M., Weinberger, K.Q., Blitzer, J.: Co-training for domain adaptation. In: NIPS (2011)
4. Deng, J., Berg, A.C., Li, K., Fei-Fei, L.: What Does Classifying More Than 10,000 Image Categories Tell Us? In: Daniilidis, K., Maragos, P., Paragios, N. (eds.) ECCV 2010, Part V. LNCS, vol. 6315, pp. 71–84. Springer, Heidelberg (2010)
5. Deng, J., Dong, W., Socher, R., Li, L., Li, K., Fei-Fei, L.: ImageNet: A Large-Scale Hierarchical Image Database. In: CVPR (2009)
6. Donahue, J., Jia, Y., Vinyals, O., Hoffman, J., Zhang, N., Tzeng, E., Darrell, T.: Decaf: A deep convolutional activation feature for generic visual recognition. arXiv preprint arXiv:1310.1531 (2013)

7. Everingham, M., Gool, L.V., Williams, C.K., Winn, J., Zisserman, A.: The Pascal Visual Object Classes (VOC) Challenge. IJCV 88(2) (2010)
8. Fang, C., Xu, Y., Rockmore, D.N.: Unbiased metric learning: On the utilization of multiple datasets and web images for softening bias. In: ICCV (2013)
9. Farhadi, A., Endres, I., Hoiem, D., Forsyth, D.: Describing objects by their attributes. In: CVPR (2009)
10. Fei-Fei, L., Fergus, R., Perona, P.: Learning generative visual models from few training examples: An incremental bayesian approach tested on 101 object categories. Comput. Vis. Image Underst. 106(1), 59–70 (2007)
11. Fernando, B., Habrard, A., Sebban, M., Tuytelaars, T.: Unsupervised visual domain adaptation using subspace alignment. In: ICCV (2013)
12. Gong, B., Sha, F., Grauman, K.: Overcoming dataset bias: An unsupervised domain adaptation approach. In: NIPS Workshop on Large Scale Visual Recognition and Retrieval (2012)
13. Gong, B., Shi, Y., Sha, F., Grauman, K.: Geodesic flow kernel for unsupervised domain adaptation. In: CVPR (2012)
14. Gong, B., Grauman, K., Sha, F.: Connecting the dots with landmarks: Discriminatively learning domain-invariant features for unsupervised domain adaptation. In: ICML (2013)
15. Gong, B., Grauman, K., Sha, F.: Reshaping visual datasets for domain adaptation. In: NIPS (2013)
16. Griffin, G., Holub, A., Perona, P.: Caltech 256 object category dataset. Tech. Rep. UCB/CSD-04-1366, California Institue of Technology (2007)
17. Hand, D.J.: Classifier Technology and the Illusion of Progress. Stat. Sci. 21, 1–15 (2006)
18. Hand, D.J.: Academic obsessions and classification realities: ignoring practicalities in supervised classification. In: Classification, Clustering, and Data Mining Applications, pp. 209–232 (2004)
19. Hoffman, J., Kulis, B., Darrell, T., Saenko, K.: Discovering Latent Domains for Multisource Domain Adaptation. In: Fitzgibbon, A., Lazebnik, S., Perona, P., Sato, Y., Schmid, C. (eds.) ECCV 2012, Part II. LNCS, vol. 7573, pp. 702–715. Springer, Heidelberg (2012)
20. Khosla, A., Zhou, T., Malisiewicz, T., Efros, A.A., Torralba, A.: Undoing the Damage of Dataset Bias. In: Fitzgibbon, A., Lazebnik, S., Perona, P., Sato, Y., Schmid, C. (eds.) ECCV 2012, Part I. LNCS, vol. 7572, pp. 158–171. Springer, Heidelberg (2012)
21. Lai, K., Bo, L., Ren, X., Fox, D.: A large-scale hierarchical multi-view rgb-d object dataset. In: ICRA (2011)
22. Lampert, C.H., Nickisch, H., Harmeling, S.: Learning to detect unseen object classes by between class attribute transfer. In: CVPR (2009)
23. Leibe, B., Schiele, B.: Analyzing appearance and contour based methods for object categorization. In: CVPR (2003)
24. Microsoft: Microsoft Research Cambridge Object Recognition Image Database. http://research.microsoft.com/en-us/downloads/b94de342-60dc-45d0-830b-9f6eff91b301/default.aspx (2005)
25. Ordonez, V., Deng, J., Choi, Y., Berg, A.C., Berg, T.L.: From large scale image categorization to entry-level categories. In: ICCV (2013)
26. Patricia, N., Caputo, B.: Learning to learn, from transfer learning to domain adaptation: A unifying perspective. In: CVPR (2014)

27. Qiu, Q., Patel, V.M., Turaga, P., Chellappa, R.: Domain Adaptive Dictionary Learning. In: Fitzgibbon, A., Lazebnik, S., Perona, P., Sato, Y., Schmid, C. (eds.) ECCV 2012, Part IV. LNCS, vol. 7575, pp. 631–645. Springer, Heidelberg (2012)
28. Rodner, E., Hoffman, J., Donahue, J., Darrell, T., Saenko, K.: Towards adapting imagenet to reality: Scalable domain adaptation with implicit low-rank transformations. CoRR abs/1308.4200 (2013)
29. Saenko, K., Kulis, B., Fritz, M., Darrell, T.: Adapting Visual Category Models to New Domains. In: Daniilidis, K., Maragos, P., Paragios, N. (eds.) ECCV 2010, Part IV. LNCS, vol. 6314, pp. 213–226. Springer, Heidelberg (2010)
30. Sanchez, J., Perronnin, F.: High-dimensional signature compression for large-scale image classification. In: CVPR (2011)
31. Tommasi, T., Caputo, B.: Frustratingly easy nbnn domain adaptation. In: ICCV (2013)
32. Tommasi, T., Quadrianto, N., Caputo, B., Lampert, C.H.: Beyond Dataset Bias: Multi-task Unaligned Shared Knowledge Transfer. In: Lee, K.M., Matsushita, Y., Rehg, J.M., Hu, Z. (eds.) ACCV 2012, Part I. LNCS, vol. 7724, pp. 1–15. Springer, Heidelberg (2013)
33. Torralba, A., Efros, A.A.: Unbiased look at dataset bias. In: CVPR (2011)
34. Xiao, J., Hays, J., Ehinger, K.A., Oliva, A., Torralba, A.: Sun database: Large-scale scene recognition from abbey to zoo. In: CVPR (2010)

Domain Adaptation with a Domain Specific Class Means Classifier

Gabriela Csurka$^{(\boxtimes)}$, Boris Chidlovskii, and Florent Perronnin

Xerox Research Centre Europe, 6 chemin Maupertuis, 38240 Meylan, France
{Gabriela.Csurka,Boris.Chidlovskii,Florent.Perronnin}@xrce.xerox.com

Abstract. We consider the problem of learning a classifier when we dispose little training data from the target domain but abundant training data from several source domains. We make two contributions to the domain adaptation problem. First we extend the Nearest Class Mean (NCM) classifier by introducing for each class domain-dependent mean parameters as well as domain-specific weights. Second, we propose a generic adaptive semi-supervised metric learning technique that iteratively curates the training set by adding unlabeled samples with high prediction confidence and by removing labeled samples for which the prediction confidence is low. These two complementary techniques are evaluated on two public benchmarks: the ImageClef Domain Adaptation Challenge and the Office-CalTech datasets. Both contributions are shown to yield improvements and to be complementary to each other.

Keywords: Domain adaptation · Self-adative metric learning · NCM

1 Introduction

The shortage of labeled data is a fundamental problem in machine learning applications. While huge amounts of unlabeled data is generated and made available in many domains, the cost of acquiring data labels remains high. Domain adaptation addresses this problem by leveraging labeled data in one or more related domains, often referred as "source" domains, when learning a classifier for unseen data in a "target" domain.

The domains are assumed to be related but not identical and when we apply directly models learned on source domains the performance can be often very poor on the target. This is especially true in computer vision applications as existing image collections used for *e.g.* object categorization present specific characteristics which often prevent a direct cross-dataset generalization. The main reason is that even when the same features are extracted in both domains, the underlying cause of the domain shift (changes in the camera, image resolution, lighting, background, viewpoint, and post-processing) can strongly affect the feature distribution and thus violate the assumptions of the classifier trained on the source domain. Therefore it is important during the learning process to infer models that adapt well to the test data they will be deployed on.

© Springer International Publishing Switzerland 2015
L. Agapito et al. (Eds.): ECCV 2014 Workshops, Part III, LNCS 8927, pp. 32–46, 2015.
DOI: 10.1007/978-3-319-16199-0_3

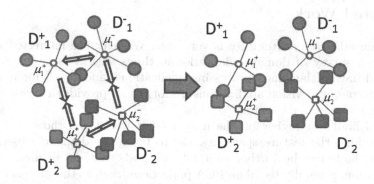

Fig. 1. Exploiting class and domain-related labels to decreased interclass distances and increase intraclass distances independently of the domain

Hence one of the main issues of domain adaptation is how to deal with data sampled from the different distributions and how to compensate this mismatch by making use of information coming from both source and target domains during the learning process to adapt automatically.

Our contributions, aiming to address these issues, are therefore two-fold:
- We extend the nearest class mean (NCM) classifier and its metric learning approach [14] to the problem of domain adaptation by introducing domain specific class means (DSCM) with domain specific weights. While this method yields surprisingly good results without any learning procedure (besides computing the per-class and per-domain means), we also show that metric learning yields further improvement. This involves learning a such transformation of the feature space that decreases interclass distances and increases intraclass distances independently of the domain (see illustration for two domains in Fig.1).
- Inspired by [19], we propose a self-adaptive metric learning domain adaptation (SaMLDa) framework where we exploit the available unlabeled target instances to better adjust the learned metric to the target domain. The idea is to use the DSCM classifier 1) to select and label unlabeled target instances to enrich the training set and 2) to remove the more ambiguous source examples from the training set. This dynamically updated training set is used to iteratively refine the learned transformation by forcing the learning process to exploit the characteristics of the unlabeled target instances. While naturally our SaMLDa framework uses the DSCM based metric learning approach, we show that other metric learning approaches can be used in the framework in order to improve the classification on the target instanced in the transformed space.

The rest of the paper is organized as follows. In section 2 we review the relevant literature. Then, in section 3 we describe the DSCM classifier and the corresponding metric learning and in section 4, the self-adaptive metric learning domain adaptation (SaMLDa) framework. Section 5 provides details about the datasets and our evaluation framework and section 6 details the results of our experiments. Finally we conclude the paper in section 7.

2   Related Work

The domain adaptation literature is very vast. We refer the interested reader to [12] for a survey of domain adaptation methods with a focus on learning theory and natural language processing applications, and to [2] for a survey focusing on computer vision applications. As for [15], it provides a review on the related topic of transfer learning.

We will limit our review on the most related works, *i.e.* those that focus on transforming the feature space in order to bring the domains closer. This class of methods can be further split into methods that do an unsupervised transformation, generally based on PCA projections, such as the subspace based domain adaptation methods in [1,6,7,9].

In contrast to these unsupervised learning of the transformation matrix, there are a set of metric learning based methods that exploits class labels (in general both in the source and in the target domain) to learn a transformation of the feature space such that in this new space the instances of the same class become closer to each other than to instances from other classes and this independently of the domain they belong to [10,13,17,21]. While the Domain Invariant Projections (DIP) in [1] are also learned without using class labels, the extended DIP+CC search for invariant projections that encourages samples with the same class labels to form a more compact cluster. The proposed DSCMML method can also be placed in this subgroup.

In addition we exploit unlabeled target instances and refine the metric accordingly. The proposed framework is inspired by [19], but the idea of using unlabeled target instance in an active supervised domain adaptation can be also found in [18]. Similarly, [5] proposes to use unlabeled target data, however they are used to measure the data distribution mismatch between the source and target domain. Their Domain Transfer SVM generalizes the sample re-weighting of Kernel Mean Matching [11] by simultaneously learning the SVM decision function and the kernel such that the difference between the means of the source and target feature distributions (including the unlabeled ones) are minimized.

3   Domain Specific Class Means Classifier

The Domain Specific Nearest Class Means (DSCM) classifier extends the NCM by considering domain based class means and it was inspired by the Nearest Class Multiple Centroids (NCMC) classifier proposed in [14]. In what follows, we first review the NCM and NCMC and then introduce the proposed DSCM.

The nearest class mean (NCM) classifier assigns an image to the class $c^* \in Y_c = \{1, \ldots, C\}$ whose mean is the closest:

$$c^* = \operatorname*{argmin}_{c \in Y_c} d_{\boldsymbol{W}}(\boldsymbol{x}_i, \boldsymbol{\mu}_c), \quad \text{with } \boldsymbol{\mu}_c = \frac{1}{C} \sum_{i:y_i=c} \boldsymbol{x}_i, \tag{1}$$

where y_i is the ground-truth label of the image x_i, N^c is the number of training examples from the class c and $d_W(x_i, \mu_c) = ||W(x_i - \mu_c)||^2$ is the squared Euclidean distance between an instance x_i and the class mean μ_c in some projected feature space given by the transformation matrix W. If W is the identity (I), this corresponds to the Euclidean distance in the original feature space.

We can easily reformulate Eq. 1 as a multi-class softmax assignment using a mixture model (with equal weights), where the probability that an image x belongs to the class c is defined as follows (see also [14]):

$$p(c|x_i) = \frac{\exp\left(-\frac{1}{2}d_W(x_i, \mu_c)\right)}{\sum_{c'=1}^{N_C} \exp\left(-\frac{1}{2}d_W(x_i, \mu_{c'})\right)}. \tag{2}$$

and the final assignment is done by $c^* = \operatorname{argmax}_{c \in Y_c} p(c|x_i)$. This definition may also be interpreted as the posterior probabilities of a Gaussian generative model $p(x_i|c) = \mathcal{N}(x_i, \mu^c, |\Sigma)$ with the mean μ^c and class independent covariance matrix $\Sigma = (W^\top W)^{-1}$.

Note that, once the metric d_W is known, learning the mean parameters of this classifier is very efficient as it only involves summing the image descriptors for each class and domain. A great advantage is that, if the metric is fixed, we can easily add new classes, new domains or new training images to existing classes and domains at almost zero cost [14].

The Nearest Class Multiple Centroids (NCMC) classifier [14] extends the NCM classifier by representing each class by a set of centroids $\{m_c^j\}_{j=1}^k$ obtained by clustering images within each class, instead of a single class mean (NCM corresponds to $k = 1$ and $m_c^1 = \mu_c$). The posterior probability for the class c is then defined as:

$$p(c|x) = \frac{1}{Z} \sum_{j=1}^{k} \exp\left(-\frac{1}{2}d_W(x, m_c^j)\right), \tag{3}$$

where $Z = \sum_c \sum_j \exp\left(-\frac{1}{2}d_W(x, m_c^j)\right)$ is the normalizer and the model for each class becomes an equal weighted Gaussian mixture distribution with m_c^j as means and $\Sigma = (W^\top W)^{-1}$ being the shared covariance matrix.

The Proposed Domain Specific Class Means (DSCM) Classifier. The NCMC classifier can be naturally extended to the case of multiple domains where instead of selecting centroids in an unsupervised manner, for each class we consider domain specific class means:

$$\mu_d^c = \frac{1}{N_d^c} \sum_{i:y_i=c, x_i \in \mathcal{D}_d} x_i, \tag{4}$$

where N_d^c is the number of images from class c in domain $\mathcal{D}_d$. In such a case, the class assignment can be written as:

$$p(c|x_i) = \frac{\sum_d w_d \exp\left(-\frac{1}{2}d_W(x_i, \mu_d^c)\right)}{\sum_{c'} \sum_d w_d \exp\left(-\frac{1}{2}d_W(x_i, \mu_d^{c'})\right)} = \frac{\sum_d w_d p(x_i|c, d)}{\sum_{c'} \sum_d w_d p(x_i|c', d)} \tag{5}$$

This model also corresponds to a generative model, where the probability for an image $\boldsymbol{x}_i$ to be generated by class c is given by a Gaussian mixture distribution $p(\boldsymbol{x}_i|c) = \sum_d w_d p(x_i|c,d) = \sum_d w_d \mathcal{N}(\boldsymbol{x}_i, \mu_d^c, |\Sigma)$, with the mixing weights w_d, the domain specific class means μ_d^c and the class and domain independent covariance matrix $\Sigma = (\boldsymbol{W}^\top \boldsymbol{W})^{-1}$. Again, if $\boldsymbol{W} = \boldsymbol{I}$, the distances are computed in the original feature space, and $\Sigma = \boldsymbol{I}$.

Domain specific weights w_d in Eq. 5 allows to express different importance of different domains. These weights can be manually fixed (if we have some prior knowledge about the sources), learned (*e.g.* cross validated) or deduced directly from the data. If we denote the target domain by $\mathcal{T}$ and the source domains by $\mathcal{S}_i$, one possibility to define w_{s_i} is to measure how well the source domain $\mathcal{S}_i$ is aligned with the target domain $\mathcal{T}$ in the space projected by $\boldsymbol{W}$. This can be done by *e.g.* using target density around source ($TDAS$) proposed in [6]:

$$TDAS = \frac{1}{N_s} \sum_{\boldsymbol{x}_i^s \in \mathcal{S}} |\{\boldsymbol{x}^t | d_{\boldsymbol{W}}(\boldsymbol{x}^t, \boldsymbol{x}_i^s)| \le \epsilon|, \tag{6}$$

where ϵ is set to the half of the mean distance between the source sample and the nearest target sample.

Alternatively, in the semi-supervised setting, where a small set of labeled instances are available from the target domain (denoted by $\mathcal{T}_l$), we can proceed as follows. We consider the class means for each source $\mathcal{S}_i$ individually and use them within Eq. 2 to predict the labels for instances in $\mathcal{T}_l$. The average classification accuracy of this classifier can be used directly as w_{s_i}.

Note that in the case of large datasets, Eq. 5 can be further extended by considering a set of domain specific prototypes for each class by clustering the N_d^c domain specific images from class c and domain d. Another possible extension is to consider domain and class specific weights w_d^c in Eq. 5, where both, the TDAS measure and the NCM accuracy can be also computed for each class individually. However these extensions being more suitable for larger datasets will not be considered in the paper.

3.1 Metric Learning for DSCM

The aim of metric learning is to find a projection matrix $\boldsymbol{W}$, such that the log-likelihood of the correct DSCM class predictions are maximized on X:

$$\mathcal{L} = \sum_{\boldsymbol{x}_i \in X} \ln p(c = y_i | \boldsymbol{x}_i) = \sum_{\boldsymbol{x}_i \in X} \left[\ln \sum_d w_d p(\boldsymbol{x}_i | y_i, d) - \ln Z_i \right]$$

where $Z_i = \sum_{c'} \sum_d w_d p(\boldsymbol{x}_i | c', d)$

Similarly to [14], we optimize this log-likelihood with mini-batch stochastic gradient descend (SGD) using a fixed learning rate (η), and randomly sampled small batch, $X_b \subset X$ of the training data to update $\boldsymbol{W}$ with the gradient:

$$\nabla_W \mathcal{L} = \sum_{\boldsymbol{x}_i \in X_b} \left[\sum_{c'} \sum_d \left(\frac{g_{i,d}^{c'}}{Z_i} - [\![c' = y_i]\!] \frac{g_{i,d}^{c'}}{p(\boldsymbol{x}_i | c')} \right) \boldsymbol{W} (\mu_d^{c'} - \boldsymbol{x}_i)(\mu_d^{c'} - \boldsymbol{x}_i)^\top \right]$$

where $g^{c'}_{i,d} = w_d p(x_i|c', d)$ and $[\![\cdot]\!]$ is one if its argument is true and zero otherwise. Note that we initialize W with principal component analyses, keeping the number of eigenvectors corresponding to the desired dimension of the projected space, generally, much smaller than the initial feature space.

4   Self-adaptive Metric Learning for Domain Adaptation

Two main cases are in general distinguished in domain adaptation. Unsupervised DA refers to the case where no labeled data is available from the target domain and semi-supervised DA where there are a few labeled images from the target domain to guide the learning process. Let denote by $\mathcal{T}_l$ the set of labeled target instances (that can be empty) and by $\mathcal{T}_u$ the set of unlabeled target set. Let $\mathcal{S}_1, \ldots, \mathcal{S}_{N_S}$ denote N_S source domains and X_r a current training set containing labeled instances (that can be ground truth labels or predicted ones) from different sources. We denote by Y_c the class labels, by $Y_d = \{s_1, \ldots s_{N_S}, t\}$ the domain-related labels, where t refers to the target domain and by $\boldsymbol{w}_d = (w_{s_1}, \ldots, w_t)$ the set of domain-specific weights.

We propose a Self-adaptive Metric Learning Domain Adaptation framework (SaMLDa) inspired by the method proposed in [19] where, similarly, we add iteratively unlabeled images from the target domain and remove images from the source to refine W. The proposed framework assumes a metric learning component $f_W(X_r, \boldsymbol{W}_r, \boldsymbol{w}^r_d)$ that gets as input an initial transformation $\boldsymbol{W}_r$, a set of labeled training instances X_r and optionally a set of domain-specific weights $\boldsymbol{w}^r_d$. Then, using either only the class labels Y_c or also the domain-related labels Y_d of the instances in X_r, it outputs an updated transformation $\boldsymbol{W}_{r+1} = f_W(X_r, \boldsymbol{W}_r, \boldsymbol{w}^r_d)$.

The DSCMML described in section 3.1 is one particular case of the metric learning component, but the algorithm can use any other metric learning approach (and improve its performance as we will see in section 6). Indeed, in the case of metric learning methods not designed to handle multiple sources, the domain-related labels Y_d and weights $\boldsymbol{w}_d$ are simply ignored by f_W.

The main steps of our self-adaptive metric learning based domain adaptation algorithm (see Algorithm 1) are the followings:

- Using the initial labeled set X_1 (including labeled target instances if available), we set $\boldsymbol{W}_0$ as the first PCA directions on the training set and compute $\boldsymbol{W}_1 = f_W(X_0, \boldsymbol{W}_0, \boldsymbol{w}^0_d)$. One advantage of the dimensionality reduction is that we have fewer parameters to learn, which is especially important when only a relatively small amount of training examples are available; it also generally leads to a better performance.
- Then, we iteratively refine $\boldsymbol{W}_r$ by adding at each iteration to the current training set X_r unlabeled instances from the target with their predicted class labels and removing the less confident source instances[1]. In contrast to [19],

---

[1] Improving in general the domain specific class means as the relevant source data becomes better clustered around these means.

Algorithm 1. The SaMLDa approach

Require: The initial training set $X_0 = \{S_1, \ldots, S_{N_S}, T_l\}$.
Require: Domain-specific weights w_d^0 and an initial transformation W_0.
Ensure: A metric learning component f_W.
1: Get $W_1 = f_W(X_1, W_0, w_d^0)$.
2: **for** $r = 1, \ldots, N_R$ **do**
3:    Set $X_r = X_{r-1}$, $w_d^r = w_d^{r-1}$ and compute μ_d^c.
4:    Optionally, update w_d^r using $TDAS$ or NCM with W_r.
5:    For each $x_i \in X_{r-1}$ and each class c_j compute $p(c_j|x_i)$ using Eq. 5 with W_r.
6:    For each class c_j, add $x_i^t \in T_u$ to X_r for which $p(c^*|x_i^t) - p(c^\dagger|x_i^t)$ is the largest.
7:    For each class c_j, remove $x_j^s \in X_{r-1} \setminus T$ from X_r for which $p(c^*|x_j^s) - p(c^\dagger|x_j^s)$ is the smallest.
8:    Set $W_{r+1} = f_W(X_r, W_r, w_d^r)$.
9:    If stopping criteria is met (classification accuracy degraded or no more data available to add or remove), quit the loop.
10: **end for**
11: Output W_{r^*} where $r^* + 1$ is the iteration at stopping criteria (or $r^* = N_R$).

---

where added or removed images are selected by the distances between low-level features[2], we use the DSCM class probabilities defined in Eq. 5.

1. For each class c_j, we add the unlabeled target example $x_i^t \in T_u$ to X_r for which $p(c^*|x_i^t) - p(c^\dagger|x_i^t)$ is the largest where $c^* = c_j$ is the predicted label of x_i^t and $p(c^\dagger|x_i^t)$ is the second largest score. Note that as $\sum_{j=1}^C p(c_j|x) = 1$, these are the images for which the classifier is the most confident about the prediction c^*, which however does not mean that the label is correct.

2. Similarly, for each class we remove the source image from X_r for which $p(c^*|x_j^s) - p(c^\dagger|x_j^s)$ is the smallest, *i.e.* the classifier finds it the most ambiguous example. Note that we use one element from all sources, but alternatively we could consider one per source decreasing more rapidly the amount of source data in X_r.

3. We compute $W_{r+1} = f_W(X_r, W_r, w_d^r)$ and optionally we update w_d^r as described in section 3.

– We iterate these steps until no more target data can be added, source data can be removed or the maximum iteration is achieved. However, adding training images with predicted labels comes with the risk of adding noise (incorrect labels). Therefore we also add the following stopping criteria. At each iteration, we evaluate the classification accuracy on the original labeled set and if the classification performance in step r incurs a stronger degradation than a predefined tolerance threshold (we used 1%) compared to the accuracy obtained in step r we stop iterating and retain W_r, the metric obtained before degradation. Note that other criteria can also be considered such as measuring the variation between iterations of the $TDAS$.

---

[2] Their image-to-class distance is computed as a sum of distances between low level features extracted from the image and their closest low level feature within a class.

5 Datasets and Evaluation Framework

We used four datasets to test our framework: ICDA1 and ICDA2 from the Image-Clef Domain Adaptation Challenge[3] as well as the OffCalSS and OffCalMS built on the Office dataset + Caltech10 used in several DA papers [1,6,8,9].

ICDA2. We denote by ICDA2 the dataset that was used in the challenge to submit the results. It consists of a set of image features[4] extracted by the organizers on randomly selected images collected from five different image collections: Caltech-256, ImageNet ILSVRC2012, PASCAL VOC2012, Bing and SUN denoted by C,I,P,B and S for simplicity. The organizers selected 12 common classes present in each datasets, namely, *aeroplane, bike, bird, boat, bottle, bus, car, dog, horse, monitor, motorbike, people*. Four collections (C, I, P and B) are proposed as source domains and for each of them 600 image feature and the corresponding labels were provided. The SUN dataset served as the target domain with 60 annotated and 600 non-annotated instances. The task was to provide predictions for the non-annotated target data. Neither the images nor the low-level features were accessible by the participants.

ICDA1. The ImageClef Domain Adaptation Challenge had two phases where in the first phase the participants were provided with a similar configuration as ICDA2, but with different features. We will denote this set with ICDA1. While in the case of ICDA2 we used only the provided train/test configuration and show the results obtained on the provided test set, in the case of ICDA1 we show the average results of an 11 fold cross-validation setting, where the 600 test documents were split into 10 folds and the train set added as 11th fold. At each time one of the 11 folds was added to the source sets to train the classifier and tested on the 600 remaining target documents.

OffCalSS. The OffCalSS dataset was built following the semi-supervised settings used in [6,8,9], *i.e.* 10 common classes (*backpack, touring-bike, calculator, head-phone, computer-keyboard, laptop-101, computer-monitor, computer-mouse, coffee-mug and video-projector*) were selected from four domains Amazon, Caltech-10, DSLR and Webcam (denoted by A,C,D and W). To build the training set 8 images from each class (when the source domain was D or W) and 20 images (when the source was A or C) was considered, to which 3 target instances per class were added. The training source and target examples were randomly selected and the experiment was repeated 20 times.

OffCalMS. In OffCalSS we evaluate only one domain (source) versus one domain (target). Also, the source domain considered is relatively small, which is, in some sense, a bit contradictory to the general assumption of domain adaptation, where it is in general assumed that large labeled source instances are

---

[3] http://www.imageclef.org/2014/adaptation
[4] SIFT based bag-of-visual words [3].

available to support the learning process. Therefore, using the same dataset and features as for OffCalSS, we build a multi-source setting similar to ICDA1 to which we will refer to as OffCalMS. In this case we fix one of the dataset as target (*e.g.* A) and use several or all the others (C,D and W) as source to evaluate our multi-source framework (AMLDA). In this case, all the labeled sources documents are used to which we add 3 randomly sampled target examples per class. We repeated this experiment 10 times and report average results.

In the case of multi-source datasets (ICDA1, ICDA2 and OffCalMS), we consider different source combinations by an exhaustive enumeration of all possible subsets. For instance, in the case of ICDA1, we have $SC_i, i = 1, \ldots, N_{SC}$, where $N_{SC} = 2_S^N - 1 = 15$ and N_S is the number of sources, *e.g.* in the case of ICDA1, $SC_1 = \{\mathbf{C}\}$, $SC_6 = \{\mathbf{C}, \mathbf{P}\}$ and $SC_{15} = \{\mathbf{C}, \mathbf{I}, \mathbf{P}, \mathbf{B}\}$. Then for each source combination, we concatenate the target training set $\mathcal{T}_l$ with the selected sources SC_j to build the training set X_1. If we denote the corresponding classifier by f^{SC_j}, to improve the final classification accuracy we can further combine the predictions of all these classifiers either using a majority vote or when available by averaging the class prediction scores. In both cases we used an unweighted combination in our experiments, but weighted fusion can also be used if there is enough data to learn the weights for each SC_i combination on a validation set. As we are in a semi-supervised setting we also consider f^{SC_0} in the combination, the classifier learned using only the labeled target set $\mathcal{T}_l$. We will denote the final prediction obtained as the combinations of all $N_{SC} + 1$ classifier by FusAll in the tables.

6   Experimental Results

Our first set of experiments were done on ICDA1 and ICDA2 in the semi-supervised setting. We consider all the available labeled source datasets (given a configuration) and the labeled target set grouped together as a single training set allowing us to consider different, not necessary multi-domain, classifiers to predict labels for the unlabeled target instances.

First, we consider the original feature space, meaning that we did not apply any metric learning procedure ($\mathbf{W} = \mathbf{I}$) and we evaluate classification performance of labeling the target examples of different source combinations.

Note that when we refer to the *original features*, they are different from the provided features as the latter were from the beginning power normalized[5] [16] using $\alpha = 0.5$. This allows already to an increase of 3-5% in accuracy on the baseline SVM and on the distance based classifiers, which explains why our baseline on OffCalSS is higher than in the literature.

As the SVM main baseline, for each configuration we considered the multi-class SVM from the LIBSVM package[6] trained in the original feature space. Using an initial 11 fold cross validation on ICDA1, we found that the linear kernel with $\nu = 0.12$, $C = 0.01$, and $\mu = 0.5$ performed the best. As only few

---

[5] As the original features are L1 normalized, we ended up with L2 normalized features.
[6] http://www.csie.ntu.edu.tw/~cjlin/libsvm/

Table 1. Classification performances on ICDA1 (left) and ICDA2 (right) in the original feature space, meaning that $W = I$ in the Eqs. 2, 3 and 5

ICDA1	SVM	KNN	NCM	NCMC	DSCM	ICDA2	SVM	KNN	NCM	NCMC	DSCM
C	26.32	22.79	25.08	23.83	32.33	C	23	22.5	11.67	13.17	26
I	31.85	25.92	23.71	21.71	32.21	I	26.67	25.5	13.00	16.33	25.5
P	27.32	18.91	23.83	21.06	32.89	P	25.5	20.67	19.50	15.17	24.83
B	33.92	27.98	27.83	27.23	33.36	B	30.5	24.17	15.33	14.83	24.67
C,I	29.08	22.7	23.48	21.21	30.85	C,I	22.67	23.50	13.5.0	13.17	25.33
C,P	27.29	20.09	23.03	21.36	31.94	C,P	21.83	21.67	16.00	11.33	26.33
C,B	30	26.52	26.94	25.2	31.64	C,B	26.00	23.00	12.50	13.83	26.17
I,P	29.88	19.33	24.42	20.68	30.86	I,P	26.50	17	14.33	20.33	26.67
I,B	36.89	27.85	24.91	23.14	30.94	I,B	30	23.33	15.67	13.83	27.17
P,B	30.12	22.48	26.83	23.02	32.03	P,B	29.83	22.17	15	22.17	26.5
C,I,P	28.67	20.05	24.65	20.52	30.33	C,I,P	22	22	14.17	12.5	27.33
C,I,B	33.42	25.79	24.44	21.55	30.17	C,I,B	27.5	21.5	14.67	18.67	24.33
C,P,B	28.05	22.44	26.26	22.74	30.85	C,P,B	24.17	22.67	15.83	18.67	26.83
I,P,B	32.48	22.91	25.59	22.39	30.59	I,P,B	28.17	21.33	15.5	15.83	27.67
C,I,P,B	29.39	22.38	24.89	22.06	29.48	C,I,P,B	24.5	21.5	16	17.5	26.67
Mean	30.31	23.21	25.06	23.21	31.37	Mean	25.92	22.44	14.84	22.44	26.13

target examples are in general available for each dataset, we used these fixed values for all datasets. Other parameters, such as the learning rate and number of iterations of the metric learning, were also cross-validated on ICDA1 and used on all datasets.

Evaluation in the Original Feature Space. First, we compare the SVM with distance based classifiers, namely KNN, NCM, NCMC and DSCM. As the first three are not domain adaptation specific methods they do not use the domain specific labels Y_d but consider the union of the labeled target and source instances as a single domain training set. In contrast, the Domain Specific Class Means (DSCM) classifier considers distances to class and domain specific class means, hence it is able to take advantage of domain specific labels Y_d. In this first set of experiments we use fixed weights (where $w_t = 2$ and $w_{s_i} = 1$). In the NCMC classifier, we use the same number of cluster means per class as the number of domains ($N_S + 1$) to fairly compare[7] with DSCM. The classification results are shown in Table 1. We can see that DSNCM outperforms all three distance based non parametric classifiers (KNN, NCM and NCMC) for all source combinations; it even outperforms for most configurations (and in average) the multi-class SVM. This already shows that DSCM applied without any learning is a suitable classifier for domain adaptation.

Evaluation in the Projected Feature Space. For experiments in the projected space, we consider metric learning approaches that optimizes W for the corresponding classifiers. For KNN we consider the metric learning where the ranking loss is optimized on triplets [4,20]:

$$L_{qpn} = \max(0, [1 + d_W(\boldsymbol{x}_q, \boldsymbol{x}_p) - d_W(\boldsymbol{x}_q, \boldsymbol{x}_n)]), \qquad (7)$$

---

[7] The unsupervised clustering being does not guarantee the correspondence between clusters and domains. While different number of cluster centers might have yielded to better results, the training target dataset is rather small for cross-validation.

Table 2. Distance based classification performances on ICDA1 and ICDA2 using the features projected with W learned by the corresponding metric learning method

ICDA1	KNN +ML	NCM +ML	NCMC +ML	DSCM +ML	ICDA2	KNN +ML	NCM +ML	NCMC +ML	DSCM +ML
C	26.74	26.03	24.77	28.41	C	24.67	18.17	16.83	25.17
I	29.33	27.11	28.52	32.88	I	28.33	25.5	24.17	30.33
P	25.94	25.27	23.88	26.5	P	26.33	22.83	23.67	25.33
B	33.21	33.08	32.48	34.85	B	30.17	29	30.17	34.17
C,I	29.62	26.47	25.5	30.89	C,I	25.83	19.83	18	25.67
C,P	25.48	25.86	23.92	30.32	C,P	24.83	16.17	15	23.33
C,B	30.36	30.92	29.5	32.92	C,B	27.83	20.5	18.5	24.5
I,P	26.62	26	26.89	31.86	I,P	27.17	15	22.17	29.67
I,B	33.45	32.86	33.48	35.23	I,B	30.17	25.17	21.17	33.5
P,B	28.29	31.41	27.29	33.68	P,B	28.17	25.17	22.5	30.67
C,I,P	25.98	27.48	25.53	31.67	C,I,P	25	15.5	16.67	27.17
C,I,B	31.15	31.33	28.89	34.68	C,I,B	28.33	18.83	23.83	28.5
C,P,B	28.27	29.98	28.92	32.67	C,P,B	25.17	19.5	27.5	27.83
I,P,B	29.82	30.33	29.56	34.58	I,P,B	29.67	22	27.33	31.83
C,I,P,B	29.21	29.85	28.74	33.24	C,I,P,B	27.83	21.5	24.83	27.67
Mean	28.9	28.93	27.86	32.29	Mean	27.3	20.98	22.16	28.36

where x_p is an image from the same class as the query image x_q, and x_n an image from any other class. The Nearest Class Mean Metric Learning (NCM+ML) optimizes W according to Eq. 2 and the Nearest Class Multiple Centroids classifier based metric learning (NCMC+ML) according to Eq. 3 (see details in [14]). Finally, we consider the Domain Specific Class Means based Metric Learning (DSCM+ML) described in section 3.1. We report results in Table 2. SVM results in the projected space are not included as we observed in general a drop[8]. in performance compared to Table 1. From these results, we can see that:

- Metric learning significantly improves the classification in the target domain in all cases, even when we apply methods which are not domain specific as ML for KNN, NCM and NCMC. The reason is that on the merged dataset the learning approach is able to take advantage of the class labels to bring closer the images from the same class independently of the domains and hence the final classifier is able to better exploit labeled data from the sources in the transformed space than in the original one.
- When we compare the different metric learning approaches, DSCMML outperforms all other methods on ICDA1 and in most cases on ICDA2. The few exceptions are when KNN+ML performs better than DSCM+ML on ICDA2. Note however that for ICDA2 we have a single test set, while on ICDA1 we average on 11 folds hence we can assume that DSCM+ML is consistently better than KNN+ML. Comparing to the SVM baseline (see Table 1) we see that DSCM+ML is almost always significantly better than the results obtained with the linear multi-class SVM.

Evaluation of SaMLDa with Different Metric Learning Algorithms.
The aim of these experiments is to show that the Self-adaptive Metric Learning

---

[8] Reducing interclass and increasing intraclass distances does not mean improving linear separability between classes, especially when we decrease the dimensionality. Testing different non-linear kernels was out of the scope of the paper.

Table 3. Showing the improved accuracy for each metric learning when we refine the metric with the SaMLDa algorithm

ICDA1	KNN + ML	KNN + SaMLDa	NCM + ML	NCM + SaMLDa	NCMC + ML	NCMC + SaMLDa	DSCM+ ML	DSCM+ SaMLDa
C	26.74	27.41	26.03	27.45	24.77	25.7	28.41	28.67
I	29.33	29.67	27.11	27.89	28.52	28.56	32.88	32.68
P	25.94	26.59	25.27	26.41	23.88	24.79	26.5	27.92
B	33.21	33.83	33.08	34.35	32.48	33.12	34.85	35.55
C,I	29.62	30.09	26.47	28.42	25.5	25.98	30.89	31.21
C,P	25.48	26.42	25.86	27.79	23.92	24.86	30.32	32
C,B	30.36	31.03	30.92	32.97	29.5	29.95	32.92	34.59
I,P	26.62	27.77	26	26.92	26.89	26.65	31.86	32.33
I,B	33.45	34.02	32.86	35.27	33.48	34.02	35.23	37.42
P,B	28.29	28.58	31.41	33.32	27.29	27.8	33.68	35.3
C,I,P	25.98	27.15	27.48	29.27	25.53	26	31.67	33.77
C,I,B	31.15	31.77	31.33	32.91	28.89	29.74	34.68	36.52
C,P,B	28.27	28.21	29.98	32.03	28.92	29.15	32.67	34.8
I,P,B	29.82	30.88	30.33	33.18	29.56	31.03	34.58	36.52
C,I,P,B	29.21	30.06	29.85	32.12	28.74	29.64	33.24	35.74
Mean	28.9	29.57	28.93	30.69	27.86	28.47	32.29	33.67

Domain Adaptation (SaMLDa) described in section 4 can be used to further improve the performance of any of the previously mentioned metric learning approaches by iteratively updating the metric with unlabeled target examples. Note that in our algorithm the metric yielding the results in Table 2 correspond to the results obtained with W_1. We also tested the performance with W_0 corresponding to the PCA projection, but the results were far below the results obtained with W_1. In Table 3 we compare the classification accuracies between a given metric learning W_1 using only the initial training set X_1 and the metric W_{r^*} refined with SaMLDa, where f_W is the corresponding metric learning. We only show results on ICDA1, but similar behavior was observed on ICDA2.

The results show that if we integrate any of these metric learning approaches with the proposed SaMLDa algorithm, we are able to improve the classification accuracy in 58 out of 60 cases and for the two remaining cases the drop is not significant. When we compare SaMLDa with different metrics, best results are obtained when ML for DSCM is used.

Comparing Different Weighting Strategies. In Table 4 we compare different weighting strategies: fixed weights, weights obtained using $TDAS$ and weights using NCM accuracies. In the top 3 rows we show results when the weighting strategy was used in SaMLDa, *i.e.* we updated w_d^r at each iteration, while on the bottom 3 lines we show results when we used the manually fixed weights during the learning and used the $TDAS$ or NCM based weights with the learned metric W only at test time. In all cases we show the mean of all configuration results (as in the tables above), the results for all four sources and the results obtained as a late fusion of all SC_i source combinations (including SC_0). From Table 4 we can draw the following conclusions:

- The best weighting strategy is in general using the NCM accuracies. Using TDAS actually decreases the performance in most cases.
- Using the weighting strategy only at test time and using fix weight at training time seems to be a good compromise as the results are relatively similar and

Table 4. Different weighting strategies on ICDA1 (left) and ICDA2 (right) used during both training and test (top 3 rows) and test only (bottom 3 rows)

ICDA1	fix	TDAS	NCM
Mean	32.29	31.75	32.67
C,I,P,B	33.24	31.83	34.53
FusAll	39.18	39.29	39.86
Mean	32.29	31.69	32.88
C,I,P,B	33.24	32.73	34.56
FusAll	39.18	38.74	39.56

ICDA2	fix	TDAS	NCM
Mean	27.06	28.39	27.17
C,I,P,B	30.67	29	27.67
FusAll	38	37.17	37.5
Mean	27.06	26.72	27
C,I,P,B	30.67	28.83	33
FusAll	38	37.83	37.67

Table 5. Results on OffCalSS compared with [6] and [1], where for $\mathcal{D}_1 \rightarrow \mathcal{D}_2$, the domain $\mathcal{D}_1$ was used as source and $\mathcal{D}_2$ was the target

	SVM (ours)	DSCM	DSCM + SaMLDa	SA [6] +SVM	DIP+CC [1] +SVM		KNN (ours)	KNN + SaMLDa	SA [6] + KNN
C→A	53.66	50.64	54.14	44.7	61.8		42.01	53.02	45.3
D→A	46.37	48.76	46.77	41.6	56.9		43.08	47.34	45.8
W→A	44.72	48.43	45.66	39.3	53.4		40.33	46.52	44.8
A→C	44.6	34.89	44.21	40.6	47.8		33.75	43.96	38.4
D→C	38.5	34.24	38.62	34.8	44.2		31.58	38.73	35.8
W→C	36.79	33.42	36.59	32.6	43.6		29.19	36.8	34.1
A→D	50.94	62.05	53.07	40.9	67.5		50.87	54.09	55.1
C→D	54.57	61.57	56.97	41.1	65.8		50.71	55.51	56.6
W→D	76.81	64.65	73.27	77.6	92.6		71.65	77.2	82.3
A→W	53.68	66.08	56.81	38.2	72.5		56.77	59	60.3
C→W	54.42	65.06	59.58	82.2	69.9		58.17	58.74	60.7
D→W	83.74	71.47	81	87.1	89.1		78.79	83.53	84.8

in this way we can keep the training costs lower (no need to estimate the weights at each step).

– Note finally, that averaging the predictions from all source combinations (FusAll) improves the final results significantly in all cases compared to using the C, I, P, B source combination alone.

Evaluation on OffCalSS. We consider the OffCalSS dataset where in contrast to the other datasets we have only a single source and only a relatively small amount of training source images (20 or 8 instances from each class) to which 3 labeled target images per class were added from the target domain. For each source-target pair, we consider in the original feature space the multi-class SVM, the DSCM (with the NCM accuracy based weighting) and the KNN classifiers (with $k = 1$ as 1NN is used in general with this dataset in the literature). In addition, both for KNN and DSCM we show in Table 5 the results of the SaMLDa framework with the corresponding metric learning. As a comparison we show that our results are slightly better than the results of the unsupervised subspace alignment (SA) in [6], but they are below the current state-of-the art results on this dataset (DIP+CC) [1]. The latter also exploits the idea of bringing closer instances from the same class in the projected (latent) space, but exploits jointly with the empirical distance between the source and target domains when they learn the latent space.

Evaluation on OffCalMS. We finally evaluate the proposed methods on the OffCalMS where each dataset serve as target in turn and the others as sources

Table 6. Results on OffcalMS considering different dataset as target domains

A	SVM	DSCM	DSCM + SaMLDa	KNN	KNN + SaMLDa
A	47.53	47.07	48.38	43.32	43.32
C	56.76	50.78	59.19	43.18	54.62
D	44.11	50.54	46.24	42.46	47.35
W	41.63	47.39	42.13	39.83	44.66
C,D,W	57.22	52.59	59.44	43.5	53.79
FusAll	73.27	80.57	79.46	60.84	71.27

C	SVM	DSCM	DSCM + SaMLDa	KNN	KNN + SaMLDa
C	33.39	32.66	33.39	28.04	28.04
A	46.76	35.21	46.74	35.66	45.57
D	37.93	34.19	38.53	30.67	39.79
W	38.08	36	36.77	30.7	39.21
A,D,W	50.84	38.59	49.86	36.8	47.22
FusAll	66.4	61.48	73.9	46.44	64.85

D	SVM	DSCM	DSCM + SaMLDa	KNN	KNN + SaMLDa
D	56.61	58.82	59.45	56.06	56.06
A	46.38	60.31	50.71	52.52	47.87
C	47.48	61.5	50.87	51.26	49.84
W	87.64	68.19	85.04	88.82	88.82
A,C,W	70.71	70.47	70.16	77.95	65.04
FusAll	89.69	84.49	95.28	91.02	87.95

W	SVM	DSCM	DSCM + SaMLDa	KNN	KNN + SaMLDa
W	63.92	62.98	64.6	61.62	61.62
A	51.21	67.58	51.66	57.58	49.47
C	47.7	66.57	56.3	53.02	48.08
D	86.24	73.89	84.04	87.36	88.15
A,C,D	62.15	72.15	67.51	78.68	59.7
FusAll	90.64	92.34	95.36	96	89.74

where the whole dataset is considered for training. In Table 6 we show the results for 1) using only the labeled target set as training SC_0, 2) using each source individually $(SC_i, i = 1..3)$ as training where T_l was added to the source, 3) using the set of all sources (SC_{N_s}), and finally 4) the fusion of all combination results (FusAll). In all cases we show similarly to OffCalSS the SVM, DSCM and KNN results in the original space and the results of the SaMLDa framework with the corresponding metric learning. Note that the test sets are the same as in Table 5 (up to the randomly selected small T_l set) so we can observe an important gain in performance due to adding more source instances and especially considering more than a single source domain (FusAll).

7   Conclusion

Targeting multi-source domain adaptation we extended the Nearest Class Mean (NCM) classifier by introducing, for each class, domain-dependent mean parameters as well as domain-specific weights. We have shown that the proposed Domain Specific Class Means (DSCM) classifier is already suitable for domain adaptation without any learning and its performance can be further improved by appropriately designed metric learning. As a second contribution, which is orthogonal to the first one and therefore complementary, was a generic self-adaptive metric learning technique that iteratively curates the training set by adding unlabeled samples for which the prediction confidence was high and removing the labeled samples for which the prediction confidence was low. We have shown on two public benchmarks, the ImageClef Domain Adaptation Challenge and the Office-CalTech datasets, that the proposed self-adaptive metric learning approach can bring improvement to various metric learning approaches in the domain adaptation framework.

References

1. Baktashmotlagh, M., Harandi, M.T., Lovell, B.C., Salzmann, M.: Unsupervised domain adaptation by domain invariant projection. In: ICCV (2013)

2. Beijbom, O.: Domain adaptations for computer vision applications. University of California, San Diego (June 2012)
3. Csurka, G., Dance, C., Fan, L., Willamowski, J., Bray, C.: Visual categorization with bags of keypoints. In: SLCV (ECCV Workshop) (2004)
4. Davis, J.V., Kulis, B., Jain, P., Sra, S., Dhillon, I.S.: Information-theoretic metric learning. In: ICML (2007)
5. Duan, L., Tsang, I.W., Xu, D., Maybank, S.J.: Domain transfer SVM for video concept detection. In: CVPR (2009)
6. Fernando, B., Habrard, A., Sebban, M., Tuytelaars, T.: Unsupervised visual domain adaptation using subspace alignment. In: ICCV (2013)
7. Gong, B., Shi, Y., Sha, F., Grauman, K.: Geodesic flow kernel for unsupervised domain adaptation. In: CVPR (2012)
8. Gong, B., Grauman, K., Sha, F.: Reshaping visual datasets for domain adaptation. In: NIPS (2013)
9. Gopalan, R., Li, R., Chellappa, R.: Domain adaptation for object recognition: An unsupervised approach. In: ICCV (2011)
10. Hoffman, J., Kulis, B., Darrell, T., Saenko, K.: Discovering Latent Domains for Multisource Domain Adaptation. In: Fitzgibbon, A., Lazebnik, S., Perona, P., Sato, Y., Schmid, C. (eds.) ECCV 2012, Part II. LNCS, vol. 7573, pp. 702–715. Springer, Heidelberg (2012)
11. Huang, J., Smola, A., A., Borgwardt, K., Schoelkopf, B.: Correcting sample selection bias by unlabeled data. In: NIPS (2007)
12. Jiang, J.: A literature survey on domain adaptation of statistical classifiers. Tech. rep. (2008)
13. Kulis, B., Saenko, K., Darrell, T.: What you saw is not what you get: Domain adaptation using asymmetric kernel transforms. In: CVPR (2011)
14. Mensink, T., Verbeek, J., Perronnin, F., Csurka, G.: Distance-based image classification: Generalizing to new classes at near zero cost. PAMI 35(11), 2624–2637 (2013)
15. Pan, S.J., Yang, Q.: A survey on transfer learning. IEEE Transactions on Knowledge and Data Engineering 22(10), 1345–1359 (2010)
16. Perronnin, F., Sánchez, J., Mensink, T.: Improving the Fisher Kernel for Large-Scale Image Classification. In: Daniilidis, K., Maragos, P., Paragios, N. (eds.) ECCV 2010, Part IV. LNCS, vol. 6314, pp. 143–156. Springer, Heidelberg (2010)
17. Saenko, K., Kulis, B., Fritz, M., Darrell, T.: Adapting Visual Category Models to New Domains. In: Daniilidis, K., Maragos, P., Paragios, N. (eds.) ECCV 2010, Part IV. LNCS, vol. 6314, pp. 213–226. Springer, Heidelberg (2010)
18. Saha, A., Rai, P., Daumé III, H., Venkatasubramanian, S., DuVall, S.L.: Active Supervised Domain Adaptation. In: Gunopulos, D., Hofmann, T., Malerba, D., Vazirgiannis, M. (eds.) ECML PKDD 2011, Part III. LNCS, vol. 6913, pp. 97–112. Springer, Heidelberg (2011)
19. Tommasi, T., Caputo, B.: Frustratingly easy nbnn domain adaptation. In: ICCV (2013)
20. Weinberger, K., Saul, L.: Distance metric learning for large margin nearest neighbor classification. JMLR 10, 207–244 (2009)
21. Zha, Z.J., Mei, T., Wang, M., Wang, Z., Hua, X.S.: Robust distance metric learning with auxiliary knowledge. In: IJCAI (2009)

Nonlinear Cross-View Sample Enrichment for Action Recognition

Ling Wang$^{(\boxtimes)}$ and Hichem Sahbi

Institut Mines-Télécom, Télécom ParisTech; CNRS LTCI, Paris, France
{ling.wang,hichem.sahbi}@telecom-paristech.fr

Abstract. Advanced action recognition methods are prone to limited generalization performances when trained on insufficient amount of data. This limitation results from the high expense to label training samples and their insufficiency to capture enough variability due to viewpoint changes.

In this paper, we propose a solution that enriches training data by transferring their features across views. The proposed method is motivated by the fact that cross-view features of the same actions are highly correlated. First, we use kernel-based canonical correlation analysis (CCA) to learn nonlinear feature mappings that take multi-view data from their original feature spaces into a common latent space. Then, we transfer training samples from source to target views by back-projecting their CCA features from latent to view-dependent spaces.

We experiment this cross-view sample enrichment process for action classification and we study the impact of several factors including kernel choices as well as the dimensionality of the latent spaces.

Keywords: Action recognition · Kernel methods · Canonical correlation analysis · Viewpoint knowledge transfer · Sample enrichment

1 Introduction

Human action recognition is highly important for video understanding. In a wide range of applications (such as robotic vision, autonomous driving, video surveillance and retrieval), automatic solutions are necessary in order to recognize several categories of human actions. To achieve this goal, machine learning and classification methods are used to obtain models from existing labeled video collections. However, with the fast growth of industrial applications, action recognition solutions should handle realistic scenarios in challenging conditions including outdoor environment, moving platforms, cluttered background and viewpoint change. As learning and classification methods usually require labeled data, which are scarce and expensive to collect, making use of training data adequately becomes essential.

Under these constraints, enhancing the generalization ability of learning models is necessary, even when labeled training data are scarce. In current literature, action recognition solutions are categorized according to their data

© Springer International Publishing Switzerland 2015
L. Agapito et al. (Eds.): ECCV 2014 Workshops, Part III, LNCS 8927, pp. 47–62, 2015.
DOI: 10.1007/978-3-319-16199-0_4

representation and learning methods. These works include but not limited to designing discriminative and robust features [7,19,31], building compact and effective representations [28,37], modeling context and hierarchies [14,22] and designing kernels [4,5,33]. However, even advanced action recognition models have limited generalization power if training data are scarce; indeed, insufficient training samples do not capture enough the inherent variability due to several factors including viewpoint changes.

One possible solution to address this issue is to increase the size of training data by providing larger datasets that sufficiently cover the variability in action recognition; for instance [10,16,17,30] provided around 100 video clips for each action. As training needs to process more videos, this opens a direction to large scale video processing, where models should sufficiently cover the variability. Alternative solutions, based on transfer learning and domain adaption [26], rely on another principle; knowledge learned in one task is applied to another different task in order to make best use of current data. In this framework, no new data needs to be collected, knowledge, however, is added.

In this work, we are interested in solutions that enrich training video data by transferring knowledge about their acquisition conditions (mainly viewpoints). Inspired from the observation that cross-view video features are highly and non linearly correlated, we use a kernel version of canonical correlation analysis (CCA), in order to learn cross-view transfer mappings that take video features from existing (source) to new (target) views.

1.1   Related Work

As action recognition is usually based on appearance and motion features, it is well understood in the literature that large viewpoint change usually causes large variation in these features and reduces the generalization ability of recognition models. The issue of viewpoint change has received a particular attention in action recognition research (see for instance [1,11]) and several existing techniques [13,15,20,35,39] focus on building view invariant representations while others combine models learned for different source views [3,34]. In studies of features through different viewpoints, appearance and motion patterns are shown to be very correlated. In [23], view-dependent vocabularies are connected through corresponding action pairs to build a new dictionary which is more tolerant to view changes. Recently, existing methods make effort to transfer knowledge between viewpoints; several works [21,36,38] explore linear relationship between features in fixed source view - target view pairs. Combination models are also needed for view-independent classification. Still, these methods require large quantity of stereo vision data and adequate labeling and annotation information through different viewpoints which are very expensive. Other techniques transfer knowledge through different types of databases. For example, [8] builds a multi-view spatio-temporal AND-OR graph model from 3D human skeleton data and [32] aligns video trajectories with the projected trajectories from a large 3D motion capture database and synthesizes multi-view training data.

1.2   Motivation and Contribution

Again, recognizing actions in video is usually based on local appearance and motion features. However, the latter are subject to strong variations due to acquisition conditions (viewpoint in particular). Features, especially motion ones, are not viewpoint invariant, so models learned with insufficient training sets are clearly unable to capture the inherent viewpoint variability and thus have weak generalization power on test data. A straightforward solution to overcome this limitation, is to synthesize large training sets of videos, to better model variability due to viewpoint changes, for instance, by horizontally flipping frames with symmetric views or by using still or animated 3D models. In contrast to our proposed method (see §2), this large scale video synthesis process makes the pre-processing step (prior to train action classifiers) very time demanding as the whole feature extraction pipeline needs to be applied on all the newly generated videos. Furthermore, and regardless processing time issues, this process may hit two major limitations: i) the insufficiency of the simple flipping operations, ii) and the possible unrealistic aspect of (rendered and animated) 3D models.

Stereo vision is an alternative that provides knowledge in order to learn cross-view mappings. This knowledge is transferable to new videos and may improve classification performance. Usual methods rely on large view-specific stereo datasets to learn transfer models, but during testing, they are not scalable to general datasets whose views (or poses) are not known a priori. Indeed, view-specific data transfer methods may require a preliminary step of human pose estimation in order to decide which view-specific model to apply. Besides the issue of learning pose-specific models[1], pose estimation should also be achieved during the transfer process (i.e., during testing). In contrast, our data transfer solution, presented in this paper, neither requires pose estimation nor view-specific training models for action recognition.

Research on cross-view action recognition shows that multiple-view shots are highly correlated both in appearance and in motion; an assumption of *linear* relationship is helpful (even though insufficient) to learn cross-view transfer models [21,36,38]. However, when measuring canonical correlations between cross-view features using CCA (see a particular example in Fig. 1), we observe that they decrease fast, and only few pairs of canonical basis vectors can be found so that projected data are well correlated. With *nonlinear* (kernel-based) CCA, correlations have higher values (see again Fig. 1), and this suggests that relationships between cross-view features are nonlinear.

Considering the above motivations, we introduce in this paper a novel method that enriches video data by transferring their features from few existing training videos (taken from source views) to other views. The proposed method is based on a nonlinear version of canonical correlation analysis and it is motivated by the fact that actions observed across views are highly and non linearly correlated. Using this principle, we show that this feature transfer and enrichment process is highly effective in order to improve the performance of action recognition. This

---

[1] That may require a lot of human effort in order to label videos and their poses (which is also subject to error).

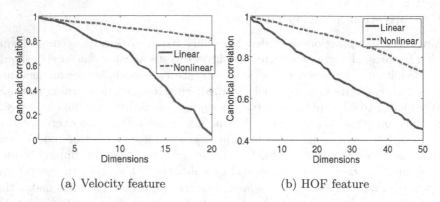

(a) Velocity feature   (b) HOF feature

Fig. 1. A comparison between linear and nonlinear canonical correlation analysis: for linear CCA, canonical correlations decrease fast and only few pairs of canonical basis vectors have highly correlated data while for nonlinear CCA, canonical correlations are high and decrease slowly

allows us to obtain more training examples that cover many viewpoints especially when the initial training data are insufficient in order to capture the variability due to viewpoint changes. Experiments conducted show the effectiveness of our method for action recognition.

The remainder of this paper is organized as follows: in §2, we propose our cross-view feature transfer using kernel-based CCA; in §3, we present some experiments on action recognition and we compare different kernels and the impact of feature transfer on action recognition. Finally, we conclude our work in §4.

2   Cross-View Feature Transfer

Consider two overlapping and synchronous video sequences, of the same scenes, taken from two camera viewpoints (referred to as source and target views). We assume that the target view (denoted by t) forms a relative angle θ with respect to the source view (denoted by s). Let $\mathcal{V}_s = \{x_1^s, \ldots, x_n^s\}$, $\mathcal{V}_t = \{x_1^t, \ldots, x_n^t\}$ be the set of features (see §3.1) extracted inside the bounding boxes surrounding moving objects of interest in the source and target views respectively; we assume that $\mathcal{V}_s$, $\mathcal{V}_t$ are ordered so $x_i^s \in \mathcal{V}_s$ is aligned with $x_i^t \in \mathcal{V}_t$, i.e., the underlying features belong to the same moving physical object. In what follows, we use canonical correlation analysis (CCA) in order to learn transformations that *maximize the expected correlation of aligned data in $\mathcal{V}_s$, $\mathcal{V}_t$ into a common latent space.* We use these learned transformations to induce (*unobserved*) features in a target view, from *observed* video features taken from a source view.

2.1   Training with Canonical Correlation Analysis

Let $\mathcal{X}$ be an input space (for instance the 96 dimensional HOG space) and consider $\mathcal{V}_s$, $\mathcal{V}_t \subseteq \mathcal{X}$ as two training sets of aligned features. The goal is to learn transformation matrices $\mathbf{P}_s$, $\mathbf{P}_t$ that characterize features in $\mathcal{V}_s$, $\mathcal{V}_t$ while being viewpoint invariant. Canonical correlation analysis finds two sets of orthogonal axes in $\mathcal{X}$ (also referred to as canonical basis vectors) such that the projection of $\mathcal{V}_s$, $\mathcal{V}_t$, on these axes, maximizes their correlation. Again, $\mathbf{P}_s$, $\mathbf{P}_t$ denote the projection matrices of these orthogonal axes which respectively correspond to views s and t. CCA finds these matrices by maximizing the following criterion [9,12]:

$$(\mathbf{P}_s, \mathbf{P}_t) = \arg\max_{\mathbf{A},\mathbf{B}} \ \mathbf{A}'C_{st}\mathbf{B}$$
$$\text{s.t.} \ \ \mathbf{A}'C_{ss}\mathbf{A} = 1$$
$$\mathbf{B}'C_{tt}\mathbf{B} = 1 \tag{1}$$

here $\mathbf{A}'$ stands for transpose of $\mathbf{A}$ and C_{st} (resp. C_{ss}, C_{tt}) is the interclass (resp. intraclass) covariance matrices of data in $\mathcal{V}_s$, $\mathcal{V}_t$. One can show (see for instance [9,12]) that (1) is equivalent to solving the following eigenproblem:

$$C_{st}C_{tt}^{-1}C_{ts}\mathbf{P}_s = \lambda^2 C_{ss}\mathbf{P}_s$$
$$\mathbf{P}_t = \tfrac{1}{\lambda}\, C_{tt}^{-1}C_{ts}\mathbf{P}_s \tag{2}$$

Projection matrices $\mathbf{P}_s$, $\mathbf{P}_t$ define a common latent space (denoted by $\mathcal{L} \subset \mathbb{R}^d$) in which the correlation between $(\mathbf{P}'_s\, x_i^s, \mathbf{P}'_t\, x_i^t) \in \mathcal{L} \times \mathcal{L}$ is maximized ($i = 1, \ldots, n$). Note that cross-view transformations might not be only related to linear geometric transformations as they include other nonlinear physical aspects including (illumination changes, etc.), so one should consider a nonlinear version of CCA using kernel mapping (see §2.2). Prior to describe the cross-view mapping method in §2.3, we will review kernel mapping via kernel principal component analysis (KPCA) in §2.2. The latter makes it possible to control dimensionality of data and helps defining new mapping spaces so that CCA transformations become nonlinear.

2.2   Kernel Mapping

Let Φ be an implicit mapping (defined via a kernel function $K(x, z) = \Phi(x)'\Phi(z)$) from the input space $\mathcal{X}$ into a high dimensional feature space $\mathcal{H}$. Assume the training set $\mathcal{V}_s$ is centered in $\mathcal{H}$, i.e., $\sum_{i=1}^n \Phi(x_i^s) = 0$. KPCA finds principal orthogonal projection axes by diagonalizing the covariance matrix $M = (1/n) \sum_{i=1}^n \Phi(x_i^s)\Phi(x_i^s)'$. The principal orthogonal axes, denoted $\{E_k\}_{k=1}^n$, can be found by solving the eigenproblem $ME_k = \lambda_k E_k$, where E_k, λ_k are, respectively, the kth eigenvector and its underlying eigenvalue. It can be shown (see for instance [29]) that the solution of the above eigenproblem lies in the span of the training data, i.e., $\forall k = 1, \ldots, n$, $\exists \alpha_{k1}, \ldots, \alpha_{kn} \in \mathbb{R}$ s.t. $E_k = \sum_{j=1}^n \alpha_{kj}\Phi(x_j^s)$, where $\alpha_k = (\alpha_{k1}, \ldots, \alpha_{kn})$ are found by solving the eigenproblem $K\alpha_k = \lambda_k\alpha_k$. Here K is the Gram matrix on the centered data in $\mathcal{V}_s$ in the feature space $\mathcal{H}$. In case the data are not centered, this matrix is defined as

$$K_{ij} = \left\langle \Phi(x_i^s) - \frac{1}{n}\sum_k \Phi(x_k^s), \Phi(x_j^s) - \frac{1}{n}\sum_k \Phi(x_k^s) \right\rangle, \tag{3}$$

Fig. 2. General action recognition videos in different viewpoints [27]

where $\langle \cdot, \cdot \rangle$ denotes the inner product. Each data $x \in \mathcal{V}_s$ is explicitly mapped into $\psi(x) \in \mathbb{R}^p$, where $\psi(x) = \big(\langle x, E_1 \rangle, \ldots, \langle x, E_p \rangle \big)' \ (p \ll n)$. The same KPCA mapping process is achieved for data in $\mathcal{V}_t$. CCA is now applied to $\psi(\mathcal{V}_s)$, $\psi(\mathcal{V}_t) \subset \mathbb{R}^p$ as shown subsequently.

2.3   Cross-View Feature Transfer Using CCA

Fig. 2 shows video examples of actions taken from different views. A hypothesis of cross-view transfer learning is that features in different views are drawn from the same distribution in the latent space $\mathcal{L}$. So, we assume that latent features capture visual characteristics of moving objects/persons while being tolerant to their viewpoint changes. Thus the features in the input space $\mathcal{X}$ (extracted directly from video data) are connected by the CCA latent features in $\mathcal{L}$. Assuming that mappings $\mathbf{P}_s$, $\mathbf{P}_t$ are invertible (or utilizing Moore-Penrose pseudoinverse [6]), we transfer features $\{\psi(x^s)\}$ (from the source view) to features $\{\psi(x^t)\}$ (in the target view) by

$$\psi(x^t) := (\mathbf{P}_s \mathbf{P}_t^{-1})' (\psi(x^s) - \bar{\psi}^s) + \bar{\psi}^t, \tag{4}$$

here $\bar{\psi}^s$, $\bar{\psi}^t$ are the estimated sample means in $\psi(\mathcal{V}_s)$, $\psi(\mathcal{V}_t)$ respectively. Notice that Eq. (4), follows the assumption that CCA projections in the latent space $\mathcal{L}$ are viewpoint invariant, i.e., $\mathbf{P}'_s(\psi(x^s) - \bar{\psi}^s) \simeq \mathbf{P}'_t(\psi(x^t) - \bar{\psi}^t)$.

In practice, we build transformation matrices $\mathbf{P}_s$, $\mathbf{P}_t$ using a dataset of "source-target" view video sequences that correspond to the same moving actors [24] (see Fig. 3; in this example, (b, c, d, e, f) correspond to the source views while (a, b, c, d, e) correspond to the target view). This dataset includes simple actions shot by 20 cameras with equiangular optical axes; the angle θ between these axes is constant and relatively small ($\theta = 18^0$) in order to avoid occlusions and to obtain enough alignments across views.

We generate abundant trajectories from video data by tracking densely sampled keypoints [31]. As frames in different views are synchronized, we obtain sets $\mathcal{V}_s$, $\mathcal{V}_t$ of aligned trajectories according to their keypoint locations in corresponding frames using SIFT matching [25]. In the learning process, we randomly sample 4000 pairs of corresponding trajectories in $\mathcal{V}_s$, $\mathcal{V}_t$ and use them to learn KPCA mapping as well as CCA transformation matrices $\mathbf{P}_s$, $\mathbf{P}_t$.

2.4 Video Set Enrichment

Using the learned transformation matrices $\mathbf{P}_s$, $\mathbf{P}_t$, we enrich the set of training videos across different views by transferring component features. We describe each video with component-based features using the method in [33] that generates and groups abundant trajectories from video data by tracking densely sampled keypoints. During video enrichment, we first map source view component features (defined as centers of their assigned trajectory features) using KPCA, then we generate new component features associated to a target view, by transferring their KPCA features using Eq. (4). Again, this transfer assumes that corresponding features in the latent space are highly correlated.

Given a set of training videos $\{V_i\}$ with unknown source view angles in $\{\alpha_i\}$, the transfer process "hallucinates" a new set of video component features *with a relative angle* θ (i.e., with target view angles in $\{\alpha_i + \theta\}$); note that generated video features inherit the same labels as original videos. Though we cannot process videos in target views (as they are not available), we can generate new training samples by the transfer process in Eq. 4. In this way, generating many training samples covering more views is very efficient and also effective for action recognition as shown in experiments.

3 Experimental Analysis

In this section, we measure the impact of our cross-view feature transfer method on action recognition. We first evaluate the ability of KPCA[2] in order to generate high dimensional and more discriminating features. Then, we apply CCA on the obtained KPCA features and evaluate its performance for cross-view feature transfer. As will be shown later in this section, the generalization power of

---

[2] With different kernel functions.

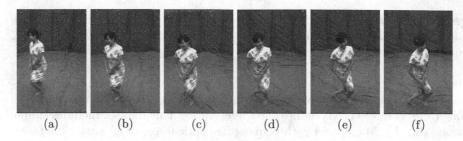

Fig. 3. Frame examples from stereo videos [24]

our feature transfer method, and its positive impact on action recognition performances, increases when the dimensions of KPCA and CCA mappings reach reasonably large values.

3.1 Evaluation Set and Setting

Dataset and features. We conduct experiments on the UCF Sport dataset [27]. The latter includes 150 videos containing 10 classes of actions shot in real environment with large viewpoint variation and background changes. In order to evaluate the results, we use the data split protocol introduced in [18]; we build support vector machine (SVM) classifiers on the training set (of 103 videos), and report the classification accuracy on the remaining test set (of 47 videos). As a preprocessing step, we first extract dense trajectories [31] from original videos and we keep only those inside the bounding boxes provided by [18], so that trajectories are roughly around the human body[3]. Then, we group these trajectories into mid-level components using the unsupervised clustering method in [33]. Finally, we represent each video by the set of its mid-level components (limited to 100 components in practice) and each one is described by five feature vectors: Velocity Shape, HOG, HOF, MBHx, MBHy (see [31] for details).

Action recognition with SVMs. We use the convolution kernel in order to evaluate the similarity between any two given videos V, V'; this kernel is defined as $K(V, V') = \sum_{c \in V, c' \in V'} k_e(c, c')$. Here two choices are considered for the elementary kernel k_e: linear and Laplacian RBF with $\gamma = 1$ (see table 1). The convolution kernel is computed between pairwise videos and plugged into SVMs for training and classification. In all these experiments, the regularization parameter C in SVMs is fixed to 10 and "one vs. all" SVMs are trained for each action class; a given test video is assigned to the action class that maximizes its SVM score. In the remainder of this section, SVM classifiers based on linear (resp. Laplacian RBF) elementary kernels will be referred to as LCK (resp. RCK).

In what follows, we study the influence of kernel choice used for KPCA on the performance of action recognition. These performances are reported for different

---

[3] Besides, according to our transfer settings, we only transfer knowledge on actions.

KPCA and CCA dimensions corresponding to the p-largest eigenvalues (of the underlying kernel matrices) and the d-largest correlations (associated to the canonical basis vectors) respectively (see §2.2, §2.1).

Table 1. Types of kernels used in the experiments

	Kernel Type	Formulation	Parameters
1	Linear	$k(x,y) = x'y$	–
2	Polynomial	$k(x,y) = (\gamma x'y + 1)^d$	$\gamma = 1, d = 2$
3	NegDist	$k(x,y) = -\|x-y\|^p$	$p = 1$
4	GHI**	$k(x,y) = \sum_i \min(|x_i|^\gamma, |y_i|^\gamma)$	$\gamma = 1$
5	Gaussian RBF*	$k(x,y) = e^{-\frac{\|x-y\|^2}{2\gamma \bar{d}^2}}$	$\gamma \in \{0.01, 1, 100\}$
6	Laplacian RBF*	$k(x,y) = e^{-\frac{\|x-y\|}{\gamma \bar{d}}}$	$\gamma \in \{0.1, 1, 10\}$

** Generalized Histogram Intersection Kernel [2]
* In RBF like kernels, $\bar{d}$ is the mean distance between all training samples.

3.2 Influence of KPCA Mapping on Action Recognition

As discussed in §2.3, KPCA is a preprocessing step that maps data from an input space $\mathcal{X}$ into a high dimensional space $\mathcal{H}$ so that cross-view CCA transformations can be learned and applied in $\mathcal{H}$. Note that KPCA mapping is used not only to make CCA transformations nonlinear, but also to make features more discriminating in $\mathcal{H}$. Thus, prior to evaluate the performance of CCA transfer (see §3.3), we evaluate in this section the ability of KPCA to produce more discriminating features in $\mathcal{H}$ by measuring its impact on the performance of action recognition (i.e., without sample enrichment). This impact is measured for different kernel choices (see again table 1) and also for different values of p (the dimension of KPCA mapping).

Table 2 shows action recognition performances for different kernel choices for KPCA (listed in table 1); these results are obtained with linear SVM classifiers (LCK). The results show that nonlinear KPCA mapping improves classification performances (w.r.t linear mapping) especially when using the generalized histogram intersection and RBF kernels. Note that Gaussian RBF kernel is more sensitive to the choice of parameters than Laplacian RBF and the latter has a similar behavior compared to NegDist kernel. These results also corroborate the fact that features in $\mathcal{H}$ are more discriminating when dimension p is sufficiently (but not very) large.

3.3 Influence of CCA Mapping on Action Recognition

Considering aligned training features $\psi(\mathcal{V}_s)$, $\psi(\mathcal{V}_t) \subset \mathbb{R}^p$ of the source and target views, we use CCA projection matrices $\mathbf{P}_s$, $\mathbf{P}_t$ (as shown in §2.1, §2.2, §2.3 and

Table 2. This table shows action recognition performance using KPCA mapping and linear SVMs: features are projected into a p dimensional space. Note that we do not explore larger values of p (i.e., $p > 128$) for the linear KPCA as the dimension of the input space is bounded by 128. Similarly, we do not explore larger values of p for the Gaussian RBF KPCA (with $\gamma = 100$) as the latter behaves as linear KPCA for large values of γ.

KPCA dim (p) — Kernels for KPCA	64	128	256	512	1024	2048
Linear (baseline)	53.2	**57.4**	–	–	–	–
Polynomial	59.6	**61.7**	61.7	61.7	61.7	61.7
NegDist	61.7	66.0	**68.1**	68.1	68.1	68.1
GHI	68.1	68.1	**72.3**	72.3	70.2	70.2
Gaussian RBF ($\gamma = 0.01$)	66.0	68.1	**72.3**	70.2	70.2	72.3
Gaussian RBF ($\gamma = 1$)	**59.6**	59.6	59.6	59.6	59.6	59.6
Gaussian RBF ($\gamma = 100$)	**59.6**	59.6	59.6	–	–	–
Laplacian RBF ($\gamma = 0.1$)	66.0	68.1	70.2	70.2	**72.3**	72.3
Laplacian RBF ($\gamma = 1$)	66.0	68.1	68.1	68.1	68.1	**70.2**
Laplacian RBF ($\gamma = 10$)	63.8	66.0	**68.1**	68.1	68.1	68.1

in Eq. (4)) in order to enrich the training set of videos. The purpose is to show the impact of this CCA-based enrichment process on action recognition.

Dimensionality and kernel choice. Tables 3, 4, 5 illustrate the impact of CCA transfer on action recognition performances for different settings of kernels in KPCA including linear, histogram intersection and Gaussian RBF respectively. These tables also report performances for different values of dimensions p, d (related to KPCA and CCA mapping respectively) and Fig. 4 shows transfer error between generated features and those in the ground truth both in target views, w.r.t p. From these results, it is clear that better performances and small transfer errors are obtained with nonlinear KPCA mappings, particularly with histogram intersection, and these performances increase as the dimensions p, d of KPCA and CCA mappings become reasonably large, both with linear and non-linear SVM classifiers. Indeed, when d is small, canonical basis vectors (in $\mathbf{P}_s$, $\mathbf{P}_t$) preserve accurate relationship between transferred features (i.e., high correlations) while less knowledge is transferred. As more dimensions are taken (i.e., as d increases), more knowledge is transferred but with more bias due to the decrease of the canonical correlations.

Motion vs. appearance features. In order to understand the importance of transferred (motion[4] and appearance[5]) features, we compare two settings: in the first one i) we transfer only motion features and we consider appearance features viewpoint invariant, while in the second setting ii) we transfer both motion and appearance features. Tables 6 – 7 compare the impact of these two settings

---

[4] Velocity Shape, HOF, MBHx, MBHy.
[5] HOG.

Table 3. This table shows action recognition performances (%) with and without the enrichment process for different values of p (related to linear KPCA mapping) and d (related to CCA)

$p \backslash d$	Linear SVMs (LCK)			Nonlinear SVMs (RCK)		
	noenrich	enrich perfs w.r.t d		noenrich	enrich perfs w.r.t d	
		$d=64$	$d=128$		$d=64$	$d=128$
$p=64$	53.2	**59.6**	-	76.6	**80.9**	-
$p=128$	57.4	55.3	**61.7**	78.7	**80.9**	80.9

Table 4. This table shows action recognition performances (%) with and without the enrichment process for different values of p (related to histogram intersection KPCA mapping) and d (related to CCA). Note that $d \leq p$ as the dimension of CCA cannot exceed that of KPCA.

$p \backslash d$	Linear SVMs (LCK)							Nonlinear SVMs (RCK)						
	noenrich	enrich perfs w.r.t d						noenrich	enrich perfs w.r.t d					
		64	128	256	512	1024	2048		64	128	256	512	1024	2048
64	68.1	59.6	–	–	–	–	–	78.7	**83.0**	–	–	–	–	–
128	68.1	**70.2**	66.0	–	–	–	–	74.5	**80.9**	76.6	–	–	–	–
256	72.3	72.3	**76.6**	68.1	–	–	–	74.5	76.6	**78.7**	78.7	–	–	–
512	72.3	**74.5**	74.5	70.2	68.1	–	–	74.5	70.2	72.3	**78.7**	70.2	–	–
1024	70.2	**74.5**	72.3	70.2	74.5	68.1	–	74.5	**76.6**	74.5	76.6	76.6	70.2	–
2048	70.2	70.2	70.2	**72.3**	72.3	70.2	72.3	74.5	72.3	72.3	74.5	72.3	66.0	66.0

Table 5. This table shows action recognition performances (%) with and without the enrichment process for different values of p (related to Gaussian RBF KPCA mapping, with $\gamma = 0.01$) and d (related to CCA). Note that $d \leq p$ as the dimension of CCA cannot exceed that of KPCA.

$p \backslash d$	Linear SVMs (LCK)							Nonlinear SVMs (RCK)						
	noenrich	enrich perfs w.r.t d						noenrich	enrich perfs w.r.t d					
		64	128	256	512	1024	2048		64	128	256	512	1024	2048
64	66.0	59.6	–	–	–	–	–	70.2	**72.3**	–	–	–	–	–
128	68.1	68.1	63.8	–	–	–	–	72.3	72.3	72.3	–	–	–	–
256	72.3	72.3	70.2	66.0	–	–	–	72.3	**76.6**	74.5	76.6	–	–	–
512	70.2	70.2	**72.3**	70.2	72.3	–	–	72.3	74.5	76.6	**80.9**	72.3	–	–
1024	70.2	**76.6**	76.6	74.5	72.3	70.2	–	72.3	**74.5**	74.5	74.5	72.3	72.3	–
2048	72.3	72.3	74.5	74.5	74.5	**76.6**	72.3	72.3	74.5	**80.9**	68.1	70.2	70.2	70.2

Table 6. This table shows a comparison between "motion and appearance transfer" vs. "motion transfer only" for different values of p, d. In these results linear kernel is used for KPCA. Note that $d \leq p$ as the dimension of CCA cannot exceed that of KPCA.

$p \backslash d$	Linear SVMs (LCK)		Nonlinear SVMs (RCK)	
	64	128	64	128
64	59.6/**61.7**	-	**80.9**/78.7	-
128	55.3/**61.7**	**61.7**/57.4	**80.9**/78.7	**80.9**/80.9

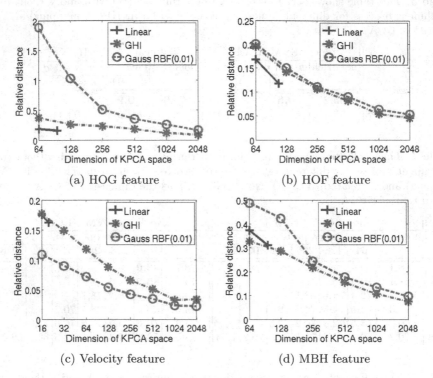

(a) HOG feature   (b) HOF feature

(c) Velocity feature   (d) MBH feature

Fig. 4. This figure shows the trend of transfer error between generated and ground truth features in target views when increasing the dimension p of KPCA mapping; for fixed p, dim d is set to obtain the full rank p. This transfer error is measured using the average relative distance defined as $dist(x, z) := \frac{1}{n} \sum_{i=1}^{n} ||x_i - z_i|| / ||z_i||$.

Table 7. This table shows a comparison between "motion and appearance transfer" vs. "motion transfer only" for different values of p, d. In these results histogram intersection kernel (top) and Gaussian RBF kernel, with $\gamma = 0.01$ (bottom) are used for KPCA. Note that $d \leq p$ as the dimension of CCA cannot exceed that of KPCA.

$p\backslash d$	64	128	256	512	1024	2048	64	128	256	512	1024	2048
	\multicolumn{6}{Linear SVMs (LCK)}			Nonlinear SVMs (RCK)					
64	59.6/59.6	–	–	–	–	–	**83.0**/80.9	–	–	–	–	–
128	**70.2**/68.1	66.0/63.8	–	–	–	–	80.9/**80.9**	76.6/76.6	–	–	–	–
256	72.3/68.1	**76.6**/68.1	68.1/66.0	–	–	–	76.6/78.7	78.7/**80.9**	78.7/78.7	–	–	–
512	**74.5**/68.1	74.5/70.2	70.2/72.3	68.1/66.0	–	–	70.2/76.6	72.3/80.9	78.7/**83.0**	70.2/74.5	–	–
1024	**74.5**/70.2	72.3/70.2	70.2/70.2	74.5/68.1	68.1/70.2	–	76.6/78.7	74.5/**80.9**	76.6/**80.9**	76.6/78.7	70.2/70.2	–
2048	70.2/**72.3**	70.2/70.2	72.3/68.1	**72.3**/66.0	70.2/68.1	72.3/72.3	72.3/76.6	72.3/74.5	74.5/**78.7**	72.3/70.2	66.0/66.0	66.0/66.0

$p\backslash d$	64	128	256	512	1024	2048	64	128	256	512	1024	2048
	\multicolumn{6}{Linear SVMs (LCK)}			Nonlinear SVMs (RCK)					
64	59.6/**66.0**	–	–	–	–	–	**72.3**/72.3	–	–	–	–	–
128	**68.1**/66.0	63.8/66.0	–	–	–	–	**72.3**/70.2	72.3/**72.3**	–	–	–	–
256	**72.3**/**72.3**	70.2/68.1	66.0/70.2	–	–	–	76.6/74.5	74.5/72.3	76.6/74.5	–	–	–
512	70.2/**72.3**	**72.3**/72.3	70.2/70.2	72.3/72.3	–	–	74.5/74.5	76.6/74.5	**80.9**/78.7	72.3/72.3	–	–
1024	**76.6**/74.5	76.6/70.2	74.5/68.1	72.3/72.3	70.2/70.2	–	74.5/74.5	74.5/**76.6**	74.5/72.3	72.3/72.3	72.3/72.3	–
2048	72.3/74.5	74.5/74.5	74.5/**76.6**	74.5/**76.6**	**76.6**/74.5	72.3/72.3	74.5/76.6	**80.9**/78.7	68.1/68.1	70.2/70.2	70.2/70.2	70.2/70.2

on the accuracy of action recognition; each cell in these tables corresponds to a pair - ("motion and appearance transfer" vs. "motion transfer only"). We observe that the setting (i) (i.e., assuming viewpoint invariant HOG features) is

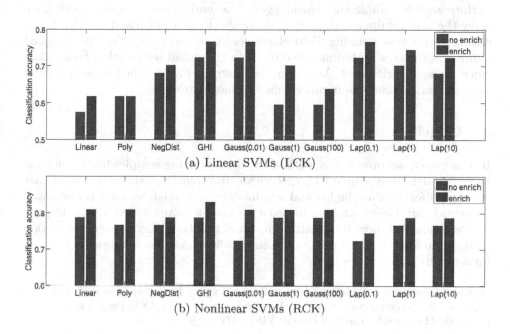

(a) Linear SVMs (LCK)

(b) Nonlinear SVMs (RCK)

Fig. 5. This figure shows action recognition performances with and without the enrichment process for different kernels

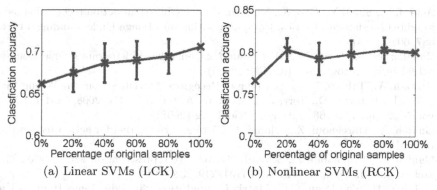

(a) Linear SVMs (LCK)   (b) Nonlinear SVMs (RCK)

Fig. 6. This figure shows the evolution of action recognition performances w.r.t the fraction k of original training data involved in enrichment ($k = 0\%$ stands for no enrichment while $k = 100\%$ means that all original data are used for enrichment, thereby the size of training set doubles). These results correspond to the average classification accuracy of 100 runs. Each run corresponds to a fraction k of random training samples used for enrichment.

relatively accurate but globally the setting (ii) is more accurate especially when dimensions p, d are not large.

Overall performances. Finally, Fig. 5 compares the overall action classification performance of sample enrichment against no enrichment. For each kernel, we show the best results (corresponding to the best setting of p and d). This figure clearly shows that training SVM classifiers for action recognition, on enriched training set makes performance better than the initial setting that trains classifier without enrichment. Moreover, as shown in Fig. 6, when enough data is used for enrichment, the improvement becomes noticeable.

4   Conclusions

In this paper, we proposed a method to enrich training samples by transferring their features from source to target views. Inspired from the observation that cross-view features are highly and non linearly correlated, we used kernel-based canonical correlation analysis in order to map features across views. Experiments conducted show the positive impact of this enrichment process on action recognition and the influence of different (mainly nonlinear) kernels on the performances.

Acknowledgments. This work was supported in part by a grant from the Research Agency ANR (Agence Nationale de la Recherche) under the MLVIS project and a grant from DIGITEO under the RELIR and VISUNET projects.

References

1. Ashraf, N., Shen, Y., Cao, X., Foroosh, H.: View invariant action recognition using weighted fundamental ratios. Computer Vision and Image Understanding **117**(6), 587–602 (2013)
2. Boughorbel, S., Tarel, J.P., Boujemaa, N.: Generalized histogram intersection kernel for image recognition. In: ICIP (2005)
3. Farhadi, A., Tabrizi, M.K.: Learning to Recognize Activities from the Wrong View Point. In: Forsyth, D., Torr, P., Zisserman, A. (eds.) ECCV 2008, Part I. LNCS, vol. 5302, pp. 154–166. Springer, Heidelberg (2008)
4. Gaidon, A., Harchaoui, Z., Schmid, C.: A time series kernel for action recognition. In: BMVC (2011)
5. Gaidon, A., Harchaoui, Z., Schmid, C.: Activity representation with motion hierarchies. Int. J. Comput. Vision **107**(3), 219–238 (2013)
6. Golub, G.H., Van Loan, C.F.: Matrix Computations, 3rd edn. Johns Hopkins University Press, Baltimore, MD, USA (1996)
7. Gorelick, L., Blank, M., Shechtman, E., Irani, M., Basri, R.: Actions as Space-Time Shapes. IEEE Trans. Pattern Anal. Mach. Intell. **29**(12), 2247–2253 (2007)
8. Gupta, A., Martinez, J., Little, J.J., Woodham, R.J.: 3D Pose from Motion for Cross-view Action Recognition via Non-linear Circulant Temporal Encoding. In: CVPR (2014)

9. Hardoon, D.R., Szedmak, S.R., Shawe-taylor, J.R.: Canonical Correlation Analysis: An Overview with Application to Learning Methods. Neural Comput. **16**(12), 2639–2664 (2004)
10. Hassner, T.: A Critical Review of Action Recognition Benchmarks. In: 1st IEEE International Workshop on Action Similarity in Unconstrained Videos (ACTS) at the IEEE Conf. on Computer Vision and Pattern Recognition (CVPR) (2013)
11. Holte, M.B., Tran, C., Trivedi, M.M., Moeslund, T.B.: Human Action Recognition Using Multiple Views: A Comparative Perspective on Recent Developments. In: Proceedings of the 2011 Joint ACM Workshop on Human Gesture and Behavior Understanding (2011)
12. Hotelling, H.: Relations Between Two Sets of Variates. Biometrika **28**(3/4), 321–377 (1936)
13. Huang, C.H., Yeh, Y.R., Wang, Y.C.F.: Recognizing Actions across Cameras by Exploring the Correlated Subspace. In: ECCV Workshops (1) (2012)
14. Jiang, Z., Lin, Z., Davis, L.: Recognizing Human Actions by Learning and Matching Shape-Motion Prototype Trees. IEEE Trans. Pattern Anal. Mach. Intell. **34**(3), 533–547 (2012)
15. Junejo, I.N., Dexter, E., Laptev, I., Pérez, P.: Cross-View Action Recognition from Temporal Self-similarities. In: Forsyth, D., Torr, P., Zisserman, A. (eds.) ECCV 2008, Part II. LNCS, vol. 5303, pp. 293–306. Springer, Heidelberg (2008)
16. Kliper-Gross, O., Hassner, T., Wolf, L.: The Action Similarity Labeling Challenge. IEEE Trans. Pattern Anal. Mach. Intell. **34**(3), 615–621 (2012)
17. Kuehne, H., Jhuang, H., Garrote, E., Poggio, T., Serre, T.: HMDB: A Large Video Database for Human Motion Recognition. In: ICCV (2011)
18. Lan, T., Wang, Y., Mori, G.: Discriminative Figure-Centric Models for Joint Action Localization and Recognition. In: ICCV (2011)
19. Laptev, I., Marszalek, M., Schmid, C., Rozenfeld, B.: Learning Realistic Human Actions from Movies. In: CVPR (2008)
20. Le, Q.V., Zou, W.Y., Yeung, S.Y., Ng, A.Y.: Learning hierarchical invariant spatio-temporal features for action recognition with independent subspace analysis. In: CVPR (2011)
21. Li, R., Zickler, T.: Discriminative virtual views for cross-view action recognition. In: CVPR (2012)
22. Liang, X., Lin, L., Cao, L.: Learning Latent Spatio-temporal Compositional Model for Human Action Recognition. In: Proceedings of the 21st ACM International Conference on Multimedia (2013)
23. Liu, J., Shah, M., Kuipers, B., Savarese, S.: Cross-view action recognition via view knowledge transfer. In: CVPR (2011)
24. Liu, Y., Dai, Q., Xu, W.: A Point-Cloud-Based Multiview Stereo Algorithm for Free-Viewpoint Video. IEEE Trans. Vis. Comput. Graph. **16**(3), 407–418 (2010)
25. Lowe, D.G.: Distinctive Image Features from Scale-Invariant Keypoints. Int. J. Comput. Vision **60**(2), 91–110 (2004)
26. Pan, Sinno Jialin and Yang, Qiang: A Survey on Transfer Learning. IEEE Trans. on Knowl. and Data Eng. 22(10), 1345–1359 (2010)
27. Rodriguez, M.D., Ahmed, J., Shah, M.: Action MACH: A Spatio-temporal Maximum Average Correlation Height Filter for Action Recognition. In: CVPR (2008)
28. Sadanand, S., Corso, J.J.: Action Bank: A High-Level Representation of Activity in Video. In: CVPR (2012)
29. Schlkopf, B., Smola, A.J., Müller, K.R.: Kernel principal component analysis. Advances in Kernel Methods: Support Vector Learning, pp. 327–352 (1999)

30. Soomro, K., Roshan Zamir, A., Shah, M.: UCF101: A dataset of 101 human actions classes from videos in the wild. In: CRCV-TR-12-01 (2012)
31. Wang, H., Kläser, A., Schmid, C., Liu, C.L.: Dense Trajectories and Motion Boundary Descriptors for Action Recognition. Int. J. Comput. Vision **103**(1), 60–79 (2013)
32. Wang, J., Nie, X., Xia, Y., Wu, Y., Zhu, S.C.: Cross-view Action Modeling, Learning and Recognition. In: CVPR (2014)
33. Wang, L., Sahbi, H.: Directed Acyclic Graph Kernels for Action Recognition. In: ICCV (2013)
34. Weinland, D., Özuysal, M., Fua, P.: Making Action Recognition Robust to Occlusions and Viewpoint Changes. In: Daniilidis, K., Maragos, P., Paragios, N. (eds.) ECCV 2010, Part III. LNCS, vol. 6313, pp. 635–648. Springer, Heidelberg (2010)
35. Weinland, D., Ronfard, R., Boyer, E.: Free viewpoint action recognition using motion history volumes. Computer Vision and Image Understanding **104**(2), 249–257 (2006)
36. Wu, X., Wang, H., Liu, C., Jia, Y.: Cross-view Action Recognition over Heterogeneous Feature Spaces. In: ICCV (2013)
37. Yang, Y., Saleemi, I., Shah, M.: Discovering Motion Primitives for Unsupervised Grouping and One-Shot Learning of Human Actions, Gestures, and Expressions. IEEE Trans. Pattern Anal. Mach. Intell. **35**(7), 1635–1648 (2013)
38. Zhang, Z., Wang, C., Xiao, B., Zhou, W., Liu, S., Shi, C.: Cross-View Action Recognition via a Continuous Virtual Path. In: CVPR (2013)
39. Zheng, J., Jiang, Z., Phillips, P.J., Chellappa, R.: Cross-View Action Recognition via a Transferable Dictionary Pair. In: BMVC (2012)

Multi-Modal Distance Metric Learning:
A Bayesian Non-parametric Approach

Behnam Babagholami-Mohamadabadi[✉], Seyed Mahdi Roostaiyan,
Ali Zarghami, and Mahdieh Soleymani Baghshah

Department of Computer Engineering, Sharif University of Technology, Tehran, Iran
babagholami@alum.sharif.edu

Abstract. In many real-world applications (e.g. social media application), data usually consists of diverse input modalities that originates
from various heterogeneous sources. Learning a similarity measure for
such data is of great importance for vast number of applications such as
classification, clustering, retrieval, etc.

Defining an appropriate distance metric between data points with
multiple modalities is a key challenge that has a great impact on the
performance of many multimedia applications. Existing approaches for
multi-modal distance metric learning only offer point estimation of the
distance matrix and/or latent features, and can therefore be unreliable
when the number of training examples is small. In this paper we present a
novel Bayesian framework for learning distance functions on multi-modal
data through Beta Process, by which we embed data of different modalities into a single latent space. Moreover, using the flexible Beta process
model, we can infer the dimensionality of the hidden space using training
data itself. We also develop a novel Variational Bayes (VB) algorithm to
compute the posterior distribution of the parameters that imposes the
constraints (similarity/dissimilarity constraints) directly on the posterior
distribution. We apply our framework to text/image data and present
empirical results on retrieval and classification to demonstrate the effectiveness of the proposed model.

Keywords: Metric learning · Multi-modal data · Beta process · Variational inference · Gibbs sampling

1 Introduction

Recently, multi-modal data has been grown explosively thanks to the ubiquity
of the social media (e.g. Facebook, Flicker, Youtube, iTuens, etc). In such data,
information comes through multiple input channels (images contain tags and
captions, videos are associated with audio signals and/or user comments). Hence,

Electronic supplementary material The online version of this chapter (doi:10.
1007/978-3-319-16199-0_5) contains supplementary material, which is available to
authorized users.

© Springer International Publishing Switzerland 2015
L. Agapito et al. (Eds.): ECCV 2014 Workshops, Part III, LNCS 8927, pp. 63–77, 2015.
DOI: 10.1007/978-3-319-16199-0_5

each modality can be characterized by different statistical features which reveals the importance of the fact that the modality corresponding to a distinct input source, carries different kinds of information.

In many applications including classification [6], retrieval [7], clustering [8], and recommendation systems [9], choosing a proper similarity measure between items is a crucial task. To address this problem, a wide range of Distance Metric Learning (DML) methods have been proposed [1],[2],[3],[4],[5]. Although the performance of DML methods have been promising on similarity search problems, most existing DML algorithms are designed to work on single-modal data, hence, they are limited in that they do not effectively handle the distance measure of multi-modal data which may originate from totally different resources.

Recently, the multi-modal distance metric learning has been received an increasing attention [11],[18]. In this paper, we propose a Bayesian framework for multi-modal distance metric learning based on the Beta process [19] that takes into account the distance supervision (similarity/dissimilarity constraints). Our method embeds data of arbitrary modalities into a single latent space with the ability to learn the dimensionality of the latent space by the data itself. Given supervisory information (labeled similar and dissimilar pairs), we develop a novel Variational Bayes (VB) algorithm which incorporates such information into the proposed Bayesian framework by imposing the constraints directly on the parameters of the posterior distribution of the latent features.

The rest of this paper is organized as follows. Section 2 introduces some related work in metric learning area. In Section 3, we briefly review the Beta process. We present the propose multi-modal distance metric learning framework based on Beta process model in Section 4. In Section 5, we introduce a novel VB algorithm to compute the posterior distribution of the parameters and the hidden variables. Experimental results are presented in Section 6. Finally, we conclude our work in Section 7.

2   Related Work

Metric Learning has become a very active research area over the last years [1],[2],[3],[4],[5]. In this problem, we intend to learn an appropriate dissimilarity measure from the data samples when some similarity and dissimilarity constraints on data points are available. Xing et al. [10] introduced a metric learning method by formulating the learning task into the following constrained convex optimization problem.

$$A^* = \underset{A}{argmin} \sum_{(x_i, x_j) \in S} (x_i - x_j)^T A (x_i - x_j),$$

$$s.t. \sum_{(x_i, x_j) \in D} (x_i - x_j)^T A (x_i - x_j) \geq 1, \ A \succeq 0, \tag{1}$$

where A is a Mahalanobis distance matrix (A must be positive semidefinite matrix to satisfy the non-negativity and triangle inequality conditions), and S and D denote the set of positive and negative constraints respectively.

Some other well-known algorithms in this area include Relevant Component Analysis (RCA) [12], Discriminative Component Analysis (DCA) [13], Information-Theoretic Metric Learning (ITML) [14], Large Margin Nearest Neighbor (LMNN) [15], Regularized Metric Learning [16], Laplacian Regularized Metric Learning (LRML) [17] that learn a Mahalanobis distance metric.

The problem with all of the above methods is that they are primarily designed for data with single modality and are not appropriate for multi-modal data. One very simple approach to remedy this problem is to join the features from different modalities into a single representation and learn an appropriate metric using that representation. Unfortunately, this naive solution does not consider the incompatibility of heterogeneous information sources and subsequently, ignores the dependency relationships between various modalities that could lead to suboptimal performance.

Attempting to address this issue, some researchers have introduced some metric learning methods for multi-modal data. McFee and Lanckriet [11] proposed a multi-modal distance metric learning method based on Multiple Kernel Learning that learns each kernel for a different modality of the data. This algorithm learns for features of each modality a Mahalanobis distance metric in the reproducing kernel Hilbert space (RKHS), that can be solved by semidefinite programming. Very recently, Xie and Xing [18] have combined multi-wing harmonium model (MVH) [20] for multimodel integration and the metric learning method introduced in [10] for incorporating supervisory information into the proposed model. More precisely, this method tries to embed data of different modalities into a single latent space by imposing the similarity/dissimilarity constraints on the latent features. This is done by minimizing the distance of similar pairs while separating dissimilar pairs with a certain margin in the latent space. Although the results of this algorithm is promising, there are two problems with this method. First, this algorithm only provides point estimation of the latent features which could be sensitive to the choice of training examples, hence the algorithm tends to be unreliable when the number of training examples is small. Second, the dimensionality of the latent space must be specified a priori that could be a hard assumption.

To address the above problems, in this paper, we present a Bayesian framework for Multi-Modal Distance Metric Learning (MMDML) based on the Beta process that targets tasks where the number of training examples is limited. Indeed, using the full Bayesian treatment, the proposed framework is better suited to dealing with a small number of training examples than the non-Bayesian approaches. Moreover, using the flexible Beta process, we are able to infer the number of latent features from the observed data.

3   Beta Process

The Beta process $B \sim BP(c, B_0)$ is an example of completely random measures [22] which is defined as a distribution on positive random measures over a measurable space $(\Omega, \mathcal{F})$ [19]. It is parameterized by a base measure B_0 which is defined over Ω and a positive function $c(\omega)$ over Ω which is assumed constant for simplicity $(c(\omega) = c)$. This process is an example of a Lévy process with the Lévy measure as

$$\nu(d\pi, d\omega) = c\pi^{-1}(1 - \pi)^{c-1} d\pi B_0(d\omega). \tag{2}$$

For generating samples from $B \sim BP(c, B_0)$, first, a non-homogeneous Poisson process is defined on $\Omega \times \mathcal{R}^+$ with intensity function ν. Then, $Poisson(\lambda)$ number of points $(\pi_k, \omega_k) \in [0, 1] \times \Omega$ are drawn from the Poisson process $(\lambda = \int_{[0,1]} \int_{\Omega} \nu(d\omega, d\pi) = \infty)$. Finally, a draw from $B \sim BP(c, B_0)$ is constructed as

$$B_\omega = \sum_{k=1}^{\infty} \pi_k \delta_{\omega_k}, \tag{3}$$

where δ_{ω_k} is a unit point measure at ω_k (δ_{ω_k} equals one if $\omega = \omega_k$ and is zero otherwise) . It can be seen from equation 3, that B_ω is a discrete measure (with probability one), for which $B_\omega(A) = \sum_{k:\omega_k \in A} \pi_k$, for any set $A \subset \mathcal{F}$.

4   Proposed Method

In this section, we present our Bayesian framework for multi-modal distance metric learning which directly imposes the constraints on the posterior distribution of the latent features.

4.1   Problem Formulation

Let $T = [\bar{X}, \bar{Y}]$ be the observed bi-modal data matrix (for simplicity, we assume we have two-modal data, but our method can be easily extended to multi-modal data) where $\bar{X} = [X_1, X_2, ..., X_d]_{M \times d}$ denotes the first modality data matrix, where $X_i = [x_{1i}, ...x_{Mi}]^T$ is the i-th data point of the first modality, and $\bar{Y} = [Y_1, Y_2, ..., Y_d]_{N \times d}$ denotes the second modality data matrix, where $Y_i = [y_{1i}, ...y_{Ni}]^T$ is the i-th data point of the second modality. We also denote $\bar{H} = [H_1, H_2, ..., H_d]_{K \times d}$ as the latent feature matrix, where $H_i = [h_{1i}, ...h_{Ki}]^T$ is the latent feature for the i-th data point. We are also given two sets of pairwise constraints which are defined as

$$A = \{(i, j) \mid (X_i, Y_i) \text{ and } (X_j, Y_j) \text{ are in the same class}\},$$
$$D = \{(i, j) \mid (X_i, Y_i) \text{ and } (X_j, Y_j) \text{ are in two different class}\},$$

where A is the set of similar pairwise constraints, and D is the set of dissimilar pairwise constraints. In order to utilize the Beta process in the proposed Bayesian framework, we model the latent feature matrix $(\bar{H})$ as an element-wise multiplication of a binary matrix $(\bar{Z} = [Z_1, ..., Z_d]_{K \times d})$ and a real weight matrix $(\bar{S} = [S_1, ..., S_d]_{K \times d})$. Hence, we have $\bar{H} = \bar{Z} \odot \bar{S}$, where $\odot$ is the element-wise multiplication operator. To be fully Bayesian, we must define appropriate prior and likelihood distributions for all observed $(\bar{X}, \bar{Y})$ and latent $(\bar{Z}, \bar{S})$ variables. Based on the above definitions, the proposed generative model goes as follows:

- For each data point $(X_i, Y_i)_{i=1}^d$, first draw corresponding features Z_i, S_i from the prior distributions $p(Z_i|\beta_z)$ and $p(S_i|\beta_s)$ respectively.
- For each drawn feature $(Z_i, S_i)_{i=1}^d$, draw the data point X_i and Y_i from the likelihoods $p(X_i|Z_i, S_i, \beta_x)$ and $p(Y_i|Z_i, S_i, \beta_y)$ respectively.

where $\beta_z, \beta_s, \beta_x$ and β_y are the free parameters of the proposed generative model (to be fully Bayesian, we put appropriate prior distribution on these parameters and infer the corresponding posterior distributions from observed data). It should be noted that using the above generative process, we assume that elements of each modality are independent of other modalities given the latent features. More precisely, we have:

$$p(\bar{X}, \bar{Y}|\bar{Z}, \bar{S}, \beta_x, \beta_y) = \prod_{i=1}^d \prod_{m=1}^M p(x_{mi}|Z_i, S_i, \beta_x) \prod_{n=1}^N p(y_{ni}|Z_i, S_i, \beta_y). \quad (4)$$

We also make assumptions about the complete conditionals in the proposed model (a complete conditional is the conditional distribution of a latent variable given the other latent variables and the observations). We assume that these distributions are in the exponential family,

$$p(Z_i|\bar{Z}_{-i}, \bar{S}, \bar{X}, \bar{Y}, \beta_z, \beta_x, \beta_y) \propto p(X_i|Z_i, S_i, \beta_x)p(Y_i|Z_i, S_i, \beta_y)p(Z_i|\beta_z)$$
$$\propto exp\{\eta_z(\bar{Z}_{-i}, S_i, X_i, Y_i, \beta_z, \beta_x, \beta_y)^T t_z(Z_i)\}, \ i = 1, ..., d, \quad (5)$$

$$p(S_i|\bar{S}_{-i}, \bar{Z}, \bar{X}, \bar{Y}, \beta_s, \beta_x, \beta_y) \propto p(X_i|Z_i, S_i, \beta_x)p(Y_i|Z_i, S_i, \beta_y)p(S_i|\beta_s)$$
$$\propto exp\{\eta_s(\bar{S}_{-i}, Z_i, X_i, Y_i, \beta_s, \beta_x, \beta_y)^T t_s(S_i)\}, \ i = 1, ..., d, \quad (6)$$

where the notation $\bar{Z}_{-i}$ and $\bar{S}_{-i}$ refers to the set of columns of $\bar{Z}$ and $\bar{S}$ except the i-th column respectively, and the vector functions $\eta(.)$ and $t(.)$ are the *natural parameter* (the natural parameter is a function of the variables that are being conditioned on) and the *sufficient statistics* respectively. These assumptions on the complete conditionals imply a conjugacy relationship between the hidden variables and the observations that implies a specific form of the complete conditional for the latent features.

We put a prior distribution on the binary matrix $\bar{Z}$ using the extension of the Beta process which takes two scalar parameters a_π and b_π and was originally proposed by [21]. A sample from the extended Beta process $B \sim BP(a_\pi, b_\pi, B_0)$ with base measure B_0 may be represented as

$$B_\omega = \sum_{k=1}^K \pi_k \delta_{\omega_k}, \quad (7)$$

where,

$$\pi_k \sim Beta(a_\pi/K, b_\pi(K-1)/K), \quad \omega_k \sim B_0. \quad (8)$$

This sample will be a valid sample from the extended Beta process, if $K \to \infty$. B_ω can be considered as a vector of K probabilities that each probability π_k

corresponds to the atom ω_k. Now, we consider each latent binary feature $Z_i (i = 1, ..., d)$ to be drawn from a Bernoulli process $Be(B_\omega)$ with B_ω defined as 7 where a sample from this process can be generated as

$$Z_i = \sum_{k=1}^{K} z_{ki} \delta_{\omega_k}, \quad i = 1, ..., d, \tag{9}$$

where z_{ki} is generated by $z_{ki} \sim Bernoulli(\pi_k)$. So, we set the free parameter $\beta_z = [\pi_1, ..., \pi_K]$. By letting $K \to \infty$, the number of the atoms K (the dimensionality of the latent feature space) can be learned from the training data.

Based on the Beta-Bernoulli process prior on binary latent features $\bar{Z}$, computing the posterior distribution of $\bar{Z}$ is tractable for any likelihood function. However, for the weight latent features $\bar{S}$, the prior and the likelihood distributions must be in the conjugate exponential family as

$$p(X_i, Y_i | S_i, Z_i, \beta_x, \beta_y) =$$

$$\prod_{m=1}^{M} \prod_{n=1}^{N} \left(A(x_{mi}) A(y_{ni}) exp\{\eta(S_i, Z_i, \beta_x, \beta_y)^T t(x_{mi}, y_{ni}) - \phi(S_i, Z_i, \beta_x, \beta_y)\} \right),$$

$$\tag{10}$$

$$p(S_i | \beta_s) = \prod_{k=1}^{K} A(s_{ki}) exp\{\beta_s^T t(s_{ki}) - \phi_s(\beta_s)\}, \tag{11}$$

where the scalar functions $A(.)$ and $\phi(.)$ are the *base measure* and *log-normalizer* respectively. Using the conjugacy relationship between Eqs. 10 and 11, the sufficient statistics for s_{ki} is

$$t(s_{ki}) = (\eta_{s_{ki}}(S_i, Z_i, \beta_x, \beta_y), -\phi_{s_{ki}}(S_i, Z_i, \beta_x, \beta_y)), \tag{12}$$

where $f_x(.)$ means that we consider x as the free parameter of the function f by considering all other parameters as constant. The parameter β_s has two components $\beta_s = (\beta_s^1, \beta_s^2)$. The first component β_s^1 is a vector of the same dimension as $\eta_{s_{ki}}(S_i, Z_i, \beta_x, \beta_y)$; the second component β_s^2 is a scalar. This form will be important when we derive constrained variational inference in Section 5.1.

To be fully Bayesian, we also put conjugate prior distributions on the free parameters β_s, β_x and β_y as

$$p(\beta_s | a_s) = A(\beta_s) exp\{a_s^T t(\beta_s) - \phi_{\beta_s}(a_s)\}, \tag{13}$$

$$p(\beta_x | a_x) = A(\beta_x) exp\{a_x^T t(\beta_x) - \phi_{\beta_y}(a_x)\}, \tag{14}$$

$$p(\beta_y | a_y) = A(\beta_y) exp\{a_y^T t(\beta_y) - \phi_{\beta_x}(a_y)\}, \tag{15}$$

where

$$t(\beta_s) = (\beta_s, -\phi_s(\beta_s)), \tag{16}$$

$$t(\beta_x) = (\eta_{\beta_x}(S_i, Z_i, \beta_x, \beta_y), -\phi_{\beta_x}(S_i, Z_i, \beta_x, \beta_y)), \tag{17}$$

$$t(\beta_y) = (\eta_{\beta_y}(S_i, Z_i, \beta_x, \beta_y), -\phi_{\beta_y}(S_i, Z_i, \beta_x, \beta_y)), \tag{18}$$

where $a_\pi, b_\pi, a_s, a_x, b_y$ are the hyper-parameters of the proposed model. The graphical representation of the proposed model is demonstrated in Fig. 1.

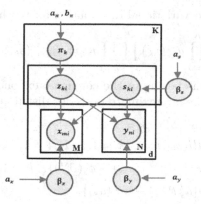

Fig. 1. The graphical representation of the proposed Bayesian model

5 Posterior Inference

Due to the fact that computing the exact posterior distribution of the latent variables given the observations is intractable, in this section, we develop a new VB algorithm, to approximate that posterior distribution.

The goal of variational inference is to approximate the true posterior distribution over the latent variables with a variational distribution which is closest in KL divergence to the true posterior distribution. A brief review of the VB algorithm for the exponential family distributions provided in the supplementary Material. In our variational inference framework, we use the finite Beta-Bernoulli approximation, in which the dimensionality of the latent space (K) is truncated and set to a finite but large number. If K is large enough, the analyzed multi-modal data using this number of latent features, will reveal less than K components.

In the following section, we introduce our VB method which incorporates the information of similarity/dissimilarity constraints into inferring the posterior distributions.

5.1 Constrained Variational Inference

In the proposed Bayesian MMDML model, the latent variables are $\varXi = \Big\{ \varPi = [\pi_1, \pi_2, ..., \pi_K], \bar{Z}, \bar{S}, \beta_s, \beta_x, \beta_y \Big\}$, and the hyper-parameters are $\varPhi = \{a_x, a_y, a_s, a_\pi, b_\pi\}$. So, the joint probability of data and unknown variables are

$$P(\bar{X}, \bar{Y}, \varXi \mid \varPhi) = \prod_{i=1}^{d} \Big(\prod_{m=1}^{M} P(x_{mi} \mid Z_i, S_i, \beta_x) \prod_{n=1}^{N} P(y_{ni} \mid Z_i, S_i, \beta_y)$$
$$\prod_{k=1}^{K} P(z_{ki} \mid \pi_k) P(s_{ki} \mid \beta_s) \Big) \prod_{k=1}^{K} P(\pi_k \mid a_\pi, b_\pi) P(\beta_x \mid a_x) P(\beta_y \mid a_y) P(\beta_s \mid a_s). \quad (19)$$

We use a fully factorized variational distribution for the hidden variables as

$$q(\Pi, \bar{Z}, \bar{S}, \beta_s, \beta_x, \beta_y) = \prod_{k=1}^{K} q_{\pi_k}(\pi_k) \prod_{i=1}^{d} \prod_{k=1}^{K} q_{z_{ki}}(z_{ki}) q_{s_{ki}}(s_{ki}) q_{\beta_s}(\beta_s) q_{\beta_x}(\beta_x) q_{\beta_y}(\beta_y).$$

Since all the distributions belong to the conjugate exponential families, we can determine the form of the approximate posterior distributions, so we have:

$$q_{\pi_k}(\pi_k) = Beta(\pi_k; a_\pi^k, b_\pi^k), \quad k = 1, ..., K,$$

$$q_{z_{ki}}(z_{ki}) = Bernoulli(z_{ki}; \nu_{ki}), \quad k = 1, ..., K, i = 1, ..., d,$$

$$q_{s_{ki}}(s_{ki}) = A(s_{ki})exp\{(\hat{\beta}_s^{ki})^T t(s_{ki}) - \phi_s(\hat{\beta}_s^{ki})\}, \quad k = 1, ..., K, i = 1, ..., d,$$

$$q_{\beta_s}(\beta_s) = A(\beta_s)exp\{\hat{a}_s^T t(\beta_s) - \phi_{\beta_s}(\hat{a}_s)\},$$

$$q_{\beta_x}(\beta_x) = A(\beta_x)exp\{\hat{a}_x^T t(\beta_x) - \phi_{\beta_y}(\hat{a}_x)\},$$

$$q_{\beta_y}(\beta_y) = A(\beta_y)exp\{\hat{a}_y^T t(\beta_y) - \phi_{\beta_x}(\hat{a}_y)\}.$$

If we denote the set of posterior parameters by Ω, the proposed constrained variational inference then involves maximizing the lower bound on the marginal likelihood ($P(\bar{X}, \bar{Y} \mid \Phi)$ by enforcing similar/dissimilar pairs to have similar/dissimilar posterior distributions over their latent features. This is equivalent to solving the following optimization problem

$$\hat{\Omega} = \underset{\Omega}{argmin} \; -\mathbb{E}_q(\log P(\bar{X}, \bar{Y}, \Xi \mid \Phi)) - H[q] + \frac{1}{|A|} \sum_{(i,j) \in A} \sum_{k=1}^{K} \left(\lambda_z(\nu_{ki} - \nu_{kj})^2\right.$$

$$\left. + \lambda_s(\hat{\beta}_s^{ki} - \hat{\beta}_s^{kj})^2\right), \quad s.t. \; \forall (i,j) \in D, \sum_{k=1}^{K}(\nu_{ki} - \nu_{kj})^2 \geq 1, \sum_{k=1}^{K}(\hat{\beta}_s^{ki} - \hat{\beta}_s^{kj})^2 \geq 1,$$

$$(20)$$

where $H[.]$ denotes the Entropy operator, and $|A|$ denotes the cardinality of the set A. In [20], the similarity and dissimilarity constraints are directly imposed on the latent features. In our Bayesian framework, instead of imposing the constraints directly on latent features ($\bar{Z}, \bar{S}$), we impose them on the parameters of the posterior distributions of the latent features. It should be noted that both $P(\bar{X}, \bar{Y}, \Xi \mid \Phi)$ and $H[q]$ are functions of posterior parameters (Ω). The VB method simply tries to minimize the above objective function using the Coordinate Descent method. $\mathbb{E}_q(\log P(\bar{X}, \bar{Y}, \Xi \mid \Phi))$ can be decomposed as

$$\mathbb{E}_q(\log P(\bar{X}, \bar{Y}, \Xi \mid \Phi)) = \sum_{k=1}^{K} \mathbb{E}_q \log P(\pi_k \mid a_\pi, b_\pi) + \sum_{i=1}^{d} \sum_{k=1}^{K} \mathbb{E}_q \log P(z_{ki} \mid \pi_k) +$$

$$\sum_{i=1}^{d} \left(\sum_{m=1}^{M} \mathbb{E}_q \log P(x_{mi} \mid Z_i, S_i, \beta_x) + \sum_{n=1}^{N} \mathbb{E}_q \log P(y_{ni} \mid Z_i, S_i, \beta_y) \right.$$

$$\left. + \sum_{k=1}^{K} \mathbb{E}_q \log P(s_{ki} \mid \beta_s) \right) + \mathbb{E}_q \log P(\beta_s \mid a_s) + \mathbb{E}_q \log P(\beta_x \mid a_x) + \mathbb{E}_q \log P(\beta_y \mid a_y).$$

$$(21)$$

The update equation for each distribution is as follows (due to the conjugacy relationship for $\Pi, \beta_s, \beta_x, \beta_y$ and the fact that these variables do not appear in the constraints, updating posterior distribution of these variables is straightforward and is omitted due to the lack of space).

Update for $\bar{Z} = [Z_1, Z_2, ..., Z_d]$:
Due to the fact that there are some constraints on the posterior parameters of the binary feature matrix $\bar{Z}$, we cannot derive the update equation for the posterior parameters of $\bar{Z}$ in the closed form. Hence, for updating the parameters in our coordinate descent framework, we reformulate the objective function of Eq. 20 as a function of the posterior parameters of $\bar{Z}$ and directly solve the obtained optimization problem (it should be noted that in expanding the objective function, we consider all parameters fixed but the parameters of the binary feature matrix $\bar{Z}$). For updating each posterior parameter $\nu_{ki}(k = 1, ..., K; i = 1, ..., d)$, first, we define function $F(\nu_{ki})$ as:

$$F(\nu_{ki}) = -\mathbb{E}_q(\log P(\bar{X}, \bar{Y}, \Xi \mid \Phi)) - H[q] + \frac{\lambda_z}{|A|} \sum_{j \in \{j \mid (i,j) \in A\}} (\nu_{ki} - \nu_{kj})^2 + c, \quad (22)$$

where c is the summation of all terms which are independent of ν_{ki}.

$$\mathbb{E}_q(\log P(\bar{X}, Y, \Xi \mid \Phi)) = \sum_{m=1}^{M} \mathbb{E}_q \log P(x_{mi} \mid Z_i, S_i, \beta_x)$$

$$+ \sum_{n=1}^{N} \mathbb{E}_q \log P(y_{ni} \mid Z_i, S_i, \beta_y) + \mathbb{E}_q \log P(z_{ki} \mid \pi_k) + c$$

$$= \sum_{m=1}^{M} f_{mi}(\nu_{ki}) + \sum_{n=1}^{N} f_{ni}(\nu_{ki}) + \langle \log \pi_k \rangle \nu_{ki} + \langle \log(1 - \pi_k) \rangle (1 - \nu_{ki}) + c, \quad (23)$$

where $f_{mi}(\nu_{ki}) = \mathbb{E}_q \log P(x_{mi} \mid Z_i, S_i, \beta_x)$ and $f_{ni}(\nu_{ki}) = \mathbb{E}_q \log P(y_{ni} \mid Z_i, S_i, \beta_y)$ and $\langle . \rangle$ indicates the expectation operator. For the entropy, we have:

$$H[q] = -\mathbb{E}_q \log q_{z_{ki}}(z_{ki}) + c = -\nu_{ki} \log \nu_{ki} - (1 - \nu_{ki}) \log(1 - \nu_{ki}) + c. \quad (24)$$

We can update the parameter ν_{ki} by solving the following optimization problem

$$\hat{\nu}_{ki} = \underset{\nu_{ki}}{arg min} \sum_{m=1}^{M} f_{mi}(\nu_{ki}) + \sum_{n=1}^{N} f_{ni}(\nu_{ki}) + \langle \log \pi_k \rangle \nu_{ki} + \langle \log(1 - \pi_k) \rangle (1 - \nu_{ki})$$

$$+ \nu_{ki} \log \nu_{ki} + (1 - \nu_{ki}) \log(1 - \nu_{ki})$$

$$s.t. \quad (\nu_{ki} - \nu_{kj})^2 \geq 1 \quad \forall j \in \{j \mid (i,j) \in D\}. \quad (25)$$

It is worth noting that the above optimization problem is a one dimensional problem that can be solved efficiently. Similarly, we can update the posterior parameters $(\{\hat{\beta}_s^{ki}\}(i = 1, ..., d; k = 1, ..., K))$ of the feature matrix $\bar{S}$ using the same procedure.

5.2 Latent Feature Prediction

After computing the posterior distribution of the latent features of the training data, in order to compute the posterior distribution of the latent feature for a new instance (X_t, Y_t), we must compute $P(H_t|X_t, Y_t, T)$ by integrating out the variables $\beta_x, \beta_y, \beta_s$, and Π as

$$P(H_t|X_t, Y_t, T) = \iiiint P(Z_t, S_t, \beta_x, \beta_y, \beta_s, \Pi|X_t, Y_t, T) d\beta_x d\beta_y d\beta_s d\Pi$$

$$= \iiiint P(Z_t, S_t|\beta_x, \beta_y, \beta_s, \Pi, X_t, Y_t, T) P(\beta_x|T, X_t, Y_t) P(\beta_y|T, X_t, Y_t) \times$$

$$P(\beta_s|T, X_t, Y_t) P(\Pi|T, X_t, Y_t) d\beta_x d\beta_y d\beta_s d\Pi. \tag{26}$$

Since the above expression cannot be computed in closed form, we resort to Gibbs sampling to approximate it. In other words, we estimate $P(Z_t, S_t|X_t, Y_t, T)$ as

$$P(Z_t, S_t|X_t, Y_t, T) \approx \frac{1}{L} \sum_{l=1}^{L} \delta_{z,s}(Z_t^l, S_t^l), \tag{27}$$

where L and r^l denote the number of samples and the l-th sample of the latent variable r. To sample from $P(Z_t, S_t|X_t, Y_t, T)$, we sample from $P(Z_t, S_t, \beta_x, \beta_y, \beta_s, \Pi|X_t, Y_t, T)$ based on the Gibbs sampling method [23]. Then, we simply ignore the values for $\beta_x, \beta_y, \beta_s, \Pi$ in each sample (it is worth noting that for generating samples for $\beta_x, \beta_y, \beta_s, \Pi$, we consider the approximate posterior distributions $q(\beta_x), q(\beta_y), q(\beta_s), q(\Pi)$ as the prior distributions for these variables respectively).

Due to assumption that the posterior distribution of the latent features belong to the exponential famiy (Eqs. 5,6,13,14,15), deriving Gibbs sampling equations is straightforward.

In order to compare a test data point (X_t, Y_t) with a training data point (X_j, Y_j) based on their latent features, we first generate L samples $(\{Z_t^l, S_t^l\}_{l=1}^{L})$ for the latent features Z_t, S_t based on the Gibbs sampling method. Then, we simply use Euclidean distance between the empirical mean of the generated samples $(\frac{1}{L} \sum_{l=1}^{L} Z_t^l \odot S_t^l)$ and the mean of the posterior distribution of the latent feature of (X_j, Y_j):

$$d((X_t, Y_t), (X_j, Y_j)) = \|\frac{1}{L} \sum_{l=1}^{L} H_t^l - \mathbb{E}_q[H_j]\|_2 = \|\frac{1}{L} \sum_{l=1}^{L} Z_t^l \odot S_t^l - \mathbb{E}_q[Z_j] \odot \mathbb{E}_q[S_j]\|_2,$$

where $d(.,.)$ and $\mathbb{E}_q[x]$ denote the distance function and the mean of the posterior distribution of the random variable x respectively.

6 Experimental Results

In this section, we verify the performance of the proposed Bayesian framework on tagged images data (images are associated with user textual tags such as title, description, comments, etc) which is ubiquitous in many photo sharing websites such as Instagram and Flickr.

Following [18], for image data modality, we first extract SIFT features from images. Then, we represent each image (X_i) using normalized bag-of-words on SIFT features. We also consider a discrete bag-of-words representation for text (Y_i) data [18].

To specialize our general Bayesian framework to tagged images data, we propose the following model for this bi-modal data:

$P(z_{ki} \mid \pi_k) \sim Bernoulli(\pi_k), \quad k = 1, ..., K, \ i = 1, ..., d,$

$P(\pi_k; a_\pi, b_\pi) \sim Beta(a_\pi/K, b_\pi(K-1)/K), \quad k = 1, ..., K,$

$P(s_{ki} \mid \gamma_s) \sim \mathcal{N}(0, \gamma_s^{-1}), \quad k = 1, ..., K, \ i = 1, ..., d,$

$P(x_{mi} \mid Z_i, S_i, W_m, \gamma_x) \sim \mathcal{N}(W_m^T(S_i \odot Z_i), \gamma_x^{-1}) \quad m = 1, ..., M, \ i = 1, ..., d,$

$P(y_{ni} \mid Z_i, S_i, U_n, \theta_n) = \dfrac{1}{1 + exp(-y_{ni}(U_n^T(S_i \odot Z_i) + \theta_n))} \quad n = 1, ..., N, \ i = 1, ..., d,$

$P(W_m \mid \gamma_w) \sim \mathcal{N}(0, \gamma_w^{-1}I), \quad m = 1, ..., M,$

$P(U_n \mid \gamma_u) \sim \mathcal{N}(0, \gamma_u^{-1}I), \quad n = 1, ..., N,$

$P(\gamma_s; a_s, b_s) \sim Gamma(a_s, b_s), \ P(\gamma_x; a_x, b_x) \sim Gamma(a_x, b_x),$

$P(\gamma_w; a_w, b_w) \sim Gamma(a_w, b_w), \ P(\gamma_u; a_u, b_u) \sim Gamma(a_u, b_u),$

$P(\theta_n) \sim \mathcal{N}(0, 1), \quad n = 1, ..., N,$

where we assume that each element of Y_i is a binary random variable with logistic function distribution ($y_{ni} = +1$ if the n-th term of a tag dictionary appears around the i-th image and $y_{ni} = -1$ otherwise). We also assume that each element x_{mi} of X_i is a Gaussian variable denoting the normalized bag-of-words representation based on the SIFT feature.

Since the non-conjugacy of sigmoid function and Gaussian function violates our conjugacy assumption of posterior distribution over latent features $\bar{S}$, we use the local lower bound to the sigmoid function [24], which states for any $x \in R$ and $\xi \in [0, +\infty]$

$$\frac{1}{1 + exp(-x)} \geq \sigma(\xi)exp\left((x - \xi)/2 - \lambda(\xi)(x^2 - \xi^2)\right), \qquad (28)$$

where,

$$\lambda(\xi) = \frac{-1}{2\xi}\left(\frac{1}{1 + exp(-\xi)} - \frac{1}{2}\right). \qquad (29)$$

So, we replace each sigmoid factor with the above lower bound, then we optimize the factorized variational distributions and free parameters ($\{\xi_{ni}\}_{n=1, i=1}^{N,d}$) using the EM algorithm (the constrained VB algorithm and the Gibbs sampling equations for this model is available in the Supplementary Material).

6.1 Experimental Setup

We report the results of the proposed method (PM) on NUS-WIDE-1.5K: a subset selected from NUS-WIDE dataset which was used in [18]. The images of this dataset is from Flicker and each image is associated with more than one user tag. For this dataset, we selected 30 classes and choose 50 images for each class (the total number of images is 1500). The 30 classes are **food, glacier, bridge, buddha, cliff, clouds, building, car, cathedral, leaf, monks, forest, computers, desert, flag, mushrooms, flowers, hills, lake, moon, motorcycle, actor, butterfly, camels, airplane, bicycle, ocean, police,** and **pyramid.** We randomly choose half of the images for training and the other half for testing. For the text modality, 1000 tags with top frequency are selected to form the tag dictionary. For image modality, we extract SIFT based bag-of-words representation with a codebook of size 1024. We need to generate side information in the forms of pairwise training instances. Following [1], we sample "similar" pairs by picking up two instances from the same class and "dissimilar" pairs by choosing two instances from different classes. We randomly sample about 10K "similar" pairs and 10K "dissimilar" pairs from the training set.

For comparison purposes, we compare our method with the **O-Xing** (we concatenate original feature vectors of text modality and image modality into a single representation and subsequently learn a Mahalanobis distance using the metric learning method proposed in [10]), **O-ITML** (we combine features of text and image into a whole and feed it to the ITML [1] method), **MVH-Xing** (we use the unsupervised MWH model to embed data from text and image modalities to the latent space and learn distance measure on the latent representations using the method proposed in [10]), **MVH-ITML** (we use ITML [1] to learn distance on the latent feature vectors obtained from MWH model), **MKE** (We compare with the multiple kernel embedding method proposed in [11]), and **SMVH-Xing** (we use the supervised MWH model based on "similar" and "dissimilar" pairs to embed data from text and image modalities to the latent space and learn distance measure on the latent representations using the method proposed in [18].

In the experiment, all Gamma priors are set as Gamma $(10^{-6}, 10^{-6})$ to make the prior distributions uninformative. The parameters a_π, b_π of the Beta distribution are set to $a_\pi = K$ and $b_\pi = K/2$. A preset large dimensionality of the latent features $K = 120$ is used for this dataset. The regularization parameters are also set as $\lambda_z = 1000$; $\lambda_s = 1000$. For the Gibbs sampling inference, we discard the initial 200 samples (burn-in period), and collect the next 300 samples to present the posterior distribution over the latent feature of a test instance.

6.2   Classification and Retrieval Experiments

We apply the learned distance measure for k-nearest neighbor (k-NN) classification on the dataset. Table 1 summarizes the classification accuracy for $k = 1, 3, 5, 10, 20$.

This table shows three major points. First, the proposed method (PM), SMVH-Xing, MVH-Xing, and MVH-ITML significantly outperform the two other methods, because these methods capture the correlation and complementary relationships between the modalities by transferring two different modalities into a shared single modality (latent space).

Table 1. k-NN classification accuracy on NUS-WIDE-1.5K dataset

Method	O-Xing	O-ITML	MVH-Xing	MVH-ITML	MKE	SMVH-Xing	PM
1-NN	87.34	89.74	89.60	92.67	81.20	92.80	**95.34**
3-NN	82.26	68.27	87.47	89.07	70.94	90.54	**93.07**
5-NN	67.46	49.87	84.53	84.94	57.60	88.13	**90.14**
10-NN	46.27	26.14	74.40	71.74	46.14	84.93	**88.26**
20-NN	13.74	7.07	60.53	46.80	19.07	71.86	**77.74**

Table 2. Average precision (AP) of image retrieval on NUS-WIDE-1.5K dataset

Method	O-Xing	O-ITML	MVH-Xing	MVH-ITML	MKE	SMVH-Xing	PM
AP	52.24	42.48	74.85	68.89	51.26	84.42	**88.61**

Second, MVH-Xing, and MVH-ITML are less accurate than SMVH-Xing, and PM. The reason is that in MVH-Xing, and MVH-ITML, feature embedding and metric learning are performed separately, while SMVH-Xing, and PM embed multi-modal data into the latent space and learn distance metric simultaneously to achieve the overall optimality that leads to better performance.

Third, our method has better performance than the SMVH-Xing due to the fact that the number of the training data points are small. More precisely, SMVH-Xing uses Maximum Likelihood (MAP estimation from probabilistic point of view) which can overfit to small-size training data. In contrast, the proposed method uses Bayesian learning that is relatively immune to overfitting.

In order to demonstrate the ability of the proposed method to learn the dimensionality of the latent space as well as the latent features, we plot the sorted values of $\langle \Pi \rangle$ for the NUS-WIDE-1.5K dataset, inferred by the algorithm (Fig. 2). As it can be seen, the algorithm inferred approximately 83 number of features, fewer than the 120 initially provided.

For the retrieval task, we treat each test image as query and we rank the other images of the test set according to their distances with the given query. We consider an image relevant to query if both images share the same class label. We use the standard Average Precision (AP) [18] to evaluate the retrieval result. The AP value is the area under precision-recall curve for a query.

The **recall** is the ratio of the relevant examples retrieved over the total relevant examples, and the precision value is the ratio of relevant examples over the total retrieved examples in the database.

The AP result is summarized in Table 2 from which, we can see that our methods have better performance than the other methods.

6.3 Sensitivity Analysis

We test the sensitivity of the proposed method to different choices of the parameter λ_z. Fig. 2 shows the variation of average precision (AP) with varying λ_z (while evaluating λ_z, the parameter λ_s is fixed). As can be seen, by increasing λ_z from 0.1 to 1000, AP is improved. Moreover, further increasing λ_z reduces the

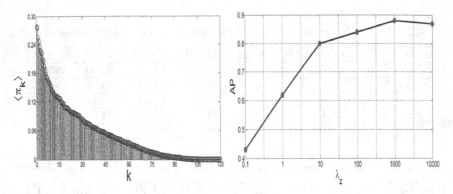

Fig. 2. Left: Inferred $\langle \Pi \rangle$ for the NUS-WIDE-1.5K dataset, Right: Retrieval performance sensitivity with respect to λ_z

average score mildly (the AP drops from 88.61 to 87.78). The possible reason is that using Bayesian learning prevents the model from overfitting to the training data.

7   Conclusion

In this paper, we propose a general Bayesian framework of multi-modal distance metric learning. This framework embed arbitrary number of data modalities into a single latent space with the ability of learning the dimensionality of the latent space from observed data itself. Moreover, a new Varitional Inference algorithm is introduced that is capable of encoding distance supervision of data points. Empirical results on tagged image retrieval and classification applications demonstrated the benefits inherited from the proposed fully-Bayesian method.

References

1. Davis, J.V., Kulis, B., Jain, P., Sra, S., Dhillon, I.S.: Information-theoretic metric learning. In: ICML (2007)
2. Globerson, A., Roweis, S.: Metric learning by collapsing classes. In: NIPS (2006)
3. Guillaumin, M., Verbeek, J., Schmid, C.: Is that you? Metric learning approaches for face identification. In: ICCV (2009)
4. McFee, B., Lanckriet, G.: Metric learning to rank. In: ICML (2010)
5. Nguyen, N., Guo, Y.: Metric Learning: A Support Vector Approach. In: Daelemans, W., Goethals, B., Morik, K. (eds.) ECML PKDD 2008, Part II. LNCS (LNAI), vol. 5212, pp. 125–136. Springer, Heidelberg (2008)
6. Nishida, K., Hoshide, T., Fujimura, K.: Improving tweet stream classification by detecting changes in word probability. In: Proceedings of the 35th International ACM SIGIR Conference on Research and Development in Information Retrieval (2012)
7. Zhen, Y., Yeung, D.Y.: A probabilistic model for multi-modal hash function learning. In: KDD (2012)

8. Qi, G.J., Aggarwal, C.C., Huang, T.S.: On clustering heterogeneous social media objects with outlier links. In: Proceedings of the Fifth ACM International Conference on Web Search and Data Mining (2012)

9. Aizenberg, N, Koren, Y., Somekh, O.: Build your own music recommender by modeling internet radio streams. In: Proceedings of the 21st International Conference on World Wide Web (2012)

10. Xing, E., Ng, A.Y., Jordan, M.I., Russell, S.: Distance metric learning with application to clustering with side information. In: NIPS (2003)

11. McFee, B., Lanckriet, G.: Learning multi-modal similarity. The Journal of Machine Learning Research (2011)

12. Bar-Hillel, A., Hertz, T., Shental, N., Weinshall, D.: Learning a mahalanobis metric from equivalence constraints. Journal of Machine Learning Research (2005)

13. Hoi, S.C.H., Liu, W., Lyu, M.R., Ma, W.Y.: Learning distance metrics with contextual constraints for image retrieval. In: IEEE Conference on Computer Vision and Pattern Recognition (2006)

14. Jain, P., Kulis, B., Davis, J.V., Dhillon, I.S.: Metric and kernel learning using a linear transformation. Journal of Machine Learning Research (2012)

15. Weinberger, K., Blitzer, J., Saul, L.: Distance metric learning for large margin nearest neighbor classification. In: NIPS (2006)

16. Si, L., Jin, R., Hoi, S.C.H., Lyu, M.R.: Collaborative image retrieval via regularized metric learning. ACM Multimedia Systems Journal (2006)

17. Hoi, S.C.H., Liu, W., Chang, S.F.: Semi-supervised distance metric learning for collaborative image retrieval and clustering. ACM Trans. Multimedia Comput. Commun. Appl. (2010)

18. Xie, P., Xing, E.P.: Multi-Modal Distance Metric Learning. In: IJCAI (2013)

19. Hjor, N.L.: Nonparametric bayes estimators based on beta processes in models for life history data. Annals of Statistics (1990)

20. Xing, E.P., Yan, R., Hauptmann, A: Mining associated text and images with dual-wing harmoniums (2005)

21. Paisley, J., Carin, L.: Nonparametric factor analysis with beta process priors. In: ICML (2009)

22. Kingman, J. F. C.: Completely random measures. Pacific Journal of Mathematics (1967)

23. Robert, C.P., Casella, G.: Monte carlo statistical methods. Springer (2004)

24. Jaakkola, T., Jordan, M.I.: Bayesian parameter estimation via variational methods. Statistics and Computing (2000)

Multi-Task Multi-Sample Learning

Yusuf Aytar[✉] and Andrew Zisserman

Visual Geometry Group, Department of Engineering Science, University of Oxford,
Oxford, UK
yusuf@robots.ox.ac.uk

Abstract. In the exemplar SVM (E-SVM) approach of Malisiewicz
et al., ICCV 2011, an ensemble of SVMs is learnt, with each SVM trained
independently using only a single positive sample and all negative samples for the class. In this paper we develop a *multi-sample learning* (MSL)
model which enables joint regularization of the E-SVMs without any
additional cost over the original ensemble learning. The advantage of
the MSL model is that the degree of sharing between positive samples
can be controlled, such that the classification performance of either an
ensemble of E-SVMs (sample independence) or a standard SVM (all positive samples used) is reproduced. However, between these two limits the
model can exceed the performance of either. This MSL framework is
inspired by multi-task learning approaches.

We also introduce a multi-task extension to MSL and develop a *multi-
task multi-sample learning* (MTMSL) model that encourages both sharing between classes and sharing between sample specific classifiers within
each class. Both MSL and MTMSL have convex objective functions.

The MSL and MTMSL models are evaluated on standard benchmarks
including the MNIST, 'Animals with attributes' and the PASCAL VOC
2007 datasets. They achieve a significant performance improvement over
both a standard SVM and an ensemble of E-SVMs.

Keywords: Multi-task learning · Exemplar SVMs

1 Introduction

A number of recent papers in computer vision [11,15] have explored the use of a
mixture of linear SVM classifiers [13,30] and locally linear SVMs [12,19]. In cases
where there is a large diversity in positive training samples, for example artic-
ulations of a human [15] or viewpoints of an object [11], superior performance
is achieved by multiple linear classifiers, compared to limiting the classifier to a
single linear SVM. This is because each linear SVM can learn a template for a
tight cluster ('components' or 'aspects') of visual appearances. Motivated by this
success, Malisiewicz *et al.* [23] investigated the limit of the idea and introduced
the exemplar SVMs (E-SVMs), where a SVM is trained for each positive sample
together with all the negative samples, and the final classifier is defined as an
ensemble of exemplar SVMs.

© Springer International Publishing Switzerland 2015
L. Agapito et al. (Eds.): ECCV 2014 Workshops, Part III, LNCS 8927, pp. 78–91, 2015.
DOI: 10.1007/978-3-319-16199-0_6

In this paper we introduce models to explore the spectrum between a single linear SVM and an ensemble of E-SVMs. The single linear SVM may not have the capacity to model all per sample variations, but has the possibility of generalizing across multiple positive samples. At the other end of the spectrum, an ensemble of E-SVMs can certainly accommodate sample specific variation, but has no possibility of learning across positive samples, since each E-SVM is a sample specific classifier learnt independently from a single positive sample. We introduce here *multi-sample learning* (MSL), for jointly learning multiple E-SVMs. This has the flexibility to travel between the two ends of the learning spectrum (i.e. single SVM and ensemble of E-SVMs) without any extra cost over E-SVMs. The advantages of MSL are that (i) a sweet spot can be chosen between the two ends which improves classification performance, and (ii) compared to a mixture of linear SVMs, the formulation is convex.

The MSL formulation is inspired by multi-task learning (MTL) [5,10,26] approaches. In MTL, different classification tasks are jointly regularized, though in general only a loose relation between tasks is encouraged as the tasks might be very different from each other. In contrast, in MSL, sample specific classifiers for the same class are learnt simultaneously and the classifiers can be very close to one another. Thus, depending on the amount of similarity (or diversity) between the positive samples, the coupling between the classifiers can be encouraged more strongly. While diversity in the positive training samples are modeled with the sample specific classifiers, common features are favoured by joint regularization of these classifiers.

Moreover, we also introduce a multi-task extension to MSL which is termed *multi-task multi-sample learning* (MTMSL). This model encourages the sharing between classes and between sample specific classifiers within each class.

First, we present the formulations for MSL and MTMSL. Then, we describe the optimization procedure and implementation details. Finally, we illustrate the power of MSL and MTMSL on three example datasets, and discuss possible extensions to these methods.

2   Multi-Sample Learning

In this section we define the MSL objective for learning sample specific classifiers in a joint regularization framework. Assume we have a binary classification problem where N is the number of training samples, $X = \{x_i\}_{i=1}^{N}$ are the features, and $Y = \{y_i\}_{i=1}^{N}$ are the corresponding binary labels chosen from the set $y_i \in \{-1, 1\}$. Then the standard SVM objective for solving this classification problem is:

$$\min_{w} \quad \lambda ||w||^2 + \sum_{i}^{N} \max\left(0, 1 - y_i(w^\mathsf{T} x_i)\right) \qquad (1)$$

where w is the classifier vector, λ controls the trade off between the hinge loss and regularization, and the bias term is included by appending a constant number to the end of each x_i and extending the w vector accordingly.

In contrast to the 'classical' SVM, where all positive samples are used to train a single vector w, MSL increases the capacity of the model by defining sample specific classifiers for each positive sample. However, unlike exemplar SVMs [23], in order to enable sharing between classifiers, MSL jointly regularizes the sample specific classifiers such that the objective can be tuned to behave as an SVM or ensemble of exemplar SVMs, or any point in between. The formulation is:

$$\min_{u,\mathbf{w}} \quad \lambda||u||^2 + \beta \sum_{i\,|\,y_i=1}^{N} ||w_i - u||^2 + \sum_{i\,|\,y_i=1}^{N} L_e(w_i; X, Y) \tag{2}$$

$$\text{where} \quad L_e(w_i; X, Y) = \max\left(0, 1 - w_i^{\mathsf{T}} x_i\right) +$$

$$\frac{1}{N^+} \sum_{j\,|\,y_j \neq 1}^{N} \max\left(0, 1 + w_i^{\mathsf{T}} x_j\right), \tag{3}$$

N^+ is the number of positive samples, u is the shared base vector, and the w_i's are sample specific classifiers defined for each positive sample. L_e represents the hinge loss for the given exemplar SVM. The hyperparameters λ and β control the trade off between the hinge loss and regularization, as well as the balance between individual sample specific regularization and joint regularization. With the appropriate setting of the hyperparameters (2) will converge to a classical SVM or an ensemble of exemplar SVMs.

As $\beta \to \infty$, the regularizer $\sum_i^N ||w_i - u||^2$ acts as the hard constraint $w_i = u, \forall i$. Thus each w_i is forced to be same as u and equation (2) becomes the classical SVM formulation (1). Note that in the loss function (3) the loss coming from negative samples are multiplied with $\frac{1}{N^+}$, this ensures exact equivalence with the SVM formulation in (1) since L_e is summed over each positive sample exactly N^+ times.

As $\lambda \to \infty$, u will be forced to a zero vector, the regularization term $\sum_i^N ||w_i - u||^2$ will become $\sum_i^N ||w_i||^2$, and the formulation is equivalent to learning each sample specific classifier individually (i.e. an ensemble of exemplar SVMs). In this case the multiplier $\frac{1}{N^+}$ for the negative loss terms becomes a balancing factor between a single positive and many negative samples. Stronger weighting for the positive loss term is also applied in the ensemble of exemplar SVMs [23] setting and is noted as a factor for improving the success of E-SVMs.

Note that the formulation (2) is convex and the global optimum can be found through standard convex optimization methods (section 4). [18] also uses a similar convex formulation, though targeting dataset bias.

Discussion. There are two main types of formulations for multi-task learning. In the first group, classifier vectors for each task are coupled by minimizing the Frobenius norms of the classifier vector differences [10,22,25] or by sharing a common prior [7,21,27]. In the second, the model parameters are generated from a common latent feature representation which is provided by different forms of nuclear norm regularization [1–5,24].

MSL encourages joint learning over samples through a shared vector u, in a similar manner to the multi-task learning framework of [10] from the first group. Different forms and anaysis of this particular type of regularization are investigated in [9,10] thoroughly including analysis of the dual form and the kernelization.

Considering that $w_{mean} = \frac{1}{N^+} \sum_i w_i = \arg\min_u \sum_i ||w_i - u||^2$, the regularizer that encourages the sharing in MSL, i.e. the term $\sum_i ||w_i - u||^2$, can also be written as $\sum_i ||w_i - w_{mean}||^2$ if there is no penalization on the norm of u (i.e. $\lambda = 0$). Since:

$$\sum_i ||w_i - w_{mean}||^2 = \frac{1}{2N^+} \sum_{i,j} ||w_i - w_j||^2 \tag{4}$$

it can be seen that this corresponds to a fully connected pairwise regularization structure between the sample specific classifiers, Therefore we can also write the regularization term as $\sum_{i,j} ||w_i - w_j||^2$, however in this form we lose the flexibility of imposing additional penalization on the shared vector (since there is no longer a term in u).

Convex approaches [1,3,4,24] from the second group, which are based on nuclear norm regularization, can also be used for encouraging the task relatedness. However, this is not suitable for our problem as we now discuss. The nuclear norm regularization induces low rank solutions and encourages the classifiers to be composed from a smaller set of latent basis vectors, It can be applied to softly enforce joint learning between the sample specific classifiers using a formulation such as:

$$\min_W \quad \lambda||W||_* + \sum_{i \,|\, y_i=1}^{N} L_e(w_i; X, Y) \tag{5}$$

where the columns of the matrix W are sample specific classifiers w_i, and λ controls the trade off between regularization and hinge loss. Since the nuclear norm encourages low rank solutions for the matrix W, with a sufficiently strong regularization (i.e. very large λ) a rank 1 solution for W can be obtained. If W is rank 1, then each w_i will have the same direction in the feature space (their magnitudes may differ but this does not effect the *ranking* order of test samples). Thus by a heavy nuclear norm penalization of W, each w_i will converge to a single classifier vector, in a similar manner to the convergence of MSL (2) to the classical SVM limit as $\beta \to \infty$. However, since $||W||_F \leq ||W||_*$, heavily penalizing $||W||_*$ also imposes a strong l_2 regularization on each w_i. The outcome is that w_i becomes over regularized (i.e. a very small magnitude vector), and consequently the performance drastically decreases. Therefore, using nuclear norm regularization, it is not possible to converge to a single classifier solution without a substantial loss in performance. This is the reason that we based the MSL on the first type of multi-task learning, rather than the second.

3   Multi-Task Multi-Sample Learning

In this section multi-task learning is incorporated with MSL in a joint formulation. This method again builds on the regularized multi-task learning approach of [10] which encourages sharing between tasks by minimizing the squared l_2 norms of classifier vector differences.

Unlike the binary classification problem, here we have multiple classes and the objective is to solve either a multi-class classification problem or multiple one-versus-all classification tasks trained simultaneously. In the first place we introduce a multi-class classification formulation and then describe learning multiple one-versus-all classifiers jointly.

In the **multi-class classification** setting, each sample belongs to a single class and the goal is to classify test samples into one of the existing classes. In the MSL formulation we have a single u which is shared across all sample specific classifiers w_i. In multi-task multi-sample learning (MTMSL), we have multiple u's, one for each class denoted as u_t. In addition to regularizing sample specific classifiers with the shared base vector u_t as in (2), we additionally regularize all the u_t's with another shared vector v which encourages sharing between u_t's. The formulation for MTMSL for the multi-class classification problem is:

$$\min_{v,u,w} \quad \gamma||v||^2 + \lambda \sum_t^T ||u_t - v||^2 + \tag{6}$$

$$\beta \sum_i^N ||w_i - u_{c(i)}||^2 + \sum_t^T \sum_{i \mid y_i^t = 1}^N L_e(w_i; X, Y^t)$$

where the w_i's are the sample specific classifiers, T is the number of classes, $c(i)$ is the class index of the ith training sample, y_j^t is the binary label of the jth sample for the class t, and similarly $Y^t = \{y_j^t\}_{j=1}^N$ is the set of binary labels for class t. The hyperparameters γ, λ and β determine the behavior of the formulation:

- As $\gamma \to \infty$, v will be forced to a zero vector, consequently the regularization term $\sum_t^T ||u_t - v||^2$ becomes $\sum_t^T ||u_t||^2$ and the formulation (6) is equivalent to T separate MSL (2) formulations each learning a classifier independently (i.e. there is no sharing across classes).
- As $\beta \to \infty$, each w_i will be forced to be equal to its class level shared vector $u_{c(i)}$, thus the formulation converges to the multi-task learning objective introduced in [10] (i.e. there is no multi-sample sharing).
- As both $\gamma \to \infty$ and $\beta \to \infty$, formulation learns T individual SVMs (1), one for each particular class (i.e. no multi-task or multi-sample sharing).

In the **multiple one-versus-all classification** setting, each training sample can have none (i.e. background) or several class labels, and the target is to classify the test sample as positive or negative for each class separately. With a slight change in the formulation MTMSL can support this setting:

$$\min_{v,u,w} \quad \gamma||v||^2 + \lambda \sum_{t}^{T} ||u_t - v||^2 + \tag{7}$$

$$\beta \sum_{t}^{T} \sum_{i \,|\, y_i^t=1}^{N} ||w_i^t - u_t||^2 + \sum_{t}^{T} \sum_{i \,|\, y_i^t=1}^{N} L_e(w_i^t; X, Y^t)$$

where w_i^t is the sample specific classifier of the ith sample for class t. Note that both formulations (6) and (7) are convex.

Discussion. In the multi-task setting, unlike MSL where we might need strong coupling between E-SVMs, a nuclear norm based regularization [1,3,4,24] can also be used for encouraging the class-level task relatedness since we don't need very strong coupling between class level classifiers.

4   Optimization and Implementation Details

In this section we describe the optimization procedure used for minimizing our objective functions and the calibration of E-SVMs.

Since both MSL (2) and MTMSL (6, 7) are convex problems they can be minimized globally using convex optimization techniques. Particularly we use stochastic subgradient descent algorithm for optimizing our objectives. The optimization procedure will be described on the formulation (6) and it can be easily adapted to the other described formulations.

For convenience we cast the objective in (6) as:

$$\min_{v, \Delta u, \Delta w} \quad \gamma||v||^2 + \lambda \sum_{t}^{T} ||\Delta u_t||^2 + \beta \sum_{i}^{N} ||\Delta w_i||^2 +$$

$$\sum_{t}^{T} \sum_{i \,|\, y_i^t=1}^{N} L_e(v + \Delta u_{c(i)} + \Delta w_i; X, Y^t) \tag{8}$$

At each iteration an E-SVM w_i and a sample x_j are randomly selected and the parameters $v, \Delta u_t, \Delta w_i$ are updated using the subgradients below:

$$v' = \gamma v - L_{ij} x_j, \qquad \Delta u_t' = \lambda \Delta u_t - L_{ij} x_j,$$
$$\Delta w_i' = \beta \Delta w_i - L_{ij} x_j$$

$$L_{ij} = \begin{cases} -1, & if \quad y_j = -1 \quad and \quad w_i^T x_j > -1 \\ 1, & if \quad i = j \quad and \quad w_i^T x_j < 1 \\ 0, & otherwise \end{cases}$$

A decreasing learning rate is used inverse proportional to the iteration number.

One important step for the success of ensemble of E-SVMs [23] is the post calibration of sample specific classifiers. Even though learning E-SVMs jointly in

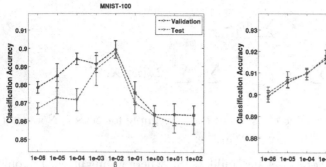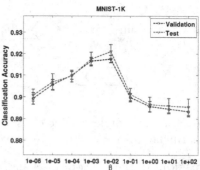

Fig. 1. The effect of the hyperparameter β in MSL on the MNIST dataset.
The hyperparameter λ is fixed and the performance on both validation and test sets
are shown. The multi-class classification accuracy as a function of the hyperparameter
β is displayed. With a large enough β, the MSL gives the same result as the single
class SVM. Moving towards the single class SVM (from left to right) the performance
increases and then decreases back. Thus for an optimum β MSL outperforms both
ensemble of E-SVMs and single class SVM.

the MSL framework provides a certain level of calibration, we also apply a post
calibration step on a validation set such that the responses of each w_i on the
validation set has zero mean and unit variance. The final classification score for
any sample x is then obtained by a max over the calibrated E-SVMs weighted
by the individual confidences:

$$f(x) = max_i^{N^+} c_i \frac{w_i^\mathsf{T} x - \mu_i}{\sigma_i}, \tag{9}$$

where μ_i is the mean and the σ_i is the standard deviation of the scores of w_i
on the validation set, and c_i is the confidence of the w_i measured as the average
precision (AP) of w_i evaluated on the validation set.

5   Experiments

In this section we present evaluation of our methods on three datasets: (a)
MNIST digits dataset, (b) Animals with Attributes dataset [20], (c) PASCAL
VOC 2007 dataset [8]. Datasets are separated into training, validation and test
sets. The methods are trained on the training set and the hyperparameters λ, β,
γ and calibration are determined using the validation set. The following methods are compared: SVM, ensemble of exemplar SVMs (EE-SVM), the proposed
multi-sample learning (MSL), multi-task learning of [10] (MTL), and the proposed multi-task multi-sample learning (MTMSL)

In the first two experiments (i.e. MNIST and Animals with Attributes), the
methods are evaluated on a *multi-class classification* setting, where the task is to
classify each test sample into one of the existing classes. All the experiments are
conducted 5 times with 5 different random selections of training, validation and

test sets from the entire dataset. The mean multi-class classification accuracy and one standard error (i.e. defined as standard deviation of accuracies scaled by $1/\sqrt{5}$) is reported for each method. The PASCAL VOC 2007 dataset is particularly used for category detection experiments, where the task is to identify if each test sample belongs to the target category or not.

Since SVM, EE-SVM and MSL are binary classifiers, in order to use them in a multiclass classification setting, a one against all classifier is trained for each class using each method. The SVM classifiers are calibrated such that each one will give zero mean unit variance score on the validation set. For EE-SVM and MSL, each sample specific classifier is calibrated as described in (9) and class level scores are obtained. The final classification is performed by classifying each test sample into the maximum scoring class.

5.1   MNIST Dataset

MNIST dataset consists of 70K samples of 10 handwritten digits and the task is to classify each test sample into one of the digit classes. We extracted two subsets from this dataset. The first subset is extracted using the exact same setting described in [16]. The images are preprocessed with PCA and the dimensionality is reduced to 64 so as to retain $\sim 95\%$ of the total variance. This subset, referred as *MNIST-100*, consists of 100 training, 50 validation and 50 test samples per class. In order to observe the results for larger number of training samples we also evaluated on a second subset, referred as *MNIST 1K*, which uses 1000 training, 500 validation and 500 test samples per class.

Table 1 displays the classification accuracy results comparing all the methods on MNIST dataset. Using the same setting with [16] on MNIST-100, our SVM baseline is slightly better than their reported results. Since the randomizations might be different slight variations are expected. Among the binary classification methods MSL performs significantly better than the SVM and EE-SVM. It achieves at least 2% improvement over the other two methods on both subsets. In order to better visualize the behavior of MSL, we display the performance of the method as a function of the β parameter. Note that as $\beta \to \infty$, MSL converges to the SVM solution, and for very small β values it behaves closer to EE-SVM (it would behave exactly as EE-SVM if $\lambda = \infty$). As is shown in figure 1 on both of the subsets, moving from EE-SVM to SVM (from left to right) the performance increases and then decreases, finally reaching the SVM solution (large β values). This result demonstrates that combining the generalization of SVM and specification of EE-SVM can lead to much better results. With only 100 positive training samples per class, MSL reaches the accuracy of an SVM trained with 1000 positive samples (see table 1).

Note that the EE-SVM performance is not as good as SVM. In [23] it is clearly stated that in order to obtain a good performance from EE-SVM method each E-SVM needs to be trained against a very large number of negative training samples. Unfortunately in the classification problems we don't have as many negative samples as we have in object detection tasks where the negatives are unlimited (i.e. any subwindow of any image). This observation from [23] explains

Table 1. The multi-class classification accuracy comparison of methods on MNIST dataset. Note that MSL with 100 positive samples per class (MNIST-100) performs as well as SVM with 1000 positive samples per class (MNIST-1K). Note, the first row shows the individual task learning results from [16], and the MTL result in the first row is the learned grouping MTL of [16].

	SVM	EESVM	MSL	MTL	MTMSL
Animal-19	33.25±0.29	13.54±0.48	34.60±0.25	34.64±0.28	34.82±0.27
Animal-43	15.52±0.35	5.79±0.23	16.56±0.31	16.38±0.18	16.71±0.36

Table 2. The multi-class classification accuracy comparison of methods on Animal dataset

	SVM	EESVM	MSL	MTL	MTMSL
MNIST-100 of [16]	84.10±0.30*	n/a	n/a	84.80±0.30*	n/a
MNIST-100	85.84±0.55	78.12±0.99	89.68±0.22	85.72±0.47	89.44±0.16
MNIST-1K	89.57±0.37	82.70±0.40	92.10±0.32	89.55±0.34	92.04±0.32

the inferior behavior of EE-SVM method in our experiments. Nevertheless when learnt jointly, as in MSL, ensemble of these sample specific SVMs manages to outperform SVM solution.

As [16] noted as well, multi-task learning for MNIST dataset doesn't help much for improving the classification accuracy. Nevertheless, MTMSL method clearly outperforms the MTL approach for both of the subsets of MNIST dataset.

5.2   Animal Dataset

Animals with Attributes dataset [20], which will be referred as Animal dataset from here on, consists of 50 animal classes and $\sim 30K$ samples in total. For each sample, 2000 dimensional SIFT bag of words (BOW) features are kindly provided by the dataset creators [20]. As a preprocessing step we reduced the dimensionality of the features from 2000 to 500 using PCA. Some classes in the dataset have a small number of samples. In order to analyse the performance with different number of classes and samples we extracted two subsets from the Animal dataset. *Animal-43* subset consists of 43 classes which have more than 300 samples, and *Animal-19* consists of 19 classes which have more than 700 samples. *Animal-43* organized as 100 training, 100 validation and 100 test samples per class, and *Animal-19* organized as 500 training, 100 validation and 100 test samples per class. Similar to the previous problem the task is a multi-class classification problem and the same settings are used for calibration and evaluation.

The results on the Animal dataset is shown in table 2. Similar to the MNIST experiments MSL approach significantly outperform the EE-SVM and SVM by a margin of at least 1% improvement. Figure 2 shows the performance of MSL as a function of β parameter. It shows a similar behavior to MNIST experiments and gives an optimum result somewhere in between EE-SVM and SVM. Note

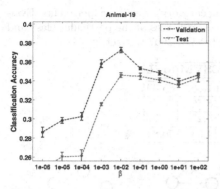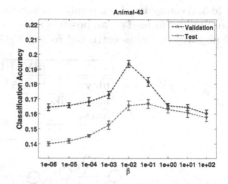

Fig. 2.   The effect of the hyperparameter β in MSL on the Animal dataset.
Note the increase in performance before reaching to the single class SVM limit (i.e.
$\beta = 1e + 2$). See caption of figure 1.

the performance gap between the validation and test sets in figure 2. This gap
suggests that we need more training samples for more stable results. Nevertheless
it doesn't change the behavior of β parameter. Since calibration is performed
on the validation set, MSL gives a better performance on the validation set
compared to the test set. EE-SVM has a similar performance behavior as in
MNIST experiment due to the reason explained in the previous section.

MTMSL only had a small gain over MSL for this dataset. As shown in table 1,
MTL improves the results $\sim 1\%$ over the SVM result on both of the subsets. And
MSL, which doesn't even use the multi-task learning or task relations, performs
as well as MTL in the Animal-19 subset and better than MTL in the Animal-43
subset. Similar to the MNIST experiments, the multi-task extension of MSL, i.e.
MTMSL, outperforms MTL on both of the subsets.

5.3   PASCAL VOC Category Detection

These experiments are performed on PASCAL VOC2007 dataset which contains 9,963 images. The dataset is arranged as 2501 training, 2510 validation
and 4952 testing images. We picked bicycle, motorbike, horse and cow classes
for our detection experiments as their side-facing examples have similar aspect
ratios. For each category the mean bounding box(BB) is computed by taking
the mean of each coordinate seperately across all the positive BBs belonging
to the category. Then all the positive BBs are warped to the mean BB as we
need the training samples to have same feature dimensionality. Histogram of
oriented gradients (HOGs) [6] are used as the features. Training and validation
is performed using all positive side-facing examples of the category together
with 5000 random negative BBs cropped from the negative images. Similarly
tests are performed on all positive side-facing examples and 20K negative BBs
from the test set of PASCAL VOC2007 dataset. In these experiments MSL is
compared against SVM and EE-SVM. As is shown in table 3, MSL constantly
outperformed EE-SVM and SVM results.

Table 3. Average Precision results on side-facing category detection experiments. Evaluations are performed on all positive (side-facing) instances of the particular class and 20K negative instances extracted from PASCAL VOC 2007 test set.

	SVM	EESVM	MSL
bicycle	84.25	61.88	85.09
motorbike	75.81	18.56	76.36
horse	82.97	15.29	83.77
cow	70.14	14.53	70.84

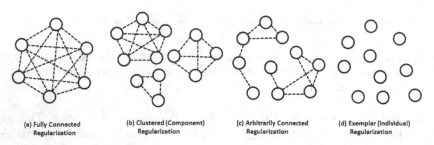

(a) Fully Connected Regularization   (b) Clustered (Component) Regularization   (c) Arbitrarily Connected Regularization   (d) Exemplar (Individual) Regularization

Fig. 3.   Different models of joint regularization can be explored via regularization graphs. Each node represents a sample specific classifier and the links represent the weights of the joint regularization terms $||w_i - w_j||^2$ $\forall i, j$ This paper particularly explores a type of fully connected regularization displayed in (a) with different levels of uniform weights on the edges which can be thought as springs. As the weight of edges increase classifiers are all forced to be as close as possible which in the limit reaches to a single class SVM, or if the weights become looser the classifiers become independent and in the limit reaches to the ensemble of exemplar svms displayed in (d). However, in between these two ends there are many other structural choices of the regularization graph to be explored as displayed in (b) and (c).

6   Conclusion and Future Directions

In this paper we introduced the multi-sample learning framework which combines the generalization ability of SVM with specialization property of EE-SVMs and provides a balanced learning framework which can travel between the two ends of the learning spectrum (i.e. SVM and EE-SVM).

We extended our approach to multi-task multi-sample learning which enables sharing between the classes as well as the sample specific classifiers within each class. By setting the hyperparameters appropriately, MTMSL can be tuned to behave as multiple SVMs, multiple EE-SVMs, multiple SVMs with MTL, multiple EE-SVMs with MTL or any sweet spot between these endpoints. We presented significant performance improvements in two datasets with varying sample sizes for both the MSL and MTMSL approaches.

Some recent MTL approaches take account of the task relationships in the MTL formulation [9, 14, 16, 17, 28, 29] using the structure between tasks in the regularization. Relationships of this type can also be applied to MSL, We can define a joint regularization graph via defining relations between classifier pairs, and regularize the sample specific classifiers accordingly. We sketch this extension here.

Assuming that there is no penalization on the norm of u, then, as already mentioned in section 2, $\sum_i ||w_i - u||^2$ can be re-cast as pairwise difference regularizations $\frac{1}{2N^+} \sum_{i,j} ||w_i - w_j||^2$. If we represent the joint regularization relations as a graph whose nodes are the sample specific classifiers, then the regularization term $\sum_{i,j} ||w_i - w_j||^2$ corresponds to a fully connected graph structure (see figure 3). Furthermore, if we introduce weights for the joint regularization terms as $\sum_{i,j} A_{ij} ||w_i - w_j||^2$ where A encodes the graph structure, then the fully connected regularization becomes a special case of this new regularization term where $A_{ij} = 1$, $\forall i, j$. Subsequently we can encode any graph structure (e.g. clusters, hierarchies, or arbitrary regularization relations) by setting the adjacency matrix A accordingly. A few example structural choices of A are displayed in figure 3. Assuming that the relation matrix A is non-negative, then the regularizer will be convex. A regularization term can also be represented in the spectral form as below:

$$\sum_{ij} A_{ij} ||w_i - w_j||^2 = trace(WLW^\top) \tag{10}$$

$$where \quad L = D - A, \quad D_{ii} - \sum_{j \,|\, i \neq j}^{N^+} A_{ij}$$

where L is the graph laplacian of the regularization graph and the columns of the matrix W are sample specific classifiers w_i. The regularizer (10) is biconvex in L and W and it can be optimized by fixing one and optimizing the other iteratively.

Learning both classifiers and the graph structure from the data by additionally imposing regularizers on L opens many other possibilities of joint regularization. For instance, if we perform nuclear norm regularization on L it will provide us sparsity in the eigenvalues (same with the singular values in this case) of L. Since it is known that the number of zeros in the eigenvalues of the graph laplacian L defines the number of connected components in the graph, we naturally obtain a convex regularizer that encourages automated clustering of sample specific classifiers that will be jointly regularized.

References

1. Amit, Y., Fink, M., Srebro, N., Ullman, S.: Uncovering shared structures in multiclass classification. In: ICML, pp. 17–24 (2007)
2. Ando, R.K., Zhang, T.: A framework for learning predictive structures from multiple tasks and unlabeled data. Journal of Machine Learning Research **6**, 1817–1853 (2005)
3. Argyriou, A., Evgeniou, T., Pontil, M.: Multi-task feature learning. In: NIPS, pp. 41–48 (2006)

4. Argyriou, A., Evgeniou, T., Pontil, M.: Convex multi-task feature learning. Machine Learning **73**(3), 243–272 (2008)
5. Caruana, R.: Multitask learning. Machine Learning **28**(1), 41–75 (1997)
6. Dalal, N., Triggs, B.: Histogram of Oriented Gradients for Human Detection. Proc. CVPR. **2**, 886–893 (2005)
7. Daumé III, H.: Frustratingly easy domain adaptation. CoRR (2009)
8. Everingham, M., Van Gool, L., Williams, C.K.I., Winn, J., Zisserman, A.: The PASCAL Visual Object Classes Challenge 2007 (VOC2007) Results (2007). http://www.pascal-network.org/challenges/VOC/voc2007/workshop/index.html
9. Evgeniou, T., Micchelli, C.A., Pontil, M.: Learning multiple tasks with kernel methods. Journal of Machine Learning Research **6**, 615–637 (2005)
10. Evgeniou, T., Pontil, M.: Regularized multi-task learning. In: KDD 2004: Proceedings of the Tenth ACM SIGKDD International Conference on Knowledge Discovery and Data Mining, pp. 109–117. ACM, New York (2004)
11. Felzenszwalb, P., Mcallester, D., Ramanan, D.: A discriminatively trained, multi-scale, deformable part model. In: Proc. CVPR (2008)
12. Fornoni, M., Caputo, B., Orabona, F.: Multiclass latent locally linear support vector machines. In: ACML, pp. 229–244 (2013)
13. Fu, Z., Robles-Kelly, A., Zhou, J.: Mixing linear svms for nonlinear classification. IEEE Transactions on Neural Networks **21**(12), 1963–1975 (2010)
14. Jacob, L., Bach, F., Vert, J.: Clustered multi-task learning: A convex formulation. In: NIPS, pp. 745–752 (2008)
15. Johnson, S., Everingham, M.: Learning effective human pose estimation from inaccurate annotation. In: Proc. CVPR, pp. 1465–1472 (2011)
16. Kang, Z., Grauman, K., Sha, F.: Learning with whom to share in multi-task feature learning. In: ICML, pp. 521–528 (2011)
17. Kato, T., Kashima, H., Sugiyama, M., Asai, K.: Multi-task learning via conic programming. In: NIPS (2007)
18. Khosla, A., Zhou, T., Malisiewicz, T., Efros, A.A., Torralba, A.: Undoing the damage of dataset bias. In: Fitzgibbon, A., Lazebnik, S., Perona, P., Sato, Y., Schmid, C. (eds.) ECCV 2012, Part I. LNCS, vol. 7572, pp. 158–171. Springer, Heidelberg (2012)
19. Ladicky, L., Torr, P.H.S.: Locally linear support vector machines. In: Proc. ICML, pp. 985–992 (2011)
20. Lampert, C.H., Blaschko, M.B.: Structured prediction by joint kernel support estimation. Machine Learning (2009)
21. Lee, S., Chatalbashev, V., Vickrey, D., Koller, D.: Learning a meta-level prior for feature relevance from multiple related tasks. In: ICML 2007: Proceedings of the 24th International Conference on Machine Learning, pp. 489–496. ACM, New York (2007)
22. Liu, J., Sun, J., Shum, H.: Paint selection. In: Proc. ACM SIGGRAPH (2009)
23. Malisiewicz, T., Gupta, A., Efros, A.A.: Ensemble of exemplar-SVMs for object detection and beyond. In: Proc. ICCV (2011)
24. Obozinski, G., Taskar, B., Jordan, M.I.: Joint covariate selection and joint subspace selection for multiple classification problems. Statistics and Computing **20**(2), 231–252 (2010)
25. Parameswaran, S., Weinberger, K.Q.: Large margin multi-task metric learning. In: NIPS, pp. 1867–1875 (2010)

26. Thrun, S.: Learning to learn: Introduction. Kluwer Academic Publishers (1996)
27. Yu, K., Tresp, V., Schwaighofer, A.: Learning gaussian processes from multiple tasks. In: ICML, pp. 1012–1019 (2005)
28. Zhang, Y., Yeung, D.: A convex formulation for learning task relationships in multi-task learning. CoRR abs/1203.3536 (2012)
29. Zhou, J., Chen, J., Ye, J.: Clustered multi-task learning via alternating structure optimization. In: NIPS, pp. 702–710 (2011)
30. Zhu, X., Vondrick, C., Ramanan, D., Fowlkes, C.: Do we need more training data or better models for object detection? In: Proc. BMVC, pp. 445–458 (2012)

W19 - Surveillance and Re-Identification

Learning Action Primitives for Multi-level Video Event Understanding

Tian Lan[1]([✉]), Lei Chen[2], Zhiwei Deng[2], Guang-Tong Zhou[2], and Greg Mori[2]

[1] Stanford University, Stanford, USA
taranlan@cs.stanford.edu
[2] Simon Fraser University, Burnaby, Canada

Abstract. Human action categories exhibit significant intra-class variation. Changes in viewpoint, human appearance, and the temporal evolution of an action confound recognition algorithms. In order to address this, we present an approach to discover action primitives, sub-categories of action classes, that allow us to model this intra-class variation. We learn action primitives and their interrelations in a multi-level spatio-temporal model for action recognition. Action primitives are discovered via a data-driven clustering approach that focuses on repeatable, discriminative sub-categories. Higher-level interactions between action primitives and the actions of a set of people present in a scene are learned. Empirical results demonstrate that these action primitives can be effectively localized, and using them to model action classes improves action recognition performance on challenging datasets.

1 Introduction

In recent years, the understanding of complex video events has drawn increased interest in the computer vision community. A complex video event usually involves multiple inter-related people and contains rich spatio-temporal structures at various granularities. Fig. 1 shows an example video event in a long-term care facility. In terms of understanding this type of event, there is a variety of questions one can ask: Is there a fall in the scene? Where is the fallen person? When and how did the person fall? Are there any people coming to help? These potential queries often involve multiple levels of details ranging from the overarching event to the fine-grained details of individuals (*where, when and how*).

In this paper, we develop a novel framework for a complete understanding of video events, including: *event classification* (e.g. fall in nursing home), *action recognition and localization* (e.g. standing, squatting), *fine-grained action primitive discovery* (e.g. pushing a wheelchair, squatting and facing right) and spatio-temporal structure extraction (e.g. squatting beside a person who just fell a few seconds ago).

Understanding complex video events is an extremely challenging problem. It shares all of the difficulties of person detection and action recognition, in addition to significant difficulties unique to event classification. The use of hierarchical models integrating multiple semantics such as actions and/or social roles has

L. Agapito et al. (Eds.): ECCV 2014 Workshops, Part III, LNCS 8927, pp. 95–110, 2015.
DOI: 10.1007/978-3-319-16199-0_7

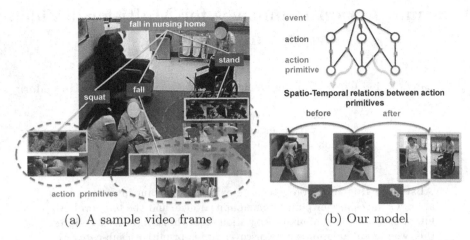

(a) A sample video frame   (b) Our model

Fig. 1. A multi-level video event representation. In the left we show a sample video frame and the goal is to decide whether it is a fall scene or not. We found several actions (e.g. squatting, falling, standing, etc), and each action is recognized using fine-grained action primitives as shown in the yellow rectangles (e.g. squat facing right, stand to push wheelchair, etc). We jointly model the action primitives, actions and event, while considering the spatio-temporal interactions between action primitives. The model for describing the video frame is illustrated in the right side.

been shown to boost event classification performance in realistic videos [1–5]. Despite these successes, there are two important issues not well addressed - localizing the actions and interpreting their fine-grained appearance. The former, usually achieved by generic person detectors (e.g. [6]), brings considerable input noise to the higher-level models, while the latter prevents a deeper level event understanding. We address these problems by modeling *action primitives*, which contain fine-grained information that can not be captured by the basic action categories.

Traditional human detectors are known to have difficulties in capturing the wide range of appearance of human actions in realistic, unconstrained videos. In this paper, we argue that the fine-grained action primitives are key to resolving appearance variations within the action categories. Considering the difficulties in obtaining such labelings, we advocate a weakly supervised setting where the action categories are provided in training, and the action primitives are automatically discovered from the training data. We propose a discriminative spatio-temporal clustering algorithm to discover the action primitives. The action primitives are then treated as mixture components in a latent SVM framework, and refined during learning. Our method detects possibly multiple person instances in each video frame and generates detailed fine-grained action primitives for each instance.

Further, the action primitives naturally contain a rich set of spatial-temporal relations. For example, as shown in Fig. 1, the action primitives: "losing balance", "lying on the floor" and "pushing wheelchair" are in strict temporal ordering and form typical spatial patterns. These spatio-temporal relations are important to distinguish between different events, such as fall and non-fall. Our model captures these relations, and allows flexible inference of different levels of semantics and their dependencies in a video.

2 Previous Work

The literature on human activity recognition is extensive, and covers a large number of aspects of the problem. A comprehensive review of the field was done by Turaga et al. [7]. In this section we review a selection of closely related research, focusing on spatial and temporal representations and action category learning.

Representations for Individuals: A variety of approaches has been developed for representing the action of an individual. Bag-of-words approaches based on local features [8] form the basis for many systems. Recent approaches have pushed toward using a higher-level representation, often by learning mid-level patch representations. Kovashka and Grauman [9] consider higher-order relations between visual words, discriminatively selecting important spatial arrangements. Maji et al. [10] use *poselet* activations, the presence of mid-level body parts indicative of a particular action. Jain et al. [11] learn mid-level discriminative spatio-temporal patches in a data-driven fashion, not relying on poselet-type body part labels.

Many approaches follow a similar vein, analyzing spatio-temporal data to represent human actions in video. Wang et al. [12] track moving points densely over subjects, leading to a dense trajectory feature capturing detailed motion of entire subjects in a scene. Raptis et al. [13] build upon this direction, grouping low-level trajectory-type features into mid-level parts via latent variables. Tian et al. [14] extend the deformable part model to temporal data, modeling the changes in spatio-temporal positions of body parts throughout a sequence. Ma et al. [15] describe a novel multi-scale representation for a person over time, with large and small-scale patches.

Spatio-Temporal Structures in Action Recognition: In our work we discover action primitives and model their spatio-temporal relations. Temporal modeling of human actions in terms of lower-level primitives has a long history in computer vision research. The work by Yamato et al. [16] used hidden Markov models (HMMs) and discovered temporal evolution of actions such as tennis swings. Moore and Essa [17] built stochastic grammars to represent components of actions. Bobick and Wilson [18] described state-based representations of gestures. Bregler [19] discovered low-level primitives, again using HMMs, and showed the ability to detect primitives such as states in a gait cycle.

Larger-scale structures, relating the actions of all the individuals in a scene, have been studied previously. Medioni et al. [20] utilized the relative positions and directions of movement of interacting objects such as vehicles and checkpoints. A recent body of work has developed related techniques, trying to infer interactions in video sequences and model arrangements of groups of people. Lan et al. [1, 2] examine latent interaction models at levels of individual actions, social roles, and group activities. Choi et al. [3] unify the problem of inferring activities with tracking individuals. Amer et al. [4] develop a model for multi-scale activity analysis, using AND-OR graphs with efficient inference techniques. Ramanathan et al. [5] learn social roles from weakly labeled data in complex internet videos.

Action Localization: Localizing an action in space and time is likely a crucial step in order to reason about group activities. Methods that perform explicit spatio-temporal localization include Ke et al. [21], who develop segmentation-based features for detecting actions in videos with complex, moving background clutter. Klaser et al. [22] track individuals and build features for describing each trajectory before final classification. Lan et al. [23] reason about tracking as a latent variable, and select discriminative sub-regions of a video for classification. Tran and Yuan [24] phrase localization as a regression problem, and learn a structured output model for producing human action bounding boxes in video. As mentioned above, Tian et al. [14] develop deformable part models, which can localize actions spatio-temporally.

Sub-category recognition: A contribution of our work is developing an algorithm for discovering action primitives, sub-categories of the original action classes. In the action recognition literature, this problem has been largely unaddressed. Basic latent variable models have been used, typically modeling aspect or appearance, such as the work of Yao and Fei-Fei [25]. Kitani et al. [26] use a probabilistic latent variable model for discovering action categories. A local feature representation is used, latent action categories are learned over spatial and temporal low-level features. Hoai and Zisserman [27] develop a discriminative approach for sub-category discovery.

In the object recognition community, there exists related work on modeling objects and their subcategories, for instance the work of Lan et al. [28], Gu and Ren [29], and Todorovic and Ahuja [30]. We bridge this line of work to action recognition and develop novel methods for spatio-temporal action sub-category analysis.

3   Action Primitive Based Action Localization

Given a set of training videos with annotations of basic-level action categories and bounding boxes in each frame, our goal is to discover the action primitives and learn action detectors. Our approach is inspired by the recent success of subcategory based object detection [28, 29, 31]. A standard pipeline of this line of work is to first partition the examples of an object category into different subcategories and then learn a multi-component object detector as a mixture of subcategory models. The multi-component object models can handle the intra-class variations and thus improve the object detection performance.

We adapt the multi-component object detectors to the video domain and learn multi-component action detectors. Different from static images, actions in the same video tend to have large correlations, especially when they are temporally close to each other. We propose a novel hierarchical discriminative clustering scheme, to discover action primitives from videos. These action primitives are treated as

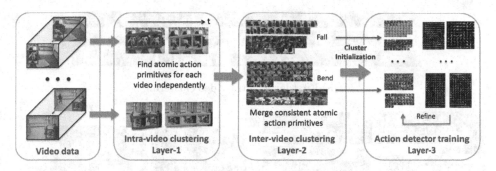

Fig. 2. A general pipeline of our action primitive based action localization model. Details are described in the text.

mixture components in the object model, and further refined during learning. An overview of our approach is illustrated in Fig. 2.

Now we introduce the discriminative action clustering algorithm. The algorithm starts by clustering examples in each individual video and then gradually merges consistent clusters from multiple videos. Next, we present each layer in detail.

3.1   First Layer: Intra Video Clustering

The first layer finds highly homogeneous action clusters for each video independently. Action examples in a video naturally form into multiple spatio-temporal clusters: examples within a small spatio-temporal volume tend to be consistent in appearance. Based on this intuition, we define the similarity between examples as an integration of appearance, spatial and temporal cues.

For the appearance similarity, we use a recently proposed exemplar-SVM based metric [28]. An exemplar SVM detector is trained for each positive example, and negative examples are randomly sampled from all video frames excluding the regions correspond to person. We use HOG as the feature descriptor. For each example, we run the detector on all other examples of the same action class in the video. We consider the top K scoring detections. The appearance similarity between a pair of examples i and j is defined as $d(i,j) = s(I_i, I_j)$, where I_i denotes the indices of the examples which are selected as the top K firings by the detector i. s measures how many times the detectors i and j are fired on the same window.

For the spatial similarity, we use the Euclidean distance between a pair of examples. The temporal similarity is defined as the number of frames between a pair of examples. We integrate these three similarities into the Medoid Shift clustering framework [32].

Fig. 3 (a) shows a visualization of several example clusters. Note that, due to our strategy of discriminative clustering and incorporating spatio-temporal relations between examples, most of the examples in the same cluster correspond to the same person in neighboring frames and are highly consistent in appearance.

(a) First layer: intra-video clustering

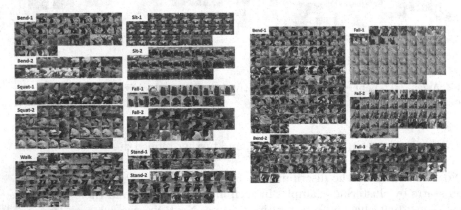

(b) Second layer: inter-video clustering   (c) Third layer: action detector training

Fig. 3. Sample clusters in each layer. The first layer clusters actions within the same video. The second layer clusters actions in between videos. Finally, the third learns strong action detectors for further processing. Please refer to the text for details.

3.2   Second Layer: Inter-Video Clustering

We have obtained a large collection of atomic clusters, where each cluster contains highly consistent examples from the same video. The next step is to merge consistent atomic clusters from different videos. This step also relies on the same discriminative clustering scheme.

We train a linear SVM for each atomic cluster, where we use all examples in the atomic cluster as positive examples, and negative examples are randomly sampled from all video frames excluding the regions corresponding to a person. Similar to the intra-video clustering scheme, we run the detectors on all other examples of the same action class. Then we compute the affinity matrix, where the (i, j) entry of the matrix denotes the appearance similarity $d(i, j)$ (defined in the previous section) between atomic clusters i and j.

In this layer, we only use appearance cues to measure the similarity between pairs of atomic clusters. Once we have the affinity matrix, we do another level of clustering via the standard affinity propagation [33]. In this way, consistent atomic clusters from different videos are merged into one cluster. These clusters are used as our initial set of action primitives. Visualizations of example clusters in the second layer are shown in Fig. 3 (b).

3.3   Third Layer: Action Primitive Refining and Detector Training

The first two layers of our clustering framework automatically partition the person instances in each action class into a set of action primitives that are consistent in appearance, space and time. Now our goal is to train action detectors that can simultaneously recognize the action and localize the person who is performing the action. Modeling the action primitives that corresponds to the subcategories of the original action class will significantly reduce the intra-class variations and improve the detection performance. However, including noisy action primitives can cause the detector to become unreliable and thus hurt the action detection performance. In this work, we train the action detectors in the latent SVM framework, which iteratively learn the action detectors and refine the action primitives.

Object Detector Learning: We learn a multi-component action detector based on the DPM mixture model [6], where the mixture components are initialized by the action primitives discovered through our multi-layer clustering algorithm. We treat the action primitive labels as latent variables and allow them to refine during the latent step. Note that in standard DPM framework, the mixture components are initialized according to the examples' aspect ratios. However, the aspect ratio heuristic does not generalize well to a large number of subcategories, and thus often fails to provide a good initialization.

Action Primitive Pruning: There is no guarantee that all of the action primitive templates are discriminative. Weak templates can potentially put negative effects on detection results. We introduce a procedure to prune the templates that are not discriminative. We quantify this criterion with the average precision measure of action detection. We compute a precision-recall curve for each action primitive template; if its average precision is less than a threshold (0.5), we remove it. We compute precision with all positive examples, and a subset of 500 negative examples. The surviving action primitives are again used to initialize the multi-component action detector.

In our experiments, we used two iterations, as most good action primitives did not need more to converge (i.e. stop changing). We visualize the person examples in several sample action primitives in Fig. 3 (c).

4   Multi-level Event Model

Our goal is to learn an event model that jointly considers persons' actions and action primitives, as well as the spatio-temporal interactions between them. We start with an example (Fig. 1) that illustrates modeling a fall event in a nursing home surveillance video. This scene includes a few actions like squat, fall and stand. Each action is fine-grained, represented by a certain action primitive, e.g. squat facing right, fall and sit on the floor, stand to push wheelchair, etc. We believe recognizing these actions helps to determine the event label, since it is common to find persons squatting, falling, standing, or running in a fall scene. Furthermore, the spatio-temporal interactions between these persons could also provide valuable information. For example, "losing balance", "falling on the floor", "squatting besides the fallen person" and "pushing wheelchair toward the fallen person" are in strict temporal ordering and form typical spatial patterns. We explicitly formulate spatio-temporal interactions in our model. Note that the interactions are between action primitives, rather than basic action categories. This is to remove ambiguity in generic actions – a fallen person sitting on the floor is likely interacting with a person standing to push a wheelchair, instead of a person standing still. Using action primitives enables us to discover these fine-grained cues for better video understanding.

To use our model in video recognition tasks, we employ the follow pipeline. During training, we have labeled frames where the event labels and action labels are provided, and we discover action primitives as described in Section 3. The frames are then represented by the multi-level event model, which is further learned in a max-margin framework to recognize events. During testing, we are given a test frame and we would like to decide the event label. We run our action primitive detectors to obtain candidate person detections, and reason about the event label from the detected actions, action primitives, spatio-temporal interactions, as well as the learned event model. Next, in Section 4.1, we formulate our multi-level event model. We then introduce the max-margin learning in Section 4.2.

4.1   Formulation

We first describe the multi-level labeling. Each video frame $\mathbf{x}$ is associated with an event label $y \in \mathcal{Y}$, where $\mathcal{Y}$ is the set of all possible event labels. Each person is associated with two labels: basic level action and action primitive. We use $\mathcal{H}$ and $\mathcal{Z}$ to denote the sets of all possible action and action primitive labels, respectively.

We encode three types of temporal information in our model: co-occurrence, before and after. We say that an action co-occurs with a video frame if the action takes place in the same temporal segment as that frame. Otherwise, the action is before or after the video frame. In our experiments, we consider the actions detected on that video frame as co-occurring. The before (or after) actions are those detected at most 20 sampled frames[1] before (or after) the given frame. We ignore the actions further away when modeling the current video frame. We denote a type of temporal information as $t \in \mathcal{T}$, where t equals to c, b and a representing co-occurrence, before and after, respectively.

To interpret $\mathbf{x}$ with the multi-level event representation, we find a candidate person x_i^t in each temporal segment t, and for each basic action category $i \in \mathcal{H}$, where $\mathcal{H}$ is the set of action labels. In our experiments, the candidate person x_i^t is simply set as the highest responding detection for action i in temporal segment t. However, we could easily extend our model to perform latent search over a set of candidate detections. Note that x_i^t is also associated with an action primitive label $z_i^t \in \mathcal{Z}$ with $\mathcal{Z}$ denotes all possible action primitives.

---

[1] In the nursing home dataset, 20 sampled frames account for roughly 10 seconds.

We now define the score of interpreting a video frame $\mathbf{x}$ with the multi-level event representation as:

$$F_\theta(\mathbf{x}, y) = \sum_{i \in \mathcal{H}, t \in \mathcal{T}} \alpha_{y,i,t} \cdot x_i^t + \sum_{i \in \mathcal{H}, j \in \mathcal{H}, t \in \mathcal{T}} \beta_{y, z_i^t, z_j^t, t}^\top \cdot [x_i^c, x_j^t, d_{ij}^t] \tag{1}$$

where we use x_i^t interchangeably to denote the feature extracted from the bounding box of the person x_i^t. In our model, we set x_i^t as the scalar output of the action primitive detector for computational efficiency. Besides, $\theta = [\{\alpha\}, \{\beta\}]$ are the model parameters to be learned in the max-margin framework. We describe in detail each component in Eq. 1 in the following.

Unary event-action potential $\alpha_{y,i,t} \cdot x_i^t$: This potential captures the compatibility between the event y of the frame and each action i taking place in a given temporal segment. $\alpha_{y,i,t}$ is a scalar parameter that weights action i in temporal segment t for event y – high weights indicate discriminative actions.

Pairwise Action Primitive Potential. $\beta_{y, z_i^t, z_j^t, t}^\top \cdot [x_i^c, x_j^t, d_{ij}^t]$: This potential captures the compatibility between the event and pairs of action primitives. We fix the first person x_i^c to perform a co-occurring action since we target on modeling the current video frame. The second person x_i^t could be in any temporal segment to interact with person x_i^c. The term d_{ij}^t is a spatial feature computed based on the relative position and scale of person x_j^t's bounding box w.r.t. person x_i^c's bounding box. Note that d_{ij}^t is with respect to the second person's temporal segment t, which could be co-occurrence, before or after. Details of the spatial feature will be introduced in the following.

A straightforward way is to consider the interaction between every pair of action primitives. However, the model will become intractable and including irrelevant interactions will have negative effects on the event model. To handle this problem, we only consider a sparse set of interactions, by removing action primitive pairs that are infrequent (fewer than ten appearances) in the training data. For each selected action primitive pair, we follow [28] to extract the spatial feature. We start by fitting a two component Gaussian mixture model (GMM) to (the bounding boxes of) the pairs of action primitives. The GMM helps us to model various scale and spatial aspects of the action primitive pair. Moreover, we can produce a hypothesis for a bounding box by conditioning the learned GMM on the bounding box of a contextual person. We use the GMM output as the spatial feature. Formally, d_{ij}^t is the GMM score for person x_j^t's bounding box conditioned on person x_i^c's bounding box, where the GMM is trained for the action primitive pair (z_i^c, z_j^t).

Note that this pairwise potential accounts for spatio-temporal interactions between action primitives. The parameter $\beta_{y, z_i^t, z_j^t, t}$ identifies discriminative spatio-temporal interactions by assigning high weights.

4.2 Learning

We now describe how to learn the multi-level event model for video event recognition. Given a set of labeled training video frames $\{\mathbf{x}_i, y_i\}_{i=1}^N$, we would like to train the model parameters θ that tend to produce the correct event label for a new test video frame. A natural way of learning the model is to adopt the multi-class SVM formulation [34] as follows:

$$\min_{\theta, \xi \geq 0} \frac{\lambda}{2} \|\theta\|^2 + \sum_{i=1}^{N} \xi_i, \quad \text{s.t. } F_\theta(\mathbf{x}_i, y_i) - F_\theta(\mathbf{x}_i, y) \geq 1 - \xi_i, \quad \forall i, y \neq y_i \quad (2)$$

where $\xi = \{\xi_i\}_{i=1}^{N}$ are the slack variables to allow soft margin, and λ is a trade-off parameter. The constraint enforces that scoring a video frame $\mathbf{x}_i$ with the ground-truth label y_i is marginally larger than that with any other label $y \neq y_i$. The objective can be optimized using off-the-shelf solvers. In our experiments, we use a cutting-plane based solver implemented by [35].

5   Experiments

The focus of this work is on analyzing complex video events at multiple levels of granularity, including human actions and fine-grained primitives, spatio-temporal relations among multiple people and over-arching scene-level events. This type of structure widely exists in realistic multi-person scenes with rich social interactions. We demonstrate the effectiveness our approach with a challenging real-word application: fall detection in long-term care facilities. We have collected a large dataset of surveillance video footage from a nursing home facility – un-choreographed activity that contains substantial intra-class variation in action categories, and a natural setting to verify the efficacy of modeling complex activity structures.

5.1   Video Event Recognition

Understanding video events performed by multiple people has drawn lots of attention recently. However, the standard benchmark datasets on multi-person (group) activities (e.g. [4,36]) are usually limited to pedestrian activities, such as walking together, talking, queueing, etc. In this work, we have collected a new challenging dataset for understanding multi-person activities in surveillance videos. Our dataset contains a diverse set of actions and primitives with large intra-class variations and thus presents lots of challenges in action recognition and localization. Focusing on the videos containing falls, this dataset naturally contains a rich set of realistic social interactions that form interesting spatio-temporal structures (e.g. squat beside a fallen person, lose balance, push wheelchair towards a person, etc). In the following, we first introduce the details of the dataset and experimental settings and then report the results.

Nursing Home Event Dataset: Our dataset consists of 125 video sequences (**in total 8 hours**) captured from fixed surveillance cameras mounted in a variety of rooms of a nursing home, including dining rooms, living areas, and corridors. Videos are recorded at 640 by 480 pixels at 24 frames per second. See Fig. 4 for example frames from the dataset.

Fig. 4. Nursing Home Event Dataset. Our dataset contains 125 video sequences with six actions: walking, standing, sitting, bending, squatting, and falling. There are two event labels including fall (shown in the first two rows) and non-fall (shown in the last row). These video sequences are collected from a real-world nursing home surveillance project.

Table 1. Video event recognition performance on the nursing home dataset

	Unary		Unary+Pairwise		
Model:	DPM	Primitive	Spatial	Temporal	Full model
AP (in%):	62.5	66.1	68.1	68.4	**68.6**

We split the dataset by using 104 short video clips for training (3 mins on average), and 21 relatively longer video clips for testing (8 mins on average). We annotated a subset (34769 frames) of all the frames in the training videos. Note that in this type of surveillance footage, it is common that there are no persons (or only static persons) appearing in the camera view over a relatively long period of time. Thus we skip annotating these frames. Our annotations include bounding boxes around the true location of the people in each frame (in the subset), action labels for each person, as well as the per-frame event labels. We define six action classes: walking, standing, sitting, bending, squatting, and falling, and two event classes: fall and non-fall. In order to remove redundancy, we sample 1 in every 10 frames for evaluation.

Baselines: We have designed four baselines to compare with our full model. The first DPM baseline runs DPM based action detectors [6], and detects actions for each video. The detection scores are then used in the unary model of Eq. 1, disregarding the temporal term t. Note that this method shares a similar principle to Action Bank [37]. The second baseline is the same as the first, but using the proposed action primitive detectors instead. We combine the action primitive detectors with the unary model of Eq. 1, which results in a hierarchical structured (event and actions) model. This is an example of a standard structured model for action recognition. The third spatial baseline uses the spatial information only by disregarding the other temporal segments (i.e. setting $\mathcal{T} = \{c\}$). Finally, the last temporal baseline considers only the temporal information by removing the spatial feature d_{ij}^t from our full model. Note that the spatial baseline, the temporal

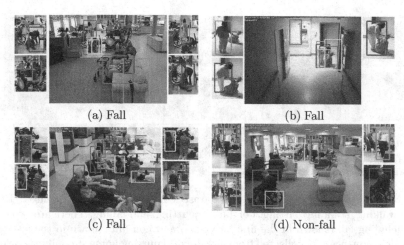

(a) Fall   (b) Fall

(c) Fall   (d) Non-fall

Fig. 5. Visualizations of our result. We select four frames, and show the detected actions in each frame. Each bounding box is marked by a color, which denotes the predicted action class. We use green, red, purple, blue, yellow and cyan to represent walking, standing, sitting, bending, squatting, and falling respectively. The actions used in the before and after segments are listed in the left and right of the frame, respectively. Our model captures the spatio-temporal interactions among these actions to predict the event labels (as captioned below each frame): the first three frames are all believed to be fall scenes with the last being non-fall.

baseline, and our full method learn with both the unary event-action potential and the pairwise action primitive potential.

For a fair comparison, we use the same solver for learning all these methods. The trade-off parameter λ in Eq. 2 is simply set as 1 for all experiments. The recognition performance is measured by average precision (AP) of fall detection.

Results: The results are listed in Table 1. We first compare the two baselines using unary models only. The action primitive based baseline outperforms the DPM based method. This validates the usage of our learned action primitives. Furthermore, adding the pairwise model to the unary model improves the overall recognition performance. Specifically, our full model outperforms all other baseline methods including the temporal model and the spatial model. This result verifies that the pairwise potentials capture useful spatio-temporal information for recognizing video events. We have proposed a unified framework that builds over low-level action primitives and mid-level actions to analyze high-level video events. Intuitively, one can model spatio-temporal interactions among action primitives to capture useful cues. The result shows that the unified framework can be effective on a challenging dataset, and performs better than standard approaches using Action Bank-type representations and other structured models.

Visualizations of our results are shown in Fig. 5, which shows that our model captures spatio-temporal interactions between action primitives to reason about the event label. For example, in Fig. 5 (a), the nurse in red stood to push the

Table 2. Action localization performance on the UCF-Sports dataset. Action-ness stands for the first baseline that runs on all the action bounding boxes, and DPM is the second baseline that trains a DPM for each action class.

Model:	Action-ness	DPM	Ours
mAP (in%):	37.1	49.8	**55.8**

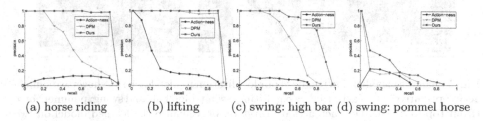

(a) horse riding   (b) lifting   (c) swing: high bar (d) swing: pommel horse

Fig. 6. Precision-recall curves of four sample action classes on the UCF-Sports dataset. These action classes have obvious action sub-categories and thus benefit from our action primitive based model.

wheelchair when she saw the fallen person, and then walked out to call for help. Another man in a black shirt stayed right beside to help the fallen person by performing a series of actions (bending-squatting-bending). These are obvious cues for a fall scene. Moreover, in the scene of Fig. 5 (h), a nurse walked toward the fallen person, and then bent to help. Note that the actions detected in the before and after segments compensate for the noisy detections in the video frame, and together are used to interpret this as a "fall" scene. In Fig. 5 (d), we correctly recognize this non-fall scene although there is a false detection of a falling action. This is because this scene has no spatio-temporal interactions between bending, squatting and falling that are commonly seen in fall scenes.

5.2   Action Localization

Higher-level modeling of structured human activities is aided by accurate action localization. In order to verify the performance of our action primitives, we use them for action localization on the popular UCF-Sports dataset [38].

Dataset: The UCF-Sports dataset consists of 150 broadcast videos from 10 action classes ranging from diving, golf swinging, kicking, lifting, horse riding, running, skating, swinging (on the pommel horse and on the floor), and swinging (at the high bar), to walking. We follow the training/testing split proposed in [23] and use 103 videos for training and 47 for test. We use the ground-truth bounding annotations provided in the training data.

Baseline: We compare our action primitive based action localization model with the following baselines. The first baseline is an "action-ness" detector (c.f. [39]) that is simply a DPM trained on all bounding boxes without considering the action class.

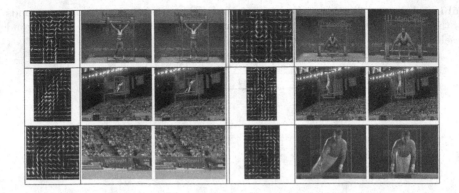

Fig. 7. Sample visualization results of our localization model. Each row shows two sample action primitives of an action class, e.g. lifting, swing: high bar, and swing: pommel horse (from top to down). For each action primitive, we visualize the learned model on two sample video frames, where the highest responding detections are shown in red rectangles. For comparison, we also plot the ground-truth bounding boxes in blue rectangles.

The second baseline executes a standard DPM detector for each action class. As for our model, we follow the steps described in Section 3 to generate action primitives. After learning, an average of 4 action primitives are discovered for each action class.

For performance evaluation, we run each compared model on the test videos. We assume that the action recognition is perfectly done so we use the corresponding action detector for each action class, for the DPM model and ours. We collect the detector responses on each frame, and measure the mean average precision according to the PASCAL VOC criterion [40].

Results: The mAP results are reported in Table 2, which shows that our model outperforms all the baselines. We have also selected sample action classes and plotted the precision-recall curve in Fig. 6. These results again validate the utility of action primitives in localizing actions. We visualize sample localization results in Fig. 7. As can be seen, the action primitives are well-localized in many instances. Detailed, accurate localization of this form can permit the type of high-level activity reasoning that our full model can produce.

6   Conclusion

We presented an algorithm for learning a multi-level representation for the actions of people in a scene. In order to address the intra-class variation of an action category, we developed a data-driven approach to discover action primitives. These action primitives model specific appearance, viewpoint, and temporal stage variants of an action category. An algorithm for automatically discovering these primitives from only action-level supervision was presented, based on clustering and discriminative selection of primitives. A multi-level model for the actions of people in a scene was built around these primitives, allowing us to model detailed inter-relations among action primitives. Empirical results showed that these primitives permit effective localization of actions, improved recognition of human actions, and a detailed explanation of human behaviour in an entire scene-level event.

References

1. Lan, T., Wang, Y., Yang, W., Mori, G.: Beyond actions: discriminative models for contextual group activities. In: NIPS (2010)
2. Lan, T., Sigal, L., Mori, G.: Social roles in hierarchical models for human activity recognition. In: CVPR (2012)
3. Choi, W., Savarese, S.: A unified framework for multi-target tracking and collective activity recognition. In: Fitzgibbon, A., Lazebnik, S., Perona, P., Sato, Y., Schmid, C. (eds.) ECCV 2012, Part IV. LNCS, vol. 7575, pp. 215–230. Springer, Heidelberg (2012)
4. Amer, M.R., Xie, D., Zhao, M., Todorovic, S., Zhu, S.-C.: Cost-sensitive top-down/bottom-up inference for multiscale activity recognition. In: Fitzgibbon, A., Lazebnik, S., Perona, P., Sato, Y., Schmid, C. (eds.) ECCV 2012, Part IV. LNCS, vol. 7575, pp. 187–200. Springer, Heidelberg (2012)
5. Ramanathan, V., Yao, B., Fei-Fei, L.: Social role discovery in human events. In: CVPR (2013)
6. Felzenszwalb, P.F., Girshick, R.B., McAllester, D., Ramanan, D.: Object detection with discriminatively trained part based models. T-PAMI 32, 1672–1645 (2010)
7. Turaga, P., Chellappa, R., Subrahmanian, V.S., Udrea, O.: Machine recognition of human activities: A survey. T-CSVT (2008)
8. Schuldt, C., Laptev, I., Caputo, B.: Recognizing human actions: a local SVM approach. In: ICPR (2004)
9. Kovashka, A., Grauman, K.: Learning a hierarchy of discriminative space-time neighborhood features for human action recognition. In: CVPR (2010)
10. Maji, S., Bourdev, L., Malik, J.: Action recognition from a distributed representation of pose and appearance. In: CVPR (2011)
11. Jain, A., Gupta, A., Rodriguez, M., Davis, L.S.: Representing videos using mid-level discriminative patches. In: CVPR (2013)
12. Wang, H., Kläser, A., C.Schmid, Liu, C.L.: Action recognition by dense trajectories. In: CVPR (2011)
13. Raptis, M., Kokkinos, I., Soatto, S.: Discovering discriminative action parts from mid-level video representations. In: CVPR (2012)
14. Tian, Y., Sukthankar, R., Shah, M.: Spatiotemporal deformable part models for action detection. In: CVPR (2013)
15. Shugao Ma, Jianming Zhang, N.I.C., Sclaroff, S.: Action recognition and localization by hierarchical space-time segments. In: ICCV (2013)
16. Yamato, J., Ohya, J., Ishii, K.: Recognizing human action in time-sequential images using hidden markov model. In: CVPR (1992)
17. Moore, D., Essa, I.: Recognizing multitasked activities from video using stochastic context-free grammar. In: AAAI (2002)
18. Bobick, A., Wilson, A.: A state-based technique for the summarization and recognition of gesture. In: ICCV (1995)
19. Bregler, C.: Learning and recognizing human dynamics in video sequences. In: CVPR (1997)

20. Médioni, G., Cohen, I., Brémond, F., Hongeng, S., Nevatia, R.: Event detection and analysis from video streams. T-PAMI **23**, 873–889 (2001)
21. Ke, Y., Sukthankar, R., Hebert, M.: Event detection in crowded videos. In: ICCV (2007)
22. Kläser, A., Marszałek, M., Schmid, C., Zisserman, A.: Human focused action localization in video. In: International Workshop on Sign, Gesture, Activity (2010)
23. Lan, T., Wang, Y., Mori, G.: Discriminative figure-centric models for joint action localization and recognition. In: ICCV (2011)
24. Tran, D., Yuan, J.: Max-margin structured output regression for spatio-temporal action localization. In: NIPS (2012)
25. Yao, B., Fei-Fei, L.: Modeling mutual context of object and human pose in human-object interaction activities. In: CVPR (2010)
26. Kitani, K.M., Okabe, T., Sato, Y., Sugimoto, A.: Discovering primitive action categories by leveraging relevant visual context. In: ECCV Workshop on Visual Surveillance (2008)
27. Hoai, M., Zisserman, A.: Discriminative sub-categorization. In: CVPR (2013)
28. Lan, T., Sigal, L., Raptis, M., Mori, G.: From subcategories to visual composites: a multi-level framework for object detection. In: ICCV (2013)
29. Gu, C., Ren, X.: Discriminative mixture-of-templates for viewpoint classification. In: Daniilidis, K., Maragos, P., Paragios, N. (eds.) ECCV 2010, Part V. LNCS, vol. 6315, pp. 408–421. Springer, Heidelberg (2010)
30. Todorovic, S., Ahuja, N.: Learning subcategory relevances for category recognition. In: CVPR (2008)
31. Gu, C., Arbeláez, P., Lin, Y., Yu, K., Malik, J.: Multi-component Models for object detection. In: Fitzgibbon, A., Lazebnik, S., Perona, P., Sato, Y., Schmid, C. (eds.) ECCV 2012, Part IV. LNCS, vol. 7575, pp. 445–458. Springer, Heidelberg (2012)
32. Sheikh, Y.A., Khan, E.A., Kanade, T.: Mode-seeking via medoidshifts. In: ICCV (2007)
33. Frey, B.J., Dueck, D.: Clustering by passing messages between data points. Science (2007)
34. Crammer, K., Singer, Y.: On the algorithmic implementation of multiclass kernel-based vector machines. JMLR **2**, 265–292 (2001)
35. Do, T.M.T., Artieres, T.: Large margin training for hidden markov models with partially observed states. In: ICML (2009)
36. Choi, W., Shahid, K., Savarese, S.: What are they doing?: collective activity classification using spatial-temporal relationship among people. In: International Workshop on Visual Surveillance (2009)
37. Sadanand, S., Corso, J.J.: Action Bank: a high-level representation of activity in video. In: CVPR (2012)
38. Rodriguez, M.D., Ahmed, J., Shah, M.: Action MACH: a spatial-temporal maximum average correlation height filter for action recognition. In: CVPR (2008)
39. Alexe, B., Deselares, T., Ferrari, V.: What is an object?. In: CVPR (2010)
40. Everingham, M., Van Gool, L., Williams, C.K.I., Winn, J., Zisserman, A.: The PASCAL visual object classes (VOC) challenge. IJCV **88**, 303–338 (2010)

Learning Skeleton Stream Patterns with Slow Feature Analysis for Action Recognition

Yanhu Shan, Zhang Zhang, and Kaiqi Huang[(✉)]

Institute of Automation, CAS, Beijing, China
{yanhu.shan,zzhang,kqhuang}@nlpr.ia.ac.cn

Abstract. Previous studies on MoCap (Motion Capturing (MoCap) System tracks the key points which are marked with conspicuous color or other materials (such as LED lights). The motion sequences are collected into MoCap action datasets, e.g., 1973 [3] and CMU [4] MoCap action datasets.) action data suggest that skeleton joint streams contain sufficient intrinsic information for understanding human body actions. With the advancement in depth sensors, e.g., Kinect, pose estimation with depth image provides more available realistic skeleton stream data. However, the locations of joints are always unstable due to noises. Moreover, as the estimated skeletons of different persons are not the same, the variance of intra-class is large. In this paper, we first expand the coordinate stream of each joint into multi-order streams by fusing hierarchical global information to improve the stability of joint streams. Then, Slow Feature Analysis is applied to learn the visual pattern of each joint, and the high-level information in the learnt general patterns is encoded into each skeleton to reduce the intra-variance of the skeletons. Temporal pyramid of posture word histograms is used to describe the global temporal information of action sequence. Our approach is verified with Support Vector Machine (SVM) classifier on MSR Action3D dataset, and the experimental results demonstrate that our approach achieves the state-of-the-art level.

Keywords: Action recognition · Skeleton · Joint stream · Multi-order streams · Slow feature analysis

1 Introduction

Recently, human action recognition has been an important domain of computer vision because of its great application prospects in intelligent visual surveillance, human-computer interaction, smart home, etc. Human action can be treated as a 3D space-time volume concatenated by images. Low-level and mid-level features [7][2][5][20] are extracted for action description, and the results on several realistic action datasets [15][6][12] demonstrate its promise. However, the lack of high-level semantic information makes this kind of methods not handle complex actions. Several previous studies [3][1] use skeleton of human body for gesture/action representation, and these work suggest that skeleton provides enough

© Springer International Publishing Switzerland 2015
L. Agapito et al. (Eds.): ECCV 2014 Workshops, Part III, LNCS 8927, pp. 111–121, 2015.
DOI: 10.1007/978-3-319-16199-0_8

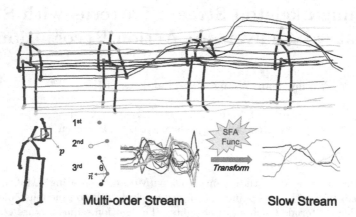

Multi-order Stream   **Slow Stream**

Fig. 1. (Best viewed in color) Kinetic stream pattern learning and transformation. The slow streams are the transformed 5 slowest streams.

information to describe human body actions. However, skeletons estimated from RGB image sequence are not accurate enough for action representation. Fortunately, motion capturing technique [14] can estimate the 3D skeleton joints easily with data from depth camera and help us to avoid the influence of the limits from preprocessing techniques.

Recent studies [21][8] employ both 3D skeleton joints and depth images to improve the capability of feature representation. Skeleton visualization intuitively demonstrates that although the skeleton sequences are unstable, skeletons contain sufficient information of human body actions. Thus, our work focuses on action representation with only skeleton joint streams, i.e., 3D skeleton joint trajectories as shown in Fig. 1.

Earlier work of Campbel and Bolick [1] represents action sequence by projecting pre-existing 3D joints trajectories to curves in subspaces of phase space. The poses in an action form a curve. Although the work can only recognize limited motions with simple descriptors, this work provides a new thinking of action recognition with joint streams. In order to obtain a better action representation, Lv et al. [11] model the dynamics of single joints in the skeleton with Hidden Markov Model (HMM), and the HMM models are combined to form a strong multi-class AdaBoost classifier. This approach can effectively improve the discrimination of action representation in data from Motion Capture (MoCap) system, however, it is still a challenging work to model joint streams with HMM due to lots of noises in the estimation of 3D skeleton sequences. Moreover, modeling a HMM for each class with single joint exists the risk of overfitting when the data volume is small. Zhao et al. [26] learn a vocabulary for each normalized distance stream of a pairwise joints, which reduces the noises in 3D skeleton sequences, and a gesture is represented by combining the corresponding words in different vocabularies. Nevertheless, high-level information is lacked in the feature description.

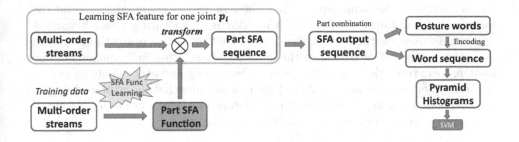

Fig. 2. The framework of our approach

Slow Feature Analysis (SFA) is a method for learning the invariant patterns from visual data. Researches [22] in neuroscience suggest that high-level visual perceptions vary more slowly over time in contrast to input signal. Thus, SFA has been employed in several previous work [25][16] to describe the dynamic of video on realistic datasets.

Inspired by this, we propose an approach to learning high-level patterns from skeleton joint streams with SFA and encoding the high-level information into skeleton postures for action representation. Fig. 2 shows the framework of our approach. Firstly, we construct a multi-order kinetic stream for each key joint by applying the original skeleton sequence. The new streams contain not only the local dynamic of joints but also the dynamic of the center joints relative to others. Secondly, we learn a pattern of each multi-order stream with SFA and encode the high-level dynamic pattern into the original skeleton stream as a part SFA sequence of the joint. The part SFA sequences of all joints are combined into a SFA posture sequence. Then, a dictionary of postures is learned, and the posture sequence is encoded with the posture words in the dictionary. To incorporate the global temporal order information, temporal pyramid is applied for action representation. The classifier we used is SVM.

2   Method

The main stages of our method is threefold: Section 2.1 presents how to generate the multi-order streams from original skeleton sequence data. Then, the SFA is introduced in Section 2.2. In Section 2.3, we propose the method of action representation and classification.

2.1   Multi-order Streams

With the motion capturing technique [14], 20 joints in each frame are estimated from depth video. The position of joint p at frame t has 3 coordinates $p(t) = [x(t), y(t), z(t)]$. The position changes of p over time form a point stream shown in Fig. 1. As the intra-class variance for one action performed by different subject (or even the same subject but different times) is always large and the joint streams contain lots of noises, it is challenging to learn a invariable action pattern. To disperse the intra-variance and avoid the risk of overfitting, we learn an action pattern of each joint in the human body skeleton individually. For one joint p, we extract the high-order streams between p and other joints as well as the first-order position stream of the joint to make sure that the combined stream contain both local and body structural information. The multi-order stream of one joint contains three parts as shown in Fig. 1:

$1^{st} Order$: The first-order stream is the split of the original joint shift in 3 coordinate over time, i.e.,

$$s^{1st} = [x(1{:}T), y(1{:}T), z(1{:}T)]^{\top}, s^{1st} \in R^{3 \times T} \tag{1}$$

where

$$x(1{:}T) = [x(1), x(2), ..., x(T)] \tag{2}$$

is the stream in x coordinate, and T is the number of frames in the sequence. Similarly, $y(1{:}T)$ and $z(1{:}T)$ are the streams of the other two coordinates.

$2^{nd} Order$: The second-order stream describe the variations of the distances between joint p and the other joints, i.e.,

$$s^{2nd} = \{D_{pq}(1{:}T)\}, q \in \mathcal{J} \mid q \neq p, s^{2nd} \in R^{19 \times T} \tag{3}$$

where $D_{pq}(1{:}T)$ is the distance sequence of p and q over time and $\mathcal{J}$ denotes the 20 joint set. The distance sequence of pairwise joints can reflect the dynamic information of joint p relative to others, and the body structural information of human action is naturally encoded into the distance streams. Euclidean distance is used in our work to measure the distance between two joints. For joint p, a 19-d stream is generated as the second-order stream.

$3^{rd} Order$: As shown in Fig. 1, the third-order streams are composed of two parts. One is the angle sequence $\theta(1{:}T)$ over time, where θ is the angle of two skeleton segments (segment is the link between two joints in the skeleton) centering on joint p. The other is a sequence formed by the normal vector $\boldsymbol{n}_i$ of the plane determined by the above two segments in frame i. The normal vector sequence $n(1{:}T)$ can be decomposed into 3 streams by considering 3 coordinates of the vector respectively. As these 4 streams are determined by three points, they are combined as the third-order stream and denoted as s^{3rd} in space $R^{4 \times T}$.

Streams of all the three orders are combined as the final multi-order stream

$$\mathbf{s} = [s^{1st}, s^{2nd}, s^{3rd}]^{\top}, s \in R^{26 \times T} \tag{4}$$

of joint p. The sequence of each dimension in $\mathbf{s}$ is normalized to zero mean and unit variance to reduce the variances among skeletons of different subjects. Note that some terminal joints connected with only one joint (such as head, hands and feet) are not processed, because there is no angle on these points.

Moreover, the joints shared by more than two segments are employed repeatedly to form different multi-order streams containing different 3rd-order streams. To distinguish the multi-order streams sharing the same joint center, we call the joint p connecting two certain segments a joint unit.

2.2   SFA Function Learning

Slow Feature Analysis (SFA) have been used for learning the invariant patterns from visual data. It can extract high-level visual perceptions vary more slowly over time compared with multi-dimensional input signal and thus can be applied to describe the dynamic changes of human action with temporal sequence. The method is mathematically defined as follows:

Given a multi-dimensional input signal $s(t)$ from training data, the SFA is to learn a function set $g(s) = [g_1(s), ..., g_M(s)]^\top$ which makes the M-dimensional output $o(t) = [o_1(t), ..., o_M(t)]^\top$ vary as slow as possible, where $o_j(t) = g_j(s(t))$. The function learning process can be described as an optimization problem

$$\min_{g_j(t)} \langle \dot{o}_j^2 \rangle_t \tag{5}$$

subject to

$$\langle o_j \rangle_t = 0 \quad (zero\ mean) \tag{6}$$

$$\langle o_j^2 \rangle_t = 1 \quad (unit\ variance) \tag{7}$$

$$\forall j < j' : \langle o_j, o_{j'} \rangle_t = 0 \quad (decorrelation), \tag{8}$$

where $\langle\ \rangle_t$ is a mean function over time, $\langle o_j \rangle_t$ and $\dot{o}_j$ are the temporal average and the first order derivative of the j-th dimension signal sequence, respectively. The objective of Eqn.(5) is to minimize the temporal variance measured by the average square of the first order derivative. Eqn.(6) is a normalization for convenience, and Eqn.(7) is to avoid the trivial solution $o_j = const$ which means that the output signal carries no information of changes. The constraint in Eqn.(8) has two roles: ensuring that different dimension output signals carry different types of information and sorting the order of different dimension signals from slowest to fastest.

The transformation function can be unified as

$$g_j(s) = w_j^\top h(s) = \sum_{k=1}^{K} w_{jk} h_k(s). \tag{9}$$

When g_j is linear function, $h(s) = s$, and in the case of nonlinear, $h(s) = [h_1(s), ..., h_K(s)]^\top$ is a set of polynomial (usually quadratic) expansion functions for linearization. Note that $h(s)$ is centralized by minus $\langle h(s) \rangle_t$, i.e., $h(s) = h(s) - \langle h(s) \rangle_t$. Thus, the objective function of Eqn.(5) can be rewritten as

$$\langle \dot{o}_j^2 \rangle_t = w_j^\top \left\langle \dot{h}(s)\dot{h}(s)^\top \right\rangle_t w_j = w_j^\top A w_j, \tag{10}$$

and
$$\langle o_j, o_{j'} \rangle_t = \mathbf{w}_j^\top \langle \mathbf{h}(\mathbf{s})\mathbf{h}(\mathbf{s})^\top \rangle_t \mathbf{w}_{j'} = \mathbf{w}_j^\top \mathbf{B} \mathbf{w}_{j'}. \tag{11}$$

Considering constraint in Eqn.(7), the objective function can be evolved into

$$\langle \dot{o}_j^2 \rangle_t = \frac{\langle \dot{o}_j^2 \rangle_t}{\langle o_j, o_j \rangle_t} = \frac{\mathbf{w}_j^\top \mathbf{A} \mathbf{w}_j}{\mathbf{w}_j^\top \mathbf{B} \mathbf{w}_j}. \tag{12}$$

The optimization problem can be solved by the generalized eigenvalue approach

$$\mathbf{A}\mathbf{W} = \mathbf{B}\mathbf{W}\mathbf{\Lambda} \tag{13}$$

The eigenvectors $[\mathbf{w}_1, \mathbf{w}_2, ..., \mathbf{w}_M]$ corresponding to the M smallest eigenvalues sorted in ascending order are the weights of SFA function $\mathbf{g}(\mathbf{s}) = [g_1(\mathbf{s}), g_2(\mathbf{s}), ..., g_M(\mathbf{s})]$ in Eqn.(9).

2.3   Action Representation and Classification

For each joint unit, we can learn a set of SFA functions, and the SFA function sets of all joint units are combined as $\mathbf{G} = [\mathbf{g}^1, \mathbf{g}^2, ..., \mathbf{g}^N]^\top$, where $\mathbf{g}^i$ is the SFA function set of joint units i. With the learnt SFA function $\mathbf{G}$, the multi-order stream $\mathbf{s}^i$ of joint i can be transformed into a new slow stream feature $\hat{\mathbf{s}}^i = \mathbf{g}^i(\mathbf{s}^i)$ with the size of $M \times T$. Combination $\mathbf{S}(t) = [\hat{\mathbf{s}}^1(t), \hat{\mathbf{s}}^2(t), ..., \hat{\mathbf{s}}^N(t)]^\top$ is used as a stable expression of action sequence. The dimension of $\mathbf{S}(t)$ is $d' = M \times N$.

A posture can be described with the d' dimension vector at the corresponding time/frame, and each action is a posture sequence over time. Although the sequence contains lots of postures, some postures in a short time are very similar. Moreover, several actions share many postures. To describe the action sequence robustly with some key postures, we quantize the postures by clustering the observed posture vectors into a posture dictionary. K-means is employed here to cluster K centers as posture words, and 1-NN is used to label observational vectors with the posture words. Thus, each action can be transformed as a sequence of posture words corresponding to the observational postures.

As known that temporal information is very important for action representation. In order to encode the temporal information of one action into the final action descriptor, we apply a three-tier temporal pyramid with partitions 4×1, 2×1 and 1×1. For each subregions, we count the numbers of different posture words to obtain a histogram, then, the histograms generated from all 7 subregions are concatenated as the final action representation.

Multi-class Support Vector Machine (SVM) with RBF kernel is utilized for action classification. Parameter cost term and kernel bandwidth are optimized using a greedy search with a 5-fold cross-validation on the training data.

3   Experimental Results and Analysis

In this section, we show the verification of our approach on the public MSR Action3D dataset [8], and the experimental results demonstrate that the proposed method can achieve the state-of-the-art level.

MSR Action3D dataset contains 20 actions: *high arm wave, horizontal arm wave, hammer, hand catch, forward punch, high throw, draw x, draw tick, draw circle, hand clap, two hand wave, side-boxing, bend, forward kick, side kick, jogging, tennis swing, tennis serve, golf swing, pickup & throw*. Each action was performed by 10 subjects for two or three times. The dataset contains 557 action samples, and the frame rate of sequences is 15 f/s. The original action data of this dataset consists of depth image sequences. 20 3D skeleton joint positions are estimated from each depth image by applying the real time skeleton tracking technique [14].

Due to the large amount of computation for classifying all the actions, the dataset is divided into 3 subsets: AS1, AS2 and AS3, and each subset contains 8 actions. The partition follows the rule that AS1 and AS2 group actions with similar movement, while AS3 groups complex actions together. The actions in the three subsets are:

AS1: *Horizontal arm wave, Hammer, Forward punch, High throw, Hand clap, Bend, Tennis serve, Pickup & throw*
AS2: *High arm wave, Hand catch, Draw x, Draw tick, Draw circle, Two hand wave, Slide boxing, Forward kick*
AS3: *High throw, Forward kick, Side kick, Jogging, Tennis swing, Tennis serve, Golf swing, Pickup & throw*

We evaluate our method on MSR Action3D dataset by using the 2-fold cross-subject test setting following the benchmark system [8], i.e., subjects 1,3,5,7,9 are used for training and 2,4,6,8,10 are used for testing. We do not compare with some methods [9,10] which just simply split data into two parts, because the performance of various 2-fold divisions vary widely. As mentioned in Section 2.1, some joint units share one joint center. The number of joint units can be confirmed by the existing angles between two connected segments in the skeleton. The joint of shoulder center connects with 4 segments, and we use the smallest 4 angles in the 3D space to form joint units. Removing the angles connected to hands and feet, the remaining 16 angles in the skeleton are used in our experiments. Thus, N mentioned in Section 2.3 is equal to 16. The number of SFA function M is empirically set to 15. We use the quadratic expansion function $h(d) = [d_1, d_2, ..., d_n, d_1 d_1, d_1 d_2, ..., d_n d_n]^\top$ to expand the d-dimension of stream feature s in Eqn.(9).

Table 1 compares the results between our approach and the state-of-the-art methods published in recent years. We can see from the results that our method achieves good performance on the three action sets of MSR Action3D dataset, and the average accuracy outperforms those of state-of-the-art methods.

Fig. 3 shows the confusion matrixes for the three action scenes of MSR Action3D dataset. The method works well on AS1 and AS3 action sets while the performance is relatively poor on AS2 set. Contrasting the actions in the three sets, some actions in AS2, e.g. {*High arm wave, Hand catch, Slide boxing*} and {*Draw X, Draw circle*}, are more similar than others, moreover, these actions are always with short durations where the high-level visual patterns are hard to learn by SFA. The highest performance on complex AS3 action set demonstrates that

Table 1. Result comparison with other published methods. 'D' and 'S' in the 'Data' column represent depth and skeleton information respectively.

Method	Year	Data	Accuracy (%)			
			AS1	AS2	AS3	Average
Li et al. [8]	2010	D	72.9	71.9	79.2	74.7
Xia et al. [23]	2012	D	87.98	**85.48**	63.46	78.97
Yang et al. [24]	2012	D	74.5	76.1	96.4	82.33
Vieira et al. [18]	2012	D	84.70	81.30	88.40	84.8
Wang et al. [21]	2012	D + S	-	-	-	88.20
Zhao et al. [26]	2013	S	-	-	-	81.70
Oreifej et al. [13]	2013	D	-	-	-	88.36
Wang et al. [19]	2013	S	-	-	-	90.22
Vemulapalli et al. [17]	2014	S	-	-	-	89.48
Our method		S	**92.47**	82.14	**97.17**	**90.59**

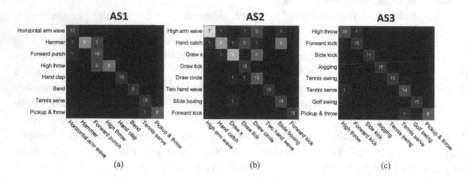

(a)   (b)   (c)

Fig. 3. The confusion matrixes for the three action sets of MSR Action3D dataset

the learnt high-level patterns by SFA contribute to recognizing complex human actions.

In order to have a deep insight of the proposed approach, comparison experiments are done to analyze the contributions of multi-order stream and SFA transformation, and the results are laid out in Table 2. It's obvious that high-order (2nd and 3rd) streams contain more action information, and multi-order streams can improve the performance of recognition accuracies on all subsets. Moreover, the description capability of each type of streams can be improved with SFA transformation. Combined with the slow streams shown in Fig. 1, we can know that SFA can be used to learn the intrinsic information from streams with noise, and the transformed streams are more stable. Note that the SFA function number M is empirically set by considering all actions in the three subsets, thus, some learned relative faster functions will influent the pow of SFA stream feature and make the performance reduce in some subsets.

Table 2. Result comparison of stream orders and SFA transformation

Method	Accuracy (%)			
	AS1	AS2	AS3	Average
1st Order	59.14	61.61	76.42	65.72
2nd Order	75.26	62.50	87.74	75.17
3rd Order	74.19	64.29	87.74	75.41
Multi-Order	83.49	74.54	90.29	82.78
1st Order + SFA	64.52	60.71	73.58	66.27
2nd Order + SFA	69.89	72.32	88.68	76.96
3rd Order + SFA	78.49	68.75	90.57	79.27
Multi-Order + SFA	**92.47**	**82.14**	**97.17**	**90.59**

4 Conclusion

This paper has proposed an approach to recognize human actions with skeleton joint streams. We generate multi-order streams from original data to improve the description capability of skeleton joint streams. Then, the SFA is employed to decrease the intra-variance of data. Temporal pyramid of posture word histograms is used to describe the global temporal information of action sequence. The experimental results demonstrate that both multi-order streams and the SFA contribute to the recognition accuracy. Compared to the state-of-the-art methods, the part of action representation in our system has big room of improvement by employing discriminative information of action sequence. Moreover, online action recognition with skeleton point information will be more widely used in applications such as human-computer interaction, entertainment or even robot control. Thus, we can optimize our method from these aspects.

Acknowledgments. This work is supported by the National Basic Research Program of China (Grant No. 2012CB316302), National Natural Science Foundation of China (Grant No. 61105009 and Grant No. 61175007).

References

1. Campbell, L., Bobick, A.: Recognition of human body motion using phase space constraints. In: Proceedings of the Fifth International Conference on Computer Vision, 1995, pp. 624–630 (1995)
2. Dollar, P., Rabaud, V., Cottrell, G., Belongie, S.: Behavior recognition via sparse spatio-temporal features. In: 2nd Joint IEEE International Workshop on Visual Surveillance and Performance Evaluation of Tracking and Surveillance, 2005, pp. 65–72 (2005)

3. Gunnar, J.: Discriminative video pattern search for efficient action detection. Perception and Psychophysics **14**(2), 201–211 (1973)
4. Han, L., Wu, X., Liang, W., Hou, G., Jia, Y.: Discriminative human action recognition in the learned hierarchical manifold space. Image and Vision Computing **28**(5), 836–849 (2010)
5. Kovashka, A., Grauman, K.: Learning a hierarchy of discriminative space-time neighborhood features for human action recognition. In: 2010 IEEE Conference on Computer Vision and Pattern Recognition (CVPR), pp. 2046–2053 (2010)
6. Kuehne, H., Jhuang, H., Garrote, E., Poggio, T., Serre, T.: Hmdb: a large video database for human motion recognition. In: Proc. Int. Conf. Comput. Vis. (November 2011)
7. Laptev, I., Lindeberg, T.: Space-time interest points. In: Proceedings of the Ninth IEEE International Conference on Computer Vision, 2003, vol. 1, pp. 432–439 (2003)
8. Li, W., Zhang, Z., Liu, Z.: Action recognition based on a bag of 3d points. In: 2010 IEEE Computer Society Conference on Computer Vision and Pattern Recognition Workshops (CVPRW), pp. 9–14 (2010)
9. Lu, C., Jia, J., Tang, C.K.: Range-sample depth feature for action recognition. In: 2014 IEEE Conference on Computer Vision and Pattern Recognition (CVPR) (2014)
10. Luo, J., Wang, W., Qi, H.: Group sparsity and geometry constrained dictionary learning for action recognition from depth maps. In: 2013 IEEE International Conference on Computer Vision (ICCV), pp. 1809–1816. IEEE (2013)
11. Lv, F., Nevatia, R.: Recognition and segmentation of 3-D human action using HMM and multi-class AdaBoost. In: Leonardis, A., Bischof, H., Pinz, A. (eds.) ECCV 2006. LNCS, vol. 3954, pp. 359–372. Springer, Heidelberg (2006)
12. Marszalek, M., Laptev, I., Schmid, C.: Actions in context. In: Proc. Conf. Comput. Vis. Pattern Recognit. (June 2009)
13. Oreifej, O., Liu, Z.: Hon4d: Histogram of oriented 4d normals for activity recognition from depth sequences. In: 2013 IEEE Conference on Computer Vision and Pattern Recognition (CVPR), pp. 716–723 (2013)
14. Shotton, J., Fitzgibbon, A., Cook, M., Sharp, T., Finocchio, M., Moore, R., Kipman, A., Blake, A.: Real-time human pose recognition in parts from single depth images. In: 2011 IEEE Conference on Computer Vision and Pattern Recognition (CVPR), pp. 1297–1304 (2011)
15. Soomro, K., Zamir, A.R., Shah, M.: Ucf101: A dataset of 101 human actions classes from videos in the wild. CoRR abs/1212.0402 (2012)
16. Theriault, C., Thome, N., Cord, M.: Dynamic scene classification: Learning motion descriptors with slow features analysis. In: 2013 IEEE Conference on Computer Vision and Pattern Recognition (CVPR), pp. 2603–2610 (2013)
17. Vemulapalli, R., Arrate, F., Chellappa, R.: Human action recognition by representing 3d skeletons as points in a lie group. In: 2014 IEEE Conference on Computer Vision and Pattern Recognition (CVPR) (2014)
18. Vieira, A.W., Nascimento, E.R., Oliveira, G.L., Liu, Z., Campos, M.F.M.: STOP: space-time occupancy patterns for 3D action recognition from depth map sequences. In: Alvarez, L., Mejail, M., Gomez, L., Jacobo, J. (eds.) CIARP 2012. LNCS, vol. 7441, pp. 252–259. Springer, Heidelberg (2012)
19. Wang, C., Wang, Y., Yuille, A.: An approach to pose-based action recognition. In: 2013 IEEE Conference on Computer Vision and Pattern Recognition (CVPR), pp. 915–922 (2013)

20. Wang, H., Kläser, A., Schmid, C., Liu, C.L.: Dense trajectories and motion boundary descriptors for action recognition. International Journal of Computer Vision, March 2013
21. Wang, J., Liu, Z., Wu, Y., Yuan, J.: Mining actionlet ensemble for action recognition with depth cameras. In: 2012 IEEE Conference on Computer Vision and Pattern Recognition (CVPR), pp. 1290–1297 (2012)
22. Wiskott, L., Sejnowski, T.: Slow feature analysis: Unsupervised learning of invariances. Neural Computation **14**(4), 715–770 (2002)
23. Xia, L., Chen, C.C., Aggarwal, J.: View invariant human action recognition using histograms of 3d joints. In: 2012 IEEE Computer Society Conference on Computer Vision and Pattern Recognition Workshops (CVPRW), pp. 20–27 (2012)
24. Yang, X., Tian, Y.: Eigenjoints-based action recognition using naive-bayes-nearest-neighbor. In: 2012 IEEE Computer Society Conference on Computer Vision and Pattern Recognition Workshops (CVPRW), pp. 14–19 (2012)
25. Zhang, Z., Tao, D.: Slow feature analysis for human action recognition. IEEE Transactions on Pattern Analysis and Machine Intelligence **34**(3), 436–450 (2012)
26. Zhao, X., Li, X., Pang, C., Zhu, X., Sheng, Q.Z.: Online human gesture recognition from motion data streams. In: Proceedings of the 21st ACM International Conference on Multimedia, MM 2013, pp. 23–32. ACM, New York (2013)

A Novel Visual Word Co-occurrence Model for Person Re-identification

Ziming Zhang$^{(\boxtimes)}$, Yuting Chen, and Venkatesh Saligrama

Boston University, Boston, MA 02215, USA
{zzhang14,yutingch,srv}@bu.edu

Abstract. Person re-identification aims to maintain the identity of an individual in diverse locations through different non-overlapping camera views. The problem is fundamentally challenging due to appearance variations resulting from differing poses, illumination and configurations of camera views. To deal with these difficulties, we propose a novel visual word co-occurrence model. We first map each pixel of an image to a visual word using a codebook, which is learned in an unsupervised manner. The appearance transformation between camera views is encoded by a co-occurrence matrix of visual word joint distributions in probe and gallery images. Our appearance model naturally accounts for spatial similarities and variations caused by pose, illumination & configuration change across camera views. Linear SVMs are then trained as classifiers using these co-occurrence descriptors. On the VIPeR [1] and CUHK Campus [2] benchmark datasets, our method achieves 83.86% and 85.49% at rank-15 on the Cumulative Match Characteristic (CMC) curves, and beats the state-of-the-art results by 10.44% and 22.27%.

1 Introduction

In intelligent surveillance systems, *person re-identification* (*re-id*) is emerging as a key problem. *Re-id* deals with maintaining identities of individuals traversing different cameras. As in the literature we consider *re-id* for two cameras and focus on the problem of matching probe images of individuals in Camera 1 with gallery images from Camera 2. The problem is challenging for several reasons. Cameras views are non-overlapping so conventional tracking methods may fail. Illumination, view angles and configurations for different cameras are generally non-consistent, leading to significant appearance variations to the point that features seen in one camera are often distorted or missing in the other. Finer bio-metrics like face and gait thus often become unreliable [3].

The existing papers mainly focus on designing distinctive signature to represent a person under different cameras, or learning an effective matching methodology to predict if two images describe the same person. Our proposed method diverts from the literature by aiming to learn an appearance model that is based on *co-occurrence statistics* of visual patterns in different camera views. Namely, our appearance model captures the appearance "transformation" across cameras instead of some unknown invariant property among different views. Particularly,

© Springer International Publishing Switzerland 2015
L. Agapito et al. (Eds.): ECCV 2014 Workshops, Part III, LNCS 8927, pp. 122–133, 2015.
DOI: 10.1007/978-3-319-16199-0_9

Fig. 1. Illustration of codeword co-occurrence in positive image pairs (*i.e.* two images from different camera views per column belong to a *same* person) and negative image pairs (*i.e.* two images from different camera views per column belong to *different* persons). For positive (or negative) pairs, in each row the enclosed regions are assigned the same codeword.

our method does not assume any smooth appearance transformation across different cameras. Instead, our method learns the visual word co-occurrence pattens statistically in different camera views to predict the identities of persons.

While co-occurrence based statistics has been used in some other works [4] [5] [6], ours has a different purpose. We are largely motivated by the observation that the co-occurrence patterns of visual codewords behave similar for images from different views. In other words, the transformation of target appearances can be statistically inferred through these co-occurrence patterns. As seen in Fig. 1, we observe that some regions are distributed similarly in images from different views and robustly in the presence of large cross-view variations. These regions provide important discriminant co-occurrence patterns for matching image pairs. For instance, statistically speaking, the first column of positive image pairs shows that "white" color in Camera 1 can change to "light blue" in Camera 2. However, "light blue" in Camera 1 can hardly change to "black" in Camera 2, as shown in the first column of negative image pairs.

Thus we propose a novel visual word co-occurrence model to capture such important patterns between images. We first encode images with a sufficiently large codebook to account for different visual patterns. Pixels are then matched into codewords or visual words, and the resulting spatial distribution for each codeword is embedded to a kernel space through *kernel mean embedding* [7] with latent-variable conditional densities [8] as kernels. The fact that we incorporate the spatial distribution of codewords into appearance models provides us with locality sensitive co-occurrence measures. Our approach can be also interpreted as a means to *transfer* the information (*e.g.* pose, illumination, and appearance) in image pairs to a common latent space for meaningful comparison.

To conduct re-identification, we employ linear support vector machines (SVMs) as our classifier trained by the appearance descriptors. On the VIPeR [1] and CUHK Campus [2] benchmark datasets, our method achieves 83.86%

and 85.49% at rank-15 on the Cumulative Match Characteristic (CMC) curves, and beats the state-of-the-art results by 10.44% and 22.27%.

1.1   Related Work

The theme of local features for matching is related to our kernel-based similarity measures. To ensure locality, [9] models the appearances of individuals using features from horizontal strips. [10] clusters pixels into similar groups and the scores are matched based on correspondences of the clustered groups. Histogram features that encode both local and global appearance are proposed in [11]. Saliency matching [2,12], one of the-state-of-the-art methods for *re-id* uses patch-level matching to serve as masks in images to localize discriminative patches. More generally low-level features such as color, texture, interest points, co-variance matrices and their combinations have also been proposed [10,13–19]. In addition high-level structured features that utilize concatenation of low-level features [18] or deformable part models (DPMs) [20] have been proposed. Metric learning methods have been proposed for *re-id* (*e.g.* [21–24]). In [25,26] distance metrics are derived through brightness transfer functions that associate color-levels in the two cameras. [27] proposes distance metrics that lend importance to features in matched images over the wrongly matched pairs without assuming presence of universally distinctive features. Low-dimensional embeddings using PCA and local FDA have also been proposed [28]. Supervised methods that select relevant features for *re-id* have been proposed by [14] using Boosting and by [15] using RankSVMs.

2   Visual Word Co-occurrence Models

We generally face two issues in visual recognition problems: (1) *visual ambiguity* [29] (*i.e.* the appearance of instances which belong to the same thing semantically can vary dramatically in different scenarios), (2) *spatial displacement* [30] of visual patterns.

While visual ambiguity can be somewhat handled through codebook construction and quantization of images into visual words, our goal of matching humans in *re-id* imposes additional challenges. Humans body parts exhibit distinctive local visual patterns and these patterns systematically change appearance locally. Our goal is to account for this inherent variability in appearance models through co-occurrence matrices that quantify spatial and visual changes in appearance.

2.1   Locally Sensitive Co-occurrence Designs

We need co-occurrence models that not only account for the locality of appearance changes but also the random spatial & visual ambiguity inherent in vision problems. Therefore, we first construct a codebook $\mathcal{Z} = \{\mathbf{z}\} \subset \mathbb{R}^D$ with M codewords. Our codebook construction is global and thus only carries information about distinctive visual patterns. Nevertheless, for a sufficiently large codebook distinctive visual patterns are mapped to different elements of the codebook, which has the effect of preserving local visual patterns. Specifically, we map each pixel at 2D location $\pi \in \Pi$ of image $\mathcal{I}$ into (at least one) codewords to cluster pixels.

To emphasize local appearance changes, we look at the spatial distribution of each codeword. Concretely, we let $C(\mathcal{I}, \mathbf{z}) \subseteq \Pi$ denote the set of pixel locations associated with codeword $\mathbf{z}$ in image $\mathcal{I}$ and associate a spatial probability distribution, $p(\pi | \mathbf{z}, \mathcal{I})$, over this observed collection. In this way visual words are embedded into a family of spatial distributions. Intuitively it should now be clear that we can use the similarity (or distance) of two corresponding spatial distributions to quantify the pairwise relationship between two visual words. This makes sense because our visual words are spatially locally distributed and small distance between spatial distributions implies spatial locality. Together this leads to a model that accounts for local appearance changes.

While we can quantify the similarity between two distributions in a number of ways, the kernel mean embedding method is particularly convenient for our task. The basic idea to map the distribution, p, into a reproducing kernel Hilbert space (RKHS), $\mathcal{H}$, namely, $p \to \mu_p(\cdot) = \sum K(\cdot, \pi) p(\pi) \stackrel{\Delta}{=} E_p(K(\cdot, \pi))$. For universal kernels, such as RBF kernels, this mapping is injective, $i.e.$, the mapping preserves the information about the distribution [7]. In addition we can exploit the reproducing property to express inner products in terms of expected values, namely, $\langle \mu_p, \Phi \rangle = E_p(\Phi), \forall \Phi \in \mathcal{H}$ and obtain simple expressions for similarity between two distributions (and hence two visual words) because $\mu_p(\cdot) \in \mathcal{H}$.

To this end, consider the codeword $\mathbf{z}_m$ in image $\mathcal{I}_i^{(1)}$ and codeword $\mathbf{z}_n$ in image $\mathcal{I}_j^{(2)}$. The co-occurrence matrix (and hence the appearance model) is the inner product of visual words in the RKHS space, namely,

$$
\begin{aligned}
\phi(\mathbf{x}_{ij})_{mn} &= \left\langle \mu_{p(\cdot | \mathbf{z}_m, \mathcal{I}_i^{(1)})}, \mu_{p(\cdot | \mathbf{z}_n, \mathcal{I}_j^{(2)})} \right\rangle \\
&= \sum_{\pi_u} \sum_{\pi_v} K(\pi_u, \pi_v) p(\pi_u | \mathbf{z}_m, \mathcal{I}_i^{(1)}) p(\pi_v | \mathbf{z}_n, \mathcal{I}_j^{(2)}),
\end{aligned}
\tag{1}
$$

where we have used the reproducing property in the last equality. We now have several choices for the kernel $K(\pi_u, \pi_v)$ above. We list some of them here:

Identity: $K(\cdot, \pi) = \mathbf{e}_\pi$, where $\mathbf{e}_\pi$ is the usual unit vector at location π. We get the following appearance model:

$$
\phi(\mathbf{x}_{ij})_{mn} \propto \left| C(\mathcal{I}_i^{(1)}, \mathbf{z}_m) \bigcap C(\mathcal{I}_j^{(2)}, \mathbf{z}_n) \right|,
\tag{2}
$$

where $| \cdot |$ denotes set cardinality. This choice often leads to poor performance in $re\text{-}id$ because it is not robust to spatial displacements of visual words, which we commonly encounter in $re\text{-}id$.

Radial Appearance Model (RBF): This leads to the following appearance model:

$$\phi(\mathbf{x}_{ij})_{mn} = \sum_{\boldsymbol{\pi}_u} \sum_{\boldsymbol{\pi}_v} \exp\left(\frac{\|\boldsymbol{\pi}_u - \boldsymbol{\pi}_v\|_2^2}{2\sigma^2}\right) p(\boldsymbol{\pi}_u|\mathbf{z}_m, \mathcal{I}_i^{(1)}) p(\boldsymbol{\pi}_v|\mathbf{z}_n, \mathcal{I}_j^{(2)}) \qquad (3)$$

$$\leq \sum_{\boldsymbol{\pi}_u} \max_{\boldsymbol{\pi}_v} \left\{ \exp\left(\frac{\|\boldsymbol{\pi}_u - \boldsymbol{\pi}_v\|_2^2}{2\sigma^2}\right) p(\boldsymbol{\pi}_v|\mathbf{z}_n, \mathcal{I}_j^{(2)}) \right\} p(\boldsymbol{\pi}_u|\mathbf{z}_m, \mathcal{I}_i^{(1)}).$$

The upper bound above is used for efficiently computing our appearance model by removing the summation over $\boldsymbol{\pi}_v$. This appearance model is often a better choice than the previous one because RBF accounts for some spatial displacements of visual words for appropriate choice of σ.

Latent Spatial Kernel: This is a type of probability product kernel that has been previously proposed [8] to encode generative structures into discriminative learning methods. In our context we can view the presence of a codeword $\mathbf{z}_m$ at location $\boldsymbol{\pi}_u$ as a noisy displacement of a true latent location $\mathbf{h} \in \Pi$. The key insight here is that the spatial activation of the two codewords $\mathbf{z}_m$ and $\mathbf{z}_n$ in the two image views $\mathcal{I}_i^{(1)}$ and $\mathcal{I}_j^{(2)}$ are conditionally independent when conditioned on the true latent location $\mathbf{h}$, namely, the joint probability factorizes into $Pr\{\boldsymbol{\pi}_u, \boldsymbol{\pi}_v \mid \mathbf{h}, \mathcal{I}_i^{(1)}, \mathcal{I}_j^{(2)}\} = Pr\{\boldsymbol{\pi}_u \mid \mathbf{h}, \mathcal{I}_i^{(1)}\}Pr\{\boldsymbol{\pi}_v \mid \mathbf{h}, \mathcal{I}_j^{(2)}\}$. We denote the noisy displacement likelihoods, $Pr\{\boldsymbol{\pi}_u \mid \mathbf{h}, \mathcal{I}_i^{(1)}\} = \kappa_1(\boldsymbol{\pi}_u, \mathbf{h})$ and $Pr\{\boldsymbol{\pi}_v \mid \mathbf{h}, \mathcal{I}_j^{(2)}\} = \kappa_2(\boldsymbol{\pi}_v, \mathbf{h})$ for simplicity. This leads us to $K(\boldsymbol{\pi}_u, \boldsymbol{\pi}_v) = \sum_{\mathbf{h}} \kappa_1(\boldsymbol{\pi}_u, \mathbf{h})\kappa_2(\boldsymbol{\pi}_v, \mathbf{h})p(\mathbf{h})$, where $p(\mathbf{h})$ denotes the spatial probability at $\mathbf{h}$, which we assume here to be uniform. By plugging this new K into Eq. 1, we have

$$\phi(\mathbf{x}_{ij})_{mn} = \sum_{\boldsymbol{\pi}_u} \sum_{\boldsymbol{\pi}_v} \sum_{\mathbf{h}} \kappa_1(\boldsymbol{\pi}_u, \mathbf{h})\kappa_2(\boldsymbol{\pi}_v, \mathbf{h})p(\mathbf{h})p(\boldsymbol{\pi}_u|\mathbf{z}_m, \mathcal{I}_i^{(1)})p(\boldsymbol{\pi}_v|\mathbf{z}_n, \mathcal{I}_j^{(2)})$$

$$\leq \sum_{\mathbf{h}} \max_{\boldsymbol{\pi}_u} \left\{ \kappa_1(\boldsymbol{\pi}_u, \mathbf{h})p(\boldsymbol{\pi}_u|\mathbf{z}_m, \mathcal{I}_i^{(1)}) \right\} \max_{\boldsymbol{\pi}_v} \left\{ \kappa_2(\boldsymbol{\pi}_v, \mathbf{h})p(\boldsymbol{\pi}_v|\mathbf{z}_n, \mathcal{I}_j^{(2)}) \right\} p(\mathbf{h}),$$

$$(4)$$

where the inequality follows by rearranging the summations and standard upper bounding techniques. Again we use an upper bound for computational efficiency, and assume that $\mathcal{P}_{\mathcal{H}}$ is a uniform distribution for simplicity without further learning. The main idea here is that by introducing the latent displacement variables, we have a handle on view-specific distortions observed in the two cameras. We only show the performance using the latent kernel in our experimental section, since it produces much better performance than the other two in our preliminary results.

2.2   Implementation of Latent Spatial Kernels

Fig. 2 illustrates the whole process of generating the latent spatial kernel based appearance model given the codeword images, each of which is represented as

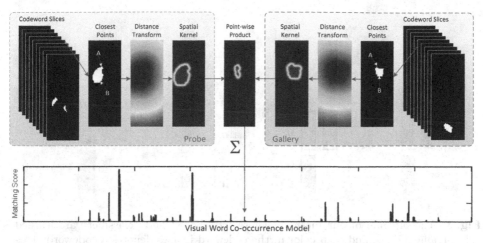

Fig. 2. Illustration of our visual word co-occurrence model generation process. Here, the white regions in the codeword slices indicate the pixel locations with the same codeword. "A" and "B" denote two arbitrary pixel locations in the image domain. And "Σ" denotes a sum operation which sums up all the values in the point-wise product matrix into a single value $\phi(\mathbf{x}_{ij})_{mn}$ in our model.

a collection of codeword slices. For each codeword slice, the max operation is performed at every pixel location to search for the spatially closest codeword in the slice. This procedure forms a distance transform image, which is further mapped to a spatial kernel image. It allows each peak at the presence of a codeword to be propagated smoothly and uniformly. To calculate the matching score for a codeword co-occurrence, the spatial kernel from a probe image and another from a gallery image are multiplied element-wise and then summed over all latent locations. This step guarantees that our descriptor is insensitive to the noise data in the codeword images. This value is a single entry at the bin indexing the codeword co-occurrence in our descriptor for matching the probe and gallery images. As a result, we have generated a high dimensional sparse appearance descriptor.

3   Experiments

We test our method on two benchmark datasets, VIPeR [1] and CUHK Campus [2]. For each dataset, images from separate camera views are split into a gallery set and a probe set. Images from the probe set are treated as queries and compared with every person in the gallery set. For each query, our method produces a ranking of matching individuals in the gallery set. Performance can be evaluated with these resultant rankings, since the identity label of each image is known. The rankings for every possible query is combined into a Cumulative Match Characteristic (CMC) curve, which is a standard metric for re-identification performance. The CMC curve displays an algorithm's recognition rate as a function of rank. For instance, a recognition rate at rank-r on the CMC curve denotes

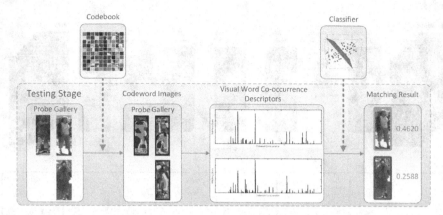

Fig. 3. The pipeline of our method, where "codebook" and "classifier" are learned using training data, and each color in the codeword images denotes a codeword. This figure is best viewed in color.

what proportion of queries were correctly matched to a corresponding gallery individual at rank-r or better. Experimental results are reported as the average CMC curve over 3 trials.

3.1 Implementation

We illustrate the schematics of our method in Fig. 3. At training stage, we extract low-level feature vectors from randomly sampled patches in training images, and then cluster them into codewords to form a codebook, which is used to encode every image into a codeword image. Each pixel in a codeword image represents the centroid of a patch that has been mapped to a codeword. Further, a visual word co-occurrence model (descriptor) is calculated for every pair of gallery and probe images, and the descriptors from training data are utilized to train our classifier, performing re-identification on the test data.

Specifically, for each image a 672-dim ColorSIFT [2][1] feature vector is extracted for a 10×10 pixel patch centered at every possible pixel. Further, we decorrelate each feature using the statistics learned from training data, as suggested in [31].

For codebook construction, we randomly sample 1000 patch features per image in the training set, and cluster these features into a codebook using K-Means. Then we encode each patch feature in images from the probe and gallery sets into a codeword whose Euclidean distance to the patch feature is the minimum among all the codewords. As a result, each image is mapped into a codeword image whose pixels are represented by the indices of the corresponding encoded codewords. We also normalize our appearance descriptors using min-max normalization. The min value is for our descriptors is always 0, and the max value is the maximum among all the codeword co-occurrence bins over every training descriptor. This max value is saved during training and utilized for normalization during testing.

---

[1] The authors' code can be downloaded at http://www.ee.cuhk.edu.hk/~rzhao/.

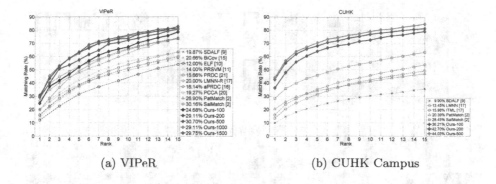

(a) VIPeR   (b) CUHK Campus

Fig. 4. Matching rate comparison between different methods on (a) VIPeR and (b) CUHK Campus datasets. Numbers following "Ours-" in the legends denote the size of the codebook used in each experiment. Expect for our results, the other CMC curves are cited from [2]. This figure is best viewed in color.

In the end for classifiers, we employ LIBLINEAR [32], an efficient linear SVMs solver, with the ℓ_2 norm regularizer. The trade-off parameter c in LIBLINEAR is set using cross-validation.

3.2 VIPeR

Since introduced in [33], the VIPeR dataset has been utilized by most person re-identification approaches as a benchmark. VIPeR is comprised of 632 different pedestrians captured in two different camera views, denoted by CAM-A and CAM-B, respectively. Many cross-camera image pairs in the dataset have significant variations in illumination, pose, and viewpoint, and each image is normalized to 128×48 pixels.

In order to compare with other person re-identification methods, we followed the experimental set up described in [2]. The dataset is split in half randomly, one partition for training and the other for testing. In addition, samples from CAM-A form the probe set, and samples from CAM-B form the gallery set. The parameter σ in the spatial kernel function is set to 3 for this dataset.

Fig. 4(a) shows our matching rate comparison with other methods on this dataset. When the codebook size is 100, which is pretty small, our performance is close to that of SalMatch [2]. With increase of the codebook size, our performance is improved significantly, and has outperformed that of SalMatch by large margins. For instance, at rank-15, our best matching rate is 10.44% higher. Using larger sizes of codebooks, the codeword representation of each image is finer by reducing the quantization error in the feature space. However, it seems that when the codebook size is beyond 500, our performance is saturated. Therefore, in the following experiments, we only test our method using 100/200/500 codewords.

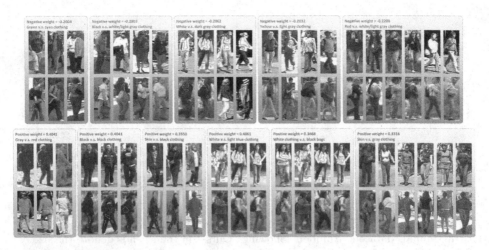

Fig. 5. Examples of codeword co-occurrence with relatively high positive/negative weights in the learned weighting matrix. Same as Fig. 1, in each row the regions enclosed by red (or cyan) color indicate that the codeword per pixel location in these regions is the same. This figure is best viewed in color.

Fig. 5 illustrates some codeword co-occurrence examples with relatively high positive/negative weights in the learned weighting matrix. These examples strongly support our intuition of learning codeword co-occurrence based features in Section 1.

3.3 CUHK Campus

The CUHK Campus dataset is a relatively new person re-identification dataset explored by two state-of-the-art approaches outlined in [2] and [34]. This dataset consists of 1816 people captured from five different camera pairs, labeled P1 to P5. Each image contains 160×60 pixels. Following the experimental settings from [2] and [34], we use only images captured from P1 as our dataset. This subset contains 971 people in two camera views, with two images per view per person. One camera view, which we call CAM-1, captures people either facing towards or away from the camera. The other view, CAM-2, captures the side view of each person.

For our experiments, we adopt the settings described in [2] for comparison[2]. We randomly select 485 individuals from the dataset and use their 4 images for training, and the rest are used for testing. The gallery and probe sets are formed by CAM-1 and CAM-2, respectively. To re-identify a person, we compare the probe image with every gallery image, leading to 486×2=972 decision scores. Then per person in the gallery set, we average the 2 decision scores belonging to this person as the final score for ranking later. The parameter σ in the spatial kernel function is set to 6 for this dataset, since the image size is larger.

---

[2] We thank the authors for the response to their experimental settings.

Fig. 4(b) summarizes our matching rate comparison with some other methods. Clearly, using only 100 codewords, our method has already outperformed others dramatically, and it works better when using larger sizes of codebooks, similar to the behavior in Fig. 4(a). At rank-15, our best performance is 22.27% better than that of SalMatch.

4   Conclusion

In this paper, we propose a novel visual word co-occurrence model for person re-identification. The intuition behind our model is that the codeword co-occurrence patterns behave similarly and consistently in pairs of gallery/probe images and robustly to the changes in images. To generate our descriptor, each image is mapped to a codeword image, and the spatial distribution for each codeword is embedded to a kernel space through *kernel mean embedding* with latent spatial kernels. To conduct re-identification, we employ linear SVMs as our classifier trained by the descriptors. We test our method on two benchmark datasets, VIPeR and CUHK Campus. On both datasets, our method consistently outperforms other methods. At rank-15, our method achieves matching rates of 83.86% and 85.49%, respectively, which are significantly better than the state-of-the-art results by 10.44% and 22.27%.

Several questions will be considered as our future work. It would be useful to reduce the computational complexity of calculating our pair-wise latent spatial kernels. One possibility is to modify the learning algorithm by decomposing the weight matrix into two separable parameters, because our appearance model can be decomposed into two parts, one from the probe image and the other from the gallery image. Such decomposition will accelerate the computation. Second, in our preliminary experiments, latent spatial kernel yields significantly better results over the other two choices. It would be interesting to explore other selection of kernels (or even learn the optimal kernels) and how they affect the behavior of our visual word co-occurrence model. Building a *re-id* system for natural images using object proposal algorithms (*e.g.* [35,36]) and our model with different classifiers (*e.g.* [37–39]) would be interesting as well.

Acknowledgments. This work is supported by the U.S. DHS Grant 2013-ST-061-ED0001 and ONR award N00014-13-C-0288 respectively. The views and conclusions contained in this document are those of the authors and should not be interpreted as necessarily representing the official policies, either expressed or implied, of the agencies.

References

1. Gray, D., Brennan, S., Tao, H.: Evaluating appearance models for recognition, reacquisition, and tracking. In: 10th IEEE International Workshop on Performance Evaluation of Tracking and Surveillance (PETS) (September 2007)
2. Zhao, R., Ouyang, W., Wang, X.: Person re-identification by salience matching. In: ICCV (2013)

3. Vezzani, R., Baltieri, D., Cucchiara, R.: People reidentification in surveillance and forensics: A survey. ACM Comput. Surv. 46(2), 29:1–29:37 (2013)
4. Banerjee, P., Nevatia, R.: Learning neighborhood cooccurrence statistics of sparse features for human activity recognition. In: AVSS, pp. 212–217 (2011)
5. Galleguillos, C., Rabinovich, A., Belongie, S.: Object categorization using co-occurrence, location and appearance. In: CVPR (June 2008)
6. Ladicky, L., Russell, C., Kohli, P., Torr, P.H.S.: Graph Cut Based Inference with Co-occurrence Statistics. In: Daniilidis, K., Maragos, P., Paragios, N. (eds.) ECCV 2010, Part V. LNCS, vol. 6315, pp. 239–253. Springer, Heidelberg (2010)
7. Smola, A.J., Gretton, A., Song, L., Schölkopf, B.: A Hilbert Space Embedding for Distributions. In: Hutter, M., Servedio, R.A., Takimoto, E. (eds.) ALT 2007. LNCS (LNAI), vol. 4754, pp. 13–31. Springer, Heidelberg (2007)
8. Jebara, T., Kondor, R., Howard, A.: Probability product kernels. JMLR 5, 819–844 (2004)
9. Bird, N.D., Masoud, O., Papanikolopoulos, N.P., Isaacs, A.: Detection of loitering individuals in public transportation areas. Trans. Intell. Transport. Sys. 6(2), 167–177 (2005)
10. Gheissari, N., Sebastian, T.B., Hartley, R.: Person reidentification using spatiotemporal appearance. CVPR 2, 1528–1535 (2006)
11. Bazzani, L., Cristani, M., Perina, A., Murino, V.: Multiple-shot person re-identification by chromatic and epitomic analyses. Pattern Recogn. Lett. 33(7), 898–903 (2012)
12. Zhao, R., Ouyang, W., Wang, X.: Unsupervised salience learning for person re-identification. In: CVPR, pp. 3586–3593 (2013)
13. Farenzena, M., Bazzani, L., Perina, A., Murino, V., Cristani, M.: Person re-identification by symmetry-driven accumulation of local features. In: CVPR, pp. 2360–2367 (2010)
14. Gray, D., Tao, H.: Viewpoint Invariant Pedestrian Recognition with an Ensemble of Localized Features. In: Forsyth, D., Torr, P., Zisserman, A. (eds.) ECCV 2008, Part I. LNCS, vol. 5302, pp. 262–275. Springer, Heidelberg (2008)
15. Prosser, B., Zheng, W.S., Gong, S., Xiang, T., Mary, Q.: Person re-identification by support vector ranking. In: BMVC, vol. 1, p. 5 (2010)
16. Bauml, M., Stiefelhagen, R.: Evaluation of local features for person re-identification in image sequences. In: AVSS, pp. 291–296 (2011)
17. Bak, S., Corvee, E., Bremond, F., Thonnat, M.: Multiple-shot human re-identification by mean riemannian covariance grid. In: AVSS, pp. 179–184 (2011)
18. Ma, B., Su, Y., Jurie, F.: Bicov: a novel image representation for person re-identification and face verification. In: BMVC (2012)
19. Liu, C., Gong, S., Loy, C.C., Lin, X.: Person Re-identification: What Features Are Important? In: Fusiello, A., Murino, V., Cucchiara, R. (eds.) ECCV 2012 Ws/Demos, Part I. LNCS, vol. 7583, pp. 391–401. Springer, Heidelberg (2012)
20. Nguyen, V.-H., Nguyen, K., Le, D.-D., Duong, D.A., Satoh, S.: Person Re-identification Using Deformable Part Models. In: Lee, M., Hirose, A., Hou, Z.-G., Kil, R.M. (eds.) ICONIP 2013, Part III. LNCS, vol. 8228, pp. 616–623. Springer, Heidelberg (2013)
21. Dikmen, M., Akbas, E., Huang, T.S., Ahuja, N.: Pedestrian Recognition with a Learned Metric. In: Kimmel, R., Klette, R., Sugimoto, A. (eds.) ACCV 2010, Part IV. LNCS, vol. 6495, pp. 501–512. Springer, Heidelberg (2011)
22. Li, W., Zhao, R., Wang, X.: Human Reidentification with Transferred Metric Learning. In: Lee, K.M., Matsushita, Y., Rehg, J.M., Hu, Z. (eds.) ACCV 2012, Part I. LNCS, vol. 7724, pp. 31–44. Springer, Heidelberg (2013)

23. Mignon, A., Jurie, F.: PCCA: a new approach for distance learning from sparse pairwise constraints. In: CVPR, pp. 2666–2672 (2012)
24. Zheng, W.S., Gong, S., Xiang, T.: Person re-identification by probabilistic relative distance comparison. In: CVPR, pp. 649–656 (2011)
25. Porikli, F.: Inter-camera color calibration by correlation model function. In: ICIP, vol 2. pp. II-133 (2003)
26. Javed, O., Shafique, K., Rasheed, Z., Shah, M.: Modeling inter-camera space-time and appearance relationships for tracking across non-overlapping views. Comput. Vis. Image Underst. 109(2), 146–162 (2008)
27. Zheng, W.S., Gong, S., Xiang, T.: Re-identification by relative distance comparison. IEEE TPAMI 35(3), 653–668 (2013)
28. Pedagadi, S., Orwell, J., Velastin, S., Boghossian, B.: Local fisher discriminant analysis for pedestrian re-identification. In: CVPR, pp. 3318–3325 (2013)
29. van Gemert, J., Veenman, C.J., Smeulders, A.W.M., Geusebroek, J.M.: Visual word ambiguity. IEEE Trans. Pattern Anal. Mach. Intell. 32(7), 1271–1283 (2010)
30. Felzenszwalb, P.F., Girshick, R.B., McAllester, D.A., Ramanan, D.: Object detection with discriminatively trained part-based models. TPAMI 32(9), 1627–1645 (2010)
31. Hariharan, B., Malik, J., Ramanan, D.: Discriminative Decorrelation for Clustering and Classification. In: Fitzgibbon, A., Lazebnik, S., Perona, P., Sato, Y., Schmid, C. (eds.) ECCV 2012, Part IV. LNCS, vol. 7575, pp. 459–472. Springer, Heidelberg (2012)
32. Fan, R.E., Chang, K.W., Hsieh, C.J., Wang, X.R., Lin, C.J.: LIBLINEAR: A library for large linear classification. JMLR 9, 1871–1874 (2008)
33. Gray, D., Brennan, S., Tao, H.: Evaluating appearance models for recognition, reacquisition, and tracking. In: PETS, pp. 47–47 (2007)
34. Li, W., Wang, X.: Locally aligned feature transforms across views. In: CVPR, pp. 3594–3601 (June 2013)
35. Zhang, Z., Warrell, J., Torr, P.H.S.: Proposal generation for object detection using cascaded ranking svms. In: IEEE CVPR, pp. 1497–1504 (2011)
36. Cheng, M.M., Zhang, Z., Lin, W.Y., Torr, P.H.S.: Bing: Binarized normed gradients for objectness estimation at 300fps. In: IEEE CVPR (2014)
37. Zhang, Z., Li, Z.N., Drew, M.S.: Adamkl: A novel biconvex multiple kernel learning approach. In: IEEE 2010 20th International Conference on Pattern Recognition (ICPR), pp. 2126–2129 (2010)
38. Zhang, Z., Sturgess, P., Sengupta, S., Crook, N., Torr, P.H.: Efficient discriminative learning of parametric nearest neighbor classifiers. In: 2012 IEEE Conference on Computer Vision and Pattern Recognition (CVPR), pp. 2232–2239. IEEE (2012)
39. Zhang, Z., Ladicky, L., Torr, P., Saffari, A.: Learning anchor planes for classification. In: Advances in Neural Information Processing Systems, pp. 1611–1619 (2011)

Joint Learning for Attribute-Consistent Person Re-Identification

Sameh Khamis[1]([⊠]), Cheng-Hao Kuo[2], Vivek K. Singh[3], Vinay D. Shet[4],
and Larry S. Davis[1]

[1] University of Maryland, College Park, MD, USA
sameh@umiacs.umd.edu
[2] Amazon.com, Seattle, USA
[3] Siemens Corporate Research, Princeton, USA
[4] Google, Mountain View, USA

Abstract. Person re-identification has recently attracted a lot of attention in the computer vision community. This is in part due to the challenging nature of matching people across cameras with different viewpoints and lighting conditions, as well as across human pose variations. The literature has since devised several approaches to tackle these challenges, but the vast majority of the work has been concerned with appearance-based methods. We propose an approach that goes beyond appearance by integrating a semantic aspect into the model. We jointly learn a discriminative projection to a joint appearance-attribute subspace, effectively leveraging the interaction between attributes and appearance for matching. Our experimental results support our model and demonstrate the performance gain yielded by coupling both tasks. Our results outperform several state-of-the-art methods on VIPeR, a standard re-identification dataset. Finally, we report similar results on a new large-scale dataset we collected and labeled for our task.

1 Introduction

Person re-identification is the problem of matching people across multiple, typically non-overlapping, cameras [8]. Matching is complicated by variations in lighting conditions, camera viewpoints, backgrounds, and human poses. Research in person re-identification has been motivated by increasing safety and security concerns in public spaces, where face recognition and other fine biometric cues are not available because of the insufficient image resolution [9].

Approaches addressing this problem usually focus on either representation, where better descriptors or features are used to specifically address this problem [6–8,10], or learning, where a better similarity or distance function is proposed [1,11,12,20,31]. Our work falls into the latter category. While some recent approaches use one or more standard distance metrics (*e.g.* Euclidean distance or

---

This work was done while the authors were at Siemens Corporate Research, Princeton, NJ.

L. Agapito et al. (Eds.): ECCV 2014 Workshops, Part III, LNCS 8927, pp. 134–146, 2015.
DOI: 10.1007/978-3-319-16199-0_10

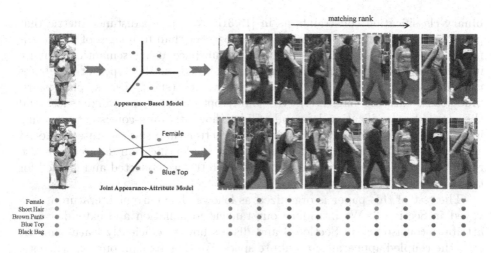

Fig. 1. Overview of our approach. An image of a person of interest on the left (the probe) is used to rank images from a gallery according to how closely they match that person. The correct match, highlighted in a green box, can be difficult even for humans to find given the severe lighting and pose differences between the two images. Similarly, approaches that model only appearance are likely to suffer from these challenges. Our main contribution, on the other hand, is the integration of a semantic aspect, through attributes, into the matching process. We jointly learn a distance metric that optimizes matching and attribute classification by projecting the image descriptors to a coupled appearance-attribute space. Leveraging this representation, our approach gains some invariance to lighting and pose and achieves better performance on the re-identification task.

Bhattacharyya distance) for matching [13, 15, 21], approaches that instead learn a distance metric for the problem have had better success.

We illustrate our approach to person re-identification in Figure 1. Given an image of a person of interest (the probe), we are interested in a list of subjects images (the gallery), ranked according to how well they match the probe. It can be quite challenging even for a human to find the correct match for the probe image in the figure. Consequently, appearance-based models, represented at the top of the figure, tend to suffer from the severe lighting and pose changes. We instead approach this by augmenting appearance with a semantic attribute-based description of the subject and jointly optimize both ranking and attribute classification. As shown in the figure, the semantic representation in our model imposes an attribute-consistent matching, introducing invariance to the extreme lighting and pose changes, and at the same time the resulting attribute classifiers are better tuned because of the regularization imposed by the matching constraints. We validate both claims empirically. It is noteworthy that our approach is not limited to person re-identification and applies to any matching problem.

We first demonstrate how learning a distance metric optimized over ranking loss, which is a natural aspect of the re-id problem, outperforms one subject to binary classification constraints as in [19,31]. We learn a distance metric that projects images of the same person closer together than to images of a different person. We then augment the projection subspace using semantic attribute information. Our semantic representation is based on the types of attributes that humans might use in describing appearance (short sleeves, plain shirt, blue jeans, carrying bag, etc.). We jointly optimize for the ranking loss and the attribute classification loss and validate how attribute-consistent matching in this coupled space achieves performance better than several state-of-the-art approaches on VIPeR [9], a standard person re-identification dataset. We also report our results on a new dataset (Indoor-ReID) we collected and labeled for this task.

The rest of this paper is organized as follows. The current literature is surveyed in Section 2. We introduce our ranking formulation and extend it with attribute-consistency in Section 3 and discuss how to efficiently learn a metric over the coupled appearance-attribute space. We then explain our experimental setup and evaluate our approach in Section 4. Finally, we conclude and summarize our work in Section 5.

2   Related Work

Approaches for person re-identification are generally composed of an appearance descriptor to represent the person and a matching function to compare those appearance descriptors. Over the years, several contributions have been made to improve both the representation as well as the matching algorithm in order to increase robustness to the variations in pose, lighting, and background inherent to the problem. Many researchers addressed the problem by proposing better feature representations for the images. Ma et al. [18] use local descriptors based on color and gradient information and encode them using high dimensional Fisher vectors. Liu et al. [17] use different feature weights for each probe image based on how unique these features are to the subject. Zhao et al. [30] use unsupervised saliency estimation and dense patch matching to match subjects, which can even be augmented with a supervised approach.

Several approaches also exploit the prior knowledge of the person geometry or body structure to obtain a pose invariant representation. Farenzena et al. [7] accumulate features based on the symmetry of the human body. Gheissari et al. [8] match fitted triangulated meshes over segmented images of subjects. Bak et al. [2] use body parts detectors with spatial pyramid matching. Similarly, Cheng et al. [6] utilize Pictorial Structures (PS) to localize the body parts and match their descriptors. However, these approaches tend to suffer if the pose variations are too extreme, which can invalidate symmetry or break part-based detectors.

Given feature based representations of a pair of images, an intuitive approach is to compute the geodesic distance between the descriptors, for instance, using the Bhattacharyya distance between the histogram-based descriptors or L2-norm between descriptors in a Euclidean space. However some features may be more relevant for appearance matching than others. To this end, several approaches have been proposed to learn a matching function in a supervised manner from a dataset of image pairs. For instance, Gray et al. [10] use boosting to find the best ensemble of localized features for matching. Prosser et al. [22] propose ensemble RankSVM to solve person re-identification as a ranking problem, while Wu et al. [29] solved a ranking problem subject to a listwise loss instead of a pairwise loss in an effort to realize results closer to what a human would generate.

On the other hand, approaches that learn a distance metric on the feature descriptors have had better success on standard benchmark datasets. Zheng et al. [31] learn a metric by maximizing the probability of a true match to have a smaller distance as compared to a wrong match. Köstinger et al. [12] learn a Mahalanobis metric that also reflects the properties of log-likelihood ratio test and reports better performance over traditional metric learning. Hirzer et al. [11] propose a distance learning approach which is not guaranteed to learn a pseudo-metric, but nonetheless achieves expected performance with a reduced computational cost. Pedagadi et al. [20] extract very high dimensional features from the subject images, which then go through multiple stages of unsupervised and supervised dimensionality reduction to estimate a final distance metric. An et al. [1] learn a distance metric using Regularized Canonical Correlation Analysis (RCCA) after projecting the features to a kernelized space. Finally, Mignon et al. [19] learns a PCA-like projection to a low-dimensional space while preserving pairwise constraints imposed by positive and negative image pairs. We extend the latter's work to a joint optimization framework and learn a projection to a coupled appearance-attribute subspace, and we successfully report a significant performance improvement. The integration of attribute-consistency into the matching process, which is the main thesis of our work, is also applicable to other metric learning approaches.

With the recent success of attribute-based modeling approaches [4,5,14], earlier attempts have also been made to overcome the lighting and pose variations by integrating attributes into the matching process. However, the existing approaches simply augment the extracted feature descriptors with attribute labels obtained independently and thus fail to capture the interactions between the attributes and the identities [15,16,27]. Our work attempts to simultaneously learn matching and attribute classification, and through the coupled process improve the performance of both tasks.

Our approach also does not require access to the attribute labels at test time. In that aspect our work is also related to matching with privileged information. Learning Using Privileged Information (LUPI) is a learning framework where additional information, in our case the attribute labels, is available at training time but is not provided at the test stage [26]. Recent work investigated using attributes in a two stage approach, where the result of the attribute classifiers is used to scale SVM margins in the second stage [24]. We instead integrate both attributes and matching in a single objective function and optimize them jointly.

3   Approach

3.1   Attribute-Consistent Matching

Most work on person re-identification focuses on appearance-based methods, which intuitively suffer from the lighting and pose changes inherent to any matching problem. We instead propose to complement appearance models, which are nonetheless crucial to matching, with a semantic aspect. The semantic representation in our approach is introduced through the integration of attributes into the matching process. We jointly learn a discriminative projection to a joint appearance-attribute subspace. Unlike LMNN [28], this subspace is of lower dimensionality and is discriminatively learned for the purpose of matching [19]. By performing matching in this space, our model exhibits some invariance to the lighting and pose conditions that impede models which rely only on appearance.

We start by introducing our notation. We initially extract a set of feature vectors $\mathbf{x}$ for the subjects in the dataset. We index the features as triplets, where first two vectors $\mathbf{x}_{(i,1)}$ and $\mathbf{x}_{(i,2)}$ corresponds to images of the same subject, while the third vector $\mathbf{x}_{(i,3)}$ corresponds an image of a different subject. We are also given attribute labels $\mathbf{y}$ for the same subjects, where y_{jk} denotes the attribute value of image j for attribute k. To this end, we optimize the joint regularized risk function:

$$\min_{\mathbf{A},\mathbf{B}} \quad F(\mathbf{A},\mathbf{B}) =$$

$$\min_{\mathbf{A},\mathbf{B}} \quad \frac{\lambda_A}{2}\|\mathbf{A}\|_F^2 + \frac{\lambda_B}{2}\|\mathbf{B}\|_F^2 +$$

$$\sum_i \ell(1 + D_{AB}^2(\mathbf{x}_{(i,1)}, \mathbf{x}_{(i,2)}) - D_{AB}^2(\mathbf{x}_{(i,1)}, \mathbf{x}_{(i,3)})) +$$

$$C\sum_j \sum_k \ell(1 - y_{jk}\mathbf{b}_k\mathbf{x}_j), \tag{1}$$

where the two linear mappings $\mathbf{A}$ and $\mathbf{B}$ map input vectors $\mathbf{x}$ into the joint subspace defined by the two projections, and ℓ is a loss function. The projection is learnt so as to satisfy the joint constraint set. The subspace defined by $\mathbf{A}$ only imposes ranking constraints on feature vector triplets; distances between images of the same subject are smaller than those between images of different subjects. The subspace defined by $\mathbf{B}$ includes additional classification constraints that encode the semantic aspect of our model, where each dimension in this subspace represents an attribute, and each row $\mathbf{b}_k$ of the matrix $\mathbf{B}$ is basically a linear classifier for that attribute.

The objective function in Equation 1 is jointly minimizing two loss functions: the ranking loss for the matching and the classification loss for the attribute subspace. Optimizing a ranking loss is arguably more appropriate for person re-identification where ranking is performed at test time. One advantage of this formulation is that both the distance constraints and the attribute classification constraints can be sparse. We explicitly included a regularization term for both matrices to avoid trivial solutions and to achieve a faster convergence rate.

The squared distance between two images in this coupled space can be defined as:

$$D^2_{AB}(x_i, x_j) = \left\| \begin{bmatrix} \mathbf{A} \\ \mathbf{B} \end{bmatrix} (x_i - x_j) \right\|^2_2$$
$$= \|\mathbf{A}(x_i - x_j)\|^2_2 + \|\mathbf{B}(x_i - x_j)\|^2_2, \qquad (2)$$

which is also the sum of the squared distances in the subspaces defined by the two linear mappings $\mathbf{A}$ and $\mathbf{B}$.

To empirically validate our claim that our attribute-consistent model is more discriminative, we strip our model of the attribute classification constraints. The resulting model is parameterized only by the linear operator $\mathbf{A}$ which projects the input vectors $\mathbf{x}$ to the same dimensionality as our original model in Equation 1. This allows us to isolate the effect of the attribute classification constraints on the matching process. This stripped baseline model is then defined as follows:

$$\min_{\mathbf{A}} G(\mathbf{A}) = \min_{\mathbf{A}} \frac{\lambda}{2} \|\mathbf{A}\|^2_F +$$
$$\sum_i \ell(1 + D^2_A(\mathbf{x}_{(i,1)}, \mathbf{x}_{(i,2)}) - D^2_A(\mathbf{x}_{(i,1)}, \mathbf{x}_{(i,3)})) \qquad (3)$$

where the distance in the low dimensional space is defined as

$$D^2_A(x_i, x_j) = \|\mathbf{A}(x_i - x_j)\|^2_2. \qquad (4)$$

3.2   Optimization

To this point we set the loss function in our experiments to the hinge loss:

$$\ell(x) = \max(0, x), \qquad (5)$$

which is convex but not differentiable. There are many smooth approximations of the hinge loss (*e.g.*, the generalized logistic function [19]), but given that we regularize our objective explicitly, convergence rate was not an issue. Under the hinge loss our distance constraints are similar to those in LMNN [28], while our classification constraints correspond to the constraints of a linear SVM. This means that the distance constraints in the objective function are not convex with respect to $\mathbf{A}$ or $\mathbf{B}$. However, an iterative subgradient descent approach on the parameters of both matrices has been shown to converge to good local optima [25,28].

We can now compute a subgradient of the objective with respect to the variables $\mathbf{A}$ and $\mathbf{B}$. A subgradient with respect to $\mathbf{A}$ is:

$$\frac{\partial H(\mathbf{A}, \mathbf{B})}{\partial \mathbf{A}} = \lambda_A \mathbf{A} + 2\mathbf{A} \sum_{i \in I(\mathbf{A}, \mathbf{B})} (\mathbf{C}_{(i,1),(i,2)} - \mathbf{C}_{(i,1),(i,3)}) \qquad (6)$$

where the set I is the subset of triplets $\mathcal{T}$ that violate the distance constraints and is defined formally as:

$$I(\mathbf{A}, \mathbf{B}) = \{ i \in \mathcal{T} : D_{AB}^2(\mathbf{x}_{(i,1)}, \mathbf{x}_{(i,3)}) - $$
$$D_{AB}^2(\mathbf{x}_{(i,1)}, \mathbf{x}_{(i,2)}) < 1 \}, \tag{7}$$

and $\mathbf{C}_{i,j}$ is the outer product matrix for the difference between two feature vectors $\mathbf{x}_i$ and $\mathbf{x}_j$:

$$\mathbf{C}_{i,j} = (\mathbf{x}_i - \mathbf{x}_j)(\mathbf{x}_i - \mathbf{x}_j)^T. \tag{8}$$

Similarly, a subgradient with respect to row $\mathbf{b}_k$ in $\mathbf{B}$ is:

$$\frac{\partial H(\mathbf{A}, \mathbf{B})}{\partial \mathbf{b}_k} = \lambda_B \mathbf{b}_k + 2C \sum_{j \in J_k(\mathbf{B})} y_{jk} \mathbf{x}_j^T + $$
$$2\mathbf{b}_k \sum_{i \in I} (\mathbf{C}_{(i,1),(i,2)} - \mathbf{C}_{(i,1),(i,3)}) \tag{9}$$

where the set J_k is the subset of feature vector indices that are misclassified by attribute classifier k, which is represented by row $\mathbf{b}_k$:

$$J_k(\mathbf{B}) = \{ j \in \mathcal{L} : y_{jk} \mathbf{b}_k^T \mathbf{x}_j < 1 \} \tag{10}$$

To learn the linear mappings we then use a projected subgradient descent algorithm [23]. The iterative projections to the constrained Frobenius norms dramatically sped up the convergence rate for the learning procedure. We also employ restarts to avoid local minima. The details of the approach are provided in Algorithm 1.

4   Experiments

4.1   Setup

We evaluated our model on VIPeR [9], a standard person re-identification dataset, as well as the new dataset, Indoor-ReID, which we collected and labeled. VIPeR contains 632 images of 316 subjects captured from 2 cameras. The images are captured outdoors and have significant lighting and viewpoint variations. We use the 15 binary attributes annotated by [15]. The dataset is split randomly into a training set and a testing set. In one set of experiments the splits are of equal sizes (316 subjects each) and in another set the training set has only 100 subjects and the test set has 532 subjects. Testing is done by considering images from Camera A as probe and evaluating their matches from images in Camera B. All the benchmarking results are averages of 10 runs.

Indoor-ReID was collected in an indoor office environment, using 4 different cameras at varying angle and under different lighting conditions. It contains over 28,000 images from 290 different subjects. The images were generated by sampling images from several trajectories obtained over a few hours of surveillance

Algorithm 1. Learning Attribute-Consistent Matching

1: **INPUT: x, y,** $\mathcal{T}, \mathcal{L}, \lambda_A, \lambda_B, C, T$
2: Initialize $\mathbf{A}_1$ and $\mathbf{B}_1$ randomly
3: **for** $t = 1 \ldots T$ **do**
4:     Find the violating triplets $I(\mathbf{A}_t, \mathbf{B}_t)$ (Equation 7)
5:     Calculate $\frac{\partial H(\mathbf{A}_t, \mathbf{B}_t)}{\partial \mathbf{A}_t}$ (Equation 6)
6:     Set $\eta_A = \frac{1}{\lambda_A t}$
7:     Set $\mathbf{A}_{t+\frac{1}{2}} = (1 - \eta_A \lambda_A)\mathbf{A}_t + \eta_A \frac{\partial H(\mathbf{A}_t, \mathbf{B}_t)}{\partial \mathbf{A}_t}$
8:     Set $\mathbf{A}_{t+1} = \min \left\{ 1, \frac{1}{\sqrt{\lambda_A}\|\mathbf{A}\|_F} \right\} \mathbf{A}_{t+\frac{1}{2}}$
9:     Find the violating indices $J_k(\mathbf{A}_t, \mathbf{B}_t)$ for each k (Equation 10)
10:    Calculate $\frac{\partial H(\mathbf{A}_t, \mathbf{B}_t)}{\partial \mathbf{B}_t}$ (Equation 9 for each k)
11:    Set $\eta_B = \frac{1}{\lambda_B t}$
12:    Set $\mathbf{B}_{t+\frac{1}{2}} = (1 - \eta_B \lambda_B)\mathbf{B}_t + \eta_B \frac{\partial H(\mathbf{A}_t, \mathbf{B}_t)}{\partial \mathbf{B}_t}$
13:    Set $\mathbf{B}_{t+1} = \min \left\{ 1, \frac{1}{\sqrt{\lambda_B}\|\mathbf{B}\|_F} \right\} \mathbf{B}_{t+\frac{1}{2}}$
14: **end for**
15: **OUTPUT:** $\mathbf{A}_{T+1}$ and $\mathbf{B}_{T+1}$

data. Since a subject may appear several times over different tracks, we manually annotated the identities across tracks. We also annotated 16 attributes for each subject, which include 10 attributes for attire description (sleeve length, pants length, hair length, top color, pants color, hair color, top pattern, hat, facial hair, glasses), 3 attributes for non-attire description (gender, build, complexion), and 3 attributes for carry-on objects (bag, backpack, handheld). Some of the collected attributes are multivalued, *e.g.* color is chosen to be the dominant color and is selected out of the 11 universal color names in Berlin and Kay [3]. Figure 2 illustrates some samples from our dataset. To evaluate our approach we split the dataset into a training set and a testing set of equal size with almost identical attribute distributions. At test time we calculate the distances between two tracks as the distance between two randomly sampled representative images, one from each track. The same sampled images are used for all the benchmarks to ensure a fair comparison. We also average the results for both setups over 10 runs.

We extract the same features used in recent benchmarks [1,11,20] for both VIPeR and Indoor-ReID. We divide each image into overlapping patches of size 8×8 with 50% overlap in both directions, which results in 341 patches. From each patch we collect 8-bin color histograms for YUV and HSV color spaces, and additionally LBP histograms using a grayscale representation of the image. We then concatenate each feature type separately for all the patches in each image as in [20] and proceed to perform unsupervised dimensionality reduction using PCA to project the three feature sets to 100, 20, and 40 dimensions respectively. Our approach would then discriminatively project this down to an even lower dimensional subspace of only 50 dimensions.

Fig. 2. Sample images from our dataset (Indoor-ReID). The dataset contains over 28,000 images of over 290 different subjects captured under diverse lighting and viewpoint conditions. The dataset is also annotated with 16 different attributes for each subject.

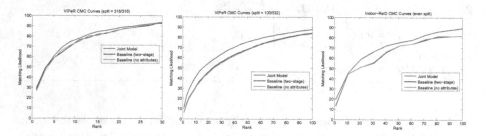

Fig. 3. CMC Curves for VIPeR and Indoor-ReID. The curve for the joint model using the coupled appearance-attribute space dominates the two baseline curves in all graphs. The first graph for VIPeR was created with an even training/test split (316/316), while the second graph figure was created with a split of 100 training subjects and 532 test subjects. For Indoor-ReID the dataset was split evenly.

To evaluate the contribution of the coupling, we report the results against two baselines. The first baseline represents the stripped ranking formulation in Equation 3, where the data is basically just projected to a lower dimensional subspace. As a second baseline we report the results using a two-stage approach, where we augment our extracted features using the output of separately trained attribute classifiers before optimizing the ranking formulation. This baseline validates that the performance gain in the joint model is due to using a coupled appearance-attribute subspace and not just due to utilizing attribute information. We finally report our attribute classification accuracies on both datasets using the 50/50 split. On Indoor-ReID the multi-class attributes were expanded to n-binary valued attributes for the training, and the predicted attribute value at test time is the one with the highest score. We finally compare the attribute classification results on VIPeR to those reported in [15]. The model parameters λ_A, λ_B, and C are set by cross validation to 10^{-2}, 10^{-2}, 10^{-3} respectively for all our experiments.

Table 1. Re-identification quantitative results on VIPeR using two different splits. The numbers are the percentage of correct matches at rank r, i.e. in the top ranked r images. In our results we note specifically that augmenting the subspace with the attributes in the joint model significantly improved the results, given a fixed subspace dimensionality.

VIPeR Ranks (split = 316/316)				
Approach	$r=1$	$r=5$	$r=10$	$r=20$
Joint Model	29.54	60.34	75.95	87.34
Baseline (two-stage)	27.85	58.65	73.42	86.92
Baseline (no attributes)	26.58	58.23	73.00	85.65
RCCA [1]	30.00	-	75.00	87.00
RPLM [11]	27.00	-	69.00	83.00
sLDFV [18]	26.53	56.38	70.88	84.63
eSDC [30]	26.74	50.70	62.37	76.36
LFDA [20]	24.18	-	67.12	-
CPS [6]	21.84	44.64	57.21	71.23
PCCA (χ^2_{RBF}) [19]	19.27	48.89	64.91	80.28
SDLAF+AIR [15]	17.40	39.04	50.84	67.27

VIPeR Ranks (split = 100/532)				
Approach	$r=1$	$r=5$	$r=10$	$r=20$
Joint Model	11.05	28.91	41.30	54.83
Baseline (two-stage)	6.35	20.81	31.24	46.17
Baseline (no attributes)	5.94	19.89	30.60	45.15
PCCA (χ^2_{RFB}) [19]	9.27	24.89	37.43	52.89
PRDC [31]	9.12	24.19	34.40	48.55

4.2 Results

The Cumulative Matching Characteristic (CMC) curve has been adopted as the standard metric for evaluation for person re-identification systems. The curve illustrates the likelihood of the correct match being in the top r ranked images for each rank r. Our CMC curves for both VIPeR and Indoor-ReID are shown in Figure 3. The first graph for the VIPeR dataset uses the even training/test split (316/316) while the second graph uses the more challenging 100/532 split. The curve for our joint model dominates the two baseline curves, more clearly on the bottom figure, demonstrating the performance gain that the coupling achieves. Similarly, the third graph shows the CMC curves for the new Indoor-ReID dataset, and the joint model with the coupled subspace is also clearly dominating the two baseline curves.

We also report the numbers for comparison in Tables 1 and 2. Our joint model achieves the highest accuracies across all reported ranks. Using better feature descriptors is likely to even increase this gain, as can be seen from the two reported performances for ITML ([31] and [12]). We outperform PCCA [19] using the same kernel (sqrt), number of negative examples (10), and same subspace

Table 2. Re-identification quantitative results on Indoor-ReID. The numbers are the percentage of correct matches at rank r, *i.e.* in the top ranked r images. The joint model projecting to the coupled space significantly outperformed the baseline model, given a fixed subspace dimensionality.

Indoor-ReID Ranks (even split)				
Approach	$r=1$	$r=5$	$r=10$	$r=20$
Joint Model	19.51	35.77	45.53	59.35
Baseline (two-stage)	13.82	34.15	43.90	50.41
Baseline (no attributes)	13.01	34.15	44.72	50.41

Table 3. Attribute classification results on VIPeR and Indoor-ReID. Our classification accuracies on VIPeR are higher than those of AIR [15] on almost all attributes.

Approach	AIR [15]	Ours
Shorts	79	**88.8**
Sandals	64	**93.3**
Backpacks	**66**	64.2
Jeans	**76**	69.3
Carrying	**75**	71.0
Logo	59	**78.7**
V-neck	44	**91.6**
Open-outer	64	**76.6**
Stripes	41	**92.3**
Sunglasses	66	**76.2**
Headphones	74	**97.5**
Shorthair	**52**	50.0
Longhair	65	**66.9**
Male	**68**	49.3
Skirt	67	**95.2**
Average	64	**77.4**

Approach	Random	Ours
Sleeve Length	50.0	62.7
Pants Length	50.0	86.9
Hair Length	33.3	78.6
Hat	50.0	96.1
Top Color	9.1	22.3
Pants Color	9.1	38.0
Hair Color	9.1	47.5
Top Pattern	25.0	75.1
Bag	50.0	67.0
Backpack	50.0	91.2
Handheld	50.0	58.9
Glasses	50.0	58.2
Gender	50.0	74.0
Facial Hair	50.0	96.4
Build	33.3	62.4
Complexion	33.3	57.8
Average	37.6	67.1

dimensionality (30). Our results also demonstrate that integrating the semantic aspect by coupling attribute classification and matching significantly improved the performance across all experiments. This effect is even more pronounced in the second set of experiments on VIPeR. Similarly, on Indoor-ReID the joint model projecting to the coupled space significantly outperformed the baseline model.

We finally quantify our attribute classification results on both datasets in Table 3. For VIPeR we compare with the reported numbers from Layne *et al.* [15]. We achieve better accuracies for most attributes using the simple linear classifiers in our model. We also report our attribute classification accuracies on Indoor-ReID. Since some of the labeled attributes for Indoor-ReID are multivalued, we also report the random chance performance. During training we expanded the multivalued attributes to n-binary attributes, and at test time we predict the attribute value with the largest score.

5   Conclusion

We presented a joint learning framework for attribute-consistent matching. We integrate semantic attributes and person re-identification by projecting the input images to lower dimensional coupled appearance-attribute subspace. Matching in this subspace exhibits some invariance to the severe lighting conditions and pose variations that hinder appearance-based matching models. We evaluated our model on VIPeR, a standard benchmark dataset for person re-identification, as well as a new large scale dataset we collected and annotated with attributes relevant to the problem. We report results that outperform several state-of-the-art methods on VIPeR and demonstrate on both datasets that the performance gain by the joint model improves over the baselines and over prior art using the same input features.

Acknowledgments. This research was supported by contract N00014-13-C-0164 from the Office of Naval Research through a subcontract from United Technologies Research Center, and by a grant from Siemens Corporate Research.

References

1. An, L., Kafai, M., Yang, S., Bhanu, B.: Reference-based person re-identification. In: AVSS (2013)
2. Bak, S., Corvee, E., Bremond, F., Thonnat, M.: Person re-identification using spatial covariance regions of human body parts. In: AVSS (2010)
3. Berlin, B., Kay, P.: Basic color terms: Their universality and evolution. University of California, Berkeley (1969)
4. Bourdev, L.D., Maji, S., Malik, J.: Describing people: A poselet-based approach to attribute classification. In: ICCV (2011)
5. Chen, H., Gallagher, A., Girod, B.: Describing clothing by semantic attributes. In: Fitzgibbon, A., Lazebnik, S., Perona, P., Sato, Y., Schmid, C. (eds.) ECCV 2012, Part III. LNCS, vol. 7574, pp. 609–623. Springer, Heidelberg (2012)
6. Cheng, D.S., Cristani, M., Stoppa, M., Bazzani, L., Murino, V.: Custom pictorial structures for re-identification. In: BMVC (2011)
7. Farenzena, M., Bazzani, L., Perinal, A., Murino, V., Cristani, M.: Person re-identification by symmetry-driven accumulation of local features. In: CVPR (2010)
8. Gheissari, N., Sebastian, T.B., Tu, P.H., Rittscher, J.: Person reidentification using spatiotemporal appearance. In: CVPR (2006)
9. Gray, D., Brennan, S., Tao, H.: Evaluating appearance models for recognition, reacquisition, and tracking. In: PETS (2007)
10. Gray, D., Tao, H.: Viewpoint invariant pedestrian recognition with an ensemble of localized features. In: Forsyth, D., Torr, P., Zisserman, A. (eds.) ECCV 2008, Part I. LNCS, vol. 5302, pp. 262–275. Springer, Heidelberg (2008)

11. Hirzer, M., Roth, P.M., Köstinger, M., Bischof, H.: Relaxed pairwise learned metric for person re-identification. In: Fitzgibbon, A., Lazebnik, S., Perona, P., Sato, Y., Schmid, C. (eds.) ECCV 2012, Part VI. LNCS, vol. 7577, pp. 780–793. Springer, Heidelberg (2012)
12. Köstinger, M., Hirzer, M., Wohlhart, P., Roth, P.M., Bischof, H.: Large scale metric learning from equivalence constraints. In: CVPR (2012)
13. Kuo, C.H., Khamis, S., Shet, V.: Person re-identification using semantic color names and rankboost. In: WACV (2013)
14. Lampert, C.H., Nickisch, H., Harmeling, S.: Learning to detect unseen object classes by between-class attribute transfer. In: CVPR (2009)
15. Layne, R., Hospedales, T.M., Gong, S.: Person re-identification by attributes. In: BMVC (2012)
16. Layne, R., Hospedales, T.M., Gong, S.: Towards person identification and re-identification with attributes. In: Fusiello, A., Murino, V., Cucchiara, R. (eds.) ECCV 2012 Ws/Demos, Part I. LNCS, vol. 7583, pp. 402–412. Springer, Heidelberg (2012)
17. Liu, C., Gong, S., Loy, C.C., Lin, X.: Person re-identification: What features are important? In: Fusiello, A., Murino, V., Cucchiara, R. (eds.) ECCV 2012 Ws/Demos, Part I. LNCS, vol. 7583, pp. 391–401. Springer, Heidelberg (2012)
18. Ma, B., Su, Y., Jurie, F.: Local descriptors encoded by fisher vectors for person re-identification. In: Fusiello, A., Murino, V., Cucchiara, R. (eds.) ECCV 2012 Ws/Demos, Part I. LNCS, vol. 7583, pp. 413–422. Springer, Heidelberg (2012)
19. Mignon, A., Jurie, F.: Pcca: A new approach for distance learning from sparse pairwise constraints. In: CVPR (2012)
20. Pedagadi, S., Orwell, J., Velastin, S., Boghossian, B.: Local fisher discriminant analysis for pedestrian re-identification. In: CVPR (2013)
21. Prosser, B., Gong, S., Xiang, T.: Multi-camera matching using bi-directional cumulative brightness transfer functions. In: BMVC (2008)
22. Prosser, B., Zheng, W.S., Gong, S., Xiang, T.: Person re-identification by support vector ranking. In: BMVC (2010)
23. Shalev-Shwartz, S., Singer, Y., Srebro, N., Cotter, A.: Pegasos: Primal estimated sub-gradient solver for SVM. Mathematical Programming, Series B **127**(1), 3–30 (2011)
24. Sharmanska, V., Quadrianto, N., Lampert, C.H.: Learning to rank using privileged information. In: ICCV (2013)
25. Torresani, L., Lee, K.: Large margin component analysis. In: NIPS (2007)
26. Vapnik, V., Vashist, A.: A new learning paradigm: Learning using privileged information. In: IJCNN (2009)
27. Vaquero, D.A., Feris, R.S., Tran, D., Brown, L.M.G., Hampapur, A., Turk, M.: Attribute-based people search in surveillance environments. In: WACV (2009)
28. Weinberger, K.Q., Saul, L.K.: Distance metric learning for large margin nearest neighbor classification. JMLR (2009)
29. Wu, Y., Mukunoki, M., Funatomi, T., Minoh, M., Lao, S.: Optimizing mean reciprocal rank for person re-identification. In: AVSS (2011)
30. Zhao, R., Ouyang, W., Wang, X.: Unsupervised salience learning for person re-identification. In: CVPR (2013)
31. Zheng, W.S., Gong, S., Xiang, T.: Person re-identification by probabilistic relative distance comparison. In: CVPR (2011)

Person Re-identification by Discriminatively Selecting Parts and Features

Amran Bhuiyan[✉], Alessandro Perina, and Vittorio Murino

Pattern Analysis and Computer Vision (PAVIS),
Istituto Italiano di Tecnologia, Genova, Italy
Amran.Bhuiyan@iit.it

Abstract. This paper presents a novel appearance-based method for person re-identification. The core idea is to rank and select different body parts on the basis of the discriminating power of their characteristic features. In our approach, we first segment the pedestrian images into meaningful parts, then we extract features from such parts as well as from the whole body and finally, we perform a salience analysis based on regression coefficients. Given a set of individuals, our method is able to estimate the different importance (or salience) of each body part automatically. To prove the effectiveness of our approach, we considered two standard datasets and we demonstrated through an exhaustive experimental section how our method improves significantly upon existing approaches, especially in multiple-shot scenarios.

Keywords: Pedestrian re-identification · STEL segmentation · Lasso regression

1   Introduction

Person re-identification is becoming an important topic in Computer Vision, especially in video surveillance scenarios. Its goal is to recognize (indeed, re-identify) an individual captured in diverse locations over different non-overlapping camera views, considering a large set of candidates.

The common assumption in re-identification (re-id) is that individuals do not change their clothing so their appearance in all the views is similar. This is still a complex task due to the nonrigid structure of the human body, the different perspectives with which a pedestrian can be observed, and the highly variable illumination conditions. Re-identification approaches can be divided in two classes of algorithms: learning-based and direct methods. In the former group, a dataset of different individuals is used to learn the features and the metric space where to compare them, in order to guarantee a high re-identification rate (e.g., see [8-14,15]). In contrast, direct methods are mainly devoted to the search of the most discriminant features and their combination so to design a powerful descriptor (or signature) for each individual. Besides, re-identification algorithms can also be categorized in single-shot and multiple-shot classes of methods.

© Springer International Publishing Switzerland 2015
L. Agapito et al. (Eds.): ECCV 2014 Workshops, Part III, LNCS 8927, pp. 147–161, 2015.
DOI: 10.1007/978-3-319-16199-0_11

The former focuses on associating pairs of images for each individual, while the latter employs multiple images of the same person as the probe and/or in the gallery set, trying to exploit this additional information.

As for learning-based approaches, in [10], pairwise dissimilarity profiles between individuals are learned and adapted for nearest-neighbor classification. The approach presented in [11] uses boosting to select a combination of spatial and color information for viewpoint invariance. In [8], a high-dimensional signature composed by multiple features is projected into a low-dimensional latent space by a Partial Least Squares reduction method. In [12], contextual visual knowledge is exploited, enriching a bag-of-word-based descriptor by features derived from neighboring people, assuming that groups of persons are invariant across different camera views. Re-identification is cast as a binary classification problem (one vs. all) in [13] adopting Haar-like features and a part-based MPEG7 dominant color descriptor. In [24], re-id is considered as a relative ranking problem in a higher dimensional feature space where true and wrong matches become easily separable. Finally, re-identification is considered as a Multiple Instance Learning problem in [15], where a method of synthetically augmenting the training dataset is also proposed.

Direct methods focus more on designing novel features for capturing the most distinguishing aspects of an individual. In [16], a descriptor is proposed by subdividing the person in horizontal stripes, keeping the median color of each stripe accumulated over different frames. A spatio-temporal local feature grouping and matching is proposed in [17], where a decomposable triangular graph is built in order to capture the spatial distribution of the local descriptor over time. The method proposed in [18] segments a pedestrian image into regions, and stores the spatial relationship of the colors into a co-occurrence matrix. This technique proved to work well when pedestrians are seen from similar perspectives. In [19], SURF interest points are collected over short video sequences and used to characterize human bodies. Symmetry- and asymmetry-driven features are explored on [5,7] based on the idea that features closer to the body symmetry axes are more robust against scene clutter and body extremities. Covariance features, originally employed for pedestrian detection [20], are extracted from coarsely located body parts and tailored for re-id purposes in [21]. This work has been extended in [22] by considering the case where multiple images of the same individual are available. The authors adopt the manifold mean as surrogate of the different covariances coming from the multiple images. Similar features, i.e., MSCR and color histograms, have been also employed in [3,4], and used to match signatures based on Custom Pictorial Structures [1] to finely segment body parts and extract appearance descriptors.

In addition to color based features, there are some other features that have been proved to be promising for the re-id task, such as: textures [8,9,11], edges [8], Haar-like features [13], interest points [19], image patches [11], and segmented regions [18]. All these features can be extracted from horizontal stripes [16], triangular graphs, concentric rings [17], symmetry-driven structures [5,7], and horizontal patches [21]. Another unconventional application of re-id considers

Fig. 1. (a) Lineups of pedestrians; and (b,c) corresponding segmentations (best viewed in color).

Pan-Tilt-Zoom cameras, where distance between signatures are also computed across different scales [6] while estimating the most discriminant part.

Within this context, we propose an approach that focuses on discriminating parts and features, taking inspiration from [6]. The idea is to learn the most discriminant body parts (and associated features) able to separate (or match) at best a given a set of pedestrians. A least shrinkage and selective operator (Lasso) regression method [23] is used for this selection task adopting standard features extracted by segmented body parts, together with the generative model introduced in [2]. Performance has been evaluated by testing our method on two well recognized publicly available datasets, CAVIAR4REID and VIPeR.

Our approach, belongs to the class of the direct methods and it differs from previous works in two important aspects: i) we use Stel Component Analysis (SCA) segmentation technique which is quite effective for pedestrian segmentation, and ii) unlike [3], no manual weighting of individual parts is required for all the pedestrians, instead this is automatically carried out by exploiting regression weights.

The idea of considering parts of the body for re-id is not new. In [3,4], the authors used the pictorial models (see Fig.1c), and in the experimental section we will show that SCA yields to better results.

The rest of the paper has been organized as follows. Section 2 describes of the proposed approach in detail. Sec. 3 reports the experimental results, and concluding remarks are drawn in Sec. 4.

2   The Approach

The pipeline that characterizes our approach consists of the following steps:

Pedestrian segmentation: We segmented each image using SCA [2]. This segmentation method yields to consistent segments across images and it allowed us to discard background regions and focus the analysis on the foreground parts.

Feature extraction: We extracted standard features from each foreground segment.

Rank-to-mask strategy: We applied Lasso regression on every pedestrian in a one-vs-all fashion, and used the regression coefficients to determine the more discriminating parts and/or features.

Signature matching: We evaluated our approach using standard matching approaches.

In the following, each step is described and analyzed focusing on multi-shot re-identification.

2.1   Pedestrian Segmentation

The aim of this phase is to isolate the actual body appearance from the rest of the scene. This allows the proposed approach to focus solely on the individual and its parts, ignoring the context in which it is immersed.

We performed this separation by using Stel Component Analysis (SCA) [2]. This segmentation algorithm is based on the notion of "structure element", or stel, which can be explained as an image portion (often discontinuous) whose topology is consistent over an image class. A stel often represents a meaningful and semantic part for a class of objects, like an arm or the head for pedestrians. For example, in Fig. 1 we show few images of pedestrians and their related segmentation in stels. Each color indexes a particular stel s_i while maintaining consistent the segmentation (same color, same part of the body) across the whole dataset. This is very important as it allows us to compare consistently feature signatures extracted in the various body parts.

More formally, SCA captures the common structure of an image class by blending together multiple stels: it assumes that each pixel measurement x_i, with its 2D coordinate i, has an associated discrete variable s_i, which takes a label from the set $\{1, ..., S\}$. Such a labeling is generated from a stel prior $p(s_i)$, which captures the common structure of the set of images.

The model detects the image self-similarity within a segment: pixels with the same label s are expected to follow a tight distribution over the image measurements. Finally, while the appearance similarity is local (for each image), the model insists on consistent segmentation by means of a stel prior, which is common for all the images.

SCA has been previously considered for re-id, in particular in [5,7], where the authors used it to perform a background-foreground segmentation (S=2): an

a) SCA prior p(s)

b) Background stels are filtered out

c) Pictorial Models

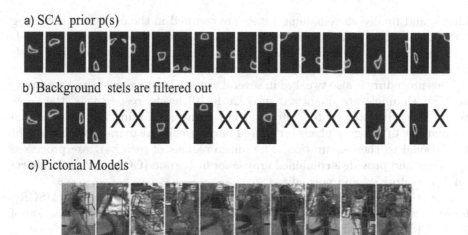

Fig. 2. a) Segmented part-masks for whole image. b) Foreground extraction procedure. c) Lineup of pedestrians and superimposed pictorial structures.

example of the segmentation prior $p(s_i)$ used is shown in Fig. 2a. Here, for the first time, we exploited SCA's segmentation in multiple parts $(S > 2)$, discarding background parts and considering the features in each each part separately. An example of a learned SCA segmentation prior is shown in Fig. 2a, where S=20. After learning the stel prior, we manually filtered out the background stels, as shown in Fig. 2b. It is worth to note that the model is learned only once and it is independent on the dataset. Furthermore the background suppression is performed once and not for each individual image, because all the images have consistent segmentation.

In our experiments, we set the number of segment to S=20 and we modeled the distribution over the image measurements as a mixture of Gaussians. To learn the segmentation prior we set the number of iterations to 50. Segmentation of new images (i.e., probe) consists in fast inference and is done in real time.

2.2 Feature Extraction

The feature extraction stage consists in distilling complementary aspects from each body part in order to encode heterogeneous information and to capture distinctive characteristics of the individuals. There are many possible cues useful for a fine visual characterization and we considered two types of features: color histograms and maximally stable color regions (MSCR) [25]. This is the same signature already used in [3–5, 7].

Color histograms represent a good compromise when they encode separately shades of gray from colored pixels. To do so, first, all RGB pixel values are converted to the HSV color space, h,s,v. Then, they are subject to the following operations: all pixels with value $v < \tau_{black}$ are counted in the bin of blacks, all pixels with saturation $s < \tau_{gray}$ are counted in the gray bins according to their value v, and finally all remaining pixels are counted in the color bins according to their hue-saturation coordinates (h,s). Basically dark and unsaturated pixels are counted separately from the others, and the brightness of the colored pixels are ignored by counting only their chromaticity in a 2D histogram.

This procedure is also tweaked in several ways to improve speed and accuracy: the HSV channels are quantized into [20,10,10] levels, respectively, the votes are (bi-)linearly interpolated into the bins to avoid aliasing and the residual chromaticity of the gray pixels is counted into the color histograms with a weight proportional to their saturation. The image regions of each part are processed separately and provide a combined gray-color histogram (GC histogram in short) which is vectorized and normalized.

The other extracted feature is the Maximally Stable Color Regions (MSCR). Here we used the full body masks independently to constrain the extraction of the MSCR blobs. The MSCR operator detects a set of blob regions by looking at the successive steps of an agglomerative clustering of the pixels. At each step, neighboring pixels with similar color are clustered, employing a threshold that represents the maximal chromatic distance between colors. The threshold is varied at each step and the regions that are stable over a range of steps constitute the maximally stable color regions of the image. As in [3,4], we extracted a signature $MSCR = \{(y_i, c_i) \mid i = 1, ..., N\}$ that contains the height (vertical size) and color of the maximum stable regions, or blobs. The algorithm is set in a way that provides many small blobs and avoids creating big ones. The rationale is to localize details of the pedestrians appearance which is more accurate for small blobs.

2.3   Discriminative Analysis: Rank-to-Mask Strategy

The second novel contribution of our approach is a discriminative analysis of parts and features, which in our case are histogram bins. Our idea is that we can identify a pedestrian by looking only to a subset of the signature features which is different for each pedestrian in the gallery. We accomplish this by ranking features and parts based on the means of a regression approach.

Given a pool of training images for N pedestrians (the gallery) we perform a sparse regression analysis using Lasso [23], which is a general form of regularization in a regression problem. In the simple linear regression problem every training image, described by the proposed feature vector and denoted with $x^{(n)}$, is associated with a target variable $z^{(n)}$ which represents the identity. The target variable can then be expressed as a linear combination of the image features as follows:

$$z^{(n)} = \left(\alpha^{(n)} \right)^{\mathsf{T}} \cdot x^{(n)} \tag{1}$$

where T represents the transposed vector.

The standard least square estimate calculates the weight vector $\alpha^{(n)}$ by minimizing the error function.

$$E\left(\boldsymbol{\alpha}\right) = \sum_{n=1}^{N} \left(z^{(n)} - \left(\boldsymbol{\alpha}^{(n)} \right)^{\mathsf{T}} \cdot x^{(n)} \right)^2 \tag{2}$$

Again, in our case N corresponds to the total number of pedestrians we have in the training set. The regularizer in the Lasso estimate is simply expressed as a threshold on the L1-norm of the weight $\boldsymbol{\alpha}$:

$$\sum_{j} \mid \alpha_j \mid \leq \mathsf{K} \tag{3}$$

This term acts as a constraint that has to be taken into account when minimizing the error function, being K a constant. After doing this, it has been proven that (depending on the parameter K), many of the coefficients α_j become exactly zero [24].

In our approach, the aim is to determine the visual characteristics of each pedestrian that discriminate him/her from all the others pedestrians present in the gallery. To this end, we performed Lasso regression for each pedestrian separately, considering all its training images has positive samples. In other words, we solved N regression problems, each one returning a pedestrian-specific weight vector $\boldsymbol{\alpha}^{(n)}$ $n = 1, \ldots, N$. Since each dimension $\alpha_j^{(n)}$ weighs a different feature in a different part, $\mathbf{j} = (p, f)$, it is possible to figure out which parts (indexed by p) or signature feature (indexed by f) are the most discriminant for a each pedestrian, and those which can be neglected.

One important consideration is that one cannot weigh the histogram comparisons directly with Lasso outputs as they are not normalized across samples. To solve this issue we used ranking. First, we sorted regression coefficients in decreasing order of their absolute value $|\alpha_{p,f}^{(n)}|$, and second, we assigned a weight to each feature j based on its ranking position $r_{p,f}^t$ as follows:

$$R_{p,f}^{(n)} = \begin{cases} 1 & \text{if} \quad r_{p,f}^t \leq P \quad \text{and} \quad \alpha_{p,f}^{(n)} > 0 \\ 0 & \text{Otherwise} \end{cases} \tag{4}$$

Where P is a position in the rank; for example if $P = 1$, only the top feature is considered, etc..

We called $R_{p,f}^{(n)}$, the *Rank-to-mask* coefficients: They filter out features which are not important to discriminate the identity of the person n, where the importance is given by the regression coefficients. Furthermore, by summing $\alpha_{p,f}^{(n)}$ over the parts, the individual color bins or/and the pedestrians, we can highlight the *individual* parts or color bins which are more important. To summarize, we introduced the following strategies:

Best parts for pedestrian - BPP. We summed over all the features for each pedestrian $\hat{\alpha}_p^{(n)} = \sum_f \alpha_{p,f}^{(n)}$ and then we applied the aforementioned procedure to $\hat{\alpha}_p^{(n)}$. The resulting $\hat{R}_p^{(n)}$ are then simply replicated for each feature f in the part p to reconstruct a mask vector of size $F \times P$ which is subsequently used in the signature matching phase. This strategy aims at highlighting the most discriminative parts for each pedestrians.

Best parts for dataset - BPD. We summed over the features and pedestrians $\hat{\alpha}_p = \sum_{f,n} \alpha_{p,f}^{(n)}$ and we proceeded likewise the previous case. This strategy aims at highlighting the most discriminative parts in the whole dataset.

Best feature for pedestrian - BFP. We summed over the parts for each pedestrian $\hat{\alpha}_f^{(n)} = \sum_p \alpha_{p,f}^{(n)}$ and we proceeded likewise the previous cases. This strategy highlights which are the best feature useful to recognize each pedestrian.

Best features for dataset - BFD. We summed over the parts and pedestrians $\hat{\alpha}_f = \sum_{p,n} \alpha_{p,f}^{(n)}$ and we proceeded likewise the previous cases. This strategy aims at highlighting the most discriminative features for each pedestrian.

As illustrative example, Fig. 3a shows the training images of pedestrian. After Lasso-based training, we compute the ranking using the **BPP** strategy resulting in *rank-to-mask* coefficients shown on the right of the figure. The pedestrian presents a white cross in the middle of torso and it is easily understandable that this should be a very discriminant part for this individual, and in fact torso is the most discriminating part. Similar considerations can be drawn by looking at the other two examples in Fig. 3b.

2.4 Feature Matching

Likewise [3], we employed color histogram and the MSCR blobs as image signature. To match two signatures $S_a = (h_a, MSCR_a)$ and $S_b = (h_b, MSCR_b)$ we calculated the distance

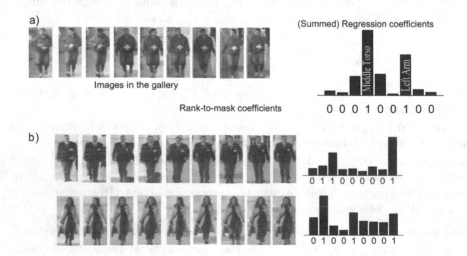

Fig. 3. a) Multiple (gallery) images of a same pedestrian. The regression coefficients summed up across the features highlight which are the most important parts to identify that pedestrian. Coefficients are then ranked and only the top P are retained. In this case $P = 2$. b) Two other examples considering P=3.

$$d\left(S_a, S_b\right) = \beta \cdot d_h\left(R \odot h_a, R \odot h_b\right) + (1 - \beta) \cdot d_{MSCR}\left(MSCR_a, MSCR_b\right) \quad (5)$$

where

$$d_h\left(R \odot h_a, R \odot h_b\right) = \log\left(\sqrt{R \odot h_a}^{\mathsf{T}} \cdot \sqrt{R \odot h_b}\right) \quad (6)$$

is the Bhattacharyya distance ($\odot$ represent point-wise multiplications), and

$$d_{MSCR}\left(MSCR_a, MSCR_b\right) = \frac{1}{|M_a \cup M_b|} \sum_{(i,j) \in M_a \cup M_b} \delta_{ij} \quad (7)$$

is the MSCR distance. Rs are the *rank-to-mask* coefficients introduced in the previous section (at some rank P), and β balances the two distances defined by Eq. 6 and Eq. 7. The latter is obtained by first computing the set of distances between all blobs $(y_i, c_i) \in MSCR_a$ and $(y_j, c_j) \in MSCR_b$:

$$\delta_{ij} = \gamma \cdot d_y\left(y_i, y_j\right) + (1 - \gamma) \cdot d_{lab}\left(c_i, c_j\right) \quad (8)$$

where γ balances the height distance $d_y = \frac{|y_i - y_j|}{H}$, and $d_{lab} = \frac{\|lab(c_i) - lab(c_j)\|}{200}$ is the Euclidean distance in the CIELAB color space. Then, the sets $M_a = \{(i,j) \mid \delta_{ij} \leq \delta_{ik}\}$ and $M_b = \{(i,j) \mid \delta_{ij} \leq \delta_{kj}\}$ of minimum distances are calculated from the two point of views, and finally we calculate their average as shown in Eq. 7.

The normalization factor H for the height distance is set to the height of the images in the dataset, while the parameters β and γ are tuned through cross-validation.

3 Experimental Results

The aims of the experimental section are *i)* to compare the SCA segmentation with pictorial models [3,4] and with the BG-FG segmentation (based on SCA) used in [5], and *ii)* to show to which extent the *rank-to-mask* strategy works.

As comparisons, we considered [3–5] because the three methods use exactly the same features, thus making the comparison fair. We compared our results with the best performance obtained by [3].

We considered two public available datasets, CAVIAR4REID [4,28] and VIPeR [26,27]. In particular, CAVIAR4REID covers almost all the challenging aspects of the person re-identification problem, such as shape deformation, illumination changes, occlusions, image blurring, low resolution images, etc.

The most important performance evaluation report tool for re-id is the Cumulative Matching Characteristic (CMC) curve, which is a plot of the recognition performance vs. the re-id ranking score and it represents the expectation of finding the correct match in the top n matches. Higher curves represent better performance. The performance can also be evaluated by computing the ranked matching rates, and these results are shown in the following tables.

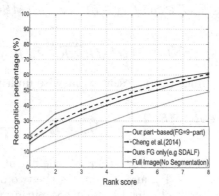

Fig. 4. CMC curves for multiple-shot trials on CAVIAR4REID.

CAVIAR4REID Dataset : It contains images of pedestrians extracted from the CAVIAR repository [4], providing a challenging real world setup. From the 72 identified different individuals (with images varying from 17×39 to 72×144), 50 are captured by two cameras and 22 from only one camera and each pedestrian has 10 images from each camera. Here we restricted to the subjects taken from 2 cameras, and selected M=5 images from the first camera for the probe set and M=5 images from the second camera as gallery set. Then, we performed multi-shot re-id (multi-vs-multi or CMvsM strategy); this is actually the same setup used in [3]. All images are re-sized to 32×96 pixels.

From the experimental findings shown in Fig.4-6, it will be evident that our approach outperforms convincingly the methods in the literature at different ranks.

As a first test we evaluated SCA segmentation for S>2. Fig. 4 reports the recognition accuracies: SCA segmentation clearly outperforms pictorial models used in [3,4] and the background-foreground segmentation used in SDALF which correspond to SCA run with S=2. We also reported the re-id performance obtained by considering the full image (without any segmentation): despite in this dataset all the pedestrians appear in the same environment, this actually affects the accuracy.

In the second part of the experiments we evaluated the *rank-to-mask* strategy, varying the rank P (see Eq.4). We set Lasso constant K (see Eq. 3) to 50, however the performance of the method has not changed much by varying this parameter.

In Fig. 5 and Tables 1 and 2, we reported the result of the *rank-to-mask* strategy based on the pedestrian specific parts-based (BPP) and the dataset specific parts-based (BPD) ranking scenarios, for different ranking (P) values, respectively.

Although the top-1 part for BPD shows better performance than the same ranking for BPP, still, considering all the instances, it is evident BPP scenario works better than BPD scenario.

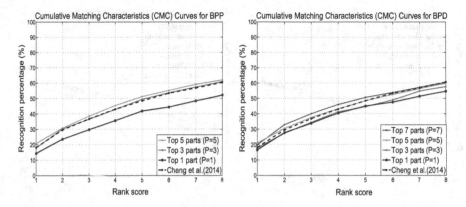

Fig. 5. Comparative plots between best-part for pedestrians (BPP) scenario and best-part for dataset (BPD) scenario on CAVIAR4REID.

Table 1. Comparison with Cheng et al.(2014) [3] methods for top-ranked matching rate (%) on the CAVIAR4REID dataset using best-part for pedestrian (BPP) scenario

Methods	r=2	r=4	r=6	r=8
Top 5 parts (P=5)	30.8	45.4	55.2	62.2
Top 3 parts (P=3)	30.2	42.8	53.8	61.0
Top 1 part (P=1)	23.6	35.6	44.4	52.2
Cheng et al.(2014)	29.6	43.0	53.4	60.6

Table 2. Comparison with Cheng et al.(2014) [3] methods by top-ranked matching rate (%) on the CAVIAR4REID dataset using best-part for database (BPD) scenario

Methods	r=2	r=4	r=6	r=8
Top 7 parts (P=7)	33.0	46.0	53.8	60.6
Top 5 parts (P=5)	30.6	43.0	52.6	59.8
Top 3 parts (P=3)	27.8	41.4	49.0	57.8
Top 1 parts (P=1)	27.8	40.4	47.6	54.6
Cheng et al.(2014)	29.6	43.0	53.4	60.6

In Fig.6 and Table 3,4, the result of the *rank-to-mask* strategy based on the pedestrian specific feature-based (BFP) and the dataset specific feature-based (BFD) ranking scenarios, for different ranking (P) values have been reported, respectively. The BFP scenario based top-1 feature showed almost equivalent accuracy of BFD based on the top-5 features. In general, we reached the results of [3] by considering only the top-10 features in BFP ranking scenario, while for the BFD ranking scenario it took about 35 top features.

From all the above analysis, we can confirm how the Lasso regression method introduced here is able to extract a significant ranking of features and improve re-id performance. It is also worth mentioning that the performance gets saturated after considering a certain number of top features ranking scores, i.e., after that, it does not show considerable variations.

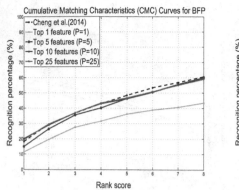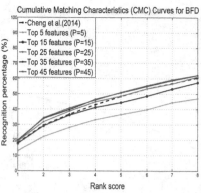

Fig. 6. CMC curves comparing best-feature for pedestrians (BFP) and best-feature for dataset (BFD) scenarios on CAVIAR4REID.

Table 3. Comparison with Cheng et al.(2014) [3] methods by top ranked matching rate (%) on the CAVIAR4REID dataset using best-feature for pedestrians (BFP) scenario

Methods	r=2	r=4	r=6	r=8
Top 25 features (P=25)	29.6	43.4	50.8	59.0
Top 10 feature (P=10)	29.0	43.0	50.8	59.2
Top 5 features (P=5)	26.4	40.2	50.8	60.0
Top 1 feature (P=1)	19.6	31.6	38.8	43.4
Cheng et al.(2014)	29.6	43.0	53.4	60.6

Table 4. Comparison with Cheng et al.(2014) [3] methods by top ranked matching rate (%) on the CAVIAR4REID dataset using best-feature for database (BFD) scenario

Methods	r=2	r=4	r=6	r=8
Top 45 features (P=45)	34.4	46.0	55.4	62.2
Top 35 features (P=35)	34.2	46.4	55.0	62.2
Top 25 features (P=25)	31.8	44.6	53.8	61.2
Top 15 features (P=15)	29.2	41.2	48.6	57.4
Top 5 features (P=5)	22.2	33.2	39.8	47.0
Cheng et al.(2014)	29.6	43.0	53.4	60.6

VIPeR Dataset : This dataset contains two views of 632 pedestrians. Each pair is made up of image of same pedestrians taken from arbitrary viewpoints under varying illumination conditions. Each image is 128 × 48 pixels and presents a centered unoccluded human figure, although cropped short at the feet in some side views. In the literature, results on VIPeR are typically produced by mediating over ten runs, each consisting in a partition of randomly selected 316 image pairs. For this dataset, we reported the results by computing the normalized area under curve (nAUC) value.

Fig. 7 reports the comparison of the recognition accuracy of our part-based approach with pictorial structure (PS) part-based model of Cheng et al. [3].

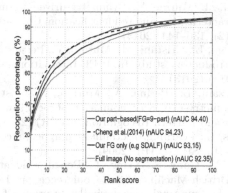

Fig. 7. CMC curves for single-shot trials on VIPeR.

In this dataset, SCA segmentation only works slightly better than pictorial models used in [3,4], but definitely works better than the background-foreground segmentation used in SDALF. Finally, our *rank-to-mask* strategy has not improved the results because the regressors overtrained. Here, in fact, we are in a single shot case and we have only a single positive instance for training.

4   Conclusions

In this work, we have proposed a discriminatively masked part-based re-identification method. For the first time, we exploited the segmentation provided by stel component analysis using a large number of parts. As second contribution, we proposed a method based on Lasso regression to rank the body parts and/or the features which makes our approach quite effective and efficient in multiple-shot scenarios while showing slightly poorer performance in the single-shot case for the datasets analyzed. Empirical results suggest that specific ranking of human body parts and associated features is a promising strategy for re-identification.

References

1. Andriluka, M., Roth, S., Schiele, B.: Pictorial structures revisited: People detection and articulated pose estimation. In: IEEE Conference on Computer Vision and Pattern Recognition, pp. 1014–1021 (2009)
2. Jojic, N., Perina, A., Cristani, M., Murino, V., Frey, B.: Stel component analysis: Modeling spatial correlations in image class structure. In: IEEE Conference on Computer Vision and Pattern Recognition, pp. 2044–2051 (2009)
3. Cheng, D.S., Cristani, M.: Person Re-identification by articulated appearance matching. In: Person Re-Identification. Springer (2014) ISBN 978-1-4471-6295-7
4. Cheng, D.S., Cristani, M., Stoppa, M., Bazzani, L., Murino, V.: Custom pictorial structures for re-identification. In: British Machine Vision Conference (BMVC) (2011)

5. Bazzani, L., Cristani, M., Murino, V.: Symmetry-driven accumulation of local features for human characterization and re-identification. Computer Vision and Image Understanding **117**(2), 130–144 (2013)
6. Salvagnini, P., Bazzani, L., Cristani, M., Murino, V.: Person re-identification with a ptz camera: An introductory study. In: IEEE International Conference on Image Processing (ICIP 2013) (2013)
7. Farenzena, M., Bazzani, L., Perina, A., Murino, V., Cristani, M.: Person re-identification by symmetry-driven accumulation of local features. In: IEEE Conf. on Computer Vision and Pattern Recognition (CVPR) (2010)
8. Schwartz, W., Davis, L.: Learning discriminative appearance-based models using partial least squares. In: SIBGRAPI (2009)
9. Prosser, B., Zheng, W., Gong, S., Xiang, T.: Person re-identification by support vector ranking. In: British Machine Vision Conference, pp. 1–11 (2010)
10. Lin, Z., Davis, L.S.: Learning pairwise dissimilarity profiles for appearance recognition in visual surveillance. In: Bebis, G., Boyle, R., Parvin, B., Koracin, D., Remagnino, P., Porikli, F., Peters, J., Klosowski, J., Arns, L., Chun, Y.K., Rhyne, T.-M., Monroe, L. (eds.) ISVC 2008, Part I. LNCS, vol. 5358, pp. 23–34. Springer, Heidelberg (2008)
11. Gray, D., Tao, H.: Viewpoint invariant pedestrian recognition with an ensemble of localized features. In: Forsyth, D., Torr, P., Zisserman, A. (eds.) ECCV 2008, Part I. LNCS, vol. 5302, pp. 262–275. Springer, Heidelberg (2008)
12. Zheng, W., Gong, S., Xiang, T.: Associating groups of people. In: British Machine Vision Conference (2009)
13. Bak, S., Corvee, E., Bremond, F., Thonnat, M.: Person re-identification using haarbased and DCD-based signature. In: Workshop on Activity Monitoring by Multi-Camera Surveillance Systems (2010)
14. Sivic, J., Zitnick, C.L., Szeliski, R.: Finding people in repeated shots of the same scene. In: Proceedings of the British Machine Vision Conference (2006)
15. Satta, R., Fumera, G., Roli, F., Cristani, M., Murino, V.: A multiple component matching framework for person re-identification. In: Maino, G., Foresti, G.L. (eds.) ICIAP 2011, Part II. LNCS, vol. 6979, pp. 140–149. Springer, Heidelberg (2011)
16. Bird, N., Masoud, O., Papanikolopoulos, N., Isaacs, A.: Detection of loitering individuals in public transportation areas. IEEE Trans. Intell. Transp. Syst. **6**(2), 167–177 (2005)
17. Gheissari, N., Sebastian, T.B., Tu, P.H., Rittscher, J., Hartley, R.: Person reidentification using spatiotemporal appearance. In: IEEE Conf. on Computer Vision and Pattern Recognition (CVPR), vol. 2, pp. 1528–1535 (2006)
18. Wang, X., Doretto, G., Sebastian, T.B., Rittscher, J., Tu, P.H.: Shape and appearance context modeling. In: IEEE Intl. Conf. on Computer Vision (ICCV), pp. 1–8 (2007)
19. Hamdoun, O., Moutarde, F., Stanciulescu, B., Steux, B.: Person re-identification in multicamera system by signature based on interest point descriptors collected on short video sequences. In: ACM/IEEE Intl. Conf. on Distributed Smart Cameras (ICDSC), pp. 1–6 (2008)
20. Tuzel, O., Porikli, F., Meer, P.: Pedestrian detection via classification on riemannian manifolds. IEEE Trans. PAMI, 1713–1727 (2008)
21. Bak, S., Corvee, E., Bremond, F., Thonnat, M.: Person re-identification using spatial covariance regions of human body parts. In: AVSS (2010)
22. Bak, S., Corvee, E., Bremond, F., Thonnat, M.: Multiple-shot human reidentification by mean riemannian covariance grid. In: Advanced Video and Signal-Based Surveillance, Klagenfurt, Autriche (2011)

23. TibShirani, R.: Regression Shrinkage and Selection via the Lasso. Journal of the Royal Statistics Society. Series B(Methodological) **58**(1), 267–288 (1996)
24. Prosser, B., Zheng, W., Gong, S., Xiang, T.: Person re-identification by support vector ranking. In: British Machine Vision Conference, pp. 1–11 (2010)
25. Forssén, P.E.: Maximally stable colour regions for recognition and matching. In: IEEE Conf. on Computer Vision and Pattern Recognition (CVPR) (2007)
26. Gray, D., Brennan, S., Tao, H.: Evaluating appearance models for recognition, reacquisition and tracking. In: IEEE Intl. Workshop on Performance Evaluation for Tracking and Surveillance (PETS) (2007)
27. VIPeR Dataset. http://vision.soe.ucsc.edu/?q=node/178
28. Caviar dataset (2004). http://homepages.inf.ed.ac.uk/rbf/CAVIAR/

Calibration Methodology for Distant Surveillance Cameras

Peter Gemeiner[(⊠)], Branislav Micusik, and Roman Pflugfelder

AIT Austrian Institute of Technology GmbH, Vienna, Austria
peter.gemeiner@ait.ac.at

Abstract. We present a practical method for video surveillance networks to calibrate their cameras which have mostly non-overlapping field of views and might be tens of meters apart. The calibration or estimating the camera pose, focal length and radial distortion is an essential requirement in video surveillance systems for any further automated tasks like person tracking or flow monitoring. The proposed methodology casts the calibration as a localization problem of an image with respect to a 3D model which is built a priori with a moving camera. The method comprises state-of-the-art functioning blocks, the Structure from Motion (SfM) and minimal Perspective-n-Point (PnP) solvers, which were proved stable in 3D computer vision community and applies them in context of video surveillance. We demonstrate that the calibration method is effective in difficult repetitive, reflective and texture less large indoor environments like an airport.

Keywords: Video surveillance · Networked cameras · Calibration

1 Introduction

Surveillance camera networks of environments like airports, train stations, shopping malls etc, are backbones of security and monitoring systems to prevent hazardous situations and to guarantee smooth operation and people flow. The networks consist of high number of cameras, in magnitude thousands, in heavily non-overlapping setup, tens of meters apart cameras. The non-overlapping setup reflects the fact that typically all entrance and exit points are covered, but not entire areas which would yield enormous number of the cameras. Tasks like automatic visual tracking of people, person re-identification, people flow monitoring across such networked cameras are tasks which on one side would automate the operation processes significantly, but on the other, still represent substantial scientific challenges.

The aforementioned tasks can be solved better when the spatial mutual positions of all the cameras are available. Estimating position and orientation of

This research has been supported by funding from the Austrian Research Promotion Agency (FFG) project LOLOG nº 3579656 and PAMON nº 835916 and from EU FP7 under grant agreement nº 257906.

© Springer International Publishing Switzerland 2015
L. Agapito et al. (Eds.): ECCV 2014 Workshops, Part III, LNCS 8927, pp. 162–173, 2015.
DOI: 10.1007/978-3-319-16199-0_12

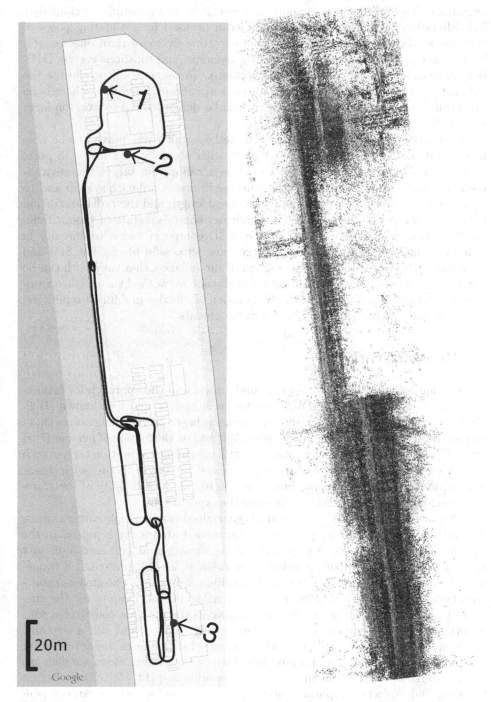

Fig. 1. Left side depicts three positions of calibrated surveillance cameras within the map of an airport terminal. Right side displays the reconstructed point cloud. This image is best viewed in color.

cameras which are tens meters apart, however, represent a significant challenge. No calibration target like a checkerboard can be used for estimating poses of cameras as the target cannot be seen in one time by more than one camera. To measure physically the distances of the cameras, and rotations e.g. by IMU, is cumbersome, very laborious and inaccurate. To use moving people for the calibration is rather theoretical than a practical concept. Therefore, there is no practically feasible methodology which would be demonstrated to work on large scale with acceptable effort of a user.

In this paper, we propose a practical method which was proved to be able to calibrate cameras which are 200m apart with accuracy of 1 meter in pose, as Fig. 1 shows. The main idea is to use as a calibration target the environment itself. It allows to bring all the cameras in one coordinate system and to estimate their internal parameters like the focal length and the radial distortion parameter in one go. The proposed methodology comprises state-of-the-art functioning blocks which were proved stable in 3D computer vision community in different context. In this paper, we merge those successful blocks, the SfM and minimal PnP solvers, and show in context of surveillance, that they both can be advantageously used for the calibration of distant networked surveillance cameras. Especially we demonstrate that calibration is effective in difficult repetitive, reflective and texture less large indoor environments.

2   Related Work

Calibration is theoretically sufficiently understood and the approach for estimation based on point and line correspondences is mature and well known [1][2]. Derived techniques for single surveillance cameras based on vanishing points [3][4], on foot-head homologies of visible persons [5][6] and on the motion of persons [7][8] exist. Nevertheless, surveillance companies still use simple calibration targets such as checkerboards in various sizes and sophisticated rigid rigs together with classic techniques based on point correspondences [9][10], as the reliability of the aforementioned techniques ist still not meeting the expectations.

This basic correspondence approach is generalisable to multiple camera views. A solution based on a laser pointer that is carried around by a person in the environment was shown by Svoboda et al. [11]. Funiak et al. [12] used a distinct marker carried by a person or robot. Deverajan et al. [13] presented a framework that takes the whole environment as calibration target. The environment's structure is assumed rigid and rich of matchable points. Despite all the success of these work, calibrating distant cameras, as the problem constitutes with a network of surveillance cameras, is surprisingly difficult and still a scientific challenge. The basic approach fails when cameras become more distant as either the point detection and matching breaks down or the camera views are disjoint.

To overcome these problems, a recent new approach [14][15][16] uses person tracking and exploits temporal continuity of the trajectory which can compensate the lack of correspondence. Unfortunately, it turned out that smoothness is a rather weak constraint compared to correspondence, hence the approach becomes for larger distances between cameras infeasible (larger times persons are immeasurable), a situation that happens frequently in surveillance applications.

The proposed approach combines Deverajan's idea to use the whole environment as calibration target, but instead of solely using the images of distant cameras which clearly limits reliable matching, the approach enriches the set of images by a large collection taken with a portable camera. Similar work has been done in 3D reconstruction where techniques for camera localisation based on sparse 3D point clouds exist [17][18][19].

3   Approach

The methodology works as follows. First, we reconstruct the environment by visiting a place with an additional calibrated camera, acquiring a sequence in a free walk, loop like, trajectory. This step employs a standard SfM pipeline and reconstructs the scene as a sparse cloud of 3D points. Second, the surveillance cameras are stitched to the 3D model by the re-sectioning PnP (Perspective-n-Point) algorithm from 2D-3D correspondences.

3.1   Portable Camera

Before calibrating surveillance cameras in a new environment an image acquisition with a portable camera has to take place. This portable camera has known internal parameters and is equipped with 180° FOV optics as depicted in Fig. 2. This wide FOV proved to have two following advantages comparing to a standard camera. First, it can deliver longer feature tracks, which is important in poorly textured environments. Second, it provides well spatially distributed projective rays, which helps for estimating the epipolar geometry much more robustly.

Fig. 2. Portable camera equipped with wide FOV optics

3.2   Structure from Motion

After capturing the image sequence of the new environment with the portable camera the next step is the reconstruction of this environment. However, due to the fact that the portable camera moved freely in space, without the usage of any additional sensors, its poses are unknown as well. Therefore the reconstruction of the unknown scene together with the camera poses leads to the classical SfM problem.

In recent years, several open-source SfM software packages appeared, e.g. Snavely's 'Bundler', which has roots in 'Photo tourism' [20] and the impressive 'Rome in a Day' project [21]. However, most of these SfM software packages include only perspective camera models, which is a dominant constraint for indoor spaces. The inclusion of an omni-directional camera model was the main reason why a custom SfM package has been developed within this work.

The custom SfM software used here contains the typical functional blocks:

- feature detection,
- establishing point correspondences,
- estimating pose between pairs of consecutive cameras,
- registration of all camera poses,
- triangulation of projective rays from point correspondences,
- loop-closing and
- non-linear optimization.

For feature detection several interest points together with their descriptors are selected (e.g. SIFT [22] and MSER [23]). The feature points are matched automatically in order to establish point correspondences, which are concatenated in tracks for more views. The matching process is assuming that the sequence of images is taken consecutively, which can help to reduce the amount of outliers in indoor spaces. However, the amount of outliers is still large and an epipolar geometry constraint is needed to validate them. For this validation the known five-point [24] algorithm is used and as a result the relative orientation and translation between a pair of images is obtained. With the help of these relative orientations and translations the projection matrices of all cameras are registered to the initial frame with linear method. In parallel to this, the reconstruction of the projective rays using the validated point correspondences is also linearly computed. To minimize the drift in scale, which typically appears in all odometry problems, the essential loop closing step is implemented as next step. With the help of this step additional point correspondences are found in images far apart from each other. In the last functional block, the linearly reconstructed points and camera poses are used for initialization for the non-linear optimization procedure. For this non-linear optimization the large framework called Bundle adjustment [25] is used, where as a cost function the reprojection error is selected.

3.3   Camera Calibration

Once the environment is reconstructed and represented as a sparse cloud of 3D points, the surveillance cameras are stitched to the 3D model with a re-sectioning algorithm. The re-sectioning, called also PnP (Perspective-n-Point) or absolute positioning, stands for determining the absolute position and orientation of a camera from a set of 2D-to-3D point correspondences. It is one of the most important problems in computer vision with a solid theoretical background and a broad range of applications.

In context of surveillance, the following PnP algorithms are of interest. In most general case, where no information about the cameras is available, minimal non-linear P4Pfr [26,27] or non-minimal linear P5Pfr [28] solvers estimating camera position, orientation, focal length and radial distortion from four or five 2D-to-3D correspondences, respectively, can be utilized. If the internal calibration of the surveillance cameras is known, e.g. obtained by one of the checkerboard methods or through vanishing point estimation, then the P3P [29] is applicable. If e.g. a vertical vanishing point is detectable in the images of the surveillance cameras or a gravity vector of the camera is known, then vP3Pf [30] or gP3Pf [31], respectively, can be employed. In general, more information about the cameras is available, more accurate result can be achieved. In all our experiments we consider the most general P4Pfr case where no information about the cameras is available, showing thus the upper limit of the inaccuracy in calibration.

An important step in using the PnP algorithms is to establish the 2D-to-3D correspondences between the image of the surveillance camera and the 3D model. Typically, the sequence of a moving camera is acquired between one to two meters above the floor level. The surveillance cameras, however, are mounted couple of meters above the floor level to observe better the area from an elevated location and not to be reachable by people. This results in a very wide baseline setting of the cameras which reconstructed the 3D model and the surveillance cameras. Our experience showed that the difference in a viewpoint is mostly so large that none of the available image descriptors, e.g. [32], is invariant enough to handle it. To confirm that, we evaluated state-of-the-art approaches [17] [18] [19] for the large scale image based localization. They use effective strategies like visual words, vocabulary trees, prioritized search, virtual cameras, and perform reasonably well for localizing images which are spatially close to the images used for building the 3D model. However, in case of surveillance cameras the methods were ineffective in all our experiments. A fully automatic matching in this application domain therefore still remains a challenge.

Instead, we designed a simple GUI for establishing those 2D-to-3D correspondences manually. Experiments showed that only 6 to 10 correspondences are sufficient to get reasonable estimate and it is rather fast and not very laborious task. Despite that the matching is done manually, the whole concept shows its very high potential for calibrating purposes, indicating sufficient accuracy for following automated surveillance application like person tracking and people flow monitoring.

4   Experimental Results

The methodology presented here can be used for the calibration of surveillance cameras, which are mounted at larger distances from each other in different environments, outdoor or indoor. In this paper, however, we show the most difficult case, the indoor scenario, as very difficult for SfM and PnP algorithms. Humans typically design indoor spaces so that they contain reflective surfaces, glass elements, narrow corridors, and almost no texture. In general, these properties cause problems to establishing point correspondences and bring most of the matching algorithms into failure. Despite that we demonstrate on real hard environments the possibility to cope with these problems and present a working method composed of our developed custom SfM software based on large FOV optics and of available PnP algorithms.

The custom SfM software has been tested in different indoor environments: two international airports and two office buildings. The image acquisition of these

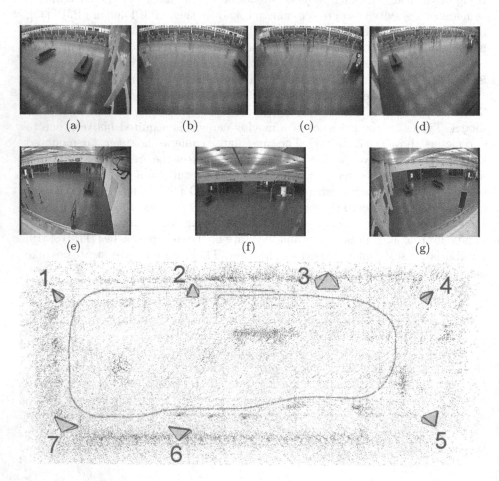

Fig. 3. The two top rows show seven views from the surveillance cameras at the Airport Vienna. The bottom image depicts the reconstructed environment as a sparse point cloud, the trajectory of the portable camera as a red line and the seven surveillance cameras calibrated with the presented methodology. This image is best viewed in color.

environments contains single loop captured in continues shutter mode with an partial overlap of the captured images and baseline of roughly 30cm. Ground Truth is not available for the presented sequences, therefore, as a way to quantitatively judge the result, we compare the estimated positions of the surveillance cameras to the wall or ceiling which are visible in the sparse 3D models. We roughly know where all the cameras are and how they align to each other. Moreover, for the airport sequence (see Fig. 1), to even better judge the results, we overlay the reconstructed trajectory and the position of the surveillance cameras with the Google Maps.

The first presented sequence is the Terminal from an airport. Fig. 1 shows the estimated position of the surveillance cameras and the sparse cloud of 3D points. This is the largest reconstruction in this paper, it contains eight partial reconstructions, stitched semi-automatically together. The covered area is about 40m x 200m. One can notice that the estimated trajectory of the moving camera is correctly estimated as it does not cross the walls and mainly follows the open space. We calibrate three surveillance cameras which are 200m apart and whose estimated poses roughly correspond to their true locations in the map. Due to security reasons, no screenshots from the surveillance cameras can be published.

The second sequence is from the international airport of Vienna, see Fig.3. This environment similarly to the previous sequence contains reflective surfaces,

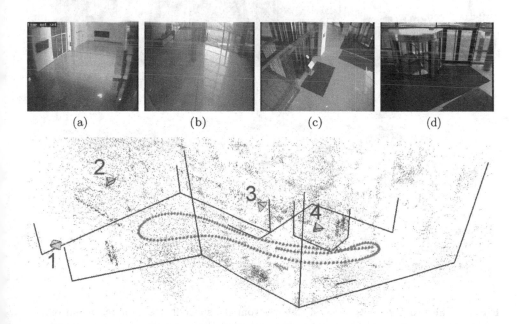

(a)   (b)   (c)   (d)

Fig. 4. The top row shows four views from the surveillance cameras in an office environment. The bottom image depicts the reconstructed environment as a sparse point cloud, the trajectory of the portable camera as a red line, and four surveillance cameras calibrated with the presented methodology. This image is best viewed in color.

very few textured objects, and almost one color floor, which make it very difficult for the SfM and calibration. We calibrated 7 cameras which are mounted in a way that the camera centers lie on two parallel lines aligned with two opposite walls. This was correctly reconstructed, as can be seen in Fig.3.

The next sequence is a hall of a modern office building depicted in Fig. 4 which is very similar to the large infrastructure buildings as e.g. airports or train stations. All the lines in the 3D model were additionally reconstructed through manual correspondences in order to improve visualization and better judge the estimated poses of the four surveillance cameras. All these cameras

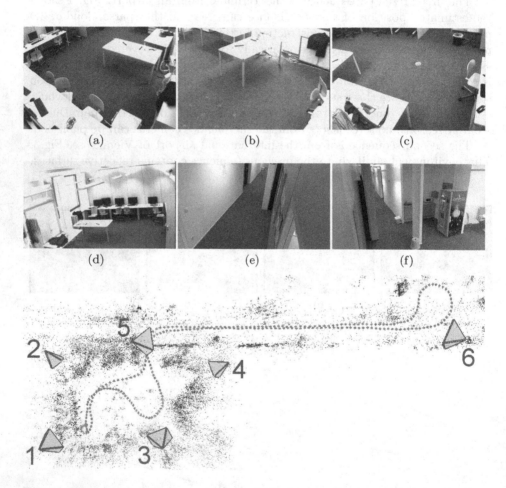

Fig. 5. The two top rows show six views from the surveillance cameras in an office / corridor environment. The bottom image depicts the reconstructed environment as a sparse point cloud, the trajectory of the portable camera as a red line, and six surveillance cameras calibrated with the presented methodology. This image is best viewed in color.

are aligned in reality but also in the estimation with the walls bounded by the reconstructed lines.

The last sequence is a narrow office corridor, shown in Fig. 5. Here, we had to visit one of the rooms as the surveillance cameras were mounted along the corridor and in the room as well. We had to enter and leave again the room through a door which is one of the most difficult situations in indoor SfM and SLAM community. The door causes separation of the room and the corridor spaces and it is hard to keep necessary amount of tracks for successful pose estimation. However, as the result shows, the reconstructed 3D structure is feasible and useful for further calibration of 6 cameras. The estimated positions of the six cameras visually align with their true locations.

To summarize, for all the sequences from various environments, our comparisons indicate accuracy in the pose estimation of the surveillance cameras to be under 1m. This is far sufficient for further tasks like multi cameras person tracking, people flow monitoring across networks of distant cameras.

5   Conclusions

We presented a practical methodology for calibrating very distant surveillance cameras, apart tens of meters, in difficult indoor environments, poorly textured, full of repetitiveness, and reflections. We show that building on well researched parts in geometry community of computer vision area, namely Structure from Motion and Perspective-and-Point algorithms, a sufficiently accurate and practically interesting method can be brought into the video surveillance field. The method does not require a laborious placement of any calibration target, and when managing fully automatic matching, a large number of cameras could be conveniently calibrated. To the best of our knowledge, this is the first work which demonstrates a calibration method on large airport scenario with cameras hundreds meters apart.

Acknowledgements. Authors would like to thank Gustavo Fernandez and Georg Nebehay for the help with the image acquisition. Authors are also gratefull to the smart camera lab at University of Klagenfurt for their help with the experiments.

References

1. Faugeras, O., Luong, Q.T., Papadopoulou, T.: The Geometry of Multiple Images: The Laws That Govern The Formation of Images of A Scene and Some of Their Applications. MIT Press (2001)
2. Hartley, R.I., Zisserman, A.: Multiple View Geometry in Computer Vision, 2nd edn. Cambridge University Press (2004)
3. Wildenauer, H., Hanbury, A.: Robust camera self-calibration from monocular images of manhattan worlds. In: Proc. CVPR (2012)
4. Wildenauer, H., Micusik, B.: Closed form solution for radial distortion estimation from a single vanishing point. In: Proc. BMVC (2013)

5. Krahnstoever, N., Mendonca, P.: Bayesian autocalibration for surveillance. In: Proc. ICCV (2005)
6. Micusik, B., Pajdla, T.: Simultaneous surveillance camera calibration and foot-head homology estimation from human detections. In: Proc. CVPR (2010)
7. Rahimi, A., Dunagan, B., Darrell, T.: Tracking people with a sparse network of bearing sensors. In: Pajdla, T., Matas, J.G. (eds.) ECCV 2004. LNCS, vol. 3024, pp. 507–518. Springer, Heidelberg (2004)
8. Krahnstoever, N., Mendona, P.R.S.: Autocalibration from tracks of walking people. In: Proc. BMVC (2006)
9. Heikkila, J., Silven, O.: A four-step camera calibration procedure with implicit image correction. In: Proc. CVPR (1997)
10. Zhang, Z., Zhang, Z.: A flexible new technique for camera calibration. IEEE Transactions on Pattern Analysis and Machine Intelligence 22, 1330–1334 (1998)
11. Svoboda, T., Martinec, D., Pajdla, T.: A convenient multicamera self-calibration for virtual environments. Presence: Teleoperators and Virtual Environments 14(4), 407–422 (2005)
12. Funiak, S., Guestrin, C., Paskin, M., Sukthankar, R.: Distributed localization of networked cameras. In: Proc. IPSN (2006)
13. Devarajan, D., Cheng, Z., Radke, R.: Calibrating distributed camera networks. Proceedings of the IEEE 96(10), 1625–1639 (2008)
14. Rahimi, A., Dunagan, B., Darrell, T.: Simultaneous calibration and tracking with a network of non-overlapping sensors. In: Proc. CVPR (2004)
15. Rudoy, M., Rohrs, C.: Enhanced simultaneous camera calibration and path estimation. In: Proc. ACSSC (2006)
16. Picus, C., Pflugfelder, R., Micusik, B.: Auto-calibration of non-overlapping multi-camera CCTV systems. In: Shan, C., Porikli, F., Xiang, T., Gong, S. (eds.) Video Analytics for Business Intelligence. SCI, vol. 409, pp. 43–67. Springer, Heidelberg (2012)
17. Irschara, A., Zach, C., Frahm, J.M., Bischof, H.: From structure-from-motion point clouds to fast location recognition. In: Proc. CVPR (2009)
18. Sattler, T., Leibe, B., Kobbelt, L.: Fast image-based localization using direct 2D-to-3D matching. In: Proc. ICCV (2011)
19. Sattler, T., Leibe, B., Kobbelt, L.: Improving image-based localization by active correspondence search. In: Fitzgibbon, A., Lazebnik, S., Perona, P., Sato, Y., Schmid, C. (eds.) ECCV 2012, Part I. LNCS, vol. 7572, pp. 752–765. Springer, Heidelberg (2012)
20. Snavely, N., Seitz, S.M., Szeliski, R.: Photo tourism: Exploring photo collections in 3D. ACM Transactions on Graphics (SIGGRAPH Proceedings) 25(3), 835–846 (2006)
21. Agarwal, S., Snavely, N., Simon, I., Seitz, S., Szeliski, R.: Building rome in a day. In: International Conference on Computer Vision (2009)
22. Lowe, D.G.: Distinctive image features from scale-invariant keypoints. International Journal of Computer Vision 60, 91–110 (2004)
23. Matas, J., Chum, O., Urban, M., Pajdla, T.: Robust wide baseline stereo from maximally stable extremal regions. In: British Machine Vision Conference, pp. 384–393 (2002)
24. Nister, D.: An efficient solution to the five-point relative pose problem. IEEE Pattern Analysis and Machine Intelligence 26(6), 756–770 (2004)
25. Triggs, B., McLauchlan, P.F., Hartley, R.I., Fitzgibbon, A.W.: Bundle adjustment – a modern synthesis. In: Triggs, B., Zisserman, A., Szeliski, R. (eds.) ICCV-WS 1999. LNCS, vol. 1883, pp. 298–372. Springer, Heidelberg (2000)

26. Josephson, K., Byröd, M.: Pose estimation with radial distortion and unknown focal length. In: Proc. CVPR (2009)
27. Bujnak, M., Kukelova, Z., Pajdla, T.: New efficient solution to the absolute pose problem for camera with unknown focal length and radial distortion. In: Kimmel, R., Klette, R., Sugimoto, A. (eds.) ACCV 2010, Part I. LNCS, vol. 6492, pp. 11–24. Springer, Heidelberg (2011)
28. Kukelova, Z., Bujnak, M., Pajdla, T.: Real-time solution to the absolute pose problem with unknown radial distortion and focal length. In: Proc. ICCV (2013)
29. Kneip, L., Scaramuzza, D., Siegwart, R.: A novel parametrization of the perspective-three-point problem for a direct computation of absolute camera position and orientation. In: Proc. CVPR (2011)
30. Micusik, B., Wildenauer, H.: Minimal solution for uncalibrated absolute pose problem with a known vanishing point. In: Proc. 3DV (2013)
31. Kukelova, Z., Bujnak, M., Pajdla, T.: Closed-form solutions to minimal absolute pose problems with known vertical direction. In: Kimmel, R., Klette, R., Sugimoto, A. (eds.) ACCV 2010, Part II. LNCS, vol. 6493, pp. 216–229. Springer, Heidelberg (2011)
32. Lowe, D.G.: Distinctive image features from scale-invariant keypoints. IJCV 60(2), 91–110 (2004)

Improving Global Multi-target Tracking
with Local Updates

Anton Milan[1]([⊠]), Rikke Gade[2], Anthony Dick[1], Thomas B. Moeslund[2],
and Ian Reid[1]

[1] University of Adelaide, Adelaide, Australia
anton.milan@adelaide.edu.au
[2] Aalborg University, Aalborg, Denmark

Abstract. We propose a scheme to explicitly detect and resolve ambiguous situations in multiple target tracking. During periods of uncertainty, our method applies multiple local single target trackers to hypothesise short term tracks. These tracks are combined with the tracks obtained by a global multi-target tracker, if they result in a reduction in the global cost function. Since tracking failures typically arise when targets become occluded, we propose a local data association scheme to maintain the target identities in these situations. We demonstrate a reduction of up to 50 % in the global cost function, which in turn leads to superior performance on several challenging benchmark sequences. Additionally, we show tracking results in sports videos where poor video quality and frequent and severe occlusions between multiple players pose difficulties for state-of-the-art trackers.

Keywords: Multi-target tracking · Data association

1 Introduction

Tracking multiple objects in a dynamic environment is crucial for visual scene understanding. Some of the most relevant applications for this task include driver assistance, visual surveillance, and sports analysis. The problem itself consists of localising each target in every single time instance *as well as* correctly maintaining each target's identity over time. This latter task is often referred to as *data association* and can be solved by existing methods as long as all targets remain sufficiently far apart from one another. However, challenges arise when several targets come close together causing intersecting or intertwined trajectories. In such situations, recovering each individual's identity has a combinatorial complexity in the number of tracks and measurements, and thus quickly becomes

Electronic supplementary material The online version of this chapter (doi:10.1007/978-3-319-16199-0_13) contains supplementary material, which is available to authorized users. Videos can also be accessed at http://www.springerimages.com/videos/978-3-319-16198-3.

L. Agapito et al. (Eds.): ECCV 2014 Workshops, Part III, LNCS 8927, pp. 174–190, 2015.
DOI: 10.1007/978-3-319-16199-0_13

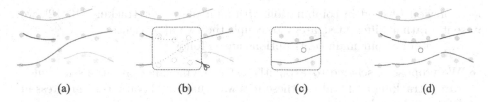

(a)   (b)   (c)   (d)

Fig. 1. Overview of our optimisation algorithm. Given a possibly erroneous solution *(a)*, we locate each error *(b)* and perform a local optimisation within its neighbourhood *(c)*. The newly obtained solution is inserted back into the original one if and only if it increases the overall likelihood considering all remaining frames and targets *(d)*.

infeasible. In addition, the task is complicated further by noisy sensor data with imprecise localisation, false alarms, and missing measurements.

Most current approaches to multi-target tracking are based on *tracking by detection* [1–6]. Here, tracks are formed by linking detections obtained independently in each frame in a preprocessing step. This helps to avoid tracker drift, but usually depends on a pre-defined target model which is trained offline. When tracking by detection, more accurate results have been obtained by so-called *global* methods that consider a batch of several frames (or even an entire video sequence) jointly as opposed to determining the state based only on previous observations [7,8]. The rationale here is that potential ambiguities may be resolved more easily once more evidence is acquired. However one must accept a delay in the output as a tradeoff for better accuracy.

Although tracking by detection approaches achieve state-of-the-art results, they struggle in those situations where the detector provides little to no evidence for the presence of a target. Detector failures may arise for numerous reasons, such as low image contrast, partial or complete occlusions, or abrupt and significant change in appearance due to lighting, posture, or object size. Even though short detection dropouts in certain, unambiguous areas can usually be bridged robustly by global optimisation techniques, correctly resolving data association remains challenging in cases where several targets merge on the image plane obstructing each other's line of sight. Long term occlusions or ambiguities are even more challenging, as the number of feasible association combinations increases with the time interval considered.

We propose to exploit the power of *model-free visual trackers* to 'untangle' tracks in such challenging situations (see Fig. 1 for an illustration). Model-free trackers do not rely on pre-existing detections, instead building an online model of target appearance based purely on an instance of the target appearing in a single frame. The performance of visual object trackers has increased dramatically in recent years [9] making them robust to appearance change and partial occlusion, which is a desirable property for solving the problem at hand. Moreover, we propose a strategy to integrate model-free visual object tracking into a multi-target tracking setting. Although visual trackers have, in one way or another, been previously used in combination with multiple target tracking [10–12], we present a rather different strategy to couple the two approaches.

In particular, our main contributions are as follows:

- We propose a scheme to explicitly detect challenging situations in multi-target tracking and address these in a way that builds on recent progress in both single and multi-target tracking.
- We apply model-free visual trackers to several targets simultaneously in order to resolve difficult situations locally.
- We integrate visual trackers into a multi-target tracking framework to find improved optima of the objective function by making local changes.
- We demonstrate the validity of our approach on particularly challenging sports videos.

We argue that our approach is able to drive the optimisation much quicker towards improved local minima leading to a substantial increase in performance both visually and quantitatively. Our experiments show superior performance on several challenging benchmark sequences.

2   Related Work

The popularity of multi-target tracking in computer vision has increased dramatically in the recent past leading to a large amount of related literature. In this section we will concentrate on the most important work related mainly to offline multi-target tracking approaches. Despite their limitation of a delayed output, offline approaches to multi-target tracking have become increasingly popular due to their superior accuracy. The main difference to online (or recursive) approaches, such as Kalman filters [13,14] or particle filters [7,8] is that instead of processing each frame as soon as it is obtained, the optimisation of an objective function is performed on a batch of consecutive frames simultaneously. These methods are usually more robust at dealing with false positives or occlusions.

Offline Multi-target Tracking. The main difference between approaches lies in the exact formulation of the objective function and its optimisation strategy. Jiang *et al.* [15] solve an integer linear program using LP-relaxation to obtain a (nearly) optimal solution. However, the number of targets in the scene needs to be fixed a-priori. Zhang *et al.* [1] reformulate the task as a network flow problem, which can be solved in polynomial time using min-cost flow algorithms. Occlusions are handled by inserting target hypotheses in a greedy fashion. Their approach served as a starting point for a similar strategy [16], which followed a greedy optimisation scheme and was thus much more efficient. Another globally optimal approach, which explicitly models merged measurements is presented in [17]. Individual tracks are however resolved using a simple shortest paths strategy, which may result in intersecting paths. More recently, Liu *et al.* [5]

use a network-flow approach to recover long-term trajectories of sports players using context-aware motion models, while Butt and Collins [18] integrate high-order dynamic terms. A coupling of object detection and tracking has been proposed in [19,20] with a quadratic and linear objective, respectively. Further formulations to solve for data association include graph-based approaches, such maximum weight independent set [21] set-cover [22] and generalised minimum clique graphs [4].

A slightly different way to solve the task is to concentrate on reconstructing trajectories rather than on data association and only implicitly handle the latter. A regularly discretised space allows one to pose the problem as an integer linear program, which is solved to global optimality by LP-relaxation [23] or by the k-shortest paths algorithm [2]. To overcome the limitation imposed by the discrete grid, a purely continuous state space is used in [6]. However, such an accurate description of the complex task leads to a highly non-convex optimisation problem which is minimised locally by gradient descent augmented with heuristic discontinuous jumps. A more elegant discrete-continuous energy was later proposed in [24], where both trajectory estimation and data association are handled simultaneously by minimising a single objective.

The main motivation for designing such complex objective functions [6,19,21, 24] is to describe the problem at hand as accurately as possible. Although they obtain state of the art results, they are difficult to optimise and often become trapped in local minima. In practice, this manifests in tracking errors such as fragmented trajectories or confused target identities. In this work we focus on overcoming these errors by applying recent results from single target tracking.

Model-Free Tracking. Recent advances in visual single object tracking [25–27] have also adopted the tracking by detection paradigm. However, rather than train the detector offline, so-called *model-free* trackers train a classifier to separate the target from its background, using positive and negative training examples gathered while tracking. This has the advantage of requiring only initialisation in a single frame and of training a detector specifically for the current appearance of the target. Several methods have been applied to the task, including multiple instance learning [28], structured output learning [26], metric learning [29] and kernel methods [27].

In general, model-free tracking methods are successful over short time periods but their performance degrades over longer time spans, or when target appearance changes significantly. By using them to correct short term errors in long term tracks obtained by global methods, we play to the strength of these two different approaches. Because the model-free tracker operates only on the output of the global tracker, it is independent of its implementation and can therefore be combined with any of the above tracking frameworks. The final result is still obtained by optimising the global objective function; the short term tracks are simply used to generate plausible hypotheses, which the optimiser can use to break out of local minima.

Other recent work has also demonstrated the use of single target visual trackers within multi-target tracking. In [10], contours of multiple objects of arbitrary shape are represented using level-sets and an underlying generative model determines location, depth ordering and segmentation of each target. Similarly, a level-set tracker is also applied in the context of pedestrian tracking from a moving camera in [11], where sparse person detections are augmented with the temporally varying target contours provided by the low-level tracker. Izadinia *et al.* [30] detect pedestrians using the deformable part-based model [31] and in addition to tracking entire people, trajectories of their individual body parts are recovered. In [12], multi-target tracking is based on both, detections from an offline object detector and a visual tracker output. The decision on which cue to use is made based on a pre-trained model using several features such as detector response or optic flow. Zhang *et al.* [32] also propose to couple several individual trackers by enforcing to preserve the spatial structure between all targets over time. While this may help to resolve data association in certain cases where objects tend to exhibit similar motion patterns, it is not generally applicable to arbitrary people tracking, in particular sports videos with abrupt and erratic target motion.

Our method is different from previous work in the following aspects: (i) We exploit the power of visual trackers explicitly in difficult situations. To this end, we localise difficult situations in the space-time volume and use the output of multiple coupled single target trackers to generate a strong set of local hypotheses. (ii) We present a local data association scheme for single target trackers. To avoid clumping and identity switching between individual trackers, we follow a simple, yet effective technique based on bipartite graph matching. (iii) We integrate the output of single target trackers into a global energy minimisation method. To avoid potential drift caused by online learned trackers, the local solution is verified in the global context using a robust multiple target objective.

3   Multi-target Tracking by Energy Minimisation

In this work, we follow the recent trend and address multi-target tracking by minimising a highly complex energy function. We use the discrete-continuous formulation proposed in [24]. Note, however, that our method is generic and does not rely on any specific formulation of the underlying objective function.

A weakness of any non-convex global objective is that it may become trapped in local minima, which results in fragmented or incorrectly associated tracks. To remedy this, we propose to focus explicitly on those solution regions that are most likely to be erroneous and to guide the optimisation toward alternative solutions using single target tracking with local data association. The entire algorithm is summarised in Algorithm 1, and the individual steps are illustrated in Figure 1.

We now describe in more detail each of the steps in the algorithm.

Algorithm 1. Tracking multiple targets by local and global optimisation

input : Initial global solution S (Sec. 3.1)
output: Final trajectories
while ¬ *converged* **do**

    Find next error Ξ in current solution S (Section 3.2)
    Optimise locally within spatio-temporal neighbourhood of Ξ to obtain $\hat{S}$
    (Sec. 3.3, 3.4)
    Stitch partial solution $\hat{S}$ into global solution S, if global cost is reduced
    (Sec. 3.5)

end

3.1 Global Data Association

In our formulation, multi-target tracking is performed by optimising a discrete-continuous objective, where both data association and trajectory estimation are solved for by minimising a single energy function. Given a set of target detections $\mathbf{D} = d_1, \ldots, d_D$ within a video sequence of F frames, the goal is to find the most likely solution for assigning a unique target identifier to each detection, and at the same time to estimate a continuous trajectory for each target.

Following the notation of [24], we represent the state space by two sets of variables. A discrete set $\mathbf{f} = f_1, \ldots, f_D$ determines the data association, where each variable takes on a label l from the label set $\mathbf{L} = \{1, \ldots, L, \varnothing\}$ which corresponds to a specific target (or a false alarm). A set of continuous variables $\mathcal{T}$ describes the shape of all trajectories under consideration, where each trajectory is represented by piecewise polynomials.

The discrete part of the energy is posed as a graphical model with unary and pairwise potentials and label costs [33]:

$$E(\mathbf{f}) = \phi_d + \psi_{d,d'} + h_{\mathbf{f}} + h_{\mathbf{f}}^{\mathsf{X}}, \tag{1}$$

while the continuous part controls the trajectories:

$$E(\mathcal{T}) = \phi_{\mathcal{T}} + h_{\mathbf{f}} + h_{\mathbf{f}}^{\mathsf{X}}. \tag{2}$$

In a nutshell, the unary (or data) terms ϕ measure how well the trajectory hypotheses fit the observations, the pairwise terms ψ enforce spatio-temporal smoothness in the labelling, and the label cost models a prior on individual trajectories ($h_{\mathbf{f}}$), such as target dynamics or track persistence, as well as on pairs of tracks ($h_{\mathbf{f}}^{\mathsf{X}}$) to suppress implausible solutions with strongly overlapping trajectories. The complete energy is then minimised by alternately fixing one set of variables at a time, generating the initial solution S. For more details, we refer the reader to [24].

3.2 Error Detection

Given an initial solution hypothesis S, our goal is to localise errors within this solution and correct them. Several types of local error may exist, including split tracks, swapped identities and merged trajectories. The importance of each error type is application specific, but to demonstrate our approach, we focus only on the most obvious error type that is also convenient to detect, namely an interrupted trajectory. Under the assumption that the scene does not contain any doors or large scene occluders where people may disappear indefinitely, a target that enters the field of view must ideally remain tracked until it leaves the scene. Therefore, any trajectory T_i that terminates prematurely and not close to the image border is considered a candidate for improvement. In practice, this is likely to overestimate the number of locations at which errors may occur. This does not detract from the final solution as, in the case of a genuine track endpoint, all hypothesised track joins are likely to result in a higher overall cost, and therefore the initial solution will be unchanged.

Let $\mathbf{x}_i^t$ be the (x, y) location of target i in frame t. Further, let t_i^* denote either the first or the last frame in which target i exists. An error $\Xi = \{x_i, y_i, t_i^*\}$ is possibly present at the spatio-temporal location $\mathbf{x}_i^{t_i^*}$ if and only if $1 < t < F$ and $\beta(\mathbf{x}_i^{t_i^*}) > \tau$. $\beta(\cdot)$ computes the distance to the closest image border and τ is a margin where trajectories are allowed to terminate, which is set to 100 pixels in our experiments.

3.3 Choosing the Local Optimisation Region

To optimise the solution locally, we consider a spatio-temporal window around each detected error. In particular, we optimise over the temporal window $\Omega = \{t - k, \ldots, t + k\}$, where k is fixed to 10 frames in our experiments. This time span is usually long enough to resolve an ambiguity, but still local enough to rely on the output of a visual tracker.

It remains to determine which existing trajectories are involved in the current error and should be re-estimated within Ω. On one hand, it is desirable to reduce the current problem to the smallest possible subset to enable efficient optimisation. On the other hand, discarding too many concurrent trajectories may lead to conflicts in the later step when the two solutions are to be merged. In a typical setting, trajectories that are far apart from one another are independent. A reasonable trade off therefore is to only consider a small subset of trajectories $T^* \subset T$ which is within a neighbourhood Σ of the error Ξ. To determine the neighbourhood, we create a short auxiliary trajectory $\hat{T}$ by tracking the target back and forth within the temporal window Ω, initialised from the error Ξ. To reduce the state space for the optimisation while at the same time not ignoring important dependencies, we consider only those detections d_i that are within a certain radius of $\hat{T}$ during the local optimisation (*cf.* Fig. 1 (c)). Formally, the set of target candidates is reduced to

$$\hat{\mathbf{D}} = \{d_i | t_i \in \Omega, \|\mathbf{d}_i - \hat{T}^{t_i}\| < 2s\}, \tag{3}$$

where $\mathbf{d}_i$ denotes the spatial and t_i the temporal location of detection i, respectively, and s is the target size.

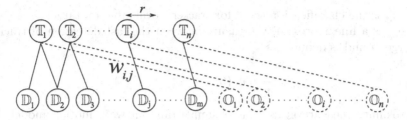

Fig. 2. Example of the bipartite graph that must be solved for each frame. Each tracker $\mathbb{T}_i$ is connected to all detections $\mathbb{D}_j$ that lie within its search radius and to one occlusion node $\mathbb{O}_i$.

3.4 Local Optimisation

In principle, any existing method can be used to find a plausible solution within the spatio-temporal neighbourhood of the detected error. To guide the optimisation into more promising regions, we exploit single target visual trackers in combination with local data association to generate likely trajectory hypotheses. To this end, we initiate a tracker $\mathbb{T}_i$ from each terminating point of each trajectory $\mathcal{T}_i$ in $\mathcal{T}^*$ that is involved in the error $\varXi$. In our experiments we employ a recent tracker by Henriques *et al.* [27]. We use the implementation distributed by the authors. In practice, its high robustness and speed make it feasible to quickly generate many short term track hypotheses, although again other single target trackers could also be used. The resulting tracks form a set of strong candidates for selection in the optimisation procedure.

Traditional single target tracking-by-detection algorithms consider only the single detection in each frame with maximum classification score. In order to solve ambiguous situations where several trackers may detect the same target, we extend this approach by including other possible targets. We include all non-overlapping detections whose classification score is more than 10% of the maximum classification score for the individual tracker. The task of local data association is then to optimise the associations between a set of individually trained trackers $\mathbb{T}$ and the set of detections $\mathbb{D}$ for each frame. By representing this association problem in a bipartite graph we are able to find an optimal solution using the Hungarian algorithm. In order to handle occlusions we also introduce an occlusion node for each tracker, which accounts for fully occluded targets. Figure 2 illustrates an example of the bipartite graph for one frame.

Each tracker $\mathbb{T}_i$, $i = 1, \ldots, n$, is initialised, and linked to m detections $\mathbb{D}_1, \ldots, \mathbb{D}_m$ and its respective occlusion node $\mathbb{O}_i$. Edges between trackers and detections with a distance larger than the search radius r have weights zero and are therefore omitted in Figure 2. The size of r is chosen as the mean of the height and width of the target. The weight assigned to each edge combines the appearance measure given by the classification score and a proximity measure that penalises large spatial jumps between consecutive frames:

$$w_{i,j} = s_{i,j} \cdot p_{i,j}, \tag{4}$$

where $s_{i,j}$ is the classification score for tracker i evaluated on target j, scaled to $[0, 1]$. $p_{i,j}$ is a linear proximity measure between the last detection of tracker i and target j and is defined as

$$p_{i,j} = \frac{1}{r} \max \left(0, r - \|\mathbb{T}_i^{t-1} - \mathbb{D}_j\|\right). \tag{5}$$

The proximity measure is used as a simple random walk motion model. Particularly in sports the motion may be abrupt, therefore, we choose this zero displacement model rather than assuming constant velocity.

Edges connecting a tracker to its occlusion node are assigned a low weight, which is empirically chosen as 8% of the maximum classification score in order to be lower than real detections.

3.5   Combining Local and Global Solutions

To stay consistent with the overall formulation, we minimise the same discrete-continuous objective function as is used to evaluate the quality of the complete solution on the spatio-temporal subset $\{\Sigma, \Omega\}$ using track hypotheses from Section 3.4. After the optimisation, the resulting solution $\hat{S}$ replaces the original solution within $\{\Sigma, \Omega\}$ if the overall energy $E(\hat{S} \cup \tilde{S})$ is decreased. $\tilde{S}$ is obtained by simply removing all partial trajectories from S that lie within the spatio-temporal neighbourhood $\{\Sigma, \Omega\}$ of the error.

4   Experiments

Datasets. We demonstrate our approach on eight different sequences. The first set consists of six publicly available videos including the PETS 2009 benchmark [34][1] and TUD Stadtmitte [35]. All videos show pedestrians in a single view but they exhibit a large variation in person count, camera viewpoint and motion patterns. Since the camera calibration is available for this dataset, we perform tracking on the ground plane in world coordinates.

As well as evaluating on standard benchmarks, we also demonstrate the performance on difficult sports tracking data. In particular we show tracking on two sequences in the challenging sport of Australian Rules Football (AFL), in which there is regular and frequent crowding of players and contact between them, making it a very difficult tracking problem. We make this new dataset including the ground truth annotations and the detections used in this work publicly available[2].

Metrics. Quantifying performance of multiple target tracking is a notoriously difficult task [36]. Ambiguities in annotations, assignments strategies and metric descriptions prohibit a purely objective evaluation. Here we follow the most

---

[1] Sequences: S2L1, S2L2, S2L3, S1L1-2, S1L2-1.
[2] http://research.milanton.net/data

widely used strategy and report several metrics for all our experiments. Next to standard precision and recall figures we report the CLEAR MOT metrics [37], which consists of tracking accuracy (MOTA) and tracking precision (MOTP). The former combines three error types: false positives, missed targets and identity switches, into a single number such that zero errors corresponds to 100%. The latter measures the localisation error of the tracker w.r.t. the annotated ground truth. Moreover, we also show the number of correctly recovered trajectories as proposed in [38]. A target is considered mostly tracked (MT), if it is correctly detected in over 80% of frames within its time span. Similarly, a mostly lost (ML) trajectory is only recover in 20% of frames or less. Finally, the numbers of track fragmentations and identity switches are stated for completeness.

Before presenting the overall tracking performance of our system, we discuss the importance of local data association for single target trackers and illustrate the potential of our locally driven optimisation scheme measured by the reduction of the total cost. We then provide an extensive quantitative evaluation on various challenging sequences and compare our results to several state-of-the-art methods.

4.1 Local Data Association

Let us first qualitatively demonstrate the effect of local data association using multiple model free trackers in situations with a high presence of occlusions.

Figure 3 shows two comparisons between tracking with and without local data association. The first sequence is from the PETS 2009 S2L2 dataset, and the second one is a challenging situation from an AFL game. The images are cropped for better visibility. In all cases model-free trackers are initialised for each target depicted with bounding boxes in the left most image. The 1st and 3rd rows show the results of running the two, respectively three trackers individually, without local data association. In rows two and four the results are obtained by including the Hungarian data association described in Section 3.4. The results show clearly that the individual trackers are prone to drift in settings with multiple persons. In row 1 the identity switches and the blue target is lost after occlusion. By including local data association these situations are resolved, and the two targets are correctly tracked even after full occlusions. In the 3rd row without data association the three trackers clump together and follow the same person which yields the highest classifier score for each of the trackers after the occlusion. The local data association shown in the 4th row again resolves this situation and keeps tracking the three individual persons while maintaining their correct identities.

To quantify the importance of multiple tracker reasoning, we minimise the global objective with and without explicit local data association (no LDA) for proposal generation. Experimental results are reported in the following sections.

Fig. 3. Visual trackers without (1st and 3rd rows) and with (2nd and 4th rows) local data association. See text for details.

4.2   Energy Minimisation

To verify the potential of our approach, we compare the magnitude of the initial solution S of the overall energy to the final solution obtained after including local tracks. Figure 4 shows the relative energy decrease for various sequences. The energy is scaled in each case such that the initial point, which is obtained by [24], corresponds to 100%. It is important to note that we minimise the exact same energy without introducing new detections. By focusing on erroneous regions and by exploiting model-free trackers for better hypothesis generation, our proposed local optimisation can find a lower global cost in nearly every iteration and an overall reduction of over 50% in some cases. Dotted lines for the AFL sequences show the energy reduction using proposals of independent single target trackers without local data association. One iteration takes approximately one second to compute on a standard PC. We set the maximum number of iteration to 150 in all our experiments.

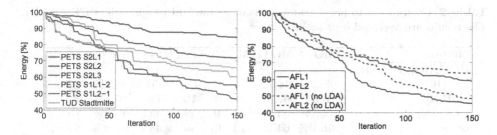

Fig. 4. Minimising a global energy function by focusing on local optimisation windows. The dotted plots on the right hand side depict the energy minimised by our scheme by only using independent single target trackers *without* local data association (no LDA).

Table 1. Quantitative results on two AFL sequences. Best result across all methods is highlighted in bold face for each measure.

Method	MOTA	MOTP	MT	ML	Frag.	ID sw.	Precision	Recall
FFP Detector [39]	–	–	–	–	–	–	65.4%	55.0%
SMOT [40]	16.7%	60.8%	2	3	**38**	**14**	59.8%	52.0%
DCO [24]	29.7%	63.3%	3	**2**	93	97	70.9%	56.3%
ours (no init)	32.0%	**64.1%**	6	**2**	54	54	67.4%	64.5%
ours (no LDA)	39.0%	63.6%	6	**2**	44	27	72.1%	64.2%
ours (full)	**41.4%**	63.6%	**7**	**2**	39	22	**73.2%**	**65.8%**

4.3 Quantitative Evaluation

AFL Sports Data. We first demonstrate quantitative performance of our approach on the two sports sequences. To obtain candidate detections, we trained a person detector based on fast feature pyramids [39] using only one single image as training data resulting in moderate precision and recall. Table 1 shows the detector's performance as well as tracking results from two recent multi-target tracking methods. The similar-appearance multiple object tracker (SMOT) [40] is specifically designed to address situations shown in these sports sequences with similar target appearance by relying only on motion similarity and using a generalised linear assignment to reconstruct long-term tracks. While this method shows excellent performance with no or little detection noise, it struggles to correctly infer plausible trajectories in a realistic challenging setting. The second baseline is a recent energy minimisation-based method (DCO) [24], which can eliminate many false positive detections. However, due to the complex formulation of its objective, the optimisation reaches only a moderate local minimum with many short tracks leading to a high number of interrupted trajectories and identity switches.

The second part shows three variants of our proposed method. The first one (no init) is our optimisation strategy starting from the trivial solution, where each detection is considered an error (or equivalently a single-frame track). Note that we are able to outperform other methods by appying our customized optimisation scheme. The second strategy (no LDA) uses [24] as initialisation but

Table 2. Comparison to previous methods on a standard benchmark (PETS, TUD). The results are averaged over six sequences.

Method	MOTA	MOTP	MT	ML	Frag.	ID sw.	Precision	Recall
HOG/HOF Det. [41,42]	–	–	–	–	–	–	79.5%	62.2%
DP [16]	46.0%	**64.7%**	8	11	165	204	91.7%	55.8%
KSP [2]	41.7%	62.8%	8	20	**10**	**18**	91.6%	46.8%
DCO [24]	55.7%	63.6%	11	**9**	49	43	93.0%	61.6%
ours	**56.9%**	64.1%	**13**	10	40	48	**93.4%**	**62.8%**

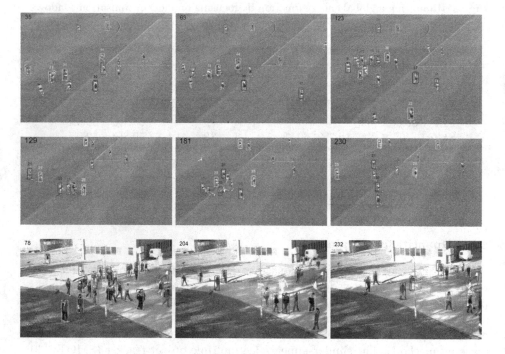

Fig. 5. Exemplar frames from two AFL clips and the PETS S2L2 sequence. Note that using model-free trackers allows one to maintain the identity of a player even during severe deformations and pose changes (*cf.* the blue target (ID 20) in the second row).

does not involve local data association for hypothesis generation as described in Section 3. Finally, by applying our full method using localised optimisation with visual trackers, we are able to further minimise the objective function, which is also reflected in the superior tracking performance.

Public Benchmark. Our second set of experiments involves a public tracking benchmark. Table 2 shows a quantitative comparison of our proposed strategy to previous methods: A network flow-based approach solved with dynamic programming (DP) [16], globally optimal tracking on a discrete grid (KSP) [2] and the same energy minimisation formulation as before [24]. All numbers are computed using code provided by the authors, publicly available detections, ground truth and evaluation scripts[3]. Note that the slightly higher absolute number of ID switches is a result of incorrectly bridging or extending interrupted trajectories. However, the positive effect of recovering more tracks (MT) and thereby increasing the recall outweighs, yielding higher overall accuracy.

Although we outperform state-of-the-art methods on this benchmark, the improvement is less prominent than in the AFL case. One reason for this behaviour may be that the detection quality is poorer on the sports sequences due to large deformations and small target size (cf. Tab. 1 and Fig. 5), yielding a more complex optimisation problem with more local minima. It is also possible that [24] finds a solution much closer to the global optimum on the public sequences, which may indicate that it is well suited to the benchmark but shows limitations on novel data.

4.4   Qualitative Results

Finally, Figure 5 illustrates qualitative results on three sequences. Each row shows three frames from AFL1, AFL2, and PETS S2L2, respectively. Note that our method is able to correctly identify nearly all targets even in extremely challenging conditions with substantial levels of multiple occlusions. Also note how the potential of using visual model-free trackers within a traditional multi-person tracking setting is unfolded in situations with extensive pose variation, such as demonstrated by the cyan (ID 33) and the blue (ID 20) targets in the first and second row, respectively. Please refer to the supplemental video for further visual results.

5   Conclusion

We proposed a simple yet effective method to optimise highly complex objectives for multiple target tracking by focusing explicitly on correcting errors locally. A local data association technique combined with a set of visual object trackers is able to drive the optimisation into much better minima reducing the energy by over 50% and consequently leading to superior solutions. We demonstrate the validity of our approach on particularly challenging sports sequences and public benchmark data achieving state of the art performance.

In future work we plan to more thoroughly investigate different error types and their influence on the final solution. It may also be possible to design even more accurate and more complex objective functions that better approximate the true state but still remain tractable using our local optimisation strategy.

Acknowledgments. We gratefully acknowledge the financial support of the Australian Research Council through Laureate Fellowship FL130100102 to IDR.

---

[3] Note that the corrected numbers are reported for [24], which differ from the original publication.

References

1. Zhang, L., Li, Y., Nevatia, R.: Global data association for multi-object tracking using network flows. In: CVPR 2008 (2008)
2. Berclaz, J., Fleuret, F., Türetken, E., Fua, P.: Multiple object tracking using k-shortest paths optimization. IEEE T. Pattern Anal. Mach. Intell. 33(9), 1806–1819 (2011)
3. Yang, B., Nevatia, R.: An online learned CRF model for multi-target tracking. In: CVPR 2012, pp. 2034–2041 (2012)
4. Roshan Zamir, A., Dehghan, A., Shah, M.: GMCP-Tracker: global multi-object tracking using generalized minimum clique graphs. In: Fitzgibbon, A., Lazebnik, S., Perona, P., Sato, Y., Schmid, C. (eds.) ECCV 2012, Part II. LNCS, vol. 7573, pp. 343–356. Springer, Heidelberg (2012)
5. Liu, J., Carr, P., Collins, R.T., Liu, Y.: Tracking sports players with context-conditioned motion models. In: CVPR 2013, pp. 1830–1837 (2013)
6. Milan, A., Roth, S., Schindler, K.: Continuous energy minimization for multitarget tracking. IEEE T. Pattern Anal. Mach. Intell. 36(1), 58–72 (2014)
7. Vermaak, J., Doucet, A., Pérez, P.: Maintaining multi-modality through mixture tracking. In: ICCV 2003, pp. 1110–1116 (2003)
8. Breitenstein, M.D., Reichlin, F., Leibe, B., Koller-Meier, E., Van Gool, L.: Robust tracking-by-detection using a detector confidence particle filter. In: ICCV 2009 (2009)
9. Wu, Y., Lim, J., Yang, M.H.: Online object tracking: A benchmark. In: CVPR 2013, pp. 2411–2418 (2013)
10. Bibby, C., Reid, I.: Real-time tracking of multiple occluding objects using level sets. In: CVPR 2010, pp. 1307–1314 (2010)
11. Mitzel, D., Horbert, E., Ess, A., Leibe, B.: Multi-person tracking with sparse detection and continuous segmentation. In: Daniilidis, K., Maragos, P., Paragios, N. (eds.) ECCV 2010, Part I. LNCS, vol. 6311, pp. 397–410. Springer, Heidelberg (2010)
12. Yan, X., Wu, X., Kakadiaris, I.A., Shah, S.K.: To track or to detect? an ensemble framework for optimal selection. In: Fitzgibbon, A., Lazebnik, S., Perona, P., Sato, Y., Schmid, C. (eds.) ECCV 2012, Part V. LNCS, vol. 7576, pp. 594–607. Springer, Heidelberg (2012)
13. Kalman, R.E.: A new approach to linear filtering and prediction problems. Transactions of the ASME-Journal of Basic Engineering 82(Series D), 35–45 (1960)
14. Julier, S.J., Uhlmann, J.K.: A new extension of the kalman filter to nonlinear systems. In: International Symposium on Aerospace and Defense Sensing, Simulation and Controls, pp. 182–193 (1997)
15. Jiang, H., Fels, S., Little, J.J.: A linear programming approach for multiple object tracking. In: CVPR 2007 (2007)
16. Pirsiavash, H., Ramanan, D., Fowlkes, C.C.: Globally-optimal greedy algorithms for tracking a variable number of objects. In: CVPR 2011 (2011)
17. Henriques, J.A., Caseiro, R., Batista, J.: Globally optimal solution to multi-object tracking with merged measurements. In: ICCV 2011 (2011)
18. Butt, A.A., Collins, R.T.: Multi-target tracking by lagrangian relaxation to min-cost network flow. In: CVPR 2013 (2013)

19. Leibe, B., Schindler, K., Van Gool, L.: Coupled detection and trajectory estimation for multi-object tracking. In: ICCV 2007 (2007)
20. Wu, Z., Thangali, A., Sclaroff, S., Betke, M.: Coupling detection and data association for multiple object tracking. In: CVPR 2012 (2012)
21. Brendel, W., Amer, M.R., Todorovic, S.: Multiobject tracking as maximum weight independent set. In: CVPR 2011 (2011)
22. Wu, Z., Kunz, T.H., Betke, M.: Efficient track linking methods for track graphs using network-flow and set-cover techniques. In: CVPR 2011 (2011)
23. Berclaz, J., Fleuret, F., Fua, P.: Multiple object tracking using flow linear programming. In: 12th IEEE International Workshop on Performance Evaluation of Tracking and Surveillance (Winter-PETS) (December 2009)
24. Milan, A., Schindler, K., Roth, S.: Detection- and trajectory-level exclusion in multiple object tracking. In: CVPR 2013 (2013)
25. Kalal, Z., Matas, J., Mikolajczyk, K.: P-N Learning: Bootstrapping binary classifiers from unlabeled data by structural constraint. In: CVPR 2010 (2010)
26. Hare, S., Saffari, A., Torr, P.H.S.: Struck: Structured output tracking with kernels. In: ICCV 2011, pp. 263–270 (2011)
27. Henriques, J.F., Caseiro, R., Martins, P., Batista, J.: Exploiting the circulant structure of tracking-by-detection with kernels. In: Fitzgibbon, A., Lazebnik, S., Perona, P., Sato, Y., Schmid, C. (eds.) ECCV 2012, Part IV. LNCS, vol. 7575, pp. 702–715. Springer, Heidelberg (2012)
28. Babenko, B., Yang, M.H., Belongie, S.: Visual tracking with online multiple instance learning. In: CVPR 2009 (2009)
29. Li, X., Shen, C., Shi, Q., Dick, A., van den Hengel, A.: Non-sparse linear representations for visual tracking with online reservoir metric learning. In: CVPR 2012, pp. 1760–1767 (2012)
30. Izadinia, H., Saleemi, I., Li, W., Shah, M.: (MP)^{2}T: Multiple people multiple parts tracker. In: Fitzgibbon, A., Lazebnik, S., Perona, P., Sato, Y., Schmid, C. (eds.) ECCV 2012, Part VI. LNCS, vol. 7577, pp. 100–114. Springer, Heidelberg (2012)
31. Felzenszwalb, P.F., Girshick, R.B., McAllester, D., Ramanan, D.: Object detection with discriminatively trained part based models. IEEE T. Pattern Anal. Mach. Intell. 32(9), 1627–1645 (2010)
32. Zhang, L., van der Maaten, L.: Structure preserving object tracking. In: CVPR 2013, pp. 1838–1845 (2013)
33. Delong, A., Osokin, A., Isack, H.N., Boykov, Y.: Fast approximate energy minimization with label costs. Int. J. Comput. Vision 96(1), 1–27 (2012)
34. Ferryman, J., Shahrokni, A.: PETS2009: Dataset and challenge. In: 11th IEEE International Workshop on Performance Evaluation of Tracking and Surveillance (PETS) (December 2009)
35. Andriluka, M., Roth, S., Schiele, B.: Monocular 3D pose estimation and tracking by detection. In: CVPR 2010 (2010)
36. Milan, A., Schindler, K., Roth, S.: Challenges of ground truth evaluation of multi-target tracking. In: 2013 IEEE CVPR Workshops (CVPRW), pp. 735–742 (June 2013)
37. Bernardin, K., Stiefelhagen, R.: Evaluating multiple object tracking performance: The CLEAR MOT metrics. Image and Video Processing 2008(1), 1–10 (2008)

38. Li, Y., Huang, C., Nevatia, R.: Learning to associate: Hybridboosted multi-target tracker for crowded scene. In: CVPR 2009 (2009)
39. Dollár, P., Appel, R., Belongie, S., Perona, P.: Fast feature pyramids for object detection. IEEE T. Pattern Anal. Mach. Intell. (2014) (to appear)
40. Dicle, C., Sznaier, M., Camps, O.: The way they move: Tracking multiple targets with similar appearance. In: ICCV 2013 (2013)
41. Dalal, N., Triggs, B.: Histograms of oriented gradients for human detection. In: CVPR 2005, pp. 886–893 (2005)
42. Walk, S., Majer, N., Schindler, K., Schiele, B.: New features and insights for pedestrian detection. In: CVPR 2010 (2010)

Saliency Weighted Features for Person Re-identification

Niki Martinel[✉], Christian Micheloni, and Gian Luca Foresti

Department of Mathematics and Computer Science,
University of Udine, 33100 Udine, Italy
niki.martinel@uniud.it

Abstract. In this work we propose a novel person re-identification approach. The solution, inspired by human gazing capabilities, wants to identify the salient regions of a given person. Such regions are used as a weighting tool in the image feature extraction process. Then, such novel representation is combined with a set of other visual features in a pairwise-based multiple metric learning framework. Finally, the learned metrics are fused to get the distance between image pairs and to re-identify a person. The proposed method is evaluated on three different benchmark datasets and compared with best state-of-the-art approaches to show its overall superior performance.

1 Introduction

The person re-identification problem, i.e. identifying an individual across non-overlapping camera views, is becoming one of the most interesting tasks in computer vision. Many different applications, such as situational awareness [41], wide area scene analysis [40], etc. would benefit from it. This is supported by the relevant number of works presented by the community [7,47].

The person re-identification problem is challenging due to different issues like variations on viewpoints and illumination conditions as well as persons poses and appearances. The non-rigid shape of the human body, background clutter and occlusions contribute to make the task non-trivial.

The computer vision community is addressing person re-identification by proposing both biometric-based (e.g. [18,33,46,53]) and appearance-based methods (e.g. [26,32,44,50]). Biometric-based methods exploit characteristic features (e.g. gait, face, etc.) of the person that are invariant in time but require a precise setup of the sensors (e.g. lateral or frontal view with relatively high spatial resolution). On the other hand, features extracted by appearance-based methods carry information about the appearance (i.e. clothes, carried on objects, etc.) which invariance is limited in time. But, these methods do not require a specific sensors configuration and deployment thus they are more suitable in context of wide area camera networks.

Solutions in the literature for re-identification can be further organized in three categories: (i) *Discriminative signature based methods* (e.g. [18,26,30,34])

© Springer International Publishing Switzerland 2015
L. Agapito et al. (Eds.): ECCV 2014 Workshops, Part III, LNCS 8927, pp. 191–208, 2015.
DOI: 10.1007/978-3-319-16199-0_14

exploit human-defined person models that are matched using distance measures like L^2, χ^2, etc., or a combination of those. (ii) *Features transformation based methods* compute linear [15] and nonlinear [9,10,24,46] transformation functions that are used to project features between different camera-dependent spaces. (iii) *Metric learning based algorithms* (e.g. [25,33,44,50]) learn non-Euclidean distances that are used for the classification phase.

Motivation: Our solution builds upon three main considerations about the limits of current approaches:

- Most of the existing works compute the signature either directly from the whole image or silhouette, or by fusing local features extracted from dense image patches. This way each point of the person has the same importance in the computation of the signature. As [51,52] we believe that the importance of the points is not uniform.
- Assuming we can compute the importance of points, it is not guaranteed that the same point is captured by all different views.
- Feature transformation functions are both highly non-linear [9,10,24] and depending on the class of the features, i.e., every feature transformation is modeled by a different function.

Contribution: We propose an approach that introduces three main novelties:

- A new kernelized graph-based technique to compute the importance of the points on the person, i.e., the saliency.
- The computed saliency is used as a weight in the feature extraction process: the higher the "saliency" the higher the importance of the feature for the re-identification and vice versa. This is combined with a set of local features to reduce the dependence on the saliency.
- A pairwise multiple metric learning framework used to model each feature space separately rather than jointly.

2   Related Work

Discriminative signature based methods seek for highly distinctive representations to describe a person's appearance under varying conditions. In [14], a region-based segmented image was used to extract spatio-temporal local features from multiple consecutive frames. In [13], a 2D rigid part based color appearance model was used to localize and match individuals in 3D system computed by means of the structure-from-motion technique. In [6,8,31,37,38], multiple local features were used to compute discriminative signatures for each person using multiple images. In [49], frames were used to build a collaborative representation that best approximates the query frames. In [4], Mean Riemannian Covariance patches extracted from individuals were used in a boosting scheme. In [26], re-identification was performed by matching shape descriptors of color distributions projected in the log-chromaticity space. In [52], an adjacency constrained patch matching strategy based on an unsupervised salient feature learning framework was used to improve re-identification accuracy. In [1], similarity with a reference set of persons was used in a Regularized Canonical Correlation Analysis framework. In [34], Biologically Inspired Features and covariance descriptors were used to compute the similarity between person images.

These methods addressed the problem by using human-defined person representations that are distinctive under changing conditions between different cameras. However, the exploited visual features are not be invariant to every variation that may affect the images acquired by disjoint cameras.

Features transformation based methods have addressed the re-identification problem by finding the transformation functions that affect the visual features acquired by disjoint cameras. In [24], a learned subspace of the computed brightness transfer function (BTF) between the appearance features was used to match persons across camera pairs. An incremental learning framework to model linear color variations between cameras has been proposed in [15]. In [9], the BTF was used to compensate the color difference between camera views. Tangent transfer functions derived by the homography between two cameras were also exploited to compensate the perspective difference. Usually the modeled functions are used to transform the feature space of one camera to the feature space of the other one. The re-identification then is performed in the so transformed feature space. Only recently, a few methods [2,12,28,36,39] had also considered the fact that the transformation is not unique and it depends on several factors.

Metric learning based algorithms lie in between the two above categories as they still rely on particular features but they also advantage of a training phase to learn non-Euclidean distances used to compute the match in a different feature space. In [21], a relaxation of the positivity constraint of the Mahalanobis metric was proposed. In [11], unfamiliar matches were given less importance in the optimization problem in a Large Margin Nearest Neighbor framework. Multiple metrics specific to different candidate sets were learned in a transfer learning set up in [29]. In [50], the re-identification problem was formulated as a local distance comparison problem introducing an energy-based loss function that measures the similarity between appearance instances. In [25], a metric just based on equivalence constraints was learned. In [44], regularized Local Fisher Discriminant Analysis was introduced to maximize the between-class separability and preserve multi-class modality. In [32], it has been shown that user feedback solicited on-the-fly during the deployment stage for re-ranking boosts the re-identification performance over metric learning methods.

Recently, human saliency has also been explored in [51,52]. However, in [51, 52] a reference set has been used, and, as claimed by the authors, the reference set is robust as long as its distribution well reflects the test scenario. To avoid this, we consider only neighborhood of pixels to compute the saliency. This brings three main benefits: (*a*) no need to find the best reference set for each context; (*b*) performance are not dependent from the reference set; (*c*) lower computational costs.

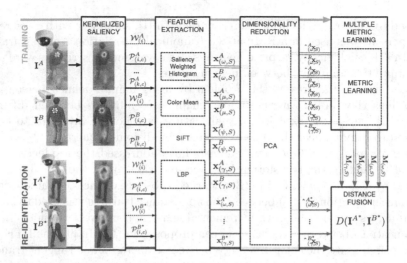

Fig. 1. Proposed system architecture based on five main stages: kernelized saliency computation, feature extraction, dimensionality reduction, multiple metric learning and distance fusion.

3   The Approach

As shown in Fig. 1, the proposed re-identification approach consists of five phases: (1) kernelized saliency computation, (2) feature extraction, (3) dimensionality reduction, (4) multiple metric learning, and (5) distance fusion.

During training each image is given to the kernelized saliency detection module to compute the saliency of each pixel, i.e. a saliency map. Then, both the saliency map and the image are split into patches that are given to the feature extraction module. This module exploits the saliency as a weighting tool for the feature computation. Four different kind of features are extracted from all the patches and for each color component of the selected color spaces. Features of the same kind, extracted from the same color space, are concatenated and input to the dimensionality reduction module that applies Principal Component Analysis (PCA). Finally, the whole training set of PCA reduced features is given to the multiple metric learning module. This is in charge to learn a separate metric between two cameras for each feature type and color space.

During the re-identification phase, the same reduced representation computed for images coming from disjoint cameras, is given to the distance fusion module together with the learned metrics to compute the final dissimilarity.

3.1   Kernelized Saliency

Using our visual sensing field we are able to focus our limited perceptual and cognitive resources on the most pertinent subset of the available sensory data. We usually tell that a portion of the image is "salient" if it is "different" from its surroundings. However, being our goal to re-identify a target across disjoint cameras we have to deal with background clutter that may induce state-of-the-art saliency detection algorithms [3,16,22,23,27,45,48] to label "salient" a background region. But, we want only points on the person's silhouette to have high saliency.

Let $\mathbf{I} \in \mathbb{R}^{m \times n}$ be the image of a person and let assume that the silhouette stands somewhere in the center of it. Then, given a feature map $\mathbf{F} \in \mathbb{R}^{m \times n}$ we want to compute an activation map $\mathbf{A} \in \mathbb{R}^{m \times n}$ such that features at coordinates (x, y), denoted as $\mathbf{F}_{(x,y)}$, which are "different" in their neighborhood and are close to the center of the image lead to high values of $\mathbf{A}_{(x,y)}$.

To achieve such objective the graph-based algorithm in [19] has been extended as follows. A fully-connected directed graph $G_\mathbf{A}$ is built by connecting every node (x, y) of $\mathbf{F}$ with all the other ones. The weight of each directed edge from node (x, y) to (p, q) is computed as

$$w((x,y),(p,q))_\mathbf{A} = \left| \log \left(\frac{\mathbf{F}_{(x,y)}}{\mathbf{F}_{(p,q)}} \right) \right| K_\mathbf{F} \left([x,y]^T, [p,q]^T \right) \qquad (1)$$

where we have taken the standard definition of dissimilarity between the two feature values and weighted it by a kernel function $K_\mathbf{F}$ computed between the node locations. Once $G_\mathbf{A}$ has been computed, a Markov chain is defined over it in such a way that its equilibrium distribution accumulates mass at nodes that have high dissimilarities with their surroundings.

However, considering a single feature map $\mathbf{F}$ only limits the generality of the activation map. On the other hand, if multiple $\mathbf{A}$'s are computed we need to finally combine them into a single master activation map. This can be trivially solved using an additive combination. But, if each single activation map does not have similar mass at closer nodes, we may end up with a uniform and uninformative master map. Thus another fully connected graph $G_{\hat{\mathbf{A}}}$ is computed to concentrate the mass of each $\mathbf{A}$'s into nodes with high activation values. Let the weight between two nodes (x, y) and (p, q) be computed as

$$w((x,y),(p,q))_{\hat{\mathbf{A}}} = \mathbf{A}_{(p,q)} K_\mathbf{A} \left([x,y]^T, [p,q]^T \right) \qquad (2)$$

where, as before, $K_\mathbf{A}$ is a kernel function. By defining a Markov chain over $G_{\hat{\mathbf{A}}}$ and normalizing the outbound edges to unity we can find the equilibrium distribution. As a result of this, we have that each concentrated activation map $\hat{\mathbf{A}}$ has most of the mass around nodes of $\mathbf{A}$ that have high activation values.

Now, let $\hat{\mathbf{A}}^j$ be the j-th activation map computed related to the $\mathbf{F}^j$ feature map, for $j = 1, 2, \ldots, J$. The final saliency map is defined as $\boldsymbol{\Omega} = \sum_{j=1}^J \alpha_j \hat{\mathbf{A}}^j$ where $\boldsymbol{\alpha}$ is a vector of weights.

Three important characteristics have been achieved by introducing the kernel function in the above formulation: (i) the approach proposed in [19] has been generalized such that any kernel can be used to control the weight of the two graphs edges; (ii) the weight of the edge from node (x, y) to node (p, q) is kept proportional to their dissimilarity and to their closeness in the domain of $\mathbf{F}$; (iii) on average, nodes closer to the center have higher activation values than any particular point along the image boundaries. This means that lower mass is assigned to the nodes that will most probably belong to the background, which is compliant to the assumption that the person silhouette somehow lies in the middle of the image.

3.2 Feature Extraction and Dimensionality Reduction

In the previous sections we introduced the idea that the points of a person's silhouette have different importance. However, it is not guaranteed that a very salient point acquired by a camera maintains the same property in a different camera (e.g. occluded point, change of pose, etc.). Nevertheless, if the same point is viewed by the two cameras and maintains the saliency properties then, it probably represents a good point in the re-identification process. To deal with both cases the saliency is used as a weight for a subset of features while the others are computed independently from the saliency.

As most state-of-the-algorithm methods the color, shape and texture features are considered in the proposed work. Before extracting such features, the RGB image $\mathbf{I}$ is projected into each color space $S \in \{HSV, Lab, YUV, rgs^1\}$. Then, the resulting image color channels $\mathbf{I}_{(c)}$, $c = 1, \ldots, 12$, and the saliency map Ω are divided into a set of k patches of equal size denoted $\mathcal{P}_{(i,c)}$ and $\mathcal{W}_{(i)}$ respectively, where $i = 1, \ldots, k$ denotes the patch index.

For each patch i and color channel c the following features are extracted: (a) the saliency weighted color histogram ω computed as

$$\omega_{(i,c)}^{l,u} = \sum_{(x,y) \in \mathcal{P}_{(i,c)}} \begin{cases} \mathcal{W}_{(i,x,y)} & \text{if} \quad l < \mathcal{P}_{(i,c,x,y)} \leq u \\ 0 & \text{otherwise} \end{cases} \tag{3}$$

where $\mathcal{W}_{(i,x,y)}$ and $\mathcal{P}_{(i,c,x,y)}$ are the saliency value and the pixel value at location (x,y) of patch i and color channel c. l and u are the lower and upper bin limits. (b) the color mean μ and (c) the 128-dimensional SIFT descriptor ψ. We also compute (d) the Local Binary Pattern (LBP) [43] γ from a grayscale representation of each patch i. Features of the same type extracted from all the k patches belonging to the same color space S are finally concatenated to get the corresponding feature vectors $\mathbf{x}_{(\omega,S)}$, $\mathbf{x}_{(\mu,S)}$, $\mathbf{x}_{(\psi,S)}$ and $\mathbf{x}_{(\gamma,gray)}$.

Notice that the saliency weight has been used in the extraction of histogram features only. This is due to the following reason. If we consider the task of re-identify a target across disjoint cameras, we are not guaranteed that a particular object/image region that has been assigned high saliency by one camera is visible by a different one. That is, we cannot rely on features extracted from those regions only to re-identify the target. Hence, we decided to weight only histogram features to balance this issue.

Due to the patch division the resulting feature vectors can be very high dimensional and each component may not have the same discriminative power. Principal Component Analysis is applied to each feature vector separately to get the vector of PCA coefficients $\hat{\mathbf{x}}_{(f,S)}$ where $f \in \{\omega, \mu, \psi, \gamma\}$ denotes the

---

^{1} $r = R/(R + G + B)$, $g = G/(R + G + B)$, $s = (R + G + B)/3$

feature type. To ease the notation, here and in the following, we use $S \in \{HSV, Lab, YUV, rgs, gray\}$. Notice that, while ω, μ and ψ are extracted from all the four selected color space, γ is computed only in the grayscale domain.

3.3   Multiple Metric Learning and Distance Fusion

For re-identification tasks, the input to metric learning algorithms is generally given by a vector representation of the image formed by concatenating multiple features (e.g. [21,25,44,50]). Existing approaches have not considered that different kinds of features extracted from disjoint cameras may not be modeled by the same transformation function. The joint feature space may also be too complex to be robustly handled by a single metric. So, we propose to model each feature space separately. While any metric learning may be a suitable choice, in this work we exploit the algorithm proposed in [25] as it has no parameters that need to be optimized. We will introduce it briefly and show how the learned metrics can be fused to get the final dissimilarity.

The idea is to exploit statistical inference to find the optimal decision to establish whether a pair of features is dissimilar or not. This is achieved by setting the problem as a likelihood ratio test. As suggested in [25], by assuming that the feature space of pairwise differences is governed by a normal distribution (with zero mean) we can write the ration test as

$$\delta_{(f,S)}^{(A,B)} = \log \left(\frac{\mathcal{N}\left(\hat{\mathbf{x}}_{(f,S)}^{A} \ \ \hat{\mathbf{x}}_{(f,S)}^{B}, \mathbf{0}, \Sigma_{(A,B)=0} \right)}{\mathcal{N}\left(\hat{\mathbf{x}}_{(f,S)}^{A} - \hat{\mathbf{x}}_{(f,S)}^{B}, \mathbf{0}, \Sigma_{(A,B)=1} \right)} \right) \tag{4}$$

where $\Sigma_{(A,B)=1}$ and $\Sigma_{(A,B)=0}$ are the sum of outer products computed for all the pairwise feature differences, $\hat{\mathbf{x}}_{(f,S)}^{A} - \hat{\mathbf{x}}_{(f,S)}^{B}$, that respectively belongs to the same person or to a different one.

Now, by taking the log of eq.(4) and discarding the constant terms that provide an offset, we can learn the Mahalanobis metric $\mathbf{M}_{(f,S)}$ by clipping the spectrum of $\hat{\mathbf{M}}_{(f,S)} = (\Sigma_{(A,B)=1}^{-1} - \Sigma_{(A,B)=0}^{-1})$ computed through eigenanalysis. Then, the Mahalanobis distance metric between the feature f extracted from the color space S of the images $\mathbf{I}^A$ and $\mathbf{I}^B$ is given by

$$d_{(f,S)}^2(\mathbf{I}^A, \mathbf{I}^B) = \left(\hat{\mathbf{x}}_{(f,S)}^{A} - \hat{\mathbf{x}}_{(f,S)}^{B} \right)^T \mathbf{M}_{(f,S)} \left(\hat{\mathbf{x}}_{(f,S)}^{A} - \hat{\mathbf{x}}_{(f,S)}^{B} \right). \tag{5}$$

The learned Mahalanobis distance metrics can then be fused to compute the final distance between person A and person B as

$$D(\mathbf{I}^A, \mathbf{I}^B) = \sum_f \sum_S \beta_{(f,S)} d_{(f,s)}^2(\mathbf{I}^A, \mathbf{I}^B) \tag{6}$$

where $\beta_{(f,S)}$ is a vector of distance weights.

3.4   Multiple Shot Extension

The re-identification community assumes that two sets of pedestrian images are available: the gallery set $\mathcal{G}$ (for which labels are known) and the probe set $\mathcal{T}$ (the set of pedestrians we want to re-identify). Let N be the number of images of each person in the two sets. Dependently on the value of N two matching philosophies are identified: i) single-shot ($N = 1$); ii) multiple-shot ($N > 1$). To extend our method to the multiple-shot scenario we take each feature f extracted from the color space S on N observations of a same person and pool them (mean operator). The reason for doing this is that the average of all observations is likely to be an estimate of the centroid for all samples and hence should be a valuable representation for each person.

4   Experimental Results

We evaluated our approach on three publicly available benchmark datasets: the VIPeR dataset [17], the 3DPeS dataset [5] and the CHUK02 dataset [29]. We chose these datasets as they provide many challenges faced in real world scenarios, i.e., viewpoint, pose and illumination changes, different backgrounds, image resolutions, occlusions, etc. More details about each dataset are discussed below.

Evaluation Criteria: We report the results for both a single-shot strategy and a multiple-shot strategy. All the results are shown in terms of recognition rate by the Cumulative Matching Characteristic (CMC) curve and normalized Area Under Curve (nAUC) values. The CMC curve is a plot of the recognition performance versus the rank score and represents the expectation of finding the correct match inside top k matches. On the other hand, the nAUC describes how well a method performs irrespectively of the dataset size. For each dataset, the evaluation procedure is repeated 10 times using independent random splits.

Implementation Details: To compute and fuse the saliency maps of an image we have taken the same settings in [19] and set both the kernel function $K_\mathbf{F}$ and $K_\mathbf{A}$ to be the standard Radial Basis Function with free parameter $\sigma = 1$. Each element of $\boldsymbol{\alpha}$ has been set to 1. We have sampled image patches of size 8×16 with a stride of 8×8 pixels to compute the weighted color histograms, each with 24 bins per channel. Similarly we have taken image patches of size 8×16 with a stride of 4×8 to compute the color mean and the LBP features. SIFT features have been extracted from 50% overlapping patches of size 16×16. Features have been reduced to $24, 46, 23, 21, 33, 33, 33, 33, 40, 26, 50, 34, 40$ dimensions. First 4 values are for histograms, second 4 are for the color means and the next 4 are for SIFT features extracted from the HSV (1st, 5th and 9th values), Lab (2nd, 6th and 10th values), YUV and rgs color spaces. Last value is for LBP features. Similarly, we set $\boldsymbol{\beta} = [0.06, 0.06, 0.01, 0.1, 0.1, 0.1, 0.1, 0.08, 0.02, 0.05, 0.1, 0.1, 0.1]$. All the parameters have been selected by 4-fold cross validation. Notice that, while these may have been separately estimated for each dataset, we have taken their average to provide a more general framework.

Fig. 2. 15 image pairs from the VIPeR dataset. The two rows show the different appearances of the same person viewed by two disjoint cameras.

4.1   VIPeR Dataset[2]

The VIPeR dataset [17] is one of the most challenging datasets for person re-identification due to the changes in illumination and pose, and the low spatial resolution of images. This dataset contains images of 632 persons viewed by two different cameras in an outdoor environment. Most of the image pairs show viewpoint changes larger than 90 degrees (see Fig. 2). To evaluate our method we followed the common protocol [1,21,44,52] resizing all the images to 48×128.

Table 1. Comparison with state-of-the-art methods on the VIPeR dataset. Best results for each rank are in boldface font. (*) Only results reported to 2 rounded digits are available. (**) The best run was reported, which cannot be directly compared to the other results.

Rank →	1	10	20	50	100	nAUC
Proposed	**32.97**	**75.63**	86.87	96.17	98.96	**0.9701**
SalMatch [51]	30.16	65.54	79.15	91.49	98.10	0.9542
RCCA(*) [1]	30	75	**87**	96	**99**	0.9682
LAFT [28]	29.60	69.30	81.34	**96.80**	-	-
RPLM(*) [21]	27	69	83	95	**99**	0.9625
PatMatch [51]	26.90	62.34	75.63	90.51	97.47	0.9496
eSDC.ocsvm [52]	26.74	62.37	76.36	-	-	-
eSDC.knn [52]	26.31	58.86	72.77	-	-	-
LF [44]	24.18	67.12	81.38	94.12	-	-
eLDFV [35]	22.34	60.04	71.00	88.92	**99**	0.9447
IBML(*) [20]	22	63	78	93	98	0.9516
CPS [8]	21.84	57.21	71.00	88.10	91.77	0.9360
eBiCOV [34]	20.66	56.18	68.00	84.90	88.66	0.9105
LMNN-R(**) [11]	20	68	80	93	**99**	0.9572

In Table 1 we compare our results to the state-of-the-art methods. Here we considered the scenario where half of the dataset is used for training and

---

[2] Available at http://soe.ucsc.edu/~dgray/

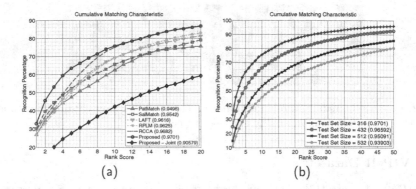

Fig. 3. Results on the VIPeR dataset reported as averaged CMC curves. In (a) comparisons with state-of-the-art methods are shown. In b results are shown as a function of the test set size.

the remaining half is used for re-identification [3]. As shown, our method achieves the highest rank 1 score by reaching a recognition rate of 32.97% thus outperforming very recent and more complicated methods like SalMatch [51], RCCA [1] and LAFT [28]. We outperform the second runner up by more than 2.8%, which is a very important result on this dataset. From rank 1 to 10 we outperform all other methods by more than 6%. RCCA [1] is the only one, that, as our method, achieves a recognition percentage higher than 70% at rank 10. More interestingly, SalMatch [51], that has the second highest rank 1 score, achieves a recognition percentage of 65.54% for the same rank. For higher ranks (50 and 100) our method has very similar performance to the recent state-of-the-art methods. In general we achieve the best overall performance with an nAUC value of 0.9701.

In Fig. 3(a) we show the comparison of our method to the five top rank 1 approaches in terms of CMC curves. We also show that learning multiple metrics enables us to achieve better performance than learning a single metric for the joint feature space (black curve). To obtain the such result all the features have been concatenated, then PCA has been applied to reduce the feature space dimensions to 79 (best results found by cross-validation). At rank 10 a recognition rate of 75.63% is achieved by learning multiple metrics, while concatenating the same features in a single vector and learning only one metric results in a recognition percentage of 42.16%.

In Fig. 3(b) we report the results of our method on the VIPeR dataset using different test set sizes. In Table 2, we also compare our method with RCCA [1], RPLM [21], PRDC [54], MCC [54], LAFT [28] and PCCA [42]. When the test set size contains 432 individuals we have the best performance on all the reported ranks. In particular we outperform the second runner up by more than 2.5% at rank 1 and by more than 7% when the considered rank is either 10 or 20.

---

[3] Notice that some approaches are not using any training data as they're discriminative signature based methods (e.g. CPS [8], eBiCOV [34], etc.).

Table 2. Comparisons on the VIPeR dataset. Recognition rates per rank score as a function of the test set size.

| Test Set Size | 432 | | | 512 | | | | 532 | | |
Rank →	1	10	20	1	5	10	20	1	10	20
Proposed	**24.72**	**66.29**	**82.70**	**14.77**	**38.06**	**53.29**	**68.32**	10.67	45.46	**65.95**
RCCA [1]	22	59	75	-	-	-	-	**15**	**47**	60
RPLM [21]	20	56	71	-	-	-	-	11	38	52
PRDC [54]	13	44	60	9.12	24.19	34.40	48.55	9	34	49
MCC [54]	-	-	-	5.00	16.32	25.92	39.64	-	-	-
LAFT [28]	-	-	-	12.90	30.30	42.73	58.02	-	-	-
PCCA [42]	-	-	-	9.27	24.89	37.43	52.89	-	-	-

Fig. 4. 15 image pairs from the 3DPeS dataset. The two rows show the different appearances of the same person viewed by two disjoint cameras.

The same applies when the test set contains 512 individuals. We outperform all existing methods by more than 10% for rank 10 and 20. Finally, if we consider 532 persons as the test set, we achieve lower performance than RCCA [1] at rank 1. For higher ranks we achieve similar and superior performance than it and all other methods.

4.2 3DPeS Dataset[4]

The 3DPeS dataset [5] contains different sequences of 191 people taken from a multi-camera distributed surveillance system. There are 8 outdoor cameras and each one is presented with different light conditions and calibration parameters, so the persons were detected multiple times with different viewpoints. They were also captured at different time instants during the course of different days, in clear light and in shadowy areas. This results in a challenging dataset with strong variation of light conditions (see Fig. 4).

We compare our results to the ones reported in [44]. However, as in [44] no much details were given about how the results had been computed, we follow a similar approach to the one used in the VIPeR dataset and resize all the images to 48 × 128 pixels. As this dataset comes with more than a single image per person per camera, we considered that all images have been used to compute

---

[4] Available at www.openvisor.org

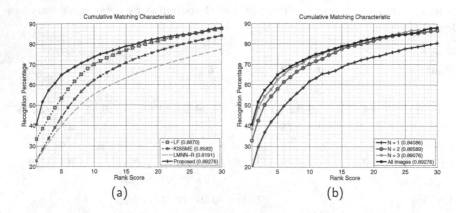

Fig. 5. Results on the 3DPeS dataset reported as averaged CMC curves. In (a) we compare our results to state-of-the-art methods: LF [44], KISSME [25] and LMNN-R [11]. In (b) we show the performance as a function of the number of shots used during both the training and the re-identification phase.

Table 3. Comparison of the proposed method on the 3DPeS dataset. Best results are in boldface font.

Rank →	1	10	25	50	nAUC
Proposed	**40.74**	**73.58**	84.64	94.90	**0.8928**
LF [44]	33.43	69.98	**84.80**	**95.07**	0.8870
KISSME [25]	22.94	62.21	80.74	93.21	0.8582
LMNN-R [11]	23.03	55.23	73.44	88.92	0.8191

the results in [44]. Then, as in [44] we randomly split the dataset into a training set and a test set containing 95 persons each.

In Fig. 5(a) we report the comparison of our method to three state-of-the-art approaches, namely LF [44], KISSME [25] and LMNN-R [11]. Our method achieves superior performance than all the others ones for ranks from 1 to 20. In particular at rank 1 we achieve a correct recognition rate of 40.74% while, LF [44], KISSME [25] and LMNN-R [11] achieve a recognition rate of 33.43%, 22.94% and 23.03% respectively.

In Table 3 we report the comparison only for a subset of all the possible rank values. As shown, for lower ranks, our method outperforms the others. For higher ones, similar performance to LF [44] are achieved. Notice that the difference in performance for ranks 25 and 50 is less than 0.2%. As for the VIPeR dataset we reach the best overall performance with an nAUC value of 0.8928.

As the 3DPeS dataset comes with multiple images of the same pedestrian, in Fig. 5(b) we report the performance of our method as a function of N. In particular, as not all the persons come with an equal number of images, if the selected value of N is higher than the actual number of available images we take the maximum allowable number of images for that person. As shown in

Fig. 6. 15 image pairs from the CUHK02 dataset. The two rows show the different appearances of the same person viewed by two disjoint cameras.

Fig. 5(b) when the single shot approach is considered ($N = 1$), our method achieves a recognition percentage of 19.05% at rank 1 and a recognition percentage of 73.68% when the considered rank is 20. At this rank our method outperforms LMNN-R [11] and meets the performance of KISSME [25] which have a recognition rate of 68.95% and 76.54% respectively. For these results LMNN-R [11] and KISSME [25] require to use all the available images while we use a single one. Considering a multiple-shot modality, our method keeps constant the performance either using $N = 2$, $N = 3$ or all the available images. This is confirmed by the fact that the reported nAUC values change by less than 0.07 among all the three cases. However, by considering $N = 3$ (or all the available images) the rank 1 performance increases of about 6% with respect to the $N = 2$ scenario.

4.3   CUHK Campus Dataset[5]

The CUHK Campus dataset [29] has images acquired by disjoint camera views in a campus environment. The dataset comes with 1,816 persons and five camera pairs denoted P1–P5 each of which is composed by different sensors (i.e. the dataset has images from ten camera views). The five camera pairs have 971, 306, 107, 193 and 239 persons respectively. Each person has two images in each camera. Other than being challenging for pose variations that occurs between camera pairs, this dataset is the one that has the highest number of persons collected by a single camera pair, thus it is the most representative for a real scenario. To evaluate our method and compare it to the state-of-the-art we follow the same protocol used in [29,51]. Results are reported for camera pair P1 when $N = 2$ images per person are considered. In this camera pair, images from the first camera are captured from lateral view, while images from the second camera are acquired from a frontal view or back view (see Fig. 6). All the 3,884 images have been resized to 60 × 160. The dataset as been split into a training set containing 485 pedestrians and a test having images for the remaining 486.

In Fig. 7 we compare the results of our method to four state-of-the-art approaches, namely, SDALF [6], TML [29], PatMatch [51] and SalMatch [51]. At rank 1 our method performs better than all other ones by reaching a correct recognition rate of 31.05%, which improves the performance of SalMatch [51]

---

[5] Available at http://www.ee.cuhk.edu.hk/~xgwang/CUHK_identification.html

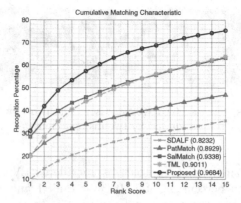

Fig. 7. Results on the CUHK02 Campus dataset (Camera P1) reported as averaged CMC curves. We show our superior performance to state-of-the-art approaches: SDALF [6], TML [29], PatMatch [51] and SalMatch [51].

Table 4. Comparison with state-of-the-art methods on the CUHK02 dataset (camera pair P1). Best results for each rank are in boldface font.

Rank →	1	5	10	20	50	100	200	nAUC
Proposed	**31.05**	**57.34**	**68.74**	**79.50**	**91.26**	**96.92**	**99.32**	**0.9684**
SalMatch [51]	28.45	45.85	55.67	67.95	83.52	92.10	98.10	0.9338
PatMatch [51]	20.39	34.12	41.09	51.56	68.42	82.00	93.23	0.8929
TML [29]	20.00	44.02	56.07	69.47	74.51	81.64	91.69	0.9011
SDALF [6]	9.90	22.57	30.33	41.03	55.99	67.39	84.12	0.8684

by about 3%. Then, as the rank score increases our method outperforms all the other ones and, at rank 10, it achieves a recognition rate of 68.74%.

As shown in Table 4, for the same rank SDALF [6], TML [29], PatMatch [51] and SalMatch [51] reach a recognition rate of 30.33%, 56.07%, 41.09% and 55.67%, respectively. Thus, for rank 10, we improve the state-of-the-art performance by more than 13%.

From the analysis of all the reported results, we can conclude that, in general, our method has superior performance than state-of-the-art approaches. This is supported by the fact that we achieve the best overall performance in terms of nAUC values for all the three considered datasets.

5   Conclusion

In this work we proposed to achieve the re-identification goal introducing a novel algorithm to identify the salient regions of a person. This is achieved by introducing a kernelized saliency that gives higher weights to the regions that are in the center of the image. Then, we used the computed saliency as a weight in a feature extraction process and combine it with other feature representations that do not consider it. The extracted features are used in a novel pairwise-based multiple metric learning framework. The learned metrics are finally fused to get the distance between image pairs and to re-identify a person. The novelty of the approach is also supported by the provided results. Our approach overall outperforms the best state-of-the-art solutions on the three most challenging benchmark datasets.

References

1. An, L., Kafai, M., Yang, S., Bhanu, B.: Reference-Based Person Re-Identification. In: Advanced Video and Signal-Based Surveillance (2013)
2. Avraham, T., Gurvich, I., Lindenbaum, M., Markovitch, S.: Learning implicit transfer for person re-identification. In: Fusiello, A., Murino, V., Cucchiara, R. (eds.) ECCV 2012 Ws/Demos, Part I. LNCS, vol. 7583, pp. 381–390. Springer, Heidelberg (2012)
3. Avraham, T., Lindenbaum, M.: Esaliency (extended saliency): meaningful attention using stochastic image modeling. IEEE Transactions on Pattern Analysis and Machine Intelligence 32(4), 693–708 (2010)
4. Bak, S., Corvée, E., Brémond, F., Thonnat, M.: Boosted human re-identification using Riemannian manifolds. Image and Vision Computing 30(6-7), 443–452 (2012)
5. Baltieri, D., Vezzani, R., Cucchiara, R.: 3DPeS: 3D People dataset for surveillance and forensics. In: International ACM Workshop on Multimedia Access to 3D Human Objects, pp. 59–64 (2011)
6. Bazzani, L., Cristani, M., Murino, V.: Symmetry-driven accumulation of local features for human characterization and re-identification. Computer Vision and Image Understanding 117(2), 130–144 (2013)
7. Bedagkar-Gala, A., Shah, S.K.: A Survey of Approaches and Trends in Person Re-identification. Image and Vision Computing (February 2014)
8. Cheng, D.S., Cristani, M., Stoppa, M., Bazzani, L., Murino, V.: Custom pictorial structures for re-identification. In: Procedings of the British Machine Vision Conference, pp. 68.1–68.11. British Machine Vision Association (2011)
9. Chu, C.T., Hwang, J.N., Lan, K.M., Wang, S.Z.: Tracking across multiple cameras with overlapping views based on brightness and tangent transfer functions. In: International Conference on Distributed Smart Cameras, vol. (1), pp. 1–6. IEEE (August 2011)
10. Datta, A., Brown, L.M., Feris, R., Pankanti, S.: Appearance modeling for person re-identification using weighted brightness transfer functions. In: International Conference on Pattern Recognition, ICPR (2012)
11. Dikmen, M., Akbas, E., Huang, T.S., Ahuja, N.: Pedestrian recognition with a learned metric. In: Kimmel, R., Klette, R., Sugimoto, A. (eds.) ACCV 2010, Part IV. LNCS, vol. 6495, pp. 501–512. Springer, Heidelberg (2011)
12. Garcia, J., Martinel, N., Foresti, G.L., Gardel, A., Micheloni, C.: Person orientation and feature distances boost re-identification. In: International Conference on Pattern Recognition (2014)

13. Garg, R., Seitz, S.M., Ramanan, D., Snavely, N.: Where's Waldo: Matching people in images of crowds. In: International Conference on Computer Vision and Pattern Recognition (CVPR), pp. 1793–1800. IEEE (June 2011)
14. Gheissari, N., Sebastian, T., Hartley, R.: Person reidentification using spatiotemporal appearance. In: International Conference on Computer Vision and Pattern Recognition, vol. 2, pp. 1528–1535. IEEE (2006)
15. Gilbert, A., Bowden, R.: Tracking objects across cameras by incrementally learning inter-camera colour calibration and patterns of activity. In: Leonardis, A., Bischof, H., Pinz, A. (eds.) ECCV 2006. LNCS, vol. 3952, pp. 125–136. Springer, Heidelberg (2006)
16. Goferman, S., Zelnik-Manor, L., Tal, A.: Context-aware saliency detection. IEEE Transactions on Pattern Analysis and Machine Intelligence 34(10), 1915–1926 (2012)
17. Gray, D., Brennan, S., Tao, H.: Evaluating appearance models for recongnition, reacquisition and tracking. In: IEEE International Workshop on Performance Evaluation of Tracking and Surveillance (PETS), Rio De Janeiro, Brazil (October 2007)
18. Han, J., Bhanu, B.: Individual recognition using gait energy image. IEEE Transactions on Pattern Analysis and Machine Intelligence 28(2), 316–322 (2006)
19. Harel, J., Koch, C., Perona, P.: Graph-based visual saliency. In: Advances in Neural Information Processing Systems, Vancouver, pp. 554–552 (2007)
20. Hirzer, M., Roth, P.M., Bischof, H.: Person re-identification by efficient impostor-based metric learning. In: Advanced Video and Signal-Based Surveillance, pp. 203–208 (2012)
21. Hirzer, M., Roth, P.M., Köstinger, M., Bischof, H.: Relaxed pairwise learned metric for person re-identification. In: Fitzgibbon, A., Lazebnik, S., Perona, P., Sato, Y., Schmid, C. (eds.) ECCV 2012, Part VI. LNCS, vol. 7577, pp. 780–793. Springer, Heidelberg (2012)
22. Hou, X., Harel, J., Koch, C.: Image Signature: Highlighting Sparse Salient Regions. IEEE Transactions on Pattern Analysis and Machine Intelligence 34(1), 194–201 (2011)
23. Itti, L., Koch, C.: Computational modelling of visual attention. Nature Reviews. Neuroscience 2(3), 194–203 (2001)
24. Javed, O., Shafique, K., Rasheed, Z., Shah, M.: Modeling inter-camera spacetime and appearance relationships for tracking across non-overlapping views. Computer Vision and Image Understanding 109(2), 146–162 (2008)
25. Kostinger, M., Hirzer, M., Wohlhart, P., Roth, P.M., Bischof, H.: Large scale metric learning from equivalence constraints. In: International Conference on Computer Vision and Pattern Recognition, pp. 2288–2295 (2012)
26. Kviatkovsky, I., Adam, A., Rivlin, E.: Color Invariants for Person Re-Identification. IEEE Transactions on Pattern Analysis and Machine Intelligence 35(7), 1622–1634 (2013)
27. Li, J., Levine, M.D., An, X., Xu, X., He, H.: Visual saliency based on scale-space analysis in the frequency domain. IEEE Transactions on Pattern Analysis and Machine Intelligence 35(4), 996–1010 (2013)
28. Li, W., Wang, X.: Locally aligned feature transforms across views. In: International Conference on Computer Vision and Pattern Recognition, pp. 3594–3601. IEEE (June 2013)
29. Li, W., Zhao, R., Wang, X.: Human reidentification with transferred metric learning. In: Lee, K.M., Matsushita, Y., Rehg, J.M., Hu, Z. (eds.) ACCV 2012, Part I. LNCS, vol. 7724, pp. 31–44. Springer, Heidelberg (2013)

30. Liu, C., Gong, S., Loy, C.C.: On-the-fly Feature Importance Mining for Person Re-Identification. Pattern Recognition (November 2013)
31. Liu, C., Gong, S., Loy, C.C., Lin, X.: Person re-identification: what features are important? In: Fusiello, A., Murino, V., Cucchiara, R. (eds.) ECCV 2012 Ws/Demos, Part I. LNCS, vol. 7583, pp. 391–401. Springer, Heidelberg (2012)
32. Liu, C., Loy, C.C., Gong, S., Wang, G.: POP: person re-identification post-rank optimisation. In: International Conference on Computer Vision (2013)
33. Lombardi, S., K, N., Makihara, Y., Yagi, Y.: Two-point gait: decoupling gait from body shape. In: International Conference on Computer Vision, pp. 1041–1048 (2013)
34. Ma, B., Su, Y., Jurie, F.: BiCov: a novel image representation for person re-identification and face verification. In: British Machine Vision Conference, pp. 57.1–57.11 (2012)
35. Ma, B., Su, Y., Jurie, F.: Local descriptors encoded by fisher vectors for person re-identification. In: Fusiello, A., Murino, V., Cucchiara, R. (eds.) ECCV 2012 Ws/Demos, Part I. LNCS, vol. 7583, pp. 413–422. Springer, Heidelberg (2012)
36. Martinel, N., Micheloni, C.: Person re-identification by modelling principal component analysis coefficients of image dissimilarities. Electronics Letters 50(14), 1000–1001 (2014)
37. Martinel, N., Foresti, G.L.: Multi-signature based person re-identification. Electronics Letters 48(13), 765 (2012)
38. Martinel, N., Micheloni, C.: Re-identify people in wide area camera network. In: International Conference on Computer Vision and Pattern Recognition Workshops, pp. 31–36. IEEE, Providence (2012)
39. Martinel, N., Micheloni, C., Piciarelli, C.: Learning pairwise feature dissimilarities for person re-identification. In: International Conference on Distributed Smart Cameras, pp. 1–6. IEEE, Palm Springs (2013)
40. Martinel, N., Micheloni, C., Piciarelli, C., Foresti, G.L.: Camera Selection for Adaptive Human-Computer Interface. IEEE Transactions on Systems, Man, and Cybernetics: Systems 44(5), 653–664 (2014)
41. Micheloni, C., Remagnino, P., Eng, H.L., Geng, J.: Intelligent Monitoring of Complex Environments. IEEE Intelligent Systems 25(3), 12–14 (2010)
42. Mignon, A., Jurie, F.: PCCA: A new approach for distance learning from sparse pairwise constraints. In: IEEE Conference on Computer Vision and Pattern Recognition, pp. 2666–2672. IEEE (June 2012)
43. Ojala, T., Pietikainen, M., Maenpaa, T.: Multiresolution gray-scale and rotation invariant texture classification with local binary patterns. IEEE Transactions on Pattern Analysis and Machine Intelligence 24(7), 971–987 (2002)
44. Pedagadi, S., Orwell, J., Velastin, S.: Local fisher discriminant analysis for pedestrian re-identification. In: International Conference on Computer Vision and Pattern Recognition, pp. 3318–3325 (2013)
45. Perazzi, F., Krahenbuhl, P., Pritch, Y., Hornung, A.: Saliency filters: contrast based filtering for salient region detection. In: International Conference on Computer Vision and Pattern Recognition, pp. 733–740. IEEE (June 2012)
46. Veeraraghavan, A., Roy-Chowdhury, A.K., Chellappa, R.: Matching shape sequences in video with applications in human movement analysis. IEEE Transactions on Pattern Analysis and Machine Intelligence 27(12), 1896–1909 (2005)
47. Vezzani, R., Baltieri, D., Cucchiara, R.: People Re-identification in Surveillance and Forensics: a Survey. ACM Computing Surveys 46(2) (2014)

48. Wang, W., Wang, Y., Huang, Q., Gao, W.: Measuring visual saliency by site entropy rate. In: International Conference on Computer Vision and Pattern Recognition, vol (2), pp. 2368–2375. IEEE (June 2010)
49. Wu, Y., Minoh, M., Mukunoki, M., Li, W., Lao, S.: Collaborative sparse approximation for multiple-shot across-camera person re-identification. In: Advanced Video and Signal-Based Surveillance, pp. 209–214. IEEE (September 2012)
50. Zhang, G., Wang, Y., Kato, J., Marutani, T., Mase, K.: Local distance comparison for multiple-shot people re-identification. In: Lee, K.M., Matsushita, Y., Rehg, J.M., Hu, Z. (eds.) ACCV 2012, Part III. LNCS, vol. 7726, pp. 677–690. Springer, Heidelberg (2013)
51. Zhao, R., Ouyang, W., Wang, X.: Person re-identification by salience matching. In: International Conference on Computer Vision, pp. 2528–2535. IEEE (December 2013)
52. Zhao, R., Ouyang, W., Wang, X.: Unsupervised salience learning for person re-identification. In: IEEE Conference on Computer Vision and Pattern Recognition, pp. 3586–3593. IEEE (June 2013)
53. Zhao, W., Chellappa, R., Phillips, P.J., Rosenfeld, A.: Face Recognition: A Literature Survey. ACM Computing Surveys 35(4), 399–458 (2003)
54. Zheng, W.S., Gong, S., Xiang, T.: Re-identification by Relative Distance Comparison. IEEE Transactions on Pattern Analysis and Machine Intelligence 35(3), 653–668 (2013)

Regularized Bayesian Metric Learning
for Person Re-identification

Venice Erin Liong[1], Jiwen Lu[1], and Yongxin Ge[2,3]($\boxtimes$)

[1] Advanced Digital Sciences Center, Singapore, Singapore
{venice.l,jiwen.lu}@adsc.com.sg
[2] Key Laboratory of Dependable Service Computing in Cyber Physical Society
Ministry of Education, Chongqing 400044, China
yongxinge@cqu.edu.cn
[3] School of Software Engineering, Chongqing University, Chongqing 400044, China

Abstract. Person re-identification across disjoint cameras has attracted increasing interest in computer vision due to its wide potential applications in visual surveillance. In this paper, we propose a new regularized Bayesian metric learning (RBML) method for person re-identification. While numerous metric learning methods have been proposed for person re-identification in recent years, most of them suffer from the small sample size (SSS) problem because there are not enough training samples in most practical person re-identification systems, so that the within-class and between-class variations can be well estimated to learn the distance metric. To address this, we propose a RBML method to model and regulate the eigen spectrums of these two covariance matrices in a parametric manner, so that discriminative information can be better exploited. Experimental results on three widely used datasets demonstrate the advantage of our proposed RBML over the state-of-the-art person re-identification methods.

Keywords: Person re-identification · Metric learning · Regularization

1 Introduction

Person re-identification aims to match and recognize persons who have been observed over different disjoint cameras, and it has many potential applications such as information retrieval and visual surveillance. Over the past decade, many person re-identification methods have been proposed in the literature, and they can be mainly classified into two categories: feature-based [8,17] and model-based [16,38,42]. Feature-based approach aims to extract robust and discriminative features to characterize the appearance of human body images [1,2,8,12,17,21,41], and model-based approach learns a classifier or ranker to recognize the query body image.

Recent years have witnessed that metric learning has been one of most popular methods in person re-identification [3,20,23,24,26–31,35,40]. Metric learning aims to learn a Mahalanobis distance metric to transform samples from

© Springer International Publishing Switzerland 2015
L. Agapito et al. (Eds.): ECCV 2014 Workshops, Part III, LNCS 8927, pp. 209–224, 2015.
DOI: 10.1007/978-3-319-16199-0_15

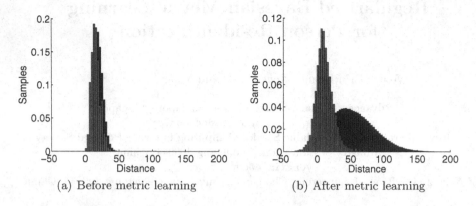

(a) Before metric learning   (b) After metric learning

Fig. 1. Similarity distribution over 3160 positive and 3160 randomly sampled negative pairs from the VIPeR dataset. (a) The original distribution in the Euclidean space. (b) The new distribution in the learned metric space. The histograms with the red color and the blue color represent the matched (same person) and mismatched (different person) image pairs, respectively. Before metric learning, the similarity of matched and mismatched pairs overlaps heavily, which is more challenging for re-identification. However, these two similarity distribution histograms become more separate in the learned distance metric, so that more discriminative information is exploited.

the original space to another feature space by exploiting the between-class and within-class variations. Representative metric learning algorithms include large margin nearest neighbor (LMNN) [39], information theoretic metric learning (ITML) [5], and neighborhood component analysis (NCA) [10]. The objective of metric learning is to learn a discriminative similarity to better measure the similarity of human body images by making use of some prior knowledge. Fig. 1 illustrates an example to show the advantage of metric learning for person re-identification. While metric learning methods have shown promising performance in person re-identification, most of them suffer from the small sample size (SSS) problem because there are usually not enough training samples to estimate the within-class and between-class variations.

In this paper, we propose a new regularized Bayesian metric learning (RBML) method for person re-identification. Our method models the difference of each positive pair and that of each negative pair as a Gaussian distribution model under the Bayesian framework, and optimizes their probability ratio to learn a discriminative distance metric. To better estimate the intra-class and inter-class variations when there are small number of training samples, we decompose the eigen-spectrum of each covariance matrix into two subspaces and regularize them in a parametric manner. By doing so, the learned distance metric can extract more relevant information. Our method is evaluated on three widely used person re-identification datasets and experimental results demonstrate the efficacy of the proposed method.

2   Related Work

Person Re-identification: Existing person re-identification methods can be categorized into two classes: feature-based and model-based. Feature-based methods extract visual signatures to differentiate different persons. For example, Farenzena *et al.* [8] developed a symmetry driven accumulation of local feature (SDALF) for body appearance modeling. Jungling *et al.* [15] designed a codebook learning approach to cluster local features for implicit body shape matching. Ma *et al.* [32] developed a BiCov descriptor which combines biologically-inspired features and covariance features for human body representation. Ma *et al.* [33] used local descriptors from pixel intensities and encoded them into higher-order Fisher vectors for feature representation. Gray *et al.* [12] selected a subset of color and texture features for person body representation. Schwartz *et al.* [37] performed partial least squares (PLS) to adaptively weight different local features for body representation. Model-based methods learn a classification or ranking model to recognize the query body image from the gallery set. Representative methods include support vector machine [36], transfer learning [18], manifold ranking [22] and metric learning [6,10,16,34]. In this work, we contribute to the second category and propose a new metric learning approach for person re-identification.

Metric Learning: Metric learning aims to learn a Mahalanobis distance metric to transform samples to another feature space by exploiting the between-class and within-class variations. In recent years, metric learning has been widely used in person re-identification and has also achieved the state-of-the-art performance. For example, Hirzer *et al.* [13] proposed a relaxed pairwise metric leaning approach. Kostinger *et al.* [16] learned a Mahalanobis distance metric based on the statistical inference over the ratio of similar and similar pairs in the training set. Zheng *et al.* [44] proposed a relative distance comparison (PRDC) metric learning to maximize the probability of a positive pair having a smaller distance than a negative pair. However, there are still two shortcomings among these methods: 1) most of them rely on a large number of training samples and may not perform well when the training set is small; 2) most of them perform an iterative optimization procedure for training, which increases the computational complexity. To address this, we propose a simple yet effective metric learning method for person re-identification, where the difference of each pair of positive and negative pairs are represented as a Bayesian model, respectively, and the ratio of positive pairs over negative pairs is minimized. Since the number of training samples is usually small, we regularize the covariance matrices in a parametric manner to make them well-estimated and stable. By doing so, relevant information can be extracted from the learned distance metric.

3   Regularized Bayesian Metric Learning

Let $x \in R^d$ be the feature representation of a body image, S and D two sets of similar and dissimilar pairs, where $(x_i, x_j) \in S$ is a feature pair from the same person and $(x_i, x_j) \in \mathcal{D}$ is a pair from different persons. We compute the following ratio:

$$\delta(x_i, x_j) = \log\left(\frac{\Pr[(x_i, x_j) \in \mathcal{D}]}{\Pr[(x_i, x_j) \in \mathcal{S}]}\right) \tag{1}$$

where $\Pr[\cdot]$ is a probability distribution function to measure the likelihood of whether (x_i, x_j) is from the same person. Specifically, $\delta(x_i, x_j)$ is high if they are from different persons, and low from the same person. We model the probability distribution function as a single Gaussian distribution of $(x_{ij} = x_i - x_j)$ with zero mean as follows:

$$\Pr[\cdot] = \frac{1}{\sqrt{2\pi\,|\,\Sigma\,|}} \exp\left(-\frac{1}{2}x_{ij}^T \Sigma^{-1} x_{ij}\right) \tag{2}$$

Then, (1) can be simplified as follows by removing the log operator and the constant term:

$$\begin{aligned}
\delta(x_i, x_j) &= x_{ij}^T \Sigma_1^{-1} x_{ij} + \log(|\Sigma_1|) - x_{ij}^T \Sigma_0^{-1} x_{ij} - \log(|\Sigma_0|) \\
&= x_{ij}^T(\Sigma_1^{-1} - \Sigma_0^{-1})x_{ij}
\end{aligned} \tag{3}$$

where

$$\Sigma_1 = \sum_{(x_i, x_j) \in \mathcal{S}} (x_i - x_j)(x_i - x_j)^T \tag{4}$$

$$\Sigma_0 = \sum_{(x_i, x_j) \in \mathcal{D}} (x_i - x_j)(x_i - x_j)^T \tag{5}$$

These two covariance matrices cannot be well estimated if there are not enough training samples. To address this, we regulate each of them. We first obtain the eigen-spectrum of each covariance matrix as follows:

$$\Sigma = \Phi\Lambda\Phi^T \tag{6}$$

where $\Lambda = \mathrm{diag}(\lambda_1, \lambda_2, \cdots, \lambda_d)$ denotes the eigenvalues of Σ, which is sorted in a descending order, and $\Phi = [\phi_1, \phi_2, \cdots, \phi_d]$ is the corresponding eigenvector.

The eigen-spectrum obtained with small number of training samples is usually biased because the energy of the spectrum is concentrated at a few principal components corresponding to the largest eigenvalues and those corresponding to smaller eigenvalues are unreliable. To better estimate the eigen-spectrum in the whole space, we divide the original eigen-spectrum of Λ into two subspaces, called principal (P) and noise (N) space and regulate each of them separately:

$$\lambda_t \in \begin{cases} P, & t \leq c \\ N, & c+1 \leq t \leq d \end{cases} \tag{7}$$

where c is a pre-specified energy percentage parameter which is computed as follows:

$$c = \min\{c | (\sum_{t=1}^{c} \lambda_t / \sum_{t=1}^{d} \lambda_t) \geq \zeta\} \tag{8}$$

To better estimate the eigen-spectrum, we present a new regularization model which reduces the effect of larger eigenvalues in P and enhances the effect of smaller eigenvalues in N as follows:

$$\lambda'_t = \begin{cases} \left(\dfrac{a}{t+b}\right)^{\alpha} + K & \text{for } t \le c \\ \dfrac{a}{t+b} & \text{for } c+1 < t < d \end{cases} \quad (9)$$

In (9), we regularize the whole eigen-spectrum in a parametric manner by using the $1/f$ function because this function fits well to the decaying nature of the eigen-spectrum [14,25]. Since the eigenvalues in P are much larger than those in N, we further shrink and suppress them by using an exponential function using parameter α, where $0 < \alpha < 1$. The parameter K in (9) is used to make the eigen-spectrum continuous in the whole space so that a smooth eigen-spectrum can be obtained in the whole space, where

$$K = \frac{a}{c+b} - \left(\frac{a}{c+b}\right)^{\alpha} \quad (10)$$

Let $\lambda_1 = \frac{a}{1+b}$ and $\lambda_c = \frac{a}{c+b}$. The coefficients a and b are computed as:

$$a = \frac{\lambda_1 \lambda_c (c-1)}{\lambda_1 - \lambda_c} \quad (11)$$

$$b = \frac{c\lambda_c - \lambda_1}{\lambda_1 - \lambda_c} \quad (12)$$

Having obtained the modeled eigen-spectrum, we compute the modeled covariance matrix as follows:

$$\Sigma' = \Phi \Lambda' \Phi^T \quad (13)$$

where $\Lambda' = \text{diag}(\lambda'_1, \lambda'_2, \cdots, \lambda'_d)$ are the eigenvalues which are sorted in a decreasing order. Now, the Mahalanobis distance metric in (3) can be computed as follows:

$$\delta(x_{ij}) = x_{ij}^T (\Sigma_1'^{-1} - \Sigma_0'^{-1}) x_{ij}$$
$$= (x_i - x_j)^T \mathbf{M}(x_i - x_j) \quad (14)$$

where $\mathbf{M} \triangleq \Sigma_1'^{-1} - \Sigma_0'^{-1}$.

Fig. 2 show the estimated and original eigen-spectrum of one covariance matrix, and we see that effect of the eigenvalues in the N space is enhanced in the modeled space. **Algorithm 1** summarizes the proposed RBML method.

4   Experiments

We evaluate the proposed RBML method on three widely used person re-identification datasets, namely the VIPeR [11], ETHZ [7] and i-LIDS [43] databases. The following describe the details of our experiments and results.

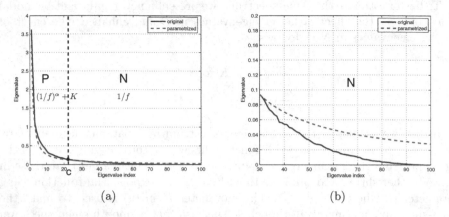

(a)   (b)

Fig. 2. (a) The basic idea of our proposed RBML, where the eigen-spectrum of the covariance matrix is decomposed into two subspaces and regularized with different models. (b) Zooming in of the original and modeled noise spaces.

Input: Positive and negative training sample pairs and parameters α and ζ.
Output: Mahalanobis distance metric **M**.
Step 1 (Initialization):
      1.1. Compute covariance matrices for similar and dissimilar pairs, respectively.
Step 2 (Regularization and Modeling):
      For each covariance matrix, repeat
      2.1. Perform eigendecomposition using (6).
      2.2. Compute for parametric c using (8).
      2.3. Estimate the new eigenspectrum using (9).
      2.4. Compute the new covariance using (13).
Step 3 (Output):
      Output the matrix **M** using (14).

Algorithm 1: RBML

4.1   Settings

For each person image, we extracted a mixture of color and texture histogram features by following the detailed settings in [12, 42]. Each person image is represented by a 2784-dimensional feature vector. Specifically, we divided the person image into six horizontal stripes. For each stripe, the RGB, YCbCr, HSV color features and texture features (Schmid and Gabor) were extracted and represented as a histogram feature. We applied PCA to project the feature representation into a 100-dimensional feature vector to remove the redundancy of the high-dimensional feature space.

Having extracted the feature of each image, we learned a discriminative distance metric by using the proposed RBML method. Finally, the nearest neighbor is used for ranking.

Fig. 3. Sample images of the VIPeR dataset. The images from each column are body images captured from different cameras and belong to the same person.

Table 1. Matching rates (%) of different metric learning methods on the VIPeR dataset

Method	$p = 316$				$p = 100$			
Rank	1	10	25	50	1	10	25	50
RBML	**27.22**	**72.78**	**89.08**	**95.89**	**13.06**	**47.46**	**64.94**	**79.70**
KISSME[16]	22.15	66.77	82.91	92.41	1.41	7.14	12.78	21.24
RS-KISSME [38]	22.31	67.41	86.23	94.62	10.71	40.98	59.30	76.79
Mahalanobis	13.29	48.58	71.04	84.02	8.93	34.49	52.82	67.86
Identity	4.43	16.93	27.06	42.56	1.41	7.42	12.69	21.43
ITML [5]	0.95	8.23	18.20	32.28	3.67	11.94	20.39	30.08
LMNN [39]	18.04	59.34	78.16	89.72	8.08	34.40	51.60	66.82

4.2 Evaluation on the VIPeR Dataset

The VIPeR dataset [11] consists of 632 persons and each person has two images captured from two different cameras in an outdoor environment. Most image pairs in this dataset have a viewpoint change of 90 degrees, where one is from the front/back view and the other is from the side view. There are large variations of illumination, viewpoint and pose in these captured images. Fig. 3 shows some sample images in the VIPeR dataset.

We followed the experimental settings in [12,42]. In our experiments, we randomly selected p persons for training and the remaining persons were used for testing. We repeated this selection 10 times and took the average as the final re-identification accuracy. In the training phase, two images from the same person form a positive pair, and two images from different persons form a negative pair. In the testing phase, we used the single-shot testing where one image per person was randomly selected to form the gallery set and the remaining images were used to form the probe set.

We used the cumulative matching curve (CMC) as the evaluation metric in our experiments, where a match is found at the top-n ranks. The parameters ζ and α were empirically set to 90% and 0.9, respectively.

Probe   Rank 15 Gallery Images   True
                                                                  Match

Fig. 4. Examples of person re-identification on the VIPeR dataset using our proposed RBML. The first column indicates the probe images, the middle area shows the top-15 ranked results from the gallery image with a highlighted red box for the correct match with our method, and the last column shows the true match.

Comparison with Existing Metric Learning Algorithms: Table 1 tabulates the matching rates of different metric learning methods, which includes LMNN, ITML, KISSME and RS-KISSME, as well as the widely used Mahalanobis and Identity (Euclidean) distance metrics on the VIPeR dataset. We see that our proposed RBML method consistently outperforms all metric learning methods with as high as 5% and 2% Rank-1 accuracy at $p = 316$ and $p = 100$, respectively. Fig. 4 shows the matching examples of our RBML method on the VIPeR dataset.

Comparison with State-of-the-Art Person Re-identification Methods: We also compared our RBML with the state-of-the-art person re-identification methods on the VIPeR dataset. Tables 2 and 3 tabulate the matching accuracies on this dataset when p is set to 316 and 100, respectively. We see that RBML outperforms all the state-of-the-art person re-identification across several ranks. Particularly, the rank-1 matching rate of our method improves the current state-of-the-art methods by 0.8% and 2.1% when p is set as 316 an 100, respectively.

Parameter Analysis: We also investigated the individual contributions of our RBML model. We define three variations of our method to study their different importance: 1) RBML1: regularizing the noise space only; 2) RBML2: regularizing without the suppression in the principal space; and 3) RBML3: regularizing the noise and principal space without continuity. RBML1 was implemented by regularizing the noise space with the $1/f$ function only and the principal space is not regularized. RBML2 ignored the suppression in the principal space, which is equivalent to setting the parameter α as 1 in RBML. RBML3 performed the same modeling method as RBML for both the principal and noise spaces but discarded the continuity parameter K in the principal space. Fig. 5

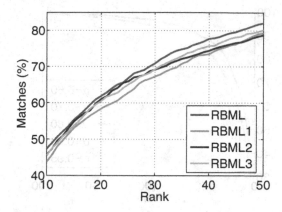

Fig. 5. CMC curves for different types of regularization methods in our model at $p = 100$ on the VIPeR dataset

Table 2. Matching rates (%) of our method and the state-of-the-art person re-identification methods on the VIPeR dataset when p is set as 316

Method	r=1	r=5	r=10	r=20
RBML	**27.53**	**58.23**	**71.52**	**84.65**
eSDC [41]	26.74	50.70	62.37	76.36
eLDFV [33]	22.34	47.00	67.04	71.00
eBiCov [32]	20.66	42.00	56.18	68.00
CPS [4]	21.84	44.00	57.21	71.00
SDALF [8]	19.87	38.89	49.37	65.73
ELF [12]	12.00	31.00	41.00	58.00
PRDC [42]	15.66	38.42	53.86	70.09
aPRDC [19]	16.14	37.72	50.98	65.95
PCCA [34]	19.27	48.89	64.91	80.28

shows the matching rates of different types of regularization model in our RBML on the VIPeR dataset. It can be seen that removing a portion of our model degrades the whole re-identification performance. Moreover, the regularization in the noise space is the most important in our method and the suppression in the principal space also contributes to the overall performance. Lastly, the continuity of the eigen-spectrum is also useful to improve the re-identification result.

We also investigated the performance of our method versus varying values of α. Fig. 6 shows the CMC curves versus varying values of α. We see that the performance of our method degrades heavily when α is smaller than 0.9.

Computational Time: We investigated the computational time of different methods on the VIPeR dataset. Our hardware configuration comprises a 2.4-GHz CPU and a 8GB RAM. Table 4 shows the average training time of different methods on the VIPeR dataset when the number of p is set as 316. We see that

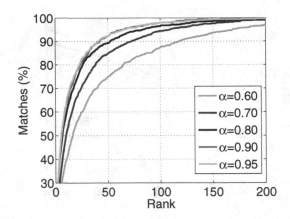

Fig. 6. CMC curves of our method versus varying values of α at $p = 316$ on the VIPeR dataset

Table 3. Matching rates (%) of our method and the state-of-the-art person re-identification methods on the VIPeR dataset when p is set as 100.

Method	r=1	r=5	r=10	r=20
RBML	**13.16**	**34.12**	**46.71**	**60.62**
Hirzer's [13]	11.00	-	38.00	52.00
PRDC [42]	9.12	24.19	34.40	48.55
PCCA [34]	9.27	24.89	37.43	52.89
MCC [10]	5.00	16.32	25.92	39.64

our RBML method is more efficient than other popular metric learning methods such as ITML and LMNN, and as efficient as KISSME. That is because our regularization operation doesn't require any complex optimization and iteration.

Comparison with Other Regularization Methods: We also compared our method with other regularization models such as smoothing and shrinkage. For smoothing regularization, the noise space of the eigen-spectrum of the covariance matrix is defined by a constant, $\beta = \frac{1}{d-c} \sum_{t=c+1}^{d} \lambda_t$. The shrinkage regularization model [9] regulates the model as: $\Sigma' = (1 - \gamma)\Sigma + \gamma\tau\mathbf{I}$, where γ is the shrinkage parameter which ranges from 0 to 1, and $\tau = (1/d)\text{tr}(\Sigma)$. Table 5 shows the matching rates of different regularization methods on the VIPeR dataset. As shown in the table, our method outperforms the smoothing and shrinkage regularization techniques at varying sizes of training set. This indicates that our method is the most effective in estimating the covariance matrix correctly.

Performance of Different Sizes of Training Set: We investigated the performance of our method with varying sizes of training set. As shown in Table 6, our method outperforms other metric learning methods at different training sizes, especially when the size of training set is small.

Table 4. Average training time (seconds) of different metric learning methods on the VIPeR dataset

Method	Time
RBML	0.0020
KISSME	0.0006
RS-KISSME	0.0020
Mahalanobis	0.0002
Identity	0.000001
ITML	6.5100
LMNN	10.2200

Table 5. Matching rates (%) of different regularization methods on the VIPeR dataset

Training Size	$p = 316$				$p = 100$			
Rank	1	5	10	20	1	5	10	20
RBML	**27.53**	**57.6**	**73.3**	**86.4**	**13.5**	**33.6**	**45.7**	**60.0**
Smoothing	21.8	51.9	66.1	77.2	9.9	26.5	38.0	52.4
Shrinkage	26.3	55.9	70.3	84.7	11.1	30.3	41.2	54.2

4.3   Evaluation on the ETHZ Dataset

The ETHZ dataset [37] consists of 8555 images of 146 persons. The images are obtained from 3 video sequences captured from a moving camera. Since the persons are captured in one single camera, the pose and viewpoint variations in this dataset are smaller than those in the VIPeR dataset. However, there are larger variations in illumination and occlusions in this dataset. Fig. 7 shows some samples from the ETHZ dataset. We randomly selected p persons and for each person, we also randomly choose 6 images for training. In the testing phase, we also used the single-shot testing where one image per person was randomly selected to form the gallery set and the remaining images were used to form the probe set. Table 7 shows the matching rates of different metric learning methods on the ETHZ dataset. As can be shown, our RBML achieves comparable results with existing metric learning when p is set to 76, and outperforms other methods when p is set to 26. Fig. 8 shows the matching examples of our RBML method on the ETHZ dataset.

Table 6. Rank 1 matching rates (%) at varying p on the VIPeR dataset

Method	p=500	p=300	p=200	p=100
RBML	**43.2**	**28.3**	**19.2**	**13.6**
KISSME	40.9	23.2	15.1	1.3
RSKISSME	41.7	24.4	18.1	10.9
Mahalanobis	20.4	13.3	3.9	3.5

Fig. 7. Sample images of the ETHZ dataset. Each column show the original image of the same person with different pose captured from a moving camera

Probe
Image
Rank 15 Gallery Images
True
Match

Fig. 8. Examples of person re-identification on the ETHZ dataset using our proposed RBML

Table 7. Matching rates (%) of different metric learning methods on the ETHZ dataset

Method	$p = 76$				$p = 26$			
Rank	1	5	10	20	1	5	10	20
RBML	**71.65**	**89.00**	**94.39**	**97.74**	62.30	**82.46**	**88.23**	**93.79**
KISSME[16]	70.93	87.11	93.52	97.31	42.67	72.62	82.85	92.1
RS-KISSME [38]	70.47	88.57	93.81	97.34	60.10	79.40	86.43	92.57
Mahalanobis	71.28	88.38	94.33	97.47	**62.42**	79.42	86.31	93.35
Identity	56.29	79.48	88.18	93.87	51.24	72.07	80.69	88.58
ITML [5]	43.92	70.85	82.09	99.31	53.92	75.63	84.45	91.97
LMNN [39]	65.76	85.78	92.23	96.22	60.32	80.01	87.20	93.02

Fig. 9. Sample images of the i-LIDS MCTS dataset. Each column show the original image of the same person captured from different cameras.

Probe Image   Rank 15 Gallery Images   True Match

Fig. 10. Examples of person re-identification on the i-LIDS dataset using our proposed RBML

4.4 Evaluation on the i-LIDS Dataset

The i-LIDS Multiple-Camera Tracking Scenario (MCTS) dataset [43] contains 476 images from 119 persons, where each person has an average of 4 images. This dataset was captured at a busy airport arrival hall by using multiple non-overlapping cameras. It is one of the more difficult datasets for person re-identification because there are heavy occlusions caused by the busy crowd and large illumination and pose variations caused by different camera views. Fig. 9 shows some samples in the dataset. We randomly selected p persons for training and used the single-shot testing for the remaining subjects. Table 8 shows the matching rates of different metric learning methods on the i-LIDS MCTS dataset. We see that our RBML outperforms other metric learning methods. Fig. 10 shows the matching examples of our RBML method on the i-LIDS dataset.

Table 8. Matching rates (%) of different metric learning methods on the i-LIDS dataset

Training Size	$p = 89$				$p = 39$			
Rank	1	5	10	20	1	5	10	20
RBML	**32.78**	**63.07**	**81.25**	**94.15**	**20.24**	**44.07**	**55.58**	**72.27**
KISSME[16]	31.24	57.54	75.91	92.84	10.72	26.95	37.10	51.79
RS-KISSME [38]	30.58	61.93	80.11	**94.15**	18.51	39.83	53.46	69.97
Mahalanobis	29.44	50.37	68.13	89.76	12.77	29.86	41.11	53.91
Identity	18.73	46.64	64.76	89.42	13.69	30.60	44.79	58.99
ITML [5]	6.63	25.15	48.17	81.14	6.07	18.42	29.25	49.58
LMNN [39]	23.63	57.18	76.12	92.28	17.79	38.19	51.10	65.45

4.5   Discussion

The above experimental results suggest the following two observations:

1. RBML consistently outperforms the other metric learning methods, especially when the size of the training set is relatively small. That is because the noise space is much larger when the size of the training set is small, and our regularization model plays an important role for such scenarios.
2. Each individual part of our regularization model contributes to the improvement of the identification performance. Moreover, our method obtains better performance than other existing regularization methods. This is because the RBML estimates the eigen-spectrum in a parametric manner so that a stable eigen-spectrum can be obtained.

5   Conclusion

In this paper, we have proposed a regularized Bayesian metric learning (RBML) for person re-identification. The proposed method learns a Mahalanobis distance metric by measuring the probability ratio between similar and dissimilar pairs modeled with a Bayesian model, where the covariance matrices are regularized in a parametric manner so that they are well-estimated. Experimental results on three widely used re-identification datasets have shown the the efficacy of the proposed method.

Acknowledgments. This study is partially supported by the research grant for the Human Cyber Security Systems (HCSS) Program at the Advanced Digital Sciences Center (ADSC) from the Agency for Science, Technology and Research (A*STAR) of Singapore, and the Specialized Research Fund for the Doctoral Program of Higher Education (Grant no. 20130191120033).

References

1. Ahonen, T., Hadid, A., Pietikainen, M.: Face description with local binary patterns: Application to face recognition. PAMI **28**(12), 2037–2041 (2006)

2. Bay, H., Tuytelaars, T., Van Gool, L.: SURF: Speeded up robust features. In: Leonardis, A., Bischof, H., Pinz, A. (eds.) ECCV 2006, Part I. LNCS, vol. 3951, pp. 404–417. Springer, Heidelberg (2006)
3. Chen, Y.-C., Patel, V.M., Phillips, P.J., Chellappa, R.: Dictionary-based face recognition from video. In: Fitzgibbon, A., Lazebnik, S., Perona, P., Sato, Y., Schmid, C. (eds.) ECCV 2012, Part VI. LNCS, vol. 7577, pp. 766–779. Springer, Heidelberg (2012)
4. Cheng, D.S., Cristani, M., Stoppa, M., Bazzani, L., Murino, V.: Custom pictorial structures for re-identification. In: BMVC, pp. 1–6 (2011)
5. Davis, J.V., Kulis, B., Jain, P., Sra, S., Dhillon, I.S.: Information-theoretic metric learning. In: ICML, pp. 209–216 (2007)
6. Dikmen, M., Akbas, E., Huang, T.S., Ahuja, N.: Pedestrian recognition with a learned metric. In: Kimmel, R., Klette, R., Sugimoto, A. (eds.) ACCV 2010, Part IV. LNCS, vol. 6495, pp. 501–512. Springer, Heidelberg (2011)
7. Ess, A., Leibe, B., Van Gool, L.: Depth and appearance for mobile scene analysis. In: ICCV, pp. 1–8 (2007)
8. Farenzena, M., Bazzani, L., Perina, A., Murino, V., Cristani, M.: Person re-identification by symmetry-driven accumulation of local features. In: CVPR, pp. 2360–2367 (2010)
9. Friedman, J.H.: Regularized discriminant analysis. Journal of the American Statistical Association 84(405), 165–175 (1989)
10. Globerson, A., Roweis, S.: Metric learning by collapsing classes. In: NIPS, pp. 451–458 (2005)
11. Gray, D., Brennan, S., Tao, H.: Evaluating appearance models for recognition, reacquisition, and tracking. In: PETS (2007)
12. Gray, D., Tao, H.: Viewpoint invariant pedestrian recognition with an ensemble of localized features. In: Forsyth, D., Torr, P., Zisserman, A. (eds.) ECCV 2008, Part I. LNCS, vol. 5302, pp. 262–275. Springer, Heidelberg (2008)
13. Hirzer, M., Roth, P.M., Köstinger, M., Bischof, H.: Relaxed pairwise learned metric for person re-identification. In: Fitzgibbon, A., Lazebnik, S., Perona, P., Sato, Y., Schmid, C. (eds.) ECCV 2012, Part VI. LNCS, vol. 7577, pp. 780–793. Springer, Heidelberg (2012)
14. Jiang, X., Mandal, B., Kot, A.: Eigenfeature regularization and extraction in face recognition. PAMI 30(3), 383–394 (2008)
15. Jungling, K., Bodensteiner, C., Arens, M.: Person re-identification in multi-camera networks. In: CVPRW, pp. 55–61 (2011)
16. Kostinger, M., Hirzer, M., Wohlhart, P., Roth, P.M., Bischof, H.: Large scale metric learning from equivalence constraints. In: CVPR, pp. 2288–2295 (2012)
17. Kviatkovsky, I., Adam, A., Rivlin, E.: Color invariants for person re-identification. PAMI 35(7), 1622–1634 (2012)
18. Li, W., Zhao, R., Wang, X.: Human reidentification with transferred metric learning. In: Lee, K.M., Matsushita, Y., Rehg, J.M., Hu, Z. (eds.) ACCV 2012, Part I. LNCS, vol. 7724, pp. 31–44. Springer, Heidelberg (2013)
19. Liu, C., Gong, S., Loy, C.C., Lin, X.: Person re-identification: what features are important? In: Fusiello, A., Murino, V., Cucchiara, R. (eds.) ECCV 2012 Ws/Demos, Part I. LNCS, vol. 7583, pp. 391–401. Springer, Heidelberg (2012)
20. Liu, N., Lu, J., Tan, Y.P.: Joint subspace learning for view-invariant gait recognition. IEEE Signal Processing Letters 18(7), 431–434 (2011)
21. Lowe, D.G.: Distinctive image features from scale-invariant keypoints. IJCV 60(2), 91–110 (2004)
22. Loy, C.C., Liu, C., Gong, S.: Person re-identification by manifold ranking. In: ICIP, pp. 3567–3571 (2013)

23. Lu, J., Tan, Y.P.: Gait-based human age estimation. IEEE Transactions on Information Forensics and Security **5**(4), 761–770 (2010)
24. Lu, J., Tan, Y.: Uncorrelated discriminant simplex analysis for view-invariant gait signal computing. Pattern Recognition Letters **31**(5), 382–393 (2010)
25. Lu, J., Tan, Y.P.: Regularized locality preserving projections and its extensions for face recognition. TSMC Part B **40**(3), 958–963 (2010)
26. Lu, J., Tan, Y.P.: Ordinary preserving manifold analysis for human age and head pose estimation. IEEE Transactions on Human-Machine Systems **43**(2), 249–258 (2013)
27. Lu, J., Tan, Y.P., Wang, G.: Discriminative multimanifold analysis for face recognition from a single training sample per person. IEEE Transactions on Pattern Analysis and Machine Intelligence **35**(1), 39–51 (2013)
28. Lu, J., Wang, G., Moulin, P.: Image set classification using holistic multiple order statistics features and localized multi-kernel metric learning. In: IEEE International Conference on Computer Vision, pp. 329–336 (2013)
29. Lu, J., Wang, G., Moulin, P.: Human identity and gender recognition from gait sequences with arbitrary walking directions. IEEE Transactions on Information Forensics and Security **9**(1), 51–61 (2014)
30. Lu, J., Zhang, E.: Gait recognition for human identification based on ica and fuzzy svm through multiple views fusion. Pattern Recognition Letters **28**(16), 2401–2411 (2007)
31. Lu, J., Zhou, X., Tan, Y.P., Shang, Y., Wang, G.: Neighborhood repulsed metric learning for kinship verification. IEEE Transactions on Pattern Analysis and Machine Intelligence **36**(2), 331–345 (2014)
32. Ma, B., Su, Y., Jurie, F.: Bicov: a novel image representation for person re-identification and face verification. In: BMVC, pp. 1–6 (2012)
33. Ma, B., Su, Y., Jurie, F.: Local descriptors encoded by fisher vectors for person re-identification. In: Fusiello, A., Murino, V., Cucchiara, R. (eds.) ECCV 2012 Ws/Demos, Part I. LNCS, vol. 7583, pp. 413–422. Springer, Heidelberg (2012)
34. Mignon, A., Jurie, F.: Pcca: A new approach for distance learning from sparse pairwise constraints. In: CVPR, pp. 2666–2672 (2012)
35. Moghaddam, B., Jebara, T., Pentland, A.: Bayesian face recognition. Pattern Recognition **33**(11), 1771–1782 (2000)
36. Prosser, B., Zheng, W.S., Gong, S., Xiang, T., Mary, Q.: Person re-identification by support vector ranking. In: BMVC, pp. 1–11 (2010)
37. Schwartz, W.R., Davis, L.S.: Learning discriminative appearance-based models using partial least squares. In: SIBGRAPI, pp. 322–329 (2009)
38. Tao, D., Jin, L., Wang, Y., Yuan, Y., Li, X.: Person re-identification by regularized smoothing kiss metric learning. TCSVT **23**(10), 1675–1685 (2013)
39. Weinberger, K., Saul, L.: Distance metric learning for large margin nearest neighbor classification. JMLR **10**, 207–244 (2009)
40. Yan, H., Lu, J., Deng, W., Zhou, X.: Discriminative multimetric learning for kinship verification. IEEE Transactions on Information Forensics and Security **9**(7), 1169–1178 (2014)
41. Zhao, R., Ouyang, W., Wang, X.: Unsupervised salience learning for person re-identification. In: CVPR, pp. 3586–3593 (2013)
42. Zheng, W., Gong, S., Xiang, T.: Re-identification by relative distance comparison. PAMI **35**(3), 653–668 (2013)
43. Zheng, W.S., Gong, S., Xiang, T.: Associating groups of people. In: BMVC, pp. 1–11 (2009)
44. Zheng, W.S., Gong, S., Xiang, T.: Person re-identification by probabilistic relative distance comparison. In: CVPR, pp. 649–656 (2011)

Investigating Open-World Person Re-identification Using a Drone

Ryan Layne$^{(\boxtimes)}$, Timothy M. Hospedales, and Shaogang Gong

Vision Group, School of EECS, Queen Mary University of London, London, UK
r.d.c.layne@qmul.ac.uk

Abstract. Person re-identification is now one of the most topical and intensively studied problems in computer vision due to its challenging nature and its critical role in underpinning many multi-camera surveillance tasks. A fundamental assumption in almost all existing re-identification research is that cameras are in fixed emplacements, allowing the explicit modelling of camera and inter-camera properties in order to improve re-identification. In this paper, we present an introductory study pushing re-identification in a different direction: re-identification on a mobile platform, such as a drone. We formalise some variants of the standard formulation for re-identification that are more relevant for mobile re-identification. We introduce the first dataset for mobile re-identification, and we use this to elucidate the unique challenges of mobile re-identification. Finally, we re-evaluate some conventional wisdom about re-id models in the light of these challenges and suggest future avenues for research in this area.

1 Introduction

Person re-identification has been extensively and aggressively studied in recent years by the computer vision community due to its challenging nature and critical role in underpinning many security and business-intelligence tasks in multi-camera surveillance [9]. This has resulted in continued improvements in performance on increasingly challenging benchmark datasets. In essence re-identification is about successfully retrieving people by *identity*, enabling security operators or higher-level software components to locate individuals. Nevertheless, it is conventionally formulated as a one-to-one set-matching problem between two fixed cameras, for which an effective model can be learned. In this paper we present an introductory study that relaxes this core assumption and investigates how re-identification generalises to mobile surveillance platforms as realised by quadrocopter drones [5].

Despite the successes of static CCTV cameras, we argue that considering alternative surveillance equipment not only opens up exciting new research areas, but also new ways of thinking about re-identification and particularly, how re-identification fits into real-world applications and links with other research fields. New technology such as remotely-operated vehicles and wearable visual sensing equipment is becoming increasingly accessible in terms of cost and availability to

© Springer International Publishing Switzerland 2015
L. Agapito et al. (Eds.): ECCV 2014 Workshops, Part III, LNCS 8927, pp. 225–240, 2015.
DOI: 10.1007/978-3-319-16199-0_16

the general public. In many cases, quickly deployable mobile visual systems rival currently predominant static CCTV cameras in terms of resolution and frame-rate. More critically, they intrinsically have a qualitative flexibility advantage – in terms of being mobile – and are thus able to dynamically adapt their viewing position and direction without being constrained by the emplaced locations of a CCTV camera.

We term any piece of equipment that can perform video surveillance in a portable sense, a *mobile re-identification platform* or, MRP.

While generalising re-identification to MRPs provides many new capabilities and research avenues, it introduces some significant differences and new challenges compared to the standard formulation of the re-identification problem. These broadly relate to the interrelated issues of (1) view ambiguity, (2) view variability and (3) open-world re-id.

Within-view Ambiguity: The first major contrast between MRP and standard fixed camera re-id relates to the number of views. That is, the standard setting is typically defined across a pair of camera views, and within-camera tracking is typically assumed to fully disambiguate detections within-view. In contrast for MRPs 'within camera' re-id is itself non-trivial because the camera's positional and orientational mobility means that even stationary people frequently enter and exit the view area due solely to self-motion of the platform. This further generalises the so called 'MvsAll' scenario described in [14] to 'AllvsAll'.

View Variability: The second major contrast is the continually varying view-stream of a MRP compared to the conventional fixed position CCTV camera. This is significant because most of the recent performance gains in the state of the art re-id methods have come from supervised learning of *view* or *view-pair specific* models [10]. In the MRP case the *continually* varying view parameters – including range, lighting, self induced motion blur and detection alignment – precludes learning such models (see Figure 1).

Open-World: Most existing re-id studies make the simplifying assumption of closed-world conditions. That is that there is a one-to-one set match, where everyone in the first camera re-appears in the second camera. No one disappears, and no extra people appear. Although convenient for modelling and benchmarking purposes, this is clearly an extremely strong assumption in practice. In the case of MRP with within-camera re-id ambiguity, and the mobile nature of the platform, closed-world is clearly an inappropriate assumption – meaning that re-id with MRP is significantly more ambiguous than the conventional setting.

Despite the challenges identified above, MRPs provide a compelling new ground to break for re-identification science both in terms of broadening the application area as well as providing the opportunity to reconsider several implicit but strong assumptions made in most existing re-id research. In this work, we make four main contributions: (i) We present a case for the pursuit and development of a new research area using mobile re-identification platforms (MRPs); (ii) We formalise three novel MRP-related variants on the classic re-identification

Fig. 1. Illustrating key differences in person detection quality when automatically detected from mobile re-identification platform video (MRP, left), compared to detections in a standard re-identification dataset, VIPeR (right). Notably, the VIPeR images (i) are in perfect register, (ii) feature standard walking poses from a limited number of relative angles. Contrastingly, the MRP images are unregistered, feature more varied pose and also occasionally heavy motion-blur because of the relative motion of the MRP to the target person during transit.

scenario; as well as associated evaluation metrics for each; (iii) We collect the first public dataset for MRP re-id and establish benchmarks for each of the identified tasks; (iv) We elucidate the unique challenges posed by MRP re-id and discuss their implications for general re-id research going forward.

2   Related Work

Re-identification: There is now an extensive body of research on conventional re-identification, broadly split into contributing effective feature representations [7,33], discriminative matching models [1,2], or both [18]. The other major design axis typically considered is 'single-shot' [1,2,33] (exactly one image per person) versus 'multi-shot' [7,15,26] (exploiting multiple images per person where available to improve results). For a broad background of research to this paper we suggest [10] and [31]. Going beyond conventional re-identification, we next discuss a few recently identified research areas that are relevant to our MRP context.

Open-world Re-Id: At its most general, open world re-identification [4,9] addresses relaxing several assumptions: one-to-one set-match (that is, that every person in the probe set appears in the gallery set and vice-versa) [13]; the assumption of matching between only two cameras [13]; the assumption of a known number of people; or that multi-shot grouping is known a-priori [14]. A few studies have begun to work toward this including [13,14]. However, these have generally considered only a couple of these relaxations at once. In contrast, the MRP re-id scenario is intrinsically open-world: self movement in a potentially open-space means one-to-one match situations are unlikely, self-motion means that tracking cannot provide multi-shot grouping, and clearly the person count of an arbitrarily surveilled space is not known in advance.

Generalised-view Re-Id: The conventional approach to maximising re-id performance is learning a discriminative model to maximise re-id rate for a specific pair of fixed camera views [1, 2]. A few studies have started to consider how re-identification models generalise across views [19] and generally found that they don't – achieving good re-id rate requires view specific discriminative training. This reflects analogous conclusions drawn more broadly in computer vision recognition [30]. As a result, studies have begun to develop transfer strategies that allow models learned from 'source' view pair(s) to be adapted to better apply in a new 'target' view [3, 19, 22] which may have different position, lighting, etc. These studies have generally considered combining [3] or adapting [19, 22] source model(s) to construct the model for a new domain – with the general aim of reducing or eliminating the need for collecting annotated training data for every pair of cameras. The important contrast with our MRP context is that domains/camera pairs as described above are *discrete*. In contrast, the video feed from a MRP is a *continuously varying* domain. This means that for previous approaches to view generalisation it is still assumed that enough data to model a specific view or view pair can be collected and a discriminative model learned. This is no longer feasible for MRP, since the constantly varying view means that collecting (let alone annotating) extensive view-specific data is impossible, and the conventional strategy of learning a discriminative model is called into question.

Drones: A full discussion of background research in drone technology is out of the scope of this paper, but see [5] for an introduction and background to drones and their capabilities. The central issue for drones to become more useful for surveillance tasks is for them to become increasingly autonomous, and a significant component of this is learning to maintain consistent person identity estimates over time, which we address here.

3   Re-identification Problem Variants and Metrics

Conventional re-identification is used as a forensic search tool, or as a module by higher-level software – such as inter-camera tracking [25]. For ease of model formulation (e.g., metric learning, SVM ranking), evaluation and establishing benchmarks, most studies formalise re-id as a closed-world set match between two specific cameras. As a result the typical evaluation metric is Rank 1 accuracy (the % of perfect gallery matches for each probe image), or the CMC curve (the % of correct matches within the top N ranked matches, for varying N) [32]. In this section we describe three distinct variants of the re-identification problem that naturally arise with MRPs – each based on intuitive application scenarios for a MRP. Table 1 summarises the problem variants proposed and compares them with classical approaches to re-id.

3.1   Watchlist Verification

In the *watchlist* task, the MRP is patrolling an area and the goal is to detect if any person encountered is somebody on a pre-defined watch-list. For the moment we make no assumption on whether the MRP is manually controlled, has a pre-programmed travel path or autonomously wanders. However, we assume that the scenario is *passive sensing* – the MRP is not going to to take action based on any detected matches. The watchlist itself could come from a variety of sources: a pre-defined mug-shot gallery; a transmitted detection from another MRP or CCTV camera; or a previous detection saved by the current MRP on a previous flight or earlier in this patrol. For example the MRP may be trying to track down a specific person previously identified performing a suspicious action of interest.

In this case, the 'probe' is a single person from the watch list, and the 'gallery' is all people observed in a patrol. In contrast to conventional re-id, this is a more open world problem in that: (i) the probe person may not appear anywhere in the patrol video (no match is an option), (ii) (most) people in the patrol video are not on the watchlist (many background distractors), and (iii) the total number of detected instances of the true match if present in the gallery/patrol video is unknown (not one-to-one). In Table 1 this is illustrated under match by [N] and [M] reflecting multiple potential *ungrouped* matches and distractors respectively.

Given these considerations, the right evaluation metrics for this problem are information-retrieval style metrics, thus we use a suite of them: (i) the rank of the true matches, and (ii) precision-recall curves and associated summary – average-precision.

3.2   Within-Flight Re-identification

In the *within-flight* re-identification task, the MRP's goal is to maintain consistent identity of person detections recorded throughout the flight.

Due to both platform and target motion, a particular target may enter the view once, or enter and exit the view multiple times throughout the flight. In this case there is only one "camera view" as compared to conventional re-id setting of two fixed cameras. However, it means that: (i) the platform motion can create potentially more view-variation over time than occurs between two fixed CCTV cameras, so "within-view" re-identification can become even harder than conventional re-id; (ii) as before, there is a general open-world identity inference problem.

The general identity inference problem here means that there is no-longer a notion of probe and gallery. Instead there is a list of N detections, which each need to be assigned one of $K \leq N$ unique identities. However K (the number of unique people in the scene) is itself unknown. In Table 1 this is illustrated under match by [N] – the single set of detections with unknown grouping – and an unknown person count.

Evaluating this open world identity assignment is non-trivial compared to closed world. To fully evaluate the performance, we use statistical analysis on all pairs of detections to measure pairwise Precision and Recall. Specifically given all true $\mathcal{L}_{gt}$ and estimated $\mathcal{L}_{est}$ labels of the N detections. A 'true' pair i, j has the same label, and a 'false' pair have different labels. Thus true-positive, true-negative, false positive and false-negative rates can be computed as in Eq. (2);

Table 1. Contrasting re-identification problem variants. Match: $N : N$ reflects closed world one-to-one mapping among N people in view 1 : view 2. $[N]$ indicates unknown within-camera grouping. M represents the unknown fraction of the people to be matched who are distractors in that they do not occur in the other view or the watchlist.

Setting	Cameras	Match	Person Count	View-specific	Multi-shot	Evaluation
Singleshot [1,2,7,33]	2	$N : N$	Known	Yes	No	Rank 1, CMC
Multishot [7,15]	2	$N : N$	Known	Yes	Grouped	Rank 1, CMC
Karaman [14]	2	$N : [N]$	Known	Yes	Group : No group	Accuracy
John [13]	2	$N + M_1 : N + M_2$	Known	Yes	No	Rank 1
Watchlist	1	$1 : [N] + [M]$	N/A	No	No group	Rank, Prec+Recall
Within	1	$[N]$	Unknown	No	No group	F-measure
Across	2	$[N] + [M_1] : [N] + [M_2]$	Unknown	No	No group	F-measure

which can in turn be summarised in terms of Precision, Recall, Specificity, and Accuracy as in Eq. (1).

$$TP = \sum_{ij} (\mathcal{L}_{gt}(i) = L_{gt}(j)) \wedge (\mathcal{L}_{est}(i) = \mathcal{L}_{est}(j))$$

$$Prec = TP/(TP + FP)$$
$$Rec = TP/(TP + FN)$$

$$TN = \sum_{ij} (\mathcal{L}_{gt}(i) \neq L_{gt}(j)) \wedge (\mathcal{L}_{est}(i) \neq \mathcal{L}_{est}(j))$$

$$Spec = TN/(FP + TN)$$
$$Acc = (TP + TN)/N \quad (1)$$

$$FP = \sum_{ij} (\mathcal{L}_{gt}(i) \neq L_{gt}(j)) \wedge (\mathcal{L}_{est}(i) = \mathcal{L}_{est}(j))$$

$$FN = \sum_{ij} (\mathcal{L}_{gt}(i) = L_{gt}(j)) \wedge (\mathcal{L}_{est}(i) \neq \mathcal{L}_{est}(j)) \quad (2)$$

3.3 Across-Flight Re-identification

The *across-flight* problem is somewhat more related to the classic problem of between-camera re-id. In this case identities should be matched across two separate MRP flights. This may be from either the same platform making two patrols, or two distinct and communicating platforms trying to coordinate identities. It is a fully open-world problem, given that within-flight/view tracking cannot be assumed for MRPs (ungrouped detections in Table 1), and that only an unknown subset of the total people in each view may be shared (in Table 1, N shared + M distractor people in each view). However, compared to within-flight re-identification, it may be somewhat harder because the environments across space and/or time may be even more different than the view change caused by platform motion in the previous case. Again, statistical analysis is the appropriate evaluation technique.

4 Methodology and Experimental Setting

4.1 Data Acquisition

Drone Setup. We use a standard remote-operated quadrocopter to realise our MRP for data acquisition. During data collection, a human operator controlled

Fig. 2. Flight path detail (center) and images of the drone used in our experiments indoors (left) and outdoors (right)

the drone via laptop using the Robot Operating System (ROS[1]) to ensure responsive handling with the control loop and sensor data capture operating at $\approx$ 200Hz whilst video from the quadrocopter was sampled at $\approx 1 - 5$Hz. For this particular commodity platform, flight time was limited by battery capacity to $\approx$ 10 minutes per flight at 640x360 pixels.

During flight, a heads-up-display (HUD) is overlaid on top of the video feed displaying standard sensor information (such as yaw, pitch, acceleration, battery and altitude), as well as real-time person detections and person detection confidence scores. This in some sense serves to provide the operator with the visual cues necessary to weakly simulate an active-sensing, fully autonomous (i.e. closed-loop) drone. If the drone is orientated poorly towards a person or the person is partially occluded then a poor detection will result and the operator can adjust the relative orientation and position of the drone based on this visualisation until a strong detection can be obtained. Some examples of the HUD can be seen in Figure 3.

Person Detection. Given the $1 - 5$Hz video feed, the next task is to obtain person detections. To maximise the reliability of this step, we first apply a corrective transform on each frame to correct for the 'roll' of the drone (using data recorded from the MRP's onboard accelerometer sensor), since the detection models assume people to be upright. In order to detect people fast enough for real-time visualisation so as to assist the MRP's operator, we employ [6]'s toolkit which provides excellent computational efficiency and detection quality. At extraction time, we resample detections to [128x48] pixels[2]. We threshold detections and discard any with a confidence of below 20% since the environments from which we will be detecting are extremely varied with respect to lighting and pose and we wish to limit the number of potential false-positive detections whilst retaining most true detections.

---

[1] http://www.ros.org/
[2] However, note that the original resolution and therefore resample quality will vary dramatically over time within a flight, see Figure 1.

Fig. 3. Screen captures from our mobile re-identification platform's data capture sessions; illustrating real-time person detections colour-coded by detection confidence. The top-left and top-right images illustrate typical operator views from the outdoor and indoor flights from Dataset 1; The bottom row illustrates Dataset 2.

For our visual features we employ the commonly used ensemble of local features [11] (ELF), which encodes both color and texture in 6 horizontal strips [24] for final features of 2784 dimensions.

Datasets. Using the procedure described above, we collected two multi-flight datasets. **Dataset 1:** The first dataset contains three flights worth of data, across an outdoor and indoor environment. These consisted of 436, 652, 848 video frames, from which we obtained 233, 471, and 797 person detections from 6, 7, and 10 distinct people (after thresholding). All person detections in this dataset are exhaustively annotated. **Dataset 2:** The second, significantly larger, dataset contains six flights of data in three different unconstrained and heavily crowded outdoor environments. Across each flight there are between 10,000 and 30,000 frames of video data and an average of 8,654 person detections from an unknown number of distinct people. Of this data, we selected a single flight and exhaustively annotated 28 unique identities within the 4096 detections available within a 2:06 window[3].

4.2   Classifier Training, Representation and Datasets

Training Strong Models. One of the central questions we wanted to answer is to what extent the state of the art discriminative models for standard benchmark

---

[3] All datasets and annotations will be realised on the web at http://qml.io/rlayne

datasets are effective for MRP based re-identification. This question is crucial because conditions in MRP-sourced video data continuously change during a flight thus there are many more combinations of pose and viewing angle than in the fixed view case assumed by most state of the art models – i.e. a fixed view with enough (annotated) data is sufficient to learn a model. It is therefore critical to discover if and how much performance discriminative models lose on dynamically changing data.

We investigate this by training a selection of strong discriminative models including one of the most popular: RankSVM [24]; and two recent state of the art approaches BR-SVM [1] and KISS [17]. We train these models on a variety of large benchmark datasets including VIPER [27] (632 distinct persons in [128x48] crops), PRID [12] (200 distinct persons), GRID [21] (250 persons) and CUHK [20] (971 persons). We resample all detections to match VIPeR's dimensions. For the computationally intensive discriminative methods, we reduce the dimension with PCA to $d = 200$ for BR-SVM and $d = 34$ for KISS as specified in [17].

Domain Shift. Since we assume a stationary view and the absence of live-annotation of video-feed data (as proxies for normal discriminative training on a single-view), the only way to apply trained matching models for MRPs is to train them on benchmark datasets before testing them on the MRP video feed. This potentially opens up the issue of *domain shift* [8,19,23] between the training and testing data. For example, due to additional chance of motion blur, mis-registered images and more variance in pose from the MRP detections (Figure 1), which are absent in VIPER.

As a preliminarily investigation into how to overcome this issue, we consider unsupervised domain-adaptation in order to better align the target MRP data X_t and source VIPeR training data X_s. That is, warp $p(X_t)$ so that it is more aligned with the source training data $p_{adapt}(X_t) \approx p(X_s)$, with the intuition that this should allow classifiers trained on X_s to generalise better to X_t [23]. In particular, we align the projected subspaces of the two datasets, using the geodesic flow kernel domain adaptation (DA) method [8] using $d_{DA} = 13$ dimensions..

4.3   Re-identification and Baselines for Comparison

For **Task 1: Watchlist**, we simulate this experiment by taking each person detection in turn as the watch-list, and matching it against every other detection from the flight to produce a ranked list. The ranked list of results is then evaluated for relevance with information retrieval metrics (Sec 3.1). Whether first, average or last rank; or average precision is the most relevant metric will depend on the end-user application and cost function. We evaluate this task with both Datasets 1 and 2. For **Task 2: Intra-flight re-identification** and **Task 3: Inter-flight re-identification** (Sec 3.2-3.3), the experiment is performed by matching every detection against every other detection. The resulting detection-affinity matrix is thresholded[4] and analysed for connected components [29]. Each

---

[4] The threshold is chosen to optimise F-measure for each model.

connected component defines an estimated person. The estimated $\mathcal{L}_{set}$ and true $\mathcal{L}_{gt}$ identities are compared using statistical analysis as explained in Section 3. We evaluate these tasks with Dataset 1. As algorithms to produce the matching scores for each experiment, we compare the following models:

NN-[DA]. Nearest-neighbor (NN) matching based on the detection descriptor.
BR-SVM-[DA] Binary-relation SVM with RBF concatenation kernel [1].
RankSVM-[DA]. SVM with difference feature and linear kernel [24].
KISS-[DA]. State of the art discriminative Mahalanobis metric learning [17].

In each case we compare the model with and without domain adaptation (-DA suffix). As explained earlier, we do not have annotated view-specific training data. Thus, we train the latter three discriminative models on the full VIPER dataset of 632 pairs and test them on the MRP video detections. These models obtain good results when applied within-domain on VIPER [1,17,24], however our experiment will test their ability to generalise this knowledge to a continuously varying view.

5   Experiments

5.1   Watchlist and Re-identification Evaluations

We first present the results for the three main tasks before drawing conclusions from them.

Task 1: Watchlist The results of watchlist verification are presented in Table 2(a) for Dataset 1, and Table 2(b) for Dataset 2. This task reflects how highly true matches to each particular watchlist person are ranked relative to all the other person detections in the dataset, on average. Clearly all methods perform better than random: average rank, for example, has a chance level of half the number of detections across all flights which is $500/2 = 250$ for Dataset 1 and $4046/2 = 2023$ for Dataset 2. The best methods obtain a first rank result of around 2. Surprisingly, this is the case both in the smaller Dataset 1 and the larger Dataset 2.

Task 2: Intra-flight re-identification Intra-flight re-id results for Dataset 1 are presented in Table 3(a). This task attempts un-constrained detection association across all detections within a flight.

Task 3: Inter-flight re-identification Intra-flight re-id results for Dataset 1 are presented in Table 3(b). This task attempts un-constrained detection association across all detections from a pair of flights.

5.2   Observations and Analysis

Based on the results described in the previous section and Tables 2-3, we make the following observations and conclusions.

Table 2. Watchlist verification results for each model. Top: Dataset 1, results are averages over all persons and all flights, average 500.3 total detections. Bottom: Dataset 2, results are for single annotated flight, 4046 total detections. For the rank metrics lower is better (↓) and for the average precision metric higher is better (↑).

Dataset 1	NN	NN-DA	KISS	KISS-DA	BRSVM [1]	BRSVM [1] DA	RankSVM [24]	RankSVM [24] DA
First rank ↓	2.08	4.69	4.15	5.37	12.32	15.87	9.76	17.53
Last rank ↓	167.93	162.89	156.70	150.82	166.35	160.78	177.32	170.37
Average rank ↓	56.30	56.47	54.45	57.39	65.65	68.77	76.81	81.51
Average Prec ↑	0.46	0.46	0.43	0.41	0.34	0.35	0.24	0.24
Dataset 2	NN	NN-DA	KISS	KISS-DA	BRSVM [1]	BRSVM [1] DA	RankSVM [24]	RankSVM [24] DA
First rank ↓	1.91	2.47	18.02	9.89	265.59	18.87	280.57	424.64
Last rank ↓	1864.34	2001.95	2152.18	2032.83	2841.16	2238.77	2673.06	3357.40
Average rank ↓	507.30	528.85	619.78	635.10	1256.77	753.53	1213.27	1848.23
Average Prec ↑	0.36	0.34	0.19	0.25	0.04	0.14	0.04	0.02

Table 3. Re-identification results for Dataset 1: (left) Intra flight, and (right) Inter flight. In each case Precision, Recall and F-measure are averaged across all three flights. Higher is better for all metrics.

	Precision ↑	Recall ↑	F-Measure ↑	Specificity ↑	Accuracy ↑	Precision ↑	Recall ↑	F-Measure ↑	Specificity ↑	Accuracy ↑
NN	0.83	0.29	0.39	0.99	0.88	0.34	0.49	0.29	0.63	0.60
NN DA	0.47	0.59	0.47	0.76	0.73	0.38	0.39	0.32	0.80	0.74
KISS [17]	0.32	0.30	0.28	0.82	0.74	0.15	0.93	0.26	0.09	0.21
KISS [17] DA	0.23	0.59	0.31	0.56	0.56	0.15	0.97	0.26	0.04	0.18
BRSVM [1]	0.37	0.27	0.18	0.70	0.70	0.15	1.00	0.26	0.00	0.15
BRSVM [1] DA	0.32	0.23	0.17	0.85	0.74	0.15	1.00	0.26	0.00	0.15
RANKSVM [24]	0.00	0.65	0.17	0.35	0.38	0.15	0.98	0.26	0.03	0.17
RANKSVM [24] DA	0.00	0.36	0.12	0.64	0.58	0.15	0.98	0.26	0.03	0.17

(1) NN is best overall – Surprisingly, outperforming all discriminative methods including KISS, BRSVM and RankSVM. In dramatic contrast to the standard ordering of results obtained in the literature [1, 2, 24], where discriminatively trained models significantly outperform simple nearest-neighbour; our results show that in the MRP context, the simplest NN method is generally best. This is true overall for Dataset 1 with all three tasks, as well as the significantly larger Dataset 2 for the watchlist task. This is due to the intrinsic challenge of MRP re-id that there is no possibility to learn view-specific models.

In order to apply discriminative models to our MRP data, we transferred models trained on VIPER. However, this may not be effective because the MRP video is more variable and unconstrained. Meanwhile, the strong discriminative models have evidently over fitted to the more constrained viewing conditions in VIPER. NN, in contrast, is more reliable because it doesn't train a strong discriminative model and thus cannot over fit in this sense.

(2) Simpler models are better overall. The overall ordering of the results is $NN > KISS > BRSVM$. This generally reflects the model complexity, with NN being the simplest, BRSVM being the most complex (due to RBF kernels on concatenated data), and KISS being in between. This ordering also reflects the importance of pairwise training data volume to the model, with KISS and

Table 4. Attempting to improve the performance of KISS [17] on the watchlist task by training on all available data (ED). Results are from a single flight in Dataset 1.

	First rank ↓	Last rank ↓	Mean rank ↓	Av Prec ↑
KISS (ED)	1.66	64.44	20.79	0.57
KISS-DA (ED)	3.29	60.68	21.40	0.56
KISS	1.25	81.31	25.90	0.53
KISS-DA	3.50	81.65	30.08	0.35

BRSVM both requiring fairly large volumes of training data from the same view in order to perform well.

(3) Domain adaptation can help – but it helps NN significantly more than discriminative models. Comparing the vanilla condition of each model with the domain adaptation condition (-DA suffix), we see that domain adaptation doesn't make much consistent difference for the watchlist experiment (Table 2), but it sometimes makes a significant difference in the re-identification experiment (Table 3). However, KISS for example is improved from mAP of 0.28 to 0.31 with domain adaptation; while NN is improved much more significantly from mAP of 0.39 to 0.47. That domain-adaptation can help is in one sense not surprising (the MRP video has different statistics to VIPER and aligning the distributions should help), but in another sense surprising (the MRP video is only a *domain* in a very limited sense – because the view varies so much there is hardly a consistent set of statistics $p(X_t)$ to adapt toward). Meanwhile, the fact that it helps NN more than KISS is understandable because KISS still suffers from over fitting to the particular source data (VIPER).

(4) Discriminative models cannot be "fixed" for MRP by adding more conventional training data. The significance of the previous results – with respect to limitations of the discriminative models – could be questioned on the grounds of whether VIPER data is *representative* enough for the variety of views obtained by the MRP. To test this, we re-trained the KISS model using the union of the four largest benchmark re-id datasets to date, including VIPER, CUHK, GRID and PRID, thus greatly increasing the volume and variety of data used. Table 4 compares the watchlist verification results when training KISS only on VIPER versus training on all existing datasets (ED suffix). Clearly using all the extra data makes only a minor difference to the performance.

5.3 Person Count Evaluation

As a final example application, we perform person counting on the flight videos. This is computed as a by-product of open-world re-identification: each identified connected component of the detections defines a distinct person. In general NN and NN-DA provide a near best or best estimate in each case, as seen in Table 5.

Table 5. Person counts in Dataset 1. Result for each method is shown as the average error between the estimated and true count. (Lower is better) (upper) **Intra**-flight condition, (lower) **Inter**-flight condition.

	Actual	NN	KISS	BRSVM	NN-DA	KISS-DA	BRSVM-DA	RankSVM
Flight1	6.0	±16.0	±23.0	±79.0	±7.0	±20.0	±37.0	±102.0
Flight2	7.0	±0.0	±0.0	±5.0	±1.0	±3.0	±2.0	±2.0
Flight3	10.0	±40.0	±13.0	±1.0	±6.0	±92.0	±3.0	±27.0
Average	7.7	±18.7	±12.0	±28.3	±4.0	±38.3	±14.0	±42.3
	Actual	NN	KISS	BRSVM	NN-DA	KISS-DA	BRSVM-DA	RankSVM
Flight1$\leqslant$2	7.0	±5.0	±0.0	±38.0	±0.0	±0.0	±74.0	±48.0
Flight2$\leqslant$3	10.0	±0.0	±13.0	±21.0	±6.0	±5.0	±0.0	±1.0
Flight1$\leqslant$3	10.0	±0.0	±6.0	±0.0	±3.0	±7.0	±84.0	±226.0
Average	9.0	±1.7	±6.3	±19.7	±3.0	±4.0	±52.7	±91.7

6 Discussion

6.1 Summary and Key Results

Based on the experiments and analysis in the previous section, we drew the following conclusions: 1. NN is the best method for MRP re-id, 2. In general simpler methods outperform more complex methods, 3. Unsupervised domain adaptation can improve MRP re-id, 4. The challenge is intrinsic to the nature of benchmark datasets being captured by static cameras, and the MRP dataset being captured by a dynamic camera.

6.2 Implications for Future Work

Given these insights, we highlight the following implications for future work:

1. Current re-id research has been too focused on learning dataset specific models, leading to dataset bias [30]. Analogous to research trends in more general computer vision [16], developing methods that avoid bias and generalise across datasets is necessary to fully exploit the potential of reid to MRPs.
2. Domain adaptation methods can potentially help adapt re-id methods across scenarios with different data statistics. However while most domain adaptation methods require some supervision in the target domain, it is important that DA methods used in this context are unsupervised, since live annotation of MRP detections is implausible. In the current results, a completely disjoint unsupervised DA module [8] is able to make an impact. Investigating tighter integration of the DA and re-id mechanism is likely to be fruitful.
3. Conventional re-id and DA [8] methods assume the target task is a distinct and discrete context. The continually varying nature of MRP view, and hence data statistics, means that it may be important to treat MRP as an online rather than a discrete adaptation process. This is a somewhat unique aspect of DA for re-id in contrast to more general vision problems [16,30].

4. Consideration of the MRP task highlights the intrinsically open-world nature of re-id which has largely been ignored for convenience by prior research. In this study we addressed this by a very simple strategy of threshold learning. However, more effort should be put toward developing more systematic and optimal methods to resolve open-world ambiguity.

5. Our new continuously-varying view dataset has a total of 51,922 unconstrained person detections across six flights resulting in hundreds of identities that partially overlap across three outdoor zones. This challenging MRP dataset is qualitatively different to existing re-id datasets, and will help drive the research challenges identified above.

6.3   Potential Applications

Finally, given the partial success obtained so far, we discuss some speculative applications for MRP technology.

Open vs. Closed-loop MRP: Our first re-identification case for MRP is an open-loop scenario where the re-identification task does not directly have any impact on the travel path of the vehicle; but data from the vehicle still enables analysis and detection albeit in a passive sense. In this mode of operation, the MRP will likely either be under control of a human operator, or will follow a set of preconfigured waypoints along a patrol-route, with the video sensor data available for analysis either in near real-time, or after the MRP has returned home. This is conceptually closest to the standard re-identification problem.

In contrast, closed-loop MRP control may be fully or semi-automated and critically, may permit the MRP to automatically adapt a regular patrol-route or journey for optimal performance on specific re-identification tasks. For example, re-id quality-control to move the MRP to get a better view when current re-id is too ambiguous [26]. For a given flight time or length, this then leads into an interesting trade-off between re-id accuracy of each individual versus coverage: the fraction of total people captured in a zone in total [28].

Acknowledgments. Ryan Layne is supported by a EPSRC CASE studentship supported by UK MOD SA/SD.

References

1. Avraham, T., Gurvich, I., Lindenbaum, M., Markovitch, S.: Learning implicit transfer for person re-identification. In: Fusiello, A., Murino, V., Cucchiara, R. (eds.) ECCV 2012 Ws/Demos, Part I. LNCS, vol. 7583, pp. 381–390. Springer, Heidelberg (2012)

2. Bischof, H., Roth, P.M., Hirzer, M., Wohlhart, P., Kostinger, M.: Large scale metric learning from equivalence constraints. In: IEEE Conference on Computer Vision and Pattern Recognition (2012)

3. Brand, Y., Avraham, T., Lindenbaum, M.: Transitive Re-identification. British Machine Vision Conference (3) (2013)

4. Cancella, B., Hospedales, T.M., Gong, S.: Open-World person re-identification by multi-label assignment inference. In: British Machine Vision Conference (2014)
5. Clarke, R.: Understanding the drone epidemic. Computer Law & Security Review **30**(3) (2014)
6. Dollár, P., Appel, R., Belongie, S., Perona, P., Doll, P.: Fast Feature Pyramids for Object Detection. IEEE Transactions on Pattern Analysis and Machine Intelligence (2014)
7. Farenzena, M., Bazzani, L., Perina, A., Murino, V., Cristani, M.: Person re-identification by symmetry-driven accumulation of local features. In: IEEE Conference on Computer Vision and Pattern Recognition (2010)
8. Gong, B., Shi, Y., Sha, F., Grauman, K.: Geodesic flow kernel for unsupervised domain adaptation. In: IEEE Conference on Computer Vision and Pattern Recognition. IEEE (2012)
9. Gong, S., Cristani, M., Loy, C.C., Hospedales, T.M.: Person re-identification, chap. In: The Re-Identification Challenge. Springer (2013)
10. Gong, S., Cristani, M., Yan, S., Loy, C.C. (eds.): Person Re-identification. Springer (2014)
11. Gray, D., Tao, H.: Viewpoint invariant pedestrian recognition with an ensemble of localized features. In: Forsyth, D., Torr, P., Zisserman, A. (eds.) ECCV 2008, Part I. LNCS, vol. 5302, pp. 262–275. Springer, Heidelberg (2008)
12. Hirzer, M., Beleznai, C., Roth, P.M., Bischof, H.: Person re-identification by descriptive and discriminative classification. In: Heyden, A., Kahl, F. (eds.) SCIA 2011. LNCS, vol. 6688, pp. 91–102. Springer, Heidelberg (2011)
13. John, V., Englebienne, G., Krose, B.: Solving person re-identification in non-overlapping camera using efficient gibbs sampling. In: British Machine Vision Conference (2013)
14. Karaman, S., Bagdanov, A.D.: Identity inference: generalizing person re-identification scenarios. In: Fusiello, A., Murino, V., Cucchiara, R. (eds.) ECCV 2012 Ws/Demos, Part I. LNCS, vol. 7583, pp. 443–452. Springer, Heidelberg (2012)
15. Khedhrer, M.I., el Yacoubi, M.A., Dorizzi, B.: Multi-shot surf-based person re-identification via sparse representation. In: Advanced Video Surveillance Systems (2013)
16. Khosla, A., Zhou, T., Malisiewicz, T., Efros, A.A., Torralba, A.: Undoing the damage of dataset bias. In: Fitzgibbon, A., Lazebnik, S., Perona, P., Sato, Y., Schmid, C. (eds.) ECCV 2012, Part I. LNCS, vol. 7572, pp. 158–171. Springer, Heidelberg (2012)
17. Kostinger, M., Hirzer, M., Wohlhart, P., Roth, P.M., Bischof, H.: Large scale metric learning from equivalence constraints. In: IEEE Conference on Computer Vision and Pattern Recognition (2012)
18. Layne, R., Hospedales, T.M., Gong, S.: Person re-identification by attributes. In: British Machine Vision Conference (2012)
19. Layne, R., Hospedales, T.M., Gong, S.: Domain transfer for person re-identification. In: Workshop on Analysis and Retrieval of Tracked Events and Motion in Imagery Streams (ARTEMIS). Barcelona, Spain (2013)
20. Li, W., Zhao, R., Wang, X.: Human reidentification with transferred metric learning. In: Asian Conference on Computer Vision (2012)
21. Loy, C.C., Xiang, T., Gong, S.: Time-Delayed Correlation Analysis for Multi-Camera Activity Understanding. International Journal of Computer Vision **90**(1) (2010)

22. Ma, A.J., Yuen, P.C., Li, J.: Domain transfer support vector ranking for person re-identification without target camera label information. In: IEEE International Conference on Computer Vision (2013)
23. Pan, S.J., Yang, Q.: A Survey on Transfer Learning. IEEE Transactions on Knowledge and Data Engineering **22**(10) (2010)
24. Prosser, B., Zheng, W.S., Gong, S., Xiang, T.: Person re-identification by support vector ranking. In: British Machine Vision Conference (2010)
25. Raja, Y., Gong, S.: Person re-identification, chap. In: Scalable Multi-Camera Tracking in a Metropolis. Springer (2013)
26. Salvagnini, P., Bazzani, L., Cristani, M., Murino, V.: Person re-identification with a ptz camera: an introductory study. In: IEEE International Conference on Image Processing (2013)
27. Schwartz, W., Davis, L.: Learning discriminative appearance-based models using partial least squares. In: 2009 XXII Brazilian Symposium on Computer Graphics and Image Processing (SIBGRAPI) (2009)
28. Sommerlade, E., Reid, I.: Information-theoretic active scene exploration. In: IEEE Conference on Computer Vision and Pattern Recognition (2008)
29. Tarjan, R.: Depth-First Search and Linear Graph Algorithms. SIAM Journal on Computing **1**(2) (1972)
30. Torralba, A., Efros, A.A.: Unbiased look at dataset bias. In: IEEE Conference on Computer Vision and Pattern Recognition (2011)
31. Vezzani, R., Baltieri, D., Cucchiara, R.: People Re-identification in Surveillance and Forensics: a Survey. ACM Computing Surveys **1**(1) (2013)
32. Wang, X., Zhao, R.: Person re-identification, chap. In: Person Re-identification: System Design and Evaluation Overview. Springer (2013)
33. Zhao, R., Ouyang, W., Wang, X.: Unsupervised salience learning for person re-identification. In: IEEE International Conference on Computer Vision (2013)

The HDA+ Data Set for Research on Fully Automated Re-identification Systems

Dario Figueira$^{(\boxtimes)}$, Matteo Taiana, Athira Nambiar,
Jacinto Nascimento, and Alexandre Bernardino

Institute for Systems and Robotics - Lisbon, Lisbon, Portugal
dfigueira@isr.ist.utl.pt

Abstract. There are no available datasets to evaluate integrated Pedestrian Detectors and Re-Identification systems, and the standard evaluation metric for Re-Identification (Cumulative Matching Characteristic curves) does not properly assess the errors that arise from integrating Pedestrian Detectors with Re-Identification (False Positives and Missed Detections). Real world Re-Identification systems require Pedestrian Detectors to be able to function automatically and the integration of Pedestrian Detector algorithms with Re-Identification produces errors that must be dealt with. We provide not only a dataset that allows for the evaluation of integrated Pedestrian Detector and Re-Identification systems but also sample Pedestrian Detection data and meaningful evaluation metrics and software, such as to make it "one-click easy" to test your own Re-Identification algorithm in an Integrated PD+REID system without having to implement a Pedestrian Detector algorithm yourself. We also provide body-part detection data on top of the manually labeled data and the Pedestrian Detection data, such as to make it trivial to extract your features from relevant local regions (actual body-parts). Finally we provide camera synchronization data to allow for the testing of inter-camera tracking algorithms. We expect this dataset and software to be widely used and boost research in integrated Pedestrian Detector and Re-Identification systems, bringing them closer to reality.

1 Introduction

The goal of a person re-identification system is to recognize and keep track of individuals as they appear and travel in heterogeneous scenarios covered by a camera network with non-overlapping (or low overlapping) fields-of-view. Re-identification has been subject of much research in computer vision due to its usefulness in a large number of application, e.g. surveillance, smart spaces, border control, crime prevention, and robotics, to quote a few (e.g., [1–3]). Still, it is difficult to reliably re-identify an individual in a camera network. More specifically, when a person disappears from a given view, it is difficult to differentiate it from other targets in a different view. Difficulties arise from a multitude of factors: visual similarity between different people, occlusions, poor quality of video data and varying imaging conditions (illumination, viewing angle, distance ranges, etc.).

© Springer International Publishing Switzerland 2015
L. Agapito et al. (Eds.): ECCV 2014 Workshops, Part III, LNCS 8927, pp. 241–255, 2015.
DOI: 10.1007/978-3-319-16199-0_17

Most existing re-identification systems still rely, to a large extent, on human supervision and intervention. Usually a human operator is assigned to constantly monitor a large number of cameras that must be watched, interpreted and acted upon. This has, of course, several shortcomings: it is costly, inaccurate and subject to human errors. This problem motivated research on automatic systems able to effectively reduce the overhead of a human operator in attaining the goals of a re-identification system.

In the classic strategy to re-identification, examples are manually selected from the images by cropping the regions occupied by persons. First, manual crops of persons with known identity are stored in a gallery. Such gallery can be seen as a training set for the recognition of persons in other views of the camera network. Then, in novel views of the camera network, *a priori* unknown persons (probes) are selected for re-identification. Re-identification is accomplished by using some sort of matching (e.g. nearest neighbour [4],in the simplest case) between the gallery and probes. This is usually performed by learning discriminative features followed by template matching using appropriate distance measures to assess the similarity between the gallery and probe images. Most existing works address the re-identification problem giving focus on the above aspects, *i.e.* extracting local features, learning classifiers and distance measures.

Concerning local features, existing approaches typically exploit texture [5], spatial structure [4], color [6] or a combination of them [7].

Regarding distance measures, a variety of works have been published proposing different approaches, e.g. weighted L2-norm distance metric [8] or Bhattacharyya distance [4]. The distance can also be learned to provide the optimal similarity measure between a pair of person images. Several distance learning approaches are available in the literature. In [9] it is proposed a brightness transfer function. A new relative distance comparison is proposed in [10] for maximizing the probability of a pair of true matches. Principal component analysis combined with local Fisher discriminative analysis is proposed in [11] to match visual features. Supervised [12] or unsupervised [13] approaches are also proposed to extract relevant features and combining them into a single similarity function.

Other works reformulate the problem of re-identification as a ranking problem, where the potential true match is assigned with the highest rank [14] rather than a distance metric converting, in this way, the re-identification problem into a relative ranking problem.

All the above methods assume pre-cropped images of pedestrians to perform re-identification. In this paper we present a dataset and propose methodologies to relax this assumption. We want to perform re-identification in full images without requiring manual intervention in the selection of the probe data. Our aim is to move forward on the automatization of re-identification systems to facilitate the browsing of large databases of images and simplify the task of a surveillance system operator.

More concisely, we present **in Section 2** a dataset (HDA+) acquired in a heterogeneous camera network with low overlapping fields of view particularly suited to evaluate the integration of pedestrian detectors with re-identification algorithms. The network is composed of 13 synchronized cameras of different resolutions, fields of view and perspectives. We provide **in Section 3** an evaluation framework that allows for the integration of pedestrian detectors (PD) and re-identification algorithms (RE-ID). The pedestrian detector automatically selects, from the incoming stream of images, the probe or test samples that are used as input to the re-identification algorithm, in a fully automated system (PD+REID). We provide sample data and software that allows for the evaluation of PD, RE-ID and tracking algorithms. Moreover, we provide additional features in the data set from which we highlight: (i) comparisons between classical and integrated systems (*i.e.* relying on ground truth or PD detections); (ii) evaluation metrics that take into account errors in the pedestrian detection stage; (iii) default gallery sets and pedestrian probes for easy operation; (iv) the ability to replace the default functionalities with user custom code; and (v) pre-computed body-part bounding boxes to facilitate the development of re-identification algorithms. With this dataset and tools we expect to attract newcomers and motivate established researchers to the problem of fully automated re-identification systems. **In Section 4** we focus on the integration of PD and RE-ID for which we provide sample code to evaluate the influence of different integration modalities. **In Section 5** we perform the quantitative evaluation of the proposed methodologies illustrating their advantages with respect to a naive integration. Finally **in Section 6** we conclude and suggest future developments.

2   The HDA+ Data Set

The HDA dataset[1] was acquired from 13 indoor cameras (HD-CAMNET) distributed over three floors of the ISR Lisboa facilities, recording simultaneously for nearly 30 minutes. The video recordings exhibit a high degree of variability: image resolutions include VGA, 1MPixel and 4MPixel with corresponding frame rates of 5FPS, 2FPS and 1FPS. Moreover, the cameras were set to acquire video from different points of view, affecting the geometry of the imaged scene and resulting in different distance ranges at which people are visible in each video. The different illumination conditions of the recording areas make the dataset challenging for tasks such as person detection and re-identification. Table 1 provides an overview of the details of the video sequences.

The dataset is fully labelled. Each appearance of a person in the sequences from 13 cameras was manually annotated. The annotation information consists in the position and size of the enclosing Bounding Box (BB), the unique ID for the person, the frame number, the camera index and the occlusion flag. The occlusion flag indicates whether the person is partially occluded or fully visible. The BB's were set to fully and tightly enclose each person. For partially visible people, the extent of the full body was estimated and the Bounding Box was set to enclose it. The only exception to this rule applies to truncated people,

---

[1] http://vislab.isr.ist.utl.pt/hda-dataset/

cam02   cam17   cam18   cam19   cam40   cam50   cam53

cam54   cam56   cam57   cam58   cam59   cam60

Fig. 1. Snapshots of the sequences acquired in the data set

i.e., people whose projection lies partially outside the image boundaries. In that case, the bounding box was also truncated. Some of the fully visible samples are provided as default gallery samples (default training set): three to five good quality images of each person, one image per appearance in each camera (a total of 250 cropped images). All other cropped images may be used as test data. This data constitutes the Ground Truth (GT) information for the dataset. A detailed documentation on the setting and data acquisition of the camera network, GT labelling procedure, and benchmarking of video analytics algorithms using the dataset can be found in the earlier publication by the authors in [15].

Table 1. camera information

CAM	02	17	18	19	40	50	53
640x480	✓	✓	✓	✓	✓		
1280x800						✓	✓
2560x1600							
Frame rate	5	5	5	5	5	2	2
No of frames	9819	9897	9883	9878	9861	2227	3521
Start time	11:57:52	11:57:57	11:58:02	11:58:06	11:58:20	12:12:29	12:01:07
End time	12:30:56	12:30:56	12:30:59	12:31:02	12:31:11	12:31:02	12:30:27

CAM	54	56	57	58	59	60
640x480						
1280x800	✓	✓	✓	✓	✓	
2560x1600						✓
Frame rate	2	2	2	2	2	1
No of frames	3424	3798	3780	3721	3670	1728
Start time	12:01:31	11:59:31	11:59:36	12:00:40	12:01:06	12.02.06
End time	12:30:02	12:31:09	12:31:09	12:31:42	12:31:40	12.30.53

In this updated version of the HDA dataset (HDAv1.1), we are releasing additional functionalities and auxiliary data. The dataset contains a general evaluation software which measures the performance of a RE-ID algorithm both in terms of the standard Cumulative Matching Characteristic (CMC) curve and in terms of a point in Precision/Recall (P/R) space. We argue that the P/R plot carries complementary information w.r.t. the CMC curve and that they should be used together to characterize the performance of a RE-ID system (see Section 3 for details).

We provide an evaluation mode that is the de facto standard for RE-ID algorithms: "MANUAL$_{\text{clean}}$". In this mode the test examples are hand-cropped images of fully visible people. We also provide a more challenging evaluation mode: "MANUAL$_{\text{all}}$", in which the test set comprises all of the hand-labelled persons, including the partially visible ones. These test sets are obtained from the GT labels on the test sequences (see Section 4 for details). For the user's convenience, we also provide the body-parts detections for all the cropped images in the test set. The parts detections are computed with the code from [16].

One of the main novelties in the current version of the dataset is the release of an architecture for a fully automated RE-ID system. We provide an integrated PD+REID system in which the input images for the RE-ID module are the detections computed by the PD module. The user of the dataset is allowed to plug in a custom PD module or take advantage of the auxiliary data we provide, in the form of the detections computed with the ACF [17] detector and the corresponding body parts detections. Integrating the PD and the RE-ID modules is not trivial because of the noise present in the detections. We provide two modules that help handle such noise. The user can choose whether to activate each module for one specific experiment, leading to four evaluation modes of the integrated system (see Sec. 4 for more details).

The synchronization of the various video sequences of a set is needed in many contexts. It is for instance essential for multi camera tracking as it provides the user with a coordinated information of the scene. Multi-camera tracking, in turn, provides useful information for a plethora of video analytics algorithms, including person Re-Identification algorithms. We provide a complete synchronization of the video sequences with the current release of the dataset. Figure 2 and Table 1 illustrate the start time, end time and the duration of capture for each of the 13 cameras used for data acquisition. Based on the frame rates of the cameras (1, 2 and 5FPS), we selected an optimal time unit of 0.1 seconds for the synchronization framework.

3   Evaluation of RE-ID Systems

Most works on RE-ID consider as input pre-cropped images tightly enclosing the pedestrians to be re-identified. All training and test examples are manually selected and cropped to depict one fully visible person. The RE-ID algorithm matches test samples to the training samples and outputs a ranked list of person ID's: the lower the rank, the more confidence there is in that ID being a correct match to the detected person. Evaluation is typically done using Cumulative Matching Characteristic (CMC) curves. The CMC curve shows how often, on average, the correct person ID is included in the best K matches for each test image. The overall performance is measured by the normalized Area Under the CMC curve (nAUC).

In this work we aim at systems that are able to take full images as input, and not only pre-cropped images. One solution to tackle this problem is to use a pedestrian detector (PD) to localize persons in the video frames and send these

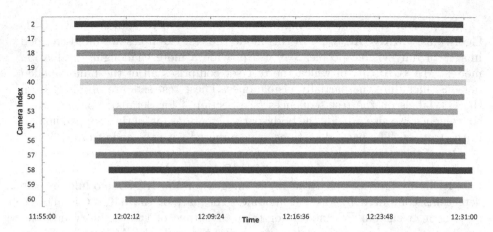

Fig. 2. The video sequences for the HDA dataset were captured for half an hour period using 13 cameras distributed in 3 floors of a building. The data acquisition was not perfectly simultaneous, being the earliest sequence frame at 11:57:52 in cam02 and the latest sequence frame at 12:31:42 in cam58.

results to a Re-ID algorithm. Such integration of a pedestrian detector with a re-identification algorithm is denoted PD+REID. From now on we concentrate on the problem of evaluating the results of PD+REID systems.

The integration of a Pedestrian Detector with a Re-Identification algorithm is not trivial, since the output of PD is prone to errors. Several types of errors may occur in the modules of the PD+REID system:

- A detected object does not correspond to a person in the image. This is termed a False Positive (FP) detection, is an error originated in the PD and it will generate a classification error at the RE-ID level because there is no correct ID for a FP.
- The system fails to detect a person. This is denoted a Missed Detection (MD) and happens whenever a ground truth Bounding Box has no corresponding detection with enough overlap. Again, this is an error of the PD module which causes a person to go unnoticed and unclassified at the RE-ID level.
- A detected object corresponds to a valid pedestrian (True Positive detection) but its rank-1 estimated class is different from the ground truth class. This is an error of the RE-ID module and we denote it an Incorrect Identification.

When a person is detected by the PD module, and is well classified by the RE-ID module we have a Correct Identification.

The CMC curve overpenalizes False Positives while ignoring Missed Detections. In order to fairly evaluate False Positives, and appreciate the effect of Missed Detections we also compute precision and recall statistics:

- $\text{Precision} = \frac{\text{Correct Identifications}}{\text{True Positive Detections} + \text{False Positive Detections}} = \frac{\text{Correct Identifications}}{\text{Number of Detections}}$
- $\text{Recall} = \frac{\text{Correct Identifications}}{\text{True Positive Detections} + \text{Missed Detections}} = \frac{\text{Correct Identifications}}{\text{Number of Person Appearances}}$

We also define two labels to take into account the possibility of re-identification algorithms able to identify persons not included in the gallery, i.e. new persons (ID-NEW), and detections not corresponding to actual people, i.e. false positives (ID-FP). In scenarios with access control it is possible to know at each time which persons exist in the surveilled space. We denote these cases as Closed Spaces. On the the other hand, there are scenarios where new persons may appear in the images (Open Spaces). If the user selects the Closed Space scenario, all persons not in the gallery set are ignored for evaluation purposes. In the Open Space scenario, persons not in the gallery set are given the special tag ID-NEW and considered in the evaluation. If the re-identification algorithm correctly identifies a person as ID-NEW, the corresponding detection counts as a Correct Identification. If a new person is attributed one of the existing ID's, then it is accounted as an Incorrect Identification. Analogously, if detections not matching the ground truth enough are passed to the RE-ID algorithm and it is able to understand that the sample is not a person, it assigns the label ID-FP and the evaluation function considers it a Correct Identification. If the label ID-FP is associated to a valid person, it is taken as an Incorrect Identification.

3.1   Using the Evaluation Tool

Here we shall describe with some detail the software tool provided. The general view of the evaluation system is show in Fig. 3. The input to the evaluation system is a list containing information about all detected objects in the test sequences and corresponding ranked list of person ID's. Each item of the input list corresponds to a detection and contains the following data:

- Camera number
- Frame number
- Localization and extent of a detection (Bounding Box information)
- List of ranked ID's

The evaluation function checks this data against the ground truth and computes the CMC curves and Precision-Recall statistics. The same data format is used to perform the classical RE-ID algorithm evaluation (RE-ID performed on manually cropped images), by using the ground truth Bounding Boxes instead of automatic detections.

While defining an evaluation experiment the user needs to specify:

- two disjoint sets of cameras, one for training and the other for testing;
- the source of the training data: the default training set provided with the data set or a user-provided one;
- the source of the test data: the ground truth hand-labelled Bounding Boxes (BB), the BB's obtained by the the automatic pedestrian detector, or BB's manually provided by the user;
- some options on whether and how to filter the test data BB's (as described in Section 4.2).

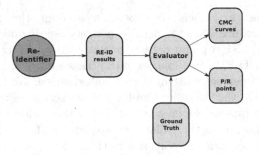

Fig. 3. The evaluation tool receives the computed detections and RE-ID ranks and produces the CMC and Precision/Recall values by comparison with the ground-truth information

When using the test data provided in HDA+, the user may employ one of three different test sets: (i) non-occluded ground truth test samples, (ii) the whole set of ground truth test samples (including the occluded ones), (iii) or a set of test samples obtained by the ACF pedestrian detector [17]. We term the evaluation modes related to the use of these test data subsets, respectively as: (i) MANUAL$_{clean}$; (ii) MANUAL$_{all}$; and (iii) DIRECT. **In Section 5** we show an experimental evaluation of these modes.

Furthermore the user should select whether to consider the special tags ID-NEW and ID-FP to correctly compute the evaluation scores according to the algorithms capabilities.

At the current state of the evaluation system, we do not allow the possibility of dynamically growing the gallery as new persons are identified in the test set. This is an important point to consider in future work.

4   Evaluation of Integrated PD+REID System

Most works on the Re-Identification (RE-ID) of people operate on manually cropped images. However, in order to achieve a fully automated RE-ID system, the automatization of the detection is needed, i.e., the cropping must be performed by a Pedestrian Detection (PD) algorithm.

The integration of PD and RE-ID poses several challenges. The False Positives (FP's) and Missed Detections (MD's) generated by the PD have an impact on the performance of the whole system: FP's lead to cropped images that are impossible to correctly associate to the ID of a person, while MD's do not generate a cropped image at all, making the identification of a missed person impossible.

Moreover, even true positive detections rather than manually selected Bounding Boxes can give rise to a more difficult RE-ID problem. First, the alignment and size of a detection bounding box with respect to the detected person are bound to be less precise than the regions selected by a user. Second, common test sets for person RE-ID consist exclusively of fully visible people, while detections can match people imaged under varying degrees of occlusion.

Connecting a PD system directly to a RE-ID one yields poor results because of the aforementioned sources of noise. In previous work [18] we introduced two improvements to the naive integration scheme: the Occlusion Filter and the use of a False Positive Class. The Occlusion Filter is a processing block which lies between the PD and RE-ID systems (see Fig. 5), its goal is to reduce the incidence of partially occluded detections in the data fed to the RE-ID system. The use of a False Positive Class stems from the observation that False Positive detections (the ones which do not correspond to a person in the image) are impossible to be correctly classified by the RE-ID system. Defining a FP class means explicitly modelling the typical FP's of a data set. This makes a correct classification of FP detections possible, which in turn allows for a coherent evaluation of the performance of the integrated system. In the current release of the HDA dataset, we distribute code and auxiliary data so that the researchers in the RE-ID field can evaluate their algorithms in different working conditions: we provide both manually cropped images and crops obtained by applying a state-of-the-art PD [17]. We provide the code that implements the Occlusion Filter and that builds the False Positive Class. All data and modules are part of an intuitive software architecture which makes it easy to integrate the user's RE-ID system and evaluate its performance in different experiments.

4.1 Naive Integration of PD and RE-ID Modules

In the classical evaluation of RE-ID systems, the input consists of a set of manually cropped images, associated with their respective person ID's. In the integrated PD+REID system a Pedestrian Detector is used to generate the cropped images which are presented as input to the RE-ID system.

In the current release of the dataset, we provide detections obtained with a state-of-the-art PD system, the ACF detector [17]. Users of the dataset can test their RE-ID algorithms in an integrated system without the need of implementing a detector. Another possibility is to plug another detector in the provided architecture, and simply select which one to use in each experiment, via the main evaluation script (please see the documentation for more details[2]).

4.2 Occlusion Filter

We showed in [18] that filtering the detections produced by a PD system based on geometrical reasoning positively affects the performance of the integrated PD+REID system. We provide the implementation of the Occlusion Filter (OF) with the HDA+ data set. The Occlusion Filter is a block which aims at filtering the detections prior to sending them to the RE-ID system, rejecting the ones which appear under a significant degree of occlusion (e.g., the woman in Fig. 4). Such detections are particularly hard to classify because the features computed

---

[2] http://vislab.isr.ist.utl.pt/hda-dataset/

Fig. 4. Example of two overlapping detections and determination of which is occluded. The two Bounding Boxes have a high degree of overlap as shown by the yellow area in the image. In a pair of overlapping detections the one with a higher positioning of its Bounding Box lower boundary (see the arrows) is the occluded one based on geometric considerations. Thus in this image, the woman is heavily occluded.

on them can be a mixture of those generated by the occluding and the occluded person. The visibility information of overlapping detections is not computed by the detection system, it is inferred instead with a heuristic based on scene geometry: in a typical surveillance scenario, with cameras mounted above the head of people and pointing downwards, the closer a person is to the camera, the lower its projection will reach on the image (see the arrows in Fig. 4).

We provide the code for the Occlusion Filter with the data set. The user can choose whether to enable it for each experiment (see details in the documentation). When the OF is active, the user needs to select the minimum amount of overlap at which we reject the occluded detection. Furthermore, the architecture allows for the user to substitute the Occlusion Filter with a different kind of filter, without compromising the functionality of the rest of the evaluation code.

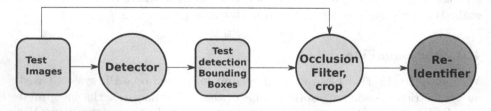

Fig. 5. Block diagram of the Detection subsystem employed in the evaluation of an integrated PD+REID system. First, a detector is run on the test images. Then, the resulting Bounding Boxes are filtered by the Occlusion Filter and the corresponding crops are generated. Such crops form the input data for the RE-ID system.

4.3 False Positives Class

We also showed in [18], that integrating a PD and a RE-ID module without appropriately managing the FP's produced by the PD, leads to inconsistencies in the evaluation. Each FP example produces an incorrect classification, leading to CMC curves which do not reach 100% accuracy (see the green line in Fig. 8). Introducing a False Positive class allows for the correct classification of a part of the FP detections and for well behaved CMC curves.

We include the code that builds the FP class in the current release of the HDA+ data set (see Fig. 6). FP examples are harvested running the detector on all images of the specified training set. Each detection with zero overlap with any Ground Truth Bounding Box is classified as a FP. In a real scenario, this would be done by computing the detections when no persons are present in the environment and creating the FP class with these detections. The set of FP's is used by the RE-ID system to create a model for the FP class. Note that the number of harvested FP's tends to be higher than the usual number of training samples for a given pedestrian.

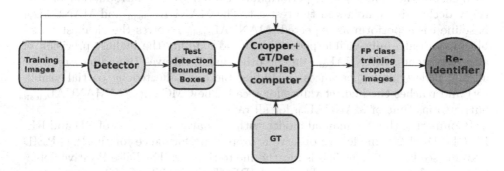

Fig. 6. Block diagram of the subsystem that computes the examples for the False Positive class. A detector is run on the training images. The detections which do not overlap at all with Ground Truth labels are deemed as False Positives. The cropped images corresponding to the False Positives are used to build a model in the RE-ID system.

5 Experimental Results

In this section we present the results obtained by applying a particular re-identification algorithm on the dataset and evaluating with the different modalities discussed in Section 3 and 4. The RE-ID algorithm is based on the Nearest Neighbour classifier, Bhattacharrya distance and HSV color histograms [6]. First we compare the RE-ID results obtained using the two manual modes, then we compare such results with those obtained by the integrated PD+REID system.

The experiments performed use the default gallery samples of cameras 50 to 59 for training, whereas camera 60 is used for testing. The annotation for camera 60 comprises 1182 Bounding Boxes, 1097 of which are of people that appear both in camera 60 and in some of the training cameras. Since we consider the Closed Space assumption in this example, the test set for the $MANUAL_{all}$ evaluation modality comprises such 1097 BB's. For the $MANUAL_{clean}$ modality, we use only the fully visible pedestrians in the test set: 467 out of 1097. For the experiments with the PD+REID system, the ACF detector produces 2579 Bounding Boxes in the test video sequence (camera 60), of which 1167 are False Positives. In the evaluation modes in which the Occlusion Filter is active, 233 detections are filtered out, leaving a total of 2309 BB's.

The results are visualized in Figure 8 (CMC curves) and Figure 7 (P/R points). Table 2 lists the corresponding numerical values: the precision and recall statistics for rank 1, including the F-score (harmonic mean of precision and recall), while CMC curves are summarized by the values of the rank 1 point and those of the normalized area under the curves (nAUC).

Comparing the $MANUAL_{all}$ with the $MANUAL_{clean}$ experiment allows us to measure the difference in performance caused by the introduction of partially occluded exemplars in the test set. The $MANUAL_{clean}$ and $MANUAL_{all}$ baseline cases perform as expected. $MANUAL_{clean}$ receives the cleanest possible input (only fully visible pedestrians) and exhibits the highest precision of all experiments. $MANUAL_{all}$, on the other hand, receives Bounding Boxes for all the pedestrian appearances (including the ones affected by partial visibility) and reaches the highest values for recall. The CMC curve of $MANUAL_{clean}$ outperforms that of $MANUAL_{all}$ for all ranks.

Comparing the two manual modes with the naive integration of PD and RE-ID (the DIRECT mode) we observe a drop in performance for the PD+REID system (see Fig. 8). This loss is mostly due to the fact that False Positive detections are always misclassified in the DIRECT mode. The CMC curve is thus limited in the highest accuracy value it can reach. Such loss is mitigated when we consider the two integration modules discussed in the previous section, the FP class and the Occlusion Filter. Figure 8 highlights the obvious improvement provided by using the FP class. This is due to two factors: (i) Adding a FP class allows all detections to be correctly identified at some rank, enabling the

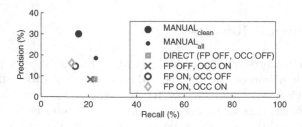

Fig. 7. Visualization of the precision-recall values as per Table 2

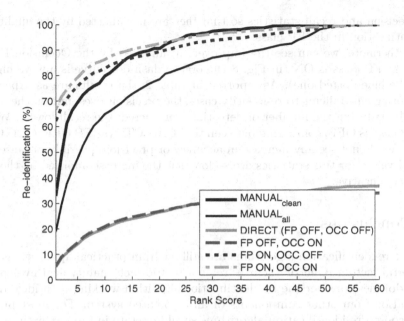

Fig. 8. CMC curves of the six Re-Identification experiments with the experimental set-ups described in the text

CMC curve to reach 100% accuracy; (ii) In this experiment, most of the False Positives are quite easy to re-identify, as they are generated by static objects in the scene (i.e, doors, fire extinguishers). This causes the low-rank part of the curve to be even higher than that of the manual modes. Note that we define

Table 2. Statistics for the different evaluation modes presented in the text. We list the number of Bounding Boxes (**# BB's**) processed in each case, and report the results in terms of **Precision, Recall, Fscore**, the CMC curves' **1st rank** and its normalized area (**nAUC**). Note that we define the precision and recall statistics so that they are not affected by the quality of re-identification in the FP class, while CMC is affected by them. This leads to the very high **1st Rank** values for the modes with FP class turned ON. These values are of little practical interest. The precision-recall values can be visualized in Fig. 7.

Exp.	# BB's	Precision (%)	Recall (%)	Fscore (%)	1st Rank (%)	nAUC (%)
MANUAL_clean	462	30.1	15.8	20.7	18.7	90.6
MANUAL_all	1097	18.6	23.1	20.6	31.2	82.4
DIRECT (FP OFF, OCC OFF)	2542	8.5	22.5	12.4	5.2	29.1
FP OFF, OCC ON	2309	8.5	20.8	12.1	5.4	27.8
FP ON, OCC OFF	2542	14.7	14.4	14.6	62.3	91.3
FP ON, OCC ON	2309	16.2	12.9	14.4	66.7	93.5

the precision and recall statistics so that they are not affected by the quality of re-identification in the FP class.

Furthermore, we can see the improvement afforded by the Occlusion Filter when the FP class is ON (in Fig. 8 the orange dash-dot curve is always higher than the blue dotted one). As reported in Table 2, the results are as expected. By filtering out difficult to re-identify cases, the precision rises, but on the other hand, by reducing the number of detections considered, the recall lowers. When the FP class is OFF, comparing between the "DIRECT" vs "FP OFF, OCC ON" modes, we do not see any increase in accuracy or precision, possibly because the general values for this statistics are so low that the increase afforded by the OF is not significative.

6   Conclusions

Current re-identification algorithms are still far from practical applications due to several factors. One of them is related to the fact that typical evaluation methodologies consider the re-identification algorithm working with ideal data, in isolation from other components of an automated system. For most practical purposes, re-identification algorithms should operate in tandem with person detectors in order to seamlessly operate using conventional video data. In this paper we proposed a few contributions towards this goal. First, a few methods were developed to improve a naive integration of pedestrian detectors and re-identification algorithms. Second, a multi-camera fully labeled dataset and associated tools was developed to facilitate the evaluation of such methods. Finally some limitations on classical evaluation metrics were identified and new ones proposed. Both the dataset and the evaluation tools are available for the scientific community. We hope these can drive interest and progress in the field. In future work we aim at developing methodologies for taking into account dynamically changing galleries, according to people entering or leaving the shared space.

Acknowledgments. This work was partially supported by the FCT project [PEst-OE/EEI/LA0009/2013], the European Commission project POETICON++ (FP7-ICT-288382), the FCT project VISTA [PTDC/EIA-EIA/105062/2008], the project High Definition Analytics (HDA), QREN - I&D em Co-Promoção 13750, Matteo Taiana was supported by the FCT doctoral grant [SFRH/BD/43840/2008] and Dario Figueira was supported by the FCT doctoral grant [SFRH/BD/48526/2008].

References

1. Doretto, G., Sebastian, T., Tu, P., Rittscher, J.: Appearance-based person reidentification in camera networks: problem overview and current approaches. Journal of Ambient Intelligence and Humanized Computing 2(2), 127–151 (2011)
2. Gong, S., Cristani, M., Yan, S.: Person Re-Identification. Springer, January 2014
3. Vezzani, R., Baltieri, D., Cucchiara, R.: People reidentification in surveillance and forensics: A survey. ACM Comput. Surv. 46(2), 29:1–29:37 (2013)

4. Farenzena, M., Bazzani, L., Perina, A., Murino, V., Cristani, M.: Person re-identification by symmetry-driven accumulation of local features. In: CVPR (2010)
5. Madden, C.S., Cheng, E.D., Piccardi, M.: Tracking people across disjoint camera views by an illumination-tolerant appearance representation. Mach. Vis. Appl. 18(3–4), 233–247 (2007)
6. Figueira, D., Bernardino, A.: Re-identification of visual targets in camera networks: a comparison of techniques. Image Analysis and Recognition, 294–303 (2011)
7. Gheissari, N., Sebastian, T., Hartley, R.: Person reidentification using spatiotemporal appearance. In: CVPR (2006)
8. Layne, R., Hospedales, T., Gong, S.: Person re-identification by attributes. In: BMVC, pp. 24.1–24.11 (2012)
9. Porikli, F.: Inter-camera color calibration using cross-correlation model function. In: ICIP (2003)
10. Zheng, W.S., Gong, S., Xiang, T.: Person re-identification by probabilistic relative distance comparison. In: CVPR (2011)
11. Pedagadi, S., Orwell, J., Velastin, S., Boghossian, B.: Local fisher discriminant analysis for pedestrian re-identification. In: CVPR (2013)
12. Gray, D., Tao, H.: Viewpoint invariant pedestrian recognition with an ensemble of localized features. In: Forsyth, D., Torr, P., Zisserman, A. (eds.) ECCV 2008, Part I. LNCS, vol. 5302, pp. 262–275. Springer, Heidelberg (2008)
13. Bashir, K., Xiang, T., Gong, S.: Feature selection on gait energy image for human identification. In: ICASSP (2008)
14. Prosser, B., Zheng, W.S., Gong, S., Xiang, T.: Person re-identification by support vector ranking. In: BMVC, pp. 21.1–21.11 (2010)
15. Nambiar, A., Taiana, M., Figueira, D., Nascimento, J., Bernardino, A.: A multi-camera video data set for research on high-definition surveillance. International Journal of Machine Intelligence and Sensory Signal Processing, Special Issue on Signal Processing for Visual Surveillance, Inderscience Journal (in press, 2014)
16. Andriluka, M., Roth, S., Schiele, B.: Pictorial structures revisited: people detection and articulated pose estimation. In: CVPR (2009)
17. Dollár, P., Appel, R., Belongie, S., Perona, P.: Fast feature pyramids for object detection. In: PAMI (2014)
18. Taiana, M., Figueira, D., Nambiar, A., Nascimento, J., Bernardino, A.: Towards fully automated person re-identification. In: VISAPP (2014)

W20 - Color and Photometry in Computer Vision

A Variational Framework for Single Image Dehazing

Adrian Galdran[1]([⊠]), Javier Vazquez-Corral[2], David Pardo[3],
and Marcelo Bertalmío[2]

[1] Tecnalia Research and Innovation, Basque Country, Spain
adrian.galdran@tecnalia.com
[2] Departament de Tecnologies de la Informació i les Comunicacions,
Universitat Pompeu Fabra, Barcelona, Spain
[3] University of the Basque Country (UPV/EHU), Basque Center
for Applied Mathematics (BCAM) and IKERBASQUE
(Basque Foundation for Sciences), Bilbao, Spain

Abstract. Images captured under adverse weather conditions, such as
haze or fog, typically exhibit low contrast and faded colors, which may
severely limit the visibility within the scene. Unveiling the image structure under the haze layer and recovering vivid colors out of a single image
remains a challenging task, since the degradation is depth-dependent and
conventional methods are unable to handle this problem.

We propose to extend a well-known perception-inspired variational
framework [1] for the task of single image dehazing. The main modification consists on the replacement of the value used by this framework for the grey-world hypothesis by an estimation of the mean of
the clean image. This allows us to devise a variational method that
requires no estimate of the depth structure of the scene, performing
a spatially-variant contrast enhancement that effectively removes haze
from far away regions. Experimental results show that our method com-
petes well with other state-of-the-art methods in typical benchmark
images, while outperforming current image dehazing methods in more
challenging scenarios.

Keywords: Image dehazing · Image defogging · Color correction ·
Contrast enhancement

1 Introduction

The effect of haze in the visibility of far away objects is a well-known physical
property that we perceive in different ways. For example, an object loses contrast as its depth in the image increases, and far away mountains present a bluish
tone [8]. Haze is produced by the presence of suspended little particles in the
atmosphere, called aerosols, which are able to absorb and scatter the light beams.
Aerosols can range from small water droplets to dust or pollution, depending
on their size. Scientific models of the propagation of light under such conditions

© Springer International Publishing Switzerland 2015
L. Agapito et al. (Eds.): ECCV 2014 Workshops, Part III, LNCS 8927, pp. 259–270, 2015.
DOI: 10.1007/978-3-319-16199-0_18

began with the observation of Koschmieder [14]. He stated that a distant object tends to vanish by the effect of the atmosphere color, which replaces the color of the object. Consequently, Koschmieder established a simple linear relationship between the luminance reflected by the object and the luminance reaching the observer. This linear relationship is based on the distance between the observer and the object. From then on, the study of interaction of light with the atmosphere as it travels from the source to the observer has continued growing as a research area in applied optics [16,17].

Restoring images captured under adverse weather conditions is of clear interest in both image processing and computer vision applications. Many vision systems operating in real-world outdoor scenarios assume that the input is the unaltered scene radiance. These techniques designed for clear weather images may suffer under bad weather conditions where, even for the human eye, discerning image content can represent a serious challenge. Therefore, robustly recovering visual information in bad weather conditions is essential for several machine vision tasks, such as autonomous robot/vehicle navigation [10] or video surveillance systems [29,32]. Aerial and remotely sensed images, related to applications as land cover classification [15,34], can also benefit from efficient dehazing techniques.

As Koschmieder stated, the problem of restoring true intensities and colors (sometimes referred to as albedo) presents an underlying ambiguity that cannot be analytically solved unless scene depth data is available [23]. For this reason, most of the previous approaches rely on physically-based analytical models of the image formation. The main goal of these approaches is to estimate the transmission, (or alternatively the depth) of the image to estimate the transmission of the image, that describes the part of the light that is not scattered and reaches the camera, and later on, to obtain the albedo based on the transmission. Alternatively, depth can also be estimated. These approaches can be later divided into multiple images ones [18–22], or single image ones [6,12]. On the other hand, there are also works that compute the albedo in the first place and obtain a depth map as a by-product. In [30], Tan estimates the albedo by imposing a local maximization of contrast, while in [5] Fattal assumes that depth and surface shading are uncorrelated. Unfortunately, both methods rely on the assumption that depth is locally constant, and the obtained images suffer from artifacts and are prone to over-enhancing.

Regarding all the previously stated, contrast enhancement of hazy images seems to be a straight-forward solution for this problem. However, conventional contrast enhancement techniques such as histogram equalization are not applicable due to the spatially variant nature of the degradation. Fortunately, recent research has presented more advanced contrast enhancement techniques that can successfully cope with spatially inhomogeneous degradations such as the one produced by haze. In this work, we rely on the perceptually inspired color enhancement framework introduced by Bertalmio et al. [1]. We propose to replace the original grey-world hypothesis by a rough estimate of the mean value of the haze-free scene. This value is softly based on Koschmieder statement [14]. A different modification of this hypothesis was already performed in previous works [7,33].

The rest of the paper is structured as follows. In the following section we review recent methods for image dehazing. Next, we formulate the image dehazing problem in a variational setting. Section 4 is devoted to experimental results and comparison to other state-of-the-art methodologies. We end up in section 5 by summarizing our approach and discussing possible extensions and improvements.

2   Background and Related Work

Most of the previous work on image dehazing is based on solving the image formation model presented by Koschmieder [14] that can be computed channel-wise as follows

$$I(x) = t(x)J(x) + (1 - t(x))A, \tag{1}$$

where x is a pixel location, $I(x)$ is the observed intensity, $J(x)$ is the scene radiance, corresponding to the non-degraded image, transmission $t(x)$ is a scalar quantity that is inversely related to the scene's depth and is normalized between 0 and 1,, while A, known as airlight, plays the role of the color of the haze, which is usually considered constant over the scene, and therefore in a channel-wise formulation it is a scalar value. Solving Eq. (1) is an under-constrained problem, i.e. there are a large number of possible solutions. To constrain this indeterminacy, extra information in different forms has been introduced in the past. For example, in [19] several instances of the same scene acquired under different weather conditions are employed to obtain a clear image. The near infra-red channel is fused with the original image in [27], and the work in [13] retrieves depth information from geo-referenced digital models, while in [28] multiple images taken through a polarizer at different orientations are used. Unfortunately, this extra information is often unavailable, difficulting the practical use of these techniques.

Dehazing is particularly challenging when only a single input image is available. In this case, the majority of existing methods are also focused on solving Eq. (1) by inferring depth information based on different means. In [4], assumptions on the geometry of hazy scenarios are made. Tarel et al. [31] estimate the atmospheric veil (equivalent to the depth map) through an optimization procedure in which they impose piecewise smoothness. The dark channel methodology [12], probably the most successful technique to date, is based on the statistical observation that haze-free images are colorful and contain textures and shadows, therefore lacking locally the presence of one of the three color components. On the contrary, hazy images present less contrast and saturation. As depth increases and the haze takes over the image, the contrast and saturation further decrease providing an estimate of the depth information based on which it becomes possible to invert Eq. (1), obtaining high-quality results. More recently, Fattal [6] elaborates on a local model of color lines to dehaze images.

Several methods that are independent of an initial estimation of the scene depth have also been devised. Tan [30] imposes a local increase of contrast in the image and a similar transmission value for neighboring pixels. Fattal [5] separates the radiance from the haze by assuming that surface shading and scene transmission are independent. Nishino et al. [23] do not compute depth in an initial stage, but rather estimate it jointly with the albedo in a Bayesian probabilistic framework.

3   Variational Image Dehazing

The majority of current dehazing algorithms are based on an estimation of the image depth (or transmission). Therefore, these methods are susceptible to fail when the physical assumptions underlying Eq. (1) are violated. This is a common phenomena both in real life, for example, when there is a source of light hidden by the haze, and in virtually-generated images that add different types of fog. Methods that do not estimate the model depth do not suffer from this problem, but they usually result in over-enhanced images due to the special characteristics of the degradation associated with haze. More conventional contrast enhancement algorithms, such as histogram equalization, are not suitable either. Fortunately, recent spatially-variant contrast enhancement techniques can be adapted to perform well for image dehazing tasks. In the following, we develop a variational framework for image dehazing that enforces contrast enhancement on hazy regions of the image throughout an iterative procedure allowing us to control the degree of restoration of the visibility in the scene.

3.1   Variational Contrast Enhancement

In 2007, Bertalmío et al. [1] presented a perceptually-inspired variational framework for contrast enhancement. Their method is based on the minimization of the following functional for each image channel I:

$$E(\mathrm{I}) = \frac{\alpha}{2} \sum_x \left(\mathrm{I}(x) - \frac{1}{2} \right) + \frac{\beta}{2} \sum_x (\mathrm{I}(x) - \mathrm{I}_0(x))^2 - \frac{\gamma}{2} \sum_{x,y} \omega(x,y)|\mathrm{I}(x) - \mathrm{I}(y)|, \quad (2)$$

where I is a color channel (red, green or blue) with values in $[0,1]$, I_0 is the original image, x, y are pixel coordinates, α, β, γ are positive parameters and $\omega(x,y)$ is a positive distance function with value decreasing as the distance between x and y increases. This method extends the idea of variational contrast enhancement presented by Sapiro and Caselles [26] and it also shows a close connection to the ACE method [25]. Bertalmío and co-authors have later revealed connections between this functional and the human visual system: they generalized it to better cope with perception results [24], and they established a very strong link with the Retinex theory of color [2,3].

The minimization of the image energy in Eq. (2) presents a competition between two positive terms and a negative one. The first positive term aims at preserving the gray-world hypothesis, by penalizing deviation of $I(x)$ from the $1/2$ value, while the second positive term prevent the solution from departing too much from the original image, by restricting output values to be relatively close to the initial $I_0(x)$. The negative competing term attempts to maximize the contrast. Focusing on this negative term of Eq. (2) we can observe a very useful relation with dehazing methods. It can be written as:

$$\sum_{x,y} \omega(x,y)|I(x) - I(y)| = \sum_{x,y} \omega(x,y)\left(\max(I(x),I(y)) - \min(I(x),I(y))\right). \quad (3)$$

We can now see that the contrast term is maximized whenever the minimum decreases or the maximum increases, corresponding to a contrast stretching. Notice that the first case, i.e., the minimization of local intensity values, is one of the premises of a haze-free image, according to the Dark Channel prior [11].

3.2   Modified Gray-World Assumption

In the image dehazing context, the Gray World hypothesis implemented in Eq. (2) is not adequate, since we want to respect the colors of the haze-free image, not to correct the illuminant of the scene. Therefore, to approximately predict which should be the mean value of a dehazed scene, we rely on the model of Eq. (1), that we rewrite here in terms of the luminance of each channel:

$$L^j = L_0^j t + (1 - t)A^j, \quad (4)$$

where $j \in \{R, G, B\}$. By rearranging, taking the average of each term and assuming that L and t are independent, we arrive to:

$$\text{mean}(L_0^j) \cdot \text{mean}(t) = \text{mean}(L^j) + (\text{mean}(t) - 1)\,\text{mean}(A^j). \quad (5)$$

Now, let us assume that the image presents regions at different depth distances, therefore, the histogram of depth values will be approximately uniformly distributed. In this way, we can set $\text{mean}(t) = \frac{1}{2}$ and approximate the previous equation by:

$$\frac{\text{mean}(L_0^j)}{2} \approx \text{mean}(L^j) + (\frac{1}{2} - 1)\,\text{mean}(A^j). \quad (6)$$

Let us note again that the airlight A is a constant value for each channel, that can be roughly approximated by the maximum intensity value on each channel, since haze regions are usually those with higher intensity.. Thus, a reasonable approximation for the mean value of the haze-free scene is given by:

$$\mu^j = \text{mean}(L_0^j) \approx 2\,\text{mean}(L^j) - A^j. \quad (7)$$

We then rewrite the energy functional as:

$$E(I^j) = \frac{\alpha}{2}\sum_x (I^j(x) - \mu^j) + \frac{\beta}{2}\sum_x (I^j(x) - I_0^j(x))^2 - \frac{\gamma}{2}\sum_{x,y}\omega(x,y)|I^j(x) - I^j(y)|. \quad (8)$$

To minimize the above energy we first need to compute its Euler-Lagrange derivative. Close details about the computation of the variational derivatives of the different terms are given in [1], where the authors find that a minimizer of (8) must satisfy:

$$\delta E(\mathbf{I}^j) = \alpha(\mathbf{I}^j(x) - \mu_j) + \beta(\mathbf{I}^j(x) - \mathbf{I}_0^j(x)) - \gamma R(\mathbf{I}^j)(x) = 0, \quad j \in \{R, G, B\} \quad (9)$$

where the function $R(\mathbf{I})$ is a contrast enhancement operator:

$$R(I)(x) = \frac{\sum_y \omega(x, y) s(\mathbf{I}(x) - I(y))}{\sum_y \omega(x, y)}, \quad (10)$$

and s is a smooth approximation of the sign function, that accounts for the first derivative of the absolute value.

We can now apply a gradient descent strategy. To this end, we solve $\frac{\delta I}{\delta t} = -\delta E(I)$, being t the evolution parameter. For the case of the energy given by Eq. (8), with the modified gray world assumption, after an explicit discretization in time, we have:

$$\mathbf{I}_{k+1}^j = \mathbf{I}_k^j(1 - \Delta t(\beta + \gamma)) + \Delta t(\beta \mu^j + \gamma \mathbf{I}_0^j) + \Delta t(\gamma R(\mathbf{I}_k^j)), \quad j \in \{R, G, B\} \quad (11)$$

The initial condition for this descent is the input image $\mathbf{I}_{k=0} = \mathbf{I}(x)$. The computations of the operator R are reformulated in terms of convolutions and computed using Fast Fourier Transforms. This brings a computational improvement to the method, since the effort to compute expression (10) falls down from $\mathcal{O}(N^2)$ to $\mathcal{O}(N \log(N))$. Details of this argument for complexity reduction can be found in [1].

4   Experimental Results

In this section we compare our proposed method versus current state-of-the-art results. In recent years, very powerful algorithms for image dehazing have appeared. When processing typical benchmark images, it is very hard to retrieve more visibility or natural colors than these methods already do although our method shows a competitive behavior in these images. However, when dealing with more realistic images, in which the fog does not follow a linear model such as Eq. (1) or the illumination is uneven, we have observed that the majority of the state-of-the-art methods tends to create severe artifacts, while ours is still able to dehaze these scenes without introducing this kind of corruption.

Let us also notice that, due to the difficulty to obtain ground-truth information of hazy/haze-free images, evaluation of dehazing methods has usually a subjective component. Quality of the results should be measured by the plausibility of the restored colors, as well as the recovered visibility in far away areas of the scene. To evaluate our results, we have run Eq. 11 with the following values: $\alpha = \beta = 0.5$, γ varied depending on the amount of enhancement we desired, η was set to 0 unless otherwise stated, and the distance function implemented was a Gaussian kernel with a standard deviation of 50 pixels. The time step was always $\Delta t = 0.15$, and we considered that a steady-state of the gradient descent

Fig. 1. (a) New York image (input). (b) to (h): Result of processing with methods of: (b) Fattal '08 [5] (c) Tan. '08 [30] (d) Kopf et al. [13] (e) Fattal '14 [6] (f) He et al. '11 [12] (g) Tarel et al. '09 [31] (h) Result of our method.

was achieved as soon as the Mean Square Error between one iteration and the next one falls below 0.02. In all the experiments, we observed convergence within 6 − 12 iterations. We have noticed that our method shows a strong robustness to slight parameter tuning.

Figure 1 displays an image of the city of New York, typically used for benchmarking of dehazing algorithms. Therein, our method is compared against the works in [5],[30], [13], [6], [12] and [31]. We see that visibility of distant objects is recovered by every method up to a reasonable degree. The very recent method of Fattal [6] and the powerful Dark Channel method [12] are possibly the ones recovering most vivid colors, although unfortunately they fail to recover the information underlying in the horizon (see upper right corner in Fig. (1e) and (1f)). Also, the method by Tan [30] suffers of noticeable over-saturation artifacts.

Figure 2 illustrates the performance of our method on an open scene image that contains a blue sky region. This is a challenging scenario for most dehazing algorithms. In fact, some of the methods perform an initial classification of pixels according to whether they belong to sky region or not. We see that only Kopf et al. method [13] maintains a natural appearance of the sky area. Unfortunately, this method needs geo-referenced data to work, and it is not usual to have

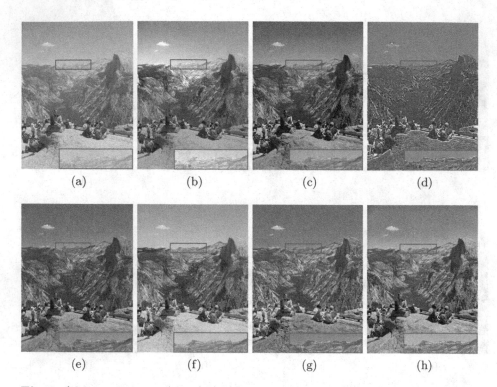

Fig. 2. a) Mountain image (input) b)-h) Result of processing with methods of b) Fattal '08 [5] c) Nishino et al. '12 [23] d) Tan '08 [30] e) He et al. '11 [12] f) Kopf et al. '08 [13] g) Tarel et al. '09 [31] h) Result of our method

this kind of input at hand. The rest of the methods, including ours, tend to over-enhance sky regions. Regarding the elimination of the distant bluish haze surrounding mountain peaks, we provide magnified detail in the right bottom corner of each image in Fig. 2, where we can observe how only Kopf et al. method, together with Fattal [5] and our algorithm are able to suppress haze without introducing an unnatural blue in far-away regions.

The previous examples demonstrate how for typical images, existing algorithms (including ours) can handle haze in an adequate manner, recovering visibility up to a reasonable degree. On the other hand, each of the methodologies restore chromatic information in a different way, although the majority of the available techniques produce rather plausible colors. Differences in the performance are subtle and only little details reveal whether a method is performing better than another in particular regions of these particular images.

Unfortunately, little research has addressed the problem of image dehazing in a more challenging and realistic scenario, such as the one depicted in Fig. 3. Let us notice that most of the state-of-the-art methodologies rely on the previous computation of a depth map of the scene. They usually resort to a physical model of the image formation under haze and bad weather conditions, such as

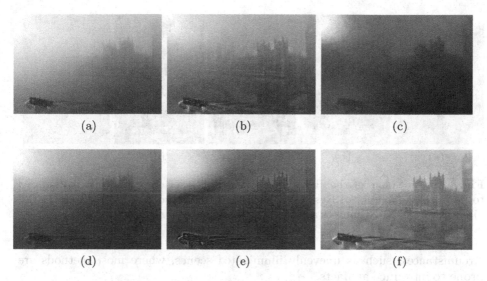

Fig. 3. a) Unevenly illuminated hazy image of the Thames river b)-f) Result of processing with methods of b) Tarel '09 [31] c) He et al. '11 [12] d) Gibson et al. '13 [9] e) Nishino et al. '12 [23] f) Result of our method.

Eq. (1). This model assumes illumination is constant in the scene. When this assumption is violated, the airlight cannot be considered to be constant. The result is a transmission underestimate or overestimate in unevenly illuminated areas, and color distortions characterized by dark blue regions appear in the restored images. This is the case for all the methods we tested, except for ours, that does not compute any depth information prior to restoration. Thanks to the attachment-to-data term, the strongly illuminated regions are handled properly, and scene structure can be recovered in the rightmost part of the image without introducing color distortion.

As a last example, let us notice that most works rely on the presence of enough chromatic information in the scene so as to recover the depth structure. When this chromatic information is weak or missing, the result is often an image with unpleasant color artifacts. Our method operates in a channel-wise manner, handling thus more robustly the lack of color cues in the input image, as can be appreciated in Fig. 4.

5   Conclusions and Future Work

In this paper, we have proposed a variational framework that can be used for image dehazing tasks. Extension of previous work on perceptual contrast enhancement allows us to devise a method that does not rely on an initial estimate of the depth information in the scene. Initial results of our method are promising, and comparable or better than state-of-the-art methods for typical benchmark images. Moreover, our algorithm performs well even in very adverse

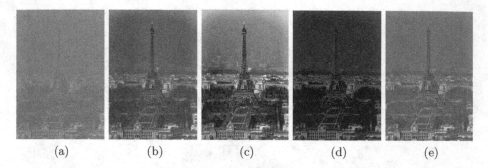

(a)   (b)   (c)   (d)   (e)

Fig. 4. a) An image of the city of Paris, with a lack of chromatic information due to haze in the scene b)-e) Result of processing with methods of b) He et al. '11 [12] c) Fattal '14 [6] d) Nishino et al. '12 [23] e) Result of our method.

circumstances, such as unevenly illuminated scenes, where most methods are prone to introduce artifacts.

We are currently developing various extensions of our methodology, such as an image-fusion approach to image dehazing, in which the iterations of the gradient descent are fused to give an improved version of the dehazed image. Further work might consist on adding extra terms to the functional, for example, Eq. (2) could be combined with a depth map coming from any of the algorithms that are able to estimate 3D structure in the scene, to enforce denoising or deblurring tasks in far away areas of the scene.

Acknowledgments. AG was partially funded by the Basque Government Project ref. IT649-13. JVC and MB were supported by European Research Council, Starting Grant ref. 306337, by the Spanish government, grant ref. TIN2012-38112, and by the Icrea Academia Award. DP was partially funded by the Project of the Spanish Ministry of Economy and Competitiveness with reference MTM2013-40824-P, the BCAM "Severo Ochoa" accreditation of excellence SEV-2013-0323, the CYTED 2011 project 712RT0449, and the Basque Government Consolidated Research Group Grant IT649-13 on "Mathematical Modeling, Simulation, and Industrial Applications (M2SI)".

References

1. Bertalmio, M., Caselles, V., Provenzi, E., Rizzi, A.: Perceptual color correction through variational techniques. IEEE Transactions on Image Processing **16**(4), 1058–1072 (2007)
2. Bertalmio, M., Caselles, V., Provenzi, E.: Issues about retinex theory and contrast enhancement. Int. J. Comput. Vis. **83**(1), 101–119 (2009)
3. Funt, B.V., Ciurea, F.: Retinex in MATLAB. J. Electronic Imaging **13**, 48–57 (2004)
4. Carr, P., Hartley, R.: Improved single image dehazing using geometry. In: Digital Image Computing: Techniques and Applications, DICTA 2009, pp. 103–110 (December 2009)

5. Fattal, R.: Single image dehazing. In: ACM SIGGRAPH Papers, SIGGRAPH 2008, pp. 72:1–72:9. ACM, New York (2008)
6. Fattal, R.: Dehazing using color-lines. ACM Transaction on Graphics (2014)
7. Ferradans, S., Bertalmio, M., Provenzi, E., Caselles, V.: An analysis of visual adaptation and contrast perception for tone mapping. IEEE Transactions on Pattern Analysis and Machine Intelligence 33(10), 2002–2012 (2011)
8. Gedzelman, S.D.: Atmospheric optics in art. Appl. Opt. 30(24), 3514–3522 (1991)
9. Gibson, K., Nguyen, T.: Fast single image fog removal using the adaptive wiener filter. In: 2013 20th IEEE International Conference on Image Processing (ICIP), pp. 714–718 (September 2013)
10. Hautiere, N., Tarel, J.P., Aubert, D.: Towards fog-free in-vehicle vision systems through contrast restoration. In: IEEE Conference on Computer Vision and Pattern Recognition, CVPR 2007, pp. 1–8 (June 2007)
11. He, K., Sun, J., Tang, X.: Single image haze removal using dark channel prior. In: IEEE Conference on Computer Vision and Pattern Recognition, CVPR 2009, pp. 1956–1963 (June 2009)
12. He, K., Sun, J., Tang, X.: Single image haze removal using dark channel prior. IEEE Transactions on Pattern Analysis and Machine Intelligence 33(12), 2341–2353 (2011)
13. Kopf, J., Neubert, B., Chen, B., Cohen, M., Cohen-Or, D., Deussen, O., Uyttendaele, M., Lischinski, D.: Deep photo: Model-based photograph enhancement and viewing. In: ACM SIGGRAPH Asia 2008 Papers, SIGGRAPH Asia 2008, pp. 116:1–116:10. ACM, New York (2008)
14. Koschmieder, H.: Theorie der horizontalen Sichtweite: Kontrast und Sichtweite. Keim & Nemnich (1925)
15. Makarau, A., Richter, R., Muller, R., Reinartz, P.: Haze detection and removal in remotely sensed multispectral imagery. IEEE Transactions on Geoscience and Remote Sensing 52(9), 5895–5905 (2014)
16. McCartney, E.J.: Optics of the Atmosphere: Scattering by Molecules and Particles. Wiley (January 1976)
17. Middleton, W.E.K.: Vision through the atmosphere. University of Toronto Press (1952)
18. Narasimhan, S., Nayar, S.: Chromatic framework for vision in bad weather. In: Proceedings of the IEEE Conference on Computer Vision and Pattern Recognition, vol. 1, pp. 598–605 (2000)
19. Narasimhan, S., Nayar, S.: Contrast restoration of weather degraded images. IEEE Transactions on Pattern Analysis and Machine Intelligence 25(6), 713–724 (2003)
20. Narasimhan, S.G., Nayar, S.K.: Vision and the atmosphere. International Journal of Computer Vision 48(3), 233–254 (2002)
21. Narasimhan, S.G., Nayar, S.K.: Interactive (de) weathering of an image using physical models. In: IEEE Workshop on Color and Photometric Methods in Computer Vision, vol. 6(6.4), p. 1 (2003)
22. Nayar, S., Narasimhan, S.: Vision in bad weather. In: The Proceedings of the Seventh IEEE International Conference on Computer Vision, vol. 2, pp. 820–827 (1999)
23. Nishino, K., Kratz, L., Lombardi, S.: Bayesian defogging. Int. J. Comput. Vis. 98(3), 263–278 (2012)
24. Palma-Amestoy, R., Provenzi, E., Bertalmio, M., Caselles, V.: A perceptually inspired variational framework for color enhancement. IEEE Transactions on Pattern Analysis and Machine Intelligence 31(3), 458–474 (2009)

25. Rizzi, A., Gatta, C., Marini, D.: A new algorithm for unsupervised global and local color correction. Pattern Recogn. Lett. **24**(11), 1663–1677 (2003)

26. Sapiro, G., Caselles, V.: Histogram modification via differential equations. Journal of Differential Equations **135**(2), 238–268 (1997)

27. Schaul, L., Fredembach, C., Susstrunk, S.: Color image dehazing using the near-infrared. In: 2009 16th IEEE International Conference on Image Processing (ICIP), pp. 1629–1632 (November 2009)

28. Schechner, Y., Narasimhan, S., Nayar, S.: Instant dehazing of images using polarization. In: Proceedings of the 2001 IEEE Computer Society Conference on Computer Vision and Pattern Recognition, CVPR 2001, vol. 1, pp. I-325–I-332 (2001)

29. Shiau, Y.H., Yang, H.Y., Chen, P.Y., Chuang, Y.Z.: Hardware implementation of a fast and efficient haze removal method. IEEE Transactions on Circuits and Systems for Video Technology **23**(8), 1369–1374 (2013)

30. Tan, R.: Visibility in bad weather from a single image. In: IEEE Conference on Computer Vision and Pattern Recognition, CVPR 2008, pp. 1–8 (June 2008)

31. Tarel, J.P., Hautiere, N.: Fast visibility restoration from a single color or gray level image. In: 2009 IEEE 12th International Conference on Computer Vision, pp. 2201–2208 (September 2009)

32. Yoon, I., Kim, S., Kim, D., Hayes, M., Paik, J.: Adaptive defogging with color correction in the HSV color space for consumer surveillance system. IEEE Transactions on Consumer Electronics **58**(1), 111–116 (2012)

33. Zamir, S., Vazquez-Corral, J., Bertalmio, M.: Gamut mapping in cinematography through perceptually-based contrast modification. IEEE Journal of Selected Topics in Signal Processing **8**(3), 490–503 (2014)

34. Zhang, Y., Guindon, B.: Quantitative assessment of a haze suppression methodology for satellite imagery: effect on land cover classification performance. IEEE Transactions on Geoscience and Remote Sensing **41**(5), 1082–1089 (2003)

Color Barcode Decoding in the Presence of Specular Reflection

Homayoun Bagherinia[✉] and Roberto Manduchi

University of California, Santa Cruz, USA
hbagheri@soe.ucsc.edu

Abstract. Color barcodes enable higher information density with respect to traditional black and white barcodes. Existing technologies use small color palettes and display the colors in the palette in the barcode itself for easy and robust decoding. This solution comes at the cost of reduced information density due to the fact that the displayed reference colors cannot be used to encode information. We introduce a new approach to color barcode decoding that uses a relatively large palettes (up to 24 colors) and a small number of reference colors (2 to 6) to be displayed in a barcode. Our decoding method specifically accounts for specular reflections using a dichromatic model. The experimental results show that our decoding algorithm achieves higher information rate with a very low probability of decoding error compared to previous approaches that use a color palette for decoding.

Keywords: Color barcode decoding · Dichromatic reflection model · Subspace classification

1 Introduction

Barcodes can be characterized by their *information rate*, that is, by the number of bits that can be encoded within a certain barcode size. One way to increase a barcode's information rate is through the use of color. By using a palette of N colors, a barcode can convey $\log_2 N$ times more bits than a traditional black and white barcode. The most successful example of color barcode is Microsoft Tag, which is based on HCCB (High Capacity Color Barcode) technology [1]. HCCB uses a grid of colored triangles with 4 colors to encode data. To ensure robust decoding, HCCB barcodes display the four colors in a set of "reference patches" at known positions in the barcode.

Displaying the reference colors in the barcode enables simple decoding strategies. For example, one may compare each color patch to the reference colors, and select the reference color that is closest to the color of the patch. At the same time, displaying all colors in the palette may be counterproductive, in terms of information rate, when large palettes are used [2]. In other words, for large palette size N, the savings produced by a large variety of color palette are offset by the need to display all colors in the palette. Based on this observation, Bagherinia and Manduchi [2] proposed the use of fairly large palettes with a limited number of reference colors displayed in the barcode. Rather than comparing

© Springer International Publishing Switzerland 2015
L. Agapito et al. (Eds.): ECCV 2014 Workshops, Part III, LNCS 8927, pp. 271–282, 2015.
DOI: 10.1007/978-3-319-16199-0_19

a color patch to a reference color, they modeled the joint color variation of the patch and of the reference colors under varying illuminant by a low-dimensional linear space. These subspaces (one per each color in the palette) can be learned offline with training images taken under multiple illuminants. When decoding a barcode image, each patch is analyzed individually, together with the reference colors. Decoding the patch color becomes a problem of associating the vector formed by the patch color and the reference colors to the closest subspace.

The linear model of [2] was built under the assumption of Lambertian surface reflectance, and thus is liable to failure when substantial specular reflection is present in the image. Since the barcode material (e.g. printed paper) is hardly Lambertian, a specular component is to be expected when the barcode is viewed from an angle. Our goal in this work was to extend the model of Bagherinia and Manduchi to explicitly account for specular reflection. We use the dichromatic model [3] to describe the appearance of a surface under specular reflection, and show how this can be included in the subspace-based decoding approach of [2], which is augmented based on the observed color of a white patch. The experimental results on images taken under a wide variety of illuminants and viewing angles show a substantial improvement (in terms of reduced decoding error rate) with respect to the original system that assumed Lambertian surface reflectance. In quantitative terms, we show that, by using a palette with $N = 20$ colors and 4 reference colors displayed in the barcode, we are able to encode a 128-bit message using 34 patches overall with 0 decoding errors in our test set. Compared to the 4-color HCCB standard that displays all 4 colors (and thus requires 68 patches to encode the same message), we achieve a reduction of the barcode size by one half.

2   Related Work

A patent by Han et al. [4], who used reference cells to provide standard colors for correct indexing, is possibly the first reported attempt to use color in a 2-D barcode This technology is marketed by Colorzip Media (colorzip.com). Later examples of color barcode technology include the method by Bulan *et al.* [5], who embed data in two different printer colorant channels via halftone-dot orientation modulation, Grillo et al. [6], who used 4 or 16 colors in a regular QR code, and Kato et al. [7] who selected colors that are maximally separated in a plane of the RGB color cube. Pei et al. used four colors in a color barcode technology named "Continuous Color Barcode Symbols" [8]. Blasinski et al. [9] proposed a framework that exploits the spectral diversity between the color channels (C, M, and Y) used in regular color printers, and the (R, G, B) color channels used in color cameras.

Several existing decoding algorithms (including HCCB [1]) include a color clustering step to identify the most representative colors in the barcode. For example, the method of Sali and Lax [10] uses a k-means classifier to assign the (R,G,B) value of a color patch to one reference color. Color clustering, however, is not guaranteed to work well with large palettes, and therefore the clustering approach is best suited to small palette sizes.

The use of large color palettes and a small number of reference colors was originally proposed by Wang and Manduchi [11], who studied the problem of information embedding via printed color. Bagherinia and Manduchi [12] attempted to decode a color barcode *without* any reference color by modeling the joint variation of the color of groups of color patches under varying illuminant. Later, the same authors [2] used a similar concept but applied to sets formed by a color patch and a set of reference color patches. As mentioned earlier, our work builds upon the algorithm described in [2].

3   Background and Definitions

A color barcode is created from a set $\mathcal{C}_N$ of N colors (*palette*) and a set $\mathcal{C}_r$ of r reference colors. A color barcode of length $K = n + r$ is defined as the arrangement of n color patches, selected from the palette $\mathcal{C}_N$ and used for information encoding, and the r reference colors of $\mathcal{C}_r$, in any spatial configuration. Decoding the bar code means assigning the color of each one of the n information-carrying patches to the index of the corresponding color in the palette $\mathcal{C}_N$. As with standard color barcodes (e.g. HCCB), we assume that the position of the reference colors in the barcode is known. In this work we will follow the approach of Bagherinia and Manduchi [2], who showed that, by carefully modeling the joint color variation as a function of the illuminant, it is possible to use $r < N$ reference colors and still obtain good decoding performance. In fact, we don't even constrain the set of reference colors $\mathcal{C}_r$ to be a subset of the color palette $\mathcal{C}_N$.

Since each color patch carries $\log_2 N$ bits of information, the barcode carries $n \log_2 N$ bits. In order to encode B bits, one needs this many color patches:

$$K = n + r = \lceil B / \log_2 N \rceil + r \tag{1}$$

Increasing the palette size N and reducing the number r of reference colors decreases the size K of the barcode, resulting in higher *information rate* [2]. For example, Fig. 1 shows the minimum length K of a color barcode that encodes a message of $B = 128$ bits as a function of the size of the color palette N and of the number of reference colors r. (Note that the HCCB standard with $N = r = 4$ would require $K = 68$ color patches for the same 128-bit message.) For a fixed number r of reference colors, the barcode length K decreases monotonically with the size of the color palettes N. In contrast, if the whole palette is represented by the reference colors ($r = N$), the plot of K at $N = 13$ ($K = 48$), after which adding colors to the palette becomes counterproductive.

While the plot in Fig. 1 suggests that large palettes with few reference colors lead to high information rate, it hides the fact that increasing the palette size typically results in larger decoding error rates, which must be offset by adding more reference colors. Let $P_E(N, r)$ is the probability of decoding error (that is, of misclassifying the color of a patch) for a given palette $\mathcal{C}_N$ and a given set of reference colors $\mathcal{C}_r$. Assuming that decoding errors are statistically independent events, the *decoding error rate*, that is, the probability of decoding error for the barcode (i.e., of decoding at least one color patch incorrectly) is equal to:

$$P_E(N, r, K) = 1 - (1 - P_E(N, r))^{K-r} \tag{2}$$

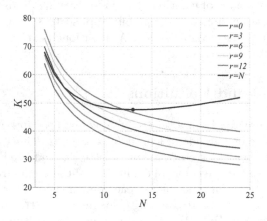

Fig. 1. The minimum number of patches K required to encode a 128-bit message versus the size of the palette N

One may expect $P_E(N, r)$ to increase with increasing N (larger palette) and decrease with increasing r (more reference colors). This was verified experimentally in [2]. This relation establishes a design trade-off between decoding error probability and information rate, mediated by the parameters N and r.

4   Subspace-Based Decoding

4.1   The Lambertian Case

We will follow the general approach of Bagherinia and Manduchi [2] for illumination-invariant color patch decoding, briefly summarized in the following. Consider a patch colored with the i-th color in the palette $\mathcal{C}_N$. The observed color $\mathbf{c}_i = [c_{i,R}, c_{i,G}, c_{i,B}]^T$ of this patch will vary as the illuminant changes (e.g., from sunlight to artificial light), making color identification difficult. The key observation of [2] is that the *joint* color variation of a set of color patches, all under the same illumination, is bound by a linear constrain. For example, consider the $3(r + 1)$-dimensional vector $\mathbf{e}_i = [\mathbf{c}_i, \mathbf{d}_1, \ldots, \mathbf{d}_r]^T$ which includes the colors of the (known) reference patches $\{\mathbf{d}_j\}$, with $\mathbf{d}_j = [d_{j,R}, d_{j,G}, d_{j,B}]^T$. If the surfaces are Lambertian, and assuming that the illuminant spectra live in a finite-dimensional subspace of dimension N_{ill}, then the vector $\mathbf{e}_i$ must live in a linear subspace S_i of dimension equal to $\min(3(r+1), N_{\text{ill}})$, which can be considered equal to N_{ill} for $r \geq 1$ [13,14]. Formally:

$$\mathbf{e}_i = \mathbf{\Phi}_i \mathbf{v} \tag{3}$$

where $\mathbf{v}$ is a N_{ill}–vector that represents the illuminant, and $\mathbf{\Phi}_i$ is a matrix that characterizes the reflectivity of the patch surface[1]. It is useful to define the *dimensionality ratio (DR)* as the ratio between the dimension of the embedding subspace S_i and the dimension of $\mathbf{e}_i$:

$$\text{DR} = \frac{N_{\text{ill}}}{3(r+1)} \tag{4}$$

This suggests a simple algorithm for decoding a generic color patch $\mathbf{c}$: (1) Build the vector $\mathbf{e}$ (by juxtaposing the observed color $\mathbf{c}$ with the observed colors of the reference patches in the same barcode); (2) Find the subspace S_i that is closest to the vector $\mathbf{e}$; (3) Decode $\mathbf{c}$ as i. Intuitively, the smaller the dimensionality ratio DR (itself an decreasing function of r), the higher the robustness of this decoding algorithm with respect to noise. This formalizes the intuitive notion that more reference colors should ensure lower decoding error rates.

The subspaces S_i for $1 \leq i \leq N$ can be learnt from observation of the colors in $C_N \cup C_r$ under a wide variety of illuminants. If multiple pictures of the color patches under different illuminants are impractical or impossible to obtain, one may "constrain" the embedding subspaces S_i by means of the diagonal (von Kries) model of color change. Indeed, under the diagonal color model, the matrix $\mathbf{\Phi}_i$ can be written as [2]

$$\mathbf{\Phi}_i^T = \begin{bmatrix} c_{i,R} & 0 & 0 & d_{1,R} & 0 & 0 & d_{2,R} \cdots \\ 0 & c_{i,G} & 0 & 0 & d_{1,G} & 0 & 0 \cdots \\ 0 & 0 & c_{i,B} & 0 & 0 & d_{1,B} & 0 \cdots \end{bmatrix} \tag{5}$$

It is easy to see that this matrix can be learnt from observation of the colors under just one illumination. However, the resulting deciding error rate are typically higher than with the "unconstrained" subspace approach [2].

4.2   The General Case

In the real world, surfaces are rarely Lambertian, and the reflected light should be expected to contain a specular component. The amount of this specular component depends on the surface characteristics and on the joint illumination/viewing geometry. For color barcodes printed on paper, the specular component can be quite noticeable [2,15].

A simple model of light reflection that accounts for specular reflection is the *dichromatic model* [3]:

$$\mathbf{c} = m^{(b)} \mathbf{c}^{(b)} + m^{(i)} \mathbf{c}^{(i)} \tag{6}$$

---

[1] Note that $\mathbf{\Phi}_i$ is also a function of the spectral sensitivities of the color filters at the camera.

The dichromatic model states that the observed color $\mathbf{c}$ of a surface is the sum of two colors, $\mathbf{c}^{(b)}$ (*body reflection*) and $\mathbf{c}^{(i)}$ (*interface reflection*), weighted by coefficients $m^{(b)}$ and $m^{(i)}$ that can take values between 0 and 1. It is normally assumed that $m^{(b)}$ (the "Lambertian component") is largely independent of changes in the viewpoint (and thus can be safely set it to 1). For most materials, the interface reflection $\mathbf{c}^{(i)}$ can be considered material-independent and equal to the color of the illuminant itself (or, equivalently, of a white surface reflecting the same illuminant). In practice, the dichromatic model predicts that the specular (interface) reflection "steers" the color of the surface towards the color of a white surface seen under the same illuminant. This observation suggests that if the barcode contains a white reference patch, the color of this white patch may be used to "remove" the specular component from the color of other patches, provided that one can somehow estimate the coefficient $m^{(i)}$ at each patch.

Formally, we can model the color of the vector $\mathbf{e}$ defined in the previous section as follows:

$$\mathbf{e}_i = \boldsymbol{\Phi}_i \mathbf{v} + \mathbf{W}\mathbf{m}^{(i)} \tag{7}$$

with

$$\mathbf{W} = \mathbf{I} \otimes \mathbf{w} = \begin{bmatrix} \mathbf{w} & 0 & 0 & \cdots \\ 0 & \mathbf{w} & 0 & \cdots \\ \vdots & \vdots & \vdots & \ddots \end{bmatrix} \tag{8}$$

where $\mathbf{I}$ is the $(r+1) \times (r+1)$ identity matrix, $\otimes$ represents the Kronecker product, $\mathbf{w}$ is the observed color of the white reference patch, and $\mathbf{m}^{(i)}$ is a $(r+1)$–vector containing the interface reflection coefficients for all patches in $\mathbf{e}$. This suggests that the subspace approach used for the Lambertian case could be extended to the general case with specularities, owing to the observed white patch. However, it should be noticed that the the presence of specular reflection increases the dimensionality[2] of the embedding space $\mathcal{S}$ to $N_{\text{ill}} + r$. With respect to the Lambertian case, the dimensionality ratio DR is thus increased by a factor of $1 + r/N_{\text{ill}}$, making decoding harder.

In order to keep the dimensionality ratio under control, in this work we assume that $m^{(i)}$ is constant across patches for a fixed illuminant. This simplifying assumption can be partly justified by the fact that, for a small sized planar barcode, the viewing geometry can be considered approximately constant for all patches. Hence, assuming constant $m^{(i)}$ across patches means neglecting the difference between interface reflection coefficients for the different patches in the barcode. This approximation allows us to rewrite Eq. (7) as follows:

$$\mathbf{e}_i = \begin{bmatrix} \boldsymbol{\Phi}_i & | & \mathbf{V} \end{bmatrix} \begin{bmatrix} \mathbf{v} \\ m^{(i)} \end{bmatrix} \tag{9}$$

---

[2] Note that the white patch is assumed to be part of the reference colors. For this patch, the specular reflection component is immaterial. This is the reason why the dimension of the embedding space is $N_{\text{ill}} + r$ rather than $N_{\text{ill}} + r + 1$.

with $\mathbf{V} = [\mathbf{w}^T, \dots, \mathbf{w}^T]^T$ obtained from the observed color of the white reference patch. With this simplification, the dimensionality ratio DR is only increased by a factor of $1 + 1/N_{\text{ill}}$ with respect to the Lambertian case.

Note that the matrix $\boldsymbol{\Phi}_i$ is computed from training data in the absence of specular reflection. In practice, this can be achieved by ensuring that, when taking training images, the color patches lie on a plane orthogonal to the camera's optical axis. Also note that, in order to compute the distance of the vector $\mathbf{e}$ to a subspace $\mathcal{S}_i$, it is useful to first derive an orthogonal column basis for $[\boldsymbol{\Phi}_i | \mathbf{V}]$, which can be achieved via QR decomposition.

5 Experimental Evaluation

We ran a number of experiments with color checkerboards printed on paper with a regular color printer. Images were taken of the checkerboards with a Canon EOS 350D camera in raw (CR2) format with a resolution of 3474x2314 pixels and 12 bits per color channel.

5.1 Training Set and Model Construction

In order to select the palette and the reference colors, we started with a "training" checkerboard with 125 colors, uniformly sampled in (R,G,B) color space. We took multiple images of this checkerboard from a constant distance of about 1.5 meters, with the camera's optical axis orthogonal to the checkerboard to minimize specular reflections, under 32 different illumination conditions. The color values within each patch were averaged together to reduce noise.

We used the method described in [2], and briefly summarized in the following, to select the color palettes $\mathcal{C}_{12} \subset \mathcal{C}_{16} \subset \mathcal{C}_{20} \subset \mathcal{C}_{24}$, together with 5 reference colors. For each illuminant, we clustered the colors of the patches using k-means with 24 clusters. We then selected the 24 cluster centers with highest occurrences among all illuminants. We repeated the same procedure to select the colors of the palettes for $N = 20$, 16 and 12, each time starting from the palette chosen in the previous step.

The reference colors were sampled from the 125-24=101 colors that were not used for the color palette $\mathcal{C}_{24}$. (Note that choosing reference colors from the palette would actually *increase* the dimensionality ratio DR from $N_{\text{ill}}/3(r+1)$ to $N_{\text{ill}}/3r$, making decoding harder.) We used a greedy recursive strategy for jointly selecting r reference colors (with $1 \leq r \leq 5$) and the dimensionality of the embedding subspaces $\{\mathcal{S}_i\}$, which was kept constant across subspaces for given r. Reference patches are added one at a time. Given the current set of r reference colors, all possible remaining $125 - 24 - r$ colors and subspace dimensions from 1 to 5 are tested using cross-validation over multiple illuminants, and the marginal error rates $P_E(N, r)$ are computed. The reference color and subspace dimension that minimize the decoding error rate are selected and added to the set. For $r = 1, 2$ the algorithm chose an embedding subspace dimension 3, while for $r = 3, 4, 5$ the chosen subspace dimension was of 4. The white patch

Fig. 2. A collage created with the chosen palette colors and reference colors, seen under three different illuminant spectra. The patches are distributed in such a way that, in lexicographic order, the first N patches form $\mathcal{C}_N$ for $N = 12, 16, 20, 24$. Following are the 5 reference colors chosen for the "unconstrained" subspace decoding algorithm, followed by the 5 reference patches chosen using the diagonal color model. The last patch is the white patch.

was then added to the reference colors when the dichromatic model was used. Note that the decoding error was computed under the assumption of Lambertian surfaces (3). Also note that we generated two sets of reference patches, one for the "unconstrained" embedding subspace model, and one for the diagonal model (5).

Along with the palette and the reference colors, we computed the embedding subspaces (represented by the matrices $\{\boldsymbol{\Phi}_i\}$ in (3)) for all combinations of palette size N and number of reference patches r, using data from all 32 illumination conditions. Additionally, we learnt the matrices $\{\boldsymbol{\Phi}_i\}$ using the diagonal model (5) for all combinations (N, r). However, since these matrices can be learnt from just one image, we created 32 versions of each $\boldsymbol{\Phi}_i$, one per illumination condition.

The color palettes and reference colors chosen with this algorithm are shown in Fig. 2.

5.2   Test Set and Results

We evaluated the performance of our proposed decoding algorithms using a 13×12 "test" color checkerboard with size of 16.5×15 cm, printed with the same color printer used for the "training" checkerboard. The first six pairs of rows each contain all 24 colors in the palette, in random order. The last row contains the five reference colors selected for the unconstrained subspace model, followed by the five reference colors chosen for the diagonal model and by two white patches. In order to facilitate automatic checkerboard detection and patch localization in our pictures, we printed a thick black edge outside the pattern, outlining a visible white frame (see Fig. 3). (This design was inspired by the ARToolKit marker concept [16].) Of course, in a real application, a smaller frame (or no frame at all) would have to be used.

Fig. 3. Examples of images with the "test" color checkerboard, used in our experimental tests. The inset at each picture shows the brightness-rescaled, zoomed-in checkerboard detail.

We took 100 images from the test checkerboard under multiple illumination conditions, multiple viewing angles (ranging from −45 to 45 degrees with respect to the normal to the checkerboard surface), and multiple distances (1 to 5 meters). Figure 3 shows some examples of our test images. Each color patch was automatically localized, and color values within the central area of the patch were averaged together to reduce noise (resulting in one color value per patch).

We evaluated the marginal error rate $P_E(N, r)$ for a combination of design choices: (a) using the unconstrained vs. the diagonal subspace model (5); (b) using the Lambertian reflection model (3) vs. the dichromatic reflection model (9). For each design choice, we considered all combinations of parameters[3] N and r. For each pair (N, r) we used the associated matrices $\{\Phi_i\}$ learnt from the "training" checkerboard as discussed above.

When using the unconstrained subspace model, the error rate $P_E(N, r)$ was given by the total number of color patches in the "test" checkerboard that were incorrectly decoded, divided by the number of images (100) and by the number of color patches in the colorchecker ($N \times 6$). The computation of the error rate using the diagonal model (5) is slightly different, as in this case there are 32 different versions of each matrix Φ_i, one per illumination condition. We tested all such matrices, and computed the error rate as the total number of color patches in the "test" checkerboard that were incorrectly decoded, divided by the number of images (100), by the number of color patches in the colorchecker ($N \times 6$), and by the number of illumination conditions in the training dataset (32).

---

[3] Note that, when using the dichromatic model, we added the white patch to the sets of reference colors used for the Lambertian reflection model, resulting in a number of reference patches larger by one.

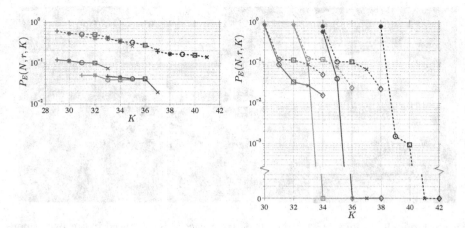

Fig. 4. The probability $P_E(N, r, K)$ of decoding error for a 128-bit message as a function of the total barcode length K, the palette size N, the number of reference colors r, and the embedding subspace type. Black: $N = 12$; Blue: $N = 16$; Green: $N = 20$; Red: $N = 24$. '+': $r = 1$; '*': $r = 2$; 'o': $r = 3$; '□': $r = 4$; '×': $r = 5$; '◇': $r = 6$. Solid line: unconstrained embedding subspace; Dotted line: diagonal model (5). Left: Assuming Lambertian reflectance (3), with r ranging from 1 to 5. Right: Using the dichromatic reflection model (9), with r ranging from 2 to 6 (the white patch was added to the chosen set of reference colors.)

The resulting error rates $P_E(N, r, K)$ for a message with $B = 128$ bits are shown in Fig. 4. As expected, the error rate decreases with increasing barcode length K. The diagonal model is also shown to perform poorly compared to the unconstrained model (as also found in [2]). Using the dichromatic model results in improved performance for large enough r. Indeed, for $N = 20$ and $r = 4$, we achieve 0 error rate for $K = 34$ in our data set. This is a very promising result, considering that the same parameters yield an error rate of 0.07 using the Lambertian reflection model. To put this result in context, consider that, as discussed in Sec. 3, a system that represents all the palette colors in the reference set ($N = r$) requires a barcode of length K equal to at least 48 (for $N = 13$) to encode 128 bits. By using a smaller number of color patches and the dichromatic model, our algorithm is able to pack the same amount of information in a barcode that is 30% smaller. With respect to the HCCB system with $N = r = 4$ (which requires $K = 68$ patches for a 128-bit message), our algorithm allows for reduction of the barcode size by half.

When using the diagonal model, an error rate of less than 0.001 is obtained only for $K \geq 40$. In this case, there is a smaller (but still significant) gain in terms of information rate with respect to the case $N = r$. As discussed earlier, the practical advantage of the diagonal model is that it requires only one picture of the color palette, rather than multiple pictures under a variety of illumination condition as needed by the unconstrained subspace model.

6 Conclusions

We have introduced a new algorithm for color barcode decoding in presence of specular reflection. Our experiments have shown that, by selecting up to 24 colors and a small number of reference colors, it is possible to achieve higher information rate than with mainstream color barcode decoding methods while ensuring low decoding error rates. Future research will consider other sources of error such as due to blur-induced color mixing from two nearby patches or to color barcodes printed from different printers.

Acknowledgements.. This material is based upon work supported by the National Science Foundation under Grant No. IIS - 0835645.

References

1. Parikh, D., Jancke, G.: Localization and segmentation of a 2D high capacity color barcode. In: IEEE Workshop on Applications of Computer Vision, WACV 2008, pp. 1–6. IEEE (2008)
2. Bagherinia, H., Manduchi, R.: High information rate and efficient color barcode decoding. In: Fusiello, A., Murino, V., Cucchiara, R. (eds.) ECCV 2012 Ws/Demos, Part II. LNCS, vol. 7584, pp. 482–491. Springer, Heidelberg (2012)
3. Shafer, S.A.: Using color to separate reflection components. Color Research & Application **10**(4), 210–218 (1985)
4. Han, T., Cheong, C., Lee, N., Shin, E.: Machine readable code image and method of encoding and decoding the same. U.S. Patent 7020327 (2000)
5. Bulan, O., Monga, V., Sharma, G.: High capacity color barcodes using dot orientation and color separability. In: Proc. SPIE-IS&T Electronic Imaging, vol. 7254 (2009)
6. Grillo, A., Lentini, A., Querini, M., Italiano, G.F.: High capacity colored two dimensional codes. In: Proc. Int. Multiconf. on Comp. Science Inf. Tech. (2010)
7. Kato, H., Tan, K.T., Chai, D.: Novel colour selection scheme for 2D barcode. In: Proc. International Symposium on Intelligent Signal Processing and Communication Systems (ISPACS 2009)(2009)
8. Pei, S. Li, G., Wu, B.: Codec system design for continuous color barcode symbols. In: Proceedings of the 2008 IEEE 8th International Conference on Computer and Information Technology Workshops, Washington, DC, USA, pp. 539–544. IEEE Computer Society (2008)
9. Blasinski, H., Bulan, O., Sharma, G.: Per-colorant-channel color barcodes for mobile applications: An interference cancellation framework. IEEE Transactions on Image Processing **22**(4), 1498–1511 (2013)
10. Sali, E., Lax, D.: Color bar code system. U.S. Patent 7210631 (2006)
11. Wang, F., Manduchi, R.: Color-constant information embedding. In: Proc. IEEE Workshop on Color and Reflectance in Imaging and Computer Vision (2010)
12. Bagherinia, H., Manduchi, R.: A theory of color barcodes. In: IEEE Color and Photometry in Computer Vision Workshop (CPCV), pp. 806–813. IEEE (2011)

13. Judd, D.B., MacAdam, D.L., Wyszecki, G., Budde, H.W., Condit, H.R., Henderson, S.T., Simonds, J.L.: Spectral distribution of typical daylight as a function of correlated color temperature. JOSA **54**(8), 1031–1040 (1964)
14. Slater, D., Healey, G.: What is the spectral dimensionality of illumination functions in outdoor scenes? In: Proc. CVPR. IEEE (1998)
15. Bagherinia, H., Manduchi, R.: Robust real-time detection of multi-color markers on a cell phone. Journal of Real-time Image Processing **8**(2), 207–223 (2013)
16. Kato, H., Billinghurst, M., Blanding, B., May, R.: Artoolkit. Hiroshima City University, Tech. Rep. (1999)

Photometric Compensation to Dynamic Surfaces in a Projector-Camera System

Panagiotis-Alexandros Bokaris[1]($\boxtimes$), Michèle Gouiffès[1],
Christian Jacquemin[1], and Jean-Marc Chomaz[2]

[1] LIMSI-CNRS, University of Paris-Sud, 91405 Orsay Cedex, France
bokaris@limsi.fr
[2] LadHyX, CNRS, École Polytechnique, 91128 Palaiseau, France

Abstract. In this paper, a novel approach that allows color compensated projection on an arbitrary surface is presented. Assuming that the geometry of the surface is known, this method can be used in dynamic environments, where the surface color is not static. A simple calibration process is performed offline and only a single input image under reference illumination is sufficient for the estimation of the compensation. The system can recover the reflectance of the surface pixel-wise and provide an accurate photometric compensation to minimize the visibility of the projection surface. The color matching between the desired appearance of the projected image and the projection on the surface is performed in the device-independent color space CIE 1931 XYZ. The results of the evaluation confirm that this method provides a robust and accurate compensation even for surfaces with saturated colors and high spatial frequency patterns. This promising method can be the cornerstone of a real time projector-camera system for dynamic scenes.

Keywords: Photometric compensation · Dynamic surface · Projector-camera system · Augmented reality · Reflectance estimation · Calibration

1 Introduction

The emerging technology of projector-camera systems is used in a wide range of applications such as augmented reality, education, cultural heritage and interactive art installations. The ability to project on arbitrary surfaces expands the limits of common multimedia and breaks new ground in human-computer interaction. Over the last decade, a significant amount of research has been done in the field of smart projection and various methods have been proposed for photometric and geometric compensation in projector-camera systems. However, a system that is able to compensate for complex dynamic surfaces still remains an open issue. The main reason is that the compensation of such a system highly depends on the projection surface. Thus, the majority of the proposed methods calibrate the system for a given surface. If the surface is not static, then the

© Springer International Publishing Switzerland 2015
L. Agapito et al. (Eds.): ECCV 2014 Workshops, Part III, LNCS 8927, pp. 283–296, 2015.
DOI: 10.1007/978-3-319-16199-0_20

system has to be recalibrated for the new surface. This leads to solutions that cannot be applied in real time and cannot handle a dynamic environment.

In general, the physical characterization of a surface requires to measure its spectral reflectance. However, obtaining such spectral data requires the use of special equipment such as a spectrophotometer or a spectral camera. This is not feasible in the majority of applications and, in addition, it is impractical to perform a significant amount of measurements for each surface.

The main contribution of this work is a robust and accurate photometric projector compensation method that can be adapted to changes on the projection surface. For this purpose, we propose a novel calibration method that does not require the projection of any calibration pattern and is entirely performed offline. Once, the system is calibrated, a single input image of the projection surface under reference illumination is sufficient for estimating the compensation. The offline calibration consists of two different procedures. The first one is to build the surface reflectance estimator using a small training set and least square data fitting. For the training set, pairs of RGB camera values and spectral reflectances are required. Thus, capturing, with the camera, a single image of a surface that has color patches with known reflectances is sufficient. The second procedure requires the measurement of the spectral responses of the RGB projector primaries. If this is not provided by the manufacturer, it can be easily obtained using a spectroradiometer. Despite requiring the use of special equipment, it has the main advantage that it is performed only once for each projector.

Once the offline calibration is achieved, the proposed method performs the color matching between the desired appearance of the projected image and the result of the projection on the surface in the independent color space CIE 1931 XYZ. Using the estimated surface spectral reflectance, the RGB values of the projector that would produce the desired image appearance are calculated.

It should be noted that since this paper focuses on the photometric compensation, it is assumed that the camera-projector correspondence has been already performed as a pre-processing step. The geometric compensation is a well studied problem. For the purposes of this research, the structured light technique proposed in [18] and applied in [12] was used for the mapping between the projector and camera pixels.

2   Previous Work

There is an increasing interest in the projector-camera systems due to their wide application range. Therefore, over the last decade, numerous methods for photometric and geometric compensation have been proposed in the literature. These methods can be separated by whether they consider the projection surface static or dynamic.

Nayar et al. [13] proposed a compensation method which is based on an offline calibration that estimates the parameters of their radiometric model. The main drawback of this method is that it requires the projection of 260 images and the a priori knowledge of the camera's response function. Grossberg et al. [7] improved this radiometric model and presented a calibration process that requires the projection of only 6 images. Even though this method provides promising results, it is only applicable in static environments since every time the projection surface changes, the projection of the calibration images has to be repeated. Bimber et al. [4] introduced the concept of smart projectors which use cameras to capture information about the environment. They provide a compensation method for projecting on arbitrary surfaces. However, their rather simple radiometrical model is not able to compensate for the complex nonlinearities in a projector or camera.

Ashdown et al. [3] proposed a compensation method that is content-dependent. The compensation image is calculated according to the values of chrominance and luminance that the system can produce. In other words, the desired appearance is fitted to the available gamut. However, CIELUV was used as the perceptually-uniform color space, which is well-known for its poor uniformity. Moreover, this approach requires a set of calibration images for each surface. Law et al. [9] introduced a perceptually based method for modifying the appearance of a surface. In their work, the physical surface is separated into patches of uniform color and an optimization process computes the compliant appearance which is the most perceptually similar to the desired appearance. This approach requires the surface to be composed of uniform color patches and has a considerably high time complexity that can be up to one hour for a complex scene.

Recently, Grundhofer [8] proposed a method that does not require projector or camera calibration. The pixel-wise mapping from projector to camera colors is generated by a sparse sampling of the projector's color gamut and a scattered data interpolation. In addition, an optional offline optimization step scales locally the input image, maximizing the achievable luminance and contrast while still preserving smooth input gradients, in order to avoid out-of-gamut artifacts. One of the main disadvantages of this approach is that it requires a considerably big set of images (125) in order to perform the necessary color mapping.

A different approach to photometric compensation is based on the acquisition of the light transport instead of projecting calibration images ([17], [14]). The use of the inverse light transport provides new possibilities for analyzing and canceling complex effects such as interreflections that cannot be compensated in a traditional photometric compensation. However, obtaining the light transport of the scene is a highly time-demanding operation that can take more than one hour. In addition, the time complexity of inverting the light transport is another constraint that limits the method to static scenes.

Besides the aforementioned methods that are limited to static surfaces, there are some methods proposed in the literature that can handle dynamic surfaces. Fujii et al. [6] presented a coaxial projector-camera system in order to avoid the problem of continuous geometrical mapping in a moving environment. Their radiometric model is similar with the one in [7] and the system can adapt to a moving surface by capturing a single frame instead of performing full recalibration. However, in order to achieve this, the surface reflectance is treated as a constant within each camera band. This is a very strong assumption and it is not valid for the majority of surface colors. Furthermore, the nonlinearities in projector and camera responses are considered to be negligible and the authors suggest an extra pre-calibration of the devices in order to be taken into account. Amano and Kato [2] introduced a coaxial system that uses a model prediction controller in order to change the appearance of a surface and was later expanded in [1]. This method requires a calibration procedure and the reflectance estimation suffers the same constraints as in [6]. Moreover, due to the use of the controller, the output requires several frames in order to be stabilized.

Park et al. [15] followed a different approach and introduced a system that continuously projects a special embedded pattern image, which allows the radiometric and geometric compensation on a dynamic surface. The embedded information used for the compensation can be encoded in the pattern either temporally or spatially. As a result, there is a tradeoff in this method between the information that can be hidden in the embedded pattern and the visibility of the pattern. Unfortunately, according to their results, the compensation starts to become acceptable only when the pattern can be perceived by the viewer.

3   Methodology

In Section 3.1, the photometric model proposed in this paper is presented. Then, the calibration procedure of the system is separated in two parts. The first one (Section 3.2) is to build the surface reflectance estimator that takes a single camera image as an input. The second part (Section 3.3) describes the linearization and calibration of the devices. Finally, once the calibration procedure has been performed offline, the compensation image can be computed online as described in Section 3.4.

3.1   Photometric Model

As it is well known, the camera and the projector are devices with non-linear responses. In a digital camera the relation between the RGB values and the illuminance impinging on its sensor, can be adequately described by a gamma function. Thus, the RGB values of the camera have to be linearized before any transformation in a linear color space, such as CIE 1931 XYZ, is performed.

$$E_c = \alpha_c (C_c)^\gamma + \beta_c \tag{1}$$

where E_c is the measured illuminance, C_c the camera color channel, α_c is a scalar that simulates the gain in the camera and β_c represents the offset due to noise. The subscript c denotes a single camera channel. Each camera channel should be addressed individually since the gain is not always identical in each channel.

The non-linear response of a projector is, usually, more complex and cannot be represented by a gamma function. However, since it is still monotonically increasing by increasing channel value, it can be inverted. The relation between the channel input value C_p and the corresponding output luminance $L_p(\lambda)$ emitted by the projector can be represented by a non-linear function $p_p()$. The result is modulated by the spectral response $q_p(\lambda)$ that is unique for each primary of the projector. The subscript p denotes a single projector channel.

$$L_p(\lambda) = p_p\left(C_p\right) q_p(\lambda) \tag{2}$$

where λ is the wavelength in the visible range of the spectrum.

The spectral illuminance $I(\lambda)$ that is reflected by a single point on the projection surface towards the direction of the camera can be formulated as follows:

$$I(\lambda) = (L(\lambda) + S(\lambda))\, r(\lambda) \tag{3}$$

where $L(\lambda)$ is the total luminance emitted by the projector, $S(\lambda)$ is the luminance of the ambient light in the room and $r(\lambda)$ is the spectral reflectance of the surface point.

The illuminance, E_c in (1), measured by the camera, which has a spectral response for each channel $q_c(\lambda)$, is given by:

$$E_c = \int (L(\lambda) + S(\lambda))\, r(\lambda)\, q_c(\lambda)\, d\lambda \tag{4}$$

Instead of working with the device-dependent digital values provided by the camera, as it is usually done in the literature ([13], [7], [6], [15]), we choose to perform the appearance matching in the device-independent color space CIE 1931 XYZ. By doing so, the matching becomes more accurate and the system more flexible since it is easier to replace the camera with another one. Therefore, the reflected illuminance of a point on the projection surface is described by its XYZ values. In other words, the spectral response of the camera is replaced by the CIE 1931 2° Standard Observer as follows:

$$X = \int_{380nm}^{780nm} (L(\lambda) + S(\lambda))\, r(\lambda)\, \bar{x}(\lambda)\, d\lambda \tag{5}$$

where $\bar{x}(\lambda)$ is one of the three CIE color matching functions. In a similar way as (5), Y and Z are given for $\bar{y}(\lambda)$ and $\bar{z}(\lambda)$, respectively.

3.2   Reflectance Estimation

As can be seen in (5), it is essential to know the spectral reflectance of the surface in order to calculate the XYZ values of the light reflected on it. Since this information is not provided, we propose a reflectance estimator that takes as an input a single camera image. All the below procedure is performed pixel-wise.

Assuming that $\{\lambda_t\}_{t=1}^{81}$ are uniformly spaced wavelengths in the interval [380, 780] nm, the camera response of (4) can be expressed in its discrete form as:

$$(x_1 x_2 x_3)^T = x \approx W_L^T r \tag{6}$$

where $r = (r(\lambda_1), \ldots, r(\lambda_{81}))^T \in \mathbb{R}^{81 \times 1}$ is the discrete spectral reflectance, $W_L = LW \in \mathbb{R}^{81 \times 3}$ corresponds to light source weighted response functions, $L \in \mathbb{R}^{81 \times 81}$ is the diagonal matrix formed by the illumination vector of the total light impinging on the surface $l = (l(\lambda_1), \ldots, l(\lambda_{81}))^T$ and $W = [s_1 s_2 s_3] \in \mathbb{R}^{81 \times 3}$ is the matrix of the camera responses, where $s_c = (s_c(\lambda_1), \ldots, s_c(\lambda_{81}))^T$ is the response function of each channel.

The aim of this section is to build a reflectance estimator using a training set and least squares data fitting. Let $x \in \mathbb{R}^k$ be a sensor measurement corresponding to a known spectral reflectance $r \in \mathbb{R}^n$. In our case, $k = 3$ and $n = 81$. The training set composed of m different reflectances is:

$$\{(x_1, r_1), \ldots, (x_m, r_m)\} \subset \mathbb{R}^k \times \mathbb{R}^n \tag{7}$$

The least squares minimization problem that minimizes the empirical loss can be written as:

$$\underset{C_r \in \mathbb{R}^{n \times N}}{\operatorname{argmin}} \sum_{i=1}^{m} \|\Phi(X)C_r^T - M\|_F^2 \tag{8}$$

where $\|.\|_F$ denotes Frobenius norm and the rows of matrix M contain the m reflectance vectors of the training set $M = [r_1 \ldots r_m]^T \in \mathbb{R}^{m \times n}$. $\Phi(X) = [\Phi(x_1) \ldots \Phi(x_m)]^T \in \mathbb{R}^{m \times N}$ is the feature map of N features and the solution C_r can be now written as:

$$C_r^T = (\Phi(X)^T \Phi(X))^{-1} \Phi(X) M \tag{9}$$

The estimation of the reflectance is provided by the following equation:

$$\hat{r} = C_r \Phi(x)^T \tag{10}$$

A third degree feature map was selected for fitting the data since through our experimentation it was found that it provides the most accurate results without over-fitting the data. Feature maps of up to fourth degree were tested.

$$\Phi(X) = (1, x_1, x_2, x_3, x_1^2, x_2^2, x_3^2, x_1 x_2, x_1 x_3, x_2 x_3,$$
$$x_1^3, x_2^3, x_3^3, x_1 x_2 x_3, x_1^2 x_2, x_1^2 x_3, x_2^2 x_1, x_2^2 x_3, x_3^2 x_1, x_3^2 x_2)^T \tag{11}$$

The training set for the reflectance estimator can be easily obtained by capturing an image of a surface that is composed of m uniform patches with known reflectance under reference illumination. The patches ideally should be Lambertian but small specularities do not affect significantly the compensation, as can be seen in the results.

3.3 Device Characterization

The characterization of a projector requires spectroradiometric or colorimetric measurements of the light emitted by the device. In order the RGB-to-XYZ transformation and the nonlinear transfer function for each primary color channel to be derived, a color ramp should be measured separately for each primary color channel. Using a spectroradiometer and measuring the radiance emitted by the device while increasing the value of each channel separately, one can obtain the spectral responses of Fig. 1(a). This figure shows the output of the projector given by (2), which consists of the spectral response of each channel weighted by a factor. As illustrated in Fig. 1(b), this weighting factor is not linear.

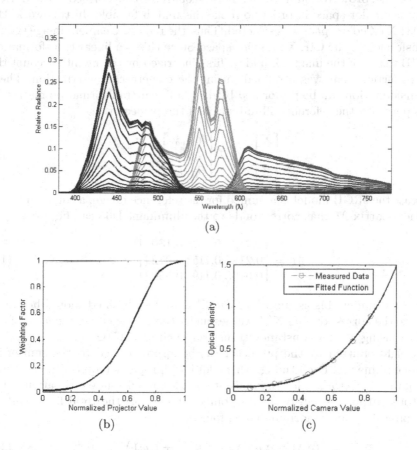

(a)

(b)   (c)

Fig. 1. (a) The spectral radiance emitted by a projector while increasing the input value of each channel individually. With blue, green and red is marked the radiance of the corresponding color channel. (b) The non-linear function of the weighting factor with respect to the projector channel value. (c) The gamma response function of the camera.

The nonlinearity of the camera can be estimated by acquiring an image of a target, such as the Macbeth ColorChecker [11], which has surfaces of varying optical density, under reference illumination. By plotting the optical density as a function of the camera values, the gamma function of the camera, as it is expressed in (1), can be derived (see Fig. 1(c)).

3.4   Photometric Compensation

The photometric compensation should create an image that once projected on the surface would produce the desired appearance. The device-dependent RGB values of the projector and the camera should be transformed to a device-independent color space in order to make this match feasible. In this work, the CIE 1931 XYZ color space was selected. Thus, the reference camera image should be transformed to the CIE XYZ color space. Since this is a linear transformation the RGB values of the image should be first linearized by taking into account the gamma function that was obtained during the camera characterization. Then, the transformation can be performed by using a linear transformation matrix M that depends on the reference illumination of the projector.

$$\begin{bmatrix} X \\ Y \\ Z \end{bmatrix} = M \begin{bmatrix} R_{linear} \\ G_{linear} \\ B_{linear} \end{bmatrix} \tag{12}$$

In case the sRGB model is assumed for the reference image, a common transformation matrix M that corresponds to the illuminant D65 can be used:

$$M = \begin{bmatrix} 0.4124\ 0.3576\ 0.1805 \\ 0.2126\ 0.7152\ 0.0722 \\ 0.0193\ 0.1192\ 0.9502 \end{bmatrix} \tag{13}$$

However, under this assumption, the XYZ values obtained should be transformed to the corresponding XYZ values under the reference illumination of the projector, using a color constancy transform, such as CAT02 [5].

The light emitted by the projector can be approximated by the sum of its individual primaries. Even though this additivity property requires the independence of the projector's color channels, it provides an adequate estimation of the projector's output, as can be seen in our results. Thus, the total light emitted by the projector can be formulated as follows:

$$E(\lambda) = a\ q_r(\lambda) + b\ q_g(\lambda) + c\ q_b(\lambda) \tag{14}$$

where $q_r(\lambda)$, $q_g(\lambda)$ and $q_b(\lambda)$ are the spectral responses of the color channels of the projector and a, b and c their weighting factors that depend on the input value (see Fig. 1(b)).

Taking into account (14) and (5), the XYZ values of the projector on the projection surface are given by:

$$X = \int_{380nm}^{780nm} (a\ q_r(\lambda) + b\ q_g(\lambda) + c\ q_b(\lambda))\ r(\lambda)\ \bar{x}(\lambda)\ d\lambda \tag{15}$$

Y and Z are similarly given for $\bar{y}(\lambda)$ and $\bar{z}(\lambda)$, respectively. Once the surface reflectance $r(\lambda)$ is estimated and the desired $XYZ_{desired}$ values of the reference images are calculated, the emitted light of the projector that would produce the same XYZ values is computed. According to (15) it is sufficient to estimate the weighting factors of (14) since the spectral responses of the primaries are known. The ambient light of the room $S(\lambda)$ is considered negligible but it can be taken into account in case it is measured.

Matching the above XYZ values with the desired ones leads to the following 3×3 system:

$$
\begin{bmatrix} a \\ b \\ c \end{bmatrix} = \begin{bmatrix} X_r & X_g & X_b \\ Y_r & Y_g & Y_b \\ Z_r & Z_g & Z_b \end{bmatrix}^{-1} \begin{bmatrix} X_{desired} \\ Y_{desired} \\ Z_{desired} \end{bmatrix} \tag{16}
$$

where

$$
X_c = \int_{380nm}^{780nm} q_c(\lambda)r(\lambda)\bar{x}(\lambda)d\lambda \tag{17}
$$

and $c = r, g, b$. Y_c and Z_c are similarly given for $\bar{y}(\lambda)$ and $\bar{z}(\lambda)$, respectively.

4   Experimental Results

After describing the details of the calibration process, some of the achieved compensations on demanding surfaces are illustrated. Finally, the quantitative evaluation of the results is concluding this section.

4.1   Characterization

The camera-projector system that was used in this paper is composed of a Nikon D90 dSLR camera and a DLP projector Christie F1+. The resolution of the camera was set to 2144 × 1424 pixels while the resolution of the projector was set to its nominal 1400 × 1050 pixels. Even though the available single-chip DLP projector has a considerably complex characterization process [16] and the channel additivity assumption does not stand completely for this projector as can be seen in Fig. 2(a), the compensation results presented in the following section state that the proposed model can still describe the system.

For the characterization of the devices, a Minolta CS-1000 spectroadiometer was used. The projector was characterized by measuring the emitted radiance for 18 uniformly distributed values in each color channel (Fig. 1(a)).

The reflectance estimator was built using the patches of the ColorChecker and 18 different uniform color sheets that were captured by the camera and their reflectances were measured by the spectroradiometer. Using only the 24 samples of the ColorChecker was not sufficient for providing accurate reflectance estimation in a wide variety of projection surfaces. However, by simply adding 18

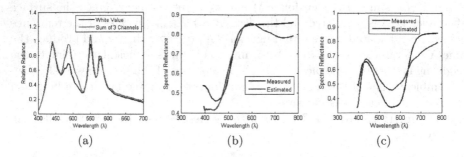

Fig. 2. (a) The spectral relative radiance of the white color and the sum of the individual color channels.(b) Estimated and measured reflectance of yellow patch. (c) Estimated and measured reflectance of purple patch.

additional patches, this small training set (42 pairs in total) was sufficient to provide accurate compensations even for surfaces with colors that were not included in the training set, as can be seen in the results. It should be noted that some specularities that were present in the color sheets do not affect dramatically the result. In order to evaluate the reflectance estimation, the reflectances of the color patches on the first surface in Fig. 4 were measured. The results for the yellow and the purple patch are shown in Figs. 2(b) and Fig. 2(c). Their corresponding CIE 2000 color difference [10] ΔE_{00} between the measured and estimated reflectance under the illuminant D65 was 1.64 and 8.24 units, respectively. Obviously, the reflectance of the surface cannot be considered constant within each projector and camera band as assumed in [6] and even small spectral differences introduce perceptible errors.

4.2 Compensations

A common problem while projecting on an arbitrary surface is that some colors of the initial image might not be reproducible. Thus, in the literature the majority of the proposed methods perform compensations on surfaces that are not saturated and the transition from one color to the next is very smooth because the human visual system is less sensitive to such low spatial frequencies. However, one of the goals of this paper is to compensate for complex surfaces without significantly constraining their context. In Fig. 4 (first row, first column), a surface that is composed by many colorful patches with strong edges and the resulting compensation for two different input images is presented. The compensation was tested on two images of characteristic difficulty. The first one is very vivid while the second one quite achromatic and of high contrast (see Fig. 3).

In case the projection surface moves or changes (e.g. moving object/projector) the compensation breaks and introduces dramatic artifacts even for a small displacement of the projection surface. The proposed method can adapt to the new surface by only capturing a new image under the reference illumination of the

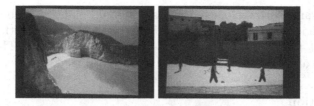

Fig. 3. The image 1 (left) and the image 2 (right) projected on a white surface

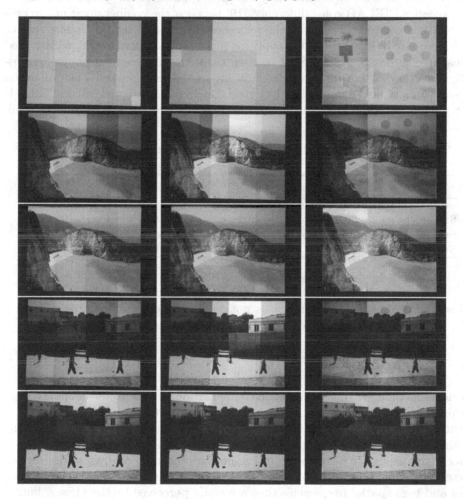

Fig. 4. From left to right: First row: The projection surface. Second row: Image 1 before compensation. Third row: Image 1 after compensation. Fourth row: Image 2 before compensation. Fifth row: Image 2 after compensation.

projector. This is illustrated in the second column of Fig. 4 (second and fourth row), where the projection surface has been changed while the compensation has remained the same with the one of the first column. Finally, the robustness of the proposed method was tested on considerably complex surfaces with high spatial frequency that make the compensation extremely challenging. The results on such a surface are presented in the third column of Fig. 4.

4.3 Evaluation

In order to evaluate quantitatively the performance of the proposed method, the mean S-CIELAB color difference [19] between the compensated image projected on a colored surface and the reference image projected on a white surface was computed. This evaluation concerns image appearance. Hence, widely used measures such as RMSE, PSNR or even CIELAB differences are not appropriate since they do not take into account any spatial information. The evaluation results for a typical monitor (72 dpi) viewed at 18 inches are presented in Table 1. It should be noted that the slight misalignement of the images due to small

Table 1. The mean S-CIELAB difference according to the desired appearance

	Image 1		Image 2	
	Non-compensated	Compensated	Non-compensated	Compensated
Surface 1	30.9	16.2	16.1	10.4
Surface 2	16.0	12.2	11.7	8.7
Surface 3	17.1	11.8	10.7	8.9

movements of the camera increases noticeably the color differences. However, the improvement using the proposed compensation is still visible.

5 Conclusions

A novel method for the photometric compensation in a projector-camera system is proposed, which enables the projection on an arbitrary surface. More importantly, this new approach estimates the reflectance of the projection surface using a single input image and can be used for applications where the projection surface is dynamic such as in the case of a moving object. In contrast with previous attempts in dynamic environments, it can compensate for surfaces with vivid colors and high spatial frequencies that are easily perceived by the viewer. Future work will seek to implement it in a real time system for dynamic scenes in order to make real time compensation on humans and moving objects feasible. Moreover, the desired appearance match will be applied in a color appearance model so that the compensation can be driven by the human visual system instead of being driven by the capture of the camera, as it is currently made. Finally, the number and variety of colors used as the training set for the reflectance estimation will be further examined.

Acknowledgments. We thank Prof. Alain Trémeau and Ass. Prof. Damien Muselet (Laboratoire Hubert Curien, Université Jean Monnet) for hosting us and providing us access to the Minolta CS-1000 spectroradiometer.

References

1. Amano, T.: Projection based real-time material appearance manipulation. In: IEEE CVPR Workshops, pp. 918–923 (2013)
2. Amano, T., Kato, H.: Appearance control using projection with model predictive control. In: ICPR, pp. 2832–2835 (2010)
3. Ashdown, M., Okabe, T., Sato, I., Sato, Y.: Robust content-dependent photometric projector compensation. In: IEEE CVPR Workshops, pp. 6–6, June 2006
4. Bimber, O., Emmerling, A., Klemmer, T.: Embedded entertainment with smart projectors. Computer **38**(1), 48–55 (2005)
5. CIE TC 8–01: A color appearance model for color management systems. Publication 159. Vienna: CIE Central Bureau (2004)
6. Fujii, K., Grossberg, M., Nayar, S.: A projector-camera system with real-time photometric adaptation for dynamic environments. In: IEEE Computer Society CVPR. vol. 2, p. 1180, June 2005
7. Grossberg, M., Peri, H., Nayar, S., Belhumeur, P.: Making one object look like another: controlling appearance using a projector-camera system. In: IEEE Computer Society CVPR. vol. 1, pp. I-452–I-459 (2004)
8. Grundhofer, A.: Practical non-linear photometric projector compensation. In: IEEE CVPR Workshops, pp. 924–929, June 2013
9. Law, A.J., Aliaga, D.G., Sajadi, B., Majumder, A., Pizlo, Z.: Perceptually based appearance modification for compliant appearance editing. Computer Graphics Forum **30**(8), 2288–2300 (2011)
10. Luo, M.R.: Cie 2000 color difference formula: Ciede 2000. Proc. SPIE **4421**, 554–559 (2002)
11. McCamy, C.S., Marcus, H., Davidson, J.G.: A color-rendition chart. J. Appl. Photogr. Eng. **2**(3), 95–99 (1976)
12. Moreno, D., Taubin, G.: Simple, accurate, and robust projector-camera calibration. In: 3DIMPVT, pp. 464–471, October 2012
13. Nayar, S.K., Peri, H., Grossberg, M.D., Belhumeur, P.N.: A projection system with radiometric compensation for screen imperfections. In: IEEE International Workshop on Projector-Camera Systems (PROCAMS) (2003)
14. Ng, T.T., Pahwa, R.S., Bai, J., Tan, K.H., Ramamoorthi, R.: From the rendering equation to stratified light transport inversion. Int. J. Comput. Vision **96**(2), 235–251 (2012)
15. Park, H., Lee, M.H., Seo, B.K., Park, J.I., Jeong, M.S., Park, T.S., Lee, Y., Kim, S.R.: Simultaneous geometric and radiometric adaptation to dynamic surfaces with a mobile projector-camera system. IEEE Transactions on Circuits and Systems for Video Technology **18**(1), 110–115 (2008)
16. Seime, L., Hardeberg, J.Y.: Colorimetric characterization of lcd and dlp projection displays. Journal of the Society for Information Display **11**(2), 349–358 (2003)

17. Wetzstein, G., Bimber, O.: Radiometric compensation through inverse light transport. In: 15th Pacific Conference on Computer Graphics and Applications, pp. 391–399, October 2007
18. Xu, Y., Aliaga, D.G.: Robust pixel classification for 3d modeling with structured light. In: Proceedings of Graphics Interface 2007. GI 2007, pp. 233–240. ACM (2007)
19. Zhang, X., Silverstein, D., Farrell, J., Wandell, B.: Color image quality metric scielab and its application on halftone texture visibility. In: IEEE Proceedings of Compcon. pp. 44–48, February 1997

A Unified Model for Image Colorization

Fabien Pierre[1,2,3,4]($\boxtimes$), Jean-François Aujol[1,2], Aurélie Bugeau[3,4],
and Vinh-Thong Ta[4,5]

[1] University of Bordeaux, IMB, UMR 5251, 33400 Talence, France
fabien.pierre@math.ubordeaux.fr
[2] CNRS, IMB, UMR 5251, 33400 Talence, France
[3] University of Bordeaux, LaBRI, UMR 5800, 33400 Talence, France
[4] CNRS, LaBRI, UMR 5800, 33400 Talence, France
[5] IPB, LaBRI, UMR 5800, 33600 Pessac, France

Abstract. This paper addresses the topic of image colorization that
consists in converting a gray-scale image into a color one. In the literature, there exist two main types of approaches to tackle this problem.
The first one is the manual methods where the color information is given
by some scribbles drawn by the user on the image. The interest of these
approaches comes from the interactions with the user that can put any
color he wants. Nevertheless, when the scene is complex many scribbles
must be drawn and the interactive process becomes tedious and time-
consuming. The second category of approaches is the exemplar-based
methods that require a color image as input. Once the example image is
given, the colorization is generally fully automatic. A limitation of these
methods is that the example image needs to contain all the desired colors in the final result. In this paper, we propose a new framework that
unifies these two categories of approaches into a joint variational model.
Our approach is able to take into account information coming from any
colorization method among these two categories. Experiments and comparisons demonstrate that the proposed approach provides competitive
colorization results compared to state-of-the-art methods.

1 Introduction

Colorization is an old subject that began with the ability of screens and devices
to display colors. The first colorization method [1] tried to map every luminance
(gray-scale) level into a color space. Obviously, all the color space can not be
recovered without injecting other information. Priors can be added in two ways:
with manual interactions or by giving a color image as an example (also called
source). In the rest of this paper, we call *target* the gray-scale image to colorize.

In the first category of methods, a user manually adds points of color (called
scribbles) on the target. Figure 1(d) shows an example of result obtained with
such priors. Generally, the image is considered as the luminance channel which
is not modified during the colorization. Only chrominance channels are computed within the algorithm. Numerous methods have been proposed based on

© Springer International Publishing Switzerland 2015
L. Agapito et al. (Eds.): ECCV 2014 Workshops, Part III, LNCS 8927, pp. 297–308, 2015.
DOI: 10.1007/978-3-319-16199-0_21

(a) Source   (b) Scribbles   (c) Exemplar   (d) Manual   (e) Our model

Fig. 1. Example of exemplar-based, manual and unified colorization. Our method is both able to work with only exemplar or only manual priors. Its novelty is the ability to combine both priors.

this principle. For instance, the method of Levin *et al.* [2] solves an optimization problem to diffuse the chrominance of the scribbles to the target with the assumption that chrominance must have small variations if the luminance has small variations. Yatziv *et al.* [3] propose a simple and fast method by using geodesic distances to blend the chrominances given by the scribbles. Heu *et al.* [4] use pixel priorities to ensure that important areas end up with the right colors. Other propagation schemes have been proposed, for instance, probabilistic distance transform [5], random walks [6], discriminative textural features [7], structure tensors [8] or non local graph regularization [9]. As often described in the literature, with these color diffusion approaches, the contours are not well preserved. In [10], the scribbles are automatically generated after segmenting the image and the user only needs to give one color to each scribble. As it is the case with all manual methods, this latter approach suffers from the following drawback: if the target represents a complex scene, then the user's interactions become very important.

In exemplar-based colorization methods, the color information is extracted from a *source* color image selected by the user. Figure 1(c) shows an example of such a method where the final result is obtained with the approach introduced in this paper. The first exemplar-based method is the one proposed by Welsh *et al.* [11] (derived from a texture synthesis algorithm [12]) that uses image patch similarities on the gray-scale channels to provide colors. [11] also proposes manual information (called swatches) to specify where to search for similar patches in the source image. Generally, exemplar-based approaches suffer from spatial consistency since each pixel is processed independently. To overcome this limitation, several works use image segmentation to improve the colorization results. For instance, Irony *et al.* [13] propose to determine the best matches between the target pixels and regions in a pre-segmented source image. With these correspondences, micro-scribbles from the source are initialized on the target image and colors are propagated as in [2]. Gupta *et al.* [14] extract different features from the superpixels [15] of the target image and match them with the source ones. The final colors are computed by imposing spatial consistency as in [2]. Charpiat *et al.* [16] ensure a spatial coherency without a segmentation but their method involves many complex steps while Chen *et al.* [17] uses image matting.

Without requiring image segmentation or superpixels extraction, Bugeau *et al.* [18] compute a set of color candidates for each target pixel by matching patches with the source image using different features. The final color is obtained by minimizing a functional including a total variation regularization on the chrominance channels. Nevertheless, despite this regularization, the contours are not always well preserved.

To summarize, the interactivity of manual methods is interesting since the user can add the color information he wants, but this task can be tedious and time-consuming. In contrast, the automatic aspect of exemplar-based methods is also interesting since they try to avoid these user's interventions by using one or several source images. However, in many cases, the user wants to add a color that is not present in the source image or to improve/correct the colorization result in one particular region by adding a scribble. The work proposed in this paper follows this idea and proposes a novel model that unifies both approaches. Up to our knowledge, this is the first method proposing this unification.

The *main contribution* of this work is the combination of the two categories of methods into a unified variational model which allows interactivity.

The paper is organized as follows. We first introduce in Section 2 a variational model for image colorization and give an efficient algorithm to compute the solution. In Section 3 we present the unified model for colorization. In section 4 comparisons with state-of-the-art methods demonstrate the improvements of the proposed approach.

2 A Variational Model for Image Colorization

In this section we propose a variational framework for image colorization. As done in most existing colorization methods, we consider the target to be a luminance image and we compute chrominances for each pixels in order to recover the final color. First, the variational model including a regularization is introduced. Next, the corresponding algorithm is given.

2.1 Penalized Variational Labelling

The color can be expressed as a value of luminance Y and two values of chrominance U and V. With these three values, it is possible to display an image on most devices. The luminance channel being given by the target, the colorization problem consists in recovering the chrominance values for each pixels. Inspired from [18], we suppose that, for each pixel x, C chrominance candidates c_i, $i = 1 \ldots C$ are available. These color candidates can both be given by extraction according texture features, by a manual method or by any colorization method. Our model consists in choosing the best color among the C.

To that end, we propose to minimize the following functional where u is the vector of chrominances ($u = (U, V)$) to compute:

$$F(u, W) := TV_c(u) + \frac{\lambda}{2} \int_\Omega \sum_{i=1}^{C} w_i \|u - c_i\|_2^2 + \chi_{\mathcal{R}}(u) + \chi_{\mathcal{E}}(W) . \qquad (1)$$

To simplify the notations, the dependence of each values to the position of the current pixel is removed. For instance, the second term of (1) is a notation for $\int_\Omega \sum_{i=1}^C w_i(\omega) \|u(\omega) - c_i(\omega)\|_2^2 \, d\omega$. We explain hereinafter the significance of each term of functional (1).

Consider the minimization of the term $\int_\Omega \sum_{i=1}^C w_i \|u - c_i\|_2^2$ with respect to u. The minimum is equal to $\sum_{i=1}^C w_i c_i$. Thus it corresponds to a weighted average of the candidates. In order to transform this minimization into a problem of labelling, we add the constraint that all weights are equal to 0 except one which corresponds to the selected label. The set of such weights is the canonical basis of $\mathbb{R}^C$ denoted as $\mathcal{E}$. This constrained problem is denoted as $\int_\Omega \sum_{i=1}^C w_i \|u - c_i\|_2^2 + \chi_\mathcal{E}(W)$ where $\chi_\mathcal{E}$ is a function which value is equal to 0 on $\mathcal{E}$ and $+\infty$ otherwise and W represents the weights $(w_1, \ldots, w_C)$.

The minimization of this term with respect to u and W provides a natural labelling where c_i are labels. Indeed, this minimum is obtained for a binary weight and the minimization of this term with respect to u is equal to c_i. Authors of [18] propose a different approach to get binary weights, but [19] shows that it is too much sensitive to the initialization. Every labelling corresponds to a local minimum (which is global) of this term. A penalization term is therefore introduced to encourage a regularized labelling. In this model, we introduce the total variation TV_c to favors images with contours but few discontinuities. λ is a parameter which controls the influence of the regularization term on the result. Finally, the term $\chi_\mathcal{R}$ requires the values to remain in the standard range for chrominance channels.

TV_c is the coupled total variation defined in the following.

2.2 Coupling the Channels

The classical total variation $\int_\Omega \sqrt{\partial_x U^2 + \partial_y U^2 + \partial_x V^2 + \partial_y V^2}$ suffers from a lack of coupling and leads to some halo effect in the colorization results [18].

We introduce a TV regularization that is able to couple the chrominance channels with the luminance one. Let TV_c be a *coupled* total variation defined as

$$TV_c(u) = \int_\Omega \sqrt{\gamma \partial_x Y^2 + \gamma \partial_y Y^2 + \partial_x U^2 + \partial_y U^2 + \partial_x V^2 + \partial_y V^2}, \quad (2)$$

where Y, U and V are the classical luminance and chrominance channels.

This formulation naturally favors images where contours in chrominance channels are at the same locations as the luminance ones. Figure 2 illustrates this effect. For the sake of clarity, assume that there is a vertical contour in the Y channel, $\partial_x Y = a > 0$ and $\partial_y Y^2 = 0$, and another one in the U channel such that $\partial_x U = b > 0$, $\partial_y U^2 = \partial_x V^2 = \partial_y V^2 = 0$. If the two contours are in the same location, the value of the total variation is equal to $TV_c(u) = \sqrt{\gamma a^2 + b^2}$ but if the contours have different locations, the value is equal to $TV_c(u) = \sqrt{\gamma a^2} + \sqrt{b^2}$. Since $\sqrt{\gamma a^2 + b^2} < \sqrt{\gamma a^2} + \sqrt{b^2}$, the minimization of TV_c favors the values of U such that the contours in the chrominance channels are in the same location

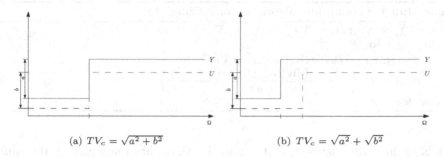

(a) $TV_c = \sqrt{a^2 + b^2}$ (b) $TV_c = \sqrt{a^2} + \sqrt{b^2}$

Fig. 2. Illustration of two situations for contours in luminance and chrominance channels with $\gamma = 1$. TV_c favors coupling of channels.

as the luminance one. We experimentally chose $\gamma = 25$ for all the experiments of the paper.

In Figure 3 we compare our model with a version without coupling. This result is provided by replacing TV_c by the classical total variation on chrominance channels, or by taking $\gamma = 0$ in our model. These results have been performed with 3(b) as target image and 3(a) as source.

(a) Source   (b) Target   (c) Without coupling   (d) Our model

Fig. 3. Comparison of our method with the classical TV

Without coupling the results are totally blurred and the colorization process fails. Thanks to TV_c, our new formulation is able to preserve contours by coupling the channel of luminance Y with the chrominance channels U and V.

2.3 Algorithm

In this section, a min-max version of (1) is proposed. A primal-dual algorithm, inspired from [20] is described to provide a local minimum of functional (1).

To this end, we rewrite the term TV_c from (2) in a dual form:

$$TV_c(U, V) = \min_{U, V} \max_{p = (p_1, p_2, p_3)} \langle \nabla U, \nabla V | p_2, p_3 \rangle + \langle \nabla Y | p_1 \rangle + \chi_{\|(p_1, p_2, p_3)\|_2 \leq 1} \quad (3)$$

where $p \in \mathbb{R}^6$ and $p_j \in \mathbb{R}^2$, $j = 1 \cdots 3$. Y is provided from the target. Minimizing (1) becomes equivalent to maximizing the dual model w.r.t. to the dual

Algorithm 1. Primal dual algorithm minimizing (1)

$u_0 \leftarrow \sum_i w_i c_i;\ (p_0)_1 \leftarrow \nabla Y\ ;\ (p_0)_{2,3} \leftarrow \nabla u_0$

for $n \geq 0$ **do**

$\quad (p_{n+1})_{1,2,3} \leftarrow P_p\left((p_n)_1, (p_n)_{2,3} + \sigma \nabla u_n\right)$

$\quad u_{n+1} \leftarrow P_u\left(\dfrac{u_n + \tau\left(\mathrm{div}((p_{n+1})_{2,3}) + \lambda S(u_n)\right)}{1 + \tau\lambda}\right)$

end for

variable p and minimizing it w.r.t. u and W. Algorithm 1 summarizes the minimization procedure.

$S(u_n)$ stands for the closest candidate of u_n, the colorized image at the nth iteration of Algorithm 1. Y is the luminance channel of the image to colorize. Parameters τ and σ are the time steps. The algorithm of [20] converges when $16\tau\sigma < 1$. The operator div stands for the divergence and ∇ the gradient defined as in [21]. The algorithm requires the projection of the two estimated data p and u. The projection P_u is necessary to ensure that the estimated image stays in the standard range of chrominance values $\mathcal{R}$ and is just a projection onto a rectangle. The computation of w_i used at initialization is described in Section 3. Finally the projection of the dual variable P_p ensures the constraint $\chi_{\|(p_1,p_2,p_3)\|_2 \leq 1}$, by projecting p onto the unit ball:

$$P_p(p) = \frac{\left(p_1 - \sigma\left(\partial_x Y, \partial_y Y\right), p_2, p_3\right)}{\max\left(\left\|\left(p_1 - \sigma\left(\partial_x Y, \partial_y Y\right), p_2, p_3\right)\right\|_2^2, 1\right)}. \tag{4}$$

3   Unifying Manual and Exemplar-Based Colorization

This section presents a simple method to unify both exemplar and manual priors for colorization of image. Although exemplar-based colorization tackles the tedious work of putting scribbles in manual colorization, the choice of the source image is rarely easy and the results contain often errors. The user may prefer to correct the result by adding a manual prior. The integration of this new prior to the exemplar-based result is not obvious. The solution of this problem is the main contribution of the paper.

Exemplar-based colorization. In our model, the exemplar-based priors are introduced *via* candidates. When a source image is provided, the first step consists in extracting for each pixel the set of candidates as done in [18]. These candidates can be provided by any colorization method. The weights w_i are then chosen as $W = 1/C$ where C is the number of candidates extracted at each pixel. The algorithm can work directly with these data.

Manual colorization. This section presents how scribbles can be directly introduced into the proposed model. The scribbles can either be given by the user before or added in an interactive and/or an iterative way. The proposed model can use the scribbles alone, the source alone or both.

The scribble information only affects the weights and the number of candidates. More precisely, for each pixel, a new candidate per scribble is added. Its value is the chrominance of the given scribble. When scribbles candidates are present, their initial weights depend on the geodesic distance. The geodesic distance map, denoted by D, is computed with the fast marching algorithm [22] and with a potential equal $\left(0.001 + \|\nabla u\|_2^2\right)^{-4}$ given in [23]. D is normalized to have a range between 0 and 1. We use the implementation of [24] to compute the geodesic distance.

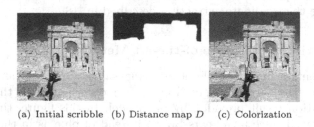

(a) Initial scribble (b) Distance map D (c) Colorization

Fig. 4. Example of color propagation with the geodesic distance. (a) represents the initial scribble, (b) the geodesic distance map from this scribble and (c) the diffusion of the color of the scribble according to this distance map. This diffusion provides a good initialization which is not perfect, but sufficient for our algorithm.

Unified colorization. The unification of the two priors is done at initialization of Algorithm 1. The variable W is initialized with $1/C$ for the candidates which come from the exemplar-based candidates extraction (in the source image) and with $1 - D$ for the candidate(s) corresponding to the scribble(s), where D is the normalized distance map. Pixels that have a low geodesic distance to a scribble get its color. At the opposite for pixels having a high geodesic distance, this new candidate will have no influence onto the colorization result.

The variable W is projected onto the simplex before running the algorithm. The projection is performed with the algorithm of [25]. The variable u is set to $\sum_i w_i c_i$ and the functional is minimized using this initialization.

Figure 4(a) shows the initial blue scribble located in the sky. The associated geodesic distance D with respect to the scribble is presented Figure 4(b) and Figure 4(c) is our colorization result. Our method is able to diffuse the color information of the scribble on constant parts of the image and at the convergence of the algorithm the coupled total variation gives more accurate results than the geodesic distance.

4   Experimental Results

In this section, we give some details about the implementation and the parameters of the unified model. We demonstrate the potential of our approach compared to state-of-the-art methods in both categories, *i.e.*, manual and exemplar-based methods.

4.1   Implementation and Parameters Setting

The implementation of Algorithm 1 has been done on GPU. The convergence takes few seconds and allows interactivity. All the presented experiments use the same set of parameters, *i.e.*, $\sigma = 0.004$, $\tau = 5$, $\lambda = 7.10^{-3}$, $\gamma = 25$ and 500 iterations. With this choice, a lot of different types of image can be colorized without tuning of parameters which is a practical advantage. For exemplar-based results, we use the candidate extraction described in [18].

4.2   Comparison with State-of-the-art Methods

Figure 5 presents a first example of our proposal. Figures 5(a) and 5(b) show the source and the target images. Figure 5(c) corresponds to the exemplar-based colorization result provided by our model. In this figure, the sky is not correctly colorized since it appears brown instead of blue as in the ruins main door. Moreover, blue colors appear on the floor. Figure 5(d) shows the results performed with only the corrections of the user where 3 scribbles are added in order to correct the first (exemplar-based) colorization result (Figure 5(c)). Figure 5(e) illustrates the advantage of the proposed unified image colorization since, the user with less effort, obtained the desired result. Finally, this result also illustrates that our model is well adapted to preserve the color contours.

Figure 6 presents results and illustrates the advantage of using a unified image colorization as compared to only using a source image or some scribbles. Manual colorization results are obtained with [2] and exemplar-based colorization results are obtained with [14]. Colorization results of the last column of Figure 6 are clearly better than the ones obtained with only the source image (fourth column)

(a) Source   (b) Scribbles   (c) Exemplar   (d) Manual   (e) Our model.

Fig. 5. First example of proposed image colorization model. Neither exemplar-based approach nor the manual one are able to properly colorize this image with the given priors. The unified method gives a suitable result.

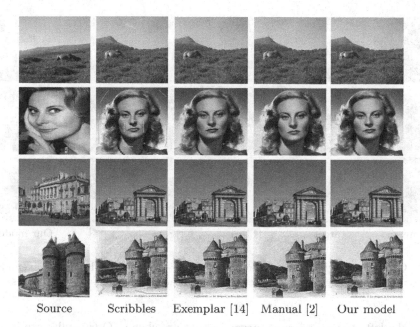

Source   Scribbles   Exemplar [14]   Manual [2]   Our model

Fig. 6. Advantage of the proposed unified model as compared to only exemplar-based or scribble-based model. From left to right: the target image to colorize, the source image, the scribbles added by the user, exemplar result of [14], manual result of [2], result with the unified approach. The unified model increases the quality of the results by taking advantages in both types of methods.

or with only the scribbles (fifth column). Actually, some objects (for instance the tramway, or the background of the portrait) are not present on the source image, thus the exemplar-based method fails. For the manual method, there is a strong lack of information, because few scribbles are provided. We remark in the fourth image that the method of [2] is not robust to noise, compared to ours. This experiment also highlights that old photographs and faces are hard to colorize as remarked, *e.g.*, in [17]. Indeed, old photographs contain a lot of noise and the texture are usually degraded. Face images contain very smooth parts (*e.g.*, the skin) and the background is rarely suitable. Nevertheless, very promising results are obtained with our method. The manual method does not colorize the hair because no scribble is given. The exemplar one does not colorize the background. Finally, the additional prior given by the scribbles of the user does not only have a local effect. Indeed, in the last result of Figure 6, the blue scribble needed to colorize the sky through the arch also improves the sky color at the bottom left of the image. Figure 9 provides additional results.

4.3   Our Model *vs.* Existing Exemplar-Based Methods

Figure 7 provides comparison of our method with existing exemplar-based colorization methods. Figure 8 is a zoom on a particular results.

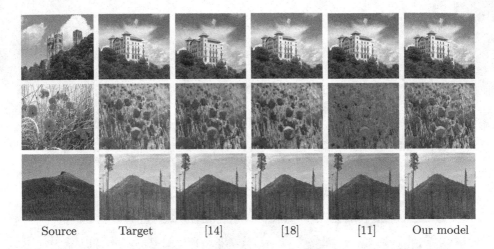

Source   Target   [14]   [18]   [11]   Our model

Fig. 7. Comparison with state-of-the-art exemplar-based methods. In the exemplar-based category, our method is competitive with other state-of-the-art approaches.

On the left, the source and target images are shown. Our results are in the third column while the other columns are results from [14], [18], and [11]. Due to the lack of regularization, images of [11] present artefacts: areas that were originally homogeneous now present irregularities (see the sky of the first image). Moreover, their method is not reliable on contours (see the third image). Our approach better preserves the contours and the homogeneous parts such as the sky. The results of [18] present halo near contours due to the lack of coupling of the classical total variation on chrominance channels. On the second image, the color are too shiny. This is due to the post-processing that does not constraint the hue to be constant. The quality of our results are comparable to [14] whereas our approach is much simpler since local segmentation like superpixels [15] is not needed. On the image with flowers, we remark that their method does not recover suitable colors. The segmentation used by [14] makes their method unable to colorize thin structures, *e.g.*, the trees on the left of the third image.

This comparison with state-of-the-art exemplar-based methods shows the reliability and the efficiency of our colorization method.

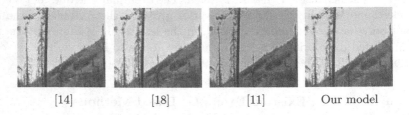

[14]   [18]   [11]   Our model

Fig. 8. Zoom on the third line of Figure 7

Source   Scribbles   Our model   Source   Scribbles   Our model

Fig. 9. Additional results

5   Conclusion

In this paper, a variational model for unified image colorization is proposed. This method combines manual and exemplar-based methods in a simple and intuitive model. Moreover, it can take into account results from any colorization methods to improve results. It opens the way to powerful interactive colorization. Our variational model includes a total variation term which couples luminance and chrominances channels. With this representation, the contours of the colorized images are well preserved. As future work, we plan to improve the results of the exemplar-based methods by studying the features to compare source and target patches. Finally, the extension to video colorization will be addressed.

Acknowledgments. This study has been carried out with financial support from the French State, managed by the French National Research Agency (ANR) in the frame of the Investments for the future Programme IdEx Bordeaux (ANR-10-IDEX-03-02). J-F. Aujol is a member of Institut Universitaire de France. The authors would like to thank Raj Kumar Gupta for providing the images presented in [14].

References

1. Gonzales, R.C., Wintz, P.: Digital Image Processing, 2nd edn. Addison-Wesley Longman Publishing Co., Inc., Boston, MA, USA (1987)
2. Levin, A., Lischinski, D., Weiss, Y.: Colorization using optimization. ACM Trans. on Graphics **23**(3), 689–694 (2004)
3. Yatziv, L., Sapiro, G.: Fast image and video colorization using chrominance blending. IEEE Trans. on Image Processing **15**(5), 1120–1129 (2006)
4. Heu, J., Hyun, D.Y., Kim, C.S., Lee, S.U.: Image and video colorization based on prioritized source propagation. In: Proc. of ICIP (2009)
5. Lagodzinski, P., Smolka, B.: Digital image colorization based on probabilistic distance transformation. Proc. of ELMAR. **2**, 495–498 (2008)

6. Kim, T.H., Lee, K.M., Lee, S.U.: Edge-preserving colorization using data-driven random walks with restart. In: Proc. of ICIP, pp. 1661–1664 (2010)
7. Kawulok, M., Kawulok, J., Smolka, B.: Discriminative textural features for image and video colorization. IEICE Trans. on Information and Systems 95(7), 1722–1730 (2012)
8. Drew, M.S., Finlayson, G.D.: Improvement of colorization realism via the structure tensor. Int. Jour. on Image Graphics 11(4), 589–609 (2011)
9. Lezoray, O., Ta, V.T., Elmoataz, A.: Nonlocal graph regularization for image colorization. In: Proc. of ICPR (2008)
10. Ding, X., Xu, Y., Deng, L., Yang, X.: Colorization using quaternion algebra with automatic scribble generation. In: Schoeffmann, K., Merialdo, B., Hauptmann, A.G., Ngo, C.-W., Andreopoulos, Y., Breiteneder, C. (eds.) MMM 2012. LNCS, vol. 7131, pp. 103–114. Springer, Heidelberg (2012)
11. Welsh, T., Ashikhmin, M., Mueller, K.: Transferring color to greyscale images. ACM Trans. on Graphics 21(3), 277–280 (2002)
12. Wei, L.Y., Levoy, M.: Fast texture synthesis using tree-structured vector quantization. In: ACM Comp. Graphics and Interactive Techniques, pp. 479–488 (2000)
13. Irony, R., Cohen-Or, D., Lischinski, D.: Colorization by example. In: Eurographics Conference on Rendering Techniques, Eurographics Association, pp. 201–210 (2005)
14. Gupta, R.K., Chia, A.Y.S., Rajan, D., Ng, E.S., Zhiyong, H.: Image colorization using similar images. In: ACM Int. Conf. on Multimedia, pp. 369–378 (2012)
15. Ren, X., Malik, J.: Learning a classification model for segmentation. In: Proc. of ICCV, pp. 10–17 (2003)
16. Charpiat, G., Hofmann, M., Schölkopf, B.: Automatic image colorization via multimodal predictions. In: Forsyth, D., Torr, P., Zisserman, A. (eds.) ECCV 2008, Part III. LNCS, vol. 5304, pp. 126–139. Springer, Heidelberg (2008)
17. Chen, T., Wang, Y., Schillings, V., Meinel, C.: Grayscale image matting and colorization. In: Proc. of ACCV, pp. 1164–1169 (2004)
18. Bugeau, A., Ta, V.T., Papadakis, N.: Variational exemplar-based image colorization. IEEE Trans. on Image Processing 23(1), 298–307 (2014)
19. Pierre, F., Aujol, J.F., Bugeau, A., Ta, V.T.: Hue constrained image colorization in the RGB space. Preprint (2014)
20. Chambolle, A., Pock, T.: A first-order primal-dual algorithm for convex problems with applications to imaging. Jour. of Math. Imag. and Vis. 40(1), 120–145 (2011)
21. Bresson, X., Chan, T.F.: Fast dual minimization of the vectorial total variation norm and applications to color image processing. Inverse Problems and Imaging 2(4), 455–484 (2008)
22. Sethian, J.A.: Level set methods and fast marching methods: evolving interfaces in computational geometry, fluid mechanics, computer vision, and materials science 3. Cambridge University Press (1999)
23. Chan, T.F., Vese, L.A.: Active contours without edges. IEEE Trans. on Image Processing 10(2), 266–277 (2001)
24. Peyré, G.: Toolbox fast marching - a toolbox for fast marching and level sets computations (2008)
25. Chen, Y., Ye, X.: Projection onto a simplex. arXiv preprint (2011). arXiv:1101.6081

Single Image Shadow Removal via Neighbor-Based Region Relighting

Tomás F. Yago Vicente[✉] and Dimitris Samaras

Image Analysis Lab, Computer Science Deptartment, Stony Brook University,
Stony Brook, NY, USA
tyagovicente@cs.stonybrook.edu

Abstract. In this paper we present a novel method for shadow removal in single images. For each shadow region we use a trained classifier to identify a neighboring lit region of the same material. Given a pair of lit-shadow regions we perform a region relighting transformation based on histogram matching of luminance values between the shadow region and the lit region. Then, we adjust the CIELAB a and b channels of the shadow region by adding constant offsets based on the difference of the median shadow and lit pixel values. We demonstrate that our approach produces results that outperform the state of the art by evaluating our method using a publicly available benchmark dataset.

Keywords: Shadow · Removal · Illumination · SVM · Histogram Matching · Texture · Recovery Image Processing

1   Introduction

Shadows are a common phenomenon in natural scenes. Shadows appear whenever an object occludes the scene's illuminant(s). Hence, shadows are an outcome of the complex interactions between geometry, albedo and illumination sources present in a scene.

Humans can derive useful visual cues from shadows to help perceive shapes, occlusions, or objects' points of contact with surfaces. However, automatically extracting these cues from images remains a challenging task. Moreover, shadows are well known to wreak havoc in a plethora of computer vision tasks such as segmentation, object detection, tracking, scene understanding or shape-from-X. Therefore, shadow-free images would help improve the performance of all these tasks. Also, shadow removal in images may be of interest for aesthetic reasons, as well as for image editing or computational photography.

There has been a growing interest in shadow detection in the past few years. Recent works using datasets of training images with labelled shadows and learning techniques have provided great advances in the state of the art [9], [11],[12] and most recently [18].

In this paper we focus on the problem of shadow removal from a single image. In earlier work, Finlayson *et al.*[7][8] remove shadows by zeroing shadow edges

© Springer International Publishing Switzerland 2015
L. Agapito et al. (Eds.): ECCV 2014 Workshops, Part III, LNCS 8927, pp. 309–320, 2015.
DOI: 10.1007/978-3-319-16199-0_22

in the gradient domain and then integrating to obtain a shadow free image. They achieve good results with high quality images, however the integration often introduces changes in color balance, global smoothness and loss of textural properties, specially in the penumbra or boundary areas. In [14], Liu *et al.* propose an integration based algorithm that attempts to improve the loss of texture that commonly accompanies integration methods. They construct a gradient field for the penumbra area to cancel out the effects of the illumination change. Their results improve in terms of texture consistency but they cannot handle non uniform shadows or complex textures. Integration based methods are highly sensitive to accurate segmentation of the shadow edges.

Shor *et al.*[15] present an affine shadow formation model with a multi scale scheme to remove shadows. They require minimal user assistance to identify shadow and lit areas of the same surface material. Based on those pairings, they obtain the constant parameters of the shadow model. Due to the assumed constant coefficient their method has problems with non uniform shadows, it also presents issues with rich textures.

Wu *et al.*[17] perform shadow matting to remove shadows. They estimate shadow intensities based on intensity ratios in the umbra region and use a Bayesian framework to regularize the shadow scale factor in the shadow regions. The umbra regions of the shadows are assumed to be roughly uniform. Guo *et al.*[9] also remove shadows based on shadow matting, they generate a soft shadow mask from the ground truth and randomly sample patches from both sides of the shadow boundary to compute the illumination ratios. Guo *et al.*[9] extensively evaluate their results on a shadow dataset that is publicly available. It is the first work to present qualitative and especially quantitative evaluation results on a somewhat large dataset as opposed to a few selected images.

We present a novel method for single image shadow removal based on region relighting. We leverage the use of a dataset with annotated shadows to train a classifier that identifies non-shadow regions that neighbor shadow regions of the same material. We propose to use a neighboring lit region to relight a shadow region. To do so, we first match the luminance values of the shadow pixels to the luminance histogram of the lit region. Then, we adjust the shadow region chromaticities by adding the difference between the median CIELAB a and b values of the lit region and the shadow region. However, the image segmentation often outputs inaccurate boundaries such that shadow(lit) pixels leak into a lit(shadow) region. Hence, we perform the relighting process only on the core pixels of the regions. That is, we ignore the outer perimeter pixels of each region. We iteratively find pairs of shadow and lit neighbors and relight the shadow regions. Finally, we process the shadow boundaries. Our results outperform the state of the art in the benchmark dataset[9]. For shadow pixels we obtain a shadow removal error, measured as Root Mean Square Error (RMSE), of 9.24, a 21% reduction compared to [10]. This article contains the following main contributions:

- A novel technique for shadow region relighting based on a neighboring lit region.

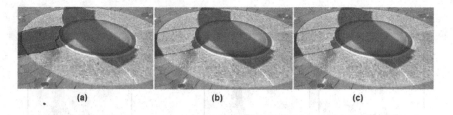

Fig. 1. a) Shadow region and lit neighbor: shadow region depicted with black boundaries, lit neighboring region depicted with yellow boundaries, common boundary drawn in blue. b) RGB reconstuction showing the result of histogram matching on L channel for the shadow region. c) Shadow region relit, results after the adjustements in a and b channels.

- A new classifier to identify pairs of shadow and lit regions of the same material.
- Extensive evaluation on the only published benchmark dataset.

The rest of the paper is organized as follows: Section 2 contains a detailed description of our method to relight a shadow region. Section 3 describes the preprocessing stage of our work. Section 4 describes the lit neighbor classifier. In Section 5 we describe the full pipeline for shadow removal. Experimental results are presented in Section 6. Finally, Section 7 concludes the paper.

2 Region Relighting

Given a shadow region R_s and a neighbor non-shadow region of the same material R_l, we look for a transformation T that relights R_s. Since the two regions are close to each other and have the same material, a transformed version of R_s should closely resemble the appearance of the lit region R_l. The relighting transformation T depends on the appearance of the lit region. We have:

$$T(R_s, R_l) = \widehat{R_s}, \ \ \text{such} \ \widehat{R_s} \approx R_l \tag{1}$$

We perform the relighting transformation in CIELab color space. First, we compute the 50 bin histogram of the luminance values, L channel, of R_l ($H_{R_l(L)}$). Then, we carry out histogram matching so that the shadow region L values match the lit region histogram [1]. Figure 2 contains an example of this step.

The resulting luminance histogram, $H_{\widehat{R_s}(L)}$, resembles that of the lit region $H_{R_l(L)}$ while still preserving a similar shape to the original shadow values $H_{R_s(L)}$. Figure 1(b) depicts the results of this step if we convert back to RGB with the adjusted luminance values for the shadow region. Figure 1(a) shows the original input image with R_l boundaries drawn in yellow and R_s boundaries drawn in black. The image segmentation often produces small inaccuracies around the

---

[1] We use Matlab's histeq function.

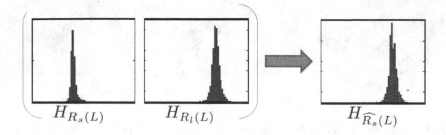

Fig. 2. Histogram matching for region relighting. L channel histograms of the shadow and lit regions depicted in figure 1(a), and the resulting matched histogram corresponding to relit region in 1(c).

regions' boundaries. That is, few shadow pixels leaking into a lit region (or vice versa) or small chunks of different material(s) are getting added to an otherwise homogeneous region. These spurious pixels modify the range of luminance values of a given region, which can severely affect the histogram matching results. Hence, we apply the relighting transformation using only the core pixels of each region. That is, we exclude the outer perimeter pixels (resulting of eroding each region with a 3 by 3 identity matrix as neighborhood structure).

As a second step, we adjust the a channel of the shadow region by adding the difference between the median a values of R_l and the median a values of R_s. Finally, the same operation is carried out for the b channel to complete the relighting process $T(R_s, R_n)$ yielding $\widehat{R_s}$. In figure 1(c), we can see the reconstructed RGB image showing the final relighting results.

3   Preprocessing

In this section we describe the initial preprocessing stages of our method. Our algorithm takes as input images containing shadows and their respective shadow masks. We begin this section by describing the segmentation of the input image into regions or superpixels. Then, we introduce the processing of the ground truth.

3.1   Region Segmentation

The quality of the region segmentation will affect the performance of our shadow removal as we operate at the region level. Ideally, we want to segment the image into superpixels that correspond to consistently illuminated regions. That is, either all pixels in a region are in shadow or all are not in shadow. Furthermore, we would like to obtain homogeneous regions in terms of material.

To segment the images into regions we use the segmentation method proposed by Yago [18], where they segment images into regions for shadow detection.

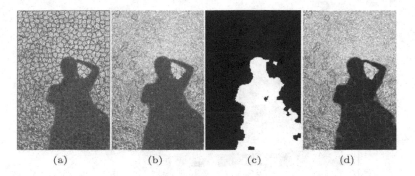

(a)   (b)   (c)   (d)

Fig. 3. a) SLIC superpixel segmentation. b) Resulting merged superpixels from a) after mean-shift clustering over mean CIELAB colors. c) Input ground truth shadow mask. d) Overlay of processed ground truth onto segmented regions.

The method consists of a two step process that is fast and robust to the choice of thresholds. First, SLIC [1] superpixel segmentation is applied to oversegment the image, obtaining an initial set of superpixels. Then, mean-shift clustering[6] over the superpixels' mean color in CIELAB color space is performed. Lastly, adjacent superpixels that belong to the same mean-shift clusters are merged into a larger region. After this second step, the final regions are considerably less than the number of superpixels in the previous step. Most of the segmented regions are consistently illuminated. In figure 3 (a) and (b) we can see example results of the first and second step of the segmentation algorithm. Once an image is segmented, we compute which regions are adjacent to which (i.e. they share a common boundary), hence defining pairs of neighboring regions.

3.2 Ground Truth Processing

The data set presented in [9] contains binary shadow masks as shadow ground truth. To generate region level shadow labels we overlay the regions segmented as described in the previous section 3.1. We label regions as shadows if they contain more than 50% shadow pixels. We implemented a Graphical User Interface in Matlab to manually annotate pairs of shadow and lit regions of the same material. With this GUI we can also refine the shadow labels.

4   Classifier for Lit Neighbors

We propose a classifier that takes as input a shadow region and a neighboring lit region. For each shadow region R_s we need to identify which of its lit neighbors R_i shares the same material with R_s. If a lit neighbor shares the same material then it can be used to relight R_s by applying the transformation T previously described in Section 2. Hence, we select features that describe: i) the similarity between R_s and R_i, ii) the transformation defined by the pair of regions

Fig. 4. GUI to annotate training data for shadow and lit regions of the same material, and to refine shadow labels

$T(R_s, R_i)$, and iii) the results of applying that transformation. If R_r and R_i, have the same material, the relit shadow region $\widehat{R_s}$ and the lit region should be similar in color and texture. We compute the following features:

– RGB color ratios between R_i and R_s: t_r, t_g, t_b encoded as $\frac{t_r + t_g + t_b}{3}$, $\frac{t_r}{t_b}$, $\frac{t_g}{t_b}$ [11].
– Earth Mover's Distance(EMD) between each region's luminance histograms.
– Median based a and b offsets defined by $T(R_s, R_i)$.
– EMD between the a and b histograms of R_i and the resulting region $\widehat{R_s}$
– χ^2 distance between the texton histogram of the relit region $\widehat{R_s}$ and the texton histogram of the combined regions $\widehat{R_s}$ and R_i.

For all the feature computations we only consider the central pixels of each region. The L, a and b histograms contain 50 bins. Positive training examples are pairs of neighboring regions sharing the same material with one being shadow and the other lit. For negative training examples the lit region is of a different material than the shadow region. We train a probabilistic SVM classifier[5] with a Gaussian RBF kernel. For model selection we perform grid search with 5-fold cross validation. We use the fast version of libSVM implemented by [13].

To generate a texton codebook we ran the full MR8 filter set [16] on the whole data set and cluster the filter responses into 128 textons using K-means.

5   Shadow Removal Pipeline

Our shadow removal method takes as input an RGB image and a binary shadow mask. As a first step, we segment the image into regions and automatically label each region as shadow or lit (as described in Section 3). For each shadow region we extract its lit neighboring regions building a set of lit-shadow pairs.

Second, we compute the features for each pair of regions, as described in the previous section, and run the classifier. The positive classifications are selected

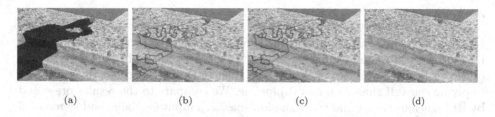

Fig. 5. Shadow removal pipeline. (a) Input image with overlaid shadow mask, boundary of segmented regions depicted in red. (b) Removal results after first iteration of our method. (c) Removal results after the second interation. (d) Final removal results after boundary areas are relit.

as candidate relighting pairs. If for a shadow region more than one lit neighbor is classified as positive we only consider the one with the highest classification confidence.

On the next stage, region relighting is performed on the candidate relighting pairs according to the process described in section 2. After that, we label the set of relit regions as lit. Hence, new pairs of lit-shadow regions are created so we can start a new cycle of identifying candidate relighting pairs using the classifier and then relighting regions based on the positive classifications. Figures 5(b) and 5(c) depict the shadow removal results after the first and second iterations of our method, respectively. As we can observe, there are three isolated shadow regions (no lit neighbors) that are successfully relit in the second round.

As a final step, we address the so far ignored boundary pixels. To remove the shadow in the outer perimeter p_s of a relit shadow region $\widehat{R}_s$, we propose a two step operation:

1. Adjust the L, a and b values of the pixels in p_s based on the core pixels of $\widehat{R}_s$. First, we compute the mean L, the median a and the median b for the core pixels and for the boundary pixels. Then, we add the differences to the pixels in p_s.
2. Smooth the new boundary pixels' values. We convert the results from the previous step to RGB. Then, we run a Gaussian filter at the locations of p_s to obtain the final values for the boundary pixels.

6   Experiments and Results

In this section we present quantitative and qualitative results of our shadow removal method using the dataset presented in [9]. This dataset contains 32 training images for which we manually annotated ground truth for our lit neighbor classifier. The testing split contains 48 shadow images for which there is a corresponding shadow-free image, considered as ground truth for shadow removal evaluation.

6.1 Quantitative Results

In table 1, we present our quantitative results compared to the state of the art by Guo *et al.*[10]. As evaluation metric we use the Root Mean Squared Error (RMSE) in CIELab space between the shadow-free images and the results of applying our full shadow removal pipeline. We compare to the results presented by [10] when using ground truth shadow masks as input for their shadow removal method. Note that we also take shadow masks as input. Furthermore, the performance of [10] deteriorates considerably when the shadow removal is applied on their shadow detection results.

As we can see in table 1, our overall error is almost half a unit lower than the state of the art, 5.96 versus 6.4. For shadow region pixels our performance reduces the error by a 21%, yielding an RMSE of 9.24 units. The performance we get on non-shadow regions is slightly worse, 4.9 versus 4.7. This is due to small faults in the segmentation such that shadow pixels leaked into lit regions (or viceversa). With no shadow removal applied, the error in non-shadow regions is 4.6.

Table 1. Shadow removal evaluation on the dataset presented in Guo *et al.*[9]. First column shows the error when no shadow removal is carried out. Second column are the state of the art results by Guo *et al.*[10], their method applies matting on the ground truth shadow mask. Third column are the results of our method.

Region Type	Original	Guo *et al.*[10]	Region Relighting(Ours)
Overall	13.7	6.4	5.96
Shadow regions	42.0	11.8	9.24
Non-shadow regions	4.6	4.7	4.9

We also evaluate our performance in shadow regions for the core pixels and for the border pixels separately, see table 2. The shadow removal error for core regions is 8.81, whereas the error in the border regions is noticeably worse at 14.09. Moreover, some shadow regions cannot be relit as no suitable lit neighbor is detected by our classifier, or does not exist in the image. The third row of the table shows the error on the core pixels of the shadow regions that were actually relit by our method. The RMSE obtained drops to 8.12.

6.2 Qualitative Results

In figure 6 we present some qualitative results. As we can observe, our method produces high quality shadow free images for a variety of materials and textures. In the first and forth images our shadow free image presents a noticeable boundary effect around the shadow regions. This is mostly due to inaccuracies in the region segmentation with respect to the actual shadows. However, the quality of the shadow removal in the inner areas is quite high. Table 3 contains the actual

Table 2. Per pixel RMSE of the shadow removal. Fist column shows the results when no shadow removal is performed. Second column are the results of our method. The core shadow regions are the shadow regions excluding their outer perimeter pixels (resulting of eroding each region with a 3 by 3 identity matrix as neighborhood). The border regions are the excluded perimeter pixels. The relit shadow regions are the shadow regions for which our method actually performed shadow removal (excluding the outer perimeters).

Region Type	Original	Region Relighting
Border Shadow Regions	36.92	14.09
Core Shadow Regions	42.45	8.81
Relit Shadow Regions	37.33	8.12

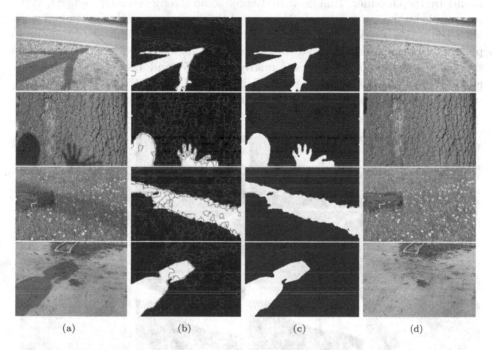

(a) (b) (c) (d)

Fig. 6. Shadow removal results. (a) Input image. (b) Ground truth shadow pixel mask with the region segmentation overlaid in blue. (c) Our shadow removal results. (d) Ground truth shadow free image.

error numbers for the images depicted in figure 6. We can appreciate how the RMSE error in the core areas of the shadow regions is particularly low.

Some interesting shadow removal cases are presented in figure 7. In these cases we can observe weaker qualitative results. In the first image we can notice some boundaries between relit regions due to poor performance by our boundary processing. The image in the second row depicts a case where some regions within the person's shadow were not able to be recovered as no suitable lit region was

Table 3. RMSE on the images shown in figure 6. First column shows the overall error. Second column depicts the error in shadow regions. The shadow core error is the error on the core shadow pixels. Core original is the error in the shadow core pixels for the original image, with no shadow removal performed.

Image	Overall Error	Shadow Error	Shadow Core	Core Original
Fig.6 1ˢᵗ row	8.88	9.91	9.81	29.64
Fig.6 2ⁿᵈ row	13.76	12.30	12.21	37.49
Fig.6 3ʳᵈ row	6.47	11.18	11.09	24.16
Fig.6 4ᵗʰ row	3.09	6.07	5.81	41.69

found by the classifier. Images 3 in 4 show some strong boundary effects, very noticeable by the human eye. In these cases the segmentation does not align well with the actual shadow boundaries. For instance, in image 3 most of the outer perimeter of the shadow leaked into adjacent lit regions. However, the error for shadow regions in these images is relative low, 6.57 and 4.84 respectively; and even lower in the core shadow pixels 6.29 and 4.58, respectively. Detailed error numbers for the images presented in figure 7 can be found in table 4.

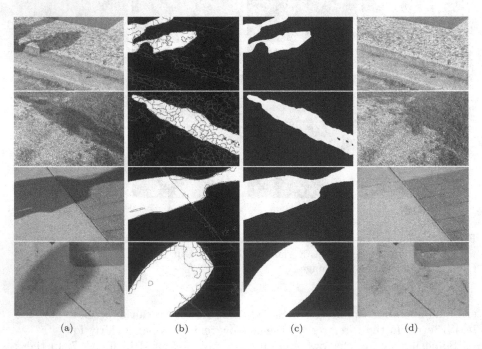

(a)   (b)   (c)   (d)

Fig. 7. Note-worthy shadow removal results. (a) Input image (b) Ground truth shadow pixel mask with the region segmentation overlaid in blue. (c) Our shadow removal results. (d) Ground truth shadow free image.

Table 4. RMSE on the images shown in figure 7. First column shows the overall error. Second column depicts the error in shadow regions. The shadow core error is the error on the core shadow pixels. Core original is the error in the shadow core pixels for the original image, with no shadow removal performed.

Image	Overall Error	Shadow Error	Shadow Core	Core Original
Fig.7 1st row	4.55	11.54	11.20	43.97
Fig.7 2nd row	6.89	12.96	12.66	28.25
Fig.7 3rd row	6.31	6.57	6.29	50.91
Fig.7 4th row	3.77	4.84	4.58	38.17

7   Conclusion and Future Work

We have presented a novel method for shadow removal in single images that outperforms the state of the art. The main contribution of our work is a new region relighting transformation based on histogram matching of luminance values between the shadow region and the neighboring lit region, plus addition of median based offsets in the a and b channels. Furthermore, we propose a new classifier to automatically identify suitable pairs of lit-shadow regions. We demonstrated that the iterative application of the proposed transformation in positively classified pairs of region is powerful enough to outperform the state of the art on the shadow removal benchmark dataset. Our results are specially accurate in the core pixels of the shadow regions.

In future work we will explore alternative ways to deal with the boundary pixels such as in-painting techniques. We are also interested in region segmentation tailored for the task of shadow removal.

Acknowledgments. This work was partially supported by NSF IIS- 1161876, IIS-1111047, NIH R21 DA034954 and the DIGITEO Institute, France.

References

1. Achanta, R., Shaji, A., Smith, K., Lucchi, A., Fua, P., Susstrunk, S.: Slic superpixels compared to state-of-the-art superpixel methods. IEEE TPAMI (2012)
2. Alpher, A., Fotheringham-Smythe, J.P.N.: Frobnication revisited. Journal of Foo **13**(1), 234–778 (2003)
3. Alpher, A., Fotheringham-Smythe, J.P.N., Gamow, G.: Can a machine frobnicate? Journal of Foo **14**(1), 234–778 (2004)
4. Alpher, A.: Frobnication. Journal of Foo **12**(1), 234–778 (2002)
5. Chang, C.C., Lin, C.J.: LIBSVM: A library for support vector machines. ACM Transactions on Intelligent Systems and Technology **2**, 27:1–27:27 (2011). software. http://www.csie.ntu.edu.tw/~cjlin/libsvm
6. Comaniciu, D., Meer, P.: Mean shift: A robust approach toward feature space analysis. IEEE Transactions on Pattern Analysis and Machine Intelligence **24**(5), 603–619 (2002)

7. Finlayson, G., Hordley, S., Lu, C., Drew, M.: On the removal of shadows from images. Pattern Analysis and Machine Intelligence. IEEE Transactions on **28**(1), 59–68 (2006)
8. Finlayson, G., Drew, M., Lu, C.: Entropy minimization for shadow removal. International Journal of Computer Vision **85**, 35–57 (2009). doi:10.1007/s11263-009-0243-z
9. Guo, R., Dai, Q., Hoiem, D.: Single-image shadow detection and removal using paired regions. In: 2011 IEEE Conference on Computer Vision and Pattern Recognition (CVPR), pp. 2033–2040 (June 2011)
10. Guo, R., Dai, Q., Hoiem, D.: Paired regions for shadow detection and removal. IEEE Transactions on Pattern Analysis and Machine Intelligence 99(PrePrints), 1 (2012)
11. Huang, X., Hua, G., Tumblin, J., Williams, L.: What characterizes a shadow boundary under the sun and sky? In: 2011 IEEE International Conference on Computer Vision (ICCV), pp. 898–905 (November 2011)
12. Lalonde, J.-F., Efros, A.A., Narasimhan, S.G.: Detecting ground shadows in outdoor consumer photographs. In: Daniilidis, K., Maragos, P., Paragios, N. (eds.) ECCV 2010, Part II. LNCS, vol. 6312, pp. 322–335. Springer, Heidelberg (2010)
13. Li, F., Carreira, J., Sminchisescu, C.: Object recognition as ranking holistic figure-ground hypotheses. In: IEEE Conference on Computer Vision and Pattern Recognition (2010)
14. Liu, F., Gleicher, M.: Texture-consistent shadow removal. In: Forsyth, D., Torr, P., Zisserman, A. (eds.) ECCV 2008, Part IV. LNCS, vol. 5305, pp. 437–450. Springer, Heidelberg (2008)
15. Shor, Y., Lischinski, D.: The shadow meets the mask: Pyramid-based shadow removal. Computer Graphics Forum **27**(2), 577–586 (2008)
16. Varma, M., Zisserman, A.: Classifying images of materials: Achieving viewpoint and illumination independence. In: Heyden, A., Sparr, G., Nielsen, M., Johansen, P. (eds.) ECCV 2002, Part III. LNCS, vol. 2352, pp. 255–271. Springer, Heidelberg (2002)
17. Wu, T.P., Tang, C.K., Brown, M.S., Shum, H.Y.: Natural shadow matting. ACM Trans. Graph. 26(2) (June 2007). http://doi.acm.org/10.1145/1243980.1243982
18. Yago Vicente, T.F., Yu, C.P., Samaras, D.: Single image shadow detection using multiple cues in a supermodular MRF. In: Proceedings of the British Machine Vision Conference. BMVA Press (2013)

Material Recognition for Efficient Acquisition of Geometry and Reflectance

Michael Weinmann[(⊠)] and Reinhard Klein

Institute of Computer Science II, University of Bonn, Bonn, Germany
mw@cs.uni-bonn.de

Abstract. Typically, 3D geometry acquisition and reflectance acquisition techniques strongly rely on some basic assumptions about the surface reflectance behavior of the sample to be measured. Methods are tailored e.g. to Lambertian reflectance, mirroring reflectance, smooth and homogeneous surfaces or surfaces exhibiting mesoscopic effects. In this paper, we analyze whether multi-view material recognition can be performed robust enough to guide a subsequent acquisition process by reliably recognizing a certain material in a database with its respective annotation regarding the reconstruction methods to be chosen. This allows selecting the appropriate geometry/reflectance reconstruction approaches and, hence, increasing the efficiency of the acquisition process. In particular, we demonstrate that considering only a few view-light configurations is sufficient for obtaining high recognition scores.

Keywords: Material recognition · Reflectance · Set-based classification

1 Introduction

The goal of accurately capturing details in surface geometry and reflectance behavior has led to a huge number of different methods and respective setups. However, current state-of-the-art acquisition procedures are rather designed regarding the expected reflectance behavior. The acquisition process is guided by the user who chooses the acquisition routines based on the impression of the material appearance he obtains when looking at the material sample.

In the domain of reflectance acquisition, it is well-known that smooth, homogeneous materials can be represented well with analytical BRDF models. These typically only depend on the direction of the incoming light and the view direction. In contrast, materials exhibiting mesoscopic effects of light exchange on surface structures imaged to a size of approximately one pixel cannot be modeled by using simple BRDF models. For such materials, current state-of-the-art techniques acquire data-driven BTFs which consider the spatial material variations in addition to the view direction and the direction of the incoming light.

In a similar way, 3D reconstruction techniques typically also depend on some basic assumptions about material reflectance. Many of the methods such as most multi-view stereo techniques, photometric stereo and structured light systems are based on assuming Lambertian reflectance behavior. Some more sophisticated extensions allow considering the wider range of opaque surfaces. In contrast,

© Springer International Publishing Switzerland 2015
L. Agapito et al. (Eds.): ECCV 2014 Workshops, Part III, LNCS 8927, pp. 321–333, 2015.
DOI: 10.1007/978-3-319-16199-0_23

other reconstruction techniques are specialized on mirroring surfaces. All the aforementioned geometry reconstruction techniques consider only a small fraction of the possible surface materials and are not tailored to consider arbitrary surface reflectance.

Without a-priori knowledge about the material properties of the material sample, the naive way would be applying several different techniques and merging their results. However, this is highly inefficient regarding acquisition time, and hardware components are stressed unnecessarily as many of the taken images do not have an influence on the final reconstruction and, thus, have to be neglected. For more efficient geometry and reflectance acquisition procedures in case of missing information about the material properties of the considered material sample or object, it is therefore desirable to automatically select only the appropriate techniques instead of applying several different methods.

In this paper, we focus on this task by investigating a-priori information in form of a database of material measurements to classify a measured material based on a small set of photos (see Fig. 1). Depending on the annotations for the closest match in the database, corresponding methods can easily be determined. For an almost mirroring metal, for instance, a shape-from-specularity approach could be used for geometry reconstruction and a BRDF measurement could be started for measuring the surface reflectance. If the considered material sample is classified as a material with strong mesoscopic effects such as present in e.g. leather, a structured light based geometry acquisition in combination with a BTF acquisition could be proposed. We demonstrate that material recognition can be achieved with a high reliability by looking at the characteristic material appearance under a few viewpoints. At first sight, this problem might seem to be not as interesting any more due to the successful studies on databases such as the CUReT database [7]. However, such databases offer only a small intra-class variance in the appearance of the involved material samples. With recent, more challenging databases with larger intra-class variances of the respective material samples such as the ALOT database [12] and the database in [30], there is a need to obtain further insights into recognizing materials using multiple view-light directions for the reference/query sets.

In summary, the key contributions of our work are

- an approach to classify material instances which can serve as an initialization for an efficient acquisition process, and
- a study for using set-based classifiers to find the closest material in the database from a set of view-light configurations which might not necessarily be contained in the database.

2   Related Work

Material classification is a challenging problem due to the significant variations in material appearance under different configurations of viewpoint, illumination and surface geometry and a lot of studies have been conducted. In the following, we briefly discuss model-based and appearance-based approaches.

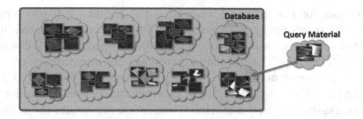

Fig. 1. Material recognition using multi-view information can be formulated as a set-based recognition task. Characteristic material traits observed in the images of a particular material instance form a respective, characteristic material space. The objective is to identify the most similar material instance within the database for an input query material by comparing the material spaces.

Model-based approaches: The inference of knowledge about the considered material surface can be approached by using certain models which capture the variations of material appearance under different view-light configurations. For analyzing physical surface models, histogram models have been used in e.g. [9] and [13] to represent the changes in appearance for materials under varying view-light conditions. In [22], recognition is approached based on a partly Lambertian and partly specular model. The studies in [5] and [10] analyzed the model-based dependency of texture features on illumination. However, such dependencies rely on certain surface characteristics which also applies for the assumed reflectance models. While analytical models might be sufficient to represent the reflectance behavior of locally smooth surfaces with homogeneous reflectance behavior, they do not reflect characteristic material traits that coin many materials with meso-scopic surface reflectance effects. Such effects take place at surface structures imaged to an area of approximately one pixel within an image. More complex material models such as bidirectional texture functions [8] can deal with such mesoscopic effects but have their limitation w.r.t. extremely specular materials. In that case, their data-driven nature requires an ideally continuous angular sampling which would significantly increase the data masses and therefore is rather impractical. Consequently, the selection of such model-based approaches is material-specific, i.e. the fitting procedures are guided by the appropriate model. In addition, the fitting involves the explicit consideration of a multitude of parameters such as the parameters of the reflectance model, the lighting, etc..

Appearance-based approaches: The key components of appearance-based material classification systems are the extraction of discriminative descriptors that reflect characteristic material traits, an efficient and appropriate modeling for the material categories and an appropriate classifier. The probably most widely used descriptors are filterbanks (e.g. [2,3,6,17,18,25,27]), color patches (e.g. [20,24,26,28,30]), denseSIFT (e.g. [20,24,30]), Local Binary Patterns (LBPs) (e.g. [3,19]), kernel descriptors [15] and combinations of multiple of these descriptors (e.g. [1,15,19,20,24,30]). Combining complimentary descriptors for material classification has been demonstrated to lead to superior results. After extracting

such descriptors for the images contained in the training set, the typical approach considers representing the appearance of a material in an individual image
based on textons as introduced in e.g. [17] and [18] and also followed in e.g.
[19,20,24,25,27,28,30]. The resulting per-image representations can then be
classified using nearest neighbor classifiers, Bayesian frameworks [20,27], MRF
classifiers [26], SVMs [3,14,19,21,30] or other classifiers such as random forests.

While single-image-based material classification represents the most focused
task, some acquisition devices also offer to easily acquire several images under
several view-light configurations which might significantly facilitate material
classification. The expected result of high performance scores is of great importance if further steps of the acquisition procedure depend on the reflectance
behavior of the material classified before. In [17] and [18], histograms have been
concatenated to form a combined vector for each particular material, which
imposes that materials are represented by a consistently handled ordering of
the configurations within the combined vector where all the individual image-
representations have to be carefully registered. For comparing the combined
vector representations, both the number and the IDs of the view-light configurations of both vectors have to coincide. In [6], bidirectional feature histogram
manifolds have been introduced. However, having a sparse set of view-light configurations represents a problem to this approach, as the reference manifolds
become coarsely sampled. In addition, linear interpolation between neighboring
view-light configurations will result in additional sources of inaccuracies which
increase with an increasing distance of the neighboring view-light configurations.

We also aim at classifying material instances using only a few images and
make use of results from the face recognition domain. For efficiency, we focus on
training-free, linear approaches as presented in [4]. In particular, our material
recognition approach yields significantly better recognition rates than previous
methods when using smaller numbers of view-light configurations.

3   Methodology

We propose an automatic assistance system for guiding the acquisition process
where the respective techniques are selected based on a prior material recognition (see Fig. 2). For a query material, we search its best representative within a
database of materials with corresponding annotations about how to acquire the
respective type of material. Hence, one core component of our system is represented by a material database which contains images of a multitude of material
samples taken under different viewing and lighting conditions which are expected
to be met during the acquisition with standard devices analyzed in [23].

For a reliable material recognition, we need to consider the spatial variations
of a material as well as its change in appearance induced by different viewing and
lighting conditions. Therefore, our approach is based on first computing state-
of-the-art descriptors to capture the characteristic material traits and the subsequent derivation of a vector-based representation for each of the given images
under individual viewing and lighting conditions (see Subsection 3.1). The set

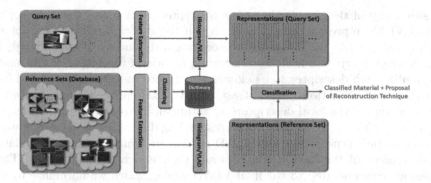

Fig. 2. Overview on the set-based material recognition scheme: After extracting descriptors, we compute a dictionary from the descriptors obtained for the reference data. This dictionary is used to quantize the representation of the content of a particular image into a vector representation. Finally, a set-to-set classification is carried out to find the closest material within the database. The attached annotations for the closest material in the database can be used to guide the subsequent reconstruction process.

of vectors resulting for an individual material sample is then used to obtain its material space. This allows to perform the comparison of different material spaces via set-to-set distances (see Subsection 3.2).

3.1 Representing Materials

In order to be representative for a certain material, material-specific properties have to be included in the set-based representation. Characteristic material traits can be identified in a huge number of different aspects such as color, surface roughness, self-occlusions, interreflections, specularities, and it has been shown beneficial to use several feature descriptors considering different types of attributes (e.g. [20]). We consider the following descriptor types which are densely sampled on a regular grid with a spacing of 5 pixels in our experiments:

– Color: We extract 3×3 color patches as in [20].
– SIFT: For considering the local spatial and directional distribution of image gradients, we extract dense SIFT descriptors as in e.g. [20]. In addition, SIFT descriptors provide robustness to variations in illumination and viewpoint.
– HOG2x2: After computing histograms of oriented gradients, neighboring descriptors are concatenated to a 124-dimensional descriptor as in [31]. As the normalization differs from the scheme used in SIFT, it captures material characteristics in a different way.
– Leung-Malik filters: LM filters [17,18] represent a filterbank with multiple orientations and multiple scales regarding the involved filters. We use 6 orientations and 3 scales.

The extracted descriptors are then used to compute a vector-based representation for each of the masked image regions. In the scope of this paper, we analyze the suitability of the popular bag-of-words representation and the more sophisticated VLAD representation [16]. Based on the descriptors extracted for the images contained in the database, we compute a dictionary of visual words for each descriptor type via k-means clustering. In case of the bag-of-words model, we quantize each descriptor to its closest visual word in the dictionary and form histogram representations. In contrast, the VLAD representation is based on first assigning all the local descriptors $\mathbf{x}_i$ within an image region to their nearest neighbor $\mathbf{c}_j$ with $j = 1, \ldots, k$ in the corresponding dictionary with k visual words for each feature type. Then, the VLAD entries are computed by accumulating the differences of the local descriptors and their assigned visual words. These entries are concatenated to the final VLAD vector, which we normalize to unit length for each of the descriptor types. These vector-based representations for the images of a particular material instance form its corresponding material space. In case of combining several descriptor representations, we simply concatenate the normalized vectors corresponding to the involved descriptor types.

3.2   Set-Based Classification

In contrast to e.g. [6] where a-priori knowledge about the considered viewing and lighting conditions is incorporated for setting up aligned training manifolds, our approach does not rely on the availability of such information. A randomly taken subset of images without knowledge about the imaging parameters should be enough to reliably recognize materials. We use the linear methods presented in [11,32] and [4], where there is no need for parameter learning. Non-linear techniques (e.g. [4]) could be employed as well at the cost of learning hyperparameters such as the kernel width.

Linear convex hull based classifier. Representing the material instances via vector representations for the respective images, we make use of the convex hull classifier presented in [4]. Here, we assume that the vector representations under the available view-light configurations chosen to represent one of the individual material samples can be represented via convex hulls. The distance between convex hulls can be calculated by using quadratic programming and is abbreviated via CHISD (Convex Hull based Image Set Distance) as in [4].

Linear affine hull based classifier. Similar to [4], we consider affine hulls for representing the material spaces. We calculate the linear affine hull parameters by computing an orthonormal basis for the affine subspace spanned by vectors representing a particular material. The distance between two linear affine hulls abbreviated via AHISD (Affine Hull based Image Set Distance) can be computed using the hyperplane which optimally separates the affine hulls.

Mutual subspace method (MSM). This type of method used in [11,32] represents each class with a subspace formed by the respective vectors, and the similarity between subspaces is determined by comparing the angles between the subspaces.

4   Experimental Results

For computing the histogram and VLAD representations respectively, we used dictionary sizes of 150 for color, 250 for SIFT, 250 for HOG2x2 and 200 for the LM filters throughout all of our experiments as used in [20,24].

In the scope of our experiments, we aim at analyzing the capabilities of the different set-based recognition techniques. We therefore perform experiments on different datasets for varying numbers of view-light configurations in the reference and query sets. We always take disjoint sets of view-light configurations for the reference/query sets of the material samples.

CUReT Database. For obtaining an intuition of the recognition performance, we use the well-established LM filters and denseSIFT for recognizing the 61 CUReT material samples (see Fig. 3, left). Using 5 randomly chosen view-light configurations for representing both reference and query materials, we already obtain high accuracies of around 95.5% for both LM filters and denseSIFT when using AHISD and CHISD with VLAD representations. MSM methods perform worse by about 5%. The benefit of the high-dimensional VLAD representation is obvious in the fact, that histograms perform significantly worse by $4\% - 11\%$. Using more view-light configurations to span the space for the different material samples, we observe that the accuracy obtained when using the individual descriptors closely approaches the 100% already for about 10 view-light configurations in reference and query sets. In general, there is a tendency that the high-dimensional VLAD description gives better accuracies than using histograms. We also combined the descriptors which additionally increases the performance.

In [6], a selection of 20 material instances of the CUReT database has been analyzed. Using 56 images per material instance for their reference manifolds, a performance of about 98% has been reached for classifying individual textures and a bit more than 70% for using 10 configurations per material. For a fair comparison, we only use LM filters as descriptors. Representing the reference sets with 10 randomly drawn view-light configurations and having a single configuration for the query material, we obtain performances of around 95% for the combination of CHISD and VLAD representations which is only slightly worse. In a direct comparison to using 10 configurations for the reference sets, this combination gives an improvement of about 20%. Using more configurations in the query sets, we already reach more than 99% starting from three configurations. DenseSIFT shows a similar performance.

The high performances reached on this database indicate that the individual material samples appear rather distinctive and that the database is not highly challenging. Additionally, as a consequence of the high performances, a real analysis of the different set-based methods w.r.t. each other is hardly possible and the need for set-based recognition is not yet clearly visible. For this reason, more insights can be obtained by using more challenging datasets with higher intra-class variances in material appearance under different view-light configurations.

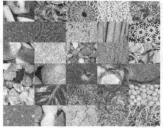

Fig. 3. Material samples in the CUReT database [8] (taken from [29]) (left) and the ALOT database [12] (right). For illustration purposes, only a subset of the 250 material samples of the ALOT database is shown.

ALOT Database. This database [12] (see Fig. 3, right) offers significantly more and also a wider range of different material types, which have additionally been observed under different illumination colors. In our experiments, we consider color patches, denseSIFT, HOG2x2, LM filters and their combination. Taking 5 view-light configurations for the reference and the query sets results in an accuracy of about 60% for color, 89% for denseSIFT, 83% for LM filters and 83% for HOG2x2 for VLADs with CHISD or AHISD and 4% less for MSM methods. Using histograms also leads to lower performances. The combination of the descriptors, however, leads to about 94% for AHISD and CHISD with VLAD and little lower accuracies for the MSM methods. Taking 10 configurations per reference/query set, the accuracies of the individual descriptors increase, and for the combination of descriptors we reach slightly above 99% using all the methods. This indicates a trend that the reliability of material recognition increases with increasing numbers of view-light configurations for reference and query sets.

Database measured for [30]. While the ALOT database [12] gives a more visible impression on the power of set-based recognition, the samples in this database still do not seem to show too extreme intra-class variations under different view-light configurations in comparison to the inter-class variances. In contrast, the material samples of the database in [30] are used to model the variance in different semantic categories. We used the measurements of the 84 material samples used in [30] and further 76 material samples in the database extension (see Fig. 4). For each of these material samples, photos have been taken under 151 different viewing directions and 151 lighting directions leading to 22,801 images per material sample. For some of the categories, several of the samples only exhibit rather subtle differences (e.g. tiles or metals). This makes the dataset challenging. Instead of grouping these samples into semantic categories as in [30], we consider the measurements per material sample individually and focus on recognizing the material samples. As illustrated in Fig. 5 and Fig. 6, the accuracy again increases for an increasing number of configurations considered in the reference/query sets. As before, we observe the trend of VLADs being more discriminative than histograms. Furthermore, the descriptors have been evaluated separately, where denseSIFTs tend to perform best. The difference to the performance of other descriptors is more visible for the histogram representations. AHISD and CHISD almost consistently outperform the MSM methods. Using the combination of different descriptors results in improvements over the accuracies obtained for the individual descriptors. These improvements are larger, if only a few configurations are available for the reference/query sets.

Fig. 4. Some of the materials measured for the database of [30] and its extension

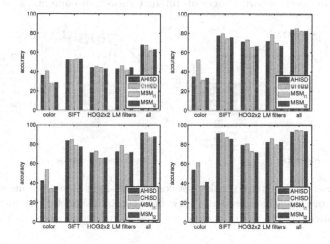

Fig. 5. Accuracies obtained for the data measured in [30] when using histograms and disjoint reference and query sets of 5 (upper left), 10 (upper right), 15 (lower left), 20 (lower right) randomly drawn images of different view-light configurations

In Fig. 7, we illustrate the dependency of the obtained accuracy on the number of view-light configurations in the query sets. We only depict this information for CHISD, which outperformed the other classifiers in the previous experiments. However, we additionally show the performances of using individual descriptors and some combinations of the descriptors. In general, the obtained accuracies increase for taking more images in the query sets and using the VLAD representation leads to accuracies superior to the ones obtained when using histograms. Furthermore, we also analyzed the accuracies obtained for using different combinations of the descriptors. The difference in the obtained accuracies indicates

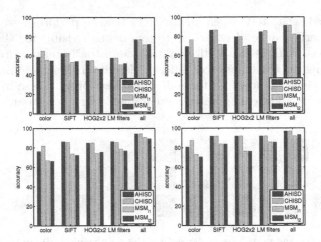

Fig. 6. Accuracies obtained for the data measured in [30] when using VLADs and disjoint reference and query sets of 5 (upper left), 10 (upper right), 15 (lower left), 20 (lower right) randomly drawn images of different view-light configurations

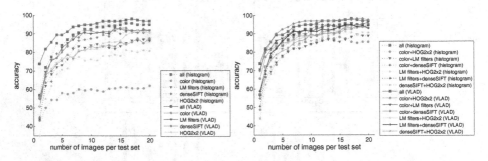

Fig. 7. Accuracies obtained for using sets of 20 view-light combinations for the reference sets and an increasing number of view-light combinations for the query materials (for the data measured in [30]). As expected, the accuracy increases with larger query sets.

that the descriptors carry different amounts of complementary information. In particular, the combination of color and denseSIFT clearly outperforms the remaining combinations of two descriptor types and even slightly outperforms the combination of all four descriptors types. Additionally, it becomes apparent that considering multiple view-light configurations leads to significant performance gains of almost 20% for using 10 configurations for the query sets in comparison to using a single configuration for the query sets when considering the combinations of descriptors. For more view-light configurations in the query set, we observe rather marginal improvements in the accuracies. When analyzing the few misclassified material samples (e.g. two of the tiles and two of the metals have not been properly distinguished) and the respective estimated material labels, we observed that the estimated material and the ground truth material indeed look rather similar and it is even hard to distinguish them as a human. In turn, this means that we still can take the stored parameters for a subsequent acquisition or reconstruction respectively due to the similarity of the materials. As a result, we also obtain a highly reliable recommendation regarding adequate acquisition and reconstruction methods.

5 Conclusions

In this paper, we have presented a study on using set-based recognition schemes in combination with standard descriptors and encodings for material recognition. Our studies demonstrate the benefit of making use of several images of a material sample for different view-light conditions regarding material recognition. There are only little performance gains possible for databases with smaller intra-class variance before reaching the saturation close to 100%, which might have lead to less interest in investigations on material recognition based on several view-light configurations in recent years. However, when considering more challenging databases with larger intra-class variances under different view-light configurations, it is still essential to provide a reliable material recognition with regard to an efficient acquisition relying on a correct recommendation of the acquisition procedure to be used. We have shown that such a material recognition can be achieved with a high reliability by looking at the characteristic material appearance under a few view-light configurations which emphasizes the significant benefit of set-based material recognition in the presence of larger variations in appearance of the individual samples.

Acknowledgments. The research leading to these results was funded by the European Commission's Seventh Framework Programme (FP7/2007-2013) under grant agreement no. 323567 (Harvest4D), 2013-2016.

References

1. Burghouts, G.J., Geusebroek, J.M.: Color textons for texture recognition. In: BMVC, pp. 1099–1108 (2006)
2. Caputo, B., Hayman, E., Fritz, M., Eklundh, J.O.: Classifying materials in the real world. Image Vision Comput. **28**(1), 150–163 (2010)
3. Caputo, B., Hayman, E., Mallikarjuna, P.: Class-specific material categorisation. In: ICCV, vol. 2, pp. 1597–1604 (2005)
4. Cevikalp, H., Triggs, B.: Face recognition based on image sets. In: CVPR, pp. 2567–2573 (2010)
5. Chantler, M., McGunnigle, G., Penirschke, A., Petrou, M.: Estimating lighting direction and classifying textures. In: BMVC, pp. 72.1–72.10 (2002)
6. Cula, O.G., Dana, K.J.: 3d texture recognition using bidirectional feature histograms. IJCV **59**(1), 33–60 (2004)
7. Dana, K.J., van Ginneken, B., Nayar, S.K., Koenderink, J.J.: Reflectance and texture of real world surfaces. Tech. rep. (1996)
8. Dana, K.J., Nayar, S.K., Ginneken, B.V., Koenderink, J.J.: Reflectance and texture of real-world surfaces. In: CVPR, pp. 151–157 (1997)

9. Dana, K.J., Nayar, S.K.: Histogram model for 3d textures. In: CVPR, pp. 618–624 (1998)
10. Drbohlav, O., Chantler, M.: Illumination-invariant texture classification using single training images. In: Texture 2005: Proceedings of the International Workshop on Texture Analysis and Synthesis, pp. 31–36 (2005)
11. Fukui, K., Yamaguchi, O.: Face recognition using multi-viewpoint patterns for robot vision. In: ISRR, pp. 192–201 (2003)
12. Geusebroek, J.M., Smeulders, A.W.M.: Amsterdam library of textures (ALOT) (June 2014). http://aloi.science.uva.nl/public_alot/
13. van Ginneken, B., Koenderink, J.J., Dana, K.J.: Texture histograms as a function of irradiation and viewing direction. IJCV 31(2–3), 169–184 (1999)
14. Hayman, E., Caputo, B., Fritz, M., Eklundh, J.-O.: On the significance of real-world conditions for material classification. In: Pajdla, T., Matas, J.G. (eds.) ECCV 2004. LNCS, vol. 3024, pp. 253–266. Springer, Heidelberg (2004)
15. Hu, D., Bo, L., Ren, X.: Toward robust material recognition for everyday objects. In: BMVC, pp. 1–11 (2011)
16. Jegou, H., Douze, M., Schmid, C., Pérez, P.: Aggregating local descriptors into a compact image representation. In: CVPR, pp. 3304–3311 (2010)
17. Leung, T., Malik, J.: Recognizing surfaces using three-dimensional textons. In: ICCV, vol. 2, pp. 1010–1017 (1999)
18. Leung, T., Malik, J.: Representing and recognizing the visual appearance of materials using three-dimensional textons. IJCV 43(1), 29–44 (2001)
19. Li, W., Fritz, M.: Recognizing materials from virtual examples. In: Fitzgibbon, A., Lazebnik, S., Perona, P., Sato, Y., Schmid, C. (eds.) ECCV 2012, Part IV. LNCS, vol. 7575, pp. 345–358. Springer, Heidelberg (2012)
20. Liu, C., Sharan, L., Adelson, E.H., Rosenholtz, R.: Exploring features in a bayesian framework for material recognition. In: CVPR, pp. 239–246 (2010)
21. Liu, C., Yang, G., Gu, J.: Learning discriminative illumination and filters for raw material classification with optimal projections of bidirectional texture functions. In: CVPR, pp. 1430–1437 (2013)
22. Osadchy, M., Jacobs, D.W., Ramamoorthi, R.: Using specularities for recognition. In: ICCV, pp. 1512–1519 (2003)
23. Schwartz, C., Sarlette, R., Weinmann, M., Rump, M., Klein, R.: Design and implementation of practical bidirectional texture function measurement devices focusing on the developments at the University of Bonn. Sensors 14(5), 7753–7819 (2014)
24. Sharan, L., Liu, C., Rosenholtz, R., Adelson, E.H.: Recognizing materials using perceptually inspired features. IJCV 103(3), 348–371 (2013)
25. Varma, M., Zisserman, A.: Classifying images of materials: achieving viewpoint and illumination independence. In: Heyden, A., Sparr, G., Nielsen, M., Johansen, P. (eds.) ECCV 2002, Part III. LNCS, vol. 2352, pp. 255–271. Springer, Heidelberg (2002)
26. Varma, M., Zisserman, A.: Texture classification: are filter banks necessary?. In: CVPR, vol. 2, pp. 691–698 (2003)
27. Varma, M., Zisserman, A.: Unifying statistical texture classification frameworks. Image and Vision Computing 22(14), 1175–1183 (2004)
28. Varma, M., Zisserman, A.: A statistical approach to material classification using image patch exemplars. PAMI 31(11), 2032–2047 (2009)
29. Visual Geometry Group (University of Oxford): Texture classification (June 2014). http://www.robots.ox.ac.uk/~vgg/research/texclass/setup.html

30. Weinmann, M., Gall, J., Klein, R.: Material classification based on training data synthesized using a BTF database. In: Fleet, D., Pajdla, T., Schiele, B., Tuytelaars, T. (eds.) ECCV 2014, Part III. LNCS, vol. 8691, pp. 156–171. Springer, Heidelberg (2014)
31. Xiao, J., Hays, J., Ehinger, K.A., Oliva, A., Torralba, A.: Sun database: Large-scale scene recognition from abbey to zoo. In: CVPR, pp. 3485–3492 (2010)
32. Yamaguchi, O., Fukui, K., Maeda, K.: Face recognition using temporal image sequence. In: Int. Conf. on Automatic Face and Gesture Recognition, pp. 318–323 (1998)

Shape in a Box

Graham D. Finlayson and Christopher Powell[⊠]

School of Computing Sciences, University of East Anglia, Norwich, UK
{G.Finlayson,Christopher.Powell}@uea.ac.uk

Abstract. Many techniques have been developed in computer vision
to recover three-dimensional shape from two-dimensional images. These
techniques impose various combinations of assumptions/restrictions of
conditions to produce a representation of shape (e.g. a depth/height
map). Although great progress has been made it is a problem which
remains far from solved, with most methods requiring a non-passive
imaging environment. In this paper we develop on a variant of photometric stereo called "Shape from color" (SFC). We remove the restriction of
known, direct light sources by exploiting mutual illumination; we simply take pictures of objects within a colourful box, hence "Shape in a
Box". We discuss the engineering process used to develop our set-up
and demonstrate experimentally that our passive imaging environment
recovers shape to the same accuracy as SFC. A second contribution of
this paper is to benchmark our approach using real objects with known
ground truth, including some 3D printed objects.

Keywords: Photometric stereo · Mutual illumination · Shape recovery

1 Introduction

Recovery of three-dimensional shape from two-dimensional images has been an
active area of research since the inception of computer vision. Common shape
recovery techniques include shape-from-X techniques, such as shape-from-stereo
(structure-from-stereo) [6,8,31] and shape-from-shading [12,18,33]. Other methods include recovery through the use of intrinsic image properties [1,2] and the
focus of this paper, photometric stereo [3,32].

Classic photometric stereo [32] recovers per-pixel surface normals of a static,
convex, Lambertian object by capturing three images (from the same camera
position) of the object illuminated by three independent lights (Fig. 1a). The
intensity of pixels in the three images forms a linear relationship with the surface
normals of the object (Fig. 1b) and thus the normals can be recovered.

We are interested in shape recovery techniques which work in a passive environment and can be performed using a single image. Our research begins with
an existing single image variant of photometric stereo, "Shape from color" [9–11]
(also known as "spectrally multiplexed photometric stereo" [14] or "photometric
stereo with colour lights" [16] - we shall hereafter refer to it as "SFC"). This
method can recover the surface normals of a Lambertian object from a single

© Springer International Publishing Switzerland 2015
L. Agapito et al. (Eds.): ECCV 2014 Workshops, Part III, LNCS 8927, pp. 334–345, 2015.
DOI: 10.1007/978-3-319-16199-0_24

colour image assuming the object is illuminated by three spectrally distinct lights simultaneously (Fig. 1d). If the colour and directions of each light source are sufficiently independent, there exists a linear relationship between the colour values of a pixel on the surface and its normal (Fig. 1e). Essentially, the three colour channels of a single image provide the same information as the three images used in classic photometric stereo. For both classic photometric stereo and SFC, recovered normals are converted to x and y derivatives and this gradient field is reintegrated to recover a height map (Fig. 1c,f).

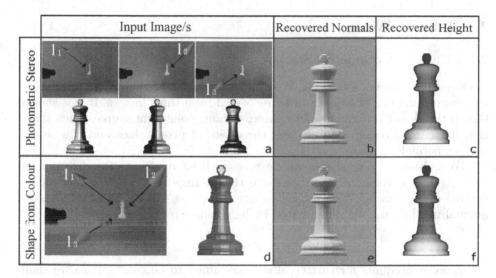

Fig. 1. In parts **a** and **d**, light sources are labelled as l_1, l_2, l_3 in the scene diagrams. In **a**, below each diagram is the image of the object. In **d**, the image is to the right of the scene diagram. Surface normals in **b** and **e** are displayed using the convention of normal maps in graphics (red = x-axis, green = y-axis, blue = z-axis). Height maps, **c** and **f** are in grayscale (white = maximum height, black = minimum height). The same colour coding is used throughout this paper.

The key contribution of this paper is to demonstrate that SFC can work without the requirement of three or more colourful lights. We make the simple observation that the light impinging on any point in a scene is often complex in nature: it is a combination of direct light sources and mutual illumination (light reflected from other surfaces). Thus we propose that the SFC method can be extended to work in any environment which provides appropriate, spectrally varying illumination. Our "Shape in a box" (SiaB) method captures the lighting environment of a specially engineered box by imaging a chrome sphere and uses this information to recover shape. The motivation for our research is to move shape recovery out of the laboratory and into a passive environment. SiaB is presented here as a first step towards achieving this goal.

Another novel contribution of this paper is that we measure shape recovery against "absolute" known ground truth 3D objects. First we use papercraft objects (available to print from many websites [1]). Second, we print objects using a 3D printer. Experiments demonstrate that SiaB achieves the same level of accuracy as SFC.

Section two contains a review of literature relevant to our work. Section three details the engineering underlying our SiaB method. Section four contains experimental results which compare the accuracy produced by SiaB with SFC by benchmarking against real 3D ground truth. Section five contains a brief conclusion and proposals for further development of our method.

2   Related Work

2.1   Classic Photometric Stereo

In classic photometric stereo [32] Woodham proposes that the surface normals of a convex, Lambertian object can be recovered from three images. It was shown that if the object is illuminated by three, distant, point light sources; then there is a linear relationship between the three sets of pixel values and the object surface normals.

To understand how shape can be recovered, let us denote the direction of each light as a vector $\mathbf{e}$, we have three (by assumption linearly independent) vectors $\mathbf{e}_1$, $\mathbf{e}_2$ and $\mathbf{e}_3$. With respect to Lambert's law, a point on a surface with normal $\mathbf{n} = [n_x \ n_y \ n_z]^t$ illuminated by light source $\mathbf{e}$ results in a pixel value p,

$$p = \alpha(\mathbf{e} \cdot \mathbf{n}), \tag{1}$$

where α accounts for surface albedo (assumed to be constant, so we shall hereafter absorb it into the $\mathbf{e}$ term). Let us use the notation $\mathbf{p}_i$ to denote the ith triple of pixel responses (one for each light) and $\mathbf{n}_i$ denote the corresponding ith scene surface normal. We group the image responses, the lighting directions and the scene surface normals into matrices P, E and N respectively,

$$P = \begin{bmatrix} \mathbf{p}_1 \ \mathbf{p}_2 \cdots \mathbf{p}_n \end{bmatrix}, E^t = \begin{bmatrix} \mathbf{e}_1 \ \mathbf{e}_2 \ \mathbf{e}_3 \end{bmatrix}, N = \begin{bmatrix} \mathbf{n}_1 \ \mathbf{n}_2 \cdots \mathbf{n}_n \end{bmatrix}. \tag{2}$$

Under the assumption that the surface in question has uniform, Lambertian reflectance, there exists a linear relationship between the light reflected at each point on the surface (captured pixel values) and the orientation of the surface at each point,

$$P = E N. \tag{3}$$

Since we know E and P, Woodham observed, we can recover N:

$$N = E^{-1} P. \tag{4}$$

Even when all the underlying assumptions hold, fine-tuning of the experimental design [4,29] is essential for the best recovery. Of course for real data

---

[1] e.g. "Paper Models of Polyhedra" - http://www.korthalsaltes.com/

the underlying assumptions may not hold, for example the presence of shadows and specular highlights are problematic. Methods exist in the literature which in essence, extend the classic Woodham approach so that shape can be recovered for more general conditions [3,17]. However, we do not comment on them further here, except to remark that the same extensions are applicable to the method developed in this paper. The focus of our work is only to present a simple algorithm for shape recovery in a passive environment.

2.2   Shape From Color (SFC)

Again let e_1, e_2, e_3 denote light direction vectors. Additionally let us denote the colour of reflected light as b_1, b_2, b_3. Values of b_i are given by

$$b_i = \int I_i(\lambda) \, S(\lambda) \, q(\lambda) \, d\lambda, \tag{5}$$

where $I_i(\lambda)$ is the spectral power distribution of the ith light, $S(\lambda)$ is the spectral reflectance function of the (Lambertian) surface and $q(\lambda)$ represents the camera sensitivities. In effect b_i is the RGB of a flat, frontally presented calibration surface with the same albedo as the object to be measured under the ith light.

Taking the values of e_i, b_i and the surface normal at a pixel n, it follows that the RGB camera response c at that pixel is given by

$$c = (e_1 \cdot n) \, b_1 + (e_2 \cdot n) \, b_2 + (e_3 \cdot n) \, b_3. \tag{6}$$

Grouping vectors e and b into matrices E and B

$$E = \begin{bmatrix} e_1 \, e_2 \, e_3 \end{bmatrix}^t, \ B = \begin{bmatrix} b_1 \, b_2 \, b_3 \end{bmatrix}. \tag{7}$$

Then equation (6) can be rewritten as

$$c = F \, n \equiv B \, E \, n. \tag{8}$$

As F and c are known, the surface normals can be recovered:

$$n = F^{-1} \, c. \tag{9}$$

Using SFC, only one image is required to recover shape. Another advantage of this method is that B and E do not have to be determined separately. Rather, a perfect Lambertian reflector of known shape can be placed in the scene and the linear relationship between recorded camera RGBs and surface normals can be recovered directly. Thus F can be found via a calibration step.

SFC can estimate shape for smooth objects and can be performed in real-time without the need for processing of temporal information. Accordingly it has found applications in face capture [30] and shape recovery in video sequences of non-rigid surfaces [5,16]. Though we note that as with photometric stereo, finely-tuned experimental design is again necessary for optimal recovery [22].

3   Shape in a Box (SiaB)

A key idea in this paper is to substitute the multiple lights used in SFC (and the related lab-based restrictions on shape measurement) using the scene illumination environment directly in a modified SFC algorithm. Crucially, we need to ensure the environment is sufficiently varying to support shape recovery. We achieve this by using the mutual illumination from the coloured walls of a simple triangular box. In section 3.3 we carry out a graphics-based simulation to determine the required geometry of the box). Our long-term ambition is to recover shape in a room with suitable mutual illumination (e.g. a room with colourful walls - see figure 3b).

3.1   Calibration

In theory calibration is simple. Like Johnson and Adelson [20] we could simply place a perfect, spherically shaped Lambertian reflector in a scene (a "spherical probe") and take an image. We could then solve for the linear transform relating the image RGBs to the surface normals of the sphere (section 2.2). However, this approach is not used directly here. No surface is perfectly Lambertian and unlike SFC we cannot choose lighting directions to - for example - minimise the appearance of specular highlights in the calibration image.

Instead we propose taking a picture of a chrome sphere to measure the light from all angles. Then we use spherical harmonic basis functions [15,26,27] to simulate the graphical model of a perfectly spherical, perfectly Lambertian reflector with the illumination environment from the chrome sphere (Fig. 2). Given the known spherical shape and synthesised image the linear transform relating image colour to surface normals is easily found [9].

It is true that the illumination environment will vary slightly according to the object placed inside the box (due to the interaction of light between the box and the object). At present our method does not account for any 'bouncing' of light rays, though the quality of our results show that in practice, the effects of this are small.

3.2   HDR Image Capture

In figure 2 we show the top of our box with the chrome sphere inside. In order to capture the full range of environment lighting we capture the image at five exposure levels. The reader can see that the light from the ambient environment (white in the middle of the sphere) is very bright. The exposures are blended into a HDR image [7,21] prior to calculating the perfect Lambertian sphere.

3.3   The Box

Light entering through the top of the box will inevitably be of higher intensity than the light reflected from the colourful interior of the box. Objects placed

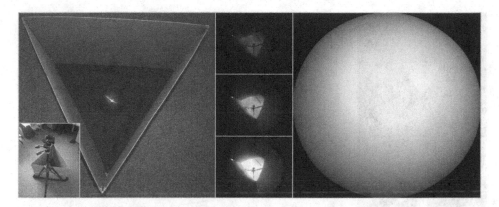

Fig. 2. Here we illustrate the scene calibration process. Left: The chrome sphere is placed inside the colourful box. Centre: Examples of bracketed exposures of the chrome sphere which are used to construct a HDR image. Right: A Lambertian sphere is synthesised under the same lighting conditions.

at the bottom need to receive sufficient mutual illumination from the sides and not have that illumination be lost in the strength of the light from the exterior environment. Equally we do not wish the box to be too deep as in this case the object placed at its bottom would be too dimly lit. So, we need a box that creates a lighting environment which meets these colour sufficiency and light intensity requirements.

To find a suitable box geometry we rendered a series of synthetic images of a chrome sphere (with 15cm diameter) placed in a box where the length and height of the triangular box walls varied. To measure the "quality" of each lighting environment we took an image of the chrome sphere and generated its Lambertian counterpart as described in section 3.1. From equation (8) we can calculate the matrix F which allows us to transform RGB values to surface normals and vice versa (i.e. $\mathbf{c} = F\mathbf{n}$). It is important that in recovering $\mathbf{n} = F^{-1}\mathbf{c}$, the inverse F^{-1} is well conditioned. That is to say, if we perturb our measured RGB values, $\mathbf{c}$, by a small amount ϵ, we would like

$$\hat{\mathbf{n}} = F^{-1}(\mathbf{c} + \epsilon) \simeq \mathbf{n}. \tag{10}$$

The condition number of a matrix F, $k(F) \in [1, \infty]$, is a measure of how good this approximation is (i.e. if $k(F) = 1$, the inverse is maximally stable). In the worst case when $k(F) \geq 10$, then $\hat{\mathbf{n}}$ can be about 10% different from $\mathbf{n}$ and this is the criteria we chose to build our box. We sought an illumination environment that supports a condition number no more than 10. The $k(F)$ generated from our synthesised boxes are shown in figure 3. As a compromise between practical considerations and condition number we settled on a box with side length 80cm and height 60cm.

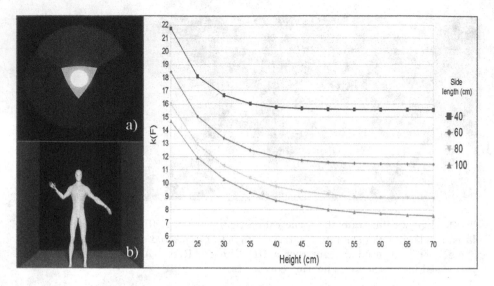

Fig. 3. a) An example of a synthetic chrome sphere from our box engineering experiments. The graph shows the results of the synthetic experiments on triangular boxes of various dimensions. Four different side lengths were each tested with the same varying heights. b) A synthetic human inside a coloured room.

3.4 Recovering Height

Once surface normals have been recovered they are converted into height maps. From equation (9) we have obtained a vector field **n** consisting of recovered surface normals. Each point in the vector field has three components, denoting the direction of the surface normal in the x,y and z axis, that is to say $\mathbf{n} = [n_x \ n_y \ n_z]$. These surface normals can be converted into a gradient field which corresponds to some surface Z by taking the ratios of the x and y components of the surface normals with their z component [19]

$$p = \frac{\partial Z}{\partial x} = -\frac{n_x}{n_z},$$
$$q = \frac{\partial Z}{\partial y} = -\frac{n_y}{n_z}.$$
(11)

For both SFC and SiaB, it is almost certain that the underlying assumptions (e.g. perfectly Lambertian reflectance) do not hold. Accordingly the gradients calculated in (11) are usually not integrable. There may not exist a height map $Z(x, y)$ which corresponds exactly to the gradients. Thus we seek the integrable surface function $\hat{Z}(x, y)$ which is the closest approximation to $Z(x, y)$, in the sense that the derivatives of $\hat{Z}(x, y)$ are as close to those in equation (11) as possible. We can find $\hat{Z}$ by solving Poisson's equation [28]

$$\nabla^2 \hat{Z} = \frac{\partial p}{\partial x} + \frac{\partial q}{\partial y} \qquad (12)$$

There have been many methods developed for the reconstruction of height from gradient fields. In this paper we present results achieved by Frankot & Chellappa's Fourier-based method [13] and Kovesi's shapelet correlation approach [23]. We also present the results of a direct "Jacobi-type" reintegrator. Specifically, since we assume that an object can be segmented from the background, we know the occluding contour of the shape. Thus, in effect our reintegration problem has Dirichlet boundary conditions of complex shape. Our "Jacobi-type" method is similar to that presented in [25]).

We do not go into further detail on the methods here but remark that gradient field reconstruction is an active area of research and direct the reader to [24] for a review of the topic.

4 Experiments

In our experiments we wished to measure the accuracy of recovered shape against ground truth. Often this is achieved through comparison against an existing shape recovery method deemed to be accurate or through the use of synthetic data. Novelly, here we benchmark on recovery of objects whose actual 3D shape is a priori known to good accuracy.

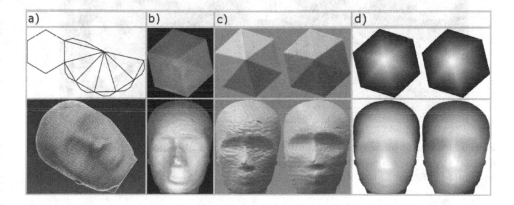

Fig. 4. Top row: a simple papercraft object. Bottom: a 3D-printed object. a) Source files, a papercraft template and a 3D model file. b) Captured images. c) left = true normal map, right = recovered normal map. d) left = true height map, right = recovered height map (using Jacobi iteration method).

4.1 Ground Truth

Our first object dataset is built from "papercraft" templates. These consist of templates which can be printed and fabricated. While the true 3D shape of the papercraft object is known, there may be some small fabrication errors. We benchmark against the perfect 3D model.

Our second ground truth set comprises of 3D printouts of custom meshes. Our ZCorp 450 3D printer prints objects by binding together successive layers of a proprietary powder (resulting in approximately Lambertian reflectance). As with the papercraft objects, there can be small discrepancies between the printed object and the source file. We benchmark against the actual 3D model source files. Examples of both types of object can be seen in figures 4 and 5.

4.2   Results

A chrome sphere is placed in the box and the linear relationship between image RGBs and sphere normals is found (section 3.1). Then an object is placed in the same location and its captured RGB values mapped to surface normals (object images can be seen in figure 5). Normals are converted to a gradient field which is reintegrated to give a height map (section 3.4).

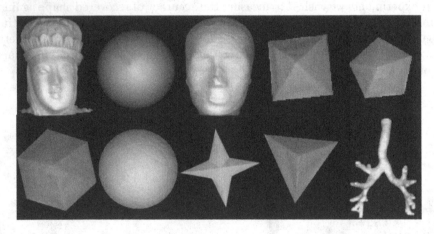

Fig. 5. Images of our experiment subjects (3D-printed objects in *italics*, papercraft in normal type). Top row, left to right: *Bust*, Cone, *Face*, Pyr4, Pyr5. Bottom row, left to right: Pyr6, Sph, Star, Tetra, *Trach*.

In table 1 ground truth and recovered height maps were both scaled to unit height and root mean squared error was calculated. The recovery percentage accuracy is calculated as shown in equation 13, where i and j refer respectively to the rows and columns of the true height map Z and the recovered height map $\hat{Z}$; m and n are the row and column lengths.

$$accuracy(\hat{Z}) = 100 - 100\sqrt{\frac{\sum\limits_{i=1}^{n}\sum\limits_{j=1}^{m}(Z_{(i,j)} - \hat{Z}_{(i,j)})^2}{nm}} \tag{13}$$

The average over all three reintegration methods yields a figure of 88.13% accurate height recovery from SiaB and 89.78% using the SFC experimental set-up. In the majority of cases, the iterative Jacobi reintegration method achieves the most accurate result of the three. An example of a recovered height map can be seen in figure 6.

Table 1. Height map accuracies as percentage values. "Shapelet" is Kovesi's method [23], "FC" is Frankot & Chellappa's algorithm [13] and "Jacobi" is our Jacobi-type method [28].

Object	SiaB Accuracy (%)			SFC Accuracy (%)		
	Shapelet	FC	Jacobi	Shapelet	FC	Jacobi
Bust	89.14	88.13	92.94	87.59	89.04	82.25
Cone	84.01	86.00	95.90	92.71	92.01	97.36
Face	92.05	89.79	85.75	88.09	88.17	80.95
Pyr4	81.47	90.85	97.18	94.45	93.19	97.44
Pyr5	85.19	88.72	97.39	93.92	92.80	97.50
Pyr6	88.41	85.25	97.09	94.72	91.06	95.78
Sph	87.51	91.06	89.42	88.41	91.14	84.03
Star	85.76	77.56	94.62	94.74	89.94	94.06
Tetra	85.26	84.23	95.38	96.08	95.03	96.54
Trach	79.63	76.71	81.45	76.84	77.29	60.32
Average	85.84	85.83	92.71	90.76	89.97	88.61

Fig. 6. Renders of recovered height maps for the *Bust* object, using the Jacobi iteration reintegration method. Left is the ground truth, centre is Shape in a Box and right is using Shape from Color.

5   Conclusion

Inferring 3D shape from images remains a much studied problem in computer vision. In this paper we have extended a photometric stereo technique, "Shape from color" [9] to achieve accurate shape recovery of Lambertian objects without the restriction of spectrally-varied, direct light sources. We have instead designed a passive imaging environment (the titular box) which generates a sufficiently spectrally-varied lighting environment through the effects of mutual illumination. We calibrate our set-up by imaging a chrome sphere inside the box and then recover the surface normals of unknown objects in the same environment. With our "Shape in a box" method we recover shape to the same accuracy as shape from color. It is expected that by enlarging the box (e.g. to the size of a small room) it will be possible to recover the shape of an entire person; indeed initial simulations show this to be a promising course for future research (Fig. 3b).

References

1. Barron, J.T., Malik, J.: Shape, albedo, and illumination from a single image of an unknown object. In: 2012 IEEE Conference on Computer Vision and Pattern Recognition (CVPR), pp. 334–341 (2012)
2. Barron, J.T., Malik, J.: Shape, illumination, and reflectance from shading. Tech. rep, UC Berkeley (2013)
3. Barsky, S., Petrou, M.: The 4-source photometric stereo technique for three-dimensional surfaces in the presence of highlights and shadows. IEEE Transactions on Pattern Analysis and Machine Intelligence 25(10), 1239–1252 (2003)
4. Barsky, S., Petrou, M.: Design issues for a colour photometric stereo system. Journal of Mathematical Imaging and Vision 24(1), 143–162 (2006)
5. Brostow, G.J., Hernández, C., Vogiatzis, G., Stenger, B., Cipolla, R.: Video normals from colored lights. IEEE Transactions on Pattern Analysis and Machine Intelligence 33(10), 2104–2114 (2011)
6. Brown, M.Z., Burschka, D., Hager, G.D.: Advances in computational stereo. IEEE Transactions on Pattern Analysis and Machine Intelligence 25(8), 993–1008 (2003)
7. Debevec, P.E., Malik, J.: Recovering high dynamic range radiance maps from photographs. Proceedings of SIGGRAPH 2007, 369–378 (2007)
8. Dhond, U.R., Aggarwal, J.K.: Structure from stereo-a review. IEEE Transactions on Systems Man and Cybernetics 19(6), 1489–1510 (1989)
9. Drew, M.S.: Shape from color. Simon Fraser University, Tech. rep. (1992)
10. Drew, M.S.: Photometric stereo without multiple images. Electronic Imaging 1997, 369–380 (1997)
11. Drew, M.S., Brill, M.H.: Color from shape from color: A simple formalism with known light sources. Journal of the Optical Society of America (JOSA) 17(8), 1371–1381 (2000)
12. Durou, J.D., Falcone, M., Sagona, M.: Numerical methods for shape-from-shading: A new survey with benchmarks. Computer Vision and Image Understanding 109(1), 22–43 (2008)
13. Frankot, R.T., Chellappa, R.: A method for enforcing integrability in shape from shading algorithms. IEEE Transactions on Pattern Analysis and Machine Intelligence 10(4), 439–451 (1988)
14. Fyffe, G., Yu, X., Debevec, P.: Single-shot photometric stereo by spectral multiplexing. In: 2011 IEEE International Conference on Computational Photography (ICCP), pp. 1–6 (2011)
15. Green, R.: Spherical harmonic lighting: the gritty details. In: Archives of the Game Developers Conference (2003)
16. Hernández, C., Vogiatzis, G., Brostow, G.J., Stenger, B., Cipolla, R.: Non-rigid photometric stereo with colored lights. In: IEEE 11th International Conference on Computer Vision (ICCV), pp. 1–8 (2007)

17. Hernández, C., Vogiatzis, G., Cipolla, R.: Shadows in three-source photometric stereo. In: Forsyth, D., Torr, P., Zisserman, A. (eds.) ECCV 2008, Part I. LNCS, vol. 5302, pp. 290–303. Springer, Heidelberg (2008)
18. Horn, B.K.: Shape from shading: A method for obtraining the shape of a smooth opaque object from one view. Tech. rep, Massachusetts Institute of Technology (1970)
19. Horn, B.K.: Understanding image intensities. Artificial Intelligence 8(2), 201–231 (1977)
20. Johnson, M.K., Adelson, E.H.: Shape estimation in natural illumination. In: 2011 IEEE Conference on Computer Vision and Pattern Recognition (CVPR), pp. 2553–2560 (2011)
21. Kirk, K., Andersen, H.J.: Noise characterization of weighting schemes for combination of multiple exposures. In: British Machine Vision Conference (BMVC), pp. 1129–1138 (2006)
22. Klaudiny, M., Hilton, A.: Error analysis of photometric stereo with colour lights. Pattern Recognition Letters (2014). http://www.sciencedirect.com/science/article/pii/S0167865513005114
23. Kovesi, P.: Shapelets correlated with surface normals produce surfaces. In: Tenth IEEE International Conference on Computer Vision (ICCV), vol. 2, pp. 994–1001 (2005)
24. Patel, V.M., Chellappa, R.: Approximation methods for the recovery of shapes and images from gradients. Applied and Numerical Harmonic Analysis, 377–398 (2013)
25. Pérez, P., Gangnet, M., Blake, A.: Poisson image editing. ACM Transactions on Graphics (TOG) 22(3), 313–318 (2003)
26. Ramamoorthi, R., Hanrahan, P.: An efficient representation for irradiance environment maps. Proceedings of SIGGRAPH 2001, 497–500 (2001)
27. Schönefeld, V.: Spherical harmonics. RWTH Aachen University, Tech. rep. (2005)
28. Simchony, T., Chellappa, R., Shao, M.: Direct analytical methods for solving poisson equations in computer vision problems. IEEE Transactions on Pattern Analysis and Machine Intelligence 12(5), 435–446 (1990)
29. Sun, J., Smith, M., Smith, L., Farooq, A.: Examining the uncertainty of the recovered surface normal in three light photometric stereo. Image and Vision Computing 25(7), 1073–1079 (2007)
30. Vogiatzis, G., Hernández, C.: Self-calibrated, multi-spectral photometric stereo for 3d face capture. International Journal of Computer Vision 97(1), 91–103 (2012)
31. Weng, J., Huang, T.S., Ahuja, N.: Motion and structure from image sequences. Springer Publishing Company (2012)
32. Woodham, R.J.: Photometric method for determining surface orientation from multiple images. Optical Engineering 19(1), 139–144 (1980)
33. Zhang, R., Tsai, P.S., Cryer, J.E., Shah, M.: Shape-from-shading: a survey. IEEE Transactions on Pattern Analysis and Machine Intelligence 21(8), 690–706 (1999)

W22 - Assistive Computer Vision and Robotics (ACVR)

Way to Go! Detecting Open Areas Ahead of a Walking Person

Boris Schauerte[✉], Daniel Koester, Manel Martinez, and Rainer Stiefelhagen

Institute for Anthropomatics and Robotics, Karlsruhe Institute of Technology,
Vincenz-Prießnitz-Str. 3, 76131 Karlsruhe, Germany
schauerte@kit.edu

Abstract. We determine the region in front of a walking person that is not blocked by obstacles. This is an important task when trying to assist visually impaired people or navigate autonomous robots in urban environments. We use conditional random fields to learn how to interpret texture and depth information for their accessibility. We demonstrate the effectiveness of the proposed approach on a novel dataset, which consists of urban outdoor and indoor scenes that were recorded with a handheld stereo camera.

1 Introduction

Being able to savely navigate and explore areas in a city is an essential aspect of our everyday lifes. Accordingly, it is also an essential ability that autonomous, humanoid robots will have to master, if we want them to seemlessly operate in our part of the world, outside of controlled factory conditions. Similarly, safe navigation and exploration in urban areas is also an essential task when aiming toward increasing the autonomy, mobility, and overall life quality of visually impaired people. While location and directionality information provided by the global positioning system (GPS) can guide people and robots toward points of interest, GPS is blind with respect to the user's immediate surroundings. Thus, complementary systems are required to recognize hindrances and warn about potential dangers along the desired path.

Many systems have been developed and can be used to detect obstacles, including the classical white cane. Most technical solutions are often targeted towards different applications, imposing specialized constraints. Furthermore, they often rely on specialized, costly hardware such as sonar, radar, or light detection and ranging (LIDAR). This hardware is incapable of perceiving information provided by, e.g., traffic lights, signs, and lane markings. Furthermore, compared to touch sensors for robots or the classical white cane for blind people, an approach based on computer vision makes it possible to smoothly go around obstacles, because obstacles can visually be perceived from a greater distance.

In this paper, we use conditional random fields (CRFs) to determine the obstacle-free area in front of a walking person. Here, in contrast to many existing approaches that model and try to detect obstacle classes, we address the dual

L. Agapito et al. (Eds.): ECCV 2014 Workshops, Part III, LNCS 8927, pp. 349–360, 2015.
DOI: 10.1007/978-3-319-16199-0_25

(a) Sidewalk   (b) Corridor   (c) Flower-box   (d) Passage   (e) Ridge

(f) Sidewalk L.   (g) Railing   (h) Car Park   (i) Alley   (j) Ladder

Fig. 1. Exemplary binary classification results (CRF with depth and visual informa-tion) overlayed over the original image illustrating the true positives (green), true negatives (blue), false positives (red), and false negatives (yellow). This graphic is best seen in color.

problem and determine the parts in an image that are not blocked by obstacles. This way, we do not solely rely on the extremely varying characteristics of obsta-cles. Instead, assuming that the user is constantly guided by our system (see, e.g., [1]) and thus the direct area in front of him is free of obstacles[1], we can leverage the ground texture and depth information directly in front of him or her. To this end, we previously introduced a heuristic that uses depth maps to predict the ground surface normals and used this information as a rough predictor [2]. In this contribution, we investigate three CRF configurations that rely on different features to predict the obstacle-free areas: First, we train a CRF without depth information, which achieves a surprisingly good performance and is suitable for application in, e.g., modern smart phones. Second, we train a CRF that solely relies on specific depth information, which is independent of obstacle texture and also can use different sensors (e.g., Kinect's depth maps). Third, we train a CRF that leverages depth and visual information (see Fig. 1), which achieves the best results in our evaluation. We recorded and annotated a novel, challenging dataset to evaluate our approach. The dataset comprises of 20 videos that were recorded with a handheld stereo camera setup and cover different urban scenes under realistic ego-motion, lighting conditions, and scene complexity.

2   Related Work

The traditional white cane has a long history as a navigational device for visually impaired, especially blind, people. Many attempts have been made to create a digital enhancement, e.g., the *GuideCane* [3]. Martinez and Ruiz [4] complement

---

[1] Please consider that it is not our intention to replace the white cane, but instead we want to complement it. Thus, a user can recover from failures by relying on the classical walking stick.

the white cane and warn of aerial obstacles, such as low hanging branches. A more radical approach, that tries to replace the walking stick, uses sonar sensors and small vibrotactile units to signal feedback to the user [5]. To provide a navigational context inside buildings, Coughlan and Maguchi [6] use colored markers placed throughout a building. These are then detected and processed by a mobile phone application. The need for specific markers is removed by Chen et al. [7] through an Inertial Measurement Unit (IMU) and an a priori known map of the building. Obstacle detection is usually constrained to a small subset, e.g., matching upper body templates of pedestrians [8] or staircases [9]. These can be based on saliency [10], hough transformation [11] or optical flow [12]. As a dual problem, ground plane detection can be achieved through plane fitting [13] using RANSAC approaches. The authors model a relationship between the ground plane disparity and image pixel coordinates. Stereo camera rigs mounted on wheeled vehicles [14,15] result in a steady camera movement and support a probabilistic model. The dependency of person detection location and size is used to generate a ground plane estimation.

Segmentation is another technique to detect the ground plane and was proposed by Lombardi [16]. In recent years, conditional random fields have achieved state-of-the-art performance for several segmentation tasks such as, e.g., semantic (scene) segmentation (e.g., [17–19]). Semantic segmentation describes the task of labeling each pixel of an image with a semantic category (e.g., "sky", "car", "street"). Accordingly, we chose conditional random fields as starting point to address our task. However, in contrast to the existing work, we are not interested in semantic object classes or types, but instead are interested in answering the question whether or not the region of an image accessible to a walking person? This naturally is related to road detection (e.g., [15,20,21]). However, detecting the walkable area in front of persons differs substantially from road detection for cars: First, we have to deal with a large amount of ego-motion that is characterized by the fact that cameras carried by a person are subject to considerably more degrees-of-freedom compared to cameras mounted on cars. Second, humans not just follow roads, they sharply change direction, often even want to cross roads (and not just on zebra crossings), and they want to walk indoors as well as outdoors. Third, roads made for cars are much wider, straighter, and smoother than the small pathes between obstacles that are common in urban scenarios, see Fig. 3.

3   Open Area Detection

3.1   Depth-Based Surface Angle Heuristic

The depth-Based surface angle heuristic builds on work done by Koester et al. [2] that determines the accessible section in front of a walking person. Using epipolar geometry, we calculate the disparity of a point and therefore its distance from the camera. Doing so for every image point, we obtain a depth map $\Delta = \{(x_i, y_i, \delta_i)\}$, which allows us to calculate gradient ∇ for small image regions. After convolution of the image in both horizontal and vertical directions, we compute the local gradient direction for each region. This results in map Φ, which consists of processed image regions and their corresponding gradient directions.

Within Φ, we calculate the accessible section by processing it in vertical bands. Such a band is a column of Φ, i.e., a vertical grouping of gradient regions. Starting with the band's bottommost block, we collect upwards all blocks that match our criteria of an aligned region. Correctly aligned regions are all blocks whose calculated angles deviate less than a certain threshold from a perfectly upright plane surface normal. Upright for this work is defined as being tilted upwards in the camera image, which prevents the algorithm from working on images where the camera is tilted above the used threshold. For our experiments this was not a problem, as the stereo camera system was mounted on a handheld carrier that was rarely tilted sideways more than 15 degrees, but to address this problem, one could simply use an Inertial Measurement Unit in combination with the cameras or estimate the dominant ground plane. When a block does not fit that criteria, the collection process stops and advances to the next vertical band. We repeat this process until the entire map has been processed, but rely on a geometric constraint in this process. When recording a real world scenario with a camera system from a persons point of view, the accessible section is usually connected to the bottom image border. This constraint allows us to focus on the accessible section that is directly in front of a person and not obstructed by any obstacles.

Due to the simplicity of the gradient calculation, the resulting algorithm works in realtime on a fairly recent computer.

3.2   Conditional Random Field.

Structure, Learning, and Prediction. In general, a CRF models the conditional probabilities of x (here, is it a walkable area?), given the observation y (i.e., features), i.e.

$$p(x|y) = \frac{1}{Z(y)} \prod_{c \in C} \psi(x_c, y) \prod_{i \in V} \psi(x_i, y) \quad , \tag{1}$$

where C is the set of cliques in the CRF's graph and i represent individual nodes. Here, ψ indicates that the value for a particular configuration x_c depends on the input y.

Naturally, our problem is a binary segmentation task, since the location depicted by a pixel can either be blocked by an obstacle or not, i.e. x_i can either be "blocked" or "non-blocked". We use a pairwise, 4-connected grid CRF structure. We linearly parametrize the CRF parameter vector Θ in unary node $u(y, i)$ (i.e., information at an image location) and edge features $v(y, i, j)$ (e.g., relating neighbored image locations). Here, it is important to consider that the cliques in a 4-connected, grid-structured graph are the sets of connected nodes, which are represented by the edges. Thus, we fit two matrices F and G such that

$$\Theta(x_i) = Fu(y, i) \tag{2}$$
$$\Theta(x_i, x_j) = Gv(y, i, j) \tag{3}$$

Here, y is the observed image and $\Theta(x_i)$ represents the parameter values for all values of x_i. Similarly, $\Theta(x_i, x_j)$ represents the parameter values for all x_i, x_j. Then, we can calculate

$$p(x; \Theta) = \exp\left[\sum_i \Theta(x_i) + \sum_j \Theta(x_i, x_j) - A(\Theta)\right] , \tag{4}$$

where $A(\Theta)$ is the log-partition function that ensures normalization.

We use tree-reweighted belief propagation (TRW) to perform approximate marginal inference, see [22]. TRW addresses the problem that it is computationally intractable to compute the log-partition function $A(\Theta)$ exactly and approximates $A(\Theta)$ with

$$\hat{A}(\Theta) = \max_{\mu \in \mathcal{L}} \Theta \cdot \mu + \hat{H}(\mu) , \tag{5}$$

where $\hat{H}$ is TRW's entropy approximation [22]. Here, $\mathcal{L}$ denotes the valid set of marginal vectors

$$\mathcal{L} = \{\mu : \sum_{x_{c \setminus i}} \mu(x_c) = \mu(x_i) \wedge \sum_{x_i} \mu(x_i) = 1\} , \tag{6}$$

where μ describes a mean vector, which equals a gradient of the log-partition function. Then, the approximate marginals $\hat{\mu}$ are the maximizing vector

$$\hat{\mu} = \arg\max_{\mu \in \mathcal{L}} \Theta \cdot \mu + \hat{H}(\mu) . \tag{7}$$

This can be approached iteratively until convergence or a maximum number of updates [23].

To train the CRF, we rely on the clique loss function, see [22],

$$L(\Theta, x) = -\sum_c \log \hat{\mu}(x_c; \Theta) . \tag{8}$$

Here, $\hat{\mu}$ indicates that the loss is implicitly defined with respect to marginal predictions – again, in our implementation these are determined by tree-reweighted belief propagation – and not the true marginals. This loss can be interpreted as empirical risk minimization of the mean Kullback-Leibler divergence of the true clique marginals to the predicted ones.

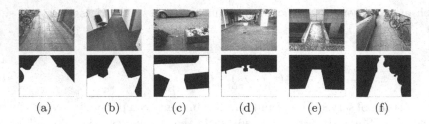

(a)　　　　(b)　　　　(c)　　　　(d)　　　　(e)　　　　(f)

Fig. 2. Exemplary key frames and binary masks of videos (a) Sidewalk, (b) Corridor, (c) Flower-box, (d) Passage, (e) Ridge, and (f) Narrow

Features. As unary depth-based features, we use the surface angle map Φ as presented in Sec. 3.1 and additionally the disparity map. As unary image-based features, we include the following information at each CRF grid point: First, we include each pixel's normalized horizontal and vertical image position in the feature vector. Second, we directly use the pixel's intensity value after scaling the image to the CRF's grid size. We expand the position and intensity information using sinusoidal expansion as described by Konidaris et al. [23,24]. Third, we append the histograms of oriented gradients (HoG) to encode the texture information.

As CRF edge features, we use a simple 1-constant and 10 thresholds to encode the difference of neighboring pixels. Then, we multiply the existing features by an indicator function for each edge type (i.e., vertical and horizontal), effectively doubling the number of features and encoding conjunctions of features and edge type. This way, we parametrize vertical and horizontal edges separately.

4   Experimental Evaluation

4.1   Dataset

We recorded a dataset to evaluate the detection of all image regions that are not blocked by obstacles [2]. This was necessary, because existing related datasets have been recorded for other use cases and mostly focus either on road scenes or people detection inside pedestrian areas (see Sec. 2). Since we target wearable sensor platforms that can assist visually impaired persons, we recorded the dataset on a handheld mobile platform carried by a pedestrian. Consequently, our dataset contains – among other challenges – realistic (camera) ego-motion on all axes. We recorded 20 videos of varying length that show common urban scenes such as, e.g., walkways and sidewalks with static obstacles (e.g. parked cars, bicycles, and street poles) and moving obstacles (e.g., cyclists and pedestrians). Some example images illustrating the dataset are shown in Fig. 2.

The videos were recorded with a stereo setup consisting of two *Point Grey Grasshopper 2* cameras, which were mounted onto a small metal carrier, axes in parallel, at a fixed distance of about 6cm with respect to the lenses' centers and the used lenses provide a field of view of 82 by 67 degrees. The metal carrier was manually held at breast height and the cameras were pointed towards the ground in front of the carrying person. Furthermore, the cameras were configured to synchronize time as well as the adaptation of gain and exposure. All videos were recorded in 8-bit monochrome mode at a resolution of 1024×768 pixels at 15 frames per second.

Overall, the dataset contains 7789 frames, out of which we labeled every fifth frame (i.e., 3 fps). We did not label the first 30 frames of each video in order to allow for proper gain and exposure synchronization. We labeled the obstacle-free section as a polygon, where we imposed the constraint that a valid region must connect to the bottom frame boundary to be reachable from the current position, otherwise obstacles could obstruct it. Examples of binary masks created from labeled frames can be seen in figure 2.

4.2 Measures

We use the human ground truth annotation of the walkable area in each labeled frame, see Sec. 4.1, to evaluate our approach with respect to two performance measures: First, we use the pixel-wise binary classification error (i.e., $1 -$ accuracy) to directly evaluate the goodness of the binary classification. In case of the depth-based heuristic, we calculate the best threshold over all training images. Second, we use the area under the receiver-operator characteristic curve (ROC AUC) to investigate the influence of the decision thresholds on the classification performance. This way, we have a measure of how well behaved the non-binary (probabilistic) prediction maps are, i.e., how far away from the truth are the predicted values typically?

To validate the statistical significance of our results, we perform paired t-tests to ensure that the compared algorithms are in fact better or worse. Here, the results of the two algorithms in question are paired for each video. We reject hypotheses at significance level $\alpha = 0.05$.

4.3 Algorithm Parameters

We use Geiger et al.'s efficient large-scale stereo matching algorithm [25] to calculate the disparity and depth maps from the stereo image pairs. For the surface angle calculation (Sec. 3.1), we use a kernel size of 32×32 pixels, tiling the original 1024×768 pixels image into 32×24 blocks. To heuristically determine the section that is not blocked by obstacles, we consider values that deviate less than $22.5°$ from an optimal perpendicular angle. We train the CRFs using a grid/feature map size of 64×48 pixels.

4.4 Results

As is apparent in Tab. 4, all CRFs outperform the heuristic baseline method on 18 out of the 20 videos in terms of prediction error. Averaged over all videos, the depth-based baseline method achieves a pixel-wise error of 0.209 and a ROC

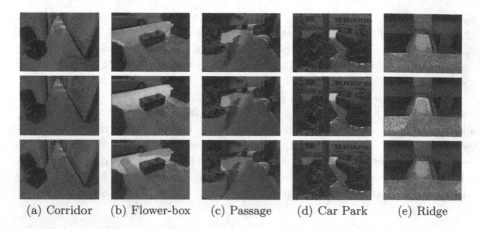

(a) Corridor   (b) Flower-box   (c) Passage   (d) Car Park   (e) Ridge

Fig. 3. Exemplary binary classifications for different CRF configurations. Top-to-bottom: No depth, depth only, and visual and depth. The binary classification is overlaid over the original image to illustrate the true positives (green), true negatives (blue), false positives (red), and false negatives (yellow). This graphic is best seen in color.

AUC of 0.852. If we train the CRF using the depth and surface angle maps exclusively, then we achieve an error of 0.126 and a ROC AUC of 0.939. Using a pairwise t-test to compare the accuracies achieved on the videos, we can reject the hypotheses of equal mean ($p_E = 0.022$) and that the heuristic approach might be better than the CRF ($p_I = 0.011$). In contrast, if we exclusively rely on image features, then we achieve an error of 0.209 and a ROC AUC of 0.937, which is better than the heuristic approach (we can reject inferiority with $p = 0.030$, but we are unable to reject equality) and very similar but slightly inferior in performance to the depth only approach (we are not able to reject any hypothesis). Finally, if we train a CRF with both depth and visual information, it achieves a pixelwise prediction error of 0.111 and a ROC AUC of 0.949. This approach provides the best performance on 16 out of the 20 videos in terms of error minimization and 14 out of 20 in terms of best ROC AUC performance. Confirmed by our statistical tests, we can safely assume that this algorithm in fact provides a better performance than the heuristic baseline (H_0: Inferior? Reject at $p_I = 0.006$; H_0: Equal? Reject at $p_E = 0.012$) and the CRF without depth information (trivially visible, because the results on all videos are better). But, contradicting our expectation given these numbers, we are unable to reject the possibility that the depth only approach is equally good or even better. Why is that? This is caused by two video sequences, namely "Corridor" and "Fence" for which the depth-only results stand out of the other results by being drastically better. If we exclude both video sequences, we can safely reject that the performance of the depth only CRF is equal or better ($p_E = 0$ and $p_I = 0$, respectively) than the performance of the CRF with depth and visual information.

The "Corridor" is an interesting case, because not just the depth-based CRF but even the depth-based heuristic outperform the CRF that uses depth and

Fig. 4. Pixel-wise binary classification error and area under the receiver operator characteristic curve achieved in a leave-one-video-out cross-validation procedure. The algorithms are: depth-based surface angle heuristic (D-based), a CRF that only uses depth features (D only), a CRF that only uses visual features (no D), and a CRF that uses depth and visual features (full). The best result for each video is marked bold. Results where D-based outperforms full are underlined.

| | ↓ Pixel-wise Error (1 − Accuracy) | | | | ↑ ROC AUC | | | |
| | heuristic | CRF | | | heuristic | CRF | | |
Sequence	D-based	D only	no D	full	D-based	D only	no D	full
Alley	0.099	0.088	0.088	**0.066**	0.928	0.971	0.972	**0.979**
Alley L.	0.138	0.124	0.073	**0.054**	0.892	0.958	0.979	**0.985**
Bicycle	0.324	0.141	**0.092**	**0.092**	0.753	0.906	0.946	**0.953**
Car	0.149	0.124	0.090	**0.065**	0.850	0.944	0.935	**0.973**
Corridor	<u>0.204</u>	**0.086**	0.365	0.316	<u>0.819</u>	**0.972**	0.702	0.753
Fence	<u>0.185</u>	**0.126**	0.284	0.260	0.855	**0.936**	0.914	0.933
Flower-box	0.276	0.169	0.160	**0.158**	0.783	0.897	0.964	**0.966**
Hedge	0.186	0.202	0.154	**0.105**	0.836	0.866	0.893	**0.917**
Ladder	0.132	0.176	0.155	**0.112**	0.836	0.920	**0.937**	0.913
Narrow	0.071	0.104	0.106	**0.058**	0.958	0.983	0.982	**0.993**
Pan	0.350	0.127	0.084	**0.063**	0.759	0.940	**0.987**	0.981
Passage	0.195	**0.125**	0.187	0.130	0.850	0.941	0.942	**0.964**
Railing	0.304	**0.189**	0.234	0.203	0.760	**0.851**	0.835	0.835
Ramp	0.269	0.163	0.164	**0.129**	0.803	0.916	**0.970**	**0.970**
Ridge	0.801	0.163	0.258	**0.140**	0.854	0.885	0.910	**0.960**
Sidewalk	0.087	0.056	0.084	**0.046**	0.929	**0.969**	0.945	0.968
Sidewalk 2	0.096	0.073	0.057	**0.043**	0.947	0.978	0.978	**0.982**
Sidewalk L.	0.088	0.110	0.087	**0.070**	0.889	0.979	0.981	**0.986**
Sign	0.146	0.099	0.079	**0.064**	0.890	0.978	0.986	**0.987**
Street	0.083	0.075	0.059	**0.044**	0.940	0.986	0.988	**0.991**
Average	0.209	0.126	0.143	**0.111**	0.852	0.939	0.937	**0.949**

visual information, see Tab. 4. However, this is most likely explained by the absence of a second indoor video that could provide suitable visual training data in our leave-one-video-out evaluation. Furthermore, it is important to note that the walls and floor in the video are nearly textureless and consequently hardly suited for HoG-like features. The case is slightly different for the "Fence" sequence, for which it is interesting to have a look at the ROC AUC. The ROC AUC of the full – i.e., visual and depth features – CRF is substantially higher (0.933 > 0.855) than the ROC AUC achieved by the depth-based heuristic and only marginally worse compared to the depth-only CRF (0.936). This stands in contrast to the considerably higher pixel-wise error (0.260 > 0.185 and 0.260 > 0.126). Accordingly, it is most likely that the actual error is caused by the final decision made by the CRF and, considering from the performance of the CRF without depth-features, might arise from the present visual features.

Overall, it is easy to conclude that depth is an important and reliable information about the accessibility of a ground section ahead. This makes sense, because while the texture of obstacles may vary substantially their main property of physically blocking a certain area is well represented in depth maps. However, if we again closely examine the results, we can see that the visual-only CRF achieves an equal or lower error compared to the depth-based CRF on 12 of the 20 sequences. Thus, it is possible to achieve an accurate prediction even with a single, monocular camera, if we have sufficient and appropriate training data. However, in many cases depth information seems more reliable and especially does not only depend on texture that can vary substantially for obstacles and scenes in general.

Although the CRF that uses depth and visual features provides the overall best performance, all algorithms have their respective use cases: First, CRFs that do not rely on depth features can use monocular cameras, which nowadays can be found in nearly all off-the-shelf mobile phones. Second, the lightweight complexity of the depth-based heuristic[2] stands in contrast to the roughly 2 fps our CRF-based implementations that are not real-time capable yet. Third, the depth-based heuristic and depth-based CRF seem to perform well in the absence of scene specific, targeted training data. Thus, they could serve as fallback in scenes or situations for which the CRFs that include visual information have not been trained.

5   Conclusion

We presented how we determine obstacle-free areas in front of a walking person or (humanoid) robot. In contrast to prior art, we focus on detecting the obstacle-free areas instead of detecting potential obstacles directly, thus addressing the dual problem to classical obstacle detection. Our evaluation dataset consists of 20 videos depicting urban scenes that we recorded using a handheld stereo camera rig. It contains realistic amounts of lighting variations, ego-motion, and scene variety in urban scenarios. Given the dataset, we can train and investigate different conditional random fields for varying sensor configurations, i.e. depth information only, stereo video recordings, and monocular video recordings. To efficiently work with depth information, we use a heuristic that predicts flat ground surfaces in front of the user that typically represent sidewalks, streets, or floors in urban environments. This algorithm also serves as a depth-only, non-CRF baseline algorithm. In summary, we are able to achieve a pixel-wise prediction accuracy of 0.874, 0.857, and 0.889 for depth-only, monocular images, and stereo images, respectively.

As part of our future work, we plan to investigate how haptic or auditory output modalities can be used to communicate the information to visually impaired users. For this purpose, we also plan to improve the computational efficiency to achieve a high system responsiveness that is essential for auditory or haptic user interfaces. Furthermore, we want to integrate self-localization and tracking to smoothly steer a blind person around obstacles.

---

[2] We exclude the time for the depth map calculation, which could be replaced by specialized sensors, e.g., Kinect.

Acknowledgments. The work presented in this paper was supported by a Google Research Award for "A Mobility and Navigational Aid for Visually Impaired Persons", the German Research Foundation (DFG) within the Collaborative Research Program SFB 588 "Humanoide Roboter", and the Quaero Programme, funded by OSEO, French State agency for innovation.

References

1. Martinez, M., Constantinescu, A., Schauerte, B., Koester, D., Stiefelhagen, R.: Cognitive evaluation of haptic and audio feedback in short range navigation tasks. In: Proc. 14th Int. Conf. Computers Helping People with Special Needs (2014)
2. Koester, D., Schauerte, B., Stiefelhagen, R.: Accessible section detection for visual guidance. In: IEEE/NSF Workshop on Multimodal and Alternative Perception for Visually Impaired People (2013)
3. Shoval, S., Ulrich, I., Borenstein, J.: Navbelt and the guide-cane (obstacle-avoidance systems for the blind and visually impaired). IEEE Robotics Automation Magazine **10**(1), 9–20 (2003)
4. Martinez, J.M.S., Ruiz, F.E., et al.: Stereo-based aerial obstacle detection for the visually impaired. In: Proc. Workshop on Computer Vision Applications for the Visually Impaired (2008)
5. Cardin, S., Thalmann, D., Vexo, F.: Wearable obstacle detection system for visually impaired people. In: Proc. VR Workshop on Haptic And Tactile Perception of Deformable Objects (2005)
6. Coughlan, J., Manduchi, R.: A mobile phone wayfinding system for visually impaired users. Assistive Technology Research Series **25**(2009), 849 (2009)
7. Chen, D., Feng, W., Zhao, Q., Hu, M., Wang, T.: An Infrastructure-Free Indoor Navigation System for Blind People. In: Su, C.-Y., Rakheja, S., Liu, H. (eds.) ICIRA 2012, Part III. LNCS, vol. 7508, pp. 552–561. Springer, Heidelberg (2012)
8. Mitzel, D., Leibe, B.: Close-range human detection and tracking for head-mounted cameras. In: Proc. British Machine Vision Conference (2012)
9. Hoon, Y., Leung, L.T.S., Medioni, G.: Real-time staircase detection from a wearable stereo system. In: Proc. Int Conf. on Pattern Recognition (2012)
10. Lee, C.H., Su, Y.C., Chen, L.G.: An intelligent depth-based obstacle detection system for visually-impaired aid applications. In: Proc. Int. Workshop Image Analysis for Multimedia Interactive Services (2012)
11. Labayrade, R., Aubert, D., Tarel, J.P.: Real time obstacle detection in stereovision on non flat road geometry through "v-disparity" representation. In: Proc. Intelligent Vehicle Symposium (2002)
12. Braillon, C., Pradalier, C., Crowley, J., Laugier, C.: Real-time moving obstacle detection using optical flow models. In: Proc. Intelligent Vehicles Symposium (2006)
13. Se, S., Brady, M.: Ground plane estimation, error analysis and applications. Robotics and Autonomous Systems **39**(2), 59–71 (2002)
14. Ess, A., Leibe, B., Schindler, K., Van Gool, L.: Moving obstacle detection in highly dynamic scenes. In: Proc. Int. Conf. Robotics and Automation (2009)
15. Ess, A., Schindler, K., Leibe, B., Van Gool, L.: Object detection and tracking for autonomous navigation in dynamic environments. The International Journal of Robotics Research **29**(14) (2010)
16. Lombardi, P., Zanin, M., Messelodi, S.: Unified stereovision for ground, road, and obstacle detection. In: Proc. Intelligent Vehicles Symposium (2005)

17. Lafferty, J.D., McCallum, A., Pereira, F.C.N.: Conditional random fields: Probabilistic models for segmenting and labeling sequence data. In: Proc. Int. Conf. Machine Learning (2001)
18. Passino, G., Patras, I., Izquierdo, E.: Latent semantics local distribution for crf-based image semantic segmentation. In: Proc. British Machine Vision Conference (2009)
19. Verbeek, J., Triggs, B.: Scene segmentation with crfs learned from partially labeled images. Advances in Neural Information Processing Systems 20, 1553–1560 (2008)
20. Kong, H., Audibert, J.Y., Ponce, J.: General road detection from a single image. IEEE Trans. Image Processing 19(8), 2211–2220 (2010)
21. Alvarez, J., Lopez, A.: Road detection based on illuminant invariance. IEEE Trans. Intelligent Transportation Systems 12(1), 184–193 (2011)
22. Wainwright, M.J., Jordan, M.I.: Graphical Models, Exponential Families, and Variational Inference. Now Publishers Inc., Hanover (2008)
23. Domke, J.: Learning graphical model parameters with approximate marginal inference. IEEE Trans. Pattern Analysis and Machine Intelligence 35(10), 2454–2467 (2013)
24. Konidaris, G., Osentoski, S., Thomas, P.S.: Value function approximation in reinforcement learning using the fourier basis. In: AAAI Conf. Artificial Intelligence (2011)
25. Geiger, A., Roser, M., Urtasun, R.: Efficient large-scale stereo matching. In: Proc. Asian Conf., Computer Vision (2011)

Road-Crossing Assistance by Traffic Flow Analysis

Adi Perry[✉] and Nahum Kiryati

School of Electrical Engineering, Tel Aviv University,
Ramat Aviv, 69978 Tel Aviv, Israel
perryad@post.tau.ac.il, adiperry@yahoo.com

Abstract. We present a system to alert visually impaired pedestrians of vehicles approaching a road-crossing without traffic control. The system is computationally efficient, requires low-cost hardware, and can be mounted on existing street infrastructure, such as sign or lighting poles. The incoming video stream, showing the approaching traffic, is transformed to a one-dimensional signal, that is forwarded to a decision module. Preliminary experimental results indicate promising probability-of-detection and false alarm rates, while providing sufficiently early warning to the pedestrian. The planned target hardware is a solar-charged low cost Android device.

Keywords: Road crossing assistance · Approaching traffic analysis · Optic flow · Blind · Visually impaired · Resource-limited system

1 Introduction

For visually impaired pedestrians, crossing a street in the absence of traffic control is a challenge. Drivers do not reliably yield to pedestrians, even those who are clearly visual impaired (holding a white cane), requiring pedestrians to cross in traffic gaps [6]. To identify traffic gaps, visually impaired pedestrians rely on hearing. The common strategy is "cross when quiet" [14]. However, relying on early detection of vehicle noise is risky, especially since the low noise level of modern cars can easily be masked by background noise. Furthermore, pedestrians with less than perfect hearing cannot follow the "cross when quiet" rule.

US data [2] indicates that the average crossing speed is 4 feet (about 1.2m) per second. A standard urban one-way single-lane street with two shoulders is 18 feet (5.5m) wide and takes 4.5 seconds to cross. A standard two-way street or one-way with two lanes is 28 feet (8.5m) wide, taking 7 seconds to cross. The traffic gap must be longer than these figures, and for safe crossing an advance warning of at least 7 seconds is necessary.

Pun *et al* [13] reviewed the field of assistive devices, especially those that use image and video processing to convert visual data to another modality, such as auditory or haptic, which can be delivered to the blind person. Several systems help locating and identifying points of interest [5] and road crossings [9,16]. Other devices provide auditory or other indications regarding traffic light status [3,4].

© Springer International Publishing Switzerland 2015
L. Agapito et al. (Eds.): ECCV 2014 Workshops, Part III, LNCS 8927, pp. 361–374, 2015.
DOI: 10.1007/978-3-319-16199-0_26

"Smart canes", employing various types of sensors, have been suggested [1,7,10], but are intended primarily for short-range obstacle detection and navigation. All these systems do not address the fundamental difficulty of crossing a road in the absence of traffic control.

An ideal solution to the road-crossing problem must reliably analyze traffic flow, detect traffic gaps, and be sufficiently robust to operate at a variety of weather conditions, day and night. Moreover, it has to be easy and cheap to install, operate and maintain. This work is intended to be a first step towards meeting this challenge.

We present a low-cost system to detect and alert pedestrians of vehicles approaching a crosswalk. When fully developed, it will be possible to mount the system on existing street infrastructure, such as traffic signs or illumination poles. The system adapts to the scene, thus minimizing installation and maintenance effort. It can detect approaching vehicles well before they reach the road crossing, thus indicating traffic gaps that are sufficient for safe crossing.

2   Hardware Platform and Installation

The input device is a video camera, capturing the incoming traffic, as illustrated in Fig. 1. The video signal is processed by low cost, lightweight computing hardware, that eventually generates the indication signal.

The hardware platform can include a compact solar panel and a rechargeable battery, to allow autonomous operation without reliance on the electric power grid. This can enhance the applicability of the system, and reduce its installation and maintenance costs. A block diagram of the system is shown in Fig. 2.

Indication of incoming traffic, or lack thereof, can be delivered to the user as an audio or tactile signal, or via a local networking interface (such as Bluetooth or WLAN) to a smartphone or a dedicated receiver.

We developed the system on a standard laptop PC, with a modified Logitech QuickCam 9000 WebCam. Targeting a low-cost solution, we implemented the algorithm as a cross-platform code, and tested it on BeagleBoard xM hardware, an open-source platform consisting of TI's OMAP 3530 (ARM processor + DSP),

Fig. 1. Mounting the system on a sign or lighting pole near a road crossing, with the camera facing the approaching traffic

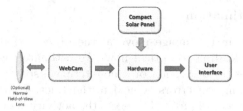

Fig. 2. The system consists of a low cost camera, streaming video to a computing device, possibly powered by a compact solar panel. User interaction options range from an auditory or visual alert to communication via a local area or cellular network. A narrow field of view lens can be used to improve the observability of distant vehicles.

suitable for rapid prototyping. With the proliferation of low-cost Android devices with built-in cameras, we are currently porting the system to Android OS.

3   Algorithm

We examined various approaches for efficient detection and evaluation of approaching traffic on a resource-limited platform. A generic approach that comes to mind is detecting any new object appearing in the field of view, tracking it, analyzing its motion and estimating its *Time to Contact* (TTC) as the basis for issuing an alert. Lee [11] observed that in a simple but typical case, the TTC can be estimated based on the incoming object's expansion rate, measured in the image plane. A newer approach for TTC estimation [8] treats the approaching vehicle as a moving plane.

In our application, the field of view (FOV) of the camera should be sufficiently wide to capture nearby vehicles (possibly leaving a parking spot). However, most approaching vehicles first appear as tiny spots near the vanishing point (VP)[1] Given the limited pixel-count of low cost video cameras, the wide FOV implies that the spatial resolution near the vanishing point is quite low. These constraints imply that the main challenge is early detection of the incoming vehicle, meeting the advance warning time requirement. Therefore, in most cases precise TTC estimation is not the issue. Also note that the approximations on which TTC algorithms rely do not hold at the most significant moment, when the vehicle is seen as a tiny, far-away spot.

We convert the space-time video processing problem to a 1-D signal analysis problem, by computing a scalar motion measure, referred to as *Activity*, reflecting the entire *relevant* motion in the scene. Objects moving along the road towards the camera induce pulses in the Activity signal, such that a significant rising Activity slope suggests an approaching vehicle. Early detection of approaching vehicles with few false alarms amounts to discrimination between a true rising Activity slope and random noise and clutter in the Activity signal.

---

[1] We use the term *vanishing point* in a loose sense, including the case of a curved road.

3.1   Activity Estimation

Brightness patterns in the image move as the objects that give rise to them move in the scene, leading to optical flow. We estimate the optical flow using a computationally-efficient version of a non-iterative sparse Lucas-Kanade [12] algorithm. The estimation errors typical to the Lucas-Kanade method can be tolerated in our application; as will be seen, the activity signal, derived from the optical flow, is an integral measure in which these errors are spatially averaged over parts of the image domain.

We employ integral images to improve the efficiency of the algorithm, as proposed by Senst et al [15], calculating integral versions of the gradient products of the image $I_x \cdot I_x$, $I_x \cdot I_y$, $I_y \cdot I_y$ and $I_x \cdot I_t$, $I_y \cdot I_t$. Evaluating a structure tensor (or a covariance matrix) is required for estimating each flow vector in the Lucas-Kanade algorithm, and each of its matrix elements can be efficiently evaluated using four simple arithmetic operations, regardless of the neighborhood size that is taken into account.

Parts of the optical flow field are associated with risk-posing approaching vehicles. Other parts might reflect distancing traffic on another lane, pedestrians crossing the road, and movements due to wind or camera vibrations. The proposed activity measure $A(t)$ is obtained by projecting the optical flow field $u(x, y; t)$ onto a *projection map*. The projection map $m(x, y)$ is a vector field supported on image regions corresponding to lanes carrying traffic towards the camera, each vector representing the local direction of approaching traffic. Formally,

$$A(t) = \sum_{x,y} m(x, y) \cdot u(x, y; t). \tag{1}$$

The scalar, time-dependent Activity is fast to compute, and quantifies the entire risk-inducing motion in the scene.

Assuming a one-way road, the projection map can be automatically generated by temporal averaging of the optical flow over a training period, see Fig. 3. The averaging process cancels the randomly oriented contributions that are due to vibrations, wind and similar phenomena, while highlighting the consistent, dominant, risk-inducing traffic motion directions in the road area alone. Slight adaptation of this procedure is necessary for dealing with two-way roads, where consistent distancing traffic is also expected within the visual field of the camera.

Variable Density and Spatially Weighted Optical Flow Computation: Maintaining minimal system cost calls for resource-limited hardware. Since optical flow computation is the most demanding element in the proposed algorithm, it is most lucrative for streamlining and optimization. Typically, large parts of the field of view, such as sidewalks and background structures, do not hold risk-posing motion. These regions, once determined, might be excluded from optical flow estimation altogether. In image regions corresponding to nearby parts of the scene, where vehicles appear quite large and expand substantially, spatially-sparse optical flow computation might be sufficient. Conversely, high density optical flow computation can be called for just where necessary, near the vanishing point, where approaching vehicles first appear as tiny spots. These considerations can be readily represented by the automatically-generated projection map. Furthermore, the *magnitude* of the projection-map vectors can be modified to emphasize motion near the vanishing point, thus improving the warning time see an example in Fig. 4. Note that the vanishing point can be readily detected during training, by back-tracking the projection-map vectors to the source of the flow.

3.2   Detecting Approaching Vehicles

In certain applications, the raw Activity signal can be delivered to the pedestrian in analog form, leaving the actual decision regarding road crossing safety in the human domain. However, in most cases we wish to provide the pedestrian with a binary signal, suggesting either that traffic is approaching ('TRAFFIC' state) or that a sufficient traffic gap occurs at that moment ('GAP' state).

Despite the substantial SNR in the Activity signal near Activity peaks, *early* detection of an approaching vehicle, at the early rising stage of the corresponding activity pulse, when the SNR is poor, is not easy. Note that the pulse shape and magnitude are generally not known in advance, as they depend on the particular vehicle characteristics, as well as on the specific scene structure and viewing conditions.

Robust detection cannot be accomplished by simple thresholding of the Activity signal; the signal should be examined within a sliding temporal window. This improves the effective SNR, the detection probability and the false alarm rate, at the cost of increased detection latency. The sliding window must therefore be short enough to maintain the warning time necessary for safe road crossing.

(a)   (b)

Fig. 3. Projection map, obtained by temporal averaging of the optical flow field over a training period. (3a) Sparse vector-field display. (3b) The flow direction in each pixel is mapped to hue, the magnitude to saturation. The color key is shown top-right.

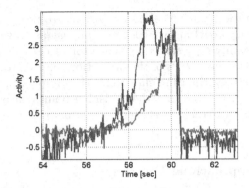

Fig. 4. Activity signal corresponding to an approaching vehicle, with (blue) and without (red) emphasizing the projection map magnitude near the vanishing point

Assume that the complete Activity pulse length is L; we wish to detect the presence of the pulse after $N \leq L$ samples are acquired. The warning is therefore delayed by N samples with respect to the first appearance of the approaching vehicle.

Within the temporal window of size N, suppose that there is either a traffic gap, such that the Activity is $A(n) = v(n)$, where $v(n)$ is a random noise process, or a vehicle initially appears, so $A(n) = s(n) + v(n)$, where $s(n)$ is the pulse shape corresponding to the specific vehicle and viewing conditions, referred to as the rising pulse. Temporal windows corresponding to earlier or later appearance of a vehicle are discussed in the sequel.

We formulate the 'TRAFFIC' and 'GAP' state hypotheses as follows:

$$
\begin{aligned}
H_1 &: A(n) = s(n) + v(n) \quad A(n) \sim \mathcal{N}\left(s(n), \sigma^2\right) \\
H_0 &: A(n) = v(n) \qquad\qquad A(n) \sim \mathcal{N}\left(0, \sigma^2\right)
\end{aligned}
\tag{2}
$$

where $A(n)$ is the Activity measurement and $v(n)$ is modelled as zero-mean additive white Gaussian noise (AWGN): $v(n) \sim \mathcal{N}\left(0, \sigma^2\right)$.

The samples $A(n)$ inside a sliding window of length N can be represented as a Gaussian random vector $\underline{y}$, with the following likelihood functions:

$$
\begin{aligned}
f_y(\underline{y}|\theta_1) &= \frac{1}{(2\pi)^{N/2}\sigma^N} \prod_{n=0}^{N-1} exp\left(-\frac{(a_n - s_n)^2}{2\sigma^2}\right) \\
f_y(\underline{y}|\theta_0) &= \frac{1}{(2\pi)^{N/2}\sigma^N} \prod_{n=0}^{N-1} exp\left(-\frac{a_n^2}{2\sigma^2}\right)
\end{aligned}
\tag{3}
$$

where we replaced the notations $A(n), S(n)$ by a_n, s_n. Applying a Likelihood Ratio Test for discriminating between the two hypotheses

$$LRT = \frac{\frac{1}{(2\pi)^{N/2}\sigma^N} \prod\limits_{n=0}^{N-1} exp\left(-\frac{(a_n - s_n)^2}{2\sigma^2}\right)}{\frac{1}{(2\pi)^{N/2}\sigma^N} \prod\limits_{n=0}^{N-1} exp\left(-\frac{a_n^2}{2\sigma^2}\right)} \gtrless \lambda \qquad (4)$$

where λ is a discriminative threshold, leads to the detection rule:

$$\sum_{n=0}^{N-1} a_n s_n \gtrless \frac{1}{2}\left(2\sigma^2 \ln\lambda + \sum_{n=0}^{N-1} s_n^2\right). \qquad (5)$$

The left hand side describes a correlator of the input Activity with the rising pulse template, and the right hand side is an application-dependent threshold. For determining the threshold, we apply the Neyman-Pearson criterion, which sets the threshold to maintain a given false-alarm probability.

The left hand side is a random Gaussian variable with variance $\sigma^2 \sum\limits_{n=0}^{N-1} s_n^2$, that we denote as $\tilde{y}$. The false-alarm probability is given by the tail distribution of the 'GAP' (θ_0) hypothesis:

$$P_{FA} = \int\limits_{\gamma}^{\infty} f_{\tilde{y}}(z|\theta_0)dz = Pr\left(\tilde{y} > \gamma|\theta_0\right) =$$

$$Pr\left(\frac{\tilde{y}}{\sigma\sqrt{\sum s_n^2}} > \gamma\frac{1}{\sigma\sqrt{\sum s_n^2}}\right) = Q\left(\frac{\gamma}{\sigma\sqrt{\sum s_n^2}}\right) = 1 - \phi\left(\frac{\gamma}{\sigma\sqrt{\sum s_n^2}}\right) \quad (6)$$

where $\phi(x)$ is the cumulative distribution function of the standard normal distribution and $Q(x)$ is its tail probability: $Q(x) = 1 - Q(-x) = 1 - \phi(x)$.

This yields a threshold $\gamma = Q^{-1}(P_{FA})\sigma\sqrt{\sum s_n^2}$ which can be determined by the SNR and the acceptable false-alarm rate. The detector can be described as

$$D(a_0, ..., a_{N-1}) \equiv \frac{\sum\limits_{n=0}^{N-1} a_n s_n}{\sum\limits_{n=0}^{N-1} s_n^2} \gtrless Q^{-1}(P_{FA})\sigma \qquad (7)$$

which is familiar as the result of applying a matched filter, correlating the input measurements with the known signal that we wish to detect. The corresponding probability of detection is:

$$P_D = Pr\left(\tilde{y} > \gamma|\theta_1\right) = ... = Q\left(Q^{-1}(P_{FA}) - \frac{\sqrt{\sum s_n^2}}{\sigma}\right) \qquad (8)$$

So far, we discussed the most challenging aspect of detection, the initial detection of an approaching vehicle. The detector is causal, hence the warning is delayed by N samples. Since the rising pulse typically increases as the vehicle approaches, once the correlator crosses the threshold, it remains above it as long as the pulse rises. To maintain continuous detection of vehicles until they reach the crossing, we extend the correlator window size beyond N as long as 'TRAFFIC' classifications are acquired, up to a maximal size not exceeding L. When vehicles appear late (e.g. leaving a parking spot close to the crossing), the rising pulse takes off at a rather high magnitude and the correlator immediately crosses the threshold.

3.3 Estimating Detector Parameters

The detector is parameterized by the noise variance (that can be estimated), and the expected shape of the activity pulse. During a training period, by the time the Projection Map is generated, the system produces Activity measurements. After sufficient training, the measurements are used to automatically generate the activity pulse model and estimate the noise variance.

The system scans the input signal acquired during training to locate its strongest local maxima, and crops a window of 10 seconds around each maximum, where most of the samples precede the maximum. The windows are batched together, and used to estimate the noise variance and activity pulse template. In practice, we model the rising pulse as the median of the cropped temporal windows. Fig. 5 illustrates the process.

4 Results

Fig. 6c shows snapshots from a day-time video sequence obtained by the system camera in a single-lane one-way street. Fig. 6a is the Activity signal corresponding to the same experimental session. Fig. 6b zooms on the time interval in which the snapshots shown in Fig. 6c were taken. The coloring of the graphs in Figs. 6a and 6b present the indication provided to the pedestrian, red meaning TRAFFIC and blue corresponding to GAP. As can be seen, TRAFFIC is declared 8-10 seconds before the vehicle reaches the camera, i.e., before the peak of the Activity signal, allowing safe crossing with substantial margin.

We recorded and annotated video taken from the system camera. For each vehicle, we noted its time of appearance t_A and its time of disappearance t_D, and calculated its apparent time interval $T_{ap} = t_D - t_A$. Obviously, T_{ap} sets an upper bound on the feasible warning time. The results were recorded with a modified USB camera and with an equivalent Point-and-Shoot camera. The USB camera is a standard webcam with its lens replaced to slightly narrow the field of view.

Ideally, a vehicle appears near the vanishing point, maximizing the feasible warning time. Note however that in certain urban or suburban scenes a vehicle can leave a parking spot within the field of view and close to the crossing, or might turn into the into the observed road from a nearby driveway. This means that while the apparent time T_{ap} of each vehicle can be more than 10 seconds, which is more than enough; however, in certain cases T_{ap} can be as short as one

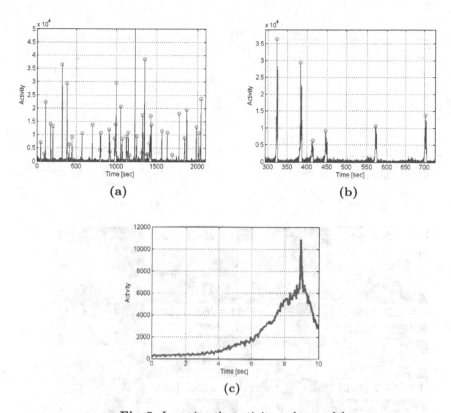

Fig. 5. Learning the activity pulse model

(5a) Activity signal over a 30 minutes training period, with the strongest local maxima detected. (5b) The same Activity results zoomed in for a few minutes of the training. (5c) The processed template that is used for correlation, generated as the median over the batch of windows.

second, allowing neither the system nor a human observer an adequate warning period.

Fig. 7 presents typical results. The activity signal is shown as a function of time. It is colored black where there is no traffic, and the system declares no warning (true negative, TN). It is colored blue where the system detects genuine incoming traffic (true positive, TP). As can be seen, practically all vehicles are detected. However, the detector is necessarily causal, inducing some latency. The time interval between the first appearance of a vehicle and the initial warning is colored green (false negative, FN). At certain points, false alarms (false positive, FP) appear, colored red. Fig. 8 demonstrates false negative and false positive events that were encountered.

For analysis, we executed the algorithm offline, on the recorded video, with various detector thresholds and settings. We register a single success per vehicle in case the detector issues a sufficiently early warning, meaning at most τ_{max}

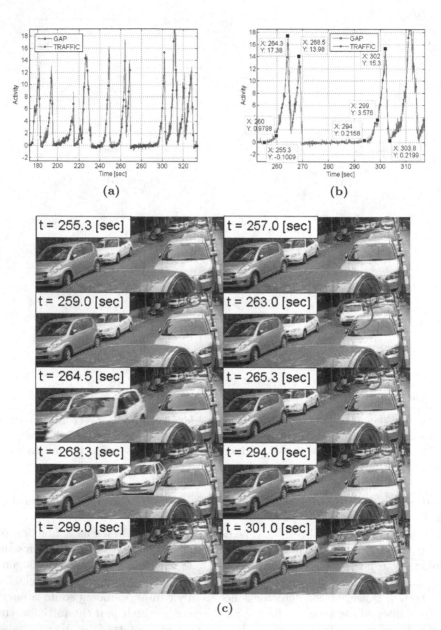

Fig. 6. Activity classification

(6a) Activity results for a typical scenario classified to TRAFFIC and GAP, colored red and blue respectively. (6b) The same Activity results expanded for a couple of approaching vehicles. (6c) Snapshots of the original video with time tags. The reader can observe that the TRAFFIC indication is declared very early, as soon as a vehicle appears.

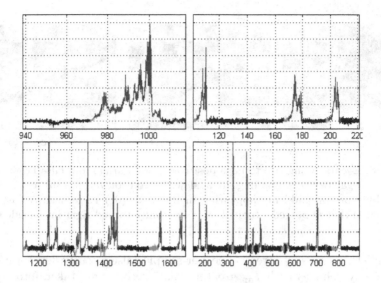

Fig. 7. Typical activity signal and classification of results

The plots describe the activity signal within four time intervals; time is labeled in seconds along the horizontal axis. The signal is colored according to the output of the system and the ground truth (true negative: black; true positive: blue; false negative: green; false positive: red).

seconds after initial appearance or at least 7 seconds before reaching the crossing. The value τ_{max} corresponds to the window size N (the minimal feasible warning time delay).

We constructed per-vehicle ROC curves based on comparison with the ground truth data. We calculate the True Positive Rate as the fraction of successes out of the total number of incoming vehicles:

$$TPR = \frac{TP}{TP + FN} = \frac{N_s}{N_{tot}} \tag{9}$$

where N_s is the number of successes and N_{tot} is the total number of vehicles. We calculate the False Positive Rate as

$$FPR = \frac{FP}{FP + TN} \tag{10}$$

where the values are previously defined and taken *per-sample* from the full recording. Note that defining the false positive rate per-sample is very severe, since even an isolated outlying false positive reading, that can easily be detected and eliminated without significant effect on the true positive rate, is registered.

Fig. 9 presents a sample of analysis results. Fig. 9a shows the per-vehicle ROC curves for a few window sizes N, corresponding to 1 to 3 second durations. Fig. 9b is the histogram (distribution) of the advance warning times over 1 hour

(a)   (b)   (c)

Fig. 8. Events giving rise to false positives (false alarms) and false negatives
(8a) False negative corresponding to a slow, distant bicyclist. (8b) False positive
induced by a person suddenly appearing in the road. (8c) False negative associated
with a vehicle that appeared, stopped, and eventually turned right into a side street.

in a single-lane one-way street. The per-sample false positive level was set to
0.01 and only vehicles with T_{ap} greater than 7 seconds are taken into account.
Short warning times corresponded to slowly driving vehicles, including bicycles.
By allowing a higher per-sample false positive level, most of the slow vehicles
can be detected substantially earlier.

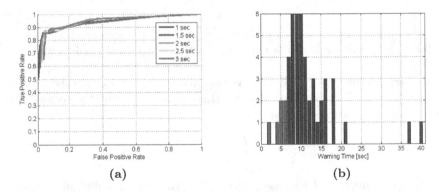

(a)   (b)

Fig. 9. Analysis results
(9a) Per-vehicle ROC curves for a few window sizes N, corresponding to intervals
between 1 second to 3 seconds. (9b) Warning times histogram covering 1 hour in a
single-lane one-way street.

5   Discussion

We presented a computationally-lean system to detect and alert pedestrians of
vehicles approaching a road-crossing. The system automatically adapts to the
scene, and can be mounted on existing street infrastructure, facilitating simple

installation. The system is designed primarily for blind and visually impaired people, but can potentially assist the young and the old, people with cognitive impairments, and others.

We implemented the system on a standard laptop PC, and also ported it on BeagleBoard xM hardware running Linux. An Android version using low-cost smartphone/tablet-like hardware is planned.

We tested the system at several locations, and achieved advance warning times approaching 9 seconds at typical day conditions with a rather wide field of view lens, slightly less at night scenarios. These results are promising, because a standard US two-lane street takes only about 7 seconds to cross. Night and poor weather conditions were examined succinctly and further experiments and analysis need to be conducted.

A single instance of the system is capable of detecting traffic approaching from a given direction and ignore distancing traffic. Full support of two-way traffic requires two instances of the system, mounted in opposite directions, preferably with a unified decision and pedestrian interface module.

Time to Contact (TTC) estimation, based on Horn *et al* [8], was also tested. As in our approach, it processes entire frames and yields a scalar signal, that could be considered as an alternative to the proposed Activity signal. The results were noisy and unstable compared to the results obtained using the suggested Activity measure.

Learning is an essential aspect of the system, including the generation of the projection map and the activity pulse model. The straightforward training and learning solutions employed in the current design leave room for sophisticated improvements.

The suggested approach is unique in being stationary and location-specific. The absence of ego-motion leads to a solution that is both robust and low-cost. Any person approaching the road crossing can take advantage of the system, with no need for a personally owned device such as a smartphone or a smart cane. This widens the potential reach of the system to weak parts of the society.

References

1. Amedi, A.: Virtual cane for the visually impaired, presented at the international presidential conference, June 2011. http://blog.imric.org/blog/sidney/virtual-cane-visually-impaired-presented-international-presidential-conference
2. American Association of State Highway and Transportation Officials: A Policy on geometric design of highways and streets. Washington, D.C. (2004)
3. Barlow, J., Bentzen, B., Tabor, L.: Accessible Pedestrian Signals: Synthesis and Guide to Best Practice. National Cooperative Highway Research Program (2003)
4. Bohonos, S., Lee, A., Malik, A., Thai, C., Manduchi, R.: Universal real-time navigational assistance (URNA): an urban bluetooth beacon for the blind. In: Proceedings of the 1st ACM SIGMOBILE International Workshop on Systems and Networking Support for Healthcare and Assisted Living Environments, HealthNet 2007, pp. 83–88. ACM, New York (2007)

5. Crandall, W., Bentzen, B., Myerss, L., Brabyn, J.: New orientation and accessibility option for persons with visual impairment: transportation applications for remote infrared audible signage. Clinical and Experimental Optometry **84**, 120–131 (2001)
6. Emerson, R., Sauerburger, D.: Detecting approaching vehicles at streets with no traffic control. Journal of Visual Impairment & Blindness **102**(12), 747 (2008)
7. Fallon, J.: Systems and methods for laser radar imaging for the blind and visually impaired (2008)
8. Horn, B., Fang, Y., Masaki, I.: Time to contact relative to a planar surface. In: Intelligent Vehicles Symposium, pp. 68–74. IEEE, June 2007
9. Ivanchenko, V., Coughlan, J., Shen, H.: Crosswatch: a camera phone system for orienting visually impaired pedestrians at traffic intersections. In: Miesenberger, K., Klaus, J., Zagler, W.L., Karshmer, A.I. (eds.) ICCHP 2008. LNCS, vol. 5105, pp. 1122–1128. Springer, Heidelberg (2008)
10. Kay, L.: A sonar aid to enhance spatial perception of the blind: engineering design and evaluation. Radio and Electronic Engineer **44** (1974)
11. Lee, D.: A theory of visual control of braking based on information about time-to-collision. Perception **5**(4), 437–459 (1976)
12. Lucas, B., Kanade, T.: An iterative image registration technique with an application to stereo vision. In: Proceedings of the 7th International Joint Conference on Artificial Intelligence, vol. 2, pp. 674–679. Morgan Kaufmann Publishers Inc., San Francisco (1981)
13. Pun, T., Roth, P., Bologna, G., Moustakas, K., Tzovaras, D.: Image and video processing for visually handicapped people. J. Image Video Process. **2007**, 4:1–4:12 (2007)
14. Sauerburger, D.: Developing criteria and judgment of safety for crossing streets with gaps in traffic. Journal of Visual Impairment & Blindness **93**(7), 447–450 (1999)
15. Senst, T., Eiselein, V., Sikora, T.: II-LK – a real-time implementation for sparse optical flow. In: Campilho, A., Kamel, M. (eds.) ICIAR 2010, Part I. LNCS, vol. 6111, pp. 240–249. Springer, Heidelberg (2010)
16. Shioyama, T., Uddin, M.: Detection of pedestrian crossings with projective invariants from image data. Measurement Science and Technology **15**(12), 2400 (2004)

Personal Shopping Assistance and Navigator System for Visually Impaired People

Paul Chippendale[1], Valeria Tomaselli[2]($\boxtimes$), Viviana D'Alto[3], Giulio Urlini[3],
Carla Maria Modena[1], Stefano Messelodi[1], Sebastiano Mauro Strano[2],
Günter Alce[4], Klas Hermodsson[4], Mathieu Razafimahazo[5], Thibaud Michel[5],
and Giovanni Maria Farinella[6]

[1] Fondazione Bruno Kessler, Trento, Italy
[2] STMicroelectronics, Catania, Italy
valeria.tomaselli@st.com
[3] STMicroelectronics, Milano, Italy
[4] Sony Mobile Communications, Lund, Sweden
[5] Inria Grenoble - Rhône-Alpes/LIG, Montbonnot-Saint-Martin, France
[6] Image Processing Laboratory (IPLAB), University of Catania, Catania, Italy

Abstract. In this paper, a personal assistant and navigator system for visually impaired people will be described. The showcase presented intends to demonstrate how partially sighted people could be aided by the technology in performing an ordinary activity, like going to a mall and moving inside it to find a specific product. We propose an Android application that integrates Pedestrian Dead Reckoning and Computer Vision algorithms, using an off-the-shelf Smartphone connected to a Smartwatch. The detection, recognition and pose estimation of specific objects or features in the scene derive an estimate of user location with sub-meter accuracy when combined with a hardware-sensor pedometer. The proposed prototype interfaces with a user by means of Augmented Reality, exploring a variety of sensorial modalities other than just visual overlay, namely audio and haptic modalities, to create a seamless immersive user experience. The interface and interaction of the preliminary platform have been studied through specific evaluation methods. The feedback gathered will be taken into consideration to further improve the proposed system.

Keywords: Assistive technology · Indoor navigation · Visually impaired · Augmented reality · Mobile devices · Wearable cameras · Quality of experience

1 Introduction

Data from the World Health Organization [1] reports that 285 million people are visually impaired worldwide: 39 million are blind and 246 million have low vision. Although about 80% of all visual impairments can be avoided or cured, as a result of increasing elderly population more people will be at risk of age-related

© Springer International Publishing Switzerland 2015
L. Agapito et al. (Eds.): ECCV 2014 Workshops, Part III, LNCS 8927, pp. 375–390, 2015.
DOI: 10.1007/978-3-319-16199-0_27

low vision. In fact, about 65% of all people who are partially sighted are aged 50 and above. Hence, systems that help with navigation in unfamiliar environments are crucial for increasing the autonomous life of visually impaired people.

We present a hardware/software platform, based on Android OS, integrating outdoor/indoor navigation, visual context awareness and Augmented Reality (AR) to demonstrate how visually impaired people could be aided by new technologies to perform ordinary activity, such as going to a mall to buy a specific product. In particular, indoor navigation poses significant challenges. The major problem is that the signals used by outdoor locating technologies (e.g. GPS) are often inadequate in this environment. Some solutions available exploit the Earth's magnetic field [9], using magnetometers available in Smartphone and relying on maps of magnetic fields; some other solutions rely on the identification of nearby WiFi access points [28], [10], but do not provide sufficient accuracy to discriminate between individual rooms in a building. An alternative approach is Pedestrian Dead Reckoning (PDR) [24], [21]. It composes an inertial navigation system based on step information to estimate the position of the pedestrian. The proposed system integrates a PDR-based system with computer vision algorithms to help people to be independent both indoor and outdoor. The implemented Pedestrian Dead Reckoning uses advanced map-matching algorithms for refining the user's trajectory and also her/his orientation, thus resulting in a significant enhancement of the final estimated position. Computer vision provides nowadays several methods for the recognition of specific objects; users with visual disabilities could benefit from this technology but, unfortunately, the success often relies upon the user being able to point the camera toward the object of interest, that must cover the major part of the image. If the object is embedded in a complex scene and its apparent size is only few pixels, the available recognition apps, usually, fail. The proposed visual target detectors can detect and localize an object of interest inside a complex scene, and also estimate its distance from the user, which is particularly helpful for the guide of a visually impaired person.

The proposed system aims also to provide an AR experience to the user; reality augmentation is not only about visual overlays, but it also encompasses other sensorial modalities. By restricting the modes of AR feedback to the user, i.e. to only non-visual means, the demonstrator leverages on audio and haptic modalities. Differently from the current AR experience which tends to be rather cumbersome and obtrusive to the user, we aim to create a seamless immersive user experience, hiding technology complexity from the user.

Another challenging goal of this project is to deliver pertinent information in a 'user' rather than a 'device' centric way. User experience understanding is essential to make assistive technology really useful, non-obtrusive and pervasive. Assistive technologies for visually impaired people cannot rely solely on design guidelines for traditional user interfaces. Quality of Experience will thus be guaranteed by iteratively performing user studies, to get insights into social acceptance and to receive feedback for further developments.

The remainder of this paper is organized as follows: Section 2 will describe the use case addressed by the proposed system, with reference to a generic storyboard and the actual implementation; in Section 3 all of the exploited hardware and software technologies will be presented; then, in Section 4, the user experience evaluation methodologies will be described, analyzing results and points to be improved; finally conclusions will be drawn in Section 5.

2 Use Case

The use case takes the form of a navigator for visually impaired people, capable of guiding a user through different elements of a mall, until she/he finds a shop to buy a specific product. The implementation of this use case requires a hardware/software platform capable of integrating the hardware-sensor pedometer with algorithms that elaborate visual inputs. Beyond the provision of a location and orientation estimate inside the mall, the system also detects possible hazards in the path of the user and is capable of routing a partially sighted user towards the desired goal. To build such a complex platform, the use case was firstly described by means of a storyboard and then it was broken down into elementary parts, each one representing a section of the path, each characterized by a specific set of algorithms (and problems) for location and navigation, in order to solve them in a tractable manner. The following subsections will describe the storyboard and the real implementation, which has been installed in a large office building to test the whole hardware/software system, which will be called VeDi.

2.1 Storyboard

The addressed use case is focused on Marc who suffers from retinitis pigments, meaning that his visual acuity has been reduced to 20/400 in his best eye. Marc finds it difficult to find exactly what he wants in the shops nowadays. It's his nephew's 12th birthday tomorrow, and he would like to buy him his favourite toy, Lego. He searches on the Internet and finds a good price at the 'Super Shopping Mall' in the Toys 'R Us shop. From 'Google directions' he knows that Bus 73 will take him from his home to the Shopping Mall. He downloads all the maps necessary for the navigation outside and inside the shopping mall onto his VeDi device. After taking the correct bus to the shopping mall Marc arrives at the bus stop nearest to it. Once he steps off the bus, as his VeDi device knew his destination and had pre-downloaded the building plan from OpenStreetMap [2], VeDi guides him to the entrance. The VeDi device drives Marc from the entrance of the mall to the elevator that will bring Marc to the floor of the mall where the toy shop is located. Marc senses there is a potential danger sign in front of him, he stops and asks the VeDi device for confirmation. The VeDi device visually detects the wet floor warning sign and provides an audio alert "walk slowly". VeDi directs Marc to the closest lift, as this is the safest path to the specific shop that VeDi believes Marc needs. VeDi guides him to the buttons using visual cues and then guides Marc's hand to make sure he presses the correct button. As Marc has had normal vision for most of his life, he has a good mental picture of the environment, but the re-assurances provided by VeDi makes his trip to the mall less stressful. The target floor in this scenario is the second floor. The lift doesn't have aural feedback but VeDi sees that Marc pressed the correct floor button, so Marc gets out of the lift on the correct floor. A lot of people are present in the mall's main thoroughfare and, as a result, VeDi replans a route for Marc that should be quieter. Marc is safely guided to the correct shop and from its entrance to the Lego shelves where he can find his gift. Once in front of the toy shelf, VeDi sees that there are several boxes close together and the platform scans the shelf and detects candidate positions where the desired toy might be. Marc orients his VeDi in front of the shelf until the desired box is found.

2.2   Use Case Implementation

For the sake of simplicity and repeatability, the demo was executed in a large office building, guiding a user from the bus stop, through the main entrance to an office located on another floor via a lift. The use case demo has been divided into several phases, which are listed below:

1. In the first phase the user is guided through the outdoor section of the route from a bus stop to the sliding doors representing the entrance of the mall; a PDR system uses the Smartphone's accelerometers to evaluate the foot-steps of the user, guiding her/him through the path;
2. The second phase guides the user through the main hall towards the lift using only a Visual Navigator, searching for specific visual beacons (like signs or environmental features) in order to identify the optimal direction and frequently making a distance estimate to them;
3. The third phase of the guidance ensures that the visually impaired person correctly uses the lift and its external and internal buttons to the first floor. It visual searches for the button panel and then tracks the user's finger to the correct button to be pressed;
4. The fourth phase restarts the navigation on the first floor and dynamically selectes the best path for the user, through an understanding of whether a corridor is crowded by people or not; a re-route then is offered in order to avoid crowded areas/corridors in favour of freer passages;
5. The fifth phase starts as soon as a free corridor is detected, and a Structure from Motion algorithm is activated for predicting the movement of the user with respect to a starting point. Any drift introduced by the algorithm is compensated by the PDR;
6. The sixth phase starts when the user is in the vicinity of the shop. The toy shop sign over the door is visually recognized as well as the logo LEGO that identifies the target shelves for the demo;
7. Finally, the demo involves the search for a specific "target box", recognizing it amongst other boxes.

3   Technologies Inside the Demonstrator

The implementation of the use case required a great integration effort, bringing together and mixing different types of algorithms to produce a refined estimate of user pose and position.

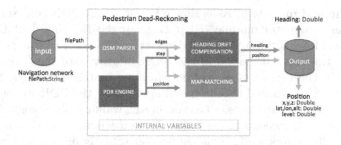

Fig. 1. Pedestrian Dead Reckoning block diagram

The system was also intended as a test-bench to assess different computer vision algorithms and user interfaces to determine user satisfaction. We were able to highlight pro and cons for each methodology and to generate guidelines for further developments.

3.1 Mobile Hardware/Software Platforms

A Sony Xperia Z device [3] was selected as the principal hardware platform, together with the Sony Smartwatch as an alternative input-output device. All of the phases of the demonstrator have been implemented as Android applications, called by a main application. To be really useful for visually impaired users, all of the implemented algorithms were tested and customized to meet real-time requirements. Aural feedback methods were evaluated by the users, fed to them in the form of alerts, suggestions, instructions, primarily through the Text To Speech (TTS) Android engine. The Smartwatch was used to trigger the various phases of the demonstration, and the display on the phone was used as an explanation for guests at demonstrations, since all instructions to the user were acoustic or vibration.

3.2 Pedestrian Dead Reckoning

PDR was used to guide the user from the bus stop to the entrance of the office block. Although in the outdoor context, GPS could have been utilised, we wanted to demonstrate how a pedometer-based system could provide sub two-metre accuracy, as urban environments often deliver poor GPS accuracy. The PDR system is based on a combination of an inertial measurement unit, map-matching and advanced positioning algorithms. Building on the PDR approach proposed in [15], the proposed PDR uses MEMS and the CPU embedded in a Smartphone. The PDR solution includes walking and standing identification, step detection, stride length estimation, and a position calculation with a heading angular sensor. The localization of the pedestrian is estimated using the tri-axial accelerometer, gyro and magnetometers. Step detection and walking distance are obtained by accelerometers while the azimuth is computed by the fusion of gyro and map data. As is shown in Fig. 1, the PDR consists of 3 main modules: the pedometer module (PDR Engine), the Heading drift Compensation and the Map matching. The pedometer counts each step a person takes by detecting the vertical motion of the centre of gravity of the body, searching for patterns in the vertical acceleration which are matched to steps. Speed and stride length are associated to a step and are used by the PDR to compute new positions [22]. Since each person has a different walking physiological model, a calibration phase is needed to estimate the step length. The calibration stage consists of a 30 meters walk. This calibration value is unique and reflects the walking characteristics of each pedestrian. Map data is also used to enhance the information provided by the PDR through a process known as map-aided positioning. Map-matching is one of the key elements to be used with a PDR module to obtain a more precise localization. Thanks to the structured indoor environment (straight lines defined by corridors and walls, with dominant directions), a user's trajectory can be matched to an edge described in the OpenStreetMap format, and a projected position can be determined. This map-matching is not widely used in PDR projects but it brings a better accuracy to CV algorithms. Because of numeric integration, the device direction computed from gyroscope attitude drifts, and hence a Heading Drift Compensation (HDC) algorithm [12], using map data, has been implemented. This algorithm uses straight-line features from the OpenStreetMap navigation network to correct, when possible, the heading derived from the gyroscope. At each detected step the HDC method finds the nearest straight-line from user's position and determines the offset to be applied to the heading.

3.3   Visual Navigator

The Visual Navigator is activated as soon as the user reaches the entrance of the building. This module coordinates one or more Visual Target Detectors and interacts with the visually impaired user to instruct her/him to safely reach a predefined destination. The interaction is managed by means of spoken messages (from the system to the user) and via a Smartwatch (bidirectional). The Visual Navigator receives, from the main application, a list of visual target detectors to be activated, in sequence or in parallel, in order to reach a set of local destinations. It notifies the user as soon as a target is detected in the scene, it communicates the direction to follow in order to reach it, and the action needed to pass from one target to the next. Moreover, the navigator warns the user in the case that dangerous situations are detected (i.e. a wet floor sign), vibrating the Smartwatch.

The Visual Target Detector module is capable of detecting and localizing a specified target within the visual range of the Smartphone camera. A target can be single- or multi-parts and its structure is encoded as a custom description file (xml format). The description file stores information about the number of sub-parts, their shape/size in the real world (represented by polylines) and the spatial relationships between them. The different parts are assumed to be co-planar. In Fig. 2a one can see a visual representation of the geometric structure

Fig. 2. (a) Geometric structure of a target, (b) Projection of the target structure on the image according to the estimated homography for the OutsideLiftButtons and (c) for the InsideLiftButtons detectors

of a multi-part target taken from an xml description. For each part, a specialized detection routine can also be specified in the xml file.

The Visual Target Detector works as follows:

- Specialized routines are applied to the input camera image to obtain a list of candidates for each part;
- Combinations of candidates are analysed in order to select the one most compatible with the target structure, taking into account the homography that maps the coordinates of the candidate regions to the real world one;
- The homography corresponding to the best combination is used to localize each part of the input image and to estimate the pose of the camera with respect to the target (using camera calibration data). The introduction of a multi-part target enables the detector to be robust to partial occlusions, a useful feature especially in the case of detecting lift buttons which can be covered by the user's hand.

Using fast template matching methods [27], text in scene algorithms [25] and skin detection techniques [20], we have developed nine detectors, seven of them are composed of a single part (WetFloor, FBK_panel, AR_Logo, LiftSign, ToyShop, LegoLogo, FingerTip) and two are composed of several parts (InsideLiftButtons, OutsideLiftButtons), see Fig. 3.

The Visual Navigator can activate Visual Target Detectors as desired. Initially in the demonstrator, it guides the user from the office entrance to the lift. Along the route, it checks for the presence of a wet floor sign (if found it warns the user). Once the first landmark (FBK_panel) is detected, the user is guided towards it by means of spoken messages with the purpose of maintaining the target in the middle part of the camera's field of view. When the estimated distance between the user and the target falls below two meters the Visual Navigator launches the AR_logo detector. In a similar way, the system looks for the target and guides the user towards it. Again, when the distance is below 0.8

Fig. 3. Example of detectable targets

meters, the LiftSign detector is activated and the user is instructed to aim the camera in the correct direction in order to look for the lift sign. When the estimated distance of the target falls below 2 meters, the user is deemed to be close to the lift. The user is then invited to turn right to search for the button pad of the lift and the corresponding detector is activated (OutsideLiftButtons). When the user is close enough, she/he is invited to touch the button pad with a finger and the FingerTip detector is enabled. The system estimates the position of the fingertip with respect to the "arrow up" button and instructs the user how to move her/his finger, until finally the finger covers the correct button. The Visual Navigator invites the user to press the button and to wait for the lift. When the user enters the lift and taps the Smartwatch confirming to be inside, the Visual Navigator enables the InsideLiftButtons detector and the FingerTip detector is used to guide the user's finger to reach and press the "Floor 1" button. The Visual Navigator is again reactivated when the user is in the proximity of the toyshop. It then launches the ToyShop detector and guides the user towards the shop entrance. Finally, when the user is confirmed to be inside the shop, by tapping the Smartwatch, the LegoLogo detector is launched, and the navigator guides the user towards the Lego boxes shelf. A template matching algorithm, exploiting local features, allows the user to find the desired box.

3.4 Scene Classification

In the scenario of indoor navigation and shopping assistance, algorithms which exploit visual cues are fundamental for recognizing some contingent events, that cannot be derived only from the map of the building and the user's position. For this reason, a visual scene classification algorithm has also been integrated into the system for detecting if a certain path is crowded, in order to perform a re-routing and help the visually impaired person to walk in a freer area, and also to detect if the user's device is facing an aisle or a shelf, inside the shop. The scene classification module can detect a set of different semantic classes, decided a priori during a training phase, extracting information from the images. Different problems should be considered in designing a scene recognition engine to be implemented on a mobile device for personal assistance: memory limitation, low computational power and very low latency, to achieve real-time recognition. In a recent work [18], the DCT-GIST image representation model has been introduced to summarize the context of the scene. Images are holistically represented starting from the statistics collected in the Discrete Cosine Transform (DCT) domain. Since the DCT coefficients are already available within the digital signal processor for the JPEG conversion, the proposed solution obtains an instant and "free of charge" image signature. This novel image representation considers the Laplacian shape of the DCT coefficient distributions, as demonstrated in [23], and summarizes the context of the scene by the scale parameters. The recognition results, obtained by classifying this image representation with Support Vector Machines [14], closely match state-of-the-art methods (such as GIST [26]) in terms of recognition accuracy, but the complexity of the scene recognition system is greatly reduced. For these reasons, this approach has been specialized for the classes needed by the defined use case. More specifically, the indoor navigation scenario could take advantage from the recognition of 4 different categories:

1. Crowded/Non-crowded;
2. Aisle/Shelf

A database has been built downloading images from the Internet and chosing about 600 samples per class; images have been chosen to represent real conditions, in terms of variety of illumination, location, etc.; then the database has been used to train 2 SVM classifiers for detecting each pair of categories. A cross-validation approach was used for assessing the performances of the algorithm on these classes. In particular, ten training and testing phases were executed for each pair of classes: at each iteration 90% of the database is used for training and the remaining 10% for testing. Finally, the global accuracy is obtained by averaging the accuracies of the ten cross-validation phases. Results are reported in Table 1.

It is quite evident that the DCT-GIST scene representation has very good performance on classes required by the indoor navigation and personal assistance system, and it is suitable for real-time applications. This algorithm was integrated with the heading information from the pedometer to provide the user with instructions for turning to her/his right and left to explore which corridor is less crowded; then the freer passage is chosen to continue the navigation.

Table 1. Scene classification results on the categories needed by the use case

	Crowded	Non-Crowded		Aisle	Shelf
Crowded	0.95	0.05	Aisle	0.93	0.07
Non-Crowded	0.04	0.96	Shelf	0.07	0.93

3.5   Structure from Motion

Navigation from the lift exit to the shop entrance is achieved by a SfM algorithm, integrated with some information from the PDR. As shown in Fig. 4, the implemented SfM pipeline consists of two main blocks. The first one processes the incoming images, in order to identify salient elements in a scene, like corners, and tracks them in the sequence to obtain a sparse optical flow. We compute a set of features per frame and generate the Optical Flow (OF) using descriptors (i.e. a vector of coefficients, able to characterize the pixels around a corner) which are compared during the matching phase, thanks to a specific function to verify an association's correctness [13]. The second block, also called the Geometry stage, uses geometric relations (like the epipolar constraint), to estimate the camera position and orientation by processing the OF produced in the previous phase. This strategy processes 2D-2D associations, finally computing a fundamental matrix thanks to a family of algorithms called N-points algorithms, where "N" indicates the number of random points engaged in the estimation of a camera pose. To obtain a robust solution, RANSAC [19] is combined with an N-points algorithm, and then the corners are triangulated to obtain a sparse 3D representation of the environment (3D Map).

A fundamental assumption, for a successful reconstruction, is the knowledge of internal camera parameters. The procedure is achieved by estimating the camera's focal length, the centre of the image and the lens distortion through the prior acquisition of a set of images framing a checkerboard. This functionality has been integrated inside the application in order to easily recalibrate the system, each time the demo is installed on a new Android device.

The SfM reconstructions are scaled in order to fit the reconstruction into the real world, this is done by fusing visual information to inertial sensor data. In this way, the SfM trajectory is rescaled using the PDR pedometer step size information, discussed in Section 3.2. This real-time rescaling enables a conversion of the user's position from euclidean space to geographical space.

4   User Experience Evaluation

Beyond the indoor navigation and augmented reality experience, it is clear that future assistive applications will also need new interaction and application mod-

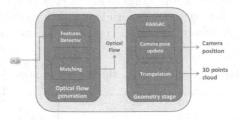

Fig. 4. Pipeline of the Structure from Motion approach

els to facilitate new forms of communication and meet increasingly high user expectations [11]. This is a huge challenge since assistive technologies for visually impaired people cannot rely on design guidelines for traditional user interfaces. New user interfaces permit interaction techniques that are often very different from standard WIMP (Windows, Icons, Menus, Pointer) based user interfaces [17]. Digital augmentation, in general, can include different senses such as sight, hearing and touch, hence they must be realized with an array of different types of input and output modalities such as gestures, eye-tracking and speech. Aspects such as: finding out how well a user performs tasks in different contexts; letting the user interact with natural interfaces; and hiding the complexity of the technology; are central to ensure good quality applications and a good user experience. In the light of these considerations, during the development of the navigator, user studies in indoor and outdoor scenario were conducted to assess social acceptance and to receive feedback for further developments. Aural guidance effectiveness was evaluated, conducting preliminary tests with blind and visually impaired people to receive proper feedback, as described in Sec. 4.1. A visualization was also created and evaluated, prior to the completion of the demonstrator, as described in Sec. 4.2. The received feedback drove the development in the last part of the implementation providing the improvement of the audio interface and the rules the device should use in these types of applications. The last evaluation, performed by experts in the field, was done when the entire system was integrated (Sec. 4.3). Ideally, the system should have been evaluated with a user study of visually impaired people. This was unfortunately not possible for all of the phases, but only for the outdoor navigation part, but it is recommended as future work to fully understand the improvements needed to fulfil the needs of the intended user group.

4.1 Evaluation of the Aural Guidance

During the development of the system, an analysis of the aural guidance technology was conducted, with several tests in the field:

1. March, 2013: Indoor and outdoor tests in Grenoble, with Alain De Borniol who is visually impaired (president of the association ACP: Accès Cible Production) and Thomas Marmol (blind son of Bruno Marmol, IT manager at INRIA);
2. April, 2013: Indoor tests at INRIA Rhône-Alpes with Christine Perey, sighted and chair of the AR Standards Community;
3. June, 2013: Indoor tests in Sugimotocho railway station and outdoor tests in Osaka city with visually impaired students from the school for the blind.

After these studies, feedback was collected:

1. Let the user choose their favourite text-to-speech engine for the navigation application;
2. Audio instructions are too long;

3. Prefer right, left, in-front or behind terms instead of using indications in degrees;
4. Make the application compliant with Google Talkback [4];
5. Interactions with the Smartphone are difficult during navigation; when possible a remote controller would be appreciated;
6. Instructions must be repeatable.

According to this feedback, some corrective actions have been implemented: first of all the application has been modified to take into account the chosen TTS engine in the general Android settings, instead of the default one (Pico TTS); guidance instructions have been focused on the nearby environment (5 meters for indoor and 20 meters for outdoor); audio instructions were changed, in accordance to feedback 3 and compliance with Talkback was guaranteed. To satisfy requirement 5, the application was modified to interact with different external devices, such as a headset, an ear set and a watch; further tests should be conducted to decide which external devices are the most suitable. Finally, to solve issue 6, the application was modified to permit the user to ask for the latest instruction by a simple pressure on the watch, the headset or the ear set.

4.2   Evaluation on the Visualization

The implemented use case consists of multiple phases. To avoid the fragmentation of the whole demonstrator, it was decided to try to visualize it before its final integration. Visualization has the objective to elicit feedback in areas that potentially require additional development. It was decided to simulate the personal assistance demonstrator using a Wizard of Oz (WOZ) approach. The WOZ prototyping method is particularly useful to explore user interfaces for pervasive, ubiquitous, or AR systems that combine complex sensing and intelligent control logic and is widely used in human-computer interaction research [16]. The idea behind this method is that a second person can simulate the missing parts of a system. Hence, it was decided to use the WOZ tool called WozARd [8], [5], to simulate the system and do a pre-evaluation prior to development completion. All phases (see Sec. 2.2) were setup at Lund University, Sweden. Two Xperia Z phones were used; one by the test leader (Wizard) and one was attached to a backpack, carried by the subject. The subject wore a Smartwatch to interact with the application. A video showing the simulation of the demonstrator can be found in [6]. The subject's eyes were covered and everything was recorded with a video camera. At the end of the experiment, suggestions and issues emerged from the video. The first suggestion was to start an application with a long press on the Smartwatch to activate a "voice menu" saying "Lego shopping", "walking home", etc.. The start of the Tour could also be initiated through scanning a NFC tag. The user should be allowed to skip assistance for a certain phase (but hazard detecting remain running), because he could be bored by excessive indications. When a new phase is started, feedback or summary might be needed; the information should tell the user what will come next from that point to the next phase. In front of the elevator, it would be better not to guide the hand but instead tell the user "you can now call the elevator" when her/his hand is on the correct button. The guidance to the correct product, requires the user to take the phone and use it to search the shelves. When the product is found, maybe it would be good to allow for product ID confirmation through a NFC or barcode scan as well as have user confirmation that she/he has completed the product navigation part. Moreover, a general improvement would be gained by a careful design interaction paradigm for watch, phone and voice input: each command on the watch (e.g. double tap, long press, swipe left, etc.) could activate a different action, but it is fundamental to avoid accidental selections.

4.3   Expert Evaluation

The VeDi system has been developed taking the recommendations in Sections 4.1 and 4.2 into account. The hardware/software platform was presented and demonstrated for expert evaluation in December 2013. The demonstrator was adapted for that location, hence the outdoor and indoor navigation would need modifications to replicate it in other locations. The evaluation was conducted through invited experts, from the Haptimap EU project [7], with extensive experience in navigation systems and with visually impaired people. As is commonly done in user experience reviews, the following review feedback concentrates solely on issues found during the demonstration, for deriving suggestions to improve the system.

1. **Tutorial/help.** The current version of the system does not have any manual or tutorial. Without an extensive tutorial or manual it is unlikely that a user that has never used the system can use it. To learn the system before using it would be important since live usage will contain situations where user misunderstandings may lead to dangerous or at least socially awkward situations, which may result in low interest in using the system again.
2. **System latency.** Some parts require the system to perform heavy computations in order to deliver instruction to the user. In these situations the instructions arrive a little late. During this delay the user moves and makes the next instruction incorrect. Each part of the system should be tested and delays measured. Viable solutions may vary depending on situations and delays. One solution could be to make the user aware of system latency and advise her/him when to move slowly. Another solution could be to change the duration and type of feedback to minimize the delay effect. In the worst case, some delays render the assistance unacceptable and the system must improve to become usable.
3. **Camera orientation.** Some algorithms need the Smartphone to be in landscape mode, whilst others require portrait. The system was designed to be worn in a chest harness so that the user has both hands available for other tasks. It is highly recommended that all algorithms can function in portrait mode to avoid the need to switch orientation.
4. **Amount and type of instructions.** The system has many audio-based instructions and feedback sounds. Visually impaired people use their hearing

to compensate for their lack of full vision. For these people, audio may cause a high cognitive workload and many visually impaired people react negatively to using heavy audio solutions. It is recommended to keep the duration and amount of audio instructions to a minimum yet on an understandable level, a clear design challenge. Users with different experience levels of the system or in different locations may require different amounts of instructions. For example, if a routine has been carried out daily for months, a user may not require the same number of confirmations that a new user would need. It is recommended that the system have different levels of verbosity and a way for the user to control it.

5. **Assistance versus instructions.** The goal of a navigation assistant for visually impaired people is to give autonomy and personal freedom to the person. If this is the case should this autonomy also be from the assistant itself? It is the experience of the reviewers that the assistance desired by the visually impaired is a case of personal preference. It is recommended that the system enables users to choose alternative paths or activities during assistance. You could think of the system as a store clerk that you can ask for recommendations but the decision is still up to the user.

5   Conclusions

A hardware/software system for guiding a visually impaired person through a building to a store shelf to find a specific item was presented. We showed an integration of vision-based with pedestrian localization systems and how we created an assistant for indoor/outdoor navigation. Building this system required a large integration effort to merge all the vision-based algorithms with hardware-sensor pedometer, to derive a constant estimate of the user's position. Algorithms were also chosen and customized to meet real-time execution requirements, which is crucial for assistive technologies on mobile devices. Many user studies were conducted during the project evolution and corrective actions were applied to the final demonstrator. Moreover, an expert review of the final demonstrator resulted in a number of recommendations that could be used to significantly improve the usability of the system. Our research has confirmed that building a technology for the assistance of the visually impaired requires a deep user study to iteratively assess user satisfaction and then to bring improvements and corrections to the system accordingly.

Acknowledgments. This research is being funded by the European 7th Framework Program, under grant VENTURI (FP7-288238). The scene classification part has been developed within the Joint Lab between IPLAB and STMicroelectronics Catania.

References

1. WHO, Fact Sheet N°282: http://www.who.int/mediacentre/factsheets/fs282/en/
2. OpenStreetMap official website: http://openstreetmap.org

3. Sony   Xperia   Z: http://www.sonymobile.com/global-en/products/phones/xperia-z/
4. Google   Talkback: https://play.google.com/store/apps/details?id=com.google.android.marvin.talkback
5. WozARd: http://youtu.be/bpSL0tLMy3w
6. Simulation of VENTURI Y2D: http://youtu.be/NNabKQIXiTc
7. HaptiMap project, FP7-ICT-224675: http://www.haptimap.org/
8. Alce, G., Hermodsson, K., Wallergård, M.: WozARd. In: Proceedings of the 15th International Conference on Human-Computer Interaction with Mobile Devices and Services - MobileHCI, pp. 600–605 (2013)
9. Angermann, M., Frassl, M., Doniec, M., Julian, B.J., Robertson, P.: Characterization of the indoor magnetic field for applications in localization and mapping. In: 2012 International Conference on Indoor Positioning and Indoor Navigation, pp. 1–9 (2012)
10. Baniukevic, A., Jensen, C.S., Hua, L.: Hybrid indoor positioning with wi-fi and bluetooth: architecture and performance. In: 14th International Conference on Mobile Data Management, vol. 1, pp. 207–216 (2013)
11. Barba, E., MacIntyre, B., Mynatt, E.D.: Here we are! Where are we? Locating mixed reality in the age of the smartphone. Proceedings of the IEEE **100**, 929–936 (2012)
12. Borenstein, J., Ojeda, L., Kwanmuang, S.: Heuristic Reduction of Gyro Drift in a Personal Dead-reckoning System. Journal of Navigation **62**(1), 41–58 (2009)
13. Brox, T., Bregler, C., Matas, J.: Large displacement optical flow. In: IEEE Conference on Computer Vision and Pattern Recognition, pp. 41–48 (2009)
14. Chang, C.C., Lin, C.J.: LIBSVM: A library for support vector machines. ACM Transactions on Intelligent Systems and Technology **2**(3), 27:1–27:27 (2011)
15. Colbrant, A., Lasorsa, Y., Lemordant, J., Liodenot, D., Razafimahazo, M.: One Idea and Three Concepts for Indoor-Outdoor Navigation, INRIA Research Report n° 7849 (2011)
16. Dow, S., Macintyre, B., Lee, J., Oezbek, C., Bolter, J.D., Gandy, M.: Wizard of Oz Support throughout an Iterative Design Process. IEEE Pervasive Computing **4**(4), 18–26 (2005)
17. Dunser, A., Billinghurst, M.: Handbook of Augmented Reality, Furht, B. (ed.) chap. 13, pp. 289–307 (2011)
18. Farinella, G.M., Ravì, D., Tomaselli, V., Guarnera, M., Battiato, S.: Representing Scenes for Real-Time Context Classification on Mobile Devices (2014). http://dx.doi.org/10.1016/j.patcog.2014.05.014
19. Fischler, M.A., Bolles, R.C.: Random Sample Consensus: A Paradigm for Model Fitting with Applications to Image Analysis and Automated Cartography. Communications of the ACM **24**, 381–395 (1981)
20. Jones, M.J., Rehg, J.M.: Statistical color models with application to skin detection. International Journal of Computer Vision **46**(1), 81–96 (2002)
21. Kurata, T., Kourogi, M., Ishikawa, T., Kameda, Y., Aoki, K., Ishikawa, J.: Indoor-outdoor navigation system for visually-impaired pedestrians: preliminary evaluation of position measurement and obstacle display. In: ISWC 2011 Proceedings of the 2011 15th Annual International Symposium on Wearable Computer, pp. 123–124 (2011)
22. Ladetto, Q.: Capteurs et Algorithmes pour la Localisation Autonome en Mode Pédestre, Phd thesis, École Polytechnique Fédérale de Lausanne (2003)

23. Lam, E., Goodman, J.W.: A mathematical analysis of the DCT coefficient distributions for images. IEEE Transactions on Image Processing **9**(10), 1661–1666 (2000)
24. Le, M.H.V., Saragas, D., Webb, N.: Indoor navigation system for handheld devices, master's thesis, Worcester Polytechnic Institute, Massachusetts, USA (2009)
25. Messelodi, S., Modena, C.M.: Scene Text Recognition and Tracking to Identify Athletes in Sport Videos. Multimedia Tools and Applications **63**(2), 521–545 (2013)
26. Oliva, A., Torralba, A.: Modeling the shape of the scene: a holistic representation of the spatial envelope. International Journal of Computer Vision **42**(3), 145–175 (2001)
27. Porzi, L., Messelodi, S., Modena, C.M., Ricci, E.: A smart watch-based gesture recognition system for assisting people with visual impairments. In: ACM International Workshop on Interactive Multimedia on Mobile and Portable Devices, pp. 19–24 (2013)
28. Xiao, W., Ni, W., Toh, Y.K.: Integrated Wi-Fi fingerprinting and inertial sensing for indoor positioning. In: 2011 International Conference on Indoor Positioning and Indoor Navigation, pp. 1–6 (2011)

Visual Interaction Including Biometrics Information for a Socially Assistive Robotic Platform

Pierluigi Carcagnì, Dario Cazzato, Marco Del Coco$^{(\boxtimes)}$, Cosimo Distante, and Marco Leo

National Research Council of Italy - Institute of Optics, Arnesano, LE, Italy
marco.delcoco@ino.it

Abstract. This work introduces biometrics as a way to improve human-robot interaction. In particular, gender and age estimation algorithms are used to provide awareness of the user biometrics to a humanoid robot (Aldebaran NAO), in order to properly react with a specific gender/age behavior. The system can also manage multiple persons at the same time, recognizing the age and gender of each participant. All the estimation algorithms employed have been validated through a k-fold test and successively practically tested in a real human-robot interaction environment, allowing for a better natural interaction. Our system is able to work at a frame rate of 13 fps with 640×480 images taken from NAO's embedded camera. The proposed application is well-suited for all assisted environments that consider the presence of a socially assistive robot like therapy with disable people, dementia, post-stroke rehabilitation, Alzheimer disease or autism.

1 Introduction

The human-robot interaction (HRI) for socially assistive robotics (SAR) applications is a new, growing, and increasingly popular research area at the intersection of a number of fields, including robotics, computer vision, medicine, psychology, ethology, neuroscience, and cognitive sciences. New applications for robots in health and education are being developed for broad populations of users [37]. In this field, the introduction of biometrics can substantially increase the level of realism perceived by potential users, since they can be used in order to give to the person the opportunity to interact with an entity that can change its behavior depending on observed peculiarities. In particular, in [21] there is a definition of *soft biometrics* as characteristics that provide some information about the individual, but such that they lack of the distinctiveness and permanence to sufficiently differentiate any two individuals. The soft biometric traits can either be continuous (e.g., height and weight) or discrete (e.g., gender, eye color, ethnicity, etc.).

Beyond realism and variance of the interaction, a system based on biometrics able to work in real-time could lead to several applications in the field of socially

© Springer International Publishing Switzerland 2015
L. Agapito et al. (Eds.): ECCV 2014 Workshops, Part III, LNCS 8927, pp. 391–406, 2015.
DOI: 10.1007/978-3-319-16199-0_28

assistive robotics, like the numerous existing application fields as autistic children, considering their well-known interest on computers and electronic devices [31], as well as people in rehabilitation in cases of dementia [39] or post-stroke [38], and generally for elderly care [4]. Moreover, a robot that bases its behavior on the recognized soft biometrics could be used to autonomously start a specific task.

Soft biometrics have been employed for filtering a large biometric database [43], as a way to improve the speed or the search efficiency of the biometric system, but they have been very rarely taken into account for HRI and artificial intelligence application. For example, in [30] user's non-verbal communication is taken into account in the design of a social robot, but a endless range of alternative biometrics could be considered for the design.

As a preliminary step, especially in order to create a fully automatic face analysis system, facial images of men and women must be extracted. The well-known Viola-Jones [41] algorithm introduces a robust cascade detector (based on AdaBoost [15] and Haar features) for the face detection in image, and is actually considered as a state-of-art approach.

Gender recognition can be viewed as a two-class classification problem, and methods can be roughly divided in feature-based and appearance-based. Mäkinen and Raisamo [29] and Sakarkaya et al. [34] introduced two wide interesting surveys that exhaustively cover the topic. The very first results were simultaneously shown in [13] and [17], in 1990. A following study, that investigated the use of geometrical features in order to achieve gender recognition, was performed by Brunelli and Poggio [7] (1995), while Abdi at al.[18], in the same year, applied pixel based methods and used a radial-basis function (RBF) network. Lyons at al. used Gabor wavelets with PCA and Linear discriminant analysis (LDA) [28]. In 2002, Sun at al. showed the importance of features selection for generic algorithms [36] first and, successively, tested the efficiency of Local Binary Pattern (LBP) for gender classification[35]. Seetci at al. applied Active Apparence Models (AAM) to this scope [33], with the support of an SVM classifier. Recently, Ihsan et al. showed the performance of a Spatial Weber Local Descriptor (SWLD)[40].

Aging estimation is one of the most investigated and not trivial biometric issue. Indeed people with the same calendar age could exhibit highly different biological age because of an harder or relaxed lifestyle. AAM is a widely used techniques for age group classification used for instance by Liu at al.[24]. Doung at al. combine Active Appearance Models (AAMs) technique and LBP local facial features in combination, while Ylioinas at al. exploit the variant of LBP features to encode facial micro-patterns [44, 45].

The problem of gender estimation, together with all the other information extractable from facial images, as a concept to enhance HRI applications has been taken into account already in [42], but gender has been considered only for the design of humanoid faces, and not as a possibility of improving social interaction thanks to the possibility to perform a recognition task on the user's face. Recently, in [23], performances comparison of gender and age group recognition to carry out robot's application service for HRI has been proposed, but with the usage of audio information only. The work of [27] addresses the same problem, but using a RGB-D device and basing its processing on the body shape.

Although several works on the topic of gender recognition have been proposed over the years, in both academia and industry, it seems that very few applications of it in the field of human-robot interaction have been taken into account. Moreover, the only work of this kind in the state of the art does not explore 2D visual information. About age recognition, the work of [16] is a first attempt to process images coming from a camera installed on a robot. Authors use genetic algorithms and self-organizing maps in order to achieve the estimation, without dealing with all related problems of unconstrained environments. In the work in [26], the age estimation is given by using radial basis function and support vector machines, but very few faces are used for training and results can not be generalized.

To overcome to these limitations, this work presents a real-time system that processes data coming from a camera on board the robot to estimate gender and age group of the subjects in the scene. This way, the robot gets awareness of the interacting person and it can rapidly adapt its behavior to the subject category in order to reach the predefined assistive goal. The system can manage multiple persons at the same time, recognizing gender and age group of each person, customizing its response in each case. All privacy principles in the field of biometrics and ambient intelligence have been taken into account [6]. The manuscript is organized as follows: in section 2, our system is presented. After introducing the overall scheme, we will focus on the two used estimation algorithms. Section 3 shows experimental results. Finally, obtained results and future developments are discussed in section 4.

2   NAO Biometrics Based Behavior System

2.1   Overview of the System

In Fig. 1 a scheme of the proposed system is shown. It is composed by two main units: the first unit is the Aldebaran NAO humanoid robot, while the second one is a Remote Computational Unit (RCU) aimed to perform all the computational tasks. RCU and NAO are connected by a local network. This architecture allows to work in real-time (avoiding an overload on the low computational power of the robot's ATOM Z530 CPU), that is a fundamental requirement in the case of assistive applications.

Video frames, coming from the camera mounted on the top of the head of the robot, are taken by means of the API (Application Programming Interface) provided with the NAO Software Development Kit. Captured video frames are sent to the Biometric Engine (BE) subsystem in order to detect the presence of a human being and predict his/her gender and age group. Biometric predictions are then sent to the Behavior Decision Module (BDM) that sends a message to the robot in order to activate gender/age specific behaviors.

Communication between NAO and the RCU has been achieved using the NAOqi framework, that allows homogeneous communication between different

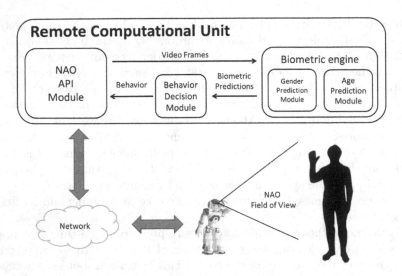

Fig. 1. A scheme of the proposed NAO biometric based behavior system

modules (motion, audio, video), homogeneous programming and homogeneous information sharing. After connecting to the robot using an IP address and a port, it is then possible to call all the NAO's API methods as with a local method. For further information, refer to the official documentation [1].

2.2   Biometric Engine

The system core is the *biometric engine*. It uses the raw video frames as input to detect the presence of a human being and predict, through the specific *gender prediction module* and *age prediction module*, his/her gender and age group respectively. Both modules follow the scheme illustrated in Fig.2, where the first step is aimed at detecting the presence of a human face in the scene and, eventually, at cropping and normalizing the detected region. The *face detection and normalization* process is performed by means of the procedure proposed by Castrillon et al. in [9] that allows the system to detect and track also multiple faces making it, in this way, able to properly match the robot behavior to each specific person. Once the normalized face patch is available, the *features extraction* phase is performed. Taking under consideration a preliminary comparative study of various feature descriptors for gender and age group estimation [8], we choose to work with Histogram of Oriented Gradients (HOG) for gender estimation and Spatial Weber Local Descriptor (SWLD) for age problem. To achieve both biometric classifications, the `features data vector` is projected into a lower dimensional subspace through the Linear Discriminant Analysis (LDA)[3] approach. Successively, the `reduced features data vector` is given as input to the *SVM prediction* block, that predicts the biometric characteristic of interest. Both LDA and SVM approaches are trained using a dataset of thousands of

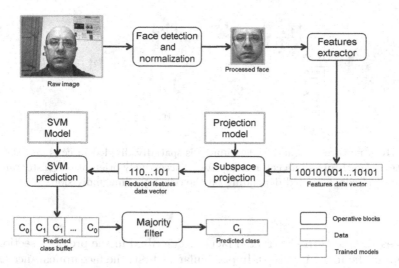

Fig. 2. The block diagram of the class prediction algorithm: the raw frames are processed in order to obtain a reliable class-prediction of the people in the scene

Fig. 3. The face detection and normalization step: the face is cropped and aligned in order to guarantee a standard pose to the *features extraction* step

faces that is freely available on line. The predicted classes are stored, frame by frame, in a circular *predicted class buffer* and finally the temporal consistency of class predictions is used to filter isolated errors: this is done by a *majority filter* that determines the gender and age group class (**predicted class**), for each person, as the class getting the greatest occurrences in the relative buffer.

Face Detection and Normalization. The detection and normalization of the face in the scene are illustrated in Fig. 3. The normalization is a fundamental preprocessing step since the subsequent algorithms work better if they evaluate input faces with predefined size and pose. At first, the well known Viola-Jones face detector [41] is applied on the frame under investigation. When a frontal face is detected, the skin color model is used to detect the face blob boundaries and then the system heuristically removes elements that are not part of the face, e.g. neck, and fits an ellipse to the blob, rotating it to a vertical position. The Viola-Jones based eye detector is then applied. Eye positions, if detected, provide a measure to normalize the frontal face candidate to a standard size of 65×59 pixels.

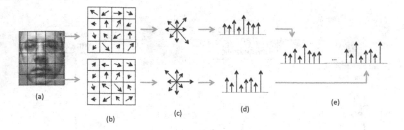

Fig. 4. HOG features extraction: the image is spatially divided in cells and the pixel orientation of each pixel in a cell is computed. Successively orientations histograms are computed and concatenated depending on the cell-space image division.

Features Extraction. Extracted faces as described in the previous section are the input of the following steps. In particular, at first, the face appearance has to be encoded by using some descriptors able to emphasizes the most discriminative features for the classification problem to be faced. The choice of the descriptor is strictly related to the specific biometric information of interest as each descriptor catches a feature set that can exhibit different capabilities to discriminate different biometric aspects.

Taking under consideration a preliminary comparative study of various feature descriptors for gender and age group estimation [8], we choose to work with Histogram of Oriented Gradients (HOG) for gender estimation and Spatial Weber Local Descriptor (SWLD) for age problem.

HOG is a well known feature descriptor based on the accumulation of gradient directions over the pixel of a small spatial region referred as a "cell", and in the consequent construction of a 1D histogram. Even thought HOG has many precursors, it has been used in its mature form in Scale Invariant Features Transformation [25] and widely analyzed in human detection by Dalal and Triggs [14]. This method is based on evaluating well-normalized local histograms of image gradient orientations in a dense grid. Let L be the image to analyze. The image is divided in cells (Fig. 4 (a)) of size $N \times N$ pixels and the orientation θ of each pixel $x = (x_x, x_y)$ is computed (Fig. 4 (b)) by means of the following rule:

$$\theta(x) = \tan^{-1} \frac{L(x_x, x_y + 1) - L(x_x, x_y - 1)}{L(x_x + 1, x_y) - L(x_x - 1, x_y)} \tag{1}$$

The orientations are accumulated in an histogram of a predetermined number of bins (Fig. 4 (c-d)). Finally histograms of each cell are concatenated in a single spatial HOG histogram (Fig. 4 (e)). In order to achieve a better invariance to disturbs, it is also useful to contrast-normalize the local responses before using them. This can be done by accumulating a measure of local histogram energy over larger spatial regions, named blocks, and using the results to normalize all of the cells in the block. The normalized descriptor blocks will represent the HOG descriptors.

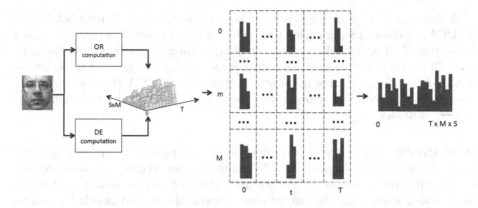

Fig. 5. WLD histogram construction process: the algorithm compute the DE and OR values for each pixel and construct the 2D histogram. The 2D histogram is split in a $M \times T$ matrix where each element is an histogram of S bins. Finally the whole 1D histogram is composed by the concatenation of the previous matrix rows.

Weber Local Descriptor (WLD) [11] is a robust and powerful descriptor inspired to Weber's law. It is based on the fact that the human perception of a pattern depends not only on the amount of change in intensity of the stimulus but also on the original stimulus intensity. The proposed descriptor consist of two components: differential excitation (DE) and gradient orientation(OR). Differential excitation allow to detect the local salient pattern by means of a ratio between the relative intensity difference of the current pixel against its neighbor and the intensity of the current pixel. Moreover the OR of the single pixel is considered. When DE and OR are computed for each pixel in the image we construct a 2D histogram of T columns and $M \times S$ rows where the T is the number of orientation and $M \times S$ the number of bins for the DE quantization with the meaning of [11]. Fig. 5 showes how 2D histogram is mixed in such a way to obtain a 1D histogram more suitable for successive operation.

With the aim to take into account the spatial information, we choose to use the Spatial WLD approach (SWLD) [40] that splits the image in sub-regions and computes an histogram for each of them. Finally, histograms are concatenated in an ordered way.

Subspace Projection. In order to improve the computational efficiency and the accuracy of the age and gender classification, a feature reduction step is then performed. To this end, Linear Discriminant Analysis (LDA) [3] is used. In LDA, within-class and between-class scatters are used to formulate criteria for class separability. The optimizing criterion in LDA is the ratio of between-class scatter to the within-class scatter. The solution obtained by maximizing this criterion defines the axes of the transformed space. Moreover, in LDA analysis, the dimension of the projection subspace is $c - 1$, where c represents the number of class.

A more classical approach is represented by the Principal Component Analysis (PCA). It chooses a dimensionality reducing linear projection that maximizes the scatter of all projected samples. Simply speaking, the more informative subspace directions are selected for the subspace reduction. Anyway our tests showed that LDA, as discriminative approach, outperform the PCA. This is a straightforward result since LDA involves the labels information in the estimation of the projection model.

SVM Prediction. After data projection, in the proposed approach age and gender classification are performed by using Support Vector Machines (SVM). In particular two different SVMs are used: the first one is trained to discriminate among three different age groups whereas the second one is trained to discriminate between male and female human gender.

SVM is a discriminative classifier defined by a separating hyperplane. Given a set of labeled training data (supervised learning), the algorithm computes an optimal hyperplane (the trained model) which categorizes new examples in the right class. In particular the C-support vector classification (C-SVC) learning task implemented in the well-known LIBSVM[10] has been used. Given training vectors $x_i \in \mathbb{R}^n, i = 1, \cdots, l$, in two classes, and an label vector $y \in \mathbb{R}^l$ such that $y_i \in \{1, -1\}$, C-SVC [5,12] solves the following primal optimization problem:

$$\min_{w,b,\xi} \quad \frac{1}{2} w^T w + C \sum_{i=1}^{l} \xi_i$$
$$\text{subject to} \quad y_i(w^T \phi(x_i) + b) \geq 1 - \xi_i,$$
$$\xi_i \geq 0, i = 1, \cdots, l,$$

where $\phi(x_i)$ maps x_i into a higher-dimensional space and $C > 0$ is the regularization parameter. Due to the possible high dimensionality of the vector variable w, usually the following dual problem is solved:

$$\min_{\alpha} \quad \frac{1}{2} \alpha^T Q \alpha - e^T \alpha$$
$$\text{subject to} \quad y^T \alpha = 0,$$
$$0 \leq \alpha_i \leq C, i = 1, \cdots, l,$$

where $e = [1, \cdots, 1]^T$ is the vector of all ones, Q is an $l \times l$ positive semidenite matrix, $Q_{ij} y_i y_j K(x_i, , x_j)$, and $K(x_i, , x_j) \equiv \phi(x_i)^T \phi(x_j)$ is the kernel function. After the dual problem is solved, the next step is to compute the optimal w as:

$$w = \sum_{i=1}^{l} y_i \alpha_i \phi(x_i) \tag{2}$$

Finally the decision function is

$$\text{sgn}(w^T \phi(x) + b) = \text{sgn}\left(\sum_{i=1}^{l} y_i \alpha_i K(x_i, x) + b \right) \tag{3}$$

Such an approach is suitable only for the two classes gender problemw. For age group classification a multi-class approach has been used. It can be treated through the "one-against-one" [22]. Let k be the number of classes, then $k(k-1)/2$ classifiers are constructed where each one trains data from two classes. The final prediction is returned by a voting system among all the classifiers. Many other methods are available for multi-class SVM classification, anyway in [20] a detailed comparison is given with the conclusion that "one-against-one" is a competitive approach.

3   Experimental Results

The experimental session consists of two main steps. The first one aims at evaluating the *biometric prediction accuracy* and it has been performed off-line (without the NAO) over a large set of faces collected in a database and it allows to validate the robustness of age and gender classification algorithms. Successively, *on line tests* involving the complete framework (NAO + RCU) have been performed in order to validate the HRI environment.

3.1   Off-line Biometric Prediction Accuracy Estimation

The evaluation of the accuracy of both *gender prediction module* and *age prediction module* has been realized with a k-fold test over the whole model estimation and prediction process. Experiments have been carried out on a fusion of two of the most representative datasets used for face classification problems: the Morph [2] and the Feret [32] datasets. Both datasets consist of face images of people of different gender, ethnicity and age and to each image is associated a descriptive CVS file containing related information. The total number of face images used in the experimental phase has been 65341 (55915 males and 9246 females). The age distribution in the considered dataset is represented in Fig. 6.

The accuracy estimation of the proposed prediction algorithms has been performed following the procedure, showed in Fig.7. It consists of two steps: a model estimation and a prediction estimation. The whole dataset has been randomly split in k sub-folds. For each of the k validation steps, $k-1$ sub-fold for the training and 1 sub-fold for the prediction/validation process have been used. Face detection and normalization has been the performed on each image of the selected k-1 training sub-fold and then the features data vectors have been extracted. The set of features data vectors has been then used to train, in sequence, the feature reduction algorithm and the SVMs. Finally the one-out fold has been finally tested by using the available models.

The process is repeated over each of 5 to one-out sub-fold combination and the accuracy results is averaged.

For HOG operator, the *VLFeat library*[1] has been used using standard parameters as in [14] that lead to a features vector of 2016 elements. On the other hand

---

[1] http:www.vlfeat.org

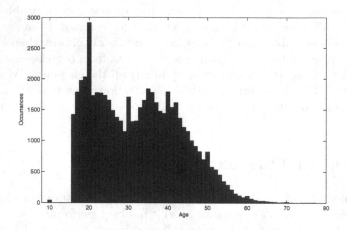

Fig. 6. Histogram for the age distribution in the Fusion dataset: the age is highly unbalancend toward the mean age range and this can affects the prediction accuracy

the SWLD operator has been developed following the line of [40] and used with value of T, M, S that are respectively of 8, 4 and 4 over a 4 × 4 grid of the image with a final features vector of 2048 elements.

The SVM classification problem has been treated by means of the publicly available LIBSVM library [10]. More precisely, we used a radial basis function (RBF) that, in the opinion of the authors of [19] as well as in our experience, seems to be the most reasonable choice. Usually a grid search for penalty parameters C and the others RBF parameters could be desirable. Anyway, our tests does not arise any significant difference in the results as the parameters change. More specifically, we set $C = 1$ and $\gamma = 1/N_f$ where N_f is the number of features.

The class separation for gender task is straightforward. On the other hand, the ages have been split in three categories: *young* (people with an age ≤ 25), *middle* (people with an age > 25 and ≤ 50) and *mature* (people with an age > 50). This splitting was thought in order to take into account generics assistive applications, as well as general purpose customized activities during rehabilitation.

We obtained a total accuracy of 90% for gender classification (developed with the SWLD descriptor) and 64.2% for age group classification (developed with the HOG descriptor). Moreover the results are presented in form of confusion tables (see Table 1) that allow a clear point of view of the real performance of each estimator where M, F, YG, MD, MT, mean male, female, young, middle and mature respectively the subfixs P and T stay for predicted and true. About gender recognition performances, it is quite evident that the imbalance among male and female true positive rate is a consequence of the insufficient female entries on the dataset.

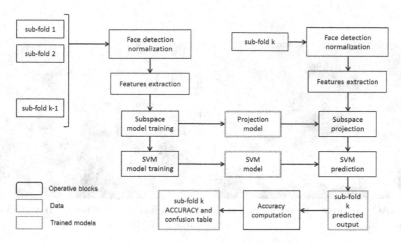

Fig. 7. Test procedure for accuracy estimation: the procedure is done k times in order to obtain the best estimation of total accuracy and confusion table

Table 1. Confusion table for gender (a) and age group (b) estimation (k-fold = 5)

(a)

	M_P	F_P
M_T	97.7%	2.3%
F_T	17.7%	82.3%

(b)

	YG_P	MD_P	MT_P
YG_T	72.3%	27.7%	0%
MD_T	11.5%	86.7%	1.8%
MT_T	0.4%	66%	33.6%

3.2 On Line Tests of the Whole Framework

The whole architecture (presented in section 2) has been tested also in a real scenario where people directly interacted with the robot. No constraints about appearance nor background were given to the participants. Persons entered the scene in the field of view of the NAO robot and when their faces were detected, the algorithms running on the remote processing units predicted their gender and age group and consequently the robot acted in the proper way. For testing purposes, i.e. in order to show the actual possibility to adapt the robot's behavior to the the user biometrics, a set of behaviors was defined and associated to the predicted biometrics as summed up in Table 2.

For example, first row shows the behavior to be taken in the presence of a male or a woman classified as young: in both cases, the robot highs five, but in case of man, it says the sentence "Hello bro!", while in case of a girl, the sentence is "Hello sister!". The behaviors related to the case of predicted presence of middle aged people are instead reported in the second row. In this case, if a woman is in the scene, NAO bows down, while in the presence of a man, the robot greets with his right hand. Fig. 8 illustrates the NAO point of view and the recognition step and the subsequent action taken depending on the gender prediction. Finally, the third row shows the behavior to be taken in the case of

(a) NAO gender recognition step (male/middle)

(b) Behavior after recognition (male/middle)

(c) NAO gender recognition step (female/middle)

(d) Behavior after recognition (female/middle)

(e) NAO gender recognition step (male/mature)

(f) Behavior after recognition (male/mature)

Fig. 8. A test of the interaction between the NAO and humans being. The NAO recognizes gender and age group of the interacting subject (a,c,e) and reacts with a customized behavior (it prostrates for middle aged woman, it greets with its right hand in the presence of middle aged male and shakes hand with a mature man).

Table 2. Behavior table: depending on the predicted gender and age group, the robot reacts with a specific and predefined behavior

	M	F
YG	High five+*Hi bro*	High five+*Hi sister*
MD	Hello	Bow down
MT	Handshake	Hand clap

older people: in the case of a man, the robot proposes an handshake to the user, otherwise it starts the hand clap game. Even a sentence to be pronounced by the robot has been customized depending on the sex and the age. In the presence of a mixed group, when a detection occur, the robot can say the exact number of men and women in the scene, as well as the age group of each participant. Since given a person each prediction is independent from the possible presence of other faces in the same image, it was possible to estimate the error of the system evaluating the interaction with the robot of one person at time. With our real scenario, we tested the algorithm on 20 persons. More precisely, 10 men and 10 women participated to the experiment covering all the age groups accounted in the experiment (from 20 to 65 years old). The test reports 3 errors for the gender, while 4 misclassifications occurred in the case of age.

About computational remarks, the system was tested on a local network in order to avoid latency errors in the evaluation of the frame rate. The RCU was a CPU i7@3.20GHz with a RAM of 16 GB DDR3. Images were processed at a resolution of 640 × 480. In these conditions, our system was able to work at a frame rate of 13 fps. This is a very encouraging result since it allowed to use the predicted gender buffer in order to strengthen the prediction.

4   Conclusions

With this work, the idea of using biometrics as a way to improve human-robot interaction has been investigated. In particular, gender and age estimation algorithms have been used to provide awareness of the user biometrics to a humanoid robot (Aldebaran NAO), in order to properly react with a specific gender/age behavior. The system can also manage multiple persons at the same time, recognizing the age and gender of each participant. The system is particularly suited for HRI applications requiring a natural level of interaction like training, rehabilitation, home-care and so on. Future works will further investigate the use of more distinctive features in order to improve the accuracy in gender and age group classification, as well as for the face detection algorithm in order to overcome the state of the art drawbacks concerning the handling of non-frontal face pose and of the strong illumination variations. About the unbalanced performance on the gender recognition task, a balanced dataset will be employed. Finally, a larger set of robot's behaviors is going to be developed in conjunction with a statistical model able to take decision about the mapping between the outcomes of the algorithmic procedures and the robot actions.

Acknowledgments. This work has been supported in part by the "2007-2013 NOP for Research and Competitiveness for the Convergence Regions (Calabria, Campania, Puglia and Sicilia)" with code PON04a3_00201 and in part by the PON Baitah, with code PON01_980.

References

1. May 2014. https://community.aldebaran-robotics.com/doc/1-14/index.html
2. May 2014. http://www.faceaginggroup.com/morph/
3. Belhumeur, P., Hespanha, J., Kriegman, D.: Eigenfaces vs. fisherfaces: recognition using class specific linear projection. IEEE Transactions on Pattern Analysis and Machine Intelligence **19**(7), 711–720 (1997)
4. Bemelmans, R., Gelderblom, G.J., Jonker, P., De Witte, L.: Socially assistive robots in elderly care: A systematic review into effects and effectiveness. Journal of the American Medical Directors Association **13**(2), 114–120 (2012)
5. Boser, B.E., Guyon, I.M., Vapnik, V.N.: A training algorithm for optimal margin classifiers. In: Proceedings of the Fifth Annual Workshop on Computational Learning Theory, COLT 1992, pp. 144–152. ACM, New York (1992). http://doi.acm.org/10.1145/130385.130401
6. Brey, P.: Freedom and privacy in ambient intelligence. Ethics and Information Technology **7**(3), 157–166 (2005)
7. Brunelli, R., Poggio, T.: Hyberbf networks for gender classification (1995)
8. Carcagnì, P., Del Coco, M., Mazzeo, P.L., Testa, A., Distante, C.: Features descriptors for demographic estimation: a comparative study. In: Distante, C., Battiato, S., Cavallaro, A. (eds.) VAAM 2014. LNCS, vol. 8811, pp. 66–85. Springer, Heidelberg (2014)
9. Castrillón, M., Déniz, O., Guerra, C., Hernández, M.: Encara2: real-time detection of multiple faces at different resolutions in video streams. Journal of Visual Communication and Image Representation **18**(2), 130–140 (2007)
10. Chang, C.C., Lin, C.J.: LIBSVM: A library for support vector machines. ACM Transactions on Intelligent Systems and Technology **2**, 27:1–27:27 (2011). http://www.csie.ntu.edu.tw/~cjlin/libsvm
11. Chen, J., Shan, S., He, C., Zhao, G., Pietikainen, M., Chen, X., Gao, W.: Wld: A robust local image descriptor. IEEE Transactions on Pattern Analysis and Machine Intelligence **32**(9), 1705–1720 (2010)
12. Cortes, C., Vapnik, V.: Support-vector networks. Machine Learning **20**(3), 273–297 (1995). http://dx.doi.org/10.1023/A%3A1022627411411
13. Cottrell, G.W., Metcalfe, J.: Empath: face, emotion, and gender recognition using holons. In: Advances in Neural Information Processing Systems, pp. 564–571 (1990)
14. Dalal, N., Triggs, B.: Histograms of oriented gradients for human detection. In: IEEE Computer Society Conference on Computer Vision and Pattern Recognition, CVPR 2005, vol. 1, pp. 886–893, June 2005
15. Freund, Y., Schapire, R.E.: A decision-theoretic generalization of on-line learning and an application to boosting. J. Comput. Syst. Sci. **55**(1), 119–139 (1997)
16. Fukai, H., Nishie, Y., Abiko, K., Mitsukura, Y., Fukumi, M., Tanaka, M.: An age estimation system on the aibo. In: International Conference on Control, Automation and Systems, ICCAS 2008, pp. 2551–2554, October 2008

17. Golomb, B.A., Lawrence, D.T., Sejnowski, T.J.: Sexnet: a neural network identifies sex from human faces. In: NIPS, pp. 572–579 (1990)
18. Abdi, H., Valentine, D., Edelman, B., O'Toole, A.J.: More about the difference between men and women: evidence from linear neural networks and the principal-component approach. Neural Comput. **7**(6), 1160–1164 (1995)
19. Hsu, C.W., Chang, C.C., Lin, C.J., et al.: A practical guide to support vector classification (2003)
20. Hsu, C.W., Lin, C.J.: A comparison of methods for multiclass support vector machines. IEEE Transactions on Neural Networks **13**(2), 415–425 (2002)
21. Jain, A.K., Dass, S.C., Nandakumar, K.: Soft biometric traits for personal recognition systems. In: Zhang, D., Jain, A.K. (eds.) ICBA 2004. LNCS, vol. 3072, pp. 731–738. Springer, Heidelberg (2004)
22. Knerr, S., Personnaz, L., Dreyfus, G.: Single-layer learning revisited: a stepwise procedure for building and training a neural network. In: Soulié, F., Hérault, J. (eds.) Neurocomputing, NATO ASI Series, vol. 68, pp. 41–50. Springer, Berlin Heidelberg (1990). http://dx.doi.org/10.1007/978-3-642-76153-9-5
23. Lee, M.W., Kwak, K.C.: Performance comparison of gender and age group recognition for human-robot interaction. International Journal of Advanced Computer Science & Applications **3**(12) (2012)
24. Liu, L., Liu, J., Cheng, J.: Age-group classification of facial images. In: 2012 11th International Conference on Machine Learning and Applications (ICMLA), vol. 1, pp. 693–696, December 2012
25. Lowe, D.G.: Distinctive image features from scale-invariant keypoints. Int. J. Comput. Vision **60**(2), 91–110 (2004)
26. Luo, R., Chang, L.W., Chou, S.C.: Human age classification using appearance images for human-robot interaction. In: Industrial Electronics Society, IECON 2013 39th Annual Conference of the IEEE, pp. 2426–2431, November 2013
27. Luo, R.C., Wu, X.: Real-time gender recognition based on 3d human body shape for human-robot interaction. In: Proceedings of the 2014 ACM/IEEE International Conference on Human-Robot Interaction, pp. 236–237. ACM (2014)
28. Lyons, M.J., Budynek, J., Plante, A., Akamatsu, S.: Classifying facial attributes using a 2-d gabor wavelet representation and discriminant analysis. In: Proceedings of the Fourth IEEE International Conference on Automatic Face and Gesture Recognition, pp. 202–207 (2000)
29. Mäkinen, E., Raisamo, R.: An experimental comparison of gender classification methods. Pattern Recognition Letters **29**(10), 1544–1556 (2008). http://www.sciencedirect.com/science/article/pii/S0167865508001116
30. McColl, D., Zhang, Z., Nejat, G.: Human body pose interpretation and classification for social human-robot interaction. International Journal of Social Robotics **3**(3), 313–332 (2011)
31. Moore, D.: Computers and people with autism. Asperger Syndrome, pp. 20–21 (1998)
32. Phillips, P., Moon, H., Rizvi, S., Rauss, P.: The feret evaluation methodology for face-recognition algorithms. IEEE Transactions on Pattern Analysis and Machine Intelligence **22**(10), 1090–1104 (2000)
33. Saatci, Y., Town, C.: Cascaded classification of gender and facial expression using active appearance models. In: 7th International Conference on Automatic Face and Gesture Recognition, FGR 2006, pp. 393–398, April 2006
34. Sakarkaya, M., Yanbol, F., Kurt, Z.: Comparison of several classification algorithms for gender recognition from face images. In: 2012 IEEE 16th International Conference on Intelligent Engineering Systems (INES), pp. 97–101, June 2012

35. Sun, N., Zheng, W., Sun, C., Zou, C., Zhao, L.: Gender classification based on boosting local binary pattern. In: Wang, J., Yi, Z., Żurada, J.M., Lu, B.-L., Yin, H. (eds.) ISNN 2006. LNCS, vol. 3972, pp. 194–201. Springer, Heidelberg (2006)

36. Sun, Z., Bebis, G., Yuan, X., Louis, S.J.: Genetic feature subset selection for gender classification: a comparison study. In: IEEE Workshop on Applications of Computer Vision, pp. 165–170 (2002)

37. Tapus, A., Maja, M., et al.: Towards socially assistive robotics. International Journal of the Robotics Society of Japan (JRSJ) **24**(5), 576–578 (2006)

38. Tapus, A., Tăpuş, C., Matarić, M.J.: User-robot personality matching and assistive robot behavior adaptation for post-stroke rehabilitation therapy. Intelligent Service Robotics **1**(2), 169–183 (2008)

39. Tapus, A., Tapus, C., Mataric, M.J.: The use of socially assistive robots in the design of intelligent cognitive therapies for people with dementia. In: IEEE International Conference on Rehabilitation Robotics, ICORR 2009, pp. 924–929. IEEE (2009)

40. Ullah, I., Hussain, M., Muhammad, G., Aboalsamh, H., Bebis, G., Mirza, A.: Gender recognition from face images with local wld descriptor. In: 2012 19th International Conference on Systems, Signals and Image Processing (IWSSIP), pp. 417–420, April 2012

41. Viola, P., Jones, M.: Rapid object detection using a boosted cascade of simple features. In: Proceedings of the 2001 IEEE Computer Society Conference on Computer Vision and Pattern Recognition, CVPR 2001, vol. 1, pp. I-511. IEEE (2001)

42. Walker, J.H., Sproull, L., Subramani, R.: Using a human face in an interface. In: Proceedings of the SIGCHI Conference on Human Factors in Computing Systems, pp. 85–91. ACM (1994)

43. Wayman, J.L.: Large-scale civilian biometrics system - issues and feasibility. In: Proceedings of the CardTech/SecureTech Government, Washington DC (1997)

44. Ylioinas, J., Hadid, A., Pietikainen, M.: Age classification in unconstrained conditions using lbp variants. In: 2012 21st International Conference on Pattern Recognition (ICPR), pp. 1257–1260, November 2012

45. Ylioinas, J., Hadid, A., Hong, X., Pietikäinen, M.: Age estimation using local binary pattern kernel density estimate. In: Petrosino, A. (ed.) ICIAP 2013, Part I. LNCS, vol. 8156, pp. 141–150. Springer, Heidelberg (2013)

Vision-Based SLAM and Moving Objects Tracking for the Perceptual Support of a Smart Walker Platform

Paschalis Panteleris[1]([✉]) and Antonis A. Argyros[1,2]

[1] Institute of Computer Science (ICS), Foundation for Research and Technology - Hellas (FORTH), N. Plastira 100, Vassilika Vouton, 70013 Heraklion, Crete, Greece
[2] Department of Computer Science, University of Crete, Heraklion, Greece
{padeler,argyros}@ics.forth.gr

Abstract. The problems of vision-based detection and tracking of independently moving objects, localization and map construction are highly interrelated, in the sense that the solution of any of them provides valuable information to the solution of the others. In this paper, rather than trying to solve each of them in isolation, we propose a method that treats all of them simultaneously. More specifically, given visual input acquired by a moving RGBD camera, the method detects independently moving objects and tracks them in time. Additionally, the method estimates the camera (ego)motion and the motion of the tracked objects in a coordinate system that is attached to the static environment, a map of which is progressively built from scratch. The loose assumptions that the method adopts with respect to the problem parameters make it a valuable component for any robotic platform that moves in a dynamic environment and requires simultaneous tracking of moving objects, egomotion estimation and map construction. The usability of the method is further enhanced by its robustness and its low computational requirements that permit real time execution even on low-end CPUs.

Keywords: Visual tracking · Human detection and tracking · Mapping · Egomotion estimation · SLAMMOT · Smart walker

1 Introduction

Tracking an unknown number of unknown objects from a camera moving in an unknown environment, is a challenging problem whose solution has important implications in robotics. In this work, we investigate how moving object tracking, ego-motion estimation and map construction can be performed simultaneously using 3D information provided by an RGBD sensor.

Our work is motivated by the perceptual requirements of the DALi c-Walker platform. The c-Walker is a device that aims to safely guide people with cognitive impairments through public spaces like airports and shopping centers. Using

---

This work was partially supported by the European Commission, through the FP7 project DALi (FP7-288917).

L. Agapito et al. (Eds.): ECCV 2014 Workshops, Part III, LNCS 8927, pp. 407–423, 2015.
DOI: 10.1007/978-3-319-16199-0_29

Fig. 1. Method overview. Top left: an RGBD frame. Top middle: The current map of the environment. Top right: A sparse set of 3D points used for egomotion estimation. Bottom left: registration of the whole point cloud with the current map of the environment. Bottom middle: a top view showing the camera position, the local environment map and the independently moving objects. Bottom right: The point cloud of the foreground moving object.

its on-board sensors, this "cognitive navigation prosthesis" monitors the environment in real time to figure out a path that poses little risk for the user. It can also perform active replanning when, for example, passages are blocked because of groups of standing people.

To create such a smart walker that can function reliably, a number of challenges associated with its perceptual capabilities must be addressed effectively and efficiently:

- Independently moving objects need to be detected and tracked so that a safe path that avoids collision can be planned.
- Egomotion needs to be estimated so that the platform can be localized in its environment.
- The map of the environment which is required for platform localization, cannot be assumed to be known a priori but must be constructed on the fly. This is because the structure of the environment may be subject to frequent changes that render an offline map construction process very impractical.
- All the above needs to be available in unprepared environments, even in the absence of other technologies. Thus, the above perceptual tasks need to be supported strictly by sensors integrated onto the platform.
- To reduce costs and energy consumption, the computational requirements of the sensory processing modules should fit low-end computers that are on-board the platform.

In this paper, we present a solution that addresses simultaneously, robustly and efficiently all the above issues. The proposed method is designed to track moving objects such as humans, estimate camera egomotion and perform map construction based on visual input provided by a single RGBD camera that is rigidly attached to the moving platform. From a computational point of view, the method performs in real time even with limited computational resources.

The proposed method (see Fig. 1) segments and tracks objects that move independently in the field of view of a moving RGBD camera. The camera is assumed to move with 6 degrees of freedom (DOFs), while moving objects in the environment are assumed to move on a planar floor. This last assumption is the only a priori knowledge made regarding the environment, and is exploited in order to reduce the computational requirements of the method since the primary goal of this work is to support perceptually an indoors smart walker platform. Motion is estimated with respect to a coordinate system attached to the static environment. In order to segment the static background from the moving foreground, we first select a small number of points of interest whose 3D positions are estimated directly from the sensory information. The camera motion is computed by fitting those points to a progressively built model of the environment. A 3D point may not match the current version of the map either because it is a noise-contaminated observation, or because it belongs to a moving object, or because it belongs to a structure attached to the static environment that is observed for the first time. A classification mechanism is used to perform this disambiguation. Based on its output, noise is filtered, points on independently moving objects are grouped to form moving object hypotheses and static points are integrated to the evolving map of the environment.

Experimental results demonstrate that the proposed method is able to track correctly moving objects. Interestingly, the performance of egomotion estimation and map construction aspects practically remains unaffected by the presence of independently moving objects, demonstrating the robustness of the ego-motion estimation module to noise as well as the capabilities of the foreground segmentation pipeline. From a computational point of view, the method performs at a frame rate of 50 fps on a laptop with an "Intel i7" CPU without the use of GPU acceleration, and can perform at near real-time speeds on ARM based embedded hardware.

2   Related Work

Our work is related to three fundamental and heavily researched problems in computer vision and robotics, that of multi-target tracking, camera egomotion estimation / localization and 3D scene structure estimation / map construction. A complete review of the related work constitutes a huge task even for any of the individual subproblems and is beyond the scope of this paper.

For the problem of object tracking in RGB images Yilmaz et al. [30] provides a comprehensive review. A number of methods try to address the problem of the changing appearance of the tracked objects through learning on-line the appearance model of a specific target and using it to track that target [4,24]. Several algorithms are specific to humans, as the detection and tracking of moving people is very important in several applications. Such algorithms [9,13,14,28,31] have improved a lot and provide reliable results when applied to simple scenes, especially from static cameras. The methods by Ferrari et al. [14] and Felzenszwalb et al. [13] are able to detect humans in non-pedestrian (i.e. sitting) poses with reasonable accuracy. However, camera motion in real-world, crowded environments which include large amounts of occlusion and clutter, as well as wide pose variation still poses a lot of challenges. Additionally, most of these methods are mainly concerned with the detection of people and not their temporal tracking. To address the challenges of tracking from a moving platform, several approaches [6,7,11,12] have recently been proposed that combine multiple detectors and work with various sensor configurations. These works perform data association to track people and are capable of estimating the camera motion. In our work we are limited to a single RGB-D sensor fixed on our target platform and thus we need to conform with the limitations of the hardware.

For the problem of simultaneous localization and mapping (SLAM), a recent review is provided in [15]. Most of the works depend on the assumption of a static environment. Deviations from this can be tolerated at different degrees, depending on the internals of the methods used. The consideration of SLAM in dynamic environments formulates the so called *SLAMMOT* problem. As stated in [21], SLAMMOT involves SLAM together with the detection and tracking of dynamic objects. SLAMMOT was introduced by Wang [5]. Their approach combines SLAM and moving object tracking that are performed based on a 2D laser scanner. Although conceptually very interesting, the practical exploitation of the method is limited by the 2D nature of laser scans and by the relatively high costs of the employed sensor. On top of the usage of a 2D laser scanner, Gate et al. [16] introduces a camera that aid the classification of moving objects. A purely vision-based method was proposed by Agrawal et al. [1] who employ a calibrated stereo configuration of conventional RGB cameras. Dense stereo 3D reconstruction builds local 3D models of the environment whose rigidity is tested in consecutive frames. Deviations are attributed to moving objects. The corresponding pixels are filtered for noise, grouped, and tracked based on Kalman filtering. The problem of deciding whether an object is static or moving has also been addressed by Sola [27] who employed contextual rules for that purpose. Wangsiripitak et al. [29] track a single, known 3D object. This information is used to safeguard an independent SLAM method from observations that are not compatible to the rigid world assumption.

The recent introduction of RGBD sensors has provided a cheap way of acquiring relatively accurate 3D structure information from a compact sensor. This has enabled the development of SLAM [10,17,18] and object tracking [20] methods with impressive results. The goal of our work is to address the combined SLAM-MOT problem by investigating the coupling of the individual subproblems under the limited computational resources of the target smart walker platform.

3   Method

The approach we propose is outlined graphically in Fig. 1 while Fig. 2 shows a detailed flow diagram. The top left images in Fig. 1 show an RGBD frame from an indoors sequence. Using the RGBD input we generate a point cloud P_c and we select a number of sparse 3D points P_g (top right) that is used for localization. Although P_g could be identical to P_c, it is shown that a limited number

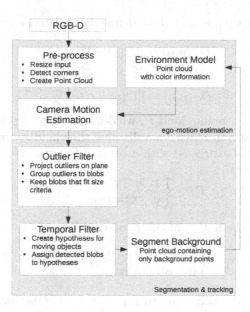

Fig. 2. Flow diagram of the method, see text for details

of carefully selected points suffice to retain the information about the structure/map of the environment, M. This allows camera localization that does not rely on expensive feature descriptors and matching. The output of the registration process is the motion of the camera (egomotion) measured in the coordinate system of M. P'_c is the registered point cloud on M (bottom left in Fig. 1). All points that do not correspond to a point on the model are considered outliers. By clustering these outliers and monitoring their temporal behavior, these are further characterized as noise, parts of independently moving objects or features that belong to the static environment. Hypotheses H about the moving objects are generated and tracked in subsequent frames. Points that belong to H are removed from P'_c and the resulting point cloud P'_{bg} is used to update M for the next frame. The rest of this section describes the steps of the employed approach in more detail.

3.1 Preliminaries

We consider point clouds P that consist of sets of colored 3D points $p = (D(p), C(p))$. $D(p)$ denotes the 3D coordinates of p in some coordinate system and $C(p)$ its associated color. Since we want to be able to compare points based on their color values, we represent color in the YUV space and perform comparisons in the UV dimensions. This reduces the influence of luminance changes to our comparisons. Contemporary RGBD cameras provide all necessary information to extract the $(D(p), C(p))$ representation for each point p they observe.

For two 3D points p and q we first define their distance in space

$$D_E(p,q) = ||D(p) - D(q)||_2$$

and in color

$$D_C(p,q) = ||C(p) - C(q)||_2.$$

Given a point p, and a point cloud P, we define p to be depth-compatible to P if there exists a point q in P within a distance threshold τ_d from p. In notation, depth-compatibility is expressed with a boolean function $DC(p,P)$ defined as

$$DC(p,P) = \begin{cases} 1 & \exists q \in P : D_E(p,q) < \tau_d \\ 0 & \text{otherwise.} \end{cases} \tag{1}$$

Similarly, we define the notion of color compatibility:

$$CC(p,P) = \begin{cases} 1 & DC(p,P) \land \exists q \in P : D_C(p,q) < \tau_c \\ 0 & \text{otherwise.} \end{cases} \tag{2}$$

It should be noted that, according to Eq.(2), color compatibility is judged only for depth-compatible points.

3.2   Camera Motion Estimation

Given a dense 3D point cloud M that represents the environment and an RGBD frame that gives rise to another dense 3D point cloud P_c, a first goal is to register P_c to M. Since P_c is measured at a camera-centered coordinate system, this registration process gives, as a result, the rigid 3D motion that relates P_c to M which is the camera egomotion. We formulate this as an optimization (maximization) problem that is solved with a generative, hypothesize-and-test optimization framework. More specifically, if the camera motion with respect to M is m_{RT} then the transformed point cloud P_c' defined as

$$P_c' = m_{RT} P_c, \tag{3}$$

should be registered to M. In Eq.(3) m_{RT} is a 4x4 transformation matrix modeling the motion of the camera with 6 degrees of freedom (3 for rotation and 3 for translation) and P_c is a 4xN matrix with the points in the observed point cloud in homogeneous coordinates. One way to evaluate the quality of a camera motion candidate solution m_{RT} is by measuring how effectively this motion registers P_c' with M. A quantification of the quality of registration is provided in the following objective function:

$$O(m_{RT}) = \sum_{p \in P_c'} DC(p,M) + \sum_{p \in P_c'} CC(p,M). \tag{4}$$

Intuitively, the first term of $O(m_{RT})$ measures the number of points in P_c' that are depth-compatible to the environment model M and the second term measures

Fig. 3. Moving in a corridor. RGB (top) and depth (bottom) input for a sequence of 3 frames. Depth appears almost identical in all the frames, making motion estimation difficult unless scene color information is taken into account.

the number of points that are also color-compatible. Thus, a motion hypothesis m_{RT} that scores higher in $O(m_{RT})$ represents a motion that brings P'_c in better registration to M.

In general, the registration process could rely only on 3D structure information. However, in certain indoor environments, this proves to be insufficient. For example, if the camera moves along a long corridor, there is not enough information to infer the egomotion just from the changes in the structure of the observed point cloud. This is illustrated in Fig. 3, where even though the RGB input obviously changes as the camera moves, the depth images look almost identical. The incorporation of color-compatibility serves to disambiguate such situations.

According to Eq.(4), the registration of P'_c to M is based on all the points of P'_c. In practice, a much smaller set of points P_g that captures the environment structure proves enough to solve the task. The points in P_g are chosen using two methods. First, we employ a corner detector [25] on the RGB part of the frame. These corners are then filtered and only the ones that have a depth value are kept. We also filter out corners that are associated with depth values but have low accuracy due to large quantization error [26]. Since the proposed method is using the scene structure in order to extract motion information and does not rely on feature matching, a simple corner detector is sufficient. Indeed exploiting cheap corners as features is one of the reasons the method requires low computational resources. Next, we choose the 3D points that are defined on a sparse (16×12) grid that is aligned to the RGBD input. This grid provides enough points in case there is not enough texture information in the observed RGB image. Using these two methods, the total number of selected points in a frame for a typical indoors scene is between 200 and 600. This represents a $0,2\%$ of the total number of points (640×480), a fact that reduces dramatically the computational requirements of the method.

The problem of egomotion estimation is now converted to the problem of finding the motion that maximizes Eq.(4). This is performed using the Particle Swarm Optimization (PSO) algorithm. It should be stressed that this top-down, generative, hypothesize-and-test solution to the problem is the one that remove the requirements for feature matches and, therefore, the need for elaborate feature extraction mechanisms.

3.3   Particle Swarm Optimization

The optimization (i.e., maximization) of the objective function defined in (Eq.(4)) is performed based on Particle Swarm Optimization (PSO) [19] which is a stochastic, evolutionary optimization method. It has been demonstrated that PSO is a very effective and efficient method for solving other vision optimization problems such as head pose estimation [23], hand articulation tracking [22] and others. PSO achieves optimization based on the collective behavior of a set of particles (candidate solutions) that evolve in runs called generations. The rules that govern the behavior of particles emulate "social interaction". Essentially, a population of particles is a set of points in the parameter space of the objective function to be optimized. PSO has a number of attractive properties. For example, it depends on very few parameters, it does not require differentiation of the objective function to be minimized and converges to the solution with a relatively limited computational budget [2].

Every particle holds its current position (current candidate solution, set of parameters) in a vector x_t and its current velocity in a vector v_t. Each particle i keeps in vector p_i the position at which it achieved, up to the current generation t, the best value of the objective function. The swarm as a whole, stores the best position p_g across all particles of the swarm. All particles are aware of the global optimum p_g. The velocity and position update equations in every generation t are

$$v_t = K(v_{t-1} + c_1 r_1(p_i - x_{t-1}) + c_2 r_2(p_g - x_{t-1})) \tag{5}$$

and

$$x_t = x_{t-1} + v_t, \tag{6}$$

where K is a constant *constriction factor* [8]. In Eqs. (5), c_1 is called the *cognitive component*, c_2 is termed the *social component* and r_1, r_2 are random samples of a uniform distribution in the range $[0..1]$. Finally, $c_1 + c_2 > 4$ must hold [8]. In all experiments the values $c_1 = 2.8$, $c_2 = 1.3$ and $K = \frac{2}{\left|2 - \psi - \sqrt{\psi^2 - 4\psi}\right|}$, with $\psi = c_1 + c_2$ were used.

In our problem formulation, the parametric space consists of the $6D$ space of camera motions m_{RT}. The rotation component of candidate camera moves is parametrized in terms of yaw (θ), pitch (ϕ), and roll (ω) angles, correspondingly yielding $R = R_x(\theta) \cdot R_y(\phi) \cdot R_z(\omega)$ for each parameter combination. Translation is parametrized by the XYZ coordinates of the camera center c. Particles are initialized at a normal distribution around the center of the search range with their velocities set to zero. Each dimension of the multidimensional parameter space is bounded in some range. During the position update, a velocity component may force a particle to move to a point outside the bounded search space. Such a component is zeroed and the particle does not move at the corresponding dimension. Since the camera motion needs to be continuously tracked in a sequence instead of being estimated in a single frame, temporal continuity is exploited. More specifically, the solution over frame t is used to restrict the search space for the initial population at frame $t + 1$. In related experiments, the search range (or the space in which particle positions are initialized) extend $\pm 150\,mm$ and $\pm 10°$ around the position estimated in the previous frame.

3.4 Handling Camera Motion Estimation Failures

A failure to estimate accurately the camera motion can be identified using the score of the objective function. If the score at a certain frame is below a threshold τ_s, then the camera motion calculated for I_t is considered inaccurate. This may occur in cases where there is not enough depth information in the scene, or when there are too many moving objects in the foreground. In our experiments we choose $\tau_s = 0.15|P_g|$ where $|P_g|$ is the number of points in P_g. If this condition holds then less than 15% of the scene features where registed during the optimization step. In this case the camera motion estimation is considered unreliable, and no tracking steps or environment update is performed.

3.5 Identifying and Tracking Foreground Objects

If the motion m_{RT} of the camera with respect to the environment model M is known, we define a point $p \in P_c$ to be an outlier when $p' = m_{RT} * p$ and p' is not color-compatible to M. Formally, the set of outliers is defined as:

$$O_c = \{p \in P_c : p' = m_{RT} * p \wedge CC(p', M) = 0\}. \tag{7}$$

The set of outliers O_c is partitioned to the following classes:

- M-class: Independently moving foreground objects (e.g., moving humans).
- S-class: Static background objects that are not yet part of the environment model. This is because as the camera moves in an unknown environment, new parts of the "static" background will become visible.
- N-class: Sensor noise. Depth measurements obtained from commercial RGBD sensors like the Microsoft Kinect and the Asus Xtion have a considerable amount of noise, especially at distances greater than 3-4 meters.

The correct assignment of outliers to these classes is very important. N-class points need to be discarded from further consideration. M-class points should support the formation of hypotheses for objects to be tracked. Finally, S-class points need to be incorporated in M. To perform this type of classification in a robust way, we capitalize on the fact that the camera moves in an environment

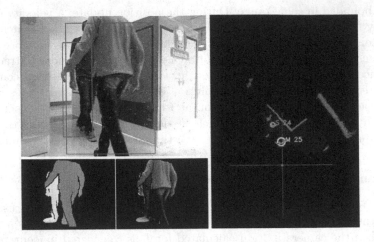

Fig. 4. Segmentation and tracking. In the floor plan view (right image), background objects are shown in purple and foreground objects in green. Foreground objects are segmented (bottom left) and tagged. The RGBD camera is mounted on a prototype smart walker during trials. The current location of the camera is on the center of the blue cross.

where objects move on the ground plane. Thus, we aggregate all observations on a floor plan F of the environment defined as

$$F = \Pi V O_c. \tag{8}$$

In Eq.(8), Π is a 4x4 orthographic projection matrix and V is the 4x4 camera view matrix for a virtual camera above the scene, while O_c is the 4xN matrix of the outlier points in homogeneous coordinates. Then, F is a 2D floor plan of the outliers which can be efficiently grouped using a blob detector and tracker. An example F is shown in Fig. 4 for one frame of an indoors sequence. For a blob B of outliers we define the following properties:

- Blob height B_h: The maximum distance of a point in the blob from the ground floor.
- Blob area B_a: The area occupied by the blob on the ground plane.
- Blob size B_s: The number of outlier points that produced the blob.

Simple rules defined over the parameters B_h, B_a and B_s suffice to identify outliers and to characterize tracking candidates for the next phase of the algorithm. When choosing the values for the blob classification parameters one must take into account that small errors in the camera motion estimation due to noise or accumulated drift can create relatively large number of outlier clusters. This limits the smallest size of a moving object that can be detected, since allowing small blobs to be considered possible candidates will result in a great number of false positive tracks.

Fig. 5. The resulting point cloud (with color) created from a sequence grabbed using the prototype smart walker. The method produces an accurate model of the environment.

In our use cases we are mainly interested in tracking human-sized objects, which is well above the size limits of the method. For our experiments the B_h was set to be between $1.0m$ and $1.8m$ while the area of the blobs, B_a, was limited between $0.19m^2$ and $0.78m^2$. The B_s parameter was empirically chosen to be less than 500, since errors on the egomotion tend to produce blobs with high number of outliers.

In order to track foreground objects, we create and maintain a number of hypotheses about moving objects in the scene. It is assumed that at the previous frame $t - 1$ there have been O_{t-1} object hypotheses with which the current set of blobs need to be associated with. This is performed with a variant of the blob tracking method proposed in [3]. The original version of that tracker was devised to track an unknown/dynamically changing number of skin coloured blobs. Instead, our own implementation of this algorithm operates on the detected blobs corresponding to moving object hypotheses.

3.6   Updating the Environment Model

The environment model is built and maintained on the fly, without any prior knowledge. In order to bootstrap the process, the point cloud P_c produced in the first frame I_0, is used as the initial model M and the location of the sensor on this frame is set to be the world origin. To update the environment model we use the background points of frame I_n created on Sec. 3.5 registered on the environment model M of frame I_{n-1} using the camera motion m_{RT} (Eq. 3).

The environment model should be updated only when there is high confidence on the quality of the calculated m_{RT}. In our experiments, we set the minimum threshold for the quality of the camera motion estimation as explained in Sec. 3.4 to be $\tau_u = 0.30|P_g|$. Choosing this value for τ_u means that when less than 30% of the scene features where registered during the optimization step, the ego-motion estimation may not be accurate enought to update the scene model.

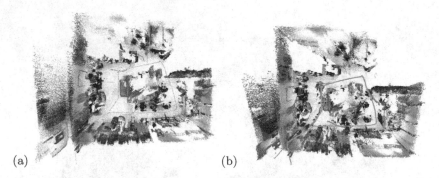

(a)   (b)

Fig. 6. (a) A floormap of an environment built in the absence of moving objects. The estimated platform trajectory shown in green. (b) The map of the environment that was built in presence of moving objects. Camera (green) and moving object (orange) trajectories are also shown.

The resulting environment model is used in order to detect moving objects in the next frame. In Fig. 5 the point cloud of a full environment model from a test dataset is shown. In practice, there is no need to keep the whole environment model in memory in order to perform object tracking. As the camera moves in the environment, older parts of the model can be discarded once they are far enough from the platform or when they get older than a pre-set age. In our experiments, the environment model is discarded every 40 frames but the knowledge about the moving objects in the scene is kept during the reset. This way, we reduce the amount of resources required to maintain a constantly expanding model, without loosing information about the foreground in the scene.

4   Experiments

The proposed approach has been evaluated quantitatively and qualitatively in a number of experiments. The experiments were performed in an indoors environment whose reconstructed top down view is shown in Fig. 6. The environment consists of a hallway and a room with a total area of $120m^2$. A number of way-points were set in order to create a closed path. The location of each way-point was measured and used to compute a ground truth trajectory that the user of the walker was asked to follow. The error on the real world location of the way-points was measured to be around $30mm$. A total of 9 way-points (marked from $W0$ to $W8$) were set creating a 9 segment closed path that goes through the corridor and around the room. That way the system was evaluated on a demanding real world scenario similar to the cluttered indoor environments that the actual device will operate in.

In a first experiment, we assessed the SLAM aspects of the proposed method, that is, we performed simultaneous localization and map construction in the absence of moving people. A user moved with the walker along the pre-planned

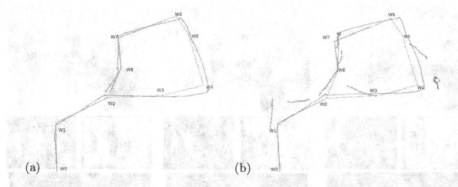

Fig. 7. View of the calculated camera trajectory (green) aligned with the ground truth trajectory (blue) in two experiments without MOT (a) and with MOT (b). The trajectories of the moving objects for the second experiment are also shown in orange. The user of the walker was asked to follow the same track in both experiments.

Table 1. Localization errors (in mm)

Segment	Average error without MO	Average error with MO
W0-W1	45	32
W1-W2	125	121
W2-W3	68	200
W3-W4	333	233
W4-W5	197	444
W5-W6	136	431
W6-W7	118	286
W7-W8	101	127
W8-W2	140	253
All	140	236

Table 2. Actual and measured distances (in mm)

Segment	Actual length	Measured without MO	Measured with MO
W0-W1	3222	3144	3121
W1-W2	3816	3886	3968
W2-W3	3643	3668	3639
W3-W4	2713	3011	3141
W4-W5	3559	3599	3719
W5-W6	1423	1183	1374
W6-W7	4032	4067	3760
W7-W8	1999	1923	1986
W8-W2	2150	1954	1877

track. The results of the reconstruction as well as the computed camera trajectory is shown in Fig. 6(a).

Figure 7(a) shows the ground truth trajectory of the walker (blue color) and the one estimated by the proposed method (green color). In the same figure, the locations of the way-points are marked along the path. Table 1 shows the ground truth measurements for the distances of these points (first column) and those estimated by the proposed method (second column). It can be verified that the estimation of these distances are rather accurate.

The same experiment was repeated in the presence of moving people. The rightmost column of Table 1 shows the estimated distances in this case. The actual reconstruction, moving object trajectories and camera trajectory are shown in Fig. 6(b). It can be verified that camera and object motion trajec-

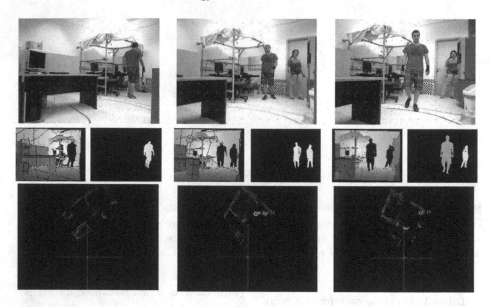

Fig. 8. Tracking moving targets. Three frames from a lab sequence. On the top row: The RGB input for each frame is shown with the points selected for the ego-motion estimation superimposed with green. Middle row: The environment model M and the foreground moving objects H from the point of view of the camera. Bottom row: The top down view of the scene. An orthographic projection of both the environment (purple) and the tracked objects (green).

tories are rather accurate. Additionally, the independently moving objects did not affect considerably the SLAM process. This is also illustrated in Fig. 7(b) that shows the estimated track of the camera and the moving objects, aligned with the ground truth trajectory. Further intermediate results are illustrated in Fig. 8.

For the whole course of the experiments, we also measured the average distance of the walker position as estimated by the method, to the corresponding line segment (ground truth). Table 2 shows these localization errors in the experiments with and without moving objects. It can be verified that, on average, the errors are comparable. A full run of the experiments is also shown on the supplementary material of this paper[1].

A prototype walker implementation has also been exhibited in the Vilnius ICT'2013 Conference[2] with great success. In that context, the DALi c-Walker had to detect and track people moving in very crowded environments.

---

[1] http://youtu.be/RnKFCypUk9U

[2] http://ec.europa.eu/digital-agenda/en/ict-2013

5   Summary

In this paper, we presented a new approach to the problem of simultaneous object tracking, localization and map construction. The proposed method exploits the visual input provided by a single RGBD camera. The method can handle an arbitrary and temporally varying number of moving objects which it localizes on a map of the environment which is progressively built from scratch. The obtained quantitative experimental results demonstrate that the method is capable of handling effectively challenging SLAMMOT scenarios. It has also been shown that the SLAM accuracy of the method is not affected significantly by the presence of moving objects which are also tracked accurately. The computational requirements of the method are rather low as its implementation on conventional contemporary architectures performs at super real time frame rates while being able to achieve near real time performance on ARM based embedded systems. Thus, with the proposed method, we achieve a robust solution to several interesting problems under loose assumptions and with limited computational resources. A practical proof of the above has been the successful deployment of the approach in use cases using the DALi c-Walker prototype.

References

1. Agrawal, M., Konolige, K., Iocchi, L.: Real-time detection of independent motion using stereo. In: IEEE WACV/MOTIONS 2005, vol. 2, pp. 207–214 (2005)
2. Angeline, P.J.: Evolutionary optimization versus particle swarm optimization: philosophy and performance differences. In: Porto, V.W., Saravanan, N., Waagen, D., Eiben, A.E. (eds.) EP 1998. LNCS, vol. 1447, pp. 601–610. Springer, Heidelberg (1998)
3. Argyros, A.A., Lourakis, M.I.A.: Real-time tracking of multiple skin-colored objects with a possibly moving camera. In: Pajdla, T., Matas, J.G. (eds.) ECCV 2004. LNCS, vol. 3023, pp. 368–379. Springer, Heidelberg (2004)
4. Bibby, C., Reid, I.: Robust real-time visual tracking using pixel-wise posteriors. In: Forsyth, D., Torr, P., Zisserman, A. (eds.) ECCV 2008, Part II. LNCS, vol. 5303, pp. 831–844. Springer, Heidelberg (2008)
5. Wang, C.C., Thorpe, C., Hebert, M., Thrun, S., Durrant-Whyte, H.: Simultaneous localization, mapping and moving object tracking. International Journal of Robotics Research (2004)
6. Choi, W., Pantofaru, C., Savarese, S.: Detecting and tracking people using an rgb-d camera via multiple detector fusion. In: ICCV Workshops, pp. 1076–1083. IEEE (2011)
7. Choi, W., Pantofaru, C., Savarese, S.: A general framework for tracking multiple people from a moving camera. IEEE Trans. Pattern Anal. Mach. Intell. **35**(7), 1577–1591 (2013)
8. Clerc, M., Kennedy, J.: The particle swarm - explosion, stability, and convergence in a multidimensional complex space. IEEE Transactions on Evolutionary Computation **6**(1), 58–73 (2002)
9. Dalal, N., Triggs, B.: Histograms of oriented gradients for human detection. In: Proceedings of the IEEE Conference on Computer Vision and Pattern Recognition, San Diego, USA (2005)

10. Endres, F., Hess, J., Sturm, J., Cremers, D., Burgard, W.: 3d mapping with an RGB-D camera. IEEE Transactions on Robotics (T-RO) (2013)
11. Ess, A., Leibe, B., Schindler, K., Van Gool, L.J.: A mobile vision system for robust multi-person tracking. In: CVPR. IEEE Computer Society (2008)
12. Ess, A., Leibe, B., Schindler, K., Van Gool, L.J.: Robust multiperson tracking from a mobile platform. IEEE Trans. Pattern Anal. Mach. Intell. **31**(10), 1831–1846 (2009)
13. Felzenszwalb, P.F., Girshick, R.B., McAllester, D.A., Ramanan, D.: Object detection with discriminatively trained part-based models. IEEE Trans. Pattern Anal. Mach. Intell. **32**(9), 1627–1645 (2010)
14. Ferrari, V., Marin-Jimenez, M., Zisserman, A.: Progressive search space reduction for human pose estimation. In: Proceedings of the IEEE Computer Vision and Pattern Recognition, Alaska (2008)
15. Fuentes-Pacheco, J., Ruiz-Ascencio, J., Rendn-Mancha, J.M.: Visual simultaneous localization and mapping: a survey. Artificial Intelligence Review, 1–27 (2012)
16. Gate, G., Breheret, A., Nashashibi, F.: Fast pedestrian detection in dense environment with a laser scanner and a camera. In: IEEE 69th Vehicular Technology Conference, VTC Spring 2009, pp. 1–6 (2009)
17. Henry, P., Krainin, M., Herbst, E., Ren, X., Fox, D.: Rgb-d mapping: Using kinect-style depth cameras for dense 3d modeling of indoor environments. Int. J. Rob. Res. **31**(5), 647–663 (2012)
18. Izadi, S., Kim, D., Hilliges, O., Molyneaux, D., Newcombe, R., Kohli, P., Shotton, J., Hodges, S., Freeman, D., Davison, A., Fitzgibbon, A.: Kinectfusion: real-time 3d reconstruction and interaction using a moving depth camera. In: Proc. UIST, pp. 559–568 (2011)
19. Kennedy, J., Eberhart, R.C., Shi, Y.: Swarm intelligence. Morgan Kaufmann Publishers (2001)
20. Luber, M., Spinello, L., Arras, K.O.: People tracking in rgb-d data with on-line boosted target models. In: Proc. of the IEEE/RSJ Int. Conf. on Intelligent Robots and Systems (IROS), San Francisco, USA (2011)
21. Márquez-Gámez, D., Devy, M.: Active visual-based detection and tracking of moving objects from clustering and classification methods. In: Blanc-Talon, J., Philips, W., Popescu, D., Scheunders, P., Zemčík, P. (eds.) ACIVS 2012. LNCS, vol. 7517, pp. 361–373. Springer, Heidelberg (2012)
22. Oikonomidis, I., Kyriazis, N., Argyros, A.A.: Tracking the articulated motion of two strongly interacting hands. In: CVPR. IEEE, June 2012
23. Padeleris, P., Zabulis, X., Argyros, A.A.: Head pose estimation on depth data based on particle swarm optimization. In: IEEE CVPRW - HAU3D 2012 (2012)
24. Ramanan, D., Forsyth, D.A., Zisserman, A.: Tracking people by learning their appearance. IEEE Trans. Pattern Anal. Mach. Intell. **29**(1), 65–81 (2007)
25. Rosten, E., Drummond, T.: Machine learning for high-speed corner detection. In: Leonardis, A., Bischof, H., Pinz, A. (eds.) ECCV 2006, Part I. LNCS, vol. 3951, pp. 430–443. Springer, Heidelberg (2006)
26. Smisek, J., Jancosek, M., Pajdla, T.: 3d with kinect. In: ICCV Workshops, pp. 1154–1160. IEEE (2011)
27. Solà, J.: Towards Visual Localization, Mapping and Moving Objects Tracking by a Mobile Robot: a Geometric and Probabilistic Approach. PhD thesis, Institut National Polytechnique de Toulouse (2007)

28. Viola, P., Jones, M., Snow, D.: Detecting pedestrians using patterns of motion and appearance. In: Proceedings of the 9th IEEE International Conference on Computer Vision, Nice, France (2003)
29. Wangsiripitak, S., Murray, D.W.: Avoiding moving outliers in visual slam by tracking moving objects. In: IEEE ICRA 2009, pp. 705–710. IEEE Press, Piscataway (2009)
30. Yilmaz, A., Javed, O., Shah, M.: Object tracking: A survey. ACM Comput. Surv. **38**(4) (2006)
31. Zhao, T., Nevatia, R.: Tracking multiple humans in crowded environment. In: CVPR(2), pp. 406–413 (2004)

Real-Time Emotion Recognition from Natural Bodily Expressions in Child-Robot Interaction

Weiyi Wang[1]([✉]), Georgios Athanasopoulos[1], Georgios Patsis[1],
Valentin Enescu[1], and Hichem Sahli[1,2]

[1] Department of Electronics and Informatics (ETRO) - AVSP,
Vrije Universiteit Brussel (VUB), Brussels, Belgium
wwang@etro.vub.ac.be
[2] Interuniversity Microelectronics Centre (IMEC), Heverlee, Belgium

Abstract. Emotion perception and interpretation is one of the key desired capabilities of assistive robots, which could largely enhance the quality and naturalness in human-robot interaction. According to psychological studies, bodily communication has an important role in human social behaviours. However, it is very challenging to model such affective bodily expressions, especially in a naturalistic setting, considering the variety of expressive patterns, as well as the difficulty of acquiring reliable data. In this paper, we investigate the spontaneous dimensional emotion prediction problem in a child-robot interaction scenario. The paper presents emotion elicitation, data acquisition, 3D skeletal representation, feature design and machine learning algorithms. Experimental results have shown good predictive performance on the variation trends of emotional dimensions, especially the arousal dimension.

Keywords: Spontaneous emotion recognition · Child-robot interaction · Bodily expressions

1   Introduction

The development of assistive robots aims at designing robots that could help humans in everyday life or on specific tasks. Among which, child companion robot is one of the major applications. Such kind of robots are designed to be able to interact autonomously with children. This requires the robots to correctly interpret the social behaviours of the children, and respond accordingly. Supported by psychological studies, affective phenomena, especially emotions, are the key information conveyed in daily communication among humans [4, 26, 30, 31]. Thus the capability of understanding the emotional states of the children, becomes an asset for child companion robots.

Emotions are multi-component responses that are delivered through various channels such as facial expressions, bodily movements, speech and physiological signals [15]. According to [12], 95% of the emotion recognition study was conducted with facial cues, the majority of the remaining 5% with audio, while

© Springer International Publishing Switzerland 2015
L. Agapito et al. (Eds.): ECCV 2014 Workshops, Part III, LNCS 8927, pp. 424–435, 2015.
DOI: 10.1007/978-3-319-16199-0_30

the bodily stimuli were relatively neglected. However, recent empirical study provided the evidence that emotional information could be not only conveyed, but also perceived, via the body as a single channel [2,3,10,35]. Encouraged by those findings, emotion recognition from bodily information attracted increasing interests in recent years, yet most of the work in the literature was focused on acted expressions of adults [6,7,9,19,20,23,32,38]. The main drawback of these studies is the loss of naturalness in the expressions, which makes them not suitable to be utilized in assistive robot applications, especially on child companion robots.

In this paper, we introduce a framework and its preliminary results, for spontaneous emotion recognition from bodily expressions in a child-robot interaction setting. The framework involves natural emotion elicitation, expressive data acquisition, emotion annotation, body feature design and learning models. The remainder of the paper is structured as following: Section 2 reviews different emotion models and gives the explanation of our choice. Section 3 describes our emotion elicitation data acquisition experiments, as well as the annotation scheme. Section 4 gives the details of the features and the recognition model for emotion prediction. We then give some experimental results in Section 5 and the discussion in Section 6.

2   Emotion Modelling

The representation of emotions could be mainly divided into two groups, referred to as *categorical models* and *dimensional models*. The categorical representations are based on selected vocabulary of emotions such as *happy, sad, feared, angry* etc [11]. These discrete labels of emotions have specific social meanings which are, to a large extent, accepted universally by people despite of the regions, cultural backgrounds or genders. Thus, they could be intuitively understood among us. Moreover, categorical models are inherently advantaged to represent simultaneous emotions that occur occasionally in real life [21]. However, the capability to describe the comprehensive emotional states is highly dependent on and constrained by the selected labels. Furthermore, categorical models normally consider the emotions as static temporal segments, which is in conflict with the intrinsic continuity of emotions, and limits the feasibility to describe the variation trends. The dimensional models, on the other hand, were advocated to meet the fact that mental states are much more complicated than the so-called basic emotions [4]. Moreover, they can better cope with the continuous nature of affect. The drawback is that those dimensions are less explicitly interpretable, compared to the categorical labels.

In this work, we use the circumplex space [29], specifically, the *arousal* and *valence* dimensions, to model the emotional states of children in their interactions with a robot. *Arousal* values indicate the external expressions between relaxed and aroused, while *valence* values reveal pleasant (positive) or unpleasant (negative) status. This choice was made mainly based on the consideration of natural interaction, by letting the robot continuously adjusting its reactions based on the perceived emotion of the child. More precisely, in our settings it is not necessary for the robot to interpret semantically the child's expressions, while it is essential that it responds quickly according to the changes (even when they are subtle) of the emotional states of the children.

3   Naturalistic Data Acquisition and Annotation

Obtaining expressive data is a vital step for spontaneous emotion modelling. This requires proper emotion elicitation protocol, well arranged recording setup, as well as reliable annotation scheme. In this section, we briefly introduce our spontaneous data acquisition and annotation framework. More details could be found in [37].

3.1   Naturalistic Emotion Elicitation of Children

In general, traditional emotion elicitation approaches employed visual and/or auditory stimuli to induce certain expressions. The most widely applied method is to ask the participants to watch film segments that were pre-selected to deliver strong feelings [14]. The main drawback of this approach lies in its static and passive nature: the participants are hardly expressing externally, especially via the body, in a non-interactive environment. Dyadic interaction tasks also attracted many research work by introducing the communication between participants [28]. A simulated Sensitive Artificial Listener (SAL) with emotional profiles were incorporated in [22] to enhance the affective engagement of the participants. However, it is relatively difficult to design the conversational scope to successfully trigger bodily expressions, specially in the case of children.

In order to deal with the above issues, we designed a child-robot interaction scenario to elicit naturalistic expressions. Each participated child was asked to play the Snakes and Ladders game against the humanoid robot NAO [24]. To better cope with the emotion elicitation purpose, we manually scripted the unfolding of four games (the child and the robot would win two of those respectively, and all the dice throws were predefined). The game steps were designed to be dramatic and therefore produce a clear reaction from the child, either positive or negative.

We hypothesize that a believable interaction should be maintained and hence the robot's verbal communication should be as natural as possible. With this in mind, we opted for a Wizard-of-Oz (WoZ) setting, where the operator's speech was streamed to the robot in real-time, with the voice being modified [34] so that it resembles the robot's voice. Moreover, the robot could display two different affective profiles while playing the game: one *competitive*, where the robot would display self-centred emotions, and one was *supportive*, focusing on the child's performance. The profiles were displayed alternatively in different games. The *competitive* profile made the robot react strongly to positive events and negative events occurring to the robot, making the robot appearing more involved in the game and eager to win it. The behaviours and gestures of the robot appeared

Fig. 1. Examples of the extracted 3D skeletons. Note that in the first and forth columns, the skeletons are well captured even some body parts are occluded.

more aroused and energetic. Following the literature on empathy and sympathy and their importance in peer bonding and fostering trust [27], using the *supportive* profile, the robot displayed and expressed behaviours suggesting a more focused interest on the outcomes for the child's. Additionally, the verbal expressions of the WoZ operator were consistent with the specific affective profile of the robot used at the time of interaction.

Before the start of the interaction, a short familiarization phase, using animated behaviours, took place so that the children would feel comfortable interacting with the robot, and to familiarize the children with the robot's movements and emotional expressions. Simple gestures (e.g., standing up, waving hello, nodding, etc.) and emotional postures (similar to the ones implemented in [5]) have been used during this phase. These behaviours were triggered by the WoZ operator via a graphical user interface.

3.2 Bodily Data Acquisition

We arranged a dual-Kinect set-up. Two Microsoft Kinect sensors were placed in 90° to record the movement of the child, at the same frame rate. The 3D skeletons were reconstructed offline from the dual recordings, using the iPi Mocap Studio software [25]. Fig. 1 gives some examples of the skeletal representations. Note that even when some body parts were occluded, the skeletons were still well tracked.

For the purpose of our current research on multi-modal emotion recognition [13,17,36], we also recorded high-definition face and frontal body videos, audio from both the robot and the child, and the child-robot interactions. All recordings were synchronized.

3.3 Dimensional Emotion Annotation

A three-view video for each recording session (see Fig.2 as an example), was generated for annotation purposes. Such three-view videos give the raters a better

Fig. 2. The synchronised three-view videos (with audio) for annotation purpose

perception of the interaction, hence a more reliable annotation. Moreover, the raters had the possibility to preview the videos as well as repeat the annotation as many times as required. Fig.3 depicts some annotations.

4 Feature Design and Recognition Model

4.1 Feature Extraction

Psychological experiments and statistical analysis conducted in [35] revealed some general relations between the bodily expressive patterns and the emotions. Although this work used the categorical emotion labels, it actually inspired us to design the feature set.

From the 3D skeletal representation, we extracted both low-level postural features and high-level kinematic and geometrical features. Human motions could be thought of as being composed of different physical segments. Each segment can move independently and exhibit an independent degree of activity [1]. These body segments have a hierarchical structure. For instance, the upper body consists of two arms, head, neck and torso. And the left arm is further composed of left hand, left lower arm and left upper arm. [35] has shown that the upper body, especially arms and head, plays the most important role for emotional expressions. Therefore, we calculate the spatial distances among hands, elbows and shoulders in each of the three dimensions, as well as the angles of the two elbows and the angles between the spine and the upper arms. Moreover, we also calculate the distance between the feet, the orientation of the feet, and the orientation of the shoulders. All these lead to 28 postural features in total.

As for the high-level features, they are designed to represent the abstract characteristics of bodily expressions, such as movement power, body spatial extension, head bending etc. in [35]:

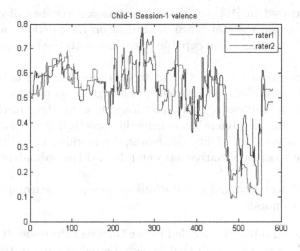

Fig. 3. Example of annotations made by two raters

- *Body movement activity and power:* Using the above described hierarchical structure, along with the mass of each body segment, estimated using the ergonomic definitions of [18], we further calculate the force, kinetic energy and momentum of the movements in a hierarchical manner (from the smallest segment to the whole body):

$$Force_{segment} = Mass_{segment} \times Acceleration_{segment} \qquad (1)$$

$$KineticEnergy_{segment} = 0.5 \times Mass_{segment} \times Velocity^2_{segment} \qquad (2)$$

$$Momentum_{segment} = Mass_{segment} \times Velocity_{segment} \qquad (3)$$

- *Body spatial extension:* From the positions of the body joints, we calculate the bounding box of the whole body. The spatial extension is calculated by considering the length proportions of the edges, i.e. $\frac{x}{y}$, $\frac{x}{z}$ and $\frac{y}{z}$.

- *Symmetry index:* We calculate symmetry/asymmetry index in x, y, z axis, respectively, based on the positions of two hands. These features highlight the importance of the hands behaviours in emotional expressions.

In total, ten high-level features are extracted. Together with the postural features, we obtain a per-frame-based feature vector of the dimension 38. The features calculation is very computationally efficient and could be done in real-time, provided the skeleton stream.

4.2 Recognition Model

Our prediction task could be abstracted as a time-series regression problem, with the following requirements:

- As demonstrated in [16], each bodily expression consists of different temporal phases, and the states are dependent on the previous ones. Thus the prediction model has to be capable of dealing with the temporal memories.

- Due to our objective to predict effective values continuously in time, sequence segmentation is undesired. This leads to a huge amount of frame-based data to be handled. Therefore, an on-line learning algorithm, instead of batch-based algorithms, is preferable, considering practical issues such as memory and computational capability. Moreover, the learning model has to be able to select the most informative data and discard the redundant ones.

- As both skeleton data and annotations are noisy, the learning model should be tolerant to noise.

Bearing these in mind, we decided to use Gaussian Processes (GP), a kernel-based non-parametric algorithm that achieved great success in time series prediction problems. Specifically, the recursive kernel is used to model the temporal dynamics. In the following, we give a brief description of the GP algorithm, more details could be found in [33].

4.3   Online Recursive Gaussian Processes

A GP is a stochastic process which can be fully determined by its mean function

$$\mu(\mathbf{x}) = \mathbb{E}[Y(\mathbf{x})] \tag{4}$$

and its covariance function

$$k(\mathbf{x}, \mathbf{x}') = \mathbb{E}[(Y(\mathbf{x}) - \mu(\mathbf{x}))(Y(\mathbf{x}') - \mu(\mathbf{x}'))] \tag{5}$$

where $\mathbf{x} \in \mathbf{X}$ is the input vector, $Y(\mathbf{x})$ is the random function on $\mathbf{x}$. Normally we assume that $\mu(\mathbf{x}) \equiv 0$, so the GP is only specified by the covariance function $k(\mathbf{x}, \mathbf{x}')$, which has a kernel form. We can then write the GP as:

$$Y(\mathbf{x}) \sim \mathcal{N}(0, k(\mathbf{x}, \mathbf{x}')) \tag{6}$$

Given the training samples $(\mathbf{x}_i, y_i) \in \mathcal{D}$, where y_i is the target value at data point i, the matrix of covariances between the training points $\mathbf{K} = [k(\mathbf{x}_i, \mathbf{x}_j)]$ is called *Gram Matrix*. We also define $\mathbf{k}(\mathbf{x}') = [k(\mathbf{x}_i, \mathbf{x}')]_{i=1}^{N}$, N being the number of training samples. Then, for a new input data point $\mathbf{x}^*$, the distribution of the prediction is:

$$p(Y^*|\mathbf{x}^*, \mathcal{D}) \sim \mathcal{N}(Y^*|\mu^*, \sigma^{*2}) \tag{7}$$

where

$$\mu^* = \mathbf{k}(\mathbf{x}^*)^T(\mathbf{K} + \sigma^2\mathbf{I}_N)^{-1}\mathbf{y} \tag{8}$$

$$\sigma^{*2} = k(\mathbf{x}^*, \mathbf{x}^*) - \mathbf{k}(\mathbf{x}^*)^T(\mathbf{K} + \sigma^2\mathbf{I}_N)^{-1}\mathbf{k}(\mathbf{x}^*) \tag{9}$$

The variance of the prediction σ^{*2} could be used as the uncertainty measure.

In order to update the GP with sequentially arriving data points, [8] proposed a sparse on-line GP algorithm. The main idea is to keep the size of the model by controlling the number of data points that are used for prediction. Those remained data points are called "*Basic Vectors*". Each sample is scored by a "novelty" measure:

$$\gamma(\mathbf{x}^\star) = k(\mathbf{x}^\star, \mathbf{x}^\star) - \mathbf{k}_\mathcal{B}^{\star T} \mathbf{K}_\mathcal{B}^{-1} \mathbf{k}_\mathcal{B}^\star \tag{10}$$

where $\mathbf{k}_\mathcal{B}^{\star T} = [k(\mathbf{b}_i, \mathbf{x}^\star)]$ and $\mathbf{K}_\mathcal{B} = [k(\mathbf{b}_i, \mathbf{b}_j)]$, with $\mathbf{b}_i, \mathbf{b}_j \in \mathcal{B}$, the basic vectors. The highly scored new sample will be absorbed in the set of basic vectors, while the lowest scored one will be discarded from the set. The number of basic vectors, as a global hyperparameter, plays the role to balance the prediction strength and the computational efficiency, which is generally determined by the calculation capacity. Refer to [8] for more details.

To cope with the temporal dynamics in a systematic way, a recursive kernel is applied on the GP, to form a recursive GP [33]. For the widely used squared exponential kernel:

$$k_{SE}(\mathbf{x}, \mathbf{x}') = exp(-\frac{||\mathbf{x} - \mathbf{x}'||^2}{2l^2}) \tag{11}$$

the corresponding recursive version is:

$$\kappa^{(t)}(\mathbf{x}, \mathbf{x}') = exp(-\frac{||\mathbf{x}^{(t)} - \mathbf{x}'^{(t)}||^2}{\sigma^2})exp(\frac{(\kappa^{(t-1)}(\mathbf{x}, \mathbf{x}') - 1)}{\rho^2}) \tag{12}$$

5   Experimental Results

The 3D skeletal frames, annotations (arousal and valence separately), as well as the video recordings of face and frontal body, were synchronised and temporally aligned to have the same frame rate of $30Hz$. The feature vectors, as described in section 4.1 were generated from the skeletal frames, on a frame basis, and all values of the features were normalised to have the same order of magnitude.

Firstly, we evaluated the emotion prediction model with same-subject sequence. The model was trained with a full recording sequence, using the on-line updating. Then the same sequence was tested on the model. The size of the GP *basic vector* was set to 300 (maximally 300 samples in the training set were kept in the model for prediction calculation). The results are shown in Fig. 4.

As it can be seen, both the arousal and valence dimensions were well predicted, with the 300 training samples stored in the GP. This result proved the effectiveness of the proposed features to describe bodily expressions.

To evaluate the generalization ability of our approach, we applied the trained model on a sequence performed by another child. Fig. 5 illustrates the obtained results. For the arousal dimension, as shown in the first sub-figure, the trends were well followed. The vertical shifts could be explained by the slightly different scales used for the annotations of the two sequences. As for the valence dimension, the result was less good compared to the arousal predictions. There were several opposite predictions. For instance, around point D in the figure, the annotated negative expression was predicted as positive. However, if we review the

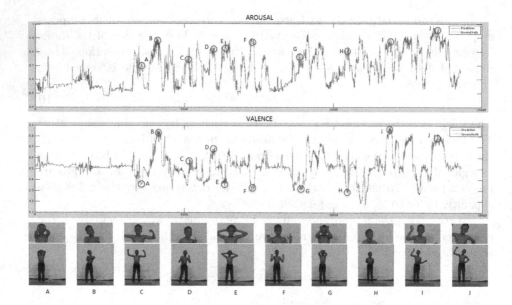

Fig. 4. Same-subject prediction. The solid and dashed curves are the prediction and the annotation, respectively. The first and second sub-figures are arousal and valence dimension, respectively. Ten frames (A-J) are marked, the corresponding facial and bodily expressions are given in the third sub-figure.

recorded videos, the negative emotion was actually delivered via the facial and vocal expressions, while the "jump and turn-around" body motion alone could be interpreted as a positive expression, that happened occasionally in other recordings. Another interesting pattern in both the arousal and valence prediction is that we can see a clear lag between the ground-truth and the prediction. This is due to the delay of the annotation (normally less than one second) reported by the raters. This delay had been compensated by the model during the prediction, which is a merit in real-time applications, as child-robot interaction.

6   Discussion

In this work, we present our initial attempt to recognize children's affective states from their spontaneous bodily expressions, in child-robot interactions. The predicted child's arousal and valence values, are used by the robot's behavioural control system, so as to achieve a more natural and comfortable interaction. We designed an emotion elicitation scenario. The preliminary experiments have shown encouraging results for both arousal and valence predictions from the stand-alone bodily cues, which has been widely recognised as a very challenging problem, especially under naturalistic settings. Moreover, our experiments further demonstrated the importance of bodily information in emotion modelling tasks. For example, position E in Fig. 5, where the face shows a positive

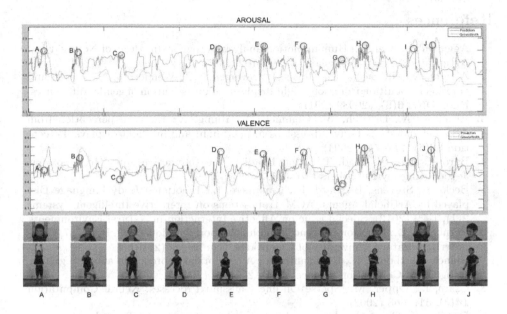

Fig. 5. Cross-subject prediction. The layout is the same as in Fig. 4.

expression that is similar to the one at position H, while the body displays a strongly negative state, which is consistent with the interaction circumstance at that moment.

Similar to the conclusion in [23], the valence dimension is much more difficult to model, as shown in our preliminary results. Therefore, in future work we planed to fuse different modalities including bodily, facial and vocal/verbal signals. Additionally, considering the fact that spontaneous emotion annotation is a very subjective task that has strong dependency on individual's perception, modelling the emotional changes instead of the absolute values might be more practical. Last but not least, a more sophisticated sample selection algorithm, could benefit the predictive performance, by keeping the most informative and contributing data frames in the model.

Acknowledgments. This work has been made under the EU-FP7 ALIZ-E Project (No. 248116), also supported by the CSC grant 2011688012. We also would like to thank the members of Beeldenstorm and KIK project in Brussels, Belgium, who provided us the opportunity to implement our data acquisition scenario. We also thank the participated children and their parents.

References

1. Aggarwal, J., Cai, Q.: Human motion analysis: a review. In: Proc. of Nonrigid and Articulated Motion Workshop, pp. 90–102 (1997)
2. Alaerts, K., Nackaerts, E., Meyns, P., Swinnen, S.P., Wenderoth, N.: Action and emotion recognition from point light displays: an investigation of gender differences. PLoS ONE **6**(6), e20989 (2011)
3. Atkinson, A., Dittrich, W., Gemmell, A., Young, A.: Emotion perception from dynamic and static body expressions in point-light and full-light displays. Perception **33**(6), 717–746 (2004)
4. Baron-Cohen, S., Tead, T.: Mind Reading: the Interactive Guide to Emotions. Jessica Kingsley Publishers Ltd. (2003)
5. Beck, A., Stevens, B., Bard, K., Canamero, L.: Emotional Body Language Displayed by Artificial Agents. ACM Transactions on Interactive Intelligent Systems **2**(1), 1–29 (2012). Special issue on Affective Interaction in Natural Environments
6. Bernhardt, D.: Emotion inference from human body motion. Tech. Rep. 787, Computer Laboratory, University of Cambridge, Cambridge (2010)
7. Bianchi-Berthouze, N., Kleinsmith, A.: A categorical approach to affective gesture recognition. Connection Science **15**(4), 259–269 (2003)
8. Csato, L., Opper, M.: Sparse On-line Gaussian Processes. Neural Computation **14**(3), 641–668 (2002)
9. De Silva, P., Osano, M., Marasinghe, A., Madurapperuma, A.: Towards recognizing emotion with affective dimensions through body gestures. In: Proceedings of 7th International Conference on Automatic Face and Gesture Recognition (FG 2006), pp. 269–274. IEEE (2006)
10. Dittrich, W., Troscianko, T., Lea, S., Morgan, D.: Perception of emotion from dynamic point-light displays represented in dance. Perception **25**(6), 727–738 (1996)
11. Ekman, P.: Basic emotions. In: Handbook of Cognition and Emotion, chap. 3. No. 1992 (1999)
12. de Gelder, B.: Why bodies? Twelve reasons for including bodily expressions in affective neuroscience. Philosophical Tran. of the Royal Society B: Biological Sciences **364**, 3475–3484 (2009)
13. Gonzalez, I., Sahli, H., Enescu, V., Verhelst, W.: Context-independent facial action unit recognition using shape and gabor phase information. In: D'Mello, S., Graesser, A., Schuller, B., Martin, J.-C. (eds.) ACII 2011, Part I. LNCS, vol. 6974, pp. 548–557. Springer, Heidelberg (2011)
14. Gross, J.J., Levenson, R.W.: Emotion Elicitation Using Films. Cognition and Emotion **9**(1), 87–108 (1995)
15. Gross, M.M., Crane, E.A., Fredrickson, B.L.: Methodology for Assessing Bodily Expression of Emotion. Journal of Nonverbal Behavior **34**(4), 223–248 (2010)
16. Gunes, H., Piccardi, M.: Automatic temporal segment detection and affect recognition from face and body display. IEEE Transactions on Systems, Man, and Cybernetics. Part B, Cybernetics: A Publication of the IEEE Systems, Man, and Cybernetics Society **39**(1), 64–84 (2009)
17. Jiang, D., Cui, Y., Zhang, X., Fan, P., Ganzalez, I., Sahli, H.: Audio visual emotion recognition based on triple-stream dynamic bayesian network models. In: D'Mello, S., Graesser, A., Schuller, B., Martin, J.-C. (eds.) ACII 2011, Part I. LNCS, vol. 6974, pp. 609–618. Springer, Heidelberg (2011)
18. Kahol, K., Tripathi, P., Panchanathan, S.: Gesture segmentation in complex motion sequences. In: Proc. of International Conference on Image Processing (ICIP 2003) (2003)

19. Kapur, A., Kapur, A., Virji-Babul, N., Tzanetakis, G., Driessen, P.F.: Gesture-based affective computing on motion capture data. In: Tao, J., Tan, T., Picard, R.W. (eds.) ACII 2005. LNCS, vol. 3784, pp. 1–7. Springer, Heidelberg (2005)
20. Kleinsmith, A., Bianchi-Berthouze, N.: Affective Body Expression Perception and Recognition: A Survey. IEEE Transactions on Affective Computing 4(1), 15–33 (2013)
21. Larsen, J.T., McGraw, A.P.: Further evidence for mixed emotions. Journal of Personality and Social Psychology 100(6), 1095–1110 (2011)
22. Mckeown, G., Valstar, M., Cowie, R., Pantic, M., Member, S., Schr, M.: The SEMAINE database: annotated multimodal records of emotionally coloured conversations between a person and a limited agent. IEEE Transactions on Affective Computing 3(1), 5–17 (2012)
23. Metallinou, A., Katsamanis, A., Narayanan, S.: Tracking continuous emotional trends of participants during affective dyadic interactions using body language and speech information. Image and Vision Computing, September 2012
24. N/A: Aldebaran Robotics. http://www.aldebaran.com
25. N/A: Ipi Mocap Studio. http://ipisoft.com/
26. Picard, R.: Affective computing. Tech. Rep. 321, MIT (1995)
27. Preston, S., de Waal, F.: Empathy: Its Ultimate and Proximate. Behavioral and Brian Sciences 252, 1–72 (2002)
28. Roberts, N.A., Tsai, J.L., Coan, J.A.: Emotion elicitation using dyadic interaction tasks. In: Handbook of Emotion Elicitation and Assessment, pp. 106–123 (2007)
29. Russell, J.A.: A Circumplex Model of Affect. Journal of Personality & Social Psychology 39, 1161–1178 (1980)
30. Russell, J.A.: Core affect and the psychological construction of emotion. Psychological Review 110(1), 145–172 (2003)
31. Scherer, K.R.: What Are Emotions? And How Can They Be Measured. Social Science Information 44(4), 695–729 (2005)
32. Schindler, K., Van Gool, L., de Gelder, B.: Recognizing emotions expressed by body pose: a biologically inspired neural model. Neural Networks: The Official Journal of the International Neural Network Society 21(9), 1238–1246 (2008)
33. Soh, H.: Online spatio-temporal gaussian process experts with application to tactile classification. In: IEEE/RSJ International Conference on Intelligent Robots and Systems (2012)
34. Verhelst, W., Roelands, M.: An overlap-add technique based on waveform similarity (wsola) for high quality time-scale modification of speech. In: ICASSP 1993, vol. 2, pp. 554–557 (1993)
35. Wallbott, H.G.: Bodily Expression of Emotion. European Journal of Social Psychology 28(6), 879–896 (1998)
36. Wang, F., Verhelst, W., Sahli, H.: Relevance vector machine based speech emotion recognition. In: D'Mello, S., Graesser, A., Schuller, B., Martin, J.-C. (eds.) ACII 2011, Part II. LNCS, vol. 6975, pp. 111–120. Springer, Heidelberg (2011)
37. Wang, W., Athanasopoulos, G., Yilmazyildiz, S., Patsis, G., Enescu, V., Sahli, H., Verhelst, W., Hiolle, A., Lewis, M., Cañamero, L.: Natural emotion elicitation for emotion modeling in child-robot interactions. In: Proc. of Workshop on Child Computer Interaction (WOCCI 2014) (2014, to appear)
38. Wang, W., Enescu, V., Sahli, H.: Towards real-time continuous emotion recognition from body movements. In: Salah, A.A., Hung, H., Aran, O., Gunes, H. (eds.) HBU 2013. LNCS, vol. 8212, pp. 235–245. Springer, Heidelberg (2013)

Eye Blink Detection Using Variance of Motion Vectors

Tomas Drutarovsky and Andrej Fogelton[✉]

Vision and Graphics Group, Faculty of Informatics and Information Technologies,
Slovak University of Technology in Bratislava, Bratislava, Slovakia
{xdrutarovsky,andrej.fogelton}@stuba.sk

Abstract. A new eye blink detection algorithm is proposed. It is based on analyzing the variance of the vertical motions in the eye region. The face and eyes are detected with a Viola–Jones type algorithm. Next, a flock of KLT trackers is placed over the eye region. For each eye, region is divided into 3×3 cells. For each cell an average "cell" motion is calculated. Simple state machines analyse the variances for each eye. The proposed method has lower false positive rate compared to other methods based on tracking. We introduce a new challenging dataset *Eyeblink8*. Our method achieves the best reported mean accuracy 99 % on the Talking dataset and state-of-the-art results on the ZJU dataset.

Keywords: Eye blink detection · Statistical variance · Motion vectors · Outlier detection · Global movement compensation

1 Introduction

Eye blink detection has different uses e.g. driver fatigue detection [1], a user monitoring for dry eye syndrome prevention [6], helping disabled people to interact with a computer [9] or face liveness detection [17].

Eye blink is defined as rapid closing and reopening of the eyelid. We focus on detection of endegenous eye blinks. Partial closed eye is called an incomplete blink. Eye blink in general lasts from 150 to 300ms [15]. Thus a standard camera with 25–30 frames per second (fps) is sufficient for eye blink monitoring. A real-time performance is desired. Published methods can be categorized into two groups: appearance and sequential based. Sequential methods are based on a motion tracking in the eye region [6] or computing difference between frames (pixels values [11], descriptors [4], etc.). Appearance based methods estimate the state of the eye (open, closed [12] or the eye closure [8]) for individual frames.

In our experience, appearance based methods have often difficulties with different conditions as the presence of glasses with a thick frame, a strong eyebrow or an eye openness (race dependent) etc. Tracking based [6] detector with no appearance knowledge achieves one of the best true positive rates on publicly available datasets, on the other side the false positive rate is higher due to face mimics and head movements.

© Springer International Publishing Switzerland 2015
L. Agapito et al. (Eds.): ECCV 2014 Workshops, Part III, LNCS 8927, pp. 436–448, 2015.
DOI: 10.1007/978-3-319-16199-0_31

We focused on tracking based method with the aim to decrease the false positive rate. Instead of the head movement compensation (which provide insufficient accuracy), we obtain the movement information from statistical variance of motion vectors.

The proposed eye blink detection algorithm consists of four steps. In the first step a flock of KLT trackers [18] is placed over the eye region. The second step uses the local motion vectors to estimate "cell" motions. The third one calculates the variance of the vertical components of these motion vectors. The variance is the input for the state machine which is the last step to detect blinks. There is a separate procedure for each eye. Blink state in one of the state machines indicates an eye blink. The method is reinitialised by a Viola–Jones type algorithm [19] to detect face and eye regions after each detected blink. This can be considered as an interplay between the flocks of trackers in the eye region and the eye detector.

The rest of the paper is structured as follows; Section 2 reviews related work. Section 3 describes the proposed method. Section 4 presents the evaluation on the publicly available datasets and discusses the results.

2 Related Work

The majority of methods are initialized with a Viola–Jones type algorithm to detect the face and eyes e.g. [3,8]. Based on circumstances, the detector is not able to detect non frontal faces/eyes, which is often compensated with region tracking [2,12]. Different approaches are used to detect eye blinks.

2.1 Appearance Based

Intensity Vertical Projection (IVP) [4] is the total pixel intensity in a frame row. The method uses the fact that an iris has a lower intensity vertical projection values compared to other regions. IVP function has two local minima representing an open eye. Blink is detected based on the changes of the IVP curve.

The method in [1] measures ocular parameters by fitting two ellipses to eye pupils using the modification of the algebraic distance algorithm for conics approximation [7]. The degree of an eye openness is characterized by the pupil shape. To eliminate the inaccuracy of the algorithm for fitting ellipses, a state machine is defined to detect eye blinks. In [8] the percentage of closure is calculated from the ratio between the iris height in the frame and the nominal value assigned during a ten-second calibration. This detector reaches 90% recall and low false positive rate on the author's own database consisting of 25 hours of driving records.

The best precision on ZJU dataset is achieved in [12]. The authors introduce two features using binarized image; $F1$ as the cumulative difference of black pixels in a detected eye region, estimated from the binary image from consecutive frames. The authors observed that the number of black pixels in a closed eye image is higher compared to an open eye image. The number of black pixels is, however, also influenced by the distance from the camera. To avoid it, the method uses an adaptive threshold based on a cumulative difference. The second feature $F2$ represents a ratio of eye height to eye width. To calculate $F2$, a binarized eye region is processed through an erosion and dilation filters. The eye state (open, closed) is estimated by a maximal vertical projection of black pixels. An open eye has greater value of this ratio, because it has higher maximal projection value. To estimate eye openness precisely, the authors use the features $F1$ and $F2$ as input values to a SVM. Three SVM classifiers are used for three different rotation angles to determine the eye state of the subject.

In [16] eyelids are detected as follows: first, an image is divided into several vertical sections. In each section, candidates for upper and lower eyelids are defined as the maximal and minimal differential values of the gray level distribution. These candidates are grouped in five sections, two of them are chosen to represent the upper and lower eyelid. All five sections are then used to calculate the *eye gap* – an average of distances between eyelid candidates. The eye gap is the degree of eye openness. Over time, it represents a blink waveform. The eye gap decreases rapidly when eye blinks. After the eye gap reaches the minimum value (eye is considered closed), it increases gradually.

In [3], a neural network-based detector is used for precise eye pupil localization. The head rotation angle is calculated using vertical positions of both pupils. The region of interest is analyzed using horizontal symmetry to determine whether the eye is open or closed. The region is divided in two halves using the axial symmetry around the line crossing centers of both pupils. Created halves represent the upper and lower eyelid regions. These halves are horizontally flipped. If the eye is open, then the horizontally flipped fragment preserves symmetry, unlike the closed eye, because of eyelashes. Therefore the difference between the upper and lower half is used as the discriminative feature to detect closed eye. The algorithm is tested on the ZJU[1] dataset and it achieves 94.8% of mean accuracy.

In [9,10], eyes are detected using the correlation coefficient over time. Open eye template is learned to estimate the eye closure and detect eye blinks. Reinitialization is triggered by the correlation coeficient falling under a defined threshold. According to the changing correlation between the eye and its open eye template, an eye blink waveform is established. The correlation score is binarized: open and closed eye.

One of the most successful methods is Weighted Gradient Descriptor [13], which calculates partial derivatives per each pixel in the eye region not only in vertical direction but also over time. Two vectors are calculated and the distance in between them over time is used as a feature function. Using zero crossing on this function eye blinks are detected. Evaluation on ZJU dataset achieves just one false positive and very high Recall 98.8%. We do not include these results in our comparison, because the authors tuned the parameters per dataset (their own and ZJU) and reported the best achieved results.

---

[1] http://www.cs.zju.edu.cn/~gpan/database/db_blink.html [accessed: 27.8.2014]

2.2 Sequential Based

Eyelid motion is used to detect blinks in [5]. Eye detection runs every 5th frame. Features are detected using FAST [14] and tracked with a KLT tracker. Features are classified based on their location; face, left and right eye. Eye and face regions are tracked based on the features. The authors calculate normal flow of the regions in the direction of intensity gradients. Eyelid motion also includes head movements, thus compensation based on the already extracted head movement is provided. Dominant orientations of the local motion vectors for the individual classes are extracted from a histogram of orientations, due to which partial invariance to eye orientation is achieved. To filter the eyelid motion, only the flow in the direction perpendicular to the line segment between the eyes is considered. The angle between this line and the horizon is calculated and flow vectors are transformed correspondingly. Corrected and normalized flow is used to calculate a mean flow magnitude of the eye regions. The dominant flow direction is recognized based on the individual orientation of local motion vectors (optical flow) in a histogram with 36 bins, each bin represents 10 degrees. Normal flow orientation and magnitude is used as the input parameter for state machines. Evaluation of the method on publicly available datasets can be found in [6].

3 Eye Blink Detection Using Variance of Motion Vectors

The proposed eye blink detection method assumes that the face and eye regions are localised. In the experiments reported in Section 4, the OpenCV implementation of a Viola–Jones type algorithm (we use cascade files: the frontal face and eye pair) is used. The detected eye region (both eyes) is enlarged in height (1.5×) to approximately half of the interocular distance to cover a larger area and thus to compensate the inaccuracy of the eye region detection. If the eyes are not detected, the frame is skipped. The region is divided into halves to separate individual eye regions. The method runs separatly for each eye. A flock of KLT trackers is placed over a regular grid (Fig. 1) spaced with 1/15 of the region dimensions (all together around 225 trackers, that count depends on the region size). Next, local motion vectors are extracted and averaged based on their locations. An average variance of vertical components of the 6 upper motion vectors is the input to a state machine, which detects an eye blink.

3.1 Eye Regions

The tracked person can move towards and backwards from the camera thus the eyes change their size and locations. The initial eye regions are obtained and a flock of trackers are placed regularly over them. Until the next reinitialization, the eye regions are re-estimated using the trackers for each frame.

Some of the trackers are lost over time. The trackers which fail to establish their new locations are omitted from further processing. The OpenCV KLT

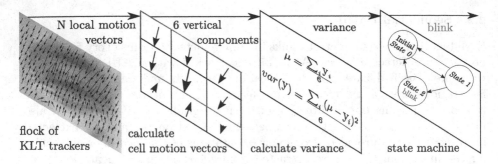

Fig. 1. Workflow of the proposed eye blink detection method

tracker implementation with an image pyramid enabled is used, from which highly unprobable new locations (major shifts across image) can occur. Therefore we omit trackers that change their location by more than a half of the image height.

KLT trackers are attracted by strong edges and corners from which some trackers diverge from the eye. We do not want to use those trackers in order to calculate motion vectors but we still keep them because there is a high probability they will return closer to the eye in future. We filter these trackers based on the estimated eye region.

The eye region is defined as a square, placed in the eye center, which is calculated as the average location of trackers in the frame for each eye. A histogram of euclidean distances of individual trackers from the eye center is created. We experimentaly evaluated a distance threshold T_d that is the beginning of the interval of 3 bins in a row with count below the threshold T_b after detected the global maximum (Fig. 2). The global maximum condition is just a precaution because the flock of trackers behavior can also cause low counts to appear at the

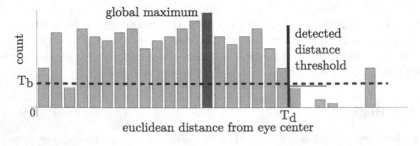

Fig. 2. Histogram of tracker euclidean distances from the eye center. The histogram is used to filter out the trackers, which are probably not in the eye region anymore. In our case, the histogram bins represent pixel distances. The distance threshold T_d is defined as the beginning of the interval of the 3 bins with count below the threshold T_b (5 in our experiments) after the global maximum is detected.

beginning of the histogram. In our experiments we use $T_b = 5$. The eye region square side length is defined as $1.6 \times T_d$.

3.2 Motion Vectors

The eye region is divided into 3×3 cells (Fig. 3). An average ("cell") motion vector is calculated for a cell from the individual local motion vectors belonging to the cell based on their locations. Eye blink causes a significant vertical move in the cells of middle row, but only a minor move in the top or bottom row. Motion vectors have different characteristics during head movements or other facial mimics. The vertical components of the middle and top rows are sufficient for further computation. From these 6 motion vectors the variance $var(y)$ (Eq. 1) is calculated. The vertical component is sufficient because there is a strong predisposition that the person's face does not rotate significantly.

Fig. 3. The eye region with flock of KLT trackers shown before and during an eyelid moves down. The region is divided into 3×3 cells. For the given cell the average tracker locations are calculated. Vertical components of the first 6 motion vectors are sufficient for further computation. The gray dots represent trackers which are used to compute motion vectors.

$$\mu = \frac{\sum_i y_i}{6}, \qquad var(y) = \frac{\sum_i (\mu - y_i)^2}{6} \qquad (1)$$

Statistical variance of the 6 upper cells represents the diversity across moves. If the variance is higher than the variance threshold T_v, it will indicate an eyelid movement. Variance is invariant to position changes of the person's face, and therefore no head movement compensation is necessary. The variance threshold is evaluated empirically on our dataset as $T_v = \kappa \times \frac{d}{fps}$, where:

- κ: Based on the tests on our dataset, the constant value is 0.02.
- d: The interocular distance is directly proportional to the subject distance from the camera. The eye size affects the size of motion vectors.
- fps: The frame rate of the input video sequence also influences the size of motion vectors. Higher frame rate means lower variance of motion vectors.

Motion vectors represent local move in the eye region which is a sign of an eye blink or possibly other moves as facial mimics, eyebrow or pupil. To eliminate detection of non blink moves a simple state machine is setup (Fig. 4). We consider eye blink as the combination of two movements – down and up move. After move down detection, the state changes from *State 0* (the initial one) into *State 1*. If the state machine is in *State 1* for about 100ms (3 frames while 30fps) and then move up is detected, the state will change into *State 2* – blink occurred. If there is no move for more than 150ms (5 frames while 30fps), the state machine will change from *State 1* back to *State 0*. We follow the assumption that an average eye blink takes from 150 to 300ms.

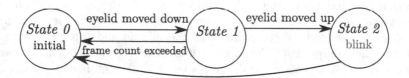

Fig. 4. The state machine of eye blink detection. After move down detection, the state changes from *State 0* into *State 1*. While in *State 1* and move up detection, the state changes into *State 2* – blink occurred. *State 1* changes back to *State 0* if there is no move for given amount of time.

Different sizes of the vertical components of the motion vectors across cells are shown in Fig. 5. Based on our observation we define move down as $(y_4 > 0)$ & $(y_4 > y_1)$ & $(var(y) > T_v)$ and move up as $(y_4 < 0)$ & $(y_4 < y_1)$ & $(var(y) > T_v)$. Algorithm 1 presents the state machine pseudo code for the eye blink detection. There are two state machines established, one for each eye. Blink state in either of the state machines defines an eye blink.

80%	100%	63%		49%	100%	-8%		-133%	-100%	-80%		-161%	-100%	-221%
66%	86%	66%		270%	301%	71%		-98%	-96%	-67%		-83%	-940%	-683%
	(a)				(b)				(c)				(d)	

Fig. 5. Difference of vertical moves in the upper 6 cells (y_0 ... y_5) during head and eye blink movements. y_1 is used as the reference to normalize the sample data only for better visualization: (a) head moves down, all motion vectors have similar size, (b) eyelid moves down, the middle row has bigger positive change, (c) head moves up, all motion vectors have again similar size, (d) eyelid moves up, the middle row has bigger negative change. Most of the time y_1 captures the head move and y_4 the eyelid move, due to which they help to define eyelid down and up move.

3.3   Reinitialization

A uniform distribution of flock of trackers is negatively affected (Fig. 6) by motion in general. A uniform distribution is important to acquire representative data of average motion vectors. We reinitialize our algorithm with face and eye detection in case of following events:

Alg. 1. State machine detecting eye blink based on variance of vertical component of motion vectors

INPUT: 6 vertical components of motion vectors(y), current state of the state machine (state), distance between eye centers (d), fps
OUTPUT: eye blink state

```
 1: procedure GET_EYE_BLINK_STATUS(y, state, d, fps)
 2:     T_v ← 0.02 * d/fps                                         ▷ variance threshold
 3:     if state = 2 then
 4:         state ← 0
 5:     end if
 6:     if state = 0 then
 7:         if ((y_4 > 0) & (y_4 > y_1) & (var(y) > T_v)) then     ▷ move down detected
 8:             state ← 1
 9:             time = current_time()
10:         end if
11:     else if (state = 1) & (100ms < (current_time() − time)) then
12:         if ((current_time() − time) < 150ms) then
13:             if ((y_4 < 0) & (y_4 < y_1) & (var(y) > T_v)) then ▷ move up detected
14:                 state ← 2                                      ▷ eye blink occurred
15:             end if
16:         else
17:             state ← 0                                         ▷ eye blink did not occur
18:         end if
19:     end if
20:     return state
21: end procedure
```

- after blink occurred,
- large number of lost trackers: more than half of the trackers are lost between two frames or the remaining number of trackers is less than 20,
- over time, after constant number of frames (in our implementation every 200 frames).

Reinitialization restores parameters to their initial values. However, it is necessary to preserve the current states of the state machines and blink frames counters, which preserve the information of how many frames in a row with no movement were observed during the *State 1*. This way the reinitialization will not interrupt the eye blink detection process.

4   Evaluation

We introduce a new dataset called *Eyeblink8*, which consists of 8 videos (Fig. 8) with 4 individuals (1 wearing glasses). Videos are recorded under different conditions with faces mostly oriented directly to the camera. It contains many natural face movements, facial mimics and other intensive non-blink moves. The dataset

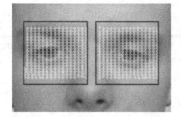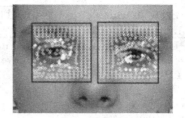

Fig. 6. Left figure shows initial flock of KLT trackers over a regular grid. Right figure represents their positions after 3 blinks. Many trackers are snapped to corners and edges disrupting the uniform distribution. Reinitialization is necessary because motion vectors rely on uniform distribution.

contains over 82600 frames (640×480) with 353 blinks. All videos are recorded using Logitech C905 camera with 30fps acquisition.

The annotation to individual videos consists of two files; the first file contains the frame numbers with the acquisition time and the second file are manually annotated states of the eye. We recognize 3 states: open, half and close. When the blink starts, *half* tags are assigned to individual frames until is fully closed. Fully closed eye is defined as 90–100% of the eye is covered with the eyelid. Fully closed eyes are tagged with *close* and openning eye is again tagged with *half* until it is fully open. Also not fully closed eye blinks can be annotated this way (consisting only from "halfs"). If only one eye is visible (or blinks) the tag *Left/Right* is added to the eye state, based on the location of the visible blink. Sample annotation is in Fig. 7. Eye blink is considered as detected if there is any intersection interval between the detected blink and anotation. For now, we do not use the information about the start of the eye blink from the state machine, we create an artificial interval around the frame with the detected eye blink with 3 frames on each side (7 frames interval with the detected eye blink in the middle). The intersection interval with the ground truth can be counted just once as *True Positive*.

We evaluated our method also on the 2 publicly available datasets (Talking Face video, ZJU). *Talking*[2] (Fig. 9) contains 5000 frames (720×576) with 61 eye blinks. A tested subject is a man taking conversation during the record. His face is mostly oriented directly to the camera and slightly turned aside. We created a new annotation compatible with our evaluation framework described above. Results are compared with the existing methods in Table 1. We failed to detect only two blinks, which happened during the downward sight, therefore the size of the vertical component of motion vectors is not significant enough.

The ZJU dataset (Fig. 10) consists of 80 short videos (10876 frames) of 20 individuals with and without glasses (insignificant small frame) captured with 30fps and size of 320 × 240. The ZJU contains together 255 eye blinks collected indoor, some of them are voluntary longer eye blinks. It is interesting

---

[2] http://www-prima.inrialpes.fr/FGnet/data/01-TalkingFace/talking_face.html [accessed: 22.7.2014]

frame number	acquisition time	frame number	state	frame number	state
2036	72.5077	8433	half	3643	halfRight
2037	72.5392	8434	half	3644	halfRight
2038	72.5712	8435	close	3645	halfRight
2039	72.6032	8436	close	3646	closeRight
2040	72.6356	8437	half	3647	closeRight
2041	72.6672	8438	half	3648	halfRight
2042	72.6994	8439	half	3649	halfRight

Fig. 7. Sample annotations for the dataset *eyeblink8*

Fig. 8. Sample snapshots from our dataset the *Eyeblink8*

that the annotation to this dataset from [3] contains even 272 eye blinks. We also manually annotated this dataset and based on our eyeblink definition there is 264 eye blinks. This dataset contains also one frame blinks and sometimes people blink twice very fast, we consider these double blinks as two. It is possible that the original annotator did consider these events differently. In Table 1 the number next to the ZJU is the number of ground true eye blinks.

Comparison on the available datasets is presented in Table 1. Methods we compare with do not mention how they calculated *false positive rate* and *mean accuracy*. We assume that the number of images with open eyes is used as *Negatives* (N). In our opinion this is not accurate, based on the study [15], an average blink takes 150–300ms (5–10 frames while 30fps). We divided the num-

Fig. 9. Sample snapshots from the *Talking face* dataset

Fig. 10. Sample snapshots from the *ZJU* dataset

ber of frames with open eyes in datasets by the average blink duration (7 frames) and this is used as negative (number of non eye blinks). From our annotation of the ZJU dataset can be read, that 2482 frames capture some part of eye blink moves. This is used to calculate more precise *False Positive* (FP) rate and *Mean accuracy* (MA). We use the following equations: $Precision = \frac{TP}{TP+FP}$, $Recall(TPrate) = \frac{TP}{TP+FN}$, $FPrate = \frac{FP}{N}$, $MA = \frac{TP+TN}{P+N}$.

Table 1. Comparison of our method on the eyeblink8, ZJU and Talking dataset. The number next to ZJU represents the number of the ground true eye blinks. There are two results in FP rate and Mean accuracy, because as true negative we consider a non blink action and not an image with open eyes (the result in brackets), which we assume is used to calculate the results in papers we compare to.

	Dataset	Precision	Recall	FP rate	Mean accuracy
Divjak & Bischof [6]	Talking	-	95%	19%	88%
Divjak & Bischof[3]	Talking	-	92%	6%	93%
Lee et al. [12]	Talking	83.3%	91.2%	-	-
Our method	Talking	**92.2%**	**96.7%**	**0.7% (0.1%)**	**99%(99.8%)**
Divjak & Bischof [6]	ZJU 255	-	**95%**	2%	97%
Lee et al. [12]	ZJU 255	**94.4%**	91.7%	-	-
Danisman et al. [3]	ZJU 272	90.7%	71.4%	1%	94.8%
Our method	ZJU 264	91%	73.1%	1.58%(**0.17%**)	93.45%(**99.8%**)
Our method	eyeblink8	79%	85.27%	0.7%(0.1%)	99.5% (99.9%)

4.1   Discussion

Our method achieves the best results in all metrics on the Talking face dataset, but lower *Recall* on the ZJU dataset. We are unable to detect 71 eye blinks on the ZJU. One third is caused by an inaccuracy of Viola–Jones type algorithm. Around 20 blinks are not complete, because the video starts with a person with closed eyes. Other failures occur mostly because of very fast eye blinks so the state machine is not registering it. If the video is not recorded properly, some

---

[3] http://www.icg.tugraz.at/Members/divjak/prework/PreWork-Results [last access: 27.6.2014]

eye blinks are only seen in one or two frames. The fastest eye blink last at least 150ms [15] and therefore should be on 5 frames (while 30fps).

Divjak & Bischof [6] have quite high false positive rate on the Talking face video. They have very low false positive rate in the ZJU dataset, where people are calm and not using face mimics and movements as in the Talking face.

Our method is invariant to shifting and thus we do not face the problem of head move compensation. It has to be stated that very fast head nodding is still detected as false positive mostly because of motion blur.

Lee et al. [12] achieves the best precision on the ZJU dataset but by 10% lower on the Talking. Their method is an apearance based and we assume that is capable of detecting the 20 incomplete eye blinks which are in the beginning of the videos. We notice that low precision in Talking dataset could be caused by significant eye brows of the person, which are closer to the eye as in the ZJU dataset. The Talking face is European person and the ZJU dataset consists of Asian people mostly whose eye brows are in average further from the eye. Their method was trained on their own dataset consisting of Asian type people facing to the camera. In *Talking face* the person often looks down, which also decreases the precision.

Our method is implemented in C++ using OpenCV achieving real-time performance on Intel Core i5 (4 cores) 3.1Ghz with 20% of CPU utilization.

5   Conclusions

There is an increase attentation on eye blink detection algorithms for different purposes as driver fatigue detection or face liveness detection etc. We present a simple method based on flock of trackers and variance of motion vectors. Standard camera with 25–30fps is sufficient. By using the statistical variance of vertical component of the motion vectors as the input for the state machine, we created a robust method and achieve invariance to common head moves and facial mimics.

We introduce our new challenging dataset *Eyeblink8* with available annotations. We achieve the best results on the *Talking face* dataset, 99% of mean accuracy. We propose a different way to compute false positives and mean accuracy based on the number of non eye blinks and not the number of images containing an open eye. We achieve state-of-the-art results on *ZJU* dataset.

Acknowledgments. This work was partially supported by VEGA 1/0625/14. My thanks belongs to Matej Makula and professor Jiří Matas for the wonderful comments which helped to improve this paper.

References

1. Bergasa, L., Nuevo, J., Sotelo, M., Barea, R., Lopez, M.: Real-time system for monitoring driver vigilance. IEEE Transactions on Intelligent Transportation Systems **7**(1), 63–77 (2006)

2. Brandt, T., Stemmer, R., Rakotonirainy, A.: Affordable visual driver monitoring system for fatigue and monotony. In: IEEE International Conference on Systems, Man and Cybernetics 2004, vol. 7, pp. 6451–6456 (2004)

3. Danisman, T., Bilasco, I., Djeraba, C., Ihaddadene, N.: Drowsy driver detection system using eye blink patterns. In: 2010 International Conference on Machine and Web Intelligence (ICMWI), pp. 230–233 (2010)

4. Dinh, H., Jovanov, E., Adhami, R.: Eye blink detection using intensity vertical projection. In: International Multi-Conference on Engineering and Technological Innovation: IMETI 2012 (2012)

5. Divjak, M., Bischof, H.: Real-time video-based eye blink analysis for detection of low blink-rate during computer use. In: First International Workshop on Tracking Humans for the Evaluation of their Motion in Image Sequences (THEMIS), pp. 99–107 (2008)

6. Divjak, M., Bischof, H.: Eye blink based fatigue detection for prevention of computer vision syndrome. In: IAPR Conference on Machine Vision Applications, pp. 350–353 (2009)

7. Fitzgibbon, A.W., Fisher, R.B.: A buyer's guide to conic fitting. In: Proceedings of the 6th British Conference on Machine Vision, vol. 2, pp. 513–522 (1995)

8. Garcia, I., Bronte, S., Bergasa, L., Almazan, J., Yebes, J.: Vision-based drowsiness detector for real driving conditions. In: 2012 IEEE Intelligent Vehicles Symposium (IV), pp. 618–623 (2012)

9. Grauman, K., Betke, M., Lombardi, J., Gips, J., Bradski, G.: Communication via eye blinks and eyebrow raises: video-based human-computer interfaces. Universal Access in the Information Society 2(4), 359–373 (2003)

10. Królak, A., Strumiłło, P.: Eye-blink detection system for human computer interaction. Universal Access in the Information Society 11(4), 409–419 (2012)

11. Kurylyak, Y., Lamonaca, F., Mirabelli, G.: Detection of the eye blinks for human's fatigue monitoring. In: IEEE International Symposium on Medical Measurements and Applications Proceedings, pp. 1–4 (2012)

12. Lee, W.O., Lee, E.C., Park, K.R.: Blink detection robust to various facial poses. Journal of Neuroscience Methods (2010)

13. Radlak, K., Smolka, B.: Blink detection based on the weighted gradient descriptor. In: Burduk, R., Jackowski, K., Kurzynski, M., Wozniak, M., Zolnierek, A. (eds.) CORES 2013. AISC, vol. 226, pp. 691–700. Springer, Heidelberg (2013)

14. Rosten, E., Drummond, T.W.: Machine learning for high-speed corner detection. In: Leonardis, A., Bischof, H., Pinz, A. (eds.) ECCV 2006, Part I. LNCS, vol. 3951, pp. 430–443. Springer, Heidelberg (2006)

15. Stern, J.A., Walrath, L.C., Goldstein, R.: The endogenous eyeblink. Psychophysiology 21(1), 22–33 (1984)

16. Suzuki, M., Yamamoto, N., Yamamoto, O., Nakano, T., Yamamoto, S.: Measurement of driver's consciousness by image processing - a method for presuming driver's drowsiness by eye-blinks coping with individual differences. IEEE ICSMC. 4, 2891–2896 (2006)

17. Szwoch, M., Pieniążek, P.: Eye blink based detection of liveness in biometric authentication systems using conditional random fields. In: Bolc, L., Tadeusiewicz, R., Chmielewski, L.J., Wojciechowski, K. (eds.) ICCVG 2012. LNCS, vol. 7594, pp. 669–676. Springer, Heidelberg (2012)

18. Tomasi, C., Kanade, T.: Detection and tracking of point features. Computer Science Department, Carnegie Mellon University, Tech. rep. (April 1991)

19. Viola, P., Jones, M.J.: Robust real-time face detection. Int. J. Comput. Vision 57(2), 137–154 (2004)

Detection and Modelling of Staircases Using a Wearable Depth Sensor

Alejandro Pérez-Yus[✉], Gonzalo López-Nicolás, and José J. Guerrero

Instituto de Investigación en Ingeniería de Aragón,Universidad de Zaragoza,
Zaragoza, Spain
{alperez,gonlopez,josechu.guerrero}@unizar.es

Abstract. In this paper we deal with the perception task of a wearable navigation assistant. Specifically, we have focused on the detection of staircases because of the important role they play in indoor navigation due to the multi-floor reaching possibilities they bring and the lack of security they cause, specially for those who suffer from visual deficiencies. We use the depth sensing capacities of the modern RGB-D cameras to segment and classify the different elements that integrate the scene and then carry out the stair detection and modelling algorithm to retrieve all the information that might interest the user, i.e. the location and orientation of the staircase, the number of steps and the step dimensions. Experiments prove that the system is able to perform in real-time and works even under partial occlusions of the stairway.

Keywords: Stair detection · Obstacle detection · Segmentation · Visually impaired · RGB-D

1 Introduction

The ability of navigating effectively in the environment is natural for people, but not easy to complete under certain circumstances, such as the case of visually impaired people or when moving at unknown and intricate environments. A personal guidance system must keep the subject away from hazards, but it should also point out specific features of the environment the user might want to interact with. In this paper we propose an algorithm which solves the detection of one of the most common features any person can come across during his daily life: the stairs. Finding stairs along the path has the double benefit of preventing falls and advertising the possibility of reaching another floor in the building.

To accomplish that we use a RGB-D sensor mounted on the chest, able to provide simultaneously color and depth information of the scene. The algorithm takes advantage of the depth perception to find the ground automatically and to dynamically recalibrate the ground position in order to project the 3D coordinates to a user-centered system. There is a segmentation process of the projected scene where the resulting segments are tentatively classified among floor, walls, random shapes and possible steps. Then the stairs detection algorithm outputs

© Springer International Publishing Switzerland 2015
L. Agapito et al. (Eds.): ECCV 2014 Workshops, Part III, LNCS 8927, pp. 449–463, 2015.
DOI: 10.1007/978-3-319-16199-0_32

if the step candidates constitute a stairway, a single step or none. If a stairway is found, the algorithm retrieves how it is positioned with respect to the subject, how many steps can be seen and their approximate dimensions.

What we present here is a new algorithm for human navigation in indoor environments that serve as base for future add-ons to help us to understand better the scene. Our main contribution is a new stair detection and modelling module that provides full information of the staircases present before the subject. Experiments with video recordings in different indoor environments have accomplished great results in terms of accuracy and time response. Besides, a comparison of our results with the ones from other publications like [16,17] has been performed, showing that the algorithm not only reaches state of the art performance but also includes further improvements. Specifically, our algorithm is the first known to the authors to be able to obtain the measurements of staircases even with people obstructing the view, allowing the extension of the information of the few steps detected to complete the staircase.

2   Related Work

Stairways are inevitably present in human-made environments and constitute a major problem in robot and human navigation. Many different types of sensors e.g. monocular and stereo cameras or laser scanning have been used for detecting stairs, all of them having intrinsic advantages and disadvantages. Some of the most outstanding publications on stairs detection using conventional cameras are [3], [6,7] and [15], and using stereo vision [9] and [14]. Other authors preferred the use of laser scanning for stairs finding, most of them focused on robot navigation, such as [2], [11] and [13].

In recent years, RGB-D cameras, such as Microsoft Kinect or Asus Xtion Pro Live, have entered the consumer market at a reduced price (around 150€) causing great impact on the fields of computer vision and robotics. Their main feature is that they capture color and depth information of the scene simultaneously. The depth sensor can help perceiving the shape of a staircase more easily and as a consequence it can help performing a more robust detection. Moreover, the depth perception is independent of textures and lightning conditions. On the other hand, depth cameras do not work well outdoors or even indoors with strong sun reflections. In our recent work we have mostly focused on the depth sensing capacities of the RGB-D camera, but the combined use of color and depth information would overcome most limitations, and will be subject for further research [1]. Some authors who choose RGB-D as main sensor use machine learning algorithms to perform staircase detection [5], [18] while others prefer using geometrical reasoning, like [16,17] and [4]. The later is the approach we also consider to solve this problem.

We believe that the existing algorithms using this technology are incomplete and can be improved. In [16] it is not taken into account the possibility of one or two steps, quite common in doorways or other special constructions. In both [16,17] they do not model and retrieve the actual measurements of the steps, information which can be used to verify the detection, to give indications to the user or to analyse the traversability of the staircase. They use a RANSAC approach for finding planes in the scene that outcomes of each step a set of points at certain height (which in [16] even extends beyond the actual step) not using any other shape constraint but the sum of sufficient points. Also, our algorithm uses no other sensor than the RGB-D camera itself, instead of an accelerometer to calculate the relative position and orientation of the scene. Our automatic floor finding algorithm is able to find the floor with one single frame and then orient the scene accordingly for the succeeding stages not being deceived by other possible dominant planes in the scene.

Delmerico et al. proposed an ascending stairway modelling that introduces some interesting ideas [4]. Their goal is to localize and model stairways to check for traversability and enable autonomous multi-floor exploration. In order to build up a complete model of the stairway they align the point clouds from different views relying on the robot's estimated pose, which is complicated in human navigation. In addition, the stair edge detection, which is the starting point of their algorithm, is based on abrupt changes in depth that only appears in ascending staircases when the sensor is lower than the steps, i.e. a small robot. However, that collapses with our idea of a chest-mounted sensor. Moreover, the incapacity of the algorithm to detect descending stairs and their requirement of a minimum of three steps for detecting a stairway leaves a margin of improvement.

3   System Setup and Floor Detection

The first module of the proposed algorithm is presented in this section. In Section 3.1 it is explained how the system is intended to be worn and the data acquired. The floor finding algorithm and the coordinates projection is the subject of the Section 3.2.

3.1   Setup Configuration and Data Acquisition

There are different options to locate the camera in a wearable navigation system. Mayol-Cuevas et al. [10] presented an extensive research about this topic. The two most common choices are head-mounted and chest-mounted. The first one has the advantages of being intuitive as it resembles the eyes location, allows the subject to simply stand and scan the environment and makes harder to have the field of view obstructed. On the other hand, it is continuously moving and it adds more complexity to implement a robust and stable navigation system. Moreover, it is less secure as the user might be looking away from his most immediate hazards, as it cannot be controlled. A chest-mounted system remains fixed to the body in a comfortable and secure manner, allowing the user to move freely knowing that the assistant will warn of any danger along the path. For these considerations we have chosen a chest-mounted system as the best option.

The camera will be slightly pointing downwards, at approximately 45° down. As the RGB-D sensor employed has a 45° of vertical field of view, it should be

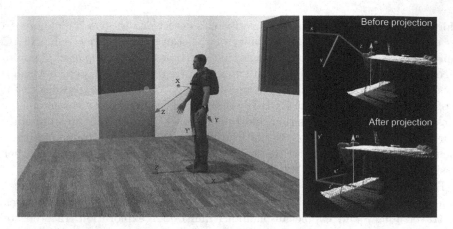

Fig. 1. Wearable camera location and axis position before (XYZ) and after $(X'Y'Z')$ the projection to the ground in a 3D render (left). Point clouds from a real case scenario, where the white points on the floor are those which form the best floor candidate plane and the yellow arrow is the corresponding normal (right).

enough to locate the obstacle-free path in front of the subject and to easily detect stairs in the scene. Currently, all the computations are operated on a laptop which could be carried in a backpack. A scheme of the configuration is shown in Fig. 1 (left).

The basic type of data used by our system are the so-called *point clouds*, consisting on a set of data of each pixel which contains the 3D location with respect to the camera and the RGB information. We have used Robot Operating System (ROS) as framework and the Point-Cloud Library (PCL) as our main library to deal with this type of data. Video sequences or single point clouds can also be stored to work offline. Capturing the data once the system is running is not highly time-consuming (about 30 Hz).

The amount of data generated by each point cloud is too large to be entirely used and thus the first operation will be filtering. For this we use a 3D voxel grid filter, a common algorithm widely used for downsampling point clouds, which also helps removing noise and smoothing the surfaces. The sizes of the edges of the voxels are determined by balancing time consumption and accuracy of the data. The filtered cloud will be used in the remaining stages.

3.2 Floor Detection

The point clouds have 3D Euclidean measurements of its location in front of the camera, but it is necessary to calculate the relative position between the sensor and the subject in order to convert the raw information acquired to oriented data that would help knowing the absolute position of the objects in the scene. The axis of the coordinate system will be transformed as shown in Fig. 1.

This projection requires to find the plane that most likely corresponds to the floor, which may not be the most dominant. No other sensor has been used for this task, so the only previous knowledge is the approximate location of the camera on the chest, which can vary due to the movement and the height of the subject. A RANSAC procedure is used to find planes, and the relative distance and orientation of each plane with respect to the camera are then tested to determine whether it is floor or not. A pass-through filter in $z - axis$ can additionally be used to restrict the search to the proximity of the user (Fig. 1 in the right). If the floor is not found with the first cloud, a new one will be captured and the process will be repeated. As the camera is pointing downwards and the user is supposed to be standing on the floor, the process should not last long.

Once a set of points belonging to a good floor candidate plane are found, the transformation matrix is computed. The normal of the plane has to be parallel to the direction of the $y - axis$, and the origin of coordinates is placed on the floor, at height 0. The fundamental plane equation is $Ax + By + Cz + D = 0$, being the normal vector $n = (A, B, C)$ and D the perpendicular distance from the origin to the plane. The rotation angles of interest are those corresponding to the $x - axis$ (α) and to the $z - axis$ (γ). It is possible to get those angles by computing the rotation needed to make n parallel to $j = (0, 1, 0)$ as shown in (1). The entire transformation matrix is shown in (2).

$$R_z R_x n^T = \begin{pmatrix} \cos\gamma & -\sin\gamma & 0 \\ \sin\gamma & \cos\gamma & 0 \\ 0 & 0 & 1 \end{pmatrix} \begin{pmatrix} 1 & 0 & 0 \\ 0 & \cos\alpha & -\sin\alpha \\ 0 & \sin\alpha & \cos\alpha \end{pmatrix} \begin{pmatrix} A \\ B \\ C \end{pmatrix} = \begin{pmatrix} 0 \\ 1 \\ 0 \end{pmatrix} = j \quad (1)$$

$$T = \begin{pmatrix} \cos\gamma & -\sin\gamma\cos\alpha & \sin\gamma\sin\alpha & 0 \\ \sin\gamma & \cos\gamma\cos\alpha & -\cos\gamma\sin\alpha & -D \\ 0 & \sin\alpha & \cos\alpha & 0 \\ 0 & 0 & 0 & 1 \end{pmatrix} \quad (2)$$

4   Segmentation of the Scene

Segmentation has been an essential issue in robot and human navigation through the years. In order to perform any relatively complex task it is necessary to recognize the features of your surroundings. Our case of study is indoor environments, where, like in most human-made scenarios, the basic structure of the scene is a combination of planes at different orientations. Range sensors have proven to be extremely helpful for this mission, and many different algorithms have been developed to perform the segmentation [8].

In this work a region-growing strategy has been used, enhanced with some refinement functions. Regions are afterwards classified as planar and non-planar using a RANSAC algorithm. We prefer this approach instead of using directly plane detection algorithms, such as RANSAC or Hough transform, because with region-growing the planes found form already a closed region corresponding to one single element and are not a set of uncorrelated points scattered in the scene [16]. The remaining points are later merged into existing planes or associated to

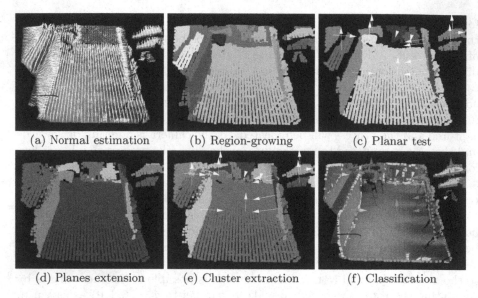

(a) Normal estimation   (b) Region-growing   (c) Planar test

(d) Planes extension   (e) Cluster extraction   (f) Classification

Fig. 2. Example of segmentation and classification from a single frame

different clusters of points. In particular, the segmentation module is divided in the following stages:

Normal estimation (Fig. 2a): The normal estimation problem is solved using an algorithm derived from the Principal Component Analysis. For each point and a group of K neighbours, the third component obtained from the analysis corresponds to the normal direction, flipped towards the viewpoint. In this process the curvature of the surfaces is also computed.

Region-growing (Fig. 2b): This algorithm starts from a *seed*, which is the point with minimum curvature, and then expands the region towards the neighbouring points that have small angle between the normals and similar curvature value. The neighbouring points which satisfy the normal and curvature threshold became the new seeds and repeats until the region cannot expand anymore. Then, a new initial seed is chosen among the remaining points, and the process starts over until the regions are smaller than a certain threshold.

Planar test (Fig. 2c): Because of how the region-growing algorithm works, most regions are planes or have a high degree of flatness, but they can also be a curved surface with smooth transitions. As the ground, walls, doors or steps are all planes, it is important to test this condition. A RANSAC algorithm looks for the biggest plane in each region and, if most of the points are inliers, it will be considered a planar surface with the plane equation obtained. Otherwise, the regions will be considered as arbitrary obstacles of the scene.

Planes extension (Fig. 2d): The points not belonging to any region are included in a planar region if they have small angle between their normal and the plane normal, they have a small perpendicular distance to the plane and they are situated near the region.

Euclidean cluster extraction (Fig. 2e): The points not belonging to any region go through a cluster extraction algorithm which establish connections and form separate entities, considered obstacles.

Plane classification (Fig. 2f): Once the segmentation stage has succeeded the planes are classified among different classes according to the orientation and the relative position of the planes. The orientation of the plane normals is compared to the normal vector of the floor. If the angle between the planes and the ground is close to $90°$, they are tentatively classified as *walls*, whereas planes whose angles are close to $0°$ are considered horizontal. Any other circumstance is considered obstacle. In this case the term *walls* simply defines a vertical planar structure as no further reasoning has been done yet.

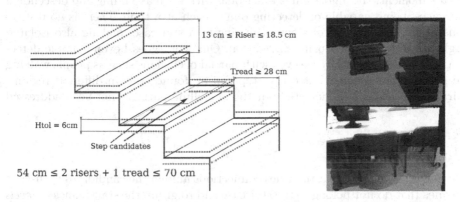

Fig. 3. Representation of the measurements of a step according to the Technical Edification Code from Spain (left). In green, the portion of the ground which can be walked over as it has no obstacles above (right).

Horizontal planes can be ground, steps or other obstacles that should be avoided (e.g. a table). It is common that the floor or steps are composed by more than one planar region as occlusions can happen. The height of the centroid of the planes is then considered: The regions with height close to zero are classified as floor, whereas the regions with positive or negative height are classified as *step candidates* if they satisfy the minimum height requirements regulated by the current Technical Edification Code valid in Spain [12] (see Fig. 3 left). According to the Code, the height of the steps ranges from a minimum $H_{min} = 13$cm to a maximum $H_{max} = 18.5$cm. Horizontal regions will be considered as *step candidates* if they are situated above (in ascending stairways) or below (in descending ones) $H_{min} - H_{tol}/2 = 10$cm from the ground. It is necessary to add a tolerance as the measurements can be too noisy. The existence of a set of at least one *step candidate* activates the stair detection algorithm. Other size and shape restrictions are kept to a minimum at this point because they could discard valid portions of steps which might be useful for a better modelling of staircases.

As a result of the segmentation and classification algorithm, the obstacles position can be projected to the ground to remove the non-walkable area from the ground detected (Fig. 3, right). Additionally, if the floor plane equation has significantly changed, a new transformation matrix is computed to not lose track of the orientation of the scene.

5   Stair Detection and Modelling Algorithm

In Section 4 it has been explained how the *step candidates* are obtained. Our stair detection and modelling algorithm is the next phase, using these *step candidates* as input, and providing the full characteristics of the staircase as output. At this moment, the algorithm is functional with both ascending and descending staircases, being capable of detecting one of each at a time. There is no restrictions about the number of steps belonging to a staircase, making also isolated single steps detectable during navigation. Our work goes beyond simple detection and models the staircase even with partial occlusions such as people walking the stairs. That means that every step can be found split in different regions. Spiral staircases can be detected but the modelling part has not been addressed yet.

5.1   Stair Detection

The detection algorithm establishes connections among the candidates to discard the ones that do not belong to the staircase and to group the stair planes in *levels* according to the distance in steps to the floor. The candidates are analysed one by one in a bottom-up strategy, for which it is necessary to select a *first step*. The candidates whose centroid is closer than $H_{max} + H_{tol}/2 = 21.5cm$ to the ground constitute *first step candidates*. If there are more than one, the connectivity to the levels above and below must be tested, otherwise it is immediate. The connectivity between regions has been computed using neighbour search and Kd-trees. The first step must also be connected to the floor if it is present in the image, i.e. if the user has not walked too close to the staircase. In a live video sequence, when there is no floor in sight, as the relative position of the camera and the user has already been computed and we know where the ground is, the connection to the ground does not need to be tested. If no first step candidate satisfies neighbouring conditions, the algorithm determines there is no staircase.

A special case occurs when there is only one possible step. It might either actually be the first step of a staircase, or be just a single step on the way. But it also can be an object which should be considered an obstacle. Here, strict area and shape conditions can be applied in order to determine in which case we are. In Fig. 4a we show an example where the ground at another level is detected.

Once there is a first step, the algorithm takes the remaining step candidates by height and starts testing connectivity and height conditions to determine whether they belong to the current or to a new level. If they have no connection to previous levels (e.g. a horizontal plane correspondent to a table) they are

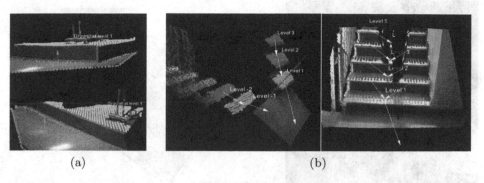

(a)   (b)

Fig. 4. (a) Floor at another level examples. (b) Connectivity between step candidates to previous levels: Ascending and descending staircases (left), more than one region per level (right).

classified as obstacles. As a result, a set of connected regions corresponding to different levels is obtained (Fig. 4b). When all the candidates have been checked, if the number of levels is greater than one, the algorithm starts the modelling of the staircase.

5.2   Stair Modelling

For modelling staircases we consider the following global geometric parameters: the width of the steps, the length of the tread, the height of the riser and the number of steps. To achieve that we use the Principal Component Analysis (PCA). This analysis is applied to each set of points corresponding to the tread of the step in each level of the staircase. Usual staircases have rectangular steps with much more width than length. The first component obtained from the PCA corresponds to the longitudinal direction (width), the second component follows the direction along the length of the step and the third component is orthogonal to the previous two, matching the normal direction of the tread (Fig. 5 left).

Mathematically, it consists in calculating the centroid of the data points, which is the mean value on each axis $\mu_{\mathbf{x}} = (\mu_x, \mu_y, \mu_z)$ and the covariance matrix of the data Σ, which is a 3×3 matrix as we are in 3D coordinates. The eigenvectors of the covariance matrix are the principal components ϕ_1, ϕ_2 and ϕ_3, being the correspondent to the highest eigenvalue the first component (width), the second highest the second component (length) and the lowest eigenvalue the third component (vertical). If we form a matrix with these vectors in columns we obtain the transformation matrix $\Phi = [\phi_1, \phi_2, \phi_3]$ which transforms our points $P_{\mathbf{x}}$ from the initial $\mathbf{x} = (x, y, z)$ axis system to P_ϕ in the principal direction axis (ϕ_1, ϕ_2, ϕ_3) with the equation:

$$P_\phi = (P_{\mathbf{x}} - \mu_{\mathbf{x}}) \cdot \Phi \tag{3}$$

Once we have our cloud transformed to the new axes it is easy to get the minimum and maximum coordinate in each direction to obtain the oriented

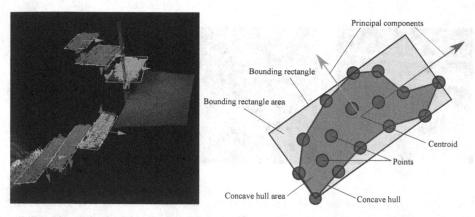

Fig. 5. Principal components for each step coloured in order (blue-green-red) and bounding rectangle in white (left). Illustrative sketch of the different components (right).

bounding box of the step. As the height is small it can be considered negligible, considering the step as a two-dimensional rectangular bounding box (Fig. 5 right). The difference between the maximum and the minimum in the first and second component are the width and the length respectively. We define *extent* as the ratio of the area of the concave hull including the points and the area of the rectangle. The extent is used to measure the quality of the detected step as it relates the area occupied by the points with respect to the area they are supposed to occupy.

The process is repeated with all steps, considering the addition of clouds at the same level as the cloud of the step. Each step has different dimensions and orientations depending on the quality of the measurements, the position of the steps with respect to the camera or the filters performance. We will choose the best step as the one with higher extent value among the steps within the valid width range, and its principal components and width will be considered as initial best guess for the model. The valid width range we choose ranges from the maximum width value detected to that maximum value minus 25cm. The principal direction of the staircase is corrected in two ways. Firstly, by forcing the third principal component to be parallel to the vertical axis. Secondly, by minimizing the sum of the area of the bounding rectangles of every step by rotating the two principal directions of the best step.

The obtention of the bounding boxes and dimensions is repeated for each step with the definitive staircase orientation. The steps will be modelled as parallelograms whose width is the width of the best step, the height is the average vertical distance between consecutive steps and the length the mean horizontal distance between the edge of every two consecutive steps. The definitive length of the steps is computed this way because the vertical projection of the bounding rectangles of two consecutive steps usually overlaps in ascending staircases (due to inclining or non-existent risers) or leaves a gap in descending staircases (due

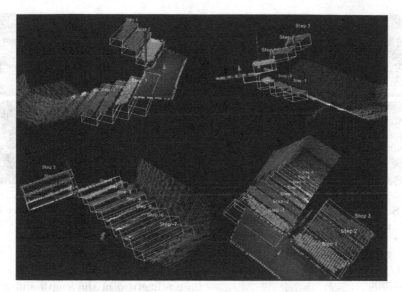

Fig. 6. Estimated model of the staircase. Top images only draws the parallelograms corresponding to the steps found, whereas at the bottom all the steps are displayed.

to self occlusions). Once we have all the parameters, we can use them to validate the staircase detection or discard it, and in case of positive results we can trace the model and even extend the information to non-detected steps (Fig. 6).

6   Experimental Evaluation

The experiments were carried out in a 3.4Ghz computer with 16 Gb of RAM running Ubuntu 12.04, ROS Hydro and the library PCL version 1.7.1. With this framework we were able to capture 640 × 480 3D point clouds in real-time and record video sequences and single frames for later experiments. Although we already had our own recordings from previous research,[1] new scenarios including stairs were also recorded to conduct specific experiments. With our own datasets we could observe that the performance of the system improves when it is used in a real-time video sequence, live or recorded. In this mode, the floor detection algorithm is only used once, and as a result its presence in the image is not required all the time.

Tang et al. compiled a dataset in [16] which includes 148 captures made with a Microsoft Kinect sensor. 90 of them include RGB and depth snapshots of a set of staircases from different poses and the other 58 are normal indoor scenes to test for false positives. The accelerometer measurements of the sensor position were also included but they are not used in our work. From the RGB and disparity range image the point cloud was calculated in each case, using previous

---

[1] http://webdiis.unizar.es/%7Eglopez/dataset.html

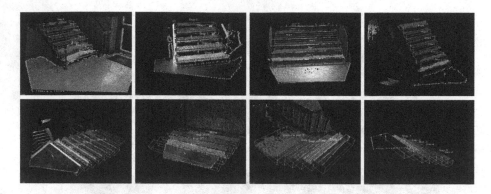

Fig. 7. Some examples of results obtained with the dataset. The last column are from captures made in darkness.

Table 1. Average time of the stages of the algorithm

Stage	Time
Filtering	15ms
Ground extraction	3ms
Normal extraction	13ms
Region-growing	16ms
Plane extension	20ms
Cluster extraction	5ms
Classification	16ms
1 stair detection	5ms

Table 2. Average and standard deviation (in centimetres) of the length and height measured with and without obstacles.

	No obstacles		Obstacles		Real
	$\bar{x}$	σ	$\bar{x}$	σ	x_r
Length	29	2.01	29.39	1.89	30
Height	15.4	1.36	15.56	0.59	17

information about the calibration parameters of the camera. The results of the test with this dataset were successful even in total darkness (Fig. 7). We tested for false positives and false negatives using this dataset and compared our results with the ones from [16] and [17] (Fig. 8a). We achieve better results with the 0% of false negatives as in [17] but also reaching a 0% of false positives.

It is also interesting to look at the step detection ratio according to the position of the step in the staircase (Fig. 8b). The behaviour changes when we are facing an ascending staircase or a descending one. Due to the orientation of the chest-mounted sensor, standing before a descending staircase allow us to see the whole staircase but the self occlusion of consecutive steps and quality of the measurements decreasing with the distance harms the detection of steps farther than the third position. In ascending staircases the ratio of detection diminishes in a less prominent way, because the steps remain almost as close to the subject as they rise, although with the penalty of having less and less visual angle. Steps higher than the seventh position are out of the field of view of the camera.

The computing time was also tested to analyse the performance of the system and to compare it to the state of the art. The complete loop iteration time

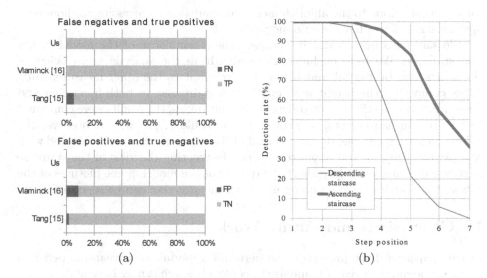

Fig. 8. (a) Comparison of false negatives and false positives between our work and the presented by [16,17]. (b) Step detection rate with the step position in the staircase.

Fig. 9. Example of a person partially blocking the view of the staircase during ascent or descent

ranges from 50 to 150ms, giving a rate of $7 - 20$Hz. The variation depends on the scene itself: close up captures provides good quality clouds and the segmentation algorithm provide less regions and as a consequence, faster results. On the other hand, a capture taken to a scene situated far from the camera adds more noise and less smooth surfaces. In general, this timing should be considered fast enough for indoor navigation assuming walking speeds around $1 - 1.5$m/s. A breakdown of the time distribution is shown in Table 1. This rate could be improved adding some optimizations to the algorithm or using multi-core processing, although no optimization efforts have been done yet.

We have also quantitatively analysed the resemblance of the model to the real staircase. We have excluded the width from the analysis as the view of the stairs may be partial and it is not as relevant as the other measurements. After computing the height and length of a staircases, in both ascending and descending perspectives, from different viewing angles, the results were compared to the real measurements, as shown in the Table 2. As we can observe, the values do not have strong deviation. Half of the experiments were conducted with real people going up and down the stairs. Obstructing the view of the staircase partially does not adversely affect the quality of the model. Some pictures of the experiments with people climbing up/down the staircase can be seen in Fig. 9.

7   Conclusions and Future Work

In this paper we have presented the perception module of a wearable personal assistant oriented to visually impaired people, although it may have applications in other fields such as robotics or special cases of human navigation. Our main contribution is the stair detection algorithm, which is not only able to detect but also to model staircases with their complete dimensions and position with respect to the user. That would provide the subject with multi-floor navigation possibilities. The experiments prove that the model quality and the computing time are good enough to be used in real-time. The algorithm overcomes some limitations existing in related works, such as the possibility of single step detection or full modelling with partial occlusions caused mainly by other people traversing the staircases.

More detection features are expected to be developed and added to the personal assistant, such as door detection, text sign recognition or people detection. But first we would like to extend the possibilities that a RGB-D sensor can bring to stair detection by combining the depth information with color images. RGB data would help improving the model, counting the steps to extend the staircase model, detecting possible staircases from farther distances where depth measurements are not reliable or when the sun rays affect negatively the depth sensing. It is also required to test the system by users in real scenarios in order to receive feedback for improving our work.

Acknowledgments. This work was supported by Ministerio de Economía y Competitividad and European Union under FPI grant BES-2013-065834 and project DPI2012-31781.

References

1. Aladren, A., Lopez-Nicolas, G., Puig, L., Guerrero, J.: Navigation assistance for the visually impaired using RGB-D sensor with range expansion. IEEE Systems Journal, Special Issue on Robotics & Automation for Human Health PP(99), 1–11 (2014)

2. Albert, A., Suppa, M., Gerth, W.: Detection of stair dimensions for the path planning of a bipedal robot. In: IEEE International Conference on Advanced Intelligent Mechatronics (AIM), vol. 2, pp. 1291–1296 (2001)
3. Cong, Y., Li, X., Liu, J., Tang, Y.: A stairway detection algorithm based on vision for UGV stair climbing. In: IEEE International Conference on Networking, Sensing and Control (ICNSC), pp. 1806–1811 (2008)
4. Delmerico, J.A., Baran, D., David, P., Ryde, J., Corso, J.J.: Ascending stairway modeling from dense depth imagery for traversability analysis. In: International Conference on Robotics and Automation (ICRA), pp. 2283–2290 (2013)
5. Filipe, V., Fernandes, F., Fernandes, H., Sousa, A., Paredes, H., Barroso, J.: Blind navigation support system based on Microsoft Kinect. Procedia Computer Science 14, 94–101 (2012)
6. Hernández, D.C., Jo, K.H.: Stairway tracking based on automatic target selection using directional filters. In: Frontiers of Computer Vision (FCV), pp. 1–6 (2011)
7. Hesch, J.A., Mariottini, G.L., Roumeliotis, S.I.: Descending-stair detection, approach, and traversal with an autonomous tracked vehicle. In: Intelligent Robots and Systems (IROS), pp. 5525–5531. IEEE (2010)
8. Hoover, A., Jean-Baptiste, G., Jiang, X., Flynn, P.J., Bunke, H., Goldgof, D.B., Bowyer, K., Eggert, D.W., Fitzgibbon, A., Fisher, R.B.: An experimental comparison of range image segmentation algorithms. Pattern Analysis and Machine Intelligence 18(7), 673–689 (1996)
9. Lu, X., Manduchi, R.: Detection and localization of curbs and stairways using stereo vision. In: International Conference on Robotics and Automation (ICRA), vol. 4, p. 4648 (2005)
10. Mayol-Cuevas, W.W., Tordoff, B.J., Murray, D.W.: On the choice and placement of wearable vision sensors. Systems, Man and Cybernetics, Part A: Systems and Humans 39(2), 414–425 (2009)
11. Mihankhah, E., Kalantari, A., Aboosaeedan, E., Taghirad, H.D., Ali, S., Moosavian, A.: Autonomous staircase detection and stair climbing for a tracked mobile robot using fuzzy controller. In: International Conference on Robotics and Biomimetics (ROBIO), pp. 1980–1985 (2009)
12. Ministerio de Fomento. Gobierno de España: Código Técnico de la Edificación, Documento Básico de Seguridad de Utilización y Accesibilidad (DB-SUA, Section 4.2) (2014)
13. Oßwald, S., Hornung, A., Bennewitz, M.: Improved proposals for highly accurate localization using range and vision data. In: International Conference on Intelligent Robots and Systems (IROS), pp. 1809–1814 (2012)
14. Pradeep, V., Medioni, G., Weiland, J., et al.: Piecewise planar modeling for step detection using stereo vision. In: Workshop on Computer Vision Applications for the Visually Impaired (2008)
15. Se, S., Brady, M.: Vision-based detection of staircases. In: Asian Conference on Computer Vision (ACCV), vol. 1, pp. 535–540 (2000)
16. Tang, T.J.J., Lui, W.L.D., Li, W.H.: Plane-based detection of staircases using inverse depth. In: Australasian Conference on Robotics and Automation (ACRA) (2012)
17. Vlaminck, M., Jovanov, L., Van Hese, P., Goossens, B., Philips, W., Pizurica, A.: Obstacle detection for pedestrians with a visual impairment based on 3D imaging. In: International Conference on 3D Imaging (IC3D) (2013)
18. Wang, S., Tian, Y.: Detecting stairs and pedestrian crosswalks for the blind by RGBD camera. In: International Conference on Bioinformatics and Biomedicine Workshops (BIBMW), pp. 732–739 (2012)

A New Application of Smart Walker for Quantitative Analysis of Human Walking

Ting Wang[1]([✉]), Claire Dune[1,2], Jean-Pierre Merlet[1], Philippe Gorce[2],
Guillaume Sacco[3], Philippe Robert[3], Jean-Michel Turpin[3], Bernard Teboul[3],
Audrey Marteu[3], and Olivier Guerin[3]

[1] Hephaistos, INRIA Sophia Antipolis, 06902 Valbonne, France
{ting.wang,Jean-Pierre.Merlet}@inria.fr
[2] HandiBio EA 4322, Université de Toulon, 83957 La Garde, France
{claire.dune,philippe.gorce}@univ-tln.fr
[3] CHU de Nice, 06000 Nice, France
bernard.teboul@libertysurf.fr
{sacco.g,robert.ph,turpin.jm,marteu.a,guerin.o}@chu-nice.fr

Abstract. This paper presents a new nonintrusive device for everyday gait analysis and health monitoring. The system is a standard rollator equipped with encoders and inertial sensors. The assisted walking of 25 healthy elderly and 23 young adults are compared to develop walking quality index. The subjects were asked to walk on a straight trajectory and an L-shaped trajectory respectively. The walking trajectory, which is missing in other gait analysis methods, is calculated based on the encoder data. The obtained trajectory and steps are compared with the results of a motion capture system. The gait analysis results show that new index obtained by using the walker measurements, and not available otherwise, are very discriminating, *e.g.*, the elderly have larger lateral motion and maneuver area, smaller angular velocity during turning, their walking accuracy is lower and turning ability is weaker although they have almost the same walking velocity as the young people.

Keywords: Smart walker · Gait analysis · Step detection · Turning · Elderly

1 Introduction

Ageing in society is a worldwide issue that especially impacts developed countries. In France, due to the high care cost and the limited number of rooms in care institution, the solution that has been chosen by care givers, frail people and their family is to maintain elderly at home and in the best conditions by giving them an adapted assistance. Among the possible assistance devices, the walkers have large number of users because of their simplicity while using the person's remaining locomotion capability.

Advances in robotics make it possible to develop more intelligent walkers by adding sensors and actuators. According to the user's needs, the functions of the

© Springer International Publishing Switzerland 2015
L. Agapito et al. (Eds.): ECCV 2014 Workshops, Part III, LNCS 8927, pp. 464–480, 2015.
DOI: 10.1007/978-3-319-16199-0_33

proposed walkers are not restricted to their primary tasks, i.e. physical support and mobility assistance [1], [2], [3]. There are other functions such as sensorial assistance, cognitive assistance and health monitoring [4], [5]. Some walkers also focus on sit-to-stand transfer [6], [7], navigation help [8], [9], obstacle avoidance and fall detection [10].

To study the extension of the functions of walkers we have developed our own family of walking aids based on the walker presented in [11]. Our walkers can perform multi-functions such as navigation, street mapping, fall detection/prevention and autonomous object recovery. In this work we use the simplest version (Fig. 1), which is based on a commercially available 3-wheels Rollator. It was instrumented with encoders at the two fixed rear wheels and a 3D accelerometer/gyrometer at the front with the purpose of determining the walker's trajectory on a 24/24 basis. A small, low energy consumption fit-pc computer manages the measurements and records all the data. Compared with the walkers proposed above, our walker is low cost, simple to be used at home and its functions can be easily extended. This paper will present how it can be used for medical monitoring of walking patterns.

Many studies have examined the effect of age on the walking by comparing younger with older adults [12], [13], [14], [15], [16], [17], [18], [19]. These studies calculated some gait parameters, such as step length, gait cycle, step width, cadence and gait speed [19], [20], [21], [22]. Some studies have considered also gait variability [15], [23], [16], [24]. However, these usual gait parameters are not sufficient and sensitive enough to evaluate the health state of elderly people, and the results of previous studies are often inconsistent according to the conditions of experiment. Another drawback of most studies is that these measures are obtained on a reduced space with specialized laboratory equipment such as motion capture systems and instrumented walkways, which may not be available in many clinics and certainly not during daily activities. Thus the recent studies used the wearable inertial sensors to analyze the fall risk of elderly people [25], [26], [27]. Thanks to encoders and a 3D accelerometer/gyrometer, by using the smart walker we can not only calculate accurately all the classical gait parameters proposed above, but also avoid imposing constraints on the end-users. We also can obtain the trajectory of the walker and therefore compare it with the reference trajectory. This comparison will allow to establish several original gait parameters which have not been considered in previous studies. Overall, using our walker the gait characteristics can be described more comprehensively.

2   Methods

This section will explain how the walker can obtain the walking trajectory and determine the stride while the subject is walking along a straight line. In addition, in order to validate our method, the obtained gait features will be compared with the data given by a 6-camera motion capture system which is used for biomechanical analysis [28].

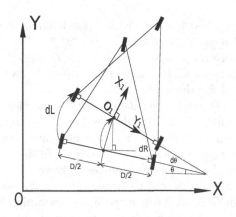

Fig. 1. The instrumented walking aid

Fig. 2. Simple kinematic model of the walker

2.1   Calculation of the Trajectory

As shown in Fig. 2, the origin of the walker frame $O_1X_1Y_1$ is supposed to be the position of the middle point between the two rear wheels. The position of the walker in a reference frame OXY is described by $[x, y, \theta]$, where θ describes the walking direction of the rollator and represents the angle between the horizontal axis of two rear wheels and the X axis. In our experiment of $10m$ straight line walk test, as the reference trajectory was directed along the Y axis we have $\theta = 0$ at the beginning of the walker's trajectory. The trajectory of the walker is determined by using the encoders. Assuming that at the $(k+1)_{th}$ time sample moment the measurement of the encoders of two rear wheels are Δ_L and Δ_R, the displacement of the left and right wheel are obtained by using (1):

$$dL = \frac{2\pi r}{4C \cdot 360}\Delta_L, \quad dR = \frac{2\pi r}{4C \cdot 360}\Delta_R \tag{1}$$

where r is the radius of the rear wheel and C is a constant parameter of the transformation between the value of encoder and the wheel radius. The change of the direction angle θ during the $(k+1)_{th}$ sampling time can be estimated as:

$$d\theta = (dL - dR)/D, \tag{2}$$

where D is the distance between the two rear wheels.

According to the kinematic model shown in Fig. 2, the changes of the walker's position can be obtained as follows [29]:

$$dx = \frac{dL + dR}{2}sin(\theta_k + \frac{d\theta}{2}), \quad dy = \frac{dL + dR}{2}cos(\theta_k + \frac{d\theta}{2}) \tag{3}$$

Finally, the new position of the walker can be calculated by using:

$$x_{k+1} = x_k + dx, \quad y_{k+1} = y_k + dy, \quad \theta_{k+1} = \theta_k + d\theta. \tag{4}$$

Using the above equations, the trajectory of the walker can be determined by using the encoders. The experiments have shown that after a straight line walking of 10 meters the estimated positioning has an absolute accuracy better than $1cm$.

2.2 Step Detection

Accelerometers are utilized to detect the walking stride in many studies [30], [31]. Most of methods use the peak value of forward acceleration to detect the walking cycle. However, some steps do not lead to a high-peak forward acceleration, and hence they are not counted although there is displacement during these periods. A recent study [32] used thresholds on the magnitude of the gyroscope and accelerometer signals to identify the zero velocity instant and regarded it as the end of a step. Our walker also uses the gyrometer data to detect the walking stride. An interesting contribution is that it allows one to differentiate the right and left steps when the subject walks along a straight line. Indeed when the subject is on the left (right) support phase the walking aid rotates on the left (right). Hence the rotational velocity of the walker around the vertical axis, which can be easily obtained by the gyrometer, is used to detect the walking stride. Its zero value instant is regarded as the end of a step.

An example of measured rotational velocity after a low pass filtering for an elderly people during walking along a $10m$ straight line is shown in Fig. 3. Since

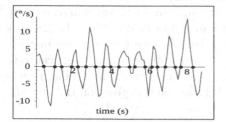

Fig. 3. Yaw angular velocity of the walker when the subject walks along a straight reference trajectory with $10m$. One step is finished when it passes zero.

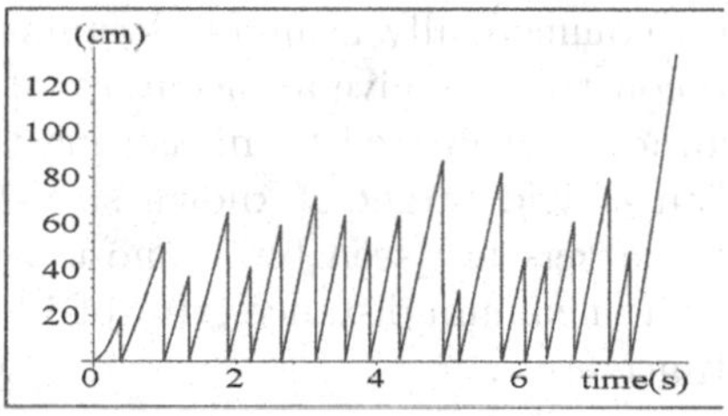

Fig. 4. Displacement of the walker during every step. The results of left steps and right steps were put together and they appeared alternately.

the position of the walker at every moment has been calculated by using the method presented in Section 2.1, the displacement of the walker during every step, which is regarded as the step length of the subject, can be easily calculated as soon as all the steps are detected, as shown in Fig. 4. Accordingly, all gait speed characteristics (such as mean value, minimum and maximum value) can be obtained for each step. With a sampling time of $1ms$ for the encoders and $4.8ms$ for the gyrometer, we may obtain a quiet reasonable accuracy on these parameters.

2.3   Validation

The proposed methods are tested on a standard 4-wheels rollator equipped with sensors and monitored by a motion capture system, as shown in Fig. 5. We attached 10 optical markers on the walker frame, wheel axis and handle. The motion capture gives the 3D trajectory of the markers at a framerate of 200Hz.

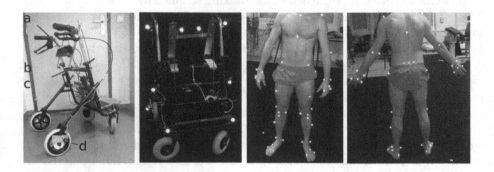

Fig. 5. Walker and motion capture optical markers set-up [33]

The motion capture system is a high cost, whole body motion analysis system widely used for bio-mechanical analysis. Its accuracy is studied in [28] among other commercially available systems for the measurement of human motion. The constructors give an accuracy of $0.6cm$ in a 3-m field of view. In [28], the accuracy is evaluated by measuring the relative distance between two markers set on a rigid target of known size ($9cm$) that rotates around a vertical axis. The markers are seen by at most 3 cameras at each time frame. The results show a maximum distance error of $1.2cm$. Yet, no result is given on the absolute distance error.

Validation of Trajectory Calculation. Fig. 6 a. and Fig. 6 c. compare two walker trajectories (straight line and U-turn) that are estimated using the encoder values with the trajectories obtained using the motion capture system. The instantaneous velocity can also be estimated by mapping the time frames to these measurements (Fig. 6 b. and Fig. 6 d.).

The straight line experiment shows that the distance estimation given by the odometers and the motion capture system are similar. The encoders are able to capture small deviations from the straight line. The U-turn experiment also shows that the trajectory of the walker is well described, even when performing maneuver. Then, the encoders' values can be used to describe the walker trajectory and they give similar results as the motion capture system.

Validation of Step Detection. The motion capture system tracks a marker set attached to the feet of the person. It gives the Cartesian position of the feet in a fixed Cartesian reference frame, which can be used to detect the steps. The velocity of the feet can also be used to determine the number of steps and their length. For example, the step starts when the velocity increases while it ends when the velocity is below an arbitrary threshold, as shown in Fig. 7.

The number of steps obtained using this method was compared with the result of the method proposed in Section. 2.2, as shown in Fig. 7. The first graph depicts the step detection by finding the zero value of the rotational velocity. The second graph represents the step detection by finding the sagital velocity changes. The third graph, at the bottom, compares the results of the two methods.

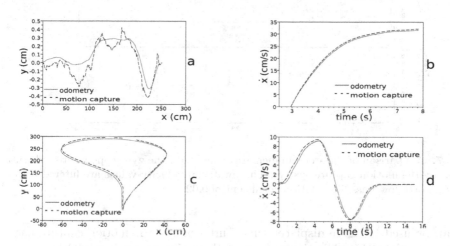

Fig. 6. Walker's trajectory and velocity estimation using the encoder (odometry) and the motion capture system for two experiments: walking on a straight line (a. trajectory and b. velocity) and U-turn (c. trajectory and d. velocity)

It is worth mentioning that the number of steps shown in the first graph depends on the parameter of the low pass filter used for the angular velocity. If the parameter is well chosen, the number of steps is quite the same as measured with the motion capture system (see Fig. 7). If the low pass filter is not correctly tuned, the starting moment of the steps is not accurately found and that will impact the calculated step length and cadence.

In summary, our smart rollator gives results that are similar to motion capture data while being cheaper, more convenient to use and faster to set up. Indeed, the motion capture has to be calibrated for each experiment, the marker set up takes time and is sensible to skin motion, it is also dependent from the abilities of the system operator and it is restricted to a small area (3-m field of view for whole body tracking with a 6-camera system) with good illumination condition. On the opposite, the walker only needs to be turned on, no calibration is required, the measurements are totally independent from the system operator, the user does not need to wear any marker and it is insensitive to condition while

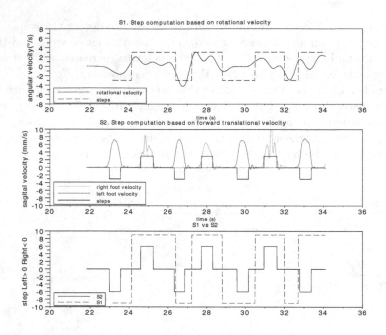

Fig. 7. Comparison of the step numbers estimated with the gyroscope vs ground truth given by the motion capture system. The rotational velocity values are filtered with a Butterworth low pass filter with a coefficient of 0.02.

it can be used for large displacements. Furthermore, the motion capture has a framerate of 200Hz, while the encoders and inertial sensors are 1000Hz.

3   Gait Analysis of a 10m Walk Test

Several classical tests used to assess the mobility of elderly people are the $10m$ walk test (10mWT) (measure: time duration) [34], Timed Up and Go test (TUG) (measure: time duration) [35], Tinetti Test (TT) (analysis of gait parameters through a video) [36]. Such tests are easy to implement but are basically global (the time for the 10mWT and the TUG may be identical for two subjects which have however very different walking patterns) or are subjective (for the TT [37]). Furthermore these tests are performed only during medical visits and consequently are not appropriate to detect abnormal events in the walking patterns. Our objective was to examine if the measurements of our walking aid allow one to refine the output of the above walking tests.

For that purpose we have led a large scale experiment that was approved by the regional ethical committee (Comité de Protection des Personnes). Each subject was asked to walk along two specific trajectories while using the walker. One is a $10m$ straight line and another is an inverted L-shaped trajectory (see Fig. 12). The subjects are a group of young adults of INRIA (with age between 25 and 65 years, mean value 32) and a group of elderly people (age over 65 years) of Nice hospital. No subject has pathological walking diseases and all of them were asked to perform twice the trajectory with the walking aid.

3.1 Results

There were 23 young adults and 25 elderly people that participated to the 10mWT. The trajectories of all the subjects for the 10mWT are presented in Fig. 8. The reference trajectory is the horizontal axis and the vertical axis is scaled to illustrate the lateral deviations between the real and reference trajectories. Fig. 8 clearly shows that the elderly subjects have larger deviations than the young subjects. The maximum lateral deviation between the real and reference trajectory of the two groups is presented in Fig. 9. It illustrates that the results of the elderly have a significantly larger deviation than that of the young subjects. For example, the mean value of the maximum lateral deviation for the elderly is 11.048 ± 5.99 cm while that for the young people is only 3.963 ± 2.301 cm.

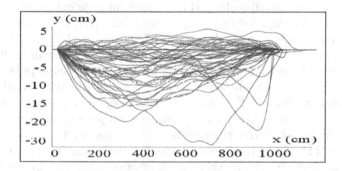

Fig. 8. Trajectory of the subjects in the xy plane, where the blue color denotes the elderly subjects and the red one denotes the young subjects. The reference trajectory is the horizontal line: $y = 0$.

In addition, several other walking indicators calculated from a trajectory, *e.g.*, the area between the real and reference trajectory, the traveled Manhattan distance and the orientation angle of the walker also reveal that the lateral motion of the elderly is larger than the younger. It has been has shown that there exists significant group difference in the medio-lateral displacement of the center of mass between healthy elderly adults and elderly patients [38] . It is consistent with our result and they reveal that walking accuracy can be regarded as a pertinent walking quality index.

Since the user's step can be detected by using our walker, most of gait parameters presented in the usual walking tests can be calculated or estimated, such as step length, step period, gait speed, cadence, forward acceleration and variability of these gait parameters. Although the step width cannot be calculated accurately, the analysis of the walker's lateral motion in the previous section can reflect the characteristic of the subjects' step width.

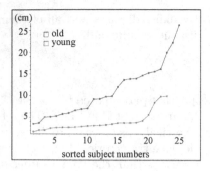 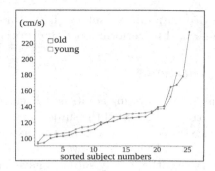

Fig. 9. Maximum lateral deviation between the real and reference trajectory. The results are sorted in ascending order.

Fig. 10. Maximum instantaneous walking velocity of the two groups. The results are sorted in ascending order.

Usually gait speed or walking velocity is regarded as a very important indicator of health. Some studies claimed that older subjects exhibited significantly reduced gait speed compared to younger adults [12], [13], [19] while other studies showed that there were little or no differences in that [16], [17]. It has been shown that the gait speed depends on age, sex [20], use of mobility aids, chronic conditions, smoking history, blood pressure, body mass index, and hospitalization [22]. The instantaneous walking velocity can be derived from the encoder measurements and Fig. 10 gives their maximum values. It shows that the maximum walking velocity of the younger subjects is a little larger than that of the elderly. For the elderly the mean value of the maximum walking velocity is 117.969 ± 15.851 cm/s and for the young people this value is 119.967 ± 16.019 cm/s. Hence there is no obvious difference between the two groups, which is consistent with the result of [16], [17].

We have also compared step period, step length and their variability for the two groups. Again, there is almost no difference between the two groups, which explains why the two groups have similar walking speed. The mean values of step period and step length of the elderly are 0.526 ± 0.1 s and 54.862 ± 11.643 cm, and 0.537 ± 0.095 s and 55.050 ± 8.605 cm for the young people.

4   Gait Analysis of an Inverted L-Shaped Trajectory Test

An inverted L-shaped reference trajectory is described in Fig. 12. During the test, the subject was asked to walk along a $5m$ straight line, turn right (or left), walk along a $5m$ straight line again, turn $180°$ and return to the starting point. Hence the total traveled distance is $20m$. The inverted L-shaped trajectory test is considered because walking with turning is a common activity in our daily life. Turning frequently causes loss of balance in all gait disorders [39], and it is associated with increased risk of falling in elderly adults [40], [41].

Many analysis of turning are considered in TUG test or figure-of-eight walking test. These studies examined the usual gait parameters such as used time

[42], gait speed, stride length, cadence, double-limb support duration during the turning [43]. Other methods assess accelerometer-derived parameters [44], [26] and gyroscope-derived parameters [45]. Our objective is to find new quality index during turning phase by using the walker instrumented with an accelerometer/gyrometer, which may help doctors to evaluate the fall risk of the elderly.

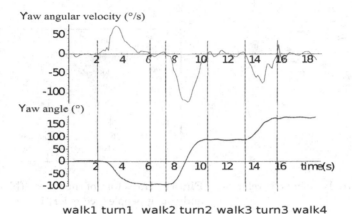

Fig. 11. Yaw angle and yaw angular velocity of an elderly subject during the inverted L-shaped trajectory test

4.1   Detection of Distinct Phases

Since the inverted L-shaped trajectory test consists of a sequence of activities such as walking, 90° turning and 180° turning, it is necessary to evaluate the user's ability in distinct phases or activities to make the test more sensitive. Several studies use wearable inertial sensors to detect the phases in TUG test by using the Euler angles or angular velocity signals that had been processed by filters [25], [26]. Some specific algorithms used to filter out the noise of the sensors for the detection are presented in [27], [46]. Here we use filtered yaw angle and yaw angular velocity to detect each activity and the test was divided into seven phases in sequence: walk 1, turn 1 (walking with 90° turning), walk 2, turn 2 (walking with 180° turning), walk 3, turn 3 (walking with 90° turning) and walk 4, as shown in Fig. 11 and Fig. 12. For example, Fig. 11 presents both yaw angle and yaw angular velocity signals of an elderly subject during the test. In order to follow the reference trajectory shown in Fig. 12, the yaw angle of the walker changes from 0° to a nearby value of −90°, 90° and 180° respectively at the end of turn 1, turn 2 and turn 3. When the yaw angular velocity passes zero and the yaw angle signal starts to increase or decrease suddenly, the turn phase starts. From this moment when the yaw angular velocity passes zero again, the turn phase ends.

As soon as the onset and offset of the three turn phases are detected, the duration of all the seven phases are obtained. During the four walk phases, the yaw angular velocity passes zero several times although the yaw angle almost keeps a constant value, and these zero-pass moments can be used to detect the user's steps, which has been presented in the previous section.

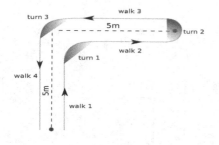

Fig. 12. Inverted L-shaped reference trajectory

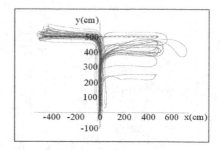

Fig. 13. Trajectory of the elderly (blue color) and young people (red color) in the xy plane

4.2   Results

There were 25 young adults (between 25 and 65 years, mean value 32) and 12 elderly people (> 69 years) that participated to the inverted L-shaped trajectory test. The walking trajectories of the two groups using the walker are presented in Fig. 13, which clearly shows that most of the elder subjects cannot follow exactly the reference trajectory. This is consistent with the result of 10mWT (see Fig. 8 and Fig. 9), meaning that the deviation between the reference trajectory and the followed trajectory can be always regarded as a walking indicator.

Turning duration is always an important index to be examined in the TUG test. It has been claimed that the elderly or people that has higher fall risk use more time during turning [25], [26], [27]. Fig. 14 presents the duration of each phase for the two groups. It clearly shows that the duration of all turning phases for the elderly is longer than that of the younger group, which is consistent with the result of previous studies. However, during the walking phases without turning, the elderly use less time. One reason which could explain this is shorter walking distance of the elderly (see Fig. 13) , with similar walking velocity of two groups, as presented in the previous section.

Using only the time parameter to evaluate the fall risk of the subject is obviously not sufficient. To further investigate this issue, other gait parameters derived from the walker will be assessed. From the walking trajectories shown in Fig. 13, we can see that the elderly need larger space to complete a turn. Hence it is interesting to compare the maneuver area, which is surrounded by a turning trajectory and a straight line that connects the start and end of the turning,

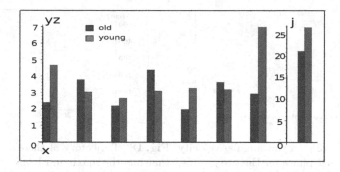

Fig. 14. Comparison of the duration of each phase for young and elderly people

as shown in green shadings of Fig. 12. Fig. 15 indicates that the maneuver area of the elderly is significantly larger. Hence it can be regarded as an important indicator to quantify the maneuvering ability of subjects.

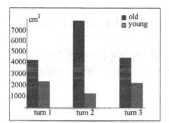
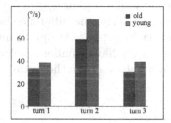

Fig. 15. Comparison of the maneuver area of each turning phase for the two groups

Fig. 16. Comparison of the RMS value of yaw angular velocity for the two groups

Root mean square (RMS) is a statistical measure of the magnitude of a varying quantity and is especially useful for sinusoids. We compared the RMS value of yaw angular velocity during turning phases between the two groups (Fig. 16). It clearly shows that during turning phases the young people has a higher RMS value of yaw angular velocity. The value of every subject during the turn around phase (turn 2) is presented in Fig. 17. It indicates that almost all members of the elderly group has lower RMS value of yaw angular velocity except for one member ($92.54°/s$). In addition, the trajectory of this subject, presented in Fig. 18, shows that the maneuver area during turn 2 phase is very small, and almost equal to the one of the young people. In order to further investigate this issue, Fig. 19 presents the maneuver area and yaw angular velocity during turn 2 phase for all subjects. It shows that during the turning phase the young people has high RMS value of yaw angular velocity and a small maneuver area. This indicates that the two groups can almost be discriminated only by using these two indicators. Moreover, for the one subject that has the maximum RMS value of yaw angular velocity ($92.54°/s$) in the elderly group, the maneuver area is

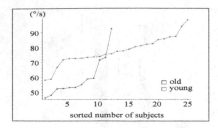

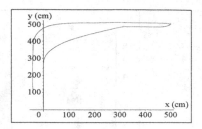

Fig. 17. RMS value of yaw angular velocity during the turn 2 phase for the two groups. The results are sorted in ascending order.

Fig. 18. Trajectory of the elderly subject that has the maximum RMS value of yaw angular velocity during the turn 2 phase

only 857.4 cm^2. Thus in Fig. 19 this point can be classified into the young group, which can explain the abnormality of Fig. 17. The RMS value of acceleration during each phase is compared for the two groups in Fig. 20. It reveals:

- all the subjects exhibit a larger acceleration during turning phases than during walking phases,
- for the elderly, the difference between the acceleration during turning phase and walking phase is significantly smaller,
- the elderly have smaller acceleration than the young people during the turn around phase while they exhibit a larger acceleration during walking phases.

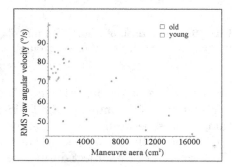

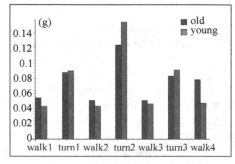

Fig. 19. RMS value of yaw angular velocity as a function of the maneuver area during the turn around phase (turn 2)

Fig. 20. RMS value of acceleration during each phase for young and elderly people

In summary, by using the smart walker instrumented with inertial sensors, the subject's gait can be assessed by the above indicators. Besides, we also compared other parameters for the two groups. Derived indicators during the 10 m straight line test and the turn around phase of inverted L-shaped trajectory test are summarized in Table 1.

Table 1. Gait indicators obtained during 10mWT and turn around phase of the inverted L-shaped trajectory test by using the walker, where **S** means *small* and **L** means *large*

10m straight trajectory			Inverted L-shaped trajectory		
Indicators	Old	Young	Indicators	Old	Young
Lateral deviation	L	S	Turning duration	L	S
Manhattan distance	L	S	Maneuver area	L	S
Orientation angle	L	S	RMS value of angular velocity	S	L
Forward acceleration	L	S	Amplitude of angular velocity	S	L
Percentage of forward support	S	L	RMS value of acceleration	S	L

5   Conclusions

This paper proposed a gait analysis method by using an instrumented walker. The results of a 10 m straight line test and an inverted L-shaped trajectory test for a group of young adults and a group of elderly people were compared comprehensively. The gait of the two groups were analyzed during both walking phases and turning phases. Several indicators that exhibit significant difference between the two groups were obtained, such as the maximum lateral deviations, the orientation angle and the traveled Manhattan distance. For the elderly these indicators are much larger than that of the young people, which indicates that the walking accuracy of the elderly is lower. Moreover, we found there is no obvious difference in step length, step period and walking speed between two groups, which is consistent with some previous studies. It reveals that these classical gait indicators are neither sufficient nor sensitive enough to evaluate the fall risk of the elderly.

For the inverted L-shaped trajectory test we found that indicators derived form the walker's sensors can be used to classify the gait quality of subjects. For example, during the turning phases for the elderly the maneuver area is larger and the RMS value of angular velocity is smaller than that of the young people. In addition, for the elderly during turning phases the RMS value of acceleration is lower than that of the young people while during the walking phases it is larger than that of young people. Surprisingly this is inconsistent with previous studies [25], [26], which claimed that during both walking phases and turning phases the RMS values of acceleration for the group with high fall risk are smaller than that of the group with lower fall risk. However, during the 10mWT we also found that the elderly have larger forward acceleration and the walking velocity of the two groups are similar. Our interpretation is that elderly people are more familiar with walking aids and have walking patterns that benefit from such an aid, while younger people have a more dynamic pattern that is jeopardized by the aid. An open issue is to deduce the gait indicators for natural gait without the walker from the measurements obtained with the walker.

References

1. Alwan, M., et al.: Stability margin monitoring in steering-controlled intelligent walkers for the elderly. In: AAAI Fall Symposium, Arlington, November 4-6, pp. 1509–1514 (2005)
2. Bostelman, R., Albus, J.: Robotic patient transfer and rehabilitation device for patient care facilities or the home. Advanced Robotics **22**(12), 1287–1307 (2008)
3. Glover, J., et al.: A robotically-augmented walker for older adults. Technical Report CMU-CS-03-170, CMU, Pittsburgh, August 1 (2003)
4. Frizera, A., Ceres, R., Pons, J., Abellanas, A., Raya, R.: The smart walkers as geriatric assistive device. The simbiosis purpose. Gerontechnology **7**(2), 108–113 (2008)
5. Spenko, M., Yu, H., Dubowsky, S.: Robotic personal aids for mobility and monitoring for the elderly. IEEE Transactions on Neural Systems and Rehabilitation Engineering **14**(3), 344–351 (2006)
6. Chugo, D., et al.: A moving control of a robotic walker for standing, walking and seating assistance. In: Int. Conf. on Robotics and Biomimetics, Bangkok, February 21-26, pp. 692–697 (2008)
7. Médéric, P., Pasqui, V., Plumet, F., Bidaud, P., Guinot, J.C.: Elderly people sit to stand transfer experimental analysis. In: 8th Int. Conf. on Climbing and Walking Robots (CLAWAR), London (2005)
8. Grasse, R., Morère, Y., Pruski, A.: Assisted navigation for persons with reduced mobility: path recognition through particle filtering (condensation algorithm). J. of Intelligent and Robotic Systems **60**(1), 19–57 (2010)
9. Kulyukin, V., et al.: iWalker: toward a rollator mounted wayfinding system for the elderly. In: IEEE Int. Conf. on RFID, Las Vegas, April 16–17, pp. 303–311 (2008)
10. Hirata, Y., Komatsuda, S., Kosuge, K.: Fall prevention of passive intelligent walker based on human model. In: IEEE Int. Conf. on Intelligent Robots and Systems (IROS), Nice, September 22–26, pp. 1222–1228 (2008)
11. Merlet, J.P.: ANG, a family of multi-mode, low cost walking aid. In: IEEE Int. Conf. on Intelligent Robots and Systems (IROS), Workshop Assistance and Service Robotics in a Human Environment, Vilamoura (October 2012)
12. Hollman, J., Kovash, F., Kubik, J.J., Linbo, R.: Age-related differences in spatiotemporal markers of gait stability during dual task walking. Gait & Posture **26**(1), 113–119 (2007)
13. Menz, H., Lord, S., Fitzpatrick, R.: Age-related differences in walking stability. Age Ageing **32**(2), 137–142 (2003)
14. Woledge, R., Birtles, D., Newham, D.: The variable component of lateral body sway during walking in young and older humans. The Journals of Gerontology: Series A **60**(11), 1463–1468 (2005)
15. Owings, T., Grabiner, M.: Variability of step kinematics in young and older adults. Gait & Posture **20**(1), 26–35 (2004)
16. Grabiner, P., Biswas, S., Grabiner, M.: Age-related changes in spatial and temporal gait variables. Archives of Physical Medicine and Rehabilitation **82**(1), 31–36 (2001)
17. Hausdorff, J.M., Edelberg, H., Mitchell, S., Goldberger, A., Wei, J.: Increased gait unsteadiness in community-dwelling elderly fallers. Archives of Physical Medicine and Rehabilitation **78**(3), 278–283 (1997)
18. Barbara, R., Freitas, S., Bagesteiro, L., Perracini, M., Alouche, S.: Gait characteristics of younger-old and older-old adults walking overground and on a compliant surface. Brazilian Journal of Physical Therapy **16**(5), 375–380 (2012)

19. Ko, S.U., Hausdorff, J., Ferrucci, L.: Age-associated differences in the gait pattern changes of older adults during fast-speed and fatigue conditions: results from the baltimore longitudinal study of ageing. Age & Ageing 39(6), 688–694 (2010)
20. Callisaya, M., Blizzard, L., Schmidt, M., McGinley, J., Srikanth, V.K.: Sex modifies the relationship between age and gait: a population-based study of older adults. The Journals of Gerontology: Series A 63(2), 165–170 (2008)
21. Zijlstra, W., Hof, A.: Assessment of spatio-temporal gait parameters from trunk accelerations during human walking. Gait & Posture 18(2), 1–10 (2003)
22. Studenski, S., Perera, S., Patel, K., et al.: Gait speed and survival in older adults. The Journal of American Medical Association Network 305(1), 50–58 (2011)
23. Callisaya, M., Blizzard, L., Schmidt, M., McGinley, J., Srikanth, V.K.: Ageing and gait variability-a population-based study of older people. Age Ageing 39(2), 191–197 (2010)
24. Hausdorff, J., Rios, D., Edelberg, H.: Gait variability and fall risk in community-living older adults: a 1-year prospective study. Archives of Physical Medicine and Rehabilitation 82(8), 1050–1056 (2001)
25. Higashi, Y., Yamakoshi, K., Fujimoto, T., Sekine, M., Tamura, T.: Quantitative evaluation of movement using the timed up-and-go test. IEEE Engineering in Medicine and Biology Magazine 27(4), 38–46 (2008)
26. Zakaria, N.A., Kuwae, Y., Tamura, T., Minato, K., Kanaya, S.: Quantitative analysis of fall risk using tug test. Compute Methods in Biomechanics and Biomechnical Engineering, 1–13 (2013)
27. Salarian, A., Zampieri, C., Horak, F.B., Carlson-Kuhta, P., Nutt, J.G., Aminian, K.: Analyzing 180 degrees turns using an inertial system reveals early signs of progression of parkinson's disease. In: 31st Annual International Conference of the IEEE Eng. Med. Biol. Soc., pp. 224–227 (2009)
28. Richards, J.G.: The measurement of human motion: A comparison of commercially available systems. Human Movement Science 18(5), 589–602 (1999)
29. Lee, K., Jung, C.B., Chung, W.J.: Accurate calibration of kinematic parameters for two wheel differential mobile robots. Journal of Mechanical Science and Technology 26(5), 1603–1611 (2011)
30. Zijlstra, W.: Assessment of spatio-temporal parameters during unconstrained walking. European Journal of Applied Physiology 92(1–2), 39–44 (2004)
31. Huang, Y., Zheng, H., Nugent, C., et al.: An orientation free adaptive step detection algorithm using a smart phone in physical activity monitoring. Health and Technology (2), 249–258 (2012)
32. Rebula, J., Ojeda, L., Adamczyk, P., Kuo, A.: Measurement of foot placement and its variability with inertial sensors. Gait & Posture 38(4), 974–980 (2013)
33. Wu, G., Cavanagh, P.R.: ISB recommendations for standardization in the reporting of kinematic data. Journal of Biomechanics 28(10), 1257–1261 (1995)
34. Salbach, N., Mayo, N., Higgins, J., Ahmed, S., Finch, L., Richards, C.: Responsiveness and predictability of gait speed and other disability measures in acute stroke. Archives of Physical Medicine and Rehabilitation 82(9), 1204–1212 (2001)
35. Podsiadlo, D., Richardson, S.: The timed 'up & go': a test of basic functional mobility for frail elderly persons. Journal of American Geriatrics Society 39(2), 142–148 (1991)
36. Tinetti, M.: Performance-oriented assessment of mobility problems in elderly patients. Journal of American Geriatrics Society 34(2), 119–126 (1986)
37. Panella, L., Lombardi, R., Buizza, A., Gandolfi, R., Pizzagalli, P.: Towards objective quantification of the tinetti test. Functional Neurology 17(1), 25–30 (2002)

38. Hahn, M., Chou, L.: Can motion of individual body segments identify dynamic instability in the elderly. Clinical Biomechanics **18**(8), 737–744 (2003)
39. Joseph, H.F.: Gait in the elderly. Medicine and Health Rhode Island, 134–135 (2008)
40. Tinetti, M.E., Speechley, M., Ginter, S.F.: Risk factors for falls among elderly persons living in the community. The New England Journal of Medicine **319**(26), 1101–1107 (1988)
41. Tinetti, M.E., Williams, T.F., Mayewski, R.: Fall risk index for elderly patients based on number of chronic disabilities. The American Journal of Medicine **80**(3), 429–434 (1986)
42. Beauchet, O., Annweiler, C., Assal, F., Bridenbaugh, S., Herrmann, F.R., Kressig, R.W., Allali, G.: Imagined timed up & go test: a new tool to assess higher-level gait and balance disorders in older adults? Journal of the Neurological Sciences **294**(1–2), 102–106 (2010)
43. Shkuratova, N., Morris, M.E., Huxham, F.: Effects of age on balance control during walking. Archives of Physical Medicine and Rehabilitation **85**(4), 582–588 (2004)
44. Weiss, A., Herman, T., Plotnik, M., Brozgol, M., Maidan, I., Giladi, N., Gurevich, T., Hausdorff, J.M.: Can an accelerometer enhance the utility of the timed up & go test when evaluating patients with parkinson's disease? Medical Engineering & Physics **32**(2), 119–125 (2010)
45. Greene, B.R., O'Donovan, A., Romero-Ortuno, R., Cogan, L., Scanaill, C.N., Kenny, R.A.: Quantitative falls risk assessment using the timed up and go test. IEEE Transactions on Bio-medical Engineering **57**(12), 2918–2926 (2010)
46. Al-Jawad, A., Adame, M.R., Romanovas, M., Hobert, M., Maetzler, W., Traechtler, M., Moeller, K., Manoli, Y.: Using multi-dimensional dynamic time warping for tug test instrumentation with inertial sensors. In: IEEE International Conference on Multisensor Fusion and Integration for Intelligent Systems (MFI), pp. 212–218 (2012)

Multi-User Egocentric Online System for Unsupervised Assistance on Object Usage

Dima Damen[✉], Osian Haines, Teesid Leelasawassuk, Andrew Calway, and Walterio Mayol-Cuevas

Department of Computer Science, University of Bristol, Bristol, UK
Dima.Damen@bristol.ac.uk

Abstract. We present an online fully unsupervised approach for automatically extracting video guides of how objects are used from wearable gaze trackers worn by multiple users. Given egocentric video and eye gaze from multiple users performing tasks, the system discovers task-relevant objects and automatically extracts guidance videos on how these objects have been used. In the *assistive mode*, the paper proposes a method for selecting a suitable video guide to be displayed to a novice user indicating how to use an object, purely triggered by the user's gaze. The approach is tested on a variety of daily tasks ranging from opening a door, to preparing coffee and operating a gym machine.

Keywords: Video guidance · Wearable computing · Real-time computer vision · Assistive computing · Object discovery · Object usage

1 Introduction

With the advent of wearable devices, systems able to provide guidance to users remain a possibility and a challenge. In particular in industrial settings (e.g. assembly, repair), operations using augmented reality or video-based manuals have been promised for a while. One of the key limitations to realize such systems is the need for authoring the content by e.g. manually segmenting and annotating videos or creating three-dimensional models that represent meaningful guidance [16],[1]. Authoring is time consuming and evidently limiting. Approaches that can provide guidance without the need for any manual intervention would enable a wider adoption of assistive wearable systems.

In this paper we present a fully automated, online and real-time approach for providing video-based guidance on object usage from egocentric video and eye gaze. The system has two modes, a *learning mode* where video snippets are automatically extracted from videos of multiple users performing tasks around a shared environment, and an *assistive mode* where a 'suitable' video snippet from the automatically collected video guides is selected, triggered by gaze. In strong contrast to most previous work on assistive egocentric guidance, we require no pre-training of the objects involved in tasks, nor knowledge of the tasks' scripts or the knowledge of how many objects will be used or interacted with. The

© Springer International Publishing Switzerland 2015
L. Agapito et al. (Eds.): ECCV 2014 Workshops, Part III, LNCS 8927, pp. 481–492, 2015.
DOI: 10.1007/978-3-319-16199-0_34

approach is able to harvest video snippets for objects of interest as a precursor for cognitive assistance. The system selects a short assistive snippet or *video guide* to be shown when a gazed-at object is recognised, to illustrate how the object was used before. This paper presents a prototype for the system and concentrates on evaluating the extraction of objects and their use. We illustrate the annotation of test videos with the automatically extracted video guides[1], and leave the evaluation of the effectiveness of the *assistive mode* with real users for future work.

The setup uses a single wearable gaze-tracker eyepiece which features a camera that looks out towards the scene and a pupil tracker that indicates where the eye is looking.

2   Related Work

Related systems to the problem we are aiming to address expect the objects to have visual markers (e.g. [18]), use model-based tracking(e.g. [16]) or be specified in advance of task performance (e.g. [1]). This review focuses on the ability to find objects of interest, i.e. task-relevant objects (TRO), from egocentric video during task performance. Common approaches include i) segmenting the area surrounding the user's hand [7],[6],[12], ii) extracting foreground regions through frame stabilisation or scene planarity assumptions [17],[21] or iii) detecting 'object-like' regions [15].

One uniquely rich source of information in egocentric sensing is eye gaze. Eye gaze has been studied for hundreds of years and more intensively since the 19th century [23]. There are two principal eye behaviours: fast motion transitions (aka saccades) and eye fixations. Importantly, studies of eye fixations during everyday tasks show substantial similarities in the locations and number of fixations by different operators, that gaze rarely visits irrelevant objects and that fixations precede actions [11],[8].

However, eye gaze has been rarely considered as part of wearable systems, perhaps due to the scarcity of *mobile* gaze tracking hardware. Exceptions include [5] which exemplifies how gaze can assist in predicting the current action, and how the predicted action can be used to estimate the forthcoming gaze position. In [20], a wearable gaze-controlled camera provides a cropped image dictated by eye gaze locations to enhance object tracking and in [4], interest points are extracted around the gaze point and matched to pre-learnt highly textured objects. None of these approaches discover objects using gaze. In [14], object segmentation using gaze is attempted from annotated short clips containing action, though the work focuses on gaze estimation.

Our recent work [3] has compared the influence of gaze, position, appearance and motion *using offline processing* on the extraction of objects in egocentric video. Results prove that 80% of objects were correctly extracted by localising gaze within a 3D map. In this work, we use the same dataset but propose an *online* incremental algorithm that learns objects and extracts video help

---

[1]   http://www.cs.bris.ac.uk/~damen/You-Do-I-Learn

guides incrementally from multiple operators. An online approach would scale with more users without the need for re-training, and data can be processed on the fly avoiding the need to store lengthy hours of egocentric video collected from multiple users. To enable real-time processing, we learn objects using the shape-based real-time object learning and detection method [2], which is capable of accommodating multiple objects in a scalable manner using constellations of edgelets. The algorithm is also capable of detecting 'moveable' objects and distinguishing them from 'static' objects that remain fixed in the 3D map.

3   Proposed Method

Our method is based on four principles:

- Spatio-temporally consistent gaze fixations indicate an observation of a task-relevant object (TRO).
- Each observation represents a candidate video snippet for assistive guidance.
- Spatially consistent observations correspond to a fixed TRO (i.e. an object with a fixed location in the scene).
- Appearance-consistent observations, observed in different locations, correspond to a moveable TRO.

The input to the system is real-time egocentric video with 2D gaze fixations. In the *learning mode* (Sec 3.1), the system aims to learn objects of interest as well as extract video snippets on how these objects are used. In the *assistive mode* (Sec 3.2), the system aims to recognise gazed-at objects and select a suitable video snippet for guidance from the automatically extracted snippets in the learning mode. The approach is completely unsupervised, and details of both modes are discussed next.

3.1   Learning Mode

First, we follow the velocity-based approach from [19] to distinguish saccades from fixations, and position the 2D fixation relative to the scene using sparse Simultaneous Localisation and Mapping (SLAM) [9]. Given the 6D pose of the scene camera, a 3D gaze ray links the direction of the gaze to a point in the scene. A dense depth map is estimated, using a triangular tessellation on the tracked interest points that are visible on the scene camera (similar to [22]). To distinguish between the 2D fixation at time t and its corresponding 3D position within the map, we refer to these as f_t^2 and f_t^3 respectively.

Next, objects are discovered using online clustering, as explained below and in Algo. 1. We define a *gaze cluster (GC)* as a collection of 'at least' ξ spatially-close consecutive gaze fixations, and use this to learn objects. Two consecutive fixations, f_t^3 and f_{t-1}^3 belong to the same GC if $||f_t^3 - f_{t-1}^3|| < \epsilon$, where ϵ is the distance threshold selected to accept clustering consecutive fixations and $||.||$ is the Euclidean distance. Notice that the temporal difference between t and $t - 1$ might not correspond to one frame, as some frames have missing gaze

---

input : fixations $\{(f_t^2, f_t^3)\}$, images $\{I_t\}; t = 1..T$
output: TROs $\{(A_k, U_k, m_k, \nu_k); 1 \le k \le K\}$
A_k learnt view-based appearance model for TRO i
U_k video snippets for TRO i
$\nu_k \in \{$fixed, moveable$\}$ type of TRO
m_k segmented 3D model for TRO k

1 $K = previousK = 0$
2 $stableGC = 0$
3 **for** $t = 1..T$ **do**
4 $\quad$ find closest gaze cluster k: min $\arg_k ||f_t^3 - \mu_k||_{\Sigma_k}$
5 $\quad$ Extract window w_t centred around f_t^2 from I_t

$\quad$ // Object Discovery
6 $\quad$ **if** $||f_t^3 - \mu_k||_{\Sigma_k} \le 1$ **then**
7 $\quad\quad$ ⌊ Update $\mu_k(Eq\ 1), \Sigma_k(Eq\ 2)$
8 $\quad$ **else**
9 $\quad\quad$ **if** $||f_t^3 - f_{t-1}^3|| < \epsilon$ **then**
10 $\quad\quad\quad$ $stableGC = stableGC + 1$
11 $\quad\quad\quad$ **if** $stableGC \ge \xi$ **then**
12 $\quad\quad\quad\quad$ $K = K + 1$
13 $\quad\quad\quad\quad$ Add a new gaze cluster $k = K$
14 $\quad\quad\quad\quad$ Learn the first view of a new object
15 $\quad\quad\quad\quad$ ⌊ $\nu_k = $ 'fixed'
16 $\quad\quad$ **else**
17 $\quad\quad\quad$ ⌊ $stableGC = 0$

$\quad$ // Learn Appearance
18 $\quad$ Detect an object within the window w_t
19 $\quad$ **if** *recognised as TRO j* **then**
20 $\quad\quad$ **if** $j \ne k$ **then**
21 $\quad\quad\quad$ **if** *confirmed from several detections* **then**
22 $\quad\quad\quad\quad$ ⌊ $\nu_k = $ 'moveable'
23 $\quad$ **else**
24 $\quad\quad$ **if** *Object was not detected in last δ frames* **then**
25 $\quad\quad\quad$ ⌊ Learn a new view for object k

$\quad$ // Video Snippets and Model
26 $\quad$ **if** $k \ne previousK$ **then**
27 $\quad\quad$ add *video snippet* u_i^k to U_k (Eq. 3)
28 $\quad\quad$ ⌊ build 3D model m_k

$\quad$ // Keep track of current GC
29 $\quad$ $previousK = k$

Algorithm 1. Proposed algorithm for *learning mode*

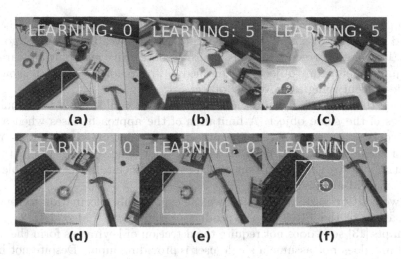

Fig. 1. Two TROs were discovered (a,b). Later, the tape was moved (c). A new fixation is spatially close to TRO '0' (d). Initially, further views were collected for TRO '0' (d,e). A few frames later, the object is consistently recognised as TRO '5' by appearance matching. Both TRO '0' and '5' are marked as 'moveable' (f).

information, or the gaze might have been discarded as a saccade. If and only if ζ consecutive fixations are within the same GC, an observation of a TRO k is discovered (Algo. 1 L. 9-15). The mean and covariance of GC are updated incrementally as further fixations are located within the threshold ϵ. Equations 1 and 2 show the incremental update for the mean and covariance of a GC.

$$\|f_t^3 - f_{t-1}^3\| < \epsilon \to \mu_t^k = \frac{\mu_{t-1}^k \times (n-1) + f_t^3}{n} \tag{1}$$

$$\to \Sigma_t^k = \frac{n-2}{n-1}\Sigma_{t-1}^k + \frac{1}{n}(f_t^3 - \mu_{n-1})^T(f_t^3 - \mu_{n-1}) \tag{2}$$

where μ_t^k is the mean, Σ_t^k is the covariance matrix and n is the number of clustered fixations at time t.

Attention is believed to have moved to another location when $\|f_t^3 - f_{t-1}^3\| \geq \epsilon$. At a future point in time $t + \rho$, further fixations can belong to the same TRO k if it is within one standard deviation from the mean of the TRO k according to the Mahalanobis distance (Algo. 1 L. 6-7). This clustering enables both small-sized and large TROs to be discovered, as it does not limit or pre-define the size of the GC. However, it assumes that the object is fixed, i.e. remains within the same 3D location.

To accommodate for moveable objects, appearance matching is considered. For every TRO k, views around the object are learnt using the real-time method from [2]. Only novel views are added to the appearance model - a view is added if the object fails to be recognised in the past δ frames (Algo. 1 L. 24-25). The gazed-at object is compared to the previously learnt K objects $\{A_k; k = 1..K\}$.

If the appearance matches a learnt TRO, at a different location, the object is believed to have moved, and is thus identified as a 'moveable' object (Algo. 1 L. 19-22). To avoid incorrect detections, multiple consecutive matching appearances are required before an object is identified as 'moveable'. Figure 1 shows an example of identifying a 'moveable' object.

Notice that identifying an object as 'moveable' could result from multiple instances of the same object. A limitation of the approach arises when a new object replaces a learnt TRO. The object is then incorrectly learnt as novel views of the previously learnt TRO. This does not affect the assistive nature of the method, as we use the current object's appearance to select a suitable *help snippet* as will be explained next.

As we position gaze in 3D space, we can exploit this information to generate visualisations of the TROs as a byproduct of the process (Algo. 1 L. 28). This step adapts [13] so it does not require the detection of keyframes form the user's motion and does not assume a single user is providing input. Despite not being perfect models, due to the fact that they are created during an action, the resulting models are useful visualisations of what objects the system has discovered. Ultimately, having a 3D model facilitates applications such as augmented reality guidance which we leave for future work.

Given consecutive fixations $(f_t^2, f_{t+1}^2, ..., f_{t+\rho}^2); \rho \geq \xi$ belonging to the same TRO, a **video snippet** u_i^k for TRO k is defined as

$$u_i^k = \{\Psi(I_j, \Delta(j), \omega) \tag{3}$$

where Ψ crops a window of size ω from Image I_j around the interpolated fixation $\Delta(j)$ as gaze information is missing in some frames (Algo. 1 L. 27). The collection of all video snippets U_k shows different ways in which the object k was used or interacted with.

As multiple operators with different heights and interaction behaviours use the same object, the method is capable of expanding the learnt views, the 3D model m_k and gather further interaction video snippets U_k. Figure 2 shows the advantages of learning from multiple users.

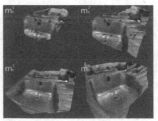

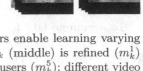

Fig. 2. For the same discovered object (sink): multiple users enable learning varying views in the appearance model A_k (left); the 3D model m_k (middle) is refined (m_k^1) shows the model for one user, two users (m_k^2) as well as five users (m_k^5); different video snippets U_k show multiple interactions with the same object (right).

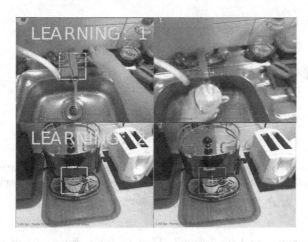

Fig. 3. During discovery (left), edges within a window around the gaze are captured as object views, and represented using affine-invariant descriptors. These are used to detect objects around the gaze point in real-time (right).

3.2   Assistive Mode

In the assistive mode, *video snippets* $\{U_k; k = 1..K\}$ can be used to provide automatic assistance for novice operators. First, the system needs to identify which object the person intends to use next, then the system would select a *video snippet*, from the potentially many snippets collected from multiple operators using the object one or more times, to be displayed to the novice operator.

We recognise objects based on the learnt views in an image patch around the gaze point using the scalable real-time texture-minimal object detector from [2]. By using the combination of fixed paths and a hierarchical hash table, the method is scalable, and can reliably detect objects at frame rate. The descriptor is affine-invariant, and the method is tolerant to a level of occlusion but is also view-dependant. Figure 3 shows the method learning (left column) and subsequently recognising (right column) objects from our experiments. Notice that the assistive mode does not require 3D tracking, and objects are recognised around the 2D gaze point.

Upon recognition, a *help snippet* is displayed to show how this object was previously used. From the possibly many *video snippets* featuring the TRO, collected in learning mode, we chose the *help snippet* h_t as a video guide at time t such that the appearance of the first frame in the snippet, is closest to the recognised view. If the object changes state, the initial appearance is a good indicator of which video snippet to show. An additional advantage is to avoid showing a snippet observing the object from a different viewpoint, so the user can easily map what they see to what they could do.

A *help snippet* is displayed each time a new object is detected. As some objects can be gazed-at multiple times during the task, we employ temporal

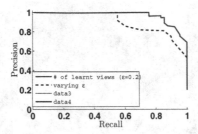

Fig. 4. Precision-Recall curve for discovering TROs as ϵ (Eq. 1) varies. For $\epsilon=0.2$ metres, discovered objects are filtered based on the number of learnt views - at 76% recall, 100% precision was achieved.

ordering in choosing the *help snippet*. That is, for a given object we choose its snippets in order, starting first from all the first encounters of that object in all training sequences. When the same object is gazed-at again, a snippet from the set from all the second encounters in the training sequences is displayed and so on.

4   Experiments and Results

Setup & Dataset. We use the dataset from [3] which was recorded using the wearable gaze tracker hardware [10]. After calibration, the scene images are synchronised with, if available, 2D gaze points. Twenty objects were ground-truthed, of which 5 are moveable objects.

To evaluate the ability of online clustering to find TROs, a 3D bounding box around fixations from one discovered TRO is compared to the manually labelled 3D bounding box on the map's point cloud. The PASCAL overlap criterion (adapted for 3D) of 20% is used for a true positive discovery, using the algorithm detailed above (parameter choices in Tab. 1). The main parameter for clustering is the threshold for 3D distances (ϵ). As ϵ (Eq. 1) varies, the number of discovered objects changes. The recall-precision results are shown in Fig. 4.

For $\epsilon = 0.2$, Tab. 2 shows the mean and standard deviation for the number of discovered, merged and split objects in one and all sequences. Since the clustering is online, different runs would result in a different set of discovered objects depending on the ordering of sequences. We run the experiments multiple times

Table 1. Parameter choices for object discovery

Eq. 1		Algo. 1	
k	10 frames	δ	5 frames
ϵ	20 cm	w	150×150

Fig. 5. [**Best seen in colour**] 22 objects were discovered within the four maps (W, D, P and K) listed from left to right by order of discovery. Out of these, 14 ground-truth objects are found (with 3 splits), and 5 are task-irrelevant (red rectangles). The 'cup' was missed at this iteration. Three objects were classified as 'moveable' (blue ellipses), out of possible 4. The charger was discovered twice and the sugar jar was discovered as three different objects.

(5 times), starting from a different sequence, and record the results. As the table shows, when trained using a single operator, precision of 79% is achieved alongside 86% of recall. When training on all operators, on average, 97% recall was achieved, with an increase in the total number of discovered objects. The number of false positives can be dropped by filtering for the number of learnt views, as operators observe TROs for longer than other objects in the scene (Fig. 4). The approach also separates fixed from moveable TROs. Recall that a TRO is 'moveable' if it is detected in different locations, using appearance matching. On average, 77% of TROs were correctly classified. The set of discovered objects from a single run is shown in Fig 5. Examples of learnt views for the discovered objects can be found in Fig 6.

Assistive Mode: To assess the ability of the approach to provide video guides, the approach is run using leave-one-out. For every operator, the *learning mode* is run on the remainder sequences to discover TROs and collect video guides. The appearance models of discovered TROs are then used to recognise objects in the 'left' sequence (i.e. not used for discovery), within patches around the 2D gaze. When an object is recognised, an insert is added indicating a suggestive

Table 2. At $\epsilon = 0.2$ metres, from one and all operators, the avg. (μ) and std dev. (σ) of the # of discovered TROs, the # of true TROs (ground-truth=20), the # of merged objects (ground-truthed as two separate objects), the # of split objects. For distinguishing moveable from fixed objects, the # of correctly classified objects.

Op		total	gt TROs	merged	split	type
1	μ	21.6	17.2	0.7	1.5	-
	σ	1.5	0.9	0.5	0.8	-
All	μ	33.2	19.3	0.2	3.8	15.5
	σ	2.0	0.8	0.4	1.6	0.9

Fig. 6. Learnt views from training sequences of multiple users for a variety of objects: coffee machine, tap, seat adjustor and screwdriver

Fig. 7. In the assistive mode, when a TRO is detected, a video snippet is inserted showing the most relevant video guide based on the initial appearance

way of how the object can be used. A *help snippet* h_t is displayed each time a new object is recognised. We showcase video help guides using inserts on a pre-recorded video. Figure 7 shows frames from the help videos and a full sequence is provided[2]. Recall that these inserts are *extracted, selected and shown* fully automatically. These could in principle be shown on a head-mounted display, but is not considered in this study. We believe this highlights the success and potentials of the work in this paper.

5   Conclusions and Future Work

In this paper we develop an online real-time system based on egocentric video with gaze. In its *learning mode*, the system discovers task-relevant objects and automatically collects video snippets from multiple users on how they used the

---

[2] http://www.cs.bris.ac.uk/~damen/You-Do-I-Learn

discovered object. In the *assistive mode*, video guides are shown on how objects have been used before, triggered by recognising the gazed-at object. This could be useful to novice users exploring the same environment and objects. This paper explains a complete online prototype, and future work aims to evaluate the benefits of the assistive mode on the performance of novice users.

References

1. Bleser, G., Almeida, L., Behera, A., Calway, A., Cohn, A., Damen, D., Domingues, H., Gee, A., Gorecky, D., Hogg, D., Kraly, M., Macaes, G., Marin, F., Mayol-Cuevas, W., Miezal, M., Mura, K., Petersen, N., Vignais, N., Santos, L., Spaas, G., Stricker, D.: Cognitive workflow capturing and rendering with on- body sensor networks (cognito). German Research Center for Artificial Intelligence, DFKI Research Reports (RR) (2013)
2. Damen, D., Bunnun, P., Calway, A., Mayol-Cuevas, W.: Real-time learning and detection of 3D texture-less objects: A scalable approach. In: British Machine Vision Conference (BMVC) (2012)
3. Damen, D., Leelasawassuk, T., Haines, O., Calway, A., Mayol-Cuevas, W.: Youdo, i-learn: Discovering task relevant objects and their modes of interaction from multi-user egocentric video. In: British Machine Vision Conference (BMVC) (2014)
4. De Beugher, S., Ichiche, Y., Brone, G., Geodeme, T.: Automatic analysis of eye-tracking data using object detection algorithms. In: Workshop on Perasive Eye Traking and Mobile Eye-based Interaction (PETMEI) (2012)
5. Fathi, A., Li, Y., Rehg, J.M.: Learning to recognize daily actions using gaze. In: Fitzgibbon, A., Lazebnik, S., Perona, P., Sato, Y., Schmid, C. (eds.) ECCV 2012, Part I. LNCS, vol. 7572, pp. 314–327. Springer, Heidelberg (2012)
6. Fathi, A., Rehg, J.: Modeling actions through state changes. In: Computer Vision and Pattern Recognition (CVPR) (2013)
7. Fathi, A., Ren, X., Rehg, J.: Learning to recognise objects in egocentric activities. In: Computer Vision and Pattern Recognition (CVPR) (2011)
8. Henderson, J.: Human gaze control during real-world scene perception. Trends in Cognitive Sciences 7(11) (2003)
9. Klein, G., Murray, D.: Parallel tracking and mapping for small AR workspaces. In: Int. Sym. on Mixed and Augmented Reality (ISMAR) (2007)
10. Laboratories, A.S.: Mobile Eye-XG. http://www.asleyetracking.com/
11. Land, M.: Eye movements and the control of actions in everyday life. Progress in Retinal and Eye Research (2006)
12. Lee, Y., Ghosh, J., Grauman, K.: Discovering important people and objects for egocentric video summarization. In: Computer Vision and Pattern Recognition (CVPR) (2012)
13. Leelasawassuk, T., Mayol-Cuevas, W.: 3D from looking: Using wearable gaze tracking for hands-free and feedback-free object modelling. In: Int. Sym. on Wearable Computers (ISWC) (2013)
14. Li, Y., Fathi, A., Rehg, J.: Learning to predict gaze in egocentric video. In: Int. Conf. on Computer Vision (ICCV) (2013)
15. Lu, Z., Grauman, K.: Story-driven summarization for egocentric video. In: Computer Vision and Pattern Recognition (CVPR) (2013)
16. Petersen, N., Stricker, D.: Learning task structure from video examples for workflow tracking and authoring. In: International Symposium on Mixed and Augmented Reality (ISMAR) (2012)

17. Ren, X., Gu, C.: Figure-ground segmentation improves handled object recognition in egocentric video. In: Computer Vision and Pattern Recognition (CVPR) (2010)
18. Rosten, E., Reitmayr, G., Drummond, T.: Real-Time video annotations for augmented reality. In: Bebis, G., Boyle, R., Koracin, D., Parvin, B. (eds.) ISVC 2005. LNCS, vol. 3804, pp. 294–302. Springer, Heidelberg (2005)
19. Salvucci, D., Goldberg, J.: Identifying fixations and saccades in eye-tracking protocols. In: Sym. on Eye Tracking Research & Applications (2000)
20. Sun, L., Klank, U., Beetz, M.: EyeWatchMe - 3D hand and object tracking for inside out activity analysis. In: Computer Vision and Pattern Recognition Workshop (CVPRW) (2009)
21. Sundaram, S., Mayol-Cuevas, W.: What are we doing here? egocentric activity recognition on the move for contextual mapping. In: Int. Conf. on Robotics and Automation (ICRA) (2012)
22. Takemura, K., Kohashi, Y., Suenaga, T., Takamatsu, J., Ogasawara, T.: Estimating 3D point-of-regard and visualizing gaze trajectories under natural head movements. In: Sym. on Eye-Tracking Research & Applications (ETRA) (2010)
23. Wade, N., Tatler, B.: The moving tablet of the eye: the origins of modern eye movement research. Oxford University Press (2005)

Wearable RGBD Indoor Navigation System for the Blind

Young Hoon Lee[✉] and Gérard Medioni

Institute for Robotics and Intelligent Systems, University of Southern California,
Los Angeles, CA, USA
{lee126,medioni}@usc.edu

Abstract. In this paper, we present a novel wearable RGBD camera based navigation system for the visually impaired. The system is composed of a smartphone user interface, a glass-mounted RGBD camera device, a real-time navigation algorithm, and haptic feedback system. A smartphone interface provides an effective way to communicate to the system using audio and haptic feedback. In order to extract orientational information of the blind users, the navigation algorithm performs real-time 6-DOF feature based visual odometry using a glass-mounted RGBD camera as an input device. The navigation algorithm also builds a 3D voxel map of the environment and analyzes 3D traversability. A path planner of the navigation algorithm integrates information from the egomotion estimation and mapping and generates a safe and an efficient path to a waypoint delivered to the haptic feedback system. The haptic feedback system consisting of four micro-vibration motors is designed to guide the visually impaired user along the computed path and to minimize cognitive loads. The proposed system achieves real-time performance at 28.4Hz in average on a laptop, and helps the visually impaired extends the range of their activities and improve the mobility performance in a cluttered environment. The experiment results show that navigation in indoor environments with the proposed system avoids collisions successfully and improves mobility performance of the user compared to conventional and state-of-the-art mobility aid devices.

1 Introduction

Visual perception plays a very important role in everyday life, and hence visual impairment adversely affects several daily activities such as ambulating familiar and unfamiliar environments[27]. Researches have proved that vision loss severely lowers the mobility of the visually impaired [4, 26, 27]. As a result, approximately more than 30% of the blind population do not ambulate autonomously outdoors [3]. Visual impairment also increases the risk of unintentional injuries which often result in medical consequences [15, 17].

Long canes and the guide dogs have been the most popular mobility aids among the blind for navigation and collision avoidance purposes. An interview

L. Agapito et al. (Eds.): ECCV 2014 Workshops, Part III, LNCS 8927, pp. 493–508, 2015.
DOI: 10.1007/978-3-319-16199-0_35

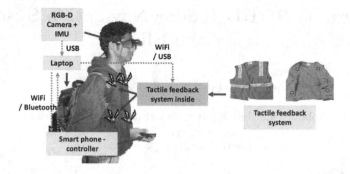

Fig. 1. Overview of the proposed system: A glass-mounted camera+IMU sensor, a smartphone user interface, and tactile interface system

in [17] also indicated that 12% and 55% of the visually impaired interviewees have used the guide dog and the long cane as a primary mobility aid, respectively. According to the 2011 National Health Interview Survey, 21.2 million American adults age 18 and older reported experiencing vision loss [24]. However, the guide dog has very limited availabilities as only about 1,500 individuals are estimated to graduate from a dog-guide user program [25] every year. The relatively small coverage range and a reactive nature of the long cane still accompany a high risk of collision, because the visually impaired can avoid obstacles only when they make contact with obstacles. Moreover, the long canes can cover the lower body portion of a blind user only.

To reduce risks from mobility-related activities and improve the mobility of people with vision loss, researchers have proposed Electronic Travel Aids (ETA) utilizing various types of sensors including GPS and laser sensors to replace the white cane [1,30].

Computer vision provides rich information of surrounding environments that can be exploited for developing sophisticated applications towards real-time applications at an affordable cost, light weight, and low power consumption. Hence, the authors believe it is appropriate to transfer computer vision techniques to develop more effective wearable mobility aids for the visually impaired.

In this paper, we present a novel glass-mounted wearable RGBD camera based navigation system for the visually impaired built on the Lee's work [14]. A glass-mounted design has become a popular form factor for wearable device applications [5]. The glass-mounted platform is ideal for the wearable navigation algorithms for the following reasons. The glass-mounted design is ideal for scanning around surrounding environments as the visually impaired user traverse to reach a goal. It also extends the range of obstacle detection by detecting obstacles located at the blind sight of the long cane. The system extended a scope of navigation tasks from directing users towards the nearest open space [14,22] to navigating to a specific destination in more robust way as presented in Section 3. In order to help the visually impaired subject navigate to a destination in an unknown environment, the proposed system analyze RGBD camera inputs to estimate 6-DOF motion of the blind subject and to perform traversability analysis. Based on the output of the navigation system, the tactile feedback system generates a cue to guide a visually impaired user along the computed path and to alert the presence of obstacles. We present experimental results showing that the system improves the mobility performance of the blind subjects and is able to guide the blind subject to a designated goal in unknown environments without colliding to obstacles in a reasonable completion time.

The rest of this paper consists of four sections as follows. Section 2 covers recent vision based mobility devices. The proposed system with all building blocks is described in Section 3. In Section 4, experimental results are presented and we finish with conclusions and future work in Section 5.

2   Literature Review

Recently, Microsoft and Primesense introduced an affordable RGB-D camera called Kinect that provides dense 3-D information registered with an RGB image at a faster rate than that of sensors used in the past. The release of the Kinect has drawn enormous attentions among researchers and caused a surge in researches in 3D SLAM. RGBD camera based mobility aid systems are described [2,31]. However, they were close to Proof-of-Concept platforms conducting obstacle avoidance tasks without egomotion estimation or building a global map of surroundings which is a key component of navigation system. In [18,23], the authors proposed a stereo vision based system that estimates a camera trajectory to predict user motion and build the vicinity 3D maps. The described system, however, detects only overhead obstacles and being shoulder-mounted, does not have the advantages described in Section 1. Researchers have proposed utilizing various types of sensors to replace the white cane [1,30]. However, such Electronic Travel Aids (ETA) designed to replace or to be attached to the long cane do not prevent head-level (chest level or higher) accidents effectively. Mobility aids based on Global Positioning System (GPS) devices [7,16] cannot perform collision avoidance and are not specifically useful indoors.

In [22], Pradeep et al. proposed real-time head mounted stereo-vision based navigation system for the visually impaired. The system is known to be the first complete wearable navigation system that adopted head mounted vision system and tactile feedback prototype which brings many advantages in mobility aids applications for the blind. The head-mounted sensor design enables the visually impaired to stand and scan surroundings easier than waist- or shoulder-mounted designs that require body rotations. The head mounted device also matches the frame of reference of the person, allowing relative position commands. The tactile interface device helps the blind users receive a resulting cue generated by the algorithms at a reasonable cognitive load through a wireless network for guidance along the safe path. The navigation system extends the coverage range and is able to detect obstacles located at the blind sight of the long cane. The experiment results indicate that the tactile vest system combined with the white cane is more efficient at alerting blind users to the presence of obstacles and

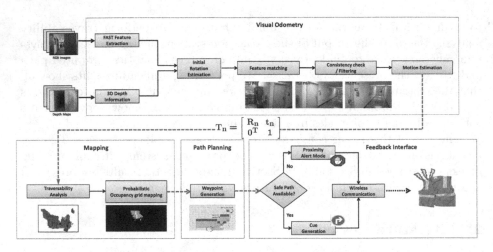

Fig. 2. Navigation algorithm overview

helping blind subjects steer away from obstacles than the white cane alone. The navigation performance was proved successful by showing trajectories generated by the proposed navigation system are the closest to the ideal trajectories from sighted subjects [22]. In [14], Lee *et. al* extended [22] and introduced a real-time wearable RGB-D camera based indoor navigation aid for the visually impaired that uses a Primesense RGB-D camera as an input device to overcome some limitations of a passive stereo camera system.

A main difference of the proposed system from [14,22] is that a blind user is able to specify the destination for a navigation task using a smartphone application, which enables the proposed system to extend a scope of navigation tasks from a local obstacle avoidance task, that is directing a blind user towards the nearest open space without collision, to a global navigation task, guiding to a designated location. And the proposed system also adopted a probabilistic grid mapping framework which helps the system to maintain accurate and up-to-date information of surrounding environment for more robust navigation performance.

3   Navigation Algorithm

In this section, we provide an overview of the navigation algorithm as illustrated in Fig. 2. The system consists of a head-mounted RGBD camera and a vest-type interface device with four tactile feedback effectors. The wearable navigation system runs a real-time egomotion estimation, mapping, obstacle detection, and route-planning algorithm.

3.1   Initialization

The system is equipped with a small 9 DOF MEMS IMU sensor on top of RGB-D sensor for an initialization purpose. Roll and Pitch angle of the camera

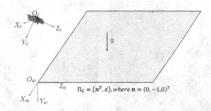

Fig. 3. (Left) Shaded areas in green color are points having a normal vector parallel to the gravity vector and used to extract the ground plane Π_G. (Right) The ground plane model is represented in the global reference frame.

orientation is initialized to be parallel to the ground plane of the world coordinate frame. Using IMU sensor readings as an orientation prior and normals of point clouds obtained using real-time normal estimation algorithm [9], we first obtain the major point clouds that have normals parallel to the gravity vector. From the set of point of clouds, we find a the plane coefficients using a RANSAC-based least square method and find the major plane $\Pi_G = (\mathbf{n}, D)$, where $\mathbf{n} = (A, B, C)^T$ is a normal vector of a plane. We then find a $\mathbf{R_0}$ such that $\mathbf{R_0} \cdot \mathbf{n} = (0, -1, 0)^T$. Yaw angle is initialized using the magnetometer reading in order to maintain an orientation with respect to the global reference frame. The pose of the blind user is represented by $\mathbf{T_n}$ where n represents the frame number.

$$\mathbf{T_0} = \begin{bmatrix} \mathbf{R_0} & \mathbf{t_0} \\ \mathbf{0^T} & 1 \end{bmatrix}, \text{ where } \mathbf{t_0} = (0, 0, 0)^T$$

The initialization step helps the visually impaired maintain consistent orientation with respect to surroundings as the blind is assumed to move on the ground plane. This is not a critical issue for offline map building applications which requires simple 3D rotations to align a model or online applications where the initial pose is always identical, for example, a ground vehicles navigation. This initialization process, however, is essential for real-time wearable navigation system because incremental mapping methods usually build a map with respect to the camera pose of the first frame. Failures to maintain the initial orientation with respect to the world often causes the navigation system to create incorrect traversability map by converting the ground plane into obstacles. Every cell of the 2D global traversability map (GTM) is also initialized to have a uniform prior probability of $P(n) = 0.5$.

3.2 Visual Odometry

In order to maintain a sense of egocentricity of a blind user, we continuously estimate the camera pose in the world coordinate frame. We adopt the **F**ast **O**dometry from **VIS**ion (FOVIS) [12] visual odometry algorithm to achieve a real-time visual odometry. Every frame begins with an RGB and depth image capture from the camera. The RGB image is converted to grayscale and smoothed using a fixed size Gaussian kernel. Then a Gaussian pyramid is constructed to

Fig. 4. FAST corners and their correspondences from the last key-frame after refinement

detect robust features at each Gaussian pyramid level. At each Gaussian pyramid level, FAST corners are extracted. In order to guarantee uniform distribution of features, images at each level is divided into 80×80 sub-images. the 25 strongest FAST corners are selected from each sub-image. Fast corners associated with invalid depth are discarded. Generally, the features motion in the image plane is caused by 3D rotation for continuous motion estimation applications. An algorithm proposed by Mei *et al.* [19] to compute an initial rotation by directly minimizing the sum of squared pixel errors between downsampled versions of the current and previous frames is used. This initial rotation estimation helps to constrain the search area for feature matching. 80 byte descriptor pixel patch, the last pixel omitted from 9×9, around a feature is normalized around zero mean. Then features are matched across frames using sum-of-absolute differences (SAD) as a match score. A graph of consistent feature matches is constructed using Howards approach [11]. The graph consists of vertices, a pair of feature matches, and edges that connects vertices. Rigid motions should preserve the Euclidean distance between two features matches over time in a static scene. The 3D Euclidean distance between features matches does not change drastically between consecutive frame. Hence, the set of inliers make up the maximal clique of consistent matches in a static scene. Then the maximal clique in the graph is found using a greedy algorithm [8,11]. Initial estimation of $6-$DOF motion is calculated using Horn's absolute orientation method [10] given the inliers by minimizing the Euclidean distances between the inlier feature matches. The initial motion estimation is further refined by minimizing reprojection errors. Matches with a reprojection error above a threshold will be discarded from the inlier set and the motion estimate is refined once again to obtain the final motion estimate. Some of visual odometry results are shown in Fig. 4.

3.3   Mapping and Traversability Analysis

A 3D local voxel grid map (LVGM), a quantized representation of 3D point clouds, is generated with respect to the camera reference frame as represented in Fig. 5. Even though path planning is performed on 2D space to reduce computation complexity in a subsequent stage, traversability is analyzed in 3D space. This allows the visually impaired to prevent collisions, since the system is able

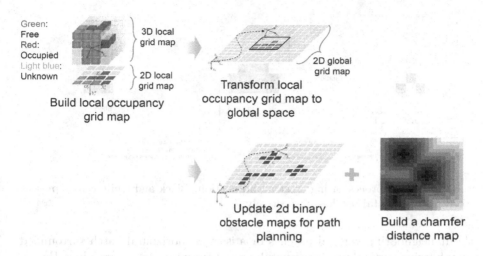

Green:
Free
Red:
Occupied
Light blue:
Unknown

3D local
grid map

2D local
grid map

Build local occupancy
grid map

Transform local
occupancy grid map to
global space

2D global
grid map

Update 2d binary
obstacle maps for path
planning

Build a chamfer
distance map

Fig. 5. Local 3D voxels is displayed with respect to the world reference frame. Local traversability is calculated O_w and O_c represent the origin of the world reference frame and the camera reference frame, respectively.

to also detect obstacles in 3D space that may be located in blind spots of the long cane.

Using the estimated camera orientation, we align the 3D LVGM in Fig. 5 with respect to the global reference frame at each frame as shown in Fig. 5. The aligned 3D LVGM is classified into occupied, free, and unknown states. Invisible voxels that are out of field of view of the camera or obstructed by another voxel are classified as unknown states. The state of the rest voxels, either occupied or free, is determined based on the number of point clouds in each voxel. Green and red voxels in a upper left corner of Fig. 5 represent free and occupied state voxels, respectively while light blue colored voxels are the voxel with unknown states. These voxels are further classified into vertical and horizontal patches which is a projection onto the local traversability map (LTM), local 2D local grid space parallel to the ground plane, centered at O'_c as shown in a upper left corner of Fig. 5. If one or more occupied voxels projected onto a cell on the LTM, the cell is registered as a vertical patch. On the other hands, cells that free voxels fall into are registered as a horizontal patch. Green cells and red cells in the bottom of a upper left corner in Fig. 5 indicate horizontal patch and vertical patches on LTM, respectively.

Glass-mounted cameras for the navigation often faces an spatial configuration where the most of point clouds from a RGBD sensor are located beyond a certain distance as the goal of the system is to guide the visually impaired to steer the subject away from possible collision threats such as walls and obstacles which act as a reliable source when estimating motion of the camera. Hence, depth values from the glass-mounted platform tend to be quite noisy since the noise characteristic of the RGB-D sensors is proportional to the quadratic of distance to a point [21] We have empirically found out that a single vertical patch

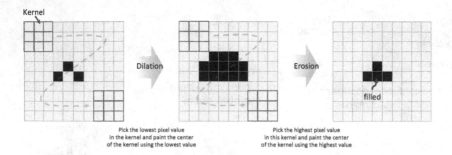

Pick the lowest pixel value
in the kernel and paint the center
of the kernel using the lowest value

Pick the highest pixel value
in this kernel and paint the center
of the kernel using the highest value

Fig. 6. A filtering process using erosion and dilation. Black and white cells represent vertical and horizontal patches, respectively.

without neighboring vertical patches or a isolated horizontal patch surrounded by neighboring vertical patches generally result from noisy sensor reading. Hence, we apply a simple filtering algorithm using 2D image processing techniques, erosion and dilation, for noise reductions on LTM. Fig. 6 shows a simple example how this erosion and dilation process fills a hole on a local grid map that is likely to be misinterpretation of the environment introduced by sensor noise.

Then the vertical and horizontal patches in the LTM are transformed to the world reference frame to update the occupancy probabilities of the 2D GTM as displayed in 5. The occupancy probability of each cell of GTM is updated by occupancy grid mapping rule suggested by Moravec[20].

$$P(n|z_{1:t}) = \left[1 + \frac{1 - P(n|z_t)}{P(n|z_t)} \frac{1 - P(n|z_{1:t-1})}{P(n|z_{1:t-1})} \frac{P(n)}{1 - P(n)}\right]^{-1} \tag{1}$$

For efficient computation in updating, we use $logOdds()$ notation which can be directly converted into probabilistic values when needed. As stated in [28], this notation replaces multiplication with addition which is more efficient in computation.

$$L(n|z_{1:t}) = L(n|z_{1:t-1}) + L(n|z_t) \tag{2}$$

One disadvantage of the update policy represented in (2) is that it requires as many observation as had been integrated before to obtain the current state. In order for the system to respond to dynamic changes in the environment immediately and overcome the overconfidence in the map, the upper and lower bound, l_{max} and l_{min}, of the $logodds$ values is enforced using clamping update policy proposed by Yguel [29].

$$L(n|z_{1:t}) = max(min(L(n|z_{1:t-1}) + L(n|z_t), l_{max}), l_{min}) \tag{3}$$

Cells on the probabilistic global traversability map whose occupancy probability is lower than $P(l_{min})$ are registered as traversable while cells with higher occupancy probability than $P(l_{max})$ are registered as non-traversable, where $P(l_{min})$ and $P(l_{max})$ are corresponding probability value of l_{min} and l_{max}, respectively. As stated 3.1, all cells are initialized to have unknown state. Once the state of a cell changed to either traversable or non-traversable from unknown, cells whose occupancy probability value falls between $P(l_{max})$ and $P(l_{min})$, are registered as unknown areas.

3.4   Path Planning

The blind subject is assumed to travel on a ground plane. Therefore, the path planning is performed on the global 2D traversability map for computational efficiency. We also build and update a chamfer distance array that stores distance to the closest obstacle corresponding to the global 2D traversability map which is used to verify a direct measure of risk of collision instantaneously. The shortest path is produced using the $D^{\star}$ Lite Algorithm as suggested by [13] from the current location to the destination. $D^{\star}$ algorithm can handle dynamic changes of the surrounding very efficiently. However, subtle changes in the map sometimes result in changes of the generated path in high frequency, which confuses the blind subject. The shortest path produced is a set of cells, DL, on the grid map which connects the current location to the destination without using untraversable cells. Instead of directly following DL, we generate a reliable waypoint, W, that are confirmed to be traversable and located at least some distance from obstacles. In order to generate a waypoint, we find the furthest point in DL which is directly visible and traversable from the current location, D_1, and another cell, D_2, located furthest in the set DL which is directly visible and traversable from D_1. Then search the neighborhood of D_1 limited by a predefined radius and find a cell that minimize the cost function, f, given in (5). $C_{i,j}$ and $CF_{i,j}$ represent a cell in i^{th} row and j^{th} column and Chamfer distance value of $C_{i,j}$, respectively. $d(C_1, C_2)$ indicates distance between two cell, C_1 and C_2.

$$W = \operatorname*{argmin}_{i,j} f_{i,j} \,, \tag{4}$$

where $f_{i,j} = w_1 \times [d(C_{i,j}, D_1) + d(C_{i,j}, D_2)] + w_2 \times CF_{i,j}$

The temporary waypoint is updated when there is motion or rotation greater than a certain threshold , when the current waypoint is not visible from the

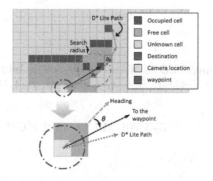

Fig. 7. An example of a waypoint update scenario

current location, or the blind subject arrives the vicinity of the waypoint to avoid frequent updates of the generated path and redundant computation.

3.5   Cue Generation and Haptic Feedback

The tactile feedback instead of audio feedback was used in order to reduce the amount of cognitive loads from hearing, which most blind users rely on for various other tasks. This system has intuitive 4 different cues for a user as followings:

- Straight (no tactile sensors on)
- Stop & Scan: Proximity Alert (all tactile sensors on)
- Turn left (top-left sensor on)
- Turn right (top-right sensor on)

The cue is generated simply based on a relative angle between a direction obtained by drawing a line from the current position to the waypoint and the current heading. In order to prevent frequent changes in cues which often causes confusions from the visually impaired subject, we utilize a hysteresis loop equation that takes the current status of a cue into account as well as a rotation angle required to reach the waypoint, W, as follows.

$$
\text{New Cue} = \begin{cases}
\text{Turn Left if} & -180° < \theta \leq -\theta_2, \\
\text{Curr. Cue if} & -\theta_2 < \theta < -\theta_1, \\
\text{Straight if} & -\theta_1 \leq \theta \leq \theta_1, \\
\text{Curr. Cue if} & \theta_1 < \theta < \theta_2, \\
\text{Turn Right if} & \theta_2 \leq \theta < 180°.
\end{cases}
$$

For example, let us assume a rotation angle, θ, falls somewhere between θ_1 and θ_2. If the current cue is **Straight**, a new cue will still be **Straight**. On the other hands, if the current cue is **Turn right**, a new cue will be **Turn right** until a subject completes rotation so that $\theta < \theta_1$. In our application, θ_1 and θ_2 are defined as 5° and 15°, respectively. The generated cue is transmitted through the wireless transmitter to the vest interface that has four vibration motors as provided in Fig. 1. Each vibration motor delivers a specific cue such as turn left, turn right, and so on.

4   Experiments

We present the experimental details and results of mobility experiments of the proposed system . Our navigation system runs at 28.4 Hz on average on the following configuration.

- CPU: Intel(R) Core(TM) i7-3630QM CPU @ 2.40GHz
- RAM: 8.00 GB
- OS: Windows 7 - 64 bit

The breakdown of processing timing is represented in Fig. 8.

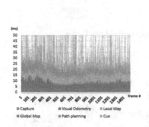

Floor plan of the experiment location

Fig. 8. Timings of each process over 1500 frames

Fig. 9. A floor plan of the mobility experiments. Red boxes and lines indicates obstacles that are not reflected in the floor plan.

Fig. 10. Snapshots of smartphone interface for a blind user

4.1   Mobility Experiments (vs. Conventional Aids)

These experiments are designed to test an ability of the system to guide a blind user in a cluttered environment. In this environment, there exist many obstacles such as tables, chairs, cublcle walls, and a fridge that are not present on the floorplan, which is a primary reason that the system does not rely entirely on the floorplan for mapping and planning and performs a real-time probabilistic map update. 4 subjects are blind-folded and asked to reach a destination in 3 different scenarios, 3 times per each scenario. In the first scenario, the subjects are asked to travel to a destination whose location is known using the white cane and provided the initial orientation towards the destination. This scenario is very similar to what one experiences in an office or at home where you spend most of your time. In the second scenario, the subjects are asked to travel to a destination whose location is known using the white cane and does not know the initial orientation towards the destination. This scenario is designed to simulate a situation often happening in a daily basis even in a very familiar environment when a subject loses a sense of the orientation or gets confused by some changes in the spatial configuration. The last scenario has the same configuration to the second scenario except that the subjects are provided with the proposed navigation system in addition to the white cane. For the last scenario, a database that contains location of interests in the building is assumed to be available at the beginning for all experiments. The database only stores 2D location of interests of a building which is very concise and can be easily appended on top of existing maps, an indoor google map for example. We extract the location of rooms and some points of interests such as elevators, exits, printers, and a fridge from using floor plan as shown in Fig. 9 aligning them to a grid where the north points up and store them in a database. You provide the system with the destination and the current location, for example to a printer room from Room 101C, to start a navigation task.

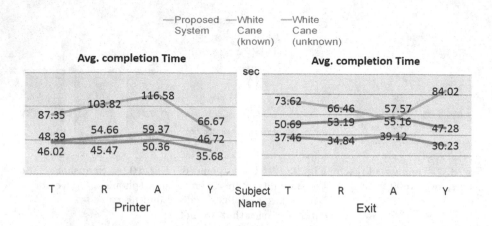

Fig. 11. The average elapsed time to complete a navigation task for different scenarios

It is obvious that you will get to a destination the fastest when you know the surrounding environments and orientation very well which is not always the case when you travel to different places. One thing to note is that losing a sense of orientation can decrease the mobility performance by about a half in terms of the completion time to reach a goal even in familiar environments which will get probably worse in unfamiliar environments. As you can see in Fig 11, the proposed system improved the mobility performance by 57.77% on average, 79.0% and 36.5% for each destination. This results from an ability of the system that can initialize the orientation using magnetometer reading and help the subjects to align themselves to the existing map.

4.2   Mobility Experiments (vs. the State-of-the-Art ETA)

It is difficult to directly compare performance of the navigation systems to other existing mobility aids than the white canes quantitatively since there are no standard courses to complete nor metrics to measure. However, walking speed is a good indicator how efficient the mobility aids is in helping the blind subject navigate around. A recent research reported $0.2m/s$ of walking speed of blind-folded subject in a non-cluttered environment [6] which can serve as a baseline for a performance comparison purpose. Hence, we set up an testing environment to perform a quantitative comparison, which contains 3 sharp curves and the width of the narrowest corridor was 0.9m. 3 blind-folded subjects were asked to follow cues from the navigation system to reach a goal, an exit door of a building whose location is unknown in advance to the subject, in an unknown environment. This test is to simulate to a case where a blind user arrives a building (unknown environments) and has a limited information such as the approximate current location, an entrance for example, and the destination in the building. Total travel distance was approximately $25m$ and the course includes obstacles including doors, chairs, as shown in Fig. 12. As shown in Fig. 12, the blind-folded subjects were able to finish the course successfully without colliding to obstacles. The subjects completed the course in 89 seconds on average resulting in $0.28m/s$ of walking speed in a non-cluttered environment, which proves the navigation system works very effectively in an unknown environment. Note is that the ability of the proposed system to guide blind subjects in an unknown environment indicates that the system is scalable to multiple buildings as a building can be easily identified by either building name or GPS information from your smartphone. Since the system builds the map of surrounding environments online, the system does not need to know all structures such as walls and so on in advance and one can generate a location database of a building and share it easily on the web.

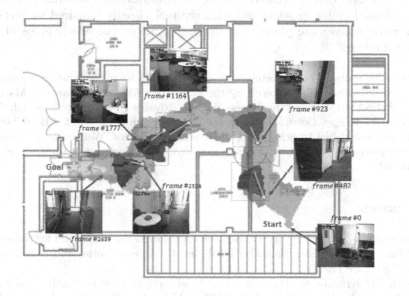

Fig. 12. A 2D GTM map generate when traveling in a non-cluttered environment: Green and red regions are horizontal and vertical patches, respectively. Yellow dots in darker areas represent a pose of the blind subject at n^{th} frame. Orange bars in darker indicate direction to the temporary goals.

5   Conclusion and Future Works

We have presented an integrated framework using RGBD sensor as an input to operate real-time navigation algorithms for an application in a mobility aids for the blind. We have also shown that an intelligent set of tactile feedback cues can guide visually impaired subjects through obstacles at a reasonable cognitive load. The mobility experiment results suggest that the system improves the mobility performance of the blind-folded users by about 58% than the blind-folded users did using their white canes when the orientation is unknown in the beginning of the navigation tasks. We also compared performance of the system in terms of the completion time of a navigation task with respect to one of the state of state-of-the-art technique [6] and we proved that the effectiveness of the system. We are planning on adopting a loop closure algorithm because in many cases people visit a few places multiple times and a loop closure detection helps to mitigate an error accumulation problem and to optimize pose estimation when you revisit a place. We have encountered severe image blurs or poor feature matching led by rapid head rotations sometimes, which caused inaccurate visual odometry results. Inertia-visual sensor fusion has been proven to provide much more robust tracking results due to complementary characteristics of an IMU sensor and cameras. For this reason, we plan to extend the range of an IMU sensor integration that is utilized only at the initialization stage under the proposed system. Finally, experiments with the real visually impaired subjects in various environments are planned in order to evaluate the effectiveness of the navigation system.

Acknowledgments. This research was made possible by a cooperative agreement that was awarded and administered by the U.S. Army Medical Research & Materiel Command (USAMRMC) and the Telemedicine & Advanced Technology Research Center (TATRC), at Fort Detrick, MD under Contract Number: W81XWH-10-2-0076. The authors would like to acknowledge Nii Mante and Prof. Weiland in Biomedical Engineering department at USC for contributions to development of the smartphone application.

References

1. Borenstein, J., Ulrich, I.: The GuideCane - A computerized travel aid for the active guidance of blind pedestrians. In: IEEE Int. Conf. on Robotics and Automation. pp. 1283–1288 (1997)
2. Brock, M., Kristensson, P.: Supporting blind navigation using depth sensing and sonification. In: Proceedings of the 2013 ACM Conference on Pervasive and Ubiquitous Computing Adjunct Publication, pp. 255–258 (2013)
3. Clark-Carter, D., Heyes, A., Howarth, C.: The efficiency and walking speed of visually impaired people. Ergonomics **29**(6), 779–789 (1986)
4. Golledge, R.G., Marston, J.R., Costanzo, C.M.: Attituds of visually imparied persons towards the use of public transportation. Journal of Visual Impairment Blindness **91**(5), 446–459 (1997)
5. Google: Google glass (2013). http://www.google.com/glass
6. Guerrero, L., Vasquez, F., Ochoa, S.: An indoor navigation system for the visually impaired. Sensors **12**(6), 8236–8258 (2012)
7. Helal, A., Moore, S., Ramachandran, B.: Drishti: An integrated navigation system for visually impaired and disabled. In: Proceedings Fifth International Symposium on Wearable Computers, pp. 149–156. IEEE (2001)
8. Hirschmuller, H., Innocent, P., Garibaldi, J.: Fast, unconstrained camera motion estimation from stereo without tracking and robust statistics. In: 7th International Conference on Control, Automation, Robotics and Vision. ICARCV 2002. vol. 2, pp. 1099–1104. IEEE (2002)

9. Holzer, S., Rusu, R., Dixon, M., Gedikli, S., Navab, N.: Adaptive neighbor-hood selection for real-time surface normal estimation from organized point cloud data using integral images. In: IEEE/RSJ International Conference on Intelligent Robots and Systems (IROS), pp. 2684–2689. IEEE (2012)
10. Horn, B.: Closed-form solution of absolute orientation using unit quaternions. JOSA A 4(4), 629–642 (1987)
11. Howard, A.: Real-time stereo visual odometry for autonomous ground vehicles. In: IEEE/RSJ International Conference on Intelligent Robots and Systems. IROS 2008, pp. 3946–3952. IEEE (2008)
12. Huang, A., Bachrach, A., Henry, P., Krainin, M., Maturana, D., Fox, D., Roy, N.: Visual odometry and mapping for autonomous flight using an rgb-d camera. In: International Symposium on Robotics Research (ISRR), pp. 1–16 (2011)
13. Koenig, S., Likhachev, M.: Fast replanning for navigation in unknown terrain. IEEE Transactions on Robotics 3(21), 354–363 (2005)
14. Lee, Y., Medioni, G.: A RGB-D camera based navigation for the visually impaired. In: RSS 2011 RGB-D: Advanced Reasoning with Depth Camera Workshop, pp. 1–6 (2011)
15. Legood, R., Scuffham, P., Cryer, C.: Are we blind to injuries in the visually impaired? a review of the literature. Injury Prevention 8(2), 155–160 (2002)
16. Loomis, J., Golledge, R., Klatzky, R.: Gps-based navigation systems for the visually impaired. Fundamentals of Wearable Computers and Augmented Reality 429(46) (2001)
17. Manduchi, R., Kurniawan, S.: Mobility-related accidents experienced by people with visual impairment. Insight: Research & Practice in Visual Impairment & Blindness 4(2), 44–54 (2011)
18. Martinez, J., Ruiz, F., et al.: Stereo-based aerial obstacle detection for the visually impaired. In: Workshop on Computer Vision Applications for the Visually Impaired (2008)
19. Mei, C., Sibley, G., Cummins, M., Newman, P., Reid, I.: A constant-time efficient stereo slam system. In: BMVC, pp. 1–11 (2009)
20. Moravec, H., Elfes, A.: High resolution maps from wide angle sonar. In: Proceedings 1985 IEEE International Conference on Robotics and Automation. vol. 2, pp. 116–121. IEEE (1985)
21. Nguyen, C., Izadi, S., Lovell, D.: Modeling kinect sensor noise for improved 3d reconstruction and tracking. In: 2012 Second International Conference on 3D Imaging, Modeling, Processing, Visualization and Transmission (3DIMPVT), pp. 524–530. IEEE (2012)
22. Pradeep, V., Medioni, G., Weiland, J.: Robot vision for the visually impaired. In: Computer Vision Applications for the Visually Impaired, pp. 15–22 (2010)
23. Sáez, J., Escolano, F.: 6dof entropy minimization slam for stereo-based wearable devices. Computer Vision and Image Understanding 115(2), 270–285 (2011)
24. Schiller, J., Peregoy, J.: Provisional report: Summary health statistics for u.s. adults: National health interview survey, 2011. National Center for Health Statistics 10(256) (2012)
25. JVIB news service: Demographics update: Alternate estimate of the number of guide dog users. Journal of Visual Impairment Blindness 89(2), 4–6 (1995)
26. Turano, K., Broman, A., Bandeen-Roche, K., Munoz, B., Rubin, G., West, S., SEE PROJECT TEAM: Association of visual field loss and mobility performance in older adults: Salisbury eye evaluation study. Optometry & Vision Science 81(5), 298–307 (2004)

27. West, S., Rubin, G., Broman, A., Munoz, B., Bandeen-Roche, K., Turano, K., THE SEE PROJECT: How does visual impairment affect performance on tasks of everyday life? Archives of Ophthalmology **120**(6), 774–780 (2002)
28. Wurm, K., Hornung, A., Bennewitz, M., Stachniss, C., Burgard, W.: Octomap: A probabilistic, flexible, and compact 3d map representation for robotic systems. In: Proc. of the ICRA 2010 workshop on best practice in 3D perception and modeling for mobile manipulation. vol. 2 (2010)
29. Yguel, M., Aycard, O., Laugier, C.: Update policy of dense maps: Efficient algorithms and sparse representation. In: Field and Service Robotics. pp. 23–33. Springer (2008)
30. Yuan, D., Manduchi, R.: Dynamic environment exploration using a virtual white cane. In: IEEE Conf. on Computer Vision and Pattern Recognition, pp. 243–249 (2005)
31. Zöllner, M., Huber, S., Jetter, H.-C., Reiterer, H.: NAVI – a proof-of-concept of a mobile navigational aid for visually impaired based on the microsoft kinect. In: Campos, P., Graham, N., Jorge, J., Nunes, N., Palanque, P., Winckler, M. (eds.) INTERACT 2011, Part IV. LNCS, vol. 6949, pp. 584–587. Springer, Heidelberg (2011)

Polly: Telepresence from a Guide's Shoulder

Don Kimber[1]([✉]), Patrick Proppe[1], Sven Kratz[1], Jim Vaughan[1], Bee Liew[1],
Don Severns[1,2], and Weiqing Su[2]

[1] FX Palo Alto Lab, California, USA
donkimber@gmail.com
[2] University of California, San Diego, San Diego, USA

Abstract. Polly is an inexpensive, portable telepresence device based
on the metaphor of a parrot riding a guide's shoulder and acting as proxy
for remote participants. Although remote users may be anyone with a
desire for 'tele-visits', we focus on limited mobility users. We present a
series of prototypes and field tests that informed design iterations. Our
current implementations utilize a smartphone on a stabilized, remotely
controlled gimbal that can be hand held, placed on perches or carried by
wearable frame. We describe findings from trials at campus, museum and
faire tours with remote users, including quadriplegics. We found guides
were more comfortable using Polly than a phone and that Polly was
accepted by other people. Remote participants appreciated stabilized
video and having control of the camera. One challenge is negotiation
of movement and view control. Our tests suggest Polly is an effective
alternative to telepresence robots, phones or fixed cameras.

Keywords: Telepresence · Image stabilization · Remote guiding ·
Wearable · Gimbal · User feedback · Iterative design

1 Introduction

According to Ryan and Deci's [1] research, human's intrinsic motivation to thrive
is based on psychological needs. Sheldon et al. list ten basic psychological needs,
including two "most fundamental" needs of *pleasure-stimulation* and *relatedness*
[2]. Pleasure-stimulation is addressed by finding sources for new experiences of
sensations and activities which cause pleasure and enjoyment. Relatedness is
the need to be close to people who are important to yourself and loved ones.
This might be one psychological reason why most people have a desire to go
outside and visit interesting locations (e.g. museums, zoos or parks) and also
to experience events such as family gatherings or music concerts together with
other people. However, not everyone is able to fulfill their wishes to explore or
be able to be close to their kin. Reasons for this may be that these persons are
physically immobile, sick in a hospital or simply very far away from where they
would like to be.

To address this issue of mobility and presence, we have developed a wearable
system called *Polly*, motivated by the metaphor of a remotely controlled parrot
which could rest on someone's shoulder and look around independently of the

© Springer International Publishing Switzerland 2015
L. Agapito et al. (Eds.): ECCV 2014 Workshops, Part III, LNCS 8927, pp. 509–523, 2015.
DOI: 10.1007/978-3-319-16199-0_36

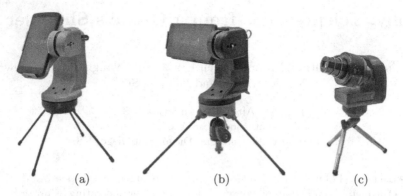

Fig. 1. From left to right: (a) Portrait Polly, (b) Landscape Polly, (c) Sony LensCam Polly. All prototypes are based on a three-axis brush-less gimbal that can be carried, placed on perches or flat surfaces, or worn by the guide at shoulder level.

view of the person carrying it. [1] We have developed a series of Polly prototypes and our current version consists of a three-axis stabilization gimbal driven by brush-less motors holding a mobile phone that provides the audio and video feed and a connection to the internet. Polly can be carried by hand, can be placed on 'perches', can rest on surfaces, or be worn by way of a backpack frame with an attachment holding Polly near the shoulder of its wearer. We implemented applications that let remote users control the gimbal orientation (pitch and yaw) from their location. We used Skype, Vidyo and Google Hangouts for audio and video transmission, but any suitable software with a mobile client suffice. [2]

We chose a wearable solution since mobile robots are difficult to control and lack mobility over terrain that is not adapted to their style of locomotion (e.g. staircases). The solution we believe that works best with the current level of technology is to use a human 'guide' at the location a remote person wishes to visit.[3] Having a human guide who carries or wears the Polly device has the following advantages: (1) the guide is in constant communication with the remote user and can easily understand their wishes, (2) humans are extremely mobile and agile, especially in environments built by and for humans, (3) the guide can mediate conversations between the remote operator and other people encountered and (4) the social interaction between the guide and remote person may be a positive part of the overall experience.

The phone is stabilized by a gimbal and can be worn on the shoulder for the following reasons. Firstly, we thought it would be advantageous for the guide to have two free hands and, secondly, not worry about pointing the camera, but allow the remote operator to do this. Finally, we found that if the mobile

---

[1] Also motivated by the remarkably stabilized head pose of many birds. http://www.youtube.com/watch?v=UytSNlHw8J8

[2] http://www.skype.com, http://www.vidyo.com, http://www.google.com/hangouts/

[3] The term *guide* is for expositional brevity. In some scenarios, the remote person may be more familiar with and knowledgeable about the space being explored.

phone is worn on a lanyard or mounted rigidly to the wearer, the video quality is significantly reduced while the guide is walking, due to excessive movement in the image. The brush-less gimbal uses an IMU for active rotation compensation and leveling resulting in a very smooth video feed, much like a Steadicam rig, but much smaller in size and weight.

After a review of related work in Section 2, Section 3 describes the design process of Polly from initial prototype to its current form, followed in Section 4 by the evolution of the User Interface. Section 5 describes field tests, including five tests with Henry Evans, a quadriplegic experienced with assistive and telepresence robotics who used and helped critique our system and one test with another quadriplegic familiar with telepresence technology. Although Sections 3–5 are presented sequentially they describe aspects of a cyclical interactive design process. In Section 6 we contribute design guidelines for builders of such systems as well as a set of practical recommendations based on our experience, followed by a discussion of further work, and finally our conclusions.

2   Related Work

Drugge et al. proposed a wearable telepresence system consisting of an HMD (Head Mounted Display) and a head-mounted camera [3]. In contrast to Polly, this does not afford the remote participant the same degree of control, since view direction cannot be changed, as it is the case using Polly's gimbal. Mayol et al. describe a wearable camera system and discuss benefits of decoupling the camera orientation from body pose of the wearer, but the control paradigm is based on active vision rather than remote control [4,5]. Similarly, systems such as Google Glass streaming to a Hangouts, or the Tele-actor system [6] do not give the remote user any direct control over view. The MH2 [7] is a shoulder-worn humanoid telepresence robot with a focus on conveying gestures and poses made by the remote remote participant. Polly, on the other hand, is not based on physical representation. Rather, a camera image of the remote participant, displayed via a smartphone, is used to represent him or her. TEROOS [8] is a shoulder-mounted wearable telepresence system, that is perhaps the wearable telepresence system with the closest resemblance to Polly, as it uses servo motors that are controllable by the remote operator. There are, however, two main differences: Firstly, the platform of TEROOS camera does not appear to be stabilized, which, as we found out during initial tests of Polly, produces low quality video while the local operator is walking. Secondly, TEROOS follows the avatar concept, similar to MH2 and uses an abstracted form of representation involving the shape of a decorated camera. Again, we believe that showing the remote operator directly may be advantageous, for example where the mobile user knows the person he is interacting with personally. The MeBot [9] is a small expressive robotic device that does include a display, but is not intended as a wearable device.

There are many telepresence robot systems (see [10] for a survey) and it is becoming more common to use these for providing access to the disabled [11].

(a)   (b)   (c)   (d)

Fig. 2. Polly Prototypes: (a) first frame mounted version, (b) first stabilized version, (c) portrait phone, (d) current landscape version

Some museums are starting to use these systems for telepresence tours, available to limited mobility visitors [12]. These systems are typically many thousands or tens of thousands of dollars and not well suited for outside tours, steps, crowded spaces, etc. By contrast, the cost for a Polly-type device is a few hundreds of dollars and being human carried, they are suitable for outside use. Another project with similar goals to Polly is Virtual Photowalks [13] which matches up photographers able to provide photo walks through beautiful or interesting locations, to remote participants, particularly but not exclusively those constrained by physical disabilities. The remote participants may talk with the photographer and request photos to be taken.

3   Design Evolution of Polly Prototypes

A design goal for Polly was to produce relatively inexpensive devices, costing several hundreds of dollars, to experiment with scenarios allowing one person to provide a video view for a remote person. The baseline case for these scenarios is what people currently do when no specialized solution is available - they run a videoconferencing app on a phone, tablet or laptop and walk around carrying these devices while trying to communicate with their remote friends. Our baseline experience consisted of using a phone in this manner, where the phone was hand held, or held by a simple strap. The videoconferencing apps we tried were Skype, Vidyo and Google Hangouts. Although none of the apps clearly dominated the others in all respects, overall we had better success in terms of video quality and persistence of connections using Skype. On the other hand we found Google hangouts slightly more convenient in terms of supporting new users, providing an integrated remote control interface and supporting multiple video clients.

3.1   First Frame Mounted Version

The first body-mounted prototype (Figure 2(a)) consisted of a fixed shoulder mount frame with no stabilization gimbal and a small daypack that could carry a tablet, digitization hardware and a battery. We created two versions, one using a Logitech 920C webcam, connected to a Microsoft surface running Skype. The other version used a GoPro camera which could record HD video onto a SD card, while simultaneously outputting analog video, which was digitized using a USB video capture device. We tried several vendors, including Diamond and Hauppauge but none of them worked directly as a video input for Skype. However, we found that using third party virtual camera programs such as XSplit or ManyCam [4] enabled us to use video from the GoPro as an input to Skype.

3.2   First Stabilized Version

We found two main drawbacks to the baseline and first mounted version. One was the lack of camera direction control by the remote participant. The second was that during walking the video was very shaky and unpleasant to watch. To address these, the next version (Figure 2(b)) used a gimbal which provides a sort of Steadicam type stabilization and for which the camera can be pointed remotely. The gimbal used was a three axis brush-less motor gimbal, designed for a GoPro camera on a small UAV (Unmanned aerial vehicle) and using the 8bit version of the SimpleBGC[5] board. The camera direction control inputs to the gimbal are provided as PWM (Pulse Width Modulation) signals, which output from a Pololu USB to PWM device[6].

As with our first frame mounted prototype, the stabilized GoPro version requires a separate device for running Skype and because the GoPro output was analog, the video needed to be digitized. (GoPro also outputs HDMI, but we could not find a portable solution for making this available as Skype input.) One limitation is that wires carrying video signals from the cameras must cross three stabilization motor axes, so it is not possible to get full travel for the motors. Furthermore, the PWM signals from the Pololu device needed to cross the yaw axis. We considered a modified version to address this problem with slip rings, but found problems with high frequency noise caused by the slip rings.

3.3   Second Stabilized Version - Portrait Mode Smartphone Polly

The main deficiency of the first stabilized version was the complexity of the system requiring the camera, gimbal, multiple USB devices and MS Surface tablet, in addition to workaround programs such as XSplit that were necessary together with basic videoconferencing programs. We decided a simpler more usable device would be an entirely self-contained unit consisting only of the gimbal and a smartphone in portrait orientation (Figures 1 and 2(c)). In this design, the camera, videoconferencing software and all necessary control software runs on the phone. The 3D-printed gimbal case contains a battery, a SimpleBGC board, and a Bluetooth 4.0 BLE-PWM device, allowing a Polly control app running on

---

[4] http://www.xsplit.com/, http://www.manycam.com/
[5] http://www.basecamelectronics.com/SimpleBGC/
[6] A Pololu Micro Maestro 6-Channel USB Servo Controller was used.

the phone to receive messages sent from remote users and control the gimbal via bluetooth. We also included an external bluetooth loudspeaker/microphone which can be worn or mounted to the carrying rig. Another advantage of the self-contained unit is modularity. Polly can be easily carried by snapping it onto a shoulder mounted rig, but can also be carried by hand, or can rest on its own 'feet', all while remaining fully functional and being remotely controlled.

Once this second Portrait Polly iteration was implemented, we started using it in field tests with outside people. We discovered two major issues with this Polly version. First, the maximum range of motion (240 degrees for yaw and 75 degrees for pitch) limited the users feeling of control (e.g. one comment was "I wanted to look down into the ravine.") Second, the phone's camera is in portrait orientation, resulting in video with smaller width than height, in contrast to common cinematic aspect ratios where the with is always greater than the height. This narrow horizontal field of view 'wastes' a lot of pixels on height and does not mimic peripheral vision.

3.4   Current version - landscape mode smartphone Polly

To address the issues of the small range of motion and narrow field of view, we incorporated a landscape mounted phone and different approach to send control commands to the SimpleBGC board into the next and current Polly iteration.

Redesigning a landscape mode gimbal was straightforward due to the modularity and 3D-printed parts, and provided greater pitch axis travel, because the vertical backing of the gimbal case restricts the phone from extreme pitch values in portrait mode, but not in landscape mode. To utilize the increased range of motion, we adjusted the SimpleBGC settings, replaced the BLE-PWM device with a Bluetooth serial module, and implemented simpleBGC's serial command protocol into our Polly control app. The serial protocol now allows a bidirectional communication path and therefore we are able to access the gimbal IMU values and board settings on the android phone. The range of motion was increased up to full 360 degrees in yaw and 180 degrees in pitch, depending on the mode used (see Section 4.2). We have also incorporated a multipurpose mount with an adjustable ball joint, and are in the final stages of implementing a special charging 'perch' which can provide power, allowing permanent operation, instead of a 90 minute battery limitation.

In our field tests, we found that in noisy or windy environments, the external bluetooth loudspeaker and microphone combination is not powerful enough for those settings, and have replaced them with a higher powered speaker.

3.5   Experimental Version

During several experiments with Polly, users expressed the desire to view distant objects. The devices used in these experiments did not have optical zoom capabilities. Video streaming quality was also often poor, regardless of which videoconferencing software we used. We found no solution capable of streaming clear and real-time low latency HD video (via 3G/4G). Our experimental Polly approach is based on the Sony DSC-QX10, which is a smartphone attachable lens-style camera with up to 10x zoom. This device is capable of live-streaming low latency video over WiFi, while simultaneously recording video in Full HD resolution onto a SD card. Newer Sony cameras, like the DSC-QX10, can be accessed and controlled via a dedicated API. Unfortunately, there is no to make the live-streamed images from the Sony camera available as video input to Skype or Hangouts apps on the phone, particularly without rooting the phone. Furthermore, the camera can only stream images on its own dedicated WiFi, and the android phone can not simultaneously access this WiFi and maintain internet connectivity. To address these limitations, we added a Linux laptop to our setup, running a kernel module to create a V4L2 loopback device [7] accessible as a 'virtual web-camera' to make the Sony camera video stream available as input to Skype or Hangouts on Linux. The laptop uses two wireless adapters to access the camera and internet simultaneously.

We have built this version of Polly, but not yet begun field tests. Although it requires a laptop or other Linux device, it has several attractive features beyond optical zoom and recording capability. It is much smaller in size and weight (0.5kg *vs* 1.0kg, see Figure1(c)) and gives us the capability of running computer vision algorithms such as tracking or object recognition on the video stream.

4   User Interface, Use Modes and Participant Interaction

We describe our approaches and choices for designing the user interfaces, the modes of operation and the way to communicate and negotiate between guide and remote participant, in terms of directions and route planning. This is still one of the biggest issues we are facing while using our prototypes in field tests.

4.1   User Interfaces

One control interface design challenge for Polly is latency, both of control signals and video. This impacts the design choice between 'proportional control' in which a slider or mouse position directly specify camera angle, and 'differential control' in which angular velocity is controlled. We found that for low latency both methods feel natural, but for higher or sporadic latency, differential control is much more difficult to use. In the lab with Polly, servers and control machines all on a single LAN we could assure latency of under .1sec., but over the internet, latencies were larger and sporadic, and were sometimes over a second. So our subsequent interfaces were based on proportional control.

Our first control UI consisted of a Python based GUI with sliders for controlling pitch and yaw, used in conjunction with Skype. We also implemented an Oculus Rift based interface where the remote user would see streamed video on a head mounted display and head orientation controlled the Polly camera view. The Oculus view was not stereo, but seeing the video in an HMD and controlling

---

[7] https://github.com/umlaeute/v4l2loopback

the camera by head motion felt natural when latency was low, as within a single LAN. However we were concerned that latency over the internet would make it unusable. Also a project priority was easy access to Polly by remote participants, so our subsequent remote interfaces have been exclusively web based.

Our web UI used an HTML5 page with sliders for yaw and pitch, controllable by mouse or arrow keys. The page could be placed next to a Skype window, or in the case of Vidyo or Google hangouts, could be included in the same web page as the video view. After several tests and experience with other users, we found that using Google Hangouts, with our web interface included as a 'Hangouts Extension app' was most expedient. (Figure 3.) We also replaced separate yaw and pitch sliders with a *'panorama view control'* having a draggable view rectangle representing current view within a larger rectangle representing possible views, similar to the interface used in [14]. Potentially in future Polly devices with panoramic cameras, this larger rectangle would show a panoramic image. Our interface also includes a *'bird's eye view'* showing Polly's orientation and current view relative to the guide. Mouse movement in this view can be used to control the Polly yaw axis. Another natural control method that was requested was to have mouse clicks within the Hangouts video window move the camera to recenter on the clicked position. Unfortunately, mouse events are not currently available in the Hangouts API.

Remote participants also requested a way to know where Polly was located and what it was looking at, so for outdoor usage where GPS data is available from the Polly phone, we added a Google Maps interface. The Polly position is shown as a green circle, with a cone indicating the camera heading. Because the streamed video quality is limited by network connectivity, and because taking photos is a natural activity and produces a keepsakes of the experience, we added a 'take-photo' action which captures a full resolution image on the phone, that shows up in the Hangouts app and is stored in a Dropbox folder. Figure 3 also shows that more than one Polly can be used and controlled through our interface.

4.2   Gimbal Usage Modes

The gimbal and SimpleBGC controller provide several operation modes for camera orientation control. One modal distinction is between proportional or differential control, and for the reasons discussed above, we use proportional control. Another modal distinction is between *heading lock* mode and *follow* mode. In heading lock mode, the camera points always in a fixed direction (although this direction may be controlled by the remote operator) *independently* of how the camera is held or the orientation of the frame of the person carrying it. In follow mode, outside of a small "deadband", the camera will gradually orient itself to maintain a fixed angle relative to the carrying frame. Pitch, roll and yaw can all be controlled in either mode, but for pitch and roll, heading lock is nearly always the natural choice and the only mode we support. For yaw however, both modes are useful. Heading lock mode is useful when the remote participant wants to look at something or control their view independently of the motion or orientation of the carrier. Follow mode is useful when the remote viewer wants to

Fig. 3. Polly Hangouts Application

keep looking in the same direction relative to the carrier, e.g. to look forward, matching the forward direction of the carrier, or look sideways to carry on a discussion with him or her.

4.3 "Look at That!" - Interaction Between Local and Remote Participants

A unique aspect of Polly in comparison to many telepresence systems is that the camera view is not only controlled by the remote participants, but also since Polly is mostly operated in follow mode, it is somehow "collaboratively" controlled by the local guide and the remote persons. Thus, the need arises for an easy way to express, even with a bad audio channel, that the remote person would like to keep looking at a particular direction. Another important issue we encountered during all of the tests is to communicate where to look at with Polly. The guide tends to say "Look at that to your left!", but since Polly's camera feed does not provide a good spatial perception of the surroundings and where the guide is looking or perhaps pointing at, it is hard to determine where exactly to look. Usually in our tests this resulted in several instructions back and forth. We recently implemented a new additional interface for the local guide, using Google Glass (See Figure 4). It not only enables the remote operators to request a stop resulting in an alert being shown, but also it displays the bird's eye view, which shows both Polly's and the guide's heading. Future studies are planned to test the effectiveness of the methods described here.

Fig. 4. Google Glass Interface

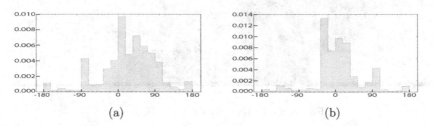

| (a) | (b) |

Fig. 5. Histograms of Polly yaw relative to frame. (a) Stanford campus tour, (b) Cantor art museum visit.

5   Polly Evaluation and Field Tests

In this section we first describe early experiments with a few common mobile telepresence scenarios using phones or early versions of Polly. These experiments assessed the feasibility of Polly in comparison to just holding a phone. We then describe tests using Polly to provide tours or remote visits for disabled users.

5.1   Initial Phone and Polly Experiments

The intention of the initial experiments was to gain understanding of the benefits of a Polly-style device compared to the base-line of a smartphone running video-conferencing software. These are summarized as the first 10 tests in Table 1. Six of these tests were performed with just a smartphone, and four with a smartphone on a Polly device.

For video communication, Skype was used on seven occasions and Vidyo, Google Hangouts and Ustream were each used once. We found that Ustream provided good video quality, but its high buffering resulted in latency on the order of 30 seconds, making it unusable for remotely controlled scenarios. The phone's internal data connection (all phones were 4G-capable) was used on six occasions and the publicly accessible WiFi at the remote location was used on the other four occasions.

After each of these tests, we asked the remote participants and the Polly guide to jointly fill out an online questionnaire and to provide free-form comments and qualitative statements on a five point Likert scale. Although the sample size is

Table 1. Initial field tests of mobile telepresence scenarios using smartphone or Polly (tests 1-10) and Polly field tests with senior or disabled remote participants (11-16)

Test	Location Type	Scenario	Dur.	Device	Software	Net.
T1	Warehouse club	remote shopping	15	phone	Skype	3G
T2	Costume fair	event visit	60	phone	Skype	3G
T3	Conference	remote attendance	20	phone	Skype	WiFi
T4	Hospital	hospital visit	10	phone	Skype	3G
T5	Aviation museum	museum visit	40	phone	Ustream	WiFi
T6	Lab office building	in-office test	45	Polly v1	Skype	3G
T7	Aviation museum	museum visit	24	phone	Vidyo	WiFi
T8	Computer store	remote shopping	15	Polly v2	Skype	WiFi
T9	Aviation museum	museum visit	45	Polly v2	Skype	3G
T10	Maker faire	event tour	40	Polly v3	Hangouts	3G
T11	Senior center	neighborhood walk	20	Polly v2	Skype	3G
T12	Senior center	remote shopping	25	Polly v2	Skype	3G
T13	Research lab	lab tour	45	Polly v2	Hangouts	3G
T14	Stanford	school tour	60	Polly v3	Hangouts	4G
T15	Stanford campus	campus tour	60	Polly v3	Hangouts	4G
T16	Park	bicycle tour	60	Polly v3	Hangouts	4G
T17	Art museum	museum visit	65	Polly v3	Hangouts	WiFi

too small for meaningful statistical analysis, the results did reinforce some of our observations during the tests. For one, the most negatively rated aspect of the Polly-style interactions was the audio-video connection quality, with a median rating of 2.5. This is also reflected in several user comments, e.g., *"The real number one problem is poor video quality and dropout."*. Another thing we note is that the median physical comfort rating for the guide was higher when using Polly than when holding a phone (4.5 vs. 3.5). The subject in test T1 commented *"As my hands became more engaged with shopping, I wished I had a Polly mount with me!"*.

We had some very compelling positive comments, for example: *"I was able to buy exactly what Anya wanted, she was happy to be included in the shopping experience and was happy with the results."* (T1), and *"It was fun seeing the museum and it was fun being able to look around. I enjoyed being able to switch between looking forward or at objects and being able to look at Steve [the guide]."* (T9).

Reactions from people at the remote locations were generally positive, e.g., *"They seemed amused and interested in seeing Polly. Patrick and Larry had brief polite conversations with Gwen [the guide]."* The guide in test T1 reported, *"People were generally interested and asked about the device"*. Another guide commented: *"Got a couple of looks like 'what's that guy doing?'"* (T8).

Table 2. Summary of Stanford Campus and Cantor Art Museum tours

Test	Name	Num Actions	Avg. Dur	Pct. Control	Avg. Yaw	Avg. Pitch	Pct. Collisions
Campus	Harry	89	10.8s	24.8	99.1	44.2	0.3
(T15)	Steve	50	4.3s	5.5	99.2	43.1	2.7
Cantor	Harry	71	8.4s	13.0	82.1	41.9	0.2
(T17)	Jim	6	8.0s	1.0	131.8	36.3	0.0

One behavior frequently observed was that the remote user would move the camera between looking forward in the direction Polly was being carried and looking towards the person carrying Polly. The activity of moving the camera view could sometimes be tedious, but made the experience feel less passive. During discussions involving a few people at the Polly location, the remote viewer would often try to point the camera towards the person talking. This was fairly easy with only a couple of people staying relatively fixed, but could be confusing with more people or when people were moving.

5.2   Tests with Disabled and Elderly Users

Once we were a little further along in the evolution of Polly, we tried to broaden our tests to assess how useful Polly would be as an assistive technology for people with limited mobility.

For our initial investigation, we engaged with the staff and patients in a local senior center. We conducted two field tests as a result of this engagement, T11 and T12. It became clear that while using Polly was interesting to this population, the use of technology that was not familiar presented some additional challenges. Subsequent field tests were with people who had suffered catastrophic events that had caused mobility limiting disability, in some cases as severe as quadriplegia.

The remote participants in field test T13 were a quadriplegic, Henry, who is mute, and communicates primarily by spelling words out to his wife Jane by looking at letters on a letter board. Henry was also able to operate the Polly interface using eye tracking for mouse movements and one finger to click. This test provided us with much useful feedback, such as the suggestion to mount the camera in a landscape orientation, and some comments about usability, that prompted us to develop the Google Hangouts app for controlling Polly. Henry and Jane were also participants in test T15, and were joined by Stuart, who is quadriplegic, but able to speak. Henry and Stuart were able to take turns controlling the position of the camera. Henry remarked "Sharing a Polly turned out to be great fun because of the social aspects - I actually preferred it."

As the user interactions with Polly had become more complex, we instrumented the interface to collect data about turn-taking. Table 2 summarizes this. Turns are times of continuous adjustment by one user, either through mouse or arrow keys. During test T15, one participant, Henry, took 89 turns, controlling Polly 24.8% of the time, with an average duration per turn of 10.8 seconds. On the average he changed the yaw by 82.1 degrees and the pitch by 44.2. Collisions did not seem to be much problem, as one user trying to get control when another user had control happened less than 3% of the time. The yaw histogram (Fig 5(a)) shows that the most common yaw placement for Polly was forward, but it was also frequently oriented towards the guide.

In a departure from our usual body-mounted configuration, T16 was performed with Polly attached to the handlebar stem of a bicycle, with the guide riding the bicycle. At this point, the Polly Hangouts plugin now contained a map. The remote participants pointed out that the map would be more useful if we could indicate view direction in it, a suggestion we have now incorporated.

T17 took place at the Stanford Cantor Art Museum, with three remote participants, A summary of the adjustment behavior, and histogram of yaw orientation are shown in Table 2 and Figure 5 (b). This test used campus WiFi rather than the phone's data network, and we had more connectivity problems, with five disconnections during the 65 minute session. This test included a museum curator providing expert commentary on the artwork, and a third person not associated with the Polly project as the 'guide' (i.e. carrying Polly.) It highlighted a number of difficulties we still must address. One was interaction between the guide and remote participants. In one case the guide suggested, "Look down at the label under that vase." When the camera did not point down, the guide tried to provide the intended view by leaning forward. However, because Polly compensates for pitch and roll, this had no effect on the camera orientation. A more subtle interaction was when the guide suggested, "Look at the picture to your right. No, further to the right." and then after a few seconds turned his body to point the camera in that direction. Because Polly was in yaw follow mode, this did cause the camera to point in that direction, but can be disorienting to the remote user because the camera is being controlled both locally and remotely. These difficulties suggest that it would be useful to have a simple way for the guide or the remote participant, to request Polly to look in the direction chosen by the guide. Based on the experiences at Cantor museum, the remote participants reported the experience as enjoyable, but it also highlighted the importance of a consistent network connection. It was also suggested that Polly is well suited to outdoor tours, but telepresence robots have some advantages for indoor tours.

6   Discussion and Future Work

Our field tests suggest that Polly type devices can provide an enjoyable mobile telepresence experience, particularly to users restricted by limited mobility, and that the social aspects of Polly use are a positive aspect of that experience.

The biggest current difficulty in using Polly is getting adequate network connectivity to maintain good video and audio quality. However, we expect that over the next few years this will become less of an issue and devices like Polly will find increased use. Furthermore, the capability of taking photos or recording high quality video while streaming at whatever quality is supported by the wireless network allows for the production of high quality video after the fact. Our GoPro based prototype had this capability and we are including it in next Polly version.

Our field trial experience reinforces several hypotheses. These include: (1) Stabilized camera motion is much more pleasing than jerky motion from unstabilized hand held or head mounted views, particularly for bandwidth limited streamed video, (2) The ability to control the camera gives a sense of engagement, even when it is not being exercised, (3) Bad audio can lead to the remote person feeling 'left out' of the experience even when they feel in control of their camera view, and (4) Communication about views and shared camera control between guide and remote participants can be challenging and requires improved user interfaces.

The decision to use a smartphone and commercial streaming apps such as Skype and Hangouts for our current Polly versions allowed us to make it relatively inexpensive and easy to operate, but constrained our use of computer vision. While the streaming apps are running, other apps do not have access to the raw images. Our next Polly version will use Linux with a loopback video device which will allow us to run computer vision algorithms on the video streams, and still use commercial streaming. [8] There are several ways that computer vision could be helpful for Polly. One is the use of QR code or object recognition to provide metadata for museum artifacts. That could also be helpful for localization indoors where GPS is not reliable. Optical flow and tracking could also be helpful for camera control, for example to keep the camera centered on an object of interest selected by the user. Feature matching could also provide better alignment than IMU sensors alone, between the Polly view and a view from Google Glass worn by a guide.

Based on our positive experiences with field trials, we believe devices like Polly will become popular as wireless network coverage improves, processor power increases, and high resolution wide field of view image sensors become available, enabling non-mechanical versions of Polly which use addressable viewports from panoramic cameras.

Acknowledgements. The authors thank Henry and Jane Evans, Adoph Smith, Stuart Turner, Mantvydas Juozapavicius, Steve Cousins, Patience Young and Michael Fischer for participating in trials and providing valuable feedback. We also thank Gwen Gordon, Tony Dunnigan, John Doherty, Susan Roberts-Manganelli and the Fremont High School Robotics team for various contributions and useful discussions.

---

[8] This may also be possible on our current phone based versions, when a native Android WebRTC client becomes available.

References

1. Ryan, R.M., Deci, E.L.: Self-determination theory and the facilitation of intrinsic motivation, social development, and well-being. American Psychologist (1) 68–78
2. Sheldon, K.M., Elliot, A.J., Kim, Y., Kasser, T.: What is satisfying about satisfying events? testing 10 candidate psychological needs. Journal of Personality and Social Psychology **80**(2), 325–339 (2001)
3. Drugge, M., Nilsson, M., Parviainen, R., Parnes, P.: Experiences of using wearable computers for ambient telepresence and remote interaction. In: Proc. 2004 ACM SIGMM Workshop on Effective Telepresence, pp. 2–11. ACM (2004)
4. Mayol, W.W., Tordoff, B.J., Murray, D.W.: Wearable visual robots. Personal Ubiquitous Comput. **6**(1), 37–48 (2002)
5. Mayol-Cuevas, W., Kurata, T.: Tutorial: Computer vision for wearable visual interface. Workingpaperimportmodel: Workingpaperimportmodel University of Bristol Other page information: - Other identifier: 2000803 (2005)
6. Goldberg, K.Y., Song, D., Khor, Y.N., Pescovitz, D., Levandowski, A., Himmelstein, J.C., Shih, J., Ho, A., Paulos, E., Donath, J.S.: Collaborative online teleoperation with spatial dynamic voting and a human "tele-actor". In: ICRA, pp. 1179–1184. IEEE (2002)
7. Tsumaki, Y., Ono, F., Tsukuda, T.: The 20-DOF miniature humanoid MH-2: A wearable communication system. In: ICRA, pp. 3930–3935 (2012)
8. Kashiwabara, T., Osawa, H., Shinozawa, K., Imai, M.: Teroos: a wearable avatar to enhance joint activities. In: Proc. 2012 ACM Annual Conference on Human Factors in Computing Systems, pp. 2001–2004. ACM (2012)
9. Adalgeirsson, S.O., Breazeal, C.: Mebot: A robotic platform for socially embodied presence. In: Proceedings of the 5th ACM/IEEE International Conference on Human-Robot Interaction. HRI 2010, pp. 15–22, Piscataway. IEEE Press (2010)
10. Kristoffersson, A., Coradeschi, S., Loutfi, A.: A review of mobile robotic telepresence. Adv. in Hum.-Comp. Int. 2013, 3:3–3:3, January 2013
11. Cousins, S., Evans, H.: Ros expands the world for quadriplegics. IEEE Robotics Automation Magazine **21**(2), 14–17 (2014)
12. Merritt, E.: Center for the future of museums blog, May 2014. http://futureofmuseums.blogspot.com/2014/05/exploring-robots-for-accessibility-in.html
13. Butterill, J.: Virtual Photowalks (2013). http://www.virtualphotowalks.org/
14. Liu, Q., Kimber, D., Foote, J., Wilcox, L., Boreczky, J.: Flyspec: A multi-user video camera system with hybrid human and automatic control. In: Proceedings of the Tenth ACM International Conference on Multimedia. MULTIMEDIA 2002, pp. 484–492, New York. ACM (2002)

Vision Correcting Displays Based on Inverse Blurring and Aberration Compensation

Brian A. Barsky[1,2]([✉]), Fu-Chung Huang[1,4], Douglas Lanman[3,5],
Gordon Wetzstein[3], and Ramesh Raskar[3]

[1] Computer Science Division, UC Berkeley, Berkeley, USA
barsky@berkeley.edu
[2] School of Optometry, UC Berkeley, Berkeley, USA
[3] MIT Media Lab, Providence, USA
[4] Microsoft, Berkeley, USA
[5] Oculus VR, Irvine, USA

Abstract. The concept of a vision correcting display involves digitally modifying the content of a display using measurements of the optical aberrations of the viewer's eye so that the display can be seen in sharp focus by the user without requiring the use of eyeglasses or contact lenses. Our first approach inversely blurs the image content on a single layer. After identifying fundamental limitations of this approach, we propose the multilayer concept. We then develop a fractional frequency separation method to enhance the image contrast and build a multilayer prototype comprising transparent LCDs. Finally, we combine our viewer-adaptive inverse blurring with off-the-shelf lenslets or parallax barriers and demonstrate that the resulting vision-correcting computational display system facilitates significantly higher contrast and resolution as compared to previous solutions. We also demonstrate the capability to correct higher order aberrations.

Keywords: Aberrations · Visual correction · Multilayer display · Deconvolution · Transparent LCDs · Light field display

1 Introduction

This work presents an alternative to eyeglasses, contact lenses, and refractive surgeries for addressing the problem of blurred human vision. The idea is to "digitally" modify the content on a display device so that when viewed by a particular user it will appear in sharp focus for this individual. This process comprises both algorithmic operations that are functions of the particular user's optical aberrations and modified display optics at a hardware level that are the same for all users. Once the display device is built, the refractive errors are corrected digitally; no further adjustment to the optical hardware component is required for different users. We correct for myopia or hyperopia and also consider more complicated blur induced by higher order aberrations.

Using an eyeglasses prescription [14] or aberration measurements from a Hartmann-Shack wavefront aberrometer [2,3] to identify the Point Spread

© Springer International Publishing Switzerland 2015
L. Agapito et al. (Eds.): ECCV 2014 Workshops, Part III, LNCS 8927, pp. 524–538, 2015.
DOI: 10.1007/978-3-319-16199-0_37

Function (PSF) of the user's eye, we inversely blur the image content such that when it will be viewed by this individual, it will appear in sharp focus.

Considering the sharp image as the result of the inverse blurred image convolved with the blurring kernel that represents the individuals PSF, the inverse blurred image can be computed by convolving the sharp image with the inverse of the blurring kernel that represents the individuals PSF.

This approach has two fundamental limitations due to the nature of blur kernels. First, blur kernels are usually interspersed with zero frequency responses and this results in some loss of frequencies which introduces some blurring and ringing artifacts in the final perceived image. Second, blur kernels are generally low-pass and consequently the frequency inversion in the prefiltering tends to amplify the higher frequencies creating expanded dynamic range requirements; to be able to show the preprocessed image on a conventional display, an image with very low contrast is produced by applying dynamic range compression to the preprocessed image.

To overcome these limitations requires going beyond using only the two-dimensional sharp image and developing higher dimensional methods. We have developed both a multilayer display that comprises a stack of 2D images as well as a light field based method requiring 4D light rays. We performed the conditioning rank analysis, which we showed is equivalent to the modulation transfer function (MTF) zeros analysis. The rank analysis revealed the design parameters of the hardware, and lightly modified hardware provides enough degrees of freedom to achieve the goal of correcting vision. Physical prototype hardware was built to illustrate these benefits. Our light field prefiltering prototype uses an iPhone 4/ iPod Touch 4, and our experimental results demonstrate that it corrects significant defocus blur.

2 Preliminary Ideas with Deconvolution

Since the Fourier transform is linear, *the modulation transfer function is the unsorted singular values, and therefore the zero-valued spatial frequencies match the zero singular values.* The inverse filter and the Wiener filter are like the pseudo-inverse approximation. Since inverting zero singular values is undefined, similarly, inverting the lost frequencies is undefined and thus some regularization strategies must be applied.

These zero-valued spatial frequencies lead to the first theoretical limitation of ringing artifacts and slight blurriness. *The lost frequencies or singular-values cannot be recovered since the blurring kernel is applied at the last step of the process*; generally, this information loss causes blurriness. The lack of certain frequencies at sharp edges generates some ringing artifacts, as shown in Figure 1.

The second problem with inverting the blurring kernel is the extremely expanded dynamic range. Due to the heavily attenuated frequency responses that are close to zero, their inversions are close to infinity, causing these frequencies to exhibit dominating sinusoidal structures in the spatial domain images, and generating negative and overwhelmingly positive pixel states; intensity re-normalization is required to show the prefiltered image on the display, but this results in reduced contrast.

Thus, there are two fundamental limitations of the prefiltering method using a traditional display:

– Frequency loss causes slight blurriness and ringing artifacts.
– Expanded dynamic range and negative pixel values require intensity re-normalization which causes reduced contrast.

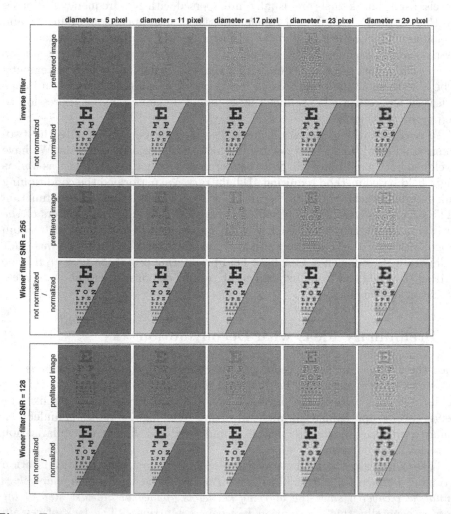

Fig. 1. Frequency domain prefiltering solutions using the inverse filter and the Wiener filter. This type of solvers generally have contrast loss problem. Depending on the regularization, the ringing artifacts can be attenuated and the contrast can be enhanced, but the image can also become more blurry.

Although these drawbacks are lightly documented in the paper by Alonso and Barreto [2], no theoretical improvement has been proposed. With the theoretical analysis for the prefiltering method on a traditional display, we conclude that the traditional display should be modified and new hardware should be built. In the next section, we will introduce the prefiltering method with a "multilayer" type of display that addresses the fundamental limitations.

3   Multilayer Displays

In this section, we develop inverse prefiltering for emerging multilayer displays. Following the limitations on image prefiltering using the conventional display, as discussed in the previous sections, the multilayer display enables an "all-pass kernel": there will be no zero-valued frequency responses [5]. We will first discuss the observations and intuitions behind the idea, and then develop the theory of multilayer prefiltering [6]; a contrast optimization will be introduced, and finally we will discuss the hardware design alternatives and our prototypes.

3.1   Frequency Preservation via Multilayer Prefiltering

For the case of image prefiltering using a conventional display, we will now refer to the case where only one display panel is used as "single-layer prefiltering." The point spread function is a *disk* function of diameter r and of the distance from the eye to the plane of focus. The closer the display is to the plane of focus, the smaller the point spread function is. This is shown on the left side of Figure 2 which illustrates two cases of defocus blur: Depicted in blue is the display closer to the plane of focus and the resulting smaller point spread function, and shown in green is the display farther from the plane of focus and the resulting larger point spread function.

On the right of Figure 2, we plot the modulation transfer functions (MTFs) of the two PSFs. Since their MTFs are both *jinc* functions with periods determined by the diameter of their PSFs, they both inevitably have the zero-valued problem.

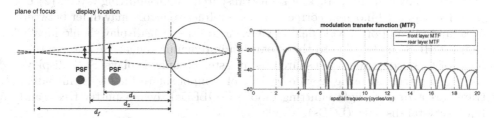

Fig. 2. Observation of multilayer PSFs and their MTFs

However, an important observation is that these zero-valued frequencies generally do not align. By using a carefully chosen separation between the two layers, the coincident frequency will not happen within human perceivable frequencies

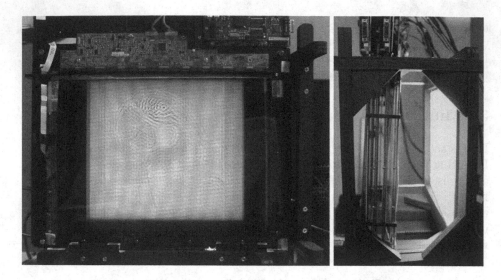

Fig. 3. Prototype multilayer display, front view and side view

(around 60 cycles per degree). This raises the engineering question of how to make both layers visible to the eye and have the two layers still maintain the properties of two different point spread functions. Fortunately, nowadays there are transparent display panels, and they are capable of refreshing at high speed (120Hz panel are commercially available). By utilizing the critical flickering rate (around 40Hz) limiting the temporal integration of the eye, we quickly interchange contents on the two displays, and the eye will fuse the two images on the retina; this is the fundamental idea of our multilayer inverse prefiltering.

3.2   Building a Multilayer Display

Any practical multilayer display must meet four design criteria. It should: (1) be optically equivalent to a stack of semi-transparent, light-emitting layers, (2) be thin, (3) support binocular correction, since refractive errors may differ between eyes, and (4) support a wide field of view. In addition, the display should ideally support HDR modes, due to the expansion in dynamic range. We observe that most of these constraints are shared by autostereoscopic displays. Such displays can be constructed using a wide variety of component technologies, including transparent organic light-emitting diodes (TOLEDs), beam-splitter trees, and liquid-crystal displays (LCDs).

We built an early prototype using a beam-splitter tree, similar to the construction by Akeley et al. [1]: viewing multiple LCDs through a set of half-silvered mirrors (i.e., beam splitters) is optically equivalent to a stack of semi-transparent, light-emitting layers. However, the form factor and field of view of this prototype was not satisfying.

A more practical construction using multilayer LCDs employing the design of Lanman et al. [10] is shown in Figure 3. This prototype comprises four modified 40.8cm-by-30.6cm Barco E-2320 PA LCD panels, supporting 8-bit grayscale display with a resolution of 1600-by-1200 pixels and a refresh rate of 60 Hz. The stack is operated in a time-multiplexed manner such that only one panel displays content at any given time. With a sufficiently long exposure (i.e., $\geq N/60$ seconds when N layers are used), the prototype appears as a semitransparent stack of light-emitting layers.

We record color images by simulating a field sequential color (FSC) backlight (i.e., a strobed backlight that illuminates the stack with time-varying color sources); for the results in Figure 6, we combine three separate photographs, each recorded while displaying a different color channel of the prefiltered images.

3.3   Experimental Results with Multilayer Display

Simulated results. We first show some simulated corrections using both single-layer prefiltering and two-layer prefiltering. The results shown in Figure 4 are

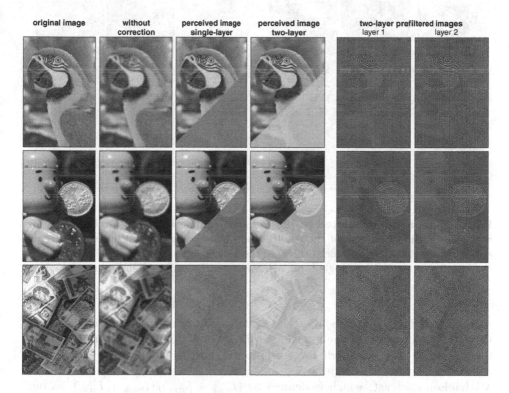

Fig. 4. Comparing simulated single-layer prefiltering results with multilayer prefiltering results. For the first two rows, we also show the comparison with negative light assumed to delineate the ringing artifacts due to the lost frequencies.

simulated with a 50mm f/1.8 lens with object at a distance 100cm, and the camera focuses at 84cm; the separation between layers is 3.4cm. By comparing with the blurred images, clearly the perceived images preprocessed with the prefiltering algorithms are sharper. For the first two examples, we show both the negative light simulation and the real perceived images. The negative light simulation enables us to see more clearly how the ringing artifacts are successfully removed with multilayer prefiltering. In the meantime, the image contrast are greatly improved, as shown in the third row. On the right of Figure 4, the corresponding prefiltered layer images are shown.

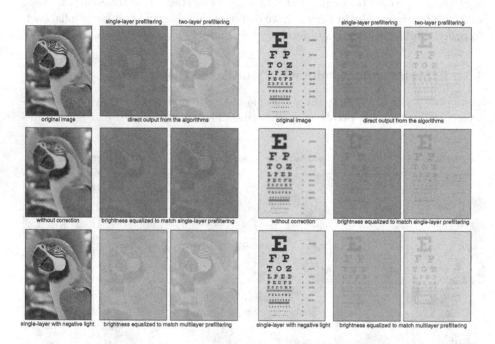

Fig. 5. Comparing simulated results when brightness are equalized. For a fair comparison, the brightness of the results from single-layer and multilayer prefiltering are equalized to match with each other. On the bottom left of each example, we manifest the ringing artifacts from single-layer prefiltering with negative light assumed.

Comparisons with equal brightness. As one might argue that the brightness setting (dynamic range) of the multilayer display may be different from a conventional display used for single-layer prefiltering, in Figure 5 we also show direct comparisons when the brightnesses are equalized to match each other. With the Michaelson contrast, which is defined as $(I_{max} - I_{min})/(I_{max} + I_{min})$, as our evaluation metric, the perceived image contrast is thus "independent" of display brightness. In both examples, the multilayer prefiltering results are still better than the single-layer prefiltering results in the image contrast, and as discussed in Section 3.1, this is achieved by avoiding the zero-valued/weak spatial frequencies and greedy contrast optimization. On the bottom left of Figure 5, we also show the ringing artifacts in the single-layer prefiltering due to the zero-valued spatial frequencies and the weak frequencies affected by the regularization. These problems are eliminated by inverting the "all-pass-kernel" of the multilayer prefiltering algorithm.

Figure 6 summarizes experimental results achieved with the multilayer LCD. A digital camera was separated by 100 cm from the front layer of the prototype and focused at 16cm in front of the display, with the minimum f-number setting of f/1.8, resulting in an aperture diameter of 2.8cm. Figure 6 confirms the predicted contrast enhancement and elimination of ringing artifacts. For example, the inset region of the bird appears brighter and with higher contrast using multilayer prefiltering, rather than the prior single-layer prefiltering algorithm. Also note that the outline of the eye and the black stripes appear with less distortion using multilayer prefiltering. Ringing artifacts, visible on the left-hand side of the face of the blue toy, are eliminated.

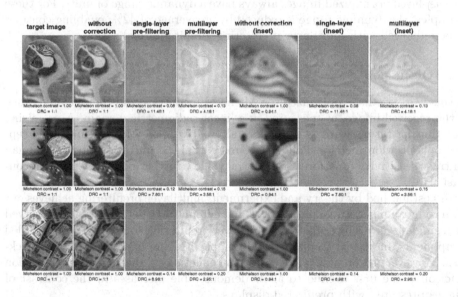

Fig. 6. Camera photographs of prefiltering results. Multilayer (two-layer) prefiltering improves image contrast. Remaining ringing artifacts are due to the spatially varying point spread function, spherical aberration, non-circular camera aperture, and offsets due to the non-linear gamma correction and diffraction.

Experimental results also reveal limitations of the linear spatially invariant (LSI) model. First, the medical display panels used in the prototype do not produce a linear radiometric response; gamma compression was applied to the displayed images, with a calibrated gamma value 2.2, to approximate a radiometrically linear display. Remaining radiometric non-linearities contribute to ringing artifacts in the experimental imagery. Second, the lens produces a spatially-varying PSF, as analyzed by Kee et al. [9]; as seen in the bottom left of the currency image, differences between the modeled and experimental PSFs result in ringing artifacts in the periphery. However, the central region is well approximated by the defocused camera model. The camera lens aperture, consisting of several blades, does not produce a circular point spread function, and thus the optical transfer functions are different. Finally, the camera lens has some spherical aberration, which is not modeled in the current experiments.

We quantitatively assess the received image using the Michelson contrast metric, given by the ratio of the difference of the maximum and minimum values, divided by their sum. Michelson contrast is increased by an average of 44% using multilayer prefiltering rather than single-layer prefiltering. Prefiltering expands the dynamic range both above and below the range of radiance values that are physically supported by the display. We quantify this effect by evaluating the dynamic range compression (DRC) of the prefiltered images, given by the difference of the maximum and minimum values before normalization. By convention, the displayed normalized images always have a dynamic range of unity. For these examples, the dynamic range is reduced by an average of 42%, enabling contrast to be enhanced with multilayer prefiltering, despite normalization.

3.4   Discussion

In this work, we have optimized the Michaelson contrast and the dynamic range of the received image, as measured in a linear radiometric domain. A promising direction for future work is to explore alternative, possibly non-linear, perceptual optimization metrics. Following Grosse et al. [4], incorporating the human contrast sensitivity function (CSF) [8] may allow further perceived gains in contrast.

As established by theory and experiment, multilayer prefiltering achieves our primary goal: mitigating contrast loss and eliminating ringing artifacts observed with single-layer prefiltering. Yet, multilayer prefiltering comes at a cost of added components, increased computational complexity, and expanded display thickness. However, to our knowledge, our introduction of the multilayer partition function is the first avenue to allow demonstrable increases in the contrast of images presented with prefiltered displays.

4   Light Field Displays

Multilayer displays have previously been proposed as compressive light field displays [12,13]. These displays as well as Huang et al.'s [6] proposal to use them for vision correction all use some form of optimization to compute the optimal—in a least-squared error sense—pixel states for the problem at hand. An alternative implementation using conventional parallax barrier or microlens-based light field displays was recently proposed as well [7]. Although any of these display architectures can be used for the application of vision correction,

Huang et al [7] showed that even these simple light field displays, when driven by appropriate prefiltering algorithms, achieve superior contrast and resolution compared to all other implementations.

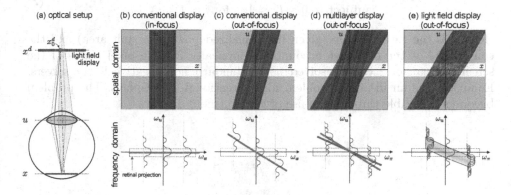

Fig. 7. Light field analysis for different displays. The light field emitted by a display is parameterized by its coordinates on the screen x^d, on the pupil u, and on the retina x (a). This light field propagates through the pupil and is projected into a 2D image on the retina. For an in-focus display, the light field incident on the retina is a horizontal line in the frequency domain (b). For a displayed image outside the accommodation range of the observer, the corresponding light field is slanted and energy is lost at some spatial frequencies (c). Multilayer displays utilize an additional display layer to preserve all spatial frequencies (d). With light field displays, frequency loss is also avoided; the perceived image frequencies are a combination of all spatio-angular frequencies of the incident light field (e). Each pixel on the screen (e.g., x_0^d) emits different intensities toward different regions on the pupil, allowing the same pixel to appear differently when observed from different locations on the retina (red arrows).

To understand how images are formed on the retina for an observed light field display, let us define the lateral position on the retina as x and that on the pupil as u (see Figure 7). Photoreceptors in the retina average over radiance incident from all angles; therefore, the perceived intensity $i(x)$ is modeled as:

$$i(x) = \int_{-\infty}^{\infty} l^d(\phi(x, u), u) A(u) \, du, \qquad (1)$$

where $\phi : \mathbb{R} \times \mathbb{R} \to \mathbb{R}$ is a mapping function that models refractions and aberrations in the eye from the spatio-angular coordinates inside the eye to a location on the screen, such that $x^d = \phi(x, u)$. The effect of the finite pupil diameter r is a multiplication of the light field with the pupil function $A(u) = rect\left(\frac{u}{r}\right)$. In the full 4D case, the $rect$ function is replaced by a circular function modeling the shape of the pupil. In discrete form, Equation 1 becomes $i = \mathbf{P}l^d$.

The objective of an aberration-correcting display is to present a 4D light field to the observer, such that a desired 2D retinal projection is perceived. Assuming that viewing distance, pupil size, and other parameters are known, the emitted light field can be found by optimizing the following objective function:

$$\arg\min l^d \ \|i - Pl^d\|_2$$
$$\text{subject to } 0 \le l^d_i \le 1, \quad \text{for } i = 1 \ldots N \tag{2}$$

Here, i is the target image (given in normalized power per unit area) and the constraints of the objective account for physically feasible pixel states of the screen. Equation 2 can be solved using standard non-negative linear solvers. Equation 2 is an ill-posed problem for conventional 2D displays. The problem becomes invertible through the use of 4D light field displays.

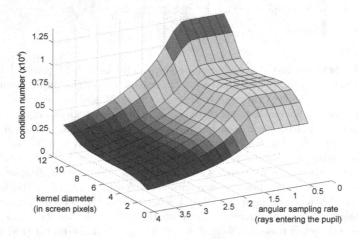

Fig. 8. The light field projection matrix corresponding to a defocused eye is ill-conditioned, implying that vision correction cannot be successful. With more angular resolution available in the emitted light field, more degrees of freedom are added to the system, resulting in lower condition numbers (lower is better), thereby making vision correcting at a high quality feasible. Even as few as 1.5 angular light field samples entering the pupil of an observer decrease the condition number.

To validate this argument, the condition number of the light field projection matrix P can be analyzed. Figure 8 shows the matrix conditioning for varying amounts of defocus and angular light field resolution (lower condition number is better). Increasing the angular resolution of the light field passing through the observer's pupil significantly decreases the condition number of the projection matrix for all amounts of defocus. This experiment demonstrates that the invertibility of Equation 2 is significantly increased (i.e. condition number is decreased) when multiple light rays emitted by the same location on the display surface enter the pupil. Only in this case is the problem of correcting refractive errors actually feasible to be solved.

conventional display   [Pamplona et al.2012]   [Huang et al. 2014]   [Huang et al. 2014]
    photograph   photograph   photograph   simulation

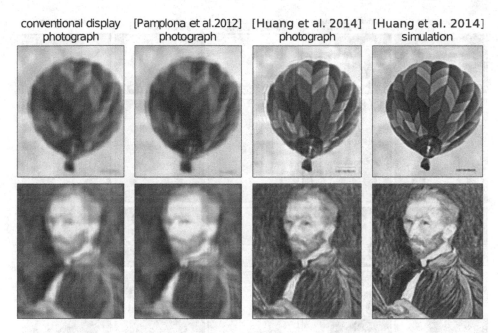

Fig. 9. Images shown on a conventional screen are blurred (first column). While direct light field display theoretically facilitates increased image sharpness (second column), achievable resolution is fundamentally limited by the spatio-angular resolution trade-off of the required light field display. Light field prefiltering allows for significantly increased resolutions (third column). (From top, source images courtesy of dfbphotos (flickr), Vincent van Gogh, Houang Stephane (flickr), JFXie (flickr), Jameziecakes (flickr), Paul Cezanne, Pablo Picasso, Henri Matisse)

Figure 9 shows results captured with a pre-filtered light field display proto-type (center right column). Photographs are captured with a camera equipped with a 50 mm lens at f/8. The display is placed at a distance of 25 cm to the camera. The camera is focused at 38 cm, placing the screen 13 cm away from the focal plane. This camera closely resembles a -6D hyperopic human eye. The results captured from the prototype (Figure 9, third column) closely resemble these simulations but contain minor artifacts that are due to moiré between the barrier mask and the display pixels. Compared to conventional 2D images shown on the screen (Figure 9, first column), image sharpness is significantly improved without requiring the observer to wear glasses. We also compare our approach to the method proposed by Pamplona et al. [11] for the same display resolution and spatio-angular tradeoff (Figure 9, second column). Basically, their approach uses the same display setup as ours but a direct solution rather than the proposed prefilter. Light field prefiltering outperforms the direct solution and allows for significantly increased resolution.

The quality achieved with all discussed vision-correcting display technologies is evaluated in Figure 10. A 10 inch tablet with a 300 PPI panel is simulated for this experiment; for the light field display approaches, a pinhole-based parallax

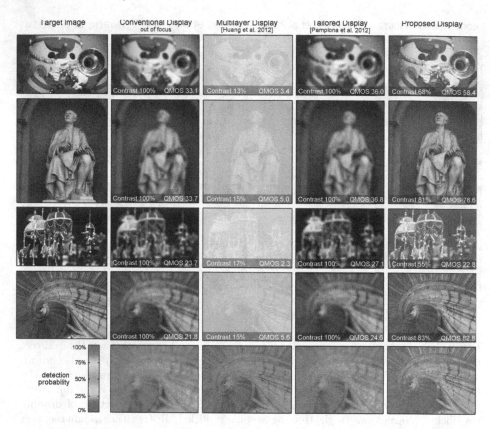

Fig. 10. Evaluation of vision-correcting displays. We compare simulations both qualitatively and quantitatively using contrast and quality-mean-opinion-square (QMOS) error metrics. A conventional out-of-focus display always appears blurred (second column). Multilayer displays with prefiltering improve image sharpness but at a much lower contrast (third column). Light field displays without prefiltering require high angular resolutions, hence provide a low spatial resolution (fourth column). The proposed method combines prefiltering and light field display to optimize image contrast and sharpness (right column). The QMOS error metric is a perceptually linear metric, predicting perceived quality for a human observer. We also plot maps that illustrate the probability of an observer detecting the difference of a displayed image to the target image (bottom row). Our method performs best in most cases. (Source images courtesy of flickr users Jameziecakes, KarHan Tan, Mostaque Chowdhury, Thomas Quine (from top))

barrier with 6.5 mm offset is simulated. The tablet is held at a distance of 30 cm and viewed with a -6.75D hyperopic eye; images are shown on the center of the display in a 10.8 cm × 10.8 cm area. Target contrast for prefiltering methods is manually adjusted to achieve the best PSNR for each example.

5   Conclusions

This is the first work to demonstrate focusing at more than one plane; although the eye has its natural focus plane, the device plane is also capable of generating a sharp image on the retina or the camera sensor. This is useful for heads-up-displays (HUDs), projecting useful information onto cars or objects when the windshield or Google glasses are close to the observer.

The near-field display is also useful in some real world applications, where wearing double glasses is cumbersome; the vision correcting display accomplishes two tasks with one device. There are some potential future directions that might engender interesting research, such as the vergences and the convergences problem of the eye when accommodating 3D content for entertainment applications.

Since some visual impairments involve high order optical aberrations, which are impossible to correct with eyeglasses unless gaze direction is restricted to be fixed, this work could improve the quality of life for people suffering from these ocular conditions. In this work, we show a promising framework for correcting higher order aberrations using a computational light field display approach; we fundamentally avoid the problem of making irregular-shaped optical elements. Through simulation, we demonstrate that the proposed prefiltering algorithm successfully compensates for different terms of the Zernike polynomials in the wavefront aberrations; however, physical experiments still need to be performed. In addition, it is unclear how the projection system behaves theoretically, and how the hardware works in practical uses.

For future work, we anticipate the condition analysis for the higher order aberrations would reveal insights on the hardware construction. We also expect higher order aberrations could have a potential impact on the off-axis viewing optimization.

Acknowledgments. This research was supported in part by the National Science Foundation at the University of California, Berkeley under grant number IIS-1219241, "Individualized Inverse-Blurring and Aberration Compensated Displays for Personalized Vision Correction with Applications for Mobile Devices."

References

1. Akeley, K., Watt, S.J., Girshick, A.R., Banks, M.S.: A stereo display prototype with multiple focal distances. ACM Trans. Graph. **23**(3), 804–813 (2004). http://doi.acm.org/10.1145/1015706.1015804
2. Alonso Jr, M., Barreto, A.B.: Pre-compensation for high-order aberrations of the human eye using on-screen image deconvolution. IEEE Engineering in Medicine and Biology Society. **1**, 556–559 (2003)
3. Archand, P., Pite, E., Guillemet, H., Trocme, L.: Systems and methods for rendering a display to compensate for a viewer's visual impairment. International Patent Application PCT/US2011/039993 (2011)
4. Grosse, M., Wetzstein, G., Grundhöfer, A., Bimber, O.: Coded aperture projection. ACM Trans. Graph. (2010). http://doi.acm.org/10.1145/1805964.1805966

5. Huang, F.C., Barsky, B.A.: A framework for aberration compensated displays. Tech. Rep. UCB/EECS-2011-162, EECS Department, University of California, Berkeley, December 2011. http://www.eecs.berkeley.edu/Pubs/TechRpts/2011/EECS-2011-162.html

6. Huang, F.C., Lanman, D., Barsky, B.A., Raskar, R.: Correcting for optical aberrations using multilayer displays. ACM Trans. Graph. **31**(6), 185:1–185:12 (2012). http://doi.acm.org/10.1145/2366145.2366204

7. Huang, F.C., Wetzstein, G., Barsky, B.A., Raskar, R.: Eyeglasses-free display: Towards correcting visual aberrations with computational light field displays. ACM Transaction on Graphics xx, 0 August 2014. http://graphics.berkeley.edu/papers/Huang-EFD-2014-08/

8. Kaufman, P., Alm, A.: Adler's Physiology of the Eye (Tenth Edition). Mosby (2002)

9. Kee, E., Paris, S., Chen, S., Wang, J.: Modeling and removing spatially-varying optical blur. In: IEEE International Conference on Computational Photography (2011)

10. Lanman, D., Wetzstein, G., Hirsch, M., Heidrich, W., Raskar, R.: Polarization fields: dynamic light field display using multi-layer LCDs. ACM Trans. Graph. 30(6) (2011). http://doi.acm.org/10.1145/2070781.2024220

11. Pamplona, V.F., Oliveira, M.M., Aliaga, D.G., Raskar, R.: Tailored displays to compensate for visual aberrations. ACM Trans. Graph. **31**(4), 81:1–81:12 (2012). http://doi.acm.org/10.1145/2185520.2185577

12. Wetzstein, G., Lanman, D., Heidrich, W., Raskar, R.: Layered 3d: Tomographic image synthesis for attenuation-based light field and high dynamic range displays. ACM Trans. Graph. (SIGGRAPH) **30**(4), 95:1–95:12 (2011)

13. Wetzstein, G., Lanman, D., Hirsch, M., Raskar, R.: Tensor displays: Compressive light field synthesis using multilayer displays with directional backlighting. ACM Trans. Graph. (SIGGRAPH) **31**(4), 80:1–80:11 (2012)

14. Yellott, J.I., Yellott, J.W.: Correcting spurious resolution in defocused images. Proc. SPIE 6492 (2007)

3D Glasses as Mobility Aid for Visually Impaired People

Stefano Mattoccia$^{(\boxtimes)}$ and Paolo Macrì'

Department of Computer Science and Engineering (DISI), University of Bologna,
Viale Risorgimento 2, 40136 Bologna, Italy
stefano.mattoccia@unibo.it, paolo.macri@studio.unibo.it

Abstract. This paper proposes an effective and wearable mobility aid
aimed at improving the quality of life of people suffering for visual disabilities by enabling autonomous and safe navigation in unknown environments. Our system relies on dense and accurate depth maps, provided
in real-time by a compact stereo vision system mapped into an FPGA,
in order to detect obstacles in front of the user and to provide accordingly vibration feedbacks as well as audio information by means of a
bone-conductive speakers. Compared to most approaches with similar
purposes, even in the current prototype arrangement deployed for testing, our system is extremely compact, lightweight and energy efficient
thus enabling hours of safe and autonomous navigation with standard
batteries avoiding the need to carry cumbersome devices. Moreover, by
conceiving the 3D sensing device as a replacement of standard glasses
typically worn by visually impaired people and by using intuitive feedbacks provided by means of lightweight actuators, our system provides
an ergonomic and comfortable user interface with a fast learning curve
for its effective deployment. This fact has been extensively verified on
the field by means of an experimental evaluation, in indoor as well as in
outdoor environments, with different users simulating visual impairment
including a blind person.

Keywords: Wearable · Visually impaired · 3D · Stereo vision · Obstacle
detection

1 Introduction

For people suffering of visual impairments even common everyday tasks, such as
freely walking on a sidewalk to reach a well-known destination, can represent a
serious problem due to the potential dangerous situations encountered along the
path. In the context figured out, hazards can be represented by other pedestrians, animals or objects (boxes, traffic signals, cars, waste containers, etc). Some
of these hazards can be *learned* by the user day by day, however many obstacle are not stationary and hence must be detected dynamically. Remaining in
the specific context figured out, other dangerous hazards can be represented by
moving cars, motorbikes, bikes at cross-roads. Although for the former hazards

© Springer International Publishing Switzerland 2015
L. Agapito et al. (Eds.): ECCV 2014 Workshops, Part III, LNCS 8927, pp. 539–554, 2015.
DOI: 10.1007/978-3-319-16199-0_38

the white cane can be effective (but quite intrusive requiring physical contacts with the "sensed" people/objects), in the latter cases it is almost useless. In fact, even when using a white cane, the visually impaired is not aware, excluding the audio perception of the surrounding, if vehicles/objects are approaching him/her, at what speed and from which directions. These facts, according to our discussions with blind people, create a sense of fear that is constantly perceived by the user. Specific signals for visually impaired available in some urban environments, such as road markers, can provide additional cues for people suffering of visually impairments. However, these signals can't help in dynamic context such as that previously highlighted. Appropriately trained guided dogs can help in such contexts but they also have some well-know limitations (e.g. the short life of a dog, costs and efforts for training, etc).

The social relevance of the the problem and the large amount of people suffering of visual impairments has lead to the development of interesting mobility aids by means of various technologies such as GPS, sonar, vision sensors that will be thoroughly reviewed in the next sections. Among these technologies, vision based approaches have the potential to overcome all other technologies but so far these systems haven't found practical deployment. The reason can be found in two key factors. The first is the actual effectiveness provided by the mobility aid in typical contexts required by people suffering of visual impairments. The other key factor is the limited usability; existing systems are in most cases cumbersome and not suited for everyday deployment for many hours as would be required for an effective practical deployment.

Our proposal aims at overcoming these limitations by using an effective methodology for obstacle detection based on robust and dense 3D data that, thanks to a 3D camera with on board FPGA processing capable of delivering very accurate depth maps according to state-of-the-art stereo vision algorithms, can be implemented on embedded devices with minimal energy and computational requirements. For these reasons, the overall system proposed in this paper is truly wearable and lightweight. Moreover, we propose in this paper a very intuitive and effective user interface that enables to perceive the surrounding environments without reducing the already limited perception capability of the visual impaired.

2   Related Work

The dramatic technology progress, mainly driven by the mobile/embedded market, nowadays enables the deployment of very powerful computing devices characterized by limited energy requirements. This fact has lead many researchers, with different degrees of effectiveness, to propose mobility aids for people suffering of visual disability. These systems can be broadly categorized in two, not mutually exclusive, categories:

- Electronic Travel Support (ETS): systems aimed at enabling autonomous navigation typically by means of obstacle detection methodologies. Sometimes these systems also enable path planning.

– Self Localization Support (SLS): systems aimed at providing to the user the capability to localize himself according to different technologies. An example, available as a mobile phone application, is "Blindsquare"[1] that provides to the user, by means of audio messages, navigation and localization information according to the position retrieved by the GPS receiver of a mobile phone.

We'd like also to point out that exist other interesting aids for visually impaired that do not strictly fall into one of the two highlighted categories. Among these we'd like to remember the ORCAM system[2] that, by means of machine learning algorithms applied to a small camera linked to the glasses, enables to identify learned objects or to infer the status of traffic lights at cross roads. Another interesting system that does not strictly fall into one of the two previous categories is the "Lend an eye" device[3] that enables to stream to the mobile phone of a remote human assistant what is seen by a camera worn by the visually impaired in order to receive suggestions.

Our system, in its current development stage, being aimed at enabling autonomous navigation by means of obstacle detection methodologies falls in the category of ETS systems. Despite this fact, it could be deployed in conjunction with SLS systems or other systems reviewed so far.

ETS systems rely on sensors, based on different technologies, in order to sense the surrounding environment and, by inferring relevant features, to provide a feedback to the user. Therefore three factors are crucial in ETS systems: effective sensing capability, robust algorithms for obstacle detection (or path planning) and intuitive feedback to the user. Three further crucial factors of an ETS system, essentials for a practical deployment, are weight, size and fast responsiveness. Excluding these latter underlying factors, we can further classify ETS according to two notable features: the sensing technology adopted and the feedback perceived by the user.

2.1 Sensing

For ETS system the sensing device used to perceive the environment is crucial to obtain robust and accurate suggestions with a *safe* amount of time before any potential collision. In the literature we can identify two broad classes of sensing technologies used for this purpose: non vision based and vision based devices.

– Non-Vision Based
  Systems based on this kind of sensing devices mostly rely on ultrasound or laser scanners technologies, often coupled with Inertial Measurements Unit (IMU) [1], GPS signals [2,3] and/or RFID [4]. These latter technologies are often used in conjunction with vision based sensing devices. Ultrasound technology provides a *localized* measure of the distance, in the form of an

---

[1] www.blindsquare.com
[2] www.orcam.com
[3] www.lendaneye.com

electrical signal, between the sensor and the area where it is pointed. Positive aspects of this technology are the limited cost and the small size. On the other hand, ultrasound sensors are directional, thus covering only a small area of the scene and can't provide an image of the sensed area. Laser scanners (e.g. [5]) enable sensing in larger areas but they are typically cumbersome and, as for ultrasound sensors, do not provide images of the sensed area. In [6], [7] and [8] are described ETS systems based on ultrasound sensors for directional depth measurements. The same technology coupled with optical sensors in order to cover a larger area was proposed in [9]. Other ETS systems, such as [5] and [9], rely on GPS coupled with optical sensors to detect obstacles.

– Vision Based

Vision, and in particular vision devices for depth perception, have been widely used for ETS systems. In [10–16] the sensing technology used consists in stereo vision. The same technology was adopted by [17]; however, in this cases, the reference image of the stereo camera is also used to detect specific markers put on the road in order to define a pre-configured path. It is worth observing that most of these stereo vision systems rely on the conventional fixed window algorithm [18] for stereo matching that, as well-known, is not very accurate near depth discontinuities and provides unreliable results in poorly textured regions. Moreover, these stereo vision systems often have a very low frame rate. Despite the widespread deployment of stereo vision technology for ETS systems, other sensing technologies have been used by other researchers; [5] uses a laser scanner coupled with two monocular camera while [9] relies on a Kinect and ultrasound sensors. Of course, due to the structured pattern projected by the Kinect, the latter system is suited only for indoor environments.

Compared to these systems, mainly based on heavy and cumbersome devices, the 3D sensing device proposed in this paper has several advantage: it is extremely lightweight, has minimal energy requirements and provides very accurate depth maps according to a state-of-the-art processing pipeline at high frame rate (about 18 fps in the configuration reported in this paper). Moreover, compared to most previous approaches, the computing platform for obstacle detection, thank to the FPGA implementation of the stereo matching algorithm, can be a compact embedded device as in the current prototype or a smartphone/tablet.

2.2   Feedback

People suffering of visual disability often improve their capability to perceive through other senses. In [19] and [20] was highlighted that visually impaired users mostly rely on touch and hearing to compensate for their visual loss and for this reason most ETS systems provide feedback according to these two senses.

– Haptic

The sense of touch, frequently not fully exploited by normally sighted people, is on the other hand essential for visually impaired. For this reason this sense has been widely used to provide feedback in ETS systems. In [6] a hand held cylinder containing moving rings provides a tactile feedback of the sensed area. Two gloves with *transcutaneous electrical nerve stimulation* (TENS) on each finger were proposed for depth perception in [21]. The sensed area is divided in ten regions and for each region a finger receives a stimulation proportional to the depth sensed in that area. Vibrotactile devices (vibration actuators), placed on sensitive parts of the human body such as hands or arms are widely used to provide haptic feedback. In [9] an array of vibrotactile devices is used to identify regions without obstacles while [17] relies on this stimulation to provide modification to the detected trajectory. A glove with a vibrotactile device for each finger was proposed in [11] in order to provide a feedback for five not overlapping regions of the sensed area. A similar approach, enhanced by a vibration modulated according to the perceived depth in each area, can be found in [22]. Array of vibration actuators with modulation proportional to the distance are reported in [16] and [8]. However, it is worth observing that [19] and [20] reported that increasing the number of vibration actuators can reduce the overall effectiveness of the feedback device. Another feedback approach consists in constraining a finger of the visually impaired by means of actuated wires as reported in [10] and [7].

Audio

The sense of hearing is also crucial for people suffering of visual disabilities and for this reason it has been exploited by means of two main approaches: audio information and *sonification*. In the first case the information consists in audio messages that can help the user to better understanding the surrounding environment according to a localization system such as a GPS (e.g. "you are at this location") or the perception module (e.g. "there is an obstacle in front of you"). Examples of systems based on this approach are [5], [9],[17], [23], [2], [14] and [1]. The other strategy, referred to as sonification, consists in encoding information concerned with the sensed area in audio signals. For instance by changing the frequency of the audio signal according to the sensed distance. Examples of systems based on this strategy are [15], [13] and [12].

We conclude this section observing that this latter strategy requires a significant amount of training and, similarly to the former approach based on standard audio information, isolates the user from the environment. Moreover, the audio signal should be used only when it is strictly requested by the user (e.g. "Where am I?") or triggered by potentially dangerous situations (e.g. obstacles). For these reasons, in our system we deploy a bone conductive headset to provide standard audio messages triggered by specific events (e.g. an obstacle in front of the user).

3 Overview of the Proposed ETS System

Our proposal aims at enabling people suffering of visual impairments to move autonomously in unknown environments in presence of dynamic objects/people

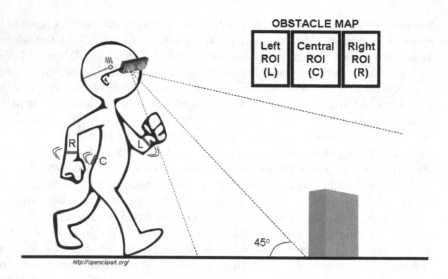

Fig. 1. Overview of the proposed system, shown in details in Figure 2, with the embedded 3D camera mounted on conventional glasses frames as shown in Figure 3. In red the three vibrotactile actuators and in blue the bone conductive headset for audio messages. The sensed area is divided in three regions, each one corresponding to a vibrotactile actuator.

by wearing *glasses* with 3D sensing capability and an effective feedback approach as depicted in Figure 1. Our system, reported in details in Figure 2, consists of a compact 3D sensor mounted on conventional glasses frames, worn as a pair of conventional glasses and tilted of about 45 degrees downward looking as shown in Figure 3, an embedded PC that detects obstacles in the area sensed by the 3D camera. The user perceives the feedback according to three vibrotactile actuators depicted in red in Figure 1 (the small armband/bracelet worn around each arm and a further armband put in another location of the human body such as the back of the neck) and a bone conductive headset according to a strategy that will be discussed in the remainder.

Observing Figure 2 we can notice the 3D camera (worn as in Figure 3), the bone conductive headset, two of the armband containing the vibrotactile actuators (the other vibrotactile device in this configuration is mounted on the back of the belt and hence not visible in the figure) and a belt containing the processing units and a battery. Concerning the processing units: the obstacle detection algorithm has been implemented on the Odroid U3 [24] platform (on the left of figure, enclosed with a plastic case) while the Arduino Due board [25], connected by means of a serial communication to the Odroid, merely controls the vibrotactile actuators. The battery, at the right, provides energy to the entire system for hours. The weight of all the electronic devices shown in Figure 2 including the camera, the headset, vibrotactile actuators and battery is about 300 g. The processing module shown in the figure can be worn as a conventional belt, as

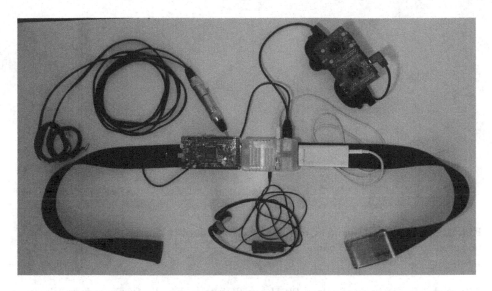

Fig. 2. Components of the proposed ETS system: 3D camera with FPGA on board processing, Odroid U3 computing platform, Arduino Due, three vibrotactile actuators, bone conductive headset and battery. The overall weight of all the components is about 300 g (3D camera + glasses + lenses + holders account for about 110 g).

depicted in Figure 5, and this fact coupled with the embedded 3D camera makes our system truly wearable. Finally we observe that, although in the currently development stage the prototype is composed of multiple distinct modules plus a battery, a smartphone or a tablet coupled with the 3D sensor could be used in place of all the processing devices (i.e. the embedded system and the Arduino board) in order to further increase compactness and usability of the proposed ETS system.

4 Hardware

In this section we describe the hardware components of our current prototype focusing our attention on the 3D sensing device at the core of our proposal.

4.1 3D Camera

The key component of our system is an embedded stereo vision camera with on board FPGA processing shown in Figure 3 that allows us to obtain accurate and robust depth maps of the scene in front of the user at almost 20 fps without introducing any computational overhead to the processing modules implemented on the Odroid CPU board [24].

The embedded 3D camera [26,27] can be configured with monochrome or color sensors at a maximum resolution of 752×480 and 60 fps. In the experiments reported in this paper the camera is configured with a resolution of $320\times$

Fig. 3. Embedded 3D camera mounted on conventional glasses. The camera is self powered through the USB cable.

240 and a frame rate of about 20 Hz, sufficient to handle fast moving object in sensed area. As will be shown in the experimental results section, the camera provides very accurate and dense depth maps according to a state-of-the-art stereo vision processing pipeline fully implemented into the FPGA that, in this specific case, is a Spartan 6 model 75. The processing pipeline consists of the following three main components: pre-processing based on the Census transform [28], rectification of the stereo pair and matching according to the Hamming distance. In particular, stereo matching algorithm mapped into the FPGA is a memory efficient implementation of the SGM algorithm [29] and the processing pipeline also includes an effective outliers detection module and a $\frac{1}{8}$ subpixel depth interpolation module. The overall processing pipeline, thank to a stream processing methodology [26], relies only on the internal memory of the FPGA. The reduced power consumption of the embedded 3D camera (about 2 Watt at 640×480 image resolution and processing stereo pairs at 40+ fps), enables us to provide power supply by means of the same USB connector used for the data and connected to the Odroid platform. The weight of the current overall camera shown in Figure 3 is about 90 g, including the M12 lenses and holders, and for this reason it does not result uncomfortable to the user wearing the 3D glasses. The camera is configured with a baseline of about 6 cm that, with the lenses adopted in our experimental validation and the hardware configuration mapped into the FPGA, enables to infer depth from 1 m to 5 m.

4.2 Embedded Processing

The data streamed by the 3D camera are sent, via USB, to the Odroid U3 [24] processing platform in order to detect the ground plane and thus potential obstacles in the sensed area. This device, one completed this task, performs a reasoning on the outcome of the obstacle detection module and accordingly sends audio messages, by means of its audio interface, to the speakers and commands, by means of a serial link, to the Arduino Due board to activate the vibrotactile actuators.

The Odroid U3 contains an ARM SoC, model Exynos 4412, Cortex A9 architecture with four cores clocked at 1.7 Ghz, 1 MB level 2 cache, 2 GB of LP-DDR2 880 Mhz RAM, a Mali-400 graphic processor at 440 Mhz developed by ARM, an USB controller and an Ethernet controller. The input/output ports provided by the Odroid board are: 3 USB, 1 Micro HDMI, 1 Ethernet. The Odroid has a size of 83 x 48 mm and weights 48 g including the heat sink. The operating system installed is Linux, specifically the distribution used for our tests was Xubuntu 13.10. The energy requirement of this platform is below 10 W (typically around 5 W), making this device an ideal candidate for our compact and lightweight ETS system.

The Arduino Due [25] board is connected, through a serial interface mapped on the USB interface, to the Odroid U3 in order to receive command to activate the vibrotactile actuators according to the outcome of the obstacle detection module. However, it is worth observing that the Arduino Due board wouldn't be strictly required being available I/O ports on the Odroid platform. Nevertheless, it has minimal weight, size and power consumption and for these reasons it was adopted to speed-up the development phase of our prototype.

5   Obstacle Detection

Once completed the description of the sensing device and of the processing modules, let's take a look to the algorithm for obstacle detection implemented into the Odroid U3. Our approach consists in the first and crucial stage in determining, for each frame, the ground plane from the disparity maps provided by the 3D camera under the hypothesis that a significant portion of the ground plane is observed in the sensed area. To accomplish this task there are two possible alternatives: processing the point-cloud associated to the disparity map or detecting the ground plane directly in the disparity domain. Although the former solution is completely invariant to camera tilting, after an appropriate experimental evaluation we decided to compute the ground plane directly in the disparity domain. The reason for this choice is twofold: efficiency and specific application domain constraints. Concerning the first fact, working in the disparity domain is less demanding in terms of computational requirements than working in the point-cloud domain. The second reason is concerned with the specific application tackled in our project: in fact in the envisioned system the user, in normal conditions, can tilt the camera on the left or on the right side of few degrees and this fact can be easily managed by a roll-detection algorithm implemented in software and/or by means of an IMU (currently not used in our system). Finally, we observe that tilting the camera by moving the head up and down would not create any problem to the plane detection algorithm working in the disparity domain.

Our algorithm, starting from the disparity map provided by the stereo camera, detects the ground plane applying a robust RANSAC-based approach [30] in the *v-disparity* domain [31]. In order to obtain a robust detection of the ground plane in the v-disparity histogram, we have implemented and tested variants of the RANSAC approach, recently reviewed an evaluated in [32], and aimed at improving efficiency and robustness to outliers. Our final framework, used for the experimental results reported in this paper, includes the following modifications to the original RANSAC framework:

- A degeneracy check in the sampling phase that enables to avoid degenerate model hypotheses such as, in our specific case, collinear vertical points. This strategy quickly allows us to discard a model hypothesis in the first stage of the RANSAC approach without any further computationally demanding verification stage.
- An R-RANSAC $T_{d,d}$ test switch, as proposed in [33], that can be optionally triggered in the sampling stage, enabling a further pre-verification stage for fast rejection of bad hypotheses. This strategy enables to verify the model considering only a small subset of randomly selected points. If these contain outliers the model is quickly discarded with a minimal amount of computation being the verification process performed on a small subset of points. Otherwise, the model is validated according to the remaining points. Although, this strategy requires more hypotheses compared to a standard RANSAC approach, this fast pre-verification phase enables in most cases a significant runtime reduction according to our evaluation.
- An effective cost function as proposed in [34]. Compared to the original RANSAC approach that assigns to all inliers the same cost, this method weights each inlier according on how the point fits with the model. In our experimental evaluation, this strategy effectively enabled to improve plane detection accuracy as well as to deal with noisy disparity measurements.
- An optional adaptive termination criteria that enables to determine the maximum number of iterations at every cycle [35] in order to minimize the runtime.

Our software processing module implemented on the Odroid, handles small lateral tilting of the camera, determining this parameter and rotate the image accordingly before the ground detection approach previously outlined in order to avoid ground plane mis-detection. The roll-detection algorithm, similarly to the plane detection algorithm, works in the v-disparity histogram domain and relies on the enhanced RANSAC framework previously outlined. Specifically, this approach determines the *mode* of the disparity in regions of the disparity map where the ground plane is more likely to be found (e.g. those areas of the disparity map that were identified as belonging to the ground plane in the previous frame) or more simply in prefixed areas in the disparity map combined by means of a voting scheme. Once determined the most frequent disparity in these regions (i.e. the mode), we build the v-disparity space considering only those points with disparity values similar to the detected mode and apply a robust linear regression based on the RANSAC framework. This allows us to determine the tilting angle and thus to compensate for lateral tilting before the ground detection algorithm. It is worth to note that for small lateral tilting, as frequently occurs in the considered application domain, the roll-detection wouldn't be required at all being the v-disparity approach invariant to small misalignments between the camera and the ground plane. Moreover, we point out that our approach does not rely, in the current stage of development, on IMUs or a Kalman filter that could further improve the robustness of our ground plane detection approach.

Once detected the ground plane we set as obstacle those points that do not lie on this surface according to a prefixed tolerance threshold and to the resulting *obstacle map* we provide feedback to the user.

6   User Feedback

By analyzing the lower portion of disparity map, the subsystem implemented on the embedded CPU board provides vibrotactile and audio messages to the user. In order to design a comfortable and effective system we decided to minimize the feedbacks according to a strategy outlined in the reminder. Moreover, we observe that the proposed system let hands and arms free; this fact is extremely important because enables exploration by touch and/or enables the deployment of the conventional white cane (e.g. for balancing).

6.1   Tactile Feedback

To accomplish an effective tactile perception, we divide the lower portion of the disparity map in three regions as depicted in Figure 1 and link each region to a vibrotactile actuator (the two associated to L and R ROIs are visible in Figure 2, the one associated to the central ROI is positioned on the back of the belt). The relationship between the actuators and the regions of the obstacle map is as follows:

- obstacle in ROI-L: left vibrotactile motor enabled
- obstacle in ROI-C: central vibrotactile motor enabled
- obstacle in ROI-R: right vibrotactile motor enabled

For each of the three regions we trigger an alarm only if there are a sufficient number of points marked as obstacle. An example of the described approach on real-images is shown in Figure 5; green means no obstacle and red means obstacle detected in that specific region. This setup allows the user to obtain an intuitive perception of the obstacle detected in the field-of-view of the camera. Moreover, the user can easily explore the surrounding area by simpling rotating the head in order to detect obstacle in the area pointed by the glasses These operations, for a constrained area around the user, are typically carried out by means of a white cane.

It is worth observing that we deliberately decided to use only three vibro-tactile actuators to design a simple and effective interface that requires only few minutes for training. Moreover, we decided to avoid modulation of the tactile feedback (e.g. proportional to the distance from the average obstacle detected in one of the sensed areas shown in Figure 1) since our evaluation clearly highlighted that this strategy requires a longer training period and, more importantly, the modulated vibration is difficult to perceive and thus less effective compared to the simpler, yet effective, solution proposed in this paper.

6.2   Audio Feedback

When an obstacle is detected in the central ROI shown in Figures 1 and 5, an audio message containing the average distance to the object is provided to the user. In order to not provide excessive and counterproductive feedbacks, the audio message is sent again only if the user/obstacle moves of at least 1 m with respect to the position of the previous obstacle. The audio feedbacks are provided according to an headset based on the bone conduction technology. This fact, as previously pointed out, is very important in order to not acoustically isolate the visually impaired from the surrounding environment. For the same reasons outlined in the previous section, concerned with usability factors, we deliberately decided to avoid sonification in our system.

7   Experimental Validation

We have extensively tested, in indoor and outdoor scenarios, the proposed ETS system shown in Figure 1 with about ten users (three of them are shown in Figure 4) including a person visually impaired that has suggested specific feedbacks during the development stage and proposed some effective modifications to our initial prototype. For normally sighted users we simulated visual impairments by covering their eyes. Experimental results concerned with three normally sighted users and a visually impaired person are available at this link[4]. It is worth noting that experimental results reported in the videos are concerned with a preliminary prototype of the proposed ETS system. Compared to the current prototype shown in Figures 2, 3 and in the rightmost image of Figure 4, the main differences are basically in the larger camera case and battery. Figure 4 shows at the left and at the center two users testing the preliminary prototype.

During our evaluation all the users agreed on the fact that the current prototype is truly *wearable* and that the proposed user interface is extremely intuitive and effective. In fact, they were able to effectively deploy the system after only few minutes it was worn. Only the visually impaired person required a slightly longer period to be fully accustomed to the system because in his daily living he heavily relies on the white cane for perception and balance. For these reasons, he initially didn't trust on the additional feedbacks provided by our system. Despite this fact, after a training period of about 30 minutes he was ready to use the proposed system and, mainly for balancing, his white cane. This latter fact is not a problem being, in our proposal, arms and hands free to move

---

[4] www.vision.deis.unibo.it/smatt

Fig. 4. Experimental evaluation with three users. The rightmost image is concerned with latest prototype shown in Figures 2 and 3 while the left and center images are concerned with the initial prototype of the system.

without constraints. After this short training period and an extensive evaluation in an urban scenario his feedback on our ETS system was extremely positive. He also highlighted that a notable feature that currently is not available in our system is a GPS-based audio navigation support that would provide a direction during obstacle detection. Nevertheless, it is worth pointing out that during the development stage described in this paper we focused our attention on the more challenging obstacle detection task because the highlighted GPS feature could be eventually added to our system by using a standard navigator (such as Google Maps or similar), available nowadays even in cheapest smart phones, or by using a GPS module attached or connected via Bluetooth to the Odroid board.

In Figure 5 are depicted three screenshot taken in an outdoor urban scenario. The upper portion of the figure contains the reference images acquired by the stereo camera and the lower portion the obstacle maps (in white the detected ground plane and in black the detected obstacle points). Superimposed to the obstacle maps are shown, for each image reported, the three sensed regions with green encoding *no obstacle* and red *obstacle detected*. In this latter case super-imposed to the image we can read the average distance from the camera to the detected obstacle. From the figure we can notice that the disparity maps provided by the 3D camera are quite accurate; in fact, the obstacle detection algorithm, processing these disparity maps accurately detects obstacles and ground plane in the real application scenarios reported in the figure. Despite these positive aspects, during our experimental evaluation we have detected some failures; these facts mainly occur in indoor environments when the sensed area is completely uniform or made of transparent objects. Nevertheless, in these circumstances the resulting disparity map tends to be very noisy and thus, in most cases, these areas are correctly identified as obstacles.

Fig. 5. Outcome of the obstacle detection algorithm in an urban scenario processing the 3D data provided by the camera worn by an user during the experimental evaluation

Finally, we observe that compared to most ETS systems proposed in literature our prototype is extremely compact and lightweight. Moreover, thank to reliable depth map and the high frame rate (about 18 fps) our system is effective even when the sensed scene contains fast moving objects/people.

8   Conclusions and Future Work

In this paper we have proposed an effective and wearable system aimed at improving the autonomous mobility of people suffering of visual impairments. Our proposal relies for depth sensing on an embedded stereo camera mounted on a pair of glasses that enables, by means of a robust obstacle detection algorithm implemented into an embedded device, to provide effective and intuitive feedbacks to the user according to vibrotactile and audio actuators. Thank to the FPGA-based 3D camera and the embedded devices used the overall system, even in the current form, is extremely compact, lightweight and with a standard battery can work for hours.

Future work is aimed at porting the obstacle detection algorithm from the embedded Odroid U3 to mobile phones or tablet in order to implement the whole software system into a single device as well as to take advantage of the GPS receiver available in most of these devices. Moreover, we are going to apply machine learning techniques for object categorization that would allow to provide further audio information concerning the kind of obstacle sensed by our system.

References

1. Loomis, J.M., Golledge, R.G., Klatzky, R.L.: Navigation system for the blind - auditory display modes and guidance. Presence **7**(2), 193–203 (1998)
2. Ran, L., Helal, S., Moore, S.: Drishti: an integrated indoor/outdoor blind navigation system and service. In: Proc. of the Second IEEE Annual Conference on Pervasive Computing and Communications (2004)
3. Helal, A.S., Moore, S.E., Ramachandran, B.: Drishti: An Integrated Navigation System for Visually Impaired and Disabled. In: ISWC 2001: Proceedings of the 5th IEEE International Symposium on Wearable Computers (2001)
4. Ceipidor, B.U., Medaglia, C.M., Rizzo, F., Serbanati, A.: RadioVirgilio/Scsamonct:an RFID-based navigation system for visually impaired. In: MobileGuide (2006). http://mobileguide06.di.unito.it/programma.html
5. Bourbakis, N.G., Kavraki, D.: An intelligent assistant for navigation of visually impaired people. In: Proceedings of the 2nd IEEE International Symposium on Bioinformatics and Bioengineering (2001)
6. Shah, C., Bouzit, M., Youssef, M., Vasquez, L.: Evaluation of ru-netra - tactile feedback navigation system for the visually impaired. In: 2006 International Workshop on Virtual Rehabilitation, pp. 72–77 (2006)
7. Ito, K., Okamoto, M., Akita, J., Ono, T., Gyobu, I., Takagi, T., Hoshi, T., Mishima, Y.: Cyarm: an alternative aid device for blind persons. In: CHI 2005 (2005)
8. Cardin, S., Thalmann, D., Vexo, F.: Wearable system for mobility improvement of visually impaired people. In: In Visual Computer journal (2006)
9. Ni, D., Wang, L., Ding, Y., Zhang, J., Song, A., Wu, J.: The design and implementation of a walking assistant system with vibrotactile indication and voice prompt for the visually impaired. In: ROBIO (2013)
10. Arcara, P., Di Stefano, L., Mattoccia, S., Melchiorri, C., Vassura, G.: Perception of depth information by means of a wire-actuated haptic interface. In: In IEEE Int. Conf. on Robotics and Automation (2000)
11. Zelek, J., Audette, R., Balthazaar, J., Dunk, C.: A stereo-vision system for the visually impaired. University of Waterloo, Technical report (2000)
12. Balakrishnan, G., Sainarayanan, G., Nagarajan, R., Yaacob, S.: Wearable real-time stereo vision for the visually impaired
13. Sanz, P.R., Mezcua, B.R., Pena, J.M.S., Walker, B.N., Tipton, S.J., White II, D.J., Sershon, C., Choi, Y.B., Yu, F., Zhang, J., et al.: 1 evaluation of the sonification protocol of an artificial vision system for the visually impaired. Evaluation (2014)
14. Hub, A., Diepstraten, J., Ertl, T.: Augmented indoor modeling for navigation support for the blind. In: Conference Proceedings: CPSN 2005 - The International Conference on Computers for People with Special Needs, Las Vegas (2005)
15. Rodríguez, A., Bergasa, L., Alcantarilla, P., Yebes, J., Cela, A.: Obstacle avoidance system for assisting visually impaired people. In: IEEE Intelligent Vehicles Symposium, Proceedings of Workshop Perception in Robotics (2012)
16. Dakopoulos, D., Boddhu, S.K., Bourbakis, N.G.: A 2d vibration array as an assistive device for visually impaired. In: BIBE (2007)
17. Fernandes, H., Costa, P., Filipe, V., Hadjileontiadis, L., Barroso, J.F.: Stereo vision in blind navigation assistance. In: 2010 World Automation Congress, WAC 2010 (2010)
18. Szeliski, R.: Computer Vision: Algorithms and Applications, 1st edn. Springer-Verlag New York Inc., New York, NY, USA (2010)

19. Velázquez, R.: Wearable Assistive Devices for the Blind. Issues and Characterization, Wearable and Autonomous Biomedical Devices and Systems for Smart Environment (2010)
20. Kaczmarek, K.A., Webster, J.G., Bach-y Rita, P., Tompkins, W.J.: Electrotactile and vibrotactile displays for sensory substitution systems. IEEE Transactions on Biomedical Engineering (1991)
21. Meers, S., Ward, K.: A vision system for providing 3d perception of the environment via transcutaneous electro-neural stimulation. In: IV (2004)
22. Johnson, L.A., Higgins, C.M.: A navigation aid for the blind using tactile-visual sensory substitution. Conf Proc IEEE Eng Med Biol Soc (2006)
23. Huang, B., Liu, N.: Mobile navigation guide for the visually disabled. Journal of the Transportation Research Board **2004**, 28–34 (1885)
24. Hard-Kernel: Odroid u3. http://hardkernel.com/main/main.php
25. Arduino: Arduino due. http://www.arduino.cc
26. Mattoccia, S.: Stereo vision algorithms for fpgas. In: The 9th IEEE Embedded Vision Workshop, CVPR 2013 Workshop (2013)
27. Mattoccia, S., Marchio, I., Casadio, M.: A compact 3d camera suited for mobile and embedded vision applications. In: The Fourth IEEE Workshop on Mobile Vision, CVPR 2014 Workshop (2014)
28. Zabih, R., Woodfill, J.: Non-parametric local transforms for computing visual correspondence. In: Proceedings of the Third European Conference-Volume II on Computer Vision - Volume II, pp. 151–158. ECCV 1994 (1994)
29. Hirschmüller, H.: Stereo processing by semiglobal matching and mutual information. IEEE Trans. Pattern Anal. Mach. Intell. **30**(2), 328–341 (2008)
30. Fischler, M.A., Bolles, R.C.: Random sample consensus: A paradigm for model fitting with applications to image analysis and automated cartography. Communications of the ACM **24**(6), 381–395 (1981)
31. Labayrade, R., Aubert, D.: In-vehicle obstacles detection and characterization by stereovision. In: Proceedings the 1st International Workshop on In-Vehicle Cognitive Computer Vision Systems, pp. 13–19 (2003)
32. Raguram, R., Chum, O., Pollefeys, M., Matas, J., Frahm, J.M.: Usac: A universal framework for random sample consensus. IEEE Trans. Pattern Anal. Mach. Intell. **35**(8), 2022–2038 (2013)
33. Matas, J., Chum, O.: Randomized ransac with td, d test. Image Vision Comput. **22**(10), 837–842 (2004)
34. Torr, P.H.S., Zisserman, A.: Mlesac: A new robust estimator with application to estimating image geometry. Computer Vision and Image Understanding **78**, 2000 (2000)
35. Choi, S., Kim, T., Yu, W.: Performance evaluation of ransac family. In: BMVC (2009)

A Robust Vision-Based Framework for Screen Readers

Michael Cormier[✉], Robin Cohen, Richard Mann, Kamal Rahim,
and Donglin Wang

Cheriton School of Computer Science, University of Waterloo, Waterloo, Canada
{m4cormie,rcohen,mannr,krahim,d35wang}@uwaterloo.ca

Abstract. With the increasingly rich display of media on the Internet,
screen reading technology that mainly considers website source code can
become ineffective. We aim to present a solution that remains robust in
the face of dynamically displayed web content, regardless of the underlying web framework. To do this, we consider techniques used in computer
vision to determine semantic information about the web pages. We consider existing screen reading technologies to see where such techniques
can help, and discuss our analytical model to show how this approach
can benefit low vision users.

Keywords: Computer vision · Screen reader · Visually impaired · Sensory substitution

1   Introduction

Modern web pages are complex, and include dynamic content and content in a
wide variety of languages and frameworks. While this provides a rich experience
for most users, it can degrade the experience of low-vision or visually impaired
users. Low vision users are users who have limited visual acuity despite using
the best lenses that are available. These users typically use screen readers, which
are applications that take the standard output generated from other programs,
interpret it, and read it to the user in a meaningful way. Existing screen readers
designed for use on web content typically use the page source code structure to
determine the best way to present the content (*e.g.* ChromeVox [8] and VoiceOver
[1]); the incorporation of rich media makes this much more difficult because of
the complexity of the underlying page source code. The resulting output is very
difficult for users to interpret.

    We use methods from computer vision to help create a semantically rich
landscape for users with low vision. By rendering the web page and emulating
how humans inspect web pages, we hope to reduce the reliance on high verbosity
screen readers, thus providing a better user experience. Verbosity settings on
screen readers can be used to read when a frame begins, or when images appear
on web pages, along with other formatting features of the web page. However, we
acknowledge that some users enjoy a high verbosity screen reader because it can

© Springer International Publishing Switzerland 2015
L. Agapito et al. (Eds.): ECCV 2014 Workshops, Part III, LNCS 8927, pp. 555–569, 2015.
DOI: 10.1007/978-3-319-16199-0_39

help to create a mental model of the web page in their minds. It may be valuable to think of low vision users performing web page rendering in their mind, using the output of a screen reader as their own "source code" to generate the display of the web page in their mental model. Since current screen reading technology mainly looks at web source code to determine where features lie in websites [8] [1], there is room for improvement using solutions from computer vision, such as edge detection and general feature extraction to more accurately report to users where content and formatting lies relative to one another. In contrast to other efforts, we propose an approach to the problem designed to more closely emulate the ways that sighted users perceive a web page, as a way of improving robustness.

This work proposes augmented or alternative communication for users who are attempting to view online webpages. Whether completely blind or simply visually impaired (either due to disability or to age), our methods would enable an audio conveying of webpage content for the user, as an additional option. This work therefore also constitutes sensory substitution (where visual display is prepared to instead be provided as audio output). Our proposed solution leverages techniques from computer vision in order to decide what to present as output.

This paper is divided into four sections, of which this introduction is the first. Section 2 describes our proposed approach to the problem. The advantages and disadvantages of our approach relative to other methods are discussed in Section 3. Finally, Section 4 consists of concluding remarks and proposed directions for future research.

2   Proposed Solution

We propose that a screen reader can make use of the high-level structure of a web page in much the same way that a human user does: by the appearance of the rendered page itself. While specific languages and frameworks for web design will inevitably evolve or be replaced over time, the web pages that they are used to produce are likely to remain consistent. There are common patterns in web design which are well established. Our intention is to respect these patterns; to fundamentally change these design patterns may be confusing for users. Figure 1 shows an example of one common pattern of organization for a web page. It is immediately clear that the top field is likely to contain a title and possibly links to major sections of the website, the left-side field is likely to contain links or incidental information, and the larger field occupying the central, right, and lower regions probably contains the primary contents of the page.

Not all web page layouts are this simple, but in general web pages are designed to organize information in an intuitive way that makes it as easy as possible to find the primary content, incidental content (such as contact information), and links to other sections of the website. Despite the often considerable complexity of a web page's code, a well-designed web page has a clear, simple structure.

We describe a combination of computer vision techniques and models which can be used to divide a web page into semantically meaningful regions, to classify

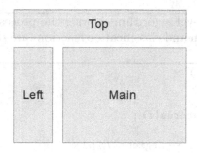

Fig. 1. Schematic example of a website structure. It is natural to assume that the main content is in the cention marked "Main," the sidebar ("Left") contains links, and the top bar contains a title and possibly some links.

these regions according to their semantic role in the page, and to read the text as the user navigates through the page. Our framework is designed to be resilient with respect to changes in the languages used to present web content and to allow visually-impaired users to navigate web sites in the same way that a sighted user would. The flowchart shown in Figure 2 shows the organization of our proposed system, with references to the sections of the text describing the major components. Likewise, Algorithm 1 describes the process of reading a page.

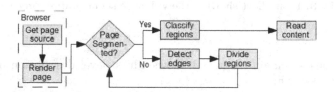

Fig. 2. Flow chart showing the high-level organization of our proposed screen reader and segmentation framework

2.1 Segmentation

Unlike previous work on segmentation for screen readers [6] [9] [12], our proposed framework uses a top-down approach to page segmentation. We believe that this is advantageous because, like a human observer seeing a page from too great a distance to see details, a top-down system can produce a reasonable large-scale segmentation even if the details are unclear or computational resources are insufficient to produce a detailed segmentation in a reasonable time. Top-down page segmentation methods have a precedent in, for example, OCR applications [3]. Our segmentation algorithm produces a hierarchical segmentation by beginning with a region corresponding to the entire page and recursively dividing regions along logical boundaries in the visual structure of each region until no such

---

Algorithm 1. High-level algorithm showing the process of reading a web page. The segmentation and classification functions are shown in algorithms 2 and 3, respectively.

---

1 **Function** ReadPage(I)
    | **Input**: Page image I
2 | $v_{img} \leftarrow I$;
3 | $v_{feat} \leftarrow$ RegionFeatures(I) ;
4 | $T_{init} \leftarrow (\{v\}, \emptyset)$;
5 | Segmentation tree $T \leftarrow$ Segment(T_{init}) ;
6 | Classification tree $L \leftarrow$ Classify(T) ;
7 | Read regions in the order specified by the user ;

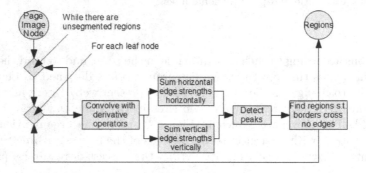

Fig. 3. Flow chart showing the web page segmentation process

logical boundaries remain. Figure 3 shows a high-level description of the page segmentation algorithm.

The first step in subdividing a region is edge detection. The process of edge detection is described in detail by Castleman [2]; here we summarize the aspects of the problem applicable to our system. An edge detection algorithm treats the image as a two-dimensional discrete function I, where $I(x, y)$ is the value of the pixel at row x and column y. The simplest definition of an edge is a point at which the magnitude of the gradient is very large; that is, the image changes very quickly (since the image function is discrete, its derivatives can only be approximated). The orientation of the edge is perpendicular to the gradient, so a vertical edge has a strong horizontal gradient. Partial derivatives of the image function ($\frac{\partial I}{\partial x}$ and $\frac{\partial I}{\partial y}$) can be calculated to specifically detect edges which are approximately vertical or horizontal, respectively. One common way to calculate the gradient or derivative is to convolve the image with a discrete kernel K; different kernels perform differently in actual edge detection. Our method uses separate horizontal and vertical edge detection (using the partial derivative kernels K_h and K_v) to produce a horizontal "edge strength" function $S_h = K_v * I$ and a vertical equivalent $S_v = K_h * I$. The edge strengths, calculated by this method, represent the magnitude of partial derivatives of brightness with respect to image position. These edge strengths are converted to binary edge maps E_h and E_v using a threshold t: $E_h(x,y) = \begin{cases} 1 & S_h(x,y) \geq t \\ 0 & S_h(x,y) < t \end{cases}$; E_v is defined analogously. The threshold is a parameter of the edge detection algorithm and can be tuned for a specific application such as our screen reader system. These edge maps are likely to have edges several pixels wide; these edges can be thinned down to more accurately locate the true edges in the image; Castleman describes [2] methods for performing this operation, but in the interest of clarity we will not discuss these methods in detail here.

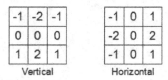

-1	-2	-1
0	0	0
1	2	1

Vertical

-1	0	1
-2	0	2
-1	0	1

Horizontal

Fig. 4. Sobel kernel functions for the vertical (left) and horizontal (right) partial derivatives of the image function. The vertical partial derivative is high across horizontal edges, and the horizontal partial derivative is high for vertical edges.

Since edge detection is so well studied, there are many algorithms that can be used. We use the Sobel edge detection operators [2], shown in Figure 4. Our initial results use the MATLAB Image Processing Toolbox implementation of the Sobel edge detection method, which automatically determines a threshold and thins the detected edges to a single pixel.

The features that our system intends to detect *may* correspond to long edges in the image, but may also correspond to aligned short edges. A sidebar with a distinct background colour, for example, will have long, continuous edges where the background colour changes, but while two columns of text against the same background colour should be separated, there is no continuous edge between them. Objects such as characters or images aligned to a horizontal or vertical line implicitly define a line which may be frequently interrupted by spaces between the objects. For the alignment to be visible, however, each object must have at least a short edge along the line to which they are aligned; furthermore, this edge must have a component parallel to the line of alignment. Our feature extraction system finds the estimated strength of vertical and horizontal division lines—both those formed by long edges and those formed by alignments—by summation of the edge map horizontally or vertically. The estimated vertical boundary strength in a specific column of the image is the total number of edge pixels in the column, and similarly for horizontal edges and rows in the image. It is reasonable to use only horizontal and vertical divisions between regions because the elements of a web page are likely to be vertically and horizontally organized. Once these features have been found for rows and columns in the image, isolated peaks are selected as candidate region boundaries. The edges of the image are also considered to be possible region boundaries.

The row-based and column-based boundary strengths are shown for an example image of the Facebook home page in Figure 5. It consists of the original image with aligned graphs of horizontal and vertical boundary strengths. Note that the highest boundary strengths (the peaks in the graphs above and to the side) correspond to natural divisions in the image of the web site.

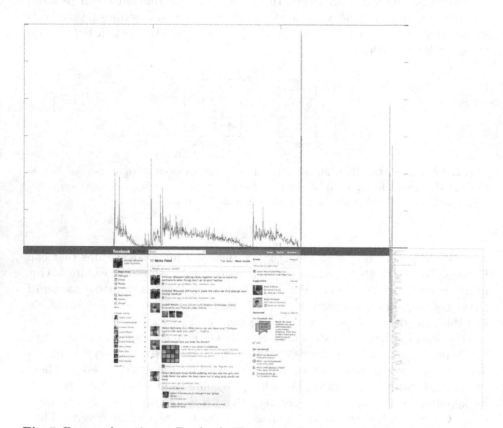

Fig. 5. Feature detection on Facebook. The top graph corresponds to vertical boundary strengths in the page image shown, and the graph on the right to horizontal boundary strengths. The vertical axis of the graph of vertical boundary strengths represents the sum of edge strengths in each column, and the horizontal axis represents position in the image and is aligned with the corresponding columns in the image of the web page. The graph of horizontal boundary strengths is similar, but rotated: replace "columns" in the previous description with "rows," and exchange the axes. Note that the strongest peaks in boundary strength are aligned with natural divisions in the page.

Once the candidate sub-region boundaries have been found, it is necessary to find the optimal set R of sub-regions that correspond to natural divisions in the current region. Each sub-region is an axis-aligned rectangle whose sides correspond to segments of the identified sub-region boundaries. Furthermore, these sub-regions must also obey the following properties:

1. No two sub-regions may overlap
2. No sub-region may include the entire current region
3. Every part of the region must be a part of some sub-region

These properties may not yield a unique segmentation. In this case, a cost function $C(R)$ can be used to guide the segmentation process. The cost function can be used to enforce a wide variety of preferences, including the number of regions, the internal properties of regions, and the relationships between regions. It may also prove useful to use domain-specific cost functions for different web pages. The requirement that the sides of the rectangle correspond to candidate region boundaries dramatically reduces the number of possible segmentations that must be searched to find an optimal solution. If valid sub-regions are found, these sub-regions are the children of the current region is the hierarchical segmentation; otherwise, the current region is a leaf node in the segmentation tree.

Figure 6 shows an example segmentation performed manually. This is an ideal segmentation, of course, but it demonstrates the objective of the segmentation algorithm. In practice, the program would segment further, but the depth of the segmentation is limited here for clarity.

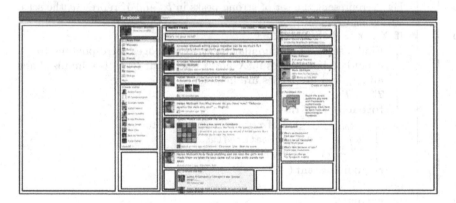

Fig. 6. Example of a manual segmentation (to a tree depth of 4) showing an ideal segmentation of a Facebook page

As in page segmentation for OCR (*e.g.* [3]), our objective is to produce a segmented page using only visual information, not code. This contrasts with typical approaches taken in web page segmentation systems (*e.g.* [4], [9]); even web page segmentation systems that use visual information typically apply bounding boxes and text properties derived from the HTML and CSS source code of the web page. Avoiding reliance on this information is intended to both ensure independence from underlying technologies (*e.g.* HTML, HTML 5, Flash, or Silverlight) and to more closely emulate the visual methods used by sighted users.

Our segmentation algorithm, representing the culmination of the methods described in this subsection, is displayed as Algorithm 2. It accepts as input an image of a rendered web page and outputs a segmentation tree of unlabelled regions in the page. The edge detection process is shown in context as part of the segmentation process.

Algorithm 2. Algorithm for producing a segmentation tree of a page image.

---

1 **Function Segment**(T)

    Input: Segmentation tree $T = (V, E)$

    Output: Segmentation tree $T' = (V', E')$

2   **foreach** $v \in V$ such that v is a leaf node **do**

3      $S_h \leftarrow v_{img} * K_h$;

4      $S_v \leftarrow v_{img} * K_v$;

5      $E_h(x, y) \leftarrow \begin{cases} 1 & S_h(x,y) \geq t \\ 0 & S_h(x,y) < t \end{cases}$;

6      $E_v(x, y) \leftarrow \begin{cases} 1 & S_v(x,y) \geq t \\ 0 & S_v(x,y) < t \end{cases}$;

7      $b_h(y) \leftarrow \sum_x E_h(x, y)$;

8      $b_v(x) \leftarrow \sum_y E_v(x, y)$;

9   Let X represent the set of strong peaks in b_v and Y represent the set of strong peaks in b_h ;

10   **if** $X \cup Y \neq \emptyset$ **then**

11   Find a set R of rectangular regions with edges corresponding to candidate boundaries in X and Y such that $C(R)$ is minimized and all required properties are maintained ;

12       $T' \leftarrow T$;

13   **foreach** $r \in R$ **do**

14         $w_{img} \leftarrow$ region of v_{img} corresponding to r ;

15         $w_{feat} \leftarrow$ **RegionFeatures**(w_{img}) ;

16         $T' \leftarrow (V' \cup \{w\}, E' \cup \{(v, w)\})$;

17   **return** **Segment**(T')

18   **else**

19   **return** T

2.2 Classification

After the web page has been segmented, the regions must be classified according to their semantic role in the page in order to present the structure of the page to the user in a comprehensible way. The classification system should have three key properties. First, the classifications of regions should account for their context in the page, not just the appearance of the specific region. Second, the structure of the classification should reflect the hierarchical structure of the segmented regions. Finally, the classification system should be flexible and adaptable to account for unusual web page designs. We propose to use a classification system based on a hidden Markov tree (HMT), a type of probabilistic graphical model originally developed for wavelet-domain signal processing [5]. Much like a hidden Markov model (HMM), an HMT contains two types of node: observations and hidden states. Whereas hidden states in an HMM have a simple sequence-based dependency structure, however, the hidden states in an HMT have a tree-based dependency structure. This model is depicted as a Bayesian network in Figure 7.

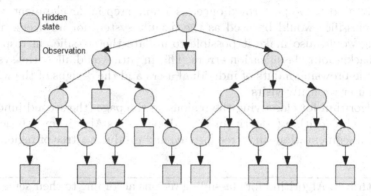

Fig. 7. A hidden Markov tree (HMT) with hidden states (circles) and observations (squares)

The tree structure of the hierarchical segmentation corresponds to the structure of the HMT. The hidden states in the HMT represent the labels of the regions in the segmentation, and the observations in the HMT represent feature vectors describing the regions.

Region labels should correspond to structures perceived by a human user—such as headers and sidebars—rather than plain structural descriptions such as "vertically-oriented container." This is critical because it is these classifications that will be used to generate the descriptions of the page layout that the user will use to navigate the page.

The choice of features used as observations in the HMT is critical to the success of the classification system. We propose to use a combination of visual features (colour and texture, for example) and position features. The visual features allow the system to distinguish between, for example, text and images. Position features allow the classification system to account for the broader context in which a region occurs.

The combination of visual features, position features, and the label of the parent region allow the classification system to respect broad patterns (which is similar to the rules used in Project ABBA [9]). Consider, for example, the case of a pattern consisting of a header, a left sidebar, and a body (as shown in Figure 1). There will be, *a priori*, a probability of $\frac{1}{3}$ that each child node will have the given pattern, but the observations of positions and sizes will clarify the matter: the left sidebar is on the left, the header at the top, and the body occupies a large percentage of the page. The observations, and the requirement that child regions be non-overlapping and jointly cover an entire parent region, capture dependencies among sibling regions, allowing the use of a simple HMT model for classification.

The classifier would be initially trained from a hand-labelled data set consisting of segmented web pages, since the web page source code would not reliably provide clear evidence of the semantic roles of regions. This training process would only need to be performed once, as a final step in development, and the resulting classifier would be used as the default system for all users. The use of learning would also make it possible to update the classifier in response to user feedback about classification errors. This in turn would allow the system to adapt to the browsing habits of individual users and the designs of the web sites that each user typically visits.

The algorithm for classifying the regions on the page (the second function in our high level algorithm (Algorithm 1)) is displayed as Algorithm 3. It accepts a hierarchical segmentation (in a tree format) and produces a tree of region labels.

Algorithm 3. Algorithm for classifying regions according to their semantic roles.

---

1 **Function Classify**(T)

    Input: Segmentation tree $T = (V, E)$
    Output: Classification tree $T' = (V', E')$

2   Let $H = (S, O, F)$ be an HMT, where S is the set of states, O is the set of observations, and F is the set of edges ;

3   For each node $v_i \in V$, let $s_i \in S$ represent the label of the region corresponding to v_i ;

4   For each node $v_i \in V$, let $o_i \in O$ represent the observations (extracted features) for v_i ;

5     $F \leftarrow \{(s_i, s_j) : (v_i, v_j) \in E\} \cup \{(s_k, o_k) : s_k \in S\}$;

6   Calculate the most likely set S' of states given the observations O and learned conditional probabilities ;

7     $T' \leftarrow (S', E)$ **return** T'

2.3 Reading

Robustness is the key concern in reading the page contents. When reading a block that has been identified as a text-containing block, the system will attempt to detect text in the image. When text has been found, the system attempts to match the text in the image of the block with text embedded in the page source code. A successful match allows the system to simply read the text found in the page source. If no match is found—for example, if the text is embedded in an image—the system can fall back to existing OCR techniques (see Figure 8).

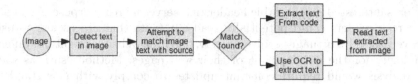

Fig. 8. Flow chart showing the output process

In use, the system would provide a brief description of the page to the user, who would select the region to read. If the region can be read immediately, the system does so; otherwise, the system describes the structure of the region to the user, who selects a sub-region to read. This continues until a simple text region is reached, which is then read to the user. Navigation of the page is in terms of the classified regions rather than in terms of the code hierarchy.

2.4 Next Steps

The choice of cost functions in segmentation is a significant outstanding question. A good cost function should reflect beliefs about the typical structure of a segmentation tree. It could be used to place approximate limits on the number of divisions at each step, encourage internal similarity within regions, or encourage regions to be of similar sizes. Empirical testing will be required to find an effective cost function.

The system presented here uses two stages—segmentation and classification—to produce the tree used to navigate the structure of the web page. It is worth considering if the labels determined at the classification stage could be used to modify the tree structure. This may allow the system to recover from a poor initial segmentation, increasing robustness and making the details of the segmentation cost function less important.

Practical issues such as implementation and interface design also merit further consideration. Integration with the web browser as an extension is a natural way to implement a screen reader system, although other options may be viable. The interface should be carefully designed to present information about page layout quickly (so that the user is not slowed down significantly) but clearly (so that the user can apply the information effectively). A method for selecting regions to read should also be quick and simple to use.

3 Discussion

There are various screen readers available today. Many of the existing screen readers such as ChromeVox [8] and VoiceOver [1] are based on the source code of web pages, i.e. HTML code, to retrieve the content of web pages. However, such a method has drawbacks. It is difficult to identify the main content solely based on source code. Some text under a "<div>" tag could be a meaningful sentence that a reader is interested in, or a table header that serves no real purpose. As a result, such screen readers could potentially read out texts that are useless to users. Moreover, as web languages evolve quickly, different websites might use different technologies for the development of their web pages. Methods such as source code analysis would require constant updates to comply with new standards, which is not scalable. Also, many web pages today support dynamically loaded content using scripting languages such as Javascript. Content generated by these scripts may not be found in the HTML source code which limits the usability of such methods.

Our solution differs from the above mentioned method in two areas. First of all, our solution is mainly based on the layout of a web page to identify where the main content is. This is similar to how humans interpret a web page when he or she sees it. Users see a web page as merely an image with static objects. They can quickly identify where useful information is by decomposing the image into segments. This is the aim of our solution: by using techniques such as edge detection, our solution divides a web page into regions, providing a clear indication of the semantic structure of the page. This helps label regions on the page. For example, once the main content area is identified, the user can tell the program to read out only the content from the main section using, for instance, a keyboard shortcut. This has significant advantages over existing screen readers. Many existing screen readers do not discriminate contents of different regions and they often read out the entire page. From a user's perspective, this is not appropriate because many web pages have the same header across multiple pages. Reading out these contents every time a user visits a web page is redundant. Furthermore, labelling the regions on pages can help users navigate through the website. For example once a left side bar is identified, a user can tell the program to read out the left bar so that he can interact with the links on the page.

Another area of difference our solution has over existing methods is that we use a visual model for segmenting the page and classifying regions. This more closely resembles the way in which a sighted user perceives a web page. Since web pages are often designed specifically for sighted users, we believe that this is a significant advantage over existing screen reader software.

In ChromeVox, a user needs to navigate the code hierarchy to the desired content in order to reach the information he or she is interested in [8] [11]. On the contrary, our solution does not search for content based on a code hierarchy, but rather makes use of computer vision techniques to jump directly to the content inside the code. Another common screen reader is Apple's VoiceOver. This screen reader is natively built into Mac OSX, and iOS devices [1]. This screen reader performs well on native applications, in part because Apple can couple the development of their products with the VoiceOver application, ensuring the output is up to specification. However, on the web, where content is not controlled by Apple, VoiceOver may not perform as well. Basing the OCR output on source code also has the challenge of trying to offer a coherent depiction for users. An example of this problem can be seen in the demonstration performed by Youtube user "kwhawell" [10]. This demonstration of Apple's VoiceOver system compares the fairly good performance on Facebook's simple mobile web site to the poor performance on the sophisticated desktop version. On the desktop version, VoiceOver jumps between regions which appear visually distinct and it is difficult to reach the status update form field. Our vision-based system, on the other hand, would be able to reflect the visual organization of the page in the structure it generates for navigation.

Project ABBA [12] has produced screen reader software that uses the visual properties of web site regions. Our system differs in its approach in the following areas:

- Our system is designed specifically to handle content presented in formats other than HTML and CSS gracefully, rather than to rely on the page source code.
- Our system is designed to reproduce the experience of sighted uses insofar as that is possible, rather than using a specialized navigation model.
- Our system uses a learned probabilistic graphical model to classify blocks in the page rather than manually-defined rules; this allows online learning to adapt the system to individual users' browsing habits

These differences make our approach complementary to existing work.

The primary disadvantage of our solution is speed. Vision algorithms can be computationally intensive [7], and a complete web page corresponds to a very large image. This disadvantage is mitigated by the increasing speed of modern hardware, however, so this need not be a fatal flaw. Web pages that rely on animation or the use of large numbers of complex images may confuse the segmentation algorithm, although web pages where images and animations dominate text content are less likely to be useful to visually-impaired users in any case.

It is important to note that our design was inspired by certain existing research on segmentation and classification for information retrieval and optical character recognition, though there as well some fundamental differences. Page segmentation methods in OCR—as in the system proposed by Cesarini *et al.* [3]—are designed to divide the page into regions suitable as input for the OCR algorithm, not input suitable for a human navigating the page. These segmentation algorithms do not need to label regions. Information retrieval methods (such as the system described by Chen, Zhong, and Cook [4] based on a generalized hidden Markov model), in contrast, produce very fined-grained segmentations and classifications which isolate specific fields and values (such as phone numbers or prices) for an automated system. The goal of web page segmentation for human users is distinct; unlike segmentation for OCR, regions must be labelled, and the desired labelled regions are coarser and at a higher level than for IR methods.

4   Conclusion

We believe that the visual structure of a rendered web page is the most natural source of information about the large-scale organization of information in the web page, since the rendered page is designed to be easy to interpret visually. We believe that our proposed method can provide a significant advantage over screen readers that do not use visual information. Furthermore, our approach differs in many respects from existing work to develop a screen reader which uses visual information. Because our system has minimal reliance on the semantics of the page source code, it can readily handle new web technologies without fundamental changes to the system itself.

Next steps with this research include proceeding with a validation. We envisage a user study, for example comparing the proposed method with a direct translation of webpages (e.g. VoiceOver [1]), as one component. We are also interested in more detailed specification of the execution times of the proposed method and its inherent computational complexity.

Future work may also include extending the method to user interfaces other than web pages (such as office software interfaces) and providing finer-grained control over the types of information the system uses. Other valuable directions for future work include providing more opportunities for personalized solutions for users and investigating in greater depth the specific needs that arise in social networking environments, such as Facebook, with a large number of messages. As the users who are interested in our proposed framework may have varying levels of sight, the output that we produce may possibly be complementary to existing displays (rather than replacing them entirely). It would be interesting to enable users to specify certain subsets of content that they would like to serve as the input to our algorithms. In addition, if users can indicate which elements they are not particularly interested in, the output that is delivered from our system can be reduced. User preferences may also motivate an extension to our system, where the visual representation driving our production of output is first of all cast in terms that focus best on what the user is most interested in knowing about. As for additional exploration of the context of social networks, we can imagine that social networks may evolve over time in order to be more welcoming of visually impaired participants; we may be able to propose certain adjustments to the gathering of information streams in these networks, to then proceed from these representations to more effective output for our users.

References

1. Apple: Apple - accessibility - OS x - VoiceOver. http://www.apple.com/accessibility/osx/voiceover/ (accessed March 16, 2014)
2. Castleman, K.R.: Digital Image Processing, chap. 18. Prentice Hall (1996)
3. Cesarini, F., Gori, M., Marinai, S., Soda, G.: Structured document segmentation and representation by the modified x-y tree. In: Proceedings of the Fifth International Conference on Document Analysis and Recognition. ICDAR 1999, pp. 563–566, September 1999
4. Chen, J., Zhong, P., Cook, T.: Detecting web content function using generalized hidden markov model. In: 5th International Conference on Machine Learning and Applications. ICMLA 2006, pp. 279–284, December 2006

5. Crouse, M., Baraniuk, R., Nowak, R.: Hidden markov models for wavelet-based signal processing. In: Conference Record of the Thirtieth Asilomar Conference on Signals, Systems and Computers, pp. 1029–1035, vol. 2, November 1996
6. Fayzrahmanov, R.R., Göbel, M.C., Holzinger, W., Krüpl, B., Baumgartner, R.: A unified ontology-based web page model for improving accessibility. In: Proceedings of the 19th International Conference on World Wide Web. WWW 2010, pp. 1087–1088. ACM, New York (2010). http://doi.acm.org/10.1145/1772690.1772817
7. Forsyth, D.A., Ponce, J.: Computer vision: a modern approach. Prentice Hall Professional Technical Reference
8. Google: ChromeVox. http://www.chromevox.com/ (accessed March 16, 2014)
9. Krüpl-Sypien, B., Fayzrakhmanov, R.R., Holzinger, W., Panzenböck, M., Baumgartner, R.: A versatile model for web page representation, information extraction and content re-packaging. In: Proceedings of the 11th ACM Symposium on Document Engineering. DocEng 2011, pp. 129–138. ACM, New York (2011). http://doi.acm.org/10.1145/2034691.2034721
10. "kwhawell": introducing a screen reader what it is how it works (2010). https://www.youtube.com/watch?v=mklnYoge7pk (accessed June 16, 2014)
11. Raman, T.V., Chen, C.L., Mazzoni, D., Shearer, R., Gharpure, C., DeBoer, J., Tseng, D.: Chromevox a screen reader built using web technology. Google technical report (2012). http://google-axs-chrome.googlecode.com/svn-history/r165/trunk/developer/chromevox-overview-2012/paper.pdf
12. TUWIEN Database and Artificial Intelligence Group: TUWIEN Project ABBA: Web Accessibility. http://www.dbai.tuwien.ac.at/proj/ABBA/ (accessed June 4, 2014)

Calculating Reachable Workspace Volume for Use in Quantitative Medicine

Robert Peter Matthew[1]([✉]), Gregorij Kurillo[1],
Jay J. Han[2], and Ruzena Bajcsy[1]

[1] Department of Electrical Engineering and Computer Science,
University of California, Berkeley, Berkeley, CA, USA
{rpmatthew,gregorij,bajcsy}@eecs.berkeley.edu
[2] Department of Physical Medicine and Rehabilitation, University of California,
Davis, Sacramento, CA, USA
jay.han@ucdmc.ucdavis.edu

Abstract. Quantitative measures of the space an individual can reach is essential for tracking the progression of a disease and the effects of therapeutic intervention. The reachable workspace can be used to track an individuals' ability to perform activities of daily living, such as feeding and grooming. There are few methods for quantifying upper limb performance, none of which are able to generate a reachable workspace volume from motion capture data. We introduce a method to estimate the reachable workspace volume for an individual by capturing their observed joint limits using a low cost depth camera. This method is then tested on seven individuals with varying upper limb performance. Based on these initial trials, we found that the reachable workspace volume decreased as muscular impairment increased. This shows the potential for this method to be used as a quantitative clinical assessment tool.

Keywords: Kinect · Muscular dystrophy · Functional workspace · Rehabilitation · Assessment · Diagnosis · Goniometry · Skeletal modelling

1 Introduction

Injury to the skeletal and muscular structure of an individual can occur through a variety of conditions ranging from traumatic accidents to genetic disorders. Monitoring the improvement of an individual's performance through medical treatments such as pharmaceuticals and rehabilitation, as well as tracking degeneration are key for customising medical treatment to an individual.

Traditional methods to track an individual's performance often relies on a series of qualitative tests administered by a clinical evaluator. These can range from recording the time to complete a specific task, to questionnaires and scored worksheets that measure quality of life.

However, a majority of these measures have focused on lower limb function, measuring an individual's performance when walking and climbing stairs.

© Springer International Publishing Switzerland 2015
L. Agapito et al. (Eds.): ECCV 2014 Workshops, Part III, LNCS 8927, pp. 570–583, 2015.
DOI: 10.1007/978-3-319-16199-0_40

There are relatively few methods for evaluating upper limb function, even though the upper limbs are critical for basic self-care activities. These activities are known as *Activities for Daily Living* or ADLs, and cover feeding, grooming, dressing and toileting care. Additionally, the need for quantitative measures for the upper limbs that are practical to implement, intuitive and scalable, has been echoed by medical practitioners.

We introduce a novel technique to quantify, the space an individual can reach using low cost sensing. By capturing an individual's upper limb motions while performing a set of arm movements that encompass cardinal shoulder range of motion, we introduce a method for creating an individualised skeleton, allowing calculation of their range of motion about each joint. These joint constraints are then used to find the region of space that the individual should be able to reach, centered at the shoulder. We call this the reachable workspace of the individual. Both the joint bounds and the volume of this reachable workspace, can be quantified and may act as usable clinical measures.

We evaluate the efficacy of these measures on a control population as well as a set of patients suffering from a degenerative neuromuscular disorder, comparing our measures to those typically used.

2 Related Work

Traditional methods for assessing limb function look at goniometry [1,2], muscle strength tests [3,4], clinical motor function scoring methods such as the Brooke, DASH and Fugl-Meyer scales [5-8] and performance based measures such as the 'nine hole peg test' and 'six minute walk test' [9-12].

The introduction of the Kinect depth camera [13] allowed for low cost, markerless motion capture with skeletal tracking. It has been used for goniometry [14,15] and tested against other motion capture devices to check its suitability for use as a clinical tool [16,17]. This has led to its use for rehabilitation measurement and exercise monitoring [18-23].

The reachable workspace of an individual has been measured for use in ergonomic design [24-26]. It has been extended for use as a clinical measure by combining it with traditional goniometry measures [27,28] and motion capture systems [29-32]. We extend this work by performing automated skeletal and goniometric measurements of the upper limb using the Kinect sensor, and calculating to creating a reachable workspace volume.

3 Mathematical Framework

In this section we introduce the mathematical tools we will use for recovering reachable workspace volume. We use techniques taken from robotics and computer graphics literature, particularly work in kinematic chains, state estimation and computational geometry [33,34]. Our method builds on the intuition that for every movement of the human arm, there is corresponding set of joint angles that describe this motion. By finding the bounds of these joint angles, we find the corresponding reachable volume in the world frame.

3.1   Kinematic Chains, Maps and Spaces

To build up the framework to describe these operations, we construct a kinematic chain that describes the arm. A kinematic chain is a set of rigid bodies, connected together by joints. Consider, the planar kinematic chain shown in Figure 1a. This chain comprises of two links, and two joints labelled J_j for $j \in [1, n]$ where n is the number of joints in the system.

We will perform our analysis based on the mappings between three separate spaces: configuration space $\mathcal{C}$, workspace $\mathcal{W}$ and outputspace $\mathcal{O}$. Our configuration space $\mathcal{C}$, is the space of all potential joint states. In our example, it is the set of angles $\theta_j \in [-\pi, +\pi]$ for $j \in [1, n]$.

For every combination of these joint angles, there is a corresponding (x, y) position of the kinematic chain. The mapping from the configuration space to the Cartesian space is given by the *forward kinematic map*, $f(\bar{\eta}, \boldsymbol{q})$ where $\bar{\eta}$ are the kinematic parameters of the model (such as joint lengths) and $\boldsymbol{q}$ is a vector of joint states. The image of f the workspace of the manipulator, denoted $\mathcal{W}$.

The manipulator workspace is contained in a larger 'output space' $\mathcal{O}$ which is the ambient space of smallest dimension that contains the workspace. We denote the m dimensional output space as $\mathcal{O}(m)$. In our example, we can take m as being either 2 or 3. $\mathcal{O}(2)$ would correspond to planar motion without orientation information $(\mathbb{R}^2)$, while $\mathcal{O}(3)$ would correspond to planar motion with orientation information $(\mathbb{R}^2 \times SO(2))$.

The relationship between the configuration, work and output spaces and the forward kinematic map can therefore be summarised by the statement:

$$f(\bar{\eta}, \boldsymbol{q}) : \mathcal{C} \to \mathcal{W} \in \mathcal{O}$$

3.2   Constrained Kinematic Chains

In our previous example, we took each joint to be perfectly revolute with its domain being the circle. We now restrict the state of each joint J_j to remain in the bounded interval $[\underline{q}_j, \overline{q}_j]$ such that every state $q_j \in [\underline{q}_j, \overline{q}_j]$ for $j \in [1, n]$. We do this for both revolute and prismatic joints constructing $\boldsymbol{Q} \in \mathbb{R}^{n \times 2}$ an array containing the bounds of each joint such that $\boldsymbol{Q}_j = [\underline{q}_j, \overline{q}_j]$.

Under the assumption that these joint bounds are capable of completely characterising the reachable workspace, we can generate a set of feasible joint angles that lie within our configuration space. For every vector $\boldsymbol{q}_r \in \mathcal{C}$, we can say:

$$\boldsymbol{q}_r = [q_{1,r}, q_{2,r}, \ldots q_{j,r}, \ldots q_{n,r}] \text{ such that } q_{j,r} \in [\underline{q}_{j,r}, \overline{q}_{j,r}]$$

We can then use our forward kinematic map to relate a point $\boldsymbol{q}_r \in \mathcal{C}$ to a point $y_r \in \mathcal{O}$.

We make the assumption that as this point satisfies our joint bounds, it lies within our valid configuration space. This means that the point y_r is a valid point in our workspace $\mathcal{W}$.

Returning to our example, we can sample 1,000 feasible points in our output space (Figure 1b)) by mapping 1,000 feasible points from our configuration space. Alpha shapes [35] can be generated for these points allowing the non-convex hull of these points to be found as shown in Figure 1c.

To compare the validity of this method, we compare our recovered workspace to one that has been created analytically[34, 36]. While the analytical solution is the ideal solution that we wish to find, the calculation becomes non-trivial for larger more complicated kinematic chains leading to use of our sampling based method.

4 Methodology

In this section, we outline the methods we used to build a skeleton for the individual and estimate the states and joint ranges for an observed motion.

We initially capture the actions of an individual performing actions relevant to ADLs. From this, we extract a kinematic model that captures the skeletal lengths and the joint range of motion. We then show how we estimate the workspace and reachable volume using these joint bounds.

4.1 Motion Capture

For our experiments, we used a Kinect depth camera to track the motions of an individual. We used the Microsoft Kinect SDK to extract the positions of several key points including the position of the head, shoulders, elbows, wrists and hips. The motion of the upper arm was recorded while the subject performed a set of prescribed movements. The 3D Cartesian coordinates for each of these points in the world frame were captured and stored.

4.2 Skeletonisation

To perform our analysis, we require a kinematic chain model of the upper arms. We used the coordinate convention outlined by the International Society of Biomechanics [37] to define a set of axes for the upper arm. This was then used to make a kinematic model of the upper arm (Figure 2).

The final model is a seven Degree of Freedom (DoF) chain, with the Glenohumeral (Gh) joint floating in space. The 6 DoF pose of the Gh centre represents the first six states in our state configuration vector q. Our final state q_7 is the rotation of the Humeroulnar (Hu) joint.

This model requires two kinematic parameters- the length between the Gh and Hu joints and the length between the Hu and wrist. These lengths were taken to be the average length between the shoulder and elbow, and elbow and wrist respectively from the Kinect dataset. Given these two parameters the position of the shoulder, elbow and wrist are functions of the seven states q.

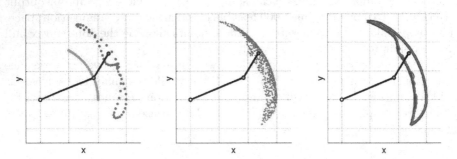

Fig. 1. Our methodology applied to a simple two link pantograph robot. Left: the robot performs an action, and the positions of the middle and end link are recorded (green and red points respectively). The joint angles corresponding to these points are found and then used to find the joint limits. Middle: These joint limits are used to find 1,000 feasible points in the output space (red). Right: The alpha-shape of these points is then found and taken to be the reachable workspace (red). This is compared to the reachable workspace calculated analytically (blue).

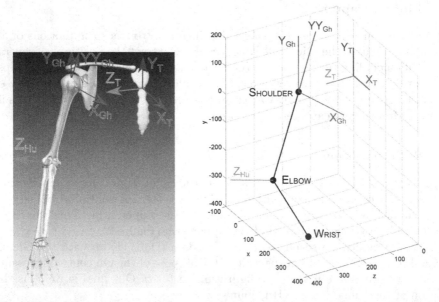

Fig. 2. Left: ISB recommendations on definitions of joint coordinates and rotational axes. Skeletal model generated using Biodigital Human[38]. Right: Our Kinematic model for the upper limbs. Y_{Gh} is parallel to Y_T, while YY_{Gh} runs parallel to the humerus. Location of the rotational centre of the Gh joint is given in Thorax (T) coordinates. Rotational pose of the Humerus is based on a Y-X-Y rotational sequence about Y_{GH}-X_{GH}-YY_{GH}. Rotation about the Hu joint is about the Hu_Z axis.

4.3 State Estimation

To capture the joint parameters of the individual, we need to find the observed range of states q. However the Kinect only provides (noisy) shoulder, elbow and wrist positions. Given these observed trajectories $y(t)$, we wish to find the corresponding state trajectories $q(t)$.

To do this, we used an Unscented Kalman Filter (UKF) [39,40] to reconstruct the joint angles from the tracked data points [41]. Given a dynamic and observation model along with uncertainty parameters, this method can be used to estimate the state of a dynamic system. The UKF takes a discrete dynamical model of the form:

$$q_{k+1} = F(q_k, v_k)$$

with the observation equation:

$$y_k = H(q_k, w_k)$$

Ordinarily, we would create a dynamical system model for F, encapsulating the masses, inertias and torques being applied to the system. However in a biological system, this is often not known a priori. While tabulated values could be used as an estimate, the masses and inertias of body segments may vary heavily with medical pathology. Similarly, joint torque estimation is non-trivial, often requiring extensive musculoskeletal modelling.

Instead we drive our dynamical system with a random walk process, modelling the higer order dynamics as an Independent and Identically Distributed (I.I.D.) process [41].

In this manner we have a system model that will estimate our joint states q_k based on our observed measurements y_{1-k}. In our experiments y is a $\mathbb{R}^{r \times 9}$ vector where r is the total number of samples, and our nine columns represent the Cartesian coordinates for the shoulder, elbow and wrist.

The UKF was run recursively on the Kinect dataset, removing segments of unreliable data. Data was deemed to be unreliable if the instantaneous change in angle exceeded 2 radians between two consecutive samples. The UKF was then reinitialised after this removal of data using the previous state values as the new starting guess.

The recovered state values were then passed through a zero-phase 3rd order lowpass Butterworth filter[42] with a normalised cutoff frequency of 0.1.

The maximum and minimum values $(\underline{q}_j, \overline{q}_j)$ for each joint j were calculated and stored as in the bounding matrix Q.

4.4 Workspace Generation

Using these bounds, we can create random joint angles respecting the bounds via an I.I.D. process. In this manner, we generate 10,000 sample points in configuration space $(q^{7 \times 10,000})$, which were then mapped into 10,000 wrist positions in our output space $(y^{3 \times 10,000})$.

While these points marked out valid regions in our workspace, we require a volumetric measurement of our reachable workspace. Using this point cloud of feasible workspace points, we used alpha-shapes[35] to create a non-convex hull marked out by this sampled data. The enclosed volume of this hull was then used as our recovered reachable workspace volume.

5   Experimental Validation

To evaluate the validity of this method, we recorded Kinect joint positions for both pathological and control test subjects. We outline our subject population and the experimental procedure and show the results from our method.

5.1   Experimental Population

Four patients diagnosed with Facioscapulohumeral muscular dystrophy (FSHD) and three healthy controls participated in this initial study. FSHD patients were diagnosed based on confirmed genetic analysis as fully described in [32]. Healthy control subjects without any musculoskeletal disorders were recruited through an approved Institutional Review Board (IRB) protocol. Consent was obtained prior to the study for all participants or their guardians and was documented via an IRB approved consent form.

FSHD is a genetic disease of skeletal muscle that stereotypically affects the skeletal muscles of the face and the shoulder girdle. Symptoms begin in early childhood with proximal upper limb muscle impairment, and progress through the teenage years. Life expectancy is unaffected, but often results in severe disabilities eventually requiring wheelchair use.

Current methods of assessing FSHD are the Brooke scale, a specific FSHD scale, shoulder-elbow strength measurements, 9-hole pegboard tests, and quality of life questionnaires. Of these, the Brooke scale is one of the most commonly used and will be used as our measure of comparison.

5.2   Experimental Procedure

Participants in the study were asked to perform a series of motions that marked out key points of their workspace. They were asked to touch six points on their body, the left and right sides of their hips, their left and right shoulders, their mouth and the top of their head while being monitored by a Kinect camera. These actions were chosen as it covers areas necessary for ADLs such as eating, grooming and toileting and covers motion in clinically relevant planes. Each pathological participant was also given a Brooke score by the study clinical evaluator.

5.3   Reachable Volume Results

We used our method for reconstructing the reachable workspace and calculating the reachable volume, one each of our participants. The results of these trials are shown in Table 1, with graphical depictions of these workspaces for a healthy subject and a subject with progressed FSHD shown in Figures 3-6.

Table 1. Comparison of computed reachable volume and Brooke Score

Subject	Reachable Volume (m^3)	Brooke Score (unitless)
Healthy 1	3.74×10^{-1}	-
Healthy 2	3.28×10^{-1}	-
Healthy 3	2.34×10^{-1}	-
Patient 1	3.58×10^{-1}	1
Patient 2	2.70×10^{-1}	2
Patient 3	1.78×10^{-1}	3
Patient 4	1.48×10^{-3}	5

6   Discussion

From the results shown in Table 1, we can see that as the Brooke score increases (showing increasing disability), the computed reachable volume decreases. Patients with low levels of disability have reachable volumes on par with that of the healthy individuals.

Looking qualitatively at the reachable workspace for the healthy and impaired subjects (Figures 3-6), we can see that there are distinct changes in the shape of the reachable workspace with change in Brooke score.

The reachable workspace for the healthy individual matches the reachable workspaces seen in previous studies [27]. The reachable space respects observed

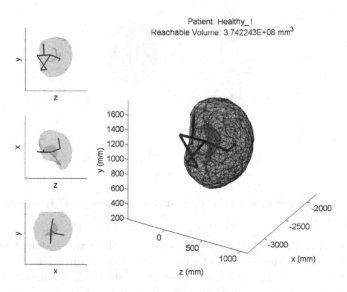

Fig. 3. Reachable workspace for a healthy subject. Upper extremities are shown in wire-frame with the reachable workspace shown in blue. Plane projected views are shown on the left.

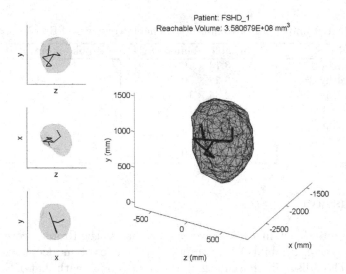

Fig. 4. Reachable workspace for Patient 1 with mild FSHD (Brooke 1)

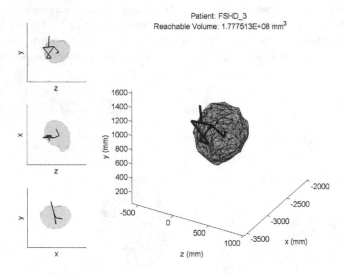

Fig. 5. Reachable workspace for Patient 3 with moderate FSHD (Brooke 3)

physiological limitations; the wrist is unable to contact the shoulder centre and there is a section of space behind the individual that is unreachable.

As the Brooke score increases, the computed reachable workspace decreases. This decrease is seen most notably in the vertical (y) direction, with the workspace no longer reaching the top of the head in Figure 5, and being level with the waist in Figure 6. This gives an indication of what is and is not possible for the individual suggesting which patients are able to perform which ADLs.

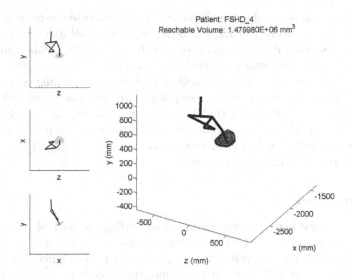

Fig. 6. Reachable workspace for patient 4 with severe FSHD (Brooke 5)

While the population size used is small, it does suggest that our quantified measure *reachable workspace volume* may be an effective method for assessing patients with FSHD and various other neuromusculoskeletal conditions, potentially characterising performance at a higher fidelity than existing methods.

6.1 Limitations

There are a number of important limitations in both our method and experimental procedure.

To generate our estimate of the reachable workspace, we make two assumptions. The first is that each joint can be taken to be independent of another. The second assumption is that the workspace is only limited by these joint bounds. These are two significant simplifications of a true system. In biological musculoskeletal structures, there are *biarticular* muscles whereby muscles span several joints. As the total length of this muscle is limited, the angles of the joints that it spans are related to each other. Similarly the shoulder complex has a number of physical constraints of the pose of the Gh centre with respect to the torso. Our second assumption works under the premise that the joint bounds can completely characterise the reachable workspace. Any workspace reduction due to muscle weakness is characterised by the respective joint angles and is independent of end point position.

We also assume that an individual reaches their joint limits when performing the motion capture task. The computed results for our healthy subjects may suggest that these joint limits were not seen, resulting in lower than expected reachable volumes.

Furthermore, these reachable volumes were not scaled to the individual. Individuals with longer arms will have a larger reachable volume given the same joint limitations. This makes the comparison between individuals using a non-normalised reachable volume potentially misleading.

Finally this is a sampling based method that relies on finding representative workspace points through random sampling. This process is computationally taxing, and does not guarantee that the found volume will accurately describe the true workspace. While the method provided representative results when compared to the analytical solution in our planar example (Figure 1), this performance needs to be accurately evaluated.

6.2   Future Work

The work presented here represents our initial findings as part of a larger study. We seek to apply these methods to a larger population set, within the FSHD community as well as for evaluating rehabilitative performance. Furthermore, the repeatability and reliability of these measures needs to be investigated as well as comparison to the conventional methods for clinical assessment.

In our method we calculated joint bounds Q that were used to represent an individuals' abilities. The study of how these angles vary with FSHD progression, as well as creating assessment measures that combine both joint angle and reachable volume may help to further quantify performance.

7   Appendix

7.1   Brooke Scale

The Brooke Scale can be summarised as showing in Table 2.

Table 2. Brooke Scoring for the Upper Limbs[5]

Brooke Score	Description
1	Starting with arms at sides, abduct arms in a full circle until they touch above the head.
2	Can raise arms above head only by shortening the arc of motion or using accessory muscles.
3	Cannot raise hands above head but can raise an 8oz. glass/cup of water to mouth (using both hands if necessary).
4	Can raise hands to mouth but cannot raise an 8 oz. glass/cup of water to mouth.
5	Cannot raise hand to mouth but can use hands to hold pen or pick up pennies from table.
6	Cannot raise hands to mouth and has no useful function of hands.

References

1. Gajdosik, R.L., Bohannon, R.W.: Clinical measurement of range of motion: Review of goniometry emphasizing reliability and validity. Physical Therapy **67**(12), 1867–1872 (1987)
2. Macedo, L.G., Magee, D.J.: Differences in range of motion between dominant and non-dominant sides of upper and lower extremities. Journal of manipulative and physiological therapeutics **31**(8), 577–582 (2008)
3. Bohannon, R.: Manual muscle test scores and dynamometer test scores of knee extension strength. Archives of physical medicine and rehabilitation **67**(6), 390–392 (1986)
4. Escolar, D., Henricson, E., Mayhew, J., Florence, J., Leshner, R., Patel, K., Clemens, P.: Clinical evaluator reliability for quantitative and manual muscle testing measures of strength in children. Muscle & nerve **24**(6), 787–793 (2001)
5. Brooke, M.H., Griggs, R.C., Mendell, J.R., Fenichel, G.M., Shumate, J.B., Pellegrino, R.J.: Clinical trial in duchenne dystrophy. i. the design of the protocol. Muscle & nerve **4**(3), 186–197 (1981)
6. Beaton, D.E., Katz, J.N., Fossel, A.H., Wright, J.G., Tarasuk, V., Bombardier, C.: Measuring the whole or the parts?: Validity, reliability, and responsiveness of the disabilities of the arm, shoulder and hand outcome measure in different regions of the upper extremity. Journal of Hand Therapy **14**(2), 128–142 (2001). The Outcome Issue
7. Lamperti, C., Fabbri, G., Vercelli, L., D'Amico, R., Frusciante, R., Bonifazi, E., Fiorillo, C., Borsato, C., Cao, M., Servida, M., et al.: A standardized clinical evaluation of patients affected by facioscapulohumeral muscular dystrophy: The fshd clinical score. Muscle & nerve **42**(2), 213–217 (2010)
8. Fugl-Meyer, A.R., Jääskö, L., Leyman, I., Olsson, S., Steglind, S.: The post-stroke hemiplegic patient. 1. a method for evaluation of physical performance. Scandinavian journal of rehabilitation medicine **7**(1), 13–31 (1974)
9. Mathiowetz, V., Weber, K., Kashman, N., Volland, G.: Adult norms for the nine hole peg test of finger dexterity. Occupational Therapy Journal of Research (1985)
10. Sharpless, J.: The nine hole peg test of finger hand coordination for the hemiplegic patient. Mossman's A Problem Orientated Approach to Stroke Rehabilitation (1982)
11. Duncan, P.W., Weiner, D.K., Chandler, J., Studenski, S.: Functional reach: A new clinical measure of balance. Journal of Gerontology **45**(6), M192–M197 (1990)
12. Enright, P.L.: The six-minute walk test. Respiratory care **48**(8), 783–785 (2003)
13. Zhang, Z.: Microsoft kinect sensor and its effect. IEEE MultiMedia **19**(2), 4–10 (2012)
14. Bo, A., Hayashibe, M., Poignet, P., et al.: Joint angle estimation in rehabilitation with inertial sensors and its integration with kinect. In: EMBC 2011: 33rd Annual International Conference of the IEEE Engineering in Medicine and Biology Society, pp. 3479–3483 (2011)
15. Fern'ndez-Baena, A., Susin, A., Lligadas, X.: Biomechanical validation of upper-body and lower-body joint movements of kinect motion capture data for rehabilitation treatments. In: 2012 4th International Conference on Intelligent Networking and Collaborative Systems (INCoS), pp. 656–661, September 2012
16. Chang, C.Y., Lange, B., Zhang, M., Koenig, S., Requejo, P., Somboon, N., Sawchuk, A., Rizzo, A.: Towards pervasive physical rehabilitation using microsoft kinect. In: 2012 6th International Conference on Pervasive Computing Technologies for Healthcare (PervasiveHealth), pp. 159–162, May 2012

17. Khoshelham, K., Elberink, S.O.: Accuracy and resolution of kinect depth data for indoor mapping applications. Sensors 12(2), 1437–1454 (2012)
18. Chang, Y.J., Chen, S.F., Huang, J.D.: A kinect-based system for physical rehabilitation: A pilot study for young adults with motor disabilities. Research in Developmental Disabilities 32(6), 2566–2570 (2011)
19. Lange, B., Chang, C.Y., Suma, E., Newman, B., Rizzo, A., Bolas, M.: Development and evaluation of low cost game-based balance rehabilitation tool using the microsoft kinect sensor. In: 2011 Annual International Conference of the IEEE Engineering in Medicine and Biology Society, EMBC, pp. 1831–1834, August 2011
20. Lange, B., Koenig, S., McConnell, E., Chang, C., Juang, R., Suma, E., Bolas, M., Rizzo, A.: Interactive game-based rehabilitation using the microsoft kinect. In: Virtual Reality Short Papers and Posters (VRW), pp. 171–172, 2012 IEEE, March 2012
21. Pastor, I., Hayes, H., Bamberg, S.: A feasibility study of an upper limb rehabilitation system using kinect and computer games. In: Engineering in Medicine and Biology Society (EMBC), 2012 Annual International Conference of the IEEE, pp. 1286–1289, August 2012
22. Uzor, S., Baillie, L.: Exploring & designing tools to enhance falls rehabilitation in the home. In: Proceedings of the SIGCHI Conference on Human Factors in Computing Systems. CHI 2013, pp. 1233–1242. ACM, New York (2013)
23. Anton, D., Goni, A., Illarramendi, A., Torres-Unda, J., Seco, J.: Kires: A kinect-based telerehabilitation system. In: 2013 IEEE 15th International Conference on e-Health Networking, Applications Services (Healthcom), pp. 444–448, October 2013
24. Li, S., Xi, Z.: The measurement of functional arm reach envelopes for young chinese males. Ergonomics 33(7), 967–978 (1990)
25. Book, A.S.: Vol. 1: Anthropometry for designers. NASA Reference Publication 1024 (1978)
26. Sengupta, A.K., Das, B.: Maximum reach envelope for the seated and standing male and female for industrial workstation design. Ergonomics 43(9), 1390–1404 (2000)
27. Klopčar, N., Lenarčič, J.: Kinematic model for determination of human arm reachable workspace. Meccanica 40(2), 203–219 (2005)
28. Klopčar, N., Tomšič, M., Lenarčič, J.: A kinematic model of the shoulder complex to evaluate the arm-reachable workspace. Journal of biomechanics 40(1), 86–91 (2007)
29. Kurillo, G., Han, J.J., Obdržálek, S., Yan, P., Abresch, R.T., Nicorici, A., Bajcsy, R.: Upper extremity reachable workspace evaluation with kinect. In: MMVR, pp. 247–253 (2013)
30. Kurillo, G., Han, J., Nicorici, A., Johnson, L., Abresch, R., Henricson, E., McDonald, C., Bajcsy, R.: Upper extremity reachable workspace evaluation in DMD using kinect. Neuromuscular Disorders 23(910), 749–750 (2013). 18th International Congress of The World Muscle Society
31. Kurillo, G., Chen, A., Bajcsy, R., Han, J.J.: Evaluation of upper extremity reachable workspace using kinect camera. Technology and Health Care 21(6), 641–656 (2013)
32. Han, J.J., Kurillo, G., Abresch, R.T., de Bie, E., Nicorici, A., Bajcsy, R.: Reachable workspace in facioscapulohumeral muscular dystrophy (fshd) by kinect. Muscle & nerve (2014)
33. Siciliano, B., Khatib, O.: Springer Handbook of Robotics. Springer (2008)

34. Khalil, W., Dombre, E.: Modeling. Butterworth-Heinemann, Identification and Control of Robots (2004)
35. Edelsbrunner, H., Mücke, E.P.: Three-dimensional alpha shapes. ACM Trans. Graph. **13**(1), 43–72 (1994)
36. Burdick, J.W.: Kinematic Analysis and Design of Redundant Robot Manipulators. PhD thesis, Stanford University (1988)
37. Wu, G., Van Der Helm, F.C., Veeger, H., Makhsous, M., Van Roy, P., Anglin, C., Nagels, J., Karduna, A.R., McQuade, K., Wang, X., et al.: Isb recommendation on definitions of joint coordinate systems of various joints for the reporting of human joint motionpart ii: Shoulder, elbow, wrist and hand. Journal of biomechanics **38**(5), 981–992 (2005)
38. Biodigital: Biodigital human (06 2014)
39. Julier, S.J., Uhlmann, J.K.: A new extension of the kalman filter to nonlinear systems. In: Int. symp. aerospace/defense sensing, simul. and controls. vol. 3, pp. 3–2, Orlando (1997)
40. Wan, E.A., Van Der Merwe, R.: The unscented kalman filter for nonlinear estimation. In: Adaptive Systems for Signal Processing, Communications, and Control Symposium 2000. AS-SPCC. The IEEE 2000, pp. 153–158. IEEE (2000)
41. Ziegler, J., Nickel, K., Stiefelhagen, R.: Tracking of the articulated upper body on multi-view stereo image sequences. In: 2006 IEEE Computer Society Conference on Computer Vision and Pattern Recognition, vol. 1, pp. 774–781, June 2006
42. Butterworth, S.: On the theory of filter amplifiers. Wireless Engineer **7**, 536–541 (1930)

A Benchmark Dataset to Study
the Representation of Food Images

Giovanni Maria Farinella[✉], Dario Allegra, and Filippo Stanco

Image Processing Laboratory, Department of Mathematics and Computer Science,
University of Catania, Catania, Italy
{gfarinella,allegra,fstanco}@dmi.unict.it

Abstract. It is well-known that people love food. However, an insane
diet can cause problems in the general health of the people. Since health
is strictly linked to the diet, advanced computer vision tools to recognize food images (e.g. acquired with mobile/wearable cameras), as well
as their properties (e.g., calories), can help the diet monitoring by providing useful information to the experts (e.g., nutritionists) to assess the
food intake of patients (e.g., to combat obesity). The food recognition is
a challenging task since the food is intrinsically deformable and presents
high variability in appearance. Image representation plays a fundamental role. To properly study the peculiarities of the image representation
in the food application context, a benchmark dataset is needed. These
facts motivate the work presented in this paper. In this work we introduce
the UNICT-FD889 dataset. It is the first food image dataset composed
by over 800 distinct plates of food which can be used as benchmark to
design and compare representation models of food images. We exploit
the UNICT-FD889 dataset for Near Duplicate Image Retrieval (NDIR)
purposes by comparing three standard state-of-the-art image descriptors: Bag of Textons, PRICoLBP and SIFT. Results confirm that both
textures and colors are fundamental properties in food representation.
Moreover the experiments point out that the Bag of Textons representation obtained considering the color domain is more accurate than the
other two approaches for NDIR.

Keywords: Food dataset · Food recognition · Near duplicate image
retrieval · Textons · PRICoLBP · SIFT

1   Introduction

Food is an essential component of human life. Nowadays, there are researches in
different fields (e.g., social, ethical and medical science) where the food has a key
role. In particular, automatic recognition of food images can provide the ability
to build monitoring systems to be embedded in wearable cameras in order to
assess the patients' diet [1,2]. The food intake monitoring can be relevant especially when patients (e.g., old people with obesity and/or diabetes, people with
food allergy) have to be assisted during their daily meals. Moreover, experts (e.g.,

© Springer International Publishing Switzerland 2015
L. Agapito et al. (Eds.): ECCV 2014 Workshops, Part III, LNCS 8927, pp. 584–599, 2015.
DOI: 10.1007/978-3-319-16199-0_41

nutritionists, psychologists) could use these monitoring applications to study the daily diet of patients to better understand their habits and/or eating disorders. Automatic food recognition could replace the traditional dietary assessment based on self-reporting in a food diary that is often inaccurate. Recent works discuss the possibility of dietary assessment through images acquired from mobile and wearable cameras [1–6]. Hence, considering the wide diffusion of mobile devices equipped with a camera, as well as the forthcoming consumer wearable cameras (e.g., Google glass), automatic food recognition is a useful resource for the assistive technology domain. Of course, the recognition of food images can let imagine many other applications (e.g., finding restaurants which serve a dish previously photographed, retrieving the list of ingredients to cook a specific dish, etc.).

Nevertheless, food has a high variability in appearance (e.g., shape, colors) due to the great assortment of existent ingredients and it is intrinsically deformable. This makes food recognition a difficult task for current state-of-the-art classification methods [7–9], and hence an important challenge for Computer Vision researchers. The image representation employed in a food recognition engine plays the most important role. Moreover, to study a representation for food it is essential to get a huge number of food images, with a high variety of dishes. In sum, representative datasets are indispensable. Although many approaches have been published, the datasets used for the tests have a limited number of classes/images. Moreover, the current datasets have not been designed with the aim of properly studying an image representation for food images; they are usually composed by images collected through the Internet, where a specific dish is present only once. For instance, considering the current food datasets, there is no way to understand if a specific type of feature is repeatable in different images of the same dish acquired under different points of view, scales or rotation angles. Hence, despite many approaches have been published, it is difficult to find papers where different techniques are compared on the same dataset. This makes difficult to understand which are the peculiarities of the different techniques and which is the best method for food recognition so far.

In this paper we introduce the first food dataset composed by 889 distinct plates of food. Each dish has been acquired with a smartphone multiple times to introduce photometric (e.g., flash vs no flash) and geometric variability (rotation, scale, point of view changes). The overall dataset contains 3583 images acquired with smartphones. The dataset is designed to push research in this application domain with the aim of finding a good way to represent food images for recognition purposes. The first question we try to answer is the following: are we able to perform a near duplicate image retrieval (NDIR) in case of food images? Note that there is no agreement on the technical definition of near-duplicates (see [10] for an in-depth discussion). The definition of near duplicate depends on the degree of variability (photometric and geometric) that is considered acceptable for each particular application. Some approaches (e.g. [11]) consider as near duplicate images the ones obtained by slightly modifying the original ones through common transformations such as changing contrast or saturation, scaling, cropping, etc. Other techniques (e.g. [12]) consider as near duplicate the images of the same scene but with different viewpoint and illumination. In this paper we consider this last definition of near duplicate food images to test different image representations on the proposed dataset. We benchmark the proposed dataset in the context of NDIR by using three standard state-of-the-art image descriptors: Bag of Textons [13], PRICoLBP [14] and SIFT [15]. Results confirm that both textures and colors are fundamental properties. The experiments performed point out that the Bag of Textons representation is more accurate than the other two approaches for NDIR.

The paper is organized as following. In Section 2 the related works on food classification are presented. A brief description of the food dataset used so far is also given. In Section 3, we describe the proposed dataset. The image representation methods used to perform Near Duplicate Food Retrieval are detailed in Section 4, whereas Section 5 reports the experimental settings and results. Finally, Section 6 concludes the paper with hints for further researches.

2   Related Works

In literature there are several works related to food recognition. Most of them address the challenging problem of health monitoring by proposing solutions for dietary assessment [1–6]. Kim et al. [3] presented a mobile user interface which provides a front-end to a client-server image recognition and portion estimation software. Chen et al. [16] proposed a three steps pipeline for calories estimation in dietary assessment: in the first step the food base plane is localized, then the food image is segmented and a 3D model is obtained; finally calories of the food are inferred using information related to the volume of the estimated 3D model. Kong et al. [1] proposed a system called "DietCam" to verify the diet assessment for obesity monitoring purposes.

In all of the aforementioned assistive technologies, a robust and effective recognition engine of food dishes is important. It can help the users in self-reporting the daily food intake. Moreover, the automatically collected information (e.g., through the system implemented in wearable smart glasses) can be also used by the experts to monitor patients over time to better understand eating disorders. A key role in food recognition engine is given to the representation models used to describe the visual content of food images. Jim?nez et al. [17] proposed a method to recognize spherical fruits in natural environments by considering variabilities such as shadows, bright areas, occlusions and overlapping fruits. To this aim a laser scanner has been used to obtain a representation based on 3D information. Joutou et al. [18] exploited multiple features together with a Multiple Kernel Learning (MKL) for food classification. Specifically they used the bag of visual words paradigm on SIFT features, color histogram, and responses to Gabor filters to encode the images. Yang et al. [8] proposed to exploit spatial relationships between the different ingredients composing a dish after a soft-labeling performed through semantic segmentation. The direction of the spatial ingredients co-occurrences and the information of the soft-labeling of the midpoint among them have been also included in the representation.

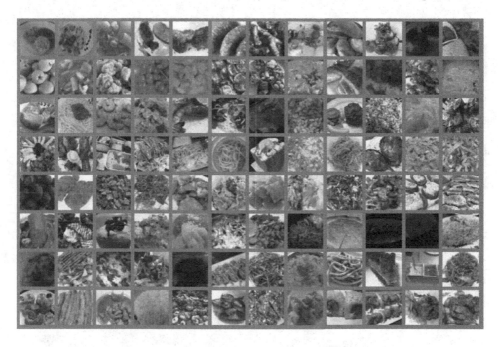

Fig. 1. Examples of 96 dishes of the proposed UNICT-FD889 dataset

To properly evaluate the performances of a food recognition method a dataset has to be used for testing purposes. Chen et al. [7] proposed the "Pittsburgh Fast-food Image Dataset" (PFID). This dataset is composed by 1098 food images belonging to 61 different categories of fast-food dishes mainly acquired in laboratory. Food pixels are labeled in order to discard background for experimental purposes. This dataset has been used in recent works to compare the performances of different food image representations [8,9]. Another dataset that can be used for food classification purposes is the one proposed by Matsuda et al. [19]. This dataset, called "UECFood100", is composed by typical asian food images collected through the internet and belonging to 100 food categories.

3   Proposed Dataset

Considering the aforementioned works it can be summarised that the main representation for food images have been obtained considering SIFT features, Textures information (e.g., obtained through Gabor filters) and color information. The bag of visual word paradigm is usually used to obtain the final feature vector to be used for food classification purpose. Moreover spatial relationship among features are employed. However, to properly study the peculiarities of the image representation in the food application context, a representative benchmark datasets is needed. These facts motivated our work. We introduce the first food images dataset composed by 3583 images related to 889 distinct dishes of food

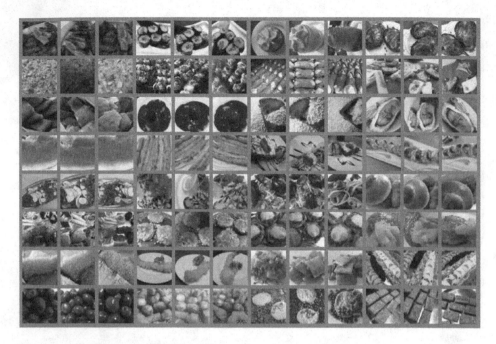

Fig. 2. An example of 32 dishes of the proposed UNICT-FD889 dataset. Three different instances for each dish are shown. The images of a dish present both geometric and photometric variabilities (e.g., see images of the first, second and third columns in the second row).

of different nationalities (e.g., Italian, English, Thai, Indian, Japanese, etc.). In Fig. 1 some instances of the different dishes within the proposed dataset are shown. We refer to this dataset as "UNICT-FD889" (UNICT Food Dataset 889) from here on. Food images have been acquired by users in the last four years during meals with a smartphone (i.e., iPhone 3GS or iPhone 4) in unconstrained settings (e.g., different backgrounds and light environmental conditions). Hence, the UNICT-FD889 dataset is a collection of food images acquired by users in real cases of meals. Each plate of food has been acquired multiple times (four in the average) to guarantee the presence of geometric and photometric variabilities (see Figs. 1 and 2). UNICT-FD889 dataset is designed to arouse research in this application domain with the aim of finding a good way to represent food images for recognition purposes. The UNICT-FD889 differs from the PFID [7] and UECFood100 [19] dataset not only because it contains a larger number of distinct food dishes. The main difference is related to how the dataset has been acquired, i.e., by users during meals, which allows to test real cases. Moreover, differently than the other two datasets, each dish is present multiple times (with variabilities) allowing to perform a more accurate study in building a representation model for food recognition. The complete set of images composing the UNICT-FD889 dataset can be visually assessed (and downloaded) at the following URI: http://iplab.dmi.unict.it/UNICT-FD889.

4 Representation Methods

In this paper we benchmark the proposed dataset considering it for Near Duplicate Image Retrieval (NDIR) purpose. We employ three standard state-of-the-art image descriptors as baseline in our tests: Bag of Textons [13], PRICoLBP [14] and SIFT features [15]. We decided to use Textons because they are powerful in representing textures and have been obtained the best results so far on the PFID dataset [8,9]. PRICoLBP descriptor has been chosen since it encodes spatial co-occurrence of local LBP features which are useful to represent textures. Finally SIFT features have been considered due their good performances in the context of near duplicate image retrieval. All the considered local descriptors are rotationally invariant. The SIFT is also scale invariant. The representation have been considered in both grayscale and color domains. The experiments reported in Section 5 pointed out that the Bag of Textons representation in color domain is more accurate than the other approaches for NDIR. In the following subsections the three baseline representations used in our experiments are briefly summarized.

4.1 Bag of Textons

Textons have been introduced by Julesz in 1981 [20] as the elementary structure for the visual perception and in particular as key atoms of textures. Textons have been used in computer vision studies in the context of texture analysis and image classification [13,21–23]. From a computational point of view, Textons are obtained as responses of the gray or color image to a bank of filters. To represent an image the filter responses of the images of a training dataset are collected and quantised through clustering procedure (e.g., K-means). Each cluster prototype is hence considered as a Textons and the collection of Textons compose the final codebook. The pixel-wise filter responses of an image (from training and testing sets) are hence associated to the different clusters (i.e., Texton prototype) considering a similarity measure (e.g., Euclidean distance). The distribution over the different Textons is hence used to represent an image. In [9] Textons have been exploited for food classification purposes obtaining good results. To obtain Textons, the feature space of the filter responses related to the training images can be clustered taking into account the classes or in a global way. When classes are considered, the quantization procedure is performed considering the responses of the different classes separately and then the Textons obtained for the different classes are taken all together to compose the final codebook. On the other hand, clustering all the filter responses independently from the different classes allows to obtain a single global Textons vocabulary to be used for classification purposes. Following the experiments performed in [9] we consider both method (class-based and global) to obtain Textons and compare them considering the UNICT-FD889 dataset for NDIR purposes. For the class-based Textons representation each dish is considered a class. So considering a quantization to obtain K Textons per dish we have a final codebook composed by $889 \times K$ Textons. In our experiments we use the rotational invariant MR4 bank of filters to extract Textons [13]. All the details on how to properly obtain the Bag of Textons representation (e.g., image intensities normalization and filter responses normalization) are available in [13] and [9]. Since the number of clusters (i.e., Textons) to be used for quantizing the filter responses space is a parameter of this approach, we have performed tests at varying of it. In our tests we have employed the χ^2 distance to measure the similarity between the Bags of Textons related to two different images.

4.2 PRICoLBP: Pairwise Rotation Invariant Co-occurrence Local Binary Pattern

PRICoLBP [14] is a descriptor to encode texture information. This descriptor considers spatial co-occurrence and pairwise orientations of the well-known LBP local features [24]. The descriptor preserves the relative angles between the orientations of LBP features pairs by obtaining rotational invariance. Given two pairs A and B, the orientation of the point A is computed and then the uniform pattern of B is obtained taking into account the orientation of A. For the co-occurrence pattern, the authors use the gradient magnitude of two points to weight the co-pattern. PRICoLBP can be extracted on both grayscale and color domain. This descriptor has been recently employed in the context of food recognition obtaining the best results with respect to others state-of-the-art methods [25]. To compute the PRICoLBP descriptor, we have used the original implementation provided by the authors which is available at the following page: http://qixianbiao.github.io/. Also in this case, we have employed the χ^2 distance to measure the similarity between two different images represented with PRICoLBP descriptor.

4.3 SIFT Features

Scale-Invariant Feature Transform (SIFT) [15] is one of the most popular descriptor used in computer vision. This descriptor has been tested in different application contexts, such as object recognition [26], image stitching [27] and near duplicate image retrieval [28,29] and food recognition [8]. SIFT is a transform able to detect keypoints invariant to scale and rotation. Moreover, it is robust to affine transformations and changes in illumination. For near duplicate image retrieval purpose the SIFT features extracted from a query image are matched to the SIFT features of the image in the training dataset. The matching is done through Euclidean-distance based nearest neighbor approach. A rejection procedure based on the ratio of the nearest neighbor distance to the second nearest neighbor distance is used to increase robustness. The query image is associated to the image of the training dataset with the highest number of matches for retrieval purposes. In our test we also tested a weighted matching score in which each match is inversely weighted taking into account the similarity between the SIFT descriptors of the matched keypoints. In our experiments we use VLFeat [30] to extract SIFT features considering both grayscale and color domain. In the case of color images the SIFT features are extracted and matched independently on each color channel. Then, given an image query, the sum of the matching over the three channels are considered to compute the most similar image on the training set.

5   Experimental Settings and Results

In this section we discuss the settings and the evaluation measures used to compare the three considered image representations on the UNICT-FD889 dataset. For testing purposes images have been resized to 320 x 240 pixels. To properly evaluate the different representation methods, the experiments have been repeated three times. At each run different approaches are executed on the same training and test sets. To this purpose, at each run we have built a training set composed by 889 images, by selecting one image of the UNICT-FD889 dataset per dish, whereas the rest of images have been used for testing purposes. The images considered for the three training sets are different. At each run, test images are used to perform queries on the corresponding training dataset used for that test. Given an image representation, the final results are obtained by averaging over the three tests. As in [12,29], the retrieval performances on each run have been evaluated with the probability of the successful retrieval $P(n)$ in a number of test queries:

$$P(n) = \frac{Q_n}{Q} \tag{1}$$

where Q_n is the number of successful queries according to $top - n$ criterion, i.e., the correct near duplicate image is among the first n retrieved images, and Q is the total number of queries. We also consider the precision/recall values at $top - n = 1$. Note that the precision and recall for $top - n = 1$ are equivalent because there is only one correct match for each query in the training set. Finally the retrieval results are evaluated through the mean average precision (mAP) measure, i.e., the area under the precision-recall curve (see [31] for further details).

As first we tested the Bag of Textons representation obtained in two modalities [9,13]: class-based and global-based. For the class-based representation each dish image within the training set has been considered as a class. Then, 10 Textons per image have been extracted by quantizing through K-means clustering the filter responses space related to the considered dish image. The final Textons vocabulary to be used for the representation has been obtained by collecting all the Textons extracted on each dish image. The size of the Textons vocabulary is hence equal to 8890. For the global-based Textons, all the filters responses related the 889 dish images of the training set have been considered in a single run of the Kmeans clustering with K=8890. Moreover the global-based representation has been considered by reducing the number of Textons composing the final vocabulary. These tests have been performed by considering gray scale version of the images. Fig. 3 shows $P(n)$ curves related to the aforementioned tests. It can be seen that all the curves are overlapped. This means that the two

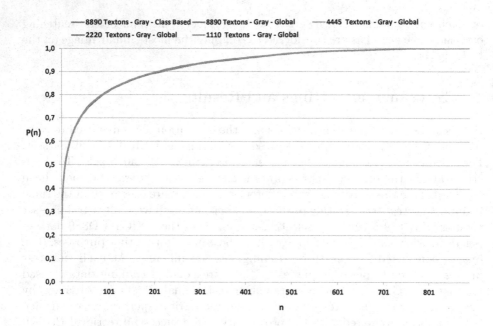

Fig. 3. Global Textons vs Class-Based Textons

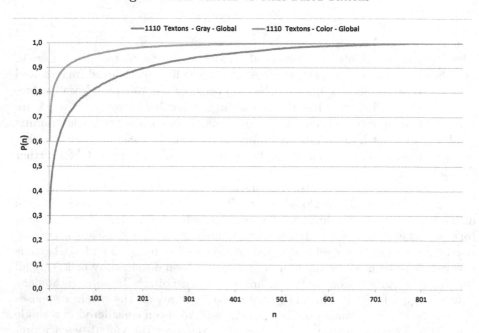

Fig. 4. Gray Textons vs Color Textons

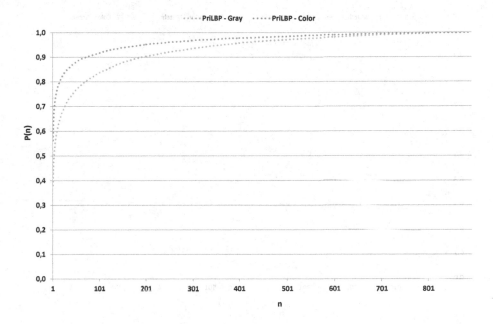

Fig. 5. Gray PRICoLBP vs Color PRICoLBP

Bag of Textons representation modalities (class-based and global) obtain similar performances. Moreover reducing the global vocabulary to 1110 does not affect the results. This differs from the results obtained by the authors of [9], where class-based Bag of Textons outperformed global one. Motivation can be due to the fact that the UNICT-FD889 dataset is bigger than the dataset used in [9]; the guess is that by increasing the number of images and classes the two representation modalities converge in performances. Finally it is interesting to note that by strongly reducing the number of the global Textons in the final vocabulary from 8890 to 1110 the performances are maintained with high reduction of both time and space resources. Note that the accuracy obtained considering a global vocabulary with 1110 Textons at $top-n = 1$ is less than 30%. To understand the influence of color information in representing food, we have compared Bag of Textons obtained in a global way in grayscale and color domains (i.e., responses of filters on the three RGB channels). The results of the comparison are reported in Fig. 4. Considering $top - n = 1$ the representation obtained in the color domain achieves more than 30% of improvement (i.e., 60.20%).

Since the results obtained with the Bag of Textons approach were promising, we considered the recent image descriptor PRICoLBP [14] for comparison purposes. This descriptor is able to encode textures and also spatial co-occurrence of local features in a rotational invariant way. It has been recently used for food classification obtaining the best results [25]. However it has never been compared with respect to Bag of Textons representation in the context of food recognition. The results obtained by PRICoLBP descriptor (both gray and color domain)

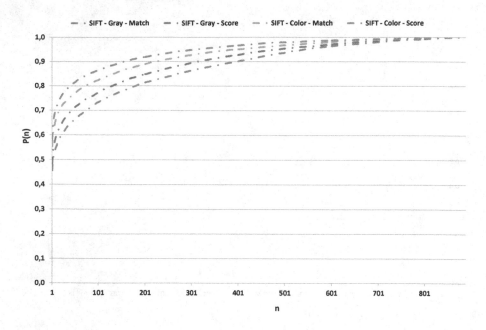

Fig. 6. Gray SIFT vs Color SIFT. The words "match" and "score" are used to identify respectively the similarity measure based on the number of matching and the weighted one.

are reported through $P(n)$ curves in Fig. 5. Despite the PRICoLBP descriptor achieves better performances than Bag of Textons in gray scale domain, it does not outperforms Bag of Textons in the color domain.

Finally we have tested SIFT which are the most popular features used for near duplicate image matching. The results obtained with the SIFT descriptor are reported in Fig. 6. In this case we have used the similarity measures based on number of matchings (with Lowe's rejection procedure) and also the one in which the matchings are inversely weighted taking into account matching distances (called score in Fig. 6). The approach with weighted similarity performs better than considering only the number of matchings. However, Bag of Textons in color domain wins the comparison again.

The best results obtained with the Bag of Textons representation, PRICoLBP and SIFT descriptors are reported in Fig. 7. By zooming the $P(n)$ curves (see Fig. 8) it can be observed that at $top-n = 1$, Bag of Textons representation obtain the best performances and SIFT matching outperform PRICoLBP. In Fig. 9 we report Precision/Recall (i.e., $top-n = 1$ since we have only one image per dish in the training set) of all tested representation. Finally in Fig. 10 the mAP results are shown.

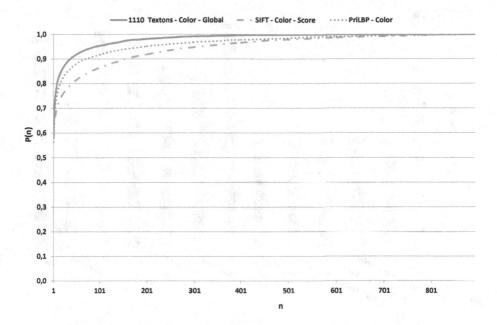

Fig. 7. Best results obtained with Bag of Textons, PRICoLBP and SIFT

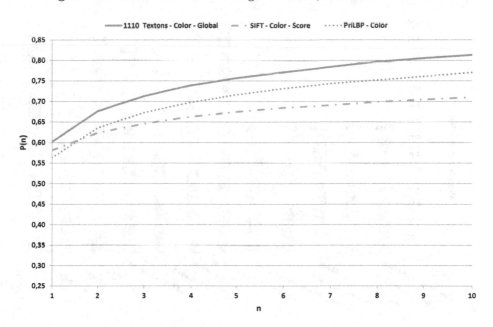

Fig. 8. Best results obtained with Bag of Textons, PRICoLBP and SIFT

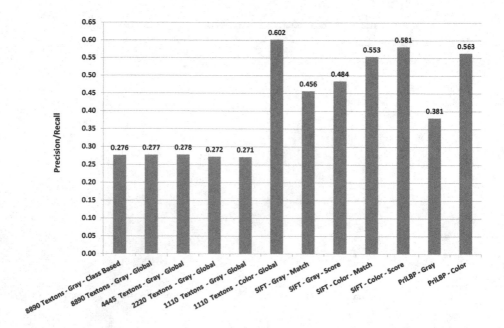

Fig. 9. Precision/Recall results (i.e., $top - n = 1$)

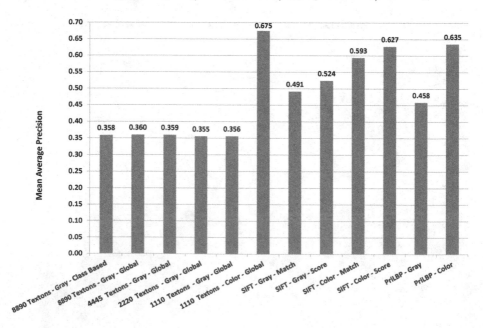

Fig. 10. mAP comparison

6   Conclusion and Future Works

In this paper we considered the problem of representation and distinguishing among different food dishes. The automatic recognition of food images is a challenging area for computer vision researchers and is fundamental for assistive technologies concerning diet monitoring. Image representation plays an important role in food recognition and, for this reason, we proposed a representative dataset called UNICT-FD889 to evaluate image representation models. The dataset contains over 800 dishes, and can be employed to study the peculiarities and weaknesses of different representation techniques. In this work we have tested Bag of Textons, PRICoLBP and SIFT representations to benchmark the dataset considering the problem of near duplicate image retrieval. Experiments pointed out that Bag of Textons representation gives the best result. Future works could be devoted to extend the proposed dataset in order to include other samples of dishes, to organize the images of the dataset in categories with different levels (e.g., main courses vs second courses, pasta vs pizza), and to label the main ingredients of each dish. Moreover classification experiments (e.g., food vs non-food, main courses vs second courses, pasta vs pizza) to assess the performances of different representation models coupled with state-of-the-art classifiers (e.g., SVM) could be done. By taking into account the results obtained in this paper, others image descriptors which consider spatial co-occurrence of Textons (e.g., Correlatons [32]) can be considered and eventually revised to address the problem of food recognition. Finally combination of different descriptors could be tested to exploit their peculiarities.

References

1. Kong, F., Tan, J.: Dietcam: Automatic dietary assessment with mobile camera phones. Pervasive and Mobile Computing 8(1), 147–163 (2012)
2. Xu, C., He, Y., Khannan, N., Parra, A., Boushey, C., Delp, E.: Image-based food volume estimation. In: International Workshop on Multimedia for Cooking and Eating Activities, pp. 75–80 (2013)
3. Kim, S., Schap, T.R., Bosch, M., Maciejewski, R., Delp, E.J., Ebert, D.S., Boushey, C.J.: Development of a mobile user interface for image-based dietary assessment. In: International Conference on Mobile and Ubiquitous Multimedia, pp. 1–13 (2010)
4. Arab, L., Estrin, D., Kim, D.H., Burke, J., Goldman, J.: Feasibility testing of an automated image-capture method to aid dietary recall (2011)
5. Zhu, F., Bosch, M., Woo, I., Kim, S., Boushey, C.J., Ebert, D.S., Delp, E.J.: The use of mobile devices in aiding dietary assessment and evaluation. Journal of Selected Topics in Signal Processing 4(4), 756–766 (2010)
6. O'Loughlin, G., Cullen, S.J., McGoldrick, A., O'Connor, S., Blain, R., O'Malley, S., Warrington, G.D.: Using a wearable camera to increase the accuracy of dietary analysis. American Journal of Preventive Medicine 44(3), 297–301 (2013)
7. Chen, M., Dhingra, K., Wu, W., Yang, L., Sukthankar, R., Yang, J.: Pfid: Pittsburgh fast-food image dataset. In: IEEE International Conference Image Processing, pp. 289–292 (2009)

8. Yang, S., Chen, M., Pomerleau, D., Sukthankar, R.: Food recognition using statistics of pairwise local features. In: IEEE Computer Vision and Pattern Recognition, pp. 2249–2256 (2010)

9. Farinella, G.M., Moltisanti, M., Battiato, S.: Classifying food images represented as Bag of Textons. in: IEEE International Conference on Image Processing (ICIP), pp. 5212–5216 (2014)

10. Oliveira, R.D., Cherubini, M., Oliver, N.: Looking at near-duplicate videos from a human-centric perspective. ACM Transaction on Multimedia Comput. Commun. Appl. 6(3), 15:1–15:22 (2010)

11. Ke, Y., Sukthankar, R., Huston, L.: Efficient near-duplicate detection and sub-image retrieval. In: ACM International Conference on Multimedia, pp. 869–876 (2004)

12. Hu, Y., Cheng, X., Chia, L.T., Xie, X., Rajan, D., Tan, A.H.: Coherent phrase model for efficient image near-duplicate retrieval. IEEE Transactions on Multimedia 11(8), 1434–1445 (2009)

13. Varma, M., Zisserman, A.: A Statistical Approach to Texture Classification from Single Images. International Journal of Computer Vision 62(1–2), 61–81 (2005)

14. Qi, X., Xiao, R., Guo, J., Zhang, L.: Pairwise rotation invariant co-occurrence local binary pattern. In: European Converence on Computer Vision, pp. 158–171 (2012)

15. Lowe, D.G.: Distinctive Image Features from Scale-Invariant Keypoints. International Journal of Computer Vision 60(2), 91–110 (2004)

16. Chen, H.C., Jia, W., Yue, Y., Li, Z., Sun, Y.N., Fernstrom, J.D., Sun, M.: Model-based measurement of food portion size for image-based dietary assessment using 3d/2d registration (2013)

17. Jimnez, A.R., Jain, A.K., Ruz, R.C., Rovira, J.L.P.: Automatic fruit recognition: a survey and new results using range/attenuation images. Pattern Recognition 32(10), 1719–1736 (1999)

18. Joutou, T., Yanai, K.: A food image recognition system with multiple kernel learning. In: IEEE International Conference on Image Processing, pp. 285–288 (2009)

19. Matsuda, Y., Hoashi, H., Yanai, K.: Recognition of multiple-food images by detecting candidate regions. In: IEEE International Conference on Multimedia and Expo, pp. 25–30 (2012)

20. Julesz, B.: Textons, the elements of texture perception, and their interactions. Nature 290(5802), 91–97 (1981)

21. Malik, J., Belongie, S., Leung, T., Shi, J.: Contour and Texture Analysis for Image Segmentation. International Journal of Computer Vision 43(1), 7–27 (2001)

22. Leung, T., Malik, J.: Representing and Recognizing the Visual Appearance of Materials using Three-dimensional Textons. Int. J. Comput. Vision 43(1), 29–44 (2001)

23. Battiato, S., Farinella, G.M., Gallo, G., Ravì, D.: Exploiting textons distributions on spatial hierarchy for scene classification. Eurasip Journal on Image and Video Processing, pp. 1–13 (2010)

24. Ojala, T., Pietikainen, M., Maenpaa, T.: Multiresolution gray-scale and rotation invariant texture classification with local binary patterns. IEEE Transactions on Pattern Analysis and Machine Intelligence 24(7), 971–987 (2002)

25. Qi, X., Xiao, R., Li, C., Qiao, Y., Guo, J., Tang, X.: Pairwise rotation invariant co-occurrence local binary pattern. IEEE Transactions on Pattern Analysis and Machine Intelligence (2014)

26. Lowe, D.G.: Object recognition from local scale-invariant features. In: IEEE International Conference on Computer Vision, pp. 1150–1157 (1999)

27. Brown, M., Lowe, D.: Automatic panoramic image stitching using invariant features. International Journal of Computer Vision **74**(1), 59–73 (2007)
28. Chum, O., Philbin, J., Zisserman, A.: Near duplicate image detection: min-hash and tf-idf weighting. In: British Machine Vision Conference, pp. 1–10 (2008)
29. Battiato, S., Farinella, G.M., Puglisi, G., Ravì, R.: Aligning codebooks for near duplicate image detection. Multimedia Tools and Applications **72**(2), 1483–1506 (2014)
30. Vedaldi, A., Fulkerson, B.: VLFeat: An open and portable libraryof computer vision algorithms (2008). http://www.vlfeat.org/
31. Philbin, J., Chum, O., Isard, M., Sivic, J., Zisserman, A.: Object retrieval with large vocabularies and fast spatial matching. In: Conference on Computer Vision and Pattern Recognition (2007)
32. Savarese, S., Winn, J., Criminisi, A.: Discriminative object class models of appearance and shape by correlatons. In: IEEE Computer Society Conference on Computer Vision and Pattern Recognition, pp. 2033–2040 (2006)

Mobile Panoramic Vision for Assisting the Blind via Indexing and Localization

Feng Hu[1]([⊠]) , Zhigang Zhu[1,2], and Jianting Zhang[1,2]

[1] Department of Computer Science, The Graduate Center, CUNY,
New York, NY 10016, USA
fhu@gradcenter.cuny.edu
[2] Department of Computer Science, The City College of New York,
New York, NY 10031, USA
zzhu@ccny.cuny.edu, jzhang@cs.ccny.cuny.edu

Abstract. In this paper, we propose a first-person localization and navigation system for helping blind and visually-impaired people navigate in indoor environments. The system consists of a mobile vision front end with a portable panoramic lens mounted on a smart phone, and a remote GPU-enabled server. Compact and effective omnidirectional video features are extracted and represented in the smart phone front end, and then transmitted to the server, where the features of an input image or a short video clip are used to search a database of an indoor environment via image-based indexing to find both the location and the orientation of the current view. To deal with the high computational cost in searching a large database for a realistic navigation application, data parallelism and task parallelism properties are identified in database indexing, and computation is accelerated by using multi-core CPUs and GPUs. Experiments on synthetic data and real data are carried out to demonstrate the capacity of the proposed system, with respect to real-time response and robustness.

Keywords: Panoramic vision · Mobile computing · Cloud computing · Blind navigation

1 Introduction

Localization and navigation in indoor environments such as school buildings, museums etc., is one of the critical tasks a visually-impaired person faces for living a convenient and normal social life. Despite a large amount of research have been carried out for robot navigation in robotic community[4][5][6], and several assistive systems are designed for blind people[15][11][1], efficient and effective portable solutions for visually impaired people are not yet available. In this paper, we intend to build an easy-to-use and robust localization and navigation system for visually-impaired people, using a portable omnidirectional lens on a mobile phone camera. Currently, the main stream solutions for localization are based on GPS signals; however, in an indoor environment these methods are not

© Springer International Publishing Switzerland 2015
L. Agapito et al. (Eds.): ECCV 2014 Workshops, Part III, LNCS 8927, pp. 600–614, 2015.
DOI: 10.1007/978-3-319-16199-0_42

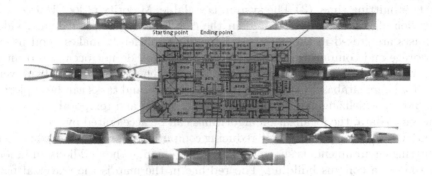

Fig. 1. One testing environment and some sample omnidirectional images. The red line in the map is the modeled path, and the dark blue line as well as the light blue line are the testing paths.

applicable since GPS signals are unavailable or inaccurate. Pose measurements using other onboard sensors such as gyroscopes, pedometers, or IMUs, are not precise enough to provide user heading information and instructions for moving around for a visually impaired person.

To provide an alternative solution to GPS-based navigation systems, RFID sensors and mobile robot based systems were developed by Kulyukin et al[9] and Cicirelli et al[3]. Although passive RFID tags can integrate local navigation measurements to achieve global navigation objectives, these systems rely heavily on the distribution of RFID sensors and specially designed robots. In our method, no extra sensors or infrastructure need to be installed in the environment, and no other complex devices are required except a daily-used smart phone (such as an iPhone) and a compact lens. Another existing solution proposed by Legge et al[10] uses a handheld sign reader and widely distributed digitally-encoded signs to give location information to the visually impaired. Again, this method also requires attaching new tags to the environment, and it can only recognize some specific locations. Our proposed system does not have any requirements for changing the environment, and the viewer can be localized in the entire interiors of a building instead of just a few individual locations.

Our system has the following characteristics that make it an appropriate assistive technology for the visually impaired navigation in the indoor context. (1) No extra requirements are needed on hardware except a daily-used smart phone and a portable lens, which is simple, inexpensive and easy to operate. Neither extra power supply is needed. (2) A cloud computing solution is utilized. Only compact features of a video clip need to be processed in the front end and then be transmitted to a server, which guarantees a real-time solution while saving a lot of bandwidth. Different from transmitting an original image or a video clip, which will cost a lot of mobile traffic and may need a long communication time, our method only transfers essential scene features, usually less than one percent of the original data and thus has very low communication cost and little transmitting time. (3) The system is scalable. Majority of localization and navigation algorithms are executed in the cloud server part, and image/video databases are stored in the cloud part too. This efficiently makes good use of the storage and computation power of the server and do not occupy too much of smart phone's resources. This also implies that the solution can scale up very well for a large database. (4) Parallelism in both data and tasks can be explored, since data parallelizing can be applied in both spatial and temporal dimensions of the video data, the localization algorithms can be accelerated by using many-core GPUs, and thus significantly reducing computational time. One example of our testing environments is shown in Fig. 1. The map in the middle is an indoor floor plan of a campus building. The red line in the map is the traversal path when modeling this environment, and the dark blue line and the light blue line are the paths used for capturing video clips for testing. Some sample omnidirectional images are shown around the map, and their geo-locations are indicated in the floor plan.

The organization of the rest of the paper is as follows. Section 2 discusses related work. Section 3 explains the main idea of the proposed solution and describes the overall approach. Section 4 illustrates the calibration and preprocessing procedure. Section 5 discusses localization by indexing as well as issues in paralleling process. Section 6 gives a conclusion and points out some possible future work.

2   Related Work

Appearance-based localization and navigation has been studied extensively in computer vision and robotics communities using a large variety of different methods and camera systems. Outdoor localization in the urban environment with panoramas captured by a multicamera system (with five side-view cameras mounted on the top of a vehicle) is proposed by Murillo et al[14]. Another appearance approach based on Simultaneous Localization and Mapping (SLAM) of a large scale road database, which is obtained by a car-mounted sensor array as well as GPS, is proposed by M. Cummins and P. Newman[4]. These systems deal with outdoor environment localization with complex camera systems. In our work, we focus on the indoor environment with simple but effective mobile sensing devices (smart phone + lens) to serve the visually-impaired community by providing a robust and easy-to-use panoramic mobile navigation system.

A visual nouns based orientation and navigation system for blind people was proposed by Molina et al[13][12], which aligns images captured by a regular camera into panoramas, and extracts three kinds of visual nouns features (signage, visual text, and visual-icons) to provide location and orientation instructions to visually-impaired people using visual noun matching and PnP localization methods. In their work, obtaining panoramas from images requires several capture actions and relatively large computation resources. Meanwhile, sign detection and text recognition procedures face a number of technical challenges in a real environment, such as illumination changes, perspective distortion, and

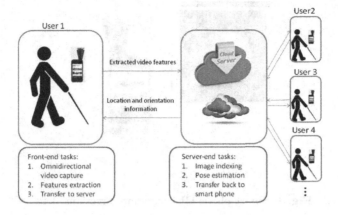

Fig. 2. System diagram

poor image resolution. In our paper, an omnidirectional lens GoPano[7] is used to capture panorama images in real time, and only one snapshot is needed to capture the entire surroundings rather than multiple captures. No extra image alignment process is required, and no sign detection or recognition is needed.

Another related navigation method in indoor environments is proposed by Aly and Bouguet[2] as part of the Google street view service, which uses six photos captured by professionals to construct an omnidirectional image of each viewpoint inside a room, and then estimates the camera pose and moving parameters between successive viewpoints. Since their inputs are unordered images, they construct minimal spanning tree among complete graph of every viewpoint to select triples for parameter estimations. In our method, since we use sequential video frames, we do not need to find such spatial relationships between images, and thus we can skip these procedures. Therefore we reduce the computation cost and pursue a real-time solution.

Representing and compressing omnidirectional images into compact rotational invariant features was proposed by Zhu et al[17], where the Fourier transform of the radial principle components of each omnidirectional image is used to represent the image. In our paper, based on the observation that an indoor environment usually includes a great number of vertical lines, we explore the omnidirectional features of these vertical lines in both the HSI space (Hue, Saturation and Intensity) and the HSI gradient space of an omnidirectional image, instead of using original RGB space only, as in [17], and generate one-dimensional omnidirectional HSI and HSI gradient projections. Then we use the Fourier transform components of these projections as the representation of omnidirectional image to reduce feature size and obtain rotation-invariant features and then find both the viewer's location and heading direction. Another major difference is that we aim to find a user's location and orientation from each omnidirectional image, where as in [17], only six road types are classified using a neural network based approach.

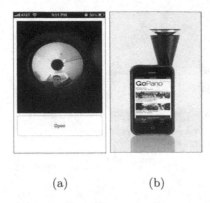

(a)   (b)

Fig. 3. Smart phone GUI and omnidirectional lens

3   Overview of Our Approach

The hardware of the system is designed with two components: the smart phone front end part and the server part. The system diagram is shown in Fig. 2. The front end part consists of a smart phone and an omnidirectional lens, which mounts on the phone with a case. In our implementation, we use an iPhone and a GoPano lens, which is shown in Fig. 3.

The software of the system includes two stages: the modeling stage and the query stage. In the modeling stage of our current implementation, the developer of the database (the model) carries the mobile phone and moves along the corridors with an even pace, covering and recording the video into a database. Geo-tags(e.g. physical locations of current frames) are manually labeled for key frames (e.g. at doors, turns, etc.) and the rest of them are linearly interpolated. In the future, motion estimation algorithms can be used to ease the constraint of linear motion. To reduce the storage need, we do some preprocessing to the data, which will be discussed in Section 4. In the querying stage, a visually impaired user can walk into the area covered in the above modeling stage and take a short video clip. The smart phone extracts video features and sends them to the server via wireless connections. The server receives the query and search the image candidates in the database, and returns the localization and orientation information to the user.

Using all the pixels in images of even a short video clip to represent a scene is too expensive for both communication and computation, and the data are also not invariant to environment variables such as illumination, user heading orientation, and other environment factors. Therefore, we propose a concise and effective representation for the omnidirectional images by using a number of robust one-dimensional omnidirectional projections (omni-projections) for each panoramic scene. We have observed that an indoor environment often has plenty of vertical lines (door edges, pillar edges, notice boards, windows, etc.), and features along vertical lines can be embedded inside of the proposed omni-projection representations, so these features can be extracted and be used to estimate viewer's

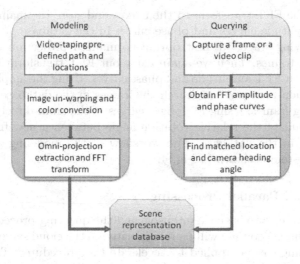

Fig. 4. Workflow of modeling and querying stages

locations. Newly extracted features of an input image are used as query keys to localize and navigate in the environment represented by the database.

Because different scenes may have similar omni-projection features, using a single frame may cause false indexing results. We adopt a multiple frame querying mechanism by extracting a sequence of omni projection features from a short video clip, which can greatly reduce the probability of false indexing. When database scales up for a large scene, it is very time consuming to sequentially match the input frame features with all the images in the database of the large scene. So we use GPGPU to parallelize the query procedure and accelerate the querying speed.

3.1   The Overall Indexing Approach

While the system server is running, a user can send a query with newly captured video frames, and their corresponding locations are searched in the database. Since frames in the database are tagged with geo-location information, the system can provide the location information to the user. Currently, only physical locations relative to the floor plan are tagged, however in the future more information can be added, such as doorplates, office names, locations of daily-used facilities(e.g. telephones, water fountains, elevators) etc.

In the modeling stage, we first traverse all the desired paths and locations in an indoor environment and capture the original panoramic video of the scene. Then we perform un-warping to obtain the cylindrical representations of the omnidirectional images, convert the images to HSI color space and carry out a number of other preprocessing operations (such as gradient operations). After that, we project the images' columns to obtain the omni-projection curves for each frame (for both H, S, I and gradients of them). All the curves are normalized.

Finally we do the FFT transform to the curves and store the main components of the FFT amplitude curves and phase curves in the database.

In the querying stage, we first obtain normalized projection curves of the newly captured frames. Then we again carry out FFT transform to the curves and compute their FFT amplitude and phase curves. Using the amplitude curves, which are rotation-invariant, we search the frames in the database and find the closest matching frames. Using the phase curves of the omni-directional images, we can also estimate the relative rotation angle between a new frame and the matched frame in the database. The workflow of the modeling and querying stages in our system is shown in Fig. 4.

3.2   Cloud and Parallel Processing

The modeling procedure is space intensive and the querying procedure could be very time consuming, so they will be manipulated in the cloud server part, where parallel processing can be applied to accelerate the procedures. The basic idea of multi-frames indexing is to use a sequence of newly captured video frames to query pre-built video frame database to increase the success rate. Even with the preprocessing step to reduce the size of the input data, the computational cost of multi-frame query in the database would be high if the database is large.

One strategy is to partition input video into individual frames and query the database with each frame. For every input query frame, a straightforward approach is to compare each frame with all the frames one-by-one. Then after all the queries return their matching candidates, which for example, top 5 matches for each frame, an aggregation step of the most consistent sequence of matches can be obtained by considering that both the input and the matched sequences are temporal sequences. In this way the querying process could have three levels of parallelisms. First, we process all the frames of a video in parallel. Second, we use multiple threads to compare each input frame with multiple database frames simultaneously, rather than comparing with them one-by-one. Third, some of the operations in obtaining rotation-invariant projection curves, such as the Fourier transform algorithm can take advantage of the parallel processing. For doing this, the original omni-projection curves will be sent from the front end to the server, which is still efficient in communication due to their low dimensionality.

Parallel acceleration is necessary in the query procedure. Without parallel speed up, the time consumed in one single query operation take hundreds of milliseconds on our current experimental database (with only several thousand frames), and it would be multiplied if the scale significantly increases for a realistic indoor environment. After using parallel acceleration, this time is reduced to several milliseconds and greatly improves the performance of the query response. Details will be provided in Section 5.

4   Calibration and Preprocessing

The original frames captured by the GoPano lens and smart phone camera is a fish-eye-like distorted image, which is shown in Fig. 5(a), and has to be rectified.

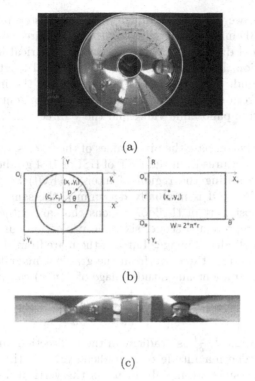

(a)

(b)

(c)

Fig. 5. (a) Original video frame and its parameters; (b) geometric relationship between the original and un-warped images; and (c) un-warped omnidirectional image

Fig. 5(c) shows the un-warped image in a cylindrical projection representation, which has planar perspective projection in the vertical direction and spherical projection in the horizontal direction. For achieving this, a calibration procedure is needed to obtain all the required camera parameters.

Assuming that the camera is held up-right and the lens's optical axis is horizontal, the relationship between the original image and un-warped image can be illustrated in Fig.5(b)[8][16]. Define the original pixel coordinate system as $X_iO_iY_i$, the un-warped image coordinate system is $X_eO_eY_e$, and the original circular image center is (C_x, C_y). Then a pixel (x_e, y_e) in the un-warped image and corresponding pixel (x_i, y_i) in the original image has the following relationship.

$$\begin{cases} x_i = (r - y_e)cos(x_e * \frac{2\pi}{W}) + C_x \\ y_i = (r - y_e)sin(x_e * \frac{2\pi}{W}) + C_y \end{cases} \quad (1)$$

where r is the radius of the outer circle of the original circular image, thus the vertical dimension (in pixels) of the cylindrical image, and $W = 2\pi r$ is the perimeter of the circle, turning to the horizontal dimension (in pixels) of the cylindrical image.

This un-warping process is applied to every frame in the database and all the input query frames. Since the un-warped images still have distortion in the vertical direction (radial direction in the original images) due to the nonlinearity of the GoPano lens, we perform an image rectification step using a calibration target with known 3D information to correct the radial direction so that the projection in the vertical direction of the un-warped cylindrical images is a linear perspective projection. By doing this, the effective focal length in the vertical direction is also found. From this point on, we assume the image coordinates (u, v) are rectified from (x_e, y_e) , and the u direction (horizontal direction) represents the 360-degree panoramic view, and the v direction (vertical direction) is perspective.

We do not directly compare the pixel values of the frames; instead, we extract rotational invariant features from the FFT of HSI or HSI gradient curves, which are obtained by projecting the region of interest (ROI) of the image frame. Currently rectangular ROI is manually determined the same for all images in order to exclude most part of th floor regions that are subject to changes in different times. To represent a scene, six omni-projection curves are extracted from each rectified cylindrical image. Three of them are from H, S and I channels of the image, and the rest three are from the gradient magnitudes of the H, S and I channels. The gradient magnitude image of $f(u,v)$ can be calculated

$$|\nabla f(u,v)| = |\frac{\delta f}{\delta u}du + \frac{\delta f}{\delta v}dv| \qquad (2)$$

where f can be H, S and I, $\frac{\delta f}{\delta u}$ is gradient in the u direction, and $\frac{\delta f}{\delta v}$ is gradient in the v direction. The magnitude of a gradient value is the L-2 norm of the $(\frac{\delta f}{\delta u}, \frac{\delta f}{\delta v})$. In practice, since we mainly focus on the vertical lines in the images as our features, we only use the horizontal gradient. From this point on, we will use a feature function g(u,v) to represent one of the six types of images (H, S, I and their gradient magnitudes, or simply gradients). Then the omni-projection curve $c(u)$ of the feature function $g(u, v)$ is generated by projecting the ROI of the image in the v direction:

$$c(u) = \sum_{v=0}^{H-1} g(u,v), u = 0, 1, 2, ..., W - 1 \qquad (3)$$

where W and H are the image width and height of the ROI (where H is smaller than r), and $u = 0, 1, 2, ..., W - 1$ are the horizontal pixel indices (corresponding angles from 0 to 360 degrees). Therefore the curve $c(u)$ is an omnidirectional projection curve (i.e., omni-projection curve). A linear normalization is applied to all the curves to turn them into the same scale. With all the six curves, we can store each and every of them into the database, and use them to compare with the new input curves to find the optimal location for a newly input frame.

5   Localization by Indexing

Localization is essential to visually-impaired people, since not only it provides the position and orientation of the user, but also it can supply additional information of the environment, e.g. locations of doors, positions of doorplates, etc.

When the database scale increases, using key features to do the indexing is necessary in order to obtain real-time performance without losing too much index accuracy. Meanwhile, sequential search is not practical when database scales is up significantly, therefore parallel searching is explored in this paper.

5.1   Indexing and Rotation Estimation

We use the major components of FFT transforms of the six omni-projection feature curves as the keys to do the indexing in this paper. For an omni-projection curve $c(u), u = 0, 1, 2, ..., W - 1$, if the camera rotates around the vertical axis, it will cause a circular shift of the cylindrical representation of the omnidirectional image, which then corresponds to a circular shift to the signal $c(u)$. If an omnidirectional image has a circular shift of u_0 to the right, this is equivalent to rotating the camera coordinate around z axes for $\Phi = -2\pi u_0/N$[17]. Suppose the signal after a right circular shift u_0 is $c'(u)$, we have the following equation:

$$c'(u) = c(u - u_0) \tag{4}$$

Define the DFT of $c(u)$ is defined as a_k, the DFT of $c'(u)$ is defined as b_k, then

$$\begin{cases} a_k = \sum_{u=0}^{W-1} x(u)e^{-je2\pi ku/W}, k = 0, 1, ..., W - 1 \\ b_k = a_k e^{-je2\pi ku_0/W}, k = 0, 1, ..., W - 1 \end{cases} \tag{5}$$

The magnitudes of the omni-projection curves are rotation-invariant, i.e., $|a_k| = |b_k|$. Therefore we use the FFT magnitudes of the six omni-projection curves of a query frame to do indexing in the database. In our current experiments, the first half of the FFT magnitudes of each curve $|a_k|$ are used in the querying stage for indexing. The distances of the six curves between a query and each database frame are calculated, and a distance metric is chosen, e.g. using one of the most discriminative curves or use the average distance of the six, and the final match is the database frame that yields the smallest distance. From our experiments, we have found that the gradient of intensity curve provides the best discrimination.

To find the rotation angle of the current image (i.e. amount of the circular shift), the problem is equivalent to finding the maximal value of the circular correlation function(CCF)

$$CCF(u_0) \sum_{u=0}^{W-1} c(n) * c(u - u_0) \tag{6}$$

where $u_0 = 0, 1, ..., W - 1$. According to the correlation theorem, we can calculate $CCF(u_0)$ as

$$CCF(u_0) = F^{-1}\{a^*(k)b(k)\} \tag{7}$$

We only carry out this task after the optimal match is found, since it is meaningless to find the shifted angle if the location is not matched correctly.

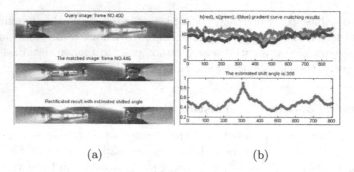

(a)   (b)

Fig. 6. (a) An example of a query image and its matched result in a database; (b) the matching scores with database frames and the estimated heading differences between the query and database frames

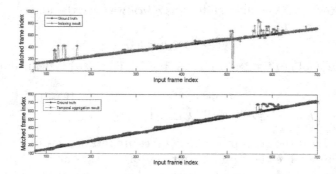

Fig. 7. Matching results of all the test database frames without (top) and with temporal aggregation(bottom)

5.2   Real Data Experiments: Accuracy and Time Performance

We carried ur a number of experiments for testing the accuracy and time performance of the indexing based localization approach. In the first experiment, we compared the accuracy of single versus multiple frame indexing with a small database of 862 frames. One example of indexing a new query frame is shown in Fig. 6 (a) and (b). Fig. 6(a) shows the input frame, the target frame, and the shifted version of the input image after finding the heading angle difference. In Fig.6(b), the first plot shows the searching results of the input frame with all the frames in the database using hue (red), saturation (green) and intensity (blue). We found that the information of intensity feature performs the best. The circular correlation function curve is shown on the bottom right, showing that the heading angle difference can be found after obtaining the correct match.

Because different scenes may have very similar omni-projection curve features, a query with only one single frame may cause false matches, as shown in Fig. 7 (top). In this figure, the horizontal axis is the index of input frames (of a new sequence) and the vertical axis is the index of database frames (of the old sequence). Both sequences cover the same area. The black curve shows the ground truth data of matching results, and the red curve shows the matched results by our system. There are a few very obvious mismatches around frame 150, 500, and 600 due to the scene similarities. This leads us to design a multiple-frame approach: if we use a short sequence of input frames instead of just one single frame to perform the query, a temporally consistent match results for all the input frames will yield a much more robust result. Fig. 7(bottom) shows the testing results with temporal aggregation, where for every frame, its nearby 25 frames' querying results are aggregated and the median index value is used as the final result. In the current implementation, we take advantage of the fact that both the query frames and the database frames are sequentially indexed, so we use a simple median filter of the 25 indexing results to obtain the temporal aggregation result. By a simple calculation, the average indexing error reduced to 14.7 frames with temporal aggregation from 25.3 frames with a single frame indexing. These correspond to 0.29 m versus 0.51 m distance error in space. But more importantly, as we can see from the curve, temporal aggregation has corrected the very obvious mismatches and generate more robust results.

In the second experiment, the entire floor of a building is modeled, as shown in Fig. 1. We first capture a video sequence of the entire floor (with a total of 3674 frames) as the training database, whose path is shown as the red line. We then capture two other short databases(along the dark blue line and the light blue line) as the testing databases. Some sample omnidirectional images used in the modeling process are shown around the map in Fig. 1, and their geo-locations are attached to the floor map too. Fig. 8 shows matching results using the two test databases against the large scale database. Fig. 8(a) shows the results using the frames near the starting and ending position. We would like to note that starting point and ending point are marked out only for visualization purpose; they are not used in the indexing process. Fig. 8(b) shows the results using frames in the middle of the loop. The black line is the ground truth, and the dashed black line is the tolerance bound with the accuracy within 2 meters. Because it is inevitable to avoid scene similarity, there are some mis-matching results. For example, in Fig. 8(c), the first image is the best matched result and the second one is the original query image, however they are images of two totally different locations. Again, these mismatches could be corrected using temporal aggregation.

If using only a single CPU to search sequentially, the amount of time consumed would increase proportional to the number of frames in the database. Therefore we use GPUs to do the query in parallel, so that we can search all the frames and compare an input frame to multiple database frames at the same time, which will greatly reduce the time used. Fig. 9 shows the time used with and without many-core GPUs for a database with the number of images changed from 1000 frames to 8000 frames. In the single CPU version, the time spent increases from 20 ms to 160 ms, whereas using a many-core GPU (Kepler K20 chip), the time is reduced by 20 times(from 1.13 ms to 8.82 ms, for databases of

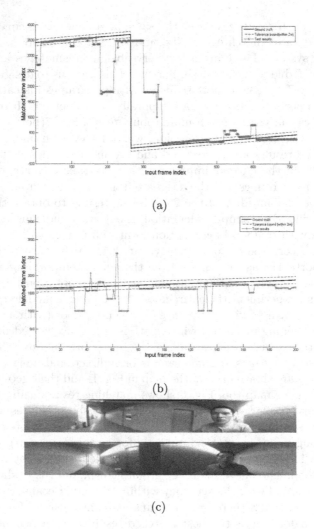

Fig. 8. (a) Matching results near the starting point of the loop; (b) matching results in the middle of the loop; (c) a pair of mismatching results

1000 to 8000 frames). Note that the current test only has a database with a few thousand frames. With a larger database of an indoor scene, the time spending on a single CPU will be prohibitive, whereas using multi-core CPUs/GPUs, the time spending can be greatly reduced. Note the current experiments have not fully used the capacity of the server. Since we can apply tens of thousands of threads in one or multiple GPUs, the acceleration rate has potential to improve.

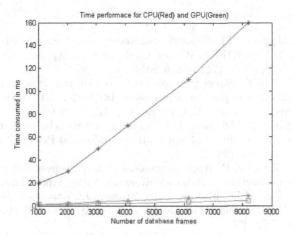

Fig. 9. Time usage with and without GPU acceleration: Red without GPU; Green with GPUs. Curves with squares are experiments using 1024 threads while curves with asterisks are experiments using 2048 threads.

6   Conclusion and Discussion

In this paper we have proposed a mobile panoramic system to help the visually impaired people to localize and navigation in indoor environments. We use a smart phone with panoramic camera and high performance server architecture to ensure the portability and mobility of the user part and take advantage of the huge storage as well as high computation power of the server part. An image indexing mechanism is used to find the rough location of an input image (or a short sequences of images), and to improve the query speed and ensure a real time performance, we use many-core GPUs to parallelize the query procedure. There are a few issues we will be dealing with in the future. First, a large scale scene database, for example, multiple floors of an entire building, or a number of buildings on campus, will be built and used to create more testing environments. Second, hierarchical and context-based methods can be used to avoiding sequential searching the entire database for every query. For example we can use GPS or WiFi to obtain rough location information and localize the user in the nearby places before we search the database around those locations. Third, user interface in communicating the localization and navigation information to a blind user, as well as implementation of the front end algorithms on the mobile phone should be optimized to make it more natural for the user to use.

Acknowledgements.. The authors would like to thank the US National Science Foundation (NSF) Emerging Frontiers in Research and Innovation (EFRI) Program for the support under Award No. EFRI 1137172. The authors are also grateful to the anonymous reviewers for their valuable comments and suggestions that have helped us revise the paper and identify future research directions.

References

1. Altwaijry, H., Moghimi, M., Belongie, S.: Recognizing locations with google glass: A case study. In: 2014 IEEE Winter Conference on Applications of Computer Vision (WACV), pp. 167–174, March 2014
2. Aly, M., Bouguet, J.Y.: Street view goes indoors: Automatic pose estimation from uncalibrated unordered spherical panoramas. In: 2012 IEEE Workshop on Applications of Computer Vision (WACV), pp. 1–8. IEEE (2012)
3. Cicirelli, G., Milella, A., Di Paola, D.: Rfid tag localization by using adaptive neuro-fuzzy inference for mobile robot applications. Industrial Robot: An International Journal **39**(4), 340–348 (2012)
4. Cummins, M., Newman, P.: Appearance-only slam at large scale with fab-map 2.0. The International Journal of Robotics Research **30**(9), 1100–1123 (2011)
5. Davison, A.J., Reid, I.D., Molton, N.D., Stasse, O.: Monoslam: Real-time single camera slam. IEEE Transactions on Pattern Analysis and Machine Intelligence **29**(6), 1052–1067 (2007)
6. Di Corato, F., Pollini, L., Innocenti, M., Indiveri, G.: An entropy-like approach to vision based autonomous navigation. In: 2011 IEEE International Conference on Robotics and Automation (ICRA), pp. 1640–1645. IEEE (2011)
7. GoPano: Gopano micro camera adapter, June 2014. http://www.gopano.com/products/gopano-micro
8. Hui, Z., Fei, L., Hui-juan, L.: Study on fisheye image correction based on cylinder model. Computer Applications **28**(10), 2664–2666 (2008)
9. Kulyukin, V., Gharpure, C., Nicholson, J., Pavithran, S.: Rfid in robot-assisted indoor navigation for the visually impaired. In: Proceedings of the 2004 IEEE/RSJ International Conference on Intelligent Robots and Systems. (IROS 2004), vol. 2, pp. 1979–1984. IEEE (2004)
10. Legge, G.E., Beckmann, P.J., Tjan, B.S., Havey, G., Kramer, K., Rolkosky, D., Gage, R., Chen, M., Puchakayala, S., Rangarajan, A.: Indoor navigation by people with visual impairment using a digital sign system. PloS one **8**(10), e76783 (2013)
11. Manduchi, R., Coughlan, J.M.: The last meter: blind visual guidance to a target. In: Proceedings of the 32nd annual ACM conference on Human factors in computing systems, pp. 3113–3122. ACM (2014)
12. Molina, E., Zhu, Z.: Visual noun navigation framework for the blind. Journal of Assistive Technologies **7**(2), 118–130 (2013)
13. Molina, E., Zhu, Z., Tian, Y.: Visual nouns for indoor/outdoor navigation. In: Miesenberger, K., Karshmer, A., Penaz, P., Zagler, W. (eds.) ICCHP 2012, Part II. LNCS, vol. 7383, pp. 33–40. Springer, Heidelberg (2012)
14. Murillo, A.C., Singh, G., Kosecka, J., Guerrero, J.J.: Localization in urban environments using a panoramic gist descriptor. IEEE Transactions on Robotics **29**(1), 146–160 (2013)
15. Rivera-Rubio, J., Idrees, S., Alexiou, I., Hadjilucas, L., Bharath, A.A.: Mobile visual assistive apps: benchmarks of vision algorithm performance. In: Petrosino, A., Maddalena, L., Pala, P. (eds.) ICIAP 2013. LNCS, vol. 8158, pp. 30–40. Springer, Heidelberg (2013)
16. Scaramuzza, D., Martinelli, A., Siegwart, R.: A flexible technique for accurate omnidirectional camera calibration and structure from motion. In: IEEE International Conference on Computer Vision Systems, ICVS 2006, pp. 45–45. IEEE (2006)
17. Zhu, Z., Yang, S., Xu, G., Lin, X., Shi, D.: Fast road classification and orientation estimation using omni-view images and neural networks. IEEE Transactions on Image Processing **7**(8), 1182–1197 (1998)

The Design and Preliminary Evaluation of a Finger-Mounted Camera and Feedback System to Enable Reading of Printed Text for the Blind

Lee Stearns[1]($\boxtimes$), Ruofei Du[1], Uran Oh[1], Yumeng Wang[2],
Leah Findlater[3], Rama Chellappa[4], and Jon E. Froehlich[1]

[1] Computer Science, University of Maryland, College Park, Maryland, USA
{lstearns,ruofei,uranoh,jonf}@umd.edu
[2] School of Architecture, University of Maryland, College Park, Maryland, USA
yumeng@umd.edu
[3] College of Information Studies, University of Maryland, College Park,
Maryland, USA
leahkf@umd.edu
[4] Electrical and Computer Engineering, University of Maryland, College Park,
Maryland, USA
chella@umd.edu

Abstract. We introduce the preliminary design of a novel vision-augmented touch system called *HandSight* intended to support activities of daily living (ADLs) by sensing and feeding back non-tactile information about the physical world *as it is touched*. Though we are interested in supporting a range of ADL applications, here we focus specifically on reading printed text. We discuss our vision for HandSight, describe its current implementation and results from an initial performance analysis of finger-based text scanning. We then present a user study with four visually impaired participants (three blind) exploring how to continuously guide a user's finger across text using three feedback conditions (haptic, audio, and both). Though preliminary, our results show that participants valued the ability to access printed material, and that, in contrast to previous findings, audio finger guidance may result in the best reading performance.

Keywords: Accessibility · Wearables · Real-time OCR · Text reading for blind

1 Introduction

Over 285 million people have visual impairments (VI) worldwide—including 39 million who are blind—that can affect their ability to perform activities of daily living [1]. In many countries, such as the US [2], VI prevalence is increasing due to aging populations. While previous research has explored combining mobile cameras and computer vision to support people with VI for at-a-distance information tasks such as navigation (*e.g.,* [3]–[8]), facial recognition (*e.g.,* [9]–[12]), and spatial perception (*e.g.,* [13]–[15]), they fail to support proximal information accessed through touch.

© Springer International Publishing Switzerland 2015
L. Agapito et al. (Eds.): ECCV 2014 Workshops, Part III, LNCS 8927, pp. 615–631, 2015.
DOI: 10.1007/978-3-319-16199-0_43

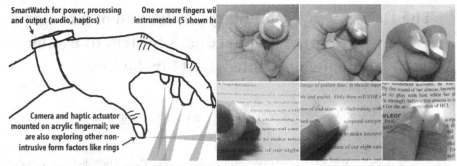

(a) Example HandSight Envisionment (w/5 instrumented fingers)   (b) Ring Form Factor   (c) Nail Form Factor   (d) 2-Finger Setup

Fig. 1. HandSight uses a $1 \times 1 \text{mm}^2$ *AWAIBA NanEye 2C* camera developed for minimally invasive surgeries (*e.g.*, endoscopies) that can capture $250 \times 250 \text{px}$ images at 44fps. The above images: (a) a design mockup and (b-d) early form factors with the NanEye camera. In this paper, we explore a single camera implementation with a ring form factor in a text reading context (see Figure 2).

We are pursuing a new approach: a vision-augmented touch system called *HandSight* that supports activities of daily living (ADLs) by sensing and feeding back non-tactile information about the physical world *as it is touched*. Although still at an early stage, our envisioned system will consist of tiny CMOS cameras ($1 \times 1 \text{mm}^2$) and micro-haptic actuators mounted on one or more fingers, computer vision and machine learning algorithms to support fingertip-based sensing, and a smartwatch for processing, power, and speech output; see Figure 1. Since touch is a primary and highly attuned means of acquiring information for people with VI [16], [17], we hypothesize that collocating the camera with the touch itself will enable new and intuitive assistive applications.

While we are interested in supporting a range of applications from object recognition to color identification, in this paper we focus on the challenge of reading printed text. Our overarching goal is to allow blind users to touch printed text and receive speech output in real-time. The user's finger is guided along each line via haptic and non-verbal audio cues. At this stage, our research questions are largely exploratory, spanning both human-computer interaction (HCI) and computer vision: How can we effectively guide the user's finger through haptic and auditory feedback to appropriately scan the target text and notify them of certain events (*e.g.*, start/end of line or paragraph reached)? How accurately can optical character recognition (OCR) be achieved at a speed that is responsive to the user's touch? How do the position, angle, and lighting of the finger-mounted camera affect OCR performance?

To begin examining these questions, we pursued two parallel approaches. For the computer vision questions, we developed an early HandSight prototype along with efficient algorithms for perspective and rotation correction, text detection and tracking, and OCR. We present preliminary evaluations and demonstrate the feasibility of our envisioned system. For the HCI-related questions, we developed a custom test apparatus on the Apple iPad that simulates the experience of using HandSight, but provides us with additional experimental control and allows us to more precisely track the user's finger in response to feedback conditions. Using this setup, we report on a preliminary evaluation with four VI participants (three blind) across three finger guidance conditions: *audio, haptics,* and *audio+haptics.* Findings suggest that audio may be the most intuitive feedback mechanism of the three.

Compared to the majority of emerging computer vision systems to support VI users, which use head- or chest-mounted cameras (*e.g.,* [4], [12], [18]), our system offers two primary advantages: (i) *collocation of touch, sensing, and feedback,* potentially enabling more intuitive interaction and taking advantage of a VI individual's high tactile acuity [16], [17]; (ii) *unobtrusive, always-available interaction* that allows for seamless switching between the physical world and vision-augmented applications. As a finger-mounted approach, our work is most similar to [19]–[21], described next.

2   Related Work

Scientists have long sought to support blind people in reading printed text (for a review, see [22], [23]). Many early so-called "reading machines for the blind" used a sensory substitution approach where the visual signals of words were converted to non-verbal auditory or tactile modalities, which were complicated to learn but accessible. Two such examples include the *Optophone,* which used musical chords or 'motifs' [24] and the *Optacon,* which used a vibro-tactile signal [25], [26]. With advances in sensing, computation, and OCR, modern approaches attempt to scan, recognize, and read aloud text in real-time. This transition to OCR and speech synthesis occurred first with specialized devices (*e.g.,* [27]–[29]), then mobile phones (*e.g.,* [30], [31]), and now wearables (*e.g.,* [12], [21]). While decades of OCR work exist (*e.g.,* [32]–[35]), even state-of-the-art reading systems become unusable in poor lighting, require careful camera framing [36], [37], and do not support complex documents and spatial data [38]. Because HandSight is self-illuminating and co-located with the user's touch, we expect that many of these problems can be mitigated or even eliminated.

As a wearable solution, HandSight is most related to *OrCam* [12] and *FingerReader* [21]. OrCam is a commercial head-mounted camera system designed to recognize objects and read printed text in real-time (currently in private beta testing). Text-to-speech is activated by a pointing gesture in the camera's field-of-view. While live demonstrations with sighted users have been impressive (*e.g.,* [39], [40]), there is no academic work examining its effectiveness with VI users for reading tasks. The primary distinctions between HandSight and OrCam are, first, hand-mounted versus head-mounted sensing, which could impact camera framing issues and overall user experience. Second, HandSight supports direct-touch scanning compared to OrCam's indirect approach, potentially allowing for increased control over what is read and reading speed as well as increased spatial understanding of a page/object. Regardless, the two approaches are complementary, and we plan to explore a hybrid in the future.

More closely related to HandSight, FingerReader [21] is a custom finger-mounted device with vibration motors designed to read printed text by direct line-by-line scanning with the finger. Reported evaluations [21] of FingerReader are limited to a very small OCR assessment under unspecified "optimal" conditions, and a qualitative user study with four blind participants. The participants preferred haptic to audio-based finger guidance; this finding is the opposite of our own preliminary results, perhaps due to differences in how the audio was implemented (theirs is not clearly described). Further, our study extends [21] in that we also present user performance results.

In terms of finger guidance, haptic and audio feedback have been used in numerous projects to guide VI users in exploring non-tactile information or tracing shapes. Crossan and Brewster [41], for example, combined pitch and stereo sonification with a force feedback controller to drag the user along a trajectory, and found that performance was higher with audio and haptic feedback than haptic feedback alone. Other approaches have included sonification and force feedback to teach handwriting to blind children [42], speech-based icons or "spearcons" [43], vowel sounds to convey radial direction [44], and use of primarily tactile feedback to transmit directional and shape data [45]–[47]. Our choice to vary pitch for audio-based line tracing feedback with HandSight is based on previous findings [41], [43], [48]. Oh *et al.* [48], *e.g.*, used sonification to support non-visual learning of touchscreen gestures; among a set of sound parameters tested (pitch, stereo, timbre, etc.), pitch was the most salient.

3   System Design

HandSight is comprised of three core components: sensors, feedback mechanisms, and a computing device for processing. Our current, early prototype is shown in Figure 2. Before describing each component in more detail, we enumerate six design goals.

3.1   Design Goals

We developed the following design goals based on prior work and our own experiences developing assistive technology: (1) *Touch-based rather than distal interaction.* Although future extensions to HandSight could examine distal interaction, our focus is on digitally augmenting the sense of touch. (2) *Should not hinder normal tactile function.* Fingers are complex tactile sensors [49], [50] that are particularly attuned in people with visual impairments [16], [17]; HandSight should not impede normal tactile sensation or hand function. (3) *Easy-to-learn/use.* Many sensory aids fail due to their complexity and high training requirements [22]; to ensure HandSight is approachable and easy to use, we employ an iterative, human-centered design approach. (4) *Always-available.* HandSight should allow for seamless transitions between its use and real-world tasks. There is limited prior work on so-called always-available input [20], [51]–[53] for blind or low-vision users. (5) *Comfortable & robust.* HandSight's physical design should support, not encumber, everyday activities. It should be easily removable, and water and impact resistant. (6) *Responsive & accurate.* HandSight should allow the user to explore the target objects (*e.g.*, utility bills, books) quickly—the computer vision and OCR algorithms should work accurately and in real-time.

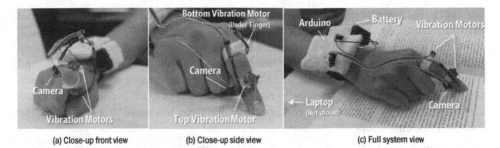

(a) Close-up front view   (b) Close-up side view   (c) Full system view

Fig. 2. The current HandSight prototype with a NanEye ring camera, two vibration motors, and an Arduino. Finger rings and mounts are constructed from custom 3D-printed designs and fabric. Processing is performed in real-time on a laptop (not shown).

3.2   Hardware

Sensing Hardware. Our current prototype uses a single $1 \times 1mm^2$ *AWAIBA NanEye 2C* camera [54] that can capture 250×250 resolution images at 44 frames per second (fps). The NanEye was originally developed for minimally invasive surgical procedures such as endoscopies and laparoscopies and is thus robust, lightweight, and precise. The camera also has four LEDs coincident with the lens (2.5mm ring), which enables dynamic illumination control. The small size allows for a variety of finger-based form factors including small rings or acrylic nail attachments. In our current prototype, the camera is attached to an adjustable velcro ring via a custom 3D-printed clip.

Processing. For processing, we use a wrist-mounted Arduino Pro Micro with an attached Bluetooth module that controls the haptic feedback cues. The video feed from the camera is currently processed in real time on a laptop computer (our experiments used a Lenovo Thinkpad X201 with an Intel Core i5 processor running a single computation thread at approximately 30fps). Later versions will use a smartwatch (*e.g.,* Samsung Galaxy Gear [55]) for power and processing.

Feedback. HandSight provides continuous finger-guidance feedback via vibration motors, pitch-controlled audio, or both. Our current implementation includes two vibration motors that are **8mm diameter disks and 3.4mm thick** (Figure 2), though we are actively looking at other solutions (see Discussion). A text-to-speech system is used to read each word as the user's finger passes over it, and distinctive audio and/or haptic cues can be used to signal other events, such as end of line, start of line, etc.

3.3   CV Algorithm Design and Evaluation

Our current HandSight implementation involves a series of frame-level processing stages followed by multi-frame merging once the complete word has been observed. Below, we describe our five stage OCR process and some preliminary experiments evaluating performance.

Stage 1: Preprocessing. We acquire grayscale video frames at ~40fps and 250x250px resolution from the NanEye camera (Figure 3). With each video frame, we apply four preprocessing algorithms: first, to correct radial and (slight) tangential distortion, we use standard camera calibration algorithms [56]. Second, to control lighting for the next frame, we optimize LED intensity using average pixel brightness and contrast. Third, to reduce noise, perform binarization necessary for OCR, and adapt to uneven lighting from the LED, we filter the frame using an adaptive threshold in a Gaussian window; finally, to reduce false positives, we perform a connected component analysis and remove components with areas too small or aspect ratios too narrow to be characters.

Stage 2: Perspective and Rotation Correction. The finger-based camera is seldom aligned perfectly with the printed text (*e.g.*, top-down, orthogonal to text). We have observed that even small amounts of perspective distortion and rotation can reduce the accuracy of our text detection and OCR algorithms. To correct perspective and rotation effects, we apply an efficient approach detailed in [56]–[58], which relies on the parallel line structure of text for rectification. We briefly describe this approach below.

To identify potential text baselines, we apply a Canny filter that highlights character edges and a randomized Hough transform that fits lines to the remaining pixels. From this, we have a noisy set of candidate baselines. Unlikely candidates are filtered (*e.g.*, vertical lines, intersections that imply severe distortion). The remaining baselines are enumerated in pairs; each pair implies a potential rectification, which is tested on the other baselines. The baseline pair that results in the lowest line angle variance is selected and the resulting rectification is applied to the complete image.

Fig. 3. A demonstration of our perspective and rotation correction algorithm.

More precisely, the intersection of each pair of baselines implies a horizontal vanishing point $V_x = l_1 \times l_2$ in homogeneous coordinates. If we assume the ideal vertical vanishing point $V_y = [0, 1, 0]^T$, then we can calculate the homography, H, that will make those lines parallel. Let $l_\infty = V_x \times V_y = [a, b, c]^T$ and calculate the perspective homography, H_p, using those values. The perspective homography makes the lines parallel, but does not align them with the x-axis. We must rotate the lines by an angle θ using a second matrix, H_r. The complete rectifying homography matrix becomes:

$$H_p = \begin{bmatrix} \cos(\theta) & -\sin(\theta) & 0 \\ \sin(\theta) & \cos(\theta) & 0 \\ 0 & 0 & 1 \end{bmatrix} \begin{bmatrix} 1 & 0 & 0 \\ 0 & 1 & 0 \\ a/c & b/c & 1 \end{bmatrix} = \begin{bmatrix} \cos(\theta) & -\sin(\theta) & 0 \\ \sin(\theta) & \cos(\theta) & 0 \\ a/c & b/c & 1 \end{bmatrix} \quad (1)$$

To investigate the effect of lateral perspective angle on performance, we performed a synthetic experiment that varied the lateral angle from -45° to 45° across five randomly selected document image patches. The raw rectification performance is shown in Figure 4a and the effect of rectification on character-level OCR is shown in Figure 4b accuracy (the algorithm for OCR is described below).

Stage 3: Text Detection. The goal of the text detection stage is to build up a hierarchy of text lines, words, and characters. This task is simplified because we assume the perspective and rotation correction in Stage 2 has made the text parallel to the x-axis. First, we split the image into lines of text by counting the number of text pixels in each row and searching for large gaps. Next, we split each line into words using an identical process on the columns of pixels. Gaps larger than 25% of the line height are classified as spaces between words. Finally, we segment each word into individual characters by searching for local minima in the number of text pixels within each column.

Stage 4: Character Classification. Real-time performance is important for responsive feedback, which prevents us from using established OCR engines such as Tesseract. Thus, we compute efficient character features (from [59]), and perform classification using a support vector machine (SVM). Each character candidate is centered and scaled to fit within a 32x32 pixel window, preserving the aspect ratio. The window is split into four horizontal and vertical strips, which are summed along the short axis to generate eight vectors of length 32 each. These vectors, along with the aspect ratio, perimeter, area, and thinness ratio make up the complete feature vector. The thinness ratio is defined as $T=4\pi(A/P^2)$ where A is the area and P is the perimeter. We compensate for the classifier's relatively low accuracy by identifying the top k most likely matches. By aggregating the results over multiple frames, we are able to boost performance.

Stage 5: Tracking and Final OCR Result Output. The camera's limited field of view means that a complete word is seldom fully within a given frame. We must track the characters between frames and wait for the end of the word to become visible before we can confidently identify it. Character tracking uses sparse low-level features for efficiency. First, we extract FAST corners [60], and apply a KLT tracker [61] at their locations. We estimate the homography relating the matched corners using the random sample consensus [62]. After determining the motion between frames, we relate the lines, words, and individual characters by projecting their locations in the previous frame to the current frame using the computed homographies. The bounding boxes with the greatest amount of overlap after projection determine the matches. When the end of a word is visible, we sort the aggregated character classifications and accept the most frequent classification. This process can be improved by incorporating a language dictionary model, albeit at the expense of efficiency. A text-to-speech engine reads back the identified word.

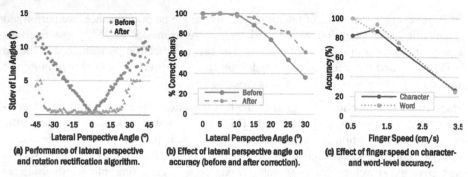

Fig. 4. Results from preliminary evaluations of our (a-b) Stage 2 algorithms and (c) the effect of finger speed on overall character- and word-level accuracy

To investigate the effect of finger movement speed on OCR accuracy, we recorded five different speeds using a single line of text. The results are presented in Figure 4c. With greater speed, motion blur is introduced, and feature tracking becomes less accurate. In our experience, a "natural" finger speed movement for sighted readers is roughly 2-3cm/s. So, with the current prototype, one must move slower than natural for good performance. We plan on compensating for this effect in the future using image stabilization and motion blur removal, as well as incorporating a higher frame rate camera (100fps).

4   User Study to Assess Audio and Haptic Feedback

Our current prototype implementation supports haptic and audio feedback, but how best to implement this feedback for efficient direct-touch reading is an open question. Ultimately, we plan to conduct a holistic user evaluation of the system to assess the combined real-time OCR and finger guidance for a variety of reading tasks. At this stage, however, our goal was to refine the finger guidance component of the system by conducting a preliminary evaluation of three types of feedback: (1) audio only, (2) haptic only, and (3) a combined audio and haptic approach. We conducted a user study with four visually impaired participants to collect subjective and performance data on these three types of feedback. To isolate the finger guidance from the current OCR approach, we used a custom iPad app that simulates the experience of using the full system.

4.1   Method

Participants. We recruited four VI participants; details are shown in Table 1. All four participants had braille experience, and three reported regular use of screen readers.

Test Apparatus. The setup simulated the experience of reading a printed sheet of paper with HandSight (Figure 5). It consisted of the hand-mounted haptic component of the HandSight system controlled by an Arduino Micro, which was in turn connected via Bluetooth to an Apple iPad running a custom experimental app. The iPad was outfitted with a thin foam rectangle as a physical boundary around the edge of the screen to simulate the edge of a sheet of paper, and was further covered by a piece of tracing paper to provide the feel of real paper and to reduce friction. The app displayed text documents, guiding the user to trace each line of the document from left to right and top to bottom. As the user traced their finger on the screen, text-to-speech audio was generated, along with the following feedback guidance cues: start and end of a line of text, end of a paragraph, and vertical guidance for when the finger strayed above or below the current line. Lines were 36 pixels in height and vertical guidance began when the finger was more than 8 pixels above or below the vertical line center.

Feedback Conditions Tested. We compared three finger guidance options:

- *Audio only.* All guidance cues were provided through non-speech audio. The start and end of line cues were each a pair of tonal percussive (xylophone) notes played in ascending or descending order, respectively. The end of paragraph sound was a soft vibrophone note. When the user's finger drifted below or above a line, a continuous audio tone would be played to indicate that proper corrective movement. A lower tone (300 Hz) was played to indicate downward corrective movement (*i.e.*, the user was above the line). The pitch decreased at a rate of 0.83Hz/pixel to a minimum of 200Hz at 127 pixels above the line. A higher tone (500 Hz) was used to indicate upward corrective movement (up to a maximum of 600Hz with the same step value as before).

- *Haptic only.* The haptic feedback consists of two finger-mounted haptic motors, one on top and one underneath the index finger (see Section 3.2). Based on piloting within the research team, the motors were placed on separate finger segments (phalanges) so that the signal from each was easily distinguishable. To cue the start of a line, two short pulses played on both motors, with the second pulse more intense than the first; the reverse pattern indicated the end of a line. For the end of a paragraph, each motor vibrated one at a time, which repeated for a total of four pulses. For vertical guidance, when the finger strayed too high, the motor underneath the finger vibrated, with the vibration increasing in intensity from a

Table 1. Background of the four user study participants.

ID	Age	Gender	Handed-ness	Level of Vision	Years of Vision Loss	Diagnosed Med. Condition	Hearing Difficulties
P1	64	Female	Left	Totally blind	Since birth	Retinopathy of prematurity	N/A
P2	61	Female	Left	Totally blind	Since birth	Retinopathy of prematurity	Slight hearing loss
P3	48	Male	Right	Totally blind	Since age 5	N/A	N/A
P4	43	Female	Right	No vision one eye, 20/400 other eye	30 years	Glaucoma	N/A

(a) iPad test apparatus   (b) Participant 1   (c) Participant 3

Fig. 5. User study setup and test apparatus: (a) overview; (b-c) in use by two participants

low perceivable value to maximum intensity, reached at 127 pixels above the line; below the line, the top motor vibrated instead (again with the maximum intensity reached at 127 pixels).

- *Combined audio-haptic.* This combined condition included all of the audio *and* haptic cues described above, allowing the two types of feedback to complement each other in case one was more salient for certain cues than the other.

Procedure. The procedure took up to 90 minutes. For each feedback condition, the process was as follows. First, we demonstrated the feedback cues for the start/end of each line, end of paragraph, and vertical guidance. Next, we loaded a training article and guided the user through the first few lines. Participants then finished reading the training article at their own pace. Finally, a test article was loaded and participants were asked to read through the text as quickly and accurately as possible. While we provided manual guidance as necessary to help participants read the *training* article (*e.g.*, adjusting their finger), no manual guidance was given during the *test* task. Four articles of approximately equivalent complexity were selected from *Voice of America* (a news organization), one for the training task and one to test each feedback condition; all articles had three paragraphs and on average 11.0 lines (*SD*=1.0) and 107.0 words (*SD*=13.5). The order of presentation for the feedback conditions was randomized per participant, while the test articles were always shown in the same order. Questions on ease of use were asked after each condition and at the end of the study. Sessions were video recorded, and all touch events were logged.

4.2   Findings

We analyzed subjective responses to the feedback conditions, and user performance based on logged touch events. Figure 6 shows a sample visualization from one participant (P1) completing the reading task in the *audio-only* and *haptic-only* conditions. Due to the small sample size, all findings in this section should be considered preliminary, but point to the potential impacts of HandSight and tradeoffs of different feedback.

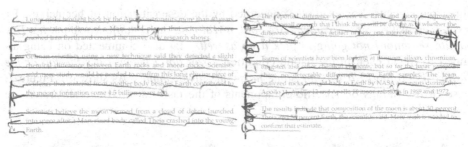

(a) Participant 1 finger trace (audio only condition)   (b) Participant 1 finger trace (haptic only condition)

Fig. 6. Our iPad test apparatus allowed us to precisely track and measure finger movement. Example trace graphs for Participant 1 (P1) across the audio- and haptic-only conditions are shown above (green is on line; red indicates off-line and guidance provided). These traces were also used to calculate a range of performance measures. For example, the average overall time to read a line for P1 took 11.3s (*SD*=3.9s) in the audio condition and 18.9s (*SD*=8.3s) in the haptic condition. The average time to find the beginning of the next line (traces not shown above for simplicity but were recorded) was 2.2s (*SD*=0.88s) in the audio condition and 2.7s (*SD*=2.4s) in the haptic condition.

In terms of overall preference, three participants preferred *audio-only* feedback; see Table 2. Reasons included that they were more familiar with audio than haptic signals (P1, P3), and that it was easier to attend to text-to-speech plus audio than to text-to-speech plus haptic (P4). P2's most preferred condition was the *combined* feedback, because she liked to have audio cues for line tracing and haptic cues for start/end of line notifications. In contrast, *haptic-only* feedback was least preferred by

Table 2. Overall preference rankings per participant. Audio feedback was the most positively received.

	Rank 1	Rank 2	Rank 3
P1	Audio	Combined	Haptic
P2	Combined	Audio	Haptic
P3	Audio	Haptic	Combined
P4	Audio	Combined	Haptic

Table 3. Ratings comparing prior text reading experiences with HandSight; 1-much worse to 5-much better

	Braille	Screen Reader	Printed Text
P1	3	3	3
P2	3	5	5
P3	4	4	4
P4	5	5	5

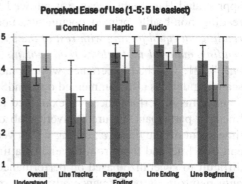

Fig. 7. Avg perceived ease of use of different text guidance attributes based on a 5-point scale (1-*very difficult*; 5-*very easy*). Error bars are stderr (*N*=4).

three participants. For example, concerned by the desensitization of her nerves, P1 expressed that: *"...if your hands are cold, a real cold air-conditioned room, it's [my tactile sensation] not going to pick it up as well."* P4 also commented on being attuned to sound even in the haptic condition: *"You don't know if it's the top or the bottom [vibrating]...It was the same noise, the same sound."* As shown in Figure 7, ease of use ratings on specific components of the task mirrored overall preference rankings.

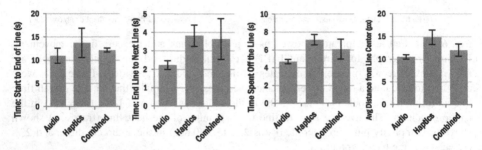

Fig. 8. Average performance data from the four user study participants across the three feedback conditions. While preliminary, these results suggest that audio-only feedback may be more effective than the other options tested. Error bars show standard error; (*N*=4).

Participants were also asked to compare their experience with HandSight to braille, screen readers and printed-text reading using 5-point scales (*1-much worse* to *5-much better*). As shown in Table 3, HandSight was perceived to be at least as good (3) or better compared to each of the other reading activities. In general, all participants appreciated HandSight because it allowed them to become more independent when reading non-braille printed documents. For example, P3 stated, *"It puts the blind reading on equal footing with rest of the society, because I am reading from the same reading material that others read, not just braille, which is limited to blind people only"*. P1, who had experience with Optacon [26], Sara CE, and other printed-text scanning devices also commented on HandSight's relative portability.

In terms of performance, we examined four primary measures averaged across all lines per participant (Figure 8): average absolute vertical distance from the line center, time spent off the line (*i.e.,* during which vertical feedback was on), time from start to end of a line, and time from the end of a line to the start of the next line. While it is difficult to generalize based on performance data from only four participants, *audio-only* may offer a performance advantage over the other two conditions. *Audio-only* resulted in the lowest average vertical distance to the line center for all participants. Compared to the *haptic-only* condition, *audio-only* reduced the amount of time spent off the line by about half. It was also faster for all participants than *haptic-only* in moving from the end of a line to the start of the next line. A larger study is needed to confirm these findings and to better assess what impact the feedback conditions have on reading speed from start to end of a line.

5   Discussion

Though preliminary, our research contributes to the growing literature on wearables to improve access to the physical world for the blind (*e.g.*, [12], [19], [21]). The design and initial algorithmic evaluation of our current HandSight prototype show the feasibility of our approach, and highlight important technical issues that we must consider. Additionally, our user study, which evaluated three finger-guidance approaches using a controlled setup (the iPad test apparatus), found that, in contrast to prior work [21], haptic feedback was the *least* preferred guidance condition. The pitch-controlled audio feedback condition was not only subjectively rated the most preferred but also appeared to improve user performance. Clearly, however, more work is needed. Below, we discuss our preliminary findings and opportunities for future work.

Haptic Feedback. Though we have created many different types of finger-mounted haptic feedback in our lab, we tested only one in the user study: when the user moved above or below the current line, s/he would feel a continuous vibration proportional in strength to the distance from the vertical line center. We plan to experiment with form factors, haptic patterns (*e.g.*, intensity, frequency, rhythm, pressure), number of haptic devices on the finger, as well as the type of actuator itself (Figure 9).

Fig. 9. We are evaluating a range of micro-haptic actuators: (a) $10\times2.7mm^2$ vibro-discs; (b) 5×0.4 mm^2 piezo discs; (c) 3×8 mm^2 vibro-motors; (d) 0.08mm Flexinol wire (shape memory alloy).

While our current haptic implementation performed the worst of the feedback conditions, we expect that, ultimately, some form of haptics will be necessary for notifications and finger guidance.

Blind Reading. Compared to current state-of-the-art reading approaches, our long-term goals are to: (1) provide more intuitive and precise control over scanning and text-to-speech; (2) increase spatial understanding of the text layout; and (3) mitigate camera framing, focus, and lighting issues. Moreover, because pointing and reading are tightly coupled, finger-based interaction intrinsically supports advanced features such as rereading (for sighted readers, rereading occurs 10-15% of the time [63] and increases comprehension and retainment [64], [65]). We focused purely on reading simple document text, but we plan to investigate more complex layouts so the user can sweep their finger over a document and sense where pictures are located, headings, and so on. We will explore a variety of documents (*e.g.*, plain text, magazines, bills) and household objects (*e.g.*, cans of food, cleaning supplies), and examine questions such as: How should feedback be provided to indicate where text/images are located? How should advanced features such as re-reading, excerpting, and annotating be supported, perhaps, through additional gestural input and voice notes?

Computer Vision. Our preliminary algorithms are efficient and reasonably accurate, but there is much room for improvement. By incorporating constraints on lower-level text features we may be able to rectify vertical perspective effects and affine skew. We can also apply deblurring and image stabilization algorithms to improve the maximum reading speed the system is able to support. Robust and efficient document mosaicking and incorporation of prior knowledge will likely be a key component for supporting a wider range of reading tasks.

Multi-sensory Approach. Currently, our prototype relies on only local information gleaned from the on-finger camera. However, in the future, we would like to combine camera streams from both a body-mounted camera (*e.g.,* Orcam [12]) and a finger-mounted camera. We expect the former could provide more global, holistic information about a scene or text which could be used to guide the finger towards a target of interest or to explore the physical document's layout. We could also use the information to improve the performance of the OCR algorithms, by dynamically training the classifier on the page fonts and creating a generative model (*e.g.,* [66]).

6 Conclusion

Our overarching vision is to transform how people with VI access visual information through touch. Though we focused specifically on reading, this workshop paper offers a first step toward providing a general platform for touch-vision applications.

References

1. Pascolini, D., Mariotti, S.P.: Global estimates of visual impairment: 2010. Br. J. Ophthalmol. **96**(5), 614–618 (2011)
2. National Eye Institute at the National Institute of Health, Blindness Statistics and Data. http://www.nei.nih.gov/eyedata/blind.asp (accessed: March 10, 2014)
3. Dakopoulos, D., Bourbakis, N.G.: Wearable Obstacle Avoidance Electronic Travel Aids for Blind: A Survey. IEEE Trans. Syst. Man, Cybern. Part C (Applications Rev.) **40**(1), 25–35 (2010)
4. Balakrishnan, G., Sainarayanan, G., Nagarajan, R., Yaacob, S.: Wearable real-time stereo vision for the visually impaired. Eng. Lett. **14**(2), 6–14 (2007)
5. Hesch, J.A., Roumeliotis, S.I.: Design and Analysis of a Portable Indoor Localization Aid for the Visually Impaired. Int. J. Rob. Res. **29**(11), 1400–1415 (2010)
6. Hub, A., Diepstraten, J., Ertl, T.: Design and Development of an Indoor Navigation and Object Identification System for the Blind. SIGACCESS Access. Comput. (77–78), 147–152 (2003)
7. Manduchi, R.: Mobile Vision as Assistive Technology for the Blind: An Experimental Study. In: Miesenberger, K., Karshmer, A., Penaz, P., Zagler, W. (eds.) ICCHP 2012, Part II. LNCS, vol. 7383, pp. 9–16. Springer, Heidelberg (2012)
8. Helal, A., Moore, S.E., Ramachandran, B.: Drishti: an integrated navigation system for visually impaired and disabled. In: Proceedings Fifth International Symposium on Wearable Computers, pp. 149–156 (2001)
9. Krishna, S., Little, G., Black, J., Panchanathan, S.: A wearable face recognition system for individuals with visual impairments. In: Proceedings of the 7th International ACM SIGACCESS Conference on Computers and Accessibility, pp. 106–113 (2005)

10. Krishna, S., Colbry, D., Black, J., Balasubramanian, V., Panchanathan, S.: A systematic requirements analysis and development of an assistive device to enhance the social interaction of people who are blind or visually. In: Impaired, Workshop on Computer Vision Applications for the Visually Impaired (CVAVI 2008), European Conference on Computer Vision ECCV 2008 (2008)
11. Gade, L., Krishna, S., Panchanathan, S.: Person localization using a wearable camera towards enhancing social interactions for individuals with visual impairment. In: Proceedings of the 1st ACM SIGMM International Workshop on Media Studies and Implementations that Help Improving Access to Disabled Users, pp. 53–62 (2009)
12. OrCam Technologies Ltd., OrCam - See for Yourself. http://www.orcam.com/ (accessed: June 23, 2014)
13. Iannacci, F., Turnquist, E., Avrahami, D., Patel, S.N.: The haptic laser: multi-sensation tactile feedback for at-a-distance physical space perception and interaction. In: Proceedings of the SIGCHI Conference on Human Factors in Computing Systems, pp. 2047–2050 (2011)
14. Khambadkar, V., Folmer, E.: GIST: A gestural interface for remote nonvisual spatial perception. In: Proceedings of the 26th Annual ACM Symposium on User Interface Software and Technology, pp. 301–310 (2013)
15. Israr, A., Bau, O., Kim, S.-C., Poupyrev, I.: Tactile feedback on flat surfaces for the visually impaired. In: CHI 2012 Extended Abstracts on Human Factors in Computing Systems, pp. 1571–1576 (2012)
16. Norman, J.F., Bartholomew, A.N.: Blindness enhances tactile acuity and haptic 3-D shape discrimination. Atten. Percept. Psychophys. 73(7), 2323–2331 (2011)
17. Goldreich, D., Kanics, I.M.: Tactile Acuity is Enhanced in Blindness. J. Neurosci. 23(8), 3439–3445 (2003)
18. Karim, S., Andjomshoaa, A., Tjoa, A.M.: Exploiting sensecam for helping the blind in business negotiations. In: Miesenberger, K., Klaus, J., Zagler, W.L., Karshmer, A.I. (eds.) ICCHP 2006. LNCS, vol. 4061, pp. 1147–1154. Springer, Heidelberg (2006)
19. Nanayakkara, S., Shilkrot, R., Yeo, K.P., Maes, P.: EyeRing: a finger-worn input device for seamless interactions with our surroundings. In: Proceedings of the 4th Augmented Human International Conference, pp. 13–20 (2013)
20. Yang, X.-D., Grossman, T., Wigdor, D., Fitzmaurice, G.: Magic finger: always-available input through finger instrumentation. In: Proceedings of the 25th Annual ACM Symposium on User Interface Software and Technology, pp. 147–156 (2012)
21. Shilkrot, R., Huber, J., Liu, C., Maes, P., Chandima, N.S.: FingerReader: a wearable device to support text reading on the go. In: CHI 2014 Ext. Abstr. Hum. Factors Comput. Syst. (Vi), pp. 2359–2364 (2014)
22. Cooper, F.S., Gaitenby, J.H., Nye, P.W.: Evolution of reading machines for the blind: Haskins Laboratories' research as a case history. Haskins Laboratories (1983)
23. Capp, M., Picton, P.: The optophone: an electronic blind aid. Eng. Sci. Educ. J. 9(3), 137–143 (2000)
24. D'Albe, E.F.: On a Type-Reading Optophone. Proc. R. Soc. London. Ser. A 90(619), 373–375 (1914)
25. Bliss, J.C.: A Relatively High-Resolution Reading Aid for the Blind. Man-Machine Syst. IEEE Trans. 10(1), 1–9 (1969)
26. Kendrick, D.: From Optacon to Oblivion: The Telesensory Story. American Foundation for the Blind AccessWorld Magazine 6(4) (2005)
27. Intel, Intel Reader. http://www.intel.com/pressroom/kits/healthcare/reader/ (accessed: January 10, 2014)
28. knfb Reading Technology Inc., knfb Reader Classic. http://www.knfbreader.com/products-classic.php (accessed: June 22, 2014)

29. Gaudissart, V., Ferreira, S., Thillou, C., Gosselin, B.: SYPOLE: mobile reading assistant for blind people. In: 9th Conference Speech and Computer (SPECOM) (2004)
30. Blindsight, Text Detective. http://blindsight.com/textdetective/ (accessed: November 01, 2013)
31. knfb Reading Technology Inc., kReader Mobile. http://www.knfbreader.com/products-kreader-mobile.php (accessed: June 24, 2014)
32. Mori, S., Suen, C.Y., Yamamoto, K.: Historical review of OCR research and development. Proc. IEEE **80**(7), 1029–1058 (1992)
33. Shen, H., Coughlan, J.M.: Towards a Real-Time System for Finding and Reading Signs for Visually Impaired Users. In: Miesenberger, K., Karshmer, A., Penaz, Petr, Zagler, W. (eds.) ICCHP 2012, Part II. LNCS, vol. 7383, pp. 41–47. Springer, Heidelberg (2012)
34. Chen, X., Yuille, A.L.: Detecting and reading text in natural scenes. In: Proceedings of the 2004 IEEE Computer Society Conference on Computer Vision and Pattern Recognition, CVPR 2004, vol. 2, pp. II–366–II–373 (2004)
35. Wang, K., Babenko, B., Belongie, S.: End-to-end scene text recognition. In: 2011 IEEE International Conference on Computer Vision (ICCV), pp. 1457–1464 (2011)
36. Jayant, C., Ji, H., White, S., Bigham, J.P.: Supporting Blind Photography. In: The Proceedings of the 13th International ACM SIGACCESS Conference on Computers and Accessibility, pp. 203–210 (2011)
37. Manduchi, R., Coughlan, J.M.: The last meter: blind visual guidance to a target. In: Proceedings of ACM SIGCHI Conference on Human Factors in Computing Systems (CHI 2014) (2014, to appear)
38. Kane, S.K., Frey, B., Wobbrock, J.O.: Access lens: a gesture-based screen reader for real-world documents. In: Proceedings of the SIGCHI Conference on Human Factors in Computing Systems, pp. 347–350 (2013)
39. OrCam as uploaded by YouTube user Amnon Shashua, OrCam at Digital-Life-Design (DLD) in Munich, Digital-Life-Design (2014). http://youtu.be/3m9ivtJI6iA?t=2m10s (accessed: June 22, 2014)
40. OrCam as uploaded by YouTube user Amnon Shashua, OrCam TED@NYC, TED@NYC (2013). http://youtu.be/_3XVsCsscyw?t=4m53s (accessed: June 22, 2014)
41. Crossan, A., Brewster, S.: Multimodal Trajectory Playback for Teaching Shape Information and Trajectories to Visually Impaired Computer Users. ACM Trans. Access. Comput. **1**(2), 12:1–12:34 (2008)
42. Plimmer, B., Reid, P., Blagojevic, R., Crossan, A., Brewster, S.: Signing on the Tactile Line: A Multimodal System for Teaching Handwriting to Blind Children. ACM Trans. Comput. Interact. **18**(3), 17:1–17:29 (2011)
43. Su, J., Rosenzweig, A., Goel, A., de Lara, E., Truong, K.N.: Timbremap: Enabling the visually-impaired to use maps on touch-enabled devices. In: Proceedings of the 12th International Conference on Human Computer Interaction with Mobile Devices and Services, pp. 17–26 (2010)
44. Harada, S., Takagi, H., Asakawa, C.: On the audio representation of radial direction. In: Proceedings of the SIGCHI Conference on Human Factors in Computing Systems, pp. 2779–2788 (2011)
45. Yatani, K., Truong, K.N.: SemFeel: a user interface with semantic tactile feedback for mobile touch-screen devices. In: Proceedings of the 22nd Annual ACM Symposium on User Interface Software and Technology, pp. 111–120 (2009)
46. Yatani, K., Banovic, N., Truong, K.: SpaceSense: representing geographical information to visually impaired people using spatial tactile feedback. In: Proceedings of the SIGCHI Conference on Human Factors in Computing Systems, pp. 415–424 (2012)
47. Noble, N., Martin, B.: Shape discovering using tactile guidance. In: Proceeding of the 6th International Conference EuroHaptics (2006)

48. Oh, U., Kane, S.K., Findlater, L.: Follow that sound: using sonification and corrective verbal feedback to teach touchscreen gestures. In: Proceedings of the ACM SIGACCESS International Conference on Computers and Accessibility (ASSETS 2013) (2013, to appear)
49. Lederman, S.J., Klatzky, R.L.: Hand movements: A window into haptic object recognition. Cogn. Psychol. **19**(3), 342–368 (1987)
50. Johnson, K.: Neural basis of haptic perception. In: Pashler, H., Yantis, S. (eds.) Stevens' Handbook of Experimental Psychology: Volume 1: Sensation and Perception, 3rd edn., pp. 537–580. Wiley Online Library (2002)
51. Saponas, T.S., Tan, D.S., Morris, D., Balakrishnan, R., Turner, J., Landay, J.A.: Enabling always-available input with muscle-computer interfaces. In: Proceedings of the 22nd Annual ACM Symposium on User Interface Software and Technology, pp. 167–176 (2009)
52. Morris, D., Saponas, T.S., Tan, D.: Emerging input technologies for always-available mobile interaction. Found. Trends Human-Computer Interact. **4**(4), 245–316 (2010)
53. Saponas, T.S.: Supporting Everyday Activities through Always-Available Mobile Computing. University of Washington (2010)
54. AWAIBA, NanEye Medical Image Sensors. http://www.awaiba.com/en/products/medical-image-sensors/ (accessed: January 10, 2014)
55. Samsung, Samsung Galaxy Gear. http://www.samsung.com/us/mobile/wearable-tech/SM-V7000ZKAXAR (accessed: January 10, 2014)
56. Hartley, R., Zisserman, A.: Multiple View Geometry in Computer Vision. Cambridge University Press (2003)
57. Jagannathan, L., Jawahar, C.: Perspective correction methods for camera based document analysis. In: Proc. First Int. Work. Camera-based Doc. Anal. Recognit., pp. 148–154 (2005)
58. Zaliva, V.: Horizontal Perspective Correction in Text Images (2012). http://notbrainsurgery.livejournal.com/40465.html
59. Abuhaiba, I.S.: Efficient OCR using Simple Features and Decision Trees with Backtracking. Arab. J. Sci. Eng., **31**(2), 223–244 (2006)
60. Rosten, E., Drummond, T.: Fusing points and lines for high performance tracking. In: Tenth IEEE International Conference on Computer Vision (ICCV 2005), vol. 1,2, pp. 1508–1515 (2005)
61. Tomasi, C., Kanade, T.: Detection and Tracking of Point Features. Carnegie Mellon University Technical Report CMU-CS-91-132 (1991)
62. Fischler, M.A., Bolles, R.C.: Random Sample Consensus: A Paradigm for Model Fitting with Applications to Image Analysis and Automated Cartography. Commun. ACM **24**(6), 381–395 (1981)
63. Keefer, R., Liu, Y., Bourbakis, N.: The Development and Evaluation of an Eyes-Free Interaction Model for Mobile Reading Devices. Human-Machine Syst. IEEE Trans. **43**(1), 76–91 (2013)
64. Dowhower, S.L.: Repeated Reading: Research into Practice. Read. Teach. **42**(7), 502–507 (1989)
65. Levy, B.A.: Text processing: Memory representations mediate fluent reading. Perspect. Hum. Mem. Cogn. aging Essays Honour Fergus Craik, 83–98 (2001)
66. Lucke, J.: Autonomous cleaning of corrupted scanned documents — a generative modeling approach. In: 2012 IEEE Conference on Computer Vision and Pattern Recognition, pp. 3338–3345 (2012)

High Dynamic Range Imaging System for the Visually Impaired

Ahmed Maalej[1]([✉]), Guillaume Tatur[2], Marie-Céline Lorenzini[2],
Christelle Delecroix[3], Gérard Dupeyron[2,3], Michel Dumas[3], and Isabelle Marc[1]

[1] LGI2P, Mines of Alès, Parc Georges Besse, Nîmes 30035, France
maalejahmed@gmail.com
[2] C.H.U of Nîmes, Place du Pr R. Debré, Nîmes 30029, France
[3] A.R.A.M.A.V Institut, 12 Chemin du Belvédère, Nîmes 30900, France

Abstract. This paper describes a portable High Dynamic Range (HDR) imaging system for visually impaired people, intended to display contrast enhanced images of real world environment. The device is composed of a digital camera and head mounted display (HMD) equipped with high resolution screens. The camera is mounted on the HMD to acquire the ambient scene, the acquired images are processed to generate HDR images through the control of local luminance information. The contrast enhancement method adopted in our system is based on pyramidal image contrast structure representation that relies on the local band-limited contrast definition. The imaging system we propose aims at displaying images that meet the visual capabilities related to contrast sensitivity of people with low vision. It also provides a solution to alleviate discomfort problem expressed by these people when they are facing real-world changing light conditions.

Keywords: High Dynamic Range (HDR) · Contrast enhancement · Assistive devices · Visually impaired · Low vision

1 Introduction

The human vision is a complex process that remains largely misunderstood, despite the great amount of studies that propose to describe and model this system. This complexity comes from the fact that the human vision is based on the eye, known as one of the most complex human organs, and regarded as the most powerful sense to collect comprehensive information on our physical world when comparing with hearing, touch, taste and smell. The eye vision

Electronic supplementary material The online version of this chapter (doi:10.1007/978-3-319-16199-0_44) contains supplementary material, which is available to authorized users. Videos can also be accessed at http://www.springerimages.com/videos/978-3-319-16198-3.

L. Agapito et al. (Eds.): ECCV 2014 Workshops, Part III, LNCS 8927, pp. 632–642, 2015.
DOI: 10.1007/978-3-319-16199-0_44

makes easy the daily living tasks, such as mobility and locomotion, reading, driving, face recognition and object manipulation. Furthermore, human eyes have extremely high visual range that can easily differentiate between very bright and dark regions in the same scene and are able to perceive a granularity with ratio on the order of 10.000.000:1 (though instantaneous sensitivity is within a range not larger than 10^2-10^3) from highlights to shadows and even greater if light sources are visible. However, visual performance is sensitive to luminance changing conditions. Under photopic (i.e daylight) luminance levels, visual functions such as acuity, contrast sensitivity, color discrimination, depth perception and motion detection are likely optimal. On the contrary, under low luminance mesopic/scotopic (i.e nightlight) conditions, performance are considerably reduced [1]. These performances severely degrade for visually impaired people who suffer from vision loss and limitation of visual capability resulting from eye diseases, such as glaucoma [2], macular degeneration [3], retinitis pigmentosa (RP) [4], diabetic retinopathy [5], and some other visual disorders.

Progressive peripheral field loss is the most important symptom of RP. At later stages of the pathology, central vision may also be reduced. But even at the earliest stages, many patients complain of difficulties or discomfort in functioning in bright light [6] and experience night blindness. For this population, the partial or total loss of vision affects the quality of life in the way that accomplishing daily activities can really be challenging. While medical and therapeutic treatments, for visual impairment, are still limited in effect, vision adaptation and rehabilitation techniques may help patients to better cope with their disabilities.

In recent years, electronic systems, namely vision aids, have also been designed for assistive applications for the visually impaired. Augmented reality appears as a promising area. Luo and Peli [7] developed a visual field expander based on an optical see-through Head Mounted Display (HMD). Their system superimposes minified edge images of the ambient scene over the wearers see through natural vision. Providing this supplemental visual information, to patients with severely restricted peripheral field (known as tunnel vision), allowed them to find targets outside their residual field of view. Molton et al. [8] propose an image processing technique using stereo-vision system to discriminate the obstacles relative to the ground. Edge enhancement on natural images is investigated as a mean of providing pertinent information to the user [9]. To the best of our knowledge, these electronic aids do not offer luminosity control in both dark and bright levels. Particularly RP users of the optical see-through devices are even more exposed to high lightening conditions because of edge enhancement, which can be painful for them.

In this work, we propose a portable High Dynamic Range (HDR) imaging system that alleviates discomfort problems faced by visually impaired people due to real world changing illumination conditions, especially toward very high or very low illuminations. The conception of this system is conducted in collaboration with low vision rehabilitation specialists (orthoptists, orientation and mobility specialists) in order to match the needs of the visually impaired. This system consists of an advanced HMD coupled with a digital camera. The camera device is used to acquire images of the ambient scene, these images are processed to generate HDR images so that the effect of light changing conditions of the real scene can be ignored, a tone mapping technique is then applied to obtain images that are visually similar to a real scene by careful mapping to a set of luminances that can be displayed on the HMD screen device. The system intend to display live HDR images of ambient scenes in a way that meets the visual capabilities of visually impaired people.

This paper is organized as follows: in Section 2 we present the HDR image generation technique we apply for our portable imaging system. In Section 3, we detail the overall architecture of our system and its application for the visually impaired, especially for people who have RP and Glaucoma. Finally, the conclusion and possible future works are given in Section 4.

2   High Dynamic Range Generation and Presentation

2.1   HDR Radiance Map

Despite recent advances in camera sensing technology, existing cameras are only capable of sensing limited dynamic range, and are still faraway from recovering the high dynamic range of light intensities within a real world scene. Several hardware and software techniques have been developed in order to capture the entire visual information present in a high dynamic range (HDR) scene[10]. When capturing any scene, digital cameras are unable to store the full dynamic range resulting in low quality images where details are concealed in shadows or washed out by bright lights. This is mainly due to the limited bit depth allocated to encode color information of each single pixel. For a true color image representation, considered to approximate natural color rendition, RGB color channels is encoded in 24-bit (8-bit per channel), which offers only 256 levels of tone. This can result in drastic dynamic range compression of the natural color/intensity and in an increase or decrease of pixel saturation toward respectively brighter or darker zones of the image, to end up with low dynamic range (LDR) image. HDR techniques were proposed to overcome this limitation, and make it possible to construct a radiance map that recovers high dynamic range from images acquired by digital cameras by combining multiple images of the same scene at different exposures. Different HDR synthesis methods exist [11–15]. The main concept of HDR image generation is based on combining multiple and differently exposed LDR images of the same subject matter. At least two LDR images are needed to build the HDR radiance map, one acquired with a short exposure time, the other with a high exposure time, respectively resulting in underexposed and overexposed images. With underexposed image, details from brighter areas of the acquired scene are captured, while for the overexposed image, details within the dark areas are highlighted. Debevec and Malik in [12] proposed a method of recovering high dynamic range radiance maps from photographs. They developed an algorithm based on exploiting the physical property of their imaging system and its response function. Knowing these characteristics is very helpful in correctly fusing pixel data from images taken from different imaging systems (photography camera, video camera, film camera, etc) regarding their different digitization processes. In their paper they elaborate the radiance equation for constructing the radiance map, given by:

$$\ln E_i = g\left(Z_{ij}\right) - \ln \Delta t_j \tag{1}$$

Where E_i is the irradiance value for a pixel i, Z_{ij} denotes the pixel value with i the spatial index over pixels and j the index over exposure times Δt_j and g is a monotonic function derived from the sensor reciprocity equation. E_i and g are recovered using a minimization approach based on a quadratic objective function.

2.2 Tone Mapping

Once calculated, radiance map poses a fundamental problem, that is how to map the large range of intensities found in such image into the limited range supported by conventional display devices (e.g. OLED,LED,LCD). The dynamic range of these various devices is much smaller than the dynamic range commonly found in real-world scenes. Therefore, when it comes to displaying an HDR image on LDR output medium, an image processing technique is applied to reduce the dynamic range, and referred to as tone mapping operator (TMO). After a step of enlarging the dynamic range of combined LDR images to generate HDR images, the principle of TMO goes in reverse direction, and it is a step of mapping the large range of intensities found in an HDR image into a limited intensity levels that meet display devices capabilities. Numerous TMO algorithms have been proposed to generate displayable HDR images [10, 16–22]. The key issue in tone mapping is then to compress an image while at the same time preserving some attributes of the image. Different TMO algorithms focus on different attributes with the result that we have a large set of algorithms which aim to preserve contrast, visible detail, brightness or even appearance.

2.3 Contrast Processing

Part of a human's ability to discern information is attributed to its capacity to perceive difference in luminance within a field of vision, Human Visual System (HVS) is mostly sensitive to relative luminance ratios (contrast) rather than absolute luminance, this can explain the fundamental adaptation ability of the HVS to real world light conditions. Contrast detection and contrast discrimination are two of the most thoroughly studied topics in vision perception literature [23,24]. Research on contrast have resulted in several definitions of contrast (e.g. simple contrast, Weber fraction, logarithmic ratio), and response of the HVS to grating stimuli (generally sinusoidal gratings) can be modelled by the contrast sensitivity function (CSF). Typically, the CSF is measured by threshold detection measurements or supra-threshold (above contrast detection threshold) contrast measurements [25]. Both permit to quantitatively evaluate variations of HVS's sensitivity over spatial frequencies. Most of contrast definitions and measurement that have been proposed in the literature were defined and derived on simple visual stimulus and simple patterns under normalized conditions, such as sinusoidal gratings or single patch of light on a uniform background. Peli [26] proposed a new definition for quantifying the contrast, designated by local band-limited contrast, which take into consideration the spatial frequency information of the contrast in images. This definition assigns a contrast value to every point in the image as a function of the spatial frequency band. The contrast is measured based on difference between selected levels of a Gaussian pyramid. Unlike the other definitions, the local band-limited contrast is suitable for complex images. However, the resulting difference of Gaussians leads to a band-pass limited measure of contrast, which tends to introduce halo artifacts at sharp edges when it is modified. Mantiuk et al.[19] developed a framework for contrast enhancement and visually appealing tone mapping demonstrated to be robust to noise and introducing no artifacts. Their work was based on the gradient domain methods which they generalized and extended to account for perceptual issues such as the sensitivity for suprathreshold contrast in HDR images. Mantiuk introduced a low-pass measure of contrast based on the logarithmic ratio G as the measure of contrast between two pixels, given by:

$$G_{i,j}^k = \log_{10}(\frac{L_i^k}{L_j^k}) \qquad (2)$$

where L_i^k and L_j^k are luminance values for neighboring pixels i and j. The first step in the tone mapping process is to use the equation (2) to transform the luminance, obtained from the radiance map calculation in section 2 to contrast. The second step is to perform the inverse operation that restores an image from modified contrast values $\widehat{G}$. This can be achieved by minimizing the objective function, given by equation 3, and that reduces the distance between a set of contrast values $\widehat{G}$ that specifies the desired contrast, and G, which is the contrast of the actual image.

$$f(x_1^1, x_2^1, \ldots, x_N^1) = \sum_{k=1}^{K} \sum_{i=1}^{N} \sum_{j \in \Phi_i} p_{i,j}^k (G_{i,j}^k - \widehat{G}_{i,j}^k)^2 \qquad (3)$$

where x_i^1 is the contrast value of the ith pixel on the finest level of the pyramid. Φ_i is the set of the neighbors of the pixel i, N is the total number of pixels, K is the number of levels in a Gaussian pyramid, and $p_{i,j}^k$ is a constant weighting factor. After getting the contrast information from pixel luminance values, it is transduced to the perceptually linearized visual response space to get response values of the HSV. A contrast mapping step is then applied on the resulting image to fit into the contrast reproduction capabilities of the display device (here the OLED HMD).

3   Application for the Visually Impaired

3.1   Visual Impairment

Visually impaired people suffer from significant limitations of visual capabilities depending on the strongly varying conditions of luminance in real-world environments. In normal vision, the retina contains two types of photoreceptors, rod and cone cells, and operates differently under distinct adaptation conditions. At high and medium average of luminance (photopic and mesopic conditions), visual functions such as acuity, contrast sensitivity and color discrimination, carried out by cones, are near optimal. At very low illumination (scotopic) level, cones do not have a sufficient sensibility and only rods are active, leading to substantially reduced acuity and contrast sensitivity. Night blindness (i.e dramatic decrease of visual acuity and contrast sensibility in mesopic and scotopic conditions) occurs when rod photoreceptors (as in retinitis pigmentosa) or optic nerve (as in glaucoma) are damaged [27]. The cone degeneration (macular degeneration and RP) strongly lowers the glare threshold and leads to photoaversion The visual adaptation to the variation of light is also slowed, as compared to normal vision : changes of luminance levels over time (from dark room to a lightened room and vice versa) can lead people to express discomfort, or even pain for a sudden and extreme change of illumination.

In order to help patients suffering from RP and Glaucoma to cope with their light sensitivity, we intend to design a new type of specialized "electronic googles" : Wear opaque glasses that completely cover the eyes allows the visually impaired to be protected against the external high luminosities. The only source of light comes from the HMD display, which can be controlled via tone mapping operator to match the user's comfort range of luminosity. On the other hand, dark areas in the real scene may be displayed with more contrast, in order to ease their comprehension.

3.2   System Architecture

The wearable aid system that we propose is composed of two major devices: a single digital camera and an advanced technology of commercialized HMD device. Fig. 1 illustrates the major components of the system. The camera is fixed on the top of the HMD, and used for data acquisition of the ambient scene. Acquired data pass through image processing pipeline build to generate HDR images. The resulting images are then displayed on the HMD screen.

Digital Camera. The camera we use is a CMOS image sensor that reaches a maximum resolution of 1920×1080 at a rate of 30 frames per second (fps) in YUY2 data output format, where YUY2 is a raw video encoding format in the family of YUV formats that encodes color images taking into account human perception, in the sense that it stores the color information the same way human brain works. Since human has finer spatial sensitivity to luminance or "luma" (black or white) differences than chromatic (color) differences, YUY2 is a type of YUV of color space representation that samples the luma (Y) once every pixel but only samples the chroma (U(Cb) and V (Cr)) once every horizontal pair of pixels. To control the exposure duration, the camera has a shutter speed that ranges from 2.10^{-4} to 1 second.

Head Mounted Display. For design prototyping we use as test platform the zSight professional head mounted display, characterized by a set of properties such as a high resolution full-color SXGA 1280×1024 pixels per eye, a 60 binocular field of view, a 24 bit of color depth encoding. The device screens are designed with the new organic light-emitting diode (OLED) technology, enabling to achieve a high contrast ratio of 10000:1 from highlights to shadows. This HMD is an occlusive device that isolates completely the user from the real wold. For better wearing comfort, the HMD is equipped with a adjustable binocular to fit the inter-pupillary distance (IPD), as well as an adjustable focus for each eye using the outer lens rings.

Using a spectrophotometer, a physical calibration procedure has been performed for light and color measurement of the HMD screens with pre-fixed parameters settings of the display (i.e brightness, contrast). This HMD profiling and calibration is needed for a better control of how this device produces colors and light energy.

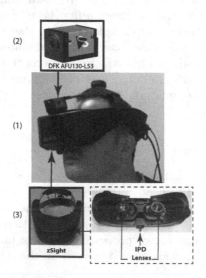

Fig. 1. (1) Portable real world HDR imaging system composed of: (2) a digital camera, (3) an OLED HMD using binocular system equipped with mechanical adjustment for inter-pupillary distance (IPD) and for focus (±4 diopters) for each eye

3.3   HDR Image Generation for the Visually Impaired

In this work we derive the Mantiuk's framework in order to perform tone mapping with a better image representation which would models the Human Visual System (HVS) performance. Simulating the HSV perceptual effects during the tone mapping process conveys a realistic impression of HDR data over a wide range of luminance, when such data are displayed on typical display devices (e.g OLED). This framework exploits Peli's study [26] which shows that contrast discrimination sensitivity, especially of complex images, is highly dependent on spatial frequency. Thus the definition of local band-limited contrast is useful for determining nonlinear threshold characteristics of spatial vision in both normal observers and the visually impaired. The contrast processing technique presented in Section 2.3, that incorporates band-limited contrast definition to measure contrast as a difference between levels of Gaussian pyramid, is applied to design a contrast enhancement method for images that improves the local image contrast by controlling the local image gradient. Since that contrast enhancement plays a very important role in increasing visual quality of an image, this method is a major part of HDR image generation pipeline. This pipeline starts from live image sensor that acquires multiple images with different exposures, the obtained images are then combined to calculate the HDR radiance map. The computed radiance map is then used to derive a contrast enhancement, as a final step, the contrast values are mapped to display LDR images on the HMD screens. This contrast mapping does not intend to only fit HDR images to LDR displays, but we want also that the displayed images meet visual capabilities of visually impaired people. The Fig. 2 illustrates three raw frames acquired with a single camera at different exposures (low, medium and high) of a scene and the obtained HDR image. The first frame is acquired with a short shutter speed resulting in an under-exposed image, where details related to illuminated areas are highlighted. The second frame is taken with medium shutter speed, useful to enlarge the set of input frames and hence a larger dynamic range of the scene luminance is considered for our HDR image generation pipeline. As for the third frame, it is taken with a high shutter speed which gives an over-exposed image where details related to shadows and poorly illuminated areas of the scene are pointed out. The resulting frame is the HDR image that is contrast-mapped for the HMD display.

The main advantage of our system is that it displays contrast-enhanced images of the ambient scene independently from its luminance conditions. Besides, the HMD encloses the eyes and the visual field of the user, fairly enough to prevent light interference of external luminance with the HMD screen radiance. Hence it will help the visually impaired to achieve optimal vision performance. To provide effective assistance, our device has to be capable of controlling the brightness emitted by the display of the HMD in order to keep it within the visual comfort range of the user, which means between a level high enough to allow detection contrasts, and a level low enough so as not to cause glare or pain. More over, transitions between different levels of luminance have to be slow enough to allow the user's visual adaptation. Accurate knowledge of

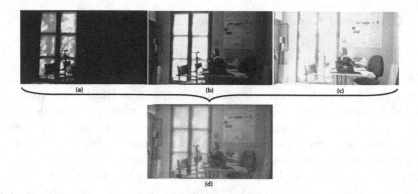

Fig. 2. (a) Under-exposed frame exploited to highlight details around the illuminated area (e.g. external tree shadow distinguished through the window door under daylight illumination), (b) frame with medium exposure used to enlarge the dynamic range inputs to the HDR image generation pipeline, (c) Over-exposed frame acquired to bring out hidden detail in the shadows and poorly illuminated areas, (d) LDR image output from our HDR image construction pipeline.

parameters such as visual comfort range of luminosity and visual adaptation speed within this comfort range, makes it possible to modify tone mapping operator to take into account visual capabilities of the user. These visual parameters are not measured quantitatively during classical orthoptic assessment, who study visual acuity, visual field, ocular motility, and color vision. Glare measurements exist [28] but are not exactly suitable for our study, as they are designed to measure visual performance under very high luminance levels. In the same way, measures of contrast sensitivity under scotopic conditions do not appear in normal procedure of low vision assessment. So we were led to design the specific psychophysical tests that allow us to measure these parameters. These test will be conducted once we have the agreement of bioethical commission.

4   Conclusion and Future Work

In this paper, we have proposed the concept of a wearable aid system for visually impaired people. The system is composed of a single digital camera and a commercialized HMD which can display realistic visual images of the environment acquired by the camera. The singularity of the displayed images is that they are the result of an HDR image generation pipeline, which combines multiple frames of the same scene at different exposures to generate an HDR image, this HDR image is the subject of a contrast mapping technique derived to obtain a displayable image on the LDR screens of the HMD. The HDR image processing technique is applied to enhance the contrast of the displayed images and intend to meet the visual capabilities of visually impaired people. These capabilities are described in terms of several parameters, assessed through specifically designed tests. To achieve contrast enhancements, local gradient luminance of images is controlled through a Gaussian pyramid representation structure.

In future, we plan to reduce the processing latency of our system, especially of the HDR image generation module which is time-consuming, in order to meet the unavoidable constraint of real time. Contrast has to be significantly enhanced for the high spatial frequencies [29] where greater reduction in sensitivity occurs. We would also like to study the color information and include a color enhancement module to our framework, using a representation similar to contrast enhancement based on the luminance information. Furthermore, technical concerns such as electrical consumption, weight and prizes of our wearable device will be investigated in a future work when proofs of efficiency are established.

Acknowledgments. This work was financially supported by Sopra Group for the larger part, and by Areva and Capgemini.

References

1. Boff, K., Kaufman, L., Thomas, J.: Handbook of Perception and Human Performance: Sensory processes and perception. Number, vol. 1 in Handbook of Perception and Human Performance. Wiley (1986)
2. Glovinsky, Y., Quigley, H.A., Drum, B., Bissett, R.A., Jampel, H.D.: A whole-field scotopic retinal sensitivity test for the detection of early glaucoma damage. Arch. Ophthalmol. **110**(4), 486–490 (1992)
3. Jackson, G.R., Owsley Jr., C., G.M.: Aging and dark adaptation. Vision Research **39**(23), 3975–3982 (1999)
4. Jacobson, S.G., Voigt, W.J., Parel, J.M., Apathy, P.P., Nghiem-Phu, L., Myers, S.W., Patella, V.M.: Automated light- and dark-adapted perimetry for evaluating retinitis pigmentosa. Ophthalmology **93**(12), 1604–16011 (1986)
5. Wolfe, K.A., Sadun, A.A.: Threshold amsler grid testing in diabetic retinopathy. Graefes Arch. Clin. Exp. Ophthalmol. **229**(3), 219–223 (1991)
6. Gawande, A.A., Donovan, W.J., Ginsburg, A.P., Marmor, M.F.: Photoaversion in retinitis pigmentosa. Br. J. Ophthalmol. **73**(2), 115–120 (1989)
7. Luo, G., Peli, E.: Development and evaluation of vision rehabilitation devices. In: EMBC, 2011 Annual International Conference of the IEEE Engineering in Medicine and Biology Society, pp. 5228–5231 (August 2011)
8. Molton, N., Se, S., Brady, J.M., Lee, D., Probert, P.: A stereo vision-based aid for the visually impaired. In: Image and Vision Computing, pp. 251–263 (1998)
9. Froissard, B., Konik, H., Trémeau, A., Dinet, E.: Contribution of augmented reality solutions to assist visually impaired people in their mobility. In: HCI (7), pp. 182–191 (2014)
10. Reinhard, E., Devlin, K.: Dynamic range reduction inspired by photoreceptor physiology. IEEE Transactions on Visualization and Computer Graphics **11**(1), 13–24 (2005)
11. Mann, P., Mann, S., Picard, R.W.: On being 'undigital' with digital cameras: Extending dynamic range by combining differently exposed pictures. In: Proceedings of IS&T, pp. 442–448 (1995)

12. Debevec, P.E., Malik, J.: Recovering high dynamic range radiance maps from photographs. In: SIGGRAPH 1997 Proceedings of the 24th Annual Conference on Computer Graphics and Interactive Techniques, pp. 369–378. ACM Press/Addison-Wesley Publishing Co, New York, NY, USA (1997)

13. Robertson, M.A., Borman, S., Stevenson, R.L.: Dynamic range improvement through multiple exposures. In: Proc. of the Int. Conf. on Image Processing (ICIP 99), pp. 159–163. IEEE (1999)

14. Mann, S.: Comparametric equations with practical applications in quantigraphic image processing. IEEE Transactions on Image Processing 9(8), 1389–1406 (2000)

15. Jinno, T., Okuda, M., Adami, N.: Acquisition and encoding of high dynamic range images using inverse tone mapping. In: ICIP 2007 IEEE International Conference on Image Processing, 4, pp. IV - 181-IV - 184 (September 2007)

16. Drago, F., Myszkowski, K., Annen, T., Chiba, N.: Adaptive logarithmic mapping for displaying high contrast scenes. Computer Graphics Forum 22, 419–426 (2003)

17. Durand, F., Dorsey, J.: Fast bilateral filtering for the display of high-dynamic-range images. In: SIGGRAPH 2002 Proceedings of the 29th Annual Conference on Computer Graphics and Interactive Techniques, pp. 257–266. ACM, New York, NY, USA (2002)

18. Fattal, R., Lischinski, D., Werman, M.: Gradient domain high dynamic range compression. ACM Trans. Graph. 21(3), 249–256 (2002)

19. Mantiuk, R., Myszkowski, K., Seidel, H.P.: A perceptual framework for contrast processing of high dynamic range images. ACM Trans. Appl. Percept. 3(3), 286–308 (2006)

20. Mantiuk, R., Daly, S., Kerofsky, L.: Display adaptive tone mapping. ACM Trans. Graph. 27(3), 68:1–68:10 (2008)

21. Pattanaik, S.N., Tumblin, J., Yee, H., Greenberg, D.P.: Time-dependent visual adaptation for fast realistic image display. In: SIGGRAPH 2000 Proceedings of the 27th Annual Conference on Computer Graphics and Interactive Techniques, pp. 47–54. ACM Press/Addison-Wesley Publishing Co., New York, NY, USA (2000)

22. Reinhard, E., Stark, M., Shirley, P., Ferwerda, J.: Photographic tone reproduction for digital images. ACM Trans. Graph. 21(3), 267–276 (2002)

23. Barten, P.: Contrast sensitivity of the human eye and its effects on image quality. Press Monographs. SPIE Optical Engineering Press (1999)

24. De Valois, R.L., De Valois, K.K.: Spatial vision. Annual Review of Psychology 31(1), 309–341 (1980)

25. Wandell, B.: Foundations of vision. Sinauer Associates (1995)

26. Peli, E.: Contrast in complex images. Journal of the Optical Society of America 7, 2032–2040 (1990)

27. Oomachi, K., Ogata, K., Sugawara, T., Hagiwara, A., Hata, A., Yamamoto, S.: Evaluation of contrast visual acuity in patients with retinitis pigmentosa. Clin. Ophthalmol. 5, 1459–1463 (2011)

28. Aslam, T.M., Haider, D., Murray, I.J.: Principles of disability glare measurement: An ophthalmological perspective. Acta Ophthalmol. Scand. 85(4), 354–360 (2007)

29. Alexander, K.R., Barnes, C.S., Fishman, G.A., Pokorny, J., Smith, V.C.: Contrast sensitivity deficits in inferred magnocellular and parvocellular pathways in retinitis pigmentosa. Invest. Ophthalmol. Vis. Sci. 45(12), 4510–4519 (2004)

A System for Assisting the Visually Impaired in Localization and Grasp of Desired Objects

Kaveri Thakoor[✉], Nii Mante, Carey Zhang, Christian Siagian,
James Weiland, Laurent Itti, and Gérard Medioni

University of Southern California, Los Angeles, CA, USA
{thakoor,mante,itti,medioni}@usc.edu,
{carey.zhang,christian.g.siagian}@gmail.com, jweiland@med.usc.edu

Abstract. A prototype wearable visual aid for helping visually impaired people find desired objects in their environment is described. The system is comprised of a head-worn camera to capture the scene, an Android phone interface to specify a desired object, and an attention-biasing-enhanced object recognition algorithm to identify three most likely object candidate regions, select the best-matching one, and pass its location to an object tracking algorithm. The object is tracked as the user's head moves, and auditory feedback is provided to help the user maintain the object in the field of view, enabling easy reach and grasp. The implementation and integration of the system leading to testing of the working prototype with visually-impaired subjects at the Braille Institute in Los Angeles (demonstration in the accompanying video) is described. Results indicate that this system has clear potential to help visually-impaired users in achieving near-real-time object localization and grasp.

Keywords: Object recognition · Attention · Tracking · Localization · Grasp · Auditory feedback · Visually impaired

1 Introduction

The World Health Organization estimates that there are 285 million visually impaired people in the world [1]. Studies by Nau et al. [2] have concluded that locating items is one of the prime tasks for which visually impaired persons continue to depend on sighted helpers. This paper describes a prototype wearable visual aid, currently under development, which provides near-real time object recognition, localization, tracking, and guidance cues to help a visually impaired user to point his or her head towards a desired object, allowing for easy reach and grasp of the target object. The system consists of an Android-phone-based

Electronic supplementary material The online version of this chapter (doi:10.1007/978-3-319-16199-0_45) contains supplementary material, which is available to authorized users. Videos can also be accessed at http://www.springerimages.com/videos/978-3-319-16198-3.

© Springer International Publishing Switzerland 2015
L. Agapito et al. (Eds.): ECCV 2014 Workshops, Part III, LNCS 8927, pp. 643–657, 2015.
DOI: 10.1007/978-3-319-16199-0_45

command module, which allows the user to query for specific items of interest via finger-touch. A two-stage computer vision algorithm next localizes and recognizes the desired item: recognition is achieved via SURF (Speeded Up Robust Features: robust local feature detector developed by Bay et al. [26]), further enhanced by an attention-biasing algorithm developed at the University of Southern California (Attention Biased Speeded Up Robust Features, AB-SURF). This algorithm [5] takes inspiration from the human cognitive system's ability to bias attention to characteristics relevant to the desired object and uses these features to locate the three most likely candidate regions in the scene where the object may be present. Next, high-performing Speeded Up Robust Features (SURF) [26] are extracted to find which one of these three possible regions best matches images of the desired object contained in the trained database; location information regarding this best region is passed to an object tracker [32]. The tracker maintains position information of the object as the user's head moves, while auditory feedback cues are provided to help the user center the object in the camera field of view for easy access. Visually impaired subjects were able to use the system to grasp desired objects within 12 to 13 seconds from the time the algorithm recognized the object, demonstrating the system's value for improving the independence and quality of life for visually impaired people.

2 Related Work: System Overview and Context

Object recognition devices for the visually impaired can be categorized into two main groups: (1) wearable, camera-based systems which process the incoming scene [6,7] and (2) smart-phone or finger-pointing based aids that recognize items within the field of view of the phone camera or region defined by the finger-point [8–11]. Of the first variety, Bjorkman et al. [6] have implemented a system which utilizes two pairs of stereo cameras, taking inspiration from the human visual process: one pair of cameras is for saccading to relevant object regions, and the other pair is for foveating (or focusing) for finer grained recognition within this relevant region. Furthermore, they utilize hue-based saliency and SIFT (Scale Invariant Feature Transform) [25] based features along with color histograms for object recognition; they also harness depth information using the stereo cameras to determine object size and filter objects based on foreground or background location. Although this approach shows good accuracy on household objects and functions quickly, its bulkiness makes it impractical for use by individuals, and there exists no means of providing guidance or feedback to a user once an object is found. On the other hand, in the work of Bigham et al. [8], the user captures an initial picture of the scene using a smartphone (though lightweight and easy to use, relies on the user's ability to frame a well-defined scene); the image is then crowd-sourced: expert sighted human annotators view the images on a website and provide back detailed segmentation and object identity information, allowing for object localization for the visually-impaired user (via auditory feedback) but relying on external annotators to obtain that goal. The OrCam [12] introduced in June of 2013 has combined both of these approaches with an eye-level camera attached to the user's glasses and basic recognition capability (of traffic lights, signs, and some objects); however, it also relies on the user having sufficient vision to point his or her finger to relevant items of interest in the surroundings. The novelty of the innovation described here lies in its combination of the best of both of the above approaches while also providing a closed loop system (that can aid even those who are completely blind, as no localization on the part of the user is required). The system utilizes only a single camera with lightweight, portable algorithms (all implemented on a single MacBook Pro I5, 2.4 GHz laptop computer), that attend, recognize, localize, track, and provide feedback to the user in near real-time from the time the user provides a tactile request for an object on an Android phone. All system components are shown in the figure below.

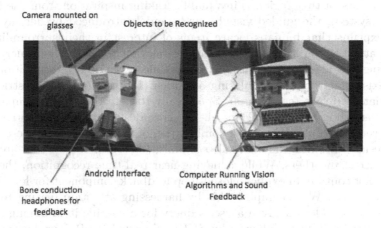

Fig. 1. All components of system shown as they are typically set during an experiment with a visually impaired subject

3   Implementation Details

3.1   Android User Command Interface

This section describes the implementation of the front-end user interface that the visually impaired user employs to provide input to the system as to which item he or she is interested in locating. A User Datagram Protocol (UDP) server-client model was chosen to allow communication between a Java-based tactile interface application on an Android phone [27], which acts as the client, and a Neuromorphic Robotics Toolkit (NRT) C++ module on the MacBook Pro laptop mentioned earlier, which acts as the server and houses all computer vision algorithms for the system (NRT is the modular toolkit developed at the University of Southern California [34] that is used for system integration throughout this paper). The Android device transmits messages in the form of strings (the name of the user's object query, e.g. "SPLENDA"), while the server module receives this string information and transforms it into a form that can be understood and processed by the rest of the object recognition chain (also built within separate NRT modules, discussed in more detail in Section 4).

3.2 Object Recognition

Alternate Recognition Techniques. Although several smart-phone based applications and electronic travel aids exist (including [9,10,12]) that provide recognition and navigation assistance to blind and low vision users, they require the user to select a 'frame' or region as input to the system. This is a real challenge for visually impaired users [2–4]. Thus, a computer vision system that can localize a desired region or object within a scene and provide recognition of the contents of that region is invaluable. Taking inspiration from the human cognitive system, the guided visual search model introduced by Jeremy Wolfe [13,14] explains that humans locate items of interest in their surroundings by focusing attention on 'targets' (key features relevant to the current query item) and paying less attention to 'distractors'. While other object recognition algorithms exist that rely on modulating attention [15], recognition is restricted to certain dataset types (cars, faces). Specifically to help the visually impaired in their grocery shopping, Winlock et al. [16] have designed a system to recognize several grocery store items using a combination of mosaicing, SURF descriptors, and Bayesian statistics; they have also established certain objects that are easier to recognize than others. While achieving near real-time recognition, their system does not contain an explicit closed-loop feedback component for localization after recognition. We accomplish this by harnessing attention biasing to fixate on regions most relevant given a user's query for a specific item among objects from a trained database, followed by SURF (Speeded Up Robust Features) for object recognition in the chosen regions. As another alternative, sensory substitution devices (SSDs) are a unique class of aids for the blind that use a modality other than vision to convey visual information to the user. An example of an SSD is the vOICe system. The vOICe SSD represents the camera-captured scene via an auditory soundscape. The vOICe conversion program [17] transforms a scene into auditory information ('soundscapes') based on three rules: the vertical axis (i.e., elevation of the object) is represented by frequency, the horizontal axis by time and stereo panning, and the brightness of the image is encoded by loudness. Although these conversion rules appear relatively simple, explicit and quite extensive training is required to learn how to interpret even simple shapes. Learning to use the vOICe SSD requires months of training before independent utility can be achieved [18].

While SSDs, electronic travel aids, and smart phone applications may provide some form of scene understanding, they suffer from various disadvantages: excessive reliance on human neuroplasticity and learning before a blind person can use them productively, inability to locate the relevant regions where desired objects may be present in a scene, and potentially uncomfortable latency times before a recognition response is provided to a user. Our work, Attention-Biased

Speeded Up Robust Features (AB-SURF), provides both localization and recognition and is optimized for integration into a closed loop system which also tracks the recognized object and provides real-time feedback, allowing the user to independently query, seek, and reach out to grasp a desired object in the surroundings.

Traditional computer vision object recognition models rely on sliding-window detectors (i.e. application of object recognition algorithms on overlapping subimages of the scene, tessellating the whole scene, a computationally intensive and time consuming process) [19,20]. To enhance efficiency, we have replaced this technique by an attention-based mechanism that narrows down regions of interest by biasing the search toward statistical features consistent with the query object. Attention mechanisms are broken into three different types: (1) those stemming from bottom-up cues [21,22], e.g. inherently conspicuous regions, (2) those influenced by top-down (task-driven) motivation, e.g. knowledge of the target item [24], and (3) those resulting from a blend of bottom-up and top down forces [23,24]. The bottom-up saliency maps are computed via the method of Itti and Koch [24]. Specifically, in our top down approach, we use 30 hues and 6 saturations within the color dimension, 12 intensities within the luminance dimension, and 8 orientations. Overall, this narrows the space over which recognition must compute, yielding a five-fold speedup as compared to SURF performance alone on 640 x 480-pixel images. In addition, we achieve object recognition accuracy with AB-SURF in simple cluttered scenes comparable to the recognition accuracy of SURF on single, isolated objects (more quantitative results discussed in next section).

Neurally-Inspired Object Recognition: Attention-Biased Speeded Up Robust Features (AB-SURF). Here we describe implementation and performance of an algorithm, Attention Biased Speeded Up Robust Features (AB-SURF), to localize as well as recognize objects contained in regions of interest. AB-SURF functions by computing a biased saliency map; unlike a bottom-up saliency map [24], which is generated by determining the most inherently salient regions in a scene by extracting features across channels of hue and orientation and weighing all features equally, a biased saliency map is generated by heavily weighing those characteristics most consistent with the item of interest, allowing for attention to be focused to regions relevant for a given query even if they are not necessarily the most conspicuous regions at first glance. Once these regions are extracted, SURF-based [26] object recognition is used to evaluate these top three regions to determine the best match given the query, outputting only the top result as the recognized object.

Complete analysis of attention-biased SURF object recognition was carried out on 382 10-object images and 655 5-object images in [5]; True Positive Rates (TPRs: number of instances when the object was correctly recognized as present out of the total number of tested images) are plotted for each object below. All five objects present in the 5-object images exhibit true positive recognition rates of greater than 80%, with three of the five objects having recognition rates of greater than 99%. Overall, the 5-object case yields excellent results. Furthermore, attention biasing significantly reduces the computation required for recognition by eliminating the need for a brute force sliding window approach to locate a desired object in the image. The sliding window approach (at 50% window overlap) would require at least 40 subwindows (or many more, if the sliding window overlap is greater than 50% to improve performance) to be recognized per frame, instead of just the 3 subwindows selected by attention-biasing, requiring 7 to 8 seconds to process.

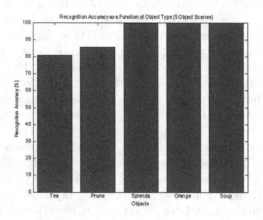

Fig. 2. Plot of true positive recognition rate for each of the five objects in 5-object scenes

Scenes with 10 household objects exhibit an expected reduction in accuracy due to the larger image area captured (by moving the camera back) to accommodate more objects, resulting in lower resolution for each object. Accuracy for 5 of the objects ranges from 63% to 96%. However, true positive recognition rates of the other 5 objects consistently remain less than 50%, with three of these below 10% chance level. Thus, attention biasing is helpful for some objects (Orange, Prune, Soup, Splenda, Cereal). These also are the largest of the 10 representative household objects chosen; hence, they fill most of the area in the recognized subwindows, making them well-matched to the subwindow size chosen (180 by 180 pixels). By contrast, the 5 objects for which attention-biased object recognition exhibits low accuracy occupy only a fraction of the chosen subwindow, suggesting that conducting these analyses with tuned subwindow sizes may improve accuracy for certain objects, as less surrounding clutter will reduce confusion for the feature-based recognition algorithm. Therefore, future extensions will benefit from harnessing depth information via input from a PrimeSense depth sensor to obtain more accurate object segmentation, in order to filter objects based on size and shape, enabling more robust, accurate object recognition.

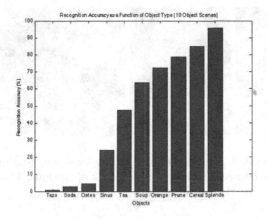

Fig. 3. Plot of true positive recognition rate for each of the ten objects in 10-object scenes. Seven of the ten objects exhibit classification accuracy above chance (ten percent).

3.3 Object Localization and Tracking System (OLTS)

In the context of this system, tracking algorithms serve as a means to detect objects in real time. Real time conditions come in to play because one of the main purposes of the system is to give dynamic feedback to human users. Thus, it was necessary to choose a state of the art tracker. There are several trackers which track objects via assuming search areas within the frame [29–31], or which use state prediction via particle filters to determine object trajectory.

The aforementioned trackers yield desirable results; however, their flaws are exposed in videos exhibiting abrupt motion, frame-cuts, or objects leaving the field of view [32]. These are all constraints necessary for the OLTS. While employing the OLTS, the user wears a head mounted camera with a 100 degree field of view (FOV); thus, abrupt motion or objects leaving the FOV may occur. These considerations led us to utilizing the Context Tracker [32].

The system utilizes the Context Tracker and an auditory feedback module, the Sound Map. The system only requires one video frame with a bounding box enclosing the object to be tracked. Once this bounding box has been provided to the tracker, the tracker continually detects the object in the following frames, and the position of the object is updated within the control loop of the program. This position is then passed to the auditory feedback algorithm. The feedback algorithm then provides speech-synthesized commands to the user based on the position of the aforementioned object. The specifics of the vision algorithm and feedback module will be explained below.

Context Tracker. The Context Tracker, which makes use of the P-N tracker [32], was the tracker of choice for the OLTS, as it is a basic target tracker. In addition to P-N learning, the Context tracker utilizes contextual information

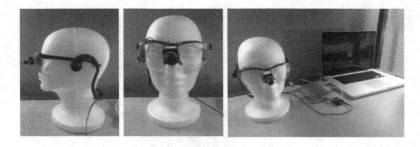

Fig. 4. OLTS hardware. A camera mounted to glasses sends visual input to the computer. The computer houses the vision and feedback algorithms. The bone conduction headphones relay information to the subject.

to robustly track objects. This contextual information is categorized into two entities: supporters and distracters. Supporters are features that consistently occur around the object; distracters are regions that have similar appearance to the actual target/object [32]. The addition of supporters and distracters allows the context tracker to deal with frame cuts, similar objects, and abrupt motion.

Auditory Feedback. The feedback algorithm, the Sound Map, yields speech-synthesized feedback to the user based on the position of the desired object. It does so by discretizing the camera field of view into 9 regions (Figure 5). Depending upon the region in which the object resides, the computer synthesizes spoken words back to the user.

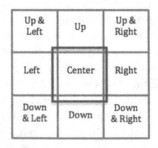

Fig. 5. Sound Map for auditory feedback mechanism. The grid represents a camera field of view (FOV). The position of the object in 3D space is mapped to the 2D FOV above. Once the object is mapped to this FOV, it falls into one of the 9 grid cells. Depending upon the grid to which the object belongs, the computer conveys the corresponding word. The size of this entire grid covers 640 x 480 pixels.

The user's goal is to listen to voice feedback, and turn his or her head based on the synthesized words. Once the object is within the "Center" region of the camera, the computer conveys the synthesized word "Center" to the user through bone conduction headphones. The user then reaches and grasps the desired object. A central angle of 23.4 degrees was chosen, as this was determined to allow for optimal grasp based on another study [33].

4 System Integration

The modular components of the system were integrated within the Neuromorphic Robotics Toolkit developed at the University of Southern California [34]. The attention-biasing, recognition, user interface, tracking, and feedback modules are shown below in Figure 6 with their corresponding input and output ports. These ensure correct information is passed between modules as needed to allow for their functionality, much like arguments can be passed from function to function in a computer program.

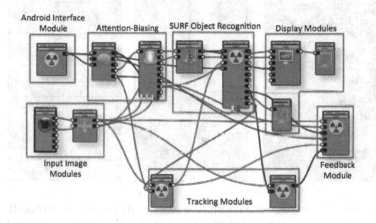

Fig. 6. System integration in Neuromorphic Robotics Toolkit; system components are labeled; links between modules represent inputs and outputs needed for functioning of each subpart based on information from other subparts.

5 Methods

The prototype system was taken to the Braille Institute in Los Angeles, California (USA) for testing with visually impaired subjects. Subjects were seated in front of one, two, or three household objects either positioned at the center, left, or right of the visual field. They were provided with an Android phone interface with the "Talk Accessibility Mode" turned on (upon one tap of a button on the screen, the function of the button is spoken out loud; two quick taps in succession are required to execute the command controlled by the button). The Android interface employs software developed in [27], which allows the user to "Find" a specific item and then shows a screen of ten possible objects (images of the Android interface screens are shown in Figure 7); we restricted search in this experiment to a box of Splenda or a carton of Orange juice. Subjects were instructed to double-tap the name of a single pre-specified object in front of them and then wait to hear cues as to where the object was located; when the 'center' or 'stay' command was given, they were instructed to reach out with their hand in a straight line from their nose until they touched the object situated approximately arm's length (0.45m to 0.61m, 1.5ft to 2ft) away. It is noteworthy that currently the computer vision algorithms are implemented on a laptop, for development and testing purposes, that may be placed in a backpack worn by the user for mobility; work is ongoing toward designing and building dedicated hardware for the vision algorithms described that is even smaller and more portable.

Fig. 7. Images of Android phone interface screens: (left) control for setting IP address and port number for communication with server module described in Section 3.1, (middle) option to 'Find' a specific object, (right) specific object query options for localization and grasp.

Fig. 8. (Left) Subject wearing the head mounted camera and bone conduction headphones. (Right) Example scene with objects and 9-region grid overlayed.

6   Results

Three visually-impaired subjects (due to Retinitis Pigmentosa, Cytomegalovirus Retinitis, and Optic Nerve Dysplasia, respectively) utilized the system and provided their evaluation using the System Usability Scale [35]. Reported scores were 82.5, 92.5, and 80.0, respectively. Time was recorded for each stage of the algorithm for two of these subjects (an optimal method of data collection was established after the first subject), including time to grasp the object and total time to use the system from the time the query was initiated. Average time is reported below in seconds for each stage (AB: Attention-Biasing). Out of the ten trials conducted for each subject, trials were excluded in cases when retraining was required mid-use due to a misunderstanding of how to use the system, and trials were excluded if the recognition algorithm failed so as not to confuse the subjects (this will be discussed in further detail in the next section).

Table 1. Time taken for Attention-Biasing (AB), Recognition, and Grasping (in seconds). Of the 10 trials conducted, 4 were excluded from subject RP and 2 from subject RT (2 of these (for RP), 1(for RT) due to subject misinterpretation of cues and 2 (for RP), 1(for RT) due to incorrect recognition result from algorithm).

Patient ID	AB	Recognition	Grasp	Total
RP (n = 6)	6.20	5.55	13.0	31.6
RT (n = 8)	7.36	7.43	12.8	41.8

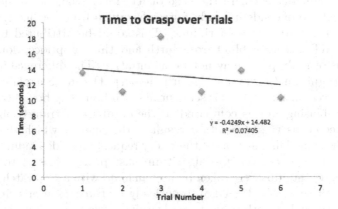

Fig. 9. Time taken to grasp object as a function of trial number for subject RP, $p = 0.602$

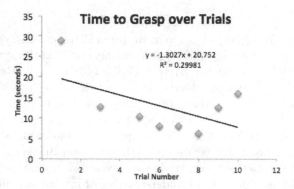

Fig. 10. Time taken to grasp object as a function of trial number for subject RT, $p = 0.160$

7 Discussion

From results shown above, we observe that subjects were able to use the system independently for a majority of the conducted trials and successfully obtain the desired object. Out of the 10 trials conducted for each subject, in 2 out of the 10 trials for subject RP and 1 out of 10 for subject RT, the recognition algorithm did not correctly recognize the presence of the object; hence these trials were excluded. In the case of RP, for 2 trials, the subject extended a hand outward higher than nose level, so these were excluded; the subject was retrained before experiments were continued. In the case of RT, for 1 trial, the subject moved a hand laterally to one side instead of straight out in front for one trial, so the subject was retrained before continuing. This could be attributed to the fact that subject RT has been blind from birth and thus proprioception of space and positions of body parts may not be as intuitive. The difference in time for achieving recognition (purely an algorithmic output) can be explained by the fact that the recognition process is sequential (each bounding box obtained from the attention-biasing step is compared to the database of trained objects; the final box selected as the recognition result is the one for which the matched object has the same label as that of the query requested, so depending on which of the three boxes is correct, the algorithm must process from 1 to 3 boxes). Furthermore, timestamps were taken by human hand with a stopwatch. In future experiments, these will be logged automatically by the computer being used to run the algorithms. For both subjects, no learning effect was observed ($p > 0.1$ in both cases) over trials with the system. This insignificant learning trend can be attributed to the extensive training completed with the subjects prior to running these experiments. Conducting experiments with more subjects and with more trials per subject will help to confirm this conclusion.

8   Conclusions

Our prototype system provides visually-impaired users the ability to query for a specific item of interest and receive explicit object recognition, localization, and feedback information to allow for ease of grasping of the desired object. To our knowledge, this is the first closed-loop system of its kind that provides explicit object localization and recognition as well as audio feedback for grasp without the need for the user to define a relevant region of the scene. The average time to grasp a desired object is between 12 to 13 seconds from recognition response (31 to 42 seconds from query initiation). These results along with the high system usability scale scores given by these three subjects indicate that this assistive computer vision tool is a promising aid for the visually-impaired, who make up nearly 5% of the global population. It is expected that the grasp response times can be improved to under 10 seconds with the incorporation of real-time hardware implementations of the algorithms described here, such as FPGA or GPU based implementations [36]. Furthermore, the computer vision algorithms described have the potential to serve not only as assistive algorithms for the blind but can also provide autonomous recognition and tracking in defense or exploratory (underwater/space) situations, that may be unfit or unsafe for human travel.

Acknowledgments. This research and development project/program/initiative was conducted by the University of Southern California and is made possible by a cooperative agreement that was awarded and administered by the U.S. Army Medical Research and Materiel Command (USAMRMC) and the Telemedicine and Advanced Technology Research Center (TATRC), at Fort Detrick, MD under Contract Number: W81XWH-10-2-0076. This research was also made possible by an Unrestricted Departmental Grant from Research to Prevent Blindness, New York, NY 10022. The authors would like to thank Dr. Sophie Marat for her essential algorithmic contributions to the development of the prototype system described in this manuscript.

References

1. Visual Impairment and Blindness Fact Sheet, World Health Organization (2012). http://www.who.int/mediacentre/factsheets/fs282/en/ (accessed: May 6, 2013)
2. Nau, A.C.: Gaps in assistive technology for the blind: understanding the needs of the disabled. In: Keynote Lecture, IEEE ICME Workshop on Multimodal and Alternative Perception for Visually Impaired People (MAP4VIP), San Jose, CA (July 2013)
3. Manduchi, R., Coughlan, J.: The last meter: blind visual guidance to a target. In: Proceedings of the SIGCHI Conference on Human Factors in Computing Systems (2014)
4. Manduchi, R., Coughlan, J.: (Computer) vision without sight. Communications of the ACM **55**(1) (2012)

5. Thakoor, K., Marat, S., Nasiatka, P.J., McIntosh, B.P., Sahin, F.E., Tanguay, A.R., Weiland, J.D., Itti, L.: Attention-Biased speeded-up robust features (AB-SURF): a neurally-inspired object recognition algorithm for a wearable aid for the visually impaired. In: IEEE ICME Workshop on Multimodal and Alternative Perception for Visually Impaired People (MAP4VIP), San Jose, CA (July 2013) (Best Student Paper Award)

6. Bjorkman, M., Eklundh, J.-O.: Vision in the Real World: Finding, Attending, and Recognizing Objects. International Journal of Imaging Systems and Technology **16**, 189–208 (2007)

7. Schauerte, B., Martinez, M., Constantinescu, A.: An assistive vision system for the blind that helps find lost things. In: Proceedings of the 13th International Conference on Computers Helping People with Special Needs, vol 2, pp. 566–572 (2012)

8. Bigham, J.P., Jayant, C., Miller, A., White, B., Yeh, T.: VizWiz: locateIt-enabling blind people to locate objects in their environment. In: IEEE Computer Society Conference on Computer Vision and Pattern Recognition Workshops (CVPRW) (2010)

9. Nanayakkara, S.C., Shilkrot, R., Maes, P.: EyeRing: a finger-worn assistant. In: International ACM SIGCHI Conference on Human Factors in Computing, Austin, TX (2012)

10. Matusiak, K., Skulimowski, P., Strurnillo, P.: Object recognition in a mobile phone application for visually impaired users. In: The 6th International Conference on Human System Interaction (HSI), pp. 479–484 (2013)

11. Recognizer, L.: Looktel (2009). http://www.looktel.com/recognizer (accessed February 23, 2013)

12. OrCam - See for Yourself. http://www.orcam.com/ (accessed: May 01, 2014)

13. Wolfe, J.M.: Guided search 2.0: a revised model of visual search. Psychonomic Bulletin and Review **1**(2), 202–238 (1994)

14. Treisman, A.M., Gelade, G.: A Feature-Integration Theory of Attention. Cognitive Psychology **12**, 97–136 (1980)

15. Gepperth, A.R.T., Rebhan, S., Hasler, S., Fritsch, J.: Biased Competition in Visual Processing Hierarchies: A Learning Approach Using Multiple Cues. Cognitive Computation **3**(1), 146–166 (2011)

16. Winlock, T., Christiansen, E., Belongie, S.: Toward real-time grocery detection for the visually impaired. In: IEEE Computer Society Conference on Computer Vision and Pattern Recognition Workshops (CVPRW), pp. 49–56 (2010)

17. Meijer, P.B.: An experimental system for auditory image representations. IEEE Transactions on Biomedical Engineering **39**(2), 112–121 (1992)

18. Striem-Amit, E., Guendelman, M., Amedi, A.: Visual Acuity of the Congenitally Blind Using Visual-to-Auditory Sensory Substitution. PLoS ONE **7**(3), March 2012

19. Papageorgiou, C., Poggio, T.: A trainable system for object detection. International Journal of Computer Vision **38**(1), 15–33 (2000)

20. Moghaddam, B., Pentland, A.: Probabilistic visual learning for object representation. IEEE Transactions on Pattern Analysis and Machine Intelligence **19**(7), 696–710 (1997)

21. Marat, S., Ho-Phuoc, T., Granjon, L., Guyader, N., Pellerin, D., Guerin-Dugue, A.: Modeling Spatio-Temporal Saliency to Predict Gaze Direction for Short Videos. International Journal of Computer Vision **82**(3), 231–243 (2009)

22. Rutishauser, U., Walther, D., Koch, C., Perona, P.: Is bottom-up attention useful for object recognition?. In: IEEE Conference on Computer Vision and Pattern Recognition (2004)

23. Navalpakkam, V., Itti, L.: Modeling the influence of task on attention. Vision Research **45**(2), 205–231 (2005)
24. Itti, L., Koch, C.: A saliency-based search mechanism for overt and covert shifts of visual attention. Vision Research **40**(10), 1489–1506 (2000)
25. Lowe, D.G.: Distinctive Image Features from Scale-Invariant Keypoints. International Journal of Computer Vision **60**(2) (2004)
26. Bay, H., Tuytelaars, T., Van Gool, L.: SURF: speeded up robust features. In: Leonardis, A., Bischof, H., Pinz, A. (eds.) ECCV 2006, Part I. LNCS, vol. 3951, pp. 404–417. Springer, Heidelberg (2006)
27. Adebiyi, A., Zhang, C., Thakoor, K., Weiland, J.D.: Feedback measures for a wearable visual aid designed for the visually impaired. Association for Research in Vision and Ophthalmology Annual Meeting, May 5–9, Seattle, Washington (2013)
28. Aly, M., Welinder, P., Munich, M., Perona, P.: Scaling object recognition: benchmark of current state of the art techniques. In: IEEE 12th International Conference on Computer Vision Workshops (ICCV Workshops) (2009)
29. Adam, A., Rivlin, E., Shimshoni, I.: Robust fragments-based tracking using the integral histogram. In: International Conference on Computer Vision and Pattern Recognition (2006)
30. Babenko, B., Yang, M.-H., Belongie, S.: Visual tracking with online multiple instance learning. In: International Conference on Computer Vision and Pattern Recognition (2009)
31. Grabner, H., Leistner, C., Bischof, H.: Semi-supervised on-line boosting for robust tracking. In: Forsyth, D., Torr, P., Zisserman, A. (eds.) ECCV 2008, Part I. LNCS, vol. 5302, pp. 234–247. Springer, Heidelberg (2008)
32. Dinh, T., Vo, N., Medioni, G.: Context tracker: exploring supporters and distracters in unconstrained environments. In: International Conference on Computer Vision and Pattern Recognition (2011)
33. Mante, N., Medioni, G., Tanguay, A., Weiland, J.: An auditory feedback study on the object localization and tracking system. In: Biomedical Engineers Society Annual Meeting (BMES Annual Meeting) (2014)
34. iLab Neuromorphic Robotics Toolkit: Get NRT. http://nrtkit.org/documentation/g_GetNRT.html (accessed: June 29, 2014)
35. Measuring Usability with the System Usability Scale (SUS): Measuring Usability. http://www.measuringusability.com/sus.php (accessed: June 29, 2014)
36. Kestur, S., Park, M.S., Sabarad, J., Dantara, D., Narayanan, V.: Emulating mammalian vision on reconfigurable hardware. In: IEEE 20th Annual International Symposium on Field-Programmable Custom Computing Machines (FCCM), pp. 141–148 (2012)

Descending Stairs Detection with Low-Power Sensors

Severine Cloix[1,2]($\boxtimes$), Guido Bologna[2], Viviana Weiss[2], Thierry Pun[2], and David Hasler[1]

[1] Centre Suisse d'Electronique et de Microtechnique, Neuchâtel, Switzerland
[2] Computer Science Department, University of Geneva, Geneva, Switzerland
Severine.Cloix@csem.ch

Abstract. With the increasing proportion of senior citizens, many mobility aid devices were developed such as the rollator. However among walker's users, 87% of their falls is attributed to rollators. The EyeWalker project aims at developing a small device for rollators to protect elderly people from such dangers. Descending stairs are ones of the potential hazards rollator users have to daily face. We propose a method to detect them in real-time using a passive stereo camera. To meet the requirements of low-power consumption, we examined the performance of our stereo vision based detector with regard to the camera resolution. It succeeds in differentiating dangerously approaching stairs from safe situations at low resolutions. In the future, our detector will be ported on an embedded platform equipped with a pair of low-resolution and high dynamic range stereo camera for both indoor and outdoor usage with a battery-life of several days.

Keywords: Descending stair detection · Stereo vision · Elderly care · Rehabilitation · Visual impairment · Low-power sensors

1 Introduction

In industrialized countries the number of mobility impaired people increases especially among the elderly [14,21]. Studies demonstrate that the population of the over 65s is growing and the governments' will is to improve the elderly's independence and home caring in order to postpone their move to an assisted living facility integration. The rollator, widely spread among elderly, aims at helping its users keep their independence and a safe mobility. However these tools can lead to falls especially in urban zones and buildings. They occur when the user misjudges the nature or the extent of some obstacles, which can happen in any kind of familiar or unknown environments. To answer these issues, various prototypes of "intelligent walkers" are motorized [17] and programmed to plan routes and to detect obstacles with active or passive sensors. However such aids are complex and thus expensive even if produced in large quantities. As a result, most users may be reluctant to use them. In practice their use is limited to indoor situations due to their weight and their short battery life.

© Springer International Publishing Switzerland 2015
L. Agapito et al. (Eds.): ECCV 2014 Workshops, Part III, LNCS 8927, pp. 658–672, 2015.
DOI: 10.1007/978-3-319-16199-0_46

Unlike the current trend, the EyeWalker project's objective is to develop a low-cost, ultra-light computer vision-based device for users with mobility problems. It is meant to be an independent accessory that can be easily fixed on a standard rollator and with a daylong autonomy. Our device will warn users of potentially hazardous situations and help locate particular items, such as everyday objects. It has to operate in miscellaneous environments and under widely varying illumination conditions. The users initially targeted by this project are elderly persons that still live independently. According to elderly care experts that we interviewed, descending sidewalks and stairs are among the most common hazards. Thus our system aims at detecting descending stairs. To meet the requirements of both low-power consumption and outdoor and indoor usage, we focused on employing methods based on 3D information obtained from a passive stereo camera.

The power consumption of a full system results from the power consumption of the hardware and the software. Since the image resolution impacts both the power consumption of the sensor and of the processing, our goal is to find a low complexity algorithm which works with the lowest acceptable image resolution. We propose a descending stair detector based on depth information obtained from a stereo vision algorithm adapted to real-time.

This paper is organized as follows: Section 2 describes relevant examples related to the state-of-the-art in stereo computer vision; Section 3 explains how to detect descending stairs from 3D sensors; The main stereo vision approaches, which allow 3D information extraction, are recalled in Section 4; Section 5 describes the hardware choices and setup built for the evaluation of our approach; The experimental results, where we look for the lowest acceptable resolution, are detailed and discussed in Section 6 before concluding on the future work in Section 7.

2 Related Works

Sidewalks and stairs are among the obstacles mobility impaired people have to daily face [27]. Even though laws and new constructions are made to improve their accessibility, there is still work to be done. Several institutions propose guidelines both for constructors [3] and users [9]. Works on stair detection have started in the robotic domain for Unmanned Ground Vehicles (UGV) [26]. The UGVs are built to navigate in buildings where security is not assured, for example for searching victims in buildings. While detecting staircases and climbing stairs/sidewalks [2,7,8,19] are subject to research, rare are the studies on detecting descending stairs in the computer vision domain. In the field of electronic travel aids (ETA), PAM-AID is the only prototype demonstrating its ability to detect descending stairs [18]. However this prototype uses an active IR sensor. To our knowledge, authors of [13] are the only ones who proposed to tackle the detection of the descending stairs using passive computer vision. In their method, once the staircase candidates are detected with texture energy measurement, one is randomly selected and used to validate the presence of descending stairs. Other computer vision based stair detectors use monocular cameras and encounter the issue of false positives raised by repetitive patterns such as zebra crossings [25].

3   Method

We are interested in the falls related to the loss of balance caused by the change of the ground elevation. We aim at measuring this change from a ground depth map. Given the acquisition of a semi-dense 3D map from a system as depicted in 1, each point (x, y) of the ground depth map can be expressed by: let (X, Y, Z) be a 3D point in the world space and R the rotation matrix that positions the depth axis vertically. Thus the new coordinate system has its Z-axis orthogonal to the floor, X-axis becomes normal to the rollator's motion and Y-axis parallel to said motion. The centre of both coordinate systems is the centre of the stereo rig, both cameras having the same focal length f, expressed in pixels. To get the

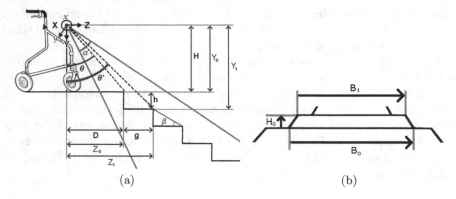

(a)   (b)

Fig. 1. (a) A rollator facing a descending stair. The stereo camera is tilt so that the beginning of the stairs and its first step give angles of θ and θ'. The latter are respectively located at a distance of Z_0 and Z_1 and a height of Y_0 and Y_1 from the camera. (b) The first step imaged by the camera as a trapezoid defined by its bases B_0, B_1 and its height H_0.

corresponding pixel coordinates of (X, Y, Z) in the ground depth map, a point in 3D space is subject to a rotation around the X-axis:

$$R \begin{pmatrix} X \\ Y \\ Z \end{pmatrix} \tag{1}$$

with

$$R = \begin{pmatrix} 1 & 0 & 0 \\ 0 & cos\theta & -sin\theta \\ 0 & sin\theta & cos\theta \end{pmatrix} , \tag{2}$$

followed by a projection according the 3x3 camera projection matrix P:

$$P = \begin{pmatrix} f & 0 & 0 \\ 0 & f & 0 \\ 0 & 0 & 1 \end{pmatrix} . \tag{3}$$

The resulting coordinates in the ground depth image are

$$x = f \frac{X}{Y sin\theta + Z cos\theta} , \tag{4}$$

$$y = f \frac{Y cos\theta - Z sin\theta}{Y sin\theta + Z cos\theta} . \tag{5}$$

Note that we used capital letters for world coordinates and lower case for image coordinates. These equations define the limits to detect the stair first. Let the floor be located at depth $Z = Z_0$ and let the first step start at $(Y, Z) = (Y_0, Z_0)$ and end at $(Y, Z) = (Y_1, Z_1)$ in the original coordinate system. We assume the stairs are centred in front of the stereo camera. The step is imaged by the camera as a trapezoid defined by its bases B_0, B_1 and its height H_0:

$$B_0 = \frac{f(Z_1 - Z_0)}{Y_0 sin\theta + Z_0 cos\theta} , \tag{6}$$

$$B_1 = \frac{f(Z_1 - Z_0)}{Y_1 sin\theta + Z_1 cos\theta} \tag{7}$$

$$H_0 = f \frac{Y_0 cos\theta - Z_0 sin\theta}{Y_0 sin\theta + Z_0 cos\theta} - f \frac{Y_1 cos\theta - Z_1 sin\theta}{Y_1 sin\theta + Z_1 cos\theta} \tag{8}$$

$$= \frac{f(Y_0 Z_1 - Z_0 Y_1)}{(Y_0 sin\theta + Z_0 cos\theta)(Y_1 sin\theta + Z_1 cos\theta)} . \tag{9}$$

The trapezoid's area of the projected step on the depth map is defined by

$$A = \frac{(B_0 + B_1)H_0}{2} , \tag{10}$$

where the area A is constrained by its sign, i.e. by

$$A > 0 \iff (\frac{Y_0}{Z_0} - \frac{Y_1}{Z_1}) > 0 , \tag{11}$$

which corresponds to tilting the camera by an angle big enough to see the first step in the lower part of the image according to

$$\theta < \theta' . \tag{12}$$

This area also defines the proportion of pixels located at a deeper level than the ground if we consider the projection of several steps. This proportion of pixels is then compared to a threshold T_D: The stair presence is predicted when the ratio of pixels located under a ground is greater than the proportion T_D. To classify each capture into one of the three classes (danger, warning or safe), the decision making strategy follows the flowchart depicted in Fig. 2 and summarized in Table 1. By defining two zones in the picture we impose the condition that the angle θ defined by the focal axis of the system is less than the angle θ' defined by the location of the first step that must be detected as a danger.

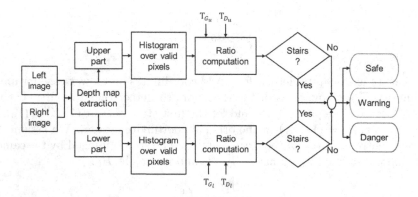

Fig. 2. Flowchart of our approach to detect descending stairs, T_{D_u}, T_{D_l}, T_{G_u} and T_{G_l} being the pixel ratio and ground depth thresholds for the upper and lower sub-images respectively

In other words, our three-bin classifier works as follows: the ground depth map is extracted from the stereo pictures and divided into the upper and lower sub-images of same size. For each sub-image we compute the histogram over valid depth values. The ratio of pixels located below a ground level T_{Gi} (i={u,l}) is then compared to a threshold T_{Di}. If this ratio is greater than T_{Di} then the sub-image is classified as a stair (positive). The final decision is made from the binary classification of the two sub-images: (i) it is safe if both sub-images are negative; (ii) it is a warning if the upper sub-image is positive and the lower one is negative; (ii) it is a danger if the lower sub-image is positive, no matter what the prediction is for the upper sub-image.

4   Stereo Vision

4.1   Stereo Matching

Stereo correspondence is a challenging field of research [20] in term of software and hardware implementation. It has to respond to the high demand of real-time execution and frame rates. From the matched points we can extract a disparity map. The disparity is the difference between the x-coordinates of the detected point in both pictures. Provided the correct matching, the depth map is built

Table 1. Three-bin classification rules according to the dangerousness of the fronting floor, T_{Du} and T_{Dl} being pixel ratio thresholds

Upper sub-image	Lower sub-image	Class prediction	Class definition
$Ratio < T_{Du}$	$Ratio < T_{Dl}$	Safe	No stairs in the whole image
$Ratio > T_{Du}$	$Ratio < T_{Dl}$	Warning	Stairs appear in the upper sub-image only i.e. far from the user
Any	$Ratio > T_{Dl}$	Danger	Stairs appear at least in the lower sub-image i.e. close to the user

from the disparity map using image geometry triangulation [12]. Assuming the pin-hole camera model [12] and the cameras having the same focal length f, separated by a baseline T, the distance of a detected point is

$$Z = \frac{f \times T}{d} \, , \tag{13}$$

where Z is expressed in meters, f in pixels, T in meters and d the disparity in pixels.

The stereo matching approaches can be categorized into two groups: sparse or dense [20]. The first approach is also known as feature-based matching and results in a sparse output. The correspondence process is applied to features such as corners, edges or key points [1]. In order to compare the different key points, we shall measure their similarity. This similarity can either result from comparing the surroundings via patches or attributes commonly called descriptors [5]. Each descriptor of the left image points is compared to the list of descriptors of the right image points and matched to the most similar one. Feature descriptors tend to be robust against orientation and intensity variation while key points are robust to perspective changes. Thus this method can be applied for real-time applications that require a very sparse depth map [6], for example in image registration applications. Besides it does not require precise calibration.

The second stereo correspondence approach relies on comparing patches of images in order to minimize a cost function. This cost function can be local or global [20]. As far as local methods are concerned, the aim is to minimize the difference between the patches located on the epipolar lines in order to finally get the disparity for every pixel of the reference image. The taxonomy of stereo matching [22] is the reference in the domain of global stereo correspondence. However the algorithms can be time, memory and power consuming. Konolige proposed a real-time stereo matching algorithm based on sum of absolute difference (SAD) and implemented on FPGA [15]. The patch centred on each pixel of the reference image is compared to a patch centred on a pixel in the other image located on the epipolar line and within a disparity range to reduce the processing time, especially when the desired depth range is known. The size of the SAD window is also a heuristic defined before processing. The algorithm used by the commercial stereo camera Bumblebee2[1] dedicated for real-time applications and used for our experiments is also SAD-based. Our problem can be solved using depth maps that are only partially dense. To compute the depth map, we apply Konolige's algorithm and keep only the values that are associated to a high matching score. Thus some of the locations of the depth map are undefined, which leads to a semi-dense depth map. The remaining valid pixels form a set of reliable depth values.

4.2   Stereo Cameras

As explained in [16], passive stereo vision suffers from matching failure on low-textured regions and repetitive patterns. Projecting a texture on the scene drastically improves the stereo matching. Projector-based systems became serious competitors to passive stereo cameras. However the main drawback of such IR-projector-based sensors is their inability to work outdoors. Authors of [11] also showed the degradation of the 3D reconstruction at different times of the day. The stronger the illuminance, the poorer the quality of the resulting 3D map. Thus passive stereo cameras keep on being employed for outdoor applications related to navigation [24] whereas active ones are leading the indoor application usage. Commercially available stereo cameras are the Microsoft Kinect[2] and the Asus Xtion[3] for the active ones.

5   Hardware Setup and Depth Map Acquisition Requirements

According to [27] and [23] level changes are considered hazardous to mobility impaired people when sidewalks are 4 cm high on flat terrain and more than 3 centimetres high on a slope. As far as stairs are concerned, the step height is often between 15 and 18 centimetres. The latter constrains the acquisition system to have a corresponding depth resolution that can be deduced from (13) as

$$\Delta Z = \Delta d \frac{fZ^2}{fT} \ . \tag{14}$$

In other words a disparity difference of one pixel (δd) must translate in a height difference smaller than a step height. Equation (14) demonstrates that for a camera located at 80 cm from the ground, the theoretical depth resolution is 6.58 mm, 10.52 mm and 21.05 mm at respectively 512 x 384, 320 x 240 and 160

---

[1] http://ww2.ptgrey.com/stereo-vision/bumblebee-2
[2] http://www.xbox.com/en-US/kinect
[3] http://www.asus.com/Multimedia/Xtion_PRO

x 120 pixel resolution. The bumblebee2 could capture steps as high as sidewalks with the assumption that the camera is laying parallel to the ground. However the surfaces shall be well textured to extract the optimal depth map.

Fig. 3. Our experimental setup mounted with the Bumblebee2 stereo camera

To evaluate our approach the stereo camera is attached on a standard three-wheel rollator (Fig. 3). The Bumblebee2, our passive stereo camera, is fixed at H_0=76 cm from the ground. For the sake of comparison, we also use the Microsoft Kinect fixed at 78 cm from the ground. Both systems are tilted with an angle of $\theta = 35$ degrees. Knowing the standard dimensions of a stair step [3], our set-up should detect the first step as a danger at Z_0-56 centimetres. The acquisition is carried out with a laptop computer. The Bumblebee images are captured at the highest resolution (512 x 384 pixels). The impact of the camera resolution is evaluated by resizing the captured frames for different intermediate resolutions from 512 x 384 pixels to 160 x 120 pixels with a pixel area relation based algorithm.

6   Experiments and Results

The evaluation is performed offline on frames captured with the Microsoft Kinect and the Bumblebee2.

6.1   Required Data

The evaluation of our approach requires a ground depth map as input, the depth being defined as the distance from the camera plan to the ground. The active camera directly gives the depth information on which we computed the ground level at each pixel according to the rotation around the X-axis. A passive stereo camera captures a pair of raw images. In order to proceed to the stereo matching that produces the disparity map followed by the depth map, the raw images have to be undistorted and rectified. This calibration process is of uttermost importance [10]. The Bumblebee2 being already calibrated, we record the rectified pairs of images. The algorithm employed to extract the depth map from the rectified pictures is the one of Konolige [4, 15]. We choose this stereo matching as opposed to the Bumblebee library in order to have a manageable code to

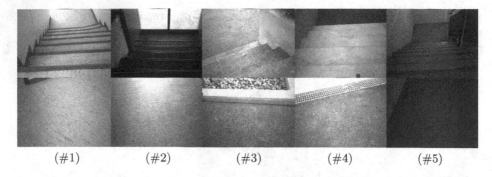

(#1)   (#2)   (#3)   (#4)   (#5)

Fig. 4. Scenes where the images were captured with both the Kinect and the Bumblebee2: indoor stair case (#1), entrance indoor stairs (#2), outdoor stairs to enter a building (#3), outdoor stairs (#4), indoor emergency stair case (#5)

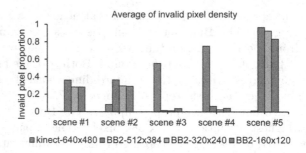

Fig. 5. Average of the proportion of pixels with unknown depth from the Kinect and the Bumblebee2 (BB2) captures at three different resolutions

further port on an embedded platform. Moreover the detection algorithm does not require accurate depth, nor does it require a fully dense map. The resulting depth map is processed according to the transformation demonstrated in Section 3. Each sub-image of a frame is annotated according to the presence of stairs.

The assessment of our approach was carried out on five scenes of descending stairs (Fig. 4): Scene #1 and scene #5 are indoor scenes; scene #2 is an indoor scene close to a glass door; scene #3 is an outdoor stair under a canopy cover; scene #4 is a scene completely outdoor close to a building that created shadow during the experiment. The scenes' illuminance is respectively 90, 430, 5000, 2200 and 8 lux, which explains the quality of the resulting depth maps. Since the active cameras are unable to work outdoor due to the powerful infrared wavelengths from sunlight, it results in very sparse depth maps (Fig. 5). The passive stereo camera gives denser depth maps, especially outdoors where the scenes are highly textured. However its performance drastically drops in poor lighting conditions, which is rarely a problem since we assume rollator users do not wander in such dark places.

In normal lighting conditions the Bumblebee2 (512 x 384) and the Kinect (640 x 480) have similar performance in term of valid depth values computed. The Kinect has a non-negligible advantage when the indoor lighting drops because of the infrared illumination it projects. The illuminance impacts the quality of the required data. This analysis confirms our choice of evaluating our approach only with a passive stereo camera.

After a training phase done with 70% of data randomly chosen from the first three scenes (cf. Fig. 4), the final detectors described in the following sections ran on two test sets: (i) the remaining 30% of scenes #1 to #3, (ii) all captures of scene #4. The results were similar for both sets. We thus present results for the second set as it is completely different from the training set.

6.2   Classification for High Accuracy

As depicted in Fig. 2 our detector needs four parameters, T_{G_u}, T_{G_l}, T_{D_u} and T_{D_l}. In order to determine their optimal values, we proceed to a training phase with 70% of data randomly chosen from the first three scenes. T_{G_i} and T_{D_i} vary from 88 to 130 (cm) and 0 to 1 respectively. The SAD window size and the disparity range were adapted to the resolution, starting from 15 pixels and 144 pixels respectively for the highest resolution. The training set performance is measured from the analysis of the true positive rate TPR (also called recall), the false positive rate FPR, the missed rate FNR (false negative rate), the true negative rate TNR, the accuracy ACC (also called recognition rate) and the precision PPV (also called positive predictive value). The recall is the ratio of true stairs correctly predicted. The false positive rate is the ratio of safe cases predicted as stairs. The missed rate is the ratio of true stairs predicted as safe situations. The accuracy is the ratio of good predictions out of all the samples. The true negative rate is the ratio of safe cases correctly predicted among all predictions of safe cases. Finally the precision is the ratio of correctly predicted stairs out of stairs prediction.

According to the training, the best accuracy scores on each detector are obtained for T_{G_l} between 88 and 92 (cm) and T_{G_u} is located around 104 cm. T_{G_l} optimal value corresponds to the distance between the floor and the first step of the stairs whereas the optimal T_{G_u} comes from the fact that the deepest pixels appearing in the top of the image do not belong to the first step but to deeper ones. The resulting optimal parameters for best accuracy values are listed in Table 4. To produce relevant feedback to the rollator users, we opted for the decision making strategy described in Section 3. The resulting three-bin classification on the second test set with the parameterisation for best accuracy scores is depicted in Fig.6. Safe and dangerous situations are rarely mixed up. At any resolutions, no safe cases are predicted as dangers and up to 0.5% of dangers are classified as safe situations.

Table 2. Performance of the descending stair detector on the lower sub-images of the training set at the best accuracy for various resolutions. These results are used to tune TG_l and TD_l for the final detector run on the test sets.

Resolution	T_{D_l}	T_{G_l}	FPR	TPR	PPV	ACC	FNR	TNR
512 x 384	0.015	92	0.001	0.944	0.997	0.980	0.056	0.999
465 x 349	0.02	92	0.000	0.941	0.999	0.979	0.059	1.000
393 x 295	0.015	98	0.002	0.944	0.996	0.979	0.056	0.998
365 x 274	0.02	92	0.001	0.942	0.997	0.979	0.058	0.999
320 x 240	0.02	92	0.003	0.940	0.995	0.977	0.060	0.997
301 x 225	0.03	92	0.000	0.929	1.000	0.975	0.071	1.000
256 x 192	0.03	90	0.002	0.927	0.996	0.973	0.073	0.998
204 x 153	0.045	90	0.007	0.918	0.986	0.967	0.082	0.993
160 x 120	0.095	88	0.009	0.875	0.981	0.950	0.125	0.991

6.3   Classification to Minimize False Alarms and Misses

To help rollator users it is important: (i) to avoid false alarms otherwise they will turn away from the device that raises irrelevant alarms; (ii) not to miss relevant alarms. Thus we looked for TG_u, TG_l, TD_u and TD_l that minimize false positives and false negatives. In other words, we looked for the best true positive rate at full precision. From the training results, we got the desired parameters listed in Table 5. The resulting performance on the test data (scene #4) is summarized in Fig. 7. Again, at any resolutions, all safe situations are never predicted as dangers. Warnings are more misclassified, mainly as safe situations than in the previous experiment. For resolutions higher than 204 x 153, less than 0.8% of dangers are missed because predicted as safe and goes up to 2.6% at the lowest resolution.

Table 3. Performance of the descending stair detector on the upper sub-images of the training set at the best accuracy for various resolutions. These results are used to tune TG_u and TD_u for the final detector run on the test sets.

Resolution	T_{D_u}	T_{G_u}	FPR	TPR	PPV	ACC	FNR	TNR
512 x 384	0.015	104	0.013	0.919	0.987	0.951	0.081	0.987
465 x 349	0.015	106	0.016	0.919	0.984	0.949	0.081	0.984
393 x 295	0.020	110	0.015	0.915	0.986	0.948	0.085	0.985
365 x 274	0.030	100	0.023	0.910	0.978	0.941	0.090	0.977
320 x 240	0.030	104	0.027	0.910	0.974	0.940	0.090	0.973
301 x 225	0.050	104	0.018	0.898	0.983	0.938	0.102	0.982
256 x 192	0.055	108	0.019	0.894	0.982	0.935	0.106	0.981
204 x 153	0.070	110	0.040	0.895	0.962	0.926	0.105	0.960
160 x 120	0.095	110	0.124	0.898	0.891	0.887	0.102	0.876

Table 4. Chosen parameters for the descending stair detector for various resolutions according to the best accuracies obtained from the training phase (70% of data from scenes #1 to #3)

Resolution	T_{D_u}	T_{G_u}	T_{D_l}	T_{G_l}
512 x 384	0.015	104	0.015	88
465 x 349	0.020	104	0.020	88
393 x 295	0.020	104	0.020	88
365 x 274	0.030	104	0.020	88
320 x 240	0.030	104	0.025	88
301 x 225	0.050	104	0.030	88
256 x 192	0.090	104	0.030	88
204 x 153	0.190	104	0.045	88
160 x 120	0.275	104	0.095	88

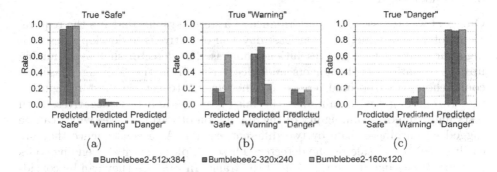

Fig. 6. Prediction on the test data (scene #4) with the parameters set according to the best accuracies obtained on training for three different resolutions

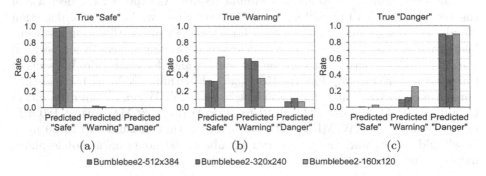

Fig. 7. Prediction on the test data (scene #4) with the parameters set according to the best minimization of false positives and false negatives obtained on training for three different resolutions

Table 5. Chosen parameters for the descending stair detector for various resolutions according to the best true positive rate at 100% precision. obtained from the training phase (70% of data from scenes #1 to #3).

Resolution	T_{D_u}	T_{G_u}	T_{D_l}	T_{G_l}
512 x 384	0.025	104	0.030	92
465 x 349	0.030	106	0.030	92
393 x 295	0.035	112	0.030	92
365 x 274	0.040	112	0.030	92
320 x 240	0.045	114	0.030	92
301 x 225	0.060	116	0.030	92
256 x 192	0.070	118	0.035	92
204 x 153	0.140	118	0.065	92
160 x 120	0.220	118	0.175	92

6.4   Discussion

Our goal was to assess the performance of a stereo system that fits the requirements of a battery lifetime of at least day. Our objective is to develop a descending stair detector with low resolutions cameras. The detector shall avoid mixing up safe situations with dangers and vice versa. From the training phase, we could choose two optimal sets of parameters: (i) to get the best recognition rate (accuracy); (ii) to minimize the false positives and false negatives. Both tests highlighted the ambiguity of the annotation of warning cases which can be tagged as warning or safe by two different experts. As a consequence they are easily predicted as safe by the detector. These samples present descending stairs that are appearing at the very top of the frame. In practice they can be considered as a safe situation since they are far enough from the user. Nevertheless, in this problem, safe situations are clearly distinct from dangerous ones.

The two parameterisations gave similar results. As expected the decrease of the resolution alters the performance. However when we look at the detection of safe and dangerous situations as a binary classification, the accuracy keeps being greater than 98.9%. We have to focus on improving the confusion between warnings and safe cases both on the annotation and detection side. In terms of time and power consumption, the Konolige's algorithm is dedicated to real-time applications and ran at 6 fps on FGPA in 1997[15]. We expect our algorithm to run on an ARM cortex-M4 at 10 fps. An Arm cortex-M4 runs at 180MHz and consumes 157 μW/MHz. With two cameras that consume up to 60 mW, we should expect our detector to run for about 160 hours on a mobile phone battery (700mAh at 3.7V).

7   Conclusions and Future Work

We proposed a reliable descending stair detector based on stereo vision. We demonstrated the robustness of our approach at low resolution. The classifier is capable of recognizing more than 98.9% of safe and dangerous situations at very low resolution and up to 99.8% at higher resolutions. Our results enable us to be highly confident in integrating our algorithm on an embedded platform equipped with low resolution sensors to reach the project's user requirements of low power consumption (several days) and real-time feedback (about 10 fps). As future steps, we will extend our experiments to sidewalks. Our detector will be embedded on an off-the-shelf hardware board connected to a pair of low resolution and high dynamic range cameras for both indoor and outdoor usage for elderly safety and self-confidence.

Acknowledgments. This project is supported by the Swiss Hasler Foundation Smart-World Program, grant Nr. 11083. We thank our end-user partners: the FSASD, "Fondation des Services d'Aide et de Soins à Domicile", Geneva, Switzerland; EMS-Charmilles, Geneva, Switzerland; and Foundation "Tulita", Bogotá, Colombia.

References

1. Bay, H., Ess, A., Tuytelaars, T., Van Gool, L.: Speeded-up robust features (SURF). Computer Vision and Image Understanding **110**(3), 346–359 (2008)
2. Bouhamed, S.A., Kallel, I.K., Masmoudi, D.S.: New electronic white cane for stair case detection and recognition using ultrasonic sensor. International Journal of Advanced Computer Science & Applications **4**(6) (2013)
3. BPA: "brochure technique escaliers" and "garde-corps base: norme sia 358", bureau de prévention des accidents (2009). http://www.bfu.ch/sites/assets/Shop/bfu_2.007.02_Escaliers.pdf, http://www.inoxconcept.ch/images/normes_sia_358.pdf (Online, accessed June 20, 2014)
4. Bradski, G., Kaehler, A.: Learning OpenCV: Computer vision with the OpenCV library, 1st edn. O'Reilly Media (September 2008)
5. Calonder, M., Lepetit, V., Ozuysal, M., Trzcinski, T., Strecha, C., Fua, P.: BRIEF: computing a local binary descriptor very fast. IEEE Transactions on Pattern Analysis and Machine Intelligence **34**(7), 1281–1298 (2012)
6. Cloix, S., Weiss, V., Bologna, G., Pun, T., Hasler, D.: Obstacle and planar object detection using sparse 3D information for a smart walker. In: 9th International Conference on Computer Vision Theory and Applications, vol. 2, pp. 305–312, Lisbon, Portugal (January 2014)
7. Cong, Y., Li, X., Liu, J., Tang, Y.: A stairway detection algorithm based on vision for ugv stair climbing. In: IEEE International Conference on Networking, Sensing and Control, ICNSC 2008, pp. 1806–1811. IEEE (2008)
8. Delmerico, J.A., Baran, D., David, P., Ryde, J., Corso, J.J.: Ascending stairway modeling from dense depth imagery for traversability analysis. In: 2013 IEEE International Conference on Robotics and Automation (ICRA), pp. 2283–2290. IEEE (2013)
9. Equiterre: "rampes, marches et escaliers" and "trottoirs" guidelines. http://www.mobilitepourtous.ch/pdf/fiche_7.pdf, http://www.mobilitepourtous.ch/pdf/fiche_1.pdf (Online, accessed June 20, 2014)
10. Furukawa, Y., Ponce, J.: Accurate camera calibration from multi-view stereo and bundle adjustment. International Journal of Computer Vision **84**(3), 257–268 (2009)

11. Gupta, M., Yin, Q., Nayar, S.K.: Structured light in sunlight. In: IEEE International Conference on Computer Vision (ICCV) (2013)
12. Hartley, R., Zisserman, A.: Multiple View Geometry in compter vision, 2nd edn. Cambridge University Press (2003)
13. Hesch, J.A., Mariottini, G.L., Roumeliotis, S.I.: Descending-stair detection, approach, and traversal with an autonomous tracked vehicle. In: 2010 IEEE/RSJ International Conference on Intelligent Robots and Systems (IROS), pp. 5525–5531. IEEE (2010)
14. Kinsella, K., He, W.: An aging world: 2008. Tech. rep. (June 2009). http://www.aicpa.org/research/cpahorizons2025/globalforces/socialandhumanresource/downloadabledocuments/agingpopulation.pdf
15. Konolige, K.: Small vision systems: hardware and implementation. In: Eighth International Symposium on Robotics Research, pp. 111–116, Hayama, Japan (1997)
16. Konolige, K.: Projected texture stereo. In: 2010 IEEE International Conference on Robotics and Automation (ICRA), pp. 148–155. IEEE (2010)
17. Lacey, G., Rodriguez-Losada, D.: The evolution of guido. IEEE Robotics & Automation Magazine 15(4), 75–83 (2008)
18. Lacey, G., Namara, S.M., Dawson-Howe, K.M.: Personal adaptive mobility aid for the infirm and elderly blind. In: Mittal, V.O., Yanco, H.A., Aronis, J., Simpson, R.C. (eds.) Assistive Technology and Artificial Intelligence. LNCS (LNAI), vol. 1458, pp. 211–220. Springer, Heidelberg (1998)
19. Lee, Y.H., Leung, T.S., Medioni, G.: Real-time staircase detection from a wearable stereo system. In: 2012 21st International Conference on Pattern Recognition (ICPR), pp. 3770–3773. IEEE (2012)
20. Nalpantidis, L., Sirakoulis, G., Gasteratos, A.: Review of stereo vision algorithms: From software to hardware. International Journal of Optomechatronics 2(4), 435–462 (2008)
21. OECD: Society at a glance. OECD Social Indicators, 2006 Ed., organization for Economic Co-operation and Development, 2009 data are available on the Web (2006)
22. Scharstein, D., Szeliski, R.: A taxonomy and evaluation of dense two-frame stereo correspondence algorithms. Int. J. Comput. Vision 47(1–3), 7–42 (2002)
23. Schmidt, E., Manser, J.A.: Directives "voies piétonnes adaptées aux handicapés" rues - chemins - places. http://www.mobilitepietonne.ch/fileadmin/redaktion/publikationen/Strassen_Wege_Plaetze__Richtlinien_fuer_behindertengerechte_Fusswegnetze_f.pdf (Online, accessed June 20, 2014)
24. Serro, M., Shahrabadi, S., Moreno, M., Jos, J.T., Rodrigues, J.I., Rodrigues, J.M.F., Buf, J.M.H.: Computer vision and GIS for the navigation of blind persons in buildings. Universal Access in the Information Society (February 2014)
25. Shahrabadi, S., Rodrigues, J.M.F., du Buf, J.M.H.: Detection of indoor and outdoor stairs. In: Sanches, J.M., Micó, L., Cardoso, J.S. (eds.) IbPRIA 2013. LNCS, vol. 7887, pp. 847–854. Springer, Heidelberg (2013)
26. Tseng, C.K., Li, I., Chien, Y.H., Chen, M.C., Wang, W.Y.: Autonomous stair detection and climbing systems for a tracked robot. In: 2013 International Conference on System Science and Engineering (ICSSE), pp. 201–204. IEEE (2013)
27. Walter, E., Cavegn, M., Scaramuzza, G., Niemann, S., Allenbach, R.: Fussverkehr unfallgeschehen, risikofaktoren und prävention (2007). http://mobilitepourtous.ch/pdf/Bpa_Pietons_accidentes_2007.pdf (Online, accessed June 20, 2014)

Model-Based Motion Tracking of Infants

Mikkel Damgaard Olsen[1]([✉]), Anna Herskind[2], Jens Bo Nielsen[2,3], and Rasmus Reinhold Paulsen[1]

[1] Department of Applied Mathematics and Computer Science,
Technical University of Denmark, Kongens Lyngby, Denmark
mdol@dtu.dk
[2] Department of Neuroscience and Pharmacology, University of Copenhagen,
Copenhagen, Denmark
[3] Department of Nutrition, Exercise and Sport, University of Copenhagen,
Copenhagen, Denmark

Abstract. Even though motion tracking is a widely used technique to analyze and measure human movements, only a few studies focus on motion tracking of infants. In recent years, a number of studies have emerged focusing on analyzing the motion pattern of infants, using computer vision. Most of these studies are based on 2D images, but few are based on 3D information. In this paper, we present a model-based approach for tracking infants in 3D. The study extends a novel study on graph-based motion tracking of infants and we show that the extension improves the tracking results. A 3D model is constructed that resembles the body surface of an infant, where the model is based on simple geometric shapes and a hierarchical skeleton model.

Keywords: 3D model fitting · Infant pose estimation · Markerless motion tracking · Depth images

1 Introduction

Motion tracking of humans has attracted considerable interest in recent years, but only few studies exist in which the methods have been used for motion tracking of infants. However, the techniques can be of great benefit in the evaluation of infant development, as they can quantify the movements of infants and might be able to improve the diagnostics of different motor related diseases, namely cerebral palsy (CP). CP is the most common motor disability among children, affecting 2-2.5 out of 1000 infants [1]. It is caused by an injury to the fetal or infant brain, and the physical impairment is in many cases accompanied by disturbances of cognition and perception [2]. Among several others, preterm birth and birth asphyxia are associated with an increased risk of CP, but frequently a clear underlying pathology is not found [3,4]. During infancy symptoms are often subtle, but early warning signs include failure to meet motor milestones such as crawling and walking [5]. Due to the lack of unequivocal symptoms, in current practice, most children with CP are not diagnosed until the age

© Springer International Publishing Switzerland 2015
L. Agapito et al. (Eds.): ECCV 2014 Workshops, Part III, LNCS 8927, pp. 673–685, 2015.
DOI: 10.1007/978-3-319-16199-0_47

of 2 years [1]. However, studies have shown that the movement patterns of infants are influenced by CP already in the months before and after birth [6]. In fetuses, the movements can be observed and analyzed using ultrasound, while the post-birth studies are often based on analyzing videos of the infants' so-called general movements, which can be observed until the age of 5 months (corrected w.r.t term). By observing and identifying the motion patterns, cerebral palsy may thus be suspected at a much earlier age. Early identification of infants at risk of CP leads to the possibility of early intervention, which may improve the development of the infants' motor and cognitive skills. However, due to the time consuming procedure of analyzing the motion patterns, it is unrealistic to manually examine all infants born at risk of CP. The method presented in this work will thus try to move closer to an automatic system. The idea is that the system should be standard equipment, e.g. located at outpatient clinics, used for analyzing movement patterns of prematurely born infants. Because of this we cannot use a complex system that requires hours of preparation and calibration, but it should be a sort of plug-and-play system. As mentioned, studies within this field of interest are limited, but some work exists on motion tracking of infants. In [7,8] the authors use 6 sensors attached to the infants' wrists, ankles, chest and head. The sensors give temporal information about position and orientation. In [9], the authors use an optical motion system, where reflective markers are attached to the infant's limbs and multiple infra-red cameras are used to reconstruct the 3D location of the markers in space. From this, a set of parameters is extracted and used for early detection of spasticity due to cerebral palsy. In [10], the authors propose a new, optical flow-based method for quantifying the motion of infants with neonatal seizures, based on an overall quantitative measure of pixel-differences between successive frames. The optical flow-based approach is also used in [11], where the authors use color images as input to an optical flow-algorithm in order to track the position of the infants' hands and feet. Here, the authors manually initialize the position of the different body parts and adjust the positions during the tracking, in order to improve robustness of the method. In [12] the authors describe a method for tracking the 3D positions of anatomical extremities(hands, feet, head) and sub-extremities(elbow, knee) of infants based on a graph-based method equivalent to the approach in [13–15]. Based on the the work of [12], the method is extended with a model-based approach as in [16,17]. This both improves the body part localization and the tracking of the infants movements over time. The data is obtained using an affordable and easy-to-use depth sensor, Microsoft Kinect, which has revolutionized research within the field of low cost motion tracking.

2   Methods

The data used in this work, are depth and color images acquired with the Kinect sensor from Microsoft. The depth images have been recorded at a resolution of 480×640 pixels and the same resolution is used for the color images. As far as the authors' knowledge, no benchmark database of dense 3D data of infants exist

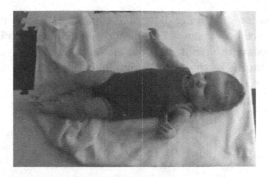

Fig. 1. Color image of one of the recorded infants. The infant wears an easily recognizable (blue) bodystocking and lies on a white blanket.

and a non-public database is used, which has been created simultaneous with this study. The participating infants are 3-8 months of age. For each infant 15-30 minutes of data have been recorded, while the infants have been laying on a flat surface e.g. a mattress or a blanket (see Figure 1). It should be noted that the pictures and data are used and published with respect to an agreement signed by the participating families. The Kinect has been positioned above the infant using a tripod for ordinary cameras. Using the depth images, a 3D point cloud representation of the infant and its surroundings can be generated. In order to make tracking easier, the fact that the infant lies on a flat surface is used to differentiate between foreground (most likely the infant) and background, by fitting a least squares plane to the surface. This is simply done by solving the linear system:

$$a(\mathbf{x} - x_c) + b(\mathbf{y} - y_c) + c(\mathbf{z} - z_c) = \mathbf{d}, \qquad (1)$$

where; $(\mathbf{x}, \mathbf{y}, \mathbf{z})$ are the observed 3D points of the underlying surface, (x_c, y_c, z_c) is a 3D point on the plane, and (a, b, c) are the elements for the normalvector of the plane. $\mathbf{d}$ defines the signed distances to the plane, but is set to zero during the fitting process. It is assumed that the viewing direction of the camera is nearly perpendicular to the flat surface and thus, the normal is corrected to point towards the camera. Given the estimated plane parameters, the signed distance from every 3D point to the plane can be calculated and this is used to discard points behind the plane $(\mathbf{d} < 0)$. In order to remove small deviations of the underlying surface, a non-zero value is used as threshold. In addition, the infant wears an easily recognizable bodystocking, which is used to locate the baby, using color-based pixel classification.

2.1 Body Model

In this work, we use a 3D model to describe the surface of the human body. The model is constructed from a predefined number of geometric shapes that are connected based on the underlying skeleton. In order to measure the distance from the body model to the observed data, a "point to shape"-distance function is defined for each shape [16,17]. Currently the geometric shapes are:

– Cylinder: Used for describing elongated body parts, such as arms, legs and feet. The distance between a 3D point and the cylinder can be found analytically, by projecting the point onto the medial axis of the cylinder and taking the thickness/radius of the cylinder into account. The distance function for at 3D point $\mathbf{p}$ is thus defined as:

$$d = \begin{cases} \|\mathbf{p} - \mathbf{a}\| & \text{if } \lambda \leq 0 \\ \|\mathbf{p} - \mathbf{b}\| & \text{if } \lambda \geq 1 \\ \|\mathbf{p} - (\mathbf{a} + \lambda(\mathbf{b} - \mathbf{a}))\| & \text{otherwise} \end{cases}, \tag{2}$$

where, $\mathbf{a}$ and $\mathbf{b}$ are the start- and endpoints of the cylinder and

$$\lambda = \frac{(\mathbf{p} - \mathbf{a}) \cdot (\mathbf{b} - \mathbf{a})}{\|\mathbf{b} - \mathbf{a}\|^2} \tag{3}$$

is the normalized length of the vector $(\mathbf{p} - \mathbf{a})$ projected onto the line $(\mathbf{b} - \mathbf{a})$. It should be noted, that this distance is only for calculating the distance from a 3D point to the medial axis of a cylinder and the radius of the cylinder should be included in order to calculate the distance to the surface. Moreover, the described distance function, represents the distance to a rounded cylinder, when the radius/thickness is included.

– Sphere: Used to describe the head of the infant. The distance is easily computed, as the distance between the center point and the 3D point. Again, the radius of the body part should be included, in order to measure the distance to the surface, rather than the distance to the center.

– Ellipsoid/Superquadratic: The torso/stomach is modeled as a combination of two superquadratics. The upper part is modeled as a round-cornered box, in order to describe the box-like shape of the shoulders, while the lower part is modeled as a simple ellipsoid. In this case, no closed form solution exists for calculating the exact euclidean distance. Instead two differnet approaches has been used, which approximates the true distance:

  1. One solution is to use a numerical method, as explained in [18], which minimizes the distance from the 3D point to a point on the surface of the ellipsoid. The method is not generalized to superquadratics, but it is also possible to use iterative methods for approximating the distance for the upper bodypart [19].

  2. Another solution is to create a distancemap of the bodypart. Once the distancemap is created, the distance from the superquadratics to a 3D point can be approximated, by mapping the 3D point to the distancemap coordinates.

Inspired by previous work [20,21], we have chosen to model the skeleton as a hierarchical model, with the root starting from the center of the body. The identification of the body center is based on the center of mass of a set of classified pixels. As the infants wear a colored bodystocking during the recording, this can be recognized and tracked in the data. The fact that the infant lies on its back, is the reason the body center is chosen as the root joint. This is because the

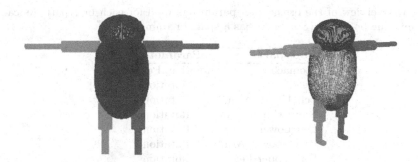

Fig. 2. Visual 2D (left) and 3D (right) representation of the model used in this study. The colors are simply to differentiate the bodyparts. Red and green are used to differentiate between left and right bodyparts, respectively.

location of the body center should be the most static part of the infant and more movement should be seen in the outer limbs. The articulated model can be seen in Figure 2, where colors are used to differentiate between left(red) and right(green) bodyparts.

In relation to the hierarchical connection between the bodyparts, the geometric shapes are oriented and positioned, using simple rotations and translations. However, instead of modeling the rotations in the global coordinate system, with euler angles, axis-angle representations are used, where rotations are limited to local coordinate systems, as the local coordinate system of each joint, changes based on the parent joints. The definition of axis-angle rotations is described widely in the literature [22,23] where the Rodriquez rotation formula can be used to construct a rotation-matrix given a axis-angle representation. Given an axis of rotation ω and a rotation angle θ, the rotation matrix can calculated as:

$$\mathbf{R} = \mathbf{I}_3 + \hat{\omega}\sin\theta + \hat{\omega}^2\left(1 - \cos\theta\right). \tag{4}$$

$\mathbf{I}_3$ is the 3×3 identity matrix and the ˆ operator constructs the skew symmetric matrix of the vector ω.

2.2 Fitting the Model

In order to fit the model to the observed data, the Levenberg Marquardt method is used, to iteratively refine the body parameters. The state vector and objective function will thus be defined in the following. An overview of the state parameters used in this study are listed in Table 1. Only the *Stomach* bodypart has a spatial parameter, which controls the global position of the model, while the position of the remaining bodyparts are constrained based on the hierachical model and the size parameters of the body.

The size parameters define the size and relative location of the bodyparts and are listed in Table 2. The size parameters are not part of the optimization but are either given prior to the optimization or estimated during an initialization

Table 1. Overview of the orientation parameters used for each bodypart. As can be seen, only one bodypart (*Stomach*) has a spatial parameter.

Bodypart	Parameters
Stomach	Rotation, Position
Head	Rotation
Left Upper Arm	Rotation
Right Upper Arm	Rotation
Left Lower Arm	Rotation
Right Lower Arm	Rotation
Left Upper Leg	Rotation
Right Upper Leg	Rotation
Left Lower Leg	Rotation
Right Lower Leg	Rotation
Left Foot	Rotation
Right Foot	Rotation

Table 2. Overview of the size parameters used for each bodypart. These parameters are not part of the optimization, but are used during the creation of the 3D model.

Bodypart	Size	Location
Stomach	Extension for the three axis	Global
Head	Radius	Relative to Stomach
Left Upper Arm	Radius + Length	Relative to Stomach
Right Upper Arm	Radius + Length	Relative to Stomach
Left Lower Arm	Radius + Length	Relative to Left Upper Arm
Right Lower Arm	Radius + Length	Relative to Right Upper Arm
Left Upper Leg	Radius + Length	Relative to Stomach
Right Upper Leg	Radius + Length	Relative to Stomach
Left Lower Leg	Radius + Length	Relative to Left Upper Leg
Right Lower Leg	Radius + Length	Relative to Right Upper Leg
Left Foot	Radius + Length	Relative to Left Lower Leg
Right Foot	Radius + Length	Relative to Right Lower Leg

step. It should be noted that symmetry is utilized and it is thus assumed that symmetric bodyparts are identical, with respect to size and relative location.

Once the state parameters are defined, the next step is to optimize on these parameters using the Levenberg-Marquardt optimization scheme, in order to fit the 3D model to the observed data. By concatenating the state parameters in a state vector $\mathbf{x}$, the optimization can be written as:

$$\min_{\mathbf{x} \in \mathbb{R}} \sum_{i=1}^{N} \| \mathbf{p}_i - \mathbf{c}\left(\mathbf{p}_i, \mathbf{x}\right) \|, \tag{5}$$

where $\mathbf{c}\left(\mathbf{p}_i, \mathbf{x}\right)$ calculates the closest 3D point on the model, given the 3D data point $\mathbf{p}_i$ and the state vector. An extension to the above minimization, is that the state vector **x** is constrained, based on the anatomical properties of the human body joints. One requirement for the Levenberg-Marquardt algorithm, is an initial starting guess. In this study, a good estimate of the starting guess is found using an existing method for detecting and locating anatomical extremities, based on graph theory [12]. Here the anatomical extremities such as head, hands and feet are located by assuming that these points are furthest away from the bodycenter, when the distance measure is based on geodesic distances over the body surface. The distance is estimated by representing the surface as a graph, where neighboring 3D points are connected by nodes. This approach is able to locate and identify both the extremities and sub-extremities such as elbows and knees. The described method is able to give an estimate on the spatial location of the extremities. In order to obtain the respective state vector, an inverse kinematics method is used.

The total body-modeling method is summarized in the following, where input is the data obtained from the Kinect sensor.

1. Apply background subtraction in order to segment the infant from the background/underlying surface.
2. Define Body Parameters either using fixed parameters or during an initialization step.
3. Use graph-based method to obtain an estimate on the location of the anatomical extremities.
4. Apply an inverse kinematics algorithm in order to obtain the state parameters, given the location of the extremities(end effectors).
5. Refine the state parameters, in order to minimize the distance between the 3D model and the observed data.

The above described approach, estimates the orientation parameters of a single frame. However, by using the optimized parameters of one frame, as starting guess for the successive frame, the human body can be tracked in time.

3   Results

In order to test and evaluate the described method, Kinect recordings of 7 infants' movements have been obtained, where each infant has been recorded for 15-30 minutes. As no ground truth data is available, a various number of frames have been manually annotated for each infant. The frames have been selected such that they cover a wide variety of poses. In Figure 3, the results from the presented method can be observed. The method is able to correctly locate and identify the different body parts and the joint angles can be extracted directly from the respective state vector. It should be noted that an offset of the 3D model has been used, to better illustrate the estimated pose.

Fig. 3. Examples of the (translated) model fitted to the observed data. The point clouds are colored for visualization purposes, but only the 3D information is used during the optimization process.

In the following, the two methods (graph-based vs. model-based) are compared. The Euclidean distance between the manually positioned 3D points and the estimated joint locations are used to evaluate the tracking approach. In Figure 4 and Figure 5, the mean and standard deviation of the residuals are shown, respectively. The reader should notice that the *Stomach* and *Chest* residuals does not differ significantly, as these locations are found almost equivalently. However, the localization of the remaining joints has improved significantly, both with respect to mean and standard deviation.

The results indicate how robust the method is to locate the different body parts. As mentioned earlier, the technique can easily be extended to motion tracking, instead of human body detection. In Figure 6 the Euclidean distances between successive frames can be observed, for four different joints. Is is noteworthy to see that the graph-based tracking contains a lot of peaks/noise, while the model-based tracking gives a more smooth tracking. The reason for this, is that the model-based approach is less sensitive to deviations in data, compared to the graph-based method.

Based on the tracking results of one of the infants, Figure 7 shows the angles of the upper arms and the thighs, during a time period of 45 seconds. It is observed that the right upper arm is less active, compared to the remaining body parts.

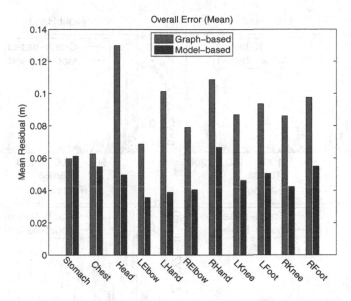

Fig. 4. The mean of the residuals listed for each body part in the model. Both the results from the graph-based approach (*red*) and the extended method (*blue*) are visualized.

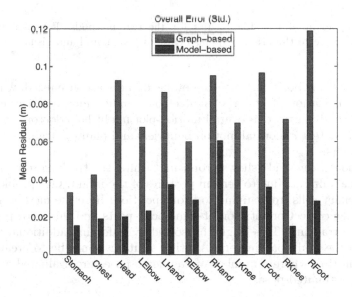

Fig. 5. The standard deviation(*right*) of the residuals listed for each body part in the model. Both the results from the graph-based approach (*red*) and the extended method (*blue*) are visualized.

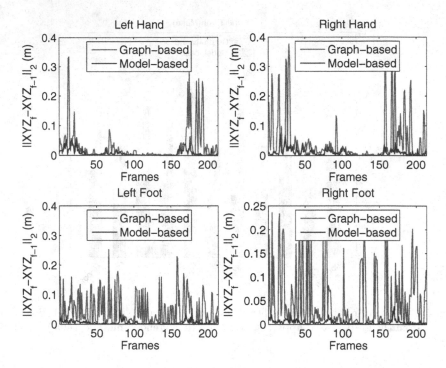

Fig. 6. Comparison of tracking results for the two methods. For each frame the Euclidean distance to the previous joint-location is calculated and visualized.

In Figure 8 the positions of the elbows and knees are visualized, which gives a better visualization of how the right elbow is much more passive, compared to the other bodyparts. This overall motion-plot might help doctors and physiotherapists to detect abnormal motion behaviors and plan the training according to these results.

Even though the study shows promising results, the tracking sometimes gets stuck in local minima, due to certain postures of the infant. One problem is e.g. when the infant rolls from supine to prone position. Here the method is unable to recover the correct orientation of some body parts and this error propagates through the tracking. This might be solved by enforcing additional temporal filtering on the body parameters. Another solution would be to create a pose library as in [16], where a number of candidate poses are evaluated and tested against the estimated pose.

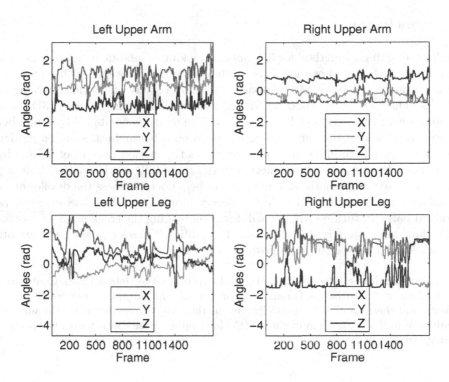

Fig. 7. The angles with respect to the local x-, y- and z-axis, for four bodyparts. It is noteworthy that the right upper arm is less active, compared to the three other bodyparts.

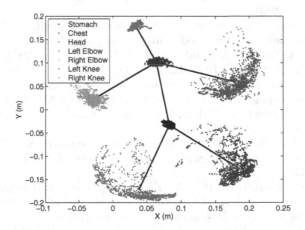

Fig. 8. Visualization of the location of 7 bodyjoints, namely; stomhach, chest, head, left/right elbows and left/right knee. The lower variation of the right elbow, shows that less movement has occurred for this joint.

4 Conclusion

We have described a method for 3D motion tracking of infants, based on a model-based approach. We show how this method gives good results, with respect to both accuracy and precision, compared to a novel study on motion tracking of infants. The method is based on fitting a 3D model to the observed 3D data, obtained with the Microsoft Kinect sensor. The model is combined by a number of geometric shapes that are connected based on a hierarchical skeleton model. We show how the results can be used to assess the motion pattern of infants by evaluating the raw motion parameters or the spatial 3D motion paths. This is a step closer to an automatic system that can help doctors assess the development of infants' motor control in order to detect motor impairing diseases such as cerebral palsy. In future work, we will focus on making the tracking more robust, such that the method is able to recover from difficult poses e.g. when the infants rolls over from supine to prone position.

Acknowledgments. The authors would like to thank the Helene Elsass Center and the Ludvig and Sara Elsass Foundation for funding the project as well as all of the infants and their families for participating in this project. Furthermore, the authors would like to thank the organization APA, for helping make contact with the participating families.

References

1. Himmelmann, K.: Epidemiology of cerebral palsy. Handbook of Clinical Neurology **111**, 163–167 (2013)
2. Bax, M., Goldstein, M., Rosenbaum, P., Leviton, A., Paneth, N., Dan, B., Jacobsson, B., Damiano, D.: Proposed definition and classification of cerebral palsy. Developmental Medicine & Child Neurology **47**(8), 571–576 (2005)
3. Goldsmith, S., Badawi, N., Blair, E., Taitz, D., Keogh, J., McIntyre, S.: A systematic review of risk factors for cerebral palsy in children born at term in developed countries. Developmental Medicine and Child Neurology **55**(6), 499–508 (2013)
4. McIntyre, S., Morgan, C., Walker, K., Novak, I.: Cerebral palsy-don't delay. Dev Disabil Res Rev **17**(2), 114–29 (2011)
5. Murphy, N., Such-Neibar, T.: Current problems in pediatric and adolescent health care. In: Cerebral Palsy Diagnosis and Management: The State of the Art, pp. 149–69 (2003)
6. Einspieler, C., Prechtl, H., Bos, A., Ferrari, F., Cioni, G.: Prechtl's Method on the Qualitative Assessment of General Movements in Preterm. Wiley, Term and Young Infants. Clinics in Developmental Medicine (2008)
7. Berg, A.: Modellbasert klassifisering av spedbarns bevegelser (2008)
8. Rahmanpour, P.: Features for movement based prediction of cerebral palsy (2009)
9. Meinecke, L., Breitbach-Faller, N., Bartz, C., Damen, R., Rau, G., Disselhorst-Klug, C.: Movement analysis in the early detection of newborns at risk for developing spasticity due to infantile cerebral palsy. Human Movement Science **25**(2), 125–144 (2006)

10. Karayiannis, N.B., Varughese, B., Tao Jr., G.: J.D.F., Wise, M.S., Mizrahi, E.M.: Quantifying motion in video recordings of neonatal seizures by regularized optical flow methods. IEEE Transactions on Image Processing 14(7), 890–903 (2005)

11. Stahl, A., Schellewald, C., Stavdahl, O., Aamo, O.M., Adde, L., Kirkerod, H.: An optical flow-based method to predict infantile cerebral palsy. IEEE Transactions on Neural Systems and Rehabilitation Engineering 20(4), 605–614 (2012)

12. Olsen, M.D., Herskind, A., Nielsen, J.B., Paulsen, R.R.: Motion tracking of infants. In: 22nd International Conference on Pattern Recognition (ICPR). (2014, to appear)

13. Plagemann, C., Ganapathi, V., Koller, D., Thrun, S.: Real-time identification and localization of body parts from depth images. In: 2010 IEEE International Conference on Robotics and Automation (ICRA), pp. 3108–3113 (2010)

14. Baak, A., Müller, M., Bharaj, G., Seidel, H.P., Theobalt, C.: A data-driven approach for real-time full body pose reconstruction from a depth camera. In: IEEE 13th International Conference on Computer Vision (ICCV), pp. 1092–1099. IEEE (November 2011)

15. Schwarz, L.A., Mkhitaryan, A., Mateus, D., Navab, N.: Estimating human 3d pose from time-of-flight images based on geodesic distances and optical flow. In: FG, pp. 700–706. IEEE (2011)

16. Ganapathi, V., Plagemann, C., Koller, D., Thrun, S.: Real-time human pose tracking from range data. In: Fitzgibbon, A., Lazebnik, S., Perona, P., Sato, Y., Schmid, C. (eds.) ECCV 2012, Part VI. LNCS, vol. 7577, pp. 738–751. Springer, Heidelberg (2012)

17. Droeschel, D., Behnke, S.: 3d body pose estimation using an adaptive person model for articulated icp. In: Jeschke, S., Liu, H., Schilberg, D. (eds.) ICIRA 2011, Part II. LNCS, vol. 7102, pp. 157–167. Springer, Heidelberg (2011)

18. Eberly, D.: Distance from a point to an ellipse, an ellipsoid, or a hyperellipsoid (2013)

19. Portal, R., Dias, J., de Sousa, L.: Contact detection between convex superquadric surfaces. Archive of Mechanical Engineering LVII 2, 165–186 (2010)

20. Mnier, C., Boyer, E., Raffin, B.: 3d skeleton-based body pose recovery. In: 3DPVT, pp. 389–396. IEEE Computer Society (2006)

21. Shen, S., Tong, M., Deng, H., Liu, Y., Wu, X., Wakabayashi, K., Koike, H.: Model based human motion tracking using probability evolutionary algorithm. Pattern Recognition Letters 29(13), 1877–1886 (2008)

22. Moeslund, T.B., Hilton, A., Krger, V., Sigal, L., eds.: Visual Analysis of Humans - Looking at People. Springer (2011)

23. Pons-Moll, G., Rosenhahn, B.: Ball joints for marker-less human motion capture. In: IEEE Workshop on Applications of Computer Vision (WACV) (2009)

A Fast and Flexible Computer Vision System for Implanted Visual Prostheses

Wai Ho Li$^{(\boxtimes)}$

Monash Vision Group, Monash University, Melbourne, Australia
wai.ho.li@monash.edu

Abstract. Implanted visual prostheses generate visual percepts by electrically stimulating the human visual pathway using an array of electrodes. The resulting bionic vision consists of a spatial-temporal pattern of bright dots called phosphenes. This patient-specific phosphene pattern has low resolution, limited dynamic range and is spatially irregular. This paper presents a computer vision system designed to deal with these limitations, especially spatial irregularity. The system uses a new mapping called the Camera Map to decouple the flexible spatial layout of image processing from the inflexible layout of phosphenes experienced by a patient. Detailed simulations of a cortical prosthesis currently in pre-clinical testing were performed to create phosphene patterns for testing. The system was tested on a wearable prototype of the cortical prosthesis. Despite having limited computational resources, the system operated in real time, taking only a few milliseconds to perform image processing and visualisations of simulated prosthetic vision.

Keywords: Visual prosthesis · Bionic eye · Cortical implant · Simulated prosthetic vision · Wearable computer vision · Integral images · Irregular · Camera maps · Real time · Phosphene maps · Image processing

1 Introduction

According to the World Health Organization, visual impairment and blindness affect nearly 300 million people worldwide[1]. Some causes of vision loss, such as cataracts, can already be treated using existing medical technology. Implanted Visual Prostheses (IVP) attempt to address currently incurable diseases, such as Retinitis Pigmentosa (RP), by electrically stimulating the still-healthy parts of a patient's visual pathway to produce prosthetic vision.

Prosthetic vision has many limitations, which are further detailed in Section 2. These limitations severely restrict the *bandwidth* of visual information that can be provided to a patient. Computer Vision provides a promising way to improve the usefulness of prosthetic vision despite its limitations. This paper presents a computer vision system for implanted visual prostheses. The system can be

---

[1] http://www.who.int/mediacentre/factsheets/fs282/en/

© Springer International Publishing Switzerland 2015
L. Agapito et al. (Eds.): ECCV 2014 Workshops, Part III, LNCS 8927, pp. 686–701, 2015.
DOI: 10.1007/978-3-319-16199-0_48

flexibly tailored in a patient-specific manner and operates in real time on a computationally limited wearable prototype. The research contributions, design and testing of the system are detailed in Section 3.

Ever since 1755, when LeRoy discharged a Leyden Jar to cause a blind patient to see "flames passing rapidly downward" [15], numerous experiments have confirmed that electrical stimulation of the human visual pathway can result in visual percepts. Modern implanted visual prosthesis (IVP) operate using the same fundamental principle. Controlled electrical stimulation is applied using small implanted electrodes to produce a bright visual percept called a *phosphene*. By apply temporally varying stimuli using an array of electrodes, the patient *sees* spatial-temporal patterns of phosphenes similar to a low resolution dot display.

In the late 1960's, Brindley and Lewin [2] developed the first IVP. The system used an array of electrodes on the visual cortex to elicit multiple phosphenes at different locations of a patient's visual field. However, the IVP was only suitable for laboratory use as the stimulation electronics were not portable. The IVP also did not include a portable camera.

From the 1970's to the early 2000's, Dobelle developed several IVP devices that used implanted cortical electrode arrays, including systems that generate electrical stimuli based on imagery captured with a headworn camera [9]. Despite a range of problems including the heaviness of the portable electronics and the use of wired transcranial connections, a patient's biography suggests that the device did provide useful vision [21].

Recent research and development have focused on IVP that electrically stimulate either the retina or the visual cortex[2]. The reason for the focus on retinal and cortical stimulation is that electrical stimulation at these two anatomical locations can give reliable spatial patterns of phosphenes. Retinal prostheses, such as the Argus II device from Second Sight, have already been implanted into several tens of human patients in clinical trials [11]. Cortical implants, such as the Monash Vision Group's Gennaris device[3], are still in the preclinical phase. However, cortical implants may be able to treat additional causes of blindness as the cortex is further *downstream* along the visual pathway. The cortex also has a larger surface area than the retina, which may allow vision with higher spatial resolution.

For a survey of IVP research and development, including many concepts in this paper, please refer to the extensive book edited by Dagnelie [8].

2   Limitations of Implanted Visual Prostheses

At a fundamental level, implanted visual prostheses operate by converting imagery from a headworn camera into spatial-temporal patterns of electrical stimulation applied to a patient's visual pathway. This is true for both cortical and retinal prostheses. The conversion process is usually performed on portable computational hardware, which is externally worn by the patient.

---

[2] http://www.eye-tuebingen.de/zrenner/retimplantlist/
[3] http://www.monash.edu.au/bioniceye/resources.html (Annual report 2013)

Figure 1 is a system overview of Monash Vision Group's cortical visual prosthesis [17], which contains stereotypical sub-systems shared by many other prostheses. Images are captured by a headworn camera and sent to a portable computer, the *Pocket Processor*. In real time, the pocket processor converts camera images into spatial-temporal patterns of electrical stimulation, which are conveyed over a wireless link. The implanted electrodes receives electrical power and signal from the wireless coil, which it uses to apply electrical stimulation to the visual cortex. A conceptual walkthrough of how the MVG device operates is available online: http://youtu.be/v9Ip8j3eca8.

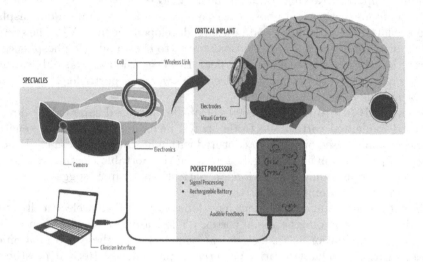

Fig. 1. Overview of the Monash Vision Group (MVG) Cortical Visual Prosthesis

2.1   Limited Spatial and Intensity Resolutions

The conversion from headworn sensor imagery to electrical stimuli is an ongoing research problem. While state-of-the-art stimulation regimes are able to reliably elicit phosphenes (bright visual percepts), the elicited phosphenes have poor dynamic range and can only be packed at low spatial resolutions. Figure 2 illustrates this using Simulated Prosthetic Vision (SPV), a technique pioneered in the early 1990's to simulate what an implanted patient may *see* [4]. The input image is converted into prosthetic vision using an adaptive thresholding approach [22] where a corresponding phosphene is enabled for bright regions of the input image. The SPV assumes the ability to generate 625 binary phosphenes, which is similar to the expected capabilities of the Monash Vision Group prosthesis [16].

The SPV image in Figure 2b clearly illustrates the severe information loss due to the limited spatial and intensity resolution of prosthetic vision. As the number of phosphenes generally corresponds to the number of implanted electrodes[4], the spatial resolution of prosthetic vision is limited by the factors such as the spread

---

[4] Coordinated activation of many electrodes may increase future phosphenes counts.

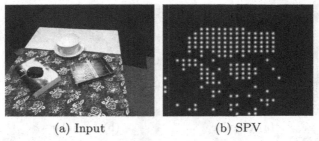

(a) Input   (b) SPV

Fig. 2. Simulated Prosthetic Vision (SPV) from an implanted visual prostheses

of electrical charge, surgical safety of implantation and electrode fabrication technology. Improvement in these areas are slow as they often require lengthy preclinical and clinical trials.

Clinical studies of retinal prostheses [10] suggest that multiple levels of phosphene brightness can be achieved but *brightness ratings are likely to vary substantially across sessions and across subjects.* There is also evidence that phosphenes of multiple levels of intensity can be produced by varying stimulation currents [20], but changes in phosphene brightness may be coupled with changes in phosphene shape and size. There is little evidence that phosphene brightness can be varied consistently with a cortical prosthesis. As such, the work presented below assumes the *worst case* of binary phosphenes.

Arguably, Dobelle was the first to consider the use of computer vision to improve the usefulness of prosthetic vision [9]. More recently, simple IVP computer vision algorithms were developed to run on wearable devices with embedded processors [23,29]. More sophisticated IVP vision algorithms have also been investigated using less portable computers. *Transformative Reality* [18] uses multiple sensing modalities to better *render* a pattern of phosphenes representing models of the world. The substantial body of work on *Vision Processing for prosthetic vision* [1] applies computer vision algorithms to improve simulated multi-intensity phosphene patterns for reading text, navigation and other tasks.

2.2   Irregular Phosphene Maps

A patient's *Phosphene Map* contains all the phosphenes that can be elicited by electrical stimulation. Older IVP research, including work on image processing and computer vision, generally assumes regular phosphene maps similar to the map shown in Figure 3a. However, there is strong clinical and biological evidence to suggest that phosphene maps are irregular and patient-specific [3,19,27]. An example of an irregular phosphene map is shown in Figure 3b.

Apart from irregular locations and sizes, there is also evidence that phosphenes can exhibit irregular *shapes.* Studies from Bionic Vision Australia[5] and Second Sight [19] show that the shape of phosphenes can be anisotropic and the shape of phosphenes may vary depending on electrical stimulation.

---

[5] http://goo.gl/LwcGwO

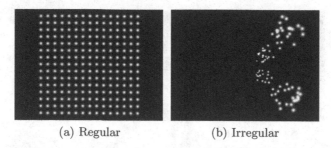

(a) Regular   (b) Irregular

Fig. 3. Example of Regular and Irregular phosphene maps

The computer vision system presented in this paper has the potential to accommodate all three aspects of phosphene map irregularity: location, size and shape. However, as the MVG device is still in the preclinical stage, the system is only tested on phosphene maps simulated based on electrical, surgical and cortical models. These models only generate irregularities in phosphene locations and sizes. The simulation assumes that phosphenes appear as isotropic Gaussians as recommended by the survey of simulated prosthetic vision by Chen *et al* [5]. Details of the simulation are available in Section 3.1.

3   Computer Vision System for IVP

Despite the reality that Implanted Visual Prostheses (IVP) produce irregular phosphene maps, very little research has been done to address the problem in full. Research that attempts to deal with irregular phosphene maps generally only do so for *near-regular* mappings where small spatial shifts in phosphene locations and electrode dropouts are modelled [25] or only irregular phosphene shapes are considered over a regular grid [14].

More importantly, many systems do not run in real time on an embedded processor suitable for a wearable medical device. Clinical trials of retinal implants [28] and cortical implants [21] suggest that prosthetic vision may have refresh rates as high as 10Hz. Simulated Prosthetic Vision trials show that low refresh rates may reduce task performance [13]. Therefore, a practical IVP requires a fast and flexible computer vision system.

Given the background above, this paper provides the following contributions:

1. Section 3.1 describes a detailed simulation of a cortical IVP device
2. Section 3.2 details a computer vision system that deals with irregular phosphene maps using a second mapping called the Camera Map to provide flexibility.
3. Section 3.3 details a fast image processing method for the vision system.
4. Section 3.4 details a simulated prosthetic vision visualisation that shows the phosphenes *seen* by a patient in real time.
5. Section 3.5 summarises the real time performance of the system.

3.1   Simulating a Cortical Implanted Visual Prosthesis

Phosphene maps were simulated in order to test the computer vision system. The simulation is based on the Monash Vision Group (MVG) cortical Implanted Visual Prothesis (IVP), which is currently undergoing preclinical trials. Parameters of the MVG IVP system were obtained from published sources [16,17].

The main components of the simulation are detailed on the left of Figure 4 (in red). The simulation starts with the definition of the spatial layout of an implanted electrode array. The array is also known as a *tile*. The MVG IVP uses multiple identical tiles. A tile contains 43 active electrodes. The MVG *Tile Layout* is shown at the top left of Figure 4 with blue dots representing electrodes.

Next, the simulation places multiple tiles onto the surface of the visual cortex. Coordinates on the visual cortex are defined on a *Cortical Plane*, which represents a flattened cortical surface. *Tile Locations* are defined using 2D affine transforms. This results in a list of *Ideal Electrode Locations* on the cortical plane. A surgical scenario proposed by a MVG Neurosurgeon is shown at the middle-left of Figure 4. The four-tile wedge-shaped arrangement avoids the Calcarine Sulcus, which is a large crevice on the visual cortex.

The simulation then applies two sources of irregularities that simulate real world issues: Electrode dropouts and the imprecise placement of electrodes. The *Dropout Rate* models implanted electrodes that fail to elicit a phosphene when stimulated electrically. For example, a dropout rate of 50% means that half of all implanted electrodes cannot be used to elicit a phosphene. Electrode dropouts have been reported in multiple IVP clinical trials [11,32], but generally at rates lower than 50%.

Spatial Error models several issues by approximating their combined effect as a normally distributed 2D random offset defined on the cortical plane. For example, electrode deformation during surgical insertion and variations in cortical anatomy are both factors that can be approximated as spatial error. The application of dropouts and spatial error results in *Irregular Electrode Locations*, an example of which can be seen at the bottom-left of Figure 4.

Finally, a *Cortical Model* is applied to estimate the locations of phosphenes in the visual field. The cortical model, also known as a visuotopic map or retinotopy, relates spatial regions on the cortical plane to corresponding regions in the visual field. For the MVG IVP, the cortical model exhibits a *log-polar* relationship, where regions in central vision are mapped to larger cortical regions than regions in peripheral vision. This phenomenon is known as *cortical magnification*. Detailed illustrations of cortical models showing magnification and retinotopy can be found in [26].

As the MVG IVP uses multiple electrode tiles implanted near the occipital lobe, the electrodes will electrically stimulate regions of the primary visual cortex (V1) primarily corresponding to central vision. As such, the simulation uses the Monopole cortical model [24]:

$$z = \exp(\frac{w}{k}) - a \qquad (1) \qquad\qquad m = \frac{E + a}{k} \qquad (2)$$

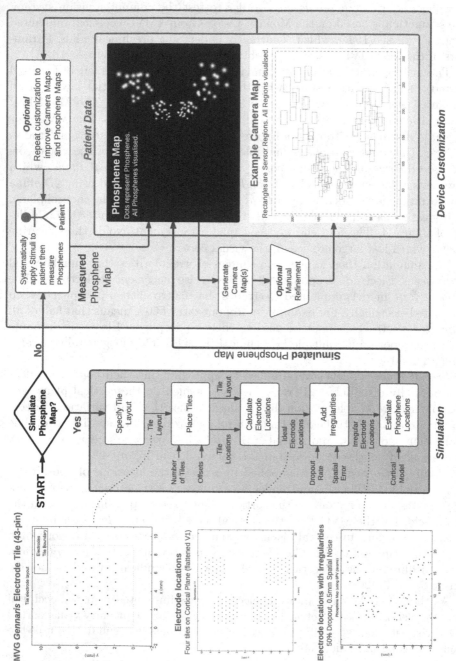

Fig. 4. System for the Simulation and Generation of Patient Data

The variable w is a complex variable representing the 2D spatial location of an electrode on the cortical plane as $w = x + iy$. z is a complex variable representing the corresponding spatial location of phosphenes in the visual field. E is the Eccentricity, which is an angle radiating from the center of the visual field. m is the cortical magnification, which increases the size of phosphenes further from the center of the visual field. k and a are constants that model the cortical magnification and the location of central vision. The values of $k = 15$ and $a = 0.7$ were selected based on typical values used in human models.

Figure 5 contains Simulated Prosthetic Vision (SPV) visualisations of simulated phosphene maps generated assuming four MVG tiles implanted on the left primary visual cortex (See middle-left of Figure 4). The locations and sizes of phosphenes in the visual field are governed by Equations 1 and 2. The SPV visualisation covers around 10 degrees of the visual field. The phosphenes are on the right visual hemisphere as the left visual cortex is being stimulated.

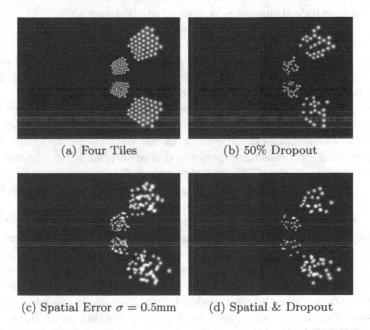

(a) Four Tiles   (b) 50% Dropout

(c) Spatial Error $\sigma = 0.5$mm   (d) Spatial & Dropout

Fig. 5. SPV visualisations of phosphene maps for the MVG IVP

3.2   Dealing with Irregular Phosphene Maps Using Camera Maps

A key innovation of the proposed IVP computer vision system is the use of **two** mappings: A Phosphene Map and a Camera Map.

Phosphene Map
   A mapping between **Stimuli** and **Phosphene**.
Camera Map
   A mapping between **Stimuli** and **Regions in the Camera Image**.

Stimuli is defined as electrical stimulation that elicits phosphenes. For the sake of simplicity, the work in this paper assumes that a single electrode can trigger a stimulus which in turn produces only one phosphene. In other words, it is assumed that one working electrode can produce one phosphene. This assumption is the norm in current IVP research. For reasons detailed in Section 2.1, only binary phosphenes are considered. Note however that the proposed system can be extended to deal with more complex assumptions, such as multi-level phosphenes or many-to-many mappings between stimuli and phosphenes.

An irregular phosphene map is visualised on the middle-right of Figure 4. In practice, a phosphene map is either obtained by simulation or psychophysics measurements performed on the implanted patient. The latter is commonly referred to as *Phosphene Mapping*, which involves the adjustment of electrical stimulation while obtaining patient feedback regarding phosphene appearance. Phosphene mapping dates back to the pioneering work of Brindley and Lewin [2]. A patient's phosphene map is expected to be nearly constant over time, but factors such as electrode dropouts may lead to small changes.

Existing IVP computer vision systems usually assume near-regular phosphene maps and also uses the phosphene map as the spatial layout for image processing. For example, Figure 2 shows a down sampling operation carried out using a spatial layout based on a regular phosphene map. Irregular phosphene maps have also been used to directly specify image processing regions [30].

However, the phosphene map is a measurement that approximates the *true* phosphenes experienced by the patient during stimulation by implanted electrodes. It basically represents the state of the patient-electrode interface. To modify how image processing is performed spatially, existing systems have to modify the phosphene map. This *one-map* approach confuses the *inflexible* phosphene map with the relatively flexible and arbitrary spatial mappings that can be used for image processing operations.

Unlike existing approaches, the proposed IVP computer vision system does not use the phosphene map to perform image processing operations. Instead, the phosphene map is only used by the system to perform real time visualisations, as detailed in Section 3.4. Image processing is performed using a *Camera Map*, which contains a set of mappings between stimuli and regions in the camera image. Figure 6 explains the relationship between a camera map and phosphene map. Essentially, the stimuli relates both maps by acting as an index into the phosphene map and the camera map.

The motivation of having two separate maps is to decouple the state of the patient-electrode interface from how image processing is performed. The system treats the phosphene map as a constant mapping measured by clinicians while the camera map can be continually redesigned by engineers. The camera map can also be modified according to patient preferences and clinician recommendations.

The bottom right of Figure 4 shows a camera map generated from the phosphene map above it. Each rectangle represents a camera image region that is processed to determine whether to activate the corresponding phosphene. Regions in the camera map can be manually moved, scaled, reshaped and even

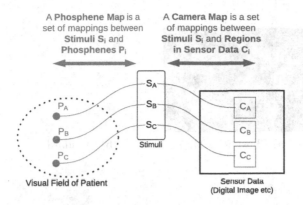

Fig. 6. Relationship between Phosphene Map and Camera Map

removed if needed; the latter can be used to disable a camera region in response to electrode dropouts. Also note that while this paper only considers rectangular regions, this two-map approach can be extended to irregularly shaped regions.

Another benefit of using a two-map approach is that while there is only one *true* phosphene map for an individual patient, there can be many possible corresponding camera maps. Figure 7 shows 3 camera maps for a two-tile phosphene map. The *Standard* camera map has image regions based on the size and location of corresponding phosphenes. The *Zoomed* camera map only covers the center of the camera image, which acts as a zoom function. The smaller regions may also be useful for the patient when viewing finer detail while panning the camera over a scene. Finally, the *Large* camera map shows the use of overlapping regions that mimic retinal receptive fields when processed using a Laplacian filter.

Image processing is performed with a camera map according to the process in Figure 8. Each region C_i in the camera map is processed independently. The results of the processing is used to decide whether to activate the corresponding phosphene P_i. For example, a system that shows bright objects can be built using a binary thresholding operation, where a phosphene is activated when the corresponding region has a mean intensity above a threshold value.

3.3   Fast Image Processing Using Integral Images

This section describes a fast thresholding method that quickly processes regions of a camera map. The method was implemented using C++ and platform-specific SIMD intrinsics for the MVG Wearable Prototype (Pocket Processor) shown in Figure 10. The thresholding method is described by Algorithm 3.1.

The inputs of the method are a gray sub-image (Region-of-Interest from headworn camera image), threshold value ("thVal"), threshold mode ("thMode") and a Stimuli Buffer where each element represents a Stimuli S_i corresponding to camera map region C_i (see Figure 6). The threshold mode can be *Manual*, where a threshold value is chosen by the patient via key presses, or *Auto*, where Otsu's method [22] is used to find a threshold automatically. The method outputs a

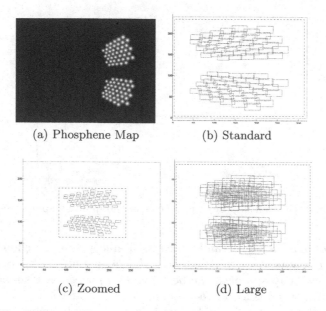

(a) Phosphene Map   (b) Standard

(c) Zoomed   (d) Large

Fig. 7. Several Camera Maps for a Two-Tile Phosphene Map

stimuli buffer where a *high* value in element S_i will produce electrical stimulation that elicits the corresponding phosphene P_i. It also outputs the threshold value ("thValUsed") when operating in automatic threshold mode.

The *integral*() function computes an integral image. Integral Images came from the Summed Area Table concept in Computer Graphics, which was first described by Crow [7]. The concept was later popularized by the work of Viola and Jones [31], who used integral images to rapidly compute the sum of pixel regions to calculate Haar-like features. The *fastmean*() function in the algorithm uses integral images to quickly calculate the mean of a region (*sum/count*).

Note that the integral image only has to be calculated once for an input image in order to allow fast mean computation for practically any number of rectangular regions. As the majority of computational time rests with the *integral*() function instead of the *fastMean*() function, the method has a predictable running time that is independent of the camera map. This is true even for Camera Maps with many overlapping regions such as the one shown in Figure 7d.

The *threshold*() function in Algorithm 3.1 takes "thSrc" as input and outputs into "thDst", both of which are small arrays with size equal to the number of enabled regions in the camera map. Regions in the camera map can be disabled in response to electrode dropouts, patient or clinician requests or algorithm-specific reasons. Elements in "thDst" are set to *high* if the corresponding element in "thSrc" is above the threshold value. Otherwise the element is set to zero.

The method described above operates within the pocket processor sub-system of the MVG device in Figure 1. The pocket processor also generates audio cues, accepts user inputs, provides a clinician interface for the modification of

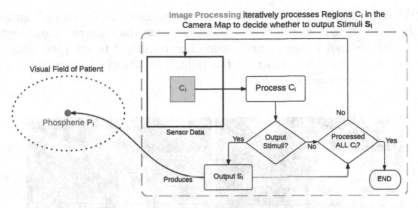

Fig. 8. Image processing using a Camera Map

Algorithm 3.1 Fast Threshold using Integral Images

Input: $graySubImage$, $thVal$, $thMode$, $stimuliBuffer$
Output: $stimuliBuffer \leftarrow array(int)$, $thValUsed$
  $stimuliBuffer \leftarrow 0$, $e \leftarrow 0$
  $integralImage \leftarrow$ integral($graySubImage$)
  for all $i \leftarrow \{0, rect.length() - 1\}$ **do**
    if $enable[i]$ **then**
      $thSrc[e] \leftarrow$ fastMean($integralImage$, $rect[i]$)
      $e \leftarrow e + 1$
  $thValUsed \leftarrow$ threshold($thSrc$, $thDst$, $thVal$, $thMode$)
  $j \leftarrow 0$
  for all $i \leftarrow \{0, numEnabled - 1\}$ **do**
    if $enable[i]$ **then**
      $stimuliBuffer[i] \leftarrow thDst[j]$
      $j \leftarrow j + 1$

---

stimulation parameters and outputs stimulation commands to the wireless system. Details of these additional functionalities are outside the scope of this paper.

3.4 Real Time SPV Visualisation Using Phosphene Map

A fast Simulated Prosthetic Vision (SPV) visualisation algorithm was also implemented in C++ for the MVG pocket processor. It uses the patient's phosphene map and the stimuli buffer output of the fast image processing method to render a 640×480 image of activated phosphenes. This provides a real time visualisation of the prosthetic vision experienced by a patient, which is useful for engineers making adjustments to image processing parameters and for clinicians modifying stimulation parameters or guiding patients through psychophysics activities. The visualisation is disabled during daily use to reduce computational and power costs as the vision impaired patient do not need this functionality.

SPV visualisations captured during system testing are shown in Figures 9a and 9b. The left side of the visualisation contains the camera image overlaid with regions defined in the camera map. The results of image processing, the activated phosphenes, are shown on the right. The phosphene map is the same as the four-tile map in Figure 5a.

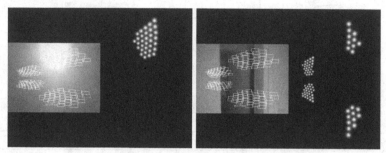

(a) Images from wearable camera

(b) Offline testing with synthetic images

Fig. 9. Real Time SPV visualisations

Phosphenes are drawn using template images that are pre-generated by the simulation described in Section 3.1. A pixel texture is copied to a region of interest in the SPV visualisation image in a similar way as the *blit* operation available in many graphics libraries.

3.5   System Testing and Results

The computer vision system was tested on the MVG wearable prototype in Figure 10. As the MVG device is still in the preclinical phase, system testing was performed using the simulated phosphene map from Figure 5a. The camera map used for testing can be seen in the SPV visualisations in Figures 9. Real time system operation and SPV visualisations for different mappings can be seen in the videos accompanying the paper[6].

---

[6] http://goo.gl/fBKpWT

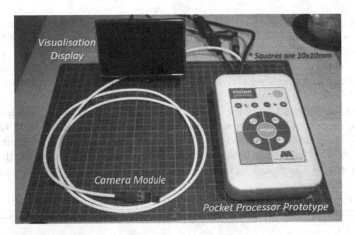

Fig. 10. Wearable Hardware Prototype for Software Development and Testing

Processing times measured over 400 images from the camera module (640×480):

	Mean (ms)	STD (ms)	Min (ms)	Max (ms)
Image Processing	2.53	0.14	2.41	2.69
SPV Visualisation	1.98	0.37	1.03	2.87

4   Discussion and Conclusions

This paper presented a real time computer vision system for implanted visual prostheses. The system uses a novel second mapping called the Camera Map, decoupling the invariant patient-electrode interface from the highly flexible pixel regions used for image processing. The system is fast, taking only several milliseconds to perform image processing and visualisation.

Future work will focus on two aspects. Firstly, the computer vision system will be integrated into ongoing psychophysics trials measuring task performance [12] and evaluating thresholding approaches [6]. Secondly, additional image processing modes will be implemented for the computer vision system.

Acknowledgements. Monash Vision Group is funded through the Australian Research Council Research in Bionic Vision Science and Technology Initiative (SR1000006). The author thanks the anonymous reviewers for their insightful comments.

References

1. Barnes, N.: An overview of vision processing in implantable prosthetic vision. In: IEEE International Conference on Image Processing, pp. 1532–1535, September 2013
2. Brindley, G.S., Lewin, W.S.: The sensations produced by electrical stimulation of the visual cortex. The Journal of Physiology **196**, 479–493 (1968)

3. Buffoni, L.X., Coulombe, J., Sawan, M.: Image processing strategies dedicated to visual cortical stimulators: a survey. Artificial Organs 29(8), 658–64 (2005). http://www.ncbi.nlm.nih.gov/pubmed/16048483

4. Cha, K., Horch, K., Normann, R.A.: Simulation of a phosphene-based visual field: visual acuity in a pixelized vision system. Annals of Biomedical Engineering 20(4), 439–449 (1992)

5. Chen, S.C., Suaning, G.J., Morley, J.W., Lovell, N.H.: Simulating prosthetic vision: I. Visual models of phosphenes. Vision Research 49(12), 1493–1506 (2009)

6. Collette, M., Horace, J., Lindsay, K., Wai Ho, L.: The Impact of Luminance Threshold Modes and Phosphene Dropout Rates in Psychophysics Testing for the Monash Vision Group's Cortical Vision Prosthesis Gennaris. Frontiers in Human Neuroscience 7 (2013)

7. Crow, F.: Summed-area tables for texture mapping. In: ACM SIGGRAPH Computer Graphics. 18, pp. 207–212, July 1984. http://dl.acm.org/citation.cfm?id=808600

8. Dagnelie, G.: Visual Prosthetics. Springer, US, Boston, MA (2011)

9. Dobelle, W.H.: Artificial vision for the blind by connecting a television camera to the visual cortex. ASAIO Journal (American Society for Artificial Internal Organs: 1992) 46(1), 3–9 (2000). http://www.ncbi.nlm.nih.gov/pubmed/10667705

10. Greenwald, S.H., Horsager, A., Humayun, M.S., Greenberg, R.J., McMahon, M.J., Fine, I.: Brightness as a function of current amplitude in human retinal electrical stimulation. Investigative Ophthalmology & Visual Science 50(11), 5017–5025 (2009)

11. Humayun, M.S., Dorn, J.D., da Cruz, L., Dagnelie, G., Sahel, J.A., Stanga, P.E., Cideciyan, A.V., Duncan, J.L., Eliott, D., Filley, E., Ho, A.C., Santos, A., Safran, A.B., Arditi, A., Del Priore, L.V., Greenberg, R.J.: Interim results from the international trial of Second Sight's visual prosthesis. Ophthalmology 119(4), 779–788 (2012)

12. Josh, H., Mann, C., Kleeman, L., Lui, W.L.D.: Psychophysics testing of bionic vision image processing algorithms using an FPGA Hatpack. In: 2013 IEEE International Conference on Image Processing, pp. 1550–1554. IEEE, September 2013, http://ieeexplore.ieee.org/lpdocs/epic03/wrapper.htm?arnumber=6738319

13. Josh, H., Yong, B., Kleeman, L.: A Real-time FPGA-based Vision System for a Bionic Eye. In: ARAA (ed.) Proceedings of Australasian Conference on Robotics and Automation. p. Online. ARAA, Melbourne, Australia (2011)

14. Kiral-Kornek, F.I., Savage, C.O., O'Sullivan-Greene, E., Burkitt, A.N., Grayden, D.B.: Embracing the irregular: A patient-specific image processing strategy for visual prostheses. In: International Conference of the IEEE Engineering in Medicine and Biology Society 2013, 3563–3566, January 2013. http://www.ncbi.nlm.nih.gov/pubmed/24110499

15. LeRoy, C.: Ou l'on rend compte de quelques tentatives que l'on a faites pour guerir plusieurs maladies par l'electricite. In: (Paris), H.A.R.S. (ed.) Memoires Math. Phys., pp. 87–89 (1755)

16. Li, W.H.: Wearable Computer Vision Systems for a Cortical Visual Prosthesis. In: 2013 IEEE International Conference on Computer Vision Workshops, pp. 428–435. IEEE, December 2013

17. Lowery, A.J.: Introducing the Monash vision group's cortical prosthesis. In: 2013 IEEE International Conference on Image Processing, pp. 1536–1539. IEEE, September 2013

18. Lui, W.L.D., Browne, D., Kleeman, L., Drummond, T., Li, W.H.: Transformative reality: Augmented reality for visual prostheses. In: 2011 10th IEEE International Symposium on Mixed and Augmented Reality, pp. 253–254. IEEE, October 2011. http://doi.ieeecomputersociety.org/10.1109/ISMAR.2011. 6092402http://youtu.be/J30uYYkDApYhttp://youtu.be/iK5ddJqNuxY

19. Nanduri, D., Humayun, M.S., Greenberg, R.J., McMahon, M.J., Weiland, J.D.: Retinal prosthesis phosphene shape analysis. In: International Conference of the IEEE Engineering in Medicine and Biology Society 2008, pp. 1785–1788, January 2008. http://www.ncbi.nlm.nih.gov/pubmed/19163027

20. Nanduri, D., Humayun, M.S., Weiland, J.D., Dorn, J., Greenberg, R.J., Fine, I.: Encoding of size and brightness of percepts in a visual prosthesis, September 2013. http://www.google.com/patents/US8527056

21. Naumann, J.: Search for Paradise: A Patient's Account of the Artificial Vision Experiment. Xlibris (2012). http://www.amazon.com/Search-Paradise-Artificial-Experiment-ebook/dp/B009A86X9K

22. Otsu, N.: A Threshold Selection Method from Gray-Level Histograms. Ieee Transactions On Systems Man And Cybernetics 9, 62–66 (1979)

23. Parikh, N., Itti, L., Weiland, J.: Saliency-based image processing for retinal prostheses. Journal of neural engineering 7(1), 16006 (2010). http://www.ncbi.nlm.nih.gov/pubmed/20075505

24. Polimeni, J.R., Balasubramanian, M., Schwartz, E.L.: Multi-area visuotopic map complexes in macaque striate and extra-striate cortex. Vision Research 46(20), 3336–3359 (2006)

25. van Rheede, J.J., Kennard, C., Hicks, S.L.: Simulating prosthetic vision: Optimizing the information content of a limited visual display. Journal of Vision 10(14), 1–14 (2010)

26. Schiller, P., Tehovnik, E.: Visual Prosthesis. Perception 37, 1529–1559 (2008)

27. Srivastava, N.R.: Simulations of Cortical Prosthetic Vision. In: Dagnelie, G. (ed.) Visual Prosthetics, pp. 355–365. Springer (2011)

28. Stingl, K.K.T., Bartz-Schmidt, K.U., Besch, D., Braun, A., Bruckmann, A., Gekeler, F., Greppmaier, U., Hipp, S., Hörtdörfer, G., Kernstock, C., Koitschev, A., Kusnyerik, A., Sachs, H., Schatz, A., Peters, T., Wilhelm, B., Zrenner, E.: Artificial vision with wirelessly powered subretinal electronic implant alpha-IMS. Proceedings. Biological sciences / The Royal Society 280(1757), 20130077 (2013). http://rspb.royalsocietypublishing.org/content/280/1757/20130077.abstract

29. Tsai, D., Morley, J.W., Suaning, G.J., Lovell, N.H.: A wearable real-time image processor for a vision prosthesis. Computer methods and programs in biomedicine 95(3), 258–69 (2009). http://www.ncbi.nlm.nih.gov/pubmed/19394713

30. Veraart, C., Wanet-Defalque, M.C., Gerard, B., Vanlierde, A., Delbeke, J.: Pattern Recognition with the Optic Nerve Visual Prosthesis. Artificial Organs 27(11), 996–1004 (2003)

31. Viola, P., Jones, M.: Rapid object detection using a boosted cascade of simple features. In: Proceedings of the 2001 IEEE Computer Society Conference on Computer Vision and Pattern Recognition, CVPR 2001, pp. 511–518. IEEE (2001). http://ieeexplore.ieee.org/lpdocs/epic03/wrapper.htm?arnumber=990517

32. Wilke, R., Gabel, V.P., Sachs, H., Bartz Schmidt, K.U., Gekeler, F., Besch, D., Szurman, P., Stett, A., Wilhelm, B., Peters, T., Harscher, A., Greppmaier, U., Kibbel, S., Benav, H., Bruckmann, A., Stingl, K., Kusnyerik, A., Zrenner, E.: Spatial resolution and perception of patterns mediated by a subretinal 16-electrode array in patients blinded by hereditary retinal dystrophies. Investigative Ophthalmology & Visual Science 52(8), 5995–6003 (2011)

An Intelligent Wheelchair to Enable Safe Mobility of the Disabled People with Motor and Cognitive Impairments

Yeounggwang Ji, Myeongjin Lee, and Eun Yi Kim[(✉)]

Visual Information Processing Laboratory, Konkuk University,
Seoul, South Korea
{ji861020,lmj5542,eykim04}@gmail.com

Abstract. In this paper, we develop an Intelligent Wheelchair (IW) system to provide safe mobility to the disabled or elderly people with cognitive and motor impairments. Our IW provides two main functions: obstacle avoidance and situation awareness. Firstly, it detects a variety of obstacles by a combination of a camera and 8 range sensors, and finds the viable paths to avoid the collisions of obstacles based on learning-based classification. Secondly, it categorizes the current situation where a user is standing on as sidewalk, roadway and traffic intersection by analyzing the texture properties and shapes of the images, thus prevents the collisions of vehicle at the traffic intersection. The proposed system was tested on various environments then the results show that the proposed system can recognize the outdoor place types with an accuracy of 98.25% and produce the viable paths with an accuracy of 92.00% on outdoors.

Keywords: Intelligent wheelchair · Obstacle avoidance · Situation awareness · learning-based path generation

1 Introduction

With the increase of elderly and disabled people, a wide range of support devices and care equipment have been developed to help improve their quality of life. Traditionally, the wheelchair, including powered and manual ones, is the most popular and important assistive device for the disabled and the elderly. In particular, Intelligent Wheelchairs (IWs) have received considerable attention as mobility aids [1-5]. Essentially, IWs are electric powered wheelchairs (EPWs) with an embedded computer and sensors, giving them intelligence. Two basic techniques have been used to develop IWs: 1) navigation techniques for automatic obstacle avoidance and 2) convenient interfaces that allow handicapped users to control the IW themselves using their limited physical abilities.

In this study, our goal is to develop the navigation techniques that allow the multiply disabled with cognitive and motor impairments for more safe mobility.

During last decades, many navigation systems have been investigated for IWs, and most of them have used a combination of bumpers, infrared (IR) sensors, ultrasonic sensors, and sonar sensors for collision avoidance [2-7]. Such sensor-based navigations

© Springer International Publishing Switzerland 2015
L. Agapito et al. (Eds.): ECCV 2014 Workshops, Part III, LNCS 8927, pp. 702–715, 2015.
DOI: 10.1007/978-3-319-16199-0_49

consider objects protruding more than a certain distance from the ground as obstacles. The NavChair was presented for the elderly people [2], which can detect various obstacles with range sensors such as IRs and ultrasonics, and help the user safely past obstacles and narrow space. The robotic wheelchair was developed by Yanco et al. [3], which provides the avoidance of obstacles and automatic following of a target specified by the user (e.g. follow a person walking in front of the wheelchair). In addition, a drive-safe-system (DSS) was developed to provide safe and independent mobility to the visually impaired [4-5]. The DSS can detect various obstacles using 2 bumpers, 5 IRs and 5 ultrasonics, and provide the wall following and door crossing in indoors. Such sensor-based navigations are simple, inexpensive and easy to install, and are thus widely used. However they suffer from specular reflections and poor angular resolution. In addition to detect various obstacles such as small or flat objects, they require many sensors with high capacity.

As an alternative method to sensor-based navigation, a method has been received a lot of attention [8-12]. The vision-based navigation is further categorized into methods using stereo and monocular vision. The methods using stereovision techniques discriminate obstacles from the backgrounds by 3D depth information. The major drawback of such methods involves high computational time and hardware costs. On the other hand, the monocular vision-based navigations have used the image processing and computer vision technique to recognize the obstacles, where obstacles are considered as objects that differ in appearance from ground. Accordingly, an appearance model to describe the visual properties of background is required, which should be robust to some situational effects such as cluttered background and illuminations. In [13], online background model is proposed that can be easily learned on real-time, which can work well on both textured and texture-less background and improve the sensitivity to illumination.

Although many navigation systems are working well on indoors and outdoors, they still have one major problem. In real outdoor environments, many accidents have occurred on the traffic intersections, which are more dangerous places to the disabled people and cognitively impaired people. To fully guarantee the safety of the wheelchair users, the mechanism to recognize the outdoor situation should be also attached to the IWs.

In this paper, we present a new intelligent wheelchair (IW) to provide safety to the people with various disabilities and the elderly people. To guarantee the safe mobility, the proposed IW supports two main functions: obstacle avoidance and situation awareness. With these functions, it can detect a variety of obstacles and dangerous situations on real environments and recommend safe paths to avoid them. Firstly, the obstacles are recognized by the combination of a camera and 8 range sensors, then viable paths are generated by learning-based algorithms such as a neural network (NN) and a support vector machine (SVM). Secondly, to prevent the collisions with vehicles on the traffic intersection, the situation awareness classifies the place types where a user is standing on as sidewalk, roadway and intersection by texture classification and shape filtering.

To evaluate the effectiveness of the proposed IW, several datasets have been collected from real environments with various illumination types and complex structures, and then the experiments were performed. Then, the results showed that the proposed system can recognize the outdoor place types with an accuracy of 98.25% and produce the viable paths with an accuracy of 92.00% on outdoors.

2   Proposed Intelligent Wheelchair

The goal of this study is to provide safe mobility to a wheelchair user while the users are controlling the wheelchair to their destination. To provide the safe mobility it should detect a variety of obstacles and dangerous situations on real environments and recommend safe paths to avoid them. For this, we present a hybrid obstacle avoidance and a situation awareness.

Figure 1 shows the architecture of the proposed IW, which is composed of an electric powered wheelchair, one camera, 8 ultrasonic sensors, laptop computer and data acquisition (DAQ) board. Through analyzing the images obtained from the CCD camera, we can recognize the upcoming obstacles and the place types where a user is standing on, so prevent the collisions of obstacles with various obstacles including the static walls, pedestrian and vehicles on the traffic intersections.

The proposed IW is composed of four main modules: 1) situation awareness, 2) vision-based obstacle avoidance, 3) sensor-based obstacle avoidance and 4) converter. While a wheelchair user is moving, IW should detect various obstacles and find the viable path to avoid them. For this, a hybrid method is adopted using both sensor values and camera, where obstacles are detected using the sensor values and background subtraction, and viable paths are determined by learning-based classification. In addition, to prevent the collisions of vehicles on the traffic intersections, the situation awareness module discriminated the user's current place as intersection and sidewalk. Finally, all the recognition results are given to the converter that determines most appropriate paths and notifies the decisions to user or directly control the wheelchair.

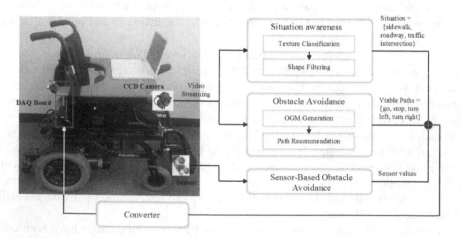

Fig. 1. Overall system architecture

3   Obstacle Avoidance

In our system, to fully guarantee the user's safety, both the camera and the range sensors are used to detect the dangerous situation such as static obstacles and moving obstacles. Then, 8 range sensors can measure only the obstacles within the distance of 2m from the wheelchair, whereas the camera can cover 0.4m to 14m. Thus, the most of the obstacles are recognized by the vision-based algorithm, and sensor-based algorithm is mainly used to recognize the stairs and the obstacles upcoming from the backside of the wheelchair.

3.1   Vision-Based Obstacle Avoidance

Occupancy Map Generation. An occupancy grid map (OGM) represents the environmental information such as the position and size of an obstacle, where each cell models the risk of the corresponding area using gray color levels. In current, we used a camera which has the same focal length of 22mm to human vision and resolution of 320×240 pixels. In this module, the image is transformed to 32×24 OGM, through background color estimation and subtraction.

In this work, the background model is estimated by simple online learning developed by Ulrich and Nourbakhsh [14]. The background color is estimated from only the reference area, that is, 1m-trapezoidal area in front of camera. The input image is filtered by 5×5 Gaussian filters, and transformed into the HSI color space. From the reference area, two color histograms are calculated for Hue and Intensity. These histograms are accumulated for recent five frames, which are used as background model. The background model is continuously updated, as a new frame is input.

Once the background model is obtained, classification is performed. For every frame, each pixel is classified as follows:

$$\begin{cases} M_t = 1 \ \ if \ (|BH_t(s) - H_t(s)|) \le T_H \ \ and \ (|BI_t(s) - I_t(s)|) < T_I \\ \\ M_t = 0 \ \ otherwise \end{cases} \tag{1}$$

where the T_H is the threshold value for hue histogram BH_t and T_I is the threshold value for intensity histogram BI_t. In this paper, the hue and intensity thresholds are set to 60 and 80, respectively

Based on the background classification results, the OGM is produced, where each cell is corresponding to one block of 10×10 pixels in the binary image M_t, and its color models the risk of the corresponding area. Here 10 gray-scales are used according to the risk. Then, the gray scale of a cell is determined by 1/10(# of pixels classified as obstacles). The brighter a grid cell, the more closely space obstacles.

Path Generation. Despite of online learning-based background estimation, the misclassification between background and obstacles can be occurred, as the vision-based system is inevitably affected by time-varying illumination. To compensate the affects by such situational effects, the learning-based path generation is developed.

Here, both a neural network (NN) and a support vector machine (SVM) are considered as the classifier, and the classifier that has the better performance is adapted.

The NN-based classifier is composed of 768 input nodes, 110 hidden nodes and 4 output nodes. It receives the gray values of pixels on 32×24 occupancy map, and outputs four floating numbers that represent the probabilities of four directions to be selected as viable path. Among four directions - Go straight, Stop, Turn Left, and Turn Right, - the direction with the highest value is determined as the viable path.

Unlike the NN that allows for multi-class classification, the standard SVM is has been designed for binary classification problems. To apply such a SVM to four-directions classification, a decision tree is designed, where each node corresponds to one binary classifier that determines if an example belongs to one specific direction class. The decision is performed by three steps: the classification is first performed to divide the current situation into move or stop, the next one is the classification of go and turn, finally the classification of turn-left and turn-right. The SVMs receive the same feature vectors with the NN and use a linear kernel.

The NN-based classifier and SVM-based one were tested with lots of test image collected from real indoors and outdoors, then the result showed the latter is better than the former, which is discussed in experiments.

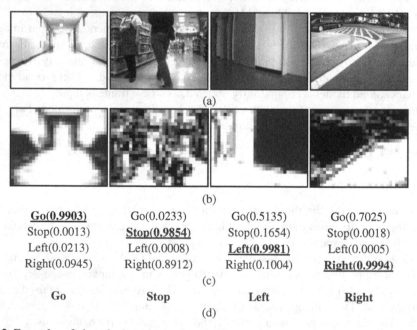

Go(**0.9903**)	Go(0.0233)	Go(0.5135)	Go(0.7025)
Stop(0.0013)	**Stop(0.9854)**	Stop(0.1654)	Stop(0.0018)
Left(0.0213)	Left(0.0008)	**Left(0.9981)**	Left(0.0005)
Right(0.0945)	Right(0.8912)	Right(0.1004)	**Right(0.9994)**

(c)

| **Go** | **Stop** | **Left** | **Right** |

(d)

Fig. 2. Examples of obstacle detection and path recommendation (a) input image, (b) generated OGMs, (c) and (d) recognition results by NN and SVM

Figure 2 shows the result of obstacle avoidance. Figure 2(a) shows the input image and Figure 2(b) shows the generated 32×24 occupancy map result. For the first and fourth images, the proposed method succeeds in correctly detecting the obstacles, while it fails to detect some obstacles in the second image. The main cause is the time-varying illumination. Then, the predicted viable paths by the NN and SVMs are shown in Figs. 2(c) and (d). As you can see, learning-based method can recommend the accurate viable paths.

3.2 Sensor-Based Obstacle Avoidance

Figure 3 shows how the sensors were positioned on the proposed IW. 4 ultrasonic sensors (I1~4) are used for emergency stop if the obstacles are detected in front of IW and find path to avoid them. Also, 4 ultrasonic sensors (I5~8) are used to detect obstacles at back of IW.

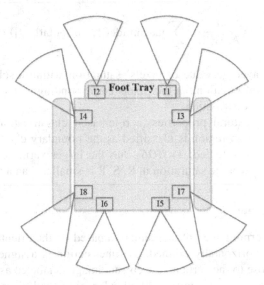

Fig. 3. Position of sensors on proposed IW

By processing the sensors' information, the sensor-based method divides the current paths as 'move' and 'stop,' and it is mainly used to recognize the stairs and the obstacles upcoming from the backside of the wheelchair.

4   Situation Awareness

In addition, through analyzing the images obtained from the CCD camera, we can recognize if the user is approaching to the traffic intersection, thereby preventing the collisions of traffic vehicles.

In this work, a situation means the type of place the user is located, which is categorized into sidewalk and intersection. For recognizing outdoor situation, texture classification and shape filtering were performed on the input image.

4.1 Texture Classification

We first apply Gaussian filter and histogram equalization to the input image in turn. Then, the input image sized at 640×480 is divided into 768 sub-regions sized at 20×20 and texture classification is performed on the respective sub-regions.

To discriminate the boundaries between sidewalks and roadways from other lines, the texture properties of sub-regions are investigated.

In this work, to characterize the variability in a texture pattern, both HOG (Histogram of Oriented Gradient) and color information are used.

The HOG is the feature descriptor to count the occurrences of gradient orientation in the sub-regions of an image, which is many used for object detection [14]. For 20×20 sized sub-region, R the HOG is calculated, which is identified as

$$HOG_R = \left\{ HOG_R(i) = \frac{1}{Area(R)} \times \sum_{j \in R} magnitude(j), \text{if orientation}(j) = i\, (1 \leq i \leq 6) \right\} \quad (2)$$

In addition, the average value of pixels' saturation within a sub-region is used to describe the color information, as the pixels corresponding to the roadway have the distinctive saturation distribution.

Based on these textural properties, a rule-based classification is performed on every sub-region. A sub-region is classified as the boundary class if both of the following conditions are satisfied: 1) HOG_R has the larger variance than a predefined threshold θ_H; 2) the average saturation in R, S_R is smaller than a threshold θ_S.

4.2 Shape Filtering

In this step, we determine the outdoor situation based on the orientations of the boundaries: if they are horizontally aligned, the intersection is assigned to the image; if they are aligned close to the vertical, the current image is labeled as side-walk.

To eliminate the affects by misclassified sub-regions and determine correct situation, the profile analysis is performed on the classified images.

Accordingly, a classified image is projected along a y-axis and x-axis and two histograms are computed: horizontal histogram and vertical one. Thereafter, the following three heuristics are applied in turn, to determine the current situation : (1) An intersection is assigned to the current image in which some horizontal his-togram values are more than a threshold; (2) An intersection is assigned to the input image in which the vertical histogram is uniformly distributed; (3) A sidewalk is assigned in which the vertical histogram has the larger variance than a threshold σ. Hence, 10 was set to σ by experiments.

Figure 4 shows the situation awareness. Figure 4 (a) shows the input image. Then texture classification result as shows in Figure 4 (b). As can be seen in Figure 4 (b), the classification results include most of the sub-regions with correct boundary class. And Figure 4 (c) and (d) illustrate how the situation is determined. Figure 4 (c) is a y-axis projection profile of a classified image, and Figure 4 (d) is an x-axis projection profile of a classified image. As you can see in Figure 4 (c), the top image has the vertical histogram with larger variance, thus its situation is considered as sidewalk. On the other hand, the bottom image has some horizontal histogram values larger than a threshold, thus its situation is determined as intersection.

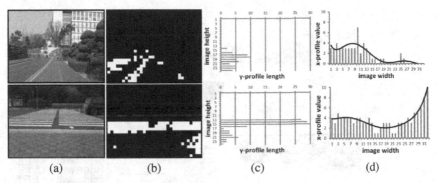

(a) (b) (c) (d)

Fig. 4. Shape filtering results (a) Input images (b) texture classification results (c) horizontal projection profiles (d) vertical projection profiles

5 Converter

The Converter receives all of the recognized results in situation awareness and vision-based and sensor-based methods, and determines more appropriate decisions to support users' safe mobility. Table 1 illustrates the decision function to select the viable paths among the results given from three modules.

Table 1. The decision function to select the viable paths in Converter

---

Input: real time image streaming I, 8 sensors values S
Output: values paths v = {go, stop, turn-left, turn-right}

```
Selecting the viable paths on converter(I, S)
{
    a = Situation awareness(I);
    b = Sensor-based obstacle avoidance (S);
    c = Vision-based obstacle avoidance (I);

    if (a== 'intersection') v ←'stop'
    else if (b=='stop') v ←'stop'
    else v ←c;

    Interface(v);
}
```

Such a decision is conveyed to the user through auditory interface or visual interface. Figure 5 shows the visual interface, where the recognized results are displayed onto the Notebook screen (see the right image of Figure 5).

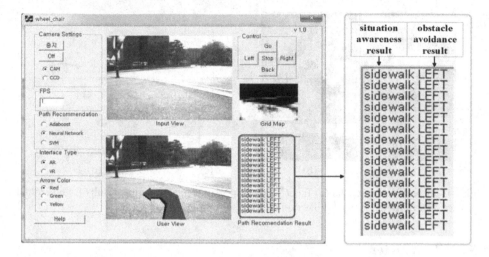

Fig. 5. Visual user interface

Some of the cognitively impaired or the elderly people has the difficulties in controlling the wheelchair in real-time, so the collisions with the dangerous obstacles can be occurred. To prevent them, the Converter allows the direct control of the wheelchair according to the recognized results from three modules.

As shown in Figure 1, our IW uses a DAQ board to translate the recognition results into control commands for the IW. Similar to a general electric powered wheelchair, which is controlled by the voltage passed to the joystick, a DAQ board (USB-6009) is used to transform the ADC function and DAC. The board is connected to a computer through a serial port and programmed using Visual Studio. The board program then controls the directions of wheelchair by modifying the voltage passing through the wheelchair.

6   Experimental Results

To assess the effectiveness of the proposed IW, experiments were performed on the images obtained from indoors and outdoors. For the practical use as mobility aids, it should be robust to environmental factors, such as different place types and lightening conditions. Therefore, 80,000 indoor and outdoor images, including official buildings, department stores, and underground areas, were collected over one year at different times. For all images, the ground-truth was manually labeled by human. Among them, some images were used for evaluating the proposed outdoor situation awareness and some were used for evaluating the performance of the obstacle detection.

6.1 Obstacle Avoidance Results

In this section, we investigated the performance of obstacle detection with a huge data. Unlike the outdoor situation awareness, this module was evaluated using images obtained from both indoors and outdoors.

Table 2 shows the dataset used for evaluating the obstacle detection module. A total of 80,000 images were collected, which were then categorized into 4 datasets, according to their illumination, background texture, and obstacles.

Table 2. The experimental data for evaluating the obstacle avoidance

Places	DB Sets	Illumination	Background texture	Obstacles
Indoor	DB I CCD daytime	- Fixed illumination (fluorescence)	- Little reflection - Weakly textured floor	- Only static obstacles
	DB II CCD daytime	- Fixed illumination with pin light	- High reflection - Marble textured or highly textured floors	- Static and dynamic obstacles
Outdoor	DB III CCD daytime	- Direct sunlight with little shadow	- Weakly textured ground with small road signs	- Static Obstacles
	DB IV CCD daytime	- Direct sunlight with complex shadow	- Reflection by sunlight - Highly textured ground	- Static and dynamic obstacles (moving people and vehicles)

To assess the validity of the proposed method, the results were compared with those of existing method using vector field histogram (VFH) [15].

Figure 6 shows results tested on various environments. Figure 6(a) to (d) show the generated OGMs and determined viable paths. As you can see, the proposed method can accurately predict the viable paths to prevent the collisions of obstacles.

(a)   (b)   (c)   (d)

Fig. 6. Obstacle avoidance results (a) – (d): the input images and OGMs determined as go-straight, stop, turn-left and turn-right

Figure 7 shows the performance summarization of obstacle detection under indoors and outdoors, for three methods – VFH-based method, NN-based method and

SVM-based method. On average, VFH-based method has accuracy of 68.00% and 68.80% on indoors and outdoors, respectively. On the other hand, the SVM-based method can generate avoidable paths in the accuracy of 88.00% and 92.00% on the respective environments, and NN-based method has accuracy of 83.80% and 89.00%.

As you can see, the learning based method showed the better performance; in particular, it can significantly improve the performance on the outdoors– improvement of 20.20%, at least. And the SVM-based classifier showed the superior accuracy to the NN-based classifier.

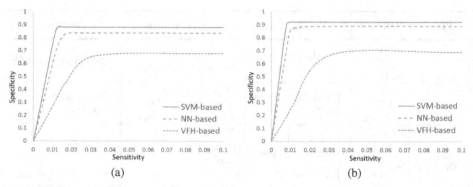

Fig. 7. Performance summarization of obstacle avoidance when using three methods (a) the accuracy on indoors (b) the accuracy on outdoors

6.2   Situation Awareness Results

A total of 2243 images were collected, which were then categorized into 6 datasets, according to their environmental complexity, as illustrated in Table 3.

Table 3. The experimental data for evaluating the situation awareness

Environmental Factors		The Number of		Usage
Illumination Type	Scene Complexity	Images		
Direct sunlight with little shadow	Highly textured ground with static obstacles	110	DB1	Training data
	Textured ground with moving obstacles (people, car)	64	DB2	
	Highly textured ground with static structures	844	DB3	Test data
	Textured ground with simple structures	256	DB4	
Direct sunlight with complex shadow	Non-textured ground with simple structures	156	DB5	
	Textured ground with simple structures	312	DB6	

Among them, 174 images were used as training data for finding optimal parameter set (θ_H, θ_S, σ), which were used for texture classification and shape filtering. And the other images were used for testing.

Figure 8 shows some recognition results for various environments. Figure 8 (a) shows the input images, where the images have the time-varying illumination, and the sidewalks have diverse patterns and colors. The input images were first enhanced through pre-processing stage, which are shown in Figure 8 (b). Then, the texture classification and shape filtering were performed. As shown in Figure 8 (c), the boundaries between side-walks and roadways were correctly extracted, despite of diverse pattern of sidewalks, however they still included some false alarms. To eliminate the affects by misclassified sub-regions and determine correct situation, the profile analysis were performed on the classified images, which are shown in Figure 8 (d). The results showed that the proposed method have a robust performance to the pattern of ground and illumination type.

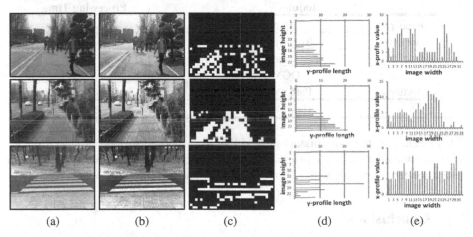

| (a) | (b) | (c) | (d) | (e) |

Fig. 8. Situation awareness results (a) input image (b) enhanced image by preprocessing (c) texture classification results (d)-(e) horizontal and vertical histograms used in shape filtering

Table 4 summarizes the performance of the situation recognition under various outdoor environments. The average accuracy was about 87.60%. For the DB1 to DB4, the proposed method showed the accuracy of above 96.00%.

Table 4. Accuracy of outdoor situation awareness (%)

	DB1	DB2	DB3	DB4	DB5	DB6	Total
Accuracy	91	95.3	100	100	94.8	97.4	96.42

6.3   Processing Time

The main purpose of the proposed system is to help the safe mobility of the user and to prevent some dangerous collisions with vehicles or obstacles. For its practical use as an assistive device, the real time processing should be supported.

Table 5 shows the average frame processing time in the respective module of wheelchair. In current system, the sensor based obstacle avoidance does not play a role in the overall time metric, as it has own processing power on sensor board. Thus, only the times taken to process the video stream were considered. The processing times were about 228.54ms for the outdoor situation awareness and were about 5.03ms for obstacle detection. As such, the proposed method can process more than 4 frames per second on low-performance computer.

Table 5. Average frame processing time (ms)

Modules		Processing Time
Outdoor situation awareness	Preprocessing	41.24
	Texture classification	181.32
	Shape filtering	5.98
Obstacle detection	OGM generation	2.95
	Path recommendation	2.08
	Total	233.57

Consequently, the experiments proved that the proposed method produced the superior accuracy for situation awareness and safe path prediction, thereby assisting safe navigation for the people with various disabilities and the elderly people in real-time.

7   Conclusions

In this paper, an intelligent wheelchair equipped situation awareness was presented to help the safe mobility of the people with various disabilities and the elderly people. The proposed system provides obstacle detection and avoidance, and situation awareness. With them, the proposed IW can detect a variety of obstacles and generate the viable paths to avoid the collisions of them. Moreover, it can recognize the outdoor situations as sidewalk, roadway and traffic intersection, thereby preventing the accidents on the traffic intersection.

To assess the effectiveness of the proposed IW, experiments were performed on the images obtained from indoors and outdoors. For the practical use as mobility aids of the elderly and disabled people, the proposed system should be robust to environmental factors, such as different place types and lightening conditions. Therefore, 80,000 indoor and outdoor images, including official buildings, department stores, and underground areas, were collected over one year at different times. Then the results showed that the proposed method can recognize the situation awareness with an accuracy of 98.25% and produce the viable paths with an accuracy of 90.00%.

Acknowledgment. This research was supported by the MSIP(Ministry of Science, ICT and Future Planning), Korea, under the ITRC(Information Technology Research Center) support program (NIPA-2014-H0301-14-1001) supervised by the NIPA(National IT Industry Promotion Agency) and Basic Science Research Program through the National Research Foundation of Korea(NRF) funded by the Ministry of Education, Science and Technology(NRF-2013R1A1A3013445).

References

1. Mihailidis, A., Elinas, P., Boger, J., Hocy, J.: An Intelligent Powered Wheelchair to Enable Mobility of Cognitively Impaired Older Adults: An Anti-Collision System. IEEE Transactions on Neural Systems & Rehabilitation Engineering **15**(1), 136–143 (2007)
2. Levine, SP., Bell, DA., Jaros, LA., Simpson RC, Koren Y, Borenstein J.: The NavChair Assistive Wheelchair Navigation System. IEEE Trans. Rehabil. Eng. **7**(4) (1999) 443–451
3. Yanco, H.A.: Wheelesley: A Robotic Wheelchair System: Indoor Navigation and User Interface. In: Mittal, V.O., Yanco, H.A., Aronis, J., Simpson, R.C. (eds.) Assistive Technology and Artificial Intelligence. LNCS (LNAI), vol. 1458, p. 256. Springer, Heidelberg (1998)
4. Sharma, V., Simpson, R.C., Lopresti, E.F., Schmeler, M.: Clinical evaluation of semiautonomous smart wheelchair architecture (Drive-Safe System) with visually impaired individuals. J. Rehabil. Res. Dev. **49**(1), 35–50 (2012)
5. Lopresti, E.F., Sharma, V., Simpson, R.C., Mostowy, L.C.: Performance testing of collision-avoidance system for power wheelchairs. J Rehabil Res Dev **48**(5), 529–44 (2011)
6. Rodríguez, A., Yebes, J.J., Alcantarilla, P.F., Bergasa, L.M., Almazán, J., Cela, A.: Assisting the Visually Impaired: Obstacle Detection and Warning System by Acoustic Feedback. Sensors **12**(12), 17476–17496 (2012)
7. Xu, X., Zhang, Y., Luo, Y., Chen, D.: Robust Bio-Signal Based Control of an Intelligent Wheelchair. Sensors **2**(4), 187–197 (2013)
8. Haigh, KZ., Yanco, HA: Automation as caregiver: A survey of issues and technologies. In: Proceedings of the AAAI-2002 Workshop on Automation as Caregiver: The Role of Intelligent Technology in Elder Care (2002)
9. Simpson, R.C.: Smart wheelchairs: A literature review. Journal of Rehabilitation Research and Development **42**(4), 423–435 (2005)
10. Goedemé, T., Nuttin, M.: Omni directional Vision-based topological navigation. Journal of Computer Vision **3**(74), 219–236 (2007)
11. Murillo, A.C., Kosecka, J., Guerrero, J.J., Sagues, C.: Visual door detection integrating appearance and shape cues. Robotics and Autonomous Systems **56**, 512–521 (2008)
12. Bellotto, N., Burn, K., Wermter, S.: Appearance-based localization for mobile robots using digital zoom and visual compass. Robotics and Autonomous Systems **56**, 143–156 (2008)
13. Ju, JS., Kim, EY.: EyeCane: Navigation with camera embedded white cane for visually impaired person. ACM Conference on SIGASSETS (2009)
14. Ulrich, I.: Appearance-based obstacle detection with monocular color vision. In: Proceedings of the Seventeenth National Conference on Artificial Intelligence and Twelfth Conference on Innovative Applications of Artificial Intelligence, pp. 866–871 (2000)
15. Borenstein, J., Koren, Y.: The vector field histogram-fast obstacle avoidance for mobile robots. Robotics and Automation **7**(3), 278–288 (1991)

A Visual SLAM System on Mobile Robot Supporting Localization Services to Visually Impaired People

Quoc-Hung Nguyen[1](✉), Hai Vu[1], Thanh-Hai Tran[1], David Van Hamme[2],
Peter Veelaert[2], Wilfried Philips[2], and Quang-Hoan Nguyen[3]

[1] International Research Institute MICA, Hanoi University of Science and
Technology, Hanoi, Vietnam
{quoc-hung.nguyen,hai.vu,thanh-hai.tran}@mica.edu.vn
[2] Ghent University/iMinds (IPI), Gent, Belgium
dvhamme@telin.ugent.be, peter.veelaert@hogent.be
wilfried.philips@ugent.be
[3] Hung Yen University of Technology and Education, Hung Yen, Vietnam
quanghoanptit@yahoo.com.vn

Abstract. This paper describes a Visual SLAM system developed on a mobile robot in order to support localization services to visually impaired people. The proposed system aims to provide services in small or mid-scale environments such as inside a building or campus of school where conventional positioning data such as GPS, WIFI signals are often not available. Toward this end, we adapt and improve existing vision-based techniques in order to handle issues in the indoor environments. We firstly design an image acquisition system to collect visual data. On one hand, a robust visual odometry method is adjusted to precisely create the routes in the environment. On the other hand, we utilize the Fast-Appearance Based Mapping algorithm that is may be the most successful for matching places in large scenarios. In order to better estimate robot's location, we utilize a Kalman Filter that combines the matching results of current observation and the estimation of robot states based on its kinematic model. The experimental results confirmed that the proposed system is feasible to navigate the visually impaired people in the indoor environments.

Keywords: Visual odometry · Place recognition · FAB-MAP algorithms · Kalman filter

1   Introduction

Autonomous localization and navigation are extreme desirable services for visually impaired people. Most commercial solutions are based on the Global Positioning System (GPS), WIFI, LIDAR, or fusion of them. iNavBelt uses ultrasonic sensors to procedure a 120-degree wide view ahead of the user [19]. GuideCane has an ultrasonic sensor head mounted on a long handle [3] The EyeRing developed by MIT's Media Lab, is a finger-won device that translates images into aural signals. Although such kind of devices are useful to blind/visually impaired people in some environments, major drawbacks are that they only give limited information, and require well-focused user control. Recent techniques in the computer vision and robotics community offer

© Springer International Publishing Switzerland 2015
L. Agapito et al. (Eds.): ECCV 2014 Workshops, Part III, LNCS 8927, pp. 716–729, 2015.
DOI: 10.1007/978-3-319-16199-0_50

substantial advantages to overcome those limitations. This paper proposes the use of visual sensors mounted on an intelligent system like a mobile robot to assist the visually impaired/blind people in indoor environments. The proposed system aims to solve two problems: 1. Understanding the current environments. 2. Robot self-location. Regarding the problem #1, the question is "What does the world look like?". Answering this question involves building a map of the environment. In contrast to this, self-location service relates to estimating a pose to a relative position on the created map, to answer the second question "Where am I?". A visual SLAM method relying on the visual appearance of distinct scenes is responsible for finding solutions to both problems: it builds and maintains a map of the robot's trajectory and the landmark positions. Recent approaches like FAB-MAP are aimed at reaching a high recall rate at 100% precision. In this work, we employ a robust FAB-MAP [4] that is reliable to recognize known places through autonomous operation in an intelligent system like a mobile robot. FAB-Map 2.0 has been applied to a 1000 km dataset and achieved a recall of 3.1% at 100% precision (14.3% at 90% precision respectively).

Although FAB-MAP approaches are reliable for recognizing places in large-scale environments, in indoor environments, repetitive structure and sensory ambiguity constitute severe challenges for any place recognition system. Our real experiments in indoor environments show that by setting a threshold on the probability for matching an observation, it is very difficult to obtain high recall rate (~ 14% at 100% precisions). Therefore, we focus on two improvements in this paper. We first clearly describe the visual dictionary of the discriminant scenes. In indoor environments, because many scenes has repetitive structure, the visual dictionary needs to include only representative scenes. Secondly, we deploy the Kalman filter to update vehicle position. This update incorporates prior knowledge of the vehicle (e.g. velocity of the mobile robot, pacing of the people).

The proposed system is implemented in two phases. The first phase is an off-line process including two main functions: building a map and learning (indexing) places in the environment. We simultaneously collect visual data for the off-line process by a self-designed image acquisition system. For building a map of the environment, we utilize a robust visual odometry proposed in [8]. This is an interesting method because it is able to build a trajectory using only one consumer-grade camera. Furthermore, in order to improve quality of the constructed map, we adapt the algorithms in [8] with contexts of the indoor environments. In order to learn places in the environment, we utilize so-called loop closure detection methods [4], [14]. The main idea for learning the visited places is that loop constraints can be found by evaluating visual similarity between the current observation and past images captured in one (or several) trials. The second phase is an online process. The current observation is matched to a place in the database. This matching procedure is similar to place recognition. A probabilistic model of FAB-MAP algorithms [4] is utilized to find the maximal likelihood. It is observed that the proposed system is not able to update new positions against the created map. We simply past new places using a simple motion model that is based on positions of the closest neighbor places.

We evaluate results of the proposed method through travels of a mobile robot which moves along corridors of a large building. The experimental results show succeful matching of places on the map with 74% precision and 88% recall. This demonstrates the possibility of guiding blind people with the mobile robot. The remainder of the paper is organized as follows: in Section 2, we briefly survey the related works. In Section 3, we present our vision-based system for automatic map building and localization tasks. We report the experimental results in Section 4. Finally, we conclude and give some ideas for future work.

2   Related Works

Localization and navigation assistance tools for visually impaired people have received much attention in the autonomous robotics community [5]. Most of the works focus on finding efficient localization solutions based on positioning data from different sensors such as GPS, laser, Radio Frequency Identification (RFID), vision or the fusion of several of them. Loomis et al. [12] surveyed efficiency of GPS-based navigation systems supporting visually impaired people. The GPS-based systems share similar problems: low accuracy in urban-environments (localization accuracy is limited to approximately 20 m), signal loss due to multi-path effect or line-of-sight restrictions due to the presence of buildings or even foliage. Kulyukin et al. [10] proposed a system based on Radio Frequency Identification (RFID) for aiding the navigation of visually impaired people in indoor environments. The system requires the design of a dense network of location identifiers. Helal et al. [9] proposed a wireless pedestrian navigation system. They integrated several signals such as voiced, wireless networks, Geographic Information System (GIS) and GPS to provide the visually impaired people with an optimized route.

Recent advanced techniques in computer vision offer substantial improvements with respect to localization and navigation services in known or unknown environments. The vision-based approaches offer not only safe navigation, but also provide a very rich and valuable description of the environment. For example, [2] develops an application named *LocateIt*, which helps blind people locate objects in indoor environments. In [22], *ShelfScanner* is a real-time grocery detector that allows online detection of items on a shopping list.

With respect to visual mapping and localization, Alcantarilla [6] utilizes well-known techniques such as Simultaneous Localization and Mapping (SLAM) and Structure from Motion (SfM) to create a 3-D Map of an indoor environment. He then utilizes visual descriptors (such as Gauge- Speeded Up Robust Features, G-SURF) to mark local coordinates on the constructed 3-D map. Instead of building a prior 3-D map, Lui et al. [11] utilize a pre-captured reference sequence of the environment. Given a new query sequence, their system attempts to find the corresponding set of indices in the reference video...

Some wearable applications based on visual SLAM have also been proposed. Pradeep et al. [17] present a head-mounted stereo-vision platform for detecting obstacles in the path and warn subjects about their presence. They incorporate visual odometry and feature based metric-topological SLAM. Murali et al. [13] estimate the users location relative to the crosswalks in the current traffic intersection. They develop a vision-based smart-phone system for providing guidance to blind and visually impaired travelers at traffic intersections. The system of Murali et al. in [13] requires supplemental images from Google Map services, therefore its applicability is limited to outdoor travel.

It is clear from these works that a SLAM-based approach is ideally suited to the task of guiding the visually impaired, because SLAM combines the two key elements required for a user-friendly and widely applicable system: map building and self-location. However, the complexity of the map building task varies in function of environment size. In some case, a map can be acquired from the visual sensor, but in other cases, the map is such that it must be constructed from other sensor modalities such as GPS, WIFI [4]. Furthermore, matching a current view to a position on the created map seems to be the hardest problem in many works [1], [7]. Important work towards appearance-based place recognition has been conducted in [20] which borrowed ideas from text retrieval systems and introduced the concept of the so called visual vocabulary. The idea was later extended to vocabulary trees by [15], allowing to efficiently use large vocabularies. [18] demonstrated city-scale place recognition using these tree structures.

Recently, Maddern et al. report an improvement to the robustness of FAB-Map by incorporating odometric information into the place recognition process. [21] propose BRIEF-Gist, a very simplistic appearance-based place recognition system based on the BRIEF descriptor. BRIEF-Gist is much easier to implement and its performance is comparable to FAB-MAP. In our point of view, an incremental map is able to support us in improving matching results. Therefore, different from the systems mentioned above, we attempt to create a rich map as good as possible through many trials. When new observations arrive, these new observations must be locally and globally consistent with the previously constructed map. To this end we employ the the loop closure algorithms from [4], [14]. Furthermore, we pay significant attention to the creation of the visual dictionary. We deploy the GIST features [16], a holistic representation of the natural scenes. Selection of the most representative frames helps to construct a robust visual dictionary of the environment.

3   The Proposed Approaches

3.1   Imaging Acquisitions System

We design a compact imaging acquisition system to capture simultaneously scenes and routes in the indoor environments.

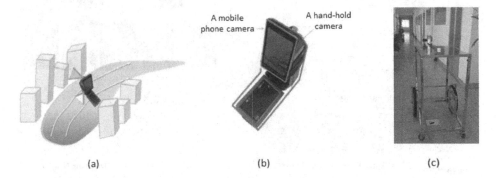

Fig. 1. (a) A schematic view of the visual data collection scheme. (b) The proposed imaging acquisition system in which a mobile phone camera is attached on rear of a hand-hold camera. (c) The image acquisition system attached on a wheel vehicle.

A schematic view of the data collection platform is shown in **Fig. 1**(a). The proposed acquisition system has two cameras. One camera captures scenes around the environment. The second one aims at capturing road on the travels. The camera setting is shown in **Fig. 1** (b). These cameras are mounted on a vehicle, as shown in **Fig. 1** (c). The details of the collected images are described in the experiments. The vehicle will be only used during the offline phase to build the map of the environment and capture scene images. Using a vehicle in the offline phase has the advantage that it avoids the vibration of the camera system. As a consequence, it allows a more accurate reconstruction of the route.

3.2   The Proposed Framework

The proposed system is shown in **Fig. 2**. Its operation consists of two phases, as described below:

- **Off-line learning**: Using the collected visual data, this phase creates trajectories and learns the places along the travels. The techniques to construct the map and learning the places are described in Sec.3.4, Sec.3.6 respectively. Because scenes and route images are captured concurrently, the constructed map contains learnt places in corresponding positions of the travel.
- **Online localization**: The current view is described using a visual dictionary. A probabilistic function attempts to match this data to the database of labeled places obtained during the offline phase. The current observation can then be matched to a corresponding position on the constructed map.

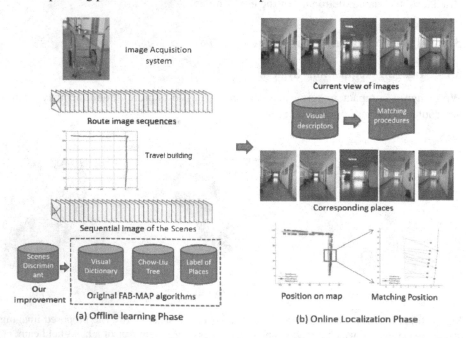

Fig. 2. The framework of the proposed system

3.3   The Map Building Based on Visual Odometry Techniques

To build route of the travel, we utilize a visual odometry method proposed by Van Hamme et al. [8]. The method is based on the tracking of ground plane features. Particularly, it is designed to take into account the uncertainty on the vehicle motion as well as uncertainty on the extracted features.

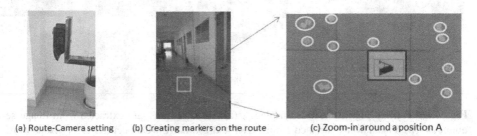

(a) Route-Camera setting   (b) Creating markers on the route   (c) Zoom-in around a position A

Fig. 3. The collection databases on Road

Our system configures the acquisition camera so that it is perpendicular to the ground plane, as shown in **Fig. 3**(a). Well-known issues for visual odometry techniques are that they need to estimate precisely correspondences between the features of consecutive frames. Once the feature correspondences have been established, we can reconstruct the trajectory of the vehicle between the two frames. Due to the floor characteristic of the corridor environment, the number of feature points detected by the original work [8] is quite limited and leads to a very poor reconstruction of the travel. To solve this issue, we manually placed additional markers over the whole journey as shown in **Fig. 3** (b-c). In future work, the odometry method should be adapted to better work in case of sparse feature distribution.

3.4   Matching Image-to-map Procedure

The places visited along the trajectory of interest will be stored in a condensed visual representation. This visual representation preferably needs to be easy to adapt to our specific indoor context and efficient at distinguishing scenes. To meet these goals, we involve the FAB-MAP technique [4] which was recently demonstrated to be successful at matching places in routes over a long period time. It is a probabilistic appearance-based approach to place recognition. Each time an image is taken, its visual descriptors are detected and extracted.

In our system, we utilize SURF extractors and descriptors for creating a visual vocabulary dictionary. A Chow Liu tree is used to approximate the probability distribution over these visual words and the correlations between them. **Fig. 4**(a)-(b) shows the extracted features and visual words to build the visual dictionary. Beyond the conventional place recognition approaches that simply compare image similarity between two visual descriptors. FAB-MAP examines co-occurrence of visual words for the same subject in the world. For example, **Fig. 4** (c) shows that for several windows, some visual words co-appearances are present.

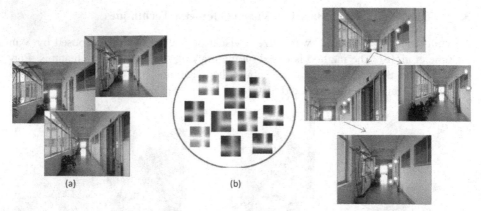

Fig. 4. FAB-MAP algorithm to learn places. (a) SURF features are extracted from image sequences. (b) Visual words defined from SURF extractors. (c). Co-occurrence of visual words corresponding to same object.

Consequently, the distinct scenes are learnt from visual training data. For updating new places, we incorporate captured images through several trials. For each new trial, we compare the images with the previously visited places which are already indexed in a place database. This procedure calls a loop closure detection, these detections are essential for building an incremental map. **Fig. 5**(a) shows only few places are marked by the first travel, whereas various places that are updated after the second travel as shown in **Fig. 5** (b).

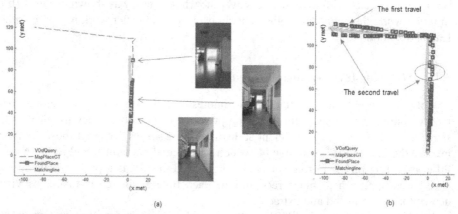

Fig. 5. (a) The places are learnt and their corresponding positions are shown in the constructed map data. (b) Many new places are updated after second trial.

3.5   Distinguishing Scenes for Improving FAB-MAP's Performances

In related works [8], [6] report that FAB-MAP obtains reasonable results for place recognition over long travels in term of both precisions and recall measurements.

However, those experiments were implemented in outdoor environments which usually contain discriminate scenes. The original FAB-MAP [2] still has unresolved problems in discriminating scenes to define visual dictionary. This issue affects the results of FAB-MAP when we deploy it in indoor environments, where scenes are continuous and not clearly distinct.

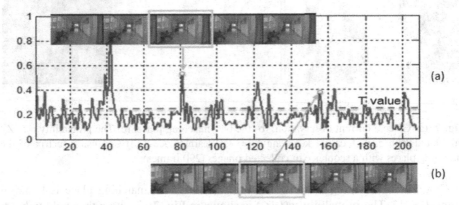

Fig. 6. (a) Dissimilarity between two consecutive frames. A threshold value T = 0.25 is preselected. (b) Two examples shows the selected key frames and their neighbor frames.

Therefore, a pre-processing step is proposed to handle these issues. Given a set of scene images S= {I₁, I₂... Iₙ} we learn key frames from S by evaluating inter-frame similarity. A feature vector F_i is extracted for each image I_j. In this work, the GIST feature [2] is utilized to build F_j. GIST presents a brief observation or a report at the first glance of a scene that summarizes the quintessential characteristics of an image. Feature vector F_i contains 512 responses which are extracted from an equivalent of model of GIST proposed in [11]. A Euclidean distance D_i between two consecutive frames is calculated to measure dissimilarity. **Fig. 6**(a) shows distance D_i of a sequence including 200 frames. The key-frame then is selected by comparing D_i with a pre-determined threshold value T. Examples of selecting two key-frames are shown in **Fig. 6**(b).

3.6   Localizing Places to Earlier Visited Ones in the Constructed Map

Given a current view, its position on the map is identified through a place recognition procedure. We evaluate the current observation at location L_i on the map by its probability when given all observations up to a location k:

$$\rho(L_i|Z^k) = \frac{\rho(z_k|L_i)\rho(L_i|Z^{k-1})}{\rho(z_k|Z^{k-1})} \qquad (1)$$

Where Z_k contains visual words appearing in all observations up to k-1; and Z^k presents visual words at current location k. These visual words are defined in the learning places phase. A probability $p(Z_k|L_i)$ infers observation likelihood as learnt in the training data. In our system, a L_i is matched at a place k∗ when $argmax(p(Z_k|L_i))$ is large enough (through a pre-determined threshold T = 0.9). The **Fig. 7** shows an example of the matching procedure.

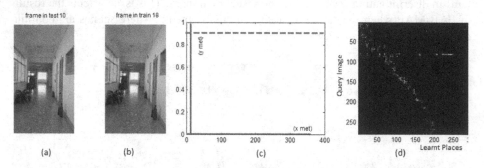

Fig. 7. (a) Given a current observation, (b) the best matching place. (c) The probability $p(L_i|Z^k)$ calculated with each location k among K = 350 learnt places. (d) Confusion matrix of the matching places with a sequence of collected images (290 frames).

Given an observation as shown in **Fig. 7**(a), the best matching place is found at *placeID* = 12. The probability $p(L_i|Z^k)$ is shown in **Fig. 7**(c) with a threshold *value* = *0.9* whose the maximal probability is *placeID = 12*. A confusion matrix of the matching places for an image sequence is shown in **Fig. 7**(d). This example shows that we can resolve most places in a testing phase.

3.7   The Kalman Filter (KF)

In our context, the observations of the robot are images captured over time, which are then converted to coordinates (x, y, z) in a predefined coordinate system using above matching procedure. However, in indoor environment, the scene does not always change significantly. Consecutive scenes could repeat when the robot moves. Therefore, the performance of image matching is not good. Sometimes, a current observation could be matched with a very far forward / backward image that makes incorrect localization of the robot. To overcome this problem, we propose to use a Kalman filter to correct the position of the robot from observation. A Kalman filter is one of the most popular techniques to improve SLAM results. In our context, we suppose that the robot moves in a flat plane, so the z coordinate of the robot is constant then we can ignore it. The *state vector* of the robot at a given time k is simply presented by its coordinates and velocity in two directions x and y. *Observation vector* is defined at each time where the image matching is found, the position of the robot could be estimated. We use this information as observation in Kalman filter. *State transition model* F_k allows to predict the state vector at time $k+1$:

$$x_{k+1} = F_k * x_k + w_k \qquad (2)$$

Where w_k is process noise, which is assumed to follow a normal distribution with covariance Q_k: $w_k \sim N (0, Q_k)$. *Observation model* H_k maps the true state space into the observed space:

$$z_k = H_k * x_k + v_k \tag{3}$$

In our case: $H = \begin{bmatrix} 1 & 0 \\ 0 & 1 \end{bmatrix}$ Where v_k is observation noise which is assumed to be zero mean Gaussian white noise with covariance R_k: $v_k \sim N(0, R_k)$

4   Experimental Results

4.1   Evaluation Environments

- *Experimental environments*: We examine the proposed method in a corridor environment of a building. The evaluation environment is shown in **Fig. 8**(c). The total length of the corridor is about 60 m.
- *Database:* Two camera devices are mounted onto a vehicle as shown in **Fig. 1**(c). The vehicle moves at a speed of 1.25 feet/second along the corridor. The total length of the corridor is about 60 m. We collect data in four times (trials), as described in **Table 1**

Table 1. Three rounds data results

Trials	Total Scene images	Total road images	Duration
L1	8930	2978	5:14
L2	10376	2978	5:30
L3	6349	2176	3:25
L4	10734	2430	4:29

4.2   Experimental Results

For map building, we use image acquisitions from L2, L3, and L4 trials. Results of the constructed map using original work of Van Hamme et al. [8] is shown in **Fig. 8**(a), whereas the reconstructed travels using proposed method are shown in **Fig. 8** (b).

As shown, the results of map building from three travels are quite stable. All of them are matched to ground truth that are plotted in green dash-line in a model 3-D of the evaluation environments, as shown in **Fig. 8** (c). Our results are a substantial improvement on the ones using original method [8] without additional markers. We believe that creating highly textures on ground plane is more efficient for detecting and matching the features. The original algorithm in [8] is designed to be robust against high uncertainty of the detected features, but requires many features to create a high quality map.

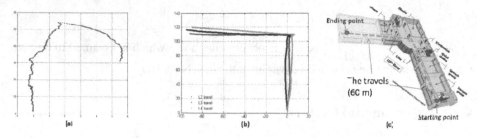

Fig. 8. (a) The travel reconstructed using original works [8]. (b) Results of three time travels (L2, L3, and L4) using proposed method. (c) A 3-D map of the evaluation environment. The actual travels also plotted in green dashed line for comparing results between (a) and (b).

We continue evaluating the proposed system with aspects of the place recognition rate on the created map. To define the visual word dictionary as described in Sec.3.4, we use collected images from L1 trial. About 1300 words are defined in our evaluation environment. We then use dataset from L4 travel to learn places along the travel. In total, K = 140 places are learnt. The visual dictionary and descriptors of these places are stored in XML files. The collected images in L2 and L3 travels are utilized for the evaluations.

Visually, some matching places results from L3 travel are shown in **Fig. 9**. Two demonstrations are shown in details in **Fig. 9** (around position A and position B). Case a shows a query image (from L3 travel) is matched to a learnt place. Therefore, its corresponding positions on the map is able to localize. A zoom-in version around position A is shown in the top panel. Case b show a *"no place found"* that query image was not found from learnt place database. For the qualitative measurement, we then evaluate the proposed system using two criteria: Precision is to measures total place detected from total query images, whereas Recall is to measure correct matching places from detected places. We setup a predetermined threshold for matching place (T = 0.9).

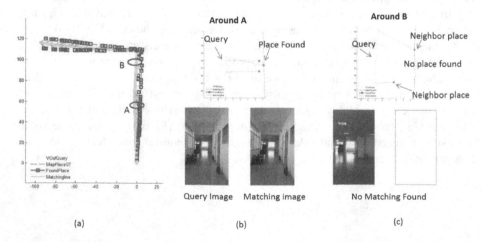

Fig. 9. (a) Results of the matching image-to-map with L3 trial. Two positions around A and B are given. (b)-(c): current view is on the left panel (query image); matching is on the right panel. Upper panel is a zoom-in around corresponding positions.

Table 2. Result of the matching places (FAB-MAP algorithms) without and with Scene discriminations

Travels	Without scene discrimination		With scene discrimination	
	Precision	Recall	Precision	Recall
L2	12%	90%	67%	82%
L3	36%	85%	**74%**	**88 %**

The **Table 2** shows precision and recall with L2 and L3 travels with/without scene discrimination step. For learning places (using original FAB-MAP, without scene discrimination), the recall of L3 travel is clearly higher than L2. The main reason is that some "new" places which were not learnt from L4 are able to update after L2 running. Therefore, more "found" places are ensured with L3 travel. **Table 2** also shows the efficiency of the scene discriminations step, the performances of image-to-map matching obviously increasing and stable for precisions measurement with scene discrimination step, whereas high confidence of the recalls is still consistent.

To show effectiveness of applying the Kalman filter, **Fig. 10** demonstrates navigation data without and with using Kalman filter. Using only the place recognition results (**Fig. 7**- left panel), the directions supporting navigation services are obviously uncontrolled. Some matching places (show in numbers) are misses and in the wrong order in this case. The main reason is the erroneous matching of some places (e.g., place ID = 11, shown in bottom panel). By using a Kalman Filter, directions supporting navigation services are correctly ordered. We can clearly observe the effectiveness on **Fig. 7**- right panel.

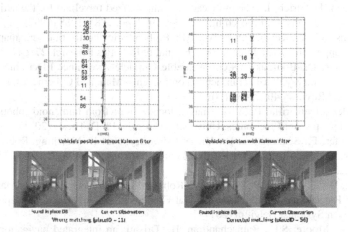

Fig. 10. Vehicle moving without/with Kalman Filter. Top row: Left panel: vehicle positios on the map using only results of the matching image-to-map procedures. The arrows show directions to guide vehicle. Numbers on left of each red box show *placeID* of the current observation. Right panel: positions of the vehicle are updated using Kalman filter. Bottom row: Left panel: This result shows wrong direction to vehicle. Right panel: is a good matching with Kalman filter.

5   Conclusions

In this paper, we presented a visual SLAM system with mobile robot supporting localization services to visually impaired people. We successfully created a map of the indoor environment using the visual odometry and learning places. The results of matching image-to-map are of high confidence for navigation service thanks to the application of a Kalman filter. The proposed system therefore is therefore feasible for deploying navigation services in indoor environments. The proposed system provides direction support for blind/visually impaired people. Further in-the-loop evaluations with the visually impaired/blind people will direct us to future work.

Acknowledgment. This work is supported by the project *"Visually impaired people assistance using multimodal technologies"* funded by the Vlaamse Interuniversitaire Raad (VLIR) in the framework of the VLIR's Own Initiatives' Program 2012 under the grant number ZEIN2012RIP19

References

1. Bailey, T., Durrant-Whyte, H.: Simultaneous Localisation and Mapping (SLAM): Part II State of the Art. IEEE Robotics & Automation Magazine **13**(2), 99–110 (2006)
2. Bigham, J.P., Jayant, C., Miller, A., White, B., Yeh, T.: VizWiz::LocateIt - enabling blind people to locate objects in their environment. In: CVPR Workshops 2010, pp. 65–72 (2010)
3. Borenstein, J., Ulrich, I.: The guidecane-a computerized travel aid for the active guidance of blind pedestrians. In: Proceeding of ICRA 1997, pp. 1283–1288 (1997)
4. Cummins, M., Newman, P.: FAB-MAP: Probabilistic localization and mapping in the space of appearance. The International Journal of Robotics Research **27**, 647–665 (2008)
5. Dakopoulos, D., Bourbakis, N.G.: Wearable Obstacle Avoidance Electronic Travel Aids for Blind: A Survey. IEEE Transactions on Systems, Man, and Cybernetics, Part C: Applications and Reviews **40**, 25–35 (2010)
6. Fernández Alcantarilla, P.: Vision based localization: from humanoid robots to visually impaired people. In: Electronics, University of Alcala, Ph.D. Thesis (2011)
7. Fraundorfer, F., Scaramuzza, D.: Visual Odometry: Part II: Matching, Robustness, Optimization, and Applications. IEEE Transaction on Robotics & Automation Magazine **19**, 78–90 (2012)
8. Hamme, D.V., Veelaert, P., Philips, W.: Robust visual odometry using uncertainty models. In: The Proceedings of 13th International Conference on Advanced Concepts for Intelligent Vision Systems, Belgium (2011)
9. Helal, A., Moore, S.E., Ramachandran, B.: Drishti: an integrated navigation system for visually impaired and disabled. In: Proceedings of the Fifth International Symposium on Wearable Computers 2001, pp.149–156 (2001)
10. Kulyukin, V., Gharpure, C., Nicholson, J., Pavithran, S.: RFID in robot-assisted indoor navigation for the visually impaired. In: The Proceeding of 2004 IEEE/RSJ IROS 2004, pp. 1979–1984 (2004)
11. Liu, J.J., Phillips, C., Daniilidis, K.: Video-based localization without 3D mapping for the visually impaired. In: The proceeding of CVPR Workshops 2010, pp. 23–30 (2010)

12. Loomis, J.M., Golledge, R.D., Klatzky, R.L.: GPS-based navigation systems for the visually impaired. In: Fundamental of Wearable Computers and Augmented Reality (2001)
13. Murali, V.N., Coughlan, J.M.: Smartphone-based crosswalk detection and localization for visually impaired pedestrians. In: Proceeding of IEEE International Conference on Multimedia and Expo Workshops (ICMEW), pp. 1–7 (2013)
14. Newman, P., Kin H.: SLAM-Loop Closing with Visually Salient Features. In: The Proceedings of the 2005 IEEE International Conference on Robotics and Automation, pp. 635–642 (2005)
15. Nister, D., Stewenius, H.: Scalable recognition with a vocabulary tree. In: The Proceeding of Computer Vision and Pattern Recognition 2006, pp. 2161–2168 (2006)
16. Oliva, A., Torralba, A.: Modeling the shape of the scene: A holistic representation of the spatial envelope. International Journal of Computer Vision **42**, 145–175 (2001)
17. Pradeep, V., Medioni, G., Weiland, J.: Robot vision for the visually impaired. In: The Proceeding of IEEE Computer Society Conference on Computer Vision and Pattern Recognition Workshops (CVPRW), pp.15–22 (2010)
18. Schindler, G., Brown, M., Szeliski, R.: City-scale location recognition. In: The Proceeding of the Computer Vision and Pattern Recognition, pp. 1–7 (2007)
19. Shoval, S., Borenstein, J., Koren, Y.: Auditory guidance with the Navbelt-a computerized travel aid for the blind. Trans. Sys. Man Cyber Part C **28**, 459–467 (1998)
20. Sivic, J., Zisserman, A.: Video Google: A text retrieval approach to object matching in videos. In: Proceedings of the 9th IEEE CVPR 2003, pp. 1470–1477 (2003)
21. Sunderhauf, N., Protzel, P.: Brief gist closing the loop by simple means. In: 2011 IEEE/RSJ International Conference on Intelligent Robots and Systems (IROS) pp. 1234–1241 (2011)
22. Winlock, T., Christiansen, E., Belongie, S.: Toward real-time grocery detection for the visually impaired. In: The Proceeding of CVPRW 2010, pp. 49–56 (2010)

Scene-Dependent Intention Recognition for Task Communication with Reduced Human-Robot Interaction

Kester Duncan[1][✉], Sudeep Sarkar[1], Redwan Alqasemi[2], and Rajiv Dubey[2]

[1] Computer Science and Engineering Department,
University of South Florida, Tampa, FL, USA
{kkduncan,sarkar}@cse.usf.edu
[2] Mechanical Engineering Department, University of South Florida, Tampa, FL, USA
{alqasemi,dubey}@usf.edu

Abstract. In order for assistive robots to collaborate effectively with humans, they must be endowed with the ability to perceive scenes and more importantly, recognize human intentions. These intentions are often inferred from observed physical actions and direct communication from fully-functional individuals. For individuals with reduced capabilities, it may be difficult or impossible to perform physical actions or easily communicate. Therefore, their intentions must be inferred differently. To this end, we propose an intention recognition framework that is appropriate for persons with limited physical capabilities. This framework determines and learns human intentions based on scene objects, the actions that can be performed on them, and past interaction history. It is based on a Markov model formulation entitled Object-Action Intention Networks, which constitute the crux of a computer vision-based human-robot collaborative system that reduces the necessary interactions for communicating tasks to a robot. Evaluations were conducted on multiple scenes comprised of multiple possible object categories and actions. We achieve approximately 81% reduction in interactions overall after learning, when compared to other intention recognition approaches.

Keywords: Intention recognition · Human robot interaction · Intelligent robots · Robot vision systems

1   Introduction

Assistive robotic technologies can provide the elderly, persons with disabilities, and injured veterans with opportunities to achieve higher levels of independence and quality of life as they reduce dependence on caregivers and increase self-sufficiency. However, there are many challenges to developing such robotic technologies. Seeing a bottle, reaching for it, and picking it up to pour its contents are relatively easy tasks for a fully-functional human; however, this task is difficult for both individuals with reduced capabilities and robots. For a robot to

L. Agapito et al. (Eds.): ECCV 2014 Workshops, Part III, LNCS 8927, pp. 730–745, 2015.
DOI: 10.1007/978-3-319-16199-0_51

complete such tasks, it must possess the perceptive ability to effectively process the individual's environment, namely the scene. This involves addressing key computer vision problems such as object segmentation, object categorization, and object pose estimation, along with manifold mechanical tasks. These issues have been considerably addressed in the computer vision and robotics literatures [13], [15], [4], [3], [16], [7] and in this work we leverage on recent advances to present a computer vision-based human robot collaborative system.

Another challenge exists when there is a lack of full communication. It is relatively easy for a fully-functional individual to directly express their intent, yet for persons with reduced capabilities, this may prove to be quite difficult or impossible depending on their communication ability. As a result, the problem of recognizing one's intention is brought to the forefront [19] as it is requisite for successful communication and collaboration [20]. These intentions are inferred from actions carried out or from changes in the environment [8], [19], [2]. In order to build robots that are competent assistants, we must endow them with this intelligent ability in order to understand the action that is to be performed on the environment, e.g. pick up the red cup vs. throw away the brown box. In so doing, we can reduce the need for direct human-robot interaction and thereby maximize robotic task performance.

As an example, consider a robot that helps a person incapable of communicating physically, choose a task to perform at a breakfast table. The robot is capable of scanning the table, and for every item that is found, a group of possible tasks that can be performed with it is recorded in a list. Subsequently, the robot asks the individual to indicate the task they want to perform. Suppose there are n possible tasks on the list. For the extreme case where the user desires the nth task, the robot would have had to prompt the user n times in order to know what to do. With intention recognition, it is possible to reduce the length of this list by only considering items the individual would most likely want performed and thereby reduce the amount of time necessary for communicating their intent.

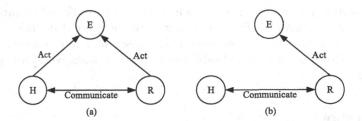

Fig. 1. Configuration of human-robot interactive systems using intention recognition. Circles with 'H' represent humans, 'R' represents robots, and 'E' represents the environment. For approaches grouped under (a), the human and robot both perform tasks on the environment whereas for (b), the environment is acted on only by the robot.

In the literature, intention recognition approaches can be classified according to two main configurations hinged on human-robot interactions as depicted in Figure 1:

1. *Intention recognition via observation of the user's physical actions and the environment* (Fig. 1a): the human and the robot may both perform tasks on the environment and there is some form of interaction between them.
2. *Intention recognition via observation of the user's environment* (Fig. 1b): the human interacts with the robot that in turn interacts with the environment.

For the first configuration (Fig. 1 (a)), the human can act directly on the environment. Therefore, both the human and the environment can be observed to infer intentions. Sensors are used to observe the user's physical actions and determine their intentions [10], [9], [22]. For example, Kelley et al. [10] presented an approach that observed an individual using an RGB-D camera and with a neural network-based method, they were able to predict their actions by analyzing their hand positions in relation to objects in the scene. Consequently, the main underlying goal of this category of approaches is to develop effective socially-interactive robotic systems and the target population is usually able-bodied individuals.

Conversely, for the second configuration, as depicted in Fig. 1 (b), the human cannot act directly on the environment; they act on it via the robot. Sensors are used to observe the environment and the robot interacts with the human for determining their intentions [6], [21], [1]. For example, Demeester et al. [6] presented a system that estimated the intent of a user using the sensor readings of their environment and the user's commands so as to take corrective action during wheelchair maneuvering. The system in turn provided assistance that was tailored to the user's driving ability.

Our survey of the state of the art finds that the second category is not fully explored. It is according to this configuration that our proposed work belongs because it is more appropriate for dealing with persons with disabilities wherein it may be quite difficult for them to perform activities on the environment. The main goal of this category of approaches is to develop robotic systems that function effectively in human environments in order to work collaboratively for achieving common goals. In light of this, we present a novel intention recognition framework used within a computer vision-based human-robot collaborative system that allows persons with disabilities to perform tasks with reduced robot interaction.

2   Overview

An activity is primarily a sequence of steps involving objects and actions carried out to accomplish a specific task. As depicted in the example of Figure 2, the activity 'Drink a soda' consists of steps whereby a soda can (*object*) is picked up (*action*) by a robotic arm and poured (*action*) into a cup (*object*) followed by moving the cup to facilitate drinking. In this work, we focus on recognizing these individual steps from captured visual data with minimum human interaction.

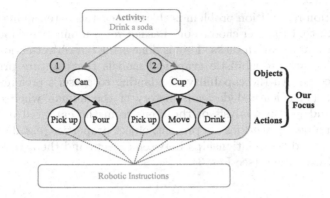

Fig. 2. Scope of our work: we determine the object-action pair that represents a user's intention at a particular step of an activity and attempt to reduce the amount of human-robot interaction necessary to accomplish this step

A schematic for our complete human-robot collaborative system is depicted in Figure 3. The system is partitioned into vision processing and intention recognition components. For vision processing, the robotic component first performs object segmentation on the captured RGB-D data to extract objects, which are represented as point cloud clusters. The position and orientation of these objects as well as their category identities are then ascertained via pose estimation and object categorization respectively. This information is required as input to our intention recognition component.

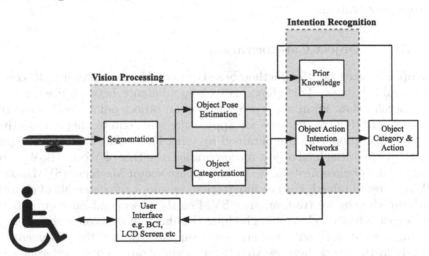

Fig. 3. Schematic of our complete human-robot collaborative system. Object category and pose information along with a user's past decision history are incorporated in our approach for intention recognition.

Our intention recognition problem is therefore cast as determining the object and action pair that the user chooses but has not yet communicated for execution by a robot for manipulation tasks. This is done using our object-action intention networks which are probabilistic graphical models that capture prior object-action knowledge with the capability of adapting to a user's preferences. They are based on: (1) a learned decision history of the human when queried by our system, and (2) an analysis of the scene from the captured RGB-D data such as which object categories are present, object properties (e.g. distance from camera, color), and the relationships between objects and the actions that can be performed with them (see Fig. 3).

3   Vision Processing

Our intention recognition framework is fully dependent on the scene content for determining the user's goal, therefore the scene must be processed accordingly. This is accomplished via object segmentation, object categorization, and object pose estimation.

3.1   Segmentation

Given an RGB-D point cloud of a scene, we first perform planar segmentation using a RANSAC-based approach, then we extract candidate object point clusters from the plane found with the largest candidate object footprint as outlined by Rusu et al. in [18]. These resultant clusters are further processed as described in subsequent sections.

3.2   RGBD Object Categorization

We employ a categorization method based on multiple cues: intensity, 2D contour shape, and 3D shape. This allows us to keep a balance between discrimination and generalization. From a 2D projection of an object point cloud, we extract SIFT [12] and HOG [5] features for appearance and contour shape respectively. The 3D shape properties are obtained by using Fast Point Feature Histograms (FPFH) [17]. For the final object representation, the Bag-of-Words (BoW) model is employed. For classification, we train Support Vector Machines (SVMs) on the BoW features obtained. For cue integration, we adopt the ensemble of classifiers paradigm whereby we train another SVM on the class confidence outputs provided by each feature classifier. The final classification decision is then made by choosing the category with the strongest support. We use the aforementioned methods in this work because they have demonstrated good performance for categorization tasks [14].

3.3   3D Object Pose Estimation Using Superquadrics

We estimate the pose (location and orientation) of object point clusters using the low latency method described by Duncan et al. in [7]. By employing superquadrics, which are compact parametric shapes with tri-axis symmetry, this method is able to determine object positions without a model base. It also recovers these superquadrics in a rapid manner by using an effective multi-scale voxelization scheme.

4   Intention Recognition Framework

An overview of our intention recognition framework is shown in Figure 4. From vision processing, object information is used as input for construction of our object-action intention network. Based on the network, a set of queries is generated and proposed to the user. The form of this proposal can vary depending on the type of human-robot interface used e.g. object bounding box for touch screen, verbal questions for speech recognition. For generalization, a query is simply a yes-or-no question. In an ideal situation, the first query proposed to the user coincides with the user's intention. If this does not occur, the query set is modified and another query is presented until the user's intention is communicated as depicted by the query loop in Figure 4. The user's selections are learned via the learning loop in order to adapt to the user's preferences. Notably, the ability of our system to simultaneously infer a user's intention and learn their preferences over time differentiates it from the state of the art. With learning, we are able to improve the intention predictions which in effect reduces the need for many rounds of user interaction. The individual components of this framework are unveiled in the following sections.

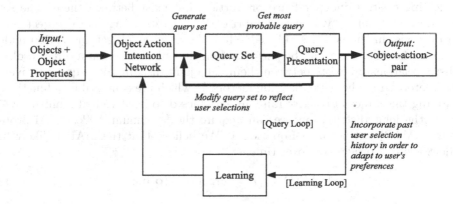

Fig. 4. An overview of our intention recognition approach which uses an object-action intention network, a set of queries for interacting with the user, and a learning process to improve predictions

4.1 Object-Action Intention Networks

We formulate our intention recognition problem by using probability theory as follows. For each 3D scene that is captured and processed, there are n objects[1]. These objects are represented by the binary random variables $\mathbf{O} = \{O_1, \ldots, O_n\}$ where their values o_i indicate whether the user wants to manipulate the object or not. Associated with each object are binary action variables $\mathbf{A} = \{A_1, \ldots, A_m\}$ whose values a_j indicate whether the user wants to perform the action on the object or not. In addition to these object and action variables are object feature variables $\mathbf{F} = \{F_1, \ldots, F_{cn}\}$, which are also binary random variables representing some intrinsic property of the object e.g distance from camera, color etc. There can be c feature variables per object and they can potentially bias an object for selection by the user, e.g. user's preference for red objects.

Under this formulation, our task is to infer the most probable object that the user wants to manipulate as well as the most probable action that the user intends to perform on the object. Thus, our goal is to find the highest-probability joint assignment of object and action variables of the form $P(o_i = yes, a_j = yes)$, which represents the intent of the user. With a joint distribution of these variables, we can answer questions about the observed scene ranging from the standard conditional probability query $P(\mathbf{O} = \mathbf{o}, \mathbf{A} = \mathbf{a} \,|\, \mathbf{F} = \mathbf{f})$, to finding the most probable assignment to some subset of variables[2]. We are particularly interested in determining the maximum a posteriori (MAP) probability, whereby the task is to infer the most likely assignment to the variables in $\mathbf{O}$ and $\mathbf{A}$ given the evidence $\mathbf{F} = \mathbf{f}$: $\arg\max_{\mathbf{o},\mathbf{a}} P(\mathbf{o}, \mathbf{a} \,|\, \mathbf{f})$.

We employ Markov Networks [11] as the foundation of our Object-Action Intention Networks so that we can model and encode the relationships between the object and action variables as directional influence between them cannot be naturally ascribed. These networks are undirected graphical models that efficiently capture the joint distribution P over the set of random variables by exploiting existing independence properties that exist between them. The set of object and action variables comprise the corresponding set of object and action nodes in the network. The edge links between an object and action node signifies that the action can be performed on the object and that a direct probabilistic relationship exists between them. The joint distribution is quantitatively parameterized in the network using factors Φ, which are compatibility functions mapping the values of a set of random variables $\mathbf{d}$ to positive real numbers $\mathbb{R}^+$. Using the joint distribution, we can acquire the Maximum A Posteriori probability (MAP) as shown in Equation 1. We believe that the MAP is likely to reflect a user's preferences over time.

$$MAP(\mathbf{O}, \mathbf{A} \,|\, \mathbf{f}) = \arg\max_{\mathbf{o},\mathbf{a}} P(\mathbf{o}, \mathbf{a}, \mathbf{f}) \tag{1}$$

---

[1] In this work, we use the term objects to refer to instances of generic object categories.

[2] We use capital letters, e.g. $\mathbf{X}$, to denote random variables and small letters e.g. $\mathbf{x}$ to denote values taken by $\mathbf{X}$.

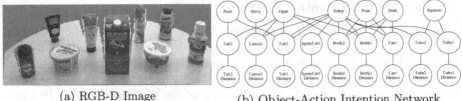

(a) RGB-D Image   (b) Object-Action Intention Network

Fig. 5. Automatically configured Object-Action Intention Network in (b) for a real 3D scene as captured by an RGB-D camera shown in (a). The object category instances present in the scene and their distances from the camera are used to automatically generate the network along with the associated actions that can be performed on them.

In this work, we only utilize an object's distance from the camera as a contributing object feature (i.e. $c = 1$) for reasoning and these variables indicate whether an object is near or far from the camera based on a dynamically-determined distance threshold. The dependencies of these object, action, and feature variables are captured by the network with the overall joint probability distribution $P(o_1, \ldots, o_n, a_1, \ldots, a_m, f_1, \ldots, f_{cn})$. Objects in the scene are resolved via object categorization and the object distances from the camera are calculated via object pose estimation as described earlier. An example of an object-action intention network is shown in Figure 5 (b) for the scene shown in Figure 5 (a). The representational complexity of these networks is $\mathcal{O}(nm)$, where n is the number of objects and m is the number of possible actions. The computational complexity is proportional to maximum size of the cliques in these networks.

Query Selection. The user is prompted with a series of *queries* based on the marginal probabilities of variables and factors in the network. A query in its most generic form is a yes-or-no question involving an object variable, an action variable, or a combination of both[3]. For every network that is constructed, there is a set of s generated queries $\mathbf{Q} = \{Q_1, \ldots, Q_s\}$ sorted according to their probabilities. The goal is to get the first query Q_1 of $\mathbf{Q}$ to match the intent of the human. For this to be achieved, the user's selections must be learned and this is described in a subsequent section. Moreover, an individual query Q_t may represent an attempt to determine if the user wants to manipulate an object $Q_t = \{O_i\}$, perform an action $Q_t = \{A_j\}$, or perform an action on a specific object $Q_t = \{O_i, A_j\}$. The user's response leads to a modification of the set $\mathbf{Q}$, eventually resulting in one that only contains the query corresponding to the user's intention. Feedback from the user is treated as observations or evidence in the network and the network is updated accordingly (see Figure 4).

---

[3] A query can be mapped to different types of human-robot interfaces that vary in terms of communication bandwidth e.g. touch screen (more queries) vs. brain computer interface (BCI) (less queries).

4.2   Incremental Intention Learning

To implement the modification of the probability distribution over all object-action pairs in response to user's preference, we cast our learning framework as a form of Recursive Bayesian Incremental Learning described as follows - Let $\boldsymbol{\theta}$ represent the collection of multinomial parameter vectors for the network factors defined over all object and action variables, hence $\theta_i = \phi_i$, where ϕ_i is the ith factor in a network. Furthermore, let $\mathcal{D}^k = \{\mathbf{x}_1, \mathbf{x}_2, \ldots, \mathbf{x}_k\}$ explicitly represent k observed user choices where $\mathbf{x}_i = \{No, No, \ldots, o_i = Yes, \ldots, No, a_j = Yes, \ldots, No\}$ indicating a user's selection of the ith object and the jth action as captured via our object action intention network (the No's coincide with the objects and actions that were not selected). Our aim is to determine the most likely object-action pair based on information we have already acquired. Therefore, by using Bayes formula, the posterior probability for the distribution over all object and action variables satisfies the recursive relation given in Equation 2.

$$P(\boldsymbol{\theta} \mid \mathcal{D}^k) \propto P(\mathbf{x}^k \mid \boldsymbol{\theta}) P(\boldsymbol{\theta} \mid \mathcal{D}^{k-1}) \tag{2}$$

Equation 2 allows us to incrementally learn a user's preferences as they repeatedly interact with our system and data are collected. Given that $P(\boldsymbol{\theta} \mid \mathcal{D}^0) = P(\boldsymbol{\theta})$, we can use this equation repeatedly to produce the sequence of probabilities $P(\boldsymbol{\theta})$, $P(\boldsymbol{\theta} \mid \mathbf{x}_1)$, $P(\boldsymbol{\theta} \mid \mathbf{x}_1, \mathbf{x}_2)$, and so on. The term $P(\mathbf{x}^k \mid \boldsymbol{\theta})$ in Eq. 2 is known as the likelihood function and it represents the probability of the observed data given the parameters values $\boldsymbol{\theta}$. Its value is given in Equation 3 whereby the probability of each datum $\mathbf{x}_i$ given the parameters $\boldsymbol{\theta}$ is proportional to the product of the factors ϕ_i defined over the subset of random variable values $\mathbf{d}_i$.

$$P(\mathbf{x}^k \mid \boldsymbol{\theta}) \propto \prod_{i=1}^{k} \phi_i(\mathbf{d}_i \mid \boldsymbol{\theta}) \tag{3}$$

$$\propto \prod_{i=1}^{k} \prod_{j=1}^{s} \theta_{ij}^{N_{ij}} \tag{4}$$

Each object-action factor ϕ_i has s values (in our case $s = 4$), therefore θ_{ij} represents the jth value of the ith factor as shown in Eq 4. N_{ij} represents the selection of the respective factor value which can be 1 or 0 in our case.

The term $P(\boldsymbol{\theta} \mid \mathcal{D}^{k-1})$ in Equation 2 represents the prior probability distribution based on the set of previously observed data samples. The prior is updated as data are collected, thereby producing the posterior distribution which then serves as the prior for the subsequent observation. We assume that the distributions under consideration are of the Dirichlet form [11]. This translates into each factor ϕ_i defined over a subset of variable values $\mathbf{d}_i$ being Dirichlet. As a result, the posterior distribution is also Dirichlet, which allows us to update them using sufficient statistics from the data. What follows is that the maximum *a posteriori* estimate for $\boldsymbol{\theta}$ is given according to sufficient statistics as shown in Eq. 5.

$$\hat{\theta}_{ij} = \frac{N_{ij} + \alpha_{ij} - 1}{\sum_{j=1}^{s} N_{ij} + \sum_{j=1}^{s}(\alpha_{ij} - 1)} \tag{5}$$

With equivalent α_{ij}'s, we are left with the form shown in Eq. 6 which is our learning equation.

$$\hat{\theta}_{ij} = \frac{\lambda N_{ij} + 1}{\sum_{j=1}^{s} \lambda N_{ij} + s} \tag{6}$$

The Dirichlet hyperparameter α_{ij} stores the prior count observed for the value j of factor ϕ_i whereas N_{ij} represents its current count and $\lambda = \frac{1}{\alpha - 1}$. Thus, the parameters θ are updated as more information becomes available. As a result, when the user selects an object to manipulate and an action to perform on that object, the value of the corresponding parameter value θ_{ij} is updated.

5   Experimental Validation

The experiments detailed in this section were performed on RGB-D scenes of common household objects captured by an RGB-D sensor where all of the objects are located on table-tops (see Figure 6). We outline the evaluation set up, outline the baseline approaches used for comparison, then we present our results.

5.1   Evaluation Set Up

To determine the user's desired intention, human-robot interaction must take place and we refer to these rounds of interactions as *sessions*. Thus, at the end of each session, the object the human wants to manipulate and the action they want to perform on that object is determined. The main performance metric we use for our evaluations is the number of human-robot interactions per session for arriving at the correct intention. The ideal scenario occurs when this value is 1, which indicates that the first query proposed to the user is their actual intent. Experiments were conducted to ascertain this value over multiple sessions using multiple instances of objects from 11 categories with at least 4 possible

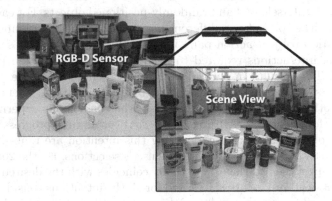

Fig. 6. Experimental set up: RGB-D scenes of common household objects are captured and processed. Objects are extracted, categorized, and their poses estimated and this is used to determine the most likely object and action that an individual desires.

Table 1. Examples of scenes used for evaluation. The scenes differ by a combination of different objects and varying object positions

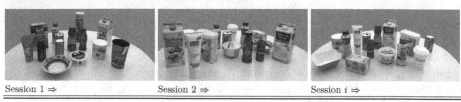

Session 1 ⇒   Session 2 ⇒   Session i ⇒

actions per object. We evaluate the performance of our framework under significant scene changes between sessions and its response after being trained with a predetermined group of intentions.

Baseline Intention Recognition Approaches. To the best of our knowledge, no algorithm exists in the state of the art with which a direct comparison can be performed. Therefore we constructed 3 approaches for this purpose:

- *Random*: randomly selects an object-action pair from the set of all possible configurations of objects and actions.
- *Scene-Random*: randomly selects an object-action pair from the set of possible configurations of objects and actions afforded by the scene.
- *Scene-Probability*: selects the highest probable object-action pair based on the total number of object-action pairs possible in the scene.

5.2   Performance Under Significant Scene changes

In this section, we demonstrate how our framework performs under considerable scene changes. As an example, consider the differences between scenes capturing a bathroom counter-top versus a kitchen counter-top. Our test scenarios involve at most 10 randomly-selected and randomly-positioned objects. For each session, each object is either placed in a different position or replaced with another. One possible intention (object-action pair) is chosen for 20 consecutive sessions and the number of interactions required to communicate this intention per session is calculated. This results in a total of 340 test scenes (see Table 1 for some examples) Consider Figure 7 which lists the top 5 queries of query sets generated for the 1st, 10th, and 20th sessions for one of the runs of this experiment. The goal intention for this run was `Drink-from-Bottle`. As time progressed, queries involving the object and action comprising this intention are ranked higher as the system learns and accomodates for the user's selections. By the 20th session, the first query proposed to the user actually coincides with the desired intention. The aforementioned procedure is followed for all the intentions considered in this work and the average number of interactions required per session is determined.

Session 1
Q1. Do you want to grasp something?
Q2. Do you want to move something?
Q3. Do you want to use **bottle**1?
Q4. Do you want to grasp **bottle**1?
Q5. Do you want to move **bottle**1?

Session 10
Q1. Do you want to use **bottle**1?
Q2. Do you want to **drink** from something?
Q3. Do you want to **drink** from **bottle**1?
Q4. Do you want to grasp **bottle**1?
Q5. Do you want to grasp **bottle**1?

Session 20
Q1. Do you want to **drink** from **bottle**1?
Q2. Do you want to **drink** from something?
Q3. Do you want to use the **bottle**1?
Q4. Do you want to grasp **bottle**1?
Q5. Do you want to grasp something?

(b) Session 1 scene after vision processing

(a) Top 5 queries for the 1st, 10th, and 20th sessions.

Fig. 7. Example run for the desired intention `Drink-from-Bottle`. Notice how queries involving both `drink` and `bottle` are ranked higher than others over time.

Figure 8 displays the result of the complete experiment and compares our results with those acquired for the baseline approaches[4]. The figure shows that despite considerable modifications to the scene, our framework manages to reduce the number of human-robot interactions over time and consistently outperforms the other methods. By the 20th session, it takes approximately 1 interaction to determine what the user desires and the number of interactions were reduced by an average of 81%. We have discovered that as a result of our intention recognition formulation, placing objects closer to the camera increased their likelihood for selection and vice versa. Therefore, by moving desired objects away from the camera, the average number of interactions increased. This phenomenom is usually observed in the first couple of sessions (see how the Scene-Probability method outperforms our method for the 1st session in Figure 8). However, this effect is significantly reduced after multiple sessions and is of negligible impact as a result of learning.

---

[4] It should be noted that for all of the experiments in this work, the object-action pairs of the constructed networks are initialized with equivalent probabilities which are then altered over time due to incremental learning. Also, multiple instances of an object category can be present in the scene at the same time.

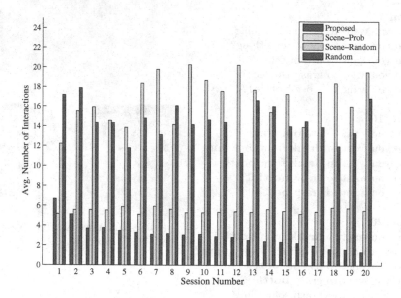

Fig. 8. Intention recognition results for significant scene changes. Each session corresponds to a different scene where the object composition of the scene varies. Notice how over time our method consistently reduces the amount of human-robot interactions required for communicating tasks to the robot.

5.3   Performance After Intention Group Training

Consider the following scenario: a person wakes up, brushes their teeth, drinks a cup of coffee, and eats a bowl of cereal before they head off to work. They repeat this sequence of events every morning. For humans, it takes relatively no effort to determine this person's morning routine after some time. For instance, if the individual's spouse wants to help them get to work faster, all they have to do is put toothpaste on the toothbrush, make coffee, and prepare the cereal ahead of time because they are cognizant of their spouse's routine. For this reason, this section presents the results of training on a group of intentions over time then determining the amount of interaction required to choose one of them from the group. This is somewhat analogous to learning the person's morning routine as previously described. Ideally, the selection likelihood of the intentions in the group should be higher than all other possible intentions, therefore the amount of interaction required to select one of them should be small.

The experiment is performed on scenes where the objects and their positions vary over the span of at least 50 sessions. Each intention in the group is selected at most 10 times in no particular order given a conducive scene. At the conclusion of this "training" period, one of these intentions is randomly chosen and the average number of interactions required for choosing it is calculated. Figure 9 illustrates the results of this experiment. It shows that our framework reduces the necessary amount of interaction for all intentions tested and that it consistently outperforms the baseline methods. This behavior is desired because we want

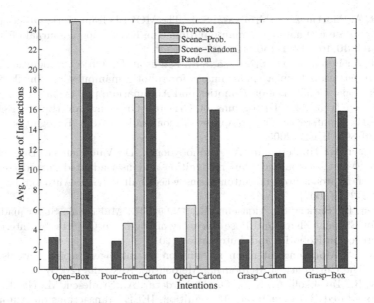

Fig. 9. Group Training: a group of intentions are learned over time then the amount of interaction required to choose one of them from the group is determined

our framework to be able to capture a user's preferences over time in order to simultaneously reduce human interaction and maximize robot task performance but at that the same time be flexible enough to adapt to new information.

6 Conclusion

In this paper, we have presented a vision-based human-robot collaborative system that enables the recognition and learning of human intentions. At the core of this system is our object-action intention recognition framework that is only dependent on scene information for inferring intentions rather than on the observation of human physical actions, which is the commonly-accepted approach. This is our principal contribution to the state-of-the-art as it is appropriate for assistive robotic systems for persons with limited physical capabilities. We have demonstrated through our evaluations that our framework is capable of adapting to a user's preferences and reduces the amount of interaction necessary for communicating tasks to a robot.

References

1. Carlson, T., Demiris, Y.: Collaborative Control for a Robotic Wheelchair: Evaluation of Performance, Attention, and Workload. IEEE Transactions on Systems, Man, and Cybernetics, Part B: Cybernetics **42**(3), 876–888 (2012)
2. Charniak, E., Goldman, R.P.: A Bayesian model of plan recognition. Artificial Intelligence **64**, 53–79 (1993)

3. Collet, A., Martinez, M., Srinivasa, S.S.: The MOPED framework: Object recognition and pose estimation for manipulation. The International Journal of Robotics Research **30**(10), 1284–1306 (2011)

4. Collet, A., Berenson, D., Srinivasa, S.S., Ferguson, D.: Object recognition and full pose registration from a single image for robotic manipulation. In: 2009 IEEE International Conference on Robotics and Automation, pp. 48–55, May 2009

5. Dalal, N., Triggs, B.: Histograms of Oriented Gradients for Human Detection. In: IEEE Conference on Computer Vision and Pattern Recognition, vol. 1, pp. 886–893. IEEE (2005)

6. Demeester, E., Huntermann, A., Vanhooydonck, D., Vanacker, G., Brussel, H.V., Nuttin, M.: User-adapted plan recognition and user-adapted shared control: A Bayesian approach to semi-autonomous wheelchair driving. Autonomous Robots **24**, 193–211 (2007)

7. Duncan, K., Sarkar, S., Alqasemi, R., Dubey, R.: Multi-scale Superquadric Fitting for Efficient Shape and Pose Recovery of Unknown Objects. In: International Conference on Robotics and Automation (2013)

8. Heinze, C.: Modelling intention recognition for intelligent agent systems. Ph.D. thesis, The University of Melbourne, Melbourne, Australia (2003)

9. Kelley, R., Tavakkoli, A., King, C., Ambardekar, A., Nicolescu, M., Nicolescu, M.: Context-Based Bayesian Intent Recognition. IEEE Transactions on Autonomous Mental Development **4**(3), 215–225 (2012)

10. Kelley, R., Wigand, L., Hamilton, B., Browne, K., Nicolescu, M., Nicolescu, M.: Deep networks for predicting human intent with respect to objects. In: Proceedings of the Seventh Annual ACM/IEEE International Conference on Human-Robot Interaction, HRI 2012, p. 171 (2012)

11. Koller, D., Friedman, N.: Probabilistic Graphical Models: Principles and Techniques, 1 edn. MIT Press (2010)

12. Lowe, D.: Distinctive image features from scale-invariant keypoints. International Journal of Computer Vision **60**(2), 91–110 (2004)

13. Madry, M., Song, D., Ek, C.H., Kragic, D.: Robot bring me something to drink from: Object Representation For Transferring Task Specific Grasps. In: IEEE International Conference on Robotics and Automation (2012)

14. Madry, M., Song, D., Kragic, D.: From Object Categories to Grasp Transfer Using Probabilistic Reasoning. In: IEEE International Conference on Robotics and Automation (2012)

15. Meger, D., Forssén, P.E., Lai, K., Helmer, S., McCann, S., Southey, T., Baumann, M., Little, J.K., Lowe, D.G.: Curious George: An attentive semantic robot. Robotics and Autonomous Systems **56**, 503–511 (2008)

16. Ramík, D.M., Madani, K., Sabourin, C.: From visual patterns to semantic description: A cognitive approach using artificial curiosity as the foundation. Pattern Recognition Letters **34**, 1577–1588 (2013)

17. Rusu, R., Blodow, N., Beetz, M.: Fast Point Feature Histograms (FPFH) for 3D Registration. In: IEEE International Conference on Robotics and Automation, pp. 3212–3217. IEEE (2009)

18. Rusu, R., Blodow, N., Marton, Z.: Close-range scene segmentation and reconstruction of 3D point cloud maps for mobile manipulation in domestic environments. In: International Conference on Intelligent Robots and Systems, pp. 3–8 (2009)

19. Tahboub, K.A.: Intelligent Human-Machine Interaction Based on Dynamic Bayesian Networks Probabilistic Intention Recognition. Journal of Intelligent and Robotic Systems **45**(1), 31–52 (2006)

20. Tavakkoli, A., Kelley, R., King, C., Nicolescu, M., Nicolescu, M., Bebis, G.: A Vision-Based Architecture for Intent Recognition. In: Bebis, G., Boyle, R., Parvin, B., Koracin, D., Paragios, N., Tanveer, S.-M., Ju, T., Liu, Z., Coquillart, S., Cruz-Neira, C., Müller, T., Malzbender, T. (eds.) ISVC 2007, Part II. LNCS, vol. 4842, pp. 173–182. Springer, Heidelberg (2007)
21. Vanhooydonck, D., Demeester, E., Nuttin, M., Brussel, H.V.: Shared Control for Intelligent Wheelchairs: An Implicit Estimation of the User Intention. In: 2003 International Workshop on Advances in Service Robotics, pp. 176–182 (2003)
22. Zhu, C., Sun, W., Sheng, W.: Wearable Sensors based Human Intention Recognition in Smart Assisted Living Systems. In: International Conference on Information and Automation, pp. 954–959 (2008)

Egocentric Object Recognition Leveraging the 3D Shape of the Grasping Hand

Yizhou Lin, Gang Hua$^{(\boxtimes)}$, and Philippos Mordohai

Department of Computer Science, Stevens Institute of Technology, Hoboken, USA
{ylin8,ghua,pmordoha}@stevens.edu

Abstract. We present a systematic study on the relationship between the 3D shape of a hand that is about to grasp an object and recognition of the object to be grasped. In this paper, we investigate the direction from the shape of the hand to object recognition for unimpaired users. Our work shows that the 3D shape of a grasping hand from an egocentric point of view can help improve recognition of the objects being grasped. Previous work has attempted to exploit hand interactions or gaze information in the egocentric setting to guide object segmentation. However, all such analyses are conducted in 2D. We hypothesize that the 3D shape of a grasping hand is highly correlated to the physical attributes of the object being grasped. Hence, it can provide very beneficial visual information for object recognition. We validate this hypothesis by first building a 3D, egocentric vision pipeline to segment and reconstruct dense 3D point clouds of the grasping hands. Then, visual descriptors are extracted from the point cloud and subsequently fed into an object recognition system to recognize the object being grasped. Our experiments demonstrate that the 3D hand shape can indeed greatly help improve the visual recognition accuracy, when compared with the baseline where only 2D image features are utilized.

Keywords: Mobile and wearable systems · Egocentric and first-person vision · Activity monitoring systems · Rehabilitation aids

1 Introduction

The motivating healthcare application of this research is the advancement of hand rehabilitation following neuromuscular injury such as stroke [10]. Typically, rehabilitation is planned based on evidence gathered in constrained clinical settings. Consequently, the usage pattern of the paretic (partially paralyzed) hand in patients' daily activities remains largely unknown, despite the importance of quantitatively measuring hand impairment in daily activities to assist the therapist. In addition to stroke, hand impairment can arise from a variety of diseases or injuries, including spinal cord injury, scleroderma, Parkinson's disease, and radial nerve damage. For stroke alone, approximately 800,000 individuals incur a cerebrovascular accident each year in the U.S. [6]. According to a survey by Nowak [14], only 40% of people who survive a stroke experience full functional

© Springer International Publishing Switzerland 2015
L. Agapito et al. (Eds.): ECCV 2014 Workshops, Part III, LNCS 8927, pp. 746–762, 2015.
DOI: 10.1007/978-3-319-16199-0_52

recovery [7]. For the remaining 60% with chronic hemiparesis, hand dysfunction is one of the most common sources of disability [11]. Occupational therapy is usually undertaken in an effort to at least partially restore function. Unfortunately, the true effectiveness of different therapy regimens is difficult to gauge. At present, the translation of clinical treatment to improved use of the affected hand remains largely unknown. Clinical assessments can be performed and user questionnaires can be administered, but objective measurements of what is actually occurring in daily life are lacking. Increasingly, therapists are encouraged to follow evidence-based practice to foster better outcomes, but the data of interest, actual functioning within the community and home, is difficult to acquire.

This paper is a step in the direction of using wearable, egocentric computer vision technology to aid hand rehabilitation. Before beginning any research with patients and therapists, however, several technical obstacles have to be overcome. Here, we address two of the relevant challenges:

- the 3D reconstruction of the grasping hand from egocentric stereo images and
- establishing that there is a correlation between the shape of the grasping hand and the identity of the object that is about to be grasped.

Having established this relationship, we can now envision the development of an approach for monitoring paretic users in their daily activities, recording information relevant to the functionality of their hands and then presenting this information to physical therapists who will determine the next steps in the users' rehabilitation. Numerous challenges will have to be addressed to realize this long-term goal. The remainder of the paper describes the current state of our approach, which has only been tested on unimpaired users so far.

Recognizing objects from an egocentric perspective is a very important task in understanding the users' daily behavior and activities. It enables continuous monitoring of the users' hands, in our cases, in natural settings and can provide potentially much more useful information than what can be collected in brief consultations with a physical therapist. We strongly believe that an egocentric approach is essential for the success of our research. An advantage of egocentric vision is that there is a large amount of contextual information centered around the user, such as hand position and gaze [5,17], to help with the recognition tasks. For example, the skin tone of the user's hand interacting with an object has been exploited by Pirsiavash and Ramanan [17] for localizing the object of attention to improve object detection. Fathi et al. [5] leveraged gaze information to help identify the object being handled by the user for daily action recognition.

Notwithstanding the demonstrated success of these previous works, two limitations are present in them. On one hand, the contextual information is more utilized as a pre-filter to scope the location of the target object to be detected or recognized. In other words, it is not an integral part of the core recognition algorithms. On the other hand, all visual reasoning in these previous works is conducted in 2D. Some important visual information that could potentially be provided by 3D information has largely been neglected.

Research in kinesiology and neuroscience reveals that the physical attributes, such as the shape, size and weight, of the object to be grasped by the user determine the posture of the grasping hand, even before contact is made [21, 22, 29]. These findings largely motivated the research conducted in this paper. We conjecture that the hand posture in an object grasping action would provide additional cues to enhance the visual recognition of the object being grasped. In this paper, we present a first systematic study to verify such a conjecture.

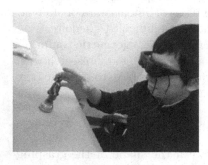

Fig. 1. A user is grasping an object, while the grasp is recorded by the egocentric stereo cameras

We begin our study by building an egocentric 3D vision pipeline to segment and recover a dense 3D point cloud of the grasping hands from egocentric stereo images. The core hardware component of our egocentric 3D vision pipeline are the Vuzix 920AR augmented reality glasses equipped with a pair of egocentric cameras [1] [2]. The dense 3D point cloud provides a non-parametric representation of the shape of the hands. Since the 3D point cloud of the hand carries implicit information of the hand posture, in this paper we focus our analysis on the point cloud, to avoid the challenging task of estimating the hand posture, which we leave as our future work.

We have collected a dataset of stereo videos involving 36 users. The users were asked to wear the AR glasses and grasp 8 objects each from a different category three times. We then conduct a systematic evaluation on an egocentric object recognition task to recognize these 8 objects engaging or not engaging the 3D features extracted from the 3D point cloud of the grasping hand. Our analysis re-validated the correlations between the physical attributes of the object and the 3D shape of the grasping hand, and manifested that 3D hand shape can indeed enhance object recognition accuracy.

This paper presents the following contributions:

1. We are the first to introduce observations from kinesiology and neuroscience, regarding the correlation between the physical attributes of the object to be grasped and the grasping hand, to the egocentric vision community.
2. To the best of our knowledge, our work presents a first systematic study to reveal how the 3D shape of a grasping hand can help improve recognition of the objects being grasped from an egocentric point of view.

---

[1] http://www.vuzix.com/

[2] The Vuzix 920AR augmented reality glasses are equipped with a near-eye display which blocks the user's field of view. Ideally it should be a see-through display for use in daily activities.

3. We have collected a labeled dataset of stereo videos involving 36 users grasping 8 different categories of objects to carry out our study, which will be shared with the community to advance research on egocentric object recognition.

2   Related Work

The core assumption behind our work, that the shape of a grasping hand can reveal information about the object about to be manipulated, is based on findings in kinesiology and neuroscience. The shape, size and weight of the object to be grasped determine the posture of the hand even before contact is made [29]. A variety of grips that can be broadly distinguished into precision or power grips and further subdivided into finer categories have been identified in the relevant literature; see [21] and references therein. Schettino et al. [22] studied hand preshaping before an object is grasped and the effects on limited vision on the modulation of hand kinematics to adjust to object contours.

A prevalent and accurate way for obtaining hand pose and articulated motion is the use of data gloves [24]. Data gloves, however, are uncomfortable and prohibitively expensive making their use in everyday activities unappealing. Here, we focus on vision-based solutions to these problems. Delamarre and Faugeras [1] used an articulated 3D model of the hand made of cones and spheres and matched it with stereo reconstructions of the hands using ICP to infer the pose of the fingers. Later, Dewaele et al. [2] presented a model-based approach for tracking the hands in stereoscopic videos that relied on motion cues in addition to shape estimates in each frame. In our current work, we have not taken advantage of the priors provided by articulated models or temporal information, but these are clearly fruitful directions for future research.

In recent years, we have observed a surge of interest in research on egocentric computer vision problems, which is the result of the combination of inspiration from early pioneering systems [16,23] and the ever growing computing power in modern wearable platforms. Here, we review recent advancement of research in egocentric visual recognition. These works can largely be put into three categories, object/scene discovery and summarization, action/activity recognition, and object recognition.

One of the major applications of egocentric visual object/scene discovery is to summarize the egocentric video for daily life logging [8,12]. Jojic et al. [8] proposed the structural epitome to summarize one's visual experiences. The STEL Epitome image produced from the egocentric video is visually similar to a panoramic image. It automatically groups the same scene and objects into tightly connected regions in the epitome image. Lee et al. [12] proposed to combine a set of egocentric features with other visual cues to build a detector for category independent important object detection. The egocentric video is then summarized based on the important objects detected.

A larger body of recent research on egocentric computer vision has been devoted to recognizing the daily actions/activities from egocentric videos

[3,5,15,17,25,27]. The CMU-MMAC database [27] built at CMU is a multi-modal activity recognition database which incorporated the videos from a head-mounted forward-looking camera as one of the modality. Spriggs *et al.* [25] acknowledged the importance of objects in activity understanding, but did not pursue object recognition at the time. Ogaki *et al.* [15] explored the use of first-person eye movement and ego-motion for indoor activity recognition. The special set-up of their equipment is that there is an inward looking camera to capture the user's eye movement. Various egocentric cues have been explored to facilitate the recognition of activity, including the skin tone of the hands [3,17] and the gaze [5].

As widely acknowledged in previous works, object recognition serves a very important role in activity understanding. The use of object recognition in ego-centric vision systems dates back to the DyPERS system of Schiele *et al.* [23]. Mayol and Murray [13] recognized manipulation activities leveraging skin color and histogram-based object classification from a shoulder-mounted camera. Ren and Philipose [18] collected a large database of egocentric videos of objects to facilitate research in egocentric object recognition. The database was used by Ren and Gu [19] who segment objects that have been grasped by the user from the background. The approaches of [4,19] rely primarily on optical flow motion cues.

Our work is different than previous research in two aspects. First, most previous egocentric vision system, if not all of them, only leveraged a monocular forward-looking camera, while our system comprises an egocentric stereo camera. Second, our proposed egocentric object recognition method benefits from the 3D hand shape derived from egocentric stereo. To the best of our knowledge, this is an egocentric cue which has never been explored before for object recognition.

3   Egocentric Object Recognition

The functional goal of our egocentric computer vision system is to recognize the object being grasped or that is about to be grasped by the user's hand. Since the egocentric vision glasses we use have a pair of stereo cameras embedded in them, we are able to reconstruct dense 3D point clouds of the grasping hand (see Section 4 for details). Therefore, our visual feature extraction incorporates two processing channels, *i.e.*, the image channel and the hand (3D point cloud) channel, as shown in Figure 2. We introduce the detailed steps of feature extraction from these two channels, followed by different strategies that the object recognition can be conducted.

Feature Extraction in the Image Channel. Given the pair of stereo images taken from the 3D egocentric camera, we densely extract SIFT descriptors from the pair of images. These SIFT descriptors are further quantized using a pre-trained visual vocabulary and subsequently aggregated to form a bag-of-features histogram. Then, recognition from the image channel can be carried out by training SVM classifiers from the bag-of-features histogram representation using linear, RBF, histogram intersection, and chi-square kernels.

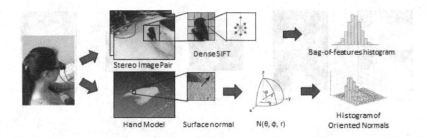

Fig. 2. The two feature processing pipelines in our egocentric object recognition system. The top row presents the feature representation from the image channel, where we extract a bag-of-words histogram as the feature representation for the object to be recognized based on densely extracted SIFT descriptor. The bottom row presents the feature representation from the 3D point clouds of the grasping hand. A histogram of oriented normals [26] is extracted to characterize the shape of the grasping hand.

Feature Extraction in the Hand Channel. As we have discussed, from the egocentric stereo image pairs, we reconstruct dense 3D point clouds of the grasping hand using the pipeline detailed in Section 4. After we obtain the dense 3D point cloud, we extract the histogram of oriented normal vectors (HONV) feature [26] from the point cloud. The HONV feature, proposed by Tang et al. [26], aggregates the surface normals into azimuth and elevation bins. It has achieved outstanding performance in recognizing objects from images with depth information. Please refer to [26] for details on the HONV feature. We adopt it here as a descriptor to characterize the shape of the grasping hand to predict the object to be grasped. The fact that HONV features are viewpoint dependent is desirable in our settings since the users observe their hands from the same vantage point when performing a given action. Subsequent recognition of the object can be conducted, once again, by training SVM classifiers on HONV features with various kernel functions.

There are two different strategies that the visual features extracted from the image channel and the 3D hand channel can be combined to build a more robust system to recognize the egocentric object, *i.e.*, the pre-fusion strategy and the post-fusion strategy.

The Pre-fusion Strategy. In pre-fusion, the features extracted from the image channel and the hand channel are concatenated together to form a larger feature vector to be used by the classification algorithm. The main challenge in the pre-fusion strategy is how to appropriately normalize features from the two different channels. We will examine the most appropriate normalization schemes in our experiments.

The Post-fusion Strategy. In post-fusion, we train two classifiers separately from features extracted from the two channels. Then the outputs from the two classifiers are linearly combined to form the final prediction by, for example, post

Fig. 3. Given a pair of images, the hand is iteratively segmented using graph cuts. Then, stereo matching, followed by bilateral filtering, is performed on the segmented images to generate point clouds which are used as inputs for recognition.

training a linear SVM on the output scores from the two classifiers. Other more sophisticated combination algorithms, such as multiple kernel learning (MKL) SVM [28] can also be leveraged. Our experiments, however, do not show any improvement in performance compared with the simple combination scheme described above, despite the considerably more computationally expensive learning process.

We will conduct a systematic evaluation of these two fusion strategies in our experiments, and carefully examine if our conjecture, that the 3D shape of the grasping hand would provide beneficial information to recognize the object being grasped, is valid.

4   3D Hand Shape from Egocentric Stereo

In this section, we present our algorithm for segmenting and reconstructing the hands given a stereo pair of images. An illustration of the steps of our current pipeline can be seen in Fig. 3. Processing begins by detecting potential skin regions using a generic color model, which is iteratively adapted to match the appearance of skin in the input frames. Stereo matching is then restricted to skin regions to improve accuracy and speed. The output of this stage is a point cloud of the hand, pre or post contact with the object, that does not contain the latter. Segmentation plays a significant role in the quality of our reconstructed models. Accurate segmentation allows us to pursue a model-free approach, unlike previous work in stereo-based hand reconstruction [1,2] that requires prior models which may have to be customized for each person.

Segmentation. First, we attempt to detect the hand by identifying potential skin regions using a generic skin-tone model [9]. We generate seeds for the hand region by selecting pixels with large probability for being skin. We also generate seeds for the background by selecting pixels that are extremely unlikely to be skin. The seeds are inserted as constraints in a binary MRF defined on a graph $G = (V \cup \{s,t\}, E)$. The weights of edges connecting nodes with the source and the sink are defined as follows:

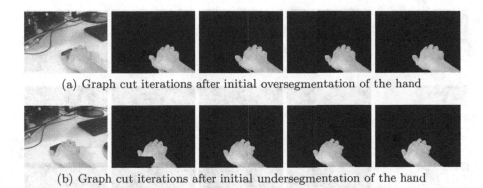

(a) Graph cut iterations after initial oversegmentation of the hand

(b) Graph cut iterations after initial undersegmentation of the hand

Fig. 4. The graph cut iterations from the initial segmentation using [9] to the final result

$$e(v, s) = \begin{cases} w_{max} & P(\text{skin}) > \Theta_s \\ 0 & \text{otherwise} \end{cases}$$

$$e(v, t) = \begin{cases} w_{max} & P(\text{skin}) < \Theta_{\bar{s}} \\ 0 & \text{otherwise} \end{cases}$$

Edge weights between neighboring nodes v_p and v_q depend on the intensity difference between the corresponding pixels.

$$e(v_p, v_q) = \max(e^{-\frac{|I_{v_p} - I_{v_q}|}{\sigma}}, k)$$

We use the QPBO algorithm [20] to segment skin from non-skin regions. If multiple connected components labeled as skin are detected, we keep the one with the largest area. Due to the use of a generic skin-tone model, the results are not perfect, but because of the conservative construction of the graph weights, the detected skin regions tend to be pure. Using the initial segmentation, we estimate unimodal Gaussian color models for skin and non-skin pixels using maximum likelihood estimation. The new appearance models are used to recompute the probabilities of pixels being in the foreground or not and the graph cut is repeated with updated edge weights. We stop iterating when the result becomes stable, or the maximum number of iterations has been reached. It should be noted that due to the inherent difficulties in skin color detection, the model of Jones and Rehg [9] requires 16 Gaussian components for each class, but after our initial segmentation, one component is sufficient for a given video. The iterations are shown in Fig. 4, and more hand segmentation results from our proposed pipeline are shown in Fig. 5.

An additional step is required in order to restrict the reconstructed model to the palm and fingers, excluding the forearm which is part of the same segment if

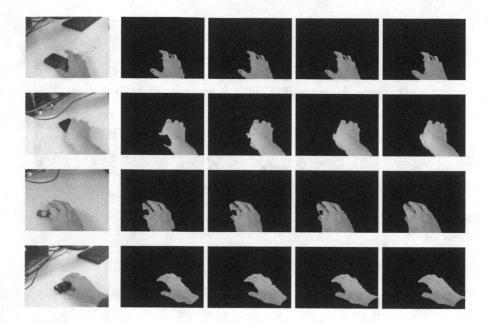

Fig. 5. Some more hand segmentation results from the iterative segmentation pipeline. From left to right, each row shows the original video frame and the segmentation results evolving with the iterations.

the person is not wearing long sleeves. We begin by detecting the orientation of the arm in the image, using the eigenvector of the hand region associated with the largest eigenvalue. Given this direction of maximum elongation, we estimate the width orthogonally to it. We then reject all pixels that are not contained in a region whose length is at most 20% larger than the width of the hand starting from the furthest point, typically a finger. This prevents inconsistent hand segments, which may or may not contain parts of the forearm, from being passed on to the 3D reconstruction, feature extraction and classification modules.

3D Reconstruction. Leveraging the skin masks to restrict the search range for stereo matches allows us to use a simple matching technique. Moreover, since we only allow skin pixels to match other skin pixels and do not attempt to match the background, matches are sought for a fraction of the pixels and only a fraction of the disparity range is valid for each pixel. This reduces the probability of error and the amount of computation.

The results shown throughout this paper are obtained using Normalized Cross Correlation (NCC) in square windows. More sophisticated methods could have been used, but stereo matching for a single surface is much easier than the general problem of stereo, even in the presence of self-occlusions as in our case.

A bilateral filter is applied on the disparity map to correct disparity errors due to differences in illumination and camera response function between the

Fig. 6. Visualizations of the reconstructed dense 3D point clouds of the grasping hand along with original video frames. From left to right, each row presents the original video frame and the dense 3D point cloud of the grasping hand viewed from different angles and at different scales.

two cameras, poor lighting, motion blur and lack of texture on the hand. The bilateral filter we use is defined according to:

$$d(\mathbf{x}) = \sum_{\mathbf{y}} w(\mathbf{x},\mathbf{y}) d(\mathbf{y}) e^{-\frac{(D(\mathbf{x},\mathbf{y}))^2}{2\sigma_s^2}} e^{-\frac{(C(\mathbf{x},\mathbf{y}))^2}{2\sigma_c^2}}, \tag{1}$$

where $w(\mathbf{x},\mathbf{y})$ is a rectangle window function, $D(\mathbf{x},\mathbf{y})$ is the distance function between $\mathbf{x}$ and $\mathbf{y}$,

$$D(\mathbf{x},\mathbf{y}) = \sqrt{(\mathbf{x}_x - \mathbf{y}_x)^2 + (\mathbf{x}_y - \mathbf{y}_y)^2},$$

$C(\mathbf{x},\mathbf{y})$ is the color difference function between $\mathbf{x}$ and $\mathbf{y}$,

$$and C(\mathbf{x},\mathbf{y}) = |\mathbf{x}_R - \mathbf{y}_R| + |\mathbf{x}_G - \mathbf{y}_G| + |\mathbf{x}_B - \mathbf{y}_B|.$$

Finally, 3D point clouds are reconstructed based on the filtered disparity map and calibration information, obtained using images of a checkerboard and standard techniques [30]. Screenshots of the dense 3D point clouds of the grasping hand extracted from our proposed pipeline are shown in Fig. 6. As can be observed, the results are quite robust to unsatisfactory illumination conditions.

5   Data Collection

Fig. 7. The objects in our dataset: cup, statue, stapler, tea can, pen, iPhone, flash disk and sunglasses

We have 8 objects from different categories in our dataset as shown in Fig. 7 and we asked 36 subjects to grasp them. For each user and each object, at least 3 grasps were performed. We did not instruct the users to grasp the objects using certain hand gestures, other than to request that they use their right hand. Between two consecutive grasps, the subject was asked to remove his or her hand completely from the object, so that every grasp could be considered independent. After all the data were collected, we manually labeled those frames in which the user's hand just touched the object, and the user's hand was about to leave from the object. Frames with heavy motion blur were not labeled.

6   Experiments

We performed a number of object recognition experiments on a dataset comprising 36 people grasping the 8 objects in a total of 767 frames. The data was split so that 25 people and 546 frames were in the training set and the remainder in the test set.

We note that in our experiments, all the frames of a single user are either in the training set or in the test set, e.g. we do not perform testing on a user's frames while different frames of the same user in the training set. Moreover, the number of video frames for each object category in the training and testing sets are shown in Table. 1.

Table 1. Number of video frames in the training and test sets

	Cup	Pen	iPhone	Flash disk	Stapler	Sunglasses	Statue	Tea can
# Training frames	27	46	86	81	71	72	89	74
# Testing frames	16	21	35	27	36	25	37	24

All experiments were performed with constant values for the parameters. For the MRF, the values used were $\Theta_s = 0.9$, $\Theta_{\bar{s}} = 0.01$, $\sigma = 25$ and $k = 0.05$. During stereo matching, we have a strong prior about the location of the hand with respect to the egocentric cameras which allows us to restrict the disparity range between 80 and 200. This interval has been effective for all subjects in our experiments. The NCC window size was 19×19 and the size of the bilateral filter was 50×50 with $\sigma_s = 30$ and $\sigma_c = 50$. To speed up the disparity calculation, we downsample the images to $\frac{1}{2}$ of their original size (305×225) and upsample them to their original size afterwards.

6.1 Baseline Results

We use SIFT and the bag-of-features (BoF) histogram as our baseline. For SIFT, we scaled the images into three different sizes and generated patches of size 16×16 every 16 pixels. For BoF, we compute a $1024 - D$ feature histogram for each frame. We use SVMs with different kernels for the classification. The results are shown in Table 3.

6.2 3D Features Only

We also did experiments on classifying the objects using only the 3D hand features. In other words, in these experiments we attempted to classify objects without extracting any features from them. Results are shown in Table 3. The confusion matrices from the two top performing kernels, namely the histogram intersection kernel and the χ^2 are shown if Figure 8(b) and Figure 9(b). We achieved nearly 35% accuracy when classifying 8 objects. This demonstrates that features from the 3D hand shape carry information about the grasped object. Although the recognition accuracy is not as high as the results obtained from the image channel, it is much better than the random guess baseline, which is 12.5%.

6.3 Pre-fusion Results

We combined features from the two processing channels using a pre-fusion strategy according to Section 3. We tried three normalization schemes: normalization 1 where we normalize each feature in the dataset to be in $[0, 1]$, normalization 2 where we normalize each feature so that its sum of squares is equal to 1, and normalization 3 where we normalize each feature to have 0 mean and sum of squares equal to 1.

After normalizing the SIFT and HONV features, we just simply combine them into a longer vector. We tested the normalization scheme in histogram intersection kernel SVM. The result is shown in Table 2. Normalization 2 is used for all other experiments. Results are shown in Table 3 and Figure 8(c) and Figure 9(c).

Table 2. Recognition accuracy using different normalization schemes

Norm	SIFT	Pre-fusion
Norm1	84.61	87.78
Norm2	85.07	89.14
Norm3	85.97	89.14
No Norm	78.33	80.54

Table 3. Recognition accuracy using different kernels

Kernel	SIFT	HONV-only	Pre-fusion
LN	78.73	30.77	83.26
HI	85.07	34.39	89.14
RBF	81.00	34.84	82.81
χ^2	82.81	35.75	87.33

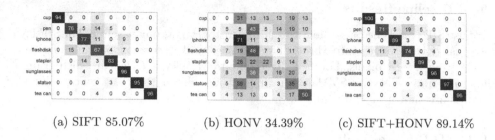

(a) SIFT 85.07%　　　　(b) HONV 34.39%　　　　(c) SIFT+HONV 89.14%

Fig. 8. The confusion matrix for the histogram intersection kernel

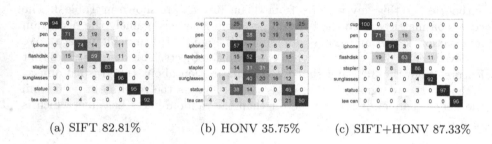

(a) SIFT 82.81%　　　　(b) HONV 35.75%　　　　(c) SIFT+HONV 87.33%

Fig. 9. The confusion matrix for the Chi-Square kernel

6.4　Discussion

From the results we can see that the additional 3D features of the hand have greatly improved the accuracy in classifying the objects. Using the histogram intersection kernel and the χ^2 kernel improved the accuracy of 7 out of the 8 categories. Our experimental results also show that post-fusion does not improve the classification results. Please refer to Fig. 8 and Fig. 9 for details. This is a strong indication that the 3D shape of the grasping hand can indeed provide beneficial complementary information to recognize the object being or about to be grasped.

We show some frames that were correctly classified after we used the additional 3D features, in Fig. 10. In these cases, the object is severely occluded by the hand, but features from the hand itself can be used to correct the errors. Some more examples that were incorrectly recognized when we only use SIFT features extracted from the video frames are shown in Fig. 11 and Fig. 12. Utilizing the HONV feature extracted from the dense 3D point cloud of the hand, our recognition system made the correct prediction on these examples.

From our experiments we also observed that a few frames were correctly classified but when we added the 3D hand features, they were assigned the wrong labels. This is mainly because not all users use a common gesture to grasp the object. Figure 13 shows an example.

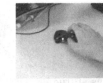

(a) Incorrectly classified as flash disk without 3D information

(b) Incorrectly classified as Stapler without 3D information

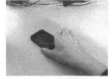

(c) Incorrectly classified as flash disk without 3D information

(d) Incorrectly classified as cup without 3D information

Fig. 10. Some example frames that were incorrectly classified when using SIFT features, but were corrected when 3D hand features were included

Fig. 11. These two frames of flash disks were incorrectly classified as stapler without using 3D features. Due to occlusion from the hand, using SIFT features only was not sufficient to classify them. The grasping shape of the hands are consistent for flash disks for almost all users, hence combining the 3D hand shape features helped to recognize them.

Fig. 12. This frame of a stapler was incorrectly classified as an iPhone. In appearance, the stapler in this frame looks like an iPhone. Because the grasping gesture of the hand is totally different when people grasp an iPone, factoring the 3D features of the grasping hand again helped to recognize it correctly.

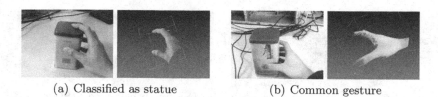

(a) Classified as statue   (b) Common gesture

Fig. 13. The left frame was incorrectly classified as a statue, because the user did not use the common gesture to grasp the object

7 Conclusion and Future Work

We have shown the first results that demonstrate that objects can be recognized indirectly by observing the shape of the hand that is about to manipulate them form an egocentric perspective. Adding features from the hand to a standard appearance based recognition engine resulted in a boost in performance, even though the hand channel does not observe the object in the frame.

This study opens up many possibilities for future work. In the short term, one direction for improvement is the use of articulated hand models which can provide strong priors for pose estimation and robustness against occlusion. We also plan to consider and exploit the temporal aspect of our data collection. The temporal continuity and redundancy of the video are virtually guaranteed to lead to performance improvements compared with our current single-frame implementation. Moreover, we plan to tie segmentation and 3D reconstruction more closely together in a feedback loop.

In the longer term, we plan to investigate the inverse direction of the relationship between hand shape and object recognition. In this scenario, the objective would be to estimate the hand shape and measure how much it deviates from the ideal grasp that corresponds to the object the user intends to manipulate. Such a system would learn the user's grasps and observe their evolution in time as a means of assessing the functionality of the user's hand. As mentioned in the introduction, this is an ambitious goal, but successful research in this direction can have tremendous impact on a large fraction of the population.

Acknowledgments. Research reported in this publication was supported by the National Institute Of Nursing Research of the National Institutes of Health under Award Number R01NR015371. The content is solely the responsibility of the authors and does not necessarily represent the official views of the National Institutes of Health. The research is also partly supported by National Science Foundation award IIS-1217797, and IIS-1350763.

References

1. Delamarre, Q., Faugeras, O.: Finding pose of hand in video images: a stereo-based approach. In: IEEE International Conference on Automatic Face and Gesture Recognition, pp. 585–590 (1998)
2. Dewaele, G., Devernay, F., Horaud, R.: Hand Motion from 3D Point Trajectories and a Smooth Surface Model. In: Pajdla, T., Matas, J.G. (eds.) ECCV 2004. LNCS, vol. 3021, pp. 495–507. Springer, Heidelberg (2004)
3. Fathi, A., Farhadi, A., Rehg, J.: Understanding egocentric activities. In: ICCV, pp. 407–414 (2011)
4. Fathi, A., Ren, X., Rehg, J.: Learning to recognize objects in egocentric activities. In: CVPR, pp. 3281–3288 (2011)
5. Fathi, A., Li, Y., Rehg, J.M.: Learning to Recognize Daily Actions Using Gaze. In: Fitzgibbon, A., Lazebnik, S., Perona, P., Sato, Y., Schmid, C. (eds.) ECCV 2012, Part I. LNCS, vol. 7572, pp. 314–327. Springer, Heidelberg (2012)
6. Go, A.S., Mozaffarian, D., Roger, V.L., Benjamin, E.J., Berry, J.D., Borden, W.B., Bravata, D.M., Dai, S., Ford, E.S., Fox, C.S., Franco, S., Fullerton, H.J., Gillespie, C., Hailpern, S.M., Heit, J.A., Howard, V.J., Huffman, M.D., Kissela, B.M., Kittner, S.J., Lackland, D.T., Lichtman, J.H., Lisabeth, L.D., Magid, D., Marcus, G.M., Marelli, A., Matchar, D.B., McGuire, D.K., Mohler, E.R., Moy, C.S., Mussolino, M.E., Nichol, G., Paynter, N.P., Schreiner, P.J., Sorlie, P.D., Stein, J., Turan, T.N., Virani, S.S., Wong, N.D., Woo, D., Turner, M.B.: Heart disease and stroke statistics 2013 update: A report from the american heart association. Circulation 127, 6–245 (2013)
7. Hankey, G.J., Jamrozik, K., Broadhurst, R.J., Forbes, S., Anderson, C.S.: Long-term disability after first-ever stroke and related prognostic factors in the perth community stroke study, 1989-1990. Stroke 33, 1034–1040 (2002)
8. Jojic, N., Perina, A., Murino, V.: Structural epitome: a way to summarize one's visual experience. In: NIPS (2010)
9. Jones, M., Rehg, J.: Statistical color models with application to skin detection. International Journal of Computer Vision 46(1), 81–96 (2002)
10. Kelly-Hayes, M., Robertson, J.T., Broderick, J.P., Duncan, P.W., Hershey, L.A., Roth, E.J., Thies, W.H., Trombly, C.A.: The American heart association stroke outcome classification: executive summary. Circulation 97, 2474–2478 (1998)
11. Kwakkel, G., Kollen, B.J., Wagenaar, R.C.: Long term effects of intensity of upper and lower limb training after stroke: a randomised trial. Journal of Neurology, Neurosurgery and Psychiatry 72, 473–479 (2002)
12. Lee, Y.J., Ghosh, J., Grauman, K.: Discovering important people and objects for egocentric video summarization. In: CVPR (2012)
13. Mayol, W., Murray, D.: Wearable hand activity recognition for event summarization. In: Ninth IEEE International Symposium on Wearable Computers, pp. 122–129 (2005)
14. Nowak, D.A.: The impact of stroke on the performance of grasping: Usefulness of kinetic and kinematic motion analysis. Neuroscience and Biobehavioral Reviews 32, 1439–1450 (2008)
15. Ogaki, K., Kitani, K., Sugano, Y., Sato, Y.: Coupling eye-motion and ego-motion features for first-person activity recognition. In: ECCV (2012)
16. Pentland, A.: Looking at people: sensing for ubiquitous and wearable computing. IEEE Transactions on Pattern Analysis and Machine Intelligence 22(1), 107–119 (2000)

17. Pirsiavash, H., Remanan, D.: Detecting activities of daily living in first-person camera views. In: Proc. IEEE Conf. on Computer Vision and Pattern Recognition (2012)
18. Ren, X., Philipose, M.: Egocentric recognition of handled objects: benchmark and analysis. In: First Workshop on Egocentric Vision (2009)
19. Ren, X., Gu, C.: Figure-ground segmentation improves handled object recognition in egocentric video. In: 2010 IEEE Conference on Computer Vision and Pattern Recognition (CVPR), pp. 3137–3144, June 2010
20. Rother, C., Kolmogorov, V., Lempitsky, V., Szummer, M.: Optimizing binary mrfs via extended roof duality. In: CVPR (2007)
21. Santello, M., Soechtino, J.F.: Gradual molding of the hand to object contours. Journal of Physiology **79**(3), 1307–1320 (1998)
22. Schettino, L.F., Adamovich, S.V., Poizner, H.: Effects of object shape and visual feedback on hand configuration during grasping. Experimental Brain Research **151**, 158–166 (2003)
23. Schiele, B., Oliver, N., Jebara, T., Pentland, A.: An Interactive Computer Vision System DyPERS: Dynamic Personal Enhanced Reality System. In: Christensen, H.I. (ed.) ICVS 1999. LNCS, vol. 1542, pp. 51–65. Springer, Heidelberg (1998)
24. Simone, L.K., Sundarrajan, N., Luo, X., Jia, Y., Kamper, D.G.: A low cost instrumented glove for extended monitoring and functional hand assessment. Journal of Neuroscience Methods **160**, 335–348 (2007)
25. Spriggs, E., De La Torre, F., Hebert, M.: Temporal segmentation and activity classification from first-person sensing. In: First Workshop on Egocentric Vision (2009)
26. Tang, S., Wang, X., Lv, X., Han, T.X., Keller, J., He, Z., Skubic, M., Lao, S.: Histogram of Oriented Normal Vectors for Object Recognition with a Depth Sensor. In: Lee, K.M., Matsushita, Y., Rehg, J.M., Hu, Z. (eds.) ACCV 2012, Part II. LNCS, vol. 7725, pp. 525–538. Springer, Heidelberg (2013)
27. la Torre, F.D., Hodgins, J., Bargteil, A., Martin, X., Macey, J.: Guide to the carnegie mellon university multimodal activity (cmu-mmac) database. Carnegie Mellon University, Tech. rep. (2008)
28. Vishwanathan, S.V.N., Sun, Z., Theera-Ampornpunt, N., Varma, M.: Multiple kernel learning and the SMO algorithm. In: Advances in Neural Information Processing Systems, December 2010
29. Winges, S.A., Weber, D.J., Santello, M.: The role of vision on hand preshaping during reach to grasp. Experimental Brain Research **152**, 489–498 (2003)
30. Zhang, Z.: A Flexible New Technique for Camera Calibration. IEEE Trans. on Pattern Analysis and Machine Intelligence 22(11), 1330–1334 (2000)

Face Recognition by 3D Registration for the Visually Impaired Using a RGB-D Sensor

Wei Li[1]([⊠]), Xudong Li[2], Martin Goldberg[3], and Zhigang Zhu[1,3]

[1] The City College of New York, New York, NY 10031, USA
lwei000@citymail.cuny.edu
[2] Beihang University, Beijing 100191, China
xdli@buaa.edu.cn
[3] The CUNY Graduate Center, New York, NY 10016, USA
mgoldberg@gradcenter.cuny.edu, zhu@cs.ccny.cuny.edu

Abstract. To help visually impaired people recognize people in their daily life, a 3D face feature registration approach is proposed with a RGB-D sensor. Compared to 2D face recognition methods, 3D data based approaches are more robust to the influence of face orientations and illumination changes. Different from most 3D data based methods, we employ a one-step ICP registration approach that is much less time consuming. The error tolerance of the 3D registration approach is analyzed with various error levels in 3D measurements. The method is tested with a Kinect sensor, by analyzing both the angular and distance errors to recognition performance. A number of other potential benefits in using 3D face data are also discussed, such as RGB image rectification, multiple-view face integration, and facial expression modeling, all useful for social interactions of visually impaired people with others.

Keywords: Face recognition · Assistive computer vision · 3D registration · RGB-D sensor

1 Introduction

Visually impaired people have difficulty in recognizing people in their daily life, therefore their visual impairment greatly limits their social lives. Without hearing voice or getting close enough to touch a person, it is hard for them to know exactly who the person is and how the person looks like. We would like to help them in this kind of situation by employing 3D computer vision based methods. By using face recognition techniques and a popular RGB-D camera, we can build computer vision system to detect and recognize people in different scenes, and then inform the visually impaired users of the recognition results.

In order to help a visually impaired person recognize people, we utilize a Kinect RGB-D sensor and propose a 3D registration based approach to face recognition. First, real-time face tracking is realized using the Kinect SDK and 3D facial feature points are extracted. The 3D pose (position and orientation) of the sensor to the observed face is estimated. Then the current 3D face (the

© Springer International Publishing Switzerland 2015
L. Agapito et al. (Eds.): ECCV 2014 Workshops, Part III, LNCS 8927, pp. 763–777, 2015.
DOI: 10.1007/978-3-319-16199-0_53

probe) is compared with all the 3D faces in a database (the gallery) by using a one-step Iterative Closest Points (ICP) approach. The *registration* errors of the probe face and the gallery faces indicate the uncertainty in face matches: the smaller the error, the more similar the two matched faces. By picking up the gallery face that has the smallest registration error with the probe face, the probe face is recognized.

The major goal of this work is to investigate what can be done with only 3D data for face recognition, and this paper has the following four contributions. 1) A highly effective ICP registration based approach is proposed for face recognition. Since a very good estimation of each face's pose is known, the initial estimation of the relative pose between the two faces (for the same person) in comparison is fairly close to the true value and therefore a one-step ICP will be able to obtain an accurate registration. For faces of different people, the approach just assume they are of the same person and the registration error of the one-step ICP indicates they are of two different faces. 2) To evaluate the robustness of the approach, an error analysis is performed by adding various degrees of errors to the *ideal* 3D face data in order to determine the required accuracy in 3D estimation of face features using the RGB-D sensor. This is compared against the accuracy of a Kinect sensor used in our experiments to evaluate the feasibility of 3D face recognition using the sensor. 3) An online recognition system prototype is built with the goal to help the visually impaired recognize people in front of them. We have also designed experiments to analyze how the system performs with various standoff distances and face orientations. 4) A number of other benefits in using 3D face information are explored, such as RGB image rectification and normalization, multiple-view face integration, and facial expression modeling, which are all useful for assisting the interactions of visually impaired people with others.

The paper is organized as follows. Section 2 introduces the background and related work. Section 3 describes the basis of our approach – 3D face feature extraction and the ICP-based face registration. In Section 4 we describe our ICP-based face recognition approach, evaluate the error tolerance of our approach, and analyze the measuring errors of the Kinect sensor. In Section 5, we provide the testing results using the proposed approach in online recognition. Then in Section 6, we discuss a number of other possible uses of the 3D face data for face modeling. Finally we conclude our work in Section 7.

2   Related Work

Face recognition has already been a topic in research for decades; researchers have gone a long way from 2D to 3D image approaches to achieve the goals of using face recognition for various applications. A lot of 2D image based face recognition methods have been proposed, and these methods have been roughly divided in to two categories: feature based and holistic based [6]. Among these methods, the LBP (Local Binary Pattern) based method [16] and Gabor based method seem to be the most outstanding ones [8] [9]. However, 2D methods face great difficulty when dealing with the problem of face pose variation in real life. Although researchers have tried to find the facial features robust to face pose variation, or align faces by using the features extracted [4] [18] [1], it is still an open problem for applications when face pose information is not available.

Another promising branch to solving the problem is using the 3D data of a RGB-D sensor. Comparing to using only 2D images, 3D data is invariant to the face pose (both position and orientation). Therefore, if we can obtain accurate 3D data, then 3D data based methods are supposed to be more appealing than 2D methods in real applications. However, due to various face poses, we may not be able to see the full view of face. The authors in [10] proposed a method to use facial symmetry to handle the face pose problem; each face is assumed to be symmetry so if part of the face is hidden, we can still obtain the full detail by using its symmetry.

Many approaches have been proposed to work on the common dataset FRGC V2[11]. In [5] both MS-LBP (Multiple scale Local Binary Patten) depth maps and Shape Index Maps are employed, then the Scale-Invariant Feature Transform (SIFT) is used to extract local features from the maps. Then the local and holistic analysis are combined to perform the matching of faces. In [12] an registration method is proposed, using an approach based on Simulated Annealing (SA) for range image registration with the Surface Interpenetration Measure (SIM). The SA starts the registration process using the M-estimator. Sample Consensus proposed in [14] is used and a final tuning is achieved by utilizing the SIM. The resulting SIM value is then used to assess the final 3D face matching. [15] uses an isogeodesic stripes graph descriptor obtained from a 3D Weighted Walk to represent a 3D face and transformed the 3D face matching to a graph matching. [2] introduces a Signed Shape Difference Map (SSDM) to compare aligned 3D faces, both the interpersonal and intrapersonal SSDMs are trained to distinguish different people and find their common features. For each test, the candidates SSDM with all the saved models are computed and matching scores are obtained by comparing with trained models to recognize the candidate.

Kinect has become a very popular RGB-D sensor, since it can provide the regular RGB images as well as Depth images in real time, therefore it is natural to integrate the two kinds of data. Using the 3D information, we can easily obtain the human face features in both 2D and 3D images. A number of researchers have worked on Kinect-based 3D face recognition. For example, [7] presents an algorithm that uses a low resolution 3D sensor for robust face recognition under challenging conditions. The method first locates the nose tip position of a face, then uses the position to find the face region. Sparse coding is used to encode the face, and then the encoded vector of the face is used as the input to a classifier to recognize the face. But due to Kinect depth measurement error, a reliable tip localization method is still in need.

3   3D Face Feature Extraction and Registration

Most of the methods discussed above can obtain good face recognition performance in experiments with well-defined datasets, but many of them have high computational cost and suffer in the cases of both non-frontal face images and changing illuminations. In our work, we would like to build a portable system that can help the visually impaired in real-time face recognition. Therefore we select Kinect as the input sensor and propose a highly effective ICP registration method. In this section, we will discuss two basic modules of the approach: face feature extraction and ICP-based face matching, before we describe our ICP-based face recognition method.

3.1   3D Facial Feature Point Extraction

The method that Kinect used for locating facial points is a regularized maximum likelihood Deformable Model Fitting (DMF) algorithm [17]. By employing this algorithm, we can obtain the 3D facial feature points of a face, as shown in Figure 1. There are 121 face feature points in total, which are distributed symmetrically on the face based on the model proposed in [17]. After we obtain the 121 feature points, we use the symmetry relations of these points to build a full view face. This is important when only part of the face is visible in the case of side views. The symmetry relationship is found by calculating the face feature position relationship with a frontal face. In Table 1, the numbers are the indices for the 121 face feature points. We list every pair of symmetric corresponding feature points as *pl* and *pr* in the heading row of the table. Some pairs of the point indices are the same because they are on the middle axis of the face.

The 121 facial feature points can be obtained in real time, even with a large rotation angle; the DMF model can track a face and obtain all the feature points, as shown in Figure 2. Having the information of the symmetry relationship, we are able to find the corresponding face patches to build a full-view face in both 3D and 2D images. This will be very useful if we want to integrate both the 3D and 2D data for face recognition, since even though the 3D face feature points are complete by using the face model, the RGB-D data of a side view is not complete, e.g. the image in the middle in Figure 2.

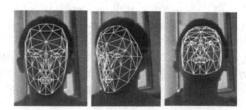

Fig. 1. 3D feature points   **Fig. 2.** Face tracker in multiple angles

3.2   3D Feature Point Registration

Different from the method proposed by others to find 3D data descriptor through very complicated computation, we directly register the 3D facial feature points

Table 1. The symmetry relationship of the facial feature points

pl	pr	pl	pr	pl	pr	pl	pr	pl	pr	pl	pr
0	0	1	34	2	2	3	3	4	4	5	5
6	6	7	7	8	8	9	9	10	10	11	44
12	45	13	46	14	47	15	48	16	49	17	50
18	51	19	52	20	53	21	54	22	55	23	56
24	57	25	58	26	59	27	60	28	61	29	62
30	63	31	64	32	65	33	66	34	1	35	35
36	36	37	37	38	38	39	39	40	40	41	41
42	42	43	43	44	11	45	12	46	13	47	14
48	15	49	16	50	17	51	18	52	19	53	20
54	21	55	22	56	23	57	24	58	25	59	26
60	27	61	28	62	29	63	30	64	31	65	32
66	33	67	69	68	70	69	67	70	68	71	73
72	74	73	71	74	72	75	76	76	75	77	78
78	77	79	80	80	79	81	82	82	81	83	84
84	83	85	86	86	85	87	87	88	89	89	88
90	91	91	90	92	93	93	92	94	94	95	96
96	95	97	98	98	97	99	100	100	99	101	102
102	101	103	104	104	103	105	106	106	105	107	108
108	107	109	110	110	109	111	112	112	111	113	117
114	118	115	119	116	120	117	113	118	114	119	115

between two faces. The inputs are two sets of 3D facial feature points of two persons. If the two sets of data are from the same person, the points can be one-to-one registered with a very small registration error, since the 3D feature points are unique facial features on the face. If the points are from two different people, the error should be much larger due to either mismatches of the two sets or the differences in the 3D structures of the two faces even with correct feature matching. For most people, their face structures are stable but are different from each other, so if the 3D measurements are accurate enough, the difference between self-matching error (of the same person) and cross-matching error (of different persons) will be obvious. We then can use the error measurements as a similarity measures of two faces to recognize different people. A commonly used method in registering 3D points is the Iterative Closet Point (ICP) approach [3]. As we have known the identities of the 121 face feature points, their correspondences can be established between two face images. Let us use P and Q to represent the two sets of feature points:

$$P = \{p_1, p_2, p_3...p_n\}$$
$$Q = \{q_1, q_2, q_3...q_n\}$$
(1)

where $p_i(i = 1, 2...n), q_i(i = 1, 2...n)$ are the 3D feature points in the two datasets, respectively. Assume the rotation matrix is R and translation vector is T, between the two datasets, then the relation between the two groups of 3D points can be represented as:

$$Q = RP + T \tag{2}$$

Denote the centers of the two sets as p and q respectively, which are:

$$p = \frac{1}{N} \sum_{i=1}^{N} p_i, q = \frac{1}{N} \sum_{i=1}^{N} q_i \tag{3}$$

the two sets of data can be represented in coordinate systems with origins as their centers:

$$p'_i = p_i - p, q'_i = q_i - q \tag{4}$$

Then we can obtain the covariance matrix H as

$$H_{(m,n)} = \sum_{i=1}^{N} p'_{(i,m)} q'_{(i,n)} \tag{5}$$

Using SVD to decompose the covariance matrix into

$$[U, D, V] = SVD(H) \tag{6}$$

the R and T can be calculated as

$$\begin{aligned} R &= VU^T \\ T &= q - Rp \end{aligned} \tag{7}$$

In the ICP algorithm, the biggest problem is finding the right initial matching point pairs. Since in a general 3D registration problem, we have no idea of the point matching relationship, we can only assume the closest points between the two datasets as the right pairs. If the initial relative pose between the two datasets is large, the iterative processing will likely converge to a local minimal and make the registration fail. However, in our face registration case, we do not have this problem since we know exactly the indexes of the 3D feature points, as shown in Figure 1. Therefore we can simply assign the point pairs and do a one-step registration, which is both robust and time efficient. By applying the one-step ICP computing, we can get the rotation matrix and the translation vector between the two sets of the points in real-time.

4 3D Registration-Based Face Recognition

4.1 ICP-Based Approach: Registration for Recognition

In Section 2, we have described the procedures in both 3D face feature point extraction and 3D face registration. The DMF algorithm is able to find the face feature points even the face has a large rotation angle to the camera. The ICP has been typically used to register multiple-view 3D data of the same object, but

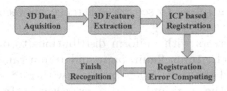

Fig. 3. Flow chart of the ICP-based face recognition

we employ it as a recognition method because the matching error is discriminative between self 3D feature matching and cross matching. The ICP-based face recognition approach has the following five steps (Figure 3):

Step 1. *3D Data Acquisition.* The 3D data is captured using and RGB-D sensor.

Step 2. *3D Feature Extraction.* Real-time face tracking is realized using the Kinect SDK and 3D facial feature points are extracted. The 3D pose (position and orientation) of the sensor to the observed face is also estimated.

Step 3. *ICP-based Registration.* The current 3D face (the probe) is compared with all the 3D faces in a database (the gallery) by using the one-step Iterative Closest Points (ICP) approach. By doing ICP, the relative pose between each pair of faces are also computed.

Step 4. *Registration Error Computing.* The registration errors of the prober face and the gallery faces are calculated as the average alignment error of the two datasets, indicating the uncertainty in face matches: the smaller the error, the more similar the two matched faces.

Step 5. *Face Recognition.* By picking up the gallery face that has the smallest registration error with the probe face, the probe face is recognized. The face recognition result can also be confirmed by the calculated relative pose between the two faces using ICP in Step 3, and the relative pose estimated from the pose estimation results in Step 2.

4.2   Robustness Analysis of the ICP-Based Approach

If the 3D face feature points are ideal data, i.e., they are accurate, the approach would be straightforward and accurate. But in reality, the 3D data have errors. In the next two subsections, we will analyze the tolerance of our approach to 3D measurement errors, and then to look into the accuracy of the Kinect sensor we use in our experiments. This will provide insights in the requirements of 3D sensors in applying in the proposed approach, and the capacity of the current Kinect sensor.

We have captured 3D facial feature points of eight people with front faces and compute every two peoples cross matching errors as well as the self matching error. We add noise to the original data at different accuracy levels. We also add rotations to the data to simulate the pose rotations; together with added errors, this simulates 3D face captures with various poses. The result would be shown in the following tables to see the difference between self matching and cross matching error.

We add random errors with uniform distributions to original data at four different accuracy levels: 1mm, 2mm, 5mm and 10mm random errors, with no rotation. Then we add the same levels of errors with rotation angles of 20, 30, and 40 degree along the x, y and z axes, respectively. In online recognition, the 3D measures could have different levels of errors depending on the sensor accuracy as well as the distances and view angles of faces. If the 3D data are captured with the same condition, for example, the same view angle, distance and resolution, high accuracy are possible to achieve whereas if the capture conditions changes, the error may increase. Different levels of measuring errors are simulated and various viewing cases are covered. We would like to note that in many practical applications the noise is not randomly distributed but follows some geometric deviation of the model polarizing the overall result in a specific direction. However we use this simplified error model as the first step to understand the tolerance of the proposed approach with noisy input.

The 3D matching errors given different levels of errors of 3D measures and view angles are summarized in Table 2 and Figure 4 .

Table 2. The average self matching error and cross matching error when applying different error and rotation

	Self ave	Sub1	Sub2	Sub3	Sub4	Sub5	Sub6	Sub7	Sub8
Err 1mm	0.0251	0.2576	0.2290	0.2117	0.3531	0.2412	0.2555	0.3488	0.2551
Err 2mm	0.0508	0.2623	0.2313	0.2072	0.3563	0.2369	0.2528	0.3462	0.2539
Err 5mm	0.1235	0.2688	0.2387	0.2128	0.3608	0.2402	0.2575	0.3466	0.2518
Err 10mm	0.2571	0.3458	0.3329	0.3059	0.4200	0.3094	0.3171	0.3884	0.3406
Err.1mm+R	0.0246	0.2578	0.2288	0.2115	0.3530	0.2409	0.2553	0.3490	0.2550
Err 2mm+R	0.0495	0.2624	0.2314	0.2112	0.3569	0.2391	0.2550	0.3425	0.2599
Err 5mm+R	0.1236	0.2861	0.2520	0.2267	0.3658	0.2505	0.2619	0.3481	0.2627
Err 10mm+R	0.2395	0.3628	0.3289	0.3039	0.4111	0.3296	0.3272	0.3900	0.3433

Table 2 shows a statistical summary with different levels of adding errors with and without rotation angles, of the comparison of self matching error and cross matching errors. The *Self ave* column shows the average of the 8 persons' self-matching error in each simulated case. Columns from Sub 1 to Sub 8 are the averages of cross-matching errors of each person to one of the eight persons. We also show the comparison in plots (Figure 4): In each of the eight cases, the first (blue) bar is the average self-matching error, and second (red) bar is the average of the smallest cross-matching error of 8 candidates. Note the recognition is achieved by choosing the smallest matching error from all the matches. The relative height shows the average matching errors. With accurate 3D measuring data (which is the case of the 1mm 3D measurement error), the discrimination using the matching error in recognition is obvious. However, when the 3D measurement error increases to 10 mm (i.e. 1 cm), even though we still see some the discrimination but the ratio between the self-matching error and cross-matching errors are not so obvious. But we observe that with an error level of 5 mm in 3D measurements, the ratio of the self-matching and cross-matching errors is still obvious, so this implies that our proposed approach can be effective with measuring data error of about 5mm. In Table 3 we list the matching results of both self matching and cross-matching of individual people with 5mm error.

Table 3. The self and cross matching error when applying error of 5mm

No.	Sub1	Sub2	Sub3	Sub4	Sub5	Sub6	Sub7	Sub8
Sub1	0.1191	0.1668	0.2638	0.4057	0.2083	0.2359	0.3978	0.2828
Sub2	0	0.1219	0.1789	0.3475	0.2306	0.2471	0.3261	0.2288
Sub3	0	0	0.1233	0.3276	0.1914	0.2272	0.2520	0.1936
Sub4	0	0	0	0.1331	0.2548	0.3222	0.5040	0.4598
Sub5	0	0	0	0	0.1244	0.2038	0.3713	0.2655
Sub6	0	0	0	0	0	0.1245	0.3507	0.2639
Sub7	0	0	0	0	0	0	0.1186	0.2488
Sub8	0	0	0	0	0	0	0	0.1254

Table 2 and Figure 4 also shows the matching results with or without rotation angles; with added rotation angles, the results have not changed much, so the approach is invariant to 3D pose rotation. This is due to the one-step ICP registration method that uses correct one-to-one face feature matching.

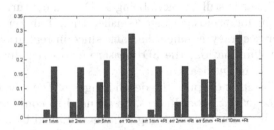

Fig. 4. The self and cross matching error under various error levels without rotations (the first four pairs) and with rotations (the last four pairs). In each pair the blue is for the self-matching error, and the red is for cross-matching error.

4.3   Kinect Calibration and Error Analysis

The RGB-D sensor we used to carry out the experiments is Kinect for Windows. It can generate depth images at a speed of 30fps with a resolution of 640x480. Since the 3D data accuracy affects the face recognition performance, we have evaluated the measurement accuracy of the device we used in our experiments. A large 66-inch LCD TV screen is used as a flat board to accomplish the evaluation. The Kinect is placed in front of the screen at 7 different positions, ranging from 60cm to 120cm, with an interval of 10cm, which is assumed the predefined working range for our system for face recognition. At each position, the 3D data of the LCD screen is obtained and is fitted with a plane. Then the distance of each measured point to the fitted plane is calculated and the standard deviation of them is used as a measure to evaluate the accuracy of the Kinect. The result is shown in Table 4.

Table 4. The accuracy evaluation of the Kinect

Nominal Distance (cm)	Average Distance (cm)	Standard Deviation of the Points to Plane Distance (cm)
120	119.41	0.89
110	109.25	0.83
100	99.10	0.68
90	88.74	0.59
80	77.56	0.42
70	67.61	0.40
60	57.99	0.38

From Table 4 we can see that the accuracy of the Kinect is better than 10 mm (i.e. 1 cm), which is from 4 mm to 9 mm. This is between the just discriminative level and the well discriminative level as we have observed in Section 4.2. This means that the Kinect is still be okay being a 3D data capturing device for the 3D face recognition for a closer range (smaller than 1 meter), but a RGB-D sensor with higher accuracy is much desirable since in real applications, due to human motion or illumination, the 3D measure errors usually are larger than the evaluation errors in an ideal case.

When using Kinect, it outputs the depth images of *Depth* values rather than point cloud data of (x, y, z) coordinates. So we need to convert the depth data into 3D data first by using the following formula obtained by a calibration procedure using targets of known distances:

$$\begin{cases} z = a_3 D \\ x = a_1(i - x_0)z \\ y = a_2(j - y_0)z \end{cases} \tag{8}$$

where D is the depth value at the position (i, j) in the output depth image. $(x_0, y_0) = (320, 240)$ is the center of the projection, $a_3 = 4.095$ and $a_1 = a_2 = 0.00175$ are the three scale parameters estimated by the calibration.

5   Online Testing and Error Analysis

From the experiments above, we know the ICP-based registration approach can be discriminative for face recognition with a relative high error tolerance, but the Kinect data error is large in real applications, in the order of 1-2cm (10 - 20 mm) at the distance of 100 cm (1 meter), a comfortable distance between two persons for a face recognition. However, we still implement the recognition system to see how well it works. To analyze the recognition error quantitatively, we design two experiments to see how distances and face angles affect the recognition results.

First we capture 3D data of 10 people standing in front of the Kinect sensor at a distance of 1 meter . Then in the online testing, we ask one person (the tester) to step into the Kinects field of view, and the tester will be captured with different distances to the Kinect and with various face angles. We save all the registration error data and plot them to show how the distances and face angles affect the recognition results.

In the first experiment, the tester stands in front of the sensor to be captured, then the tester moves back and forward smoothly, so the tester are captured at different distances. The results of matching errors are plotted in Figure 5. In this figure, the horizontal axis is the distance whereas the vertical axis is the error. The cross-matching errors of every person in the dataset are represented by a connected line segment grouping their matching error together with a specific color, and the black line is for the self-matching errors of the tester.

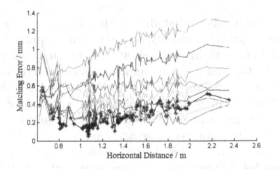

Fig. 5. Matching error plots against face distances

We can see from Figure 5, the trend of the curve is similar, and at the distance of about 1 meter, the smallest matching error provides the correct face recognition result. In most cases, within the distance range of 0.7 m to 1.4 m, the matching result for recognition is most likely to be correct, whereas in other distance ranges, the approach fail to recognize the right person.

After obtaining the relationship of distance and registration error, we also have designed the second experiment to test the angle influence on recognition results. This time we keep the tester stand at the same spot, 1m to the sensor,

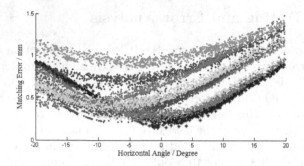

Fig. 6. Error distributions against face orientations

and ask the tester to change his facing orientation in both horizontal and vertical directions. The results are plotted in Figure 6.

In the angle error figure, the horizontal axis is the horizontal face orientation angle to front and the vertical axis is the matching error. Like Experiment 1, we use the same color to represent the cross-matching between the tester and every saved person and the black curve represent the testers self-matching. We can see that with the angle increasing the matching error is growing. In theory, the 3D data should be invariant to the pose changes, but in reality, the results show that the data captured at large angles suffer from 3D measuring errors and only the measurements in near frontal angles can indicates the right matching results.

The two experiments show that due to the 3D measurement errors of the Kinect sensor, the approach can only provide robust results when the person being viewed is within a certain distance range and with a viewing angle close to the ones saved in the face database. It cannot provide the right recognition result if the distance or angle is far from the ones when we save the dataset. However we still can use the sensor for a practical face recognition of a small pool of candidates, thanks to the real time performance of the sensor, such that we can wait the best view to be captured. Furthermore, if the error can controlled as indicated in our analysis in Section 3, the approach can tolerate large distance ranges and view angles. So the approach is promising with a better version sensor like Kinect 2 for us to implement a straightforward, efficient and robust 3D facial recognition system for the visually impaired.

6   Discussions: More Uses of 3D Face Data

In this section, we will discuss a number of other cases where 3D face data can be useful in real-time face modeling, which are all important in assisting visually impaired people in socially interacting with other people. In these cases the RGB images can also be utilized, and integrated with the pure 3D-based face recognition method proposed in the paper to improve the face recognition performance. These are our ongoing work for assisting the visually impaired people in recognizing and interacting with other people in their daily life.

6.1   2D View-Based Face Recognition

Even though the 3D face data captured by the current RGB-D sensor we used is not sufficiently accurate for 3D face recognition, the real-time estimations of 3D face poses/distances can be used to rectify and normalize the accompanying RGB images to obtain frontal faces. Or a database of faces of varying known view angles, as in Figure 7, can be bult. Then we can use the large body of 2D face recognition methods such as the eigenface approach [6], the deep face method [13], etc., to perform face recognition. The 2D face recogntition results can also be integrated with the 3D face recogntion results.

Fig. 7. Faces with varying angles   **Fig. 8.** Integrating multiple views

6.2   Multi-view Face Integration

Thanks to the real-time performance of the RGB-D sensor, we could capture a sequence of face images in real-time, and therefore build a fuller model of the 2D/3D face. We have noted the 3D face model is always complete with the 121 facial feature points, but some of the RGB views may not show the full face, such as the two side views in Figure 8. By using the real-time 3D face pose estimation and the ICP-based 3D face registration methods, an integrated view of multiple original face images can be generated. This representation can include additional features such as ears and back of the head, which are not included in the original 3D facial feature model.

6.3   Facial Expression Modeling

We can also use the real-time feature of the 3D facial features to model facial expressions, since varying views can be aligned, and all the 121 facial features can be identified and matched. Then we can create temporal trajectories of key facial features such as eyes, mouths, etc., for facial expression recognition. We could also generate various facial expressions using the 3D facial feature data and facial expression model. Figure 9 shows an interface of our current integrated demo system for 3D face tracking, recognition, multi-view integration and new view synthesis. In this figure, different face views and expressions are generated from the integrated model of multiple RGB-D face images. Even though the results are still preliminary, we believe they have very promising potentials for assisting the social interaction between visually impaired people with normal sighted people.

Fig. 9. System interface and expression synthesis

7   Conclusions

In this paper, we proposed a pure 3D feature data registration based approach to recognize people for visually impaired people. We analyze our error tolerance of our method against the current used Kinect sensors accuracy, and implement the approach with the Kinect RGB-D sensor. Although due to the Kinect measuring error the recognition is limited to distance and angle, we are confident that with sensor accuracy improvement like Kinect 2, the real-time 3D approach will have much better performance. The ongoing work includes the integration of both depth and RGB data for face recognition. Since we have obtained full-view face images of any view angles using the symmetric relations, we believe the integration of both the 3D geometric and RGB appearance features of the 121 face feature points and the integrated face images would improve the performance of our real-time face recognition system for assisting visually impaired people.

Acknowledgments. The authors would like to thank the US National Science Foundation (NSF) Emerging Frontiers in Research and Innovation Program for the support under award No. EFRI-1137172. The authors are also grateful to the anonymous reviewers of this paper for their valuable comments and suggestions.

References

1. Asthana, A., Marks, T.K., Jones, M.J., Tieu, K.H., Rohith, M.: Fully automatic pose-invariant face recognition via 3D pose normalization. In: 2011 IEEE International Conference on Computer Vision (ICCV), pp. 937–944. IEEE (2011)

2. Berretti, S., Del Bimbo, A., Pala, P.: 3D face recognition using isogeodesic stripes. IEEE Transactions on Pattern Analysis and Machine Intelligence 32(12), 2162–2177 (2010)
3. Besl, P.J., McKay, N.D.: Method for registration of 3-D shapes. In: Robotics-DL Tentative, pp. 586–606. International Society for Optics and Photonics (1992)
4. Cao, X., Wei, Y., Wen, F., Sun, J.: Face alignment by explicit shape regression. International Journal of Computer Vision 107(2), 177–190 (2014)
5. Huang, D., Zhang, G., Ardabilian, M., Wang, Y., Chen, L.: 3D face recognition using distinctiveness enhanced facial representations and local feature hybrid matching. In: 2010 Fourth IEEE International Conference on Biometrics: Theory Applications and Systems (BTAS), pp. 1–7. IEEE (2010)
6. Jafri, R., Arabnia, H.R.: A survey of face recognition techniques. JIPS 5(2), 41–68 (2009)
7. Li, B.Y., Mian, A.S., Liu, W., Krishna, A.: Using kinect for face recognition under varying poses, expressions, illumination and disguise. In: 2013 IEEE Workshop on Applications of Computer Vision (WACV), pp. 186–192. IEEE (2013)
8. Liu, C.: Gabor-based kernel pca with fractional power polynomial models for face recognition. IEEE Transactions on Pattern Analysis and Machine Intelligence 26(5), 572–581 (2004)
9. Pang, Y., Yuan, Y., Li, X.: Gabor-based region covariance matrices for face recognition. IEEE Transactions on Circuits and Systems for Video Technology 18(7), 989–993 (2008)
10. Passalis, G., Perakis, P., Theoharis, T., Kakadiaris, I.A.: Using facial symmetry to handle pose variations in real-world 3D face recognition. IEEE Transactions on Pattern Analysis and Machine Intelligence 33(10), 1938–1951 (2011)
11. Phillips, P.J., Flynn, P.J., Scruggs, T., Bowyer, K.W., Chang, J., Hoffman, K., Marques, J., Min, J., Worek, W.: Overview of the face recognition grand challenge. In: IEEE Computer Society Conference on Computer Vision and Pattern Recognition, CVPR 2005, vol. 1, pp. 947–954. IEEE (2005)
12. Queirolo, C.C., Silva, L., Bellon, O.R., Pamplona Segundo, M.: 3D face recognition using simulated annealing and the surface interpenetration measure. IEEE Transactions on Pattern Analysis and Machine Intelligence 32(2), 206–219 (2010)
13. Taigman, Y., Yang, M., Ranzato, M., Wolf, L.: Deepface: Closing the gap to human level performance in face verification. In: IEEE CVPR (2014)
14. Torr, P.H., Zisserman, A.: Mlesac: A new robust estimator with application to estimating image geometry. Computer Vision and Image Understanding 78(1), 138–156 (2000)
15. Wang, Y., Liu, J., Tang, X.: Robust 3D face recognition by local shape difference boosting. IEEE Transactions on Pattern Analysis and Machine Intelligence 32(10), 1858–1870 (2010)
16. Yang, H., Wang, Y.: A lbp-based face recognition method with hamming distance constraint. In: Fourth International Conference on Image and Graphics, ICIG 2007, pp. 645–649. IEEE (2007)
17. Zhang, Z.: Microsoft kinect sensor and its effect. IEEE MultiMedia 19(2), 4–10 (2012)
18. Zhu, X., Ramanan, D.: Face detection, pose estimation, and landmark localization in the wild. In: 2012 IEEE Conference on Computer Vision and Pattern Recognition (CVPR), pp. 2879–2886. IEEE (2012)

Learning Pain from Emotion: Transferred HoT Data Representation for Pain Intensity Estimation

Corneliu Florea$^{(\boxtimes)}$, Laura Florea, and Constantin Vertan

Image Processing and Analysis Laboratory, University "Politehnica" of Bucharest,
Bucharest, Romania
{corneliu.florea,laura.florea,constantin.vertan}@upb.ro

Abstract. Automatic monitoring for the assessment of pain can significantly improve the psychological comfort of patients. Recently introduced databases with expert annotation opened the way for pain intensity estimation from facial analysis. In this contribution, pivotal face elements are identified using the Histograms of Topographical features (HoT) which are a generalization of the topographical primal sketch. In order to improve the discrimination between different pain intensity values and respectively the generalization with respect to the monitored persons, we transfer data representation from the emotion oriented Cohn-Kanade database to the UNBC McMaster Shoulder Pain database.

Keywords: Histograms of Topographical features (HoT) · Spectral regression · Transfer learning · Pain intensity estimation

1 Introduction

When discussing the necessity of an automatic pain assessment system, several facts are to be considered: 1. Adult patients, typically, self-assess the pain intensity using a no-reference system, which leads to inconsistent properties across scale, reactivity to suggestion, efforts at impressing unit personnel etc. [10]. 2. Patients with difficulty in communication (e.g. newborns) cannot self report and assessment by specialized personnel is demanded. 3. Correct pain intensity assessment is a critical factor for psychological comfort in the periods spent waiting at emergency units [9]. A solution is an automatic appraisal of pain with choices of automatic response of medical personnel alert. Straightforward extensions envisage remote healthcare surveillance or impaired person assistance.

Although other means of investigation (e.g. bio-medical signals) were discussed [25], in the last period significant efforts have been made to identify reliable and valid facial indicators of pain [20], in an effort to develop non-invasive systems. One approach is to analyze the patients face using the Facial Action Coding Systems (FACS) [6], thus identifying action units (AUs) intensity and computing the pain score via the Prkachin - Solomon formula [21].

© Springer International Publishing Switzerland 2015
L. Agapito et al. (Eds.): ECCV 2014 Workshops, Part III, LNCS 8927, pp. 778–790, 2015.
DOI: 10.1007/978-3-319-16199-0_54

In this paper we propose a system for face analysis and, more precisely, for pain intensity estimation. To surmount the variations in the face images, we propose the use of the here–introduced Histogram of Topographical (HoT) features. The limitations of the pain annotated database are addressed within a clustering oriented transfer learning procedure that uses emotion portrait data to identify the internal representation of the face descriptors and augments the pain intensity estimation performance.

Further, in section 2 we give a short review of the face based pain intensity estimation systems. Section 3 contains the description of the used features, pointing out the difference with respect to the state of the art. The procedure for transfer learning is presented in section 5, followed by implementation details and results in section 6. The paper ends with discussions and conclusions.

2 Prior Art

The majority of the face–based pain estimation methods exploits the Action Unit (AU) face description previously used in emotion detection. A detailed review of the emotion detection methods is in the work of Zeng et al. [26].

The pain recognition from facial expressions was referred in the work of Littlewort et al. [17], who used a previously developed AU detector complemented by Gabor filters, AdaBoost and Support Vector Machines (SVM) to separate fake versus genuine cases of pain. Lucey et al. [20] used Active Appearance Models (AAM) to track and align the faces based on manually labelled key-frames and further fed them to a SVM for frame-level classification. A frame is labelled as "with pain" if any of the pain related action units found earlier by Prkachin [21] are present. Chen et al. [3] transferred information from other patients to the current patient, within the UNBC database, in order to enhance the pain classification accuracy over Local Binary Pattern (LBP) features and AAM landmarks provided by Lucey et al. [20].

Hammal and Kunz [11] measured the nasal wrinkles and used the Transferable Belief Model over subsets of the STOIC database in order to predict the pain for each frame. Kaltwang et al. [14] jointly used LBP, Discrete Cosine Transform (DCT) and AAM landmarks in order to estimate the pain intensity either via AU or directly at a sequence level processing. Werner et al. [25] fused data acquired from multiple sources and information from a head pose estimator to detect the triggering level and the maximum level of supportability of pain.

3 Histogram of Topographical Features

Global/Local Image Descriptors - State of the Art. Many types of local image descriptors are used across the plethora of computer vision applications [23]. Most of the solutions computed in the image support domain are approachable within the framework of the Taylor series expansion of the image function, namely with respect to the order of the derivative used.

Considering the zero-order coefficient of the Taylor series, i.e. the image values themselves, one of the most popular descriptors is the histogram of image values. Next, relying on the first derivative (i.e. the directional gradient), several histogram based descriptors such as HOG [4] or SIFT [18] gained popularity.

The second-order image derivative (i.e. the Hessian matrix) is stable with respect to image intensity and scale and was used in SIFT [18] and SURF [1] image key-points detectors. Deng et al. [5] used the dominant eigenvalue of the Hessian matrix to describe the regions in terms of principal curvature, while Frangi et al. [8] deployed a hard classification of the Hessian eigenvalues in each pixel (thus identifying the degree of local curviness) to describe tubular structures (e.g. blood vessels) in medical images.

Summarizing, we stress that all the mentioned state of the art systems rely on information gathered form a *single* Taylor coefficient of order zero, one or two in order to describe images globally, or locally.

The approximation of the image in terms of the first two Taylor series coefficients is the foundation of the topographical primal sketch introduced by Haralick [12], which was further used for face description by Wang and Jin [24]. In this approach, the description of the image is limited to a maximum number of 12 (or 16) classes which correspond to the basic topographical elements. Further extension lays in the work of Lee and Chen [16], who used the Hessian for locating key points and described their vicinity with the histogram of color values (order zero) and with the histogram of oriented gradients (order one).

We consider that all pixels from a region of interest carry important topographic information which can be gathered in orientation histograms or normalized magnitude histograms. In certain cases, only a combination of these may prove to be informative enough for a complete description of images.

Features. In a seminal work, Haralick et al.[12] introduced the so-called topographical primal sketch. The gray-scale image is considered as a function $I : \mathbb{R}^2 \to \mathbb{R}$. Given such a function, its approximation in any location (i, j) is done using the second-order Taylor series expansion:

$$I(i + \Delta_i, j + \Delta_j) \approx I(i,j) + \nabla I \cdot \langle \Delta_i, \Delta_j \rangle + \frac{1}{2} \begin{bmatrix} \Delta_i & \Delta_j \end{bmatrix} \mathcal{H}(i,j) \begin{bmatrix} \Delta_i \\ \Delta_j \end{bmatrix} \quad (1)$$

where ∇I is the two-dimensional gradient and $\mathcal{H}(i, j)$ is the Hessian matrix.

Eq. (1) states that a surface is composed by a continuous component and some local variation. A first order expansion uses only the ∇I term (the inclination amplitude) to detail the "local variation", while the second order expansion (i.e. the Hessian), $\mathcal{H}(i, j)$ complements with information about the curvature of the local surface. Based on the gradient and Hessian eigenvalues a region can be classified into several primal topographical features. This implies a hard classification and carries a limitation burden as it is not able to distinguish, for instance, between a deep pit or a shallow pit. We further propose a smoother and more adaptive feature set by considering the normalized local histograms extracted from Hessian eigenvalues and orientation and respectively gradient.

Derivation. Frangi et al. [8] used the concepts of linear scale space theory [7] to elegantly compute the image derivatives. Here, the image space is replaced by the scale space of an image $L(i, j, \sigma)$:

$$L(i, j, \sigma) = G(i, j, \sigma) \otimes I(i, j); \qquad (2)$$

where $G(i, j, \sigma)$ is a Gaussian kernel with variance σ^2. The differentiation is computed by a convolution with the derivative of the Gaussian kernel:

$$\frac{\partial}{\partial i} L(i, j, \sigma) = \sigma I(i, j) \cdot \frac{\partial}{\partial i} G(i, j, \sigma) \qquad (3)$$

In the scale space, the Hessian matrix $\mathcal{H}(i, j, \sigma)$ at location (i, j) and scale σ is defined as:

$$\mathcal{H}(i, j, \sigma) = \begin{pmatrix} L_{ii}(i, j, \sigma) & L_{ij}(i, j, \sigma) \\ L_{ji}(i, j, \sigma) & L_{jj}(i, j, \sigma) \end{pmatrix} \qquad (4)$$

where $L_{ii}(i, j, \sigma)$ is the convolution of the Gaussian second order derivative $\frac{\partial^2}{\partial i^2} G(i, j, \sigma)$ with the image I at location (i, j), and similarly for $L_{ij}(i, j, \sigma) = L_{ji}(i, j, \sigma)$ and $L_{jj}(i, j, \sigma)$. Further analysis requires the computation of the eigenvalues and eigenvectors of the Hessian matrix.

The decomposition of the Hessian in eigenvalue representation acquiesce the principal directions in which the local second order structure of the image can be decomposed. The second order hints to the surface curvature and, thus, to the direction of the largest/smallest bending. The two eigenvalues of the Hessian matrix $\mathcal{H}(i, j, \sigma)$ are $\lambda_1(i, j, \sigma) \leq \lambda_2(i, j, \sigma)$. The eigenvector corresponding to the largest eigenvalue is oriented in the direction with the largest local curvature; this direction of the principal curvature is denoted by $\theta_\lambda(i, j, \sigma)$.

Local Descriptors for Pain Description. In the remainder of the work, for each region of interest Ω, the following HoT descriptors will be used:

– Second order data (Hessian):
  • The histogram of hard voting of image surface curvature orientation. For each pixel in Ω, "1" is added to the orientation of the ridge/valley extracted by computing the angle of the first Hessian eigenvector, if $\lambda_2 > T_\lambda$.

$$H_1^H([\theta]) = \frac{1}{Z_1} \sum_{(i,j) \in \Omega} (\theta_\lambda(i, j) == [\theta]) \cdot (\lambda_2(i, j) > T_\lambda) \qquad (5)$$

  • The histogram of soft voting ridge orientation adds, instead of "1", the difference between the absolute values of the Hessian eigenvalues.

$$H_2^H([\theta]) = \frac{1}{Z_2} \sum_{(i,j) \in \Omega} (\theta_\lambda(i, j) == [\theta]) \cdot (\lambda_2(i, j) - \lambda_1(i, j)) \qquad (6)$$

The H_1^H and H_2^H histograms produce, each, a vector of length equal with the number of orientation bins (the preferred choice being 8) and describe the curvature strength in the image pixels.

- The range–histogram of the smallest eigenvalue, given a predefined range interval (e.g. $[0, M_{\lambda 2} = 30]$). The length of this histogram is typically constructed over $N_{bin} = 8$ bins.

$$H_3^H(k) = \frac{1}{Z_3} \sum_{(i,j) \in \Omega} \left(\lambda_2(i,j) \in \left[(k-1)\frac{M_{\lambda 2}}{N_{bin}}; \; k\frac{M_{\lambda 2}}{N_{bin}} \right] \right) \qquad (7)$$

- The range–histogram of the differences between the eigenvalues given a predefined differences range interval (e.g. $[0, M_{\lambda 12} = 50]$.

$$H_4^H(k) = \frac{1}{Z_4} \sum_{(i,j) \in \Omega} \left((\lambda_1(i,j) - \lambda_2(i,j)) \in \left[(k-1)\frac{M_{\lambda 12}}{N_{bin}}; \; k\frac{M_{\lambda 12}}{N_{bin}} \right] \right)$$

$$(8)$$

– First order data (gradient):
  - Histogram of orientation, H_1^G [4]; each pixel having a gradient larger than a threshold, T_G casts one vote;
  - Histogram of gradient magnitude, H_2^G. The magnitudes between 0 and a maximum value (100) are accumulated in 8 bins.

The constants $Z_1, \ldots, Z_4$ ensure that each histogram is normalized. Experimentally chosen values for the thresholds are: $T_\lambda = 0.1$ and $T_G = 5$.

4   Databases

Pain Database. We test the performance of the proposed system over the publicly available UNBC-McMaster Shoulder Pain Expression Archive Database [19], which contains face videos of patients suffering from shoulder pain as they perform motion tests of their arms. The movement is either voluntary, or the subject's arm is moved by the physiotherapist. Only one of the arms is affected by pain, but movements of the other arm are recorded as well to form a control set. The database contains 200 sequences of 25 subjects, totalling 48,398 frames.

The pain intensity is computed with the Prkachin-Solomon pain score [21], resulting in 16 discrete levels (0 to 15) obtained from the quantization of the elementary face AUs :

$$Pain = AU_4 + \max(AU_6, AU_7) + \max(AU_9, AU_{10}) + AU_{43} \qquad (9)$$

This score for the pain intensity is provided by the database creators, therefore acting as a reliable ground-truth for the pain intensity estimation. While in our work AUs are not computed separately for pain intensity estimation, yet eq. (9) explicitly confirms that databases build for AU recognition are relevant for pain intensity estimation.

Non Pain Database. Noting the limited number of persons available within the UNBC database, we extend the data used for learning with additional examples from a non-pain specific database, more precisely, the Cohn-Kanade database [15]. This contains 486 sequences from 97 persons and each sequence begins with a neutral expression and proceeds to a peak expression. The peak expression for each sequence is coded in the FACS system and is given an emotion label.

4.1   Landmark Localization and Areas of Interest

The UNBC-McMaster database is delivered with a set of 66 face landmarks extracted with an AAM tracker initialized in manual annotated key frames and applied on each image. In contrast, Cohn-Kanade was manually annotated[1].

We consider here that the specificity of the pain-related AUs is represented with only 22 landmarks from the given set of each of the databases. The reduced set is showed within figure 1 (a).

The UNBC landmarks are very accurate [19], yet their information is insufficient to provide robust pain estimation. In this sense, Kaltwang et al. [14] reported that using only points, for direct pain intensity estimation, a mean square error of 2.592 and a correlation coefficient of 0.363 is achieved.

Due to the specific nature of the AUs contributing to pain, and based on the 22 landmarks, we have selected 5 areas of interest, showed in figure 1 (a), as carrying potentially usefull data for pain intensity estimation.

Due to the variability of encountered head poses, we started by roughly normalizing the images: we ensured that the eyes were horizontal and the inter–ocular distance was always the same (i.e. 50). Out–of–plane rotation was not dealt with explicitly, but implicitly by the use of the histograms as features.

5   Transfer Learning

The target database of the proposed system, UNBC, is highly extensive as number of frames, but is also rather limited with respect to the number of persons (only 25) and inter-person similarity. To increase the robustness of the proposed algorithm, a new mechanism for transfer learning is proposed.

We have inspired our work from the "self-taught learning" paradigm [22]. A source database, described by the un-labelled data $\mathbf{x}_u^{(1)}; \mathbf{x}_u^{(2)}; \ldots; \mathbf{x}_u^{(k)} \in \mathbb{R}^n$ is used to learn the underlying data structure so to enhance the classification over the labelled data of the target database: $\left\{ (\mathbf{x}_l^{(1)}; y^{(1)}); (\mathbf{x}_l^{(2)}; y^{(2)}); \ldots; (\mathbf{x}_l^{(m)}; y^{(m)}) \right\}$, where $\mathbf{x}$ is the data and y are labels. According to [22], the data structure could be learned by solving the following optimization problem:

---

[1] The landmarks were made public by G. Lipori, "Manual annotations of facial fiducial points on the Cohn Kanade database", LAIV laboratory, University of Milan, web url: lipori.di.unimi.it/download/gt2.html.

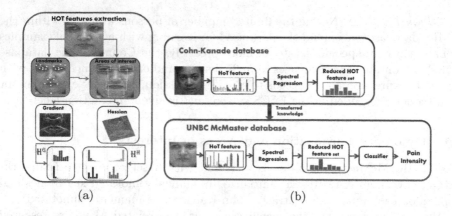

(a)   (b)

Fig. 1. (a) The features extraction procedure. (b) The transfer knowledge system. Data internal representation is computed on unlabelled data from Cohn-Kanade database to make use of the larger number of persons. The reduced data is fitted in order to predict pain intensity.

$$minimize_{\mathbf{b},a} \sum_i \left[\|\mathbf{x}_u^{(i)} - \sum_j a_j^{(i)} \mathbf{b}_j\|_2^2 + \beta\|\mathbf{a}^{(i)}\|_1 \right] ; \quad s.t. \|\mathbf{b}_j\|_2 \leq 1, \forall j \quad (10)$$

The minimization problem from eq. (10) may be interpreted as a generalization of the Principal Component Analysis concept[2] as it optimizes an overall representation, with the purpose of identifying the best minimum set of linear projections. Taking into account that the interest is in classification, we consider that: 1. the source database should be relevant to the classification task over the target database and 2. original features should form relevant clusters such that, 3. the optimization over the source database preserves local grouping. A modality to preserve the original data clustering is to compute the Locality Preserving Indexing with the similarity matrix $\mathbf{W}$:

$$W_{i,j} = \begin{cases} \frac{\mathbf{x}_i^T \mathbf{x}_j}{\|\mathbf{x}_i\|\|\mathbf{x}_j\|} & \text{if } \mathbf{x}_i \in N_p(\mathbf{x}_j) \vee \mathbf{x}_j \in N_p(\mathbf{x}_i) \\ 0 & otherwise \end{cases} \quad (11)$$

where $N_p(\mathbf{x}_i)$ contains the $p = 8$ closest neighbors of $\mathbf{x}_i$. The optimization ran over the similarity matrix, such that we solved the following regularized least squares problem over the unlabelled source database:

$$minimize_{\mathbf{B}=[\mathbf{b}_1 ... \mathbf{b}_t]} \sum_i \left(\left(\mathbf{b}_j^T \mathbf{x}_u^{(i)} - u_i^j \right)^2 + \alpha\|\mathbf{b}_j\|_2^2 \right) ; \quad i = 1, \ldots, k \quad (12)$$

---

[2] PCA is retrieved by solving $minimize_{\mathbf{b},a} \sum_i \|\mathbf{x}_u^{(i)} - \sum_j a_j^{(i)} \mathbf{b}_j\|_2^2$ s.t. $\|\mathbf{b}_j\|_2 = 1$ and $b_1, \ldots b_T$ - orthogonal.

where u_i^j is the j-th element of the eigenvector $\mathbf{u}_i$ of the symmetrical similarity matrix $\mathbf{W}$. This process of extracting the data representation (eq. (11) and (12)) is known as *spectral regression* and it was introduced by Cai et al. [2]. A similar transfer learning method was proposed by Jiang et al. [13], with two core differences: data similarity is computed using a hard assignment compared to the soft approach from eq. (11) and unsupervised clustering was performed on the target database.

Finally, the labelled new data is obtained by classification of the projected vectors $\mathbf{z}_l^{(i)}$, determined as:

$$\mathbf{z}_l^{(i)} = \mathbf{B}\mathbf{x}_l^{(i)}, \forall i = 1, \ldots m \tag{13}$$

where $\mathbf{B} = [\mathbf{b}_1 \ldots \mathbf{b}_t]$.

In our algorithm, the neutral image and respectively the images with the apex emotion from Cohn-Kanade database were the unlabelled data from the source database, while the UNBC McMaster was the target, labelled, database. The transfer learning process and the projection equation, (13), were applied independently on the Hessian based histograms, $[H_1^H, \ldots H_4^H]$ and, respectively, on the gradient based histograms $[H_1^G, H_2^G]$.

The overall proposed system, including the transfer learning procedure, is visually presented in figure 1 (b) and the method for HoT features extraction is presented in figure 1 (a).

6   Results

6.1   Testing and Training

The used training-testing scheme was the same as in the works of Lucey et al. [20] or Kaltwang et al. [14]: leave one person out cross-validation. At a time, data from 24 persons was used for training and 1 person was used for testing.

As the number of images with positive examples (with a specific AU or with Pain label) is much lower than the one containing negative data, for the actual training the two sets were made even; the negative examples used were randomly selected. To increase the robustness of the system, 3 classifiers were trained in parallel with independently drawn examples and the system output was taken as the average of the classifiers.

For the actual discrimination of the pain intensity, we used the same model as in the case of similar works, [20], [14]. We used two levels of classifiers (late fusion scheme): first, each category of features was input into a Support Vector Regressor (SVR) (with radial basis kernel function, cost 4 and $\Gamma = 2^{-5}$). Landmarks were not spectrally regressed (i.e were not re-represented with eq. (13)). The results were fused together within a second level SVR.

Given a new UNBC image and the relevant landmarks position, the query to determine the pain intensity for that image takes approximately 0.15 seconds using single thread Matlab implementation on an Intel Xeon at 3.3 GHz, with classification performed using LibSVM.

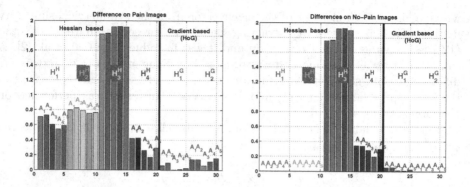

Fig. 2. Sum of absolute differences when comparing all images without pain and respectively with intense pain to a chosen no-pain reference image. Ideally, we aim for large values in the left plot and zeros in the right one. A_1 refers to the first area of interest (i.e. around the left eye), A_2 to the second one (around right eye), etc.

6.2 Experiments

First, we investigate the capabilities of the *HoT features* by considering the following *example*: we took the first frontal image without pain for each person and we considered its HoT features as reference; next, we computed the HoT features of all the images with a pain intensity higher than 5 and of all the images without pain for each person separately. We plotted the sum of absolute differences between the set considered as reference to the mentioned images with and without pain respectively. The results are presented in figure 2. Ideally, large values are aimed in the left plot and zeros in the right one. We noted that, for this particular example, the largest contribution in discriminating between pain and no-pain cases was due to Hessian based H_1^H and H_2^H histograms. Gradient based histograms lead to inconclusive differences in the case of intense pain, while H_3^H and H_4^H produced large values also for the no-pain case. The histogram type contribution on the entire database is presented in table 1.

Next, we evaluated the performance of the proposed approach for the task of continuous pain intensity estimation. The system performance was measured with the mean squared error ($\overline{\varepsilon^2}$) and with the Pearson correlation coefficient (ρ) between the predicted intensity and ground truth intensity.

The preferred implementation was by direct estimation of pain and the achieved values may be followed in table 2. Alternatively, one may consider as intermediate step the AU estimation, followed by pain prediction using equation (9); yet state of the art [14] showed that this method produced weaker results.

Feature contribution. In table 1 we reported the achieved relative accuracy increase (decrease) when only specific combinations of histogram types were used. Landmarks were not used for this experiment. As one can see, all the histograms contributed positively.

Table 1. Contribution of each of the histogram types used. We report the Pearson correlation coefficient when the mentioned type of histogram was removed. The reference is the right-most result (all histograms used). Thus, smaller is the value (i.e. larger is the decrease), higher is the contribution of the specific type of histogram.

Histogram removed	H_1^H	H_2^H	H_3^H	H_4^H	H_1^G	H_2^G	None - HoT
Correlation, ρ	0.330	0.368	0.355	0.358	0.350	0.224	0.41

Table 2. Accuracy of pain intensity estimation. We report the achieved results for various versions of features used and different methods of learning relevant features. Features used contained only Hessian based histograms (H_i^H - Hess), only gradient based histograms (H_i^G - Grad), both of them forming the so called Histogram of Topographical (HoT) features; the complete version (denoted by "All") contained landmarks and HoT. The relevant features were learned either by means of Spectral Regression (SR), or by PCA on the Cohn-Kanade database (CK) - via transfer learning or on the UNBC McMaster database. The Pain is estimated directly by the classifiers which were trained accordingly.

Learning	SR - CK				PCA-CK	SR-UNBC	PCA-UNBC	None	[14]
Feature	Hess	Grad	HoT	All	All	All	All	All	[14]
Measure	Mean Square Error ε^2								
Pain	3.76	4.67	3.35	**1.18**	1.17	1.26	1.16	1.21	*1.39*
Measure	Correlation, ρ								
Pain	0.25	0.34	0.41	0.55	0.40	0.53	0.49	0.53	*0.59*

The Influence of the Transfer Learning Method. In table 2, the overall performance, when various possibilities of transfer learning are considered, is also presented. The internal data representation was learned on the source database either by Spectral Regression (SR), or by PCA. Other considered alternatives were to perform no transfer at all, or to extract inner data representation using the data from the labelled UNBC database. The results showed that specifically relying on the similarity measure and taking into account a larger number of persons, the discrimination capability increased.

Comparison with state of art. While, as mentioned in section 2, there exist several methods that presented results on UNBC McMaster database, yet only Lucey et al. [20] and Kaltwang et al. [14] reported results on the entire database and with total separation between users when testing/trainig. However, as Lucey et al. [20] reported only binary detection results, and we are interested in intensity estimation, we will compare with the method proposed by Kaltwang et al.[14]. Their best reported performance is for the combination of DCT coefficients with histogram of LBP; the means square error was 1.386 while the correlation coefficient of 0.590. As one can see, while the correlation values are smaller, our mean square error is also smaller therefore reducing the chance for large false positives.

7   Discussion

In this paper we introduced the Histogram of Topographic features to describe faces. The addition of Hessian based terms allowed separation of various face movements and thus pain intensity levels. The robustness of the system was further enhanced by a new transfer learning method; it was inspired from the self taught learning paradigm and relied on preserving local similarity of the feature vectors as learned over a more consistent database in terms of persons, to ensure that relevant dimensions of the features are used in the subsequent classification process.

Regarding the addition of the actual features, while their individual contribution was rather small, they complemented each other well, as showed by the increase of the overall performance when all feature types were used.

The transfer learning from a database with larger number of persons increased the system robustness. More precisely, the solution that did not use the transfer procedure on some persons lead to better results, with the cost of providing smaller results on others that are more different from the remainder used for training. The transfer provided more consistent results overall, a fact which was proved by the entropy of the correlation coefficient increase from 9.01 to 9.26, enhancing the generalization with respect to person change.

The system provides indeed a number of failures. While the AU 43 (closing eyes), according to eq. (9), contributes to pain intensity, not all blinks are pain-related; the system, as in the case of [14], mistakenly associate all blinks with pain. These errors are rather small and can be easily filtered if the temporal sequence is considered. Other failures are in cases where the person's method of expressing pain is rather different from most of the others; for instance, the second person widely opens the eyes, instead of closing them, leading the system to produce false negatives. Other errors are related to the fact that the person is speaking during the test; false positives are, than, produced. At the end, we must point to the fact that an unexperienced user's opinion, if considering only individual, discontinuous, frames, produces the same kind of errors.

Acknowledgments. The work has been partially funded by the Sectoral Operational Programme Human Resources Development 2007-2013 of the Ministry of European Funds through the Financial Agreement POSDRU/159/1.5/S/134398.

References

1. Bay, H., Ess, A., Tuytelaars, T., Gool, L.V.: Speeded-up robust features (SURF). CVIU **110**(3), 346–359 (2008)
2. Cai, D., He, X., Han, J.: Spectral regression for efficient regularized subspace learning. In: ICCV, pp. 1–8 (2007)
3. Chen, J., Liu, X., Tu, P., Aragones, A.: Person-specific expression recognition with transfer learning. In: ICIP, pp. 2621–2624 (2012)

4. Dalal, N., Triggs, B.: Histograms of oriented gradients for human detection. In: CVPR, pp. 886–893 (2005)
5. Deng, H., Zhang, W., Mortensen, E., Dietterich, T., Shapiro, L.: Principal curvature-based region detector for object recognition. In: CVPR, pp. 2578–2585 (2007)
6. Ekman, P., Friesen, W., Hager, J.: Facial action coding system, 2nd edn. Research Information, Salt Lake City (2002)
7. Florack, L., Haar-Romeny, B.M., Koenderink, J., Viergever, M.: Scale and the differential structure of images. Imag. and Vis. Comp. **10**(6), 376–388 (1992)
8. Frangi, A.F., Niessen, W.J., Vincken, K.L., Viergever, M.A.: Multiscale vessel enhancement filtering. In: Wells, W.M., Colchester, A.C.F., Delp, S.L. (eds.) MICCAI 1998. LNCS, vol. 1496, pp. 130–137. Springer, Heidelberg (1998)
9. Gawande, A.: The Checklist Manifesto: How to Get Things Right. Metropolitan Books (2004)
10. Hadjistavropoulos, T., Craig, K.:Social influences and the communication of pain. In: Pain: Psychological Perspectives, pp. 87–112. Erlbaum, New York (2004)
11. Hammal, Z., Kunz, M.: Pain monitoring: A dynamic and context-sensitive system. Pat. Rec. **45**(4), 1265–1280 (1983)
12. Haralick, R., Watson, L., Laffey, T.: The topographic primal sketch. The Intl. J. of Robotics Research **2**(1), 50–71 (1983)
13. Jiang, W., Chung, F.: Transfer spectral clustering. In: Flach, P.A., De Bie, T., Cristianini, N. (eds.) ECML PKDD 2012, Part II. LNCS, vol. 7524, pp. 789–803. Springer, Heidelberg (2012)
14. Kaltwang, S., Rudovic, O., Pantic, M.: Continuous pain intensity estimation from facial expressions. In: Bebis, G., Boyle, R., Parvin, B., Koracin, D., Fowlkes, C., Wang, S., Choi, M.-H., Mantler, S., Schulze, J., Acevedo, D., Mueller, K., Papka, M. (eds.) ISVC 2012, Part II. LNCS, vol. 7432, pp. 368–377. Springer, Heidelberg (2012)
15. Kanade, T., Cohn, J.F., Tian, Y.: Comprehensive database for facial expression analysis. In: FG, pp. 46–53 (2000)
16. Lee, W.T., Chen, H.T.: Histogram-based interest point detectors. In: CVPR, pp. 1590–1596 (2009)
17. Littlewort, G., Bartlett, M., Lee, K.: Faces of pain: Automated measurement of spontaneous facial expressions of genuine and posed pain. In: ICMI, pp. 15–21 (2007)
18. Lowe, D.G.: Distinctive image features from scale-invariant keypoints. IJCV **60**(2), 91–110 (2004)
19. Lucey, P., Cohn, J., Prkachin, K., Solomon, P., Matthews, I.: Painful data: The UNBC McMaster shoulder pain expression archive database. In: FG, pp. 57–64 (2011)
20. Lucey, P., Cohn, J., Prkachin, K., Solomon, P., Chew, S., Matthews, I.: Painful monitoring: Automatic pain monitoring using the UNBC-McMaster shoulder pain expression archive database. Imag. and Vis. Comp. **30**, 197–205 (2012)
21. Prkachin, K., Solomon, P.: The structure, reliability and validity of pain expression: Evidence from patients with shoulder pain. Pain **139**, 267–274 (2008)
22. Raina, R., Battle, A., Lee, H., Packer, B., Ng, A.: Self-taught learning: Transfer learning from unlabeled data. In: ICML, pp. 759–766 (2007)
23. Tuytelaars, T., Mikolajczyk, K.: Local invariant feature detectors: A survey. Foundations and Trends in Computer Graphics and Vision **3**(3), 177–280 (2008)

24. Wang, J., Yin, L.: Static topographic modeling for facial expression recognition and analysis. CVIU **108**(1–2), 19–34 (2007)
25. Werner, P., Al-Hamadi, A., Niese, R., Walter, S., Gruss, S., Traue, H.: Towards pain monitoring: Facial expression, head pose, a new database, an automatic system and remaining challenges. In: BMVC (2013)
26. Zeng, Z., Pantic, M., Roisman, G., Huang, T.: A survey of affect recognition methods: Audio, visual, and spontaneous expressions. IEEE T. PAMI **31**(1), 39–58 (2009)

Neural Network Fusion of Color, Depth and Location for Object Instance Recognition on a Mobile Robot

Louis-Charles Caron[✉], David Filliat, and Alexander Gepperth

ENSTA ParisTech - INRIA FLOWERS team, École Nationale Supérieure des
Techniques Avancées, 828, Boulevard des Maréchaux, 91762 Palaiseau Cedex, France
louis-charles.caron@ensta-paristech.fr

Abstract. The development of mobile robots for domestic assistance
requires solving problems integrating ideas from different fields of
research like computer vision, robotic manipulation, localization and
mapping. Semantic mapping, that is, the enrichment a map with high-
level information like room and object identities, is an example of such a
complex robotic task. Solving this task requires taking into account hard
software and hardware constraints brought by the context of autonomous
mobile robots, where short processing times and low energy consumption
are mandatory. We present a light-weight scene segmentation and object
instance recognition algorithm using an RGB-D camera and demonstrate
it in a semantic mapping experiment. Our method uses a feed-forward
neural network to fuse texture, color and depth information. Running at
3 Hz on a single laptop computer, our algorithm achieves a recognition
rate of 97 % in a controlled environment, and 87 % in the adversarial conditions of a real robotic task. Our results demonstrate that state of the
art recognition rates on a database does not guarantee performance in
a real world experiment. We also show the benefit in these conditions of
fusing several recognition decisions and data from different sources. The
database we compiled for the purpose of this study is publicly available.

Keywords: Semantic mapping · Indoor scene understanding · Instance
recognition · Mobile robotics · RGB-D camera

1 Introduction

For robots to accomplish useful tasks, they must have the capacity to understand
their environment. Endowing robots with the ability to recognize previously seen
objects is one step to take them out of the labs into the real world. Our research
focuses on assistive robotics, where an autonomous robot shares the home of
its owner and helps him with his daily chores. In this context, it is important
for the robot to recognize each piece of furniture and commonplace objects in
their home. This is called object instance recognition, as opposed to object category recognition which aims at identifying an unknown object's class. The context of autonomous mobile robots brings limits on processing power and energy.

© Springer International Publishing Switzerland 2015
L. Agapito et al. (Eds.): ECCV 2014 Workshops, Part III, LNCS 8927, pp. 791–805, 2015.
DOI: 10.1007/978-3-319-16199-0_55

The lighter the algorithms, the more reactive the robot can be, and the longer it can operate without having to recharge. The algorithms described in this paper perform object instance recognition and were specifically designed to be light-weight.

Our recognition algorithm relies on data provided by an RGB-D camera (cameras providing color and depth information). These cameras have become omnipresent in robotics labs because they are affordable and give valuable information about a robot's surroundings. They are however noisy, giving imprecise distance measures, and some models can suffer from data synchronization issues, see figure 4. In our experiments, when the camera is moved quickly as happens when it is mounted on a mobile robot, a shifting occurs between the depth and color image. Images also tend to be plagued with motion blur. Common RGB-D cameras also perform very badly on reflective, transparent and dark surfaces. In real-life robotics experiments, data is further affected by partial views, occlusions, viewpoint variance and illumination changes. However, real robotic experiments allow for further processing to be done on top of single image recognition. For instance, performances can be improved by cumulating recognition scores when an object is seen several times.

The contribution of this paper is threefold. We describe an integrated RGB-D scene segmentation and object instance recognition algorithm for mobile robots. We provide the database we compiled to train the algorithm consisting of about 31200 RGB-D images of 52 common objects (600 per object). We propose a benchmark robotic experiment to evaluate the recognition of objects when they are seen in a different context as when they were learned. Our recognition method copes with all aforementioned problems and is light-weight enough to be run on an autonomous robot while it performs other tasks. In our experiment, a mobile robot performs a semantic mapping task in which it must map its environment and annotate the map with information about the objects it encountered. This experiment involves many challenges which are not encountered when using offline database for performance evaluation. As by the focus of our research, we concentrate on rather large objects lying on the ground because they can serve for navigation and indoor scene understanding. A semantic map obtained with our algorithms is shown in figure 1. This paper extends the work of [11], adding improved recognition capabilities, reliable scene segmentation and thorough analysis of performance. For the purposes of this article, our benchmarking efforts will focus on recognition. A particular interest of our investigations has been the evaluation of the fusion of color and depth information for improving recognition accuracy. The fusion is done with a feed-forward neural network.

This paper is structured as follows. The state of the art in the domains of point cloud segmentation and object recognition is presented in section 2. The database compiled for the purposes of our experiments and information about the physical implementation of our methods are detailed in section 3. Section 4 describes our segmentation and recognition algorithms. Our results are shown in section 5 and they are commented in section 6.

Fig. 1. The semantic map resulting from the online experiment

2 Related Work

Traditionally, the steps of segmentation and recognition are deemed to be essential, and this is indeed the approach we use in this article. However, segmentation-free recognition approaches have been demonstrated to be feasible and computationally efficient [14,31], though not directly in the field of robotics where recognition problems typically exhibit a very high number of object instances. Here, we will briefly review some related work for both segmentation and recognition while being aware that a field as vast as this one can only be touched lightly within the scope of this article.

2.1 Segmentation

Point cloud segmentation is a field of ongoing research, ignited by the recent advances in 3D sensing technology. The methods related here are roughly introduced in the order of the strength of the hypotheses they make on object shapes, from model-based methods to model-free ones.

Model-based techniques find prototypical shapes in an image and fit geometric models to estimate their exact pose. Such an approach is presented in [24]. Working even with partial views, they find the shape of objects by fitting geometric models like cylinders and planes. Missing data can be filled once the right shape model is found and fitted. After using a surface reconstruction technique, the final model of an object is a hybrid shape and surface description.

Depending on weaker shape hypotheses, [30] segments highly cluttered scenes by analysing point normals. First, raw depth images are spatially and temporally filtered and the point normals are computed. The scene is over-segmented into smoothly curved surfaces by thresholding the normals orientation difference of neighboring points. The segments are joined based on geometric considerations. The method is model-free, but biased to work when the scenes consist of simple box- or cylinder-shaped objects. An approach using multi-modal data is presented in [7], combining image and range data to form a hierarchy of segments and sub-segments. These segments are rated according to various "structure-ness" measures in order to retain the best object candidates. Using a similar rating concept, [15] detect multiple objects in Kinect Fusion maps of cluttered scenes. First, the scenes are over-segmented using a graph-based algorithm by [10]. Weights in the graph are computed from the dot-product of the normals of two points and the fact the they are part of a concave or convex surface. The segments are then rated for "objectness" based on different measures such as compactness and symmetry. These measures can further be used for object identification. Dubois et al. [8] propose an energy-based semantic segmentation method and compare it to a geometric method. Their method uses a Markov Random Field and relies on weak hypotheses of smoothness over appearance and labels. It is more generic than the geometric approach but its precision-recall fig-ures are not as good as those of the carefully tuned geometric method when used specifically in indoor scenarios.

Finman and Whelan [12] compute the difference between two Kintinuous maps of a given scene where in one of the maps, an object was either added or removed. Taking into account the angle of view when the scenes were shot, they can obtain the 3-D mesh of the object. Then, they train a segmentation algorithm to obtain the parameters to extract this object from the particular scene where it was seen. Once learned, the object-specific parameters can serve for object detection. This method requires to store a detailed representation of previously seen scenes to accomplish the differentiation.

2.2   3D Object Recognition

The recognition of objects from three-dimensional data is well studied in the literature, see [6,18] for survey. Many methods expect a segmented object can-didate which should be matched against templates in a database of previously registered objects. At the most fundamental level, proposed methods can be grouped into holistic and local approaches. Of the former, a prominent example is iterative closest point estimation (ICP) [34], which can match object candi-dates to templates if a rough alignment between the perceived object and at least one template exists. The Generalized Hough Transform [9] can be a useful tool, especially for simple objects like cylinders or spheres, see, e.g., [22]. Both these techniques restrict recognition to specific object types, known in advance.

If the object class is unknown, more general methods for the holistic descrip-tion of objects need to be used: an example is [32] where histograms of normal orientations between randomly chosen point pairs in the object candidate are computed, resulting in a holistic descriptor of object shape. Another notable holistic approach [20] attempts to find constant object signatures in views of object candidates that were taken from different directions. Histograms of pairs of points and normals describe very well the shape of objects and are used in the present work as one of the features fed to our learning algorithm.

Mueller et al. [19] use rules on segments size, position and alignment to merge segments into parts and parts into objects. They demonstrate good recognition results in a cluttered and disorganized scene, but with only 3 object classes.

Bo et al. [3] use unsupervised hierarchical matching pursuit to learn features suitable for object recognition. The method seems very powerful and gives excellent results for generalization over classes and instance recognition. The instance recognition evaluation is realized with objects seen from a different angle of view, but with no occlusions or change in the lighting conditions.

2.3 RGB-D Databases

Databases of RGB-D images of objects already exist. The RGB-D Object Dataset [16] and 2D3D dataset [5] are good examples. The RGB-D dataset is very similar to our own. It contains images of a large number of objects shot from different viewing angles and under controlled conditions. It additionally contains videos of scenes where a certain number of these objects can be found, under different lighting conditions and in challenging situations. The conditions in which the videos were taken however do not allow for our segmentation algorithm to be used. Also, it contains mainly small objects like bowls, bottles or cereal boxes whereas we focus on furniture like chairs and trash cans. Most of the existing methods which were tested on these database only provide performance for recognition of objects shot in controlled conditions and dismiss the video data.

2.4 Summary

For the purpose of this study, elaborate segmentation techniques are not beneficial. The most important points here being to work directly on the image provided by the RGB-D camera, and to preserve processing power. This eliminates methods working on Kinect Fusion or Kintinuous maps [12] and ones implying temporal filtering [30]. Many other techniques are simply too slow, need to be run on high-end power hungry computers or GPUs to run at a decent speed [2,3,16], or do not provide speed measures to compare with our method. Model-based segmentation techniques are too constraining for our setup. The methods measuring how much segments look like objects [15] does not aim at the detection of the kind objects that we use. Such techniques essentially prefer small, compact objects, over-segmenting human size complex objects like office chairs. It seems challenging to find measures that would work well for all everyday objects. Most techniques relying on smoothness and slowly changing curvature assumptions often are only demonstrated on very typical boxes and cylinders [17,30], which does not fit the context of our experiments. No one method focuses both on segmenting and recognizing objects in different contexts with algorithms simple enough to smoothly run on a mobile robot.

Our segmentation algorithm is very close to that of [1]. Whereas they operate in a table-top setting and rely on RANSAC to locate a plane supporting the objects in a scene, our RGB-D camera is at a known position with regard to the floor plane which can thus be identified geometrically. Once the main plane is removed, objects are found by using Euclidean clustering on the remaining points. As noted by the authors, some objects tend to be over-segmented by this procedure. To address thus issue, we project the points on the floor plane before proceeding with the clustering. [1] also follow the segmentation with an object recognition phase, but they focus on the improvement provided by the knowledge of the co-occurrence statistics of objects as learned from public databases.

3 Methodology

3.1 Database

We compiled a database of RGB-D images (and data from other robot sensors) of 52 objects, shot from 6 viewing angles. The data was collected by a robot as it autonomously moved back and forth in front of the objects. For each angle of view, 100 snapshots were taken from a distance varying between 1 and 4 meters. The objects lay on the floor, in open space. Because the robot moves during data acquisition, shifts sometimes occur between the color and the depth image and some shots are partial views of an object. As these conditions reflect the situation in which the algorithms will be tested, imperfect data were kept in the database. Only shots were the object does not appear were manually removed. The RGB-D images were processed by our segmentation algorithm, described in section 4.1, to produce appropriate data for the object recognition algorithm. This data is referred to as offline data. It was acquired with the room lights on and the windows blinds closed, during summer time. An example image of 19 objects of the database are shown in figure 2.

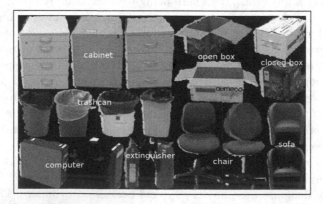

Fig. 2. Examples of cropped images of 19 objects from the offline database. Segmentation errors and sensor imperfections can be seen on the left hand side computer and the red office chair.

3.2 Robotic Experiment

A second, much smaller, database was also collected for testing purposes. We chose 22 objects from the offline database and laid them on the floor, apart from each other. The same robot that was used for building the database was, this time, manually controlled to wander around among the objects at the same time as it executed diverse tasks. These tasks are simultaneous localization and mapping, scene segmentation of the RGB-D image, object recognition of the segments, and display of the resulting semantic map (a map containing the objects found and their label). This experiment was conducted in the same room where the offline database was collected, but in a different part of the room, see figure 3. The lights were on, the window blinds open, and it was winter. This database contains a total of 135 segmented objects, with at least one occurrence of an object from 18 object instances from the offline database (due to some segmentation errors, some of the 22 selected objects are never seen). Figure 4 shows some examples of the difficulties encountered in this experiment.

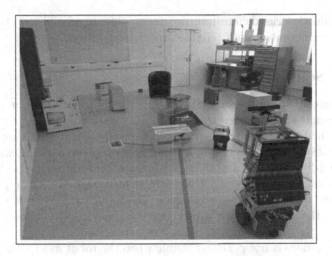

Fig. 3. The room in which the online experiment is conducted, with some of the objects from the offline database

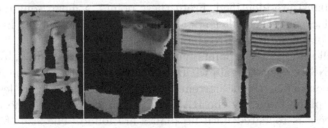

Fig. 4. Examples of difficult online object recognitions. The stool on the left hand side is blurry, and the binary mask generated from the depth segmentation is not aligned with its RGB image. The trash can in the center is occluded by an office chair. The left hand side gray air conditioner (from the online experiment) has a different color than that on the right hand side (from the database). All three objects are correctly recognized by our algorithm.

3.3   Implementation Details

We use a pioneer 3DX robot, with a Kinect RGB-D camera mounted at 1 meter from the ground and tilted slightly downward. The robot is equipped with an Hokuyo laser range finder. All software is run on a single Toshiba Tecra laptop computer (Intel Core i5, 3GB RAM) with Ubuntu 12.04. We use ROS Hydro Medusa [21] for integration, the Point Cloud Library 1.7 [25] for handling RGB-D images, OpenCV 2.4 [4] for computing color and SIFT features and PyBrain 0.3 [28] for the feed-forward neural network.

4   Algorithms

The algorithms described here improve from what is related in [11], providing more stable segmentation and reliable object recognition.

4.1   Scene Segmentation

For scene segmentation, we only use the depth information from the RGB-D camera. The image is converted to a PCL point cloud, points lying farther than 3 meters from the RGB-D camera are filtered out and point normals are computed. The segmentation procedure is split in 4 steps: floor plane removal, wall removal, clustering and filtering. As an offline calibration procedure, the position of the RGB-D camera with respect to the floor is estimated. For this purpose, we previously ran random sample consensus (RANSAC) [13] with a plane model while placing the robot in such a way that the floor covers at least half of the RGB-D image.

Since the camera is not perfectly stable when the robot moves, the floor plane position estimate must be refined for every acquired point cloud. Points lying either 20 cm above or below the estimated floor plane and having a normal perpendicular to this plane (dot-product of the point's and the floor plane's normal higher than 0.98) are identified. From these points, a mean square estimate of the current floor plane's coefficients is computed. All points lying higher than 5 cm over this plane are passed to the next processing steps.

In the wall removal step, points lying on the walls are removed. To find these points, a RANSAC is used again with the added constraint that the plane model must be perpendicular to the current floor plane. All point lying less the 5 cm away from a plane found by the RANSAC, are removed from the point cloud and the process is repeated until no planes are found. The size of each found plane is computed and if it is large enough, it is considered as a wall, otherwise it is reintegrated to the point cloud. The size threshold used in our experiments is 60 000 points.

The next step is to cluster the remaining points into groups that will be considered as objects. The clustering is done based on euclidean distance, grouping any point closer than 10 cm from each other. The clustering is a costly operation, because it has to identify each point's neighbors. The point cloud is passed through a voxel grid filter with 1 cm resolution beforehand to speed up the process. Additionally, the point cloud is projected to the ground floor. As explained in section 4.1, this is done to ensure that complex-shaped objects do not get under-segmented. The clustering is performed and groups containing more than 100 points are kept.

The last step is a filtering operation that removes groups of points that touch a border of the RGB-D image. To maintain the highest possible accuracy, each remaining cluster is "de-voxelized" (reconstructed from the original point cloud). The segmentation algorithm's outputs are the point cloud, rectangle-crop image and a pixel accurate binary mask of each object. As an example, figure 5 shows the segmentation of a part of the scene shown in figure 3.

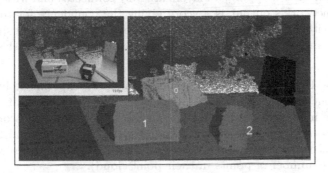

Fig. 5. Segmentation of a scene. The floor is red and the segmented objects are green. The black object on the right hand side is dismissed because it touches the border of the image.

4.2 Object Recognition

Features. The object recognition algorithm relies of features computed both on the object's point clouds and images. We use 3 different features: vocabulary of SIFT features, transformed RGB histograms [27] and point feature histograms [26].

A vocabulary of 100 SIFT features is computed by L2-clustering of the SIFT computed from the whole offline database. SIFT features computed from an object's image are matched to the vocabulary and a 100-bin histogram of word occurrence is built.

The transformed RGB histograms are normalized histograms computed on the entire masked image of an object. There are 16 bins for each RGB channel and each channel is separately normalized to zero mean and unit variance. This yields a 48-bin histogram.

The point feature histogram is computed by using 10 000 randomly selected pair of point from an object's point cloud. A point feature is computed for each pair with the distance measure normalized to the size of the object (the largest distance separating two points from the object's point cloud). The angular features and the distance are discretized to 5 levels and a 625-bin histogram is compiled.

The histograms can be used independently or concatenated to test the influence of each on performance.

Learning and Decision Making. The features computed on the training dataset serve as training data for a 3-layer feed-forward neural network. The size of the input layer depends on the features used, the hidden layer has 50 neurons and the output layer has 52, the number of objects in the database. The hidden layer has a sigmoid activation function and the output layer has a softmax activation. Neural network training is done using Rprop [23] training algorithm with early stopping, all layers are fully connected and with a bias unit. The neural network's output is a score giving the confidence for the unknown object to be either one of the 52 training instances. For offline and simple online tests, objects are given the label of the output neuron with highest score.

Map-Aware Recognition. The semantic mapping experiment brings many challenges, but has the advantage of allowing the robot to locate objects in space. In the map-aware online tests, an object's location and score is stored for accumulation. If another object is found within 30 cm of an already stored object, the recognition decision is based on the sum of their scores weighted by their size (the number of points in their point cloud).

4.3   Performance

The segmentation and object recognition algorithm runs at a rate of 3 Hz using the hardware and software setup described in section 3.3.

5   Results

Results are presented for different training and testing schemes. Four experiments were conducted: simple offline, one-angle-out offline, simple online and map-aware online recognition rates. All results are shown in table 1, comparing recognition rates obtained by using different combinations of features. All rates are computed by ignoring misclassifications induced by errors in the segmentation step.

The simple offline measure refers to the recognition rates obtained from training the neural network on 90% of the images from the database and testing on the remaining, using data from all 6 angles of view. In the one-angle-out offline experiment, the network was trained with angles of view 0°, 60°, 120°, 180° and 240° and tested on the 300° angle of view.

The online recognition rate relates to the performance of the recognition algorithm trained on the whole offline data and tested on the online data. As the online data was taken in a different situation than for the offline data, see figure 4, online recognition rates are much lower than offline recognition rates. For these tests, no data from the online database was used for training the learning algorithm. Of course, online performance measures dictated many of our high-level design choices, especially the choice of the color features. In the simple online test, each object encountered by the robot is identified individually. In the map-aware online test, the object's scores are cumulated before a decision is taken, as explained in section 4.2. Figure 6 shows the confusion of the map-aware online test when using all three features.

Table 1. Recognition rates for the simple offline, one-angle-out offline, simple online and map-aware online experiments using different combinations of features

Features			Simple offline	One-angle-out offline	Simple online	Map-aware online
SIFT	Color	Depth				
	✓		92%	72%	21%	11%
✓			79%	54%	33%	64%
✓	✓		92%	75%	39%	63%
		✓	94%	85%	**70%**	81%
✓		✓	96%	84%	62%	79%
	✓	✓	96%	**89%**	69%	**87%**
✓	✓	✓	**97%**	**89%**	**70%**	**87%**

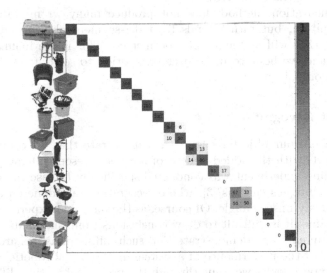

Fig. 6. Confusion matrix for the map-aware online robotic experiment using all three features. Please note that some objects present in the room do not appear in the confusion matrix because they were badly segmented.

6 Discussion

6.1 Scene Segmentation

The scene segmentation algorithm relies on the stability of the physical configuration of the robot. In an indoor laboratory or apartment setting, this assumption will hold most of the time, but it will fail in certain situations. Staircases, for example, cannot be handled with our method. Otherwise, parts of the RGB-D images belonging to the floor plane are accurately identified and removed. This is true even if the robot accelerates brusquely, bumps into obstacles and oscillates, as happens during operation.

The wall detection step of the segmentation is more problematic. If we only use RANSAC to detect these planes, the results are not reliable because aligned objects can form planes that will be labelled as walls and removed. For this reason, we use the RANSAC only to remove very big planes (with more than 60000 points), which really only appear when the robot faces a close-by wall. We had to rely on a more drastic measure to handle the smaller parts of walls: removing all points belonging to an object that touches a border of the RBG-D image (step 4 of the segmentation). This makes sure that walls and objects too big to entirely fit in a single image are not considered for object recognition. It has the drawback of also removing real objects that lie close to a wall. The RANSAC detection of wall, in a perfect setting, allowed us to detect these objects. We plan to address this issue be using information from the map to detect walls as a replacement for the RANSAC.

Our segmentation method does not produce many wrong candidates for object recognition, but rather tends to under-segment objects. Objects lying too close together will systematically be merged. This is the main problem of our method and we hope to use object recognition to solve it, as explained in the next section 6.3.

6.2 Object Recognition

The results from our object recognition demonstrate that we compare to the state of the art, with the added benefit of not being resource hungry. The one-angle-out offline experiment was conducted specifically to ease the comparison with other techniques such as [3], where recognitions are done on shots taken from a previously unseen angle. Of course, as the data and experiments are not exactly the same, it is difficult to draw conclusions from the numbers.

Our experiments also demonstrate that such offline measures are not a reliable indicator of the performance of a system during a real robotic experiment. During our experiments, we went through the process of testing different color features, inspired by the work of [27]. Even though the offline and online data we used in this paper do not differ much, the change was sufficient to make several of our attempts fail. In the end, the least discriminative color feature, also the one yielding the lowest performance on the offline experiments, gave the best results during the online tests. Still, the map-aware results show that these less discriminative features help in a real-life setting.

This is the last point we wanted to bring forward, that the fusion of texture, color, shape and position information is beneficial for recognition, especially in adversarial conditions. Table 1 shows that in our setting, it is the position fusion, done in the map-aware experiments, that is the most beneficial form of data fusion. Fusion of other modalities does not seem to ensure better results. We believe this is due to our database, in which almost every object can be distinguished based on shape only. Few objects, like the two sofas are identical but only differ in color. And in their case, we observed that the different colors affected the Kinect's depth sensor in a way that can be captured by the shape descriptor and allowed correct recognition.

6.3 Future Work

In this paper, the segmentation step is purely geometric, and cannot separate two objects if they touch each other. In the future, we are interested in exploring the use of recognition results to improve the precision of the scene segmentation. We will develop a hybrid bottom-up (geometric segmentation) and top-down (segmentation of recognized objects) to generate candidate objects and refine these segments further. As our segmentation algorithm has a tendency to provide under segmented objects and not many false candidates, we can hope to improve results in this way. Techniques based on the analysis of locally co-occurring visual words [29] or the Hough transform [33] seem promising.

Acknowledgments. The authors thank Jérôme Béchu for his help in the development of the visualization software. Louis-Charles Caron is funded by the Natural Sciences and Engineering Research Council of Canada (NSERC).

References

1. Ali, H., Shafait, F., Giannakidou, E., Vakali, A., Figueroa, N., Varvadoukas, T., Mavridis, N.: Contextual object category recognition for RGB-D scene labeling. Robotics and Autonomous Systems **62**(2), 241–256 (2014)
2. Anand, A., Koppula, H.S., Joachims, T., Saxena, A.: Contextually Guided Semantic Labeling and Search for Three-Dimensional Point Clouds. The International Journal of Robotics Research **32**(1), 19–34 (2013)
3. Bo, L., Ren, X., Fox, D.: Unsupervised feature learning for RGB-D based objectrecognition. In: Experimental Robotics, pp. 1–15 (2013)
4. Bradski, G., Kaehler, A.: Learning OpenCV: Computer vision with the OpenCV library. O'reilly (2008)
5. Browatzki, B., Fischer, J., Graf, B., Bulthoff, H.H., Wallraven, C.: Going into depth: Evaluating 2D and 3D cues for object classification on a new, large-scale object dataset. In: 2011 IEEE International Conference on Computer Vision Workshops (ICCV Workshops), pp. 1189–1195. IEEE (November 2011)
6. Campbell, R.J., Flynn, P.J.: A Survey Of Free-Form Object Representation and Recognition Techniques. Computer Vision and Image Understanding **81**(2), 166–210 (2001)

7. Collet, A., Srinivasa, S., Hebert, M.: Structure discovery in multi-modal data: A region-based approach. In: IEEE International Conference on Robotics and Automation (ICRA) (2011)

8. Dubois, M., Rozo, P.K., Gepperth, A., Gonzalez, F.A., Filliat, D.: A comparison of geometric and energy-based point cloud semantic segmentation methods. In: Proc. of the 6th European Conference on Mobile Robotics (ECMR) (2013)

9. Duda, R., Hart, P.: Use of the Hough transformation to detect lines and curves in pictures. Communications of the ACM **15**, 11–15 (1971, 1972)

10. Felzenszwalb, P.F., Huttenlocher, D.P.: Efficient Graph-Based Image Segmentation. International Journal of Computer Vision **59**(2), 167–181 (2004)

11. Filliat, D., Battesti, E., Bazeille, S., Duceux, G., Gepperth, A., Harrath, L., Jebari, I., Pereira, R., Tapus, A., Meyer, C., Ieng, S.H., Benosman, R., Cizeron, E., Mamanna, J.C., Pothier, B.: RGBD object recognition and visual texture classification for indoor semantic mapping. In: 4th Annual IEEE Conference on Technologies for Practical Robot Aplications (2011)

12. Finman, R., Whelan, T., Kaess, M., Leonard, J.J.: Toward lifelong object segmentation from change detection in dense RGB-D maps. In: 2013 European Conference on Mobile Robots (ECMR), pp. 178–185. IEEE (2013)

13. Fischler, M.A., Bolles, R.C.: Random sample consensus: A paradigm for model fitting with applications to image analysis and automated cartography. Communications of the ACM **24**(6), 381–395 (1981)

14. Gepperth, A.R.T.: Object detection and feature base learning with sparse convolutional neural networks. In: Schwenker, F., Marinai, S. (eds.) ANNPR 2006. LNCS (LNAI), vol. 4087, pp. 221–232. Springer, Heidelberg (2006)

15. Karpathy, A., Miller, S., Fei-Fei, L.: Object Discovery in 3D scenes via Shape Analysis. In: IEEE International Conference on Robotics and Automation (ICRA) (2013)

16. Lai, K., Bo, L., Ren, X., Fox, D.: A large-scale hierarchical multi-view RGB-D object dataset. In: IEEE International Conference on Robotics and Automation (ICRA), pp. 1817–1824. IEEE (May 2011)

17. Marton, Z.C., Balint-Benczedi, F., Mozos, O.M., Blodow, N., Kanezaki, A., Goron, L.C., Pangercic, D., Beetz, M.: Part-Based Geometric Categorization and Object Reconstruction in Cluttered Table-Top Scenes. Journal of Intelligent & Robotic Systems (7), January 2014

18. Mian, A.S., Bennamoun, M., Owens, R.A.: Automatic correspondence for 3D modeling: An extensive review. International Journal of Shape Modeling **11**(2) (2005)

19. Mueller, C.A., Pathak, K., Birk, A.: Object recognition in RGBD images of cluttered environments using graph-based categorization with unsupervised learning of shape parts. In: IEEE/RSJ International Conference on Intelligent Robots and Systems (IROS), pp. 2248–2255. IEEE (2013)

20. Park, I.K., Germann, M., Breitenstein, M.D., Pfister, H.: Fast and automatic object pose estimation for range images on the GPU. Machine Vision and Applications, 1–18 (2009)

21. Quigley, M., Conley, K., Gerkey, B., Faust, J., Foote, T., Leibs, J., Wheeler, R., Ng, A.Y.: Ros: An open-source robot operating system. In: ICRA Workshop on Open Source Software, vol. 3 (2009)

22. Rabbani, T., Heuvel, F.V.D.: Efficient hough transform for automatic detection of cylinders in point clouds. In: Proceedings of the 11th Annual Conference of the Advanced School for Computing and Imaging, vol. 3, pp. 60–65 (2004)

23. Reed, R.D., Marks, R.J.: Neural smithing: Supervised learning in feedforward artificial neural networks. Mit Press (1998)

24. Rusu, R.B., Blodow, N., Marton, Z.C., Beetz, M.: Close-range scene segmentation and reconstruction of 3D point cloud maps for mobile manipulation in domestic environments. In: IEEE/RSJ International Conference on Intelligent Robots and Systems (IROS), pp. 1–6. IEEE (2009)
25. Rusu, R.B., Cousins, S.: 3D is here: Point Cloud Library (PCL). In: IEEE International Conference on Robotics and Automation (ICRA), Shanghai, China, May 9–13 (2011)
26. Rusu, R., Blodow, N., Marton, Z., Beetz, M.: Aligning point cloud views using persistent feature histograms. In: IEEE/RSJ International Conference on Intelligent Robots and Systems (IROS), pp. 3384–3391. IEEE (September 2008)
27. van de Sande, K.E.A., Gevers, T., Snoek, C.G.M.: Evaluation of color descriptors for object and scene recognition. In: IEEE Conference on Computer Vision and Pattern Recognition (CVPR), vol. (1), pp. 1–8. IEEE (June 2008)
28. Schaul, T., Bayer, J., Wierstra, D., Sun, Y., Felder, M., Sehnke, F., Rückstieß, T., Schmidhuber, J.: Pybrain. The Journal of Machine Learning Research 11, 743–746 (2010)
29. Sivic, J., Russell, B.C., Efros, A.A., Zisserman, A., Freeman, W.T.: Discovering objects and their location in images. In: Tenth IEEE International Conference on Computer Vision, ICCV 2005, vol. 1, pp. 370–377. IEEE (2005)
30. Uckermann, A., Haschke, R., Ritter, H.: Real-time 3D segmentation of cluttered scenes for robot grasping. In: IEEE-RAS International Conference on Humanoid Robots (Humanoids 2012), pp. 198–203. IEEE (November 2012)
31. Viola, P.A., Jones, M.J., Snow, D.: Detecting pedestrians using patterns of motion and appearance. International Journal of Computer Vision 63(2), 153–161 (2005)
32. Wahl, F., Hillenbrand, U., Hirzinger, G.: Surflet-pair-relation histograms: A statistical 3D-shape representation for rapid classification. In: Proceedings of the Fourth International Conference on 3-D Digital Imaging and Modeling (3DIM) (2010)
33. Woodford, O.J., Pham, M.T., Maki, A., Perbet, F., Stenger, B.: Demisting the Hough Transform for 3D Shape Recognition and Registration. International Journal of Computer Vision 106(3), 332–341 (2013)
34. Zhang, Z.: Iterative point matching for registration of free-form curves and surfaces. International Journal of Computer Vision 7(3), 119–152 (1994)

An Experimental Analysis of Saliency Detection with Respect to Three Saliency Levels

Antonino Furnari[✉], Giovanni Maria Farinella, and Sebastiano Battiato

Department of Mathematics and Computer Science, University of Catania,
Catania, Italy
{furnari,gfarinella,battiato}@dmi.unict.it

Abstract. Saliency detection is a useful tool for video-based, real-time Computer Vision applications. It allows to select which locations of the scene are the most relevant and has been used in a number of related assistive technologies such as life-logging, memory augmentation and object detection for the visually impaired, as well as to study autism and the Parkinson's disease. Many works focusing on different aspects of saliency have been proposed in the literature, defining saliency in different ways depending on the task. In this paper we perform an experimental analysis focusing on three levels where saliency is defined in different ways, namely visual attention modelling, salient object detection and salient object segmentation. We review the main evaluation datasets specifying the level of saliency which they best describe. Through the experiments we show that the performances of the saliency algorithms depend on the level with respect to which they are evaluated and on the nature of the stimuli used for the benchmark. Moreover, we show that the eye fixation maps can be effectively used to perform salient object detection and segmentation, which suggests that pre-attentive bottom-up information can be still exploited to improve high level tasks such as salient object detection. Finally, we show that benchmarking a saliency detection algorithm with respect to a single dataset/saliency level, can lead to erroneous results and conclude that many datasets/saliency levels should be considered in the evaluations.

Keywords: Saliency detection · Visual attention modelling · Salient object detection · Salient object segmention · Saliency levels · Datasets for saliency evaluation

1 Introduction

During the last decades, we have observed the wide spread of affordable electronic devices capable of acquiring and processing images. This has virtually enabled a series of real-time Computer Vision applications which can rely on the large amount of data constantly gathered from the environment. Among these technologies, in particular, wearable devices provided with both computational power and a number of sensors (often including one or more cameras)

© Springer International Publishing Switzerland 2015
L. Agapito et al. (Eds.): ECCV 2014 Workshops, Part III, LNCS 8927, pp. 806–821, 2015.
DOI: 10.1007/978-3-319-16199-0_56

(a)   (b)   (c)   (d)

Fig. 1. Some sample images (a,c) and the related saliency maps (b,d)

are recently gaining more and more popularity. Since they involve egocentric vision, wearable devices are rapidly changing the way we used to intend Computer Vision and are paving the way to a number of applications tightly coupled with the user's everyday life experience. Some of these applications are related to assistive technologies such as egocentric video summarization for life-logging [1] and memory augmentation [2,3], object recognition for the visually-impaired [4], quality of life assessment and sensory substitution. Visual saliency has also been used for studying autism [5,6] and Parkinson's disease [7].

In order to be able to manage all this incoming information in real-time, a mechanism able to select the parts of the image which are the most relevant with respect to the selected task, is needed to speed up the computation. Several studies argue that such a mechanism is likely to be present in the human system of attention [8–11]. Specifically, the human attentional phenomenon is believed to happen in at least two stages: 1) pre attentive stage: is performed over the entire field-of-view (25 to 50 ms per item [9]) in order to select the locations which are sufficiently distinctive; 2) attentive stage: high level entities like objects are recognized through the combination of different features [12]. The first stage is an involuntary bottom-up process where the features automatically pop out according to their relationship with the surrounding (e.g., a red can on the grass is highly distinctive due to its red colour) [9,13]. The second stage is a volitional top down process in which many different factors, including the subject's expectations (often related to the subject's knowledge of the scene) and the given task (e.g., free-viewing vs. object-search), are involved [9,13]. These two stages of visual attention are usually modelled separately and tackled as different tasks, which gives rise to the distinction between bottom-up and top--down approaches. Methods aiming at exploiting both mechanisms fall into the class of integrated methods [14].

Building on this connection, Koch and Ullman [15] introduced the first biologically plausible model of attention, together with the concept of saliency map. A saliency map is a two dimensional topological map encoding the spatial locations conspicuousness, which can be directly exploited to select the most relevant regions of the scene (see Fig. 1 for some examples). An important result of such a connection is that weighting the importance of the acquired information using a biologically plausible model of attention allows a representation of the scene which is likely to be close to the human one. Many different approaches to visual saliency have been proposed through the last decades (see [13,14] for comprehensive reviews) and some of them have been used to model visual attention in complex systems [4]. Some saliency models are biologically plausible [16–18], some are purely computational [19,20], while others are mainly computational but still based on some biological cues [21–23].

Many different categorizations of the saliency detection methods are available in literature [13,14], but most of the authors agree on the fact that visual attention depends on the task [12–14]. Evidences of this task-dependency date back to the seminal works on eye movements and vision performed by Yarbus in the late 60s [24]. Considering that saliency detection is an useful instrument which can be integrated into a wide variety of real-time, video-based applications [1–7], we argue that attention should be paid to the level with respect to which saliency is considered. Specifically we distinguish three different levels of saliency, namely Visual Attention Modelling (VAM), Salient Object Detection (SOD) and Salient Object Segmentation (SOS). In this paper we show that algorithms designed to deal with a specific level have different performances on the other levels. This fact has to be taken into account during the testing phase of a saliency detection method. We also show that the datasets used for the evaluations should be chosen carefully in order to properly assess the algorithms' performances with respect to one or more of the selected levels. For the evaluations, we select 8 relevant saliency detection algorithms [16,19–23,25] which we divide into the three aforementioned categories: visual attention modelling, salient object detection and salient object segmentation. We assess the performances of each method against different public datasets provided with different kinds of ground truth (eye fixation maps for visual attention modelling, bounding boxes for salient object detection and pixel-wise object masks for salient object segmentation). We show the results in the form of ROC curves [13] and AUC values [13] and compare them yielding a discussion.

The contributions of our work are the following: we review the most relevant datasets which can be used to evaluate the performances of saliency detection algorithms with respect to the considered levels; we show through experimental evidences that the performances of saliency detection algorithms depend on the considered saliency level and on the nature of the stimuli; we show that eye fixation maps can be effectively used to perform salient object detection and segmentation, which suggests that bottom-up cues are important even for higher level tasks as object detection; finally we show that a given algorithm should be evaluated with respect to different datasets/saliency levels in order to obtain correct evaluations.

The remainder of the paper is organized as follows: in Section 2 we discuss the three saliency levels we focus on in this paper; in Section 3 we present some related works and review the most relevant datasets with respect to the considered saliency levels; Section 4 defines the experimental settings and the used evaluation scores; whereas in Section 5 the results are discussed. Finally Section 6 concludes the paper and gives insights about further research.

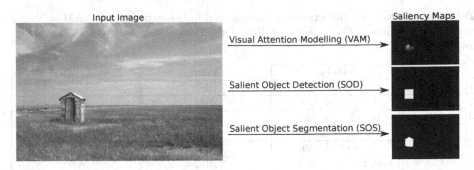

Fig. 2. An example of three different levels at which saliency should be considered in designing a saliency detection algorithm. The input image is shown on the left, whereas the "ideal" saliency maps related to the three different levels are shown on the right.

2   Saliency Levels

As already mentioned we focus on three saliency levels, which are closely related to three different tasks. In the following we describe each level discussing which stages of the attentional phenomenon are mainly involved. Fig. 2 shows some examples of saliency maps which should be computed by an algorithm with respect to different levels. Since we argue that the datasets used for the evaluation should be differentiated according to the task, we also mention which type of ground truth is best used to evaluate the algorithms' performances with respect to the considered levels.

- **Visual Attention Modelling (VAM)** refers to the ability of the saliency map to predict the human eye fixations. This level is related to the pre--attentive stage where the most distinctive spatial locations are selected in a bottom-up manner, basing on the relationship of their features with the surroundings. To benchmark this ability, the saliency maps are compared with eye fixation maps (see Fig. 3 (b) for some examples) which are acquired by tracking the eye movements of many subjects looking at the stimuli [13]. No special task, but free viewing is generally assigned to the subjects;
- **Salient Object Detection (SOD)** refers to the ability of the saliency map to detect the salient objects in the scene. Some cues from both the pre--attentive (e.g., local features distinctiveness) and the attentive (e.g., prior knowledge about the object features) stages are generally involved in this task. Algorithms aiming at salient object detection are best benchmarked against datasets provided with bounding boxes (see Fig. 3 (c) for some examples) annotating for each stimulus the position of the objects [26];
- **Salient Object Segmentation (SOS)** refers to ability of the saliency map to detect and segment the salient objects present in the scene. Also in this case, the integration of the bottom-up and top-down levels is generally involved. The performances of salient object segmentation algorithms are generally assessed using datasets containing pixel-wise object masks [21] (see Fig. 3 (c) for some examples).

Table 1. The saliency detection algorithms used in the experiments. VAM = Visual Attention Modelling, SOD = Salient Object Detection, SOS = Salient Object Segmentation.

	Acronym	Study	Year	Level
1	IT	Itti et al. [16]	1998	VAM
2	IS	Hou et al. [20]	2011	VAM
3	GB	Harel et al. [22]	2007	VAM
4	AWS	Garcia et al. [23]	2012	VAM
5	SR	Hou et al. [19]	2007	SOD
6	CA	Goferman et al. [25]	2012	SOD
7	FT	Achanta et al. [21]	2009	SOS
8	CB	Jiang et al. [27]	2011	SOS

3   Related Work

Many saliency detection algorithms are available in the literature. Here we consider some of the available methods and organize them into the three considered levels (see Section 2) taking into account what stated by the authors in the related publications or the type of the ground truth data used to assess the algorithm's performances. Moreover we review the most relevant datasets introduced in the literature, associating each dataset with one or more of the discussed levels.

3.1   Saliency Methods

We consider 8 algorithms for our analysis. We chose them according to their popularity ([16,19,21]), the variety of their approaches ([16] is biologically plausible, [19,20] are purely computational, [22] uses a probabilistic framework, [27] integrates object-level shape priors), and the performances exhibited in other benchmark papers ([22,23,25,27] have good performances in [28,29]).

The first computational model capable of producing saliency maps from input images was introduced in 1998 by Itti et al. [16]. Due to its biological plausibility, the model has been widely used as a benchmark for comparisons. In [22] Harel et al. introduce a saliency method which employs a graph-based probability model. Hou et al. have worked on spectral based approaches [19,20] exploring the connections between information redundancy and the spectral content of the input image. In [23], Garcia et al. present a visual saliency method which relies on a contextually adapted representation produced through adaptive whitening of colour and scale features. In [25], Goferman et al. introduce an approach which aims at detecting the image regions that represent the scene, building on four principles observed in the psychological literature. In [21], Achanta et al. present an approach based on the analysis of the frequency content of the image. Jiang et al. [27] concentrate on salient object segmentation considering both bottom-up cues and object-based shape priors. Table 1 summarizes the algorithms considered in this paper with the related saliency level for which they have been designed.

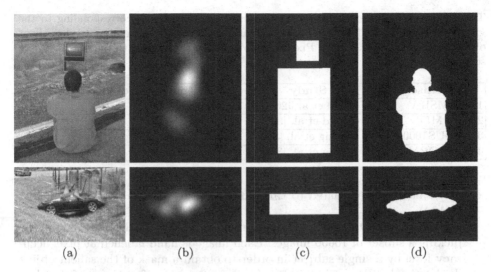

(a)   (b)   (c)   (d)

Fig. 3. Some examples of different types of Ground Truth. The stimuli (a), Eye Fixation Maps (b), Bounding Boxes annotations (c) and Pixel-Wise masks (d).

3.2   Datasets

In this subsection we review some of the most relevant datasets which have are used in the experiments. We analyse them with respect to different factors including the nature of the provided stimuli (e.g., natural images or images always containing a salient object), the nature of the ground truth and the way the ground truth is generated (e.g., how many labellers or subjects are employed). In particular we consider three types of ground truth:

- eye fixation maps, which are obtained using eye tracking data gathered from different subjects watching the stimuli;
- bounding boxes annotating the position of the salient objects of interest;
- pixel-wise masks of the salient objects depicted.

In Fig. 3 some examples of the different types of ground truth are provided. The considered datasets have been selected according to their popularity, the number of the stimuli, their diversity and the quality of the provided ground truth.

- **Microsoft Research ASIA Dataset (MSRA) [26]** is composed of 25000 images each containing a salient object of interest. The images are gathered from forums and image search engines. The dataset has been introduced for salient object detection and the ground truth consists in bounding boxes annotations. Each image is labelled by three users which are asked to draw a rectangle to specify a salient object. Considering the bounding boxes annotations, the dataset is related to the salient object detection level (SOD);
- **MIT Eye Fixations Dataset [30]** contains 1003 natural indoor and outdoor images which are viewed by 15 subjects in order to obtain eye fixations data. No particular instruction but free-viewing was given to the observers.

Table 2. The considered datasets. EF = Eye Fixation Maps (corresponding to the visual attention modelling level), BB = Bounding Boxes (corresponding to the salient object detection level), PW = Pixel Wise Masks (corresponding to the salient object segmentation level).

	Dataset	Study	Year	Images	Ground Truth	Level
1	MSRA	Liu et al. [26]	2011	10000	BB	SOD
2	MIT	Judd et al. [30]	2009	1003	EF	VAM
3	THUS10000	Cheng et al. [31]	2011	10000	PW	SOS
4	DUT-ORMON	Yang et al. [32]	2013	5168	All	All

The saliency level related to this dataset is the visual attention modelling (VAM);

- **THUS10000 Datasets [31]** is derived from the MSRA [26] dataset by picking a subset of 10000 images. Each image is hand labelled at pixel accuracy level by a single subject in order to obtain a mask of the salient object depicted. The dataset is suitable for assessing the performances of the algorithms with respect to the level of salient object segmentation (SOS);
- **DUT-ORMON Dataset [32]** contains 5168 high quality images. Three kinds of ground truth are provided with this dataset: 1) the pixel-wise masks of the salient objects, 2) the bounding boxes annotations of the salient objects and 3) the eye fixations data. The instructions given to the labellers are similar to the ones given for the other datasets. The ground truth is built employing 5 participants per image. Considering the three types of ground truth provided, the dataset is suitable for all the three considered saliency levels: visual attention modelling (VAM), salient object detection (SOD) and salient object segmentation (SOS);

Table 2 reports a summary of the considered datasets, providing information on the number of images, the type of the ground truth and the related levels.

3.3 Other Saliency Benchmark Works

At least two other saliency benchmark papers are related to the present work. In [28] the authors examine several salient object detection approaches with respect to different salient object detection and segmentation datasets. They also discuss the dataset properties, the evaluation measures to be used and the effects of the aggregation of different saliency methods. In [29] the same authors benchmark several fixation prediction algorithms against different eye fixations datasets, discussing which measures are best used for such evaluations.

Differently than the works in [28, 29], which analyse the two main levels of saliency (salient object detection and visual attention modelling) separately, in this paper we compare the results of the selected algorithms with respect to different types of ground truth. In addition, we take advantage of the DUT-ORMON dataset introduced in [32] which contains different types of ground truth for the same stimuli in order to yield more consistent and comparable evaluations of the saliency algorithms considered in this paper.

4   Experimental Settings

For the experiments we considered the 8 algorithms which have been presented in Section 3 and summarized in Table 1 and the 4 datasets which have been reviewed in Section 3.2 and reported in Table 2. In order to produce saliency maps for the evaluations, we used the original code provided by the authors, which is publicly available. For sake of fairness we don't tune the parameters of the algorithms, hence using the standard ones which are provided by the authors.

The first dataset we consider is the DUT-ORMON [32] dataset. It is useful to compare the performances of algorithms with respect to the three different saliency levels, since it contains all the three types of ground truth for the same stimuli. The second one is the MIT [30] eye fixations dataset, which we use to benchmark the algorithms with respect to the level of visual attention modelling. The third one is the MSRA [26] dataset, which has been introduced to evaluate salient object detection algorithms and contains bounding boxes annotations for each image. The fourth dataset is the THUS10000 [31] dataset which contains 10000 images taken from the MSRA dataset but provides pixel-level ground truth and is suitable to evaluate salient object segmentation algorithms. Since the THUS10000 dataset is derived from MSRA by picking a subset of the provided stimuli, for comparison sake, when benchmarking against the MSRA dataset, we consider that subset of stimuli and refer to this modified dataset as MSRA10000.

We perform three comparative experiments aimed at analysing the performances of the saliency detection algorithms at the different levels. In particular we perform tests to assess: 1) the performances of the algorithms with respect to the same stimuli but different levels, 2) the performances of the algorithms with respect to the same level, but different stimuli, and 3) to what degree there's a connection among the different levels. The final aim of this work is to show that the different levels of saliency should be taken into account when evaluating the algorithms. Consequently we want to show that considering a single saliency level or a single dataset (which is a common practice in the literature) can lead to erroneous evaluations. For each experiment we provide ROC curves and AUC scores as described in [13,14,20].

Experiment 1: in the first experiment we assess the performances of the considered algorithms with respect to the DUT-ORMON [32] dataset and its different types of ground truth. The evaluations produced by this experiments are comparable with respect to the different levels, since the stimuli are the same (i.e., the saliency maps are computed only once and benchmarked against the different types of ground truth). Nevertheless we expect the relative ranking among the algorithms could change; some algorithms should perform better on some levels than on some others;

Experiment 2: in the second experiment we evaluate the performances of the algorithms with respect to the MIT eye fixations, THUS10000 and MSRA10000 datasets. We compare the results with respect to the performances of the algorithms on the corresponding levels of the DUT-ORMON dataset. Even if the considered saliency levels are the same, we expect some different results with respect to Experiment 1, since the nature of the stimuli is different in some cases;

Experiment 3: in the third experiment, we consider the eye fixations maps included in the DUT-ORMON dataset as saliency maps and evaluate their performances on both salient object detection and segmentation on the same dataset. Since the eye fixation maps are likely to be sparse, in order to be fair with respect to the other saliency detection algorithms, we first convolve each eye fixation map with a Gaussian kernel with variance $\sigma = 15$ $pixels$. We compare the results with the performances of the other algorithms on the same dataset. This experiment tells if there is a strong connection among the different levels (e.g., if an algorithm designed for eye fixations can detect salient objects) or if the two tasks should be considered independent (e.g., if an algorithm designed for eye fixations cannot be used to detect salient objects).

5   Results and Discussion

The ROC curves related to the three experiments proposed in Section 4 are reported in Fig. 4. For each diagram, the AUC values related to the ROC curves are reported in parenthesis in the legend which is sorted in descending order to assess the algorithms' ranking. The ROC curves line styles are related to the algorithms' saliency levels: solid line for VAM, dash-dot line for SOD, dashed line for SOS. The first column of Fig. 4 contains the ROC curves related to the performances of the algorithms on the DUT-ORMON dataset with respect to different levels of saliency: visual attention modelling (a), salient object detection (c) and salient object segmentation (e). In the diagrams (c) and (d), the performances of the considered algorithms are also compared to the performances of the eye fixation maps when they are used to perform object detection and segmentation. These additional ROC curves are referred to in the legend as the "EF" series. The second column of Fig. 4 reports the ROC curves for the experiments performed on the other datasets.

In Fig. 5 a comparative diagram of the results is reported. The diagram visualizes the AUC values for each algorithm in all the evaluation settings (referred to in the form "Dataset - Level"). The line styles refer to the algorithms' saliency levels as in Fig. 4. The overall performances of the considered algorithms on all the experimental settings are measured computing the normalized area under the comparative curves through numerical integration. Those values are reported in parentheses in the legend which is sorted in descending order.

Fig. 6 shows some sample saliency maps computed on images taken from the fourth considered datasets for visual assessment. For each image the saliency maps computed by all the considered algorithms and the related ground truth data are reported.

5.1   Discussion on Experiment 1

In Fig. 5, looking at the transitions between the "DUT-VAM" configuration, the "DUT-SOD" configuration and the "DUT-SOS" configuration, it can be

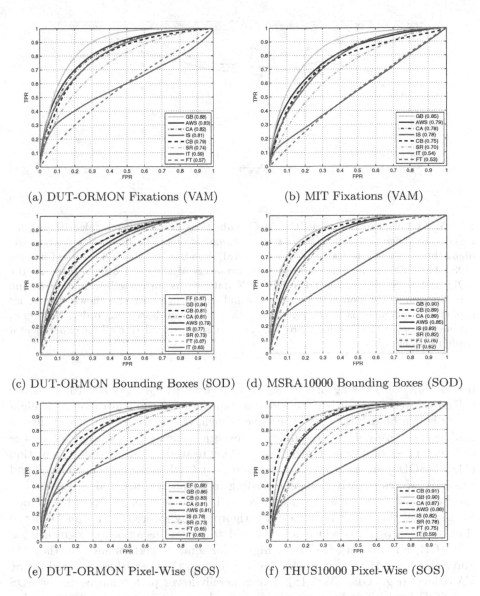

(a) DUT-ORMON Fixations (VAM)   (b) MIT Fixations (VAM)

(c) DUT-ORMON Bounding Boxes (SOD) (d) MSRA10000 Bounding Boxes (SOD)

(e) DUT-ORMON Pixel-Wise (SOS)   (f) THUS10000 Pixel-Wise (SOS)

Fig. 4. The ROC curves for the performed experiments. The ROC line styles refer to the algorithms' saliency levels: solid line for VAM, dash-dot line for SOD, dashed line for SOS. The corresponding AUC scores are reported in parenthesis in the legends. Each legend is sorted by AUC score in descending order to highlight the ranking of the algorithms in the considered settings. The first column (a, c, e) reports the performances of the same algorithms with respect to different saliency levels on the DUT-ORMON dataset. Each row (a-b, c-d, e-f) compares the performances of the same algorithms with respect to the same level but different datasets. The effects of performing salient object detection and segmentation using the ground truth fixation maps on the DUT-ORMON dataset, are reported in (c) and (e) and refer to series "EF".

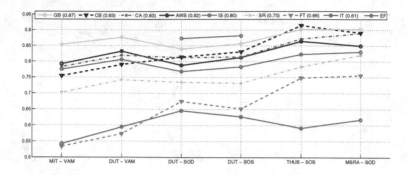

Fig. 5. The diagram visualizes the AUC evaluations of the different algorithms whit respect to different dataset/ground truth combinations. The line styles refer to the algorithms' saliency levels: solid line for VAM, dash-dot line for SOD, dashed line for SOS. The "EF" series represents the performances of the eye fixations maps on the SOD and SOS level in the DUT-ORMON dataset. As an overall evaluation among the different evaluation settings, the normalized areas under the shown curves are reported in parenthesis in the legend, which is sorted in descending order. No overall evaluation of the "EF" series is provided since it is not extended to all the experimental configurations.

noted that the ranking of the algorithms generally changes according to the saliency level. Since in the considered experimental configurations each algorithm is benchmarked against the same stimuli, we can assert that the change of ranking is entirely due to the different levels at which saliency is defined by the different types of ground truth. The ranking related to salient object detection ("DUT-SOD") and salient object segmentation ("DUT-SOS") is unchanged and the AUC scores slightly change according to the algorithms. This suggests that the SOD and SOS levels are closely related. A further analysis could be aimed at assessing this intuition in a more rigorous way. Moreover, it can be noted that some algorithms which are tailored to object detection or segmentation (e.g., CB, FT, SR and CA) have higher (or similar) performances in the SOS and SOD levels than in the VAM level. Whereas, the algorithms tailored to the VAM level (e.g., GB, AWS, IS) have generally lower performances on the SOS and SOD levels. The IT algorithm is the only exception to this scheme, giving better results on the SOD and SOS levels even if tailored to the VAM level. The GB algorithm has the best performances with respect to all the considered saliency levels on the DUT-ORMON dataset, which means that it is capable at the same time of predicting the eye fixations and performing salient object detection and segmentation. Some examples are available in Fig. 6 for visual assessment.

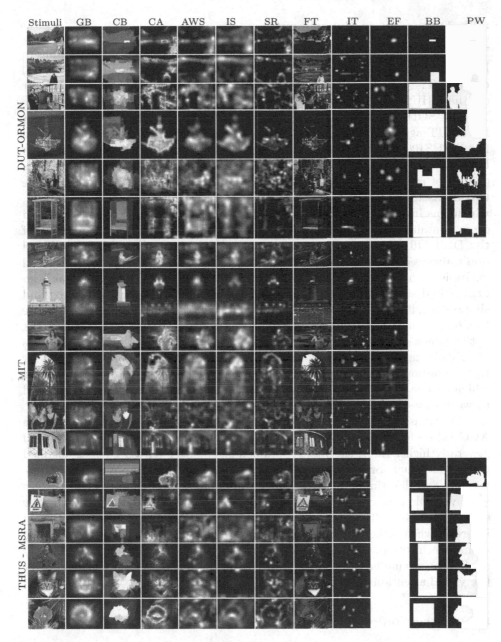

Fig. 6. Some sample saliency maps computed by the considered algorithms. Six images (first column) with the corresponding ground truths (last three columns) are reported for each dataset. The THUS and MSRA datasets are grouped since the stimuli are the same. EF = Eye Fixations maps, BB = Bounding Boxes annotations, PW = Pixel-Wise masks.

5.2   Discussion on Experiment 2

The transition between the "DUT-SOS" and the "THUS-SOS" configurations in Fig. 5, shows that most of the algorithms perform much better on the THUS1000 dataset. The only exception is the IT algorithm whose performances are lower on the THUS0000 dataset. The transition between the "DUT-SOD" and the "MSRA-SOD" datasets shows a general increase in the performances except for the IT aglorithm. Moreover the CB algorithm performs better than GB on the THUS10000 dataset, even if it performed worse with respect to the same level on the DUT-ORMON dataset (see Experiment 1). In our opinion, this change of ranking is due to the different nature of the stimuli contained in the two datasets. The THUS dataset has been derived from the MSRA dataset, which was introduced for the task of salient object segmentation, so the stimuli often contain a clearly distinguishable salient object of interest. The stimuli of the DUT-ORMON dataset are more general (and hence more "difficult") and don't always contain a clearly distinguishable salient object of interest. A visual example of this statement is provided in Fig. 7. Since the CB algorithm has been explicitly designed for salient object segmentation and makes use of context and shape prior, it is likely to work better when this information can be exploited (see Fig. 6 for visual assessment). This leads to the conclusion that, if the tackled task is the salient object detection in very controlled conditions (where the object is clearly distinguishable from its context), the THUS dataset is probably good for the evaluations, while the DUT-ORMON dataset is a more challenging dataset which can be used to assess the performances of an algorithm which is designed to work in less constrained settings.

The transition between the "MIT-VAM" and "DUT-VAM" shows that the AUC values for the eye fixations in the DUT-ORMON are consistent with (and generally higher than) the values obtained on the MIT dataset. This is justified by the fact that for both datasets the task assigned to the observer was free-viewing and the stimuli included in the two datasets are similar (natural images with variable contexts). Moreover, this finding emphasizes that predicting the eye fixations is a "less ambiguous" task than predicting the salient objects of interest, where other factors like the subject knowledge or the context of the scene are involved. Moreover the increase of the results in the "DUT-VAM" configurations underlines that the MIT dataset is generally more challenging for the visual attention modelling level.

5.3   Discussion on Experiment 3

The series "EF" in Fig. 5 shows the performances of the eye fixation maps contained in the DUT-ORMON dataset when used to perform salient object detection and salient object segmentation on the same dataset. It can be observed that the eye fixations are suitable for detecting and segmenting the salient objects of interest, performing better than all the considered algorithms. The performances of the eye fixation can be considered as an upperbound to the performances of algorithms designed for predicting the eye fixations when applied to the other

(a) DUT-ORMON   (b) THUS10000

Fig. 7. Some images from the DUT-ORMON dataset (a) and from the THUS10000 (b) dataset. As can be noted, the THUS10000 images always contain a clearly distinguishable salient object of interest, while most of the images from the DUT-ORMON dataset contain natural images where the salient objects are not always easily distinguishable.

levels of saliency. This leads us to the conclusion that there is more room for improving the results of the salient object detection/segmentation algorithms still relying on low level bottom-up cues. However it should be considered that the DUT-ORMON dataset contains natural images, where the salient objects are not always clearly distinguishable or present, and so they are more likely to correspond with the eye fixations. It would be certainly interesting to assess the performances of the eye fixations on a dataset conceived for the object detection task like the MSRA dataset, but, considering that this data is not available, this is out of the scope of the present work.

6   Conclusion

We have studied saliency at three different levels, namely visual attention modelling, salient object detection and salient object segmentation. We have shown through experimental evidence that the performances of the algorithms generally depend on the saliency level with respect to which they are benchmarked. Comparing the performances of the algorithms with respect to datasets provided with different stimuli but same type of ground truth, we have assessed that the performances also depend on the nature of the stimuli. In particular, a closer look to Fig. 5 would reveal that using a single dataset can lead to erroneous evaluations (e.g., THUS-SOS vs DUT-SOS/DUT-SOD). We have noted that visual attention modelling is a "less ambiguous task", since the evaluations agree for different eye fixation datasets. We have shown that there is a strong relationship between visual attention modelling and salient object detection and segmentation, since the eye fixation maps can be successfully used for such tasks. Considering that the eye fixation maps yield the best results with respect to the considered algorithms, we argue that there is more room for improving object detection and segmentation still relying on bottom-up pre-attentive information. Moreover, we have reviewed the main datasets available in the literature, associating them to the analysed saliency levels according to the provided ground truths. Future works will be devoted to extend our analysis to a larger number of saliency detection algorithms and datasets. We will study how saliency algorithms perform with respect to datasets composed of search arrays and psychological patterns [19]. Moreover, the level of visual attention modelling will be studied in both the dynamic and the static domain as suggested in [33].

References

1. Ghosh, J., Grauman, K.: Discovering important people and objects for egocentric video summarization. In: IEEE Conference on Computer Vision and Pattern Recognition (CVPR), pp. 1346–1353 (2012)
2. Hodges, S., Berry, E., Wood, K.: SenseCam: a wearable camera that stimulates and rehabilitates autobiographical memory. Memory **19**(7), 685–96 (2011)
3. Lu, Z., Grauman, K.: Story-driven summarization for egocentric video. In: IEEE Conference on Computer Vision and Pattern Recognition (CVPR), pp. 2714–2721 (2013)
4. Thakoor, K.A., Marat, S., Nasiatka, P.J., McIntosh, B.P., Sahin, F.E., Tanguay, A.R., Weiland, J.D., Itti, L.: Attention biased speeded up robust features (AB-SURF): A neurally-inspired object recognition algorithm for a wearable aid for the visually-impaired. In: IEEE International Conference on Multimedia and Expo Workshops (ICMEW), pp. 1–6 (2013)
5. Freeth, M., Foulsham, T., Chapman, P.: The influence of visual saliency on fixation patterns in individuals with autism spectrum disorders. Neuropsychologia **49**(1), 156–160 (2011)
6. Amso, D., Haas, S., Tenenbaum, E., Markant, J., Sheinkopf, S.J.: Bottom-up attention orienting in young children with autism. Journal of Autism and Developmental Disorders **44**(3), 664–673 (2014)
7. Mannan, S.K., Hodgson, T.L., Husain, M., Kennard, C.: Eye movements in visual search indicate impaired saliency processing in parkinson's disease. Progress in Brain Research **171**, 559–562 (2008)
8. Kastner, S., Ungerleider, L.G.: Mechanisms of visual attention in the human cortex. Annual Review of Neuroscience **23**(1), 315–341 (2000)
9. Itti, L., Koch, C.: Computational modelling of visual attention. Nature Reviews. Neuroscience **2**(3), 194–203 (2001)
10. Rolls, E.T., Deco, G.: Attention in natural scenes: neurophysiological and computational bases. Neural Networks **19**(9), 1383–1394 (2006)
11. Koch, K., McLean, J., Segev, R., Freed, M.A., Berry II, M.J., Balasubramanian, V., Sterling, P.: How much the eye tells the brain. Current Biology **16**(14), 1428–1434 (2006)
12. Treisman, A., Gelade, G.: A feature-integration theory of attention. Cognitive Psychology **136**(1), 97–136 (1980)
13. Borji, A., Itti, L.: State-of-the-art in visual attention modeling. IEEE Transactions on Pattern Analysis and Machine Intelligence (PAMI) **35**(1), 185–207 (2013)
14. Duncan, K., Sarkar, S.: Saliency in images and video: a brief survey. IET Computer Vision **6**(6), 514–523 (2012)
15. Koch, C., Ullman, S.: Shifts in selective visual attention: towards the underlying neural circuitry. Human Neurobiology **4**(4), 219–227 (1985)
16. Itti, L., Koch, C., Niebur, E.: A model of saliency-based visual attention for rapid scene analysis. IEEE Transactions on Pattern Analysis and Machine Intelligence (PAMI) **20**(11), 1254–1259 (1998)
17. Le Meur, O., Le Callet, P., Barba, D., Thoreau, D.: A coherent computational approach to model bottom-up visual attention. IEEE Transactions on Pattern Analysis and Machine Intelligence (PAMI) **28**(5), 802–817 (2006)
18. Kootstra, G., Nederveen, A., De Boer, B.: Paying attention to symmetry. In: Proceedings of the British Machine Vision Conference (BMVC), pp. 1115–1125 (2008)

19. Hou, X., Zhang, L.: Saliency detection: A spectral residual approach. In: IEEE Conference on Computer Vision and Pattern Recognition (CVPR), vol. (800), pp. 1–8 (2007)
20. Hou, X., Harel, J., Koch, C.: Image Signature: Highlighting Sparse Salient Regions. IEEE Transactions on Pattern Analysis and Machine Intelligence (PAMI) 34(1), 194–201 (2011)
21. Achanta, R., Hemami, S., Estrada, F., Susstrunk, S.: Frequency-tuned salient region detection. In: IEEE Conference on Computer Vision and Pattern Recognition (CVPR), pp. 1597–1604 (2009)
22. Harel, J., Koch, C., Perona, P.: Graph-based visual saliency. Advances in Neural Information Processing Systems 19, 545 (2007)
23. Garcia-Diaz, A., Fdez-Vidal, X.R., Pardo, X.M., Dosil, R.: Saliency from hierarchical adaptation through decorrelation and variance normalization. Image and Vision Computing 30(1), 51–64 (2012)
24. Yarbus, A.L., Haigh, B., Riggs, L.A.: Eye movements and vision (1967)
25. Goferman, S., Zelnik-Manor, L., Tal, A.: Context-aware saliency detection. IEEE Transactions on Pattern Analysis and Machine Intelligence (PAMI) 34(10), 1915–1926 (2012)
26. Liu, T., Yuan, Z., Sun, J., Wang, J., Zheng, N., Tang, X., Shum, H.Y.: Learning to detect a salient object. IEEE Transactions on Pattern Analysis and Machine Intelligence (PAMI) 33(2), 353–367 (2011)
27. Jiang, H., Wang, J., Yuan, Z., Liu, T., Zheng, N., Li, S.: Automatic salient object segmentation based on context and shape prior. In: British Machine Vision Conference (BMVC), vol. 3, p. 7 (2011)
28. Borji, A., Sihite, D.N., Itti, L.: Salient object detection: a benchmark. In: Fitzgibbon, A., Lazebnik, S., Perona, P., Sato, Y., Schmid, C. (eds.) ECCV 2012, Part II. LNCS, vol. 7573, pp. 414–429. Springer, Heidelberg (2012)
29. Borji, A., Sihite, D.N., Itti, L.: Quantitative analysis of human-model agreement in visual saliency modeling: A comparative study. IEEE Transactions on Image Processing (TIP) 22(1), 55–69 (2013)
30. Judd, T., Ehinger, K., Durand, F., Torralba, A.: Learning to predict where humans look. In: IEEE International Conference on Computer Vision (ICCV) (2009)
31. Cheng, M.M., Mitra, N.J., Huang, X., Torr, P.H.S., Hu, S.M.: Salient object detection and segmentation. Tsinghua University, Technical report(2011)
32. Yang, C., Zhang, L., Lu, H., Ruan, X., Yang, M.H.: Saliency detection via graph-based manifold ranking. In: IEEE Conference on Computer Vision and Pattern Recognition (CVPR), pp. 3166–3173 (2013)
33. Nguyen, T.V., Xu, M., Gao, G., Kankanhalli, M., Tian, Q., Yan, S.: Static saliency vs. dynamic saliency: a comparative study. In: ACM International Conference on Multimedia, pp. 987–996 (2013)

Recognizing Daily Activities in Realistic Environments Through Depth-Based User Tracking and Hidden Conditional Random Fields for MCI/AD Support

Dimitris Giakoumis[1]([✉]), Georgios Stavropoulos[1,2], Dimitrios Kikidis[1],
Manolis Vasileiadis[1], Konstantinos Votis[1], and Dimitrios Tzovaras[1]

[1] Information Technologies Institute, CERTH, Thessaloniki, Greece
stavrop@ece.upatras.gr,
{dgiakoum,dkikidis,mavasile,kvotis,tzovaras}@iti.gr
[2] University of Patras, Patras, Greece

Abstract. This paper presents a novel framework for the automatic recognition of Activities of Daily Living (ADLs), such as cooking, eating, dishwashing and watching TV, based on depth video processing and Hidden Conditional Random Fields (HCRFs). Depth video is provided by low-cost RGB-D sensors unobtrusively installed in the house. The user's location, posture, as well as point cloud -based features related to gestures are extracted; a standing/sitting posture detector, as well as novel features expressing head and hand gestures are introduced herein. To model the target activities, we employed discriminative HCRFs and compared them to HMMs. Through experimental evaluation, HCRFs outperformed HMMs in location trajectories-based ADL detection. By fusing trajectories data with posture and the proposed gesture features, ADL detection performance was found to further improve, leading to recognition rates at the level of 90.5 % for five target activities in a naturalistic home environment.

Keywords: Adl recognition · User location trajectories · Posture · Gestures · Point-cloud features · Hidden conditional random fields

1 Introduction

Automatic domestic activity recognition is a significant challenge, toward future homes equipped with robotic applications capable to monitor the resident's behaviour, identify abnormalities and assist in the establishment of daily activities [8]. This is of particular importance for cases of Mild Cognitive Impairments (MCI) or Alzheimer's Disease (AD), whereas activity monitoring can facilitate early diagnosis of cognitive decline [2]. Typically, the recognition of Activities of Daily Living (ADLs) [12] such as cooking, eating, dishwashing, has been approached through ambient sensors [3] monitoring the house environment [23], as well as locations visited from the monitored person [13][9]. During

© Springer International Publishing Switzerland 2015
L. Agapito et al. (Eds.): ECCV 2014 Workshops, Part III, LNCS 8927, pp. 822–838, 2015.
DOI: 10.1007/978-3-319-16199-0_57

the last years, relevant research efforts have focused on RGB video processing [6][5][18][31] or, especially after the emergence of the Kinect sensor, on RGB-D images [30][4].

In practical applications, where the need for robust, continuous user tracking and reduced obtrusiveness is of major importance, low-cost depth sensors (e.g. Kinect) can play a vital role; they can provide the basis for simple, low-cost sensor networks capable to track the user's silhouette throughout the house. Such networks can be rather unobtrusive in terms of input data (privacy-preserving depth images), as well as in terms of installation set-up, since limited amount of cameras (e.g. one per room) can be installed for e.g. at room roof-top corners. Although computer vision for assistive robotic applications typically considers input taken from a (depth) camera installed on the robot [29], such approaches require the robot to continuously follow the user, maintaining an appropriate view angle that allows user actions tracking. Although effective to some extent, such approaches are rather difficult to guarantee continuous user tracking in realistic scenarios, where the monitored person moves freely throughout the house. Thus, strategically and unobtrusively installed low-cost depth sensors could provide auxiliary input to the robotic system, so as to establish more detailed, continuous user tracking.

Of course, reduced cost and installation complexity of such depth sensor networks comes at a cost; that of highly varying user viewing angle, noisy user point-cloud data and occlusions that pose significant challenges in practical user posture and gesture recognition for ADL detection. Since however user location can still be robustly tracked through silhouette extraction from depth images, past approaches for user location-based ADL detection, based however on complex multi-sensorial networks [9] or RGB video [6] should be revisited, examining the potential of their rationale to advance automatic ADL detection in this new sensor context. Herein, unobtrusive continuous user location tracking is available and can be fused with robust descriptors of user pose and gestures, capable to operate under the limitations of realistic settings, toward advancing the effectiveness of future, practically applicable ADL recognition systems.

The present work follows exactly this line, introducing an ADL recognition framework based on user location trajectories and moreover, on posture and novel descriptors of the user's point cloud, capturing characteristics of head and hand gestures. The proposed framework operates on the basis of Hidden Conditional Random Fields (HCRFs), building upon the capacity of such discriminative models to provide better recognition performance, compared to their generative counterparts, i.e. Hidden Markov Model (HMM)-based models [9][24].

1.1   Related Work

As different activities typically involve different house regions that are visited by the user, with different per-activity visit frequencies, several research works have demonstrated the feasibility of detecting ADLs through the 2D trajectories generated in the house floor plan as the user moves around. Indicatively, [6] used a two-layer Hidden Semi-Markov Model, to infer ADLs such as cooking or ironing, solely based on user location trajectories taken from RGB cameras. Moving away from computer vision, in [9], state-change sensors were used, indirectly indicating among others user location, providing input to either HMMs or CRFs so as to discriminate among ADLs such as brushing teeth or cooking - preparing dinner. In [11], Semi-Markov HMM and CRF models were examined, again on the basis of state-change sensors. The work of [7], used again ambient sensors to recognize ADLs through a SVM-based detector. Although of potential toward effective ADL recognition, the above approaches, apart from [6], were based on complex multi-sensor systems. Thus, they need a large number of sensors to be installed in the house, whereas approaches based on computer vision [6], once their obtrusiveness is constrained and become privacy preserving, offer a major appealing characteristic; the fact that user activities can be tracked through only for e.g. one or two vision sensors installed in each monitored space.

Focusing on computer vision, toward incorporating apart from user location, information extracted from the user's silhouette, the work of [31] built on RGB video taken from a fisheye camera to detect activities following a three-level detection approach; the first level regarded user location and speed, the second body shape information for estimating the level of body motion and the third used primitive visual features to approach action recognition. A kNN-based detector was used to recognize cooking, brushing teeth and exercise activities. Building again upon RGB video, a system of two wide-field-of-view cameras and two narrow-field-of-view ones was employed in [18] to capture both coarse-level and fine-level activities respectively, utilizing a hierarchical Dynamic Bayesian Network (DBN). Although of potential, this line of approaches builds upon obtrusive RGB surveillance video processing.

Building upon posture and gestures, works such as [30][4] have explored RGB and depth video information fusion toward the recognition of daily actions, such as drink, pick up or sit down. In these works, features extracted from the depth video -based user's point cloud were proposed, toward 3D action representation; however, the RGB channel is still utilized, yielding privacy issues. Another line of research builds upon the depth-based markerless skeletal joints estimation method of [21]; in [28], skeleton-based body movement features were proposed for ADL recognition. Nevertheless, Kinect-based markerless skeletal joints extraction still suffer from varying view angles, occlusions and clutter in practical surveillance settings [30].

Focusing on the sole use of depth features for the detection of activities, a diverse set of approaches have been adopted by the scientific community, trying to increase the quality of the produced results while addressing specific experimental limitations. In a recent literature review on human activity recognition from 3D data [1], Aggarwall and Xia adopted a taxonomy of five types of features extracted from depth images, namely: 3D silhouettes, skeletal joints/body parts, local occupancy patterns, local spatio-temporal features and 3D optical flows. All these categories have shown promising results for the recognition of human activities but they were also found to be greatly influenced by difficulties found in real-life situations. Noise, object occlusion and camera position are some of the parameters that can dramatically degrade the results of the first three categories of features, whereas 3D optical flows and spatio-temporal features need colour information for reliable results.

Methods such as [16] have been found effective in the discrimination among different actions on rather controlled datasets (e.g. MSR Action 3D dataset [25]). However, by relying on the extraction of surface normals from the user's point cloud, they can easily become problematic in practical settings, where the user's point cloud can be highly noisy. In the present work, we focus on the recognition of daily activities in practical settings, where depth measurements are taken from un-optimal angles compared to datasets like [25] and are typically prone to occlusions and noise. In such settings, novel, more robust descriptors, capable to provide useful information to the ADL recognition system even in cases of significantly noisy user's point cloud are a significant challenge.

In the past, diverse classifiers have been used for recognizing daily activities, such as Bayesian networks [18] or SVMs [7]. As activity recognition is intrinsically a temporal classification problem [24], emphasis have been paid on Markovian state sequence models, such as HMMs [9] and their extensions employing either explicit state duration modelling [6] or hierarchical structures [10]. Relatively limited works have examined CRFs for ADL recognition [9], which can be seen as the discriminative counterparts of HMMs [24].

Conditional Random Fields are discriminative models for labelling sequences of observations. They condition on the entire observation sequence, while the features used as input can violate independence assumptions between observations, contrary to HMMs [24]. CRFs have been extensively used in the past toward gestures recognition [27][19] and motion tracking [22]. They have also been found effective in ADL detection based on state-change ambient sensors [9]. While CRFs generate per-observation labels, Hidden CRFs (HCRFs) [26] incorporate hidden states to model the underlying structure of the observations, providing a single label for the whole observation sequence. HCRFs have been successfully used in the past for gesture recognition [26], while by definition, they provide a potentially useful alternative to HMM-based approaches toward ADL recognition. Although the study of [24] indicated the potential of CRFs to drive location trajectories-based activity recognition by outperforming HMMs, to the best of our knowledge, such discriminative models and especially HCRFs, have still not been examined in the context of practical in-house ADL detection that builds upon user location trajectories.

1.2   Contribution

The present study follows the line of [9], where discriminative models, i.e. CRFs were found to have the potential to outperform generative HMMs in recognizing home ADLs through ambient state-change sensors. Considering that more fine-grained information regarding the user location, i.e. user location 2D trajectories on the house floor plan, has been found capable to drive ADL recognition through generative HMM-based models [6], this work first examines the capability of discriminative models, in particular Hidden CRFs (HCRF) [26], to advance effectiveness of ADL recognition, on the basis of user location trajectories that can be extracted from a small set of low-cost depth sensors installed unobtrusively in the house. Moreover, extending this line of research, we also incorporate user posture information in the recognition scheme, as well as novel 3D point-cloud features of the user's silhouette that are herein introduced to express head and hand gestures. Through experimental evaluation with data derived from realistic house settings, HCRFs were found to outperform HMMs in detecting the target activities from user location trajectories only. By fusing trajectory-based features with user posture and our proposed gestural features, ADL recognition performance was found to further increase, reaching precision and recall at the level of 90.52% for five target activities.

1.3   Paper Outline

Section 2 presents our proposed method for detecting standing/sitting postures and the descriptors of the user's point-cloud, which capture information related to head and hand gestures. Section 3 describes our HCRF-based activity recognition framework and Section 4 describes the process that was followed for experimental evaluation and its findings. Conclusions are drawn in Section 5.

2   Depth Video-Based User Monitoring

In order to track user movement around the house and her/his posture and actions, one must first extract the user's silhouette from the depth input images. To this end, a background image is captured prior to our system's initialization, with the monitored area empty of moving objects. For each captured frame i during runtime, the binary user silhouette $S_i, i = 1...n$ is extracted, by subtracting the depth value of each pixel (x, y) of the background image BG, from its corresponding pixel in the current frame I_i. A pixel (x, y) is considered as foreground (silhouette) if its depth value differs from the corresponding background pixel's value by more than a predefined threshold T:

$$S_i(x, y) = \begin{cases} 0 \ (Background) & \text{if } abs(I_i(x, y) - BG(x, y)) \leq T \\ 1 \ (Foreground) & \text{otherwise} \end{cases} \tag{1}$$

After the silhouette is extracted, noise induced by small changes in the background, for e.g. movement of objects like chairs or tables, is removed through post processing. This is achieved by performing connected component analysis [20] on the foreground image and taking into account the position of the user in previous frames. This way, only the area containing the user is kept.

2.1   User Location and Posture Tracking

User location with respect to the house floor plan is trivially estimated on the basis of the relative position of the silhouette and the camera, as well as the known in-house camera position. In order to estimate whether the user is standing or sitting, an approach similar to [15], albeit more robust to occlusions, is followed. Using the silhouette image as a mask, the 3D point cloud of the user is extracted and transformed from the camera coordinate system, to the coordinate system of the user, using the calibration information of the camera. Then, depending on the 3D point cloud's bounding box ratio $r = width/height$ and height h, the user's posture P_i for the frame i, is determined using a set of experimentally defined thresholds $h1, h2$(with $h1 > h2$) and $r1, r2$(with $r1 > r2$) for h and r respectively:

$$P_i = \begin{cases} Standing & \text{if } r_i < r_2 \ \& \ h_i > h_1 \\ Seated & \text{if } r_1 > r_i > r_2 \ \& \ h_1 > h_i > h_2 \end{cases} \quad (2)$$

Contrary to [15], the bounding box height is calculated in the proposed approach as the distance between the upper part of the silhouette from the floor, in the z axis of the building coordinate system. This allows robust estimation of the silhouette height, even in cases where the silhouette is occluded by objects lying between the user and the camera.

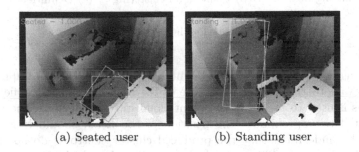

(a) Seated user   (b) Standing user

Fig. 1. Example of posture detection algorithm output

2.2   Point-Cloud Features of Upper-Body Geometry and Gestures

The present study aims to address the difficulties of activity detection algorithms when used in uncontrolled, real life environments. To this end, a robust and privacy preserving algorithm is proposed that can provide input for recognizing high-level activities, focusing on point-cloud descriptors capable to encapsulate information related to the users posture and motion. Specifically, a set of six features is defined, with special focus on the recognition of eating activity, given its importance in MCI and AD patients; AD patients at later stages can have difficulties to successfully establish eating, due to short-term memory problems.

The proposed method aims at extracting depth features that can approximate the geometry of the user's upper body but can also be minimally influenced by occlusions, changes in the orientation of the user and capable to produce reliable results independently of the camera position. The framework for the calculation of these features is summarized in Fig. 2. First, the periods when the user is seated are kept and for each frame, a bounding box is defined to include the majority of points of the user's upper body and at the same time minimize the influence of objects in the close proximity. Specifically, the horizontal dimensions of the bounding box are defined to be equal to the 2/3 of the user's arm length whereas its vertical dimension is taken as the 1/4 of the user's height. The position of the box is dynamically defined in every frame so that the centre of its upper side coincides with the highest point of the user's cloud (Fig. 2(a)).

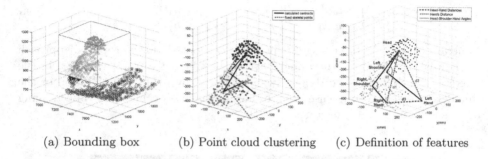

(a) Bounding box   (b) Point cloud clustering   (c) Definition of features

Fig. 2. Framework for the extraction of features

Following the extraction of the bounding box and in order to approximate points relevant to the skeletal structure of the upper body, a modified version of k-means is used to partition the point-cloud into five clusters; these clusters are expected to approximate the position of the head, shoulders and hands. It should be underlined that the produced cluster centroids do not necessarily coincide with a specific anatomical part of the human body, and that they depend on the subject's posture, the position of his/her hands and the existence of objects inside the bounding box. Nevertheless, since we are interested in obtaining information regarding the user motion and posture in uncontrolled, real-life environments, the proposed tracking algorithm can eventually approximate to some extent the user's head and hands. Therefore, from here on the five clusters of the point cloud will be labelled as head, right-shoulder, left-shoulder, right-hand and left-hand just as a naming convention for explanatory purposes.

Two are the main changes applied herein to the original k-means. First, our clustering method is initialized at each frame using the cluster centroids as produced in the previous frame, instead of using random points. This way, the algorithm converges much faster, since our frame rate is high enough (30 frames per second) to allow only small gesture changes between frames. On the other hand, in order to minimize the effects of the camera's position relatively to the occupant and increase the possibility that the clustering will comply with the expected structure of the human torso, our optimization scheme includes also the position of five fixed points as shown in Fig. 2(b). These points were defined based on the geometry of the human body in the seated position and correspond to the expected positions of head, shoulders and hands. Equation 3 summarizes our clustering optimization scheme for the partitioning of the n points in the cloud $\mathbf{X}^k = (x_1^k, x_2^k, ...x_n^k)$ of frame k, into five clusters $\mathbf{S}^k = (\mathbf{S}_1^k, \mathbf{S}_2^k, ...\mathbf{S}_5^k)$ based on their centroids $\mu^k = mean(x^k \in S_i^k)$ and the fixed points $\mathbf{Y} = (y_1, y_2, .., y_5)$.

$$\underset{\mathbf{S}}{\text{argmin}} \sum_{i=1}^{5} \sum_{x_j^k \in S_i^k} ||x_j^k - \mu_i^k||^2 * ||x_j^k - y_i||^2 \qquad (3)$$

Indicative results of our method are shown in Fig. 3 (calculated point cloud clusters and their centroids); here, it is shown how the calculated centroids follow the movement of the right hand as it approaches the user's head.

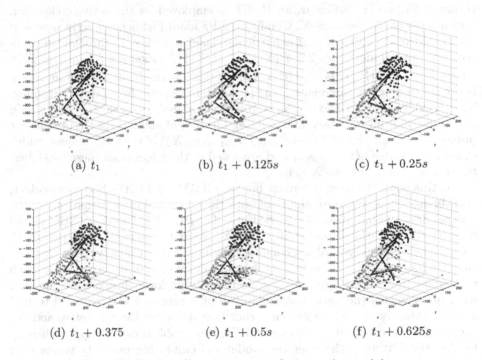

(a) t_1 (b) $t_1 + 0.125s$ (c) $t_1 + 0.25s$

(d) $t_1 + 0.375$ (e) $t_1 + 0.5s$ (f) $t_1 + 0.625s$

Fig. 3. Indicative clustering output during eating activity

Finally, the calculated centroid coordinates are used for the definition of the three first features proposed in this study, as shown in Fig. 2(c). The first feature is defined as the average of the distances of the head centroid from the two hand centroids: $f_1 = (d_1 + d_2)/2$, whereas the second regards the distance of the two hands: $f_2 = d_3$. The third feature is defined as the average of the angles between the head, shoulder and hand centroids for both sides: $f_3 = (\theta_1 + \theta_2)/2$. Finally, and in order to represent the relative movement of the user's upper body and the dynamic changes in her/his gesture, three additional features are defined as the standard deviation of 240 frame windows for each one of the above features. In order to validate the potential of these features on discriminating among eating/non-eating activities, ten periods of 10s were randomly selected from the Dataset C described at Section 4, half corresponding to eating activities and half to seated, non-eating activities (e.g. Reading). From each period, the proposed features were extracted and the Kruskal-Wallis test was employed to test the differences of the feature values distributions between the two classes (i.e. eating vs. non-eating); statistically significant ($p < 0.001$) difference was found for all features.

3 Activity Detection Framework

The activity detector of the present work is based on the theory of Conditional Random Fields; in particular, an HCRF is employed as our activity classifier. Given a set of observations X, Conditional Random Fields compactly represent the conditional probability of a particular label sequence Y through an undirected graphical model, as [24]: $P(Y|X) = (1/Z) \prod_{t=1}^{T} exp(w \times f(t, y_{t-1}, y_t, X))$, where $Z = \sum_Y \prod_{t=1}^{T} exp(w \times f(t, y_{t-1}, y_t, X))$ is a normalization constant and w is the set of weights, representing the parameters that are fitted during training. The weights are multiplied by a vector of computed features $f(t, y_{t-1}, y_t, X)$, which derive from the observations data. The weights-features set represent the potentials $\psi(t, y_{t-1}, y_t, X) = exp(w \times f(t, y_{t-1}, y_t, X))$ of the CRF cliques, which consist of an edge between y_{t-1} and y_t as well as the edges from these two labels to the set of observations X [24].

At this point the basic difference between HMMs and CRFs becomes evident; HMMs model the joint probability of both the labels and observations under the independence assumption of observations, i.e. $P(X, Y)$, whereas CRFs model directly the conditional probability $P(Y|X)$, so as to discriminate between different labels on the basis of not conditionally-independent observations. In practice, CRFs can assign a label to the features derived from observations at each time step. In our case, given for e.g. an one-minute long observation sequence, with observations (i.e. user location) taken at a rate of 1 HZ, we need to find a single label for the whole sequence that best describes the respective activity (i.e. cooking, eating, etc.). Through CRFs, this problem can be approached by finding the Viterbi path under the model and employing majority voting over the labels sequence to assign the dominant label [26]. In [26] however, HCRFs provided an alternative of significant potential to improve effectiveness in discriminating among different gestures based on user hand trajectories. As a basic aim in this work is to discriminate user trajectories on the house floor plan among different daily activities, given the similarities of our problem to the one of discriminating gestures from hand trajectories, it is reasonable to expect that HCRFs could improve performance in our context, as is further explained below.

Hidden Conditional Random Fields employ a set of hidden states to capture the certain underlying structure of each class. In particular, an HCRF models the conditional probability of a class label given a set of observations by [26]:

$$P(y|X, \theta) = \sum_s P(y, \mathbf{s}|X, \theta) = \frac{\sum_\mathbf{s} exp(\psi(y, \mathbf{s}, X; \theta))}{\sum_{y' \in Y, \mathbf{s} \in S^m} exp(\psi(y', \mathbf{s}, X; \theta))} \quad (4)$$

where $\mathbf{s} = s_1, s_2, ..., s_m$, each $s_i \in S$ captures a certain underlying structure of each class and S is the set of hidden states in the model. The potential function $\psi(y', \mathbf{s}, X; \theta) \in \rho$, parametrized by θ (parameter values of the model), measures the compatibility between a label, a set of observations and a configuration of the hidden states. By definition, HCRFs provide a modelling solution that directly addresses the needs of our problem's formulation; given an observations sequence, HCRFs build upon an underlying graphical model that captures temporal dependencies among observations, so as to derive a single label that better corresponds to the input sequence. Considering the simplest case of our specific problem, where the classifier's input is the user's location trajectory during a target activity, the HCRF employs hidden states so as to model dependencies between observations, toward recognizing the target activity being performed.

As such, a HCRF can provide more direct inference for our problem, compared to CRFs, but also to HMMs. For segmented observation sequences, each corresponding to a given activity from a set of M target activities, a set of M HMMs should be employed, each modelling trajectories of a given activity through $P(X, Y) = \prod_{t=1}^{T} P(y_t|y_{t-1}) \times P(x_t|y_t))$; the first term corresponds to pairs of labels and the second pairs each observation to its parent label. During inference, by employing the forward-backward algorithm, the probability that the respective model can produce the input trajectory can be calculated [6]. On the other hand, a single HCRF can be used so as to directly identify the most appropriate label given the input sequence, on the basis of hidden states that formulate cliques on an undirected graph between the observations and labels. Herein, a given hidden state can encode similar characteristics between two different activities that appear in segments of their observation sequences, whereas the ensemble of hidden states corresponding to each full sequence will eventually produce the required differentiation among the different labels. Moreover, long-range dependencies between observations can as well be incorporated in the HCRF, by modifying for e.g. the potential function ψ in Eq. 4, so as to include a window parameter ω that defines the amount of past and future history to be used when predicting the hidden state at each time step [26]; in this study, we follow [26], thus for window size ω, observations from $t - \omega$ to $t + \omega$ are used to compute the input features of the HCRF.

4 Experimental Evaluation

In order to experimentally evaluate our HCRF-based activity recognition framework in real-world activity monitoring scenarios, we first used the two datasets of [17]. These datasets allowed a direct comparison of our HCRF-based framework with the HMM-based approach that was followed in [17] to take place.

Moreover, in order to evaluate our approach of HCRF-based fusion of user location trajectories with information regarding the user's posture and gestures in realistic house settings, we conducted a new data collection experiment, set in a real apartment. More information regarding this dataset will be provided in what follows.

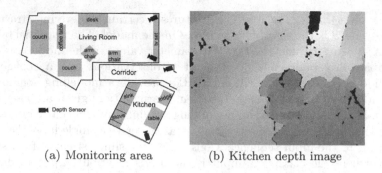

(a) Monitoring area   (b) Kitchen depth image

Fig. 4. Apartment experiment setup (Dataset C)

4.1 Datasets Description

The 1st of the datasets from [17] (Dataset A) contained user location trajectories data taken from a controlled kitchen environment, where two different persons performed three target activities in the same sequence (cooking, eating, dishwashing) for a total of nine different sessions, while being monitored from a single Kinect camera located at a kitchen's roof-top corner. In this case, four sessions were used for system training and the remaining for evaluation.

The 2nd dataset of [17] (Dataset B) concerned 24/7 monitoring of the resident of a real apartment, through three Kinect sensors, covering the apartment's living-room, the corridor and the kitchen; the resident was monitored for three days, while freely performing the target activities, i.e. cooking, eating, dishwashing and watching TV. In each day, one instance of each target activity occurred. As in the case of Dataset A, user location trajectories derived were available. In this dataset, data from the first two days were used to train the activity detection framework and the data of the third day were used for evaluation.

As mentioned earlier, a new dataset was recorded (Dataset C) from a real apartment scenario, where the resident was monitored for a period of 12 days; using 4 Kinect sensors monitoring the kitchen, corridor and living-room areas. The floor plan of the specific setting is shown in Fig. 4(a), along with the monitoring sensors' location, whereas a sample depth image taken from the apartment's kitchen is shown in Fig. 4(b). The target activities were the ones of Dataset B, with the addition of a non-eating activity, in order to describe different activities, besides eating, that take place in the area of the kitchen table such as reading or talking to the telephone. During the data collection period, 19 cooking, 10 eating, 7 non-eating, 28 dishwashing and 7 watching TV activity instances occurred. From this dataset, we used 2/3 of the activity instances as the train set and the rest were used for evaluation.

In order to train and test the examined classifiers, following the rationale of [9], we split each activity instance of the dataset into one minute-long non overlapping intervals of observations. Each interval was annotated with the label of the respective activity. With respect to each dataset, we obtained the amount of intervals per activity that is shown in Table 1.

Table 1. Number of activity intervals for training and evaluation in each dataset

Activity	Dataset A		Dataset B		Dataset C	
	Training	Evaluation	Training	Evaluation	Training	Evaluation
Cooking	20	25	48	24	37	22
Dish Washing	12	15	16	6	27	12
Eating	12	15	18	8	30	26
Non-Eating	-	-	-	-	22	20
Watching TV	-	-	110	51	40	36
Total	44	55	192	89	156	116

4.2 Results

Our framework's evaluation consisted of three different steps, involving the above datasets from the different settings. In the first step, the effectiveness of the HCRF activity detector was compared to the HMM-based one of [17], in recognizing the target activities by using solely user location trajectories data. Therefore, observations consisted in this step solely of the (x, y) timeseries of user location on the house floor plan. Evaluation at this step was performed on the basis of datasets A and B [17], while the HCRF was trained through a L-BFGS optimizer [14], using 10 hidden states and a 15sec. window.

Table 2. Detection results of the HCRF-based and HMM-based methods on datasets A and B

Activity	Dataset A				Dataset B			
	HCRF		HMM		HCRF		HMM	
	Prec.	Rec.	Prec.	Rec.	Prec.	Rec.	Prec.	Rec.
Cooking	93,48	82,70	99,34	76,15	92,00	95,83	66,07	92,50
Dish Washing	81,30	100,00	88,71	89,28	100,00	72,72	100,00	45,00
Eating	87,10	87,09	90,32	91,60	85,71	100,00	100,00	90,00
Watching TV	-	-	-	-	98,07	100,00	92,73	100,00
Average	87,30	89,93	92,79	85,67	93,95	92,14	89,70	81,88

As shown in Table 2, the HCRF was found to clearly outperform the HMM-based approach on the B dataset, while both methods produced similar results on the controlled A dataset . This was an expected result, in line with [26], given the capability of HCRFs to better learn common structures among trajectory classes and uncover the distinctive configuration that sets one trajectory class uniquely against others. In fact, our results are also in line with [9], where per timeslice ADL recognition performance was found to increase when discriminative models (CRF) were compared to generative (HMM) ones, in a state-change sensors-based monitoring context. The fact that the HMM-based approach used herein for comparison was already found in [17] to provide ADL recognition effectiveness at a better or similar level of past related works, such as [9][7] and [6], further underlines the potential of HCRFs to lead into increased ADL recognition effectiveness on the basis of user location trajectories.

Next, the HCRF-based approach was used on the C Dataset, which also included non-eating activities around the kitchen table. As can be seen in Table 3, our method performed fairly well, producing overall precision of 81.9%. However, it is clear that using only the (x, y) timeseries is not sufficient to succesfully discriminate between cooking, eating and non-eating activities that take place in the area of the kitchen table; many non-eating activity instances were detected as either cooking or eating activities.

Table 3. Detection results of the HCRF-based methods on dataset C, using only the (x, y) timeseries of user location on the house floor plan

Activity	Intervals	Detected As					Prec.	Rec.
		Cook	Dish	Eat	Non-eat	TV		
Cooking	22	14	1	1	6	0	63,64	93,33
Dish Washing	12	1	9	1	1	0	75,00	81,82
Eating	26	0	0	18	8	0	69,23	85,71
Non-Eating	20	0	1	1	18	0	90,00	54,55
Watching TV	36	0	0	0	0	36	100,00	100,00
Overall	116	15	11	21	33	36	81,90	81,90

Table 4. Detection results of the HCRF on dataset C, using the (x, y) user location trajectories, user posture and point cloud features of head and hand gestures (f_3), (f_5)

Activity	Intervals	Detected As					Prec.	Rec.
		Cook	Dish	Eat	Non-eat	TV		
Cooking	22	19	2	1	0	0	86,36	90,48
Dish Washing	12	2	10	0	0	0	83,33	71,43
Eating	26	0	0	25	1	0	96,15	86,21
Non-Eating	20	0	2	3	15	0	75,00	93,75
Watching TV	36	0	0	0	0	36	100,00	100,00
Overall	116	21	14	29	16	36	90,52	90,52

Finally, at the third step of evaluation, our proposed methods for estimating (a) user posture and (b) point-cloud features of the user's silhouette expressing head and hand gestures were also involved, so as to provide further features in the HCRF classifier. By trying different feature combinations, the use of the average of the angles between the head, shoulders and hands centroids (f_3), the deviation of the distance between the hands (f_5) and the user posture, in addition to the (x, y) timeseries, produced the best results. As can be seen in Table 4, the additional features increased the HCRF's performance by 8.6%, leading to precision at 90.52%. It is clear that the additional features improved the detection precision for eating, cooking and non-eating activities around the kitchen table. Specifically, the user posture contributed to the improvement of the discrimination rate between cooking and eating or non-eating activities, as food preparation typically involves standing postures, while the point cloud features of head and hand gestures helped in discriminating between eating and non-eating activities.

A comparison of the three detection frameworks is presented in Table 5, which shows that our proposed method produced significant increase in activity recognition performance, over both the trajectory-only HMM and HCRF.

Table 5. Comparison of activity detection results on dataset C

Activity	HMM		HCRF (x,y)		HCRF (x,y,f_3,f_5,pstr)	
	Prec.	Rec.	Prec.	Rec.	Prec.	Rec.
Cooking	85,31	83,44	63,64	93,33	86,36	90,48
Dish Washing	50,04	88,59	75,00	81,82	83,33	71,43
Eating	81,96	58,24	69,23	85,71	96,15	86,21
Non-Eating	62,78	64,10	90,00	54,55	75,00	93,75
Watching TV	89,92	86,28	100,00	100,00	100,00	100,00
Overall	80,07	76,68	81,90	81,90	90,52	90,52

5 Conclusions

This paper introduced a novel framework for automatic detection of domestic ADLs, such as cooking, dishwashing, eating and watching TV, based on the user's 3D point-cloud extracted through depth video recordings. In this context, the contribution of the present study was two-fold. First, HCRFs were introduced in the context of user location trajectories -based ADL detection and were experimentally compared to HMMs. Taking a further step forward, the present work introduced a novel approach to detecting standing-sitting user postures and more importantly, novel features extracted from the user's point-cloud, related to user head and hand gestures. Through experimental evaluation, it was found that HCRFs improved user location trajectories -based ADL recognition effectiveness compared to HMMs, whereas the inclusion of our proposed (a) standing/sitting posture detection method and (b) point cloud features of head and hand gestures led to further significant (at the level of 8%) increase in performance.

Acknowledgments. This work was supported by the Greek, nationally funded, research project "En-NOISIS".

References

1. Aggarwal, J., Xia, L.: Human activity recognition from 3d data: A review. Pattern Recognition Letters (2014)
2. Ahn, I.S., Kim, J.H., Kim, S., Chung, J.W., Kim, H., Kang, H.S., Kim, D.K.: Impairment of instrumental activities of daily living in patients with mild cognitive impairment. Psychiatry Investig 6(3), 180–184 (2009)
3. Chen, L., Hoey, J., Nugent, C., Cook, D., Yu, Z.: Sensor-based activity recognition. IEEE Transactions on Systems, Man, and Cybernetics, Part C: Applications and Reviews 42(6), 790–808 (2012)
4. Cheng, Z., Qin, L., Ye, Y., Huang, Q., Tian, Q.: Human daily action analysis with multi-view and color-depth data. In: Fusiello, A., Murino, V., Cucchiara, R. (eds.) ECCV 2012 Ws/Demos, Part II. LNCS, vol. 7584, pp. 52–61. Springer, Heidelberg (2012)
5. Daldoss, M., Piotto, N., Conci, N., De Natale, F.G.B.: Learning and matching human activities using regular expressions. In: 2010 17th IEEE International Conference on Image Processing (ICIP), pp. 4681–4684 (September 2010)
6. Duong, T., Phung, B., Bui, H., Venkatesh, S.: Efficient duration and hierarchical modeling for human activity recognition. Artificial Intelligence 173(7–8), 830–856 (2009)
7. Fleury, A., Vacher, M., Noury, N.: Svm-based multimodal classification of activities of daily living in health smart homes: Sensors, algorithms, and first experimental results. IEEE Transactions on Information Technology in Biomedicine 14(2), 274–283 (2010)
8. Hossain, M., Ahmed, D.: Virtual caregiver: An ambient-aware elderly monitoring system. IEEE Transactions on Information Technology in Biomedicine 16(6), 1024–1031 (2012)
9. van Kasteren, T., Noulas, A., Englebienne, G., Kröse, B.: Accurate activity recognition in a home setting. In: 10th Int. Conf. UbiComp 2008, pp. 1–9. ACM, New York (2008)
10. van Kasteren, T.L.M., Englebienne, G., Kröse, B.J.A.: Hierarchical activity recognition using automatically clustered actions. In: Keyson, D.V., Maher, M.L., Streitz, N., Cheok, A., Augusto, J.C., Wichert, R., Englebienne, G., Aghajan, H., Kröse, B.J.A. (eds.) AmI 2011. LNCS, vol. 7040, pp. 82–91. Springer, Heidelberg (2011)
11. van Kasteren, T., Englebienne, G., Kröse, B.J.: Activity recognition using semi-markov models on real world smart home datasets. Journal of Ambient Intelligence and Smart Environments 2(3), 311–325 (2010)
12. Lawton, M.P., Brody, E.M.: Assessment of older people: Self-maintaining and instrumental activities of daily living. The Gerontologist 9 (3 Part 1), 179–186 (1969)
13. Le, X.H.B., Di Mascolo, M., Gouin, A., Noury, N.: Health smart home for elders - a tool for automatic recognition of activities of daily living. In: 30th Annual International Conference of the Engineering in Medicine and Biology Society, EMBS 2008, pp. 3316–3319. IEEE (August 2008)
14. Liu, D.C., Nocedal, J.: On the limited memory bfgs method for large scale optimization. In: Mathematical Programming, pp. 503–528 (1989)
15. Myagmarbayar, N., Yuki, Y., Imamoglu, N., Gonzalez, J., Otake, M., Yu, W.: Human body contour data based activity recognition. In: 35th Annual International Conference of the IEEE Engineering in Medicine and Biology Society (EMBC), pp. 5634–5637 (July 2013)

16. Oreifej, O., Liu, Z.: Hon4d: Histogram of oriented 4d normals for activity recognition from depth sequences. In: 2013 IEEE Conference on Computer Vision and Pattern Recognition (CVPR), pp. 716–723 (June 2013)
17. Papamakarios, G., Giakoumis, D., Votis, K., Segouli, S., Tzovaras, D., Karagiannidis, C.: Synthetic ground truth data generation for automatic trajectory-based adl detection. In: IEEE International Conference on Biomedical and Health Informatics 2014 (BHI 2014) (June 2014)
18. Park, S., Kautz, H.: Hierarchical recognition of activities of daily living using multi-scale, multi-perspective vision and rfid. In: 2008 IET 4th International Conference on Intelligent Environments, pp. 1–4 (July 2008)
19. Ross, D.A., Osindero, S., Zemel, R.S.: Combining discriminative features to infer complex trajectories. In: Proceedings of the 23rd International Conference on Machine Learning, ICML 2006, pp. 761–768. ACM, New York (2006). http://doi.acm.org/10.1145/1143844.1143940
20. Samet, H., Tamminen, M.: Efficient component labeling of images of arbitrary dimension represented by linear bintrees. IEEE Transactions on Pattern Analysis and Machine Intelligence 10(4), 579–586 (1988)
21. Shotton, J., Girshick, R., Fitzgibbon, A., Sharp, T., Cook, M., Finocchio, M., Moore, R., Kohli, P., Criminisi, A., Kipman, A., Blake, A.: Efficient human pose estimation from single depth images. In: Criminisi, A., Shotton, J. (eds.) Decision Forests for Computer Vision and Medical Image Analysis, Advances in Computer Vision and Pattern Recognition, pp. 175–192. Springer, London (2013)
22. Sminchisescu, C., Kanaujia, A., Metaxas, D.: Conditional models for contextual human motion recognition. Computer Vision and Image Understanding 104(23), 210–220 (2006). http://www.sciencedirect.com/science/article/pii/S1077314206001093, special Issue on Modeling People: Vision-based understanding of a persons shape, appearance, movement and behaviour
23. Tapia, E.M., Intille, S.S., Larson, K.: Activity recognition in the home using simple and ubiquitous sensors. In: Ferscha, A., Mattern, F. (eds.) PERVASIVE 2004. LNCS, vol. 3001, pp. 158–175. Springer, Heidelberg (2004)
24. Vail, D.L., Veloso, M.M., Lafferty, J.D.: Conditional random fields for activity recognition. In: Proceedings of the 6th International Joint Conference on Autonomous Agents and Multiagent Systems, AAMAS 2007, pp. 235:1–235:8. ACM, New York (2007)
25. Wang, J., Liu, Z., Wu, Y., Yuan, J.: Mining actionlet ensemble for action recognition with depth cameras. In: 2012 IEEE Conference on Computer Vision and Pattern Recognition (CVPR), pp. 1290–1297 (June 2012)
26. Wang, S.B., Quattoni, A., Morency, L., Demirdjian, D., Darrell, T.: Hidden conditional random fields for gesture recognition. In: 2006 IEEE Computer Society Conference on Computer Vision and Pattern Recognition, vol. 2, pp. 1521–1527 (2006)
27. Yang, H.D., Sclaroff, S., Lee, S.W.: Sign language spotting with a threshold model based on conditional random fields. IEEE Transactions on Pattern Analysis and Machine Intelligence 31(7), 1264–1277 (2009)
28. Zhang, C., Tian, Y.: Rgb-d camera-based daily living activity recognition. Journal of Computer Vision and Image Processing 2(4), 12 (2012)

29. Zhang, H., Parker, L.: 4-dimensional local spatio-temporal features for human activity recognition. In: 2011 IEEE/RSJ International Conference on Intelligent Robots and Systems (IROS), pp. 2044–2049 (September 2011)
30. Zhao, Y., Liu, Z., Yang, L., Cheng, H.: Combing rgb and depth map features for human activity recognition. In: Proceedings of Asia-Pacific Signal and Information Processing Association Annual Summit and Conference (APSIPA ASC), pp. 3–6 (December 2012)
31. Zhou, Z., Chen, X., Chung, Y.C., He, Z., Han, T., Keller, J.: Activity analysis, summarization, and visualization for indoor human activity monitoring. IEEE Transactions on Circuits and Systems for Video Technology 18(11), 1489–1498 (2008)

3D Layout Propagation to Improve Object Recognition in Egocentric Videos

Alejandro Rituerto$^{(\boxtimes)}$, Ana C. Murillo, and José J. Guerrero

Instituto de Investigación en Ingeniería de Aragón, University of Zaragoza,
Zaragoza, Spain
{arituerto,acm,josechu.guerrero}@unizar.es

Abstract. Intelligent systems need complex and detailed models of their environment to achieve more sophisticated tasks, such as assistance to the user. Vision sensors provide rich information and are broadly used to obtain these models, for example, indoor scene modeling from monocular images has been widely studied. A common initial step in those settings is the estimation of the 3D layout of the scene. While most of the previous approaches obtain the scene layout from a single image, this work presents a novel approach to estimate the initial layout and addresses the problem of how to propagate it on a video. We propose to use a particle filter framework for this propagation process and describe how to generate and sample new layout hypotheses for the scene on each of the following frames. We present different ways to evaluate and rank these hypotheses. The experimental validation is run on two recent and publicly available datasets and shows promising results on the estimation of a basic 3D layout. Our experiments demonstrate how this layout information can be used to improve detection tasks useful for a human user, in particular sign detection, by easily rejecting false positives.

Keywords: Scene understanding · Egocentric vision · Object detection

1 Introduction

Vision systems have become an essential perception component in all kinds of autonomous and intelligent systems, including assistance oriented systems such as household robots or wearable visual assistance devices [5,29]. There is a growing interest on applications using wearable cameras for vision assistive approaches, frequently towards assistance for impaired people [4,25].

These applications are based on visual recognition systems, and it has been shown many times that context information is essential to achieve better recognition performance in real world problems [26]. Even a basic 3D model of the

We would like to thank Prof. Roberto Manduchi for his comments and suggestions, which helped us to improve the present work. This work was supported by the Spanish FPI grant BES-2010-030299 and Spanish projects DPI2012-31781, DGA-T04-FSE and TAMA.

© Springer International Publishing Switzerland 2015
L. Agapito et al. (Eds.): ECCV 2014 Workshops, Part III, LNCS 8927, pp. 839–852, 2015.
DOI: 10.1007/978-3-319-16199-0_58

Fig. 1. Our goal is to process video acquired from a wearable camera to obtain the 3D layout of the scene in each frame (Red: floor and ceiling; Green and Blue: walls from different orientations). This layout information is a strong prior to facilitate the detection of other scene details: persons, signs, doors or the traversable area.

scene provides useful information about the environment structure that facilitates automatic scene understanding. For example, it can help us identify the type of area traversed (e.g., a corridor or a room) or provide strong priors for detection and recognition of objects [14].

This work extends the work presented in [20]. Our goal is to provide a basic 3D model of the environment traversed while recording a video (Fig. 1) to enhance the performance of more complex tasks. We aim to achieve this goal without computing accurate camera motion or 3D maps of the environment.

2   Related Work

The estimation of the 3D layout of a scene from an image is a widely studied problem, as well as the advantages on using this layout information to facilitate further tasks. Prior work demonstrates the advantages of using scene layout information to improve recognition tasks. A simple 3D model of the scene or 3D spatial relationships between elements of the environment allows to better understand the content of the scene and provide strong priors for detection and recognition of objects [14,24]. Recent approaches [2,12,16] propose to solve simultaneously the problems of estimating the layout of the scene and detecting the objects that appear in it.

Earlier approaches to estimate the layout for general scenes include the work by Hoiem et al. [13], that proposed to learn appearance-based models of the scene parts (sky, floor, vertical objects) and described the scene geometry using these coarse labels. Later, Saxena et al. [23] used Markov Random Fields to infer plane parameters, such as 3D location and orientation, for homogeneous patches extracted from the image. For indoor environments, where certain additional assumptions can be made, we find the work proposed by Delage et al. [7], where a dynamic Bayesian network model is used to find the "floor-wall" boundary in the images assuming a Manhattan World [6]. Lee et al. [17] presented a method to generate interpretations of a scene from a set of line segments extracted from an indoor image. Similarly, Hedau et al. [11] proposed how to model the scene as a parametric 3D box. Gupta et al. [10] extended this idea to outdoor scenes and proposed how to create physical representations of outdoor scenes where objects have volume and mass, and their relationships describe the 3D structure and mechanical configurations.

Papers described so far analyze the structure of a single image. However, if we consider images that belong to a video sequence, we could propagate the information already obtained about the scene and obtain a better, more efficient or more robust result. Spatio-temporal restrictions between consecutive frames can provide both efficiency and accuracy improvements by accumulating the information obtained in each of them. This is one of the key ideas exploited in this work.

Most of the recent approaches taking advantage of sequential information, are based on SLAM or structure-from-motion techniques. For example, Flint et al. [8] combined geometric and photometric cues to obtain their scene model from a moving camera. They applied ideas from semantic reasoning in monocular images and 3D information obtained using structure-from-motion techniques. Similarly, Furlan et al. [9] proposed a method to estimate the 3D indoor scene layout from a moving camera. They pre-process the sequence to obtain the camera motion and a 3D map of the environment. From these results the method creates scene hypotheses that are evaluated and improved along the sequence. Tsai et al.[27] described a method to create a model of the environment using images acquired from a mobile robot. Since they focus on a robot moving indoors they can adopt constraints about the camera motion and the environment. The method uses different hypotheses describing the environment, that are updated with new details discovered while the robot moves.

Also related to our approach, we find papers on how to propagate semantic information in video sequences using different probabilistic frameworks. Badri-rananayanan et al. [1] used a probabilistic graphical model. They are able to use pixel-wise correspondences from motion estimation, image patch similarities or semantical consistent hierarchical regions to propagate the labels. Vazquez et al. [28] presented the Multiple Hypothesis Video Segmentation method for unsu-pervised segmentation of video sequences. The method works with a few frames at a time and creates, propagates and terminates the labels without supervision. Rituerto et al.[21] focused on label propagation indoors using images acquired from a mobile robot. They learn the appearance of the different regions of inter-est from some training examples and propagate them trough the sequence using a non-parametric model. Similarly, Hussain et al. [19] estimate the 3D structure of outdoor video scenes by computing different appearance, location and motion features.

Our work also proposes a probabilistic framework to propagate semantic information in a sequence, in particular, we aim to propagate the 3D layout of the environment traversed by a camera. We use a hierarchical method for single image layout estimation adapted from [18], and we then propagate and update this information making use of spatio-temporal restrictions and the lines detected in each frame.

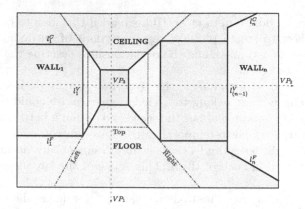

Fig. 2. Scene layout model. The *colored areas* in the image encode the different planes of the scene according to the surface orientation (red for horizontal, green and blue for vertical). The *black lines* define the scene structure and are grouped as floor (l_i^F), vertical (l_i^V) and ceiling lines (l_i^C). A scene with n planes contains n ceiling and floor lines and $n - 1$ vertical lines. *Blue dashed lines* denote the basic scene layout that originated the complete layout. *Black dashed lines* are the horizon and vertical lines defined by the vanishing points of the scene. (Best seen in color).

3   Initial 3D Scene Layout

This section presents our approach for single-view layout estimation. The proposed method provides a set of scene layout hypotheses that will be automatically evaluated, ranked and propagated accordingly. We adapt the hierarchical method proposed in [18] to compute the scene layout from an omnidirectional image. They proposed to start the process by looking for a basic scene layout: a rectangular space around the camera. Once this basic layout has been detected, they expand it by looking for plausible walls and corners. The method uses floor points as base to build and expand the hypothesis. Fig. 2 shows the scene model that we adopt inspired by those ideas. Since we are using conventional cameras, with smaller field of view than omnidirectional cameras, the basic scene layout is formed by just three walls, Left, Top and Right. As the original work, we expand the basic layout in a hierarchical process.

Lines, vanishing points and intersections. In the first step of the method line segments and vanishing points of the image are computed. To extract the image lines Canny edge detector (Kovesi [15] Matlab toolbox) is run and the vanishing points are detected following the method presented by Rother [22]. Then, intersections between the detected line segments are computed.

Building a basic room layout. Room hypotheses are randomly generated from the intersections computed. The process is shown in Fig. 3. To build a basic room, a floor intersection is randomly chosen. The vanishing lines crossing in that point are computed. To finish the hypothesis, another floor intersection

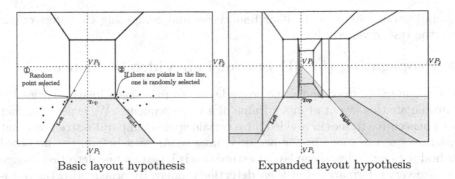

Basic layout hypothesis   Expanded layout hypothesis

Fig. 3. Basic and expanded scene layout hypotheses. In both figures, *red lines* represent the vanishing lines used to build a hypothesis and *red points* are the points used to define one hypothesis. To build a basic layout hypothesis (*black lines*), a floor intersection point is chosen randomly and vanishing lines in the directions intersecting on that point are computed. To complete the hypothesis another point is randomly selected among those where vanishing lines intersect. To expand a basic layout hypothesis (*blue lines*), we follow each of the basic room boundaries (left, top and right) and look for intersections that enlarge the room area. *Gray areas* show the expansion area where these intersections occur. (Best seen in color).

is chosen between those aligned with the computed vanishing lines. The lines crossing in those points compound the basic room hypothesis.

Expanding a basic room layout. Given a basic room hypothesis, it can be expanded to fit more complex environments. Fig. 3 shows this process. For each boundary of the basic room model, we look for intersections that could enlarge the floor area. The gray areas show where these intersections appear. The expansion process depends on the kind of boundary that we try to expand:

- *Top boundary:* we start with a random floor intersection in the Top boundary. From this point, a vanishing line is computed and another point aligned with this new line is chosen. This process is repeated until we close the area.
- *Left or Right boundaries:* in the case of Left or Right boundaries we define two ways of expanding the floor. We can choose a point aligned with the Top boundary as show for the Right boundary in Fig. 3, or choose a point in the correspondent boundary as done for the Left boundary in the same figure.

Ceiling detection. We adopt the Indoor World model that combines the Manhattan World assumption [6] and a single-floor-single-ceiling model. This model applies to most indoor environments and introduces symmetry between ceiling and floor shapes, something useful when the floor-walls boundaries are occluded. Once the floor boundaries have been defined, we look for the ceiling boundaries. We assume floor-ceiling symmetry, so we just have to detect the height of the room. We compute the first vertical line of our model, and look for ceiling intersections aligned with that line: one is randomly chosen. When we have computed the height of one vertical line, the rest of the ceiling boundaries can be computed drawing parallel lines to the floor boundaries and computing the intersections with the rest of vertical lines.

4   Propagating the 3D Layout in a Video Sequence

Once we are able to compute the scene layout from a single image, our goal is to propagate this layout at every frame of a video sequence. We exploit the fact that consecutive frames in a video have certain spatio-temporal restrictions that constrain the variations in the acquired images. As seen before, the proposed method for single-view scene layout estimation is based on line detection. Image lines are very informative, but their detection is noisy. By propagating the possible layouts computed in one frame to the next frames, we are hoping to improve the results and obtain a more robust estimation for each frame in the sequence. We adopt a particle filter based strategy to track the posterior probability of the layout given all the observations up to the current frame.

Algorithm 1 presents the main steps of our approach. I_t is the frame at time t and X_t is the layout state, compound by n layout hypotheses, $\mathbf{X}_t = \{x_1, x_2, \ldots x_n\}$. For the first frame, hypotheses are created using the single-view algorithm (Section 3). These hypotheses are evaluated and ranked as detailed in the following subsections, and the best one is selected as the solution for that frame. For next frames, new hypotheses (particles) are randomly generated depending on previous hypotheses and their evaluation score. Again, these hypotheses are evaluated in a similar manner and the best one is selected as the solution in each of the following frame

---

Algorithm 1 Particle filter based algorithm for hypothesis sampling

---

Require: Video sequence: $I_t | t = 0 \ldots \#$ frames
Ensure: 3D Scene Structure Layout: $bestHyp_t$
  $\mathbf{X}_0 = \text{generateHypothesisFromImage}(I_0)$
  $\mathbf{p}_0 = \text{evalHypotheses}(\mathbf{X}_0, I_0)$
  for $t = 1 \ldots \#$ Frames **do**
    $\mathbf{X}_t = \text{sampleNewHypotheses}(\mathbf{X}_{t-1}, \mathbf{p}_{t-1})$
    $\mathbf{p}_t = \text{evalHypotheses}(\mathbf{X}_t, I_t)$
  end for

4.1   Layout Parametrization

The model used to define the 3D scene layouts is shown in Figure 2. A room hypothesis x_i compound of n walls is parametrized as sets of floor, vertical and ceiling lines, and the vanishing points of the scene:

$$x_i = \{(l_1^F \ldots l_n^F), (l_1^V \ldots l_{(n-1)}^V), (l_1^C \ldots l_n^C), (VP_1, VP_2, VP_3)\} \qquad (1)$$

where l_i^F is the i-th floor line, l_i^V the i-th vertical line and l_i^C the i-th ceiling line, that is aligned with the same vanishing point than l_i^F (they are parallel in the scene). The model also includes the vanishing points: VP_1, VP_2 and VP_3.

Observed orientation map Hypothesis orientation map   Overlapping lines

Fig. 4. Evaluation of the hypotheses. The observed orientation map, computed from the detected lines, and the hypothesis orientation map are compared to compute S_{omap}. $S_{overlap}$ is computed as the length of overlapping (red) divided by the total length of the hypothesis lines (black). Blue lines are the detected lines that are parallel and close to the model lines. (Best seen in color).

4.2 Hypotheses Evaluation

The evaluation of the hypotheses is performed on every frame. For all the images, lines and vanishing points are computed and used to evaluate the compatibility of the layout hypotheses. We define two measurements for this evaluation computed for each layout hypothesis x_i:

- *Orientation map:* the orientation map is presented in [17]. It expresses the local belief of region orientations computed from detected line segments (Fig. 4). This orientation map, $omap(l_i)$, is compared with the orientation map defined by the hypothesis being evaluated, $omap(x_i)$ (Fig. 4). The evaluation score is computed as the number of pixels where the orientation of both maps is the same divided by the total number of image pixels, $nPix = width \times height$

$$S_{omap\ i} = \frac{\sum_{k=0}^{nPix} omap(l_i)_k = omap(x_i)_k}{nPix} \qquad (2)$$

where k is the pixel index. This score is the only evaluation used in [17] where the highest S_{omap} gives the chosen solution.

- *Observed lines overlap:* this evaluation measures the length of the overlapping between the observed lines and the lines of the hypothesis being evaluated. The layout parametrization used defines model lines delimiting the layout areas (Fig. 4). We look for lines parallel and close to these model lines and compute their overlapping length with the model lines. The score of this evaluation is computed as the total overlapping length divided by the total length of the model lin:

$$S_{overlap\ i} = \left(\frac{\sum overlap\ length}{\sum model\ lines\ length} \right)_i \qquad (3)$$

Both scores are used together to evaluate the hypotheses:

$$S_{total\ i} = mean(S_{omap\ i},\ S_{overlap\ i}) \qquad (4)$$

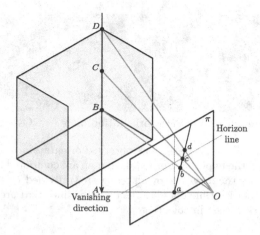

Fig. 5. The cross-ratio of the four points showed remains constant between consecutive views. This relation is used to locate the ceiling points when sampling new hypotheses. (Best seen in color).

4.3 Sampling New Hypotheses

A new set of hypotheses is created by sampling from the hypotheses of the previous frame and their evaluation score. For each hypothesis, a score has been computed, $S_{total\ i}$. The number of new hypothesis sampled from each previous hypothesis depends on this score. The probability of generating a new hypothesis, x'_i, from previous hypothesis x_i is $p_i = S_{total\ i}$. New hypotheses are created randomly, high scores will generate more new hypotheses since they are more probable, and low scores hypotheses will receive few samples or even disappear.

The model used parametrizes the layout as sets of lines describing planes. Given the camera motion, a homography relates the projection of the coplanar points between frames and the vanishing points are related by the rotation matrix. We work with a moving camera where rotation and translation are unknown. To create a new hypothesis from a previous one, we assume a random motion of the camera, with zero velocity and random noise in camera translation and rotation. Random rotation and translation are created, R and t, from 3 random angles (R $= f(roll, pitch, yaw)$ and 3 random translations ($\mathbf{t} = [t_x, t_y, t_z]^T$). The homography H relating coplanar points can be computed as

$$H = R - \frac{\mathbf{t}\, \mathbf{n}^T}{d} \tag{5}$$

where $\mathbf{n}$ is the normal of the plane where the junction points lie and d the distance between the camera and the plane. The plane used is the floor plane, where we have computed the room hypothesis. We assume d distance as unitary so the scale of the random translation t is defined by the real distance to the plane.

From hypothesis x_i, sampled hypothesis x_i' will be related by the random R and **t**. Points, pt, of the floor lines are related by a homography:

$$pt' = H \cdot pt = (\mathsf{R} - \frac{\mathbf{t}\,\mathbf{n}^T}{d})pt \quad (pt \in l_i^F | i = 1 \ldots n) \tag{6}$$

and the vanishing points are related by the rotation matrix:

$$VP_k' = \mathsf{R} \cdot VP_k \quad (k = 1 \ldots 3) \tag{7}$$

Ceiling points relation. Through the computed homography, we are able to relate the points on the floor, however we cannot relate the points in the ceiling of the scene, since they are part of a different plane. To relate the ceiling points, we assume that the distance between camera and floor remains the same between consecutive frames. We use the cross ratio to relate the height of the scene between images, Fig. 5. Given 4 collinear points, A, B, C and D, the cross ratio, C_R remains invariant for any perspective. The collinear points in our case are the two intersections defining the height of the room in the image, b and d, the vertical vanishing point, a, and the intersection between the vertical line and the line of the horizon, c. Since we consider the camera height to be the same between consecutive frames, the horizon is the same and the cross ratio remains constant. So, the cross ratio, C_R, is computed in the current image as:

$$C_R = \frac{|ac|\,|bd|}{|ad|\,|bc|} \tag{8}$$

where $|ac|$ is the signed distance between a and c. Therefore, we obtain the ceiling point from the the floor point in next image as:

$$|b'd'| = C_R \frac{|a'd'||b'c'|}{|a'c'|} \tag{9}$$

5   Experimental Validation

We have run experiments in public datasets to show the performance of the proposed method and how its use can improve object recognition tasks.

5.1   Analysis of the Method Performance

We analyze the performance of the layout estimation obtained by our method by comparing it with a well know state-of-the-art method [17] as baseline[1].

---

[1] We have used the code provided by the authors in http://www.cs.cmu.edu/~dclee/ code/index.html. This version does not include the complete environment model presented in the paper.

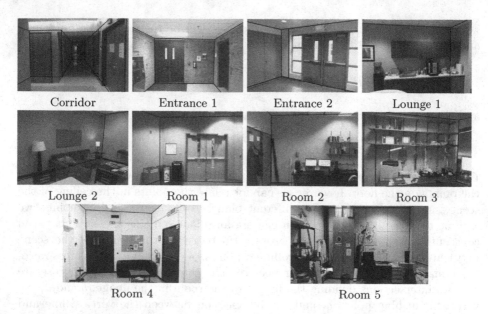

Fig. 6. Example images of all the sequences included in the dataset [9] with the best fitting layout obtained with our method

Experimental Settings. We have tested our method on the 10 sequences included in the dataset presented in [9]. These sequences have been acquired indoors with two different mobile cameras (Fig. 6) and include between 203 and 965 images. For all the sequences, the ground-truth has been manually annotated in one of each ten images. Figure 6 shows example frames of all the sequences included in the dataset and the correspondent resulting layout. Note that the Manhattan World assumption cannot be applied in some of the sequences, like Room 1 where walls are not orthogonal.

The accuracy of the solution is computed as the number of pixels where the orientation defined by the ground-truth and the orientation computed from the layout hypothesis are the same divided by the total number of pixels of the image

$$Accuracy = 100 \frac{\sum_{k=0}^{nPix} omap(GT)_k = omap(x_i)_k}{nPix} \tag{10}$$

where k is the pixel index, GT denotes the ground-truth layout, x_i is the layout hypothesis being analyzed and the number of pixels in the image is $nPix = width \times height$.

Method Evaluation. Table 1 shows the accuracy for all the sequences included in the dataset for our method and the base method [17]. The base method is intended to work on single images so we run this algorithm over all the frames of the sequence independently. For each sequence and both methods, the mean

Table 1. Mean accuracy of the layout solutions for each sequence obtained with Lee et al. method [17] and the proposed method

	Lee et al. [17]	Proposed method
Corridor	56.84	71.77
Entrance 1	80.13	72.49
Entrance 2	74.27	66.45
Lounge 1	47.40	55.43
Lounge 2	36.38	57.38
Room 1	50.73	55.99
Room 2	66.79	78.93
Room 3	36.82	74.49
Room 4	25.93	63.29
Room 5	64.70	78.85
Average	53.99	67.50

of the accuracy obtained for the solution hypothesis in all frames is shown. Our method performs better for the majority of sequences. Main performance differences correspond to Lounges 1 and 2 and Rooms 3 and 4 sequences, where the algorithm in [17] performances are low while our method produces good results. In these sequences there is more clutter than in the rest. On average, our method performs better that the baseline algorithm. Fig. 6 shows the resulting layout on one image of each sequence.

5.2   Improving Object Recognition Tasks

This subsection shows results on object recognition tasks, poster detection in this case, using an egocentric vision dataset.

Experimental Settings. The images used in this second experiment are part of a wearable vision system dataset publicly available[2]. It consists of several indoor sequences acquired with wearable vision sensors. We have selected certain frames along those sequences that contain poster or signs, our objects of interest, to be able to demonstrate how the context information provided by the layout helps to automatically discard wrong detections.

We analyze how the performance of a sign detector can be improved by using the layout information as prior information. We consider a sign detection method that detects rectangular hypothesis in the scene that could correspond to signs. We compute the Precision and Recall of the correctly detected signs given the rectangles provided by this detector, i.e., among those hypothesis given by the detector, which ones are correct or wrong after the filtering achieved thanks to the layout information.

---

[2] https://i3a.unizar.es/es/content/wearable-computer-vision-systems-dataset

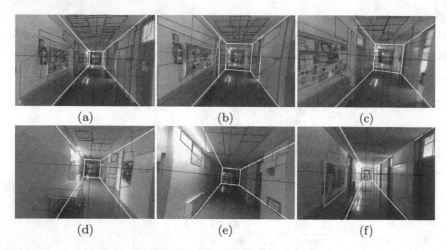

(a)   (b)   (c)

(d)   (e)   (f)

Fig. 7. We run the (rectangular) sign detector presented in [3]. We use the layout information to filter the rectangles and detect which ones are actual signs. Black rectangles show rectangles that have been correctly discarded with our filtering: they are not aligned with the scene vanishing directions or are part of more than one layout region. Blue rectangles are aligned with the layout and the vanishing directions, but they are not classified as posters by our filtering because of the relative location in the scene. Green and red show detections accepted by our filtering (correct or incorrectly respectively) and magenta rectangles are signs that have been incorrectly rejected. (Best seen in color).

Poster Detection Evaluation. Fig. 7 shows how the layout information improves the detection of posters in the images. We run the sign detector presented in [3] on a selection of images of the dataset. The detector creates detection hypotheses all over the image, but just some of them are correct. The rectangle hypothesis detected can be easily filtered using the scene layout and prior knowledge about man made environments to decide which hypothesis actually correspond to posters/signs or not:

- Scene objects are aligned with the scene vanishing points and with the vanishing points of the scene plane where they lay.
- Interesting objects, posters in our case, appear in walls, nor in floor or ceiling.
- Posters height is smaller than the wall height, they appear close to the eyes height (camera height in our case) and do not appear on top or bottom parts of the wall.

Sign detector detects 25 sign candidates per frame on average, and about 18 of these candidates are rejected (not aligned with the vanishing directions or are part of more than one layout region). The sign candidates remaining after the filtering are classified into poster or no poster. The precision of this classification is 95.24% and the recall is a bit lower 88.19%. The main reason for these high values is the filter step, where rectangles no fitting the structure are rejected. Fig. 7 shows examples of the poster detection.

6 Conclusions

This paper presents a new approach to obtain the 3D layout of a single image and propagate this layout along a video sequence. The approach is designed for indoor environments, so Manhattan World assumption is adopted. Our proposed method obtains an initial layout from a single image using certain assumptions typical for indoor environments and first-person perspective videos. Then, a particle filter framework is used to take advantage of the sequential information on video sequences and propagate the scene layout. The layout estimation method has shown better accuracy than a well known baseline and we show how to propagate the layout instead of computing all the model for each frame. Additionally, our experiments demonstrate how the 3D layout we obtain provides useful priors for recognition tasks. In particular we show how sign recognition can be improved by easily rejecting the numerous false positive detections.

References

1. Badrinarayanan, V., Galasso, F., Cipolla, R.: Label propagation in video sequences. In: IEEE Conference on Computer Vision and Pattern Recognition (CVPR), pp. 3265–3272 (2010)
2. Bao, S.Y., Sun, M., Savarese, S.: Toward coherent object detection and scene layout understanding. Image and Vision Computing 29(9), 569–579 (2011)
3. Cambra, A.B., Murillo, A.: Towards robust and efficient text sign reading from a mobile phone. In: Int. Conf. on Computer Vision Workshops, pp. 64–71 (2011)
4. Chen, L., Guo, B.L., Sun, W.: Obstacle detection system for visually impaired people based on stereo vision. In: Int. Conf. on Genetic and Evolutionary Computing, pp. 723–726 (2010)
5. Ciocarlie, M., Hsiao, K., Jones, E.G., Chitta, S., Rusu, R.B., Şucan, I.A.: Towards reliable grasping and manipulation in household environments. In: Khatib, O., Kumar, V., Sukhatme, G. (eds.) Experimental Robotics. STAR, vol. 79, pp. 241–252. Springer, Heidelberg (2012)
6. Coughlan, J.M., Yuille, A.L.: Manhattan world: Compass direction from a single image by bayesian inference. In: IEEE International Conference on Computer Vision (ICCV), pp. 941–947 (1999)
7. Delage, E., Lee, H., Ng, A.Y.: A dynamic bayesian network model for autonomous 3d reconstruction from a single indoor image. In: IEEE Computer Society Conference on Computer Vision and Pattern Recognition (CVPR), pp. 2418–2428 (2006)
8. Flint, A., Murray, D., Reid, I.: Manhattan scene understanding using monocular, stereo, and 3D features. In: IEEE International Conference on Computer Vision (ICCV), pp. 2228–2235 (2011)
9. Furlan, A., Miller, S., Sorrenti, D.G., Fei-Fei, L., Savarese, S.: Free your camera: 3d indoor scene understanding from arbitrary camera motion. In: British Machine Vision Conference (BMVC) (2013)
10. Gupta, A., Efros, A.A., Hebert, M.: Blocks world revisited: image understanding using qualitative geometry and mechanics. In: Daniilidis, K., Maragos, P., Paragios, N. (eds.) ECCV 2010, Part IV. LNCS, vol. 6314, pp. 482–496. Springer, Heidelberg (2010)
11. Hedau, V., Hoiem, D., Forsyth, D.: Recovering the spatial layout of cluttered rooms. In: IEEE International Conference on Computer Vision (ICCV), pp. 1849–1856 (2009)

12. Hedau, V., Hoiem, D., Forsyth, D.: Thinking inside the box: using appearance models and context based on room geometry. In: Daniilidis, K., Maragos, P., Paragios, N. (eds.) ECCV 2010, Part VI. LNCS, vol. 6316, pp. 224–237. Springer, Heidelberg (2010)
13. Hoiem, D., Efros, A.A., Hebert, M.: Recovering surface layout from an image. International Journal of Computer Vision 75(1), 151–172 (2007)
14. Hoiem, D., Efros, A.A., Hebert, M.: Putting objects in perspective. International Journal of Computer Vision 80(1), 3–15 (2008)
15. Kovesi, P.D.: MATLAB and Octave functions for computer vision and image processing
16. Lee, D.C., Gupta, A., Hebert, M., Kanade, T.: Estimating spatial layout of rooms using volumetric reasoning about objects and surfaces. In: Advances in Neural Information Processing Systems (NIPS) (2010)
17. Lee, D.C., Hebert, M., Kanade, T.: Geometric reasoning for single image structure recovery. In: IEEE Conference on Computer Vision and Pattern Recognition (CVPR), pp. 2136–2143 (2009)
18. López-Nicolás, G., Omedes, J., Guerrero, J.: Spatial layout recovery from a single omnidirectional image and its matching-free sequential propagation. In: Robotics and Autonomous Systems (2014)
19. Raza, S.H., Grundmann, M., Essa, I.: Geometric context from video. In: IEEE Conference on Computer Vision and Pattern Recognition (CVPR) (2013)
20. Rituerto, A., Manduchi, R., Murillo, A.C., Guerrero, J.J.: 3D Spatial layout propagation in a video sequence. In: Campilho, A., Kamel, M. (eds.) ICIAR 2014, Part II. LNCS, vol. 8815, pp. 374–382. Springer, Heidelberg (2014)
21. Rituerto, J., Murillo, A., Kosecka, J.: Label propagation in videos indoors with an incremental non-parametric model update. In: IEEE/RSJ International Conference on Intelligent Robots and Systems (IROS), pp. 2383–2389 (2011)
22. Rother, C.: A new approach to vanishing point detection in architectural environments. Image and Vision Computing 20(9), 647–655 (2002)
23. Saxena, A., Sun, M., Ng, A.Y.: Make3d: Learning 3D scene structure from a single still image. IEEE Transactions on Pattern Analysis and Machine Intelligence 31(5), 824–840 (2009)
24. Southey, T., Little, J.: 3D spatial relationships for improving object detection. In: 2013 IEEE International Conference on Robotics and Automation (ICRA), pp. 140–147 (May 2013)
25. Tapu, R., Mocanu, B., Bursuc, A., Zaharia, T.: A smartphone-based obstacle detection and classification system for assisting visually impaired people. In: Int. Conf. on Computer Vision Workshops (ICCVW), pp. 444–451 (2013)
26. Torralba, A., Murphy, K.P., Freeman, W.T.: Using the forest to see the trees: exploiting context for visual object detection and localization. Communications of the ACM 53(3), 107–114 (2010)
27. Tsai, G., Kuipers, B.: Dynamic visual understanding of the local environment for an indoor navigating robot. In: IEEE/RSJ International Conference on Intelligent Robots and Systems (IROS), pp. 4695–4701 (2012)
28. Vazquez-Reina, A., Avidan, S., Pfister, H., Miller, E.: Multiple hypothesis video segmentation from superpixel flows. In: Daniilidis, K., Maragos, P., Paragios, N. (eds.) ECCV 2010, Part V. LNCS, vol. 6315, pp. 268–281. Springer, Heidelberg (2010)
29. Wexler, Y., Shashua, A., Tadmor, O., Ehrlich, I.: User wearable visual assistance device (ORCAM), uS Patent App. 13/914,792 (2013)

Author Index

Printed in the United States
By Bookmasters